AF470556

# G. F. WATTS

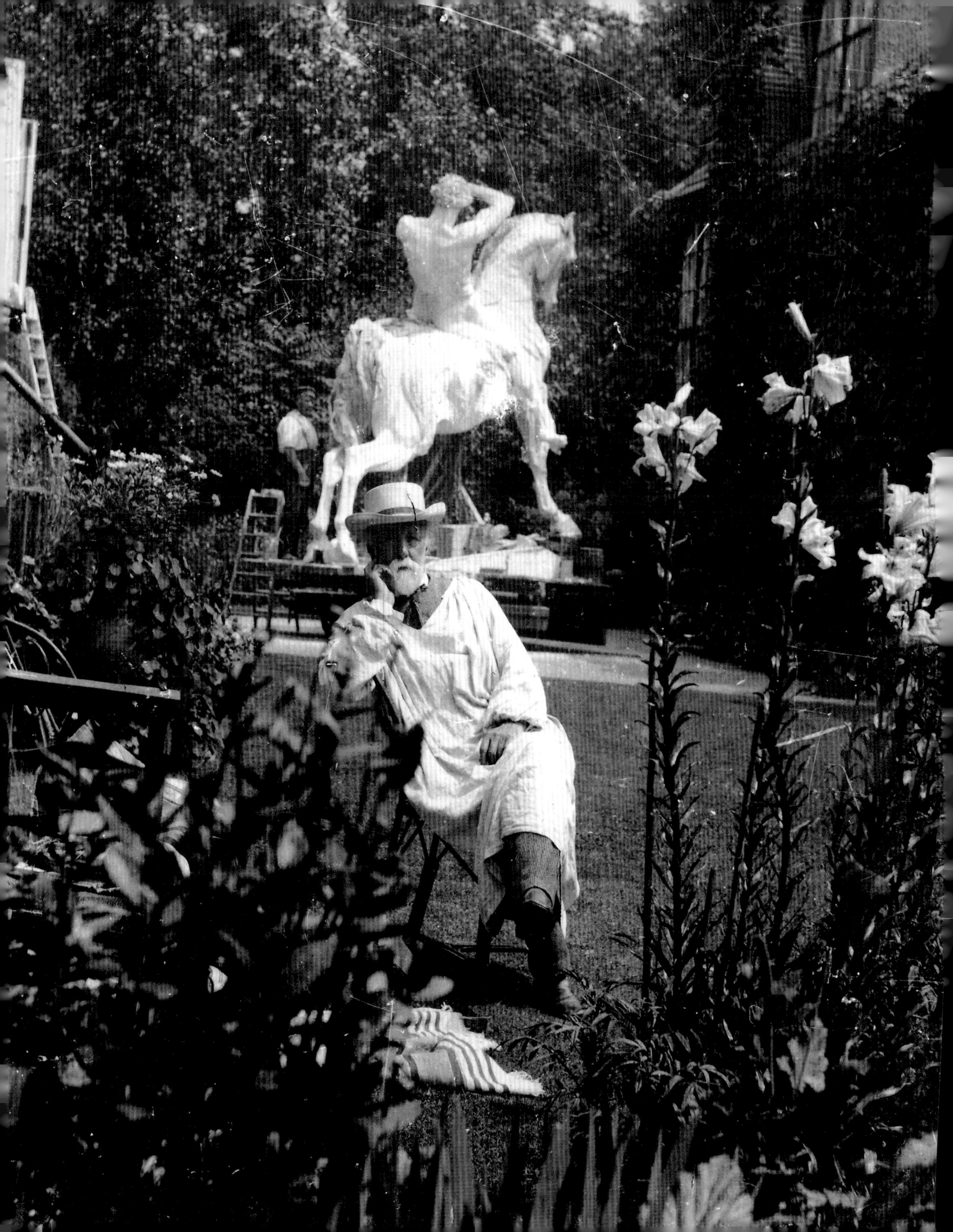

# G. F. WATTS

## The Last Great Victorian

Veronica Franklin Gould

Published for
THE PAUL MELLON CENTRE FOR STUDIES N BRITISH ART
by
YALE UNIVERSITY PRESS
New Haven and London

Designed by Gillian Malpass

Printed in Italy

**Library of Congress Cataloging-in-Publication Data**
Gould, Veronica Franklin.
  G. F. Watts : the last great Victorian / Veronica Franklin Gould.
      p. cm.
  Includes bibliographical references and index.
  ISBN 0-300-10577-0 (cl : alk. paper)
  1. Watts, George Frederick, 1817–1904. 2. Painters–England–Biography.
3. Symbolism (Art movement)–England. 1. Title: Last great Victorian. 11. Title.
  ND497.W3G68 2004
  759.2–dc22

                                        2004004214

A catalogue record for this book is available from
The British Library

*Frontispiece*   G. F. Watts in front of *Physical Energy* in the garden at Little Holland
House, Melbury Road, 1890

*Endpapers*   G. F. Watts, *Physical Energy* fronts the Rhodes Memorial (designed by Herbert
Baker 1906–16) at Groote Schuur overlooking Table Bay, South Africa.

*Page vi*   *The Utmost for the Highest*: G. F. Watts's bookplate (Watts Gallery)

*For my family*

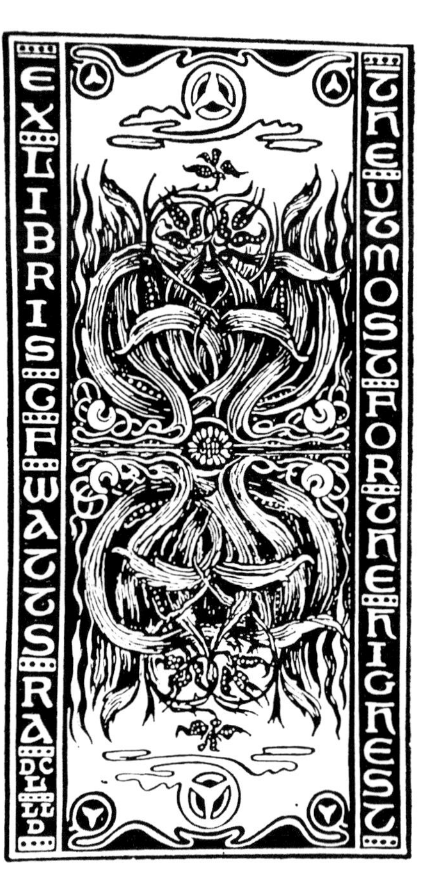

EX LIBRIS G F WATTS RA DCLLD
THE UTMOST FOR THE HIGHEST

# Contents

# Acknowledgements

MY THANKS ARE DUE TO MANY for generous hospitality and for lending invaluable material in the preparation of this book: to Douglas and Barbara Abraham, James and Olinda Adeane, Julian Agnew, the Earl and Countess of Airlie, Philip Athill, the Duke of Beaufort, Olivier Bell, Anthony Beevor, Martin Beisly, Olivier Bell, the Honourable Mrs Angus Cameron, Celia Clear, Messrs Coutts & Co, Sir Hew Hamilton-Dalrymple, William Dalrymple, Sir Andrew Duff Gordon, the Marchioness of Dufferin and Ava, Simon Edsor, Michael Estorick, Myrna Faber, Nicholas Harris, Julian Hartnoll, James Hervey-Bathurst, Sir Jack Leslie, Samantha Leslie, the Marquess of Lothian, Robin Mackenzie, Rosemary McQuorquedale, Susan Meynell, Julian Morrison-Bell, Lord Neidpath, Lady Angela Nevill, John and Anne Nevill, Mr and Mrs Stephen Norman, Belinda Norman-Butler, the Earl and Countess of Rosebery, Lord St John of Fawsley, John Schaeffer, Tim and Lindy Seago, Anne Sebba, Natalie Stutchbury, the Honourable Mrs Charlotte Townshend, the Viscount de Vesci, the Earl and Countess of Wemyss, the Grosvenor estate, the Viscount Wimborne, the Marquess of Worcester; and remembering kind help from the late Colonel Angus Cameron, Ronald and Teresa Chapman, the Earl of Balfour, John Brandon Jones and William Fredeman.

For their expert advice, I am indebted to: Daniel Briggs, Judith Bronkhurst, Stephen Calloway, John Christian, Alan Crawford, Elizabeth Cumming, Caroline Dakers, Max Donnelly, Richard Dorment, Nicholas Drummond, William Drummond, Colin Ford, Charlotte Gere, Juliet Hacking, Violet Hamilton, Brian Hinton, James Holloway, Martin Hopkinson, Simon Houfe, Alison Inglis, Chris Jordan, Dorothy Logan, Peter Lord, Joanne Lukitsch, Rupert Maas, James More Molyneux, Michael More Molyneux, Peter Nahum, Charles Noble, Richard Ormond, Linda Parry, Simon Reynolds, Jacqueline Ridge, Christopher Ridgeway, Daniel Robbins, Teresa Sladen, Alison Smith, Frances Spalding, Peter Thornton, Hilary Underwood, Michael Vickers, Philip Ward-Jackson, Jon Whiteley, Andrew Wilton, Jo Wisdom, Christopher Wood. Many thanks are due to Jenny Chatwin, Tamsin Evernden, Frank James, Jeanie James, Janet Maclean, Gemma Mason, Virginia Murray, Jane Reid, the Honourable Mrs Jane Roberts, Richard Smout, Jane Wainwright, David Wallington, Leslie Whitelaw. To Michael Barker I am indebted for his expertise with regard to the Continental Symbolists.

My grateful thanks for permission to publish or research from material are owing to: Sir Guy Acland (the papers of Sir Henry Acland); the Earl of Airlie; Balliol College (Benjamin Jowett MSS); the British Museum (letters from Sir Charles Newton); Chris Budgett; the Bodleian Library (the papers of Sir Henry Acland, William Holman Hunt, Sir Charles Newton, John Ruskin, F. G. Stephens and Sir Henry Taylor); the British Library; the Charterhouse archives (Lord Baden-Powell MSS); Trustees of the Chatsworth Settlement (Devonshire MSS); the Churchill Archives Centre (Eustace Smith); Courtauld Institute of Art, Witt Library; Fondation Custodia (Sydney Carlyle Cockerell MSS); Roy Davids (letters to Lady Davey, Harry Quilter and Theresa Sassoon); the Durham University Archives (Earl Grey MSS); Eton College Library (Lady Ritchie MSS); the Syndics of the Fitzwilliam Museum (the papers of Sir Edward Burne-Jones and of Wilfrid Scawen Blunt); Henrietta Garnett (Vanessa Bell archive); Glamorgan Record Office (Bruce family papers); the University of Glasgow (papers of J. A. M. Whistler and J. St. Loe Strachey MSS); the Grosvenor Estate (Sir Charles Dilke MSS); Hatfield House Library (Salisbury MSS); Hereford and Worcestershire Record Office (the papers of Julia Cartwright and Brian Hatton); the Hon. Simon Howard (the Castle Howard archive); the Huntington Library; the John Murray archive; King's College, Cambridge (Ashbee MSS); Leeds University Library (Sir Edmund Gosse MSS); Lincolnshire Archive (Tennyson MSS); the London Metropolitan Archive and the Ilchester estate (Holland House MSS); Leighton House Museum and the Royal Borough of Kensington and Chelsea (papers of Walter Crane, Lord Leighton and Linley Sambourne); University of Manchester, John Rylands Library (Marion Spielmann MSS); the Metropolitan Museum of Art, New York (papers relating to the 1884–85 Watts retrospective and *Love and Life*); the Honourable Society of the Middle Temple; Henry Moore Institute (the papers of Sir Alfred Gilbert and Sir William Hamo Thorneycroft); the National Portrait Gallery (G. F. Watts MSS); the National Trust (Ellen Terry MSS); the Royal Academy (Lord Leighton diaries); the Royal Archives (letters from the Viscount Knollys); Harry Ransom Humanities Research Center, The University of Texas, Schaffer Library Collection; the Tate archive; Trinity College, Cambridge (Myers MSS); Union College Schenectady; Victoria and Albert Museum (Henry Cole and G. F. Watts MSS); William Morris Museum (Mackmurdo MSS); Beinecke Rare Book and Manuscript Library, Yale University. I am indebted to the Paul Mellon Centre for Studies in British Art and the Marc Fitch Fund for generous assistance towards the cost of photographs and indexing.

I should like to thank also Gillian Malpass, Sandy Chapman and Sarah Faulks; Elizabeth Mallard-Shaw; the staff of the Art and Archive of Design, the National Art Library, the Heinz Library at the National Portrait Gallery, the Royal Academy archives and Emma Dennis; and especially Richard Jefferies, the curator of the Watts Gallery, for his constant support, guidance and humour.

Finally, to my family, thank you for all your help: to Charles Sebag-Montefiore, Harold Sebag-Montefiore, Colin Franklin, Ian and Jennifer Glynn and Hazel Carner; and to my mother, Cindy and James, this is for you.

# Foreword

As the Victorian age slowly recedes from us into more distant history, some of its great figures are curiously diminished by the widening gulf, while others are enlarged or brought into sharper focus. Hindsight makes it somewhat easier to determine their true stature, but anyone attempting to assess George Frederic Watts today is faced with peculiar difficulties. Though coming from modest origins, Watts was, by the time of his death, known and revered throughout the world. The inscription in a specially bound copy of Baron von Schleinitz's monograph of him, given to Mrs Watts reads:

> In memoriam of Mr George Frederic Watts OM RA,
> The immortal Master and one of the greatest,
> kindest and best men of all times.

The hundreds of obituaries of Watts read more like hagiographies, and it is tempting to scoff and conclude that no one could have been so good, kind and dedicated. Many have scoffed, and continue to do so, even though the fashion for deriding everyone and everything Victorian has waned.

Could so many of his contemporaries have misread him? Watts had his faults – he was human – but the most often repeated words, 'dedication to his art', 'simplicity', 'kindnes and generosity' make it seem that von Schleinitz's assessment of the man was right.

What then of Watts the artist? He is an isolated figure in English painting: a member of no group. Over-praised by his friends and savaged by his critics, he stands alone, though buttressed by his high principles and his desire to elevate art from the morass of triviality into which he found it sunk at the beginning of his career. Even his most ardent admirers must admit that the quality of his work is uneven. No one could paint, as he did, for seventy-five years without sometimes failing to reach the high standards he set himself. It is, however, his unevenness, his desire to advance the ideas of art, and his willingness to risk failure that make him so much more interesting than so many of his contemporaries who settled for a life of comfortable and lucrative mediocrity.

With much painstaking research Veronica Franklin Gould has extracted the man and his art from the clouds of malice and ignorance that have swirled about him for so long, and what emerges across the gulf that now separates us from the Victorian age, despite his small stature, is a kindly, gentle giant.

*Richard Jefferies*

# Prologue

If any artist can be said to epitomize the great reforming era of Queen Victoria, it is George Frederic Watts. A self-made man with a vision, Watts forged his way against the barbs of authority, fashion and controversy to raise the tone and status of British art, and the aspirations of the world. He provided the nation with penetrating portraits of leading thinkers, statesmen and reformers, crusaded for social and educational reform, and invented a dynamic visual language to arouse, elevate and ultimately provoke his countrymen through art. His transcendental paintings addressing the condition and progress of humanity were controversial; idealized nude figures, derided by prudes, impressed the French; his abstract surface looked, and often was, unfinished. But the magnitude of his ideas captivated viewers around the globe. Not all his compositions worked, but, 'When a man like Rembrandt or Watts paints either a portrait or a vision,' wrote one critic, 'he removes it to a sphere beyond the reach of mere physical sensation.'

As the pioneer of Symbolist Art in Britain, Watts's ambition to decorate public buildings with inspirational Michelangelesque frescoes was too avant-garde for the establishment. Nevertheless, championed by the young Ruskin as 'the only real painter of history or thought we have in England', he resolved to pursue his unique vision – painting monumental metaphysical pictures of Time, Life, Love, Death, destined for the nation. In addition to the two national series and his portrait commissions, Watts painted visionary landscapes, mythological works and, moved by the terrible poverty in London and Ireland, a key series of haunting social realist pictures. His bust of *Clytie* heralded the New Sculpture movement. No one could sway Watts from his ideals, and when full recognition came at last with the landmark opening of the Grosvenor Gallery in 1877, where he exhibited *Love and Death* – a theme he was to explore for the rest of his life – his influence spread across the Continent and to America. Such was the interest in Watts that his pictures formed the first large retrospective exhibitions devoted to a living artist held in England and at the Metropolitan Museum of Art in New York.

Seen as 'the old master in the modern man', Watts infused his paintings with poetry, musical harmony and the finest qualities of earlier masters – the form and drapery of Phidias, the painterly manner of Titian, and the monumental grandeur of Michelangelo's frescoes. Although his work reflects the age of Thomas Carlyle, John Ruskin, Charles Darwin, and the poet laureate, Alfred, Lord Tennyson, and discerning collectors hung his pictures in their Arts and Crafts houses, Watts stood apart as an artist, his haunting, almost supernatural style bypassing the constraints of his Pre-Raphaelite friends. At exhibition, his pictures were quite different: rather than glittering, they glowed. His portraits, as Tennyson famously recorded in verse, mirrored the minds of their subjects; and aristocratic young sitters felt immortalized by his brush.

Having derided his imaginative works, the Royal Academy suddenly nominated him as an associate. Uniquely, they then fast-tracked him into full membership within the year, which he accepted only after pressure from his greatest friend, future Academy president and fellow Olympian, Frederic Leighton. Though similarly inspired, their personal character and style of painting were very different. Watts did not seek what he saw as the cold perfection of Leighton's painting; he intended his pictures to be suggestive, ethereal. And whereas Leighton was firmly against art with a moral message and attacked the idea in a presidential discourse, Watts painted increasingly didactic pictures against the evils of greed, cruelty, prostitution and idleness, and images to promote progress for the twentieth century. Life was not easy, Watts demonstrated, nor should it be straight and narrow; but with justice as its mainspring it could be led by tenderness and love 'up the steeps of human conditions, the path from the baser existence to the nobler region of thought and character'. *Love and Life*, a frail nude maiden climbing the rocky path of life, was his message to the age. In this Watts sought to engage the viewer's imagination; sexual arousal was not what he had in mind. So when the Women's Christian Temperance Union protested against the hanging of this 'vulgar' picture in the White House they found themselves the subject of press ridicule.

Despite delicate health and what many saw as a reclusive lifestyle, Watts led a vigorous, colourful life. Beautiful, exuberant young women, soldiers, poets, painters and statesmen, drawn to his intellectual conversation and his aims for art and the nation, streamed into his studios at Little Holland House in Kensington and at Limnerslease, in Compton, Surrey. A visitor to Freshwater, Isle of Wight, seeing him in the company of Tennyson and the photographer Julia Margaret Cameron asked, 'Is nobody commonplace?' He had a keen sense of humour, and his warm friendships – whether these were with the great and the good or with his assistant sculptor – were enduring. Married female confidants felt special in his company and allowed him to make studies from their limbs, and aristocratic women misbehaved in his studio, but there appeared to be no hope of marriage until the teenage actress Ellen Terry burst upon the scene. Their brief union, scandalous in its break-up, yielded an enduring love affair on canvas; and the ravishing nude pictures upon which he subsequently embarked drove the statesman William Gladstone to distraction.

To counter the misery of the machine age, Watts was determined to awaken the poorest in the land to appreciate beauty, art and thought. With his second wife, Mary Fraser Tytler, the Scottish artist–craftswoman whom he married in 1886, he was a leading figure in the craft revival movement. He campaigned for educational reform and broader national reforms, and he addressed his art to the cause, for he believed that art should unite mankind and inspire an interchange of ideas between nations. 'I see the past in the present and the present in the future,' he wrote. Whatever his concerns for humanity, the state of the nation, the aspirations of the world, he expressed it in paint, and also, towards the end of his life, in the press. Watts was seen as an artist of exceptional spiritual power, and the letters, journals and memoirs of friends reveal the extraordinary impact this frail man with titanic ideals had on Victorian contemporaries. The equestrian statue *Physical Energy*, a key work of the New Sculpture movement, cast in bronze for the Cecil Rhodes memorial in Rhodesia and reworked within months of his death in 1904 for London's Hyde Park, symbolizes a man at the peak of his achievement, yet impelled to achieve even more – like Watts himself.

# Ascent to Olympus

# 1  Ambitious Young Philhellene

IMAGINATION AND AMBITION, the powerful pioneering forces that would drive Watts to revolutionize art, madden authority and attract brilliant writers, statesmen and exotic women, fermented in the piano-manufacturing workshop of his tormented father. Mr Watts, determined to rise up and make his mark, had left the cabinet-making workshop established by his father George Watts of Hereford, after whom son and grandson were named, and moved up to the capital at the end of the eighteenth century. A fiery inventor, 'George Watts, Pianoforte Maker of London' was a proud man, but clearly struggling when he advertised his 'superior' services for tuning and repairs; his imaginative experiments and desperate quest to perfect an instrument that would combine wind and string, drove him ever deeper into debt.[1] On 28 May 1816, his first wife having died – leaving three teenage children Thomas, Maria and Harriet – George Watts married twenty-nine-year-old Harriet Smith at St Mary-le-Bone parish church. Lovable, delicate Harriet became pregnant straight away.

George Frederic Watts was born above his father's workshop at 52 Queen Street, Bryanston Square, in the early hours one February morning in 1817, two years after the Battle of Waterloo and a month after marble fragments from the Parthenon went on display at the British Museum to stimulate the progress of the fine arts in Britain. Created under the guidance of the Greek master Phidias in the fifth century B.C., the age of Pericles, they had been removed by Thomas Bruce, the seventh Earl of Elgin. The artist Benjamin Haydon, who campaigned for their acquisition by the crown, felt when he first saw them 'as if a divine truth had blazed inwardly upon my mind, and I knew that they would at last rouse the art of Europe from its slumbers in the darkness.' Watts would devote his life to the cause.[2]

After a private Anglican baptism, the St Mary-le-Bone register of baptisms recorded the boy's birthday as the 22 February. Whether this was a simple mistake or evidence of how distracted his father was at this time, he would celebrate his birthday on the date inscribed in the family prayer-book, Sunday 23 February. That he shared the Christian names and birthday of the composer Handel was apposite, though he was named Frederic after his maternal grandfather and favourite uncle. Young George inherited his mother's delicate physique, slight frame and brown eyes, while he owed his Celtic passion to Mr Watts's Welsh forebears.[3] From as early as he could remember, he knew that he would be an artist.

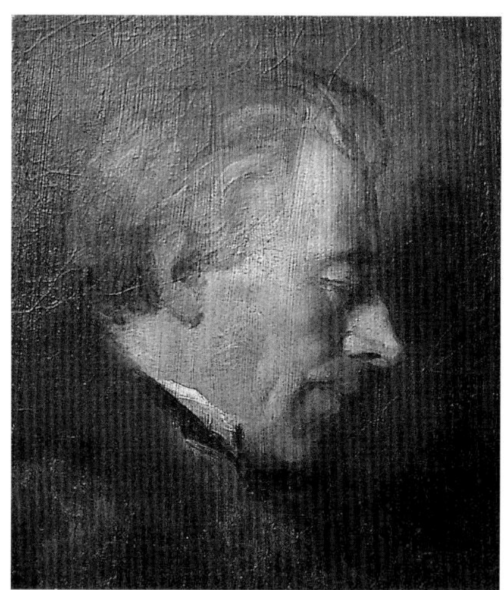

1   The artist's father, George Watts, 1834–36 (Watts Gallery).

Five-year-old George survived a measles outbreak that killed his little brothers William, Frederic and James, and precipitated his mother's death four years later from consumption. His only maternal memory – her slow, sad step – reveals a boy with a keen visual sense, and reflects dark pain and struggle in the Watts household. His father (fig. 1), who had achieved some success and been granted the citizenship of the City of Hereford, fell into decline.[4] Tormented by bereavement, the widower moved his remaining family into a smaller house in Star Street, Paddington. Mr Watts neglected his piano business, and his rages of frustration over unviable inventions created a highly charged atmosphere. Every day George dreaded a crisis. He would remember his father as 'very refined', but not quite sane. Mr Watts was devoted to the boy and taught him to read, but his tantrums caused permanent damage to his son's nerves.[5]

Loneliness and illness clouded George's life. He was brought up as though an only child; his maternal half-sisters, Maria and Harriet, did not share his intellectual, artistic spirit. Attacks of migraine and vertigo forced him to lie flat on his back for days each week and prevented him from going to school. A peculiar mystic sensation when the pain subsided made him feel as though his feet were travelling through space, and left a strangely exhilarating after-effect – even in childhood his imagination took flight. He found company in a pet sparrow, which he trained to perch on his head. One night, however, he caught its head in the cage door and to his horror the bird dropped dead at his feet. The shock of killing it haunted him for years and would underlie his artistic leitmotif of birds or feathers to symbolize Innocence.[6]

Being kept apart, deprived of competitive school activities, conscious that he looked young for his age, that he had not achieved as much as he should, and, doubtless affected by the dire state of affairs at home, spurred his ambitions. George turned to the only household luxury, his father's library, where he enjoyed Sir Roger L'Estrange's *The Fables of Aesop and other Eminent Mythologists, with Moral Reflections*, the seventeenth-century chivalric legend of *The Seven Champions of Christendom*, the Old Testament stories, and the more recent novels of Jane Austen and of Sir Walter Scott. Knights on horseback and adventures of the Greek gods and goddesses of *The Iliad* fascinated him; he made sketches of them, imagined Athene in his room 'bearing the holy aegis that knoweth neither age nor death' and the young philhellene dreamed that he too would become – through art – an aegis-bearer of the ageless language of the human mind.[7]

Sundays in his strict Sabbatarian home were dreary. Over and again he copied plates from the huge Queen Anne prayerbook. One showed the eye of the Deity: 'a realistic eye, large in the sky – from which a ray of light, solid as metal, streams upon the head of Guy Fawkes, who with his lantern is going about his evil business.' Shocked by a black-robed priest threatening wrath to come, his respect for religious teachers snapped when he read of a man who, having forgotten to read the Bible to his children, suddenly remembered, and as he reached for the book, fell back dead. If this was the hand of God, George would have none of it. Never again would he trust narrow formalized religion.[8]

He was a popular boy; playmates looked forward to his joining in their games, and as he ran out to play, he would chalk graffiti of horses on walls and gateposts[9] – the urge to decorate buildings was even then irresistible. His father, who dabbled in watercolour, recognized George's superior gifts, and dated and preserved his drawings; by 1827, within a year of his wife's death, Mr Watts had arranged, through a Hanoverian piano-manufacturer, for the ten-year-old to be apprenticed to William Behnes (later, Sculptor in Ordinary to Queen Victoria). George would informally – as he put it – 'haunt' the sculptor's studios at 91 Dean Street, Soho.[10] He studied anatomy, made outline compositions in chalk and pen, and produced monumental head studies, their sculptural form foreshadowing his mature paintings. For fine detailed studies, he learned to use silverpoint – an indelible stylus drawn on prepared paper; he worked on stone, copied engravings and etchings from Raphael, Rembrandt, Rubens, Charles Lebrun's *Espressions des Passions de l'Ame*, Greuze and Hogarth and *The Archangel Uriel and Satan*, from Milton's *Paradise Lost*. He recreated *A Lion and Tiger, Fighting*, twice the size of George Stubbs's enamel,[11] and experimented with clay. William Behnes's life outside the workshop was thoroughly dissolute; in the evenings his crippled brother Charles, a miniature-painter, introduced George to liberal intellectual thought, to the works of Shakespeare, Virgil and Ossian, and gave him his first lesson in oil painting. His copy of a portrait head of a lady by Sir Peter Lely, painted at thirteen, is an astounding testament to Watts's natural instinct for form and use of colour.[12]

Too young to notice the death of King George III, he would always recall the death of George IV in June 1830. *The Times* reflected the mood of the country in its attack on the king's 'reckless, unceasing and unbounded prodigality . . . the tawdry childishness of Carlton House and the mountebank Pavilion, or cluster of pavilions at Brighton.' King William IV, welcomed with open arms, would never equal his brother's enlightened patronage of literature, science and the arts, as the president of the Royal Academy, Sir Martin Archer Shee, discovered when his application to attend the funeral was refused. Sir Walter Scott's 'whole day of pleasure was dampd by the news of [the] King's death.' Haydon mourned the loss of 'my sincere Admirer . . . had not his wishes been perpetually thwarted, he would have given me ample and adequate employment'; a livelier diarist than painter, he added. 'The people the King liked had all *a spice of vice* in their natures . . . There was a relishing sort of abandonment about them.'[13]

George played a precocious royal trick on the Behnes. At home in the large room allotted to him as a studio, he made a flamboyant drawing of Charles I (fig. 2) in the style of van Dyck. He hid his finished picture up the chimney to let soot mellow its paint surface and then, pretending that he had stumbled on a seventeenth-century find, showed it to Behnes. The sculptor cast a critical eye over it. 'Well, I would not venture to say that it is by van Dyck, but it certainly is by no mean hand.' When the fourteen-year-old pointed out that behind the moustache and imperial matchstick beard, the face of 'Charles I' was his own self-portrait, Behnes exploded, 'Why the deuce don't you always paint like that?' The painting itself so far as is known has not survived, but the drawing exists. Ingenious boy. It is a clever likeness of both subjects. Throughout his life Watts liked to test the effects of his work, on occasion using humour to mask this serious intent.[14]

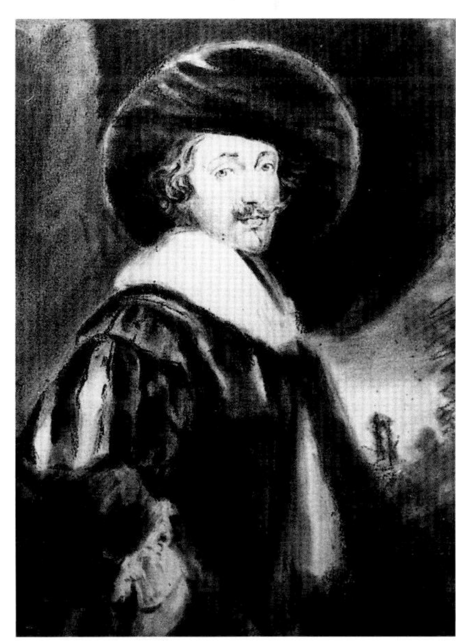

2  *Self-Portrait as Charles I, c.*1830 (Watts Gallery).

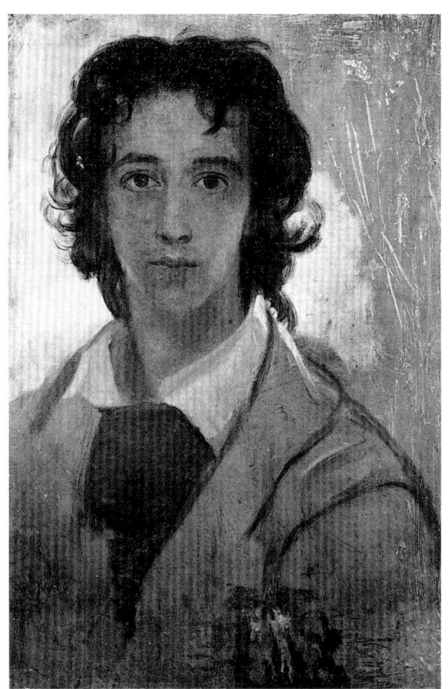

3   *Self-Portrait*, 1834 (Watts Gallery).

At about this time he was walking down the street with his sketchbook, when Haydon tapped him on the shoulder. 'May a fellow student look at your work?' The veteran painter offered encouraging words, advised the teenager to study the Elgin Marbles, and invited him to his studio. Watts did not visit Haydon, but followed his advice. He began to earn his keep, charging five shillings for portraits drawn in the Romantic style on six-inch paper, heightened with red and white chalk. Early sketchbook doodles include a splendid bonneted lady, captioned 'The Pride of the Village', women playing the piano, architecture, cricketers, gambolling children, Spartacus, knights on horseback in terrific battle scenes, all a flurry of muscular bodies, armour, spears, snorting horses.[15]

Such was his ambition that at the age of fifteen he felt overwhelmed with shame that he had not achieved greatness. He disciplined himself to wake with the sun by sleeping fully dressed rolled inside a dressing gown on the floor.[16] That sense of determination and vocation can be seen in an informal self-portrait, an oil sketch showing the seventeen-year-old with long Byronic hair, poetic face and huge, brown eyes (fig. 3). Freely painted on used canvas, the face – in shadow against a background of light – and the luminosity of the skin indicates a gentle, receptive nature and potential to capture the inner quality of other sitters, as in a portrait of his sixty-year-old father.[17] George's eloquent characterization of the still dignified, troubled man, so impressed Behnes that he hurried round to Star Street to congratulate Mr Watts on his son's first noteworthy portrait. The proud father took his son's portfolio to the president of the Royal Academy. 'I can see no reason why your son should take up the profession of art,' opined Archer Shee. Doubtless, the slim chances of success in an over-crowded profession made father and son ever more determined. Looking back, the artist appreciated how his father 'had allowed me to have my way & go on drawing when I ought to have been supporting him', which by now he was beginning to do.[18]

George Watts entered the Royal Academy Schools at Somerset Palace as a probationer on 8 January 1835 and qualified as a full student on 29 April. But, obliged to draw only from antique casts, not from life, he found the teaching unconstructive. The Keeper William Hilton singled out Watts's drawing as an example to fellow students and, when he failed to win a medal, crossed the floor and whispered, 'Never mind, you ought to have had it!' Yet he discouraged imaginative work and the schools' closure during exhibitions – for almost half the year – delayed opportunities to pass into the life-drawing class. Watts's first-recorded symbolic picture, *Undine*, which he began at this time, shows the spirit of the waters, created without a soul, turning away from the viewer. Disillusioned by the Academy, he played truant and chose to learn instead from the Elgin Marbles and would thereafter judge his own compositions according to the poetic lines, curves and drapery of Phidias.[19]

Watts studied anatomy at the Royal College of Surgeons and hired a male model for muscle action;[20] the latter, however, played little part in an extraordinary commission proposed that year by one of his sitters. The radical MP John Roebuck asked him to draw a portrait of the late Jeremy Bentham, from his Auto-Icon, 'a wax figure, which was so far curious that it covered, I believe, the philosopher's bones, and was dressed in his clothes.' Bentham had bequeathed his body to be embalmed by the College of

Physicians. Working from his Auto-Icon, in which he sits in a wideawake hat, cutaway coat, stiff gloved hands over his knees – preserved today at University College London – Watts gave him with a quizzical expression, raising one hand on to his Dapple stick, as *Jeremy Bentham in an Imaginary Landscape* (fig. 4).[21] This was a curious distraction from home troubles, concern for his father, pressure to provide for the family (Thomas having married and set himself up as a piano-manufacturer), and the ever-present obstacle of his own precarious health. He painted a small picture of a Christ-like kneeling figure, probably himself, alone and deep in prayer; while a distant grey streak glows in the wake of the dying sun, the silver shaft of light beaming over his bowed head, 'an inward vision . . . being revealed'.[22]

The dawn of the Victorian era saw the advance of Watts's career. A sense of aim and aspiration enhances the muscular power of cricketing lithographs he produced in 1837 for Nicholas 'Felix' Wanostrocht, then owner of Alfred House boys' school in Blackheath (fig. 5). The commission may have been instigated by George Watts Senior, who on occasion came to meet Felix's brother, a similarly unsuccessful inventor. While the two men paced the grounds exchanging frustrated visions, young batsmen honed their skills against the headmaster's 'Catapulta' – a novel contraption that inspired modern bowling machines – and the artist worked on a sport he grew to love. Belatedly experiencing the joys of school life, sporting companionship and choral singing, he seized the opportunity to further his education, studying French, Italian and Greek (he later taught himself German) and voice training. At work in his studio, he would often sing in a light tenor voice, which lowered when he spoke. The lithographs of Felix demonstrating *Leg Volley*, *Play*, *The Cut*, *The Draw* and *Forward*, dedicated to the Marylebone Cricket Club, were published to acclaim in July. Fuller Pilch and Alfred Mynn posed for *The Batsman* and *The Bowler*, and all seven lithographs illustrated Wanostrocht's classic *Felix on the Bat*.[23]

That spring, on Behnes's recommendation, the Greek merchant Alexander Constantine Ionides came to Watts's studio. His father, Constantine Ioannou Ipliktzis, had been painted by the fashionable painter Samuel Lane, and he wanted a copy of the portrait for the Senate Hall at the University of Athens. Ipliktzis, a textile trader, had rebuilt family fortunes in London after the Greek War of Independence and was famous for endowments to schools, universities and hospitals in Athens and Constantinople. Alexander Ionides (his surname adapted from the original Ipliktzis), had taken over the family firm and developed a thriving business in Manchester. Watts's decision to make the copy, even without permission to see the father, served him well, for the Greek preferred his ten-pound copy to the sixty-three-pound original. Ionides's unusual choice staggered friends, but, endorsed by the Rothschilds' valuer, Du Roveray, Watts's efforts led to enduring family patronage: he would paint five generations.[24]

The private view of the Royal Academy Summer Exhibition on 28 April, attended by the king and Princess Victoria shortly before his death and her accession to the throne, marked the start of the London Season. The Academy had moved into the National Gallery building in Trafalgar Square, where the twenty-year-old artist exhibited for the first time beside British masters, J. M. W. Turner, Sir David Wilkie, Sir William Beechey, Edwin Landseer and William Etty. He showed two female portraits: notably

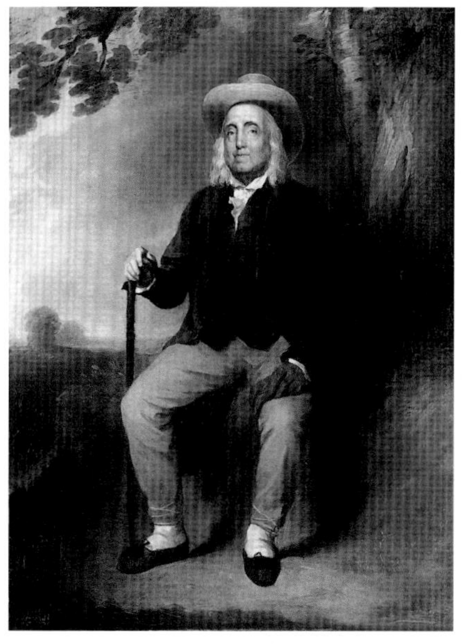

4　*Jeremy Bentham*, 1837 (Watts Gallery).

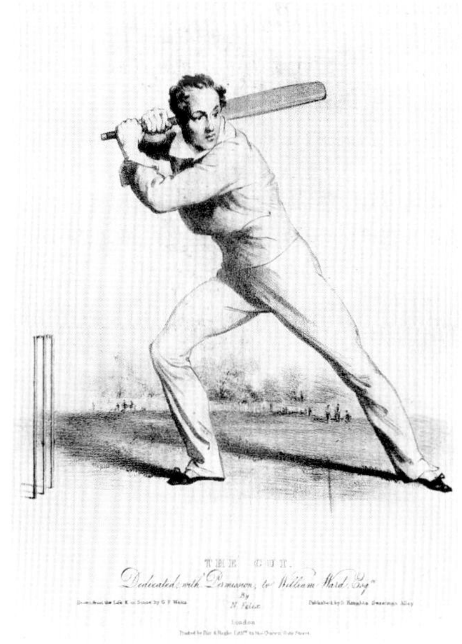


5　Felix Wanostrocht demonstrating 'The Cut' in 1837, illustrated in *Felix on the Bat*, 1845 (Watts Gallery).

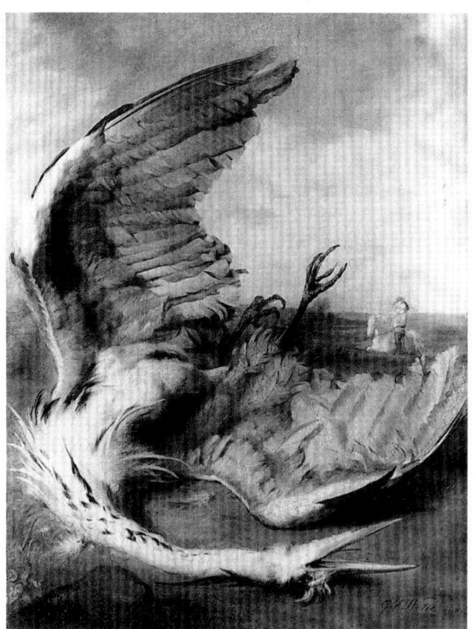

6   *The Wounded Heron*, 1837 (Watts Gallery).

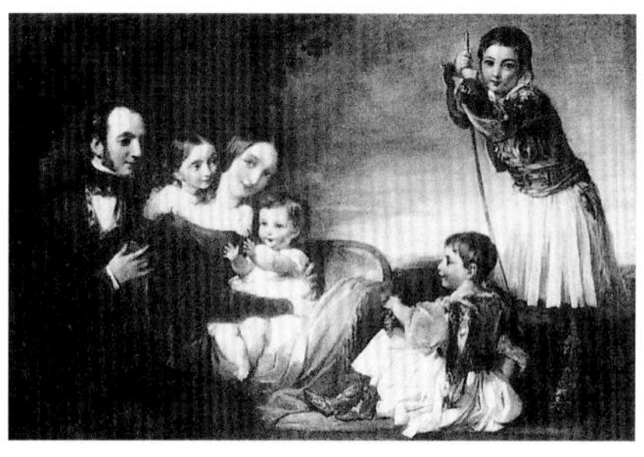

7   *The Ionides Family*, painted at Tulse Hill. From left: Alexander; his daughter, Aglaia; his wife, Euterpe; and sons, Alexander, Luke and Constantine (photo: Frederic Hollyer).

*Little Miss Hopkins*, a golden-haired, eight-year-old fingering a coral necklace; and a poignant painting, *The Wounded Heron* (fig. 6). Struck by the plumage of a dead heron hanging at a poulterer's, he had taken the bird back to his studio at 33 Upper Norton Street, Fitzroy Square, and painted it as though still alive but dying. Its silver-grey outstretched wings fill the canvas. Watts's sense of movement, observation and feeling for nature, especially in the soft, splayed neck feathers, is notable. Painted in the manner of Landseer, the heron lies on its back, the neck and open beak across the bottom, while overhead in a very English blue sky hovers a falcon, itself pursued by a huntsman on horseback below, showing the vulnerability of life in the face of violence and cruelty – as G. K. Chesterton put it, 'the pathos of dying and the greater pathos of living.' *The Wounded Heron* sold for ten pounds. The earliest known example of his preoccupation with themes of Life and Death and cruelty to birds, it was a subconscious echo of his father's anguish, but also reflected his interest in the sport of falconry.[25]

Richard Jarvis commissioned thirteen family portraits and equine paintings, among them, *The Hawking Party*, in which Watts appears leading the horse. A caricature of a distraught, long-haired, frock-coated suitor, drawn on a letter, suggests his affection for Miss Jarvis. He painted group portraits of the children of Andrew Offley Shore and William Bagshawe in Derbyshire, of Major Charles Hamilton's family and a young sculptor, John Whichelo, whose portrait attracted attention at the Academy in 1840. Whichelo brought him commissions to paint a Miss Galenga and her friend Isabella Jardine, who gave him an introduction to the Countess of Gainsborough. That year, too, Watts had a prized picture in progress of Mary Kirkpatrick Brunton standing in a fur-trimmed robe and bonnet.[26]

A hurried scrawl in the artist's tiny sketchbook notes travel instructions: 'by the Tulse Hill and Norwood omnibus from the Green Man Hill Oxford Street'. Ionides, who had moved to Tulse Hill, commissioned large group portraits (fig. 7). He posed with his wife, Euterpe, their daughter, Aglaia, baby Alecco and their elder sons, Constantine and Luke, in Greek costume, descendants of the culture never far from the artist's mind. Watts returned again and again to paint members of the brown-eyed Ionides family. Ipliktzis sat himself; his wife Mariora appears in a red and green turban, striped skirt, fur-trimmed bodice and with a splendid wart on her forehead.[27]

Expressing interest in allegory, Watts copied Angelica Kauffman's *Fame Adorning the Tomb of Shakespeare*, owned by the Marquess of Exeter, though his exhibition pictures at the Academy and the British Institution were largely portraits and literary subjects from Homer, Ovid, Boccaccio and Shakespeare. He moved from studio to studio among aspiring artists and Academicians in Clipstone Street, Fitzrovia, until in 1841 he acquired a purpose-built studio in the garden of 41 Robert Street, Hampstead Road. Here he embarked on a monumental work.[28] On 25 April 1842, the Royal Commission of the Fine Arts announced a competition for life-size fresco cartoons celebrating British achievements, scenes from English history or literature, ten to fifteen feet wide, to be exhibited at the new Palace of Westminster.[29] As head of the Commission, the Queen's consort, Prince Albert, was closely involved with the project, which was intended to stimulate a national taste for art.[30]

As a project of this scale required detailed preparation and would restrict possible earnings from portraiture, Watts made a heady proposal to Ionides, asking for a lifetime's annual allowance of three hundred pounds in return for all his work – he was painting a radiant vision of the goddess of Dawn, *Aurora*.[31] Ionides agreed to support him for the present, but rejected the youthful, short-sighted request, anticipating a successful future for the artist. A grand double portrait of Ionides' sisters, Euphrosyne at the piano with Katherine singing, suggests the musical spirit that would infuse his painting, though half a century later he would dismiss it as a potboiler and regret having to sign it. Five-year-old Luke's tutor Theophilus Kairis looked like an ancient Greek philosopher; as he was reluctant to pose, the artist had a cheval glass brought into the schoolroom at Tulse Hill, and painted from his reflection.[32]

Watts, while painting a group of the Earl of Gainsborough's children, chose to depict a defiant captive chieftain, for his Westminster cartoon, *Caractacus Led in Triumph through the Streets of Rome*. The British chieftain had been defeated on the Welsh border – a morning's ride from the Wattses of Hereford. A lion the artist had seen in the zoological gardens, throwing back its head, gave him the inspiration for the defensive pose of Caractacus, towering over the Romans. Watts, looking to the Italian old masters, transformed the humiliating march into one of glory. The 140 cartoons exhibited in Westminster Hall – the only substantial medieval building to survive the fire which had destroyed most of the original palace in 1834[33] – aroused enormous interest. Awards were announced at the private view on Saturday 1 July 1843. *Caractacus* won a top prize worth three hundred pounds (almost twenty thousand in today's currency), also awarded to Charles West Cope's *The First Trial by Jury* and to *Caesar's First Invasion of Britain* by Edward Armitage, who had enrolled at the Academy at the same time as Watts, but had left to train in Paris, where he was now chief assistant to Paul Delaroche, working on his mural *The Hemicyle*. There was no prize for Haydon, who had seen the competition as the summit of his crusade for public murals.[34]

The exhibition opened to the public on 3 July (fig. 8). A fifteen-year-old art student was exhilarated by the cartoons: to Dante Gabriel Rossetti, the prize-winners' youth disproved 'the vile snarling assertion that British Art is slowly but surely falling, never more to rise'. He admired *Caractacus* above all. A model told him that Watts had promised to pay three times the going rate for modelling fees if he won a prize, but otherwise, as sole provider for his family, he could afford to pay nothing: 'The model will now reap a rich harvest.'[35] Caractacus rose above misfortune, according to the Roman historian Tacitus, 'not a

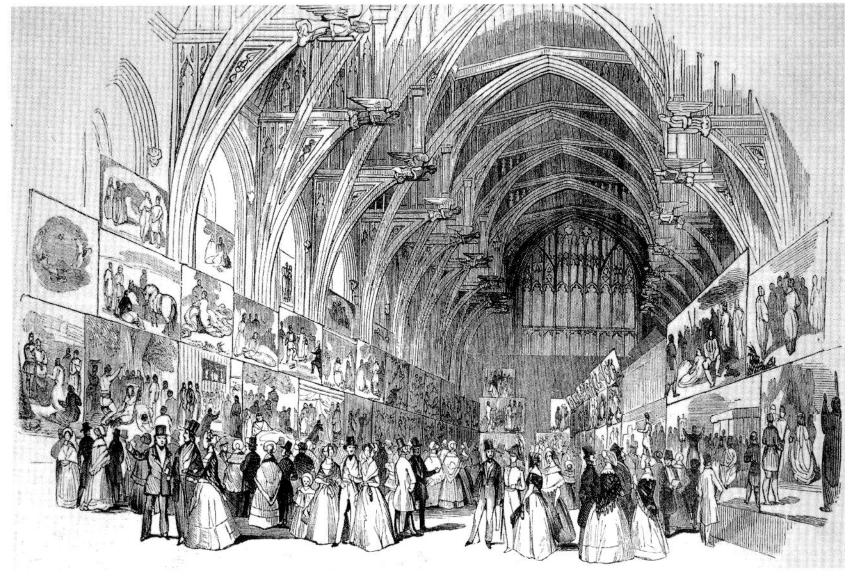

8  Exhibition of Cartoons at Westminster Hall (*Illustrated London News*, 8 July 1843).

symptom of fear appearing, no sorrow, no condescension, he behaved with dignity in ruin.' Reviewing Watts's first public achievement, the *Illustrated London News* recognized in the tall, grim figure of Caractacus the air of a conqueror.[36]

The people of Wales took Watts to their heart, yet, like Armitage, he faced nationalist criticism. For the first time he tasted the power of press controversy. The *Athenaeum* critic, happy enough with the 'highly creditable' composition of *Caractacus*, objected to the subject. 'A British captive led in triumph to "make a Roman holiday"! – Would the Delaroches and the Delacroix adorn their *Palais de Justice* with Napoleon dying under the eyes of the English sentinels!' However, the critic concluded, Watts's references to Sir Joshua Reynolds, Raphael and a trumpeter from Annibale Carracci's *Triumph of Bacchus* in the Farnese Palace in Rome, 'show taste and reading, and as such, bind us over to respect and "good construction".' [37]

Watts's ambition to tread in the footsteps of the old masters and to emulate their greatness was fuelled by an iron sense of purpose.[38] Determined never to fall into debt as his father had, he deposited the prize money in a new bank account with Messrs Coutts & Co on 14 July. The artist gave fifty pounds to his family and withdrew expenses for travel to Florence. He commissioned a childhood friend Charles Couzens to paint a watercolour and full-sized oil version of *Caractacus*, finished by himself, and arranged to sell the cartoon. As he was leaving for the Continent, he was persuaded to release it into a group sale to be exhibited with all eleven prize-winners in the provinces; albeit at a fraction of his negotiated fee, the travelling exhibition and press coverage would enhance his reputation. Watts had proved his ability to paint for and stimulate the British public. The 1843 Palace of Westminster award marked a pivotal advance that opened the door to prestige, fame and fortune.[39]

# 2 Florence

IN EARLY SEPTEMBER 1843 the idealistic twenty-six-year-old artist set out
to study High Art in Italy. Excitement carried him over a 'wretched' night
on the steamer to Boulogne and then a sixteen-hour journey by horse-
drawn *diligence* to Paris, where he stopped in the Latin quarter with
Armitage. Determined that one day his work should be considered along-
side the old masters, he argued the merits of masterpieces in the Louvre
with French art students and made watercolour sketches from Titian, Correggio, Giorgione, van Dyck, Rembrandt and Raphael. In tremendous
spirits, he continued the bracing journey to Marseilles. He and his companions on the upper bench behaved uproariously, sang at the tops of their
voices and awoke soaked to the skin after a thunderstorm.[1]

Fellow travellers were intrigued by the famous young painter, so ardent,
yet physically vulnerable. An American stranger offered to lend him
eight pounds (about five hundred pounds today).[2] Watts carried a letter of
introduction to the British minister, but planned only a short stay and was
doubtful about presenting it. 'Why should a young and poor artist want to
bother smart people?' he asked General Robert Ellice, on the steamer to
Leghorn. The general, a Florentine resident, urged him to present the letter
at the British Legation.

From Leghorn, Watts hitched a ride in an open country cart to Pisa.
Delighting in the warm Tuscan landscape, the sunlight and clusters of
purple grapes within hand's reach, he chatted in Italian to the driver. He
made tiny sketches of bulls and peasants in the Tuscan *campagna*,[3] and
from the top of the leaning tower painted watercolours of the ice-blue hills.
A day or two later, he headed for Florence, where towards the end of his
stay, having filled every moment, he met the general in the street. Ellice had
notified the British minister, Henry Fox, fourth Lord Holland, who was
expecting his call.[4] The artist presented himself at the legation in via dei
Serragli, the Casa Ferroni (known today as Palazzo Amerighi) and was
invited to dine on 3 October.[5]

Within a fortnight, the flirtatious Lady Holland, née Lady Mary Augusta
Coventry, the daughter of the Earl of Coventry, was sitting for the first
of many portraits (pl. 1). Her hair coiled at the nape of her neck, she smiled,
arousing her husband's suspicions. Day after day he recorded in his journal,
'My lady sat to Watts', noting with relief on 17 October, 'Mr Watts
improves on acquaintance.'[6] Holland had come to find him 'full of genius
and favourable, without any of the jealous, niggling, detracting vanity of

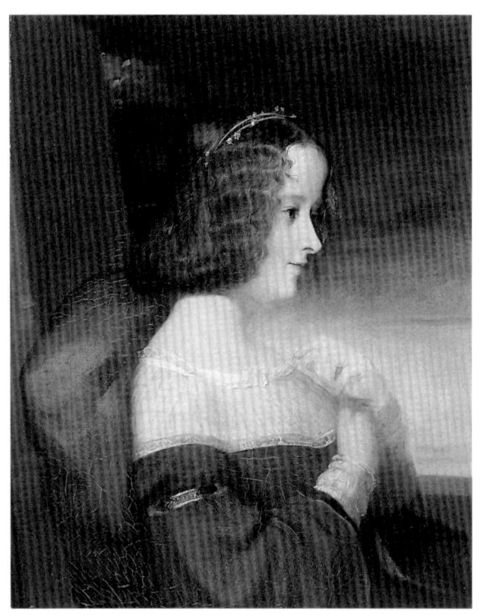

9   *Lady Dorothy Walpole*, 1844–45 (private collection).

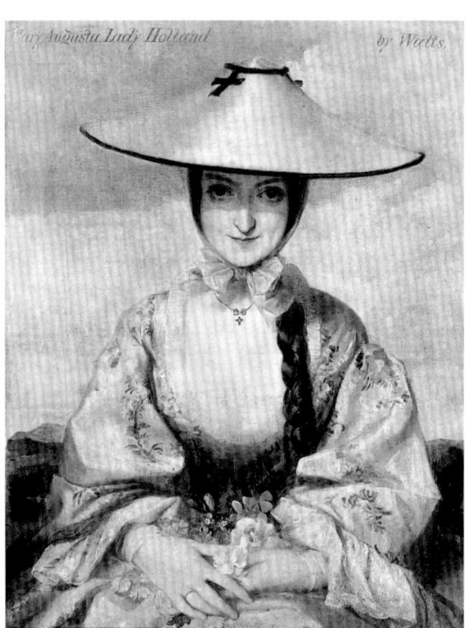

10   *Mary Augusta, Lady Holland*, c.1843 (The Royal Collection, © 2004 Her Majesty Queeen Elizabeth II)

his brother artists . . . I think he will be a great painter in his day.' Lady Dorothy Nevill, née Walpole, daughter of the Earl of Orford, claimed that her portrait predated Lady Holland's – presumably then the first in oil. It is notable as the first idealized portrait set up by Watts and painted in the Grand Manner of the Renaissance (fig. 9). He chose Lady Dorothy's red Venetian-style dress and jewelled armband and painted her against a glowing blue background. The picture completed within three weeks, he signed his name in her hair ribbon. Watts became a regular visitor to the Orfords' Palazzo San Clemente. 'Everyone was so pleased with my picture that our friend Lady Holland determined to follow my example and be painted by the young artist,' Lady Dorothy boasted. 'Her picture, however, was done simply as a portrait whilst mine was more of an idealized study, the dress, pose, everything in fact being Mr Watts's idea.'[7]

Keen to study the art of fresco in Florence, he had to find new lodgings. Lord Holland invited him to the Casa Ferroni in the meantime. On 22 October Watts moved into the hundred-room *palazzo*.[8] Struck by his precarious state of health, the minister insisted he should stay on; and Lady Holland became the first of a succession of rich married women, with obliging husbands, to be magnetized by his charisma and to take responsibility for his health and artistic welfare. The Victorian desire for genius and intellect served Watts well. 'The Great Man is the living light-fountain, which it is good and pleasant to be near,' Thomas Carlyle wrote in *On Heroes, Hero-Worship and The Heroic in History*.[9]

'We not only bind you to us, we chain you,' cried her ladyship, throwing a gold watch and chain around his neck.[10] His life was transformed at the Legation. He painted his hostess on her day bed, decorated a fan for her and drew seductive pictures, even some showing her how she would look as a coquettish old woman. One in particular provoked gossip: in it she wore a wide-brimmed Riviera hat tied beneath her dimpled cheeks, and a voluptuous auburn plait fell over her plunging neckline (fig. 10). 'Ah, nostro Paolo!' exclaimed a guest, a mischievous reference to the adulterous brother-in-law of Dante's Francesca.[11] The artist and Lady Holland were not lovers. His modest breeding and horror of adultery precluded an affair, but he happily accepted his hosts' new nickname 'Fra Paolo', making drawings and a fresco of Paolo and Francesca, seated and embracing, their knees touching.

As the Hollands' High Art protégé, Watts was launched into an aristocratic circle that could never quite be his own, but where he would be the central focus. He acquired social skills, attended balls in borrowed dress, flirted with beautiful women and secretly ridiculed society in a large sketchbook of caricatures: grotesque images of Prince Tommaso Corsini, his brother Don Neri, minister to the Grand Duke, and the pompous Baron Newmann and his wife. But he was caught off-guard by 'an Italian lady of high position' – probably Marianna Ricci[12] – who lured him to her apartment for artistic guidance. Watts saw her as a temptress. Shocked yet attracted, he was 'constantly manoeuvring to avoid situations' and inadvertently provoked one when he handed her a bouquet of flowers and watched horrified as she slipped them into her bosom. On this occasion he was saved by visitors, but he had to return the next day. 'I went as a man goes to a duel & believed myself no match for my adversary,' he would later recall, suggesting the incident as a plot for burlesque. 'With a look &

gesture I shall never forget, the flowers were drawn from their resting place . . . I took them from her hand & flung them into the fire! You may imagine what followed . . . have you ever shot a rapid in an outrigger, or . . . endeavoured to keep your seat on the back of an unbroken thoroughbred!'[13]

The great and the good came to watch the artist create a fresco of *Flora* in the palazzo courtyard.[14] Many sat for portraits, either in oil or drawn delicately in pencil by candlelight, as a record for his hosts – 'I never know my friends until you have painted them,' sighed Lady Holland.[15] Among thirty-four drawings of the Hollands' sparkling coterie were Count Walewski, the natural son of Napoleon, the Papal Nuncio Monsignor Saccone, the Prussian Count Putbus, the Corsini princes, Lord Holland's doctor, Eric Playfair, the composer Giuseppe Verdi and Lord Frederick FitzClarence, the son of William IV and his mistress Dorothea Jordan.[16] Guests felt honoured to be placed beside the artist at the sumptuous dinner table. He cut a dashing figure and had a keen wit: 'Being young, with a profusion of very good hair, a vigorous moustache & imperial – [a wilder image of his 'Charles I'] – my appearance was not against me.'[17] His ascetic diet, drinking only water, which seemed exotic and, to his amusement, encouraged Lord Holland to seek his opinion on a new wine, was probably his means of controlling his health.[18]

Despite his modest manner, the artist clearly sought fame and savoured intellectual conversation with aristocratic sitters. Many became lifelong friends. Francis Charteris MP, the newly married art collector and future Lord Elcho (later, the tenth Earl of Wemyss and March), would recall their friendship and communion in art as 'a joy and solace to me through life'.[19] Watts entered into the spirit of society and when he had had enough – effusive flattery irritated him – he would withdraw to work. A suit of armour was left in his studio after a fancy dress ball. Its symbolic chivalrous qualities appealed to the artist, who painted a self-portrait in the armour, presenting himself with a distinction and vigour that his birth and health denied him (fig. 11). On occasion he would leave the palazzo society to join artists at the Caffé Doney. Here he met the American sculptor Hiram Powers, Seymour Kirkup – both keen spiritualists – and the art dealer William Spence. Kirkup, the leader of the Florentine literary circle, had rediscovered Giotto's fresco of the poet Dante beneath the prison whitewash on the former chapel of the Palace of the Podestà (mentioned in Giorgio Vasari's *Lives of the Artists*) and talked of the night he bribed a jailer to lock him up so that he could trace the fresco.[20]

Lord Holland, noticing how constrained Watts was by his health, took charge of his artistic progress. He sought advice on fresco techniques and arranged magnificent portrait commissions. The *grande dame* of Florence, Napoleon's niece, Princess Demidoff, and her father, the exiled King of Westphalia, sat to Watts. Count Cottrell, a fellow guest at Casa Ferroni and former Chamberlain to the Grand Duke of Lucca, organized a portrait of the grand duke, who quibbled about the price – ('how shabby,' commented Lord Holland)[21] – but awarded the artist the Order of San Lodovico.[22] Major portraits undoubtedly furthered his career. However, the artist grew to despise society commissions, which infringed on his Renaissance studies. Haydon, seething with jealousy, relished his dilemma in a letter to Kirkup: 'That boy Watts . . . went out as the great student of the day. Though he came out for Art, for High Art, the first thing the English

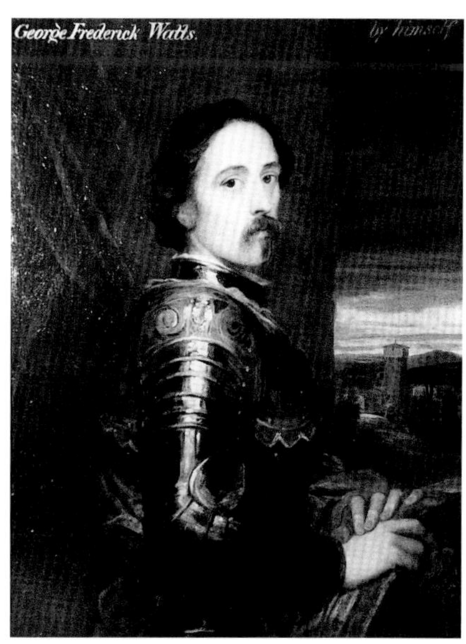


11   *Self-Portrait*, *c.*1843 (private collection).

do is to employ him on Portrait! Lord Holland, I understand, has made him paint Lady Holland!! Is this not exquisite?'[23]

The minister recognized his protégé's 'talent for really fine poetical pictures', but, as he wrote to his mother, 'Who in this age will order them and pay for them, among the few who have sense to hang them up!!?! I like him very much . . . He is very clever, well read, and wonderfully quick and intelligent; but I fear he has not the energy and qualities to ensure his prosperity in the world.'[24]

Watts was more concerned to absorb the finest qualities of the old masters. Like Jacopo Robusti Tintoretto, he aimed to combine the *colorito* of Titian and the Venetian school – the glowing effects of pigment, rather than brilliant colours[25] – with the monumental *disegno* of Michelangelo's frescoes. Less impressed by the latter's sculpture, Watts did admire his wax studies and adopted the technique, modelling figure studies in wax or clay in preparation for paintings. He would have known engravings of the Sistine Chapel when he embarked on a dynamic fresco in the *loggia* of the Hollands' summer residence, the former home of the Florentine rulers at Careggi, on the outskirts of Florence. Built for Cosimo de' Medici, the Villa Medicea, had received the poets and thinkers of the Renaissance, and grand pageants had passed through its gates. Cosimo's grandson Lorenzo the Magnificent, had died there, after being denied absolution by the monk Savonarola.[26] The walls were decorated with Renaissance frescoes and the distinctive golden balls of the Medici insignia. Inspired by the historic setting and less distracted by society, Watts set to work with new-found purpose to recreate in fresco the fate of the doctor who had failed to cure Lorenzo. *The Drowning of the Doctor* shows the Medici attendants' murderous revenge – the doctor drowned in a well (fig. 12).[27] The artist had been so excited by frescoes in the Campo Santo at Pisa – particularly, *The*

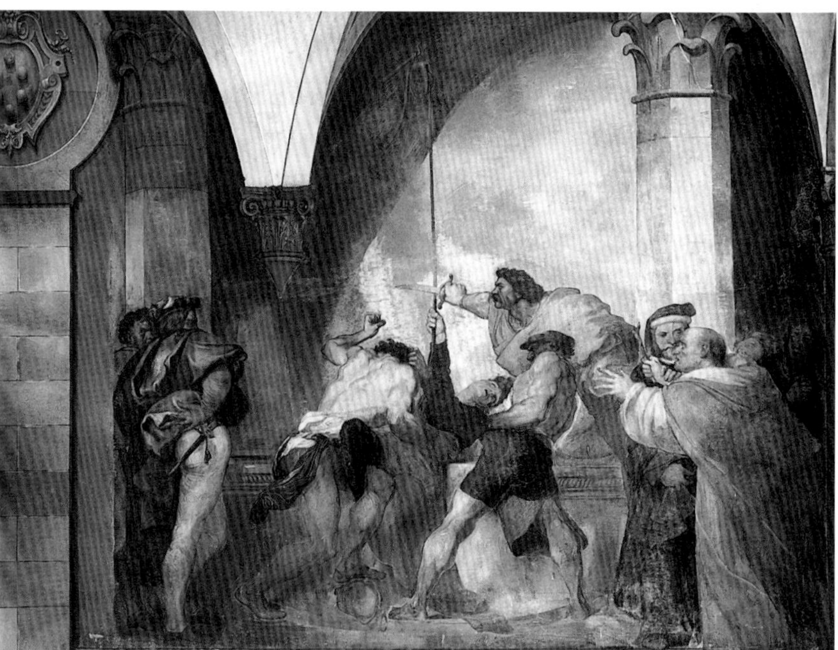

12   *The Drowning of the Doctor*, fresco, 1844–45 (Villa Medicea, Careggi).

*Triumph of Death*[28] – that Lord Holland, fearing anti-climax, postponed their visit to the poorly lit Sistine Chapel in Rome.

One night at Careggi, Watts woke to find himself on the floor, drenched with water, the bed soaked too. As the old manservant carried the bedding out to dry, he knew it could be no practical joke; and yet this ghostly re-enactment of *The Drowning of the Doctor* failed to dampen his ardour. He engaged an assistant named Peters, a model and a *muratore* to help prepare the *loggia* wall.[29]

On Friday, 16 August 1844, after almost a year in Italy, Lord Holland took Watts to Rome. It was a burning-hot day and the nervous minister hurried his impatient protégé round the architectural sights until at last they arrived inside the Sistine Chapel. As the two men looked up, they saw the 'matchless' ceiling illuminated by the evening sun. Both were exhilarated. The minister felt he had never seen the frescoes until that moment.[30] Watts determined to fill a British hall with monumental imaginative frescoes. His enthusiasm for fresco now knew no bounds.

Ideas for a national project would have been on his mind when he accompanied Lord Holland on a brief trip to London. Elizabeth, Lady Holland invited the two men to dinner. To Lord Holland's relief, for the capricious Whig hostess usually intimidated his friends, her ladyship was disarmed by Britain's aspiring Michelangelo.[31] It was during this visit to London that Watts saw his sixty-nine-year-old father for the last time. (Mr Watts's death from bronchitis a year later much affected him.) So distracted was the artist, whether by their meeting or by thoughts for fresco, that on their way back to Florence Lord Holland complained in a letter to his wife that Watts could find nothing better to sketch than a dunghill.[32]

Powerful Michelangelesque *contrapposto* in *The Drowning of the Doctor* emphasized the figures' frenzied violence and disdain – emotions Watts had never before attempted to express – and belied his struggle with the largely forgotten technique of fresco-painting. An even greater struggle for the artist – or rather, his generous host – was financing the project. Portrait commissions in Florence would cover the cost, but Watts made any excuse not to finish them. He pretended to lose his studio key, claimed not to know where the owner lived, vowed to return fees – and 'every possible humbug' until the minister drove him to the studio himself.[33] It was frustrating for both men. Watts, worried that he could not gain access to his London bank account from Italy, was too embarrassed to consult his patron. Lord Holland, observing him at work one day, engrossed but dejected, suddenly realized the problem and offered to act as his banker.[34]

Lady Holland, however, was irritated that their protégé seemed to be letting the side down and felt they should now 'break the spell'. It should be explained that he would be welcomed as a guest, 'but not a constant and *necessary* inmate,' she wrote to her husband in May 1845. 'His idleness will be laid at our door; and we shall be accused of having been the ruin of him, lucky if both of us escape with even so mild a censure.' As George Vivian, a member of the London Committee of Taste and 'an important person for Watts to court' made that very accusation, Lord Holland brought Vivian to Careggi to see the artist finishing *The Drowning of the Doctor*. 'He is just now in the fervour of historical painting', the minister reassured his wife, 'and will not be so unreasonable when the fit of glory and vision of Michael Angelo subside a little'.[35]

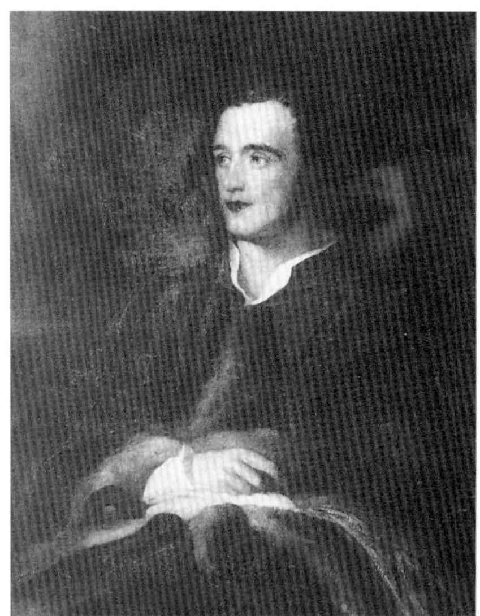

13   *Henry Edward Fox, Fourth Baron Holland*, 1843–45 (private collection; photo: Frederic Hollyer).

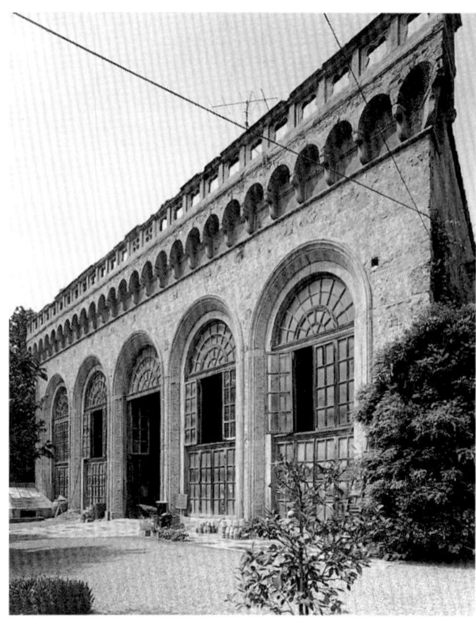

14   The Orangery, Villa Medicea, Careggi (photo: Conway Library, Courtauld Institute of Art, University of London).

A *tête-à-tête* with Watts convinced him of the artist's commitment at Careggi; he had been making landscape studies, and that autumn would be exhibiting at the Accademia dei belli Arti. Lord Holland sat to him in a red domino cloak, holding a black mask, for an informal three-quarter-length portrait (fig. 13), and let his protégé stay on.[36] Watts acquired a horse, to ride and to use as a model. A hundred-foot orangery was converted into a studio (fig. 14), where Charles Dickens noted that the 'shy young English-man' took refuge whenever visitors appeared. The artist would remember him in a splendid *manteau*, dreaming of men in chains.[37] Rather than shyness, artistic passion may have been Watts's distraction, because for the first time he was working from a female model and devoting huge canvases to themes of sexual anguish and desire. Whatever urges aristocratic sitters aroused, propriety forbade the artist to respond. His spirits were aflame after expeditions from the Hollands' villa in Naples, where he discovered the erotic frescoes at Pompeii.[38]

He began to release unspoken, pent-up desires in paint – a knight pur-suing the temptress Fata Morgana (pl. 11), symbol of Fortune or Opportu-nity, to set her prisoners free, and the thirty-foot-wide *Story from Boccaccio* in which the nude Philomena bursts out of the thicket chased by a wounded suitor and mad dogs. His painting of the spurned nymph Echo celebrated the purity and repose of the classical nude. Applying layers of tempera colours before the final oil application gave him greater flexibility over the last two larger canvases.[39] Watts exploited Marianna Ricci's sensuality for his first nude oil painting of the adulterous Paolo and Francesca floating in the dark second circle of Hell; he painted her clothed as Bice Donati, whose beauty so dazzled the medieval Guelph leader Buondelmonte that he abandoned his bride and was killed in revenge; and in a portrait before her marriage to Count Walewski, he luxuriated in her flesh tones, her full red lips, her eyes almost liquid, her shoulders bare above a pure white dress (fig. 15).[40]

Lord Holland resigned as minister in June. He returned to London to take charge of the Holland House estate after his mother's death, deposited a hundred pounds in the artist's bank account (half of which was repaid within a month) and allowed him to stay on at Careggi, where he was nego-tiating to paint a patriotic picture for Greece. In a bold calculated proposal to Ionides, Watts outlined his achievements, stoicism and moral aims: despite acquiring influential friends, he had eschewed riches from portrai-ture for High Art and fame, and painted larger-than-life designs thirty-two feet wide. Given the means, he could create pictures to inspire a nation. He suggested for Greece *Aristides Relinquishing his Right to Command to Mil-tiades*, as a striking moral message that a true hero sacrifices personal honour for the advance of his country. 'Take advantage of my enthusiasm now! I will paint you an acre of canvass for little more than the cost of the materials. Or stay, if you are not rich enough yourself get up a subscrip-tion among your friends.'[41] He would dedicate a year to a picture on the scale of the Raphael cartoons at Hampton Court, with larger-than-life figures on a twelve-by-twenty-foot canvas. Though he had received two hundred guineas for a painting one-tenth the size, of peasants with oxen in the Roman *campagna* (fig. 16), he would charge just two hundred and fifty pounds to cover the cost of models, canvas, colours and part of the studio rental and would donate his services for the privilege of painting for Greece, 'the birthplace of the Arts & Sciences'.

So infectious was his enthusiasm that Ionides, reasonably, asked for a sketch to show subscribers. The artist was indignant. Surely the Palace of Westminster award had established his capability, since augmented by observing the masters of the High Renaissance, with a view to raising art to the level of the age of Phidias? Watts's usual preparation was to make small-scale drawings, composition studies – nude, clothed and Flaxman-style outlines[42] – detailed studies in pencil, ink or watercolour, oil sketches and, for substantial works, a large-scale cartoon in charcoal and water-colour. He would invest such thought into this symbolic composition, the tone, pose and expression of each figure, to achieve elevation of character, purity of design, colour and sentiment, that he saw the request for a dry outline sketch as simplistic and insulting. 'Leave for me to paint for fame to Greece, & you will have no cause to blush for your confidence, or double the amount I named & I will undertake the work as a *commission* and will be guided (as far as reason will permit) by the views of your friends.'[43]

Lord Holland would have been amused, if not proud, to note his powers of negotiation. Even before the subject had been agreed, Watts persuaded Ionides to advance fifty pounds directly to his step-sisters, who were press-ing him for funds.[44] He made numerous preparatory drawings for *Aristides*, deferring an invitation to travel to Cannes to paint Henry, Lord Brougham, the law reformer and founder of London University, so that he could devote all his time to the picture.[45] Lord Holland, having arranged for the widowed Lady Caroline Duff Gordon and her daughters to join the artist, had left Italy in the knowledge that his protégé was negotiating to paint a moral picture of national importance and that the portrait of Brougham, who had defended Queen Caroline[46] and campaigned against the slave trade, repre-sented a positive desire to record 'certainly one of the most remarkable men of the age'. In the event neither project was carried through, but they set the tone and dual direction of Watts's lifelong mission to reinvent High Art for the betterment of mankind.

*     *     *

'Watts drank tea with us!' Lady Duff Gordon, who had been a little ruffled to find an artist occupying the ground floor of the grand Villa Medicea, was astounded that instead of wine he drank water or tea. None the less, she made full use of the artist as art tutor to her daughters and gave Watts his first opportunity to shape and stimulate the minds of albeit aristocratic students. Georgiana, at nearly twenty-eight, was just seven months younger than himself and Alice was twenty-three. That late summer of 1846 at Careggi was a delightful interlude for them all. The ladies arrived on 7 August. Each sat for her portrait and studied in his studio. Lady Duff Gordon, distracted by art and her own efforts to copy his *Bull's Head* – preferring its Italian title *Bove*[47] – did not at first notice Georgy's growing affection for their tutor. When he took them to Hiram Powers's studio, her ladyship was as excited by the sculptor's tall, handsome physique as she was by their private view of *The Greek Slave*, the marble nude that would cause a sensation at the 1851 Great Exhibition.[48] Watts was now experi-

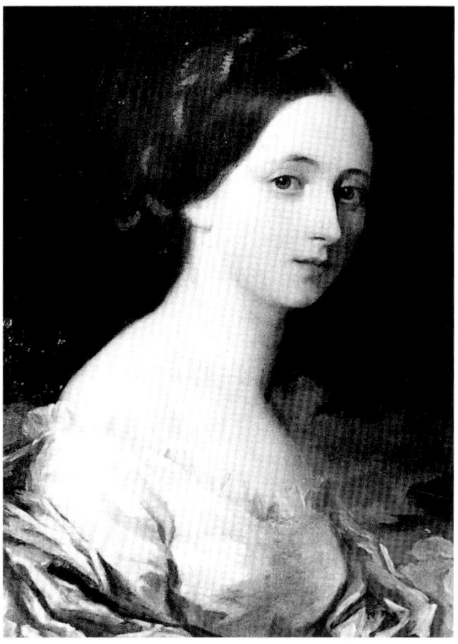

15    *Marianna Ricci*, 1846 (private collection). The portrait was made before her marriage to Count Walewski.

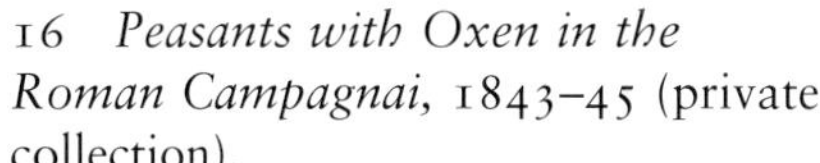

16    *Peasants with Oxen in the Roman Campagnai*, 1843–45 (private collection).

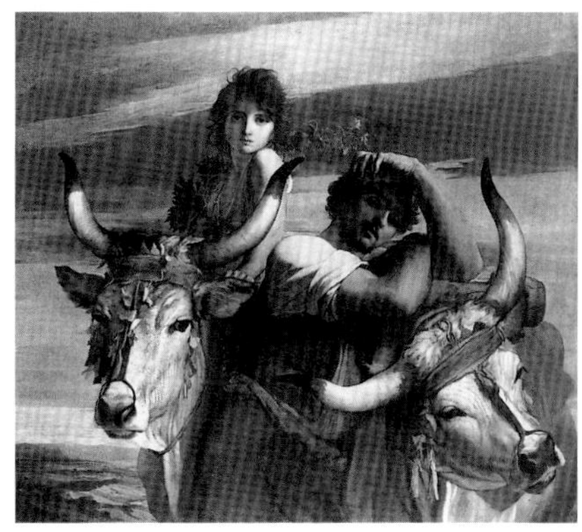

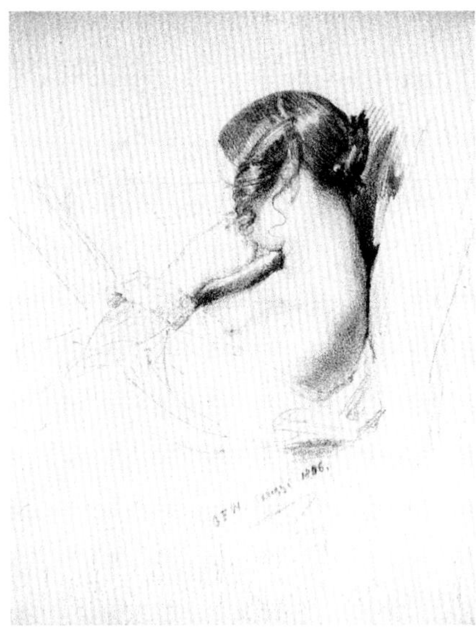

17   *Georgy Duff-Gordon Reading at the Villa Medicea*, 1846 (private collection).

menting in sculpture. Entry after entry in Lady Duff Gordon's journal celebrates his achievements, not least his 'very clever *Medusa* head as large as life', modelled in clay.[49] Proud and possessive, she noted that when sitters arrive from Florence 'we . . . lionized Mr Watts's studio' and 'showed off' his works.[50]

Georgy spent every day with the artist, learning to model clay. He made a cast from her hand and they sang duets to the accompaniment of his guitar. 'Painting, music and modelling entirely occupy our thoughts', his student wrote happily in her journal.[51] She was not an outstanding beauty, but Watts's delicate drawing, the curls at the back of her neck (fig. 17) and the dimple in her cheek, indicate tender feelings for her. He gave her studies for *The First Whisper of Love* – a cherub nuzzling a Grecian shepherd, clearly influenced by the National Gallery's recent acquisition of Correggio's *School of Love*, which he would have seen, and by Rembrandt's *Evangelist Matthew Inspired by the Angel* in the Louvre. Pen-and-ink sketches of Romeo climbing on to the balcony to kiss Juliet may also relate to this time. Disturbed only by a plague of mosquitoes, the couple strolled in the vineyard, watching the moon rise over Fiesole. For the first time Watts was enjoying romantic companionship with a woman sensitive to music, art and poetry and responsive to his teaching. Rather than sycophantic, she was strong-minded, strong enough to recognize the limit of their partnership when her mother suddenly cut short their stay at Careggi. Not only did his modest breeding preclude marriage, but, struggling to support his dependent sisters, he was in no position to provide for an aristocratic wife. Her ladyship allowed the pair one last afternoon alone while she went out with Alice. The next day, 17 November, she swept her family away to Rome, concluding as Georgy put it, 'the three happiest months I ever spent in my life.' The artist composed a farewell duet.[52]

He stayed on at Careggi and planned to spend the winter in Greece until Ionides wrote asking him to change the subject of his large picture. Its negative title may have discouraged subscribers, who could not envisage its heroic treatment in his hands. Though he had devoted much time to its composition, the artist seems to have taken the blow in his stride – in any case, he liked to have a wide range of work on the go and would often alternate in a single hour between five or six pictures, each different in subject and treatment.[53] While Ionides renegotiated, Watts turned his attention to a national work for Britain.[54] He chose a strong patriotic theme for the 1847 Palace of Westminster competition, which this time called for entries in oil; and by 21 December he had made over forty preparatory drawings and completed a small-scale study of England's first naval victory, *Alfred Inciting the Saxons to Resist the Danes*. As Watts started on the heroic twenty-foot-wide, sixteen-figure canvas, he sent Georgy a description, with a lively vignette of himself leaping about the cold orangery studio like 'a *ballerino*' to keep warm and escape swarms of mosquitos – 'Confound them!'[55]

*Alfred* carried greater pressures than he had ever known, for he had to prove that he had maintained and advanced his skills in Italy. That he had not exhibited beside his compatriots at home for four years sapped his confidence. 'Much is expected of me & many think I am losing my train,' he wrote to Ionides, assuring him that once the subject was decided he would complete the Greek picture in the summer.[56] Spurred into decision, on 28

January 1847 his patron proposed *Panthea* from Xenophon's *Cyropœdia*. 'Diavolo! Have you no conscience,' replied the artist. 'Chariots, horses, armies. Why it would cost me fifty pounds in materials & require a year to paint. But it is a fine subject & nobody shall ever accuse me of being mercenary.'[57] Without Lord Holland, Watts again found access to cash in Florence a problem. He carried out the occasional portrait commission – the young Italian tragedienne Adelaide Ristori sat to him shortly before her marriage to the Marquess del Grillo[58] – but he looked to Ionides to ease transfer of funds from his bank account.[59]

'Who the deuce can these be?' the artist wondered when his *muratore* announced the arrival of the millionaire art connoisseur Robert Holford and Reginald Cholmondeley in early March. Lady Duff Gordon's letter of introduction had miscarried; the gentlemen bowed, but their brief, stiff conversation turned into a fervent discussion of art, chiefly Giorgione. The following day he took them to a particularly fine collection. 'Mr Holford will never survive if he does not carry off one of the Giorgiones. He instantly sent to defer his departure from Florence, in the hope of being able to bring about the object he has set his heart upon.' The deed enlivened the moment and would serve him in good stead.[60]

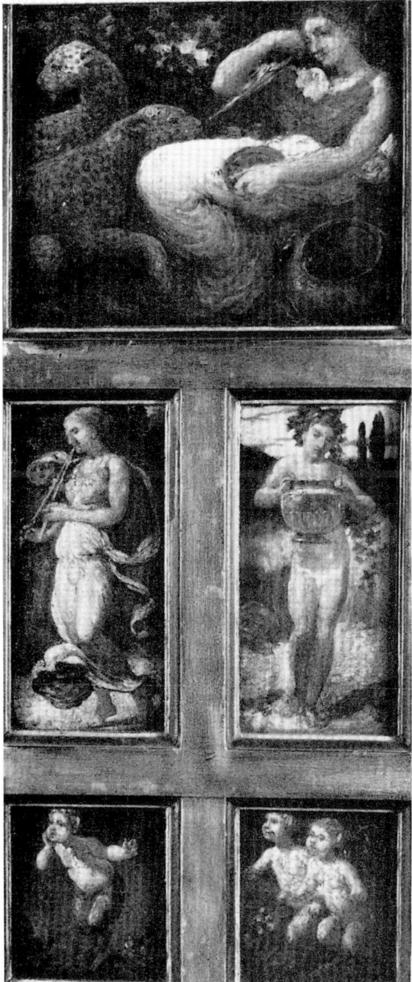

18  The door of Watts's studio in Cambridge Street.

Lonely and restless at Careggi, his aspirations soared one day, plummeted the next. 'My nature is somewhat like that of the hunting leopard,' he confided to Georgy. 'If I miss my coup I lose all spirit to pursue the chase further.'[61] On Saturday, 20 March he arrived unannounced at her door, just as she was composing a letter to him. 'Never was I so thunderstruck,' Georgy wrote in her journal. Breathless entries record an eight-day feast of art and music, devouring frescoes and ancient sculpture, climbing to the top of the Capitol tower and gazing down on moonlit views of Rome. On their last day together, he took her to the studio of Johann Friedrich Overbeck, the leader of the Nazarenes, the influential German artists working in Rome, whom he admired for their revival of monumental fresco. He drew her attention to the outlines of Overbeck's drawings and especially to the cartoon *The Triumph of the Religion in the Fine Arts*,[62] which, like Delaroche's *Hemicycle*, owed much to Raphael's *School of Athens*. Georgy saw him off at the *diligence* office: 'I wish he could have stayed a few days more.'[63]

Eighteen days later Watts set sail for England. Planning to return after the Palace of Westminster competition in June, he left his pictures in Count Cottrell's cellars and asked Georgy to write to him at Holland House,[64] the grand Jacobean mansion, where once more his loyal friend and patron made a room available. The artist soon found rooms at 48 Cambridge Street, off Edgware Road.[65] Door panels featuring allegories of the muses, surmounted by a leopard resting its chin on the lap of a muse, are believed to have come from Cambridge Street (fig. 18). Holford offered temporary studio space at his Park Lane mansion, Dorchester House.[66]

A top, five-hundred-pound award consolidated Watts's reputation at the Palace of Westminster. Luminous colouring and energy send a surge of rhythm across the life-size figures and skyscape in *Alfred Inciting the Saxons to Resist the Danes* (fig. 19). King Alfred stands in the centre with one foot on the gangplank; his body faces front, his head turns towards the people on the left, while his right arm stretches across his body and points his sword out to the right. He indicates the Danish invaders and issues the

19   *Alfred Inciting the Saxons to Resist the Danes*, 1846–47 (Palace of Westminster).

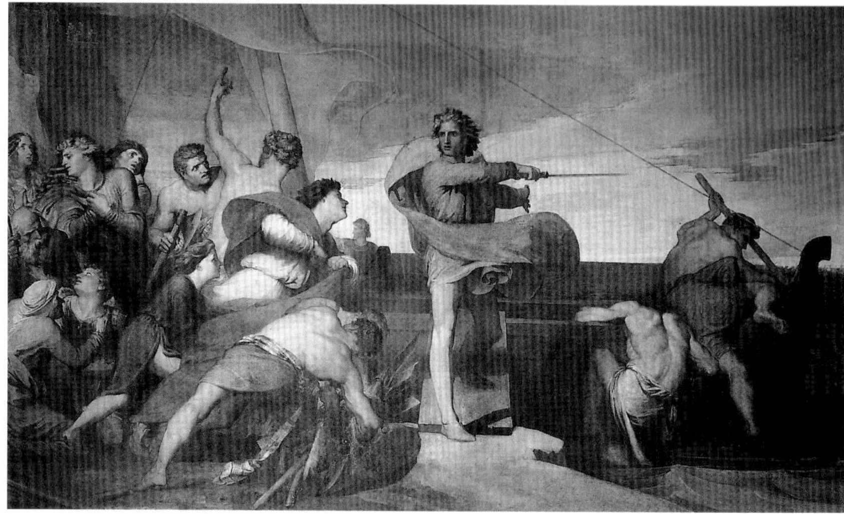

command to resist. A sail flutters up the mast indicating a sea breeze. Two muscular figures on the right scramble to action. Watts employed Tintoretto's Mannerist device of capturing the sudden movement and he looked to the Venetian for the composition of the crowd and Alfred's billowing cloak and sword. The figure of the king himself, however, is underpinned by the authority and form of Greek sculpture. His hair, modelled first in clay and given to Georgy, looks hewn. The hardy English crowd gestures in the Italian Grand Manner; Alice Duff Gordon's contemporary porcelain face and crinkled hair, added last, at the left edge, stand out in a historic scene otherwise dominated by urgent patriotic fervour. Sharp, flat outlines and broad colour suggest that Watts planned the subject as a fresco, the vivid expression of the whole established how his eyes had been opened in Italy, away from murky London fogs.

*Alfred* was the first completed work he wished to present to the nation for exhibition in a public building, but the Fine Arts Commissioners, prepared to pay thirteen hundred pounds for four pictures, pressed him to name a price. As a compromise, he agreed to take two hundred pounds, asking the Royal Commission to use the balance to offer other artists national honour and advantage.' Accepting only a fraction of the proposed fee was a patriotic blunder that would jeopardize future royal negotiations. Honour was satisfied, though; he enjoyed a healthy bank balance, and after adjustments to the king's legs, the painting was hung in the Board Room.[67] The huge competition pictures attracted ridicule – Watts's above all – when the novelist William Makepeace Thackeray caricatured him as George Rumbold ARA in *Our Street*: 'George, while at Rome, painted *Caractacus* ... *Alfred in the Neat-herd's Cottage*, 72 feet by 48 – (an idea of the gigantic size and Michael-Angelesque proportions of the picture may be formed, when I state that the mere muffin, of which the outcast king is spoiling the baking, is two feet three in diameter).'[68] Yet, unlike *Caractacus*, which a dealer had cut into three pictures, *Alfred* endured to dominate Committee Room 10 today.

## 3   A Caged Eagle

'I HAVE NOT YET MADE USE of the distempered wall in Hertford Street,' the artist wrote to Georgy. He joined the Duff Gordons at a Holland House dinner on 1 September before they left for Scotland. Their friendship remained firm and her ladyship offered him a wall at their London home for fresco experiments.[1] Watts would have read the sensational *Vestiges of the Natural History of Creation* (published anonymously, but written by Robert Chambers) that had gripped the nation ever since publication in November 1844.[2] Cheap editions of the evolutionary epic, which questioned the existence of a Creator, had been available since his return to Britain. Ranging from the formation of the cosmos to reflections on the destiny of the human race, *Vestiges* suggested that the planets had sprung from a blazing fire-mist, that life could be created in the laboratory and that humans had evolved from apes. Denounced and praised in pulpits, in periodicals and pamphlets, on railway journeys, at dinner parties and soirées,[3] it doubtless inspired Lady Duff Gordon to offer her wall. Following Carlyle's call for a 'Poet, Painter, Man of Genius' to unravel' the mystery of Time,[4] the debate arising from *Vestiges*, clearly influenced the metaphysical focus of Watts's hoped-for Michelangelesque hall of frescoes.

He resolved to design a universal epic, embodying the progress of the cosmos and civilization, cultural history and spiritual thought.[5] Subjects for this visionary scheme would preoccupy him for the rest of his life. He began by making outline sketches of a figure deep in thought – one, an amalgam of prophets from the Sistine Chapel ceiling, would be transformed decades later into his famous Symbolist painting *Hope*. On the opposite page, he drew a head at an angle, adding the body, stretched back, with legs and shoulders angled in rock formation. The sight of cracks on a wall resolved the composition of the giant figures that would suggest reposing continents.[6] Cosmic ideas mapped out in verse, thoughts that turn cynical, sow the first seed of his key theme *Love and Death* and reveal his own disillusion:

> . . . all his boasted lore & power
> An inch unto his stature cannot add
> Nor lengthen out a day his share of life,
> Nor keep him from disease, nor cause
> His mind to rise superior o'er his petty cares
> Vain are his struggles to assume the good

His Earthworm nature draws him ever down.
The sum of knowledge, the most soaring thought
And mind laborious, can acquire, reasons fail
To teach him one pride crushing truth,
His whole existence may but be a lie!
How can his pride sustain a shock so rude?
When he shall find the very senses by whose aid alone
He can acquire knowledge, make him their sport.[7]

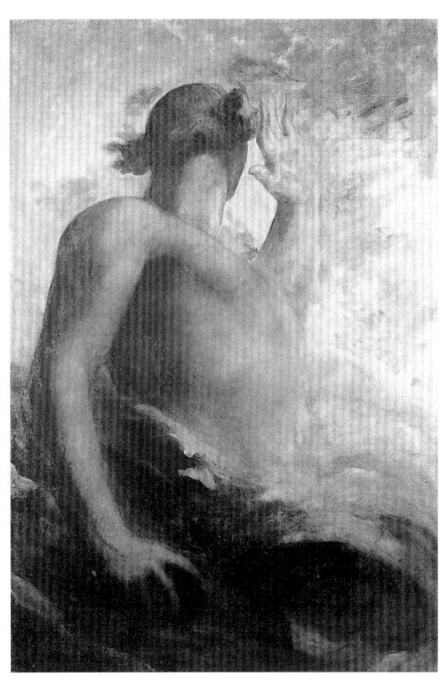

20   *Satan*, 1847 (Watts Gallery).

Watts had attracted the interest of John Ruskin, whose latest volume of his polemic *Modern Painters*, following his defence of J. M. W. Turner in the first book, established his reputation as a champion of contemporary art.[8] The critic was struck by a monumental painting of Satan in Watts's studio (fig. 20). A terrific sense of power, movement and mystery charges across the canvas, as the nude embodiment of the Evil Spirit (reminiscent of Francisco Goya's *The Colossus*), marches over the scorched earth; his head turned away from the viewer, as he shields his face from the radiance of God. In a letter inviting the artist to dine at his parents home in Denmark, Ruskin remarked, 'I don't understand the new picture, but it is glorious, and Satan has his cheekbone all right.' Sculptural, massive, fiery, painted in preparation for fresco, *Satan* was a moral and, by association with Job, social protest against greed and the tyranny of the rich over the poor.[9]

Watts was deeply troubled. After four years living in Italian palaces, painting portraits of the aristocracy and Grand Manner frescoes, he was shaken to the core by the poverty and misery in Britain. London had become a haven for refugees; catastrophic potato harvests, the staple food of the poor – particularly in Ireland – had led to mass starvation, and thousands of ragged young families were streaming in, tramping the streets in search of food and work. The River Thames, polluted with human excrement and refuse from the slaughterhouses, became a breeding ground for cholera. As he saw a poor woman turned away from the workhouse, the artist yearned to help. He decided to paint portrait commissions to raise funds for the needy, and asked to Georgy to recommend sitters. 'I will refuse *nothing*.'[10]

He enjoyed teasing a patron who had offered two guineas per figure for a crowded picture into accepting an apparently reduced (in truth, greater), fee of a shilling for the first figure, doubled and redoubled for each subsequent figure.[11] Georgy's request for his portrait prices embarrassed him, and he felt like a shopkeeper as he listed his fees, from forty guineas for a small 'kit-kat', to a hundred for 'a Bishop half length' and a hundred and twenty full-length.[12] Her brother Sir Alexander Duff Gordon sat for a portrait in charcoal. Their mother, sitting two years later, sympathized: 'a terrible task to have to paint my false hair, fat age and unshapely female.'[13]

Keen to take advantage of the young art of photography, Watts had daguerreotypes made of drapery and furniture, 'as I think the invention might be useful to Artists' and had himself photographed as an aid to self-portraiture. 'I look like a cross Lord Brougham!! . . . Heavens what a coxcomb I must have been to make myself look so picturesque in my own portrait!'[14] Photography would become popular for the study of the nude in France, where Delacroix was to write in 1851 'If a man of genius uses the Daguerreotype as it should be used, he will elevate [his art] to a height hitherto unknown.' Meanwhile in Britain, growing public distaste for the nude led the National Gallery to reject Titian's *Rape of Lucretia*.[15]

Lord Holland commissioned a portrait of Anthony Panizzi, Keeper of Printed Books at the British Museum and founder of the Reading Room, whom Watts painted at the museum,[16] and a strong, sensitive profile of François Guizot, the recently deposed prime minister of France (fig. 21). As a courtesy to his hosts, the artist decorated the Holland House ceilings with frescoes of *amorini* and scenes of medieval Florence, and the Gilt Room chimneypieces with grisaille panels and allegorical figures clothed in solid gold. Lady Holland stood for a grand seven-foot portrait, her back view and abundant coils of hair reflected in a Gilt Room mirror.[17] Watts would accept no payment from the Hollands.[18] Painting in their mansion, he was wracked by the poverty in London. The fogs affected his health and work, and he felt constricted. 'I am kept like a caged eagle', he wrote to Georgy, 'or if you think that too magnificent, like a cock-sparrow with a yard of thread tied to his leg, always thinking I can take flight and always being twitched back.'[19]

Living in lonely freedom at Cambridge Street, his ambition faltered. 'Alas for the days of Phidias and Raphael! I have not heard a stave of music since you went away. I begin to lose all perception and idea of harmony.'[20] Since the first Palace of Westminster success, his artistic vision had been geared to creating poetic beauty and harmony. Conflicting conditions threatened to erode his ambition to elevate art. Georgy accused him of 'living in an atmosphere of enchantment'. Had they been able to marry, her tough stance might have done him much good. Life, as he well knew, was not always beautiful. He had little in common with his stepsisters and though he often dined at Holland House, Lord Holland was not on hand at Cambridge Street to assuage his mood swings; and the artist was disconcerting rather than confiding in Georgy. Cut to the quick, he asked her to find him a wife:

> You talk of Fame! I am no longer to be taken in by such a pretence, but an agreeable companion in Italy would be an object worth working for . . . I take a commercial and commonsense view of the subject and therefore should not risk being deceived or disappointed and if I myself felt not violent love at least I am incapable of betraying a trust. You are probably somewhat surprised at such apparently new ideas in me, but they are not new, I have long thrown my romance to the winds.[21]

He had done nothing of the kind. 'My ambition is at an end; and my occupation is without an object,' he despaired. If he could start again, he would earn money to share with a companion, and make her happy. He insisted his affection for Georgy was 'as a sister', but contradicted himself, 'I could find it in my heart to wish you were an ill-used or overworked governess. Remember you once wished me raised.' It was she he wanted. Knowing he could not have her, and overwhelmed by loneliness, Watts was almost suicidal: 'I often think very seriously of Prussic acid!'[22] Georgy's firm reply and his formal acknowledgement enabled the artist to move on. He gave her the portrait of the Marchioness of Waterford (pl. III) and offered her any pictures he had left in the care of Count Cottrell.[23] Invited to stay in Hertfordshire with the Villiers family, whom he had met at Careggi, he made a watercolour sketch of Watford Bridge at sunset. Prussic acid was

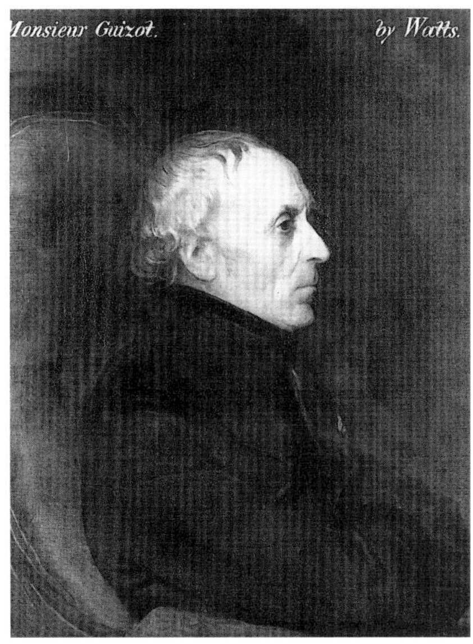


21   *François Pierre Guillaume Guizot*, 1847–48 (private collection).

as far from his mind as moral principles when Ionides asked him to recommend sights in Italy. At the top of Watts's list, above even the Sistine Chapel, was 'Pompeii! Pompeii is the greatest thing of all. I am sorry to say wander about it alone, but I remember you are a married man & probably think the less the imagination is encouraged the better.'[24]

Revolutions were breaking out in Europe, and Chartist reformers staged marches, hurling bricks into Downing Street in 1848. Amidst the turmoil, Watts resolved to paint ideal symbolic messages to inspire his fellow man. As he embarked on a solitary, lifelong crusade to raise the tone of British art, he proposed to dignify public buildings with large-scale imaginative frescoes, embodying themes outlined in his *Progress of the Cosmos* scheme. However, the art establishment could not stomach his visionary pictures, the glowing sculptural figures and bare abstract detail. While he was in Italy other Westminster prize-winners had been invited to paint frescoes in the Poets' Hall. Now his entry for the 1849 fresco competition, *The People who Sat in Darkness have Seen a Great Light*, failed to be selected.[25]

That autumn a team of radical academics, spearheaded by the British Museum archaeologist Charles Newton, instigated a campaign for a Watts fresco for Oxford University. A friend and former contemporary of Ruskin at Christ Church, Newton took Watts and Professor Charles Cockerell, architect of the new Taylorian and University Galleries (now the Ashmolean Museum), to examine the Arundel Marbles, Britain's earliest major collection of classical antiquities.[26] Cockerell had recently assisted Newton to identify the site of the Mausoleum of Halicarnassus.[27] Sifting through fragments with this scholarly duo in the university basement, the artist picked out the head of a woman whose hair was bound in a fillet like Aphrodite's on the Parthenon frieze. They were able to locate most of her remaining parts, her bust and shoulders dressed in a *chiton*, which fell in beautiful folds exposing her right breast (fig. 77). Her eyes were more prominent than characteristic idealized Greek heads. So fine was she, even in her sorry severed state – with corroded lips and missing parts of her nose and forehead – that Watts believed her to be a portrait from the age of Phidias. The archaeologist, too, thought her 'the finest bit of sculpture I know out of the Elgin Room'. In Newton, Watts found a kindred spirit and crusader for the revival of that great Hellenic school of sculpture – judged perfect in its day – to elevate modern art.[28]

Cockerell wanted Watts to paint a fresco on the Taylorian library ceiling. Newton recruited Henry Acland, a senior Christ Church contemporary and the Lee's Reader in Anatomy at Oxford, to take up the cause. 'I am sure he would do it better than anybody else', Newton enthused, pointing out that the artist offered his services free of charge. 'Now my dear Acland, you who know Oxford which I do not must tell me how to manage this matter for I have made up my mind that this fresco be painted by Watts.' While the physician pursued their controversial campaign,[29] Ruskin saw the Palace of Westminster pictures as 'the beginning of English historical art ... victorious powers of design'. The defender of Turner began to champion Watts:

Do you know Watts?' reads the first of the *Letters on Art and Literature by John Ruskin*. 'The man who is *not* employed on Houses of Parliament – to my mind the only real painter of history or thought we

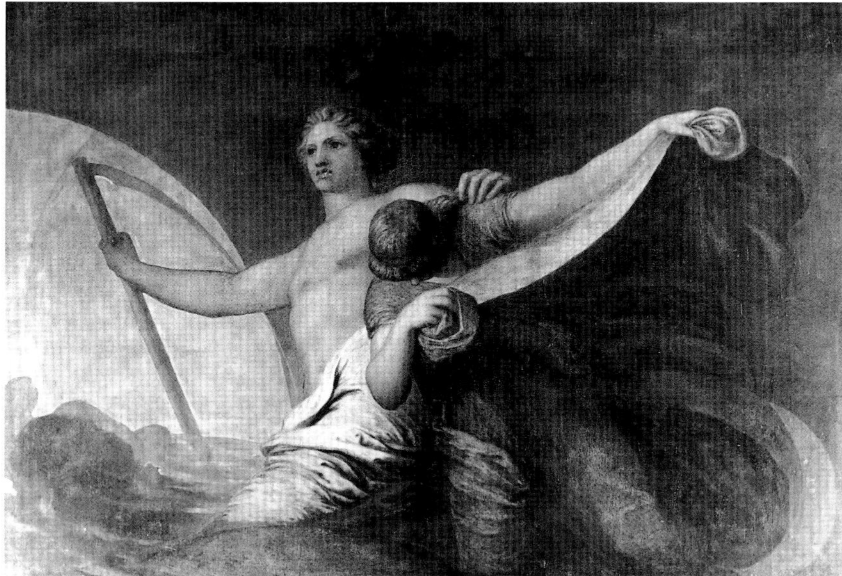

22 *Time and Oblivion* 1848 (Eastnor Castle Collection).

have in England. A great fellow, or I am much mistaken – great as one of these same Savoy knots of rock – and we suffer the clouds to lie upon him, with thunder and famine at once in the thick of them. If you have time when you come to town, and have not seen it look at the *Time and Oblivion* in his studio.[30]

*Time and Oblivion* (fig. 22), a sparse, monumental composition, was designed for the Progress of Time element of the cosmic scheme. Reinventing allegory with a modern anthropomorphic vocabulary,[31] Watts presented Time not as an old man, but as a vigorous youth, still identifiable by his scythe, while Oblivion, a cloaked figure with bowed head, speeds past. The artists of ancient Greece and the Renaissance intended their creations to inspire worship. Watts went further. By placing figures between Night and Day, showing only part of the larger, fiery sun, his aim was to stretch the viewer's imagination. 'I endeavoured to make it noble and elevated', he explained, 'for I wished to stimulate the mind and awaken large thoughts. It is solemn, sad and hard, for solemn, sad and hard are the conditions: an organ chord swelling and powerful but unmodulated'.[32]

At the same time, he painted his first moral message, *Life's Illusions* (fig. 23), a symbolic composition compressed into a sensual assault on the perils of power. Nude figures embodying Hope and Ambition, a curvaceous *femme fatale* (he had clearly seen Ary Scheffer's *Francesca Da Rimini* in Paris[33]) hover over a knight who spurs on his horse – (based perhaps on the artist's Welsh cob[34]) – to chase 'a rainbow-tinted bubble of glory'. Lovers intent on each other and a child chasing a butterfly are dangerously close to the animal whose forelegs are already over a precipice, while an old man crouching on the brink reads 'by the last rays of the dying sun'. On the ground are shattered symbols of human power. *Life's Illusions* was an unconscious self-portrait. Tantalizing aristocratic sitters were forbidden to the humble artist who aspired to ennoble the nation with High Art, but

23 *Life's Illusions*, 1849 (Tate, London).

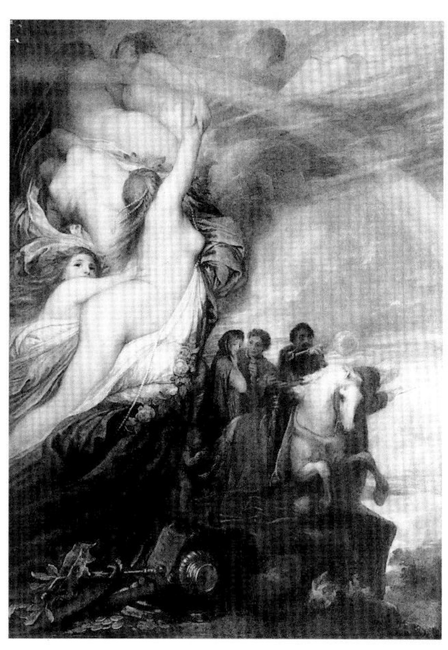

whose stature at the Palace of Westminster had been marred by ridicule. Watts had barely come to terms with his distinction as a portrait painter and the distasteful embarrassment of payment. His own nature veered from refreshing humour, to the scholarly composer of historical and symbolic paintings, to a man brought to the brink of death in winter – so it seemed – by paralysing attacks of migraine, vertigo and nausea.

Decades in advance of their time, both pictures prefigured the European Symbolism Movement, but in 1849 critics were puzzled. 'The conditions under which Mr Watts may have dreamt his dream of *Life's Illusions* it enters not into our nature to divine,' declaimed the *Athenaeum* on 19 May. Its withering review assessed his picture 'a clever combination of hues employed on masses which define no forms . . . "signifying nothing".'[35] To Watts, it seemed as though his own bubble had burst. He considered leaving Britain to settle in Athens. Yet he never quite lost hope. On 28 June he moved into new studios at 30 Charles Street, Berkeley Square.[36] He exchanged the eight-foot-high *Saxon Sentinels* for a piano and established, as his lifelong suppliers, Winsor and Newton of Rathbone Place for materials and Joseph Green of Mortimer Street for frames (his own design, a stylized Italianate acanthus leaf border surrounding wide oak flats and inner fillet of the English acorn). With Couzens on hand in his spare studio to provide copies of his pictures,[37] he blew the drips off his aspirations and let his imagination fly.

*    *    *

A mysterious sound woke Watts one night. He tiptoed out of his bedroom on to the landing above the staircase leading down to his studio. As he stood in the dark, the thirty-two-year-old artist had the impression that wings were swooping round above him, beating against the vaulted ceiling. One might assume that a bird or bat was trapped in the studio. Not George Watts, who seemed to hear a voice cry softly '*anima mia, anima mia*' before the fluttering ceased. Decades later he would relate the experience to his fiancée Mary Fraser Tytler, pointing out that it had happened in 1849, the year of her birth: 'Was it think you your soul seeking its fellow?'[38]

# 4   Crusade Against Bare Walls

WATTS YEARNED TO BROADEN THE SPECTRUM of his art, yet his reputation for portraiture attracted commissions he preferred to avoid. At Holland House, the acid tongue and *maquillage* of Henry Fleming no doubt reduced the appeal of an introduction to Virginia Pattle, whose radiant beauty was said to bring traffic to a halt. 'Oh, how in love with her we all were,' the statesman Henry Bruce, Lord Aberdare would recall.[1] Virginia lived with her married sister Sara Prinsep in Chesterfield Street, near Watts's studio. The artist was tempted, but had no time to make new social acquaintances. He would later confess that his first concentrated love 'began & encouraged & developed before I knew the living object.'[2]

Judge James Pattle, known in India as Jim Blazes, was a colourful East Indian civil servant who drank himself to death in September 1845. He and his wife, Adeline, the daughter of Queen Marie-Antoinette's page, Chevalier Antoine de l'Étang,[3] had had ten children, of whom six dynamic daughters now survived: Julia, Sarah (she preferred to drop the 'h'), Maria (known as 'Mia', grandmother of Vanessa Bell and Virginia Woolf), Louisa, Virginia and Sophia.[4] Only Virginia remained unmarried. Born in India, the Pattle sisters had been brought up by their aristocratic French grandmother near the château of Versailles and were, as Mary Watts later put it, 'Artistic to their finger-tips, with an appreciation – almost to be called a *culte* – for beauty'.[5] Passionately unconventional, they wore rich flowing robes, clustered pearls and tinkling silver and gold bangles that combined modern Parisian art with draperies of the High Renaissance and the Orient, foreshadowing the Aesthetic Movement. 'To see one of this sisterhood float into a room with sweeping robes and falling folds was almost an event in itself,' for compared to London ladies of fashion in crinolines and corsets, they looked like goddesses.[6]

One morning Watts saw two robed women with deep-lidded eyes and centre-parted hair floating, as it were, down Regent Street, leading a small boy. The artist, mesmerized, knew at once that they were Virginia, her sister and nephew. He dashed off a note to Fleming: 'You cannot be more anxious to introduce than I am to know Miss Pattle, she is beautiful.' He was to meet the sisters at Eastnor Castle in the winter of 1849.[7] The women, equally intrigued by his charisma – a piquant juxtaposition of humility and genius – became regular visitors to his studio.

Couzens's portrait of the artist at this time shows him in front of a frieze of ancient Greek elders from the Parthenon (fig. 24). Modest, yet assured,

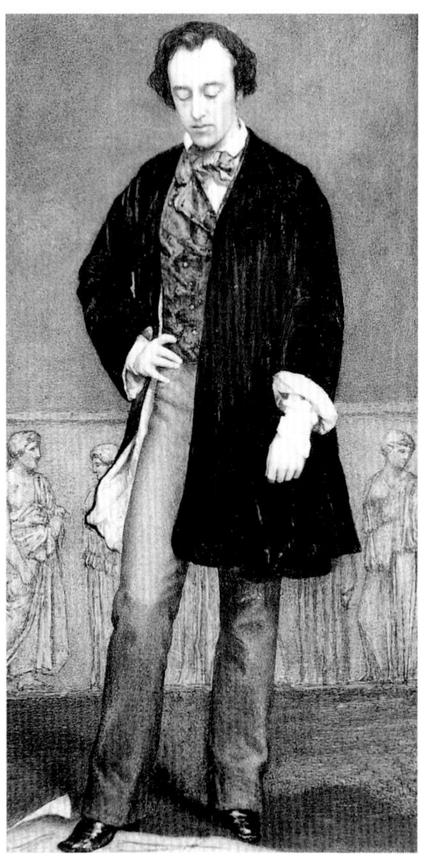

24   Charles Couzens, *G. F. Watts*, *c.*1849 (Watts Gallery; photo: Arthur Beament).

he stands clean-shaven in a flamboyant waistcoat and cravat, looking down at his own drawing curled beneath his feet. Of course Watts drew the sisters' portraits, as well as a splendid head of the octogenarian Adeline de l'Étang whom he found on her knees playing shove-halfpenny with her great-grandchildren in a corridor at Chesterfield Street.[8] Sara Prinsep, horrified by the pallor and near-paralysis that came over him that winter, took it upon herself to nurse him back to health and supervise treatment with the pioneer hydrotherapist Dr James Gully in Malvern.

In the spring of 1850, Watts exhibited drawings symbolizing Education and the Muses for the Oxford fresco.[9] That summer, on Acland's recommendation, he took on a pupil, John Roddam Spencer-Stanhope, a jovial Christ Church undergraduate, initially for the long vacation. Lady Elizabeth Spencer-Stanhope saw it as an exceptional honour that her son Roddy was to study under 'the famous Cartoon painter, who only takes pupils by great favour.'[10]

The master, deeply in love with Virginia, drew tender silverpoint studies of her in the soft grey cloak she wore that first day (fig. 25). He pared down its graceful lines for a full-length, almost monotone portrait which he exhibited in the 1850 Royal Academy Summer Exhibition[11] with a life-size symbolic painting of *The Good Samaritan* inspired by the prison philanthropist Thomas Wright. Flicking through *Chamber's Magazine* in a restaurant, he had read about Wright's activities on behalf of an ex-prisoner forced out of his job by prejudice and had painted the picture to present to Manchester Town Hall. That the Corporation accepted it within months was the first fulfilment of Watts's artistic ideal.[12] The *Art-Journal* commended his portrait of Virginia Pattle for its rare, elevated sentiment.[13] Virginia stands like a pilgrim on the stone terrace, 'her hair simply braided, and a long grey coat of nunlike simplicity falling round her,' as her great niece Laura Troubridge observed. 'She has no curls, no frills or furbelows, no jewels; she is as God made her, a perfectly beautiful woman.'[14]

Knowing that he had nothing to offer Virginia drove the artist to distraction. She encouraged him, but he believed himself to be unworthy and dared not declare himself to her. Instead, Charles, Viscount Eastnor, the future Earl Somers, enchanted by her portrait on Watts's studio dresser, proposed marriage and she accepted. Watts was devastated: 'It became wrong for me to love. I nearly died but I conquered it. My existence became a blank.'[15] He made a large chalk drawing, the strongest image yet of her oval face, heavy lidded eyes and firmly modelled throat, and painted *The Vanished Spirit*, returning for a last look upon the world, with Eastnor Castle and a book inscribed '*Finis*'. Ruskin immediately added in charcoal '*et initium*'.[16] Over the years her face would feature in some of Watts's most powerful imaginative work, but now, losing Virginia exacerbated his artistic frustration. His work was misunderstood, and all he could hope for was to pave the way for better men. In one day he painted *The Ruins*, a figure collapsed beneath a temple by the sea. 'I sit among the ruins of my aspirations watching the tide of time', he wrote to Acland.[17] Yet those broken columns were symbols of Fortitude, strength in adversity.

Watts now addressed the socio-political issue of poverty in a series of stark realist paintings.[18] *Under a Dry Arch* depicts a woman taking refuge from the cold, her shoulder hunched against her cheek, her face an expression of abject misery; behind her is St Paul's cathedral, symbolizing the formal religion that turns the other cheek. *Found Drowned*, a legal term indicating suicide, shows the body of a woman on the shore beneath Waterloo Bridge, her legs immersed in the polluted Thames; as moonlight shines on her, the Shot Tower and Brunel's new suspension footbridge loom in the background: technological progress is overshadowed by social failure – how fortunate was the woman Carlyle observed, thwarted in her attempt to drown because her crinoline inflated in the river and floated her gracefully ashore.[19] In *The Song of the Shirt*, echoing the impassioned poem by Thomas Hood, Watts protested at the plight of the desolate, overworked seamstress. As his Greek commission was unresolved, he overpainted *Panthea*[20] with a starving family to portray *The Irish Famine* (fig. 26). It is a more searing interpretation than the peasants painted by his French contemporary Jean-François Millet[21] and a rare instance in art in which Irishmen were portrayed not as coarse, but intensely human. Unique in his oeuvre, these social realist pictures were very much ahead of their time.

'You must have had a second-sight vision,' wrote the poet Aubrey de Vere, astounded that Watts had never seen Ireland. To restore his spirits after Virginia's wedding, de Vere arranged for him to stay with his brother at Curragh Chase. Watts wrote to the bridegroom, 'I am going to very different shores & shall require to remember how much happiness & excitement exists in Herefordshire to relieve the pain I must feel in witnessing the misery & degradation of Ireland.'[22] He witnessed little misery during his five-week stay. A popular guest, he romped and rode with the children and decorated the staircase at Curragh Chase with a charcoal drawing of *Dante and Beatrice*. 'He is a very remarkable man, and a very mournful one inwardly,' de Vere wrote to Alice Taylor, wife of the poet Henry Taylor. 'So do all you can to sun out what is within him, and let it creep back into its cage well warmed. His is a fine nature, but this age is wintry to it.'[23]

Refreshed and invigorated from his Irish jaunt, Watts returned to London as preparations gathered pace for the Great Exhibition of the Works of Industry of All Nations at the new Crystal Palace in Hyde Park. Masterminded by Prince Albert to promote modern produce, science and culture from around the world, it was to set the standard for international exhibitions – *expositions universelles* – throughout the century; and its profits would finance the creation of the South Kensington museums and colleges of art, science and music.[24] 'Your great card house was prodigious!' he wrote to de Vere's niece Mary. 'What a pity you could not send it to our great glass-house exhibition as a specimen of Irish industry!'[25] His ten-foot 'muffin' *The Ostracism of Aristides* stood out at the concurrent international art exhibition at Lichfield House.[26]

At that moment another house that was to cause no small stir over the ensuing years preoccupied Watts. Lord Holland suggested that he move into his dower house. The artist was in no position to take over the lease, but Sara Prinsep, who wished to expand her literary salon and needed a more spacious home outside central London, was. Watts introduced her and her husband Thoby to Lord Holland and to the '*paradisino*' where Holland's aunt Caroline Fox had received her admirer King George IV.[27] Little Holland House (fig. 27), a rambling gabled house in an idyllic rural setting, with lawns and stately arching trees, was just off Kensington High Street. An unfashionable two miles from Hyde Park Corner, it suited Sara perfectly. The Prinseps signed a twenty-one-year lease from Christmas Day

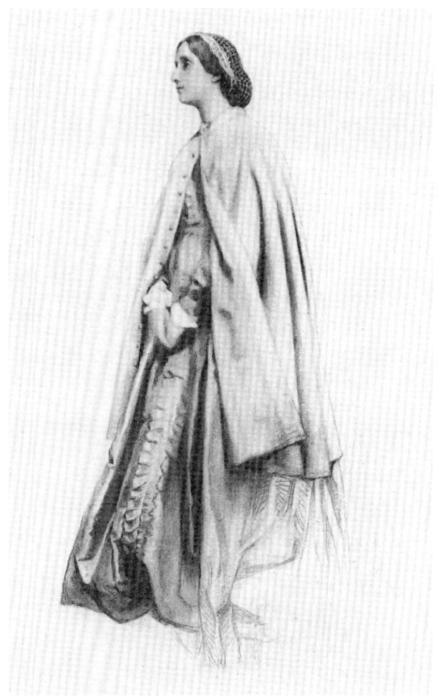

25   *Virginia Pattle*, 1849 (private collection).

26   *The Irish Famine*, 1848–50 (Watts Gallery).

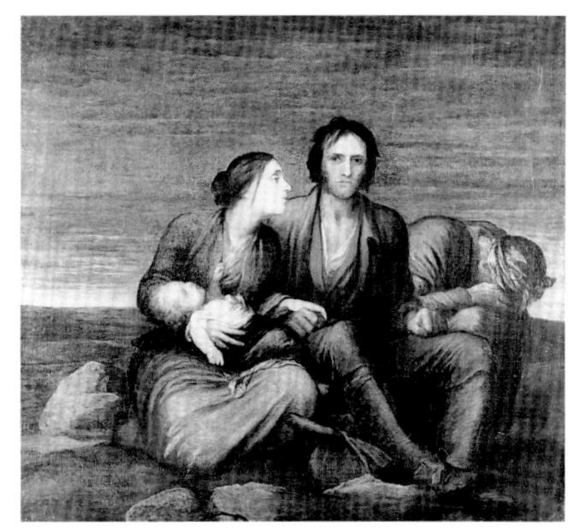

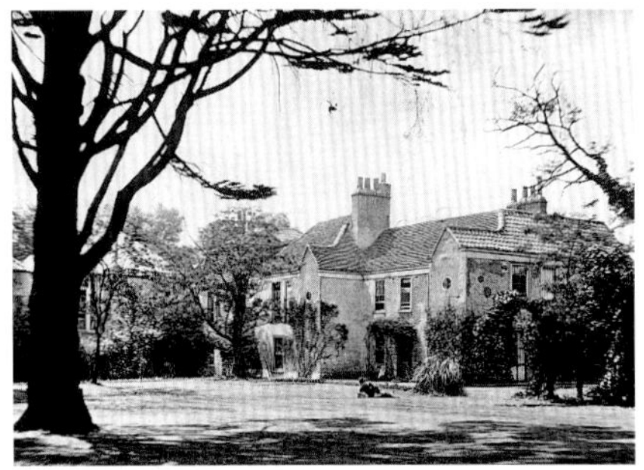

27   Little Holland House, before 1876.

1850 at two hundred pounds per annum[28] and invited Watts to stay for three days in the new year, an invitation that led to the second legendary phase in his career, lasting almost thirty years. There was mutual benefit: his intellectual friends and links with the Holland circle would elevate her literary salon and shine on her with reflected glory.[29]

Catapulted into the bosom of the Prinsep and Pattle families, Watts became the focus of their bohemian Anglo-Indian household. Sara, only a year older than himself, swamped him with maternal care. She was not especially beautiful, but worshipped beauty in others, insisting that her nieces read the Bible before they went to dances to give them 'heavenly expressions'.[30] Untidy, impulsive, chaotic, she had a warm heart, four children – Henry, aged fourteen, Valentine, twelve, Arthur, ten, and Alice, six – and a supreme talent for hospitality, though, as her granddaughter Laura observed, she was the kind of woman, 'who would have turned a convent into a scene of tumult'.[31] Virginia sat for many portraits after her marriage and regarded Watts as the finest painter of the day.[32] She too was shrewd, captivating, imperious and passionate. Few could resist her when, as Lady Henry Somerset put it, 'with all the force of a vacuum-cleaner [she] drew the secrets of the heart from the tightest bosoms.'[33]

Even more exuberant was their elder sister, Julia (fig. 28), married to Charles Hay Cameron of Lochiel, the first legal member of the Council of India. Famed for her wit and energy, she had been a prominent hostess in Calcutta, where she had entertained for the Governor-General Sir Henry Hardinge. Now living at Sheen Lodge, near Richmond Park, she was a frequent visitor to Little Holland House. Julia epitomized the Pattle family characteristics – 'doubly distilled.'[34] Watts's poetic portrait gives no hint of her energy, of how this 'woman of noble plainness'[35] was transported by visions of the beautiful and ideal into a tornado of passion. Her eyes would flash, soften and sparkle as she admonished, delighted and terrified her friends. Where her sisters were persuasive, Julia was invincible.[36] Her ecstatic praise unnerved the artist almost more than criticism until he took to deflecting it with counterattack.[37]

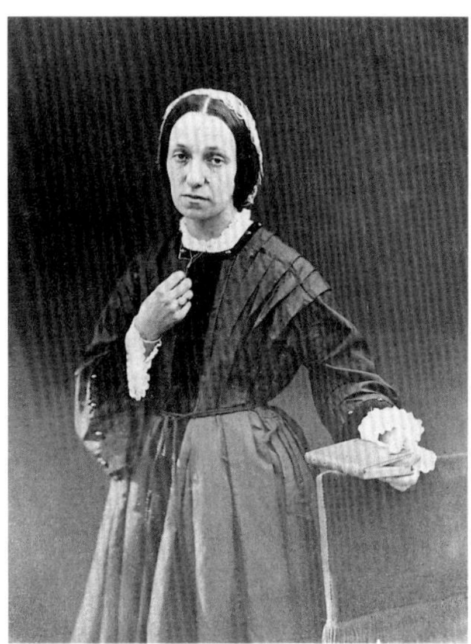

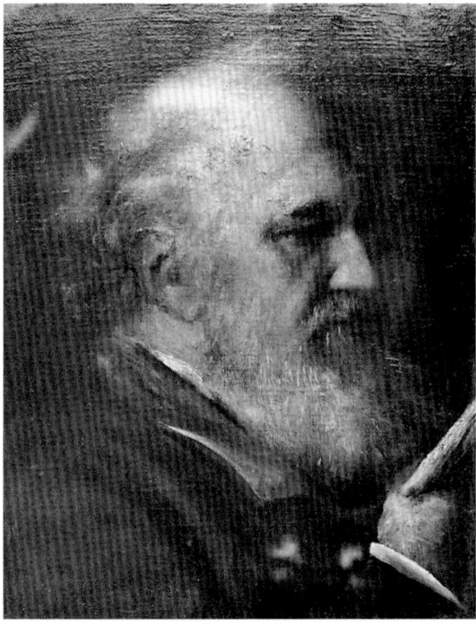

28 (*right*)   Julia Margaret Cameron, photographed by her brother-in-law Earl Somers, *c.*1862.

29 (*far right*)   *Thoby Prinsep, c.*1859 (private collection).

'Beauty', 'Dash' and 'Talent' – as Virginia, Sara and Julia were dubbed after Julia took up photography in 1863 – were extravagant mothers and devoted wives. Each appeared to eclipse their distinguished husbands. Thoby Prinsep (fig. 29) was the most refreshing person in their artistic hothouse. Grand, genial and learned, he was a director of the East India Company and provided a healthy balance of character for his wife.[38] In Thoby's company Watts enjoyed a respite from the suffocating adulation of the ladies; and his broad, encyclopaedic mind held a special appeal. 'It was just like turning the pages of a delightful book,' the artist recalled.[39] For Thoby, too, Watts was an amusing and valued companion. Now that he lived almost as one of the family they felt uncomfortable about calling him 'Mr Watts' and – as he disliked his unmusical surname and had seriously thought of changing it[40] – he gladly accepted instead the nickname chosen by Sara's youngest sister. Sophie (fig. 30), who was married to an East India Company civil servant John Dalrymple, named him 'The *Signor*'. Respectful, not over familiar, it suited the artist, indicating his reverence for Titian. In brotherly affection he nicknamed Sophie '*Sorella*'. Gradually the prefix was dropped and he became simply 'Signor', and was never again called 'George'.[41]

Living at Little Holland House, well looked after, in better health and relieved from the urgent need to earn a living, Signor was free to pursue his ideals. Portrait commissions served as his 'base for supplies';[42] and by the early 1850s he had resolved that his mission in life would be two-fold: that as well as producing symbolic public frescoes he would paint for the nation a collection of portraits to record remarkable figures of the era.[43] Viscount Mahon, the future Earl Stanhope, was pressing for a British historical portrait gallery; however, it was not until 1856 that Parliament voted to donate two thousand pounds towards its establishment, and a further four decades would pass before the National Portrait Gallery's collection of deceased celebrities hung in a permanent home.[44] Lord John Russell, the future Whig prime minister (fig. 31),[45] posing at Holland House in 1852, was the first to sit specifically for Watts's 'Hall of Fame'. He had hesitated to approach the Duke of Wellington, who died on 14 September. Half a century later, the Earl of Clanwilliam asked after 'a small skeleton hand' that the artist had been so keen to acquire that he offered to paint any picture he liked. He would recall the exchange 'not for the hand but for the mark of the Duke of Wellington at his death.'[46]

Sir Austen Henry Layard, who had recently excavated the Assyrian Bulls at Nineveh, sat for a portrait commissioned by the publisher John Murray. Watts and Layard used to meet after dinner in Bond Street, where the diplomat Robert Morier was introducing Prince Nicholas of Nassau to the literary and intellectual Englishmen of the day. Among them were the poet Robert Browning, Thackeray, the lawyer Vernon Harcourt, and James Spedding, the editor of Bacon's *Works*, the dramatist and barrister Tom Taylor, and Ruskin, whose wife Effie posed for two portraits: the first, a 'quite perfect' chalk portrait exhibited at the Academy in 1851.[47] Watts, Ruskin and Taylor were appointed to the Council of the Arundel Society, which was established to reproduce and promote knowledge of art, in order to elevate national taste. Its pioneering reduced casts from the Elgin Marbles won a medal in the Great Exhibition. Naturally, Watts bought all three examples – recumbent figures of Theseus (now believed to represent

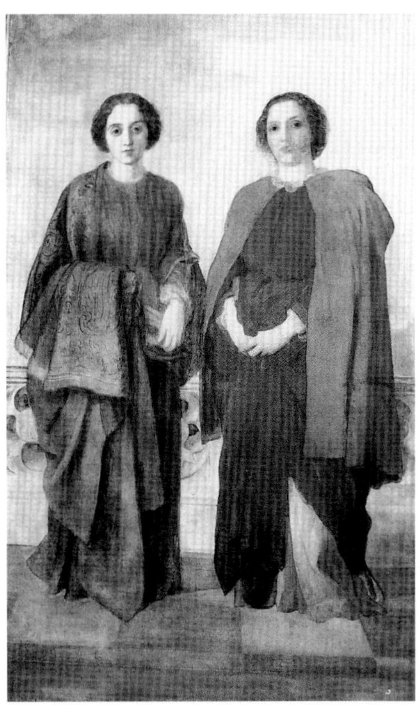

30   *Sara Prinsep and Sophie Dalrymple*, 1850 (Watts Gallery). Sara stands on the right.

31   *The Right Honourable Lord John Russell*, 1852 (photo: Frederic Hollyer).

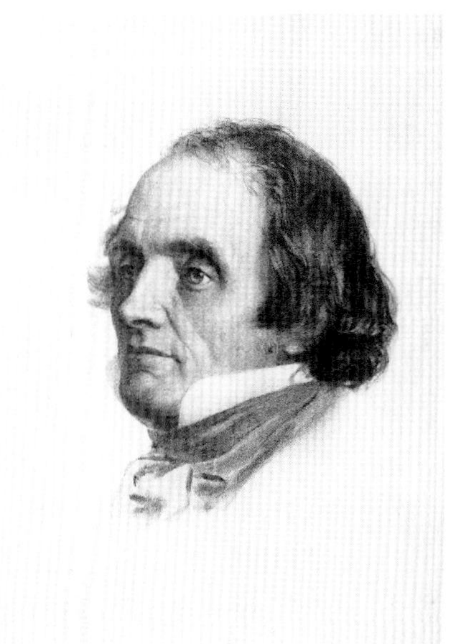

Dionysus) and Ilissus and a group of Panathenic riders – to refer to at any hour, day or night, in varied lighting and from all viewpoints, in his new studios on the upper floor of Little Holland House. When Morier was posted to Germany, Watts proposed that 'the arcanum and the Parnassus of literary swells', as the Poet Laureate Alfred Tennyson described fellow members, should meet instead at his Charles Street rooms, known thereafter as the Cosmopolitan Club, still dominated by his paintings of *Echo* and *Boccaccio*.[48]

Critics have dwelt too much on the artist's frailty and strange spiritual subject matter. He was often ill, but diets and water cures reduced attacks. Watts enjoyed the vigorous companionship of male friends, kept horses, and well into old age was a skilful rider – an innate understanding of the horse informed his art. His imaginative paintings were powerful, poetic, metaphysical images designed to suggest universal moral values. He worked alone, forging new paths. The Academy disapproved of the fresco-like technique of these allegorical, later known as Symbolist, and other subject pictures. They hung them in corners or high up – 'Oh, there's a Watts, let us sky it'[49] – and rejected his proposals to encourage High Art. After 1852 he refused to exhibit there. Preferring to develop his ideas privately, he debated his plan to reform art with distinguished Cosmopolites.

Equally dissatisfied with formal Academy convention was the younger Pre-Raphaelite Brotherhood who had formed a revolutionary new art movement in September 1848. Led by Dante Gabriel Rossetti, John Everett Millais and William Holman Hunt, they, too, were idealists, who aspired to achieve fame by reviving what they perceived to be the purity of British painting. They looked to early Italian artists and infused their work with a modern poetic spirit. Where they differed from Watts was in their medieval style and brilliant technique in pursuit of 'Truth to Nature'. Watts valued shadows; they illuminated every detail of their paintings, as though the sun shone over the entire canvas. Their realistic treatment of biblical subjects, which horrified the art establishment, attracted Ruskin, who began to transfer allegiance from the broader aspirations of Watts to those of the Pre-Raphaelites. Watts felt moved to comment on his criticisms because of the high public regard for Ruskin: 'I want you to consider well, & walk round the truth, viewing it from this distance as well as examine it with a magnifying glass lest your eye & tools becoming microscopic, fail . . . to take in the length & breadth.' He prepared two drafts of his letter to Ruskin:

> My own views are too visionary . . . too abstract . . . My instincts cause me to strive after things . . . that are rather felt than seen . . . Like you I am most interested in the progress of Art, & believe it can only be great by being true, but I am inclined to give truth a wider range, & I cannot help fearing you may become near-sighted . . . I do not agree with . . . your view of truth. It appears to me that you compound it too much with detail, & overdo properties . . . that you are less affected by falsehood of line, & absence of beauty, than you are by falsehood of line & absence of truth (yet beauty is truth, though it may not always be realized) . . . I do think that you ought to forget that Art must be divided into the imitative & the suggestive (the greater) . . . I venture to make these remarks to you because you must do all good, & no harm.[50]

As they walked back from the Academy winter exhibition, Ruskin berated him for painting not what he saw but what he wanted to see. Watts pointed to a filthy snow heap by a lamppost. 'Would you have me paint that?' 'Yes, just as you see it,' insisted the critic; their arguments always ended in humour. Watts felt constrained by the Pre-Raphaelites from developing the huge symbolic subjects Ruskin clearly valued in *The Stones of Venice*:

> We have, as far as I *know*, at present among us, only one painter, G. F. Watts, who is capable of design in colour on a large scale. He stands alone among our artists of the old school, in his perception of the value of breadth in distant masses, and in the vigour of invention by which such breadth must be sustained; and his power of expression and depth of thought are not less remarkable than his bold conception of colour effect. Very probably some of the Pre-Raphaelites have the gift also; I am nearly certain that Rossetti has it, and I think also Millais; but the experiment has yet to be tried.[51]

For Watts, working apart from the Pre-Raphaelites – a school whose vitality and momentum he respected – proved to be a tremendous obstacle and blocked public approval of his imaginative subjects for decades. Looking back, he wished that he had been born later, into a more encouraging atmosphere: 'I should certainly have joined your Fellowship, being proud to remember I always understood & acknowledged its value,' he would write to Hunt in 1897.[52] Meanwhile, with generous wall space at Little Holland House, and able to work on a wide range of subjects at any time, he moved from canvas to canvas, painting over hard, dried pigment. His need to turn from one train of thought or artistic expression to another meant that canvases stacked up unfinished, to be taken up or re-explored over the years. 'Signor! Why don't you finish one picture before you begin another?' exclaimed Thoby Prinsep. 'My dear friend,' replied the artist, 'you don't paint a picture as you would make a pair of boots.' Any thought of completion so that history could place his work in the context of the day was of minor consequence compared with the opportunity to develop and improve it.[53]

His portraits of the family lined the walls and with Stanhope's assistance Watts transformed the upper dining room into a modern Olympia, filling the arched spaces with life-size frescoes featuring the sisters and friends as symbols of scholarship and civilization. Beside the entrance, *Greece in the Lap of Egypt*, inspired by draped marble figures of *The Fates* from the Parthenon, with Virginia Somers as model, showed the world's 'unparalleled' Greek culture as a development from Egyptian art; for Watts saw the history of art as a chain, each link springing from a previous one to progress onward. *Time Unveiling Truth* glowed at one end, *Earth with the Infant Humanity* at the other. Exuding an exotic sense of maternal comfort, the women appeared individually between the windows as Muses in *The Arts*, *Science* and *Poetry*, and grouped along the side walls as *Assyria and Hindustan*, the Persian, Mongolian and Roman Empires, *Progress and Non-Progress*, *Peace and War*. The planetary system shone from the ceiling; and from the orbit of the Earth a figure gazed up towards the firmament, suggesting inspiration beyond mere worldly concerns.[54]

Visitors marvelled, but the establishment distrusted his symbolic frescoes, though he offered his design and labour free, charging only the cost of materials and scaffolding. Francis Charteris, now Lord Elcho, MP, campaigned for the cosmic scheme; he also approached the chairman of the London and North-Western Railway proposing that Watts should fresco the new Grand Hall at Euston Station. The company declined. Happy to commission symbolic sculpture and friezes, they would not risk sensation. The chairman made financial excuses, and the architect Philip Hardwick declared that he and the directors would be stoned if they sanctioned Wattsian frescoes[55] – which George Bernard Shaw later suggested were 'contemptuously refused as more likely to attract loiterers than business.'[56] The revolutionary Giuseppe Mazzini, who was planning an uprising in Italy from London, doubted a poetic picture could stimulate the intellect, until he saw *Time and Oblivion* at Little Holland House and recognized that Watts was forging a new path.[57]

'He has taken up a crusade against bare walls', Stanhope wrote to his father.[58] Watts liked to think of pupils as fellow students. He enjoyed their youthful *joie de vivre*, but the drawing discipline he set for Stanhope remained his lifelong advice to aspiring artists: 'I am at work now upon a towel, scattered in a picturesque way upon the floor, and which Watts has enjoined me to draw with as hard a pencil as I can get, and shade with the finest lines possible in order to study and imitate everything upon it, even to the blacks.' Trained to draw clear outlines, he was forbidden to rub out and warned against the standard teaching practice of copying antique sculpture because it would spoil his taste for form: 'Watts utterly condemns all conventionality and mannerisms, and says that *nothing* ought to be studied (the Elgin Marbles excepted) but nature; in studying anybody's style you lose all originality and become a mannerist, which after all is nothing but copying, thereby lowering yourself to the ranks of copy-writers, door-painters.'[59] The two men enlarged neoclassical outlines from Flaxman's Dante on to the walls of Little Holland House, and Watts painted an enlargement from *The Brethren of Saturn Delivered* for Acland.

Stanhope's dawn-to-dusk collaboration with Watts on designs denounced by the establishment and his enthusiastic tales of Little Holland House alarmed his mother. 'I went with a huge party of Pattles to see a Diorama of Calcutta,' he wrote. 'The chief amusement of the ladies being to bully poor Watts, who was in a very High Art mood at the time. We finished up with tea at the Eastnors. She is certainly A.1. for beauty.'[60] Lady Elizabeth travelled down from York to investigate Watts's influence. She found Stanhope drawing before breakfast, questioned acquaintances about his tutor's character and heard how the artists frolicked on the merry-go-round with the Prinsep boys – '*Very innocent!*' Lady Elizabeth let them paint frescos in her Harley Street drawing-room. Signor may have passed moral muster, but his artistic influence raised serious doubt. Roddy's drawing was 'decidedly wrong, and so is Watts's, with all his genius. I wish you could see the horrible, naked, mutilated figures from the Elgin Marbles with which he intends to *decorate the Governesses' Institution*. There is one as large as life, I think it is the *Theseus* – enough to frighten them all out of their wits.'[61] The Liverpool institution, set up to raise the character of governesses and improve the tone of female education, would never face a wicked Wattsian fresco.[62]

That summer of 1852, however, he embarked on *The Red Cross Knight Overcoming the Dragon* at the Palace of Westminster (fig. 32). The fresco would characterize, rather than illustrate, the theme from Spenser's poem *The Faërie Queen*. Symbolizing the triumph of Christianity, St George stands over the beast with followers of all classes. In the then dim House of Commons vestibule – now the Poets Hall – Watts used a mirror to reflect light from a high window on to each section, but could never see the entire work.[63] Compared with neighbouring frescoes, his stood up well. Rossetti may have found *The Red Cross Knight* 'truculent',[64] but its harmony with the building was singled out by Layard: 'Mr Watts is, in our opinion, the only English artist who has yet rightly understood the object and felt the importance of fresco combined with architecture.'[65]

In June, the Benchers of Lincoln's Inn accepted his offer to decorate their Great Hall. His proposal, backed by Hardwick, its architect, did not mince words in promoting art as a record of civilization. 'It is still a disgrace to us that whilst in literature, in science & in arms we are second to none, in the highest & noblest branches our painting & sculpture can lay claim to no very great excellence.' Mural decoration, he proclaimed, could 'develop those qualities which would place British artists by the side of British poets, & form a great national school . . . no man of intellect can prefer dumbness to language, & blank spaces to the elegant literature of Art.'[66]

The hall's forty-by-forty-five-foot north wall, though not a public space, afforded a noble setting for Watts's *School of Legislature*, the largest fresco hitherto attempted in England (pl. v).[67] As he began to prepare composition studies in the manner of Raphael's *School of Athens*, Tom Taylor asked for his comments on the veteran crusader of High Art fresco Benjamin Haydon and published his frank, analytical response (not initially written for publication) with Haydon's journals. In Watts's opinion, Haydon had ignored the essential role of art: to express intellectual truth intoxicated by self-glory, Haydon had achieved neither pathos nor beauty. Only his treatment of anatomy passed muster. His touch was woolly, his surface 'disagreeable'. Draperies lacked dignity and richness. Whereas Rubens was 'profuse and generous as autumn', Watts mused, 'if he is sometimes slovenly, he is so jovial and high-spirited that one forgives everything'. The same could not be said for Haydon, who even in his finest powerful work, *Solomon*, had made the chief character 'half a joker'.[68]

Authoritative and articulate, the unintended critic apologized to Sir Charles Eastlake, a friend of Haydon, and the second edition appeared with a polemic, dearer to Haydon's heart. Mural painting must be encouraged throughout Britain to awaken public taste and raise the national standard of art to the level of literature and science. The Westminster frescoes, painted by successful artists, were seldom seen by the public. Keen to instigate reform, Watts wished to inspire 'a race of workmen who . . . might become great unconsciously.' He called for the Government to decorate all public buildings, town halls, schools and railway stations with monumental intellectual frescoes and have them painted by art students, as training projects. Modern English artists, obstructed by the constraints of fashion, had no stimulus. 'Even the human form is so shut up . . . that it is only displayed to the artist under false conditions' and looked as natural as 'the Dutch garden with trees clipt into the forms of peacocks and vases'; whereas the old masters were familiar with the unconstrained beauty of the

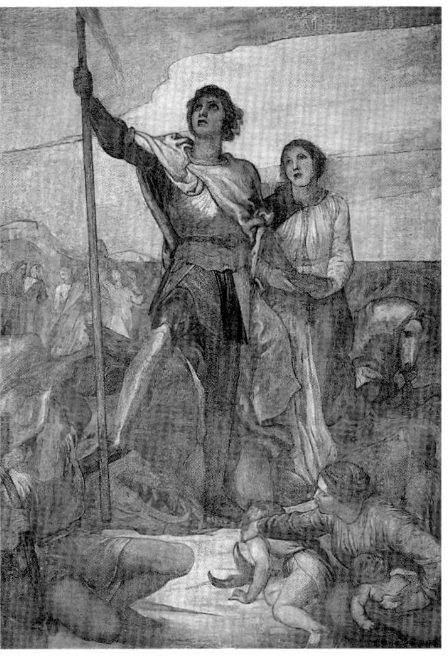

32  *The Red Cross Knight Overcoming the Dragon*, fresco, 1853 (Palace of Westminster).

human form both in and out of the studio. A visit to sunnier Italy would have afforded Haydon many a valuable lesson, he continued, grand figure groups, rich flesh colour – the key-note of the picture – and 'the out-of-door life so suggestive of breadth and brilliancy.'[69]

Newton, preparing to excavate Halicarnassus, captured the spirit as he urged the artist to join him in 'the cradle of Greek civilization', and enjoy the colouring, harmony and unity of Homer's landscape and unchanged peasant drapery: 'Why are you not here? . . . I gaze upon the landscape till my very soul seems absorbed to blend into it, till I forget material constraints of the body. No wonder that the ancients made death beautiful.' He had brought casts of *Theseus* and *Ilissus*: 'We will discourse on art & draw & read, & ride all day long to be happy.' The two philhellenes had much in common; Watts was tempted, but stayed behind to pursue fresco commitments.[70]

The Oxford campaign almost succeeded. However, by November 1852 the artist's hopes were dashed when his noble fresco designs, intended to elevate the use of art, became embroiled in scandal amid vitriolic complaints about idealized nudes. (Monumental nude figures shown under instruction from clothed educators, designed for the Taylorian Institution, clearly caused greater offence, for the university retained the sketch of the cosmic *Titans* he had made for the Radcliffe Camera.) Watts was astonished. The nude was the purest expression of High Art, as in Titian's *Sacred and Profane Love*, where the naked woman symbolizing celestial love is clearly intended to be superior to her draped companion, representing human love. 'The time must be future & real modesty when the mere absence of clothing is felt to be indecency, & I think it is one of the duties of Art to prevent such unnatural & unreal conclusions,' he wrote to Acland.[71] Embarrassed on behalf of his campaigner – 'for myself no want of taste surprises me, I only regret that the good people of Oxford are not further advanced & have such vicious ideas' – he sent Acland *The Ruins* for his trouble.[72] Lady Elizabeth turned him out of Harley Street in the spring of 1853 and ordered that before Roddy's sister Anna Maria married Percival Pickering the drawing-rooms be *'thoroughly cleaned'* of High Art.[73]

Shocked to hear from Taylor of plans to build a mortuary chapel in London, for burials *en masse*, he began to paint a majestic *Angel of Death* to dignify it. The wretched chapel was never built, but Watts's Angel – Virginia in an embroidered kimono presiding over the Court of Death (as the picture was later renamed; pl. IX) – would become one of his most important subjects, exhibited in various stages and sizes until the end of his life.[74] He drew Lady Eastlake for Murray and painted a portrait of the Hollands' adopted three-year-old daughter Marie Fox with her Spanish pointer Elia towering over her in the garden of Holland House.[75] In September, before applying colour to the wall at Lincoln's Inn, he set out with Stanhope[76] and seventeen-year-old Henry Prinsep, via Paris and Florence, to Venice.[77]

There he felt at once in harmony with the colours and movements of the Venetians. Gazing at the time-tinted stone against the sky, the bearded heads and grandly coloured chests and limbs of the figures, he saw combinations and effects that even the old masters had not reproduced. He made studies of costumes and poses, and longed for his brushes and colours. 'I can better understand now why I fail,' he wrote to Ruskin. 'Under the influence of the glowing sun every object is presented in a manner so in harmony with my own feelings that the whole language of Nature seems to me perfectly intelligible.'[78] Moved by the light effects on the mosaics and marbles, the 'reckless scattering of variety' in St Mark's Cathedral, he enthused: 'I had not imagined it possible to attain such completeness of design with apparent absence of it; largeness of whole, with its marvellous impression of unity, profusion without confusion, finish without smallness, contrasts without discords, harmonies without monotony.'[79]

From Venice, Watts took his young friends to see the frescoes painted by Giotto in Padua, admiring qualities he aimed for in his art. 'Giotto was a most wonderful man; departing from manner, dryness, and positive deformity, he displays beauty, dignity and sweetness in degrees that perhaps have never been exceeded.' He marvelled at the fourteenth-century master's 'majesty of form' and 'his original and powerful mind [that] enabled him to perceive and seize upon the noblest properties in nature.' The heads especially, and the figure of an angel seated in a boat, Watts thought as fine in Phidias in style and grandeur. 'I have seen nothing like it in the whole range of art, the dry sculpturesque qualities rendering it more like by suggesting sculpture, but less like in fact; for Phidias was eminently pictorial, stopping short exactly at that point where richness and flexibility merges into the florid. In this quality of luscious breadth and richness of surface, his style later comes out gloriously.'

He recognized Phidian texture in the drapery and flesh-painting of Giorgione and Titian: folds in every direction, close to the figure, their direction given by muscle movement. 'However voluminous and ample the drapery may be in the works of Phidias, Giorgione, or Titian, the figure never seems smothered or loaded,' he observed. 'The drapery of Raphael has been justly celebrated for its grandeur and simplicity, but excellent as it is, it looks academic and like new blanket by the side of the Greek and the Venetian.'[80]

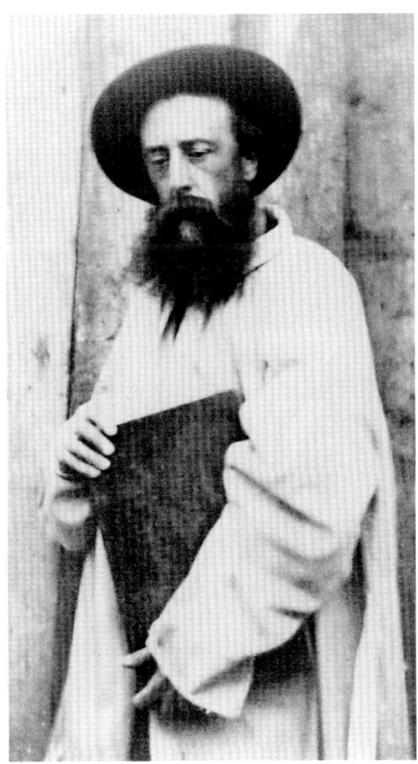

33   The artist, *c.*1853.

Watts painted himself as *A Venetian Senator* (pl. vi), humble and aspiring, light shining over his fine bone structure. His hair had thinned and he had once more a soft short beard and moustache. Presenting himself as a crimson-robed prophet, standing full-length, the exercise was useful preparation for the Lincoln's Inn composition. On his return, determined to find a moral use for his art, he found the focus, reading about 'the great truths of Christianity' – the oneness of God, the brotherhood of man, life of manly self-denial and self-sacrifice and the immortality of soul. 'Such are words that ever stir me as the trumpet stirs the soldier . . . let the future be what it may, a brave life of earnest striving after good, is what I would make my existence.'[81] His patriotic ardour was fuelled by the outbreak of the Crimean War. During his month on the Continent, the Allied British and French armies had attacked the Russian invaders at Sevastopol. Guardsmen in scarlet tunics, long grey topcoats and bearskins, and infantry with their tall black shakos marched past the Royal Academy in Trafalgar Square en route to Tilbury Docks and Balaclava. Watts yearned to be among them,[82] but his duty was to paint civilization.

Scaffolding had been erected at Lincoln's Inn, where he scratched outlines onto the wall for the vast hemicycle. Thirty law-givers, assembled beneath anthropomorphic figures of Truth, Mercy and Justice, were to represent the evolution of civilization. He wanted to create 'a grand monumental effect and pervade, so to speak, the building like a strain of Handel's music, becoming one with the architecture.' When choristers were singing in the nearby chapel, he imagined a choir of angels inspiring his creation.[83] Like Giotto, and as at Careggi, he worked in 'true fresco', painting in tempera colours, mixed with egg, onto thinly applied wet plaster; and he invited art students to assist him for their mutual benefit. He wanted artists to regard fresco painting as naturally 'as a brick-layer builds a wall', explaining to Ruskin that though experienced colleagues should not have to forgo substantial earnings from easel paintings, the laborious enterprise would develop the minds of students.[84] The Lincoln's Inn fresco was subjected to innumerable delays. As visibility on the high scaffolding would be poor during winter fogs, and as the hall was not free when the courts were sitting, it was agreed that Watts would work there only in the spring and summer vacations.

In late November, having painted giant symbolic figures at Eastnor, he embarked on an exuberant series of frescoes of *The Elements* (fig. 34) in the drawing rooms of the Somers' town house, 7 Carlton House Terrace. He had proposed to enlarge designs by Louisa, Marchioness of Waterford. Oppor-tunities for female artists were few and he wished to promote her 'transcendent talent'. Typically over-enthusiastic, he offered to magnify her best compositions 'in accordance with her grand character, thinking them greater than any things that have been produced since the time of Michel Angelo [*sic*]. It will gratify me much to make an offering of that amount of labour which a Lady cannot undertake.'[85] Chivalrous rather than sexist, the gesture was rejected, and he infused *The Elements* with the full range of Wattsian influences – flying Titianesque figures, elegant Phidian style and monumental Michelangelesque groups, Greek mythology, and ideas for his cosmic scheme.

By 1854, Watts's bank balance exceeded one thousand pounds, healthy enough for a gentleman's expenses in London. That year he received four payments of forty guineas for portrait heads – at Landseer's recommendation, he went to Brocket Hall to draw a chalk portrait of Lady Catherine Hamilton for the Queen[86] – and Lord Somers paid in a total of four hundred pounds.[87] A lingering element of guilt may have fuelled the earl's generous patronage, for it was said he never loved Virginia as Watts had done.[88] For this private commission, Watts had few qualms about incorporating semi-clad figures and, rather than employ models, he freely called upon friends for a pose, face or limb. 'I want to make use of you, don't be frightened, it is but to lend me an elbow', he wrote to Jane ('Jeanie') Senior. 'I shall call upon my friends for whatever they can with a perfect sense of propriety contribute . . . so sigh with resignation, but you promised to lend me your hair, & will I am sure add a hand or an arm occasionally.'[89] He would make studies of a wrist or elbow not only in the required position, but turning the joint about, not to make a direct copy, but to refresh his knowledge. On the same principle, when painting a frontal portrait, he would also learn the profile, so as not to depend on light and shadow for the form of the features.[90]

Jeanie was a beautiful, sensitive woman, eleven years younger than himself. She had a strong social conscience and was helping to send supplies out to the Crimea. Troubled by nerves and unhappily married to a coarse, burly barrister, Nassau Senior, son of the political economist and

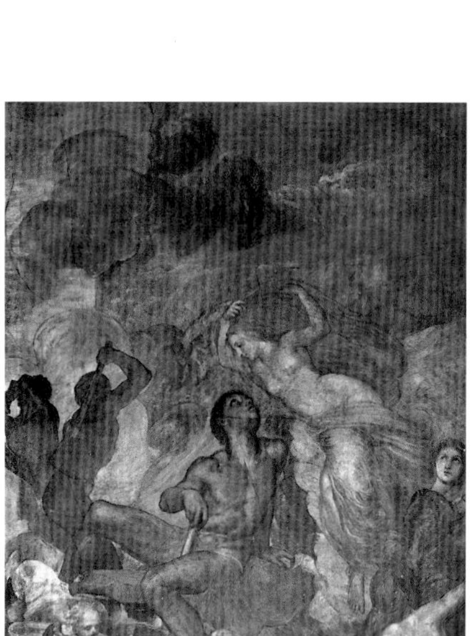

34   *The Elements* (detail), fresco, 1854–56 (Malvern College).

social reformer after whom he was named, she had become Watts's confidante and soulmate. They had met within a year of Virginia's wedding, and their intimacy meant as much to Jeanie as it did to him. She kept his letters, but to avoid prying eyes he burned hers once he had read them. He pressed her for a half-hour sitting before lunch, breaking his rule that no one was to be shown into his studio before two o'clock.[91]

As the winter drew on, painting on cold damp plaster triggered attacks of nerves and vertigo. Sara attributed his listlessness to indolence and ordered Stanhope to see he carried out his fresco commitments; this only increased his anxiety, and he asked to be left alone to complete the Somers's frescoes. Far from indolent, Watts planned to serve Britain as a war artist and to recruit friends for active service. As he wrote to Lord Somers:

> I had seriously thought of going to the Crimea . . . the excitement would afford an Artist effects & produce impressions no imaginings could shadow out or even suggest. Indeed I had a scheme & hoped to be able to induce a few young men of my acquaintance to go out & be useful in many ways, by carrying out clothing, carrying out friendly faces & perhaps even rendering assistance in the field. I feel so impressed with the greatness of the struggle there. I do not think a man should stay at home who is not called upon to remain by duties. If we fail our decline as a nation will be frightfully rapid.[92]

Painting commitments and health put paid to this patriotic plan. He was hard at work at Lincoln's Inn and Carlton House Terrace. In the new year he declined a duty that would have benefited a cause for which he cared deeply. He was invited to teach art at the Working Men's College, which had been founded by Frederick Denison Maurice and Jeanie's brother Thomas Hughes, QC MP and launched with Ruskin's help in October to enrich the lives of the adult working classes. The idea of the college was that teachers and students learned from each other. Had Watts not thought himself incapable of teaching or speaking in public, it would have done him much good. Away from the cocoon of Little Holland House, he would have enjoyed integration with students and given the kind of instruction he wanted to see in modern art schools. But the winter fogs curtailed his activities, and he replied to the invitation on 13 January 1855:

> I am impelled by the desire of making myself useful to accept the post . . . Entertaining very strong objections to the present methods of instruction, & believing that far more efficient ones might be carried into effect, I have a most ardent wish to aid in bringing favour any means of acquiring a truer perception of Art, & a greater knowledge of its principles & objects, but I distrust my capacity to fill the office of lecturer or teacher. I could only consent to work in such a character with the view of being really useful, & of effecting great reforms, & I have neither weight enough from position, nor sufficient obstinacy of disposition to inspire the confidence so necessary in the carrying out of innovation.'[93]

Instead Rossetti took the classes, with enthusiastic reciprocal satisfaction over many years.[94] He and Watts continued to boycott the Royal Academy. Millais was now an associate member, and Jeanie had modelled for his 1855 Summer Exhibition picture, *The Rescue*, shown with the first major work of Frederic Leighton. *Cimabue's Madonna*, a highly finished processional picture of over forty figures representing early Florentine culture, was bought by the queen for six hundred guineas – the sum Watts planned to charge the Marquess of Lansdowne for frescoes for the hall at Bowood House, near Calne in Wiltshire.[95]

Twenty-four-year-old Leighton had arrived from Rome to spend the early summer in England before moving to Paris. Watts received a letter of introduction from Lady Duff Gordon and rode over to call on him at Montague Square in June. Leighton, impressed by Watts's review of Haydon and his reputation for fresco painting, came out on to the pavement to greet him. The two men formed an instant rapport. Leighton was thirteen years younger and his energy and vitality appealed to Watts, who invited him back to Little Holland House and offered him studio space until he had a London base. 'Watts is a most marvellous fellow', Leighton wrote to his mother. 'If he had but decent health would whip us all, if he does not already.'[96] Having seen the Paris *Exposition Universelle* en route for London, he doubtless encouraged Watts, who was 'very desirous of seeing the various schools of art as they are now brought together in Paris', to spend the winter in the French capital.[97]

He and Jeanie had grown fond of each other and in an excitable moment before his departure she seems to have expressed the wish to escape her unhappy marriage. 'I feel anxious about you seeing how much there is in your active nature that is unsatisfied,' he wrote, 'that but for the idea of the future you would give yourself up without reserve to the gratification of the moment.' Warning her not to give in, he comforted her, '*I do* care very much, & I doubt whether any one being has a truer affection for you'[98] and in a later letter affirmed, 'As to my own influence I cannot wish it to be less than you say it is . . . it will never bring upon you difficulty or regret.'[99]

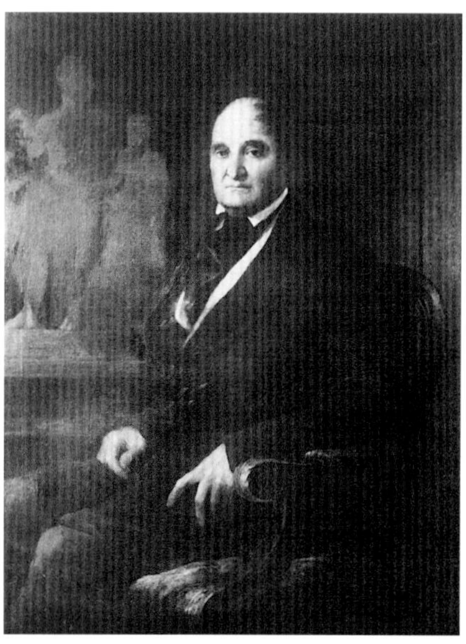

35    *Prince Jerome Bonaparte*, 1855–56 (private collection: photo Frederic Hollyer).

Travelling as a guest of Lord and Lady Holland, he now took Arthur Prinsep to Paris and rented a small studio on the left bank, at 10 rue des Saints Pères, near the Ecole des Beaux-Arts and just across the Seine from the Louvre. The studio was too small for large-scale projects, but Watts was able to prepare studies for future subjects. Taming the spirited teenager was a trial, though a wily bribe committing Arthur not to cut his frizzy fair hair until he had drawn it, yielded reference material for decades.[100] Lord Holland commissioned portraits of his distinguished Paris coterie. Prince Jérôme Bonaparte (fig. 35), now Marshal of France and Governor of the Invalides, the statesman Louis-Adolphe Thiers, and Henri d'Orléans, duc d'Aumale came to the rue des Saints Pères for sittings. The prince, bolt upright on a red velvet upholstered chair and dressed in a black frock coat, his hair brushed forward, eyes keen and alert, appears to be engaged in conversation with the artist.[101]

Thiers, engaged on a long *Histoire du Consulat et de l'Empire*, was a connoisseur of Tuscan art and admirer of Delacroix, for whom he organized magnificent mural commissions in Paris.[102] Awarded the Grand Médaille d'Honneur for his thirty-five works at the *Exposition Universelle*, Delacroix was now designing murals for the Chapelle des Anges at Saint-Sulpice. Thiers – if not Lord Elcho, who had met Delacroix in October – would have arranged for Watts to see his murals and, if possible, his studio.[103] He saw much of Leighton, whose studio in the rue Pigalle was just half an hour's walk away, up three flights of stairs[104] and came to know his warm, stately friend Adelaide Sartoris, the opera singer and the daughter and sister of the actors Charles and Fanny Kemble.[105] Watts would have seen pictures by Ingres, Ary Scheffer – a friend of Lady Duff Gordon – and the *néo-Grecs* and visited ateliers where students working from live models produced glorious nude images that were frowned upon in London. Delacroix was painting a languid *Odalisque* from a daguerreotype of a nude model with her arm raised invitingly at an angle behind her head.[106]

Jeanie, outwardly enthusiastic, a pioneer teacher in the new women's classes at the Working Men's College, feared Watts may have found new love in Paris. 'I am no more likely to marry than to become Emperor of China,' he reassured her in February 1856. 'Marrying & making money! *Jamais*!' He had eight days to paint a portrait of Princess Lieven, the brilliant, unfaithful widow of the Russian Ambassador and lover of Guizot. Her vivacity and talent for political intrigue was said to combine '*la raison de la Rochefoucault avec les manières de Madame de Sévigné*.'[107] The septuagenarian princess sat in profile on a luscious emerald-upholstered chair against a background of gilded mirrors and urns. In a black silk dress and bonnet edged with white lace, her face turned to the viewer, she appears noble and intelligent, not too formidable. Watts, daunted at first, worked at an astonishing rate to complete the detail – her fine black-lace gloves, fan and handkerchief, almost transparent above the fur-lined velvet rug warming her knees – before returning to London at the end of the month.[108]

In his extended studio at Little Holland House Watts agreed to house Leighton's neoclassical nudes *Venus and Cupid* and *Pan*, but felt that they made his own work look flat and dim. He marvelled at the younger artist's 'wonderful perception of natural effects'[109] – the Venus was daringly sinuous – and had the pictures exhibited at the Royal Manchester Institution.[110] That Leighton was virtually copying Watts's large *femme fatale* figure from *Life's Illusions* and transforming it with sensual perfection, as a private commission, into *The Fisherman and the Syren: From a Ballad by Goethe* may well have exacerbated his sense of inadequacy.

Beauty was of course paramount to both artists. However, whereas Leighton's pictures and his own pencil portraits were beautiful in themselves and much admired, Watts's visionary subjects, albeit symphonic harmonies in line and colour, were more challenging to the viewer. Painted in an abstract manner to suggest wider thought, they mystified the establishment and piled up, unfinished, at Little Holland House. Yet Ruskin stated in *Modern Painters* in 1856, three decades before the critical definition of Symbolism, that Watts and Rossetti represented 'the dawn of a new era of art, in a true unison of the grotesque with the realistic power.'[111] Watts had not achieved his desire to elevate the nation by decorating public buildings, but he had distinguished private fresco commissions under his belt, and Little Holland House visitors – poets, artists and lawyers – were now modelling for the law-givers at Lincoln's Inn.

5   Breezy Bohemia

A cosmopolitan, liberal spirit infused Mrs Prinsep's Sunday afternoon
salon at Little Holland House. Offering brilliant hospitality quite unlike the
jostle and affectation of London society gatherings, this exotic temple of
the arts in the Kensington countryside held a piquant allure for cultured
men and women. 'Nowhere else in England would it have been possible to
enter a house with such a singular variety of beautiful persons inhabiting
it,' recalled the Pre-Raphaelite painter William Holman Hunt. 'Aristocrats
there were of ministerial dignity, and generals fresh from flood and field
. . . talking with the modesty of real genius, and adding an interest to life
such as nothing else could give.'[1] Statesmen, reformers, poets, painters,
writers, and, aspiring achievers were welcomed for their individual merit.
'A breezy Bohemianism prevailed. That time of dread, the conventional
Sunday of the early Victorian era, was exchanged for the wit of cynics, the
dreams of the inspired, the thoughts of the profoundest thinkers of the
age.'[2]

Watts was prevailed upon to invite Cosmopolites.[3] Among early habitués
were Tennyson, Browning, Carlyle, Tom Taylor, Thackeray and his daughters, Anny and Minny,[4] Charles Dickens, the astronomer Sir John Herschel,
the statemen William Ewart Gladstone and Benjamin Disraeli, Jeanie and
her brother Tom Hughes who would publish *Tom Brown's School Days*
the following year, and Richard 'Dicky' Doyle, the caricaturist who
designed the *Punch* cover. Along with these were the Pre-Raphaelite artists,
the sculptor Thomas Woolner, and Sir Coutts Lindsay, a soldier, amateur
artist and intimate of Countess Somers (he was often at Eastnor with the
approval of her husband), the Austro-Hungarian violinist Joseph Joachim,
the Italian cellist Alfredo Piatti, the pianist and conductor Sir Charles Hallé
and Adelaide Sartoris, who sang arrangements of Tennyson's verses, Lord
Elcho, his neighbour the Honourable Frederick 'Poodle' Byng (the Regency
character whose curls matched his string of French poodles),[5] and the Pattle
sisters.[6]

Emma Brandling (fig. 36) was sitting for a vibrant, informal portrait
when Hunt visited for the first time in 1856. Watts regarded the future Lady
Lilford, with her perfectly proportioned features, as his most beautiful
sitter. He gave a sketch to the Pre-Raphaelite artist. 'Watts's likenesses were
not *flattered*, a phrase which always means that the real strength and character are taken out, no peculiarity was softened down. The very fullness of
personality was given; but it was the incarnation of the soul', wrote Hunt.

Emma's beauty did not extend to her voice, and Tennyson curtly advised her 'never to sing'.[7] Hunt, whose now celebrated image of Christ knocking at the barred door, *The Light of the World*, had excited hostility at the Academy two years earlier, delighted to see a modern painter with 'such dream-like opportunities and powers of exercising his genius . . . I was fain to regard Watts as an ideal Pre-Raphaelite.'[8] He brought Rossetti, who in turn lured his impoverished apprentice to Little Holland House. 'I am going with Rossetti to be introduced to a lot of swells who'll frighten me to death,' twenty-three-year-old 'Ned' Jones wrote to his father (Edward Coley Burne Jones would later prefix his third given name to his surname):

> Gabriel took me out in a cab . . . we drove and drove until I thought we should arrive at the setting sun – and he said, 'You must know these people, Ned; they are remarkable: you will see a painter there, he paints a queer sort of pictures about God and Creation.' So it was he took me to Little Holland House. It was a very strange society, foreign in its ease and brilliancy.

Introduced by Rossetti as 'the greatest genius of the age,' Ned Jones spoke little; but when he did, the young man with grey-blue eyes and fair hair straggling over his broad forehead, impressed the company. Mrs Prinsep, spotting his unease, swept him under her wing. He warmed to Watts, admired his pictures[9] and came from a similarly modest background, with a hint of Welsh blood. His father was a failed tradesman, his mother died shortly after he was born, and he himself was lovable, unassertive and delicate – William Michael Rossetti observed in *Some Reminiscences* that he suffered weak health, though, interestingly, made no such reference to Watts.

Ned, who had a light sense of humour that the two artists shared for half a century, appears in the Lincoln's Inn fresco as the royal Spartan law-giver Lycurgus. Ina King of Wessex has Hunt's camel-coloured hair and square red-gold beard, and the Persian philosopher Zoroaster owes his features to Emma Brandling. Other friends who modelled for the fresco included Tennyson, posing as Minos King of Crete, Sophie Dalrymple as Empress Theodora, Thoby Prinsep as a druid, Henry Taylor as Charlemagne, Sir Coutts Lindsay as Pythagoras, the archaeologist Charles Newton as Edward I, the barrister Vernon Harcourt as Emperor Justinian, and Armitage and the future Lord Lawrence as the Earls of Pembroke and Salisbury.[10]

Adelaide Ristori, having captivated audiences on the Continent, was now playing Lady Macbeth at Covent Garden. At Little Holland House in June, she begged to be painted once more, and was seen kissing Thoby Prinsep under the trees.[11] Conventional Victorians were unnerved by, or even disdained, Sara Prinsep's salon. Obliged to stoop under the thatched porch into a strange Anglo-Indian household, visitors faced her effusive greeting – a disarming contrast to the staid grandeur of London Society – after which they wandered at will through low, shadowy passages into rooms decorated not with Victorian wallpapers and carpets, but with frescoes painted on old gold backgrounds, pictures hung against rich red or green walls, exotic furnishings and matting. Great dishes piled high with oriental delicacies and strawberries lay on the tables; and gold-painted planets glistened from low blue ceilings. The robed Pattle sisters might be chatter-

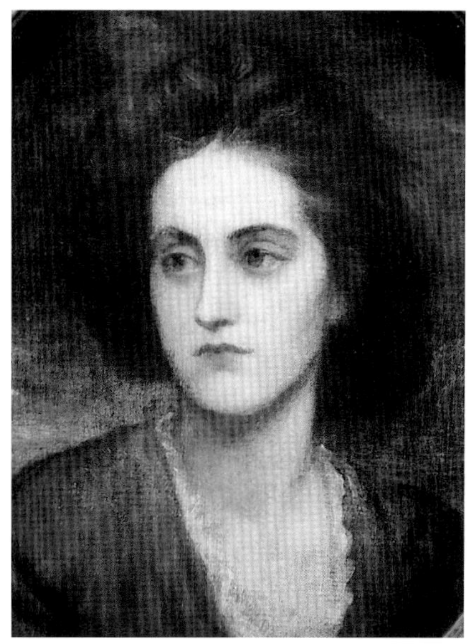

36　*Emma Brandling*, 1856–58 (Watts Gallery). This portrait was made before her marriage to Lord Lilford.

ing in Hindustani – a language ideally suited to their superabundant vitality – when the artist emerged from his studios.[12]

Mrs Fitzherbert's twenty-one-year-old granddaughter, Constance Dawson Damer, very much at home in royal circles, was awed by Watts's revered status. Introduced by her fiancé, Captain John Leslie, to 'a new world – something I had never imagined before of beauty and kindness', the autocratic Lady Constance Leslie later recalled how 'The Signor came out of his studio all spirit and so delicate, and received me very kindly as John's future wife. Thackeray was there . . . Jacob Omnium [the six-foot eight-inch campaigner against social and political abuse[13]] and Lady Somers, glorious and benevolent. Signor was the whole object of adoration and care in that house. He seemed to sanctify Little Holland House.'[14] An American visitor Ellen Twisleton, almost overcome by the intense atmosphere, was rushed into the studio to regain her composure. Watts impressed her more than any modern artist, except Turner who had died in 1851: 'Pray don't tell anyone else that I think I have discovered a genius.'[15] People felt elevated in his company. He would imbue them with his heightened sense of existence. At any moment he might tap them on the shoulder and ask, 'Oh, pray, stay where you are for a moment,' taking from his pocket a tiny sketchbook to draw a gesture or fold of drapery.

In summer guests roamed the lawns, played croquet and bowls, reclined on Indian rugs, or sank into deep sofas under the elm trees (fig. 37), treated to impromptu musical performances by Joachim, Piatti or Hallé. Janet Duff Gordon, Georgy's niece, was listening to Joachim when she felt a tap on her shoulder. 'Sit still, Janet, don't move for a few minutes,' Signor whispered before he drew a study of her intent, uplifted head.[16] Privileged friends would be invited to stay on for a sumptuous dinner. Calves' heads, lobster curry and a range of oriental dishes might be on the menu.[17] As always, Watts kept to his frugal diet of toast and butter. After dinner, the

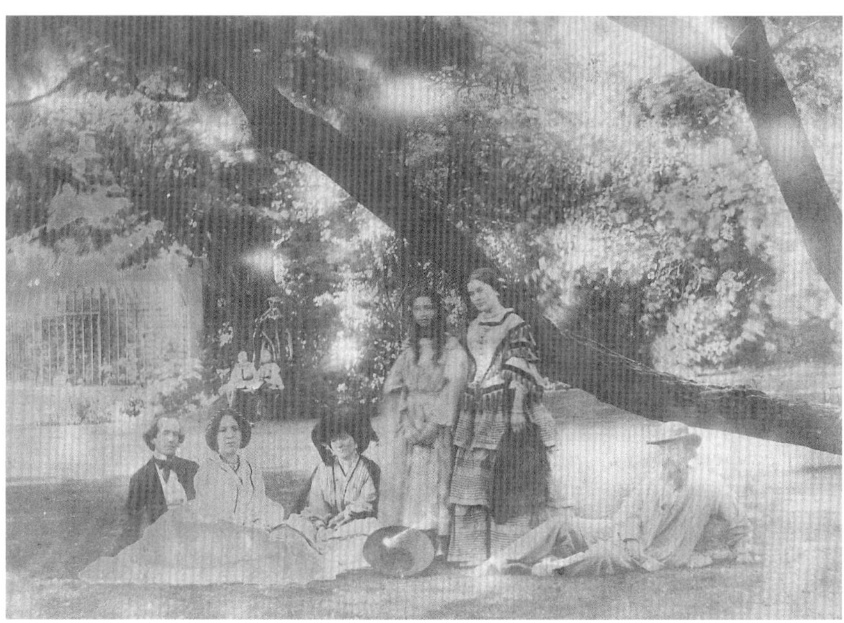

37   Sara Prinsep sits second from left in Little Holland House garden; her daughter Alice stands in the centre; and Watts reclines on the right.

musicians played by lamplight, often late into the night. The artist loved their music. Hallé was organizing an international orchestra for the 1857 Manchester Art Treasures Exhibition. 'He is so unaffected about his music,' Watts wrote to Jeanie. 'He plays for hours, & says he will play for me as long as I like!'[18]

Hearing that Tennyson was in town, Sara swept out in her brougham and forced the protesting Poet Laureate back to Kensington, where she placed him in Hunt's charge and sat him down to dinner, a defeated lion. 'In this company there ought to be Lady Somers, whose beauty I have heard much extolled. I can't see her anywhere, is she here?' Tennyson roared and crushed Hunt's discreet reply.[19] The Laureate was facing savage abuse from the public over *Maud*, his epic poem against falsehood and tyranny. He arrived, distraught, one evening, with an anonymous letter – 'Abhorred Sir, Once I worshipped you, now I loathe you, I hate you. You beast! . . . Yours in aversion' – which he showed to each guest, asking, 'What would you do if you got a letter like this?' He refused to be comforted.[20]

The bizarre behaviour of the women at the Sunday salon intensified. 'The humbug of the whole thing has become so colossal that it is ridiculous and wearying to behold,' Adelaide Sartoris complained to Leighton. 'Hallé and Joachim have been added to the menagerie of which Alfred Tennyson is still royal lion and King of beasts. The ladies of the family all attired like so many rope dancers, in various altitudes of ecstasy about all that they don't understand the first letter of – it's very funny once in a way – but I couldn't go there often now.'[21] The illustrator George du Maurier described Little Holland House as: 'A nest of proeraphaelites [sic], where . . . *tutti quanti* receive dinners and incense, and cups of tea handed to them by these women almost kneeling. Watts, who is a grand fellow, is their painter in ordinary; the best part of the house has been turned into his studio, and he lives there and is worshipped till his manliness hath almost departed, I should fancy.' Invited to dine, du Maurier was advised not to wear a dress coat. As he wrote to a friend, 'Instead of dressing for dinner there, you undress'.[22] Watts wore a velvet coat and slippers, and in the music room afterwards stretched full length on the sofa, while everyone sat in a circle and listened to du Maurier singing Schubert *lieder*. 'C'était très drôle, the worship I got. I wonder if they are sincere.'[23]

The Pattles were too highly charged to be reticent: excruciating as it may have been, their praise was genuine. Julia Cameron could be seen reciting Tennyson's latest poem to the venerable Whig statesman, the Marquess of Lansdowne under the shade of a tree.[24] Ruskin's former wife, Effie, abhorred the 'Tennyson and Watts-worship' at Little Holland House and reported that her new husband, Millais, hated the adulation he received.[25] Nevertheless, he remained an habitué, and du Maurier returned on occasion for the intellectual society.[26]

In his studios, away from the Pattle hothouse, Watts was consumed by desire and concern for Jeanie. Had she been free, he would surely have married her, but he must 'fiendishly' urge circumspection. Her nervous attacks worsened and she stopped writing, which worried him more.

> I do not help thinking you had forgotten or ceased to value the interest & attention you once wished to inspire. I do nothing by halves & if I yield to my natural sympathy for you & wish to occupy the first place in your affections it is not that I am activated by views that can make

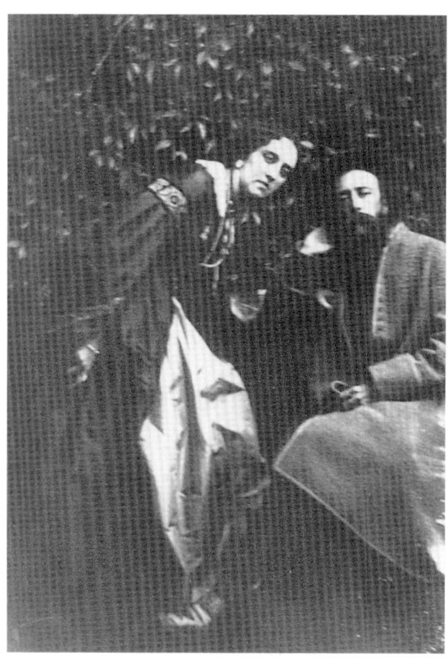

38   Watts with Sophie Dalrymple, *c*.1859.

me dangerous, whatever my impulses might have been, but I have watched you with great anxiety & grieved to see how large a place in your affections remained unoccupied.

Jeanie determined to cool their ardour, for which he respected her 'from the bottom of my soul':

Your confidence was I do think the greatest consolation I possessed – It is impossible I can ever have the hopes which you rightly say it would be wise to encourage. From the moment I was old enough to form any aspirations or objects my whole thought, my only hope was to keep my life in the society of one to whom I should be everything & she should be everything to me . . . [he details the distressing episode of his first unnamed love – presumably Virginia] . . . my mind is nerveless, boneless, crushed – Thank God I was able to conquer selfish impulses & to prove to myself that I could really love . . . I feel poorer than I was, but if possible more your friend than ever.[27]

While undergoing a three-week hydrotherapy cure with Dr Gully at Malvern in August 1856, Watts wrote that he hoped his affection would fill Jeanie's heart and reconcile her to her position. He would never give her cause for embarrassment,[28] but now his mind felt dead, its mainspring broken. He asked her to be his friend, sister, occasional nurse and helper in art, 'for you might be so', and signed himself 'at all times unchanged & unchangeable'.[29] When she questioned his love, the artist replied, 'I could love you better than anyone else now . . . I tell you my affection is jealous . . . I think although I can stop short of the madness of passion (as I well know I can never cure the madness of all absorbing love) . . . I can never fancy you but as standing upon the verge of a precipice, & can never feel that I can avert the frightful danger.' He longed to ease her,[30] but he returned to town with his mind 'like a weathercock vibrating & whirling at every gust of feeling'. Summoned to Buckingham Palace on Leighton's behalf to investigate holes in the surface of *Cimabue's Madonna*, he was then commanded to draw a portrait of the Prince of Wales's disciplinarian tutor, F. W. Gibbs.[31]

That autumn he embarked on a remarkable odyssey. Newton had discovered colossal marble lions from the ruins of Halicarnassus, built into the walls of the medieval castle of Bodrum. On leave in England, he arranged for the use of a warship for at least six months, as well as obtaining the services of an officer of the Royal Engineers and four sappers to help him excavate the mausoleum and bring the lions and other important finds to the British Museum. He invited Watts to join the expedition. To travel aboard a British man-of-war, to study the navy at close quarters and witness the excavation of one of the classical 'Wonders of the World' was an opportunity the patriotic philhellene could not refuse. Although Lincolns Inn would object to his prolonged absence, the winter fogs hampered fresco work and for the benefit of his health Dr Gully insisted on the restorative powers of the sea air.[32] On 17 October, Watts, Stanhope and Val Prinsep – now a keen art student – joined the 160-strong crew aboard the HMS *Gorgon* and set sail from Portsmouth. They picked up Newton from his residence as British Consul at Mytilene, on the island of Lesbos, and anchored in Bodrum Bay on 18 November.

Joining Newton and Watts as they inspected the castle, studying the historic Parian marble fragments – the head and forehand of the first white marble lion visible from the ramparts overlooking the harbour – was a rare privilege for Captain George Towsey. Writing in his journal, he described the expedition members as 'the most useless set of men I ever came across', except for Watts: 'a man of talent & experience but so utterly broken down for fear of his health that he requires all the care & attention of a child: cannot eat this must not eat that . . . requires cold baths half a dozen a day, warm water bottles on his feet every night – and such a man they send out to rough it on the coast of Asia Minor.' While Watts squatted on a stone recreating the distant scenery in colours more glowing and luminous than his Italian landscapes a decade earlier, Val and Stanhope, Towsey noted, appeared to do nothing but get Greek boys to model for them: 'It is quite disgusting when so many men of talent would give their ears to come.'[33] On 10 December, the digging party, uncovering a large mosaic pavement, discovered parts of a draped, winged, female torso. With a whoop of joy, they hoisted the marbles on to a cart, watched by astonished Turks, who followed the procession. To preserve accurate recordings of the ninety square feet of tessellated pavements, the three artists spent weeks colouring photographs taken by the sapper Corporal Spackman.[34]

At Christmas, Watts reduced the sailors to tears singing his favourite ballad, 'Tom Bowling', by the eighteenth-century 'Ocean Bard' Charles Dibdin.[35] He made a tiny drawing of a lion's head and paws, unearthed two days later; and on New Year's Eve, Newton found the forequarters of a life-size marble horse, a momentous discovery he believed to be a clue to the mausoleum. Subsequent digging yielded its fragments, mouldings similar to the Amazonian frieze, remains of lions, Ionic columns and large foundations. On 7 January 1857, thrilled that his name would be immortalized among antiquarians, Newton confirmed that the site was found.[36] In his absence, on 16 January, workmen summoned Watts to examine an ornamented ceiling beam, its sculpted foliage painted in vermilion, golden yellow and turquoise green. Though he ordered it to be covered at once, the 2,000-year-old decoration faded before the archaeologist could see it. Huge equestrian figures were found, one of which he suggested represented Mausolus spearing an enemy.[37]

The finds were prepared for shipment, but the firman giving permission to remove the lions was delayed. Anxious the Turks might take them, Newton sent Watts aboard HMS *Swallow* with urgent despatches to the British Ambassador to the Sublime Porte in Constantinople, Viscount Stratford de Redcliffe, who had obtained the original frieze for the British Museum. Watts took advantage of bureaucratic delays to paint two portraits for his national collection: the tall, grey-haired and amusingly indiscreet ambassador and the commander-in-chief of the Mediterranean fleet, Admiral Lord Lyons, on his flagship *The Royal Albert*. At an embassy dinner, disoriented by strange lights, sounds and odours, Watts was struck for the first time by sudden deafness.[38]

Newton, watching helplessly as the castle commandant carried out Turkish orders to remove the lions (fig. 39), ordered an overland runner to press for the firman. Meanwhile, Lord Lyons sent the artist on a Greek island cruise, jovially placing him 'in command' of the *Swallow*.[39] Gazing through the portholes, Watts marvelled at the blueness of the waters and

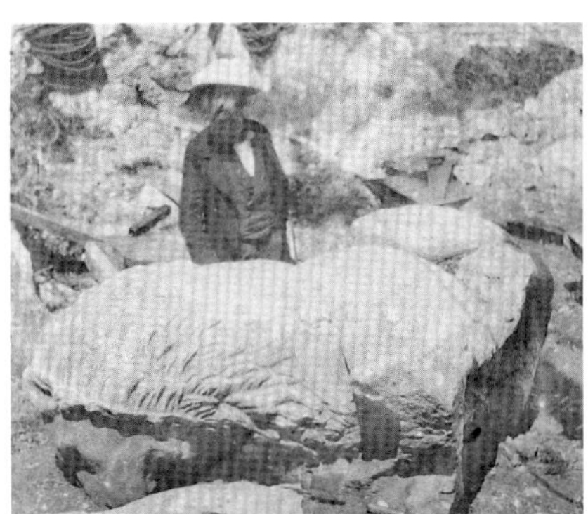

39   Charles Newton stands above excavated lion from the Mausoleum of Halicarnassus, 1856–57.

the reflected light that would inspire his *Genius of Greek Poetry*, an imaginative design he modelled in wax in the form of *Theseus* and explored in paint over two decades. On 17 March, Newton went to bed sick at heart. The lions were packed in sheepskins on a caique ready to be shipped on to a Turkish man-of-war – 'the extraction of two of my eye teeth could not have given me so great a pang.' 'At 3 this morning,' Captain Towsey noted in his journal, 'Watts brought the firman for the lions in the castle at last – just – in time.' Newton refused to believe the messenger and stayed in bed. Two hours later, a second man rushed the still sceptical archaeologist to the *Gorgon*, to find the captain pacing the quarterdeck, pointing to the caique still in harbour. It was waiting for the wind to sail. The captain was about to cast off. Newton leaped into a boat. 'Don't let that caique go,' he shouted. He sped off to the commandant, handed over the firman; and the Turkish man-of-war set sail without its prey.[40]

Watts was fascinated by the Turks, not only by their looks and manners but by the spirit of Muslim teaching: smoking was unknown to the prophet Mohammed and therefore not expressly forbidden, yet during Ramadan workmen did not smoke between sunrise and sunset; they would sit with their pipes filled, ready to light up as soon as gunfire announced sunset. The expedition dragoman sat for a splendid portrait profile.[41] Having feasted on the rediscovery of the mausoleum and its inheritors, Watts needed to return home. Too long away from fresco commitments and contemporaries, his confidence was shaky, but he was keen to discover how they had fared at the Academy. Travelling back aboard HMS *Desperate*, he arrived home in June with sketchbooks full of lions, cloudscapes, architectural details, Turkish costume, headdresses, squatting figures, nautical knots and sailors sleeping and scrubbing the decks. He was fired with energy to tackle the Lincoln's Inn wall.[42]

A cloud of fear was spreading over Little Holland House following the outbreak of the Indian Mutiny. Sixteen-year-old Arthur had left to join Henry's regiment in India, where sepoys were rebelling against their East India Company commanders. Both brothers were in danger. Watts's romantic sense of chivalry lessened his concern for Arthur, who could at least die in battle; but Henry, in a wavering native regiment, could face torture: 'Little warlike as I am, I feel like a caged wild cat when I think about it.'[43] At the Little Holland House salons, listening in rare silence to the music, fathers held their heads in their hands, tears trickling between their fingers. Thackeray wrote a poem to ease Sara's distress. Tennyson paced the lawns, composing 'Guinevere' for *Idylls of the King*, his seminal re-creation of the Arthurian legend, inspired by Sir Thomas Malory's medieval *Morte d'Arthur*. He was working on King Arthur's departure from Guinevere for battle – 'Gone – my lord! / Gone thro' my sin to slay and to be slain' – and explained as he sat for the first of several portraits, that Arthur represented conscience and his knights the sentiments, impulses, feelings, 'the more animal qualities that man has to contend with'.[44]

Arthur Prinsep was wounded. Chased by a barrage of shots, he rode for three days without food through the burning sun but, like Henry, he survived the mutiny and remained to serve in India. Watts immortalized Arthur's features in paintings of the Arthurian knight Sir Galahad, standing by his horse (pl. VIII), representing dignity, purity and chivalry, 'the characteristics of the gentleman'.[45] After the mutiny ended in June 1858, the East India Company would be disbanded, British rule appropriated by the Crown under the governorship of a viceroy and Thoby Prinsep appointed a director of the new Council of India.

Val, having decided not to follow his father into the Indian civil service, pursued art studies with Watts, whose aim to guide without imposing his style, so as not to stifle inspiration, was generous because he longed to inspire a child of his own: 'What pleasure can be greater than that of moulding the disposition and developing the intelligence! If I had such an object, such a direction of my thoughts and energies, I think I should be happy.' He confided to Jeanie, 'My last regret will be that I have no child.'[46] Riddled with self-doubt, he nevertheless had high hopes for his young Pre-Raphaelite friends. For years Little Holland House had been buzzing with their ideas; they influenced Val and Stanhope and impressed students at the Royal Academy Schools. 'We liked the anarchy of it . . . and what a contempt we had for the sleepy old conventional school' recalled William Blake Richmond. 'We all knew of Watts, and the dislike which followed him for the great efforts he was making to uplift English Art from nursery rhyme to epic poetry, from a mere academic coldness of accuracy, a kind of slick convention of painting, admirable in its way, but dull and uninspired.[47]

That summer, inspired by the Lincoln's Inn fresco, Rossetti secured approval to paint Arthurian murals in the Oxford Union Debating Hall and invited twenty-year-old Val to join Roddam Stanhope, Ned Jones, William Holman Hunt and William Morris.[48] But before he set off, Watts's latest sitter, twenty-year-old Virginia, Countess of Castiglione, treated Leighton and Val to an unexpected private view during her sitting at Holland House. As a child, the Florentine beauty had attracted the interest of Prince Louis Napoleon, and recently Count Camillo Cavour, the prime minister of Piedmont, had sent her to engage the support of the future Emperor Napoleon III for the unification of Italy – 'Succeed by whatever means you wish. But succeed!' She was the talk of Paris. Even more capricious than her cousin Countess Walewska, who had earlier tantalized Watts and now replaced her as the emperor's mistress, the Countess of Castiglione loved to thrill an audience. As the three artists entered the room, she greeted them in the nude. Watts refused to finish her portrait (fig. 40). She had posed in an off-the-shoulder red velvet gown, her famous five-strand pearl necklace falling from its oval clasp. His disgust at her 'insatiable love of flattery' tells in the blue eyes that stare with unaccustomed calm.[49]

Val left for Oxford. 'I have conscientiously abstained from inoculating [him] with my views . . . and have plunged him into the Pre-Raphaelite styx,' Watts wrote to Lady Duff Gordon. 'I don't mean to say that I held the fine young baby of six feet two by the heel, or wish to imply the power of moulding his opinions at my pleasure; but to continue my figure I found him loitering by the banks and gave him a good shove, and now his gods are Rossetti, Hunt, and Millais – to whose elbows more power.' Committed to his vision, with no desire to follow their style, Watts nevertheless felt discouraged, as he would recall in old age, 'These PRB [Pre-Raphaelite Brotherhood] played the devil with me!'[50] Outwardly he sung their praises to Lady Duff Gordon. 'The said Master Val . . . has distinguished himself by painting a picture at Oxford fourteen feet long with figures ten feet high – A muffin!'[51] However, seeing him easily influenced, Watts suggested to Ruskin that copying Rossetti's medieval style might restrict his protégé's natural instinct. The critic promised to talk to with Val and shouldered much of the blame himself:

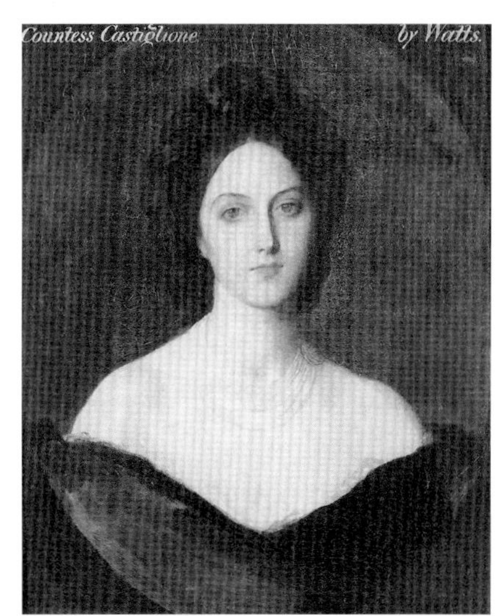


40   *Virginia, Countess de Castiglione*, 1857 (private collection).

I am answerable for a good deal of this fatal Medievalism in the beginning of it – not indeed for the principle of retrogression – but for the
stiffness and quaintness and intensity as opposed to classical grace and
tranquility – now I am suffering for so far yielding to my own likings –
I've almost got sickened of all Gothic by Rossetti's clique . . . The worst
of it is that all the fun of these fellows goes straight into their work, one
can't get them to be quiet at it, or resist a fancy; if it strikes them ever
so little a stroke on the bells of their soul, away they go to jingle, jingle,
without ever caring what o'clock it is.[52]

*    *    *

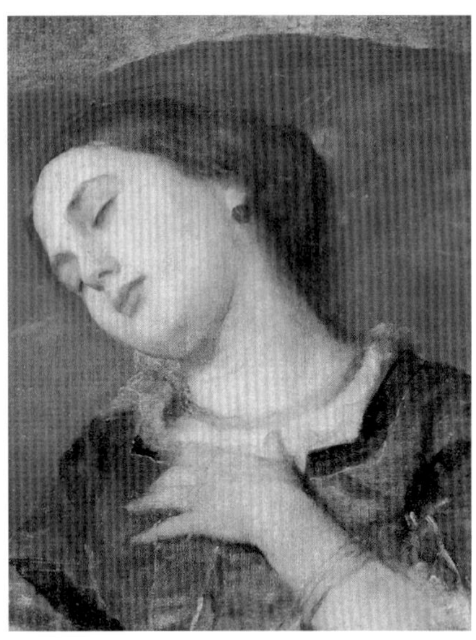

41    *Georgina Treherne* (detail),
*c.*1857–58 (Watts Gallery).

A devious little minx without a care in the world sang her way into Little
Holland House. Georgina Treherne, John Dalrymple's cousin,[53] had been
brought up in Florence, 'bristling with virtue' and banned from visiting
Casa Feroni because of her father's misgivings about Watts and Lady
Holland. Blessed with a crystal-clear soprano voice that was her passport
into society, twenty-year-old Georgina was a sexual tease. Watts, twice her
age, relished the idea of taming excitable young women. He painted
Georgina as she sang and snoozed (fig. 41). Ruskin, infuriated by one delicate drawing, accused him of making her look like an angel: 'She was not
an angel, by any means. The soft chalk translation of her did you deadly
mischief at every touch.'[54] The critic's antipathy was no doubt coloured by
his failed marriage to the forthright Effie Gray and Watts's exquisite likeness of Effie in chalk.

The artist was not taken in. Writing to Jeanie, he raised objections 'to
the same sort of things in Georgina, but now that your animal spirits do
not run away with you all that you do & say is most pleasant to me, I
should wish that you still had the spirits even.'

To raise funds for his spinster sisters, he was carrying out elaborate commissions for Jeanie's family; he had painted a full-length portrait of her
sister-in-law Mary Senior, a smaller portrait head of her mother and of
Mabel Eden and was now ready to paint Jeanie herself.[55] *Miss Senior* was
painted in his broad inimitable style and *impasto* surface texture, but he
chose, exceptionally, to paint the three other portraits in the popular Pre-
Raphaelite style. Whether or not his despair at Academy prejudice had
driven him to prove that he could, if he wished, paint exquisite Pre-
Raphaelite pictures, Watts's chief aim was to reflect his sympathy for Jeanie.
With the jewel-like clarity of a miniature, every detail of Mabel Eden's
English-rose head and of the full-length portrait of Jeanie watering lilies of
the valley (pl. VII) was in sharp focus, from the reflections in the glass pitch-
ers, the pure flesh tones, the ripples of her golden hair and fine lace trim
on her blue silk robe to the rich green wallpaper and the arum lily, orchid
and rose beneath the chair upon which she rested her knee.[56] The artist
imbued Jeanie's picture with symbolism – exceptional in his portraits at this
stage – to indicate her comforting soul. 'In making you water . . . a flower-
ing root with so much solicitude!' he explained, 'I intended by the flowers
to typify the better sentiments, aspirations and affections, which it is sometimes difficult to keep alive, or at least blooming in the crush of artificial
society'.[57]

There is no doubt about the scheming look in Georgina Treherne's eye
or the wide feathred hat she wore for her oil portrait (fig. 42).[58] The more

she played up to Signor, the more endearing was his role as her 'best friend', steering her away from vanity and deceit and from 'sipping intoxicating champagne & more intoxicating applause – pray don't indulge in both at the same time.' He chided her for neglecting his watch cry, 'Bambina, are you good?', yet became her accomplice. The artist secured an invitation from her host, Sir Thomas Sebright, who was spreading malicious gossip about Little Holland House, and astonished guests with his departing words, that he would not return.[59] Georgina tricked him into a clandestine correspondence from which he gently extricated himself, warning that her behaviour might arouse gossip among the servants or deter honourable suitors. She toyed with the idea of marrying Lord Wimborne's brother Merthyr Guest, sought Watts's advice, ignored it and announced her engagement. 'Ah Bambina would you ask if you thought I sympathized less with you?[60] He planned to spend the winter in a musical household, to hone his piano skills and distract himself from his existence '*manqué*'. Instead he took up the violin.[61]

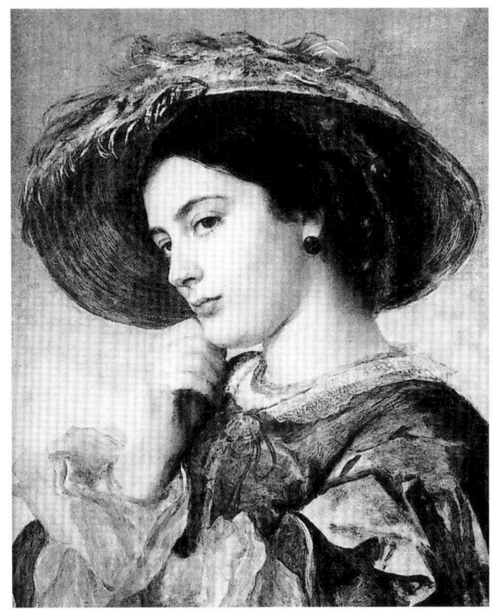

42   *Georgina Treherne, 1858* (private collection).

*     *     *

Unknown to Watts, the authorities were at last waking up to his aims. Henry Cole, the General Superintendent of the new South Kensington Museum, had been discussing plans for historical frescoes and on 11 January 1858 noted in his diary that 'Watts might begin'.[62] Jeanie tidied his studio and pasted his smaller drawings, from the earliest to recent Lincoln's Inn studies, into two albums.[63] The fresco, still in his mind an unfinished 'eyesore', hidden under wraps in his absence, was due to be completed in the spring vacation.[64] But, to the benchers' fury, he was summoned to Bowood by Lord Lansdowne, who had postponed his two frescoes until now in case scaffolding upset his visitors. In the entrance hall, Janet Duff Gordon gamely modelled in armour as Patroclus for *Achilles and Briseis* until her shoulder ached. She received a portrait in compensation. The *Genius of Greek Poetry* figure was incorporated into the Homeric fresco, which Watts was working at from seven o'clock in the morning until seven at night.[65] Occasionally he broke off early to ride Undine, the Arab mare Jeanie had found for him.[66]

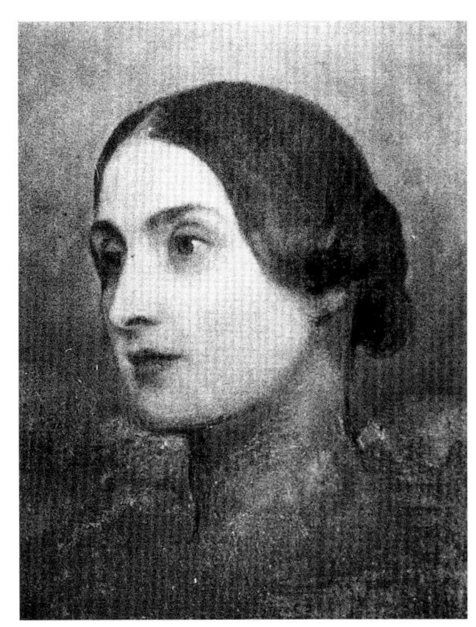

43   *The Honourable Mrs Caroline Norton, c.*1857–58 (photo Frederic Hollyer).

The flamboyant political hostess and poet Caroline Norton, who had sat to him at Holland House (fig. 43), also modelled for *Achilles*. She was an old friend of Janet's mother and of Lord Lansdowne, to whom she would dedicate her next poem, *The Lady of La Garaye*, about a woman with a tragic past. The brutality of her own husband, the Honourable George Norton, had driven her to separation and, in revenge, his suit against the prime minister, Lord Melbourne had exposed her as a scandalous woman. To retrieve her children, she had campaigned for reforms, drawing on literary skills inherited from her grandfather, the dramatist Richard Brindsley Sheridan, publishing pamphlets that led to the 1839 Infant Custody Bill and the 1857 Divorce Act. Intensely dramatic, Caroline Norton loved playing roles and sang and spoke in a deep, contralto voice. Gentlemen were captivated by her wit, intelligence and beauty, her violet-raven hair with ear-phone plaits, her large eyes, perfect nose and teeth.[67] She reminded Watts of a hunter alert to the sound of distant hounds. 'The grand flexibility of her beautiful nostril' he so admired[68] was heartily endorsed by a shopkeeper from whom Janet bought casts of limbs for drawing practice:

'There ma'am, it's the Honourable Mrs Norton's nose. Hartists do buy a lot of 'em.'[69]

Friends persuaded Watts to enter the Senior and Eden portraits for the Academy Summer Exhibition. He was understandably anxious after years of abuse. Conscious that his pictures were so unlike his contemporaries', 'not painted in a spirit or key that can make a satisfactory effect in an exhibition', he decided to test the waters by using a pseudonym 'F. W. George', which itself provoked criticism. 'So I am abused for not sending my name! …I consider contributing pictures to the Annual Exhibition like contributing an article to a series & I don't at all see why people should care about identifying Mr George with Mr Watts who is injured?'[70] He became so nervous as the exhibition approached that he could hardly climb the stairs, fearing company, solitude and even riding.[71] The Academy experiment paid off. Recognized at once, his portraits were acknowledged as the best in the exhibition, for his daring introduction of Pre-Raphaelite-style accessories rather than traditional books, curtains, pillars and landscape backgrounds. 'O remember, portrait painters, men of industry, talent, and perhaps still some faint, foolish, lurking ambition,' warned the *Athenaeum*, 'if you do not paint more like Mr George, the inevitable gravitation towards the garret of the broker's of your now applauded pictures!'[72]

While Watts was at Bowood in June, Georgina created a scandal in his studio, where she was caught alone with Lord Ward, and airily discarded Merthyr Guest. Sara, disgusted, summoned Guest's mother, Lady Charlotte Schreiber,[73] but she did not banish Georgina. A month later, James Wilson, the founder of *The Economist*, and his director elect, Walter Bagehot, heard her sing from a hammock under the trees and perform operatic duets with the baritone Graziani.[74] Finding the studio silent on his return, Watts missed her effervescence: 'I was always in a fidget about the wild little girl.'[75] (Georgina later eloped with an ineffectual Yorkshireman Harry Weldon, ran a singing academy, lured the French composer Charles Gounod with her '*voix des deux sexes*', had a lesbian affair, sued all her partners and, to the astonishment of the nuns of Gisors, spent her twilight years in their convent.[76])

The summer of 1858 was the year of the 'great stink' when fumes from sewage in the Thames caused an epidemic of marsh fever. Watts returned from Bowood to find Sara Prinsep nursing Ned Jones back to health at Little Holland House. Starved of beauty in his childhood home, he marvelled at the Kensington household where nothing was ugly and where every Sunday there were *fêtes champêtres* for guests who 'made up the "world" of England': 'the very strawberries that stood in little crimson hills upon the tables were larger and riper than others.' Louisa Herbert, a tall, shapely actress, with pale gold hair came to sit to Watts. Younger friends, captivated by her beauty – and no doubt notoriety – gathered round to draw her at the same time. She too lived apart from her stockbroker husband and fell pregnant to one of her many admirers. Little Holland House seemed remarkable to the actress. 'I never saw such men … it was being in a new world to be with them … they were different to everyone else I ever saw. And I was a holy thing to them.'[77]

To Jones, Watts was a father figure. He advised him on preparation and tools, and of course referred him to the Elgin casts. Ned felt 'compelled' to improve his drawing.[78] Inspired by a sumptuous portrait Watts was painting of Virginia Somers in Venetian rose, ochre and indigo – in itself a lesson in colour-handling – he learned to work in a broader, more Venetian manner. Both men joined the Hogarth Club, an avant-garde exhibiting society.[79] In September, persuaded by Rossetti and Morris, who deplored the luxurious atmosphere, Jones left Little Holland House.[80]

John Murray commissioned a portrait of Gladstone, at present out of office and engaged in a study of Homer. Watts explained his dual national object and the portrait collection of 'individuals whose names will be connected with the future history of the age': that 'such portraits should be as inartificial & true as possible', not necessarily pleasing. In the event, he painted two versions, one for the national collection, the other for Murray. The statesman and the artist would debate and dispute Homer for the rest of their lives. Watts believed the characters in *The Iliad* and *The Odyssey* to be different and that because Homer would not have portrayed *Ulysses* whining about death and Hades, he was not the author of *The Odyssey*.[81]

Watts's *Isabella*, a half-length portrait, its subject wearing white roses at each ear, was well hung at the 1859 Academy exhibition and hailed as 'a masterpiece of the tenderer harmonies of blonde colouring'.[82] Watts wished, nevertheless, to 'hang the Academy' for its apathy towards British art and teaching. He knew his views were extreme, but the institution must revolutionize itself. On 19 July 1859, he proposed to Lord Elcho – always a staunch supporter – that an inquiry be set up to expose the Academy's failings, to recommend improvements and to promote mural decoration. At Watts's instigation, the wheels slowly began to turn.[83]

After Gladstone's reappointment as Chancellor of the Exchequer, sittings were interrupted by affairs of state, by the artist's indisposition and by the opening of Oxford's new anthropological museum, which had been built according to the moral truths outlined by Ruskin in *The Seven Lamps of Architecture* and *The Stones of Venice*. (The critic had lectured to the workmen on site, reminding them that medieval architects did not treat their craftsmen as mere machines, encouraging them to work together as one man, yet allowing freedom of expression, principles espoused by Watts.[84]) 'An attack of diarrhoea has prevented me from doing any thing since Wednesday,' Watts apologized to the Chancellor. 'I am still very unwell & do not think it right to take your valuable time, & subject you to the trouble of sitting under the consciousness that I cannot do my best. I consider myself very unlucky, & am afraid you will be annoyed.' That the pictures were ever completed and that the statesman's respect for the artist remained intact is astonishing.[85]

At the same time, Tennyson was sitting for a second portrait (fig. 45). His family thought the first had not quite caught his poetic imagination. Watts and Tennyson aspired to interpret the highest Victorian mind in their work. This portrait afforded them an opportunity to illustrate their influence on each other. The poet asked what was in the artist's mind at the start of a new portrait and. incorporated his technique into the idyll, 'Lancelot and Elaine'. Watts aimed to show intellectual characteristics. He had no desire to highlight every wart and wrinkle. Revolutionizing the art of portraiture, he encouraged sitters to reveal their inner nature; he would talk to them, draw out each train of thought, and immerse himself in his subject to reproduce the face as 'the window of the mind':[86]

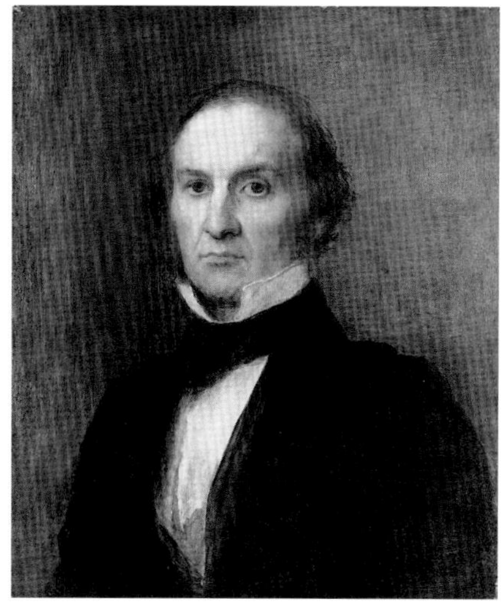

44   *The Right Honourable William Ewart Gladstone, Chancellor of the Exchequer*, 1859 (National Portrait Gallery, London).

45   *Alfred Tennyson, Poet Laureate*, 1859 (Eastnor Castle Collection).

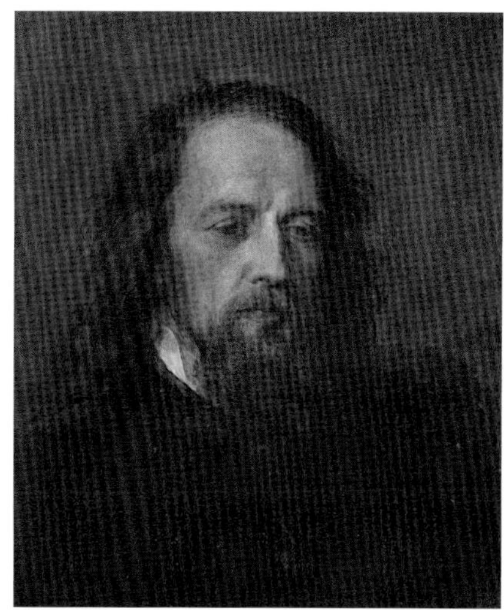

> And all night long his face before her lived,
> As when a painter, poring on a face,
> Divinely thro' all hindrance finds the man
> Behind it, and so paints him that his face,
> The shape and colour of a mind and life,
> Lives for his children, ever at its best
> And fullest; so the face before her lived,
> Dark-splendid, speaking in the silence, full
> Of noble things . . . [87]

Emily Tennyson, delighted for her husband to be in 'the Enchanted Palace', hoped it would do him good.[88] She approved the meditative portrait, which also earned Ruskin's admiration. At Little Holland House, Tennyson, overhearing the critic exclaim, 'Jones, you are gigantic!', dubbed Ned 'Gigantic Jones'. Now designing stained glass for James Powell and Sons, he was recommended by Watts to Jeanie as 'a real genius! Really a genius!', the very man to design her window (possibly, the stained-glass panel *Good Shepherd* at the United Reformed Church in Maidstone, near the home of her brother, Arthur Hughes[89]). Ruskin, who now regarded Watts as 'a man of great imagination and pathetic power', recorded an illuminating vignette of Little Holland House at the time. Watts was lying on the sofa, with the 1857 Moxon edition of Tennyson's poems open on his knee. Behind him stood the poet laureate, his face quivering with indignation as he explained, over his shoulder, why the Pre-Raphaelite illustrations did not suit the poems. Ruskin, sitting at Watts's side, looked up, deprecating Tennyson's criticisms on the artists' behalf, 'feeling very cowardly in the good cause – yet maintaining it in a low voice:

> Behind me as backer Jones . . . laughing sweetly at the faults of his own school as Tennyson declared them and glancing at me with half wet sparkling eyes, as he saw me shrink – A little in front of us – standing in the light of the window, Mrs Prinsep and her sister – two, certainly of the most beautiful women in a grand sense – (Elgin marbles with dark eyes) – that you could find in modern life – and round the room Watt's [sic] Greek-history frescoes. Tennyson . . . was maintaining that painters ought to attend to at least what the writer *said* [–] if they couldn't, to what he meant – while Watts and I both maintained that no good painter could be subservient at all: but must conceive everything in his own way, – that no poems ought to be illustrated at all – but if they were – the poet *must* be content to have his painter in partnership – not a slave.[90]

That summer, *Idylls of the King*, published at last to critical acclaim, established Tennyson among England's finest poets, as Watts acknowledged when Emily sent him a copy of the poems: 'I feel happy to have lived at the time of their production, and proud of being acquainted with the Poet.'[91]

Feeling something of a slave to his own aspirations, he put the final touch to the Lincoln's Inn fresco, *Justice: A Hemicycle of Lawgivers*, on 17 October. The *Athenaeum* reported that he had been forced to work quickly because the benchers had threatened 'over much port' to cover the fresco with whitewash. 'Mr Watts, he do work so rapid,' exclaimed the butler.[92] Layard's support was unbounded: 'We are persuaded that they will have no cause to repent their decision . . . they will boast of the greatest monument of mural as yet executed in this country.'[93] But the heroic effort left Watts drained, convinced that the *Hemicycle* was a failure. 'I shall never again have so fine a space', he despaired.[94] As ever, Julia Cameron's eulogy drove him to distraction: 'I feel as if I were practising a deception upon her, she describes a great picture, but it is hers, and not mine.' *Hemicycle* was a triumph, hailed by Millais and Rossetti as the finest modern specimen of true fresco. 'It does honour to the country', Rossetti wrote to Lord Aberdare.[95] Those words would have meant more to Watts than any other – and to his friend and patron Lord Holland, who died in Naples in December, two months after its completion. Messrs Winsor & Newton, his paint suppliers, sent a New Year gift of crystal bottles containing pure ultramarine and a rare madder, an inscription on the case urging him to pursue his noble exertions in the cause of modern art in England.[96]

Watts saw the *Hemicycle* as a prelude to an educational scheme that would see the hall filled with frescoes of historic developments in English law. Here was an opportunity for the Royal Academy to teach the noble art of mural decoration, to supply designs to be carried out by competent students, under instruction from professors, 'exactly the course of study would be pursued and experiences gained which created great artists formerly'.[97] At least the benchers overcame their irritation at his absences: 'for perfecting so important a work, no time was too extended for us'. He declined an invitation to meet the Queen, who brought Prince Arthur to see the fresco on 25 February and noted afterwards that she was 'rather disappointed'.[98]

Expenses incurred at Lincoln's Inn having taken their toll, the artist undertook further portrait commissions. John Lothrop Motley, the American historian recently introduced to the Cosmopolitan and to the Holland House circle, offered excellent conversation during sittings for two portraits.[99] With the confidence of his improved standing, Watts increased his charges to a hundred guineas for a head.[100] He informed George Cavendish Bentinck that his seven family portraits were 'valuable works of art' and, as these had to underwrite national projects, he must raise his fees 'as rapidly as prudence will permit' to match those of the fashionable portrait painter Francis Grant.[101] On 27 March 1860, Watts wrote to Bentinck: 'I am hard up. Lady Margaret [the Marquess of Clanricarde's daughter Lady Margaret Beaumont, whom he was painting full-length in shimmering silks] has got whooping cough, Lady Cork a child, the Chancellor whom I have just begun has lost his wife & Lincoln's Inn's expenses & results still sit upon me, so you see how it is.'[102]

The benchers rewarded him royally. On 25 April, they held a special dinner in his honour and presented him with an Italian Renaissance silver-gilt cup filled with five hundred new sovereigns.[103] Despite Watts's pledge not to charge for work intended to inspire the nation, the gift did not appear to trouble his conscience. He deposited five hundred pounds at Coutts the following morning and began to invest on the Stock Exchange. By June his bank balance had topped two thousand pounds. Forty years later the cup and remaining coins were to feature in his funerary picture, *Sic Transit*, as symbols of the River of Life.

Charles Darwin's seminal study, *The Origin of Species*, published in November 1859, revived the great evolution debate. The geologist had

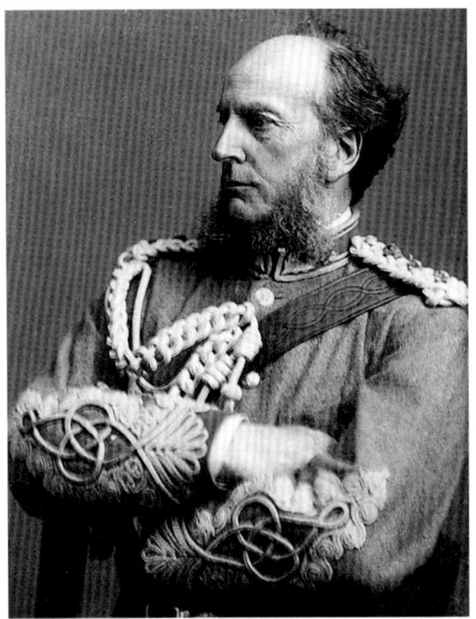

46    Lord Elcho in Volunteer uniform, *c.*1860 (photo: Fradelle and Young).

47    Watts, on the right, amongst the first privates of the Artists Rifle Volunteer Corps in 1860; William Holman Hunt is on the left (*The Artists Rifles Journal*).

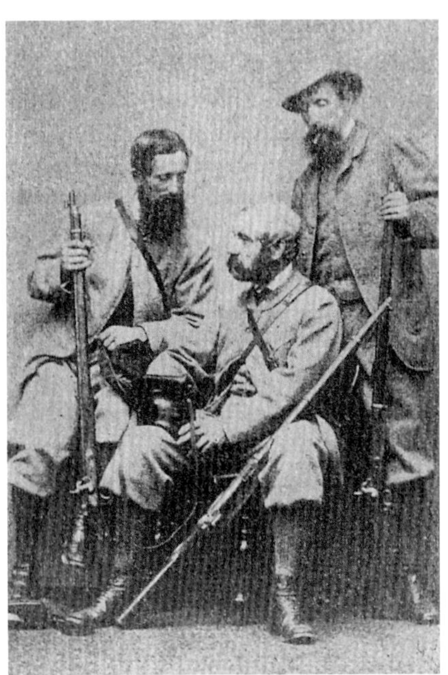

begun his research before the publication of Chambers's *Vestiges of the Natural History of Creation*,[104] which he dismissed as 'popular', whereas his science-based work, eradicating God's role in the Creation, defined the modern theory of natural evolution. 'When I view all beings not as special creations, but as the lineal descendants of some few beings,' he wrote, 'they seem to me to become ennobled.'[105] The controversy he now provoked would direct the public to look anew at Watts's imaginative subjects.

For a man driven by patriotic fervour, an opportunity to train to serve his country was not to be missed. Tennyson had published a call to arms in *The Times*[106] after ties between England and France were severed in May 1859. The War Office, fearing invasion by Napoleon III, authorized the formation of a Volunteer Force and National Rifle Association headed by Lord Elcho (fig. 46), who recruited Watts to design the Elcho Shield to be awarded to the winner of an annual competition to encourage international small-bore shooting. Asking for a sketch in January 1860, he added, 'Can I help you in getting more wall space?'[107] Lord Elcho, now MP for Haddington, had the artist's interests very much at heart. The second Bowood picture, *Coriolanus*, would not be carried out in fresco because his plasterer was not permitted to eat or sleep at Bowood, an inconvenience and discourtesy that moved Watts to paint the picture on canvas instead at Little Holland House that summer.[108]

For the Elcho shield, he supplied chalk drawings of battle scenes, of Reginald Cholmondeley resplendent in uniform and the shield itself, sized to Watts's specification – 'Let it be made in iron, and six feet high' – was made by Elkington's.[109] One of the first to enlist in the Artists Rifle Corps on 10 May, Watts is registered in the Muster Roll of the 38th Middlesex (Artists) Volunteer Corps as 'Regimental No 11, Company No 3, Watts George Fred[k], 5 ft 9 inches' (fig. 47).[110] At his suggestion, the figure of a running man was used for target practice at Wimbledon Common; and he designed the National Rifle Association logo and medals, still awarded today. William Richmond recalled that the first time he saw Watts was on horseback, his long silky beard blowing from shoulder to shoulder as he rode over the common from Kensington to join the skirmishing. Leighton, a natural leader, rose through the ranks to become Commanding Officer and Honorary Colonel of the Corps. The sight of artists in grey uniforms and pillbox caps on parade in Hyde Park had the ladies fluttering with delight.'[111]

Watts's admirers, however, were either untouchably aristocratic or married. He longed for a wife of his own, a muse and children. Just as he thought himself over the hill, another wild girl, soon herself to become a star, was about to burst into his life. What was his attraction to these vivacious youngsters? In the exalted intimacy of his studio, awestruck at first, they responded to his chivalry and understanding as they poured out their hearts and flirted with this strange, poetic artist. It was an honour to model for the Signor; he would make them feel special; he cherished their bubbly high spirits, their fiery beauty. Always conscious of his modest background, he dared not believe that, with the exception of Jeanie, women might like him for his own sake. Rather than passion he offered compassion. Young visitors were safe with him – until the flames of passion burst open the studio door.

# 6 Choosing

'YES ROSSETTI'S A GREAT, GREAT FELLOW and his wife's as charming as the reflection of a golden mountain in a crystal lake which is what she is to him', Ruskin wrote to Watts in November 1860.[1] Rossetti had married his 'stunner', muse, and model, Lizzie Siddall, herself an artist. Jones married Georgiana Macdonald, and Newton – now the Consul in Rome – was engaged to Mary Severn, an artist who recorded his archaeological finds. A wistful air tinged Watts's congratulatory note to Tom and Laura Taylor on the birth of their son: 'I think nature intended me to shine under similar circumstances, but instead I have four horses.'[2] He was painting a romantic full-length portrait of Mrs Louis Huth dressed in satin, for her husband's gallery at Possingworth in Sussex, and a sumptuous picture of Alice Prinsep seated, in a blue velvet Venetian gown, at the piano at Little Holland House (fig. 48). Her sad brown eyes stare directly at the viewer. Often snubbed by her mother, Alice was to be unhappier still in her marriage to Charles Gurney.[3]

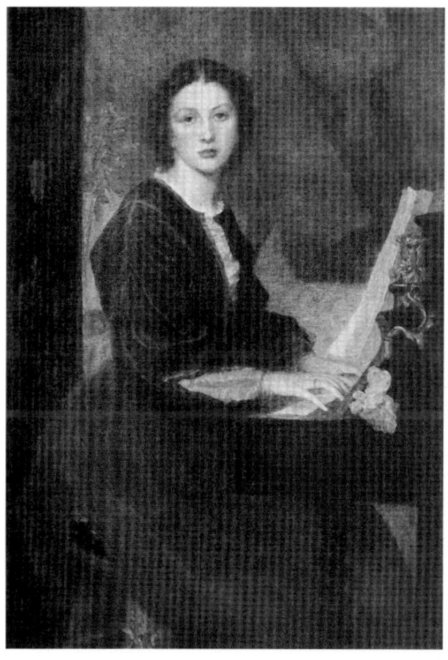

48  *Alice Prinsep*, 1860–61 (private collection).

Marie Ford, the model introduced by Rossetti in 1860, seemed to Watts 'one of the most beautiful women Nature ever formed, "finer than the Greek, because she was alive"'. He painted her as *Bianca*, offsetting her auburn hair and bloom of her flesh tones with a low-necked Florentine black dress, a bouquet of roses pressed to her breast (fig. 49). (So radiant was her complexion that when she later sat to Rossetti as the spirit of Dante's Beatrice he felt compelled to transform her into Solomon's bride, *The Beloved*.)[4] Marie Ford would reappear as *Ariadne*, but in *Bianca* Watts simply celebrated her beauty, whereas his national sitters were selected for their achievements and qualities of mind. In his portrait of George Douglas, the eighth Duke of Argyll (pl. IV), however, he challenged his fellow artists' distaste for red hair by heightening His Grace's copper sheen against a green background.[5]

To escape the winter fogs, he moved to Surrey with the Prinseps, to Sandown House in Esher, the home of Thoby's widowed sister. Watts had settled his sisters nearby, at 10 Prospect Place in Long Ditton, where he too kept a room.[6] He rode with the prince de Joinville and the duc d'Aumale, sons of the exiled French king, Louis Philippe, and, exhilarated by the thrill of the chase, hunted with the duc's Harriers. Lean as a hawk, his pony jumped like a dream and was up with the leaders to the last.[7] The artist did not consider hunting cruel, but he campaigned against docking horses' tails, which he condemned as a barbarous fashion that destroyed the har-

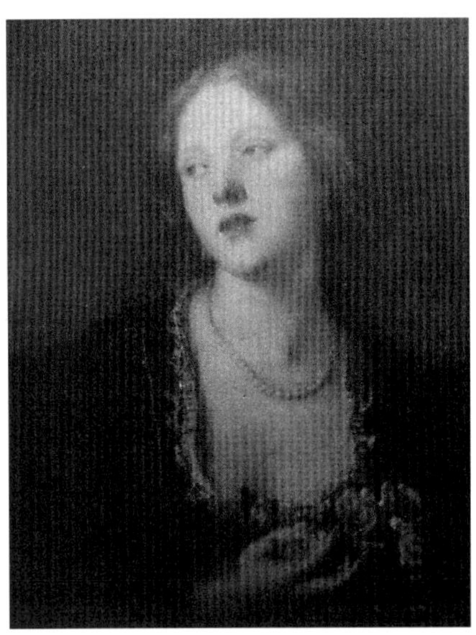

49   *Bianca*, 1860 (private collection).

monious balance of nature.[8] When Baron Carlo Marochetti showed him his statue of *Richard Coeur de Lion*, before it was erected outside the Palace of Westminster, Watts challenged the proportion of the king's thighs rather than those of his horse. The sculptor laughed, slapping his own legs: 'If it were not art I would do it again. It is because my own thighs are short!'[9]

In the spring of 1860 Watts began elaborate full-length portraits of the new lord chancellor, Lord Campbell, and the president of the Royal Society, Sir Benjamin Brodie.[10] Ruskin promised to come and sit 'whenever and wherever and as long as you like,' but Watts felt too intimidated to paint him. They corresponded at length, especially about Titian's technique, which the critic described as 'drawing with paint as tenderly as you do with chalk'. Yet Ruskin could not resist criticizing his friend's work: 'It struck me in looking at your group with child in the Academy that you depended too much on blending and too little on handling colour: that you were not simple enough, nor quick enough, to do all you felt – nevertheless it was very beautiful. I should think you were tormented a little by having too much feeling.'[11]

Far greater was Julia Cameron's all-consuming passion. She had recently moved to Freshwater on the Isle of Wight, to live near the Tennysons because her husband was often away, looking after his coffee plantations in Ceylon. She bought a pair of cottages, one to live in, the other for guests. Julia worshipped and provoked the Poet Laureate to distraction. Tearing over to his house Farringford in the middle of the night, she lured him down to the beach to gaze at the moonlit water for the good of his soul and poetry. She made him 'wed the sea' like a Venetian doge.[12] Tennyson was her finest sparring partner, but even he could not pierce her adulation for the silver-haired poet and civil servant, Henry Taylor. 'I don't see what you mean by his extraordinary beauty – why he has a smile like a fish,' he challenged Julia, who flashed back, 'Only when the Spirit of the Lord moved on the face of the waters, Alfred.'[13]

Her letter imploring Watts to paint Taylor, even after he had agreed to do so, shows her 'doubly distilled' persuasion in full flood.

> Do him immortal honor . . . I have always heard you also say that men in action were your Heroes! A silent course of forty years of *daily* devotedness to *business* . . . as well as brilliant coups d'état & successes . . . surely do make H T's life very remarkable, ranking so high as he does in all the walks of literature – & writing every [Colonial] Office Paper with as much care & perfectness of diction as he gives to an essay or to a Poem – therefore, liking his face – too – fulfil your re-reiterated intention *paint* for your gallery of great men this great head – would you? – You promised you would – Use your own incentive "Whatsoever thou findest it is in thy heart to do – do quickly" – and do find it in thy heart – for yours is the heart, the hand which *can* do it – & so there is small use in my struggling, and striving with my pen and hand which *cant* do it, to shew you how you might paint Henry Taylor as great & grand as Alfred Tennyson aye grander & greater too, I would say like the Irishman "I say Pat isn't one Man *as good* as another?" "To be soore he is *and better*!! So this being so God bless you. I commend this work to you for ever.[14]

Watts, unable to concentrate on imaginative work in the winter fogs, offered to start on Taylor's portrait in January 1861 (fig. 50) – Julia had a special shrine constructed for it in her drawing room, with a lamp perpetually burning.[15] He also began a Bohemian profile of the teenager Edith Villiers, her hair falling loosely over her robes.[16] His enthusiasm for the work of James McNeill Whistler encouraged his long-standing patron Alexander Ionides, the influential Greek Consul General, to commission work from the American artist, who now had a studio in London. Hearing that Whistler wished to meet him, Watts wrote to Ionides for an introduction; and the American became a lively habitué of Little Holland House, entertaining guests with a large mechanical male doll seated beside him at dinner.[17] Ionides, receiving quarterly payments from Watts – perhaps for extra studio rental – purchased his 1861 Academy entry, *The Window Seat*, in which the Prinseps' French maid is seen at her needlework.[18] Little Holland House still had an extraordinary attraction in the 1860s, as Ruskin demonstrated in an idiosyncratic note to Watts: 'Indeed I love you much ... so judge if I wont come & dine with you. I shall like to see you all again so much ... Not that I would dine with many people – because friends & dinner are too good to have at once – I like to eat like a bear – & hug afterwards – but to growl over my bones.' A refreshing contrast to the tutorials he usually sent the artist.[19]

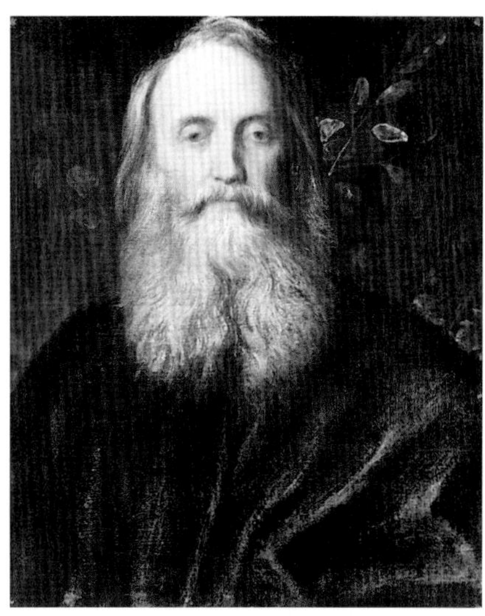

50    *Sir Henry Taylor*, 1861–70 (National Portrait Gallery, London).

Newton, prior to his appointment as the new Keeper of Greek and Roman Antiquities at the British Museum, asked Watts to send a testimonial to Dr Henry Milman, the dean of St Paul's cathedral: 'Your name would have great weight'. While writing to the dean,[20] Watts raised the controversial issue of the cathedral's interior decoration; he discussed the merits of fresco and mosaic, and offered his own services.[21] (Two years later he would be one of four artists invited to compete for the commission to design mosaics for the semi-dome behind the altar, although none was taken up;[22] in May 1863, however, he would be asked to produce designs of the Evangelists for mosaics in the four spandrels beneath the dome.[23]) Meanwhile, an exuberant new Gothic Revival church, St James the Less – built by George Edmund Street in the Westminster slums as 'a lily among the weeds' to hearten the poor – needed his help, and the monumental fresco of *Christ and the Evangelists* was the only commitment he refused to lay aside while completing *Coriolanus* for Bowood. For the text he chose 'Come unto me all ye that are heavy laden, and I will give you rest'. By July he was at work on the chancel arch.[24]

Appalled that a conservation controversy had led to the withdrawal of a donation to the National Gallery, Watts presented to the gallery a life-size, sixteenth-century Mannerist portrait of a knight in the robes of San Stefano, the military order founded by Cosimo de' Medici. With background architecture and furniture ornamented with sculpture, the picture in itself represents the fine arts. Watts believed *A Knight of San Stefano* to be by Jacopo da Pontormo, who was not yet represented in the collection. Sir Charles Eastlake, president of the Royal Academy and director of the National Gallery, had not heard of Pontormo, but accepted the gift, today attributed to Alessandro Allori.[25]

The death of the Prince Consort in December 1861 threatened the second London's International Exhibition, which was planned to exceed the Paris Exposition Universelle of 1855. Masterminded by Henry Cole, director of the South Kensington Museum, it would go ahead nevertheless, in a building designed by Captain Francis Fowke on the site of the present Natural History Museum.[26] The decision to show no new paintings amongst the works of art infuriated Watts. Paris had combined retrospective with contemporary, yet London seemed set to block artistic progress. 'What right have the committee to conclude that the pictures already exhibited are the best the English school can possibly show in 1862?'[27] His *Alfred* and *Bove*, both painted in the 1840s, had been chosen, but what angered him more was that the retrospective rule disqualified younger artists, the hitherto little-known work of Jones and Rossetti, 'productions of undoubted genius … which I believe would excite universal interest'. In a long letter to Layard, Watts lambasted the exhibition organizer, Richard Redgrave, for not treating English art with the respect given to poetry and literature.[28] In February he accepted Cole's commission to produce a sketch for a large fresco to fill the lunette at one end of the museum's South Court and recommended that Leighton be invited to design the other end.[29] This would not deter him from complaining to Layard that his bull's head was to be shown in the exhibition as 'a specimen of my early style' and that he had been asked to retouch it. Not only would the retouching be 'a deceit & a sham', he fumed on 13 March, but 'I have a great deal to do before the Nation will care a straw about my "early style".'[30] Ultimately the organizers conceded, and the rule was dropped.

The London International Exhibition opened on 1 May 1862, with heady displays of art treasures from Africa, Asia, India and Japan, and the giant gilded pyramid representing Australia's gold mines.[31] Decorative arts designs by Jones and Rossetti featured in the first public showing of William Morris's firm of artist–craftsmen, Morris, Marshall, Faulkner & Co., founded on the Ruskinian principle that hand-crafted objects restored the freedom of expression stifled by the demands of the mchine age The French sent Ingres's neoclassical nude *La Source*, yet there was still no call in Britain for Watts's imaginative work. His recent portraits, the *Tennyson* of 1859 and *Sir John Mair Lawrence*, the battle-scarred hero of the Indian mutiny – exchanged for the *Bove* – were seen to atone for the 'phantasmagoric *Alfred*'.[32] Florence Nightingale would later prize her photograph of the portrait of Lawrence. Having posed for a baron in the Lincoln's Inn fresco, he was soon to return as Lord Lawrence, viceroy and governor-general of India.[33] Watts had asked Tennyson for a signature to accompany engravings of the portrait for Colnaghi's. Autographs, prized by collectors, were a sensitive issue and neither man gave them readily. But the poet obliged, enclosing a copy of the *Idylls* with his new 'Dedication' in memory of Prince Albert. 'The stroke of the T is wanting,' Watts observed. The artist requested another: 'I don't think the Public would be satisfied with the signature of its favourite looking like Kennyson!'[34]

*Bianca, Lady Beaumont and Daughter* and his heroic, life-size painting *Sir Galahad* were warmly received at the Academy,[35] and Watts invited the philanthropic social reformer the Earl of Shaftesbury and the former lord chancellor Lord Lyndhurst to sit for the national collection. Ninety-one-year-old Lyndhurst rode out to Little Holland House for the sittings and had to sit for a second portrait because his wife complained that the first made him look old.[36]

Rossetti's wife, Lizzie, died from an overdose of laudanum and depression on 11 February 1862. As she lay in her coffin, Ruskin gave her a last sorrowful kiss, while the artist placed a manuscript of his poems in with his wife's body. (In 1869, Watts would be one of the strangely privileged

few to know of the macabre enterprise to retrieve the calf-bound manuscript, when Rossetti was keen to establish a reputation as a poet and
prepare the poems for publication.[37]) Watts had asked to meet Lizzie. 'Oh,
come and dine,' Rossetti had said; then he forgot to deliver the invitation:
'I did write to ask you to dinner, but as you did not come I thought the
letter had miscarried, and I was *partly* confirmed in that impression by
finding it in my pocket.'[38]

A commission that most deeply affected Watts was an invitation to Blickling Hall in Norfolk to paint Lord Lothian, for the thirty-year-old marquess
had begun to suffer from creeping paralysis. Watts's own attacks of near
paralysis, given the right care, lasted only a few days. The prognosis, that
his youthful sitter was doomed to premature death that no medical expertise nor love nor wealth could prevent, was to haunt the artist for years. His
later preoccupation with death in art, and the impotence of Love facing
the inexorable approach of Death – encapsulated in the metaphysical
masterpiece *Love and Death*[39] – sprang from his growing friendship with
the Lothians. During his first stay at their magnificent red-brick Jacobean
home, the Marchioness of Lothian and her sisters, Lady Gertrude and Lady
Adelaide Talbot (the future Countess of Pembroke and Countess Brownlow), posed for him, their arms entwined around each other's waists
(fig. 51). Reginald Talbot stood as the *Standard Bearer*; and in two hours
he painted a vibrant portrait of their father, the Earl of Shrewsbury, as a
lesson in oil painting from life for the recently widowed Lady Waterford.
The marchioness rode with Watts through the woods and glades, and
walked so grandly that one evening, as she approached, he and his companion exclaimed, 'O Pallas Athene!' He fascinated the women. Each
encounter with him was a high point in their lives. As the Countess of Pembroke later reminisced, 'Mr Watts was different – he had something
apart.'[40]

Happily, too, he sang with the Moray Minstrels at the home of the silk
mercer and amateur artist Arthur Lewis. On Saturday evenings, under the
direction of John Foster and the Gentlemen of the Chapel Royal, the jovial
all-male group of musical artists and writers – among them Fred Leighton,
Val Prinsep, Tom Taylor, John Millais, Dicky Doyle, and other Little
Holland House habitués – performed glees, madrigals and part songs; and
afterwards oysters were served. At Moray Lodge on Campden Hill and,
possibly, at the new Arts Club founded by Lewis in 1863, Watts would
have met artists of the St John's Wood Clique and the Belgian art dealer
Ernest Gambart, owner of the private French Gallery in Pall Mall.[41] Watts
agreed to sit to the St John's Wood artist David Wilkie Wynfield, for a series
of pioneering soft-focus, close-up photographs of painters in old master
costume. The temptation to be photographed in Titianesque pose was irresistible (fig. 52) – the robe he wore appears in Leighton's *A Noble Lady of
Venice*, completed two years later. Watts invited friends to sit to Wynfield
at Little Holland House. Ned Jones posed in Holbein costume, Leighton in
Venetian medieval, others chose Elizabethan or van Dyck.[42] As Wynfield
proposed to take a further series of literary men and 'is naturally anxious
to begin with King Alfred!' Watts invited Tennyson 'to be Photographed in
the most sublime manner'.[43] There is no record of the poet's reply or the
literary series, though he would succumb to the lens of a pioneer photographer closer to home.

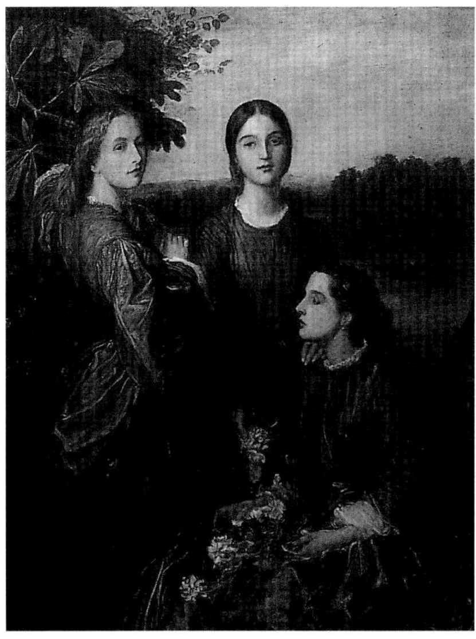

51   *The Talbot Sisters: Lady
Gertrude, Lady Adelaide and Lady
Constance, Marchioness of Lothian,*
1862 (private collection).

52   Watts posing in Venetian dress
for David Wilkie Wynfield, 1863.

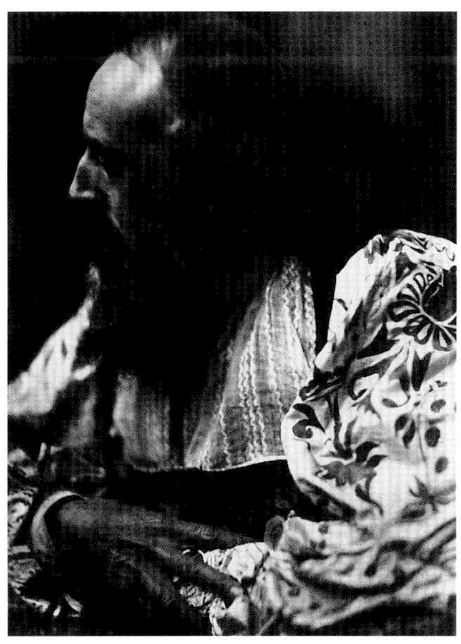

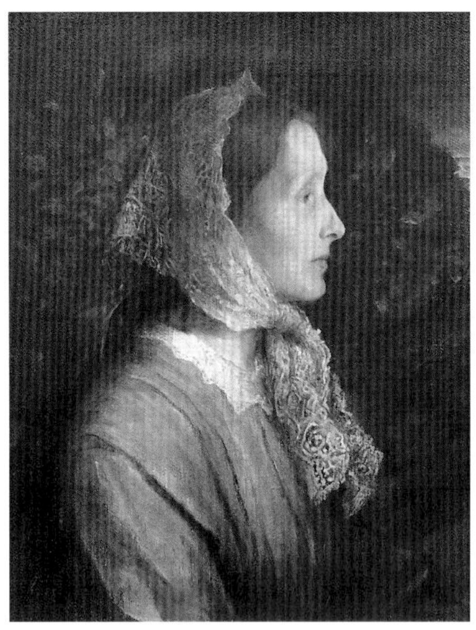

53   *Emily Tennyson*, 1862
(Tennyson Research Centre, Lincoln
County Council).

Watts spent much of November 1862 with the Tennysons at Freshwater. While the poet studied the stars through his telescope, the artist painted a surprise portrait of his wife (fig. 53); and to their delight their sons, ten-year-old Hallam and Lionel, eight, were allowed to stay up and watch. Emily Tennyson was a slight figure, physically frail; she had a delicate English rose complexion, blue eyes and a strong spiritual intellect. The artist liked to think of his pictures as poetry in paint. To present her as the wife of a poet, he gave her a laurel background (prompted, perhaps, by the *Portrait of the Poet Ariosto*, acquired by the National Gallery in 1860).[44] He painted her in profile, her lace veil folded beneath her chin. Contemporary photographs show her wearing it unfolded, which Watts may have seen as a distraction. By knotting the veil, he softened the contours of her chin to capture her powerful, yet tender spirit.[45] When the portrait was unwrapped at Farringford the following June, guests were enraptured. The Duke and Duchess of Argyll compared it to a Gainsborough, and Emily Tennyson wrote, 'I do not know how such a beautiful picture has come, but you are a subtle alchemist, a great magician, that I do know. He hopes to thank you in person tomorrow.[46]

To celebrate the publication of Anny Thackeray's first novel, *The Story of Elizabeth*, in 1863, he added a four-inch panel to her portrait, showing an open book in her hands.[47] But no magical powers could rescue the Dalziel Brothers' *Illustrated Bible* from commercial failure. Leading artists supplied designs for woodcuts in 1863. Watts rejected the 'mere costume pictures' he was asked to illustrate, suggesting instead *Moses Receiving the Tablets* or *The Brazen Serpent* or a more abstract subject from Job or Ezekiel. Eventually he sent three designs – *Esau Meeting Jacob*, *Noah Building the Ark* and *The Sacrifice of Noah*. Their request for minor adjustments seemed petty: 'My object is not to represent the phrenological characteristics of a mechanical genius, but the might and style of the inspired Patriarch.' Noah's reduced head is undoubtedly better, but he insisted on artistic licence to retain the length of limb or flexibility of joint 'commonly seen in the East . . . [I] consider myself at liberty to depart from mere correctness if necessary for my purpose'.[48]

On 17 April Watts gave evidence at the Royal Academy Inquiry (which he had proposed to Lord Elcho in 1859). Thanks to Lord Elcho, here was an official opportunity to shake the Academy from its torpor, to present effective teaching reforms and stimulate British art. The chairman, Earl Stanhope, and the commissioners had interviewed Holman Hunt and would afterwards consult Ruskin and Armitage. (Hunt had also been humiliated by the Academicians and by the time they finally offered special hanging for his *The Finding of the Saviour in the Temple*, he had sold the picture to Gambart.[49]) Watts urged the Academy to have live models in the antique school, so that instead of 'merely drawing the figure in a set position' from classical casts, students could observe natural muscle movement and proportion of the human form. Asked whether the Academy should continue to teach all three branches of art – sculpture, painting and architecture – or painting alone, he replied that all three should be connected, as they used to be 'combined in one and the same man' and should not be taught separately. He outlined schemes for training students in the highest form of art – mural-painting – on public buildings.[50] The benefits were three-fold: the exercise itself required absolute study; the murals would address serious issues ignored by English artists; and, painted throughout the country, should stimulate the public.[51]

Watts pointed out that the Royal Academy should encourage art, and cultivate and elevate national taste. Instead it was apathetic and had no influence on architecture, fashions or furniture. Worse, Academicians had opposed the new Pre-Raphaelite school: 'It appears to me to be nothing short of a phenomenon that English art should so little express the peculiar qualities of English character and history [or equal] the power and solid magnificence of English enterprise.' He proposed that art students paint Flaxman's designs as murals at public schools, 'The young men at Eton would then grow up under the influence of works of beauty of the highest excellence.' After a wide-ranging interview, he sent a letter of supplementary evidence to Lord Elcho, recommending that students be taught chemistry in relation to art and the reliability of their pigments and chosen medium, and that tests be introduced to consolidate solid practical teaching. Finally, he hoped that if the Academy moved to Burlington House (from shared space within the National Gallery), no picture should be hung above the level of the eye.[52]

The Academy took up just one of his recommendations and placed antique casts in the life and painting schools. By contrast, in Paris, the Ecole des Beaux-Arts was instituting reforms towards academic idealism, and when the avant-garde artists Edouard Manet, Camille Pissarro, Paul Cézanne, Johan Barthold Jongkind and Whistler were turned down by the Salon (the annual exhibition of the French Royal Academy), Gallic uproar prompted Napoleon III to intervene. The emperor ordered over 1,200 rejected works to be shown in an annex.[53] At the landmark Salon des Refusés in May 1863, Whistler's controversial *Symphony in White: The White Girl* – a life-size portrait of the artist's red-haired Irish model in a loose-fitting, long white gown, rejected by the Academy the previous year – was a triumph.[54] Manet's woodland picture, *Le Bain*, later known as *Le Déjeuner sur l'herbe*, outraged viewers because it featured a nude woman sitting amongst clothed gentlemen. Like Watts he was inspired by the Venetians and found his interpretations crushed by the disapproval of the authorities. He had chosen a format similar to Titian's *Concert Champêtre*,[55] but while the dubious morality of the Louvre masterpiece was superseded by Venetian grace and colour, its translation into modern French realism – *Le Bain* – appalled critics.[56] Watts kept abreast of developments in Paris; and though he would not have known that Manet was copying Titian's *Venus of Urbino* to convert into a nude *Olympia*, he too was making avant-garde nude studies and exploring classical themes. The two artists' aims and treatment were, however, quite different – apart from a rare series of erotic dancing nudes in Watts's 1863 almanac.

His first painting of *Ariadne* (see fig. 159) relates to *Olympia* insofar as both pictures show a woman whose lover is absent. Dramatic angles and abrupt tonal contrasts in Manet's picture highlight the cool, white body of the prostitute on her bed, and the black maid presenting a bouquet suggests the real and impure entry of her next client. In *Ariadne*, the Cretan princess (Marie Ford) sits in wistful, dishevelled reverie, abandoned on the island of Naxos. Watts's image of idealized beauty, taken from Ovid's *Metamorphoses*, was inspired, in form, by the Fates from the Parthenon pediment. Languidly Ariadne gazes out to sea, searching for her lover, Theseus, who is represented by the string with which she saved him from the labyrinth. The red skein falls from her hand into the playful paws of a panther at her feet. Watts softened her clothed Phidian form with drapery folds, Venetian colour and tonal gradations. Exhibited at the Academy, *Ariadne* was seen as 'a work of the highest order of imagination'.[57] The blonde model in Leighton's *A Girl Feeding Peacocks* would appear in a quite different version of *Ariadne* by Watts, and in the nude *Study with the Peacock's Feathers* – the latter as challenging to the British art establishment as *Olympia* would be to the French.[58]

Some time between March and September, a Pickwickian gentleman in pebble spectacles, a long velveteen coat and black silk knee breeches brought two teenage actresses to Little Holland House. Kate and Ellen Terry were the eldest daughters of a large itinerant theatrical family, trained almost from birth by their father, Ben, to enunciate Shakespeare to perfection. Eighteen-year-old Kate, an elegant leading lady, was the talk of the town and Nelly, irrepressibly joyful at sixteen, was London's brightest ingénue.[59] Their escort, Tom Taylor, the energetic, versatile dramatist and Secretary to the General Board of Health, knew the Terry family well. Ben and his daughters had acted in his plays for years and, like Watts, were frequent guests of the Taylors at Lavender Sweep in Clapham. The three men were exact contemporaries, forty-five years old. Although the circumstances and date of the Terry sisters' introduction to the artist are uncertain, the gist is this. Taylor, hearing that Watts had enjoyed Kate's performance at the Lyceum Theatre, took her, with Nelly as chaperone, to Watts's studio: not only would a portrait benefit her career – both their careers, if a double portrait was intended – but Kate could be an ideal partner for Watts. A talented beauty who would raise his morale, and model while he painted, she had neither husband nor aristocratic pedigree to forbid their liaison.[60]

Sara Prinsep lavished attention on Kate before leading all three into the studio.[61] Watts began a double portrait of the Terry sisters, with the elder as a Madonna figure, her head inclined over the dreamy, auburn-haired younger girl, resting on her shoulder (fig. 54). As Kate gave up sitting, Nelly, posing in an expansive Titianesque costume, began to dominate the picture. In between performances at the Haymarket Theatre, the sixteen-year-old returned again and again. Honoured to pose for the Watts, she filled his studio with joy, captivating her private audience. In *The Sisters*, the deep folds of her wide, slashed, white satin sleeves, edged with fur, her green under-sleeves and Indian shawl flying from her waist over Kate's lap suggest Nelly's generous nature; and her smoky blue eyes, absorbed in wonder at her rôle for art, express the intensity she brought to the stage.

Before the picture was finished, she posed alone for *Watchman, What of the Night?* (fig. 55), standing for hours in heavy armour as Isaiah's watchman in his vision of the fall of Babylon; her hands pressed to her breastplate, she elicits an ambiguous response – 'The morning cometh, and also the night: if ye will enquire, enquire ye: return, come.' So intent were the artist and actress that both were taken by surprise when Nelly 'fell all of a heap, nearly fainting' against his arm. To remind himself to be more considerate, Watts never removed the unintentional dash of carmine on the canvas near her heart. While her hands almost wilt with earnestness, her illuminated face, blue eyes, breastplate and the strands of her hair suggest

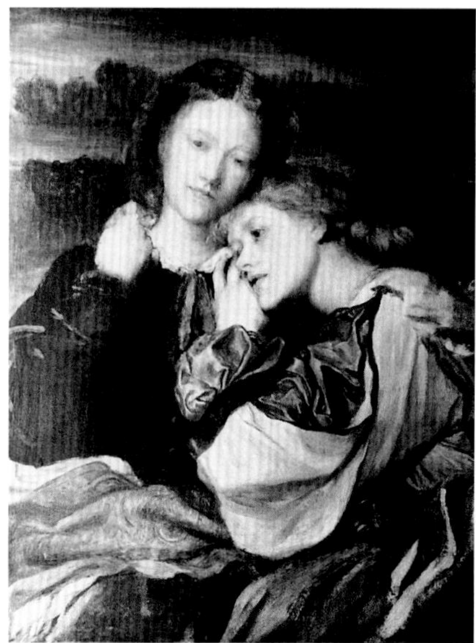

54    *The Sisters* (Kate and Ellen Terry), 1863 (Eastnor Castle Collection).

an inner vision. There is a heroic strength in this unfinished picture. Was it her idea to perform in armour as Joan of Arc, its original title?[62]

Alice Ellen Terry was born in Coventry on 27 February 1847.[63] Chosen for her first Shakespearean speaking part at the age of eight, as Mamillius in *A Winter's Tale* at the Princess's Theatre, London, Nelly had performed adult rôles from the age of thirteen. That she was able to do so she would later attribute to 'Imagination, industry, and intelligence . . . all indispensable to the actress, but of these three the greatest is, without any doubt, imagination.'[64]

The previous autumn Nelly had made her debut at the Theatre Royal, Bristol, where J. H. Chute's stock company attracted the best of the theatrical youth of the day. Dressed in a tunic 'too scanty to be quite nice', she played Cupid in the burlesque *Endymion* to rapturous applause. At a reading party in the home of the architect and critic Edward Godwin, Nelly had marvelled at the sense of design permeating the Godwins' house, in contrast to her sleazy theatrical lodgings and crowded Victorian home – 'the talk of its master and mistress made me *think*'. Godwin created a daring Greek *chiton* for her role as Titania in *A Midsummer Night's Dream*, drawing her attention to costume design. For the first time I began to appreciate beauty, to observe, to feel the splendour of things, to *aspire!*[65]

Nelly's recent performance in *The Little Treasure* at the Haymarket Theatre in London was hailed as intelligent, joyful and imbued with deep feeling, despite the patronizing antics of her leading actor, and all the deeper perhaps because 'I hated being laughed *at*!'[66] The drama critic E. L. Blanchard forecast, 'In characters illustrative of a frank and impulsive temperament, the young actress will prove a most desirable addition to the feminine strength of the dramatic corps.'[67] Nelly was therefore no lightweight when she arrived at Little Holland House. A generous-spirited, cocky tomboy, she could not help flirting, according to Laura Taylor, but 'never robbed anyone of a round of applause'. Kate could and did. She stopped sitting for Watts, however, when Nelly fell in love with him.[68] Thrilled to pose for the artist, the teenager entranced him and learned from his imaginative thoughts to develop her skills for High Art.

Little Holland House seemed to her 'a paradise, where only beautiful things were allowed to come. All the women were graceful, and all the men were gifted.'[69] The house was not unlike a stage, with monumental portraits and metaphysical paintings featuring her robed hostess and family, who would materialize out of the backdrop and shower guests with melodramatic praise. In Watts's studio the sense of drama in his allegorical works was infused with elevated thought. Earl Somers was negotiating to buy *Time and Oblivion*, which in itself symbolized his aspiration for the nation. That Watts released it is surprising. 'I don't think I should have given it up to any one but you and Lady Somers, he wrote to the earl. 'I look upon it as the only picture I have painted which represents what I might do or would have done had there been any sympathy with effort in that direction.'[70] Despite public apathy for his seminal cosmic scheme, his vision and determination remained steadfast. Even a firm of brewers refused his offer when, anticipating their demise, he asked to borrow a pair of dray horses to paint as a record. Fearful perhaps that a symbolic Watts picture might damage their image, they wanted no such advertisement. However,

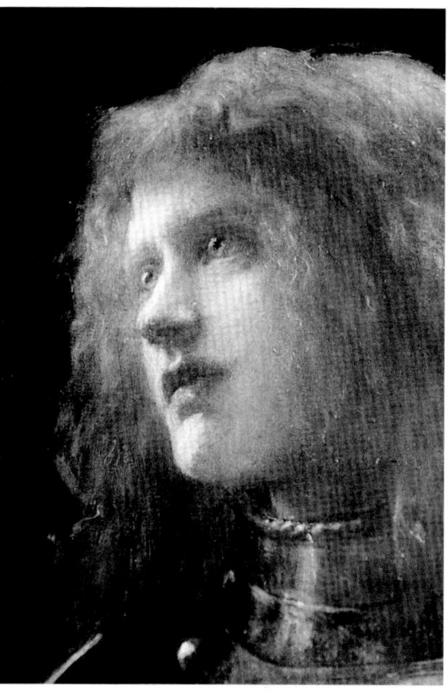

55   *Watchman, What of the Night?* (detail), 1863–64 (private collection).

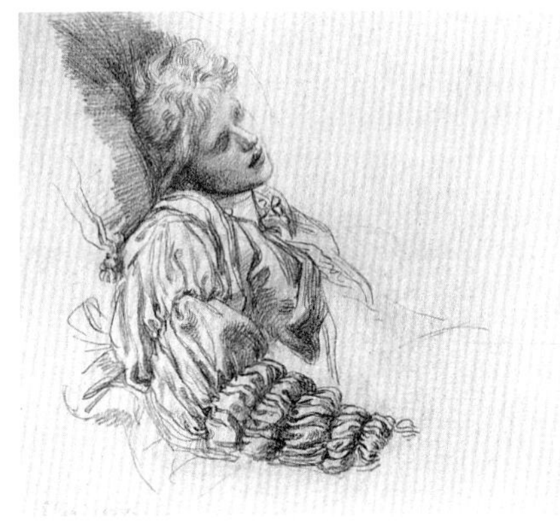

56  *Nellie Asleep*, 1864 (private collection).

Nelly would have seen the splendid pair sent from Spitalfields brewers, Messrs Truman, Hanbury and Buxton, whose dozing carman and dray horses were painted under the shade of a chestnut tree at Little Holland House, and immortalized for the nation as *The Midday Rest* – to honour the English characteristics of 'repose and latent power'.[71]

The elevated atmosphere at Little Holland House filled Nelly with wonder and, to Watts's delight, distracted her from her work. She began to find the theatre distasteful: 'To me the stage seemed a poor place when compared with the wonderful studio where Kate and I were painted as *The Sisters* . . . at the Haymarket I was not even passionately anxious to do my best . . . I was just dreaming of and aspiring after another world, a world full of pictures and music and gentle, artistic people with quiet voices and elegant manners. The reality of such a world was Little Holland House, the home of Mr Watts.'[72]

Watts longed to protect and guide her. Both were transported by their love affair in art. Awed by the epic grandeur of his pictures, Nelly sat to him for hours on end, while the artist, dazzled by her youthful beauty, made delicate studies of her face, her hair and her sleeve (fig. 56), and of her playing the piano and taking a theatrical bow. He painted portraits charged with romantic sentiment. Many excitable, impulsive young sitters had been comforted, offered guidance and made to feel special by the Signor in the intimacy of his studio. Nelly's unselfish eagerness knocked him off balance. 'Around me roots a glorious harmony, thrills all my being & fragments of a song come twisting to my lips,' he scribbled in a sketchbook. 'I know not why I am so tongue tied . . . why my hands so weak.' Unlike Georgina, Nelly performed for his art, to please him, and he saw that he could educate her for a nobler life than the stage. It was reported that his first thought was to adopt her,[73] though he would have known that her adored father, eight months his junior, was very much alive. Watts wanted not just to elevate her mind, but to marry her. Most available women of his acquaintance were above his station. Here at last was one who would not be ashamed of his origins. His distinguished commissions now included a grand full-length portrait of the Marchioness of Bath, a portrait of the Earl of Airlie, and a hundred-guinea head of Tennyson in a wideawake hat. The poet's oculist William Bowman had commissioned the latter to hang opposite Watts's refined self-portrait in black velvet painting coat and hat (fig. 57), as 'a pair of nobles answering one to the other on my walls.'[74]

For fear that Sara Prinsep might not approve of his marriage to the actress, he enlisted the help of Constance Leslie, whom he knew to be interested in the Terry sisters. He expected his letter to surprise her, as he explained his plan to remove Nelly from 'the temptations and abominations of the stage', to give her an education, and if she still felt affection for him, he would marry her. While he acknowledged their age difference, he believed that in view of prejudice against the stage – 'I share it myself' – he was offering Nelly an opportunity for a better life and a position in society. He would compensate her family for the loss of her services. 'To make the poor child what I wish her to be will take a lot of time & most likely cost a great deal of trouble & I shall want the sympathy & aid of all my friends, so I hope none of them will look coldly on my endeavours.' If Constance approved, could she commend the idea to Sara Prinsep and her family.[75]

Sara had no qualms about the marriage. Rumour has it that unknown to Watts she encouraged Nelly and may even have instigated the union. After all, a beautiful, mercurial actress would add cachet to her salon. According to the novelist Violet Hunt, 'it was all done at a lawn party' where Sara, sitting between Tom and Laura Taylor, tapped the dramatist on the knee and suggested that as Kate would not marry Signor, Nelly should. Taylor, appalled, placed a hand on each woman's knee and pleaded, 'Don't give Nelly to Watts.'[76] True or not, it was prescient. When the teenager was told that he had asked for her hand in marriage, she was stunned, stunned no doubt that the exalted artist, whose friends were leaders of society, wanted not only to paint her face, but to marry her, an actress. He was offering her the greatest Victorian female role: the wife of a genius. What she may not have known was that he longed to marry, but that his aristocratic friends and patrons would disdain his pedigree as a husband; and though he wished to protect Nelly from the degradations of the stage and, privately, to wean her of unhealthy theatrical habits, he enjoyed the company of actresses. She replied simply, 'Yes.' Though their thirty-year age difference was not uncommon, she was young to marry and, for all her theatrical experience, as innocent as a child.

Over three decades later, in a letter to the playwright George Bernard Shaw, she recalled her first kiss in Watts's studio. The artist kissed her sweetly, and she understood that she was now engaged to him. Her parents disapproved, but 'I was in Heaven for I knew I was to live with those pictures. "Always", I thought, and to sit to that gentle Mr W. and clean his brushes, and play my idiotic piano to him, and sit with him there in wonderland (the Studio).' Nelly was taken ill and invited to stay at Little Holland House. This time, he kissed her differently. She told no one for a fortnight, when she confided in her mother, saying, 'I *must* be married to him *now* because I was going to have a baby !!!! *and she* believed me . . . I was *sure* THAT kiss meant giving me a baby.[77]

The artist's campaign fanned the flames of her teenage rebellion and Nelly happily left the stage in the middle of the run of Taylor's *The American Cousin* at the end of December 1863 to devote her life to Watts. Her parents, less delighted than she professed in her memoirs, prepared for the marriage by having their children baptized *en masse* at their local church, St James, Hampstead Road.[78] As Ben's father had been a publican and Sarah's a builder, distantly related to the American artist John Singleton Copley, the Terrys had no snobbish grounds for disapproval. The Watts family may also have had misgivings: whether or not the union brought about the final rift between the artist and his half-sisters, he recalled when Harriet died in 1893 that he had not seen her for thirty years.[79]

Almost as worrying would be their marital set up. Watts had established studios on land sub-let from the Prinseps at Little Holland House,[80] and Sara made arrangements for the bubbly teenager to live there after the wedding so that his insulated life would continue as normal. But how could it? How in the eccentric joint ménage controlled by Mrs Prinsep or closeted in the poetic grandeur of his studio could they ever have a normal marriage? Even with access to Mrs Beeton's recent *Book of Household Management*,[81] Nelly would never be allowed to run the Little Holland House staff. Watts, always concerned that friends should understand his motives, talked to Jeanie. On 19 January news was relayed to Lady Duff

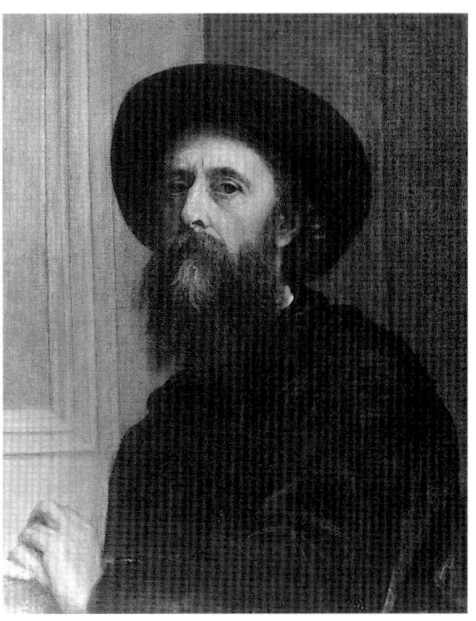

57   *Self-Portrait*, 1862–63 (Tate, London).

Gordon of the 'totally foolish marriage of Mr Watts to Miss K Terry [*sic*] of the Haymarket Theatre aged 17!!' Warmly appalled that he who had loved her daughter Georgy was to marry an actress, she noted in her journal his descent from the sublime to the ridiculous – 'I never heard of anything so silly in my whole Life!!' Writing to congratulate him, her ladyship recorded, 'I began "dear Watts" interestingly'. After Georgy herself called on him two days before the wedding, her mother's question mark and double exclamation marks are more than articulate,[82] or as the *Punch* journalist Shirley Brooks burst out when Taylor announced the nuptials at a dinner on 17 February, 'Bly fool!,[83] ' a comment that should have been directed at 'the real demon of the piece', Sara Prinsep.

George Frederic Watts, aged forty-six, married his teenage muse at St Barnabas Church, Kensington, on Saturday, 20 February 1864. The radiant bride had 'tubbed' her younger brothers and sisters and washed their fair hair before slipping into an exotic brown silk bridal gown designed for her by William Holman Hunt. It was inspired by the dress worn by the Spanish Queen Isabella d'Este in the portrait of her by Giulio Romano at Hampton Court Palace.[84] Over her auburn hair Nelly wore a white, quilted bonnet, decorated with a sprig of orange blossom, and she was wrapped in a valuable Indian shawl, without which, Constance Leslie recalled, no trousseau was complete, for it signified the bride's honourable estate.[85] Dr Francis Hussey performed the ceremony and the witnesses were Tom Taylor, Ben and Kate Terry, Val Prinsep, and Sophie Dalrymple,. Neither Thoby nor Sara Prinsep signed the marriage register. It was a cold day; and as Nelly danced back up the aisle on winged feet, Constance Leslie noticed the painfully slow pace of her 'atrabilious' bridegroom, a silver streak highlighting his profuse brown beard.[86] Lady Holland was not present at the wedding. His failure to notify her in her absence from Holland House was a shameful blunder for which he was fortunate to be forgiven.[87] Tom and Laura Taylor hosted the reception at Lavender Sweep. Nelly changed into a sealskin going-away outfit, her hair elegantly swept up into a pillbox cap over a fur-trimmed jacket with coral buttons. Overcome by emotion, she wept a great deal. 'Don't cry. It makes your nose swell,' complained the bridegroom,[88] his discomfort perhaps heightened because, as his paintings of her indicate, he was charmed by the line of her nose.

An unsubstantiated report suggests that the artist mishandled their first night – that Nelly was seen weeping on the staircase outside the marital chamber.[89] After decades of lonely pent-up desire, he may have been flummoxed by his vibrant virgin bride. Whatever happened in the bedroom, Watts was not struck with Ruskinian shock,[90] for he had already embarked on a series of nude studies of the statuesque housemaid Mary Bartley whom he had persuaded, with Sara's permission, to undress in the cause of art. He would refer to these studies of 'Long Mary' – monumental drawings on brown paper – for the rest of his life, as a writer uses a dictionary or thesaurus, looking to models for grammar, not inspiration.[91] Drawings of his voluptuous young bride relaxing in loose robes after their marriage, on the other hand, reveal tender affection. After a week's honeymoon in Hendon, at or near the home of Sara's sister Mia Jackson, she joined the Little Holland House ménage on her seventeenth birthday and felt extremely proud of her ring and new status. If only Sara had respected that with a fraction of her husband's magnanimity.[92]

On display in Leighton's studio was a picture of an auburn-haired young woman observing her artist lover at work, cheek to cheek, his hand enfolding hers: *The Painter's Honeymoon*.[93] Indeed, the Watts' sole bridal home was the studio, and here their marriage was consummated on canvas. Nelly felt that Signor was glorifying her to artistic stardom. She drew on her theatrical skills and was an inspired model, 'happy because my face was the type which the great artist who had married me loved to paint.'[94] Through his pictures, Watts played the Victorian husband to enchanted perfection, making love to his wife in pigment, tenderly training her to shape herself into submission. For *Choosing* (pl. XI), painted in jewel-like almost Pre-Raphaelite intensity, Nelly sat in her bridal gown, trimmed with black and blue ribbons, and transformed here into a deep grey colour, with an amber necklace around her neck. Attempting to smell an exotic scentless camellia, symbol of worldly vanities – the theatre – she clutches to her heart a small bunch of fragrant violets that symbolize Innocence and Love. Even today the bloom of her skin is palpable. When the picture was exhibited at the Academy, the *Athenaeum* praised 'the tone and richness of flesh-painting', whereas *Time and Oblivion*, presented as a design for sculpture, puzzled the reviewer.[95]

Nelly's charisma spurred her husband to produce outstanding work. Unlike many of his portraits, pictures of her do not appear to have been a struggle, or overworked, as Mrs Russell Barrington, who was to become well acquainted with his methods and views, would observe in *Reminiscences of G. F. Watts*. Because he tended to value his work by the amount of effort and conscious thought he had put into it, he barely recognized his more instinctive paintings: 'I doubt whether he ever realized whence came the inspiration which resulted in his most glorious visions on canvass. In *Watchman, What of the Night?* . . . it was not Isaiah, but the dramatic genius of his sitter influencing the artist's imagination in a psychic manner, which made the work what it is, a quite inspired creation.'[96]

Watts would not have discussed Nelly with Emilie Barrington. He explored the range of his wife's expression, painting her as the erotic Francesca in *Paolo and Francesca* and as the drowning Ophelia deranged by her ill-fated love for Hamlet (fig. 111). Tender idealistic sketches show a delicate young girl in the embrace of a taller middle-aged knight,[97] intending to protect her from the hazards of life. But could he really? In art, he knew where he was going, even if the public could not understand it. His ideas were strong, but his constitution was fragile and Nelly was in reality tall for her age, as strong-willed as his other female friends, yet keen to be moulded in art.

The strongest of them all, Julia Cameron, had been given her first professional camera for Christmas by her daughter and son-in-law, Julia and Charles Norman, and she photographed the newlyweds on the Normans' balcony at Cromwell Place. Watts posed in Titianesque manner, seated sideways, his noble head almost in profile and wide coat sleeve arranged into Phidian folds to break up the foreground and focus attention on his head. One photograph shows him adjusting the folds, before settling into repose, deep in thought (fig. 58). Her images of Nelly that day face the viewer. Both are disconcerting and watchful, as the monumental Byronic heroine *Medora* and as *The South West Wind*.[98] Here the photographer may have been inspired by the artist's portrait of his wife in a blue shawl, her lips

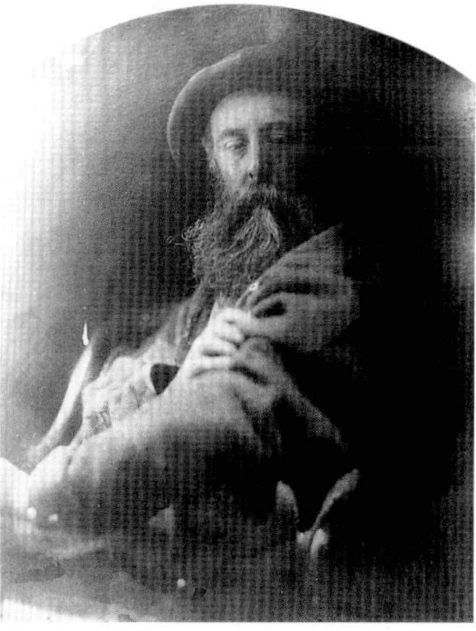

58   Arranging drapery folds before posing for Julia Margaret Cameron at Cromwell Place.

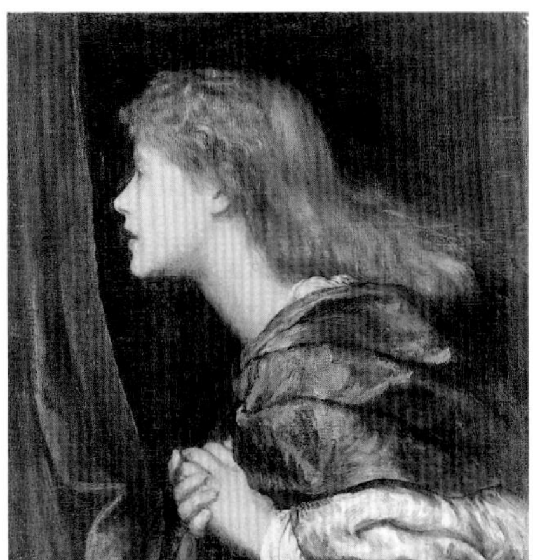

59   *Ellen Terry*, 1863–64 (National Portrait Gallery, London).

apart, hair flying and hands clasped with a sense of urgency calmed by the velvet background curtain (fig. 59). Light on the foreground drapery in *The South West Wind*, placing Nelly back in the shadows, presents her as the Breath of Life – prophetically – like a phantom floating by.

# 7   Unbridled Passion

'To the Signor to whose generosity I owe the choicest fruits of his Immortal genius I offer these my first successes in my mortal but yet divine art of photography – Julia Margaret Cameron, Fresh Water Bay Isle of Wight, Feby 22nd 64.'[1] No mere disciple, forty-eight-year-old Julia would not stop to bathe in the 'light-fountain' of heroes if she had the means to illuminate their souls. Sir John Herschel had introduced her to early developments in photography since 1839 – it was he who coined the term from Greek 'writing with light' – and her brother-in-law Lord Somers was a keen amateur photographer, but Julia had had little experience. For this highly imaginative woman who worshipped intellect, art and beauty with unbridled passion, no gift or outlet for her energy could have had greater effect. Determined to master the craft at once and transform it into a poetic High Art form, she exploited friends, strangers, beggar-maids, poets and statesmen, turning first to her 'divine artist' for advice.

Watts sent her for a training session with David Wilkie Wynfield, whose unusual photographs of colleagues focusing only on their faces were published that spring. 'If they do not, they ought to revolutionize photographic portraiture', the *Illustrated London News* proclaimed,[2] but Wynfield made little further impact and it was Julia Margaret Cameron who revolutionized the art. Her controversial soft-focus technique developed by accident as she experimented with her camera and darkroom equipment in January. Struggling to focus the lens, she discovered that instead of screwing it all the way to the sharp definition preferred by traditional photographers, she could stop as soon as she saw an image of ideal beauty.[3] It was no easy task to expose, process and print negatives, and the use of poisonous chemicals worried her, turning her hands 'as black as an Ethiopian Queen's'.[4] Yet to this impetuous, clumsy woman that augmented the creative challenge. Her diffused focus and broad modelling of form and colour through light, shadow and tone was comparable to Watts's controversial abstract technique and, like him, she felt that a greater effort heightened a picture's value.

Julia Cameron cropped her experimental efforts and pasted them into an album dedicated to Watts. On his return from honeymoon she requested his comments. Neighbours, family, friends, servants and children had been cajoled into posing in her Freshwater dining room. Once seated, they were trapped into submission. She ruffled their hair, made them hold soulful expressions while she wrestled with the lens, chemicals and exposure, then

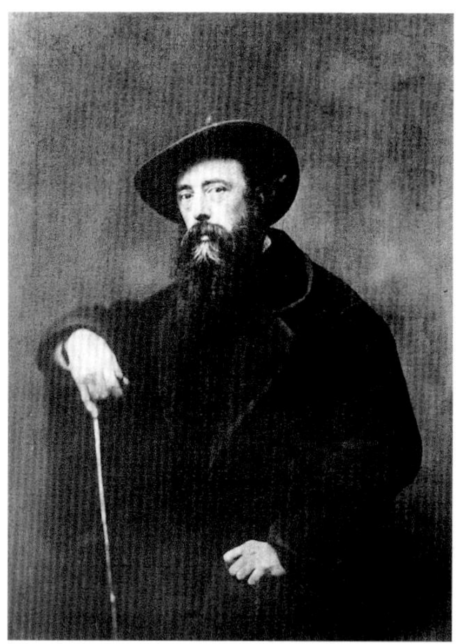

60   Watts photographed by Thoby Prinsep posing in his sealskin coat.

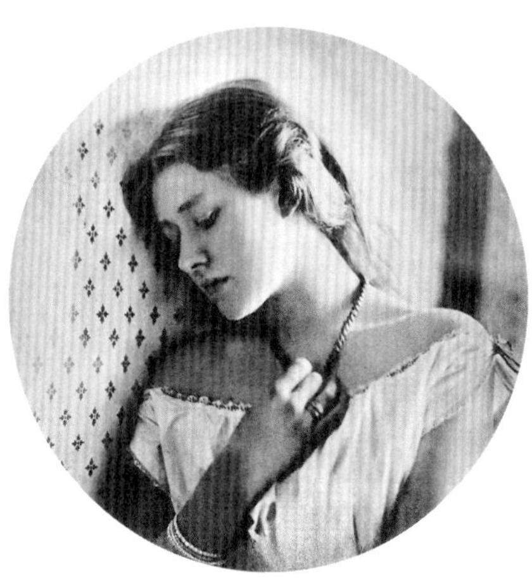

61   Julia Margaret Cameron, *Sadness*, 1864.

disappeared into her coalhouse darkroom to process, fix and tone image after image. Tousle-haired Annie Philpot sat in her buttoned coat by the window. Her soft-focus likeness could have been taken today. Tennyson's boys stood in Vandyke collars. The photographer directed light on to the long silver hair and beards of her husband Charles and of Henry Taylor, posing in Titianesque profile, and highlighted the face and neck of Mary Ryan 'My Beggar-Maid Now 15!'[5] Watts advised the photographer not to retouch or repeat the halo she had painted on to a print of her sixteen-year-old parlourmaid Mary Hillier, posing as a Madonna with children from the Freshwater fort for *The Fruits of the Spirit* series. Encouraged by his admiration for the 'large heads,' Julia forwarded the album to Herschel.[6]

Freshwater, as the home of the Poet Laureate, was a Mecca for intellectuals. It was compared with a French *salon* or with Athens in the age of Pericles. Leaders of Victorian society, poets, painters and philosophers crossed the Solent and headed for Tennyson's house, Farringford – Prince Albert, visiting from Osborne, had been an early caller. In March, the Wattses and Prinseps joined Mia Jackson and her daughter Julia for a holiday at the Camerons, where even the air was tinged with an eccentric fragrance. Chemicals mingled with the sweet smell of briar that grew amongst the ivy up to the roof and the photographer's cottages, more haphazard than Little Holland House, filled with distinguished visitors waited on by housemaid madonnas, all inveigled into sitting to her lens.[7]

Thoby Prinsep, Watts and Tennyson, dressed in distinctive broad hats and cloaks (fig. 60), presented such a striking sight as they walked down the lanes that people would stop to watch them pass.[8] The first time Nelly saw the Poet Laureate, he was seated at his library table, receiving heavy volumes from his wife. Emily Tennyson, perched on a ladder, seemed frail, 'like a slender tea-rose'. In rigorous mental health, she was physically weak and often unable to rise from her sofa to accompany her husband on his daily rambles over the Downs. He walked with Watts's teenage bride, recited poems to her, and allowed her to prepare his churchwarden pipe. Yet Nelly was happiest tumbling over gates, playing tomboy games and Knights of the Round Table with eleven-year-old Hallam and Lionel, ten.[9] Rediscovering the childhood, so long displaced by the stage, eased her restless nature. On the other hand, as Julia Cameron noticed, it emphasized the age gap between Nelly and Signor and began to undermine their marriage.

While Signor was walking or at work – on a new Tennyson portrait with poet's laurel, for the national collection, or a large picture of 'Madonna Mary' called *Charity*[10] – Julia rushed Nelly over the fields to photograph her in the poet's bathroom, ostensibly because the wallpaper was patterned with crosses. Against this unusual background, she produced the most sensual, soulful picture yet. What were her instructions to the artist's young wife as she posed in her négligé, one arm across her waist, the other fingering her necklace, showing off her wedding rings? The actress who so enlivened Watts's brush had intensified the photographic image. Registered on 30 May, it would be exhibited under the title *Sadness* (fig. 61).[11]

That spring Giuseppe Garibaldi, the conqueror of Sicily and Naples, sailed into Southampton on the first leg of a brief visit to drum up English support for the unification of Italy. Tennyson, Watts and Julia Cameron admired his campaign, and an invitation to Farringford presented an ideal opportunity to consult educated English opinion. Crowds surged forward to greet the still wounded commander when he arrived at Freshwater on 5 April. A striking figure, with a white poncho over his embroidered Red Shirt, he had a slight limp and walked with a stick. After Garibaldi had emerged from Tennyson's study and planted a wellingtonia in the garden, he was introduced to the poet's friends. Never had he met anyone like Julia Margaret Cameron. Desperate to immortalize his heroic Italian soul, she fell on her knees at his feet, threw up her black chemical-stained hands, and implored him to sit for a photograph. He mistook her for a beggar, brushed her away with a masterly gesture to which she was unaccustomed and escaped her lens.[12] Watts, however, arranged through the Duchess of Sutherland to paint his portrait in London. So tight was Garibaldi's schedule that sittings had to take place between seven and eight in the morning. The duchess brought the commander and read to him while the artist made a mystical sketch and more finished study of his head, and deputations waited below to pay him homage.[13] Both men were introduced to Florence Nightingale, who sat for a portrait, but was not well. Her face was so bloated by illness, he felt unable to do her justice, yet the unfinished sketch shows her concern and inner strength, a rare record of the prematurely ageing nurse (fig. 62).[14]

Two poignant pictures in Watts's studio caught Ruskin's eye in May: a new *Angel of Death*, and a symbolic view of haystacks and trees in the evening sun, *And All the Air a Solemn Stillness Holds*, the subject having struck the artist as he rode home one evening. A knight on horseback merges with nature in the foreground shadows.[15]

Outside the studio, the Wattses could not develop their married life. He wanted his wife to be painted by Leighton, but she despised his work.[16] Sara organized the Little Holland House staff to cater only for the needs of her beloved Signor; she treated Nelly as a child. Crushing her spirits, she insisted that the young woman, who had relinquished fame and adulation to marry him, remain silent in the company of his guests. She sat shrinking in a corner, regarded by her husband's distinguished visitors, she would recall, as more of a curiosity, or side-show than hostess. Nelly had no regrets about leaving the stage,[17] but forbidden her rôle as Mrs Watts, she was trapped as an understudy, enjoined only to observe. Benjamin Disraeli's straggling curls shook as he walked, she noticed; and Gladstone, now Leader of the House of Commons, seemed 'like a volcano at rest; his face was pale and calm . . . the calm of the grey crust of Etna. You looked into the piercing dark eyes and caught a glimpse of the red-hot crater beneath the crust.'[18]

Forced to suppress her natural exuberance, the artistry that would one day equal, if not surpass, that of her husband, Ellen Terry's spirits erupted. She could no longer refrain from entertaining her audience and threw a sponge of water on to her husband when he was admiring lilies in the garden. 'The sponge put all poetry out of his thoughts!'[19] Another afternoon, restricted to female company in the drawing room, she leaned back over the arm of her chair, released her hairpins and sat swaying from side to side as her golden hair cascaded with impropriety over her shoulders, down her body. 'Put up your hair instantly!' ordered Sara. Nelly glared, coiled it loosely above her head, stabbed in the odd pin and sat looking more ravishing and provocative than ever.[20]

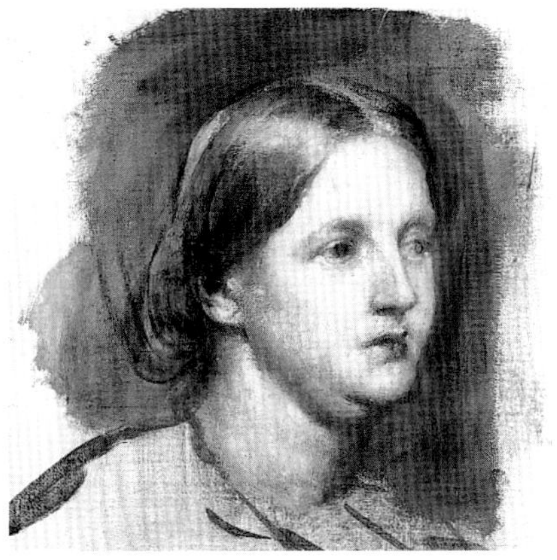

62  *Study of Florence Nightingale* (detail), 1864 (Watts Gallery).

Nelly's restlessness drained Watts, reflected badly on him and of course aroused widespread gossip. Seeing how Sara's interference undermined his wife's and his own efforts to sustain the marriage, he ordered that nobody be allowed to see him. 'This does not apply to you, but it does to a great many', he confided to Jeanie. 'I find I have to reconstruct Nelly's mind, character & habits. I wish therefore to keep her absolutely to myself & know that I am right in this.' He was determined to guide her towards a sense of calm. 'No excitement of any kind must be allowed when there is a common habit of hysteria, & a pulse of 108! Fancy what a change for me!'[21]

It was a greater task than he anticipated. Poor Nelly, discouraged from entertaining friends and constantly insulted by Sara and accused of being unworthy of the genius who had given her his name, complained to her husband. He realized that after the excitement of the stage, his comparatively secluded, scholarly world, the peace he needed in the studio was unendurable for his wife. Driven to distraction, he became impatient and could not work. On 21 August he dined at Holland House for the first time since his marriage. Nelly did not accompany him.[22] The following month he confided in Lady Lothian who, though not yet introduced to his wife, offered to help save the marriage, recognizing their particular difficulty 'as your own make of life has been rather an exceptional one, & so perhaps has hers'.[23]

For a brief moment Watts appears to have considered Nelly's return to the stage, but found the idea unpalatable and saw little possibility of a tranquil future. 'No doubt she is exactly fitted for the stage, but not for domestic life,' he wrote to Jeanie. 'If it were a profession less repugnant to my taste I would consider how it might be possible to let her have the excitement of it but it is obvious that cannot be. I really do not see how I am to get on & do my work, & if I cant I must be altogether lost.'[24] Time and again Nelly ran away.[25] He now begrudged her imaginative charms as ideas long formed from 'the exaggerated romance of sensational plays',[26] reprimanded her for 'outrageous conduct' and in the heat of the moment, told her to forget she had ever been an actress. Nelly reappeared before guests as Cupid. Never was a rôle more appropriate, except that her costume, pink tights and tunic was 'too scanty to be quite nice'.[27]

Watts had also been caught in a shaming episode. Julia Cameron, who dared to expose flesh in her photographs of the Madonna, took him on a visit to Carlyle that shocked the philosopher's wife: 'Mr C was made too late out, by an *inburst* of Mrs Cameron and Mr Watts, the former hardly to be restrained from forcing her way into Mr C's bedroom while he was changing his trousers!! – I told *her*,' Jane Carlyle complained to Lady Ashburton, 'It is a dangerous affair, rather, that you are there entering on, Mam!'[28] – less dangerous, evidently, than the scandal that followed Nelly's performance as Cupid, the official explanation for their separation. News reached the ear of Viscount Torrington, lord-in-waiting to the Queen and society gossip, who notified John Delane, the editor of *The Times* on 20 November.[29]

Half a century later, 'Lucile' Duff-Gordon, the dressmaker and wife of Georgy's nephew Sir Cosmo, revealed in *Discretions and Indiscretions*, that Ellen Terry confided that she had been thrown out after a visit to Godwin. His wife had died in May. The Wattses used to visit Godwin's Baker Street studios together, but on this occasion Nelly arrived unexpectedly and alone. She found the designer ill, nursed him throughout the night, renewing hot poultices to relieve his pain, and returned home by cab expecting her rash, albeit innocent, stay to invoke Sara's fury. She thought Signor would understand. Instead, it may have been the final straw. The Prinseps summoned her parents, accused Nelly of infidelity and cast her out as a fallen woman. The actress returned fire with the full force of the idiom learned from 'behind the lamps' and her absent husband refused to see her again.[30]

Whichever was the ultimate trigger – the Godwin episode would have been suppressed for propriety – neither party was unblameworthy, but it was Sara who destabilized their marriage. She could not relinquish her adored artist to another woman and, unable to manipulate her, she exacerbated the Wattses' difficulties and drove a spiteful wedge between man and wife. On 24 November Nelly sought refuge with the Taylors, turning up on their doorstep at seven o'clock in the evening. Signor was distraught, unable to work. Tom Taylor, incredulous at the strength of her love, persuaded her to agree to a temporary separation, for her husband's sake, but she would not countenance a permanent parting. The next day, he advised her reluctant father to have her back at home, explaining that she was 'immeasurably more sinned against than sinning . . . having turned merrily by too much love for one who has made her no return & I fear never can make her any'.[31]

Under the Prinseps' roof, Signor had neither assumed control of the marriage, nor its break-up. Nelly, devoted to their life in art, refused to acknowledge their personal torments and wished to return to the hornets' nest.[32] The artist, shamed and shattered by the loss of his wild, exuberant muse whom he could tame only in paint, retreated into his studio. He determined to destroy her pictures and wrote to Eustace Smith, a shipping magnate and Liberal MP, that as his wife had left him he wished to withdraw from his agreement to sell *Choosing*. Smith immediately ordered up his carriage, galloped over to Little Holland House and persuaded Watts to relinquish the picture, which was to be the first picture of Smith's avant-garde collection.[33] Once the artist's destructive intent was diffused, he stepped up the pace of his work, began a second, more voluptuous version of the unattainable temptress *Fata Morgana* fleeing from the knight;[34] he developed his studies from Long Mary into sensual half-length nude paintings. Those on classical themes of unfulfilled longing, notably *Clytie* and *The Wife of Pluto* (pl. XII), their faces stretched away from the viewer – the latter, in impure contrast to *Choosing*, ravished yet unsatisfied, with her nose thrust towards luxuriant silk drapery shaped like a giant scentless carnation[35] – were clearly inspired by Nelly. Only too aware that 'the perfect human being [is] not an angel', Watts believed that sensory experience should inform art.[36] One look at the flesh tones of his nudes should silence critics who doubt whether he consummated his marriage.

Signor had no desire for a divorce but under pressure, we are told, from Sara Prinsep and Virginia Somers, whose continued liaison with the newly married Sir Coutts Lindsay (fig. 63) may in itself have been open to question,[37] he agreed to a legal separation. Nelly, thunderstruck at her expulsion, at the mockery of her marriage, returned to her hideously furnished room at the Terry home, sandwiched between a tavern and a pawnbroker's in Stanhope Street.[38] Here she sat darning her brother's stockings in time

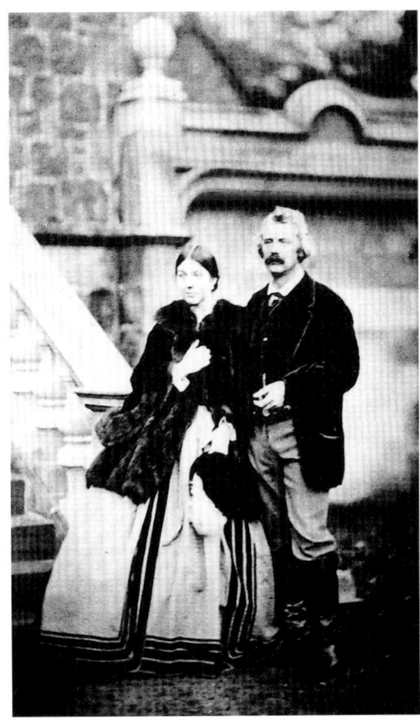

63   Sir Coutts and Lady Lindsay at Balcarras Castle, 1864 (Eastnor Castle Collection; photo: Thomas Buist).

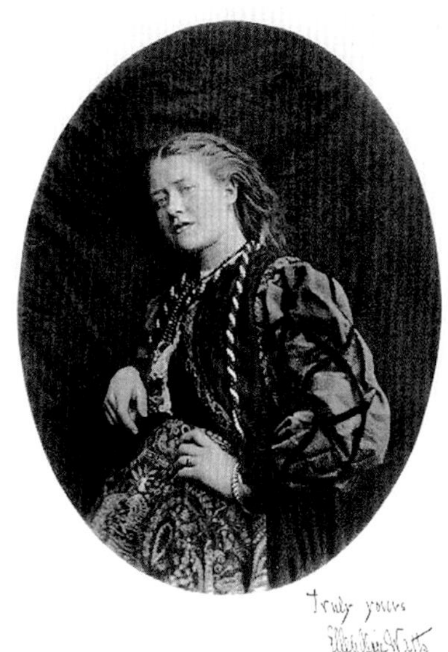

64    Nelly posing in her wedding dress for Charles Dodgson, July 1865.

to Beethoven and tried to forget 'the one dark cloud' in her young life. She burned Signor's letters, though a prayer into which he poured his guilt-ridden soul is preserved today at the Ellen Terry Memorial Museum at Smallhythe Place, near Tenterden in Kent.[39] If she received it at the time, it may have given her some heart, for she had been distressed by rumours of his ungentlemanly talk, 'things which *might* stand in my way for the future, and *also* in the way of all *my sisters*.' Generously she professed to forgive him,[40] but on 14 July, Nelly would pose defiantly in her wedding dress for a photograph by the Reverend Charles Lutwidge Dodgson, whose novel *Alice's Adventures in Wonderland* was published that year under the *nom de plume* Lewis Carroll. Bitterly, she signed the mount 'Truly yours Ellen Alice Watts' (fig. 64).[41]

Separation may have seemed less brutal, but it placed Nelly in a wretched position, degraded and open to gossip. 'Her fall is certain,' Edward Cheney reported to Lady Holland in Naples, 'and it is idle to suppose that a pretty actress in her position can remain respectable.' Cheney, a close friend of Lord Holland, who had sat to Watts in Italy and entertained him at Badger, his Staffordshire home, now sniped at the artist in letters to her ladyship – 'scandalous . . . ingratitude', 'I hear . . . he *positively loathes* her'.[42] Under the terms of the Separation Agreement – signed on 26 January 1865 and co-ordinated between Watts's solicitor John Philip Martineau[43] and barrister Vernon Harcourt[44] and Taylor acting for Nelly[45] – she was released from her husband's command and free to visit whom she liked. Clauses prevented the restitution of conjugal rights, to which he agreed 'so long as she shall lead a chaste life'; he also agreed that unless ill health stopped his professional work, he would pay maintenance of three hundred pounds per annum, to be reduced to two hundred if she returned to the stage. (In the event, he would not reduce it.)

Watts was commanded to the Isle of Wight three days later, to assist the Surveyor of the Crown Pictures, Richard Redgrave, in an examination at Osborne. Redgrave would report that the Queen showed him a fresco and some damaged paintings. Whether due to legal proceedings or his state of mind, refusing a royal command, especially with regard to fresco, was not Watts's finest move.[46]

However, as witness to the excavations at Halicarnassus, he supplied a crucial testimonial defending Newton's account of their discovery of painted sculpture, which had been challenged by the traditionalist sculptor Professor Richard Westmacott. In his *Handbook of Sculpture Ancient and Modern*, Westmacott accepted evidence of pigment on architecture and small decorative objects, but declared the few remaining spots of reddish tint on the sculpture to be 'accidental stains' incurred during burial. Watts's testimonial of 8 January 1865, published in Newton's two-volume *Travels & Discoveries in the Levant*, was supported by the British Museum Keepers of Antiquity who had seen red, brown and purple pigments on the fragments at their unpacking, established the practice of polychrome in classical sculpture. While the critic J. Beavington Atkinson later observed, 'It was a happy coincidence that the colourist of the English school should be witness to an interesting fact that goes far to settle the moot question whether the ancients were in the practice of painting statues'. The revelation provoked an international debate and fanned the flames for the contemporary use of colour in sculpture.[47]

On a meteoric path to fame, Julia Cameron was sending batch after batch of photographs. Watts criticized the *pose plastique* of her Madonna, praised her earliest pictures of Tennyson, but thought them less fine than those she had taken of himself, and he begged her to 'do justice to the noble & beautiful head, the finest you will ever have before your lens'.[48] He felt the poet's *Northern Farmer* to be 'Shakespeare's last gasp of nature. It conveys to my mind the birth, parentage, education, life and death of a whole community of rustics. Nothing could be more complete'[49] The photographer invited him to paint the Tennyson boys 'before they lose the glory of their locks' for boarding school. Asking Emily to delay their shoulder-length haircuts, he wrote 'The price shall be the pride I shall feel in giving pleasure to so great a man as Alfred Tennyson'. Hallam and Lionel sat to both Watts and Cameron that Easter.[50]

The artist's collaboration in the photographer's quest to emulate High Art 'combining the real & ideal & sacrificing nothing of Truth by all possible devotion to Poetry & *beauty*,'[51] resulted in one of her best-loved images. Watts posed with his violin and two young neighbours for *The Whisper of the Muse* (fig. 65), which, like his *First Whisper of Love*, owed much to Rembrandt's *The Evangelist Matthew Inspired by the Angel* – (The Swiss painter Arnold Böcklin, looking to Holbein more than to Rembrandt, would develop the theme in his *Self-Portrait with Death playing the Violin* of 1872.)[52] Anny and Minny Thackeray, often invited in the hope that it would raise their spirits after their father's recent death,[53] heard Watts playing when they woke up. The instrument is central to the photograph and suggests the musical harmony underlying his art. So thrilled was the photographer at having created poetic images worthy of her 'divine' artist that she inscribed the prints *The Whisper of the Muse* – A Triumph!' That day had been extraordinarily fruitful for her. The learned Thoby had posed with and without his book and Tennyson too endured several sittings, holding a folio of poetry for seminal photographs he christened, *The Dirty Monk*. Anny described their experiences:

> We came at her summons. We trembled – or we should have trembled had we dared to do so – when the round black eye of the camera was turned upon us. We felt what . . . disastrous waste of time and money and effort might ensue from any passing quiver of emotion, when the camera and the sun seemed to be running some desperate race; and when at last Tennyson walked away, Watts succeeded the Laureate in the chair, which had been moved to the verandah to catch the last rays of the light. Then came Mrs Cameron's joyful burst of triumph. She was exhausted but successful; her task was done for the day; she had accomplished her dream; a vision of the Laureate, of the Great Painter, were there, safely recorded by the lens.[54]

Anny was about to embark on her first novel. Such was the medley of visitors in Freshwater that she informed Walter Senior (Jeanie's son) that: 'everybody is either a genius, or a poet, or a painter or peculiar in some way,' quoting a friend – 'Is there *nobody* common-place?' Professor Benjamin Jowett and his students were examining a huge box of photographs brought by maids in knitted waistcoats, the poet William Allingham dropped in after a visit to Farringford, and Julia stayed up until two o'clock in the morning soaking her photographs, which she sent to Watts at Little Holland House.[55]

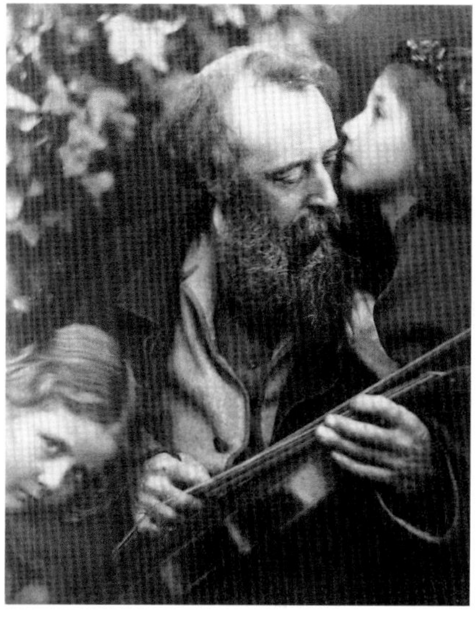

65 · Julia Margaret Cameron, *The Whisper of the Muse*, April 1865.

While he encouraged her to produce photographs that would mirror the souls of her sitters, he was only too aware of traditionalist censure and was criticized himself for not exhibiting his best pictures.[56] This was partly because he was reserving his more abstract imaginative subjects, showing them unfinished to test the effect in a gallery setting. As Cameron's painterly shadows and highlights – intended to suggest profound thoughts – were condemned as 'out of focus', and since he knew of her need to make money from her photographs in order to ease dwindling family resources, he advised her to address technical errors. 'Artists & very great lovers of the highest qualities of Art may not & perhaps do not care', he wrote, 'but the public will not care for anything that exhibits the sort of imperfection it can understand at a glance.

> Your last Tennyson is very fine but a little inky, something wrong about the eye, & rays streaking the forehead.[57] The largest of the shoulder-length Boys [no. 2] is very nearly perfect, the foot a little too large & perhaps a want of high lights. No. 1 is beautiful but somewhat burnt with flaws in the plate. The left arm & hand beautiful, he must be a grand boy! . . . you have only to take systematic trouble in the direction of your mechanical shortcomings to obtain a definite position as a Great Artist & in that object there is no better.[58]

By May 1865 Julia Cameron was winning awards at international exhibitions in Berlin and Dublin.[59] Imbued with Watts's theory that a simple dignified portrait of the head alone would expose the intellectual force of her sitters, she took her camera to Little Holland House. That month, to the 'mingled terror and delight of her friends', the photographer marched over the lawn, commandeering guests – Sir Coutts Lindsay, Tom Hughes, William Rossetti, Robert Browning. She swathed them in velvet, trying their patience as they submitted to avant-garde immortality.[60] Georgiana Burne-Jones recalled how 'Browning, the fiery and restless [was] brought to bay by her in the garden, and beguiled into sitting as she would have him, draped in strange wise, and left by her helpless in the folds of the drapery, forgotten for the time as she flew on some other quest'.[61] As Georgie was furnishing their new home in Kensington Square with Morris wallpapers and fabrics, Watts gave her a sewing machine, which her amused husband caricatured as – 'a most clever little thing that makes dresses and buys the stuff and almost pays for it.'[62]

Lady Adelaide Talbot sat for a photograph subsequently captioned *A Pensive Nun*, the subject of a picture Watts had begun in Italy, but his attempts to paint her portrait for Lord Lothian were less successful (fig. 80). Lady Adelaide had the cold classic beauty of a marble statue, better suited to Leighton's brush.[63] George Howard, heir to the Earl of Carlisle and a keen art student, took time out from his drawing lessons and sittings with Watts to pose for Julia Cameron with his sketchbook and pencil. He and his wife Rosalind watched her spend an entire afternoon at work on Lady Elcho,[64] making her sit as a Michangelesque *Cumean Sybil* and stand against an oak tree as *A Dante-esque Vision* (fig. 66); her husband posed in Volunteer uniform, hand upon sword for a single heroic image.[65]

At last an imaginative subject for Watts's cosmic scheme attracted interest at the Academy – an early sketch for *Love and Life*. While his monumental painting of *Esau*, a lean, worn huntsman resting on his spear, was

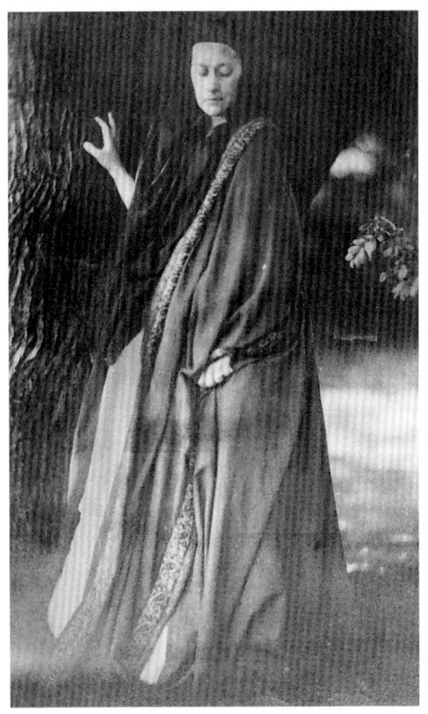

66  Julia Margaret Cameron, *Lady Elcho as a Dante-esque Vision*, May 1865.

noted for its 'dignity of conception', critics were moved by Love 'with wings of fire', who drags a strong man along a thorny path. 'There is such a flush of colour and so wealthy an idea of *chiaroscuro* . . . that all must wish to see it fully developed.'[66] Sweet nectar after nearly two decades. In his will Watts bequeathed to Countess Somers his prized original oil sketch for the 'introductory chapter' to his cosmic history of mankind. On the left of the picture ultimately named *Chaos* (fig. 138), he was planning to show violent upheaval before order was established on the planet; in the middle section, light veiled by mists, with a figure emerging from the swollen tide to mark the beginning of the strides of time and, on the right, in this detail of *The Giants*, later called *Titans* (pl. x), he proposed:

> I would then give a nearer view of the Earth; & by a number of gigantic figures stretched out at length, represent a range of mountains, & typify the bony structure of skeleton; this I would make very grand & impressive in order to imply the comparative insignificance of man.
>
> The to us most important of the constellations should shine out of the deep ultramarine firmament, Silence & Mighty Repose should be stamped upon the character & disposition of my giants; & revolving centuries & cycles should glide in the form of female figures of great beauty beneath the crags upon which the mighty forms should be; to indicate the non effect as compared with man & his works upon them.[67]

On 20 May Henry Cole went to Little Holland House to inspect Watts's oil sketch, *The Fine and Applied Arts*, for the South Kensington lunette, which was now open to wider competition. His Italianate design of groups around a central knight on horseback featured a sculptor chiselling marble, a metalworker leaning on his anvil, a goldsmith displaying his work to women whose costumes represented applied art, a potter, ships representing commerce, and an artist painting. His was the favoured choice, but he asked Cole to allow students to inlay the mosaics in his studio, and negotiations were protracted for years.[68] In the meantime, from vibrant wax-figure compositions he painted Michelangelesque cartoons of St Matthew and St John for the St Paul's cathedral spandrels.[69]

Working at a cracking pace from 6.30 in the morning until 6.30 at night, he commuted to Freshwater for further photo sessions and tutorials. '*All the heads are divine. The tone too is excellent*,' he wrote, as Cameron achieved tonal quality comparable to colour in a painting. Photographs of Mary Hillier as *The Day Spring* and *The Shunamite Woman*, leaning over a sleeping naked child, reminded him of Phidias and impressed him as 'more anti-PreRaphaelite than anything I have seen'.[70] but he reprimanded the photographer for identical shots and had severe words for a special image of her grandson, dedicated to himself: 'Do have a little shirt made of some yellowish material, the blob of formless white over the back of the large boy spoils the whole picture. What would not do in a painting will not do in a Photograph, but I am delighted with the amount of gradation you have obtained.' He explained that he was preparing his cartoon of *St John* to be executed in mosaic at St Paul's, 'so my mind is turned to a grand major key & I can well appreciate what is noblest in Art, & your last Photographs harmonize well with the effects I wish to produce but you must not be satisfied there is more to be done . . . I know your difficulties but the greatest things have been done under difficulties.' He had spent hours with a

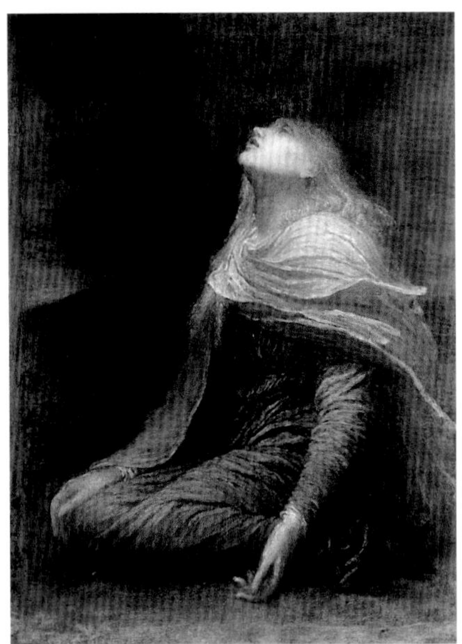

67    *Magdalen the Penitent*,
*c.*1865–84 (Museums and Galleries
on Merseyside: The Walker).

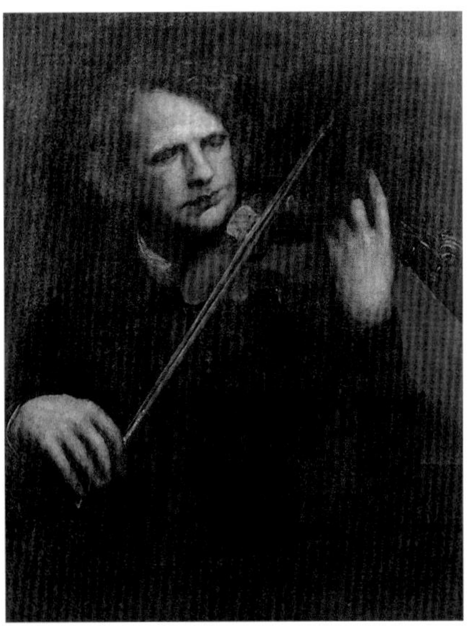

68    *Dr Joachim*, 1865–66 (Watts
Gallery).

model to achieve a 'beautiful and suggestive' arrangement for the drapery folds and he advised her to take more time. She would produce fewer photographs but each would be more valuable.[71] It was a tall order for the impetuous woman, but such was his encouragement that, 'I felt I had wings to fly with.'[72]

Her passionate, spiritual devotion to art rebounded on him. Photographs of *Magdalene*, embracing the romantic themes of sex, death and religion which especially appealed to her, do not feature in their surviving correspondence, though at about this time he embarked on *Magdalen the Penitent* (fig. 67), an extension of Cameron's theme and possibly painted as an example to her. Light shining over the face of the emotional kneeling figure, her dress arranged in multitudes of folds, highlights the upturned features of his estranged wife.

Watts was fortunate that although society was split by his marital break-up, and Jeanie ceased to correspond with him for the rest of the decade, other close friends stuck by him. His name reappeared in the Holland House dinner book and he was in increasing demand from patrons. One who treasured his friendship was the Countess of Airlie, the eldest daughter of Lord Stanley of Alderley. A well-read woman, with a rosy complexion and rapid conversational manner, Blanche Airlie chose Campden Hill as her London base in order to cultivate Watts's circle, whom she invited to intellectual breakfasts. As many friends and patrons found, his intimate confidences, correspondence and discussion, whether on artistic or spiritual matters, made the countess feel special.[73] She allowed him to use her child as a model. As she had delayed her own portrait (worth a hundred and fifty guineas) so that he could paint George Howard, who was married to her youngest sister Rosalind, Watts asked her to resume sittings on 7 July.[74] Her cousin, the new dean of Westminster, Arthur Penrhyn Stanley, commissioned a three-hundred-guinea three-quarter-length portrait, allowing his black gown to be arranged into exuberant Venetian-style folds.[75]

Inundated with requests for portraits, Watts was invited to Ashridge, Hertfordshire, in the autumn, to paint Lady Marian Alford's twenty-three-year-old son Earl Brownlow who was dying of consumption.[76] He completed the Marquess and Marchionness of Clanricarde and squeezed in a Cosmopolite, The Honourable George Fortescue,[77] before attempting to stem the tide; but then The Honourable Percy Wyndham, MP, approached him for a portrait of his wife Madeline. Watts found the warm, artistic woman too appealing to refuse. 'I really do want my time for work of a more poetic character,' he replied, but offered to start in December. Sittings did not begin for two years, but would result in an aesthetic masterpiece.[78]

In the meantime, Tom Taylor asked him to paint a portrait for a Manchester philanthropist. Keen to resume their friendship, Watts advised Charles Hilditch Rickards to arrive for sittings at nine o'clock in the morning and that although normal practice was to pay half the commission on the first day, 'I do not call myself a portrait-painter & never receive payment until the picture is finished.' Rickards, a bald, well-built man with a prominent nose and eager eyes, came for his first sitting on 19 September 1865.[79] Listening to Joachim perform at evening soirées, Watts painted a picture of the violinist playing by lamplight (fig. 68), absorbed in his music – the movement of his bow, the vibrato and resonance almost palpable in the musician's expression.

*A Study with the Peacock's Feathers* (fig. 69) and the portrait of Gladstone topped the bill and boosted the winter exhibition of Gambart's French Gallery in Pall Mall, which offered an intimate venue to show his first barebreasted picture.[80] Like Rossetti, then painting *Venus Verticordia* as a private commission – (he preferred not to exhibit) – Watts was challenging the establishment with an erotic art form decried for decades.[81] An amber necklace, identical to that Nelly wore over her wedding dress in *Choosing*, is all that his model wears; it reappears down at her finger tips; she faces the viewer and leans back against creamy silk, fur and velvet drapes whose restless folds highlight her pure flesh tones and relaxed pose; raising her other arm above and behind her head, peacock plumes curve down to her shoulder. She recalls Delacroix's *Odalisque*, Titian's *Danaë* and looks as inviting as the prostitute *Olympia* was provocative. Whereas Manet's canvas stirred an outrage at the Paris Salon (his pictures were rejected by the Royal Academy that summer, though the novelist Emile Zola had risen to his defence), Watts's model was perceived as virginal, and the beautifully balanced picture viewed as an aesthetic wonder. 'We rarely see such true Art as this,' enthused the *Athenaeum* reviewer, 'so wealthy in beauty and completeness . . . the superb treatment of the bust . . . the girlish purity of the countenance and figure, while imparting to them the glow of maturity. Notice the ineffable greys of the flesh, the tender roseate hues which permeate it, and admire the craft which has enabled the artist to model all the forms so perfectly.'[82]

The artist himself was moved by the reforming zeal of a tiny, tireless woman he invited to dine in January. Octavia Hill, granddaughter of the sanitary reformer Thomas Southwood Smith and friend of the Hughes family, was an activist for women's education, involved with the Ladies Guild, as well as the Working Men's and Working Women's Colleges. She had trained as a copyist for Ruskin, who was financing her housing projects for the poor. At Little Holland House, the twenty-seven-year-old discussed her projects with Watts while the soft twilight shone over his golden frescoes. 'He is transparently, deeply good, a quiet, sympathetic man, with large childlike heart', Octavia Hill wrote to a friend. 'There is nothing pathetic about Watts, as there is about Ruskin. Watts is a more selfcontained man, I think, but with deep and tender sensibilities, and I gather faith with which he is better satisfied . . . He had evidently taken deeply to heart all my work.'[83]

Her Working Men's College associate Rossetti invited artist friends to preview *The Beloved* in his studio at Tudor House in Cheyne Walk, Chelsea, on 19 and 20 February 1866. His Chelsea mansion was filled with props, early stringed instruments, Japanese crystal, necklaces and feathers. Outside, an eccentric menagerie of birds and beasts roamed the garden.[84] Watts, warmly dressed in a long sealskin coat, arrived with a party of 'large ladies'. Their host, working on the languorous *Lady Lilith*, pointed him out to a twenty-five-year-old art student Emilie Wilson – (the future Mrs Russell Barrington) – who watched from behind the easel as Watts examined the sumptuous picture of Marie Ford – his *Bianca* – Rossetti's Bride of Solomon draped in a green leather head-dress and kimono.[85] On the 20th, Nelly Watts, accompanying Kate on tour in the provinces, wrote to her mother:

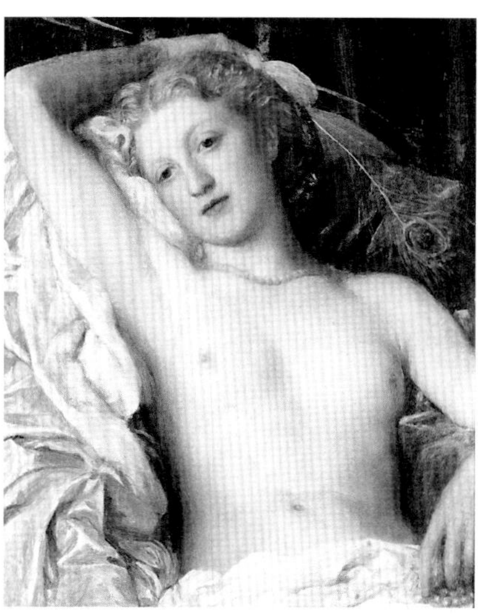

69   *A Study with Peacock's Feathers*, 1863–65 (Pre-Raphaelite Inc, by courtesy of Julian Hartnoll).

Read this to yr self!!!

To finish up the night in a pleasant manner, I went to bed and dreamed not of the Theatre (isn't that strange?) but of Mr Watts!

I dreamed he was dying, & I woke up in the greatest grief-crying!

This is the 20th of the month! My Wedding day! Married 2 years ago today! & it is such a day. *Pouring* with rain! & altogether wretched!!

Oh! . . . with all thy faults, I love thee still![86]

Nelly made a brief return to the stage for Kate's benefit on 20 June at the Olympic Theatre, appearing in *The Hunchback* as Helen in a *décolletage* that 'made Mama very angry!' while her estranged husband attracted attention at the Royal Academy Summer Exhibition with a nude sea nymph. *Thetis*, mother of Achilles, stands on the sands, binding up her golden hair. Water laps at her feet. Her long limbs and torso, her small breasts and hips, are the pure idealized form of Long Mary; a drawing inscribed 'Miss Smith' suggests that her face was taken from Ellen Smith, a Chelsea laundry maid who also posed for Rossetti. The first of a series of vertical nudes, the slender *Thetis* – a large version (pl. xxv) would stretch even higher than Ingres' *La Source* – marked a radical departure from the fleshy nudes of William Etty. The vertical format appears to ennoble and purify the figure beyond sexual desire. Inviting association with architectural form, it exemplifies the 'sensuous intellect', the Greek perception of the human figure favoured by the eighteenth-century German art historian Winckelmann. *Thetis*, seen by the *Athenaeum* as 'too girlish',[87] appealed to the Liverpool ship-owner and wealthy art patron, Frederick Leyland. Whether she was already pledged to her purchaser Lady Lothian, is uncertain. Leyland nevertheless sought an introduction to Watts through Rossetti. 'May I have the pleasure of introducing to you Mr Fredk Leyland of Liverpool, who likes your little *Thetis* so well that I could not resist showing him, if possible, that if you have not in your studio "five hundred good as she," at any rate those who are there are not her inferiors.'[88]

The mosaic of *St Matthew*, inlaid in Venice by the new glasshouse founded by Antonio Salviati, had to be substantially rearranged to match Watts's design when it was inserted into the spandrel at St Paul's that year. He painted a portrait of the dean. Although the two cartoons now hung in the nave, the demand for Watts to design mosaics for the cathedral ended after Milman's death in 1868.[89]

Browning sat for the national collection (fig. 70)[90] and the Airlies' portraits were completed. A plaid of Airlie tartan presents the earl as a Scotsman. Unusually, Watts added the countess's hands, enhancing the Venetian style of her portrait with luxuriant crimson sleeves (fig. 71). Watts explained to the earl, that the addition, 'for the benefit of the picture and for my own advantage', would not affect the agreed cost, a hundred and fifty guineas. Blanche pasted his letter on to the stretcher with a note that 'when it was hung up at Airlie Lodge in Kensington, Gladstone said it was the finest woman's portrait this century.'[91]

Watts liked his pictures to hang on a rich, dark wall, preferably red or green.[92] He advised Rickards: 'An oil picture suffers so very much if hung upon a light ground, if your walls are light it would pay you for the sake of your own pleasure in the pictures to have your room repapered, it may seem to be rather a bold request but pictures are expensive luxuries & a

70   *Robert Browning*, 1865–66 (National Portrait Gallery, London).

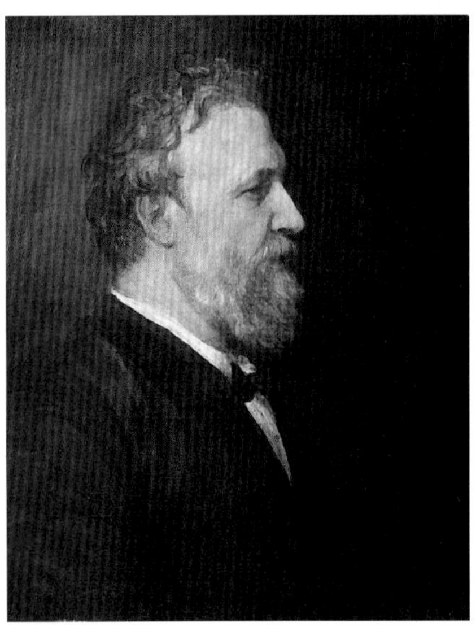

man ought to get all the satisfaction he can out of them to say nothing of justice to the artist.'[93]

Rickards bought *Bianca* and a smaller version of *Esau*. His patronage and sympathy for Watts's aspirations and aims for English art became increasingly important to the artist. As his proposals for mural-training for art students began to take effect, he steered an exploitative request from Manchester Grammar School into an educational project. The headmaster, impressed by the Lincoln's Inn fresco wanted him to paint a Roman mural and to exploit his name in school advertisements – 'Every stranger would come to see it and we should become one of the lions of the town.' Watts suggested instead that students should paint it, under professional guidance.[94]

Although studio assistance for his large South Court lunette had not materialized, he had been commissioned to paint Titian for the golden mosaic arcade along the court's upper walls, a gallery of life-size portraits of master artists and craftsmen. Designed by leading contemporary artists – (Edward Poynter, who had chosen to paint Phidias, gave the master of the fine limb bandy legs!) – they were to be set in mosaic by female art students under supervision, in Watts's case, by Minton, Hollins.[95]

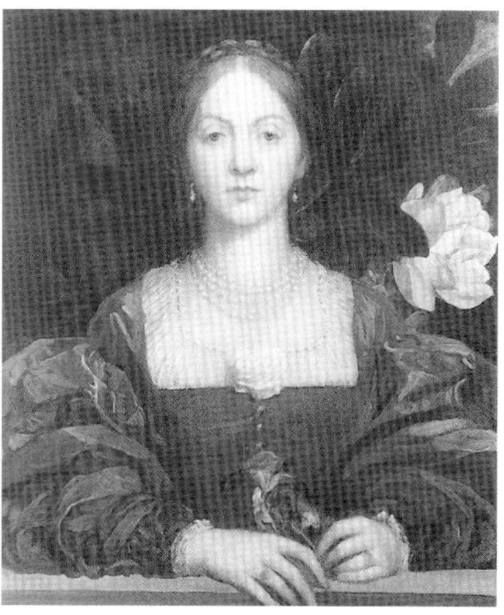

71   *Blanche Ogilvie, Countess of Airlie*, 1865–66 (private collection).

His national portraits of the two most illustrious living poets *Alfred Tennyson* and *Robert Browning* presided over the French Gallery, where the catalogue instructed viewers to learn from the artist's technique. Whereas modern practice relied on white paint, which often remained 'chalky and crude', his unusually low-toned canvases were 'loaded with colour'; the texture was rough, the lights standing out in relief and the shadows sinking into transparency, as colours were painted over each other, 'the dry are softened by the liquid, the opaque glazed into by the transparent,' to produce Venetian depth and force.[96]

Watts decided to give up portrait commissions unless the sitter was prepared to be seen as a symbolic subject.[97] The variety of sitters broadened his experience of the human character, colour and form, but the comparatively poor remuneration and stress of achieving the likeness took its toll, especially when friends and relations came to inspect the portrait. 'You stand first on one foot, then on the other, with nothing to say – waiting for the verdict. When it comes it is generally the one thing that is least bad in the painting which is most criticized.'[98] In exasperation, Watts wrote to Julia Cameron:

> Nature did not intend me for a portrait-painter . . . it has ever cost me more labour to paint a portrait than to paint a subject picture. I have given it up in sheer weariness; now come what may, my time must in future be devoted to the endeavour to carry out some of my large designs, and if I fail either to make a living or to do anything worthy of an artist . . . I fail, but I submit to the drudgery of portrait-painting no longer.[99]

Portraits of national figures, however, would remain a life-long commitment. Stimulated by variety of subject, medium and texture, he worked every daylight hour as experimental ideas cascaded from his mind, jotted down on scraps of paper, drawn and modelled in wax, to be transformed into oil and now into clay and marble.

# 8　Royal Academician



'I AM SOMETIMES TEMPTED IN MY IMPATIENCE to try if I cannot get subscriptions to carry out a project I have long had which is to erect a great statue to Unknown Worth! In the words of the eloquent author of *Felix Holt: The Radical*, "a monument to the faithful who are not famous"',[1] Watts wrote to Charles Hilditch Rickards on 17 August 1866. Had he not forfeited earnings for the two national collections, he would have funded the symbolic memorial himself. He was sculpting a life-size memorial statue and, confident that he could create a colossal bronze monument, he sought the businessman's professional opinion. 'I would give up all other work to be enabled to carry out such an idea.'[2] To Watts, sculpture, the most moral and beautiful of the arts, associated with the noble culture of ancient Greece, was the medium best suited to elevate British art and express national character. As his horizons broadened, he built up investment reserves to fund his ideals. The commission for the memorial to Sir Thomas Cholmondeley Owen of Condover reinforced his growing stature and fired him with a desire to create sculpture for the nation; and the recent publication of George Eliot's novel *Felix Holt* and the Reform Bill debate about giving the vote to working-class men,[3] spurred him to seek support for the memorial to unsung heroes, ordinary men and women. He would fight for the scheme for decades.

Before investing in substantial building works to extend his painting space and erect a sculpture studio, Watts applied for a ten-year extension to the Little Holland House lease, which was due to expire in 1871. Lady Holland had pledged the entire estate to her husband's heir, the fifth Earl of Ilchester.[4] In the meantime she was pursuing Lord Holland's programme and dividing the estate for development, selling land, albeit to his artist friends, ever closer to Little Holland House. Ionides had bought 1 Holland Park in 1864. Both Leighton, on his election as an associate member of the Royal Academy, and Val had acquired 99-year leases on farmland southwest of Little Holland House and built avant-garde red-brick studio houses in the new Holland Park Road. Val's magnificent Arts and Crafts *hôtel de peintre*, designed by Philip Webb, architect of William Morris's Red House, was number one; and George Aitchison had designed Leighton's at number two. Lady Holland's weak promise to Sara in January 1866 to 'do my best to meet your wishes' prompted Watts to apply to her in person to extend their lease. The wily widow roared with laughter, 'pooh-poohed' the need for legal formality between friends and convinced her old protégé that the lease would be secure during her lifetime. He went ahead with a two-year building programme.[5]

Leighton would drop in at dawn for a chat and critical appraisal before work. His comments were frank and constructive; and a strong alliance developed between them. Both loved music as a divine art. They sought inspiration from the finest Greek sculptors and Italian Renaissance artists and infused their own modern art with a sense of grandeur. Utterly unalike by nature and in their approach to painting – Leighton was a perfectionist, whereas to Watts technique was secondary to the idea – they remained close friends and colleagues all their lives. 'Each seemed to find in the other that which he would above all things have like to find in himself', Mary Watts later recalled. Leighton, with his splendid Olympian physique (fig. 91), was highly educated and assured; he revealed no anxiety or doubt and adopted the appearance of a suave man of the world. 'Nature got tired when she was in the middle of making me, left off, and went away and made a Leighton,' said Watts. Though self-deprecating, he was steadfast in mind and in his vision for art. Despite thinning hair, his beard remained profuse; and he was a confident horseman – he offered to teach the Countess of Airlie's children to ride. But, too often let down by ill health, he now preferred not to dine out, and had taken to wearing a hat at all times to prevent rheumatism in the head (brought on by working in cold damp conditions).[6]

The Royal Academy was courting Watts. To bring the rebel artist on board, the president, Sir Francis Grant, reformed election procedure. Up to now candidates had nominated themselves, which was humiliating for senior artists and allowed in inferiors. Grant introduced nomination by Academicians and personally recommended Watts for associate membership.[7] On 31 January Leighton came to break the news that he and Armitage had been elected, with Hunt trailing a poor third. Watts had not of course sought election, nor did he really wish it; however, while negotiations were under way, he asked Ned Burne-Jones to sound out Gabriel Rossetti, a fellow rebel. Rossetti had no desire to join himself, but counselled Watts to accept no less than full membership. He should not agree to be 'shot in' with younger, second-rate Associates to await the Academicians' pleasure:

> Had things gone as they should, you would have taken early a place suited to youth among them, and already now for some time the one which your middle life justly claims. 'Cumulative' elections are by no means unheard of in other bodies; and if they are willing to do their duty by you, the only way by which they can prove it is to make a fresh law and to elect you an Associate & Academician in one day. Nothing less, were I you, would I accept at their hands.'[8]

Events moved almost as Rossetti had outlined, although Watts, startled by the news, at first hesitated to accept the associateship in case health problems jeopardized his Academy obligations. Persuaded by Leighton and Armitage, however, that he could influence younger members and elevate public taste for art, he recognized the new liberal spirit of his election and accepted the diploma on 6 March 1867.[9] The *Illustrated London News* published a frank review of his achievements, reporting that Watts had faced 'vulgar prejudice', apathy and sneers against high art, that his sober colours and low tones appeared out of tune with the public eye. Marking

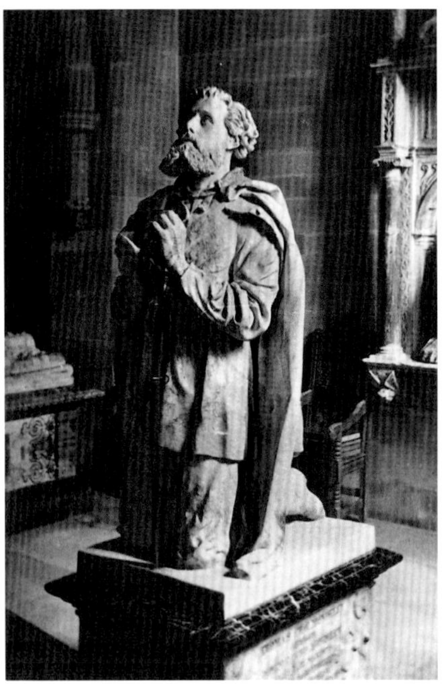

72   Memorial to Sir Thomas Cholmondeley Owen,1866–67, in the Church of St Andrew and St Mary at Condover in Shropshire.

73   May Prinsep as *Prayer*, 1867 (Manchester City Art Gallery).

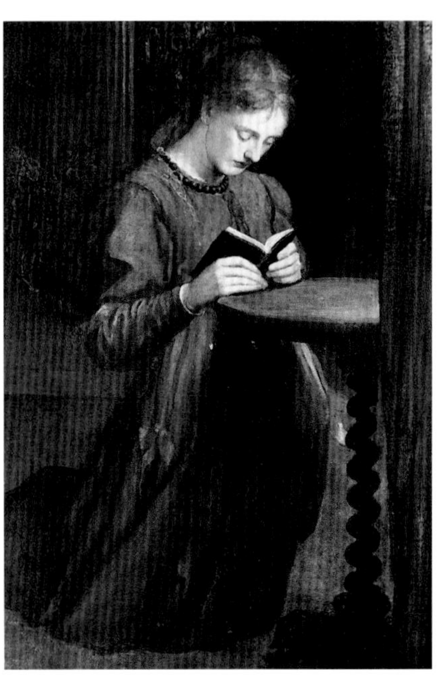

a significant breakthrough, his new forty-foot *Angel of Death* was judged 'amongst the most noble conceptions of modern art'. His genius for murals and contributions to the forthcoming Paris exhibition – *Fata Morgana* and the portrait of William Bowman – were listed, as well as his failed experiments and ambitious, unfulfilled cosmic scheme. The review, Illustrated with an engraving from one of Cameron's finest photographs, infuriated her. Watts's reply can scarcely have pacified the photographer: 'Notoriety I dislike, criticism annoys me, and praise I despise. I believe time alone can place the Poet and the Artist . . . I cannot say that I admire the copy of your photograph, but I am rejoiced to see that it is so transmogri-fied that I run no risk of being recognized.'[10] On principle he did not sign autographs for collectors,[11] but agreed, like her other eminent sitters, to sign her photograph mounts, which would double their value.[12]

The life-size marble statue of Sir Thomas Cholmondeley Owen (fig. 72) had been commissioned by his brother, Reginald Cholmondeley, for the Church of St Andrew and St Mary in Condover, Shropshire, where it was to stand in, beside an eighteenth-century monument by the French sculp-tor Louis François Roubilliac. Watts chose an unusual format, an upright kneeling figure, which he was modelling first in clay and would carve in marble – pure white for the head and red-veined for the body. Completed in 1867, the cloaked knight is seen kneeling on both knees, hands resting on his sword; his bearded face, worked from a death mask, is thrown back; the movement and folds of his cape suggest heroic action and, outstretched behind, are the wings of a guardian angel. In both painting and sculpture, Watts was developing the effect of Phidian-inspired *mouvementé* drapery to diffuse the mass – 'leaving the head and limbs free and uninterfered with, simple, massive, and important'.[13] The effect is notable in the large *Angel of Death* and in *May*, a picture of a girl kneeling at prayer (fig. 73).

Fourteen-year-old May Prinsep, Thoby's orphaned niece, had been sitting to Julia Cameron for medal-winning photographs since 1866, posing for one as a nun. She kneeled by a table for Watts, with her eyes lowered over a book, light playing over her face and hands,[14] and modelled for a figure in *The Angel of Death*. *May* (later known as *Prayer*) attracted reviewers of the Academy exhibition, where portraits of the Dean of Westminster, of the Honourable Mrs Seymour Egerton singing, and of Joachim playing the violin generally endorsed his rank. Watts's plan to challenge fellow members to a competitive gathering, to test their skills and refresh those whose art had grown rusty, was clearly too bold for a new associate. Instead, he had offered to sacrifice his exhibition entries in favour of others. 'There are many to whom it is a matter of real or fancied importance.'[15] Rickards fought off bids from John Denison, Speaker of the House of Commons[16] and Earl Grosvenor to buy *May* for three hundred guineas.[17]

With extended studio space, rising public status and Rickards's support Watts was encouraged to pursue larger symbolic pictures. By March, the first of the *Eve* series planned for the cosmic fresco scheme was well under way. 'The mother of mankind,' wrote the *Athenaeum*, 'standing as if just after the moment of creation, lost in wonder at existence, and it may be, in an ecstasy of thankfulness . . . her face upturned' (fig. 75).[18] 'Earth's archetypal Eve', Madeline Wyndham (fig. 74), began to sit for a remark-able full-length portrait in early May 1867 (pl. XVIII), her warm nature evident from the start.[19] Since his decision to abandon portraiture, Watts had declined all portrait requests from friends, but hers would nurture a lifelong rapport. Madeline was the mother of a growing, later influential family. But that month she strayed delightfully in Paris, where her husband entrusted her to the care of his cousin, the poet Wilfrid Scawen Blunt. The ever amorous Blunt feasted her on strawberries, read her poetry, kissed her feet and declared 'not quite innocent' love,[20] after which the Wyndhams returned to their London residence, 44 Belgrave Square, for the season. Blunt accompanied her to sittings at Little Holland House.

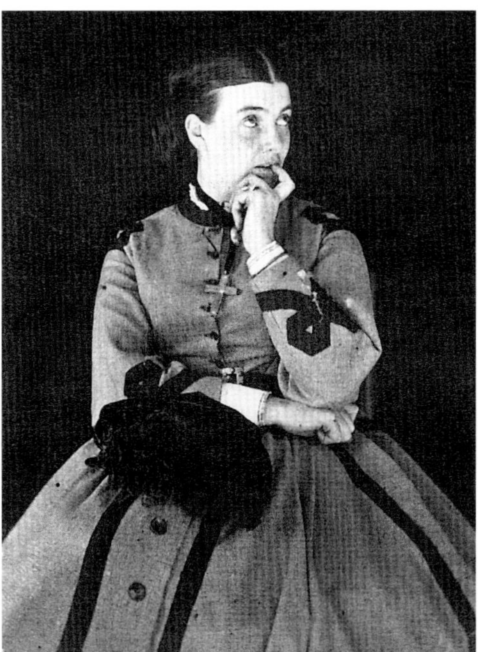

74 Madeline Wyndham, 1866.

75 (below) *She Shall Be Called Woman, c.*1867 (Courtesy of Christie's).

At thirty-two, Madeline was in the prime of womanhood. She inherited the mysterious beauty of her grandmother Pamela Fitzgerald, wife of the Irish revolutionary Lord Edward Fitzgerald.[21] She also carried the French blood of her other grandparents, Louis Philippe 'Égalité' Duc d'Orléans and his mistress, the educationalist Madame de Genlis, and she had the 'wide-minded' indulgence of her Scottish father Sir Guy Campbell.[22] Watts's oil sketch shows her standing, her dress falling in voluptuous folds and decorated with sunflowers. There is a sense of magnanimity, mystery and suppressed passion – a key Wattsian characteristic – though Madeline herself was bursting with vitality. Her 'speaking eyes' wrote Blunt, betrayed each mood – joy, melancholy, passion, wit, anger, pity.[23] She developed a lifelong rapport with the artist, recording 'remembrances' of her children in Wattsian language. Madeline would give birth to two daughters before the portrait was completed.[24]

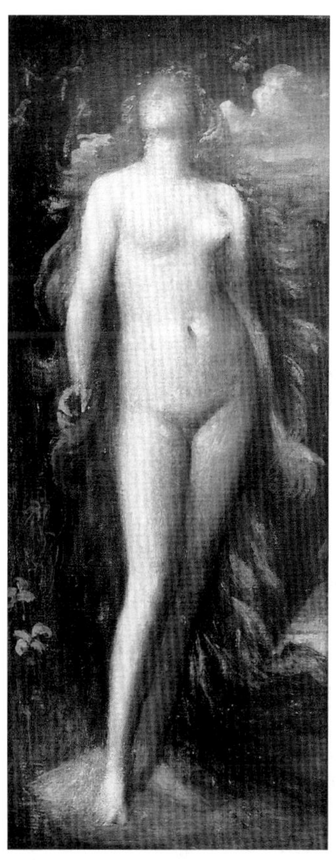

Every bit as passionate was the controversial flame-haired poet Algernon Swinburne, who came to sit for the national series in May (fig. 76). Acclaimed since 1865 for *Atalanta in Calydon* – which had been compared to Aeschylus and Sophocles and was admired by Tennyson for its tumultuous musical invention – Swinburne had consolidated his fame with the erotic *Chastelard* and *Poems and Ballads*. (The latter excited such hostility that his publisher Moxon withdrew them from circulation.) Watts would have sympathized with his ideals. Enlisted as Giuseppe Mazzini's poet in the crusade for Italian liberty, Swinburne was writing a dirge on the death of the French Symbolist poet Charles Baudelaire. Such was his inner energy that even in repose, Swinburne would turn his hands or feet[25] and he clearly struggled to suppress this in Watts's studio:

I am in the honourable agonies of portrait-sitting – to Watts. Of course it is a great honour for one to be asked to sit to him, now especially

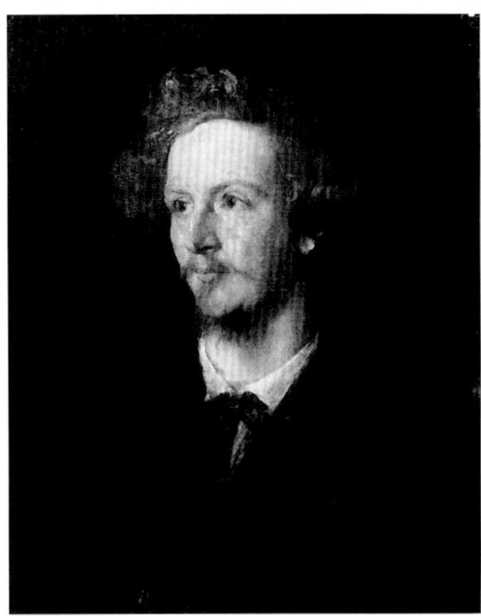

76  *Algernon Charles Swinburne*, 1867 (National Portrait Gallery, London).

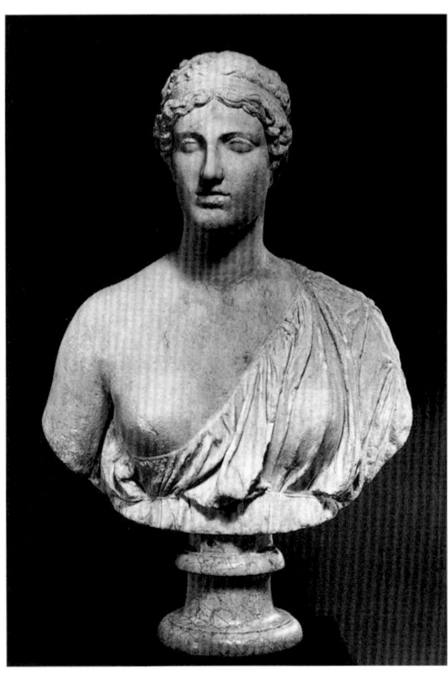

77  The Oxford Bust (Ashmolean Museum, Oxford).

that he accepts no commissions and paints portraits only for three reasons – friendship, beauty, and celebrity; having the 'world' at his feet begging to be painted. But it takes time and trouble, and he won't let me crop my hair, whose curls the British public (unlike Titian's) reviles aloud in the streets. *Il faut souffrir pour être paint*.[26]

The concept of suppressed energy fascinated Watts. Swinburne's portrait impressed colleagues from the start; the vivacity in his Titian-red hair, flaming eyes, crooked nose and wispy moustache, was seen to reflect the lyricism of his poetry, a rare combination of weakness and strength which Tom Taylor likened to 'the Duke of Argyll with the devil in him'.[27]

Oxford University Galleries, looking to Academicians for guidance for their new displays, consulted Watts about the selection of the Arundel Marbles. Now was the time to disseminate news of the bust they had found in 1849. Despite his aversion to ill-informed critics, the artist conspired with Newton to use the *Athenaeum* to present her as a recent 'discovery of considerable importance'. As her expressive features, abundant hair and slightly tilted head precluded the hand of Phidias himself, they proposed to name her 'Aspasia', after the celebrated mistress of Pericles. Despite her damage, the *Athenaeum* declared the sculpture to be invaluable. Watts painstakingly pieced her together in his studio. He adjusted her head and modelled a new nose and advised the British Museum cast-manufacturer, Domenico Brucciani, who undertook to make a mould from the 'Oxford Bust' (fig. 77).[28]

The Little Holland House salon continued to attract talented young admirers. Gertrude Jekyll, a promising twenty-three-year-old artist brought by her cousin Georgy Duff Gordon on 16 June 1867, was allowed to copy the bull's head Watts painted in Italy.[29] However, he would never be welcome at a rival salon nearby. Kate Terry deserted her London audience to marry Arthur Lewis that autumn. Her lavish salon at Moray Lodge, frequented by Little Holland House habitués, was seen as the Terrys' vengeance. Nelly had returned to full-time acting. If Sara was perturbed, Watts was in fine spirits. Promoted to full Academician with unprecedented speed on 18 December, he encountered stinging criticism from Landseer, but consolidated his elevation by extending his range of work, developing revolutionary sculptural techniques.[30] Rather than reduce his estranged wife's maintenance payments, in accordance with their settlement,[31] he channelled his desire for love and hitherto doomed passions to empower his art.

He would capture the supreme symbolic moment from an Ovidian theme, and re-create it as though for eternity. Each monumental character was charged with emotion. Turning his back on the cold neoclassical style of contemporary sculpture, he modelled a ground-breaking clay bust of *Clytie*, a subject Nelly had inspired him to paint after they parted. Spurned by Apollo, the impassioned wood nymph twists back to face the sun god and begins to metamorphose into 'a flower like a violet' – Watts had shown his bride clutching these to her heart in *Choosing*. His small languid nude *Daphne*, who rejected Apollo, was bought by the enterprising Lady Lothian and shown with *Swinburne* at the Dudley Gallery's first winter exhibition of oil paintings at the Egyptian Hall in Piccadilly.[32]

*Orpheus and Eurydice* (pl. XIII), a painted poem for which Madeline

Wyndham modelled, was hailed by the *Athenaeum* on 28 December as 'a triumph of imagination'. Leighton, after the disastrous *Triumph of Music: Orpheus, by the Power of his Art, Redeems his Wife from Hades* of 1856,[33] had recently painted Eurydice clinging to the Thracian poet, who pushes her away in order to avert his gaze. Watts chose a later moment, full of hope, but fatal. His emotive image, again echoing the flights of his lost muse, encapsulates the instant when Orpheus gazes back at his wife and in so doing loses her. In this half-length version, the poet still clutches his lyre with the single unbroken string symbolizing Hope. He clasps her breast, she falls away, her arms lose their grip, her flesh pales, her head becomes limp, and she slips back to oblivion. Her transparent *mouvementé* drapery contrasting with his vigorous, ruddy body, heightens the sense of desire and the impotence of love in the face of death.[34] Rossetti was at the time combining ecstasy and death in the figure of *Beata Beatrix*, a central Symbolist image, in which Lizzie is presented as Dante's Beatrice at the spiritual moment of death.[35] Gustave Moreau, absorbed by the subject of death, had exhibited an idealized vision of Orpheus's severed head in the 1866 Paris Salon. *Jeune fille thrace portant la tête d'Orphée* shows the poet's head juxtaposed on to his lyre carried in the limp arms of a Thracian girl, whose closed eyes intensify his fate. The Orpheus theme continued to absorb Watts and would be taken up by Moreau and the European Symbolists in the 1890s.[36]

The first of his four Apocalyptic horsemen, *The Rider on the Pale Horse* (fig. 78), representing the power to kill, was well under way by the new year. Clearly inspired by the visionary eighteenth-century poet and painter William Blake,[37] Watts's shrouded personification of Death astride its frenzied mount was more searing than Blake's swashbuckling *Death on a Pale Horse*.[38] On 7 January 1868, Henry Cole invited Watts and Leighton to fill two vast semicircular lunettes in the South Court with frescoes, for which each would be paid a handsome fifteen hundred pounds. True fresco, however, was not standing up well to the British climate – the Lincoln's Inn wall was decaying – and at Lyndhurst Church in Hampshire, Leighton had used Gambier Parry's new oil-based technique. Both officially accepted their commissions in July.[39]

Meanwhile, to achieve vigorous muscle tension for *Clytie*, Watts hired the Italian model Angelo Colarossi, who had posed for *Esau* and *The Prodigal Son*; studies from a current sitter Louise Lowther supplied the nymph's coiled hair,[40] her head, breasts and posture were taken from Long Mary, and three-year-old Margaret Burne-Jones twisting and turning in her mother's arms produced the straining pose that pushed the parameters of classicism.[41] Upon seeing the clay bust in Watts's new sculpture studio – a draughty greenhouse still under construction – the speaker of the House of Commons, John Denison, was moved to reread Ovid. Denison acknowledged, 'There lives at LHH, a Sculptor, as well as a painter.' For the marble version of *Clytie*, Watts rented studio space from the sculptor George Nelson at 8 Ravens Place, off the new Goldhawk Road in Hammersmith, and invited friends to watch the drama unfold.[42] He outlined the qualities he was aiming to achieve to Gladstone:

> Flexibility, impression of colour, & largeness of character – rather than purity – gravity, – qualities I own to be essentially necessary to sculpture

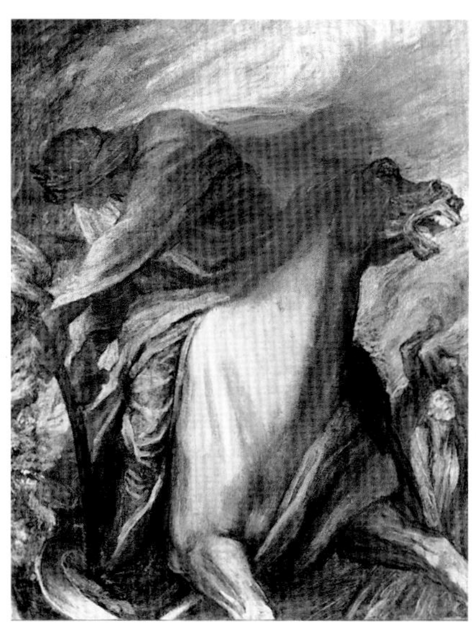

78   *The Rider on the Pale Horse*, 1867–82 (Museums and Galleries on Merseyside: The Walker).

[and echoed by his protégé Julia Cameron] but which being made as it seems to me exclusively the objects of the modern sculptor have deadened his senses & some others making part often of the glories of ancient Art, & resulted in bare & cold work.[43]

Emilie Barrington, who later watched him carve the marble *Clytie* (pl. XIV), recalled: 'He felt his own genius stronger, more peremptory, when influenced by sensuous qualities, by enthusiasm for colour and for the form which produced on him, as on the Greeks, an aesthetic feeling of delight beyond the cold, merely intellectual approval'. *Clytie* writhes in massive Michelangelesque *contrapposto*. She has none of the repose, even, of Greek sculpture. As the *Art Journal* reported, 'There is not on the surface even a tenth part of an inch that is not palpitating under vehement emotion.'[44]

Watts kept a cast of the Oxford bust in his painting studio.[45] Fascinated by colour and the interrelation between sculpture and painting, he employed Venetian colours to transform his half-draped Grecian beauty into an erotic Ovidian picture, coming to life as *The Wife of Pygmalion* (fig. 79), the ivory statue whose flesh softened at her sculptor's touch. As blood reaches her ripening lips and nipple, exposed by the folds of her *chiton*, Watts's golden-haired Galatea appears more kissable against a virginal background of lilies, than Rossetti's luscious *Venus Verticordia*, almost overpowering with her profusion of flowers and butterflies, the souls of her lovers, fluttering over the arrow pointed at her breast. Both artists celebrated the poetry of female beauty, using mythology and symbolism to recreate images of extraordinary sexual power. Promised to Eustace Smith on first refusal at two hundred guineas, *The Wife of Pygmalion, A Translation from the Greek*[46] was being prepared for the Academy's centenary summer exhibition. Such was the pressure to contribute his broadest range yet that by nightfall Watts's eyes ached. His five entries, well received, included an evening landscape, a new portrait of the British Museum librarian Sir Anthony Panizzi, painted on his retirement,[47] the unfinished marble *Clytie*, and *The Meeting of Jacob and Esau*, an enlargement from his Dalziel woodcut design, commissioned by a Dublin merchant John Wardell.[48]

*The Wife of Pygmalion* created a stir. As a work of rare poetic elevation, Galatea seemed an enigma to the critic William Michael Rossetti. Was she womanly or impassive, cold or warm?[49] She drove Gladstone to distraction. Of the many offers for her at the private view on 1 May, his was the most persistent and the Liberal leader summoned the artist to his London home, 11 Carlton House Terrace. Watts accepted, and took the opportunity to introduce Burne-Jones. As the Smiths had reserved *The Wife of Pygmalion*,[50] he invited the statesman to his studios. 'I will cure you of your love & console you for your disappointment (the picture is claimed) by showing you the fragment from which it was painted, wherein you will see all that you admire in the picture with infinite beauties altogether missed.'[51]

Swinburne, too, was impressed by *The Wife of Pygmalion*, as one of two pictures that lingered in his mind as he left the Academy.[52] During his portrait sittings, he would have seen the Oxford cast and early progress of the painting, which he clearly discussed, for in comparing her 'sweet majesty and amorous chastity' to the Venus of Melos, he encapsulated the artist's intention in his *Notes of the Royal Academy Exhibition 1868*:

The soft severity of perfect beauty might serve alike for woman or statue,

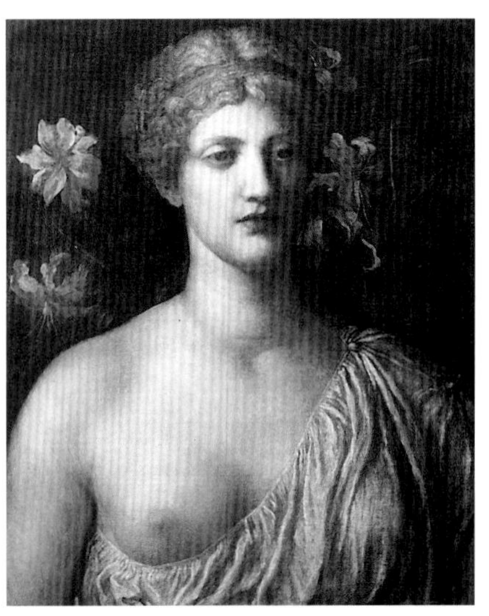

79   *The Wife of Pygmalion*, 1865–68 (The Faringdon Collection Trust, Buscot Park).

flesh or marble; but the eyes have opened already upon love, with a tender and grave wonder; her curving ripples of hair seem just warm from the touch and the breath of the goddess, moulded and quickened by lips and heads diviner than her sculptor's. So it seems a Greek painter must have painted women . . . no less than in the bust of *Clytie*, we see how in the hands of a great artist painting and sculpture may become sister arts indeed . . . how, without any forced alliance of form and colour, a picture may share the gracious grandeur of a statue, a statue may catch something of the subtle bloom of beauty proper to a picture.[53]

To have his artistic aims aired in poetic language and his sculpture promoted delighted Watts and reviews were excellent. 'Tremendous outing on my *Clytie*', he wrote to Lady Lothian.[54] The bust was in a raw unfinished state, yet Swinburne wrote:

Never was a divine legend translated into diviner likeness . . . yearning with all the life of her lips and breasts after the receding light and the removing love – this is the Clytie indeed whom sculptors loved for her love of the Sun their God . . . the splendour of her sorrow is divine . . . We seem to see the lessening sunset that she sees and fears too soon to watch that stately beauty slowly suffer change and die into flower, that solid sweetness of body sink into petal and leaf. Sculpture such as this has actual colour enough without need to borrow of an alien art.'[55]

As the 1868 National Portrait Exhibition opened at South Kensington – his reincarnation of Jeremy Bentham was on show[56] – Watts embarked on the portrait that convinced him more than ever that he was not cut out for the genre. The historian John Forster commissioned him to paint Thomas Carlyle. Painter and sitter, mutually bound by the significance of the project, found the pressure almost unendurable. A founding father of the National Portrait Gallery and himself one of the most painted Victorians, the Sage of Chelsea made it clear that he was submitting to a weary fate, 'I am to give Watts his "first sittings" (sorrow on it)', wrote on 20 May.[57]

Despite mutual respect – Carlyle talked of Watts as 'a mon of note' and the artist respected him as the first prophet of the age – there was a character clash between the two men and neither would give way. The septuagenarian, having completed his five-volume *History of Frederick the Great* in 1865, considered his literary career to be at an end,[58] whereas Watts always felt his life was just beginning. They had argued about eye colour, when Carlyle, posing for Julia Cameron at Little Holland House the previous year, had insistence that brown eyes signified an active mind and grey, contemplative. Watts countered that Guizot had distinctly recalled Napoleon's steel-cold eye;[59] and the historian had sent a bibliographic extract to prove that 'Mahomet's eyes were large, black, and full of fire', adding a patronizing note. 'For its excellence and clearness, from which *you* might paint, I have had the whole description copied for you, and send it revised with my compliments – T. Carlyle, Chelsea, June 8th 1867.'[60]

That day Cameron registered three photographs of the historian. She inscribed the full-face shot – '*Carlyle like a rough block of Michael Angelo's Sculpture*' – which had he approved as a likeness, but thought 'terrifically ugly and woe-begone'[61] and refused to face another session. 'He says it's a kind of *Inferno*!' raged the photographer. 'The *greatest* men of the age . . .

Sir John Herschel, Henry Taylor, Watts, say I have *immortalized* them . . . What is one to do – Hm?'[62] Facing Mrs Cameron's lens was undoubtedly an ordeal, but Carlyle fanned the flames. Meeting the historian after he began sitting to Watts, the Queen recorded how the 'strange-looking eccentric old Scotchman . . . held forth in a drawling, melancholy voice, with a broad Scottish accent – upon the utter degeneration of everything.'[63]

Screens and curtains were placed around the easel: 'There was much meestification,' the Sage reported to Whistler, for whom he later posed as an *Arrangement in Grey and Black*.[64] 'I was not allowed to see anything.'[65] Watts, struggling to capture the soul of his revered, cussed sitter on to canvas, could not convince him that there was more to a portrait than historical record; and Carlyle goaded him about the Elgin Marbles and insisted that none of the men was clever because of their weak jaws. His slow deliberate voice, amusing when he was witty, heightened the sting: 'Depend upon it, neither God nor man can get on without a jaw.' Watts, in turn, challenged his view that a long upper lip indicated intellect, pointing out that Napoleon, Byron and Carlyle's hero Goethe were 'remarkable for the beauty of a very short one'.[66]

By 30 June Carlyle was allowed to see the portrait. 'At last the screens were put aside and there I was,' he told Whistler. 'And I looked. And Mr Watts, a great mon, he said to me, "how do ye like it?"' Not at all. Carlyle felt he looked like a monster. 'Mon, I would have ye know I am in the hobit of wuring clean linen!' he exclaimed.[67] Carlyle tried, but failed to conceal his impatience. As he left for Scotland, he reassured Watts, 'I am anxious to neglect nothing for perfecting our mutual enterprise, in which I see in you such excellent desire after excellence.'[68] Forster saw the portrait and relayed his verdict to the sitter: 'All that your face contains is by no means there – want of softness – want of sweetness – of humour – many wants – But much that *is* there rendered very grandly indeed – a face as of a prophet – very sorrowful – very mournful – wanting the corrective I would have him give it in the refining and humanizing way – but certainly the material for the greatest picture of you that has ever been done.'[69]

*Orpheus and Eurydice* was warmly received at Wales's first major art exhibition in the new town hall at Ruthin, as 'masterly than that of, perhaps any English painter.'[70] Pressed by Thomas Hughes, he completed a portrait of the as yet anonymous author for the frontispiece of the new illustrated edition of *Tom Brown's School Days*,[71] and he painted marriage portraits of Adelbert, the third Earl Brownlow and his fiancée, Lady Adelaide Talbot (fig. 80). Seeing his distress that England was producing no great works of art, that he felt he had lost twenty years of his life (presumably, referring to lack of support for symbolic national art), Lady Adelaide wrote to Lord Lothian that 'Watts is dying to do a beautiful statue of *Britannia* to be put up to 'the faithful who are not favoured'. He had resolved the subject for his monument to everyday heroes, and the Brownlows were keen to promote it.[72]

Watts informed Lady Lothian that he was building a temporary studio – had he begun to doubt Lady Holland? – in which to sculpt a symbolic seven-foot figure. If he could realize 'a conception of the human form divine in the right of beauty', proving that '*anche io son scultore* . . . I imagine something not unworthy of a great people will be achieved! I hope this does not appear too conceited on my part!' Lady Marion Alford, Lord

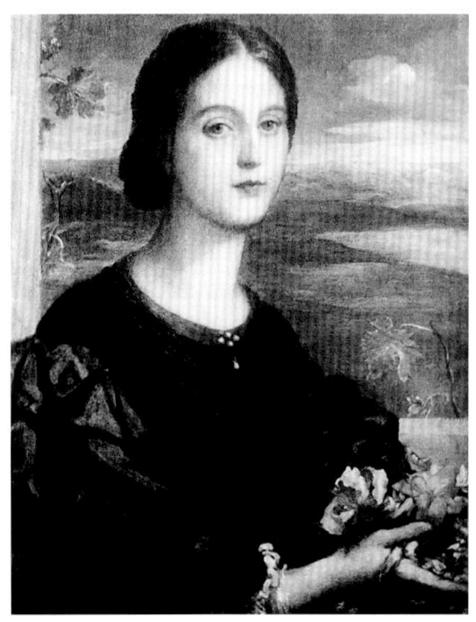

80    *Lady Adelaide Talbot*, before her marriage to Earl Brownlow in 1868 (photo: Frederic Hollyer).

Brownlow's mother, had raised his hopes for 'a bewilderingly grand project' but he believed it 'too good to be true, & I shall have to put it away among my dreams of the things that might have been.'[73] In the meantime, George Gilbert Scott invited him to sculpt an effigy of Dr John Lonsdale, the bishop of Lichfield (fig. 88). The recumbent figure would be sculpted from local alabaster and complement Scott's polychrome Gothic Revival transformation of Lichfield cathedral.[74]

In September, Watts sent Rickards a study for *Time and Death* (pl. XVI), a powerful metaphysical subject in which the stalwart youth Time, his auburn-haired head erect, advances hand in hand with Death – not a 'grinning skeleton', but a compassionate female figure. Tender rather than terrible, she looks down at flowers in her lap, while above them floats eternal Judgment, red-robed and faceless. Unusually, he had conceived the subject, complete, in a vision, and had hastily recorded the composition in chalk. As a rule, Watts built up imaginative subjects from an initial impression in his mind's eye, combined with an idea in his brain to spark a unique conception, which he would refine – barely altering the composition – over the years.[75]

He encouraged Rickards to patronize younger artists and on the Mancunian's behalf purchased a twenty-five-guinea landscape by the Frenchman Alphonse Legros, a new Little Holland House habitué and resident of Kensington. The high price he set on his own allegorical work – five hundred guineas for *The Angel of Death*, 'but I confidently hope in a few years it will be worth a 1000' – momentarily shook Rickards.[76] However, his appetite for Watts's imaginative work provided the crucial impetus that enabled him to develop major symbolic subjects. That people could accept the literary expression of ideas as similes – 'words themselves are but symbols' – but condemned allegory in art irked Watts. *Time and Death* [named '*Time Death and Judgment*' from 1869] was an example of the suggestive compositions by which he hoped to judged as an artist. 'I am very glad that you find the ring of poetry in it.'[77]

Colleagues were excited by his visionary painting of *Endymion* (fig. 81), the sleeping youth Endymion in the embrace of the moon goddess Diana, whose body, swathed in rippling pale blue draperies, their folds as fine as gossamer, surges over him in the form of a crescent moon.[78] Rossetti declared that *Endymion* 'alone should have made the year worthy to commence a new century', at which Ford Madox Brown hurried over to Little Holland House, finding 'a masterpiece that would do credit to any school in existence, or that has existed, as full of power in execution as it is poetic in conception.'[79] For Watts's imaginative style, it had an exceptionally fine finish. For the powerful half-length *Orpheus and Eurydice* he had charged Madeline Wyndham two hundred guineas; for *Endymion* he quoted five hundred.[80] It was bought by the Glasgow MP William Graham, hung upside down by the butler and, according to Graham's daughter Frances Horner, 'still looked beautiful'.[81]

In the New Year *Clytie* was to be placed in South Kensington Museum,[82] where students were completing Watts's *Titian* mosaic.[83] Appointed to the council, consolidating his Academy status, he and Leighton, now a full Academician, headed the eight-strong selection committee for the 1869 Summer Exhibition.[84] Forster wanted him to exhibit the Carlyle portrait, but more sittings were needed.[85] Nor would the self-effacing artist agree to

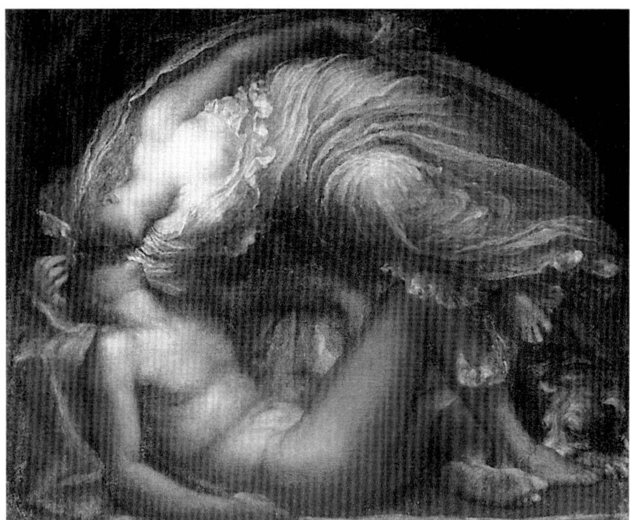

81   *Endymion*, 1869 (private collection, courtesy of Nevill Keating Pictures Ltd).

Rickards's request to show his self-portrait, because pictures of himself were experiments in method or colour.[86]

He modelled a portrait medallion to be carved in marble for the memorial to Henry Philips, and was invited to serve on a committee, headed by Earl Fortecue, to erect a monument to the Whig statesman Henry Fox, the third Lord Holland and father of his patron. Watts supported a proposal that the sculptor Joseph Edgar Boehm should design the statue and drinking fountain, but was persuaded by the committee, because of his Holland House and Kensington connections, to design the statue himself.[87] He saw to it, nevertheless, that Boehm played a prominent part. The Viennese-born Hungarian sculptor, whose portrait busts and statuettes he would have seen at the Academy, was now training Queen Victoria's talented fourth daughter Princess Louise. Boehm's first major commission, later that year, would be a portrait statue of the Queen. Meanwhile, under Watts's direction, Boehm produced the first small model of Lord Holland in his Fulham studios and the two men pulled the seated figure into shape in the garden at Little Holland House.[88]

Burlington House, the Academy's new premises in Piccadilly, with galleries designed by Sir Sidney Smirke, offered double the hanging space available at Trafalgar Square. Plans for the summer exhibition were arousing considerable interest in the art world. Watts feared dissent among the members. 'I look forward with dread to this hanging business,' he wrote to Rossetti on 30 March. 'You may be quite sure that Leighton & myself will be most desirous of doing the right thing but though the responsibility of placing the pictures rests with us & we shall be personally abused for any failure real or imagined, we are but two out of eight so that our decisions may be reversed by a majority of six votes!' Always keen to know what Rossetti was doing, Watts planned to call on him: 'I don't ask you to come & see what I have for exhibition I always dislike the whole thing, & am disgusted with my work however if you should be out this way, I need not say pray walk up & see the gems!'[89]

On 7 April, he was examining exhibition entries – 4,526 works of art, whittled down to 1,320 in four days[90] – when Ford Madox Brown called at his studio and was struck by a wide biblical seascape destined for Burlington House. In *The Return of the Dove* (fig. 82), the bird, holding an olive branch in its beak, flies in from the right, above the waves whose far-reaching ridges mark the rhythm of the water; distant hilltops tinted pale gold and rose emerge through vapour into the sky, which gradually becomes clear blue, filling the upper two-thirds of the picture. A critic would later recall *The Return of the Dove*, as 'the sensation of the Academy'.[91] The antithesis of Millais's compressed Pre-Raphaelite version, in which a girl stands inside the ark clutching the dove, which is being kissed by her companion, it was Watts's first picture to inspire a poem. As it seemed suited to engraving, he set a high value to include copyright.[92]

Julia Cameron, who registered batch upon batch of photographs may well have prompted him. No sooner had he singled out one of her symbolic profiles of Mary Hillier, registered in March, than she had it

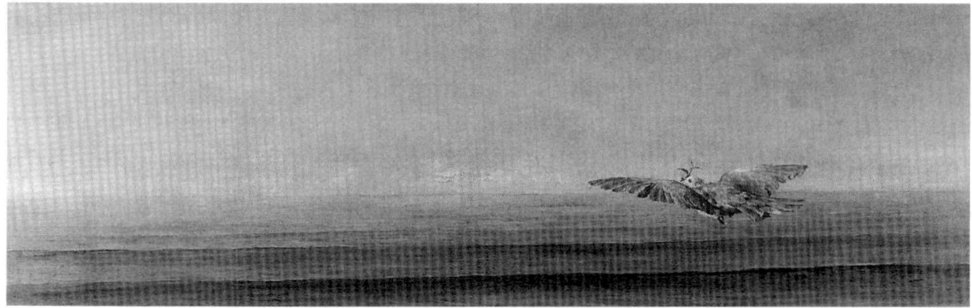

82  *The Return of the Dove*, 1868–69 (The Faringdon Collection Trust, Buscot Park).

lithographed 'The Dream – Quite Divine G F Watts's' (fig. 83).[93] The first picture Watts actually registered for copyright, on 1 April, was his spiritual Academy entry, *The Red Cross Knight and Una*, the Spenserian theme of his Palace of Westminster fresco.[94]

His commitment to the exhibition hanging took precedence over royalty. As he was engaged at Burlington House from eight in the morning until after eight at night, and unable to meet Princess Louise when she decided to pay an impromptu visit to his studios, he deputed Boehm, her modelling tutor, to act as guide.[95] That first summer exhibition he and Leighton masterminded in the grand top-lit galleries at Burlington House proved to be a seminal celebration of the emergence of classicism, idealism and an altogether broader range of modern English art. Displacing Pre-Raphaelitism, more imaginative pictures were seen to showing the influence of Continental styles.[96]

For the first time life-size canvases were placed on or below the line (eye-level); none had its base line more than twelve feet from the floor, and clear wall space separated each picture from its neighbour.[97] This provoked a furious pamphlet from Thomas Gullick, a traditionalist exhibitor who expected those 'wider intervals of crimson paper-hanging grinning between' to be filled with hundreds more paintings by 'Outsiders'. He vilified Leighton for his foreign tastes.[98] The odd Academician bristled. Two special requests from the president had been disregarded. Even so, Sir Francis recognized the Olympian triumph. 'You and Leighton acted with Roman virtue according to your judgment . . . although we have differed, it has always been done in good humour; and I can assure you as friends I value you both greatly . . . With the only trifling exception of the two pictures I think I never remember to have seen the exhibition so well hung.' Aware that Watts was again confined to bed, he suggested an encouraging remedy. 'You want another room to hang.'[99]

At the private view, Gladstone – now prime minister – determined this time to acquire *Orpheus and Eurydice*, its sense of yearning warm and erotic beside Leighton's deathly *Electra at the Tomb of Agamemnon*. 'Mindful of my craving and disappointment of last year, I went today, in the clandestine manner which becomes the like of me', he wrote to Watts.[100] But of course the picture now belonged to Madeline Wyndham.[101] To dissatisfy the prime minister was almost as frustrating for the artist as it was for Gladstone. Again, Watts invited him to the studio to give him a drawing from *Ilyssus*. Gladstone was keen to accept, 'but I shall never be quite happy until by hook or by crook I have possessed also of some little product of your brush'. He asked for a duplicate of *The Wife of Pygmalion*, which

83  Julia Margaret Cameron, *The Dream*, 1869 (Watts Gallery).

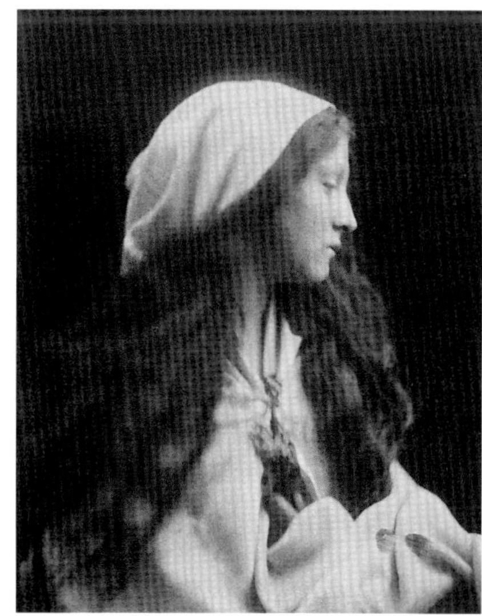

William Rossetti observed in the studio in July, with a portrait of Millais; and the drawing was forgotten, for decades.[102]

He devoted the late summer and autumn of 1869 to the life-size plaster model of the Bishop of Lichfield. In August, he borrowed a Charles II cope from Westminster Abbey. With only a death mask to refer to for the face, he concentrated on the drapery, modelling ever deeper folds, creating a dynamic whorling effect inspired by Giotto's frescoes in Padua as well as Phidias, and unique in sculpture of the day. He received five hundred pounds from Lichfield in November.[103]

The vigorous half-length portrait of Carlyle was despatched on 7 November (fig. 84).[104] The sage sits with characteristically folded hands. His expression is defiantly thoughtful, he has a fine brow, alert eyes, hair a little unkempt, the lower lip protrudes below his trimmed moustache and above a jaunty collar, the hairs of his beard establish that jaw. Forster was satisfied. Carlyle accused the artist of making him look like 'a mad labourer' and complained to his brother that this was 'decidedly the most insufferable picture that has yet been made of me, a delirious-looking mountebank full of violence, awkwardness, atrocity and stupidity.' Yet he conceded, 'The fault of Watts is a passionate pursuit of strength.'[105] G. K. Chesterton, writing in 1904, pointed out that whereas Millais had simply represented a magnificent shaggy old man, 'The uglier Carlyle of Watts has more of the truth about him, the strange combination of a score of sane and healthy visions and views, with something that was not sane, which bloodshot and embittered them all, the great tragedy of the union of a strong countryside mind and body with a disease of the vitals and something like a disease of the spirit. In fact, Watts painted Carlyle "like a mad labourer", because Carlyle was a mad labourer.' Watts regarded this important commission a failure.[106]

George Eliot was astonished to see Burne-Jones carrying a bronze cast of *Clytie* when he and Rossetti arrived for lunch on Sunday 9 January 1870. 'You have sent me the finest present I ever had in all my life', she wrote to Watts. She, too, had struggled against poor health and saw the bust as inspiration. 'You make the image you praise,' he replied. 'You are the sculptor not I, but still it is something to be "cause of wit in others".' Reflecting her radical interests in his unfulfilled aims, he went on, 'I aim at what is beyond me, and, in a wholly unsympathetic age, struggle with my half-formed conceptions; miserable in the consciousness of my incapacity. You who can not only imagine but give perfect form to your poetry, cannot fortunately realize such a struggle with phantoms.' On 5 February, he visited her at The Priory, the Regent's Park villa, where she lived boldly unmarried as 'Mrs Lewes' with the writer George Lewes. Five days later, the couple came to Little Holland House. Watts would have painted George Eliot for his national collection, but her features – large face and short-sighted look – would have dominated the expression of her visionary mind.[107]

Since his decision to give up portrait commissions, Watts had been 'besieged' by requests, which he deflected by pointing out that portraiture obstructed his plans for the nation. He expected his life to be cut short at any moment and wished to devote his remaining time and energy to 'works that will be worthy contributions to the National honour . . . to carry out the designs I have set my heart upon executing . . . I grudge every moment taken from them'. He reluctantly agreed to paint the home secretary,

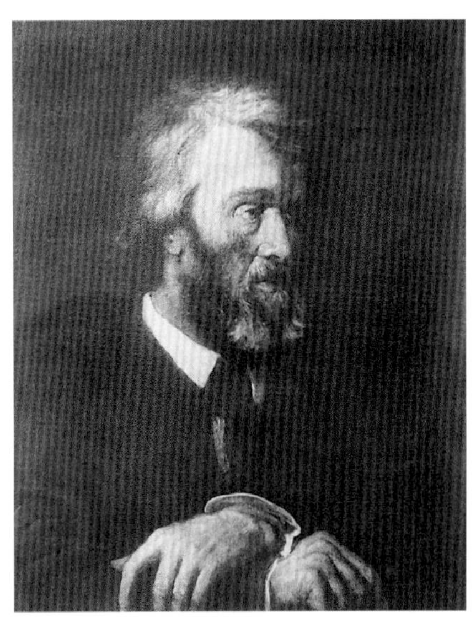

84    *Thomas Carlyle*, 1868–69 (Victoria and Albert Museum, London; photo: Frederic Hollyer).

Henry Bruce (who had bought the *Bove*), while urging him to commission Val instead: 'There is a manly strength & vigour in his pictures most uncommon in these modern times & I think him far the best colourist of the day.'[108]

In Manchester Rickards had acquired a roomful of paintings, every one framed by Green's because, wrote the Mancunian, 'brilliants are insulted unless set in the chastity of taste'. Rickards readily lent pictures to exhibitions to spread the message and would invite artists 'of the higher mental cast' to learn from them and, if they could afford it, become Watts's disciples.[109]

Having established the modern English Olympic school, Watts drew studies from the Elgin Marbles to lead Academy students towards a higher standard of art. He sent two small pictures to the Dudley Gallery, a sleeping nude *Ariadne* and a mirage-like *Island of Cos*, with nymphs swarming below the sea. While the *Illustrated London News* placed both in 'the foremost rank', the *Athenaeum*, writing of Watts as 'the figure-painter's idol of the year', dubbed *The Island of Cos* 'an aquarium', and *Ariadne*, a bold, bare-breasted contrast to Leighton's perfectly finished deathly version, 'slovenly'.[110] Watts began to transform other studies of Long Mary seated in Michelangelesque pose, one foot tucked under her thigh and her face hidden, into a nude painting, which he would later develop into his best-loved image, *Hope*.[111] Critics still talked of his 'wildness and eccentricity of manner'.[112] However, growing respect for the Academician, for his visionary sculptural works in paint and in the round, fuelled his patriotic aims and determination to create symbolic sculpture. While he would fight for decades to arouse public support for a monument to unsung heroes, *Clytie* established Watts as 'the great precursor of symbolist art in England'.[113]

## 9   'Calling off these Studios'

ON EASTER MONDAY 1870, three days after William Morris sat for his portrait, Watts wrote to Rickards of his 'strong desire' to found an art school along the lines of a medieval guild and to employ apprentices, whom he would not expect to work for the mere benefit of his instruction. To secure higher prices for his own pictures, he engaged Rossetti's colourful agent Charles Howell to act for him and asked even Rickards to negotiate through Howell: 'If I at all succeed, I shall always consider that you have helped me more than any one else by buying my pictures when very few cared to have them.'[1] From now on, he would train assistants to help with sculptural projects and allow art students to copy pictures in his painting studios.

Morris and Watts appeared to be poles apart. The burly craftsman spoke in a loud, direct manner and resented his prosperous upbringing, yet both protested against the dehumanizing effects of the machine age. They espoused the Ruskinian view that medieval-style workshops offered artists and craftsmen ideal conditions in which to work and create together. While achieving this ideal through his firm's production of wallpapers, furniture and stained glass, Morris was completing *The Earthly Paradise*, a Chaucerian epic that would become a Victorian cult volume. Tales narrated by medieval Norsemen and elders of a nameless city by a distant sea where Greek gods are worshipped, are imbued with a sense of lost love, reflecting Morris's distress at nineteenth-century moral lassitude.[2]

His private life was in turmoil. Rossetti was romancing his wife, Janey Morris, on canvas and around town; and as Burne-Jones was embroiled in an affair with the Greek sculptress Mary Zambaco, Morris turned to Burne-Jones's wounded wife. Georgie returned deep affection, but determined to remain steadfast to her distracted husband; and Morris, Rossetti and Burne-Jones, who depended upon each other professionally, kept up the semblance of friendship. They and their artist colleagues, Leighton and Millais, sat to Watts that year.

An invitation to be painted for the Hall of Fame was 'the ultimate accolade of Victorian society',[3] but Morris had a deep-seated fear of his own image and, like Rossetti, refused to face Cameron's lens. Now that he had become a public figure, and with the press clamouring for portraits, Morris accepted Watts's invitation. Nevertheless, he approached Little Holland House with a sense of distaste; and before setting out on 15 April wrote to Janey that he had 'a devil of a cold-in-the-head which don't make it very suitable'.[4] There is indeed a flush to the intense full-face portrait (pl. XXI). Morris gave just one sitting. Watts's ambitious response to that day indicates that he did engage his sitter. Warm concern in the craftsman's eyes follow the viewer; his highlighted forehead, leonine, freely painted red-tinged hair and beard, suggest his restless manner, and the silver-streaked background (perhaps added a decade later when Watts reworked the portrait) indicate his craft.

Burne-Jones, a closer friend, was invited to sit as a gift for Georgie. How much Watts knew of his affair with the flame-haired Medusa Mary Zambaco is uncertain. As Constantine Ionides's granddaughter, he had known since her birth and found her very beautiful. He had painted wedding portraits of her parents, Demetrius Cassavetti and the formidable 'Duchess' Euphrosyne Ionides; Mary had sat as a child, and again before her brief marriage to Dr Demetrius Zambaco. Her infant son, the model for the shepherd boy in *Ganymede*, caused havoc in his studio.[5] Burne-Jones pledged to spend the rest of his life with Mary, changed his mind, and the police found him rolling with her in Lord Holland's Lane (now Holland Walk), trying to stop her drinking poison.[6] The crisis had passed when Burne-Jones came to sit on 11 February. Mary was still modelling for him with large reproachful melting eyes, as Dante's Beatrice, Venus, the enchantress Vivien and the sorceress Circe. Her image as the nymph Phyllis clinging to the nude Demophoon, on show at the Old Watercolour Gallery that month, provoked such outrage – not least from Tom Taylor reviewing for *The Times* – that Burne-Jones resigned from the gallery and stopped exhibiting in public.[7] To make matters worse, Howell brought Mary to meet Georgie and was expelled from the circle. Watts wound down business with the scoundrel, preferring in future to keep a book listing pictures with their prices.[8]

At the Academy, the portrait of Burne-Jones was considered supreme (fig. 85). Watts always regarded it as one of his finest and was delighted that Georgie wanted to bequeath it to the National Gallery: 'I would rather be little among the Great than Great among the little.'[9] Peeling away the turmoil, passion and humour that characterized Burne-Jones's letters and conversation – and the wild eccentricity one reviewer anticipated[10] – it reveals the essence of the artist himself. His straight, fair hair strays over his forehead, gentle blue eyes look out from the pale face, above high cheekbones and sensitive mouth. Watts had struggled with his long beard, but it won the sitter's approval – 'What a blessed thing is painting,' wrote Burne-Jones, 'for I now have a red beard for ever'. The *Athenaeum* noted that the colour handling and drawing were 'fine enough to supply a school of portrait-painters with an admirable model', a splendid endorsement for Watts's scheme.[11]

He and Millais were responsible for hanging the 1870 exhibition. Their nudes faced each other. Millais's shockingly unclassical maiden staring into the eyes of the Knight Errant so disturbed Victorian viewers that though the Venetian flesh tones were admired, he felt compelled to produce a less flagrant head and upper torso. Even then the picture did not sell, whereas a curvaceous chained Ovidian nude with naturalistic pubic hair, *Andromeda*, exhibited by Edward Poynter was acclaimed as a sophisticated idealized subject. Poynter, the first Slade Professor at the dynamic Fine-Art School at University College, London, was about to introduce French studio

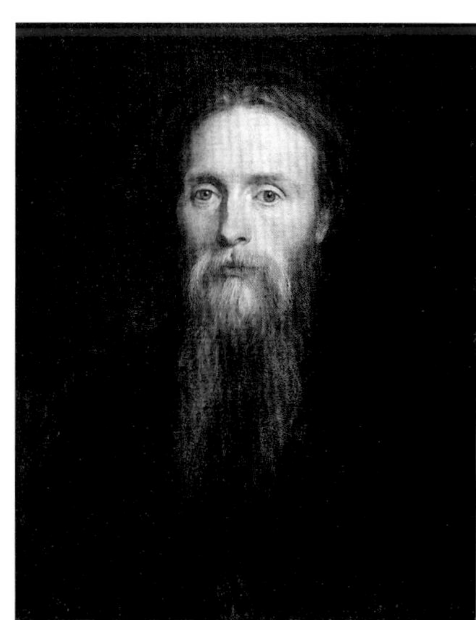

85   *Edward Coley Burne-Jones*, 1870 (Birmingham Museums and Art Gallery).

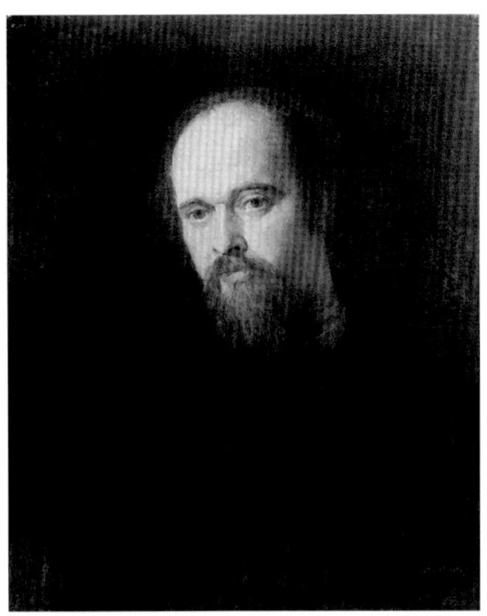

86   *Dante Gabriel Rossetti*, 1870–71 (National Portrait Gallery, London).

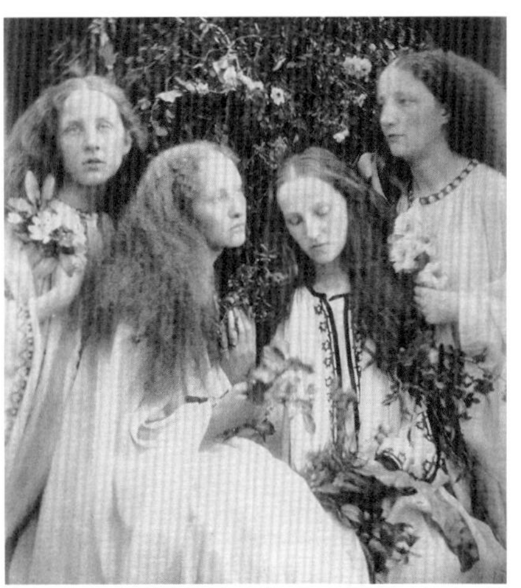

87   Julia Margaret Cameron, *The Rosebud Garden of Girls*, June 1868.

practice, with access to live models as Watts had recommended.[12] His own *Daphne* and *Fata Morgana, from Bojardo,* enlarged to six feet high, were hailed as 'caviare to the general . . . [surpassing] even Millais in their classic sweetness and perfection of female form'. Three women offered to purchase *Daphne*, but thanks to Howell's suspect activities, it remained unsold for two years.[13] Had illness and Academy commitments not delayed completion, Watts would have exhibited the grand aesthetic portrait of Madeline Wyndham. To Wilfrid Scawen Blunt, her warmth and large-limbed beauty was so suited to his imaginative works that she was for Watts what Jane Morris was for Rossetti, 'the inspirer of his noblest art, that of *The Earthly Paradise*'.[14]

Watts, who composed pictures as painted poems and lamented his literary incapacity, admired Rossetti's *Poems*, which he, like Morris, believed established the artist amongst England's greatest poets. The first sonnets of the *House of Life*, inspired by Janey, though composed as 'a complete *dramatis personae* of the soul', dealt with the mysteries of Life between Love and Death,[15] subjects Watts planned for his cosmic hall of frescoes. Shortly after the April publication, Rossetti sat for his portrait (fig. 86). A stocky figure, he generally wore a frock coat and was quite bald, though in his portrait the high-domed forehead does not detract from his dark pensive eyes and the sensuality of his full lips and untrimmed whiskers. Watts wished to represent him as a thinker, for, as Mary Watts would record in *George Frederic Watts: The Annals of an Artist's Life*, he admired Rossetti's poetry above his paintings.[16]

It was in the spring of 1870 that 20-year-old Mary paid her first visit to his studio. Her elder sisters had come to Little Holland House three years earlier, but she had been left behind at the family's highland castle. On holiday in the Isle of Wight, Ethel and Christina Fraser Tytler had posed for Julia Cameron, who insisted that her 'divine artist' must see them. Sara, enraptured by Christina's golden hair, begged the Signor to admire the 'aureole'. His gentle refusal set them at their ease: 'I am not going to pay compliments. Young ladies do not like it.' Mary Fraser Tytler had since assisted in Cameron's studio, posed with her sisters for a Tennysonian Pre-Raphaelite photograph *The Rosebud Garden of Girls* (fig. 87), and spent two years in Europe, chiefly studying art in Dresden and Rome. Their liberal-minded, spiritual father wrote treatises on the apocalypse and encouraged his daughters to develop individual skills: Christina wrote poetry and Mary painted and modelled clay. Charles Fraser Tytler had taken a house at 9 Queensgate Place, in South Kensington, near the National Art Training School where Mary now pursued her studies – a few minutes' walk from the home of the man she acknowledged at all modern exhibitions as 'the painter of painters for me'.

For the supreme step in her young career, she arrived at Little Holland House with Christina as chaperone, according to Victorian etiquette. The aesthetic pair, dressed in crinolines, their hair fashionably parted and swept back behind fine-boned aristocratic faces, presented a demure contrast to the theatrical Terry sisters eight years before. Waiting in an anteroom outside the studio, they were awed by a notice on the red-baize-covered door, 'I must beg not to be disturbed till after two o'clock.' Beside it the red-robed artist stood guard, facing them in his self-portrait *A Venetian Senator*.[17] The door swung back. 'Signor came forward to meet us . . . [His] beard was only slightly touched with grey, his hair quite brown, very fine in quality, and brushed back from the forehead . . . [he] so distinctly suggested to me the days of chivalry that I believe I should not have been surprised if, on another visit, I had found him all clad in shining armour.'[18]

As the artist guided her into his sun-filled sanctuary, the sensation must have been akin to his own some three decades earlier when he and Lord Holland first entered the Sistine Chapel. The cosmic *Titans* stood on a near easel. High overhead hung a cartoon for the mosaic decorations at St Paul's. There was the great *Angel of Death*, the first chalk drawing of *The People that have Walked in Darkness have Seen a Great Light*, portraits of the poet laureate and of the viceroy of India, and on a distant wall hung *The Return of the Dove*. Lord Elcho had lent his Giorgione, *A Shepherd Piping with Cattle*.[19] Greek casts, limbs and torsos were scattered round about. The studio was 'not merely a gallery, but a museum of ideas: thoughts struggle into utterance and art-problems await a solution', the critic J. Beavington Atkinson wrote in an essay at this time, placing Watts as a leader spearheading the advance of modern art.[20]

Hugh Lupus Grosvenor, the third Marquess of Westminster and one of the richest men in England, had commissioned Alfred Waterhouse to rebuild his vast Gothic palace, Eaton Hall in Cheshire. On 14 June, he invited Watts to create an equestrian statue of the Norman Earl of Chester, Hugh of Avranches, the first *Gros Veneur* – nicknamed 'Hugh Lupus' for his lupine ferocity in the Welsh wars. The statue, intended to impress Americans disembarking at Liverpool, would stand in front of the house, facing the Welsh hills. Lord Westminster was aware of Watts's interest, and when Landseer – the ailing sculptor of the Trafalgar Square lions – declined the commission he wrote to Watts. Honoured to be asked to design sculpture of national importance, Watts offered his services free, asking only that expenses be covered. The marquess provided assiduous research. Shocked to discover that Hugh Lupus had been a lecher 'much given to his belly', he proposed a worthier alternative, Saint Oswald. Watts would not hear of it. He stressed the old rogue's significance to the site.[21]

Preparing the small sketch model, he conceived a broader vision of a horse and rider, unconstrained by costume or date, to embody 'the human will bridling in brute force'. But Lord Westminster required a definitive historical portrait in armour. so Watts preserved sketches for the future symbolic statue – known variously as *Vital Energy*, *Active Force* and, ultimately, *Physical Energy* – that he would regard as his greatest work for the nation.[22]

In July he sought Lady Holland's permission to erect a sculpture shed. Having taken on heavy sculptural commitments, he asked for her reassurance that he would not be turned out when the Prinseps' lease expired on Christmas Day. Her ladyship apparently feigned shock at his request for a 'business' arrangement – a five-year lease extension at increased rent – reiterated her hollow promise, slithered away from legal obligation, and apparently let the shed to go up, on very shaky ground.[23]

Dissatisfied with the life-size statue of Lord Holland, which the flamboyant Boehm had modelled under his direction in Hammersmith, Watts remodelled the seated statesman, manipulating the plaster into deep folds to contrast the texture and effect of light on fabric and flesh.[24] By early October the statue was ready to be cast in bronze and erected above

Boehm's drinking fountain at the south end of Holland Park, near Kensington High Street. Seated today above a plinth at the end of the northern Rose walk, not unlike the late Marochetti's statue of the composer Rossini in Pesaro,[25] Lord Holland looks relaxed, yet alert, a genial expression on his face; his left hand rests on the arm of his chair and a walking-stick in his right hand is poised between his gaitered legs. The figure is animated by the treatment of texture and folds, which Watts was developing to an unusual degree in the effigy of Bishop Lonsdale. Here, he arranged the lawn sleeves and cope into so many folds, to attract light effects more variegated than those of the soft pink alabaster itself, that attention is drawn away from the bishop's face. This curious effigy lay on a verd-antique marble slab beneath by a twenty-foot high neo-Gothic polychrome canopy. Unusually, Watts did not aim to convey the inner character of the old Bishop, whose fatherly air once masked a shrewd, worldly nature.[26]

So intent was Watts on his portrait of Virginia Somers's eldest daughter Isabella, that he forced the wilting twenty-year-old to pose for so long in her white muslin dress, that her suitor left the room. If, as Isabella hoped, the Marquess of Lorne was waiting to ask for her hand, the chance was lost, for immediately afterwards the Queen summoned him to Balmoral to marry her daughter Princess Louise.[27]

The death of Lord Lothian at the age of thirty-eight[28] prompted Watts to exhibit at the Dudley Gallery a large oil study of the subject his friend's illness had inspired, *Love and Death*. Powerful yet tender, it was intended to embody the artist's 'vision of an idea', the passionate impotence of Love against inevitable Death, yet to divest Death of its terrors. A monumental figure draped in grey-white, with head bowed, is seen from behind as it presses open the door of a house that Love, a naked youth with broken wings, attempts to buttress. The title *Love and Death* relates to a poem by Tennyson. Except for the wings – a Wattsian leitmotif symbolizing Innocence – the imagery is extraordinarily similar to *Le Jeune Homme et la Mort* painted by Gustave Moreau after the premature death of Théodore Chasseriau and exhibited at the 1865 Paris Salon. In Moreau's picture, a young man stands in front of a doorway protected by a female nude figure of Death, with a winged cherub and scattered roses at their feet.[29] Watts's imagery, however, is unrelenting, very much his own: 'Love is not restraining Death, for it cannot do so; I wish to suggest the passionate though unavailing struggle to avert the inevitable,' he explained. He would paint a dozen versions of *Love and Death* (pl. XVII), one of his most compelling sym-bolist subjects.[30]

At the Prinseps' Brighton home in November, hard at work on Rickards's *Angel of Death*, he brooded over the poor market for his imaginative subjects and the gloomy state of the nation: 'I don't see any thing in life either of Individuals or of Nation that can compensate for the difficulties disappointments & vexation to say nothing of appalling evils. It almost seems to me it would be better if some ancestral conflagration were to clear the globe of us at once.'[31] Indeed there was an inferno.

At midday on 10 January 1871, fire broke out at Holland House. Lady Holland's sitting room was engulfed in smoke, and flames were raging up through the ceiling. Watts rushed over to the mansion, climbed on to the roof and helped remove tiles, so that buckets of water could be poured on to the blaze, keeping it in check until the fire-engines arrived. With

Leighton, Val and the house carpenter, he removed furniture, ceramics and artworks.[32] Five of his early pictures were damaged, one of a group of spaniels was destroyed and his portrait of Lord Holland was burnt beyond repair. He wrote to Lady Holland on her return from Naples and had already offered to replace it, working from a miniature,[33] when he received her distraught plea: 'Try oh try to do something. Call picture cleaners, picture restorers, incur any expense. I would starve to regain that portrait. Dear dear friend I appeal to your old affections . . . What other hand can do what you could do? I beseech you, I implore you.'[34]

Watts restored all her portraits. At the same time, Rickards had commissioned a marble version of *Medusa*, the serpent-haired Gorgon who turned beholders to stone, the obverse of his *Wife of Pygmalion* and an Italianate variant of the severed head he had modelled in clay in Italy. Rossetti's drawing of 1865, *Aspecta Medusa*, had shown her head reflected in water,[35] and Morris treated the subject in 'The Doom of King Acrisius' in *The Earthly Paradise*. Severe rheumatism prevented Watts working on the head that spring, but in the summer he was delighted by the bloom of the marble; and so taken was he by the colour and texture of the Lichfield memorial (fig. 88) that he considered sculpting *Clytie* in alabaster. Instead he would recreate its quality by staining the marble *Medusa* and carving a further head in alabaster (fig. 89).[36]

He had lent studio space to the painter George Mason, for whom Leighton had arranged commissions, offering cheery advice to lift him out of poverty on his arrival from Rome. An associate of the Academy, Mason painted pastoral landscapes celebrating the effects of sunset, moonlight and mist. His final masterpiece *Harvest Moon*, a party of reapers following their haycart home in the warm afterglow of twilight, was painted at Little Holland House. The pose of the minstrel plucking his fiddle is not unlike Watts's in *The Whisper of the Muse*, and his instrument was on hand to serve as a model.[37]

London landscapes and the effects of fog, mist and snow fascinated two Frenchman who had recently arrived in London, disheartened and penniless, as refugees from the Franco-Prussian War.[38] Twenty-nine-year-old Claude Monet and his elder compatriot Camille Pissarro painted in the open air, their style revolutionizing as they recognized shared ideals of *plein air* and the treatment of light in the landscapes of Turner and Constable. Pissarro noted, 'Watts, Rossetti, strongly interested us amongst the modern men'.[39] Monet and Pissarro exhibited in Durand-Ruel's *Society of French Artists* at the German Gallery in March and at the London International Exhibition in buildings annexed to the Albert Hall. Here they will have seen Watts's *Carlyle*, other national portraits, and a sketch for *After the Transgression*, which the *Art Journal*, generally a stern critic of his work, highlighted as 'the most daring presentiment in the exhibition;[40] Watts, too, may have noted Monet's Whistleresque *Meditation, Madame Monet au canapé*.[41]

Monet, lodging in Kensington High Street, may have been taken to Little Holland House, but Watts was very unwell that spring and tendered his resignation to the Academy – the Council persuaded him to withdraw it.[42] To Watts, the beauty of 'line' was paramount, and though he would find the Impressionists' later style distressing he was now developing variegated, impressionistic effects of light and colour in sculpture and may have been

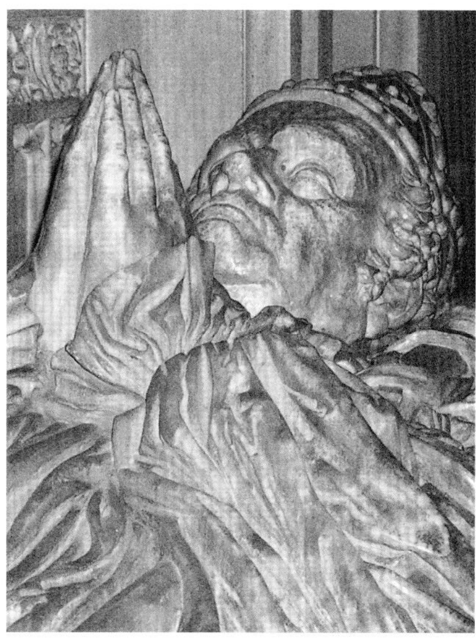

88   Memorial to Dr John Lonsdale, Bishop of Lichfield (detail), 1869–71 (Lichfield cathedral).

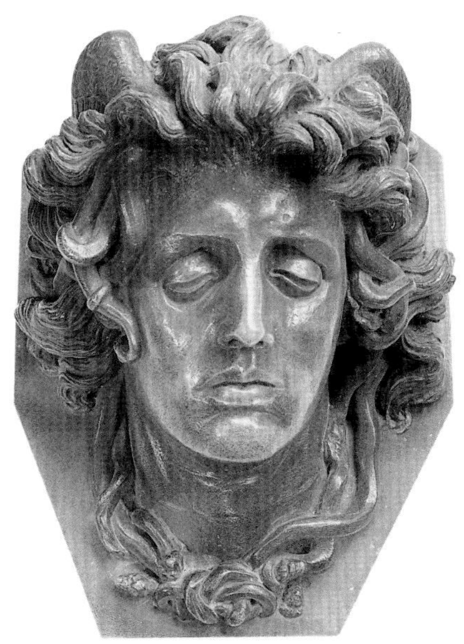

89   *Medusa*, 1871–73 (Watts Gallery).

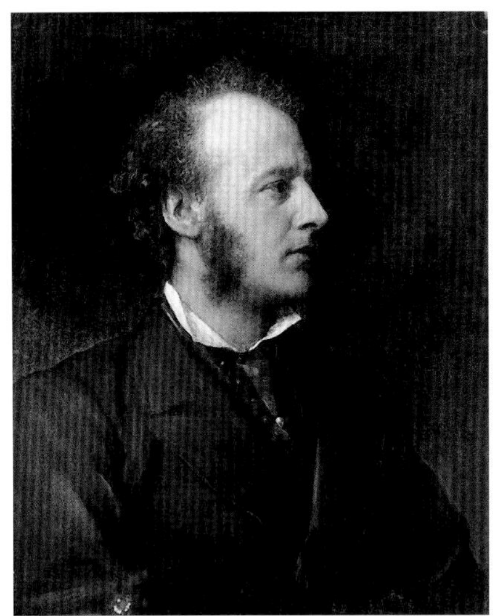

90   *John Everett Millais*, RA, 1870
(National Portrait Gallery, London).

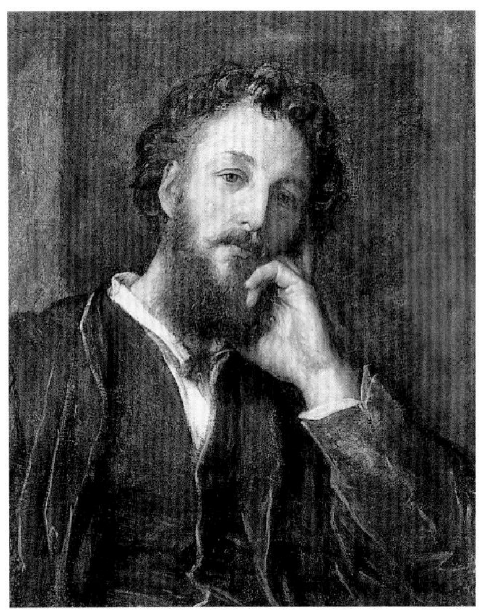

91   *Frederic Leighton*, RA, 1870
(private collection, courtesy of Nevill
Keating Pictures Ltd).

interested in their experiments. After the massacre of the Communards in June, Monet and Pissarro returned to France, as crusaders for a new movement, '*plein-air*' painting, and struggled to sell their Impressionist paintings for two to four pounds, or a triumphant eight pounds.[43]

A picture of *Venus and Cupid* was lent on Watts's behalf to the Royal Glasgow Institute of Art exhibition.[44] Prevented by illness from completing the large naked *Eve* biting the apple in Paradise – subsequently known as *Eve Tempted* – and of the Spenserian subject *Britomart and her Nurse*,[45] he sent portraits to the Academy: a waist-length profile of his self-possessed colleague J. E. Millais (fig. 90) and of the chestnut-haired Lady Isabella Somers Cocks clearly mourning the loss of Lorne (the following year she would marry Lord Henry Somerset, younger son of the Duke of Beaufort),[46] and an informal portrait of Leighton (fig. 91), painted as a gift. Now secretary of the Royal Academy, Leighton is portrayed looking at the viewer (his good friend Watts), inclining his head a little, the chin resting on his left hand, two fingers curled over his soft brown beard; the relaxed pose and natural crumpled folds of his jacket and waistcoat indicate affection between artist and sitter. While the *Athenaeum*'s review praised the 'masterly' modelling and 'triumphant' form and colour, observing that to sit to Watts was 'as was said of Tintoret, to secure immortality', the *Art-Journal* decried the *Leighton* as incomplete: 'As soon as [Watts's] idea dawns upon canvas, even dimly, he throws down his brush.'[47]

Had the reviewer been referring to an experimental subject picture, that might have been fair comment, because of the artist's desire to try out his ideas in the form of a preparatory sketch, which he painted in transparent colours over a white ground, finishing with a single, unalterable application of opaque colour.[48] In his view, repainting, which covered the tone, destroyed its brilliance and purity. His own elastic technique was transparent until the final application of colour.[49] Philip Calderon, a former Pre-Raphaelite, now a member of the St John's Wood Clique, sat to Watts and followed his advice that spring. Painting over an absorbent ground of thin whiting and size, he laid in the picture thickly with white, and a little terra verte and Venetian red. 'I am unusually pleased with it,' Calderon enthused. 'It is so luminous and bright, so dead in surface that I feel for the first time in my life I am on the way to a good thing. No more oily surface, but a bright fresco like appearance.'[50]

Watts was one of the first to answer Ruskin's call in *Fors Clavigera* 'Letters to the Workmen and Labourers of Great Britain', reprinted in *The Times* on 8 May, for contributors to a utopian society, which he planned to set up in opposition to 'iron devils'. Dedicated to natural cultivation and craftsmanship, the society would become the Guild of St George. Though sceptical of its practical success – his own drawing guild had not materialized – Watts heartily endorsed 'protest against Mammon worship' and promised Ruskin, now the Slade Professor at Oxford, a tenth of his annual earnings. He painted a poor picture of his income, only fifty pounds per year 'after satisfying just claims' should illness prevent him working,[51] and complained that people who had believed in his aims and could have underwritten his own schemes, had let him down and as a result he had been unable to fulfil his aspirations. Ruskin, grateful for his support, replied that he would proceed no further until the following year.[52]

Through Lady Airlie, Watts had offered to paint Benjamin Disraeli for the national collection. On 5 July, now in opposition between stints as Conservative prime minister, he brought his wife to the studio. He agreed to the portrait, but, unlike Gladstone, disdained having to rearrange sittings due to the painter's ill health, and refused his subsequent requests to sit for the nation.[53] Among the few secret portrait commissions Watts had been persuaded to accept were Lady Margaret Beaumont's brother-in-law, the Reverend Stopford Brooke, and Countess Spencer, the wife of the lord lieutenant of Ireland.[54]

That month, Watts was shocked to hear that Lady Holland was considering an offer for the site where he had built sculpture studios. 'You annihilate me by turning me out . . . Calling off these studios is like amputating a leg or arm,' he chastised the widow of his generous patron and friend. She had known for decades that his sole desire was to prove himself 'a true artist', that he had laboured to enrich not only the nation, but humanity – 'aspirations perhaps in me ridiculous certainly not ignoble' – and resisted popular trend and money-making, adding ignobly in parenthesis: 'to the increase of my difficulties in the present juncture'. As Lord Holland might have commented, how shabby! His father had induced this genuine fear of debt, but his own bank balance covered expenditure; he could support struggling artists and was an active investor, with rising income from shares and sculpture.[55] Certainly, living at Little Holland House – where he was relieved of the burden of running a home and his medical needs were supervised – enabled him to pursue artistic aims. He had amassed a huge amount of work and was committed to substantial sculptural projects, including a memorial to Lord Lothian, though there was no urgency for this while Blickling church was under restoration. A move would be a major undertaking and he was right to be suspicious of Lady Holland's renewed promise. Nothing was settled.

Facing an uncertain future, he pressed on with *The Angel of Death* and *The Rider on the Black Horse* in which the rider holds the scales of Justice. Watts also took on a rôle that would have delighted his father: serving on a committee for a musical instrument exhibition at the new Albert Hall.[56] *The Angel of Death*, presented as a finished design for a large picture, was his only contribution to the 1871 Dudley Gallery Winter Exhibition, because he wished to test public opinion of this supremely important subject. Veiled in shadow with attendant figures embodying Silence and Mystery, the angel presides over the court of Death. Madonna-like, she sits enthroned, nursing in her lap an infant, the beginning of Life, and receives homage from humanity, rich and poor, old and young, powerful and weak. Sickness (a study from May Prinsep) rests at her knee; an elderly earl surrenders his coronet, and a soldier lays down his sword. At the soldier's feet a crouching lion symbolizes Physical Power; and beside him a cripple begs on bended knee, and a child peers out from the grave clothes. Below them all lies the open book of Life.

The grave, grand picture hung in the place of honour at the Dudley. *The Times* linked Watts's vision to a William Blake illustration to *The Grave* by Robert Blair – presumably *The Day of Judgment*, itself inspired by the Sistine Chapel: 'Like Blake, Mr Watts has conceived the grave as "Heaven's Golden Gate" . . . The face and form of the dark-winged Angel, veiled in a shadow which is rather tender than terrible, are relieved against the golden splendour that floods the space beyond those awful portals which it is hers to open.' Neither frigid nor fantastic, with none of the terror of the Pisa frescoes *Triumph of Death* and *Last Judgment* that had excited Watts in 1844, his allegory touched the heart and kindled imagination.[57] He would have seen the 1858 reprint of *The Grave*, and there is a sense of Michelangelo in *The Angel of Death*. But Watts later wrote that, although his prophets and sibyls were not more impressive because of anatomical accuracy, this additional quality made them greater than they would have been had the anatomy been 'as in the case of Blake, defective'.[58] He would continue to work on the Dudley canvas.[59] Meanwhile, the young art student Matthew Ridley Corbett laid in the large *Angel of Death* (pl. IX) in terra verte and white.[60]

Watts learned of the Prinseps' fragile new agreement to renew their tenancy of Little Holland House each year, with a possible six months' notice to quit: 'The uncertainty of the tenure will fidget me out of the power of working.' Shamelessly, he asked Rickards to fund a new home for twenty years, taking all his pictures in exchange, so that he could complete his projects, otherwise he must hope that an artist with similar aspirations would carry out what fortune denied him: 'Now that I feel the *power* strong within me of contributing something towards the national greatness, it is very distressing to be prevented by so mean a consideration as mere money.'[61] Rickards offered kind advice, but was unable to provide financial support.

Lady Holland had been offered forty thousand pounds for the Little Holland House site, in order to build a new road that cut through the house.[62] Realizing that his future there had 'practically ceased to exist', Watts wrote to her on 3 December to withdraw his objections, hoping thereby to end hostilities, for 'it would grieve me very much to feel any coolness between so old a friend and myself'. He resolved to paint portraits to raise funds for a new studio home, but he was more troubled about lost time than expense: 'I must hope to live long enough to make that up.'[63]

He had heard that Disraeli was sitting to a more questionable brush, but the statesmen vehemently denied the rumour: 'Since busybodies have been taking liberties with both our names, I have not, & never had the slightest intention of sitting to the individual you mention.' Furthermore, 'I should be proud & justly proud, of sitting to the greatest master of our school, and whose genius I have ever admired,' but the portrait was never painted. To the statesman's frustration, Watts could find no tranquil hour for him,[64] initially, because he had embarked on his Academy diploma picture, '*My Punishment is Greater than I Can Bear*' (fig. 92), a House of Life subject. In less than four months he would have to transform a monochrome sketch of spirit figures swooping down to denounce Cain for the murder of his brother Abel, into a thirteen-foot-high canvas.[65] Concerned that it would delay Rickards's commissions, Watts offered his patron the five hundred pounds he was to receive for the bishop's effigy. 'My mind is set upon a very large work (from which of course I must expect nothing). I cannot give up my ambition to challenge the old masters, very absurd no doubt, but I can't help it . . . your pictures will become more valuable in consequence so I consider myself in this working for you.'[66]

With this ambition in mind he reminded Lady Ashburton of her interest in his large *Love and Death*, pointing out that it was one of the half dozen

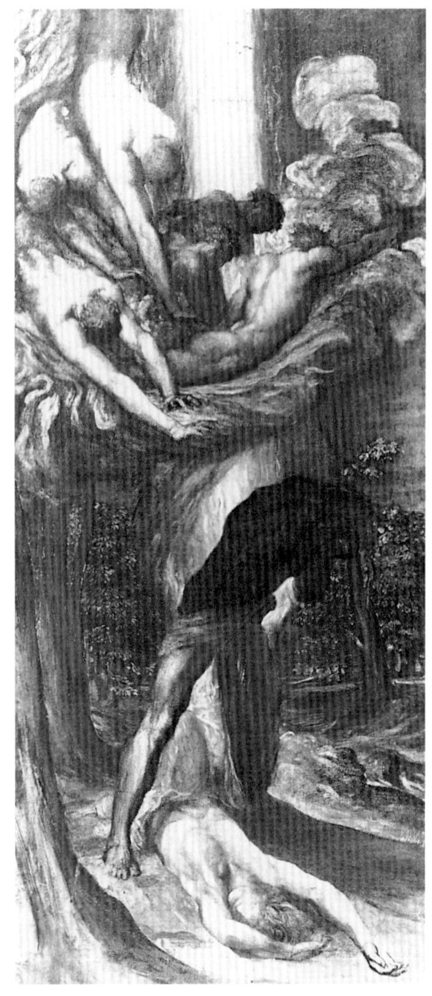

92    *The Denunciation of Cain* or '*My Punishment is Greater than I Can Bear*', 1871–72 (Watts Gallery).

designs he planned to work up to establish himself as a future old master: 'Unless I quite fail it ought to be of importance & value as it represents much labour & time & experience.' The price was fifteen hundred guineas. Lady Ashburton bought a smaller version and, as a pendant, a small *Time, Death and Judgment*, prepared by Watts's German assistant, Conrad Mansfield.[67] She had borrowed *Titans*, which the artist wished to enlarge in fresco at her home, Kent House, in Knightsbridge. The thought of Watts painting this important work in her home thrilled her, and for the artist, hoping to carry it out on the scale of the Sistine Chapel or the Stanzein the Vatican Palace, it was 'an opportunity of writing my name legibly in Time's book'. But Kent House had to be rebuilt first; and by the time works were complete, he was preoccupied with his own commissions and building works.[68]

'Come to Freshwater and live near me at Farringford!' Tennyson offered the artist a splendid solution. Watts would build a house that he could share with the Prinseps: at last he would be able to return their hospitality. Eighty-year-old Thoby was almost blind, and Sara's health was deteriorating. The Isle of Wight, with its mild climate, fresh sea breezes and dynamic friends, would suit them well. Watts bought a plot of land to the west of Farringford. In view of his respect for architecture, he would have conceived the new home as a work of art. He chose as architect Philip Webb, who had created studio mansions for Val, Stanhope and recently for the Howards at Palace Green. Each was a Ruskinian work of art designed to offset individual lifestyle and artistic needs and to reflect its location. Webb would envisage a house on site even before embarking on its design.[69] His 'sound and workmanlike' buildings were noted for their craftsmanship. On 27 February 1872 Webb accepted the brief for a three-storey studio house (fig. 93).[70]

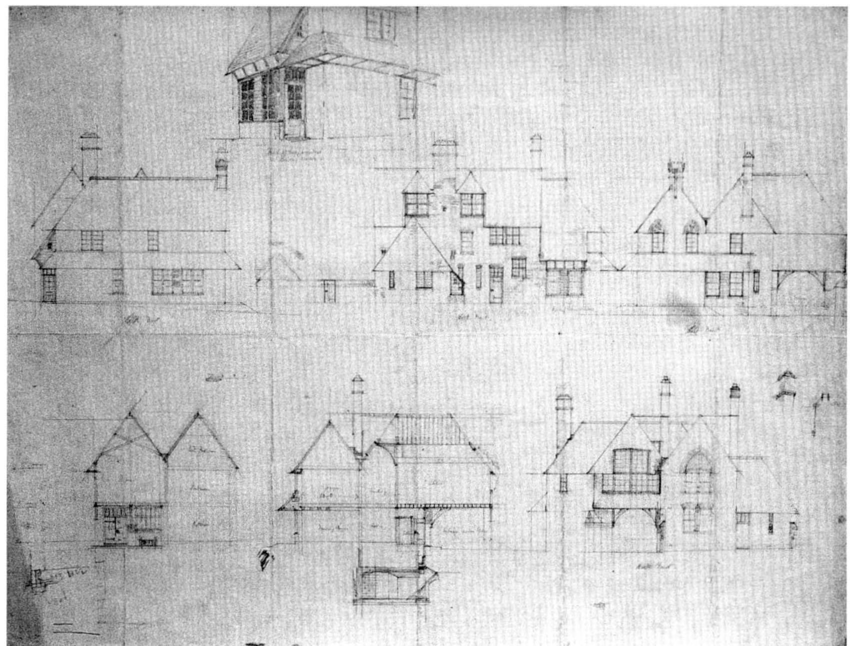

93   Philip Webb's designs for The Briary, 1872, with the studio on the first floor (private collection).

Julia Cameron, who had linked her terrace cottages with a castellated tower to form a more imposing building, later named 'Dimbola Lodge' after a Cameron estate in Ceylon,[71] gave another batch of photographs to Watts. Commenting on clarity, focus and especially tone, he advised the medal-winning photographer to acquire old master prints to improve composition. He was embarrassed by her generosity and just retained images of the Prinseps' young granddaughters, Laura Gurney as *Angel of the Nativity* and Rachel as *Cupid Considering*, seated naked with wings attached and one leg crossed over the other. Despite the child's blurred head and her feet merge into one another, which Cameron might remedy with shadow, he thought *Cupid Considering* extremely beautiful and suggestive of colour.[72]

Fundraising was going well. Rickards's Manchester associate Samuel Barlow bought *Una and the Red Cross Knight*; and the large *Daphne*, chosen with *Endymion* for the London International Exhibition in April was purchased by Louis Huth for eight hundred guineas. With others under offer, Watts enthused to Rickards, 'I run the risk of becoming a Millionaire!'[73] He signed George Lewes's pledge to send financial support to George du Maurier should blindness halt his career.[74] That summer Huth's wife, exhausted by innumerable sittings to Whistler, standing for three hours in a long black velvet dress, complained that Mr Watts did not subject her to such treatment. 'And still,' replied the American, amused, 'you come to me!'[75]

Gertrude Jekyll, again copying pictures at Little Holland House, modelled to Watts 'for arms', presumably for the diploma picture for which he prepared figure studies and modelled each section in gesso before painting. Leighton checked developments every morning.[76] Happy to entertain at lunchtime, Watts had now given up even the Academy dinner and declined Blanche Airlie's invitation with humorous regret, 'Many thousand thanks for your invitation & wish that I should come, but what should I do in the "Halls of dazzling light"?'[77]

Criticism of his portraits at the Academy was discouraging.[78] That his portraits lacked the physical force of Millais was less worrying than their assertion that he lacked the intellectual vigour of Whistler: this would have wounded him. He was facing comparison with *Arrangement in Grey and Black No.1*, the famous portrait of Whistler's mother, which he himself respected and William Richmond likened to Velasquez, 'but "without his bones" as Watts used to say.' Highly praised and admired by Watts were Leighton's *Summer Moon*, two loosely draped women asleep in the glistening moonlight, the poetic landscape painter Fred Walker's *The Old Almshouses*, which he advised Rickards to buy, and Mason's *The Harvest Moon*, bought by Eustace Smith, who sat for his portrait that year.[79]

'*My Punishment is Greater Than I Can Bear*' received mixed reviews. Watts thought it jarred with other pictures – but then to him crowded Academy exhibitions, where even Leighton's pictures suffered, were a false test. The spirit figures, voices of conscience swooping down to denounce Cain for the murder of his brother Abel seemed less effective. Adjustments he wished to make after the exhibition closed proved to be unnecessary, for on its own the picture was effective. Watts changed nothing, but the title, to *The Denunciation of Cain*. Realizing that the fratricidal incident could be developed as an epic or cantata – his notes are strikingly Wagnerian – he would later paint a sequel about *The Death of Cain* (fig. 144).[80]

Building work began at Freshwater in the summer of 1872. The new house, provisionally named Myddleton Priory after the region, was to be constructed of island brick with white-painted weather-boarding on gables and dormers to reflect the local vernacular. It was not without qualms that Webb, who liked to use local builders, engaged Stanhope's London builder, John Tyerman.[81] At Little Holland House, taking three sitters a day, Watts worked at such a pace that his eyes again became inflamed, forcing him to postpone the finishing touches to his portrait of the photographer's daughter, Julia Norman.[82] Her cousin, Sara's widowed niece Mary Clogstoun had died, and her orphaned daughters, dressed in deep mourning, were brought to the house.

In a moment of spontaneous joy, a sad little ray of sunlight pierced Watts's fatherly workaholic heart. Adeline, Blanche and Mary Clogstoun – so the story goes – were standing by the drawing-room door; Sara was wondering privately which one she would adopt, and Signor was sitting by the fire when suddenly, nine-year-old Blanche, her long blonde hair flying, ran across the room. She leaped on to his knee and threw her arms around his neck. The artist enfolded her in his and decided to adopt her himself. Sara would look after her day-to-day upbringing, but he would always look upon her as his special charge. 'I have undertaken the charge of a little orphan girl,' Watts informed Rickards on 21 September, 'so I must endeavour to do what I have not hitherto thought of doing, viz establishing a little capital.' His studios, without rules or regulations, in Kensington and in due course on the Isle of Wight would become the children's haven. Sadly, at Freshwater on 8 June, Julia Cameron, who adopted Blanche's sisters, photographed 'the lovely remains of my little Adeline', aged ten, on her deathbed. [83]

That month the statue of Lord Holland was erected in Holland Park and would be formally unveiled in October.[84] Like Leighton, Watts was shocked by the death of George Mason on the 22nd, regretting both the loss of his friendship and the poetic legacy to English Art. He advised Rickards to attend the sale Leighton was arranging to raise income for Mason's family. So many of his Manchester colleagues were sitting for their portraits that 'I must either shut up my engagement book altogether, or put . . . a prohibitive price'.[85] At the Dudley, he showed two poetic works, an unfinished sketch *Watching for the Return of Theseus* and a full-length chiaroscuro treatment of *Orpheus and Eurydice* (fig. 94), quite different from the version for which Madeline Wyndham had modelled.[86]

In November, he joined the Prinseps in Brighton, where by chance he ran into Nelly. He did not ask where she was living (with Godwin at Fallows Green, the cottage he designed in Harpenden, Hertfordshire), nor did he know that his estranged wife had two children – three-year-old Edith, and Teddy, ten months – for she had disguised her identity on their birth certificates by registering her maiden name as Watkins and giving their father's surname. Godwin – now on the council of the Royal Institute of British Architects and highly respected in the Aesthetic Movement – neglected her. Watts had not ceased to pay maintenance. Lost for words, all he could say to Nelly was how she had grown. They never met again.[87] At Brighton, he received a nasty kick on the shin while hunting to harriers and was confined to bed, with his leg raised, for a fortnight.[88] The bed curtain gave him an idea for a poetic nude ensemble, which he would paint on his return to

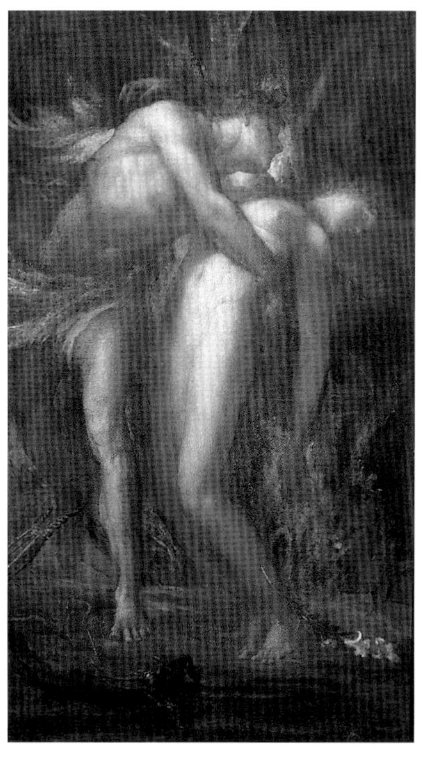

94 *Orpheus and Eurydice*, *c.*1868–72 (Watts Gallery).

town in December. Taking Long Mary studies as reference and Madeline Wyndham as model, he began *The Three Goddesses*, Pallas Athene, Juno and Venus, which would ultimately be renamed *The Judgment of Paris* and purchased by Louis Huth for eight hundred guineas.[89]

Tennyson was keeping an eye on developments at Freshwater: 'Your house here promises to be a very handsome one.' He sent Watts his latest idyll, *Gareth and Lynette*, and asked him to paint the Unitarian divine Dr James Martineau – 'a good & great metaphysician – certainly one of the note-worthy men of our time, & one of my friends, & with a head & face which . . . you alone can render justly' – for the national collection. Watts agreed. He looked forward to doing 'grave work' in Freshwater.[90]

In January 1873, the twenty-nine-year-old Sir Charles Wentworth Dilke, the Liberal MP for Chelsea and proprietor of the *Athenaeum*, and his wife Katharine sat for their portraits. Highly controversial for his republicanism, Sir Charles was secretary of the Radical Club and a disciple of the philosopher John Stuart Mill. He had helped to restore the right to vote for women ratepayers and remained an activist for female suffrage and the trades unions. Hatred of the Second Empire had led him to join the Prussian army – as an ambulance aide – on the battlefields of the Franco-Prussian war. Yet he sympathized with the French and was in Paris to witness the fall of the Empire and the oratory of the Republican dictator Leon Gambetta, whose friendship he had since courted.[91] Sir Charles's pivotal involvement in the French conflict and the birth of its Third Republic – Thiers was now president – would have fascinated Watts and must have been discussed in the studio, for the death of Napoleon III at Chislehurst in Kent on 9 January was announced as the portrait began. Dilke was asked to bring photographs 'to make me acquainted with peculiarities & shorten the sittings necessary!'[92]

Watts's use of photographs to highlight 'peculiarities' would have interested Ruskin, who wrote on 1 February. 'Your portraits are so good in points of character – though I think you always err somewhat on the resolvedly grand side – instead of giving people their little weaknesses (for which we none of us now – nor anybody in the future, should like them a whit the less) – that I wonder you cannot enjoy yourself and feel truly and rightly employed – in making such records of the existing soul-world.'[93] While the *Globe*, as it were, defended the artist, declaring that 'this gift of imagination' that drove Watts to paint the best portraits of' the age derived from the fact that 'Art to him has been a mistress, not a slave',[94] Watts attacked Ruskin's narrow vision. The critic affected not to care, but he was stung by the accusation, and wrote a tragic letter in defence, maintaining a strangely jealous respect for his flawed friends Watts and Burne-Jones, who, 'with all his power, paints still as weakly as a woman – is essentially a woman – because he paints what he *likes* in defiance of what *is*.'

> You were yourself paralysed for years by your love of the Greek style – you never made an entirely honest, complete, unaffected study of anything . . . You fancy you see more than I do in nature – you still see less – for – I, long ago, learned how impossible it was to draw what I saw – you still struggle to do so, that is to say, to draw what you like in what you see without caring about what others like – or what God likes . . . I retract nothing of what I said of my discontent with myself – nor do I

equal myself for an instant with Jones or you in personal power of thought or deed – I merely speak as a poor apothecary's boy . . . to two learned and thoughtful physicians, who had been all their lives seeking the philosopher's stone.[95]

The cosmic *Titans*, which Watts planned to keep it for life and had willed to Virginia Somers, was now bought by Richard Johnson, a colleague of Rickards. So determined was Johnson that the artist accepted his offer of one thousand guineas: 'It is my very best & greatest design, but I will sell it for this price reserving the copy right & upon the understanding that I shall be at liberty to make any replica & on any scale I please.'[96]

Watts was elected a member of the Athenaeum Club. He had been proposed by Leighton, seconded by Richard Doyle, and appointed that spring under the fast-track rule for eminent members.[97] Dilke, delighted with his portrait,[98] commissioned Watts to paint John Stuart Mill. The MP for Westminster, whose controversial speeches stirred audiences at St James's Hall, had hitherto disliked the thought of being painted, 'but I am unwilling to refuse the high compliment paid me by Mr Watts and yourself, he replied to Dilke'. When the reformer came to Little Holland House on 17 March 1873, he was fascinated by the painter's poetic ideas. The two men struck up a rapport. 'Strange it was,' Watts told William Richmond, 'but of all my pictures Mill invariably picked out the most abstract and dwelt upon these, not only with curiosity, but with evident enjoyment.' He was surprised that these intellectual subjects attracted more interest among Manchester businessmen than they did among aristocrats, whose education, wealth and leisure constricted, as Watts put it, 'the natural fosterers of the noblest aspirations in Art'.[99] The artist endorsed Mill's belief that social reform required a change of national character. Jeanie Senior's appointment as the first female poor law inspector to report on workhouse girls marked a significant advance towards breaking down barriers to women in the civil service.[100] Millicent Fawcett, the women's suffrage campaigner, saw that the portrait (fig. 95) encapsulated Mill's refined, delicate look. To Richmond, it was a masterpiece: 'Sensitive is the man he presents, an incomplete creature, sadly speculating on – even yearning for – an outlook other than the one forged by his education. All that is in Watts's portrait I found in Mill.'[101] Rapidly painted before the reformer left for France, the painting was delivered to Dilke on 8 May, the day Mills died.[102]

Shortlisted with Thomas Thornycroft and James Forsyth to create an equestrian memorial to the Earl of Mayo, the assassinated Viceroy of India, Watts was asked by the countess, Percy Wyndham's sister to take it on. Watts relinquished the commission to Thornycroft and his son Hamo.[103] So busy was he that he exhibited only portraits at the Academy in 1873.[104]

On Newton's behalf, following an appeal by Leighton, Watts sent a testimonial urging the prime minister to acquire the Castellani collection of Greek and Etruscan sculpture for the British Museum. Writing to Gladstone on 4 May, he highlighted the bronze head, which corresponded with the best Greek coins, and was of great value in retaining a nose, which rarely survived in marble sculpture. 'This is the first time I have seen that feature on any life size Greek head.[105] Whether or not the Homeric scholar needed persuasion, Watts's letter proved effective.[106]

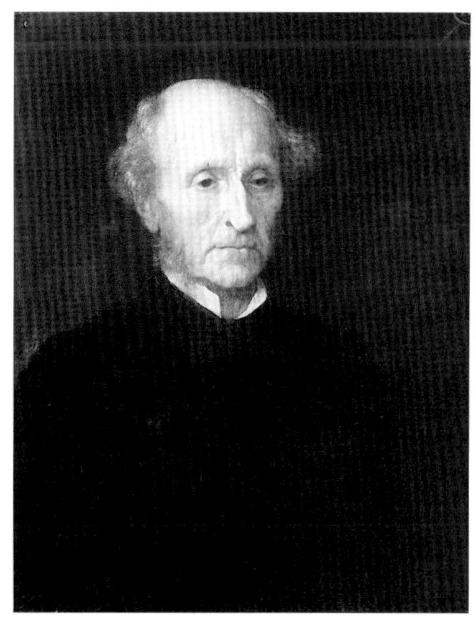

95  *John Stuart Mill*, 1873 (National Portrait Gallery, London).

In June, exhausted by overwork, Watts accepted an invitation to stay at Reigate Priory with the Somers. Virginia's face appears as Francesca in what is his finest version of *Paolo and Francesca* at this time (pl. XV). He brooded with increasing impatience over valuable time lost to portraiture, until he heard from Rickards that Johnson wished to buy, unseen, *She Shall be Called Woman* (pl. XIX).[107] As one of the three tall nudes that formed the Eve trilogy – painted to be seen together and, planned for the cosmic series, to inspire the public at large – it was not for sale. Seven feet high, the nude picture was more suited to a gallery than to a private home. 'One could not expect a household that has not been brought up in familiarity with this kind of work to escape being shocked,' Watts replied to Rickards.

He intended his single figures of Eve – *She shall be Called Woman, Eve Tempted* and *Eve Repentant* – and three compositions – *The Creation of Eve, After the transgression* (later called *The Denunciation of Adam and Eve*) and *The Denunciation of Cain* – to form part of an epic illustrating the story in Genesis and destined to be public property. 'If I could afford to do so I would paint them & present them to Manchester.' If not, Watts planned to bequeath them after his death to form part of a whole with the large *Angel of Death, Time and Death* and others. He nursed great hope in Rickards's Manchester colleagues, 'all caring for Art in the highest sense', but he was otherwise so discouraged that he doubted he would ever carry out the scheme. The artist's widow would attribute to this moment his bewildered private note at the thought of abandoning his Michelangelesque goal, the hall of cosmic frescoes, The House of Life: 'I feel as some athletic man who, awaking from a fever, finds himself reduced to half the strength of infancy; as Samson might have felt, when shaking off his lethargy, and shorn of his locks feels the wonderment of strangeness, the despair of weakness.' That *The Angel of Death* had been selected for the Vienna Universal Exhibition was hardly a sign of weakness. Watts, as ever, bounced back.[108]

Should he part with *She Shall Be Called Woman*, the price must exceed a thousand guineas.[109] He tested the unfinished canvas for pictorial effect at the Dudley winter exhibition. To the *Art-Journal*, Watts had 'never planned a nobler picture than this of our first parent'.[110] The central figure of the universe, the newly created Eve – her body vertical, her head thrown back and face drawn up towards Heaven – is seen emitting light. Golden tints fleck her neck and bosom. She represents the Greek vision of 'A line of light, straight, as a column extending through the whole heaven and through the earth in colour resembling the rainbow, only brighter and purer'.[111] In contrast, her upturned face is dark, 'for the human intuitions may take the human mind into a region where reason stops,' as Watts explained, quoting Milton's *Paradise Lost*, 'dark with excessive bright'.[112]

A payment of 260 pounds in July to Nelson – presumably for studio rental – indicates that, as he had not yet started the life-size *Hugh Lupus*, he had begun the full-size model of his memorial to Lord Lothian (fig. 96).[113] 'Watts's plaster monument to Billy,' a relative reported, 'is *very* striking, the natural attitude of the sleeping head is exceedingly life like. I think I should like the drapery more simple and unlaboured, but perhaps Watts knows best about that – It is to be in red and white mixed alabaster, which I am doubtful about.'[114] Remarkably, the *mouvementé* drapery and deep-cut Italianate hair heightens the sense of peace over the recumbent mar-

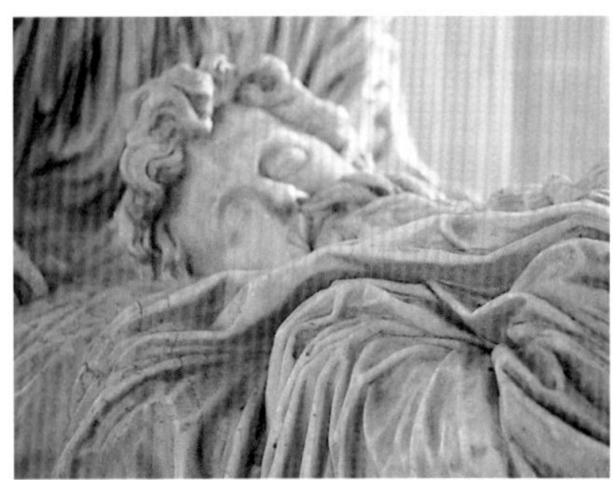

96 Memorial to William Schomberg Robert Kerr, 8th Marquess of Lothian (detail), *c.*1870–78 (Blickling church).

quess, and with life-size angels kneeling at his head and feet like Little Holland House habitués, the overall impression is of a friend asleep.[115] (The guardian angels on Henri de Triqueti's effigy of Prince Albert at Windsor are smaller than his dog.)[116] In August Watts invited Rickards to see a portrait of Blanche, probably *Little Blanche* in scarlet stockings playing on a chair. The kitten on her knee in the later *Fireside Companions*, enchanted Baron Meyer de Rothschild's daughter Hannah, who was sitting for a much-loved portrait.[117]

Webb's fears were justified. There had been trouble at Freshwater. Tyerman had not received all his dues. Local builders had caused mischief, prompting a Mr Waterfield to complain to Julia Cameron about poor workmanship at Watts's house; he then retracted his accusations in a letter to the artist, saying that he had been misinformed (probably by the Middleton 'rascal' Kennet, as Emily Tennyson referred to her builder, who also constructed Mrs Cameron's tower). Watts wanted the job finished and in early October made an appointment with Henry Saunders, a builder near Dimbola.[118] He had the head of *Medusa* sent to Rickards and after two years' record-breaking work set off with the Prinseps – both now semi-invalids – for three months' recuperation at Trinity Lodge in Bournemouth, within steamer range of the Isle of Wight.[119] Mary Fraser Tytler, holidaying in Bournemouth after her year at the Slade, bravely renewed contact with Watts.[120]

On 10 December Watts relinquished the commission for the large South Kensington lunette to Leighton, who, as Watts was doubtless aware, had recently supplied sketches for *Industrial Arts as Applied to Peace* for the companion lunette.[121] A day or two later Leighton asked for an autograph. 'If any friend of yours (nice or not) wishes to have my autograph it would surely be very ill-natured to refuse to give pleasure at so small a cost to the giver!' replied Watts. 'I confess I often take no notice of applications of the kind from people of whom I know nothing from a feeling that the thing is absurd' – He had a printed note for autograph hunters: 'Mr G F Watts regrets to say that it is against a principle he holds, with reference to the modern custom of Autograph collecting, to accede to the request just made to him.' Watts would not refuse Leighton: 'Perhaps there is more vanity in declining than there would be in granting the request. Any how I send you the illustrious signature & call in return for yours at the desire of a young Lady now staying with us here, May's sister, Annie Prinsep.'[122] He was painting a larger-than-life-size picture of May, his sweet-natured riding companion, standing in a long Ulster coat above the Hampshire coast,[123] but it was Annie who stitched his first red velvet skullcap. Made to protect his head from painful draughts, this characteristic cap gave him a Venetian air, perpetuating his image as a modern old master – an aesthetic sage, despite his uncertainties.[124]

# 10  Sweet Briary

ON MONDAY, 26 JANUARY 1874, two days after Gladstone's sudden dissolution of parliament, the treasurer of Middle Temple called at Little Holland House to commission a full-length portrait of the Prince of Wales. The artist proposed to represent His Royal Highness in his bencher's robe, with the ribbon and Star of the Order of the Garter. He asked for sittings to take place at Little Holland House, and to reserve copyright.[1] While awaiting the prince's return from St Petersburg – for the marriage of his brother Alfred, Duke of Edinburgh, to Marie Alexandrovna, the daughter of Tsar Nicholas II of Russia – Watts stayed at his new Freshwater home.

The Briary, as the house was named after the roses in its hedgerows, lay at the foot of High Down and looked across the garden towards the sea. Two cypress trees flanking the entrance to the drive recalled images of Greece and Italy.[2] Watts joined the Prinseps in early February for a fortnight. He hoped to settle there 'to make the greatest effort I am capable of, forgetting exhibitions & critics & every thing but the one object of producing works of Art worthy of a great country'. But business had to continue, and he secured Barlow's commitment to purchase *The Angel of Death* for one thousand guineas.[3]

The three-storeyed house was built of Isle of Wight red brick, with white-painted dormers. Rows of gables recalled the home Webb had designed for Val. Light shone through the south-facing dining and drawing rooms and Thoby Prinsep's ground-floor invalid suite, where windows faced south and west and family and friends liked to gather in the evenings. A covered brick path, or verandah, around the house enabled him to enjoy the air in all weathers. The artist's galleried, thirty-foot studio, with its a huge, north window, stretched the length of the butler's quarters, the housekeeper's and the kitchen. Deep eaves overhung the tall, west window through which pictures were transported, and Watts curtained off the southern section below the gallery to create a private sitting room.[4] Outside, lawns were laid out in terraces with elm trees arching overhead. Nightingales sang in the leafy glades, and soft, blustering winds blew the sea air into the garden, which gradually filled with old-fashioned flowers, lavender and sweet geranium, bordered by clipped yew hedges and climbing white and yellow roses. A magnolia grandiflora was planted at the front of the house.[5] To celebrate their freedom from London smog, Watts painted 'A Study from My Window' (fig. 97), which offered the pleasurable opportunity 'to examine

97   *A Study from My Window*, 1874 (courtesy of the Fine Art Society).

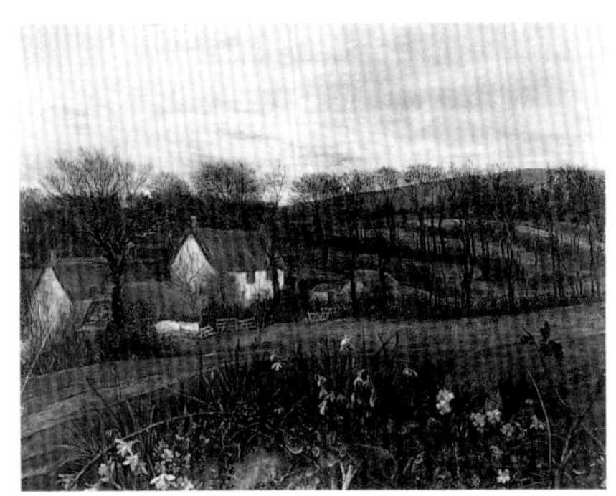

& dwell upon beauties which are ever new', and he hoped to pursue land-scape studies out of doors.[6]

Ned Burne-Jones, suffering from depression and lack of confidence, missed Signor's company and wished he could drop into the studio for a chat, especially now that Rossetti was away at Kelmscott, the Elizabethan Oxfordshire manor he shared with the Morris family.[7] 'About every fifth day I fall into despair as usual,' he wrote to Watts, who with Morris and Rossetti was still very much a father figure and seminal influence in his life.[8] Burne-Jones's efforts to ascertain the future of Little Holland House yielded a dubious response from the agent: 'Of the land I can get no news at all – I think the agent has forgotten all about it & when I stir him up invents histories for me of what he has not done in that matter'; but Val passed on news from The Briary. Relieved to hear from Signor, Ned replied by return: 'I am doing a thing I never did before in my life, answering a letter straight-away – accept the proof of my affection . . . I miss you very much for it has always been a real comfort to "run over" to Little Holland House & grumble myself out to you . . . I am really at present at the very lowest ebb of hope.' Parts of his letter, filled with news of friends and now heavily blocked out (presumably censored for posterity by the widowed Mary Watts) may have referred to William Graham's daughter Frances, to whom he was forming an attachment.[9] 'Morris I see daily but that nightly soul is dormant at present . . . Is there to be no more Little Holland House? it feels so sad as if one had come to another turn in life.'[10]

While the Prinseps established The Briary as their home,[11] Signor resumed a relentless portrait schedule at Little Holland House, finishing two full-length portraits of the Marchioness of Bath – begun over a decade earlier – and of May in her Ulster coat, for Rickards.[12] Gladstone's Liberals lost the general election, partly owing to the unpopularity of the home secretary, Robert Lowe (fig. 98), an outstanding, vigorous debater, always in conflict with Disraeli (the returning prime minister). Watts, who cannot have endorsed his opposition to the Reform Bill, was impressed by his speeches, powered as they were by classical allusions. He had met Lowe at Holland House and they used to ride with the Duchess of Cleveland in Rotten Row. After Lowe left office and on Sir John Grant's retirement as Governor of Jamaica, Watts invited both men to sit for the national collection.[13] The Royal Artillery commissioned a portrait of General Sir Edward Sabine for the officers' mess at Woolwich. An astronomer and specialist in global magnetism, he had recently retired as president of the Royal Society.[14] Sir John Hawkshaw, the engineer responsible for the rail-ways, the Thames bridges, the Clifton suspension bridge, the Amsterdam ship canal, and, currently, the Channel Tunnel Company, sat for a portrait. It was Sir John's recommendation to the doubtful Khedive that secured the construction of the Suez Canal.[15]

One of Watts's trickier fund-raising commissions was the portrait of the Lord Chief Justice Sir Alexander Cockburn, for Trinity Hall, Cambridge. The Scottish baronet, persuasive, short and dignified, but for his complexion – coloured by addiction to a less than learned frivolity and a healthier love of yachting – had presided over many a *cause célèbre*. The eccentric Tichborne inheritance case had gripped the public for months; and after its conclusion on 28 February, when he sentenced the Australian imposter, a butcher from Queensland, to fourteen years' penal servitude,[16]

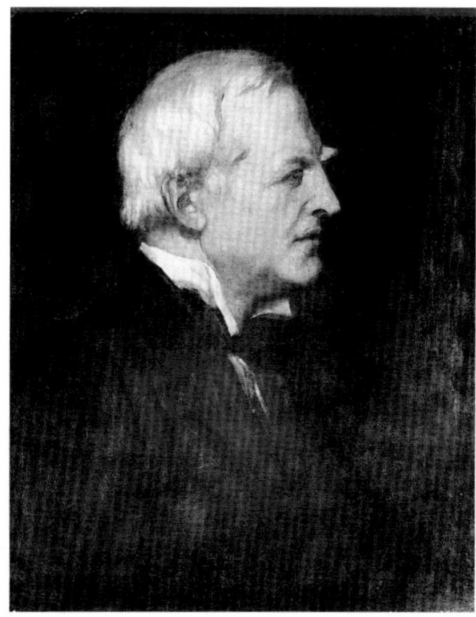

98   *The Right Honourable Robert Lowe* (afterwards Viscount Sherbrooke), before 1881 (National Portrait Gallery, London).

the lord chief justice sat to Watts. His mottled complexion frutrated the artist's efforts to mirror his mind, though the portrait was accepted by the college.[17]

The pressure of commuting back and forth to supervise workmen at The Briary placed him under considerable strain. It appears that the Prinseps had moved in before the plaster was dry, the local builder had proved inadequate and Tyerman was still working on the roof.[18] 'London workman are bad enough but in the country it is almost impossible to get any thing done at all & quite impossible to get any thing well done,' Watts complained to Rickards. 'I have been losing a good deal of time & some temper in consequence.'[19]

Alone at Little Holland House, suffering from influenza and longing for the sea air, he received a letter from Madeline Wyndham that soothed his soul and nourished his sense of genius. Her romance with Blunt consummated the previous year moved the poet to reminisce that 'her tenderness . . . was from a full cup running over, as a god might give. It glorified both giver and receiver and left her heaven no poorer than before.' Madeline was devoted to her family, friends and art. Her bountiful nature led people to compare her to a magnolia. Huge blooms appear in the foreground of her full-length aesthetic portrait (pl. XVIII).[20] Ivy fronds lie at the foot of her deep green dress, which is ornamented with giant sunflowers. Her cream silk bodice bursts through slashed sleeves and is entwined with roses at her waist, where chains fall from a large repoussé clasp she probably made herself. She leans against a classical balustrade, her left elbow resting on the pillar, her hand bent back towards her cheek; a small gold key hangs from a bracelet. The background is filled with poet's laurel growing from blue-glazed Belgrave Square jardinières. Madeline felt inspired by Watts; his art and aspirations had opened her eyes and she offered to model again when needed. Depressed at the general disinterest in his symbolic work, he valued her appreciation and rejoiced at her pleasure: 'You really are worthy of the great Art, and great nature, with which you are surrounded . . . Will you come and see me often, if it be only that we may think over these things together without saying a word!'[21]

The following day, 31 March, he notified Lady Holland that they would give up Little Holland House at the end of the year: 'It will be a fearful wrench.' She had signed the estate over to the Earl of Ilchester in January; the agreement allowed her to stay on in the Jacobean mansion, but Lord Ilchester was entitled to deal 'as he may please' with Little Holland House,[22] which was in a sorry state, increasingly damp, depleted, dilapidated, having to be patched up so often that even Watts acknowledged that no other occupant would wish to take it on. The Prinseps were clearly better off in the country.[23] By Easter, he was back at Freshwater, liasing with Alice Liddell, Dodgson's inspiration for *Alice's Adventures in Wonderland*, to discuss a portrait of her father, the Very Reverend Henry Liddell, Dean of Christ Church, Oxford, commissioned by the college to commemorate his twenty years in office.[24]

A side gate from The Briary garden opened into a lane that led over fields to the Tennysons at Faringford, half a mile away. There were frequent comings and goings between the two houses: 'Life seemed to hum like some big wheel round the Cameron household.'[25] No islander or tourist was safe from the photographer. Fishermen, people gazing at the sea or ambling down the lanes might suddenly be approached by this determined woman in dark chemical-stained clothing. 'I am Mrs Cameron, perhaps you have heard of me,' she would announce huskily. 'You would oblige me very much if you would let me photograph you.' Disarmed by her ferocious charm, unwitting models would find themselves propelled into her studio; and the 'Divine Watts' was obliged to receive her visitors. Watts loved to recall the occasion Julia's invincibility failed. She arranged to drive Tennyson, Thoby and himself to admire the view from a new house in Freshwater, only to discover that the house was inhabited. Not unnaturally, the tenant, a German count, objected to the strangers' invasion, whereupon with inexorable eloquence she introduced him to 'the greatest living poet, 'our greatest Indian legislator' and 'the greatest living painter'. This the count would not accept: 'I subscribe not to that opinion. Also in Germany have we very good painters.'[26]

That month, on 15 April, a pivotal independent exhibition opened in Paris. Pissarro, Monet and their colleagues Pierre-Auguste Renoir, Paul Cézanne, Edgar Degas and Alfred Sisley whose *plein-air* pictures had been rejected by the Salon, exhibited in the first-floor studios of the ebullient photographer Nadar. (Manet, keen for recognition by the Salon, did not participate.) Their dynamic broken touches of paint that made their canvases appear unfinished appalled critics. Seizing the title of Monet's *Impression – Sunrise*, in which the sun, reddening sky and smoking chimneys are reflected in the Seine, they derided the group as 'Impressionists'. Yet the artists embraced the term, and their first exhibition set the tone for modern art.

As the 1874 Royal Academy Summer Exhibition had reverted to discordant hanging, Watts held back the new vertical nude, *Psyche*, which he had designed as a companion to *Daphne*. He refused Rickards's requests to show the *Medusa* (designed too long ago), *Blanche* (private), and *The Rider on the Black Horse* ('quite out of place'). Instead, his portraits of Mrs L'Estrange, the Reverend James Martineau, painted 'with intense pathos, and perfect recognition of the poetry of the far-seeing eyes and sensitive lips . . . masterly and free modelling', the sole 'speaking' likeness of the late John Stuart Mill, Esq., Lady Arthur Russell, and the Reverend Harry Jones were considered 'remarkable', noted for their sense of calm and reserve. He himself admired Millais's pictures – the landscape *Winter Fuel* was the highlight.[27]

The Prince of Wales had given his assent to the Middle Temple portrait, for which the benchers agreed to pay one thousand guineas. Watts supported the prince's desire to assume a national role now that he had recovered from his near-fatal attack of typhoid, but the queen opposed the idea. His Royal Highness came to Little Holland House and the artist, struck by his thoughtfulness, made a fine chalk study of the head; but on occasion he was also obliged to transport materials to Marlborough House, where lighting conditions were different; there were interruptions; and he was obliged to retouch in the absence of his royal sitter; sittings for the full-length eight-foot canvas were delayed.[28] Watts continued to work at a furious pace, from sunrise, however early, until seven in the evening, rarely leaving the studio. He encouraged visitors to call for lunch, or after six.[29]

Problems at The Briary forced him to complain to Webb, who was furious that, after minor criticisms, he had brought in local workmen.

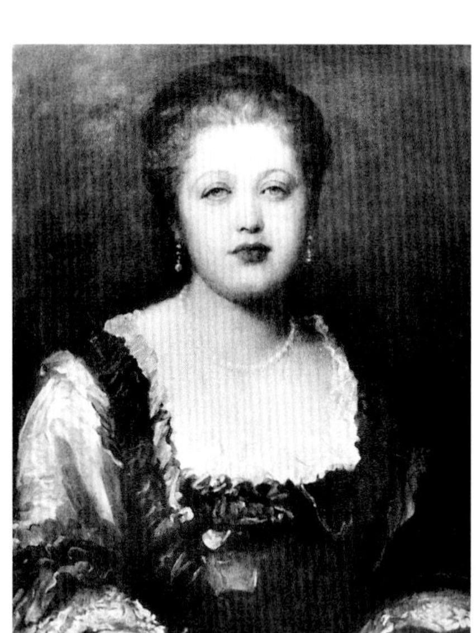

99   *Hannah de Rothschild*, 1874 (private collection: photo Frederic Hollyer).

Writing to Watts on 8 July, the architect attributed the criticisms to jealousy of their London builder, Tyerman. Disgusted at the professional discourtesy – Webb's houses are noted for fine detail – he had sought legal advice. He consulted Tyerman, who was still owed thirty or forty pounds, to ascertain his responsibility for the poor craftsmanship,[30] and he employed an independent architect named Vinall to examine the works in the presence of both Tyerman and the local tradesmen, and to oversee repairs. 'I must beg you to release me from any further interference in a matter which has been so far from satisfactory to me', Webb wrote to Watts.[31] George Howard reported to his father that the artist had worked himself into a frenzy and had again 'been made a fool of by a pack of fussy old women who want to direct his house as they did his married arrangements'.[32]

Watts soon realised that he must have a London base. The idea of living solely on the island had been a romantic, albeit healthy, whim and he could not expect patrons to cross the Solent to his studio. He was preparing pictures for exhibition in Manchester and required final sittings from Hannah de Rothschild (fig. 99). Gratefully accepting her invitation to Mentmore, he hoped to visit 'when the hounds meet there'.[33] Val acquired a 245-foot extension to his garden, and arranged to sublet to him – for sixty pounds rent – the northern end bordering the new Melbury Road, just a hundred yards from the old home.[34] To build his new studio Watts chose the architect Frederick Pepys Cockerell, who had designed Reginald Cholmondeley's Kensington home in Palace Gate,[35] and whose late father had campaigned for Watts's Oxford frescoes.

The urgency to raise further funds for the studio – his builders Jackson and Shaw received their first one-thousand-pound instalment in June[36] – fired Watts to develop visionary subjects. He laboured long at *Titans*, which Leighton and Burne-Jones persuaded him to leave as a vigorous sketch, and at *Love and Death*, which he had reworked and, though unfinished, hoped to sell handsomely at Manchester. In preparation, he had modelled a nude figure of Death from Long Mary studies and produced a harrowing full-size terracotta head of Love with young Arthur Prinsep's hair. He regarded *Love and Death* as 'my best work hitherto' and planned to paint a new version 'that may be great by the side of the greatest! I hope this does not appear too atrocious in the way of vanity,' he wrote to Rickards.[37] William Graham, having bought *The Whisper of Love*, sat for his portrait and borrowed a sketch of *Acis and Galatea*, pressed Watts for a larger version. He envisaged that *Love and Death* might one day rank with old master painting and cannily asked buy it at a discount as a sketch, 'carried out so far as you care to go with it'.[38]

*Love and Death* and Jean-Baptiste Camille Corot's *Saint Sebastien* were the chief – if controversial – highlights at the epoch-making 1874 Royal Manchester Institution exhibition of 700 modern pictures. Thanks to loans from Richard Johnson, Samuel Barlow and Rickards, Watts was represented by eight pictures, with *Love and Death* and *Angel of Death* flanking the Corot in the first room.[39] Critics declared that no modern master approached Watts in the field of allegory. Though some questioned his drawing of Love – (the artist pointed out that he was not an ordinary boy, but a symbol representing vigour and activity) – one after another they drew attention to its imaginative power.[40] A resident proposed its acquisition by the city of Manchester.[41] Gratified by this positive response, Watts wished to present *Love and Death*, *Angel of Death* and his important imaginative designs to public institutions. He had hoped that by now his income from portraiture would enable him to do so, 'but alas! several things just at this time conspire against me.'[42]

George du Maurier came to The Briary in September: 'Watts's house is very jolly'. Struck by the tall, handsome stockbroker Andrew Hichens who was courting May Prinsep, du Maurier drew cartoons for *Punch* of the pair on the beach at Freshwater (fig. 100).[43] Julia Cameron impressed him as 'the greatest character I ever met', if daunting as a neighbour. Tennyson had just asked her to provide illustrations for a cabinet edition of his *Idylls of the King*. 'Now *you* know Alfred, that *I* know that it is immortality to me to be bound up with you', she had replied and was throwing herself into the momentous project. The Yarmouth porter was summoned to model as 'King Arthur', and the photographer's husband, given to sudden fits of hilarity, as Merlin. Andrew and May, who posed for 'Gareth and Lynette',[44] sat to Watts for their wedding portraits and were married in Freshwater on 10 November.[45]

Although du Maurier found him well and happy, with the stresses of supervising and travelling between two new studio homes, the vertigo and vomiting attacks from which Watts had been free for years returned. Jeanie had acquired a house near Freshwater, at Colwell Bay. Her enlightened critical report on the influence of large barrack schools on pauper girls, published on 30 October, had taken its toll on her health; and after handing in her papers she resigned. Florence Nightingale saw her resignation as a national misfortune: 'You were arrayed almost singlehanded, a noble Army of one, against this evil.'[46] Signor suggested to Jeanie that she should come and refresh her spirits in Freshwater, where, to overcome his gout under enjoyable doctor's orders, he planned to spend much of the winter, 'traipsing over the down with Tennyson who is also recommended exercise'.[47]

Watts rode his Arab mare every day. When he and Tennyson used to visit their late friend Sir John Simeon, the poet led the way in his carriage, the artist following on horseback.[48] He planned to paint the apocalyptic *Rider on the White Horse* for Rickards, as a companion to the black rider.[49] *Dawn and Day* was given place of honour at the Dudley Gallery. In this tall mystical picture, Day, a radiant youth with gleaming eyes and purple encrusted wings, rises majestically over the deep blue of night and through the golden atmosphere above the waking figure of Dawn. Never finished, it was later purchased by the Duke of Westminster.[50] Watts's habit of exhibiting allegories unfinished so as to use the less favourable display gallery conditions to determine their final form was unpopular with critics, for, however elevated his concept, they could hardly second guess its resolution.[51]

The manager of the Lyceum Theatre offered him a private box and invited him to paint Henry Irving, whose triumphant, poignant performances as Hamlet, challenging tradition, were comparable to his own ground-breaking approach. The actor's conception of the role in terms of natural truth was revered, and the force of his personality made his modernisms acceptable, but his execution was subject to criticism. 'It would give me very great pleasure to paint a head of Mr Irving who is a real artist', Watts replied to Sidney Bateman, the manager's wife. If he undertook the portrait, it must be for the national collection, unless the Batemans

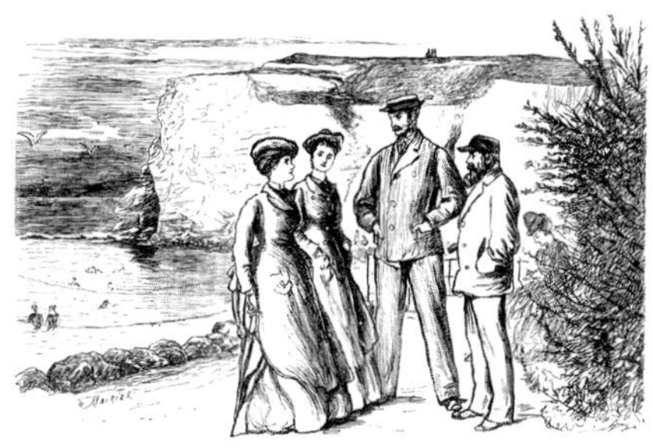

100  'Kind and Considerate', Du Maurier's caricature of May Prinsep and Andrew Hichens, centre, at Freshwater (*Punch*, 19 September 1874).

particularly wished to have it; and he would certainly see him perform, but could not do so until winter and the risk of draughts was over. 'I should like to show one who so thoroughly enters into the highest aim & aspirations my own aspirings', wrote Watts, inviting the actor to Little Holland House, but there is no record of a portrait.[52] To cheer Jeanie after a further relapse, a friend, aware of her affection for Watts, commissioned a small portrait of her, for her son Walter.[53]

According to his letter of 23 December to the Academy,[54] construction of the new house had begun. Cockerell's plans, completed in November, would not receive official approval from the surveyor until 9 January 1875, nor signed agreement until 15 July;[55] and the Memorandum of Agreement between Val Prinsep and the Earl of Ilchester, relating its construction on the 207-foot by 135-foot plot is dated 15 February.[56]

News that Rickards had been preserving his letters unnerved him. Asking his patron to keep only those relating to business, he went on to discuss his broad, liberal outlook on humanity and revealed privately that he disliked his name so much – 'Being a lover of the beautiful its want of music is distasteful to me' – and in his youth he had seriously considered changing it: 'I confess I should like to have a fine name & a great ancestry, it would have been delightful to me to feel as though a long line of worthies were looking down upon me & urging me to sustain their dignity. This I feel very strongly all the time feeling still more strongly that to do good work in the world is a better thing than an accidental place in society.'[57]

A slight contretemps followed Rickards's low offer for the large *Love and Death*. Watts replied that if Hunt's *Light of the World*, then privately owned in Manchester, could be bought for three or four hundred, he would accept that sum for *Love and Death*. But as the Mancunian well knew, it was a serious, long thought out picture painted to stimulate the public, ideally as a gift to the nation. Rickards had taken offence when he outlined his three alternatives for key symbolic works: to present them to public institutions; to earn from them a substantial income (fifteen hundred to two thousand guineas each, reflecting the value of his time, thought and experience, and comparable to doctors' and lawyers' earnings); or to preserve them as life insurance after his death, presumably for Blanche. Though his style was 'unpopular', he had absolute confidence in his high aspirations, and planned to paint an even larger version of *Love and Death*. Ever pragmatic, he doubted that the major canvases would sell and added that in order to live he would paint slighter, less time-consuming works: 'These polemical discussions make me anxious to finish my picture of the *Spirit of Religion*'.[58]

Widespread religious dissent had moved Watts to address the issue from the highest plane of thought – the spirituality of divine teaching, love and charity acceptable to all faiths – rather than present restrictive dogma. Soon to be exhibited as *Dedicated to all the Churches* (pl. XXIII), the picture appears to be as didactic as the dogma Watts despised, in its demand for religious tolerance. Symbolizing the compassionate tenderness of all Christian churches, the cloaked seated figure of the Saviour dominates the upper section of the nine-foot high canvas. (Both he and Tennyson believed that 'the poetic mind must find its religion either in the human type father, son, and brother, or in the cosmic unity . . . the world cannot get on without a personal God.')[59] Beneath his or her lap – in Watts's iconography the spirit of God is not confined by sex – cherubs, representing multi-faith humanity, nestle in the clouds. There is no cross or detail to identify creed, because Watts aimed to embrace universal faith.[60]

By contrast, Hunt's *The Shadow of Death*, showing Christ in the carpenter's shop, with Mary on her knees looking towards the shadow of his outstretched arms, was carefully tailored to the Christian narrative. Painted in Jerusalem, its completion had released the artist from a dark period of despair, and though extremists condemned it as blasphemous, *The Shadow of Death* cemented Hunt's reputation as the religious painter of the age. Despite the artificial lighting conditions under which it was now on show at Agnews, and which Watts regarded as a flattering and unfair to other artists, he admired the picture's religious poetry.[61]

Alice Gurney's father-in-law, the Right Honourable Russell Gurney, the Recorder of the City of London, sat for a celebrated portrait that year (fig. 101).[62] Her children Laura and Rachel, lived with Blanche at The Briary. They adored Signor, and used to tease him and seek refuge in his studio, which seemed a haven of peace, with no rules or chaos in the otherwise electric atmosphere charged by Sara's outbursts. If the artist's occasional hot temper or irritability did flare, it was 'harmless as summer lightning', except when the girls became over-excited and he warned them against their Pattle wilfulness and French excitability: 'You will grow up imperious women if you are not careful.' Startled by his anger, they kissed him. Their grandmother told them Signor was famous, but they regarded him as their own genius and playfellow and were enthralled by his explanations of the allegories. As they looked up at *Time and Death*, he told Laura that Time was usually shown as an old man with a scythe. (Julia Cameron, for example, had ensnared an old passing tramp; she had she rushed out, crying, 'Stop him! stop him! There goes Time!' She had him stripped, washed and shrouded in one of her best shawls to be photographed as Time.[63]) Signor explained his strong, young figure of Time, marching forward with a tread nothing could stop, not ruthless, but indifferent, which was why he had wide blank eyes; in his hand he brought Death, always beautiful, pale and mysterious, with 'a veiled head and gentle bosom where we must all lay our heads at last.'

'Darling Signor! no one had ever talked to me as he did, taking all the big facts of life and dressing them up in rainbow words like the magical colours on his palette', Laura would recall. 'He taught us values, the beauty of beauty, the joy of joy, the marvel of heroic deeds. No wonder we loved him . . . Yet with all his gentleness, he was impersonal; no one could boast of being his favourite, though it was understood that he loved Blanche best; but what he loved was the youth in all of us.' Sara suggested he should be their drawing-master. Like Titian, he painted visionary subjects directly on to the canvas. The girls felt cheated: 'Granny, Signor can't draw, he can only paint.' They sat at the table, expecting instructions for elegant landscape; he placed a wooden brick in front of them and said, 'Draw that!' They were horrified. It was far too simple. 'But the odd part was, we none of us could do it.'[64] He allowed Blanche the freedom to learn for herself, to work out her own thank-you letters. When Rickards sent her a locket, he begged him not to spoil her: 'I dread any thing in the shape of selfishness as the worst of faults. I must say she is entirely free from it at present.'[65]

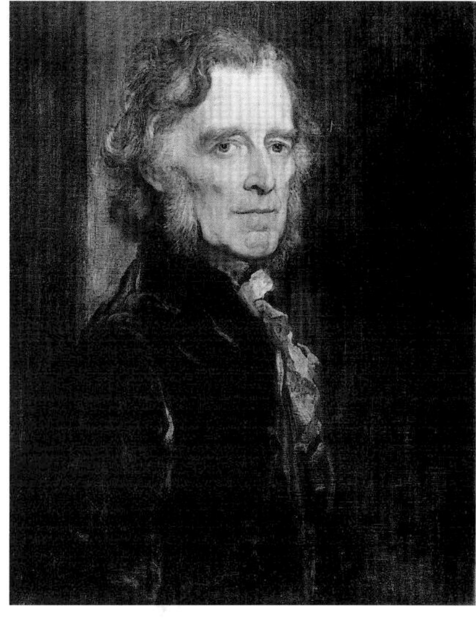

101   *The Right Honourable Russell Gurney*, QC, 1875 (Tate, London).

Trapped by influenza on his return to Kensington, he was unable to work and frustrated that he had much to oversee and still to achieve. He was allowed to stay on in the damp and depleted old Little Holland House until 25 March 1875. Wedding portraits of the younger generation – Sara's adult nieces – were under way. 'The succession of anniversaries that mark the flight of time [is] to me so dreadful', he wrote to Rickards. 'Death is nothing. But the slipping away of the power of doing is a thing I cannot contemplate without the greatest pain.'[66] He needed a final half-hour sitting from Dean Liddell, explaining to Alice that by taking out the strength of the shadows, 'the picture will be much more agreeable in expression & character'. Because of portrait commitments and storage, he secured permission to stay a few months more while the house was pulled down around him.[67]

On 17 April Ellen Terry opened as Portia in a grand aesthetic production of *The Merchant of Venice* at the Prince of Wales Theatre, which established her reputation as an actress of distinction. Godwin, as artistic director, had designed her Venetian gown of blue and white brocade. Her triumph was all the more poignant, for he had walked out of their home only weeks before. The *Daily Telegraph* reported that 'like no other Portia ever seen by Shakespeare students, so fresh and charming . . . Miss Terry, in her beautiful robes, looked as if she had stepped out of a canvas by Mr Leighton.' Amongst her audience of poets, artists and aesthetes were the young Oscar Wilde, Burne-Jones, Swinburne, and her estranged husband.[68]

*Dedicated to All the Churches* (subsequently renamed *The Spirit of Christianity*) looked awkward to Watts at the Academy. Mystifying to critics, it met with very guarded praise from Ruskin. 'Here, at least, is one picture meant to teach; nor failing of its purpose, if we read it rightly', he wrote in the Academy notes. But 'the artist concedes to himself, more and more, the privilege which none but the feeble should seek, of substituting the sublimity of mystery for that of absolute majesty of form.' That Ruskin found any aspect of the picture praiseworthy surprised the artist.[69] The portrait of Sir Edward Sabine, resplendent in the red uniform of the Royal Artillery, was admired for the modelling of the flesh and expression. Less effective was *F. W. Walker*, a painting of Johnson's son-in-law, the high master of Manchester Grammar School, and shortly, of St Paul's School, London. The *Athenaeum* favoured the portrait of thirteen-year-old *Blanche* holding her violin as she turns to face the viewer.[70]

To encourage Blanche to learn the fiddle (fig. 102), Watts took lessons himself and treated Rickards's ridiculous caution that it would damage her health, with a hearty rebuff. Joachim and Madame Neruda were 'splendid specimens of vigour' and as none of the young female violinists he knew had suffered injury, he declared the girl cited by the Mancunian in his warning must be 'constructionally defective. If not let her wear *no stays*, run, jump, play at cricket with her brothers if she have any & otherwise exercise her limbs & lungs. I will answer for the violin being innocent of harm to her.' Blanche did not live at Little Holland House. He dreaded that she might find his life dull, with only the cook Emma Graver for company. Far better for her to frolic with Laura and Rachel on the Isle of Wight, vault over five-barred gates and become 'a regular tomboy'.[71]

Emilie Barrington, armed with a letter from Jeanie, introduced herself to Watts one afternoon in June. The flame-haired[72] woman left her embar-

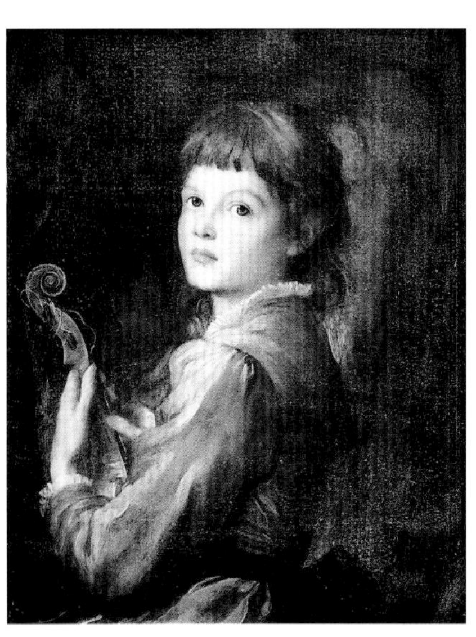

102   *Blanch Clogstoun, c.*1875 (courtesy of Christie's).

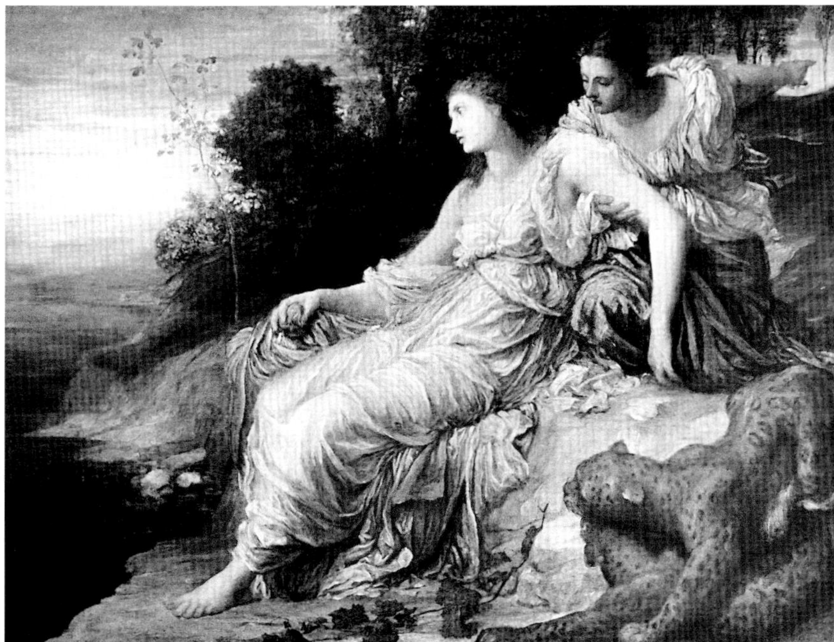

103　*Ariadne in Naxos*, 1875
(Guildhall Art Gallery).

rassed husband Russell sitting in the carriage, tottered over the rubble and
entered the isolated remains of Little Holland House. Everything except the
thatched porch and contents of the studios seemed 'to hang on its last
thread'. She returned with her sisters the following month,[73] and visited
him at The Briary. One day he opened his garden gate to find her painting
a thatched cottage in the lane; he went over to her easel and told her she
had painted the chimney as cleanly as the Venetians would have done. Flattered, if not elated – for she was well aware of her artistic failings – she
called this her first lesson. Emilie Barrington clearly interested Watts, for
he invited her to his new London studio. Though dates in her *Reminiscences* are confused, her observations are acute.[74] He liked to flatter, to
praise the best aspect of an artist's work; as Burne-Jones put it, 'Signor finds
something to admire in pictures which would make – well – very good soles
for his shoes.'[75] Excessive rather than insincere, his encouragement was
doubtless prompted by his experience of discouragement and he was
unaware how much it meant to aspiring students. Emilie Barrington would
never let their acquaintance drop.[76]

During his last hot and exhausting weeks at Little Holland House, he
painted a picture for the French Inundation Relief Fund.[77] He subscribed
to the memorial to Frederick Walker, the artist whose instinct for nature
would always move him. (Thanks to his intensive fund-raising commissions
and rising income from investment, his bank balance had almost doubled
to some eleven thousand pounds, and he would shortly invest two thousand in Great Western Railway stock.)[78] His chalk drawing of the head of
the Prince of Wales was much admired. He had repainted *Love and Death*.
'It is twice the picture it was.' In mid-August Rickards received portraits of
his niece, Mary Carver, and of Sara Prinsep, a landscape of the Carrara
Mountains (pl. XXVI) worked up from the watercolour sketches he had

made from the leaning tower of Pisa in the 1840s; and a very fine *Ariadne in Naxos* with her attendant pointing and leopards prancing to indicate the arrival of Dionysus – 'perhaps the most complete picture I have painted' (fig. 103). *Titans*, the detail from *Chaos* – as he now called the cosmic 'opening chapter' to the history of mankind – was at last on track for exhibition at Manchester, to be lent by its purchaser Johnson. Watts planned to devote the rest of his life to 'about 12 or 15 very large pictures it will be a point of conscience to paint'.[79]

Rossetti, as strong as ever in artistic ideas, poetry and paint, had suffered a mental breakdown. In August, he asked Watts for his portrait in exchange for a chalk drawing. In no state to think he might be 'straining generosity to breaking point', he had not liked the oil portrait in its early stages and did not know it was now finished, framed and destined for the nation. As he did not paint self-portraits, he wished to give it to his model Fanny Cornforth. Watts had the picture delivered to Cheyne Walk. Rossetti, astonished by 'so happy and brilliant an example of your work', acknowledged that 'I have unduly taxed your friendly feeling, & that you have responded as few would have done'. As the picture was promised to Fanny he could not return it, but to rectify the 'utter inequality of the exchange', he invited Watts to choose 'a further memento of my work'.[80] 'It gives me infinite pleasure to find that you like the picture. We will not bandy compliments or I might tell you how much I value your drawing,' Watts replied amiably. He did not consider Rossetti indebted to him, nor would he take another picture – 'that would be to rob you of your time & labour . . . though of course I should like to possess any number of your works' – and promised to visit when he was settled.[81]

The final entry for rent for 'a part of Little Holland House' was paid on 31 August 1875.[82] At the last minute, Watts ordered a 40-foot iron studio to be installed in a corner of the new plot for temporary storage; he added an extra door for Burne-Jones, whom he invited to bring in his planned chef d'oeuvre *The Story of Troy* so that they could paint together as brothers in art. Many figures in the unfinished Troy polyptych, inspired by a Mantegna altarpiece, were studies from Michelangelo, whom Burne-Jones now passionately revered; some, notably the monumental Fortune in *The Wheel of Fortune*, a favourite composition, showed the influence of Watts, who acquired a watercolour study.[83] In the event, Burne-Jones did not join him in the 'Tin-Pot', as the studio was affectionately named.[84]

As so often in Watts's life, the instrumental support of a married female admirer eased his path. Charlotte Wylie acted as manager of artworks, paymaster and keyholder at the final transition period, freeing him to spend the autumn and much of the winter at The Briary, while in the ruins of his old home she preserved some twenty frescoes of the Pattle sisters, so symbolic of Watts and their salon.[85] Thoby mourned the close of their quarter century at Little Holland House in verse.[86]

In mid-September, Watts's long-standing patron Ionides, to whom he had made a final quarterly payment in June, after fifteen years, attacked him for having kept advance payment on the Greek picture proposed in the 1840s. Whether the issue was sparked because the artist – who had forgotten that he had received all or part of the £250 fee – had asked for the return of the small *Aurora* he had lent as a deposit, or because Ionides was simply tying up loose ends on leaving Holland Park, the attack became vitriolic when his daughter Aglaia Coronio sided with Watts. The artist, whose first thought was that his long-standing patron was 'crazed!' acknowledged his debt, attempted to pacify family and friends and made an offer that was particularly generous in view of his ambitious commitments. But his proposal to repay capital plus interest owing over the decades, and for Ionides to choose one of his best large pictures for Greece or, as originally planned, have one specially painted, was rebuffed. Watts, horrified to hear that he had drawn Morris and Burne-Jones into the argument, begged Aglaia not to involve Ned. Seeking objective advice from Charles Wylie, a business acquaintance of Ionides, he incurred such bitterness and sarcasm that he asked his patron to write no more. Ionides kept *Aurora*.[87]

Fortunately, Watts was distracted by building works, 'immersed in drains, which I find equally unsalubrious and expensive,' he wrote to Charlotte Wylie on 22 September. Much as he sought to reimburse her, not least for costs, she refused remuneration for looking after his interests. She was ordering furnishings and he had asked her to keep an eye on the 'Tin-pot' studio, the works stored inside it and Conrad's activities in the new sculpture studio.[88]

Meanwhile, Mary Fraser Tytler was pursuing a sporadic master-student friendship with Watts. She received 'the greatest kindness and help' from him and grasped the chance to further their rapport in Freshwater, where her father had taken a house for August and September. Mary, too, cherished the attention he gave to what society obliged her to regard as amateur work: 'I was one of the many who brought their efforts to show him, and who, coming to learn something to enable them to draw better, went away feeling they had also learnt how to live better.'[89] By 17 September she noted in her commonplace book that she had seen 'Mr Watts' several times. She called at his new studio. The absence of 'crude newness' at The Briary surprised her. This was as much due to Webb's design in relation to the great elms and farm buildings that Watts was painting, as to the Morris furnishings, and familiar chaos of the 'household gods' from Little Holland House. Mary was thrilled and honoured by his visits to her when she was painting the portrait commissioned by her father for their highland home, Aldourie Castle.[90]

'It must be a wonderfully refined nature that can come to such greatness & remain so humble of his power – He speaks as if he were the merest beginner.' Mary was astonished that to exploit every daylight hour, Watts could be up at three o'clock in the morning. He had finished three portraits that week. 'No one knows what it costs me, yet when I take people's cheques, I feel as if I were cheating them,' he confided.[91] Looking 'very fagged', he asked, 'What is there to live for but work?' Mary shared his enthusiasm, but privately questioned such obsession.[92] He talked to her for hours about art, demonstrating his colour theories. Typically, he picked out the finest quality of any artist they discussed, responding to her admiration for the French illustrator Gustave Doré with praise while pointing out that his undoubted power and imagination were swamped by theatrical treatment. He told her sadly that there was no call for the artistic expression of the mind; and they exchanged woeful concerns about the stifling effects of the machine age on craftsmanship and the joy of creativity. Beauty had been sacrificed to convenience. 'Wonderful as photography and many mechanical art productions are,' he explained, 'still to the human mind there is lacking something that makes them touch sympathy, something human, that the mark of the hand, the mind of the artist leaves in a perhaps very inferior work of art.'[93]

He had hoped to show his latest tragically sensual *Paolo and Francesca* at the Royal Manchester Institution, but Manchester viewers were familiar with Rickards's less dynamic version. As he developed the Dante-esque floating figures over the decades, he covered Francesca in ever more *mouvementé* drapery. More pallid now, she reaches out to Paolo's hand, rather than resting her hand in his, and supports his head and shoulders, heightening the impression of the whirlwind: 'Th' Infernal hurricane, that knows no sleep, / Propels the spirits with its ruinous force, / Whirls, smites, torments them in its reckless sweep.'[94] Instead, *Titans* had its first public airing in Manchester. Beneath the deep blue firmament, monumental figures reclining over a rocky landscape to represent a mountain range – they foreshadow the twentieth-century sculptor Henry Moore; in contrast, small, luminescent female figures gliding below to represent Time, suggest man's comparative insignificance.[95] The symbolism mystified viewers. Criticism strengthened Watts's resolve not to exhibit symbolic works, whose aim the public could not see immediately. He wrote to Rickards that the critic who glanced over modern work might perceive little meaning in Beethoven's *Moonlight Sonata*, though he suggested that were the picture a fresco – as intended – its impressive effect as a noble wall decoration might inspire an intelligent spectator to find the meaning. Like Burne-Jones, he should refrain from exhibiting more thoughtful works.[96]

'One of the great objects of my life is to help forward projects for the benefit & improvement of those who so much need looking after,' Watts wrote to Jeanie on 15 October, thanking her for a letter from the philanthropic reformer Octavia Hill (presumably about the imminent foundation of the Kyrle Society, which planned to open up beautiful places and introduce colour into the lives of the poor and would be formally constituted the following year). While he pledged financial contribution and pointed out that 'Octavia Hill & yourself can do more & better, & so can Tennyson & the great intellects that work for the uplifting & improvement of human nature' and that 'my own Art would also aid in this direction', were it not for the limited opportunities afforded to art in modern times.[97]

Freshwater was in a state of turmoil over the Camerons' sudden decision to leave for Ceylon, where Charles Cameron had long planned to spend his final days. One day the silver-haired invalid, seen only in velvet robes on home ground for the last twelve years, walked down to the sea shore and decided that the time had come. Dimbola was seething with packers, packing cases, helpers and islanders lamenting their decision. 'I hope it is a wise proceeding, but doubt it,' Watts wrote to Jeanie. The photographer made a last-minute dash to London to register pictures of her heroes, Tennyson, Herschel, Darwin, Joachim and Watts before setting sail from Southampton on the 21 October.[98] Friends gathered at the docks saw two coffins amongst their luggage, a cow given by Virginia Somers to supply fresh milk and porters carrying large mounted photographs of Carlyle or Madonna Mary, which the photographer had pressed on them, crying, 'I have no money left, but take this as a remembrance.'[99]

Watts, enervated after a small operation in October, painted his surgeon Thomas Bond, his host and future surgeon Charles Macnamara and his

wife Mia (Sara's niece), and returned in fine form to The Briary.[100] Mary
Fraser Tytler came to stay as a guest of May's elder sister Anne and observed
the family scene around the luncheon table. Looking like the wife of a
Venetian doge, Sara presided at the head, with Thoby an honoured invalid
by her side; next to him, resting her hand gently on his shoulder was their
beautiful widowed niece Julia Duckworth (fig. 104). A favourite of
Cameron's lens and of Watts's brush – he had recently painted two portraits, one full-face, highlighting her determined classical features and long
throat, and the other, a more sensitive three-quarter profile, showing the
softness of her auburn hair at the nape of her neck. Beside her were May
and Andrew Hichens. Anne and Mary completed the party, with children
clamouring for a seat beside the artist, who was usually dressed in grey,
with a silk shirt, pleated frill and red ribbon tie.[101] Afterwards, in the studio,
Mary was struck by its serene sense of thought. Watts, intent on work,
stepped lightly across the vast room, courteously enduring interruptions.
One afternoon when some disinterested visitors asked to see his studio, she
was thrilled to share a moment of intimacy with her hero. Opening the
door for them, he drew back to hide 'a distinct shudder', caught Mary's
sympathetic glance and returned it with a wicked half smile.[102]

Having reassessed his aims and ambitions, Watts established that he
would earn a living from portraiture during winter months, to enable him
to carry out the large imaginative designs that had occupied his mind over
the years and wished to present to the nation. Over the last twenty-five
years he had been heartbroken by the response – not from the general
public 'who could hardly be expected to know much about the matter' –
but from the art establishment, whose rejection of his imaginative work
had inhibited his career. Resigned to their verdict, he had gone on striving
because that was his destiny. 'I have long given up the idea that my attempts
will be cared for excepting by the few who it may be rather see what I
would do, than what is done,' he wrote to Lord Wharncliffe. The artist's
amazement that he was still alive spurred him on and in December he spent
his first few nights at Melbury Road. The house was not yet finished; he
complained about drunken, idle builders – 'dishonesty is the rule' – though
he was fascinated by construction work. Under his own roof, his future
was secure and he looked forward to embarking on a new phase in his
career.[103]

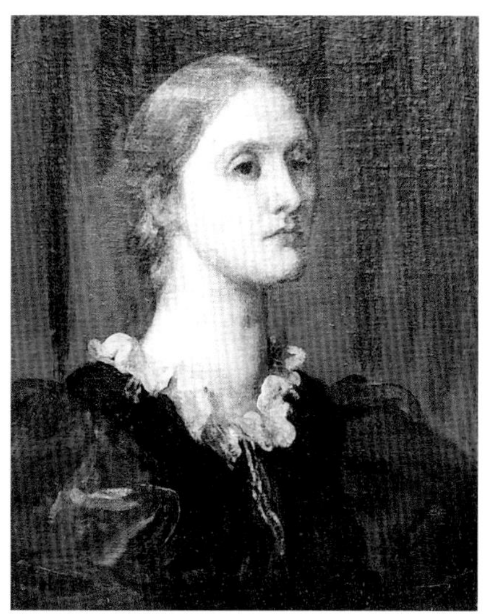

104   *Julia Duckworth, c.*1875
(courtesy of Julian Hartnoll).

11   New Little Holland House

Yet must these precincts lose the fame they won
As of high art, a seat surpassed by none
Not so, the seed hath struck deep root, & see
Four Studios rising where one used to be
Attracted hither by the master mind
That ever sought through art to elevate mankind
Still doth the Master here pursue this aim
Beneath a roof identical in name
With the demolished home we so deplore,
Spreading its fame yet wider than before.
*Julia Margaret Cameron*[1]

THE PHOENIX HAD BEGUN TO RISE long before the house turned to ashes, for it was the influence of Watts that inspired Leighton and Val Prinsep, to build studios near by, prompting art critics to refer to the School of Holland Park; and as fast as Lord Ilchester sold plots along the new Melbury Road, a colony of artists followed Watts's lead and briefed Arts and Crafts architects to build distinctive red brick studio houses, commemorated by Julia Cameron in the above verse.[2] Those 'dreadful houses' at the bottom of the garden, Lady Holland complained, frightened her swallows away.[3] Watts, permitted to retain the famous name, had settled into his new 'Little Holland House' by February. Subsequently numbered 6 Melbury Road, it was almost entirely given over to art, with double-height studios, their tall windows reaching to gabled roofs let in much more light than in the old house. This he hoped would result in more luminous pictures. The forty-nine-foot painting studio had a gallery and a twelve-foot slit for the egress of pictures at his end, with a partition and separate door for Burne-Jones. Huge wooden doors, each six feet wide, opened from the south-facing sculpture studio into the garden. There were wine cellars, but no dining room, as Watts kept to a modest medicinal diet served by Emma Graver, the Prinseps' housekeeper, who moved with him from old Little Holland House; and apart from her quarters, there was just one bedroom – 'to avoid complications' – above the sitting room, which faced south west.[4] Fired by a renewed sense of patriotism, he again vowed to give up lucrative portraiture and devote his best efforts to 'my country & my age'. Relinquishing the ease and comfort of commercial success was his protest against growing lust for wealth.[5]

As long as he could live without fear of debt, he would be satisfied. Rickards's response was to pay five hundred guineas for a 'replica' of *The Dray Horses* – painted entirely by himself, as opposed to a 'copy', partly painted by a pupil or assistant.[6] Special portraits of friends continued, especially for Virginia Somers and her younger daughter Lady Adeline Somers-Cocks, who was engaged to the Marquess of Tavistock. At Leighton's request he asked the Somers' permission to send to the Philadelphia International Exhibition *Time and Oblivion* 'the one picture which best represents my aims & feeling in Art'. In the event, he was represented by portraits of Millais and Leighton, lent by the sitters.[7] He sought to limit the number of entries per exhibitor at the Academy, though his patrons expected to see their portraits in the summer exhibition, where in 1876 he showed those of the Right Reverend Edward Harold Browne, Bishop of Ely (by then, of Winchester), and Charles Macnamara, as well as *By the Sea*.

Sir Coutts Lindsay proposed a plan to counter the unsatisfactory exhibiting conditions at the Academy. He aimed to exhibit avant-garde art in an independent gallery, to display pictures to their best advantage and to eliminate the indignity of assessment by committee. Artists would be invited to exhibit their finest work and allotted exclusive space. Charles Hallé (the musician's son, whose youthful artistic skills Watts had been asked to assess in 1862),[8] and Joseph Comyns Carr, an exuberant actor, lawyer and critic, were recruited to sound out artist friends similarly dissatisfied by the Academy. Even Burne-Jones was attracted to exhibit. Sir Coutts, seen as a modern Lorenzo the Magnificent, purchased premises in Bond Street. He commissioned William Thomas Sams to build an elegant gallery named after the Grosvenor estate, and Hallé appointed secretary.[9]

Watts, as an Academician, may not have been canvassed straight away but he felt a new urgency to pursue imaginative work: 'I have it seems to me so little time left that not a moment is to be lost, or scarcely a moment given to slighter undertakings.' He promised Rickards not to neglect his requests: 'All my work will go on together & I can hardly go to a picture now with any definite idea when I shall be able to finish it.'[10]

Emilie Barrington, who, like Mary Fraser Tytler took her work to Little Holland House and nurtured the privilege of his confidence, was an early caller at the new house.[11] She yearned to make her mark in the art world, if not in her own right, among the greatest of her day. The youngest daughter of James Wilson, the late Paymaster-General and founder of *The Economist*, Emilie was born to shine in the reflection of brilliance. Her upbringing had imbued her with the sense that her female role was to nourish male genius. Bright, brazen and impetuous, she infiltrated herself into the lives of people whose talents she admired. She had formed a bizarre friendship with Emily Faithfull, the founder of the feminist Victoria Press.[12] However, Emilie failed to play a part in the advance of professional women because she valued social position above emancipation: she married Russell Barrington, the grandson of Viscount Barrington. Her two brothers-in-law, Walter Bagehot, now editor of *The Economist*, and the essayist William Greg, who advocated female subservience to the intellectually superior male, had a strong, troubling influence on Emilie. She had manipulated her way into artists' studios, studied with Ruskin, Arthur Hughes and Ford Madox Brown. Painting up to twelve hours a day, with no exhibition success, she yearned to become a modern woman, influential in society.[13] Depressed by inadequacy, she hungered for an intellectual confidant, a father figure whose life she could organize; and when Signor, ever attracted to playing with fire, dropped a hint that he had nobody to help achieve his aims, she grasped the rôle. He replied on 7 April:

> A thousand thanks for your offer. I don't know but what you might help me with some advantage to yourself, because any one who does help me must go profoundly into the matter, and if real study has any charms for you, why, perhaps, you might be willing to undergo some stiff and stern application; but, I can tell you, help to me in the works I have proposed to myself, and indeed have plunged into, would be no child's play. If you will come and see me any day between 2.30 and 5 we may talk over possibilities.[14]

The sculptors Thomas and Mary Thornycroft were buying land to the west of Little Holland House and planned to build a pair of semi-detached studio houses. They themselves would live at 2 Melbury Road, with studios for their artistic offspring – Hamo, whose *Warrior Bearing a Wounded Youth from Battle* beat Alfred Gilbert to win the 1875 Academy Gold Medal[15] and John, who designed the first naval torpedo boats. The house next door to Watts was to be let or sold.[16] He recommended it to Emilie Barrington, who persuaded Russell to agree, in principle, to move in. In a relentless double kill, she ensnared the intimate confidence of Watts and guardianship of his genius. He introduced her to Mrs Wylie, and Jeanie approved, for Mrs Barrington would not only push Watts to achieve 'his noblest work', but she might 'stave off too many distractions (or should I say attractions)!'[17]

Mary Fraser Tytler, commuting between Scotland and Kensington, painted portraits of family and friends, and looked to Watts as her teacher. After sitting to the Scottish Academician George Paul Chalmers, however, she was somewhat distracted herself: 'It is a curious mystery how strong the similarity is between Love and Art. I believe a picture must be specially poetical to have this influence.' Watts, intent on portraying the mind of a sitter, was less successful at a female portrait where this conflicted with his appreciation of bloom and beauty. Impressed by Chalmers's female portraits, Mary compared him with Millais, who, in exchange for his portrait, was completing a picture of Hood's seamstress '*Stitch, Stitch, Stitch!*' for Watts.[18] As for male portraits, Mary remained loyal to Watts: 'it is more like comparing Titian and van Dyck. I feel strongly drawn to the Venetian now – Watts's influence no doubt.'[19] When she returned to Little Holland House in mid-May, he offered: 'I hope you will let me do anything I can that may be of use to you and that you will come and see me as often as you may feel any interest in what I may be about.'[20] Mary became his unofficial student, absorbed in art, with a confident new spring in her step.[21]

Watts's latest self-portrait showed him deep in thought as a medieval knight, his head bowed and sword lowered after battle; he holds peacock feathers, a symbol of hope in the still-troubled world. The artist was putting the finishing touches to *The Eve of Peace* (fig. 105) when Gladstone arrived on 16 May for a new portrait that Dean Liddell had commissioned for Christ Church.[22] Pressure of work meant that sittings were sporadic and, according to the statesman, distracted because the artist engaged him in

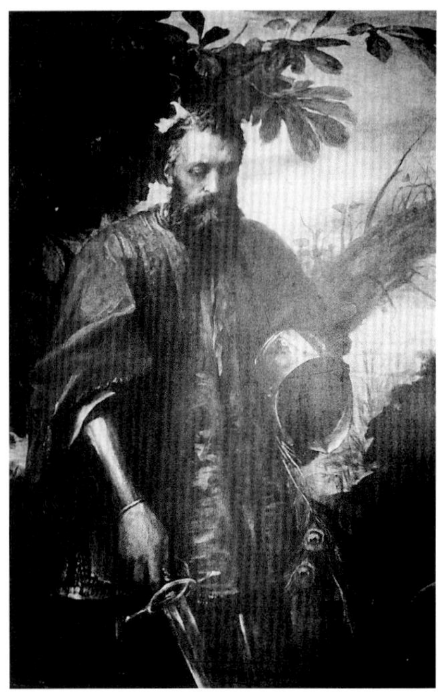

105   *The Eve of Peace*, 1863–76 (Dunedin Public Art Gallery, New Zealand; photo: Frederic Hollyer).

conversation,[23] whether about Homer, or, of immediate concern, the Eastern Question, for that month the Ottomans massacred over 12,000 Bulgarians. Disraeli dismissed the atrocities as 'coffee-house babble', talked of maintaining the 'Empire of England' – the Queen was proclaimed Empress of India on 1 May 1876[24] – and determined to support the Ottoman Empire against the Russians. British liberals and radicals were outraged. Gladstone proclaimed the Ottomans 'great anti-human species of humanity' who had violated 'the purity of matron, of maiden and of child', and published a leaflet calling on the Russians to drive the Ottomans out of Bulgaria. 'The whole country is aflame, meetings all over the place', Mary Gladstone recorded in her diary on 4 September. Carlyle, Ruskin and Burne-Jones joined the Eastern Question Association. Morris was treasurer. Watts too would be drawn in.[25]

He refused Rickards's requests for changes to his small version of *Angel of Death*, for adding a cross would impose restrictive dogma, and excluding the newborn or unborn child would reduce the poetry and significance of one of his most important 'painted poems'. *Time and Death, Love and Death* and *Angel of Death*, which he advised the Mancunian to add to his collection, must appeal purely to human sympathies, without reference to creed or dogma. He might omit the child from the replica, but never from the large composition. 'The suggestion that even the germ of life is in the lap of death I regard as the most poetic idea in the picture, the keynote of the whole.' Rickards's discomfort, argued Watts, proved that a work of such gravity was not suited to a drawing room.[26]

Ellen Terry now wished for a divorce. Tom Taylor reported that Watts would not instigate proceedings but would comply.[27] In the event he was obliged to petition for adultery: on hearing of the birth of her children, he professed that he must regretfully take action to guard against 'claims that may be made upon me to support spurious children'. He offered to shoulder the expense of both sides, made the first payment for four hundred and forty pounds on 6 July, and petitioned for divorce on 2 September.[28] In between times he was struck by severe eczema and sent to Harrogate for a three-week water cure. Itching for work, he begged Virginia Somers: 'If you know any one who wants to have a portrait (half price) now's the time. Let him or her or it, come to Harrogate. I'm desperate!'[29]

Reginald Cholmondeley lent his early version of *Paolo and Francesca* and the Turkish dragoman, *Head of a Moor*, to the Wrexham Art Treasures Exhibition in North Wales.[30] Rickards's 'most complete' *Ariadne* and *Esau* were exhibited at the Royal Manchester Institution, where a prize that Watts had rejected the previous year in favour of younger artists, was awarded in his name for 'the most poetic design, the best picture regarded from the highest point of view', to Edward Gregory's *Sir Galahad*. That autumn, the *Academy* reviewed Rickards's collection of paintings by Watts as a rare, matchless experiment and called for a public display.[31]

Watts, now painting a self-portrait for Rickards, was captivated by a twenty-one-year-old art student, Dorothy (Dolly) Tennant. He had returned to Freshwater to paint portraits of her (fig. 106) and her younger sister, Eveleen. The squirrel in Dolly's hand symbolized her inquisitive, impetuous nature. Longing to prevent his young friend running off the rails, Watts turned to Jeanie, whose nephew Gerard Hughes he was teaching: 'Your acquaintance would be of real value to her. She is a girl with a great strong

106   *Dorothy Tennant*, 1876 (Tate, London).

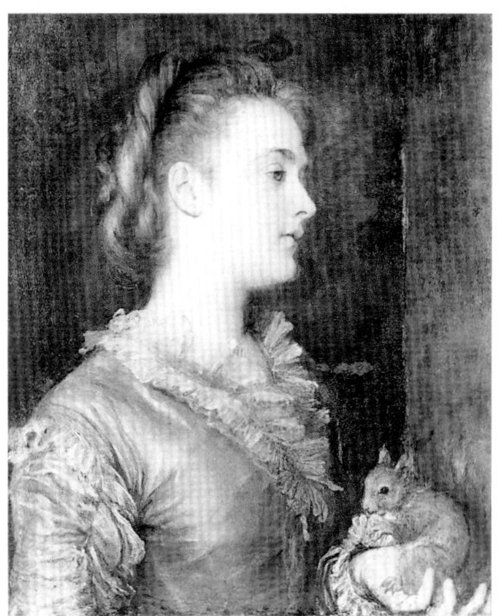

fine nature, very impulsive & ardent, a very child! with remarkable intellect & attainments, also with a singular amount of personal beauty.' As
Jeanie had never really recovered from her breakdown, he hoped calling on
her expertise might help her too.[32] He was also concerned for Blanche's
financial and moral future. Though he despised the destructive power of
money that 'can bring down the noblest spirits, & cripple the purest aspirations', he wished to give her a start in life and leave her secure. 'If I can
give her a good education & above all stimulate mental & moral qualities
that will shield her against disappointments & supply her with never fading
riches in her own mind & character', he wrote to Rickards, 'I shall not
think she will require fortune.'[33]

Striving to paint large symbolic painted poems, to 'give an impetus to art
of the highest aim' now seemed more taxing than painting from life. 'It is
an effort to grasp an intangible idea & fix it by material means, but I toil
away & only dread time the destroyer sweeping his scythe over my path
too soon.'[34] A bold triple nude composition, inspired by Long Mary's attenuated body – his ideal celebration of the female figure, seen from the front,
back and profile – was exhibited for the first time as *The Three Graces*, at
the Deschamps Galleries in New Bond Street, a venue owned by Paul
Durand-Ruel of Paris, and favoured by Whistler, Manet, Pissarro, and the
French Impressionists.[35]

Watts was preparing major exhibition pictures, which he knew would at
last define his artistic stature – 'it may be a higher or a lower one but at
any rate I shall no longer be able to feel that my best works have not been
made public'[36] – when he heard that he had been nominated to fresco a
stateroom in Manchester Town Hall. Designed by Alfred Waterhouse, the
opulent Gothic building rising on Albert Square, exemplified the city's pre-
eminence in the commercial world. Had Watts been asked a decade or so
earlier, he would have seized the opportunity. Now, he was uncertain
whether he could undertake it, partly because doctors were urging him not
to overwork, and, essentially, because his subject matter – broadly religious,
purely philosophical or poetic – might be unacceptable in Manchester, but
he wished to know more. Five rooms were proposed for fresco. Other
artists had been invited. Belgian muralists wished to provide murals using
water-glass; and Madox Brown proposed a scheme for all five rooms to be
carried out with Frederic Shields.[37]

Watts, keen to paint a picture or pictures for the Town Hall, proposed
through Rickards: *Time and Death*, *The Angel of Death*, *The Condemna-
tion of Adam and Eve*, *Cain* and *Adam and Eve in Paradise*. His overall
scheme would present the poetic, religious and philosophical view of 'the
peace & happiness that would result from the exercise of the highest human
aspirations, the degradation consequent upon disobedience to divine laws,
ending in appalling misery & murder'. With grand treatment, these subjects Watts thought fitted to the purpose exactly, whereas *Love and Death*
was more suited to a gallery, and he might sell it for four or five thousand
pounds, to an American. [38]

A long-term project in Manchester would pose serious problems. If he
could give an impulse to artistic feeling in England and create a school of
art, he would not refuse, but he had major painting and sculpture commitments.[39] He had to complete the three-figure Lothian memorial in
alabaster. The now elevated Duke of Westminster was pressing to see the

small model of *Hugh Lupus*, and Watts planned and start the full-size model of *Hugh Lupus* in the spring.[40] On Christmas Day 1876, Madox Brown informed Shields that the Committee of Decoration had decided that they, Watts, Leighton and Poynter would each paint a room. 'If this be true', wrote Madox Brown, 'you will attain your ambition of being one of the historic painters of the country, and in company with some of unquestionably the first of them.'[41]

That week the three Academicians were nominated to compete for the commission to decorate St Paul's. Stevens, who had prepared a Michelangelesque scheme had died. William Burges's neo-gothic scheme had been condemned.[42] Watts did not compete. As historical local scenes were required he declined to decorate Manchester Town Hall, and ultimately Madox Brown alone painted the twelve murals in the Great Hall.[43] Plans to build a canal linking the town with the sea, the future Manchester Ship Canal, impressed him as 'an undertaking worthy of a Great Town . . . of prodigious importance'.[44]

Watts made his last maintenance payment to Nelly's father in January. A decree *nisi* granted on 13 March 1877, citing her adultery, would be made absolute on 6 November. Within months she would marry Charles Kelly, a hearty actor with a penchant for the bottle.[45] Watts acknowledged his own failure. 'Such of us as live somewhat in the clouds are particularly liable to fall into errors.'[46] Much worse for him was the death of Jeanie on 24 March. 'A great deal is gone from me & it will be more difficult for me to carry out my objects in life missing the active sympathy that could so well comprehend the best side of them.' They had both fought against the tide to enhance people's lives and she had made material contribution to the reform of female education.[47] Watts had known and loved Jeanie with deep reciprocated affection and understanding for twenty-six years. She had been the love of his life. 'Alas, Alas. I have no words to express how I grieve.'

Jeanie's death came as he was putting final touches to exhibition pictures for the opening of the Grosvenor Gallery, as well as for the Academy summer show whose private view it had deposed as the start of the London Season. Those Academicians who were invited and unable to prevent Sir Coutts's glittering avant-garde project, clearly deemed it in their interest to take part; however, with the exception of Watts, they saved their best work for Burlington House. That they were there at all Rossetti considered contrary to the gallery's founding principle and, to the regret of critics and colleagues, he abstained; even so, in a generous letter to Hallé praising Watts and Millais, Rossetti predicted that Burne-Jones's pictures would guarantee the scheme's success.[48] So too thought Watts. 'Burne Jones will be very strong & when you have seen his works I do not think you will care much for mine, in fact I expect him to extinguish almost all the painters of the day . . . prepare yourself for being knocked off your legs,' he enthused to Rickards, warning him to buy no picture until he had been to the Grosvenor.[49]

An infusion of fresh air was breathed into the art world when Sir Coutts Lindsay's palazzo opened its Palladian doors. The most formidable rival exhibition the Academy had ever faced, the Grosvenor's spacious, stylish landmark display of modern nineteenth-century art was a sensation. Whistler arrived first at the private view on Monday 30 April, followed by

Watts in his sealskin coat, Browning, Henry James and twenty-two-year-old Oscar Wilde, making his controversial debut as an art critic. The next day 7,000 members of the public passed through the green marble vestibule to the turnstiles at the top of the broad flight of stairs, where, watched over by Whistler's *Arrangement in Grey and Black, No. 2, Portrait of Thomas Carlyle*, they paid a shilling to enter the first-floor galleries. The walls, divided by gilded cream Ionic pilasters from the old Italian Opera House in Paris, were hung with crimson silk damask from Lyons, whose colour – ideally suited to Watts's rich, low-toned paintings, though too strong for Burne-Jones's – was decried by Ruskin and relished by Wilde. Freed from the clashing patchwork squeeze of the Academy, pictures were harmoniously grouped by artist, at least six inches apart. Above a green velvet dado, there was clear crimson wall space up to blue concave panels that glistened with silver stars and the phases of the moon; above these were modern iron girders and glazing, through which light flooded into the galleries. Minton glass globes and Japanese china were displayed on gilded and marble tables, with exotic plants and sumptuous velvet couches, all arranged with exquisite taste, as if it were Sir Coutts's personal art temple.[50] Mary Fraser Tytler marvelled at the revolutionary arrangement that allowed the spectator to appreciate the significance of each painting.[51]

Watts's portraits of Lady Lindsay (fig. 106), Burne-Jones (fig. 85) and Madeline Wyndham (pl. xviii) characterized the Grosvenor Gallery and, Henry James noted, reaffirmed his position as 'the first portrait painter in England'.[52] He presented Blanche Lindsay (whom Sir Coutts had met and wooed at Little Holland House), with her violin, for the Grosvenor was also to be a musical venue; she is portrayed as a cultured, aesthetic woman metamorphosing from hostess to performer. Seen three-quarter-length from behind, turning round to face the élite viewer, Lady Lindsay begins to play, her left hand positioned well down the fingerboard, her right drawing the heel of the bow over a high string.[53] The opportunity to borrow back his portrait of Madeline Wyndham standing in her rich sunflower dress delighted Watts, for he had missed her company. The picture was their collaboration – her nature, his imagination – for as James noted in the *Galaxy*, it was a 'sumptuous' picture, large and generous in design. 'The lady looks as if she had thirty thousand a year'. But her dress would never date. 'For the art of combining the imagination and ideal element in portraiture with an extreme solidity, and separating great elegance from small elegance, Mr Watts is highly remarkable.'[54] Percy and Madeline Wyndham, a founder member of the Royal School of Art Needlework, had that year commissioned Philip Webb to design Clouds, their Wiltshire palace of art later described as 'the country house of the age'. Madeline's portrait, with its luscious aesthetic colours and textures, presented the Grosvenor as a forum for the artistic avant-garde.[55]

Hanging beside it, Watts's haunting metaphysical painted poem *Love and Death* (pl. xvii) was the first picture visitors saw on entering the main West Gallery. Here, as the young painter Graham Robertson observed, 'One wall was iridescent with the plumage of Burne-Jones's angels, one mysteriously blue with Whistler's nocturnes, one deeply glowing with the great figures of Watts, one softly radiant with the faint, flower-tinted harmonies of Albert Moore.'[56] Oscar Wilde, rusticated from Oxford after lingering in Greece and Rome and fired by Walter Pater's sensual doctrine invoking 'art for

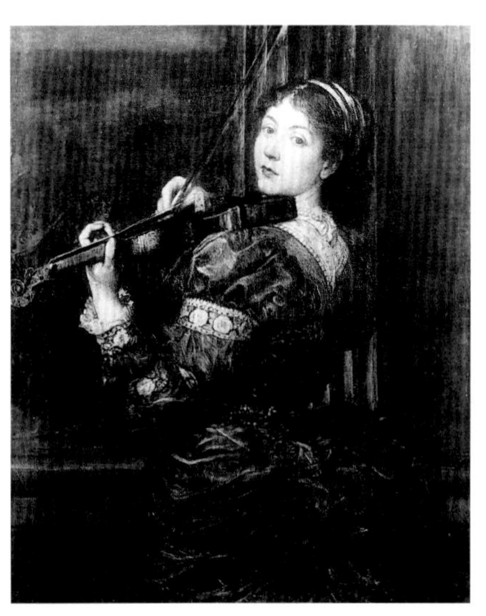

107   *Lady Lindsay*, 1877 (Tate, London).

art's sake',[57] recognized in Burne-Jones, Holman Hunt and Watts, the 'golden keys to the gate of the House Beautiful'. Whereas the first two were the finest English colourists after Turner, Watts's 'great originative and imaginative genius' reminded Wilde of Aeschylus and Michelangelo 'in the startling vividness of his conceptions'. Reporting for *Dublin University Magazine*, Wilde was struck the 'inevitable and mysterious power' of *Love and Death*: 'Except on the ceiling of the Sistine Chapel in Rome, there are perhaps few paintings to compare with this in intensity of strength and in marvel of conception. It is worthy to rank with Michael Angelo's "God dividing the Light from the Darkness." '[58] Pater, if not as gushing, concurred. James, too, usually uncomfortable with allegorical art, admired Death's 'air of majestic fatality.'

On the other side of *Love and Death* were Millais's portraits of the Duke of Westminster's daughters and, above them, '*Stitch Stitch Stitch!*', lent by Watts, who would doubtless have endorsed Wilde's impression of the 'terrible contrast . . . between this miserable pauper-seamstress and the three daughters of the richest duke in the world, which breaks through any artistic reveries by its awful vividness.'[59]

Undoubtedly, to most observers, the star of the show was Burne-Jones: having refused to exhibit elsewhere, he revealed eight pictures at the Grosvenor, notably, *The Beguiling of Merlin* (fig. 108), *The Days of Creation* and *The Mirror of Venus*. He and Watts were recognized as artists of supreme imaginative and poetic power; and Carr, reviewing the exhibition for the French periodical *L'Art*, with an etching from *Lady Lindsay* as the frontispiece, introduced them to the Continent as leaders of contemporary art. To Carr, Millais's carelessly modelled portraits paled beside Watts's richly coloured monumental compositions. 'There are few English painters of our time who have so fine an understanding of the principles of poetic design'. Less appealing, and always controversial, was Watts's abstract technique, its ambiguity intended to provoke the viewer's thought. But the strength of his conceptions, their grave simplicity, observed Carr, was rare in modern art.[60]

Neither Wilde nor James noted Gustave Moreau's visionary watercolour of Salomé dancing towards the severed head of John the Baptist, *L'Apparition*, which shared Watts's preoccupation with death, a theme that would become central to the French Symbolist painters. Like Watts, Moreau sought, through poetic, physical beauty, to reflect the timeless movements of the soul, the spirit, the heart and imagination.[61]

The picture that ruffled most feathers was *Nocturne in Black and Gold*, Whistler's atmospheric view of the explosion from a rocket's launch to its dying fall over Cremorne Gardens. Golden flecks of fire and impastoed whiffs of smoke provoked outrage. 'Certainly worth looking at for about as long as one looks at a real rocket . . . less than a quarter of a minute,' pronounced Wilde. Ruskin, condemning Sir Coutts as 'an amateur both in art and shop-keeping', fired a brutal, libellous rocket at Whistler in *Fors Clavigera*, 'I have seen, and heard, much of cockney impudence before now; but never expected to hear a coxcomb ask two hundred guineas for flinging a pot of paint in the public's face.'[62] Such denunciation by the era's most influential critic would lead Whistler – since banished by Leyland for stunningly excessive decoration in the shipowner's dining-room, a *Harmony in Blue and Gold: The Peacock Room*[63] – to sue, not only to restore his rep-

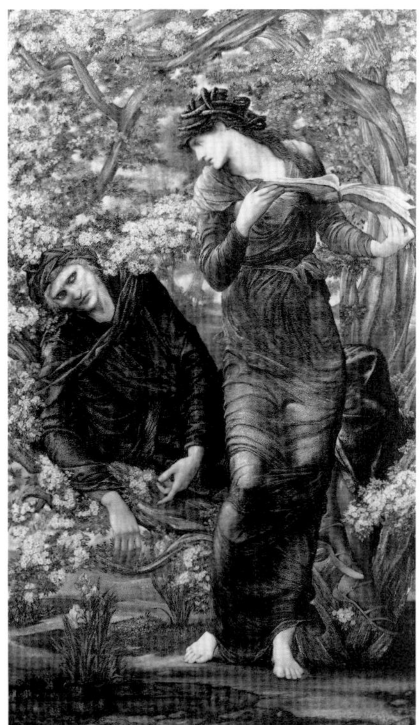

108   Edward Coley Burne-Jones, *The Beguiling of Merlin*, 1873–74 (National Museums & Galleries on Merseyside: Lady Lever Art Gallery).

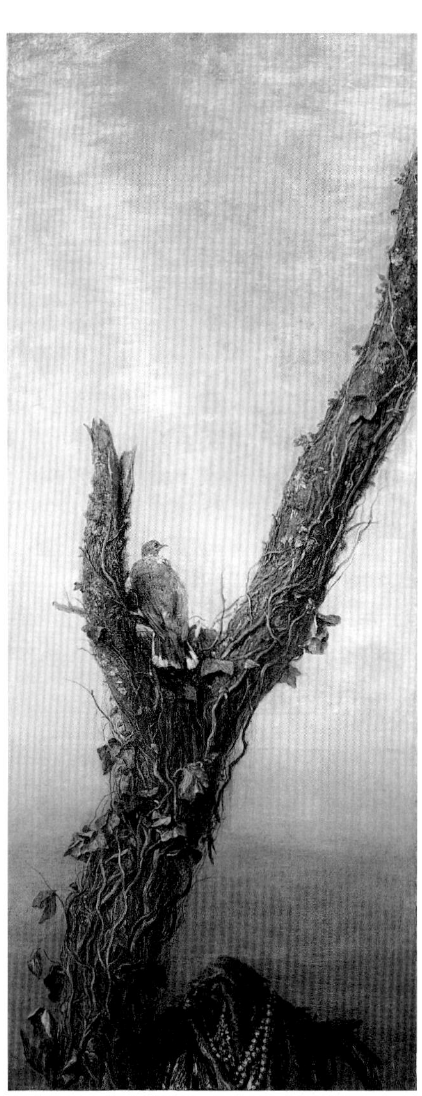

109   *The Dove Which Returned Not Again*, 1877 (private collection, courtesy of Christie's).

utation and value of his pictures, but for the sake and essence of art. Ruskin, anticipating court proceedings as an opportunity to air his views to a wider public, declared rashly that it was 'mere nuts and nectar to me'.[64]

At the Royal Academy summer exhibition, which opened six days after the Grosvenor, the key work was Leighton's life-size bronze *Athlete Strangling a Python* (later known as *An Athlete Wrestling with a Python*). Watts treasured an early sketch of the athlete. Modelled from Colarossi, the statue of a youth straining every muscle to fend off the reptile, was purchased for the nation, and would create an enormous impact throughout the century as an icon of 'The New Sculpture' movement. Aimé-Jules Dalou, a pivotal figure in the movement, who had fled from the Paris Commune and was now teaching at the National Art-Training School in South Kensington, had encouraged Leighton to execute the figure full-size.[65] Meanwhile, at the Paris Salon, a statue of a naked youth so lifelike that the anonymous sculptor was accused of casting it directly from the model, was arousing a sensation. *The Age of Bronze* was Auguste Rodin's first major work.

Watts had submitted profiles of his comely young friend Dorothy Tennant and of Earl Cowper, the Lord Lieutenant of Ireland and a six-foot-high protest against the evils of the day. The cumulative thought and the moral and artistic effects of many years that he had invested in *The Dove Which Returned Not Again* (fig. 109), set the high value he wished to receive from the picture – at least a thousand guineas – in order to underwrite national projects. Painted from nature at the Isle of Wight, it was an audacious vertical development of the calm horizontal *Return of the Dove*. The cloudless background, low horizon and subsiding floods suggest nature readjusting to a brighter future; the storm-damaged upper branch of a tree, rising diagonally in sharp focus across the foreground is disturbing. Its ivy stems have been loosened; the few remaining leaves are dead; an animated dove perches in its fork and on a broken stump below are remains of jewels and luscious drapery, symbols of the greed the floods were sent to destroy, and to the artist, a growing modern problem.[66]

That month, Wagner was conducting excerpts from his recently completed *Ring* cycle at the Royal Albert Hall. Despite warnings in the press and by Joachim about the maestro's anti-semitism, he received a 'brilliant reception'. Mary Gladstone was fascinated to watch him lead, 'quite motionless at times and then starting up in frantic excitement'. The Wagners were staying in Bayswater, as guests of Edward Dannreuther, whose wife, Ionides's daughter, Chariclea, had twice sat to Watts. Her sister, Aglaia Coronio, who had heard the entire *Ring* cycle at Wagner's new Festival Theatre in Bayreuth, asked to bring the composer's wife to Little Holland House. Cosima Wagner's response to the portrait of Joachim, who had signed a manifesto against her husband's anti-semitism, was illuminating: 'There hangs a quite amazing picture of Joachim; I can read the whole biography of this thoroughly bad person in this picture; that is not what the painter intended, but it is the very thing which reveals his talent – that he has depicted the truth without realizing it! Indeed, by trying to express something splendid.'[67]

Exactly! The artist, as much as expressing his perception of the inner spirit, the concentrated energy and resonance of the violinist, wished not just to please the eye, or follow the latest aesthetic fad 'art for art's sake', but to stimulate the viewer's imagination, which was why his equestrian statue of *Hugh Lupus* (fig. 129) could never have been an exact soldierly portrait. The Duke of Westminster sent a thumbnail sketch of the rider's legs and hindquarters of Verrocchio's monument to Bartolomeo Colleoni in Venice, marked 'toe in stirrup'. Colleoni's toes grip the stirrup as he almost stands in his saddle. Watts developed the powerful musculature and pose of the horse and the soldier's defiant glare, seating the jowelly *Hugh Lupus* well back on his charger, casting off a falcon – the *Gros Veneur* used to hawk on his Welsh campaigns – legs bent at the knee, the feet not as outstretched as he would have liked in the style of the Elgin Marbles.[68] Watts had requested a Percheron stallion to model for the statue. One May morning, Mrs Barrington was working on his designs in the iron studio when she saw through the trees 'a gorgeous white steed' led into the garden by the duke's groom. Grandly rounded and 'as white as the horse in Watts's *Sir Galahad* – with rippling, shining mane and tail', the Percheron was dressed in purple silk livery.[69]

Watts modelled the life-size equestrian statue of *Hugh Lupus* in *gesso grosso*, under the guidance of a Florentine sculptor named Fabrucci.[70] The quick-drying medieval technique was less harmful to his worsening health than damp clay, which needed constant attention in order to not to lose precision, whereas gesso – tow soaked in a mixture of size and plaster of Paris, applied in layers with the fingertips – hardened and could be cut or chiselled into form.[71] According to Emilie Barrington (not yet a neighbour, but assisting on Mondays and Thursdays), Watts began by making a large wooden framework of part of the horse, on to which he nailed sheets of brown paper and drew lines in charcoal to indicate the action he planned to express. Whether the gesso was applied to wood or – as in the later *Physical Energy* – to metal, is unclear, but both models were worked on raised pivot-table trolleys that ran on rails into the garden, where he experimented with the dry plaster, carving its variegated texture to reflect light.[72] The overriding sense of suppressed power in *Hugh Lupus* was the very quality the Prince of Wales, still thwarted of serious duty and purpose, channelled into his celebrated social whirl.

Under pressure from the treasurer of the Middle Temple, Watts invited the prince for 'one more sitting' at Little Holland House on 30 July.[73] He was courting Lillie Langtry, the wild twenty-three-year-old Phidean beauty who knocked artists, poets and aristocrats off their feet the moment they saw her. A fresh-faced goddess launched into society in the opening week of the Grosvenor, she had arrived from Jersey, with little money, a dull husband and in search of excitement. She wore no stays and dressed in simple black mourning for her brother; her hair style, unadorned and twisted into a loose knot at the nape of her neck, set a new fashion. 'All male London is going wild about the Beautiful Lady who has come to us from the Channel Islands', *Vanity Fair* declared. 'It is though some newer and more perfect creature had risen, like Aphrodite, from the sea.' Unable to resist breaking her promise to Poynter to sit to no other artist until he had finished painting her as Homer's princess Nausicaa for the Earl of Wharncliffe, and also her portrait, she was posing for Millais too. Watts, said to have met her already, was still too busy to paint the royal mistress.[74] He was charmed by the prince, who had the royal gift of appearing to listen with keen interest and desire to learn (according to his equerry Sir Frederick Ponsonby, this was quite genuine, for he would make no effort when he was bored). Though neither pompous, nor tall, his overpowering physical personality could terrify ambassadors, admirals and ministers. But in Watts's drawing of the head alone, the inner mind becomes not only apparent but dominant.[75] The *Athenaeum*'s October report that he had 'very nearly completed the colossal statue' and his 'striking likeness' of the prince was very premature.[76]

The task of infusing *Hugh Lupus* with 'human will bridling in brute force' seemed overwhelming. 'Oh! You will find out I am nothing! I have no genius!' he sighed to Mrs Barrington one evening, as they stood on the lawn outside the sculpture studio. 'One thing alone I possess, and I never remember the time I was without it – an aim towards the highest, the best, and a burning desire to reach it,'[77] a passion both desolate and exhilarating. Experimenting on the brown paper, he discovered the suggestivity of a broad curve and with great excitement summoned Mrs Barrington to discuss his theory that a good line in art should be composed from a series of flattened curves. As part of a large circle, this suggests form that extends beyond the design and stimulates the viewer 'with a sense of spring and size'; whereas a 'bad' line, tightly curved, from a small circle within the visible limit of the design, constricts both form and mind. To prove that the Greeks adopted the principle to convey the grandeur of thought and nature, he demonstrated it on his cast of *Theseus* in the iron studio porch and showed Hamo Thornycroft how it applied to the growth of vegetation and onward movement. The suggestive broad curve Watts had used in his seminal imaginative work *Time and Oblivion* and painted on the walls of old Little Holland House, now served him as a conscious aid. As Emilie Barrington observed 'Whatever suggested growth in the imagination was to Watts the keynote.'[78]

He pushed himself to the limit, refusing to compromise his rigorous dawn-to-dusk work routine. 'My life cannot possibly be long enough to enable me to do half the things I have set my heart upon doing,' he wrote to Virginia Somers. 'It makes me miserable to think of going out of the world without having really done anything for it, really achieved something.' These words echo not so much the ghost of his father as the sense of "energy suppressed", the ideas surging in his mind.[79] Blanche, taking violin lessons every day, was impressed that he played by ear. Mrs Barrington accompanied them. Almost leech-like in her attachment to genius – too demonstrative, thought Blanche – she was hungry to fill the intellectual chasm left by the death of Bagehot.[80]

In the Christmas vacation, Benjamin Jowett, the Master of Balliol College, Oxford, since 1870, began to sit for his portrait at Freshwater, taking the opportunity to stay with the Tennysons. This was a commission by the college, Jowett having declined Watts's earlier invitation to sit for the nation: 'I certainly doubt whether your time would not be better spent in great original paintings than on my portrait.' His bloated facial characteristics would present a problem.[81] Nor were the features of the historian and political philosopher W. E. H. Lecky any easier. Both men enjoyed sitting, for the opportunity to converse with Watts. Lecky sat for the national collection in early 1878. The first two volumes of his *History of England in the Eighteenth Century* were about to be published; and he was intrigued by Watts's observation, informed by studying historical portraits, that facial bones during the period from the Restoration to the end of the eighteenth century were virtually concealed, whereas modern men of note had the prominent bone structure more akin to the Elizabethan era.[82]

Thoby Prinsep died on 11 February. His thirty-year companionship meant much to Watts. Life at The Briary would never seem the same again. Sara, in her widow's cap, bore her grief nobly. The artist overcame bronchitis and threw himself into exhibition work, and on 26 March Julia Duckworth, the soulful beauty who had helped nurse her uncle Thoby, married Leslie Stephen (fig. 110), the philosopher and editor of *Cornhill Magazine*, and widower of Minny Thackeray[83]. A single two-hour sitting was sufficient for Watts to capture the troubled strands of Stephen's nature. To the critic Harry Quilter, his thin face, with long ginger hair and beard and piercing blue eyes, looked 'critical yet deprecating, sarcastic and mournful, fastidious, thoughtful, and Bohemian: not one who ranks either himself or others very high, or expects much from a life that appears to him full of errors of taste, weaknesses of intellect, and futilities of aim'.[84]

Sara decided to move to Brighton. A shorter journey for Val and Signor, it offered good educational facilities for Blanche. Her father took her on house-hunting expeditions. Their spring evenings were filled with musical soirées hosted by Leighton and by Madeline Wyndham; there was also a private concert at the Grosvenor Gallery, where Piatti played the cello unaccompanied, and Joachim and his wife performed at Little Holland House. Blanche accompanied Signor to both the Academy and Grosvenor private views.[85]

Much to Emilie Barrington's distress, Watts reworked *Ophelia* for the Grosvenor (fig. 111). One evening he took it from a pile of old canvases and held a candle over the paint surface. Ellen Terry's teenage recreation of Shakespeare's deranged drowning maiden painted with tender pathos by her husband was transformed into a macabre idealization. Eustace Smith lent his large *Sir Galahad*. In contrast, Watts sent the semi-nude *Mischief* trapping her male pursuer – Humanity – in a bramble thicket; and *Time and Death*, still so unfinished that he wished to withdraw it, presented a dynamic Wattsian challenge as visitors entered the West Gallery and excited more than a little controversy.[86]

Symbolizing 'Time must pass, and Death strike down, before justice can be done to human worth or achievement', the eight-foot canvas that had stirred the imagination of eleven-year-old Laura, was too esoteric for most visitors and provoked wide critical response, from a 'sea-sick' riddle, to 'the loftiest abstraction'. Irritated by ill-informed criticism, Watts respected *The Spectator* reviewer, who, having disliked the picture at first glance, returned to re-examine it: 'The great size of the figures, the almost passionate strength of colour, the peculiar hue of Time's body, and the ghastly face and ashen robes of Death, – all these strike one at first sight so vividly, that the impression produced is rather a distressing than a pleasing one.' After four or five visits, seeing the picture in varying lights, the reviewer judged *Time and Death* 'the most marvellous and beautiful picture of the year'.[87]

Watts acknowledged that exhibiting artists were public property and should not be offended by careful criticism. Nevertheless, he thought it might be 'amusing & instructive to collect in a publication all the different criticisms of the year with a careful summing up & judgment upon them', and his cuttings collection intensified from 1878.[88] He will have rejoiced

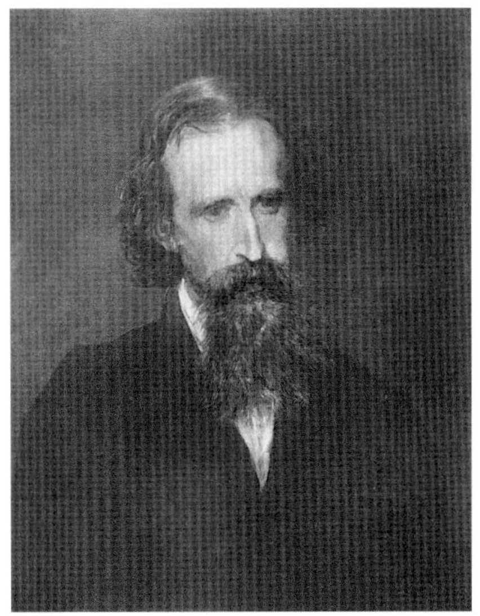

110  *Leslie Stephen*, 1878 (private collection; photo: Frederic Hollyer).

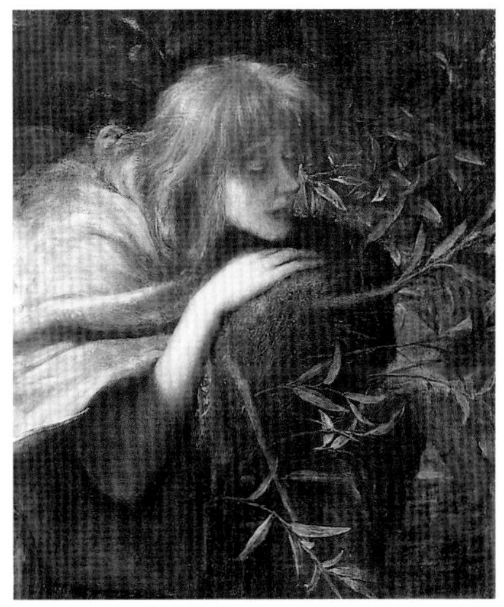

111  *Ophelia*, *c*.1863–78 (Watts Gallery).

at critical acclaim for Louisa, Marchionness of Waterford who, with Charlotte Wylie, was among the new female exhibitors in Bond Street.

Even at Burlington House, where he showed five portraits, an imaginative Spenserian picture, *Britomart and her Nurse*, attracted positive interest.[89] Poynter's contemplative portrait of the royal mistress reclining in a golden gown, *Mrs Langtry*, was trounced by the natural bloom of Millais's *Jersey Lily* standing in her black dress – the picture had to be roped off from the crowds.[90] For her presentation at Court that May, Lillie Langtry attached three of the largest ostrich plumes she could find to her headdress. One was fitted to her poke bonnet when she arrived to pose for Watts. Appalled at the suffering of the bird, 'he ruthlessly tore off the opulent ostrich feather which I regarded at that time as the glory of my head gear', Langtry recalled.[91] In retrospect, she was glad, for without the aesthetic accessory her portrait appeared timeless (fig. 112): 'I realized that he was quite right in his somewhat arbitrary ideas, for the portrait was not dated, and might have been painted yesterday or tomorrow, a quality which – Watts thought – works of all great artists should possess.' This was the first recorded step in his campaign against the cruel fashion for feathers. That he painted her as *The Dean's Daughter* in black suggests that sittings began soon after her arrival in London. Did he know that her father, the Dean of Jersey, was a philanderer? Considering the transient superficiality of her own lifestyle, what surely impressed her was that he had made her look pure and noble.[92]

Enchanted by the bloom of her complexion he made the background strong green to suggest leaves behind the roses of her skin.[93] He found Lillie Langtry's company so diverting that, she recalled, he would sometimes ignore the sitting, ring for tea and fascinate her with lectures on art. He adored colour, she wrote. How drab the London streets were without it. She sat to him for hours between social engagements over the next two years, absorbing the mysteries and splendours of the Venetian school. Later visiting the art galleries of Europe, Lillie realized 'what a debt I owed him'. Watching him in his flowing gown and skullcap, she could not resist pointing out his resemblance to Titian. He doubted her sincerity, but played along with her charm and, touched by his interest in 'the smallest details of my life', she delighted in his pleasure. 'How simple are the great!' Most artists she treated as close friends, but Signor was to her a master.[94]

Burne-Jones's growing popularity pleased, but unnerved Watts. 'It is Fairy land, & Fairy land still retains its charm', he wrote to Earl Wharncliff. People wanted instant amusement, and few, he thought, would care for his own work.[95] At the Exposition Universelle, which opened in Paris on 1 May, Millais, Watts and Leighton were seen as poet-painters; Burne-Jones's sole entry *The Beguiling of Merlin,* was acclaimed 'the most stunning picture which has come from London'. Watts exhibited ten: portraits of the Duke of Cleveland, Madeline Wyndham, Lord Lawrence, Browning, Calderon and Joachim – the marble bust of *Clytie, Love and Death* (now glazed), *Esau* and the nude Graces, lent by Louis Huth and renamed for Paris, *Pallas, Juno and Venus*, the latter, highlighted as a key example of Wattsian form, elevated sentiment and poetry. His portraits and the conception – if not the technique – of his imaginative subjects proved his 'très grande' reputation, earned Watts a gold medal and the decoration of 'Chevalier' of the Légion d'honneur.'[96]

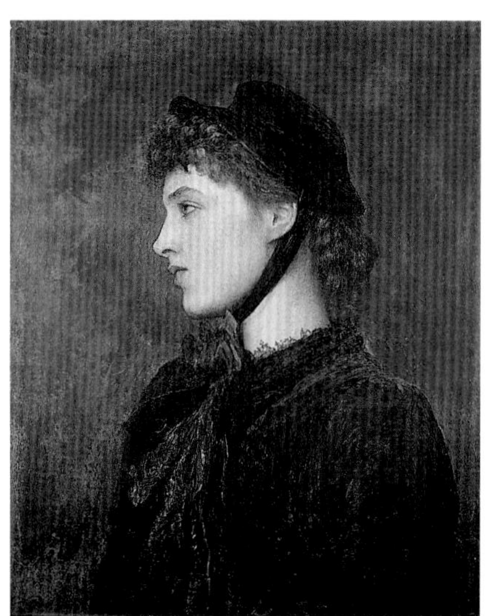

112    *The Dean's Daughter* (Lillie Langtry), 1878–80 (Watts Gallery).

During the London Season, Watts took Blanche riding in Rotten Row and to see the gymnasts at the Westminster Aquarium, which was fun for her and an opportunity for him to study the energy and movement of the human form, minimally clad.[97] Rides with Blanche were delayed by Gladstone's portrait sittings. The two men were engrossed in conversation; but to meet the college deadline, for the picture to be finished, framed and hung by 24 June, Watts had to request, 'Not a word to be spoken from the urgency of the sitting till the end!!'[98]

Such was the demand to send pictures to exhibitions at the Manchester Royal Institution and the Walker Art Gallery in Liverpool that he delegated Smith, his framer, to arrange their transfer from the Grosvenor and Burlington House.[99] At the Walker, where his noble figures Time and Death were derided as 'vulgar', 'disgusting' and 'fat monster', Watts was more interested in the controversy over Lawrence Alma-Tadema's *The Sculptor's Model*. A tall realistic nude on the Pygmalion theme, painted as instruction for John Collier, its full-frontal lack of poetic idealization caused offence. While Watts believed 'the human form divine' should never be offensive if treated with respect, he would have endorsed the Bishop of Carlisle's view that 'to exhibit a life-sized, almost photographic representation of a beautiful naked woman strikes my inartistic mind as somewhat, if not very mischievous'.[100] Nudged by Burne-Jones, he rode over to Hampstead to advise Henry Holiday on his first attempt at sculpture, a life-size reclining nude *Sleep*. Wilhelmina Stirling recalled that a policeman, seeing it in the bay window, rang the bell to warn the Holidays, 'There is a lady fainted in your dining-room and she is looking mortal bad.'[101]

Watts liked to move from one subject to another. To Burne-Jones's joy, he undertook a portrait of his daughter Margaret;[102] he had painted a ten-foot study of *Joan of Arc* from armour borrowed from Sir Coutts;[103] and he was bringing earlier pictures to completion; the warmer months Watts chiefly devoted to sculpture. Working outside on *Hugh Lupus* he got sunstroke, but struggled on, determined to achieve strength from every angle. He was also carving the marble *Clytie*, begun by Nelson; as he broke up the surface into facets to produce a more atmospheric effect and palpitating quality of surface, Emilie Barrington observed his instinctive sensibility for form, his subtle conception of planes and curves.[104] Rickards received his *Clytie* in early September, and asked for a companion bust. Watts proposed *Daphne* (fig. 113) – now under way in Nelson's studio – her head drooping over enveloping laurels, in contrast to the yearning *Clytie*. He had a new idea for a didactic public monument, *Nemesis*, a universal theme applicable to individuals and national issues; but his designs for a huge ivory and bronze statue were never heard of again. If he planned to base the statue on the *Nemesis* figure in *Time and Death*, it would have been astonishingly powerful.[105]

The scientist Thomas Huxley agreed to be painted for the national collection. Sir Francis Grant had died, in November, and Watts notified the council of the Royal Academy that he planned to paint a portrait of their new president, Sir Frederic Leighton.[106] Burne-Jones had been given the awkward task of defending Ruskin in court against Whistler at the end of the month. The case, pitting artist friends against each other, aroused a flurry of press excitement and concluded with the famous token compensation – a farthing for the insulted artist. Watts himself was often as guilty

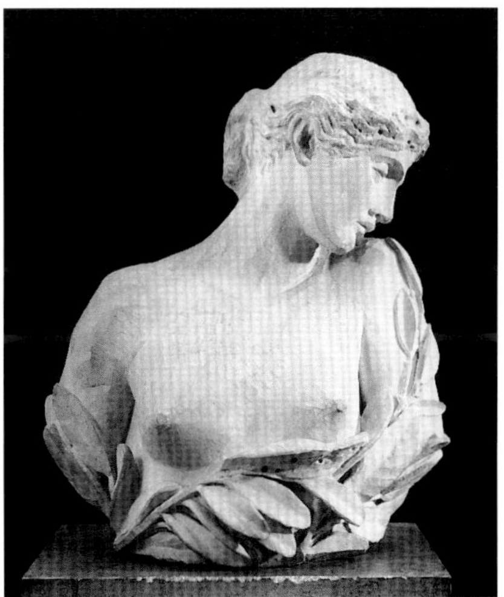

113 *Daphne* (unfinished), 1878–82 (Tate, London).

of imperfect finish – not least in his dramatic *Design for a Picture 'When Poverty Knocks at the Door, Love Flies Out of the Window'* on show at the Dudley.[107] The idea of atmospheric effect (praised by Albert Moore, testifying for Whistler), would preoccupy him increasingly in his own art.[108]

The first article devoted to Watts was one of a series, 'Our Living Artists', in the *Magazine of Art*. Wilfrid Meynell drew attention to his glowing technique, which, like Titian's blue, 'comes up *through* . . . every particle appears subtly and slightly different, and you might cut a piece from it, as from a Titian, and wear it for a jewel.'[109] To Meynell, Watts's figures, healthier than those of Burne-Jones, were strengthened by 'manliness'.[110] Facing racist criticism of the colour chosen for his universal subjects, Watts revealed his modern inclusive intent; he painted Time brown to suggest an unclothed human form exposed to the sun, rather than a clothed body protected from the elements. Even if the juxtaposition with whiter bodies appeared odd, his pictures might travel to places in greater harmony with their broad character: 'I am a painter of ideas & not realities & do not consider myself called upon to reproduce a closer resemblance to ordinary reality than is necessary for my subject, or my object in painting for all times & for all climates.'[111]

He spent the winter at Sara Prinsep's new home, 24 Lewes Crescent in Brighton. As his studio there was not large enough for ideal canvases, he had brought large platinotype prints of paintings in progress, taken by the specialist art photographer Frederic Hollyer, and worked over these in Chinese white and Indian ink in preparation for his return.[112] Resuming portraiture, because studying personal characteristics prevented mannerism, Watts invited commissions for five hundred guineas a head, for a week to ten days' sittings. Through Madeline Wyndham he agreed to paint Sir Coutts's cousin Colonel Charles Lindsay and his daughter Violet, from whom he planned to made a study for *The Angel of Death*.[113] In one sitting he sketched a fiery head of Sir Richard Burton, whose insight as the first Englishman to enter Mecca, to explore Somaliland and the sources of the Nile ought to have fascinated him, but, apparently, he could not stand the man. Burton was brilliant, blunt, cruel to his horses, and doubtless as insistent as Carlyle about his appearance – he had charged Leighton not to make him too ugly and had challenged a fellow Oxford undergraduate to a duel for criticizing his moustache. The explorer set off for the Gold Coast. Watts refused to finish his portrait, ignoring a friend's warning, 'Burton might very likely murder you for this.'[114] He now recorded Ellen Terry's *rite-de-passage* as a modern naturalistic Ophelia in Henry Irving's first production as actor-manager, which opened at the Lyceum on 30 December: in his drawing of her head, from a Window and Grove photograph, intensified her expression, the deep eyelids, glassy eyes, the waves of her fringe, her fine nose and closed lips.

In the new year, he took Blanche to the Academy for Val's long-awaited election as an associate;[115] and Evelyn Pickering – Mary Fraser Tytler's earlier contemporary at the Slade – was brought by Emilie Barrington to Little Holland House for advice on a portrait.[116] News came of the death in Ceylon of Julia Cameron on Sunday, 26 January 1879, after a short illness. A maddening, devoted friend and inspired colleague to Watts, she had been like a mother to Blanche, whose sad, telling diary entry recorded that neither she nor Signor felt the love of God. Deep religious faith – his of a wider nature than her devout Christianity – infused the work of Cameron and her 'divine' artist. Inspired by Signor, as determined and controversial, she too had achieved international status. She had immortalized as never before the famous men and fair women of her day in portraits and idealized, symbolic poses; and her mentor, respected in France as an artist of rare merit, whose imperfections even attracted interest, was seen at home as 'the old master in the modern man'.[117]

# 12   Polemicist

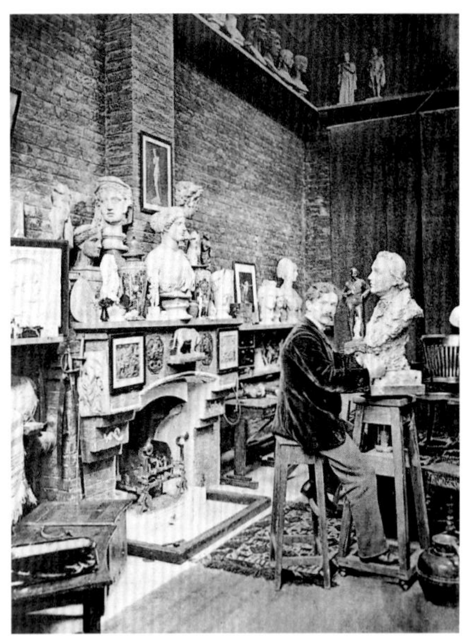

114   Hamo Thornycroft in his studio, 1884. A cast of the Oxford bust stands in the centre of his mantelpiece (photo: J. P. Mayall).

VISITORS WERE AWED BY THE ATMOSPHERE of noble simplicity at Little Holland House, by Watts's solitary life and his exalted thoughts on any subject. Although he lived simply, he was cared for like a fine-tuned race-horse to ensure that he was in the best physical condition to direct the high impulses that guided his art. He worked almost every daylight hour; on occasion he would call at Thornycroft's studio (fig. 114) to give advice – the sculptor used to test his sculpture against a prized cast of the Oxford bust on his mantelpiece.[1] In the evenings Watts relaxed, venturing out only to musical events. That he had been close to death at times heightened his desire to fulfil his aims. Attacks of ill-health were minimized through exercise and a sugar-free diet with milk or barley water, and his care rested in the well-trained hands of Emma, of his valet, Alfred, and his physician, Dr Thomas Bond, whose baby daughter had modelled for *The Spirit of Christianity*. Leading as healthy a life as possible, he would walk to Nelson's Hammersmith studio to work on *Daphne*, and his love of a good gallop earned him the Wyndham family nickname 'Jockey Watts'.[2]

His painting of Lady Godiva (fig. 115), a political interpretation of her noble ordeal, was painted as a protest against images of her as a mere sex symbol, the *Athenaeum* revealed in January 1879. 'All the feelings of womanhood surge up in her mind' as she collapses into the arms of the people of Coventry after her naked ride through the streets to compel her husband, the Earl of Mercia, to reduce taxes. Grateful residents are swathing her in white and gold drapes, while her horse nuzzles a conscientious attendant. Watts determined not only to stimulate, but to provoke his apathetic contemporaries to a higher level of thought.[3]

Sixteen-year-old Mary Wyndham spotted *The Return of Lady Godiva* in March, when her mother brought her to the studio. Regretting the Wyndhams' move to Wilbury House, near Salisbury, Watts wrote to Madeline with characteristic exaggeration, 'I have so few pleasures that I can ill afford to lose the best of all, the friendship of some few people.' He was disconcerted that, while commissioning new work from Burne-Jones, she was buying only platinotypes from his own pictures.[4] At the Grosvenor, the two artists were respected as 'kindred genius'. Burne-Jones was exhibiting the *Pygmalion* series and *The Annunciation*, for which Julia Stephen modelled 'in all the grave beauty of early pregnancy;[5] and his mystical, more mannered style was likened to the acting of Henry Irving.[6] Among Watts's eight pictures was a study of *Enid and Geraint*, presumably painted as a tribute to Julia Cameron (who had photographed the Arthurian scene for her 1874 publication of Tennyson's *Idylls*), and a refreshing, unselfconscious portrait of a child, *Dorothy*, which drew comparison with old masters. Her pale hair tumbles over her shoulders, as she stands in a claret gown, her hands are clasped together, and her frank brown eyes gaze at the viewer: 'It is as vigorous and free . . . almost as true as Leonardo, and as fresh as Rembrandt's exquisite young head of a child of the house of Orange.[7]

More controversial were the visionary final *Paolo and Francesca* (pl. xv) and full-length *Orpheus and Eurydice*, which was honoured with an etching in *L'Art*. Both subjects combine abstract ideas of love, tenderness and suffering with death. Orpheus, muscular and impassioned, runs forward and turns to clasp the pallid, wilting body of Eurydice. Her nude figure was seen as 'one of the artist's greatest achievements in the way of abstract design'.[8] Virginia Somers as Francesca cradles Paolo in a calm embrace, the contrast with her *mouvementé* drapery in the hurricane of the Inferno suggesting 'a passion too strong for death.' As one critic observed, 'we feel the change that death has wrought, a change that gives tranquillity alike to passion and to pain, and . . . the solace of reunion.'[9] Society eyebrows must have twitched at the tempestuous countess as Dante's guilty lover, cradling the semi-nude Paolo – an idealized projection of the artist's younger self.

Mary Gladstone, who admired his self-portrait of the 1860s, lent by Bowman., hated his new portrait of her father as 'a weak, peevish old man', now at the Grosvenor.[10] As Watts was determined to present 'the man, body, soul and spirit', the statesman agreed to further sittings for another version, graciously promising that 'you shall not be distracted by my yielding to the temptations which the chance of a talk with you always offers'.[11]

Bagehot had pointed out how Gladstone 'longs to pour forth his own belief; he cannot rest till he has contradicted every one else'. Like Watts, he had a playful streak that contrasted with intense gravity and 'feels the minds of his hearers as the driver the mouths of his horses'.[12] Though Mary Gladstone noted improvements in the portrait, Watts relinquished the commission and when he wrote to praise William Richmond's subsequent portrait, Dean Liddell relayed Gladstone's apologies: 'He adds slyly, that it was you who inveigled him into the conversations which caused so much distraction to you. To this no doubt you will plead guilty.'[13] The portrait itself was proof, for it was seen to depict the statesman's 'careworn look often seen in the House, but which vanishes when he speaks' – he was listening and the artist, talking.[14]

Millais's portrait of Gladstone was on show at the Royal Academy. Watts's six included portraits of the late architect F. P. Cockerell and of Sir William Armstrong, who invented the great breech-loading gun, adopted the following year as the standard for all British ordnance.[15] Still wishing to record Benjamin Disraeli, Earl of Beaconsfield, for the nation, he approached the prime minister at the Academy dinner, only to receive a rebuff. 'He supposed I did not care about painting him at the time he was willing to sit, he had given up the idea & was now too old,' Watts wrote to Lady Marion Alford, urging her to persuade him, but his time was given to Millais's fine three-quarter-length portrait.[16]

His determination never to swerve from his artistic vision enabled him to handle the impulsive women who wished to nurture his genius. He

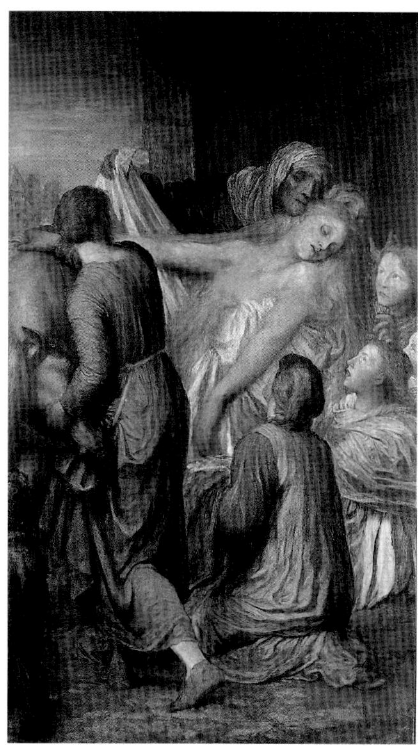

115    *The Return of Lady Godiva*, 1879–90 (Watts Gallery).

enjoyed their vitality, affection and their response to his ideas – when they were too gushing, he could retreat to his studio – and he valued their organizational skills. When the Barringtons moved into 'Melbury House' next door on 24 May, joined later by Emilie's sister Eliza, Bagehot's wealthy widow, who financed the lease,[17] he made sure that visits would not encroach on his time for receiving clients and friends. The Barringtons would be welcome between one and three o'clock or from six to eight in the evening. Emilie Barrington chose to introduce friends, amongst them the architect Halsey Riccardo, between two and three, and returned in the evening at six, followed by her husband, Russell.

In the winter, Watts would be reading in his claret velvet armchair, when Alfred announced Mrs Barrington's arrival. She found the artist secretive; the only emotion he expressed to her was artistic excitement.[18] 'Well, what's the news?' he would ask, rubbing his eyes, as he laid down his book and spectacles. He would light a candle and lead her up five steps to the double doors of the studio, through the dark passage with a window overlooking the huge, ghostly equestrian statue in the sculpture studio. A second door led into the large painting studio, lit at night by just one light and dying embers in the grate. Eager for criticism, he would point the candle to the latest detail on a canvas – he used to call his painted poems 'anthems' – Emilie Barrington was struck by the contrast of his frail hand against his monumental work.[19] One evening, seated by the fireside, arranging his long grey coat into sculptural folds, he told her he felt like 'a coarse piece of stuff' through which a golden thread ran, and he longed for that golden thread to guide his life. Until that golden thread became his, he would channel his ideas through his vigorous, articulate assistant. 'Sympathy was the leaf-mould for many of Watts's ideas', Emilie Barrington observed. 'By talking his ideas out to me in definite language he would clench thoughts that were vaguely floating in his brain, and reduce them to the state that enabled him to make use of them.[20] His visionary aiming for the highest and utmost effort to reach it, she noted, was the keynote to his art.[21]

Determined to learn from Watts, to ease his life – as she had done for her distinguished father – Emilie Barrington pushed him to achieve his artistic aims. She brought friends to see his work and introduced them to his eminent colleagues, Leighton, Burne-Jones and the craftsman Walter Crane. Intimacy with Watts brought status for herself. He even gave her the old Little Holland House frescoes, because, stacked in crates, they took up too much space in his studios and garden.[22]

He sent the portrait of Browning to the Munich International Exhibition, which opened on 4 July 1879.[23] With a six-month respite from the large equestrian model of *Hugh Lupus*, at Grosvenor House for the duke's approval,[24] but no let up in work, the artist had a very jolly August. Lillie Langtry came to sit at Little Holland House. She was also posing now as Summer, dressed in purple and gold with a basket of roses in her arms. Proud to sit for the 'gentle-mannered artist, whom I shall always regard as the greatest poetical painter of his time, she declared in her exuberant memoirs that she gave 'forty sittings' for *Summer*.[25]

Watts despatched the small version of *Love and Death* to Rickards at the end of the month. His expression 'one of the very best things I have done' – reflecting significant subject matter, hard work and keenness to please – was repeated so often that it has no value today. The bust of

*Daphne*, about to be cast in bronze, suffered damage in the casting.[26] His heroic, if less appealing, statue of *Aurora* symbolizing 'the awakening & unveiling of all that is great in resolve & perfect in life' was well advanced. The full-length female nude rises from the drapery that had covered her before dawn. To combine 'the utmost power & grandeur of form with light springiness', he used as models a Life-Guardsman, Colarossi, and drawings from Long Mary. (The combination now seems lacklustre.[27])

Emilie Barrington (fig. 116), contributed an article, 'Is a Great School of Art Possible in the Present Day?' to the erudite monthly journal *The Nineteenth Century*. Her cry against modern disregard for beauty was scholarly, but negative. The editor, James Knowles, commissioned to Watts confront the issue.[28] One morning, the artist sent bundles of jottings to Mrs Barrington and asked her to put the 'wretched scribbles' together. Her editorial role was well under way by mid-August, but the breadth and force of the ideas were his own, as he wrote and rewrote his 11,000-word polemic 'The Present Conditions of Art'.[29] He would test his opinion on any subject – political, religious or social – by setting the situation back 500 years, to sift out petty detail.[30]

Invited to write a paper on mural decoration in public buildings for discussion at the National Association for the Promotion of Social Science in Manchester, he was presented by Sir Coutts Lindsay as pre-eminent, a sage who enjoyed authority 'among all sections of artists.' Proposing a revival of church decoration – still a controversial issue amongst Protestants – he suggested that the *Te Deum* might be painted where it was sung and music rooms decorated by students, so that the camaraderie generated by part-songs and madrigals would harmonize with artistic endeavour. Contemporary subjects, such as 'Manning the Life-boat' from the *Graphic*, could be enlarged for a permanent historical record or be painted over, like a school slate. The antithesis of the monstrous machine age, this exercise, infused with musical delight, might stimulate a national school of art.[31]

Pressed by Rickards, who longed to surprise visitors with new drawing-room acquisitions, Watts was completing portraits of Blanche and of Violet Lindsay in a red dress and diaphanous scarf, gazing wide-eyed at the viewer. Violet stood in Sir Coutts's armour for the knight in *Rehearsing a Tableau* – later renamed *Joan of Arc*, it recalls Titian's *Duke of Urbino* – exhibited at the Dudley.[32] Sir Coutts Lindsay had viewed Rickards's collection that autumn and recognized that 'an Artists pictures should all be seen together'. By early December the Mancunian planned to exhibit his Watts collection, though the artist warned that exhibiting conditions were 'unsympathetic', not as harmonious as his home setting.

Watts's ambition to be viewed in the light of the old masters was achieved when the Uffizi Gallery in Florence invited him to contribute to its self-portrait gallery. Millais and Leighton were similarly honoured. In no immediate hurry to fulfil the request, Watts lent his latest self-portrait, a profile in the scullcap, seen from behind, to Rickards, who offered two hundred guineas for it. (Watts's standard price for portraiture was now five hundred guineas.) He would finish the small *Angel of Death* for the Mancunian and paint a separate self-portrait for the Uffizi, using two mirrors to achieve a new profile seen from the front.[33]

For the first time in his life, Watts felt encouraged in his visionary work: 'The wall that was ever interposed between me and the possibility of great

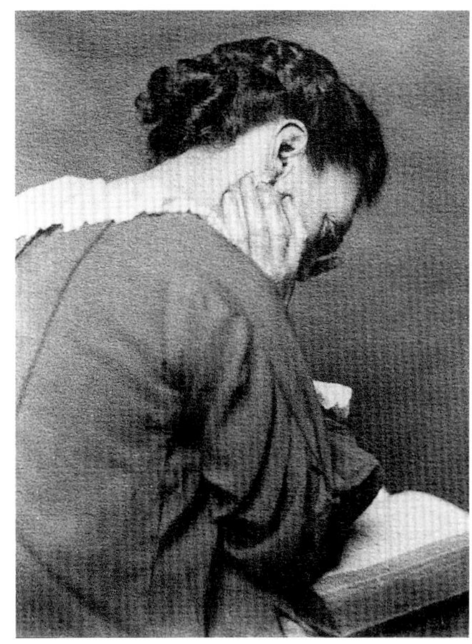

116   *Emilie Barrington Reading*, 1870s (photo Frederic Hollyer).

painting was and is thrown down!' He told Mary Wyndham that he had dreamed that Titian and Reynolds had given him a lesson and painted in front of him. 'He feels quite a fresh courage since the event, and is trying to put to practice what he learnt from them.'[34] Watts would see the Venetian in nature. In the garden with Emilie Barrington, he pointed to the evening sun weaving threads of gold through the branches of a clump of thorn trees. 'There, is that not Titian?'[35]

He sent a new presidential portrait of Leighton, resplendent in his doctoral robes, to the Grosvenor Gallery winter exhibition (pl. xx);[36] and the year closed with encouraging words from Rickards, who reported widespread interest in his exhibition to be held at the Manchester Royal Institution. 'I am as conscious for the forthcoming acknowledgment of the supremacy of your own Art as for the gratification of my own (I hope) pardonable ambition.'[37]

In 'The Present Conditions of Art', which would be published in February 1880, Watts argued how a great school of art could be achieved. 'Art is poetry manifested by science', he declared and if allowed to address serious issues it could offer a vital spark to stimulate progress, the spirit of the age. His universal message embraced wide-ranging proposals for fashion, social and education reform and the trades unions. An instinct for beauty was paramount. The eye, unlike other senses, faced ugliness comparable to 'tearing raw meat with our fingers and teeth, living in the midst of vile odours and complacently enduring abominable discords.' Tight, unhealthy waists and shoes made women appear deformed and turned the beautiful structure of the foot into 'a crippled bunch of bunions'; a gentleman's pitiful costume made his legs look like 'unshapen props'. Taste should be cultivated at public schools, because, as he pointed out, the young Etonian whose 'ridiculous get-up . . . has been a glory in his eyes since he was old enough to envy his elder brother' would one day influence the nation.

Woven through Watts's polemic is a concern for balance. Both rich and poor should be able to enjoy the 'natural loveliness' of nature. He attacked the morbidity of people who wanted to ban field sports – an activity uniting landlords, tenants and labourers – yet offered no alternative. Discouraging the natural safety-valve for superabundant national energy, this would open up the fields to manufacturing and commercial enterprise' and condemn the machine worker to drunken misery. The analytical, unsatisfied age having sapped unquestioning faith, offered no better consolation: 'Material prosperity has become our real god'.

To generate social harmony, Watts called for the leisured classes to offer resources and skills so that 'art, pressed into the service of general education . . . might again be great, and become a vital power'. Skills, achievement, wealth and position should be shared to benefit the community. Turning to trades-unionism and British trade, he urged that manual labourers should be stimulated not to outwit but to do better than each other, to aspire to quality rather than quantity. If Britain could not compete on the material front, 'we would not be beaten in the great battle of life, we must shift the contest to higher ground, where pre-eminence will be still more glorious.' Art, in harmony with these widest views, should be seen as an ennobling influence on public walls, rather than a transient 'plaything' at the Academy exhibition, which was no place to judge a grave, deliberate work of art. 'An after-dinner speech must not be an essay, still less an epic. We are elated by champagne and light buzz of talk, the room is hot, and the smell of mixed viands confounding to our senses . . . Imagine the bard or historian giving out his inspirations under these conditions . . . Yet it is art that corresponds to the highest literature . . . which must be demanded of our artists, poems painted on canvas, judged and criticized as are the poems written on paper.'

Quoting Matthew Arnold's criticism of Wordsworth – 'Noble and profound application of ideas to life is the most essential part of poetic greatness' – and Voltaire – 'No nation has treated in poetry moral ideas with more energy than the English nation' – Watts wanted that energy cultivated in the pursuit of art. 'As long as humanity is humanity, man will yearn to ascend the heights human footsteps may not tread, and long to lift the veil that shrouds the enigma of being, and he will most prize the echo of this longing in even the incoherent expression of literature, music, and art.'[38] Arnold was moved to send the latest Wordsworth, and in return Watts invited him to sit for the national collection.[39]

So dense were the fogs in February that he and his colleagues could barely see to work.[40] Watts, taken ill, was confined to his bedroom, frustrated at the delay to his work: A sketch of Blanche shows, however, that his humour remained intact. Her unkempt hair spreading over her shoulders, the teenager stands and leans forward, her palms turned to face the viewer, beseeching 'Will you be my Valentine?' He took on a young sculpture assistant, George Thompson, at the beginning of March[41] and kept a fatherly eye on Henry Holiday's, marble figure, *Sleep*. Horrified to learn that the Academy had rejected it because of nudity, Watts protested to the hanging committee, but it was too late to reinstate her.[42]

Rickards's exhibition of *The Works of G. F. Watts Esq. RA* – fifty-four paintings, predominantly imaginative subjects, with the marble head of *Medusa* and bust of *Clytie* – opened at the Royal Manchester Institution in April. Proceeds would support the new art school and children's hospital. 'I confess I dread the result of your experiment, of the effect on the public of so many pictures by the same hand', wrote Watts. He feared a critical mauling might also upset Rickards's friends and, in the imagery of his latest visionary theme *Love and Life*, he was determined not to take for rocks the ordinary stepping stones of daily life. His paintings were said to glow in the dark; and he advised Rickards to keep the light low.[43] Happily, the Mancunian reported 'great educational work' resulting from the exhibition, which the *Athenaeum* recognized as 'an extremely interesting collection'.[44]

Watts had added a hint of decorative background to William Morris's portrait, presumably to represent tapestry, which the craftsman, now weaving on a high-warp loom at his Georgian mansion Kelmscott House in Hammersmith, regarded as the summit of textile work. Flanking the portrait of Morris at the Grosvenor were two life-size idealized standing female nudes: *Daphne* sheltering within the laurel tree into which she is about to metamorphose; and *Psyche*, her head bowed in sadness as she drops the lamp that had burnt her lover, an intense aesthetic pose praised as 'pathetic'. As a favour to Sara Prinsep, he showed a portrait of the Reverend Charles Beanlands, her rector at St Michael's Church. *Watchman! What of the Night?*, described by the *Athenaeum* as 'a saintlike youth in armour' was not the Ellen Terry version, but – Watts explained in June to the art critic

Julia Cartwright – a girl from Whiteley's, who had 'gone utterly to the bad' despite his efforts to reform her in the sitter's chair.[45]

'It is curious to pass from Mr Watts's beautiful and imaginative abstractions to the intensely real life and character of Millais's *Mrs Jopling*,' a reviewer observed.[46] The two artists, however, took a similar approach to their self-portraits for the Uffizi, which were displayed either side of Henry Tanworth Wells's portrait of Princess Victoria in the great room at Burlington House. They represented themselves as painters, half-length, standing in brown coats with their palettes and brushes. While Millais faces the viewer in his larger canvas, Watts looks to his left, as though beyond the confines of the frame. Among his other portraits were of Lillie Langtry as *The Dean's Daughter*, The Right Reverend Frederick Temple, the Bishop of Exeter[47] and Evie Tennant under her parasol at Freshwater, which he completed for her marriage to the essayist, poet and psychical researcher F. W. H. Myers.[48]

He sent *Orpheus and Eurydice* to the Paris Salon, where Manet was exhibiting a portrait of the statesman Antonin Proust and Moreau was showing a languid nude, *Galatée*. The novelist Joris Karl Huysmans, reviewing the Salon for *L'Art Moderne*, was fascinated by the visionary Moreau, who like Watts employed old master influences, to create a unique mysterious style. Galatée's pose, her left hand angled behind her head as she faces front, under the watchful eye of Cyclops, echoes Delacroix's *Odalisque* and his own *Study with Peacock Feathers*.[49]

Watts was fascinated by 'Zazel', the acrobat who was fired from a large black cannon at the Aquarium and flew to the top in a terrifying, blaze of gas-light, to land in a net the other side of the building. He went behind the scenes to ask her to sit for him, in costume. The seventeen-year-old brought her sister as chaperone, but felt awkward in her low-cut circus dress: 'I couldn't have a man looking so close at my flesh, especially because when I put my head back sometimes things didn't stay where they ought to be.' Her courage and composure at each life-threatening performance had impressed him deeply. He gave her the portrait on her marriage to George Starr, the European manager of Barnum and Bailey, and in old age she would prize it as a memento of her circus days.[50]

Dean Liddell wrote on 25 May 1879 to offer Watts an honorary Oxford DCL. *The Times* reported that doctorates were to be awarded to him and to Millais, but Watts turned down the honour.[51] No doubt mindful of the failed portrait of Gladstone – again prime minister – and anxious not to be swayed by his growing reputation, he explained, 'I desire to decline everything that may be flattering to my vanity and misleading to my self judgment.'[52]

He built up a warm rapport with the great social and education reformers Cardinal Manning, the Archbishop of Westminster, and Matthew Arnold. Passionate, witty and at times disconcerting, Arnold shared the artist's urge to advance high culture to the masses; though while he considered hereditary aristocracy ill-equipped for the modern world, Watts, who valued its influence, sought to steer it for the public good. 'Culture . . . the study and pursuit of perfection . . . does not try to teach down to the level of inferior classes . . . it seeks to do away with classes,' Arnold had written in his last lecture as Professor of Poetry at Oxford. 'This is the *social idea*; and the men of culture are the true apostles of equality. The great men of culture are those who have had a passion for diffusing, for making prevail, for carrying from one end of society to the other, the best knowledge, the best ideas of their time.' Their debate during his first sitting on 1 June enabled Watts to capture his personality absolutely, thought Emilie Barrington, and that in striving further to achieve the inner man, he passed and did not quite retrieve the original inspiration when Arnold returned between breaks as a school inspector. The portraits of both Manning (pl. XXII) and Arnold (fig. 117) reflect the deep concern of the sitters; however, neither pleased their families.[53] The cardinal's efforts to house and educate the poor stirred Watts to produce a penetrating portrait and startling study of the gaunt, red-robed septuagenarian – his everyday clothes were said to be threadbare – and during the sittings he and Watts were absorbed in conversation.[54] Julia Cartwright, brought to the studio by Emilie Barrington on 30 June, recorded that Manning's 'head looks very ascetic and almost ghastly in its unfinished state'. She left her hostess sitting to Watts.[55]

He enjoyed a gay summer: tea and singing at the Wyndhams, outings to Holland House and the Grosvenor, and was determined to make *Hugh Lupus* 'a real monument of English Art'; as he explained to Rickards, 'I am giving all that I have of strength & experience & money's worth with an ardent desire to do something worthy of my country.' Seeing the great horse and rider in the garden at Little Holland House, Lady Brownlow felt 'quite struck dumb by its grandeur and beauty'.[56]

It was presumably at the Wyndhams' luncheon on 28 July, talking politics with Princess Christian, president of the Royal School of Art Needlework,[57] that Watts was persuaded to put pen to paper for the school in the *Nineteenth Century*. Knowles asked Lady Marian Alford, the school's vice-president, to contribute to his series on the employment of gentlewomen, and her daughter-in-law Adelaide Brownlow sent a copy of his letter to Watts on 6 August: 'It always does the best part of me good to see you and your works, and to hear you speak of all that is highest and noblest . . . I can only congratulate ourselves in having your pen to help the cause.'[58] The artist began to regret caving into friendly pressure. 'Why do you all persist in believing me capable of all kinds of things!' he wrote to Madeline Wyndham. 'Nobody has so little idea of writing. I wish you were in town to talk the matter over with me.' Overwork had again triggered giddiness – 'I am getting to feel something like a top, at the end of spinning and not very sure which side to fall.'[59] As he began to write, he urged her to add the views of Ruskin or Morris or, best of all, Burne-Jones: 'What you want are some eloquent, some burning words that will create a rush into the work.'[60] Meanwhile Oscar Wilde (fig. 118), who had given an sitting to Watts and had recently described him as the 'most powerful of all our living English artists', sent his latest poem on England, 'Ave Imperatrix', 'as a very poor mark of homage to one whose pictures are great poems'.[61]

On Octavia Hill's recommendation, he began an enduring association with the Reverend Samuel Barnett's ambitious scheme to cheer, enrich and educate impoverished parishioners at St Jude's Church, Whitechapel. Barnett wanted a symbolic mosaic for the outer wall of the slum church. 'Watts might be the best person to go to. He cares for idealization, personification, Time, Death, struggle between Death & Love, mistake of a woman's life, & all sorts of modern abstract & really noble ideas, cares for them earnestly, & only with the little grain of self-consciousness which

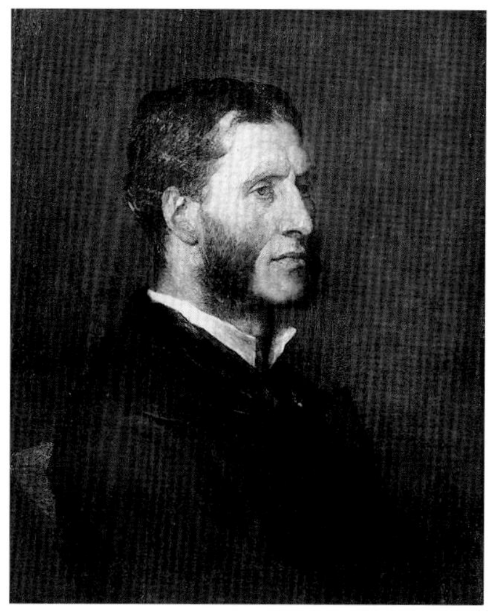

117   *Matthew Arnold*, 1880–81 (National Portrait Gallery, London).

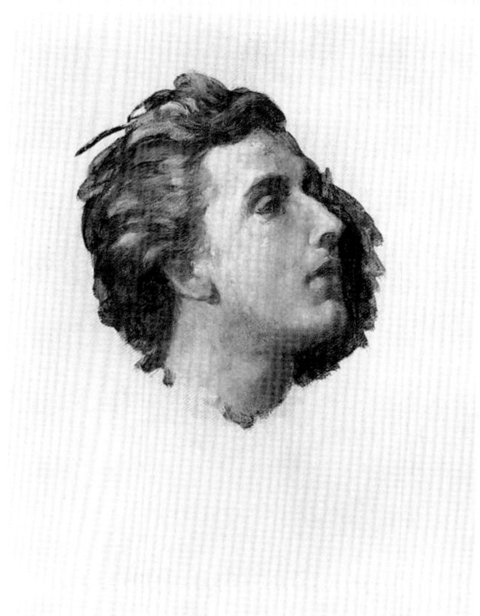

118   *Oscar Wilde*, c.1877–78 (National Portrait Gallery, London).

all people who see so far, & no farther, have', Hill had written to Barnett. 'He cares more than almost any man I know for art to be used to teach great lessons.' She pointed out that the artist had donated a new field for her scheme to preserve green open spaces for the poor. 'Show him you feel it is much you are asking, but make him feel why – he gets up at daybreak feeling life short for what he has in his thoughts, & may not help,' she advised the vicar, and warned, 'Take care he gives you nothing the world would think unfit. His high art goes towards undraped figures sometimes.'[62] *Time, Death and Judgment* – as he now named the subject – was to be carried out in the mosaic and would feature in Barnett's first art exhibition in the church schoolrooms in Commercial Road the following spring.[63] Interestingly, Watts was also advising T. C. Horsefall, who was setting up art exhibitions for Board schools in Manchester to teach the masses through the beauty of art, ideally to steer them out of poverty.[64]

Having sold no pictures for three months, and with annual household and studio expenses of over three thousand three hundred pounds – almost twice his investment income – the artist would have been relieved by commissions to paint third- and fourth-generation Ionides portraits: of Alexander's daughter, Aglaia Coronio, his son, Constantine, daughter-in-law, Agathonike, and their daughters.[65] Unable now to afford to produce a cut-price replica of the intricate fifty-figure *Titans* for less than a thousand guineas, he explained to Rickards that it should in time be worth five thousand, and that once America started buying English pictures, values would rise. It was not unusual for respected artists to earn up to seven thousand a year; and although he did not make the twelve to fifteen thousand reputedly earned by Millais, his finances were in good order. But he wanted 'a great deal more than I have, both for my own ease, & in order to help other people'.[66]

Watts was embarking on a new building project. Pictures were stacking up in his studio. He suspected the public would never care for or purchase his imaginative subjects, but as he wished nevertheless that they be seen properly he commissioned George Aitchison, the architect of Leighton's recently completed Arab Hall, to design a gallery for Little Holland House (fig. 119). By November 1880, builders had begun to lay foundations, to the west, for a lean-to picture store and twenty-eight-foot two-storey gallery, with a glass roof and protruding oriel windows to maximize space.

At his winter base in Brighton, the artist was working up *The Angel of Death* for Rickards.[67] While his avant-garde pictures became increasingly abstract in texture as he experimented with atmospheric effects, their sculptural line and form was paramount to Watts. He mistrusted French Impressionism for its momentary effect, the antithesis of his own aim for art, as he emphasized with distress to Dolly Tennant.[68]

Thomas Carlyle, the philosophical giant of the age, died on 4 February 1881. He had sat for a further portrait for the national collection (fig. 120), and had been deeply impressed by the German poet Goethe. 'No living man was ever spoken of by Carlyle as Goethe was – his mind, his intellectual power, his dominion over men,' Watts told the critic Marion Spielmann. 'I waited till he stopped. "And Shakespeare?" I asked. "Ah, Shakespeare," replied Carlyle, "he was the greatest of all!"'[69] This second portrait caught that spirit, thought the poet George Meredith when sitting himself in 1893. 'He had the look of Lear encountering a storm upon the Cornish coast,

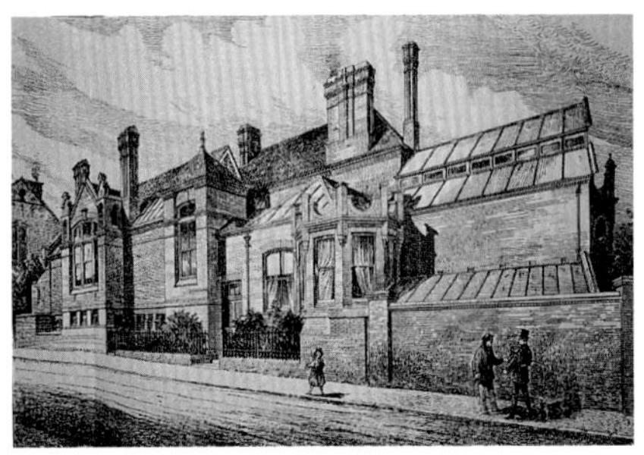

119   George Aitchison's design for the gallery extension to Little Holland House (*Building News*, 7 October 1881).

which you have given.' Sadly, the philosopher died with a gloomy vision of the future. To Watts, he had instigated the 'heroically striving' spirit of the age, but his teaching was largely negative, compared with that of Ruskin.[70]

The artist exploited negative suggestion in the letter addressed to Lady Marian Alford, published by the *Nineteenth Century* in March, summoning women to stimulate taste by sending embroidery designs to the Royal School of Art Needlework. His entreaty included a vehement protest against the cruelty and misuse of birds' feathers in dress. Warning against motifs that were unsuitable to changes of surface or direction, or that suggested decay, he suggested that embroideries for furnishings should reflect youth, light and enjoyment, creations 'beautiful in form and gorgeous in colour, birds, butterflies, beetles . . . [that] would bring about the abolition of the barbarous and abominable practice of destroying myriads of exquisite birds.' He continued:

> A whole creation of loveliness is in danger of being swept from off the face of the earth, for the object of sticking stuffed specimens about wearing apparel, where they are, notwithstanding their supreme beauty, wholly in bad taste, the extreme improbability of the real creature's presence in such places making the effect more grotesque than charming. But while the appearance of the stuffed bird perched on a lady's muff or entangled in her skirts is absurd or disagreeable, the beautiful and acknowledged imitation could be worn with perfectly good taste, and here should be a most lucrative source of employment.[71]

One guest at the Leighton soirée that Watts attended on 25 March was quite oblivious: 'Mrs Grant, wife of the President's son, is a most curious looking woman with a peacock feather hat & a rosebud jacket, pink stockings two esmeralda shoes,' noted Mary Wyndham. The performers were Piatti, Joachim and the pianist Madame Clara Schumann, who was in London for a series of triumphant Popular Concerts, as well as playing her late husband's works, performing with Joachim Brahms' new sonata for violin and piano Opus 78. Guests mingled in Leighton's spectacular Arab Hall (fig. 121). Based on the Sicilio-Norman 'Palace of Delights', La Zisa in Palermo, the walls were lined with peacock-blue Iznik and Syrian tile decorations, echoed and completed with tiles designed by William de Morgan, topped by Walter Crane's golden arabesque friezes.[72]

The artists lent the finest examples of their work to Barnett's Easter week exhibition for his impoverished parishioners, an elevating diversion from the public house, from apathy and sin. As the *Tower Hamlets Independent* declared, 'Whitechapel, it is no harm to say, is not a place where beautiful things are common.' Over 8,000 people – many of them illiterate, or criminal – visited the schoolrooms of St Jude's, where one room was filled with objects from the South Kensington Museum. Princess Louise lent art needlework, William Morris sent wallpapers and carpets, William de Morgan, a lustre vase; each was displayed with a full description. Of the pictures by Leighton, Holman Hunt, Burne-Jones, and Watts, Signor's three large symbolic works attracted most attention. Crowds gathered round Barnett as he explained *Time Death and Judgment*, the early social realist picture of the drowned woman, titled here, *One More Unfortunate*, and the Athenian general Aristides sympathizing with a shepherd. '*Aristides*

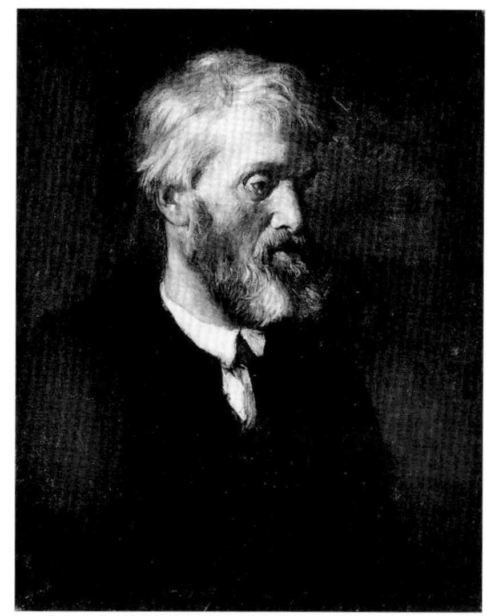

120   *Thomas Carlyle*, 1877 (National Portrait Gallery, London).

121   The Arab Hall, Leighton House.

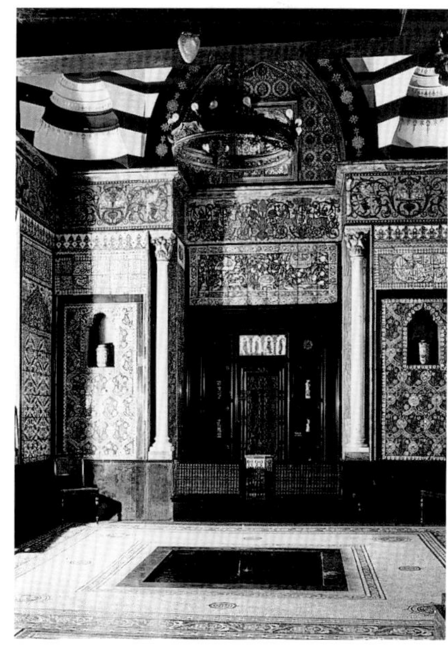

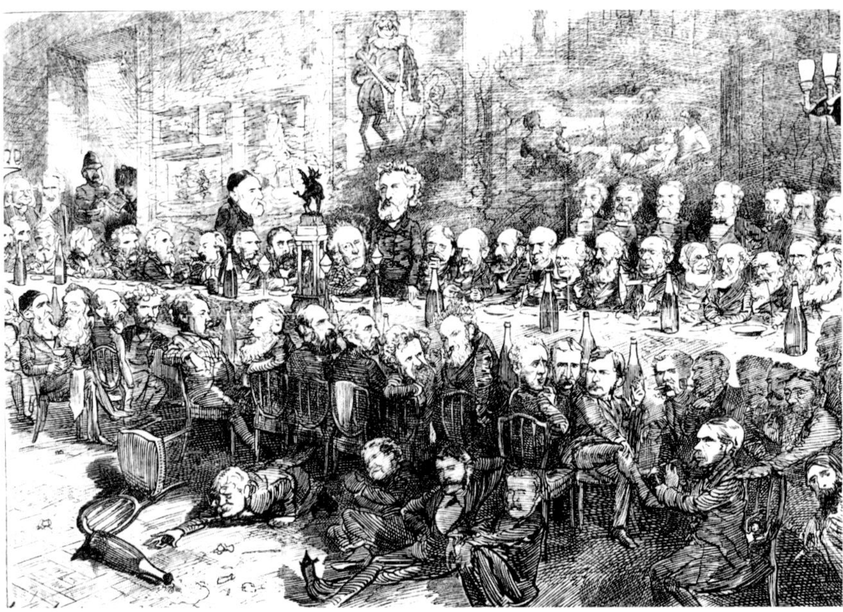

122   Watts approaching Leighton in Edward Linley Sambourne's cartoon of the Royal Academy banquet (*Punch*, May 1881).

*and the Peasant* has, we expect, helped many to feel how it is intelligence and uprightness which exalteth a man', reported the *South London Observer*.[73]

On the death of Lord Beaconsfield on 19 April, a year after a severe general election defeat, the queen ordered Millais's portrait of the statesman to be exhibited at the Royal Academy. Watts's portraits of the president, Sir Frederic Leighton (pl. xx) and of Matthew Arnold (fig. 117), his furrowed brow reflecting concerns aired in the studio, were seen as striking likenesses. Leighton invited Arnold to speak at the Academy banquet (fig. 122). His Zeus-like profile, sitting in scarlet and magenta robes and painted in an expanded format, with his palette and the bronze legs of his *Athelete Wrestling with a Python* visible in the background, celebrated the achievements of a close friend. 'Startlingly life-like to all who knew him', the picture contrasted with Leighton's own self-portrait, painted for the Uffizi, full-face and in front of the Parthenon horsemen.[74]

*Patience, or Bunthorne's Bride*, the light opera composed by Arthur Sullivan to a libretto by W. S. Gilbert satirizing high-art aestheticism, had opened at the Opéra Comique in London on 23 April 1881. 'A most intense young man . . . a soulful-eyed young man, An ultra-poetical, super-aesthetical, Out-of-the-way young man,' sang the Wilde devotee Reginald Bunthorne, 'a Greenery yallery, Grosvenor Gallery, Foot-in-the-grave young man.' Although the cult had mellowed, *Patience* was the talk of the town when the Grosvenor exhibition opened. The female chorus was based, at Luke Ionides' suggestion, on Burne-Jones's maidens descending *The Golden Stairs* – a sensation in the last exhibition. Watts would undoubtedly have attended a performance.[75]

The spirit of Hellenism infused his Grosvenor contributions, headed by *The Genius of Greek Poetry* (pl. xxiv), *Endymion* (fig. 80), *The Wife of Pygmalion* (fig. 78), a draped standing female figure of *Arcadia* and,

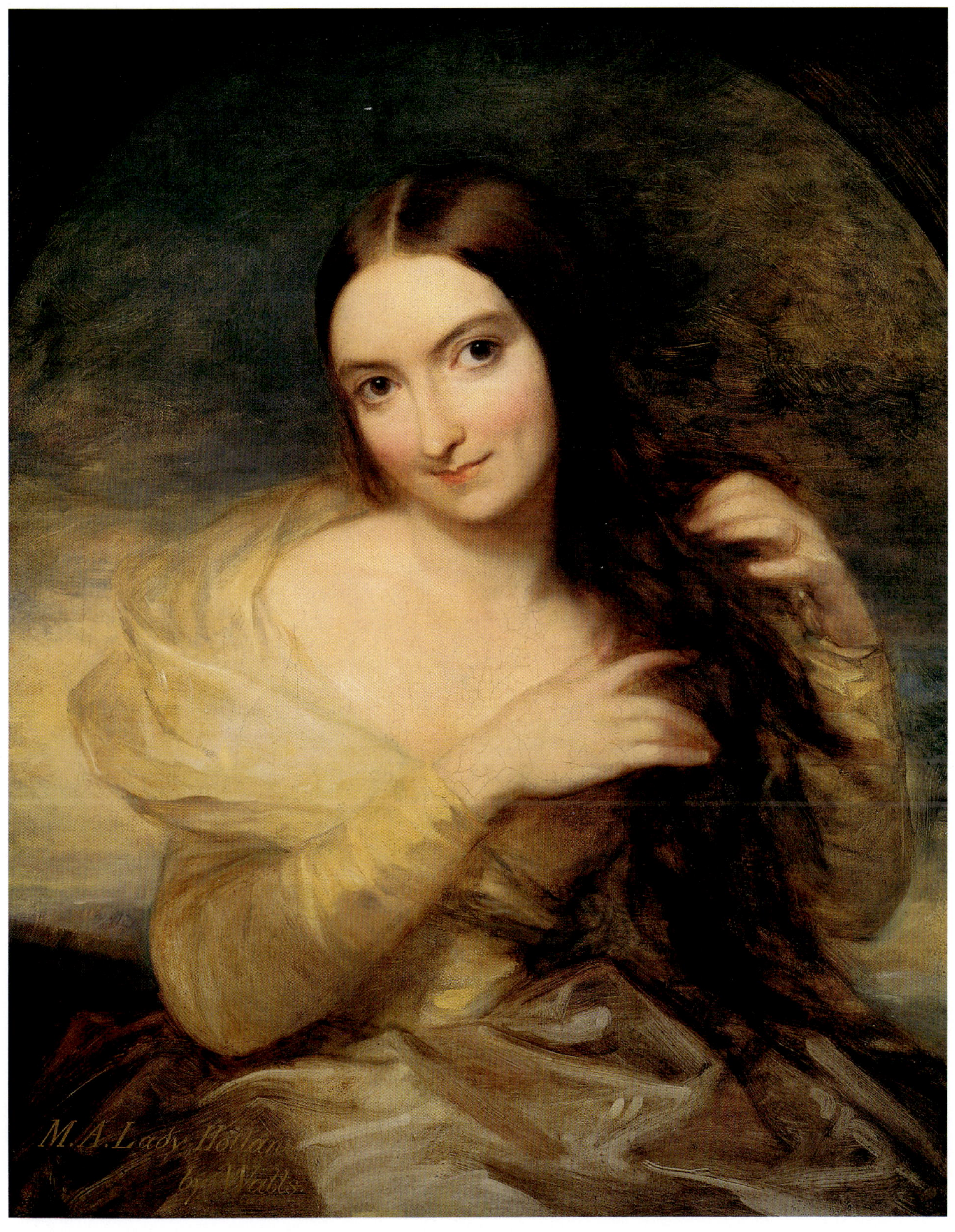

1   *Mary Augusta, Lady Holland*, 1844 (Watts Gallery).

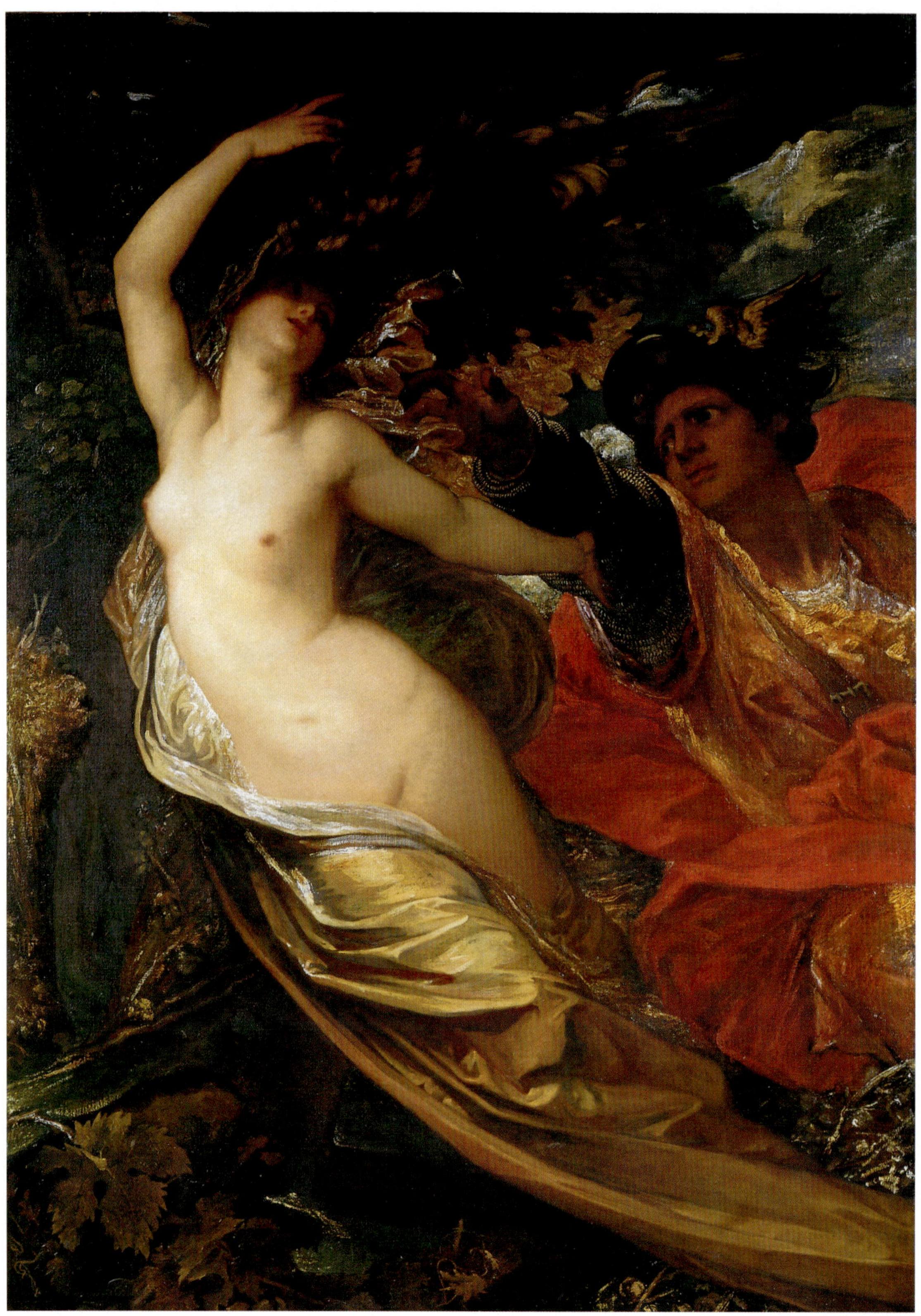

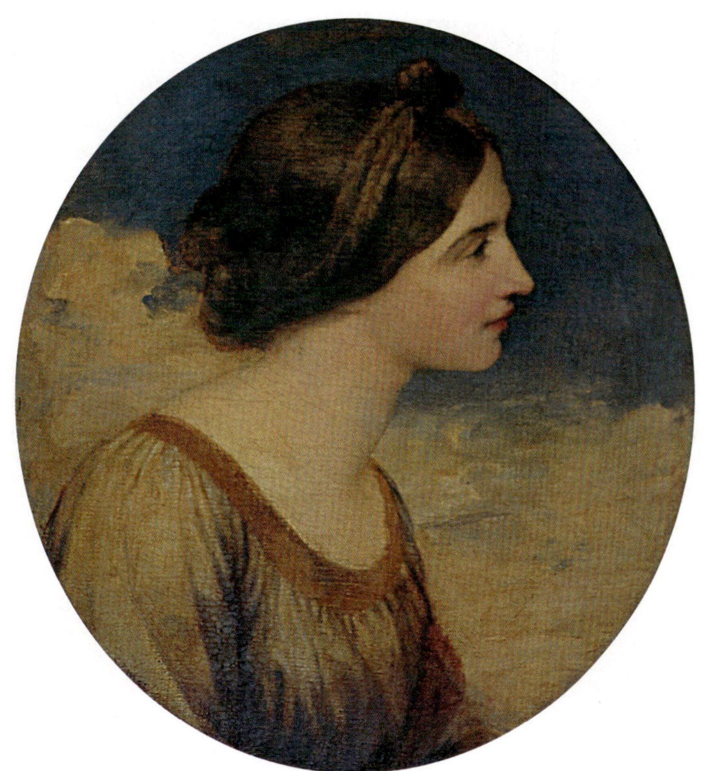



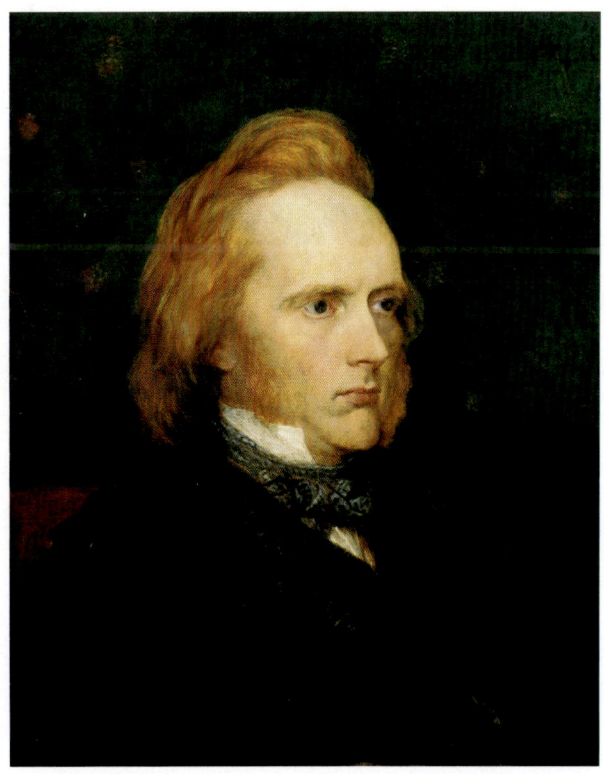

IV   *George Douglas Campbell, 8th Duke of
Argyll*, 1860 (National Portrait Gallery,
London).

II   (*facing page*)   *Fata Morgana*, 1844–47 and
1888–89 (Leicester City Museums).

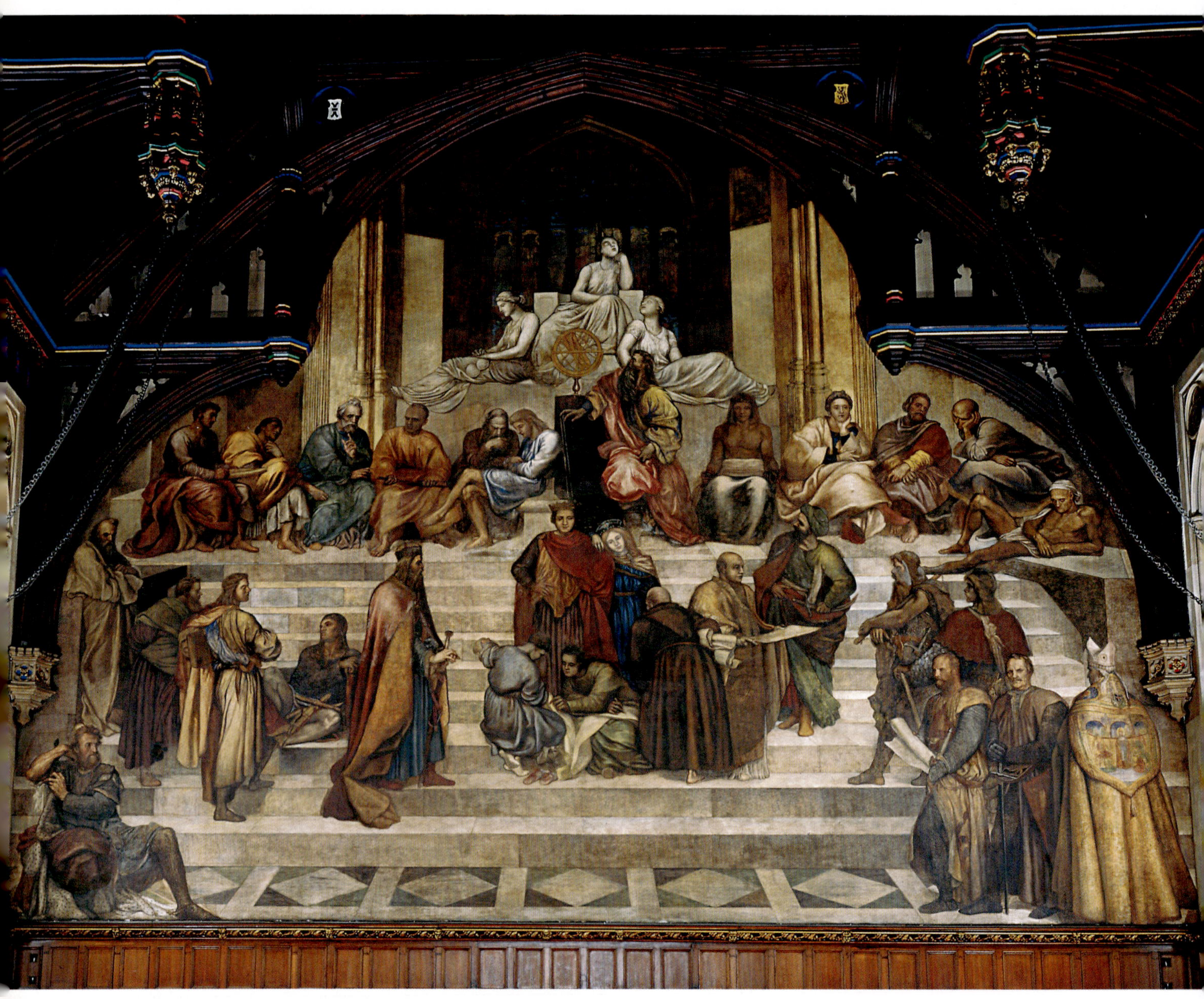

v  *Justice: A Hemicycle of
Lawgivers*, 1852–59 (Lincoln's Inn).

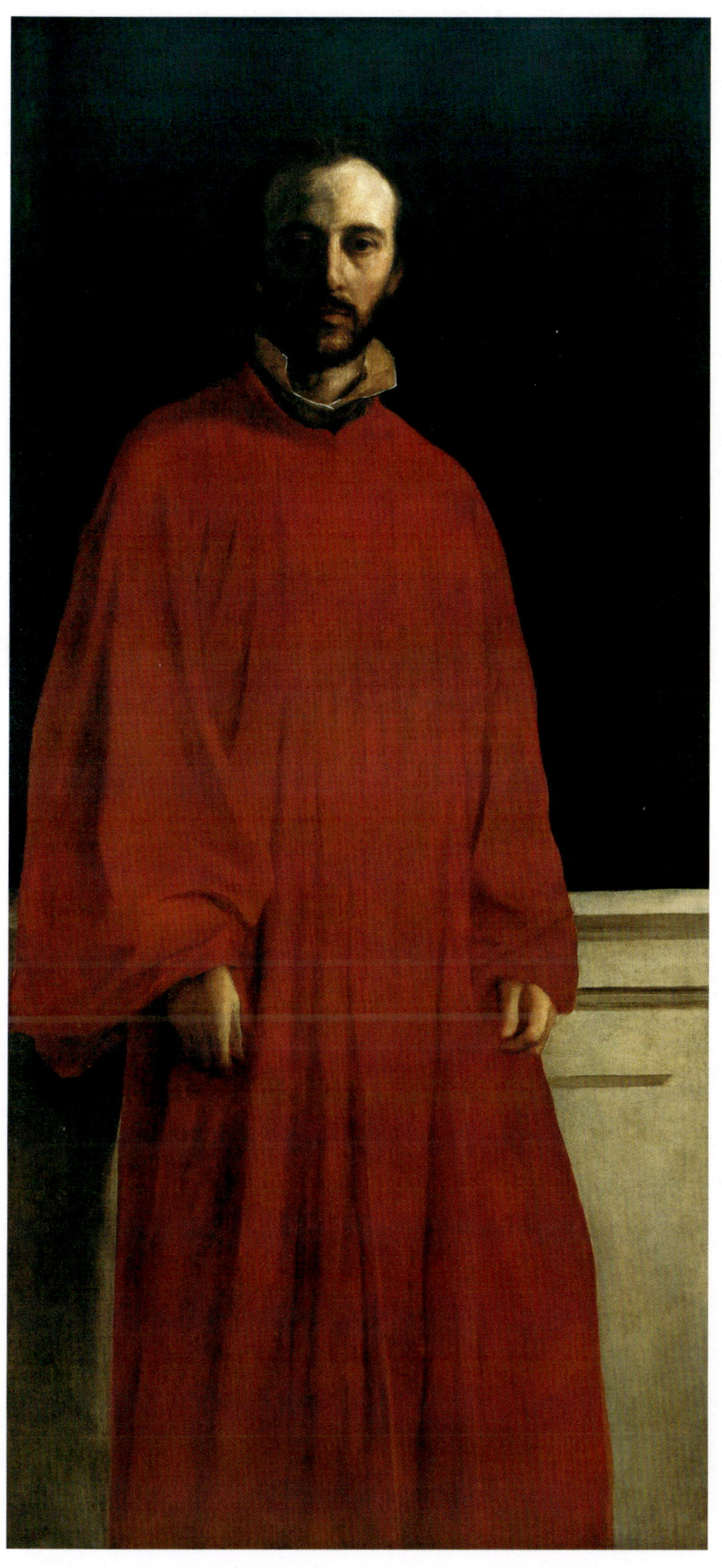

VI  *Self-Portrait as a Venetian Senator*, 1853 (private collection).

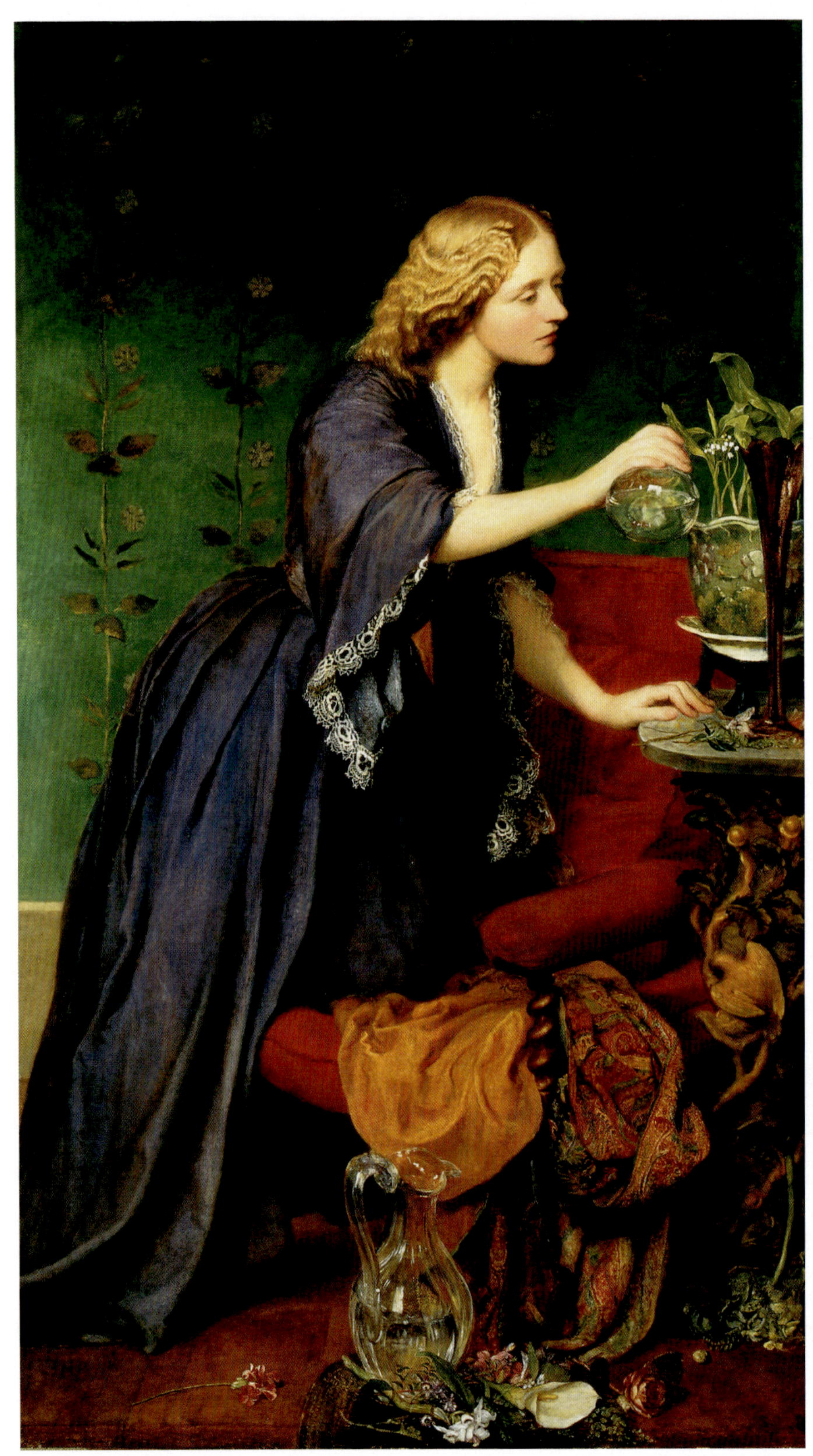

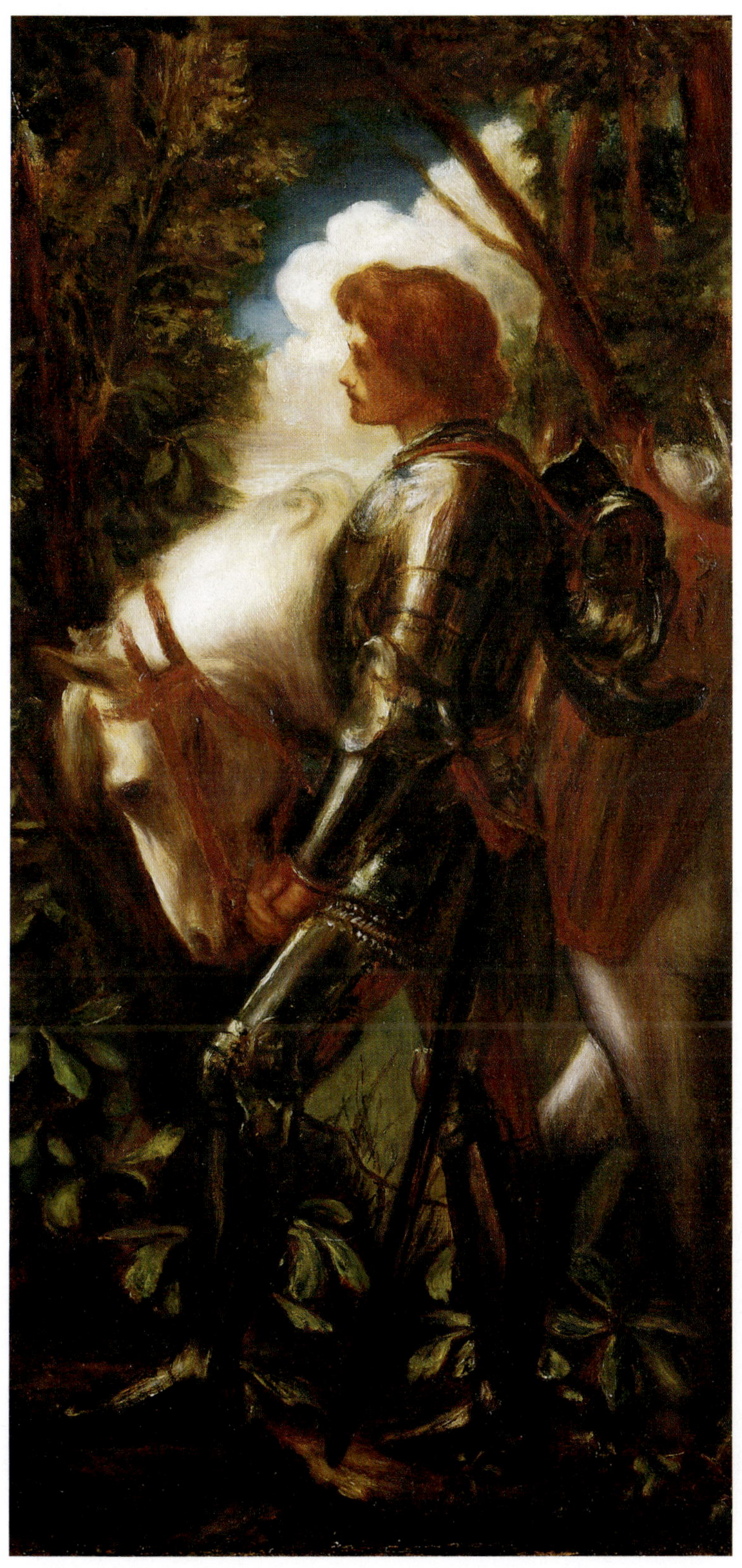

VII (*facing page*)   *Jeanie*
(Mrs Nassau Senior), 1857–58
(Wightwick Manor).

VIII   *Sir Galahad*, 1862
(private collection, courtesy of Nevill
Keating Pictures Ltd).

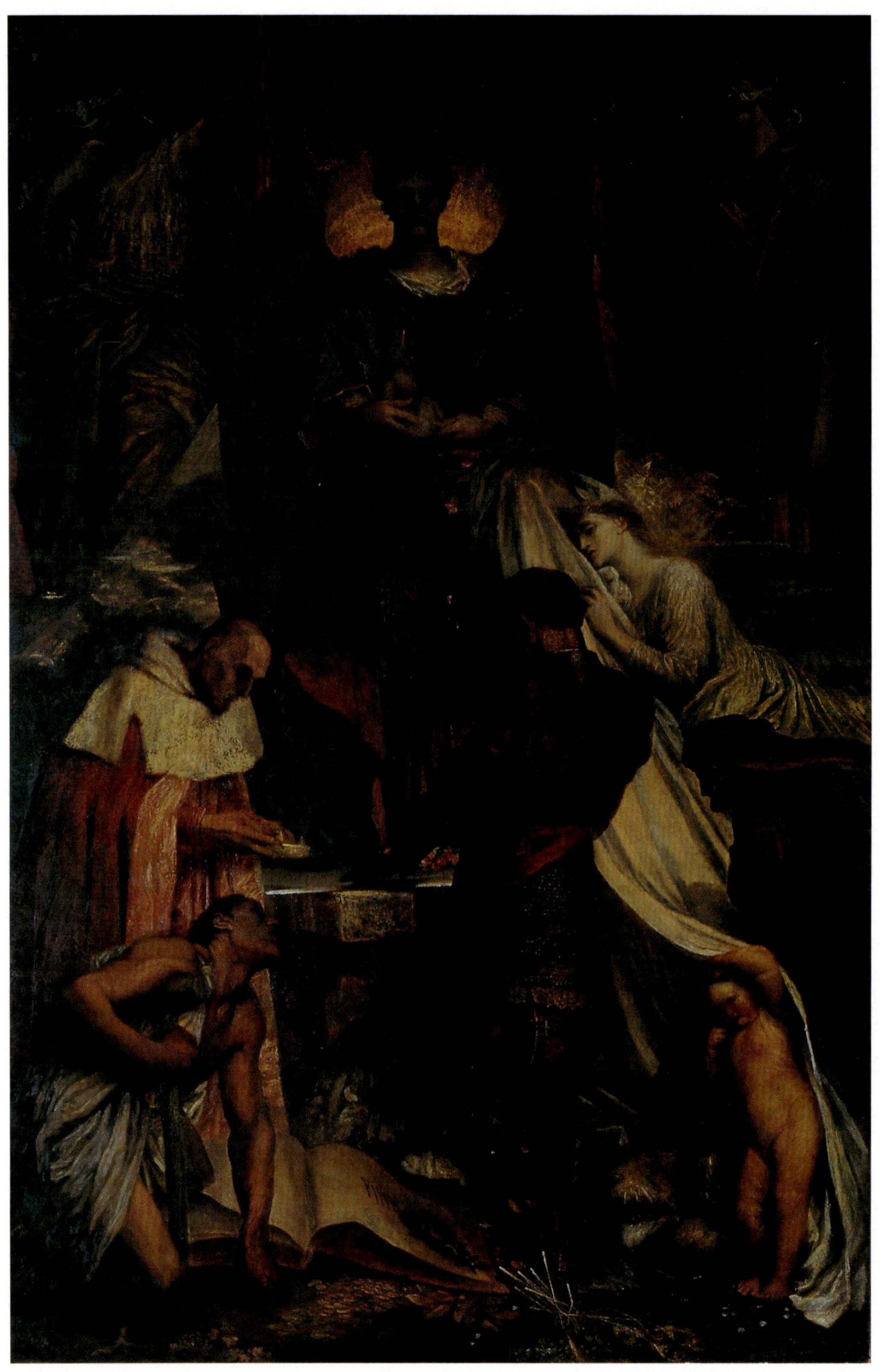

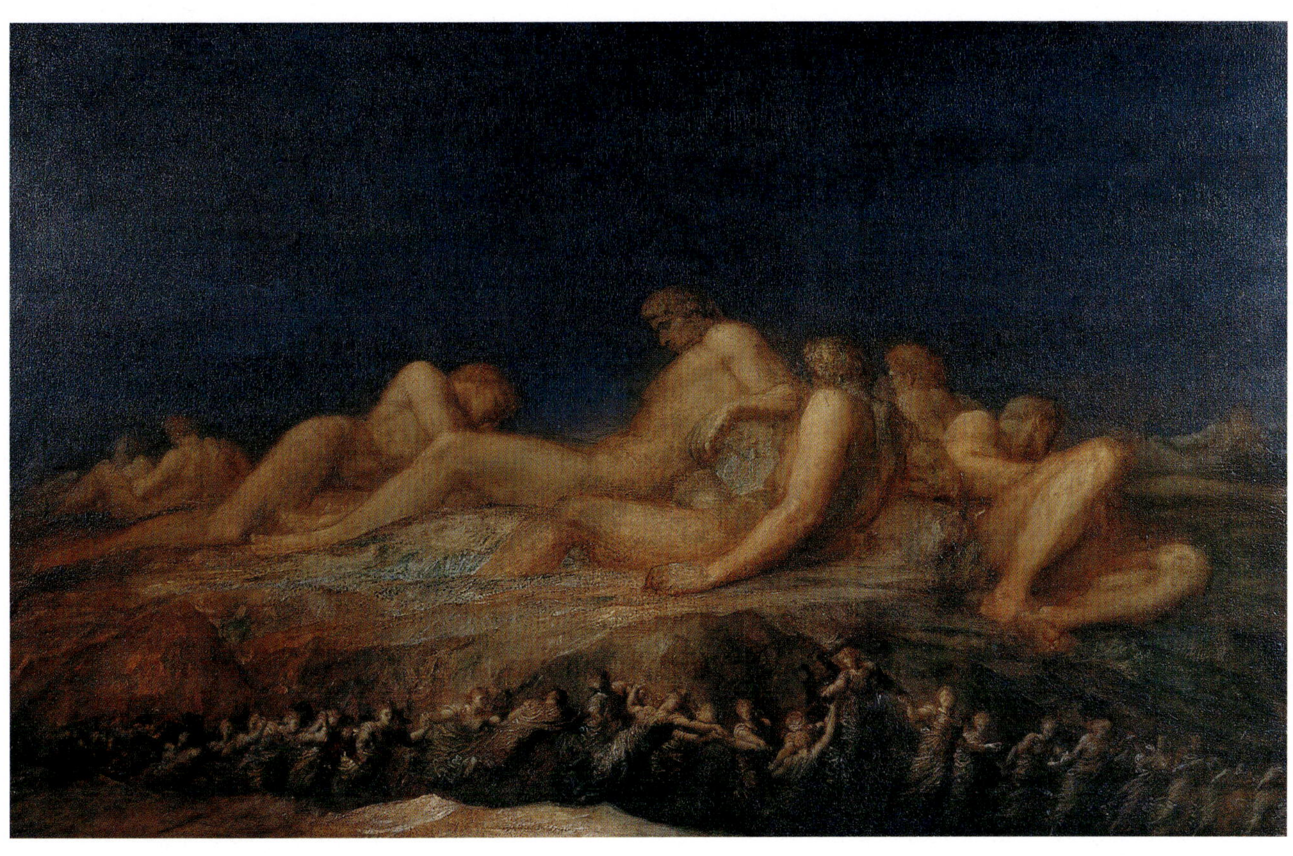

IX (*facing page*)   *The Court of Death*, 1853–1902 (Tate, London).

X (*above*)   *The Titans*, c.1848–73 (Watts Gallery).

XI (*following page*)   *Choosing*, 1864 (National Portrait Gallery, London).

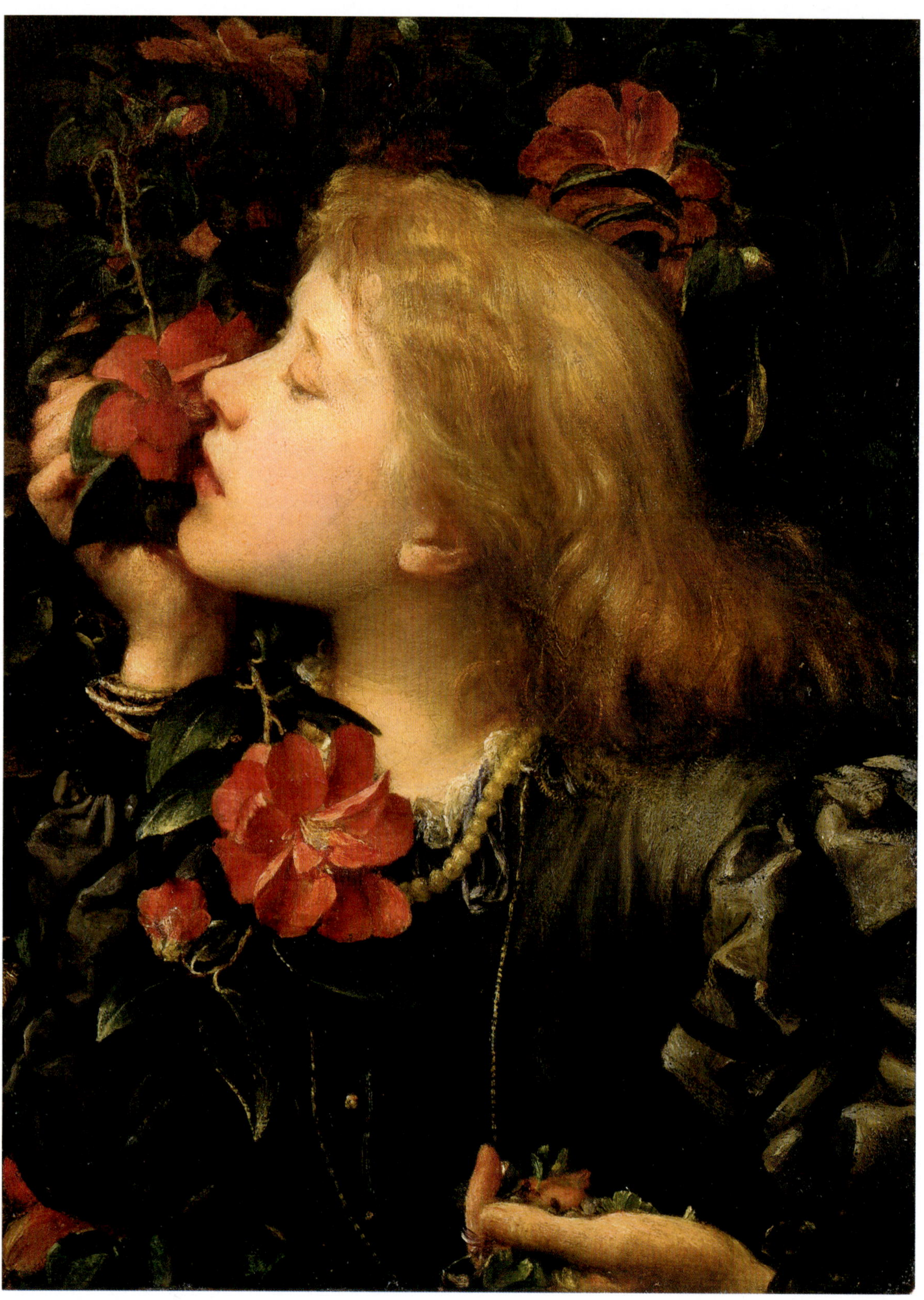

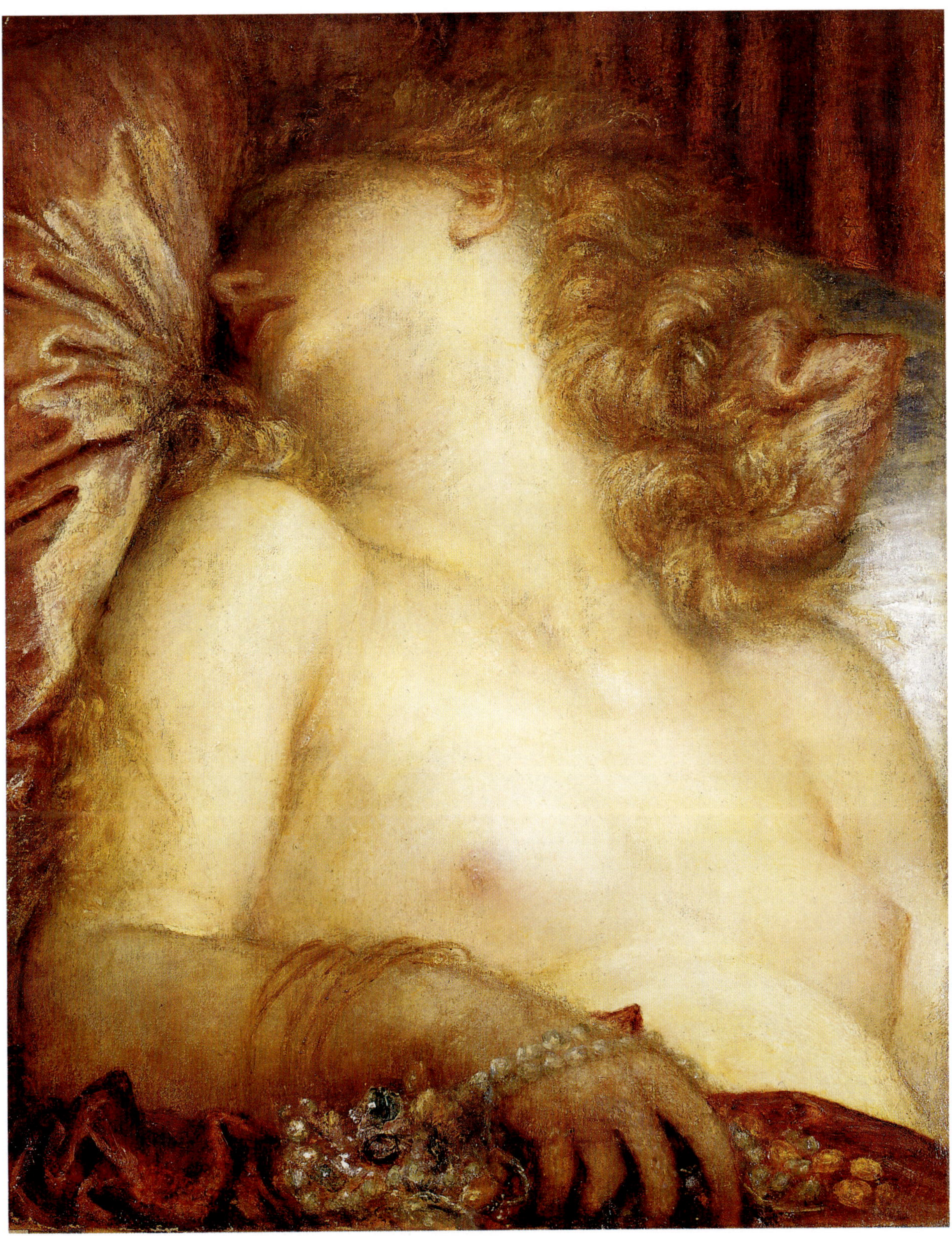

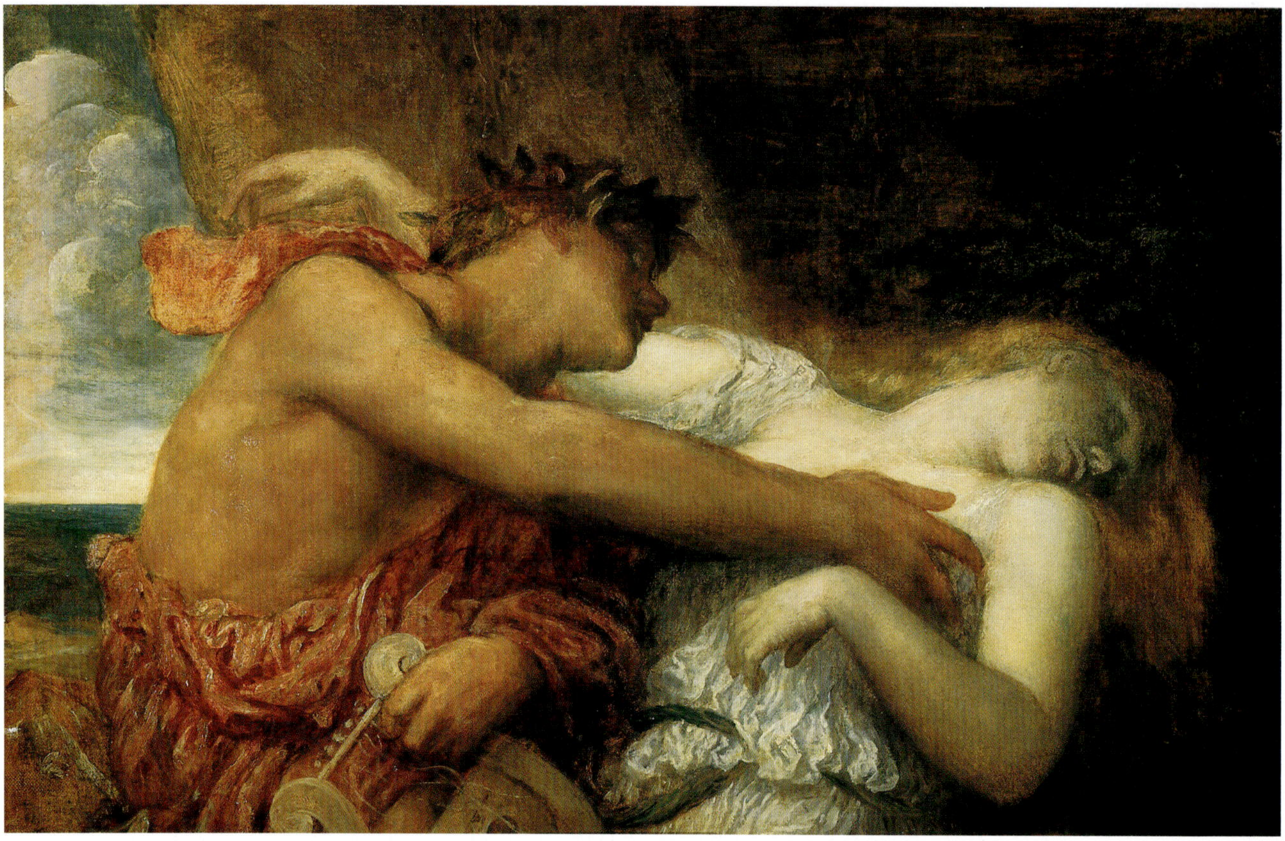

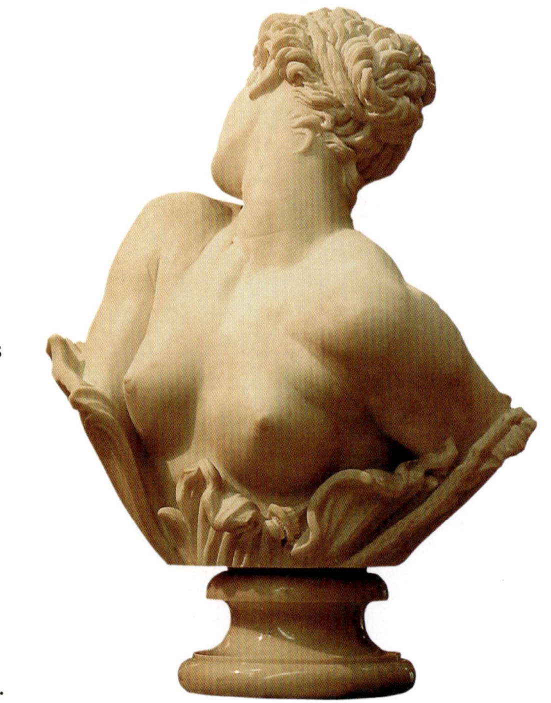

XII (*previous page*)   *The Wife of Pluto*, c.1865–89 (National Museums on Merseyside: The Walker Art Gallery).

XIII (*above*)   *Orpheus and Eurydice*, 1867–68 (private collection).

XIV (*right*)   *Clytie*, c.1867–68 (Guildhall Art Gallery, London).

XV (*facing page*)   *Paolo and Francesca*, c.1872–84 (Watts Gallery).

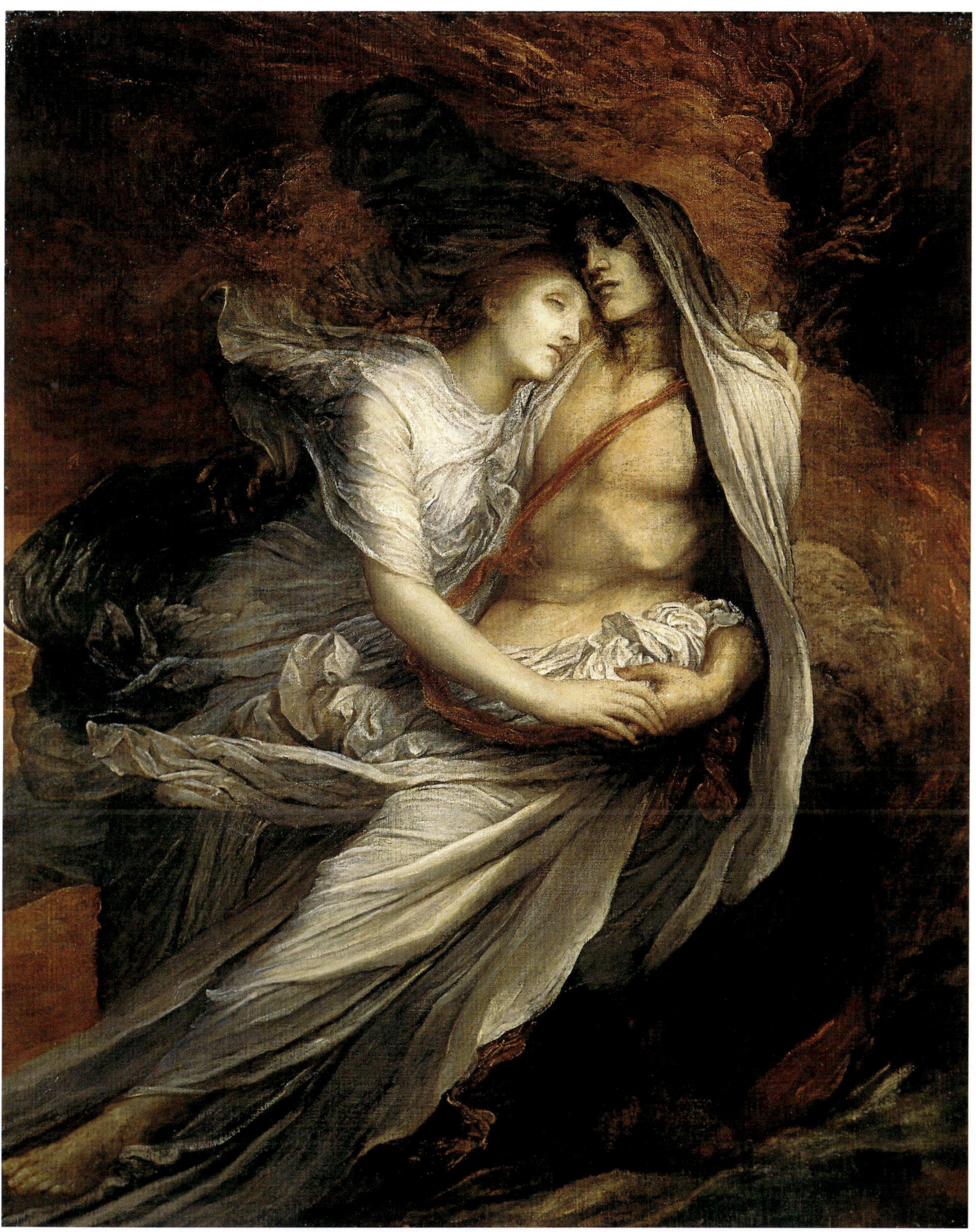

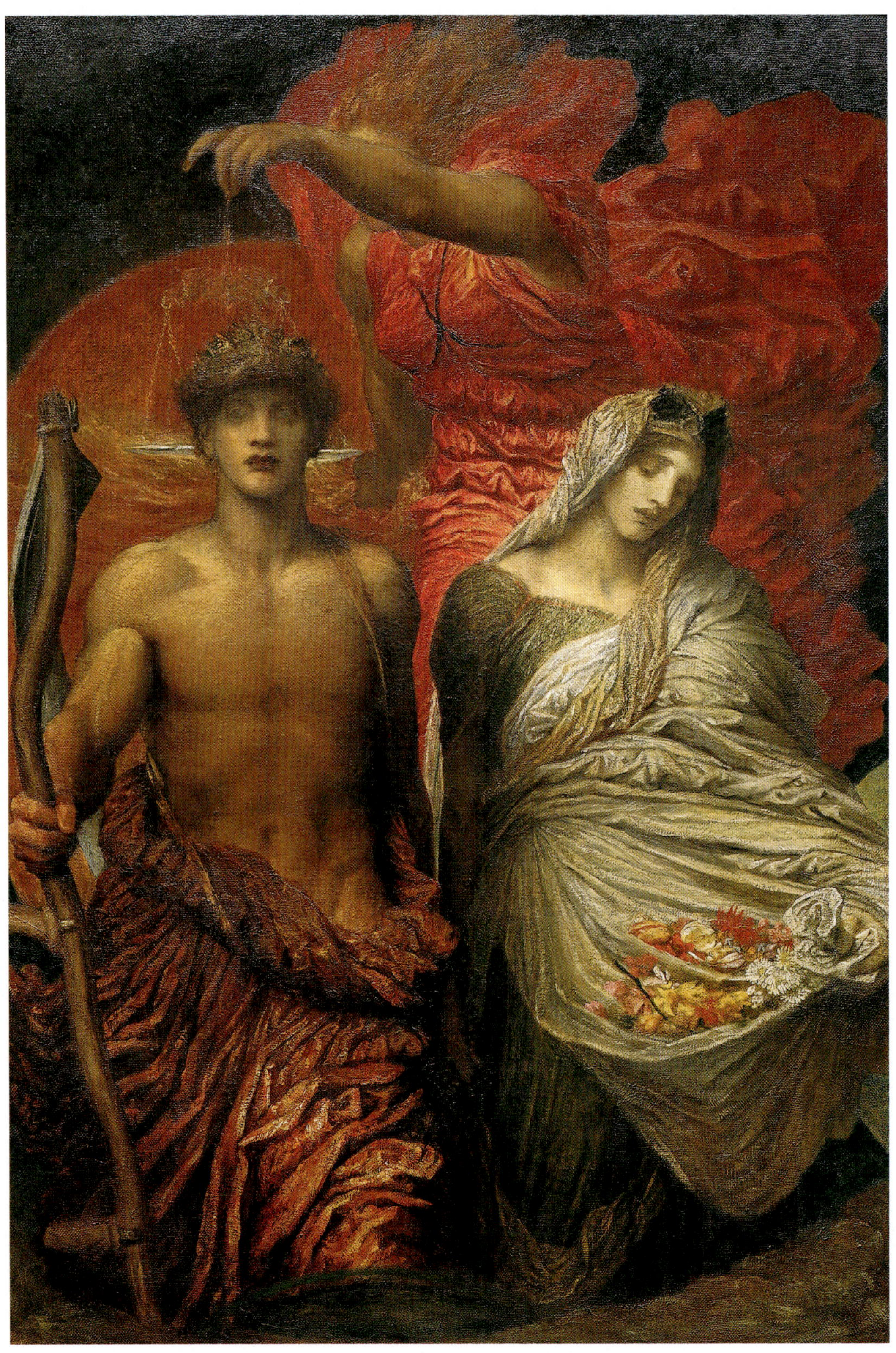

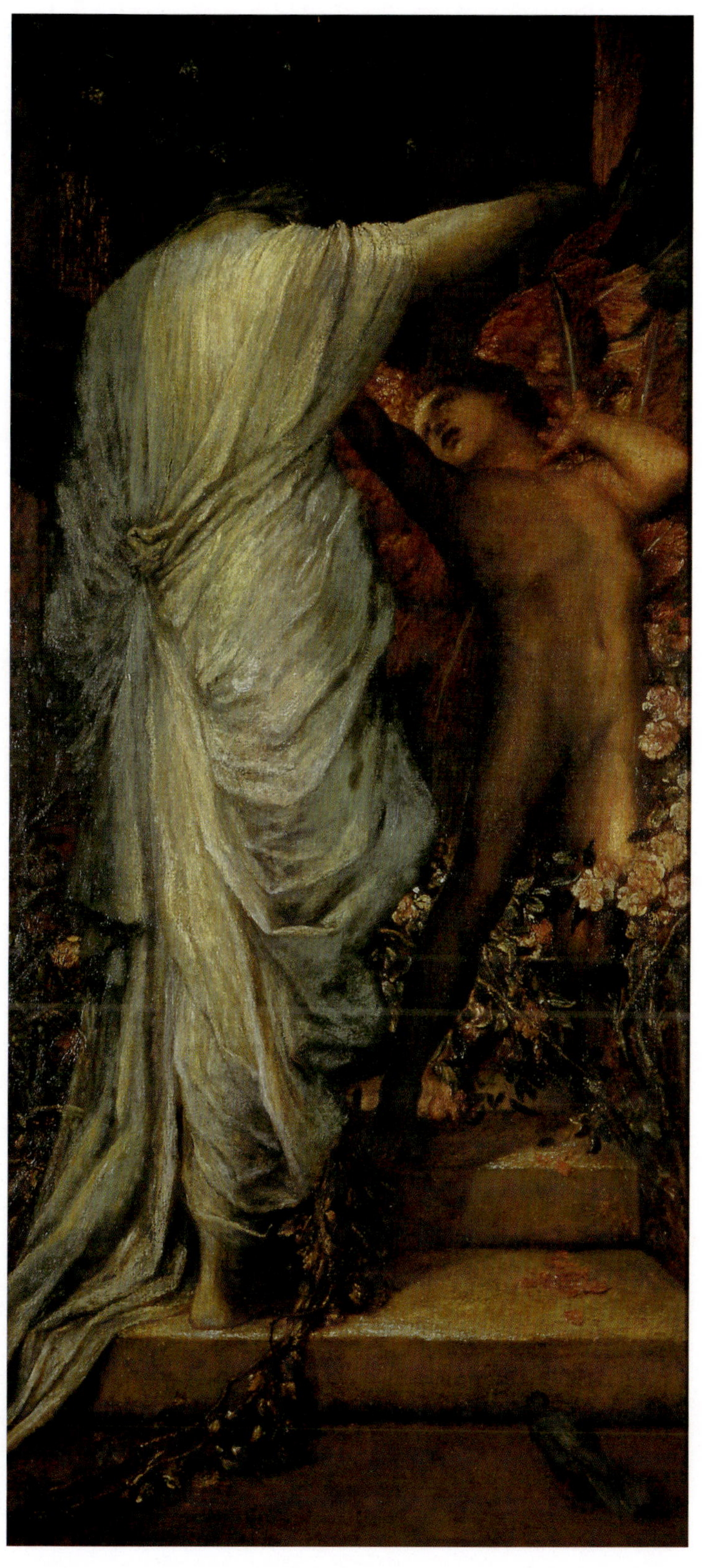

xvi (*facing page*)  *Time, Death and Judgment*, 1868–84 (St Paul's cathedral, on loan to the Watts Gallery).

xvii  *Love and Death*, 1871–87 (Tate, London).

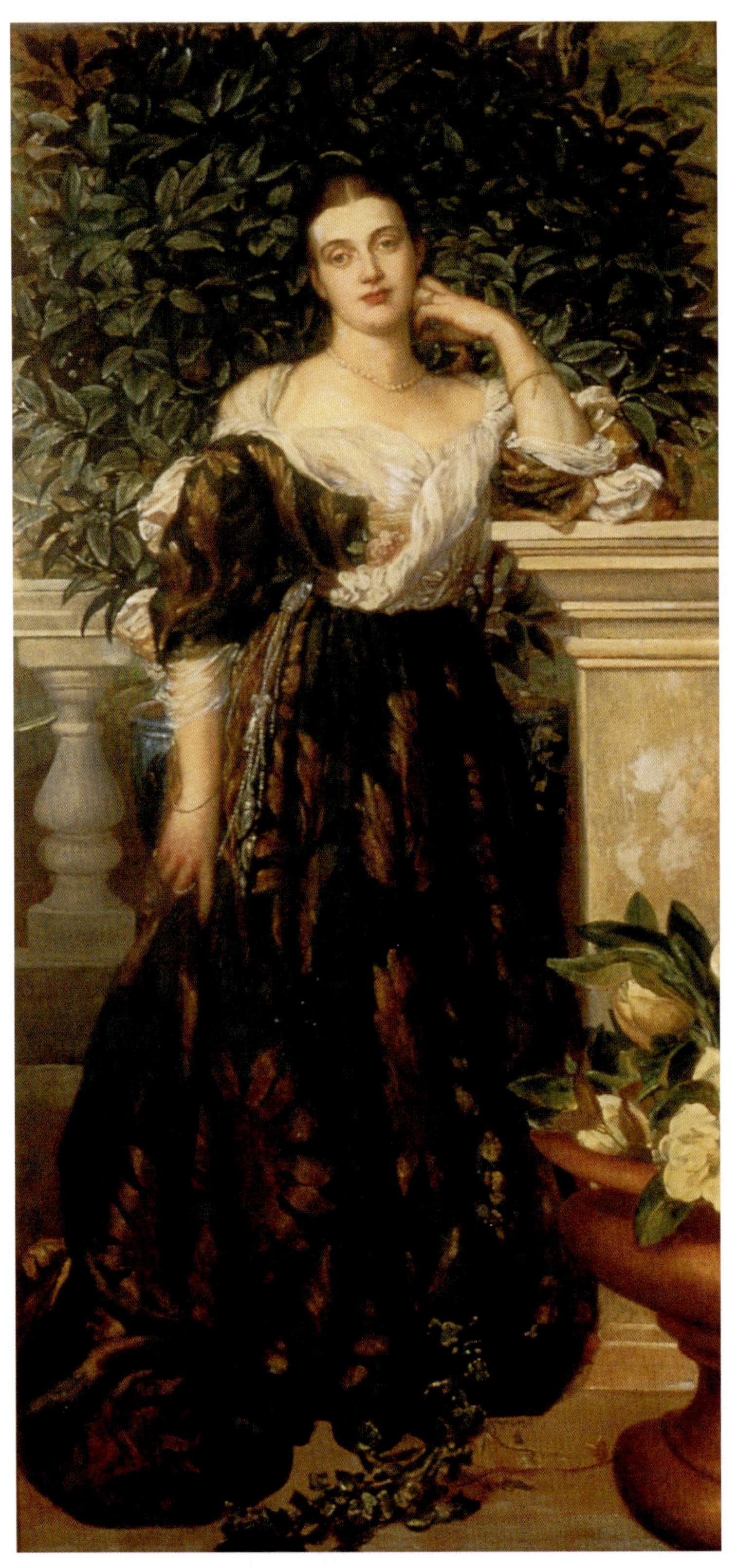

XVIII  *Madeline Wyndham*, 1867–74
(private collection).

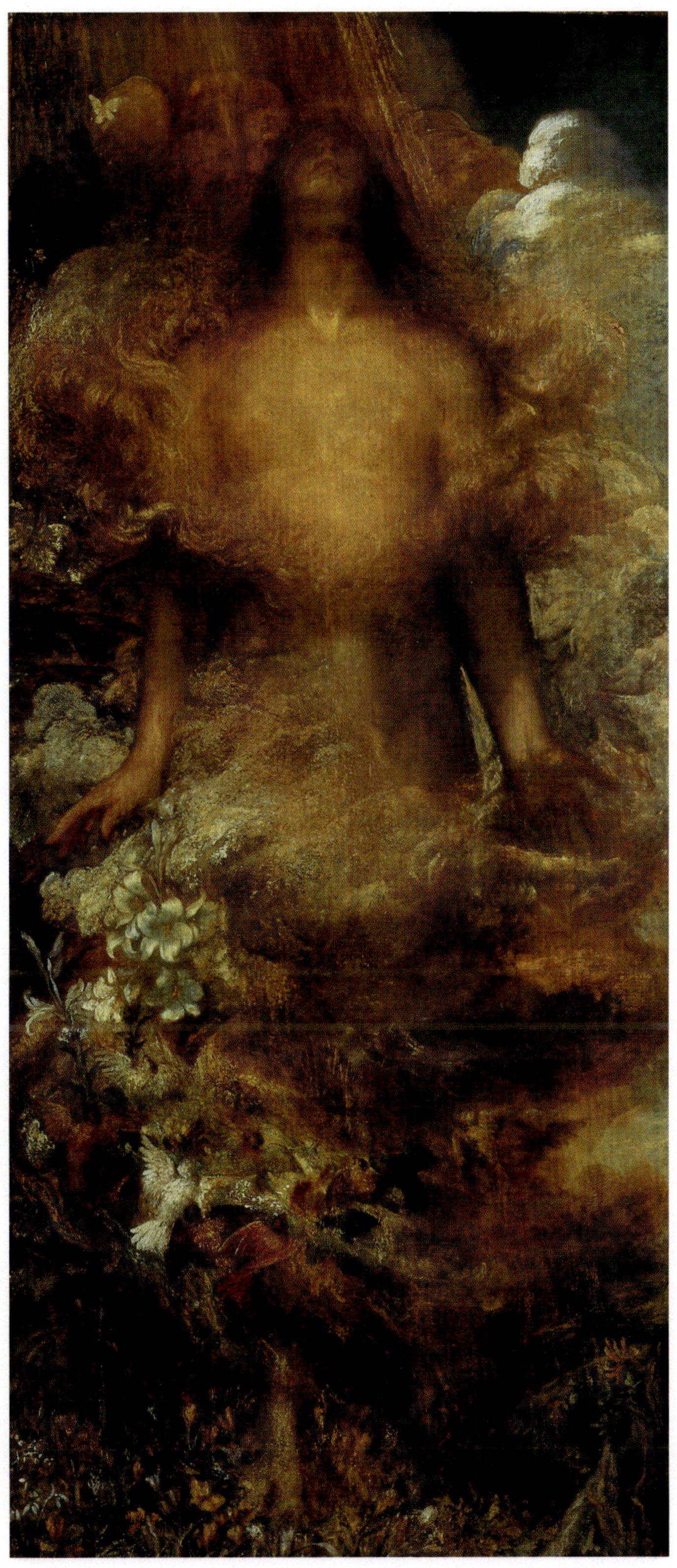

xix  *She Shall Be Called Woman*, *c.*1888–97 (Tate, London).

*following pages:*

xx  *Sir Frederic Leighton*, PRA, 1880–88 (Royal Academy of Arts, London).

xxi  *William Morris*, 1870–80 (National Portrait Gallery, London).

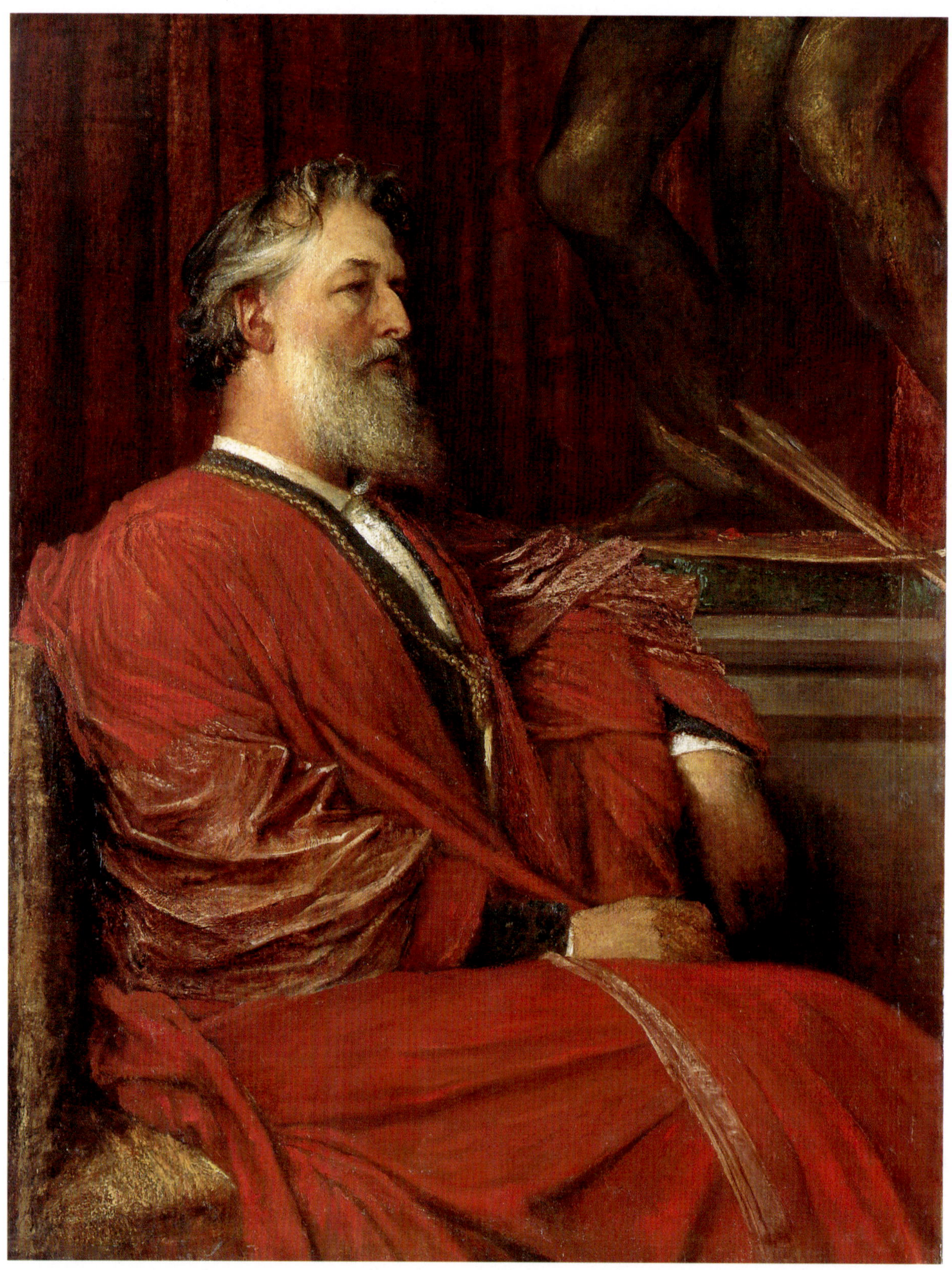

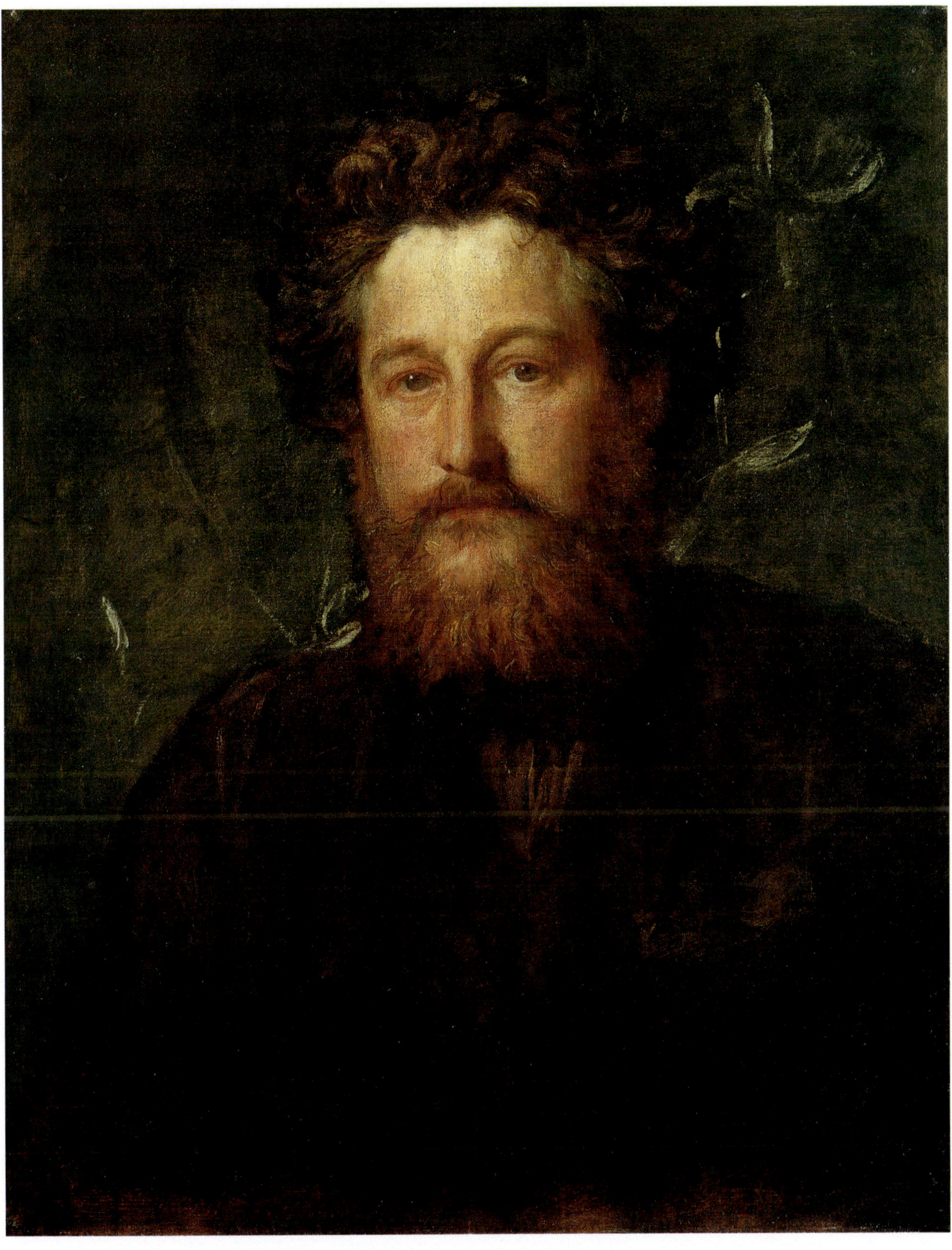

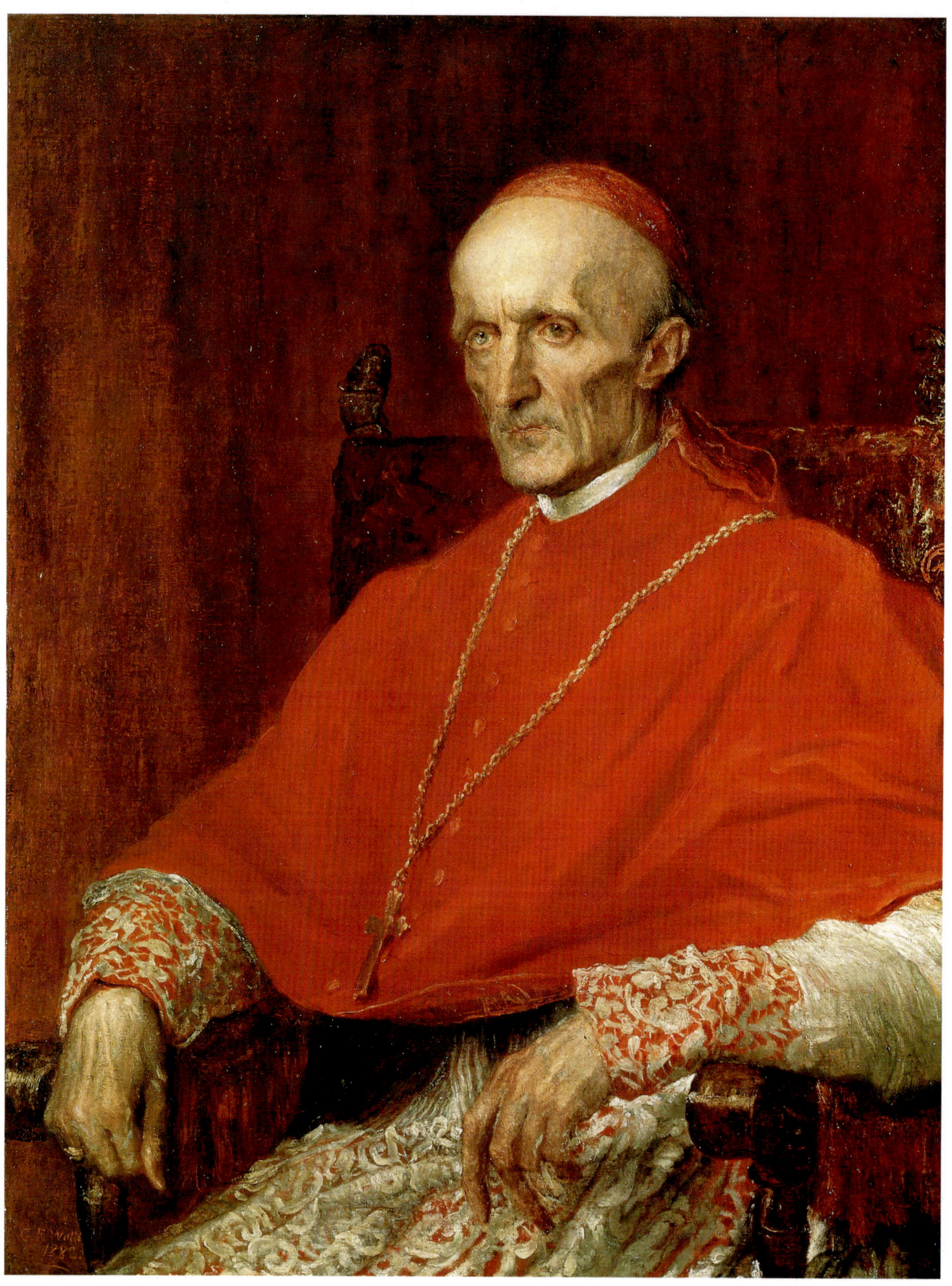

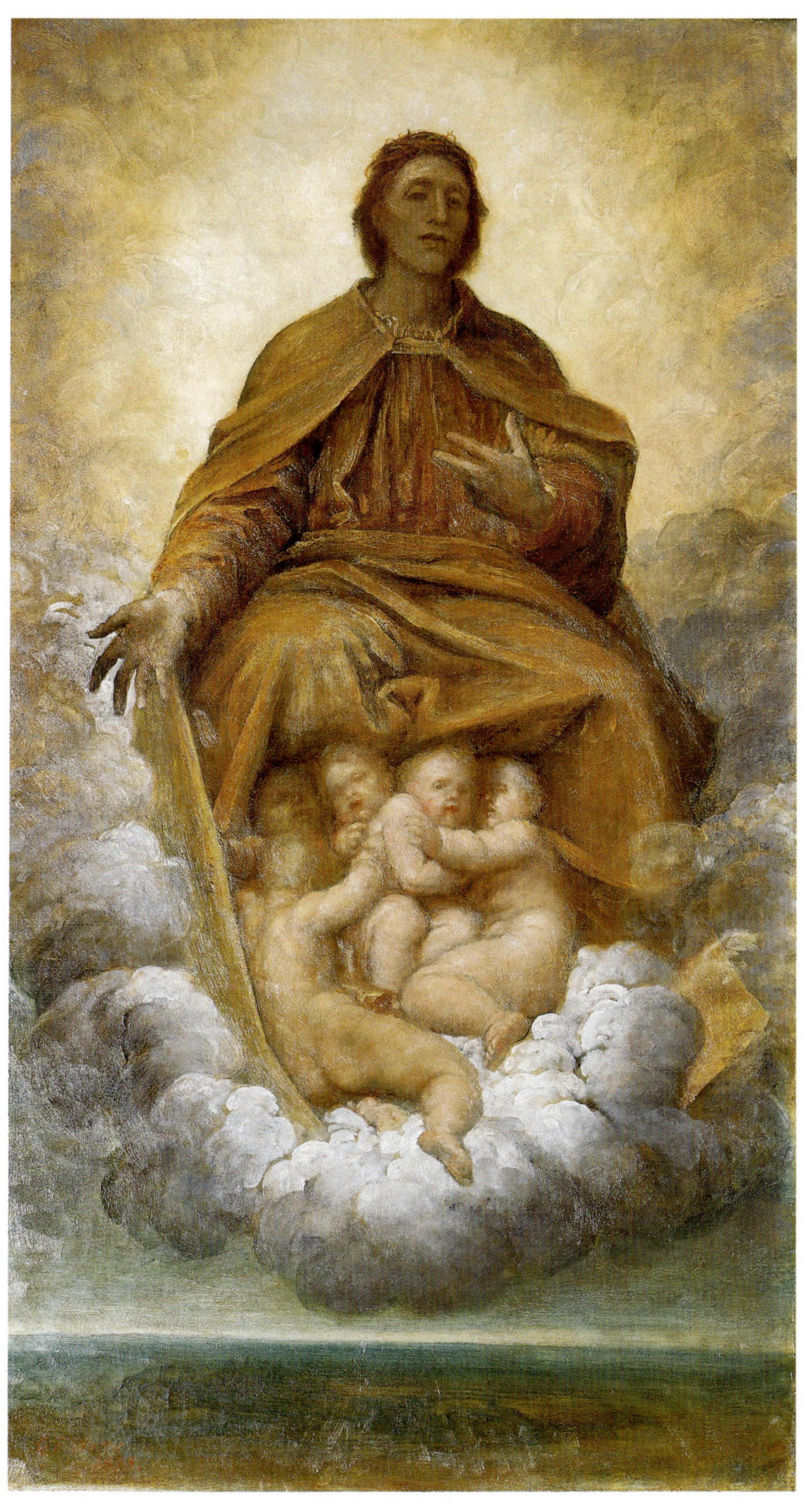

XXII (*facing page*)  *Cardinal Manning, the Archbishop of Westminster*, 1880–82 (National Portrait Gallery, London).

XXIII  *The Spirit of Christianity*, 1872–75 (private collection, courtesy of Nevill Keating Pictures Ltd).

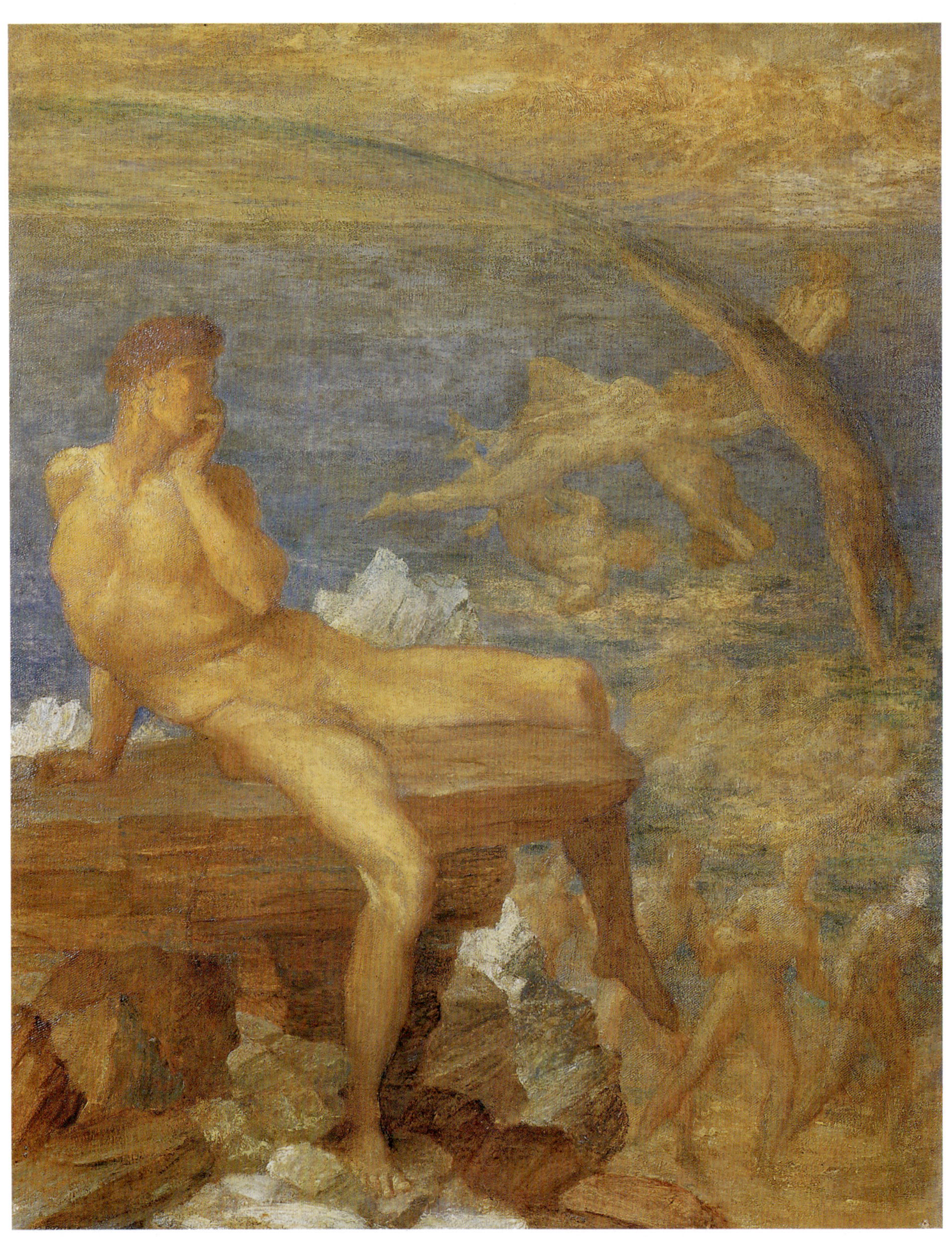

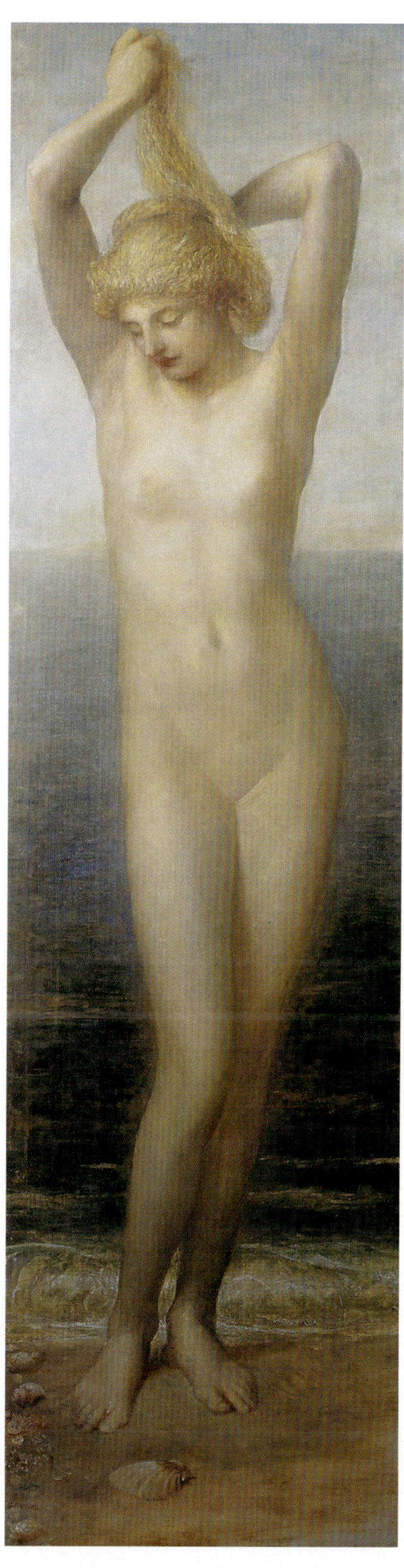

XXIV (*facing page*)  *The Genius of Greek Poetry*, c.1856–78 (Watts Gallery).

XXV  *Thetis*, 1866–93 (Watts Gallery).

XXVI (*following page top*)  *Carrara Mountains*, 1881 (private collection).

XXVII (*following page bottom*)  *The Island of Cos*, 1883 (private collection, courtesy of Christie's).

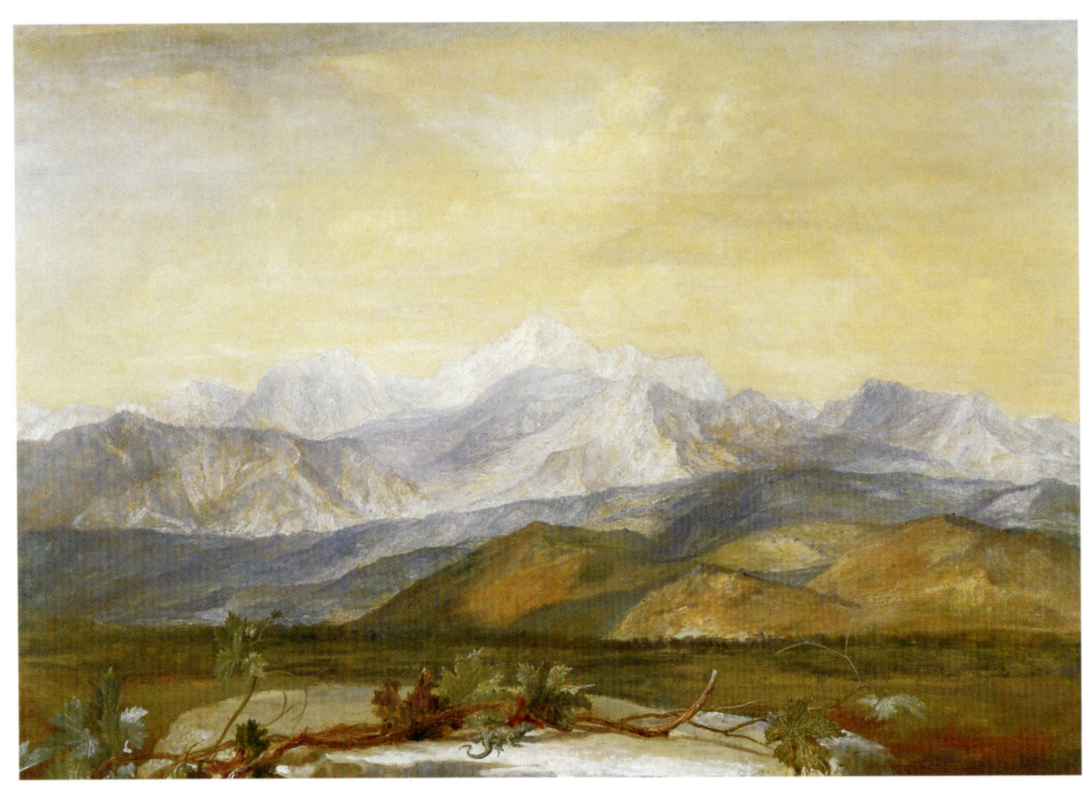

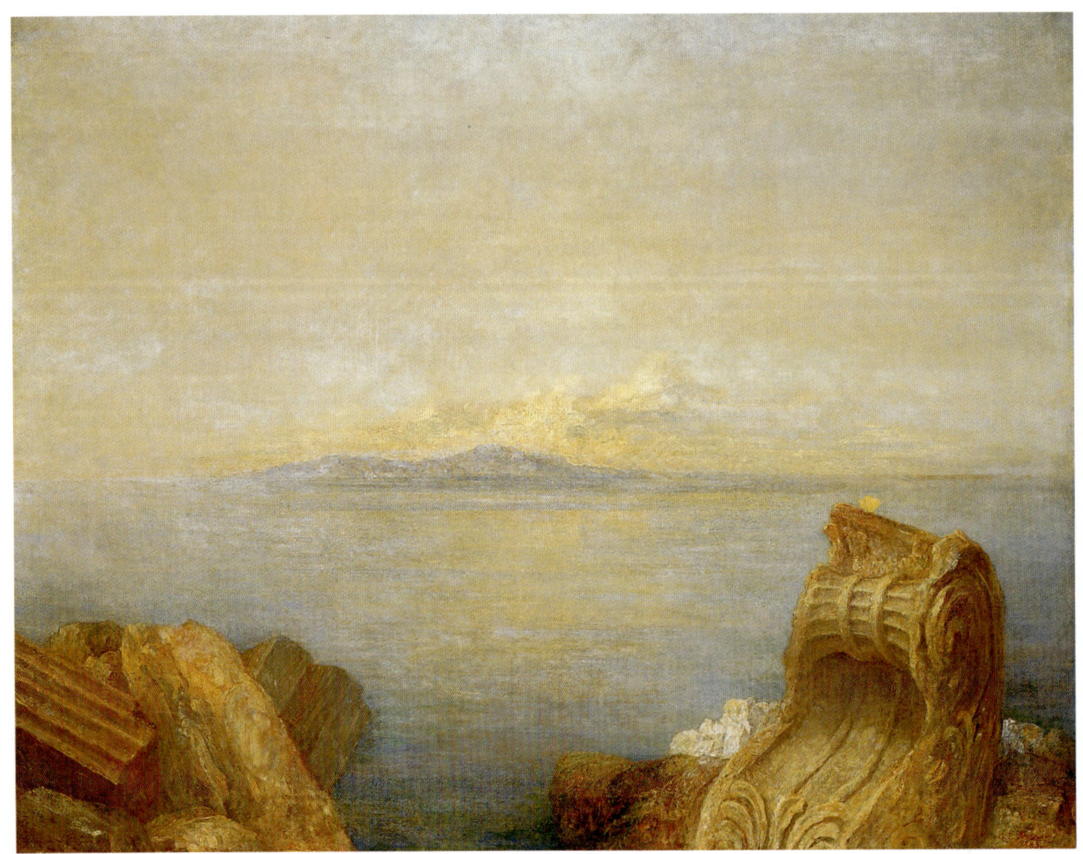

through his diplomatic protection of Greek interests, the portrait of the late Viscount Stratford de Redcliffe. To Watts, Greece was the natural home of the arts; their gods, more beautiful and larger than human beings, he wrote were 'born in the light'. So serene and harmonious were the islands, he believed their mythology resulted from constant communion with such loveliness.'[76] His *Genius of Greek Poetry*, an atmospheric anthropomorphic study in blue and gold, begun soon after his return from Halicarnassus and completed in 1878, shows a contemplative male figure on the rocks – symbolizing not a Greek man, but the Greek mind – inspired by the forces and phenomena of nature, passing in a vision before his eyes. The picture is steeped in warm, golden light, shadowed by blue haze over the sea and sky; a deeper, more glowing tone indicates the enjoyment of southern warmth, light and air.[77] While the flesh tones of *Arcadia* echo that warmth, the form of the sleeping Endymion of 1869, like the Greek genius, had developed from a Parthenon figure. The moon goddess Diana sweeping over the youth, a supreme example of the Wattsian far-reaching curve, would be seen by Chesterton as: 'the very soul of Greece . . . It is simple; it is full and free; it follows great laws of harmony, but it follows them swiftly and at will; it is headlong, and yet at rest, like the solid arch of a waterfall. It is a rushing and passionate meeting of two superb human figures.'[78]

Though not Greek, the enlarged mountain ranges of *Carrara, from the Leaning Tower of Pisa*, painted recently on silk laid over canvas, were just as visionary. Tints, warmer in the middle distance, become a celebration of blue as the mountains rise over the horizon. 'Mr Watts so rarely appears as a landscape painter that all will welcome his thoroughly pictorial and really poetical *Carrara* where the sun blanches the white hills,' the *Athenaeum* observed. Lying on the foreground marble slab representing the famous Carrara quarries, was a vine, symbolizing Immortality, and a lizard, the attribute of logic.

Venetia Cavendish Bentinck posed in red and crimson, and Violet Lindsay, herself an artist, was seen as *A Reverie*, draped in purple, a rare colour for Watts; she was also sitting for a poetic study in blue and gold to which he attached John Keats's sonnet 'Blue! Tis the life of heaven' (fig. 123 and pl. XXXIII).[79] He worked only with pure pigments, never more than two together, using transparent colour to allow the ground to show through. He used to have pigment 'field days' with Mrs Barrington, testing the effects of burnt sienna rubbed over a light red ground, and another day ultramarine over raw umber, or other combinations of earth tints. Leighton seemed sceptical of her reports. 'Oh, la cuisine, Mrs Barrington! La cuisine!'[80]

Between spells in St Petersburg and, imminently, Constantinople, the Earl of Dufferin, the brilliant, energetic ambassador, sat for the nation in May. An old friend of the artist, he interspersed Little Holland House visits with appointments with the Queen, the Foreign Office and Lansdowne House, where Sir Mountstuart Grant Duff observed, the earl's stories were 'just a shade too festive to write solemnly'.[81]

The Little Holland House Gallery was hung with pictures by the end of May. 'Rather an imposing show', Watts wrote to Rickards. He was distressed that many were unfinished. Determined to complete these, he planned to open the room to the public on Wednesday and Sunday afternoons. An early visitor, Lady Frances Balfour, wrote of their long dis-

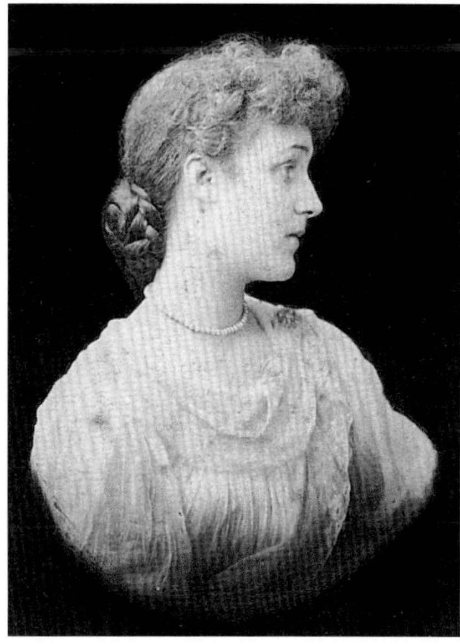

123   Marion Margaret Violet Lindsay, the future Marchioness of Granby and Duchess of Rutland.

cussion about genius: 'Watts named as the geniuses of painting in England – Burne-Jones, Turner, Rossetti, Reynolds. He refused Gainsborough a place, and I thought considered Burne-Jones first and Turner second. He dwelt a good deal on Burne-Jones's genius, saying it was remarkable for its completeness.'[82] Ned was overjoyed when Margaret's portrait was delivered to The Grange: 'What can I do in return – it looks lovely and somehow the likeness grows and I can see clearly the little face of ten years ago – that has almost passed out of recollection. I cant make out why it seems so much more like than I thought at first – but so it is – and it is an inestimable possession to me that I couldn't change for any thing I have . . . How deep I am in your debt for loving friendship now this many a year.' His intimacy and support was as valued by Watts.[83]

An Australian gold medal for *Britomart and Her Nurse* at the International Exhibition at Melbourne, was doubtless encouraging,[84] but, as he was finishing *Hugh Lupus*, he discovered a 'radical defect'. Ignoring friends' protests, he reduced the horse to a wooden frame, a drastic move vital to its improvement. Watts knew that the statue was good, but that he could make it better. It was probably now that he introduced the method he would use for *Physical Energy*. Modelling the gesso on to limb-length iron bars joined with hooks and eyes, he could turn the limbs in any direction. He simply sawed through the gesso muscle, realigned the hook and eye to change the angle, and refilled the gap.[85]

Every daylight hour now had to be devoted to *Hugh Lupus*. When Madeline Wyndham came to see the gallery on 1 June and invited him to paint her children – Mary, now nearly nineteen, George, eighteen, Guy, sixteen, Madeline, twelve, and Pamela, ten – he could not at first resist offering her a bargain, at a hundred guineas each or less. But he soon passed the project to Val, who had painted Mary as a child.[86] 'The paramount importance of pushing on my equestrian statue during the summer months has kept me slaving at it from early morning till the end of day,' he explained to Rickards. A skin irritation and weariness brought on by self-induced pressure did not help. None the less, he squeezed time for meticulous study of armour to complete the Mancunian's *Angel of Death*.[87] Watts feared that every day might be his last. 'I am like a miser who sees his coins dwindling perceptibly', he wrote to the Countess of Airlie. 'I grieve to leave so much that I intended to do, undone. When we are young we may die, when we grow old we must, so now I work as though the avenger . . . were pursuing me.'[88]

Burne-Jones entertained his Sunday guests with a tongue-in-cheek vignette of Watts's dietary restraint and gigantic physical effort to create art: 'That horse of his is getting bigger than the world, O it *is*, and too heavy for Europe to hold; if he keeps on putting more clay and stuff on it, it will go smash through into S. Africa.' And of the Little Holland House Gallery, which extended to the end of Watts's land facing Melbury Road, Ned joked to Kate Holiday, the embroiderer and wife of Henry: 'It *is* his garden and all the neighbours' gardens'.[89]

In August, the Barringtons, keen supporters of the Kyrle Society and of the Barnetts, invited the choir of St Jude's to a garden party at Melbury House, before introducing them to the more exalted studios of Leighton and Watts.[90] Access to art, Mrs Barrington noted, offered their slum visitors 'an inlet to a world of visionary beauty and noble thought', food for their spirits, which they too could share, 'a common ground for all humanity'. The benefit was mutual. Watts, seeing how eagerly these people who lived in ugly, squalid conditions, responded to his painted poems, how they listened to his explanations, reacted to his ideas and meanings, realized happily that their joy in his creations, opening their eyes to beauty, was the fulfilment of his aim, which in turn struck an inner chord in himself.[91]

On summer evenings Mrs Barrington used to play the piano, perhaps Beethoven or Handel, while he painted; and at sunset, he would put down his palette and enjoy a light song, for healthy exercise. As the warm rays fell from the high window over the glowing autumn tints on the easels, positioned to catch the light, she marvelled at the harmony and his agile mastery of his sitting cadenzas at over sixty years old.[92] He would speak of 'orchestral effects' that had flooded his mind and said he should have been a musician rather than a painter, that unlike Burne-Jones whose art grew from an inner vision, more 'revelations in sound' came to him than did actual visions for pictures. It was a fine line. Watts's vision was broader. Music was in his blood and he would have had every opportunity to compose had it moved him even more than painting did.[93]

Watts's reputation was burgeoning. His essays in the *Nineteenth Century* spurred the public to seek his views on ever wider-ranging subjects. Outstanding, if controversial, at exhibition, he had engineered unprecedented access to his work by opening his gallery to the public; and with the one-man exhibition at Manchester having repercussions in London, his voice would be heard even louder and face an unprecedented challenge at the Grosvenor Gallery.

13　Genius Exposed

In 1881 Sir Coutts Lindsay invited Watts to be the subject of the first celebrity retrospective exhibition, to inaugurate a new winter programme at the Grosvenor Gallery. It was an exceptional honour, but now that his own gallery was open to the public he was reluctant to empty its walls or to relinquish time to collate his life's work, in order to face the intimate critical assessment he most valued and feared. Sir Coutts, Hallé and Carr insisted. Watts accepted the challenge. As the first major retrospective of a living artist – 'the oldest and, broadly speaking, the greatest of our Royal Academicians'[1] – the exhibition at the Grosvenor would be of unique critical interest. (Millais had had twenty pictures exhibited at the Fine Art Society and in Paris, Gustave Courbet exhibited new works and Manet had twenty-five pictures at the gallery of *La Vie Moderne*.) Watts supplied 204 paintings, spanning four decades – portraits destined for the nation, aristocratic commissions, landscapes and imaginative conceptions of history, mythology, biblical scenes and broad universal truths, all imbued with a strong sense of sculptural form – and the marble *Clytie*. Sir Coutts Lindsay's 'bold, not to say audacious experiment' was all the more comprehensive for the artist's courage in showing subjects that did not work and were, in many cases, unfinished.[2]

Burne-Jones wrote to Rossetti for permission to loan his portrait. Weakened by chloral and deeply troubled, despite the publication that autumn of his *Ballads and Sonnets*, Rossetti suffered a stroke on 11 December. His portrait did not appear at the Grosvenor, but most owners agreed to lend. Rickards relinquished his entire collection, except for replicas and self-portraits.[3] Hallé and Mrs Barrington contacted owners, freeing Watts to paint. In the absence of Cardinal Manning, he worked from a photograph. 'If Nature writes a legible hand,' wrote Manning, 'and Photographers do not tamper with the autograph I am afraid I am not the mild old gentleman that you would have me believed to be.'[4] Serious portraits took up too much time, however, so a commission to paint George Howard was referred to William Richmond: 'My mind is so much occupied by my abstractions.' He proposed, as an enjoyable relief from grave subjects, one-sitting sketches for fifty guineas – quite a bargain, for he could achieve a fine likeness of the head at one sitting.[5]

As his pictures arrived at Bond Street, the strong gallery lighting revealed that many canvases had deteriorated, looking 'little more than pastels', Hallé recalled. Watts, with his preference for fresco, disliked a smooth oily paint surface, and used little medium. Careful to use safe colours, he would extract the oil from Winsor and Newton tubes by squeezing the paint on to a stone or blotting-paper; he reduced it under water to the texture of putty, and used it almost dry, mixed, according to Emilie Barrington, with benzine or turpentine as a medium.[6] Over the decades, the medium had evaporated, leaving the paint vulnerable. He immediately had the pictures varnished and saved by a restorer. As a result of their pure ground colour, the restored pictures appeared to be much brighter in tone than his recent unvarnished pictures looked blotchy and heavy. Concerned to explain this discrepancy, before he left for Brighton, he wrote at length to *The Times* art critic Harry Quilter, outlining his approach to imaginative subjects. Hitherto, he had felt no need to complete one before starting another, because dealers did not buy them, and he often repainted exhibited pictures. Despite their universality, he had endeavoured to convey a real feeling or mood; and he compared his use of mood, line, colour, form and surface – 'pedantic drawing purposely avoided' – to the melody and harmony employed by musicians, pointing out that neither presented actual truth.[7]

The juxtaposition of brighter, early finished works, pictures redeveloped since previous exhibitions, and unfinished, more atmospheric subjects on the walls of the two large galleries and staircase at the Grosvenor, would undoubtedly present a challenge to critics in their assessment of Watts's artistic development. Neither was the application of paint straightforward. He would wear down the outer bristles of his paintbrushes on a background, or rub them on a hard surface to create to the tiny pyramid shaped point, with which he liked to paint. Otherwise, he might use the other end of the brush, or paper, a leather stump or a filed-down toothbrush. His increasingly favoured method was to apply the putty-like pigment with a finger in distinct touches; when these were almost dry, he smeared the touches together with a paper knife and waited until the surface was quite dry before working 'partially over it', presumably with a point or fingertip, to achieve 'a bloom of atmosphere' in his painting. No mark would remain as a 'smear' on a finished canvas, which he repeatedly scorned as characteristic of the Impressionists. Ever alert to new ideas, he kept a close eye on nature, observing how various effects required different treatment.[8]

'The Collection of the Works of G. F. Watts, RA' opened to the public on Saturday 31 December 1881. As ever, most viewers, mindful of his inspiration to the Poet Laureate, were drawn to the celebrity portraits. Lady Holland had graciously lent portraits of herself in the Riviera hat, painted in 1843, and of Princess Lieven, Prince Jerome Bonaparte, Monsieur Guizot and President Thiers, all deceased. The vibrant colours of her ladyship's portrait in the Mediterranean sunlight seemed crude – the result of youthful fervour, critics suggested – beside the darker, more severe French portraits in the flatter style of Holbein; and the effects of light and shade, suggesting musical vibrations in *A Lamplight Study – Herr Joachim* and defining the 1859 portrait of Tennyson, drew comparison with Rembrandt.[9]

Watts, as 'the leader of the reformation of portrait-art in England', according to the *Magazine of Art*, had given portraiture fresh inspiration, a new point of departure; his mental and emotional adaptability in attuning to the wide variety of spiritual and intellectual forces of the Victorian age was seen as extraordinary.[10] Whereas Millais, for example, painted perfectly balanced pictures of man, mind and body, Watts presented the inner soul, the living human face. *John Stuart Mill*, the reformer's sensitive ascetic features showing strain at the end of his life – the antithesis of the exuberantly robed portrait of the late Arthur Penrhyn Stanley, Dean of Westminster and the presidential picture of Leighton – was judged the most delicately powerful historical portrait. *Thomas Carlyle*, grim and powerful, did not inspire affection, but compelled 'more than casual thought'. Recent portraits of Constantine Ionides and his wife perpetuated the family patronage.

Each was a shrewd character study, painted with the eye of an old master – who faced the viewer in the 1862 self-portrait in wide-awake hat and black velvet painting coat – and the insight of a modern man engaged with the most remarkable, wide-ranging intellects of his age. To the artist's regret, Darwin, Faraday and Disraeli had not been able to sit. Darwin, too ill to travel to London, was prepared to sit at home in Kent, but Watts, happier painting in his own studio, had never managed to go – nor had he been able to face the prospect of painting Ruskin.[11] The portrait collection attracted yards of press comment. 'It would be nothing less than a national misfortune if this splendid gallery of British worthies of the nineteenth century should eventually be dispersed', declared the *Globe*, echoed by Edmund Gosse in the *Pall Mall Gazette*. Both called for their acquisition by the State during the artist's lifetime. Quilter produced extensive coverage for *The Times* and an analysis for the *Contemporary Review*. The key to his male portraits, 'stripping the *soul-wrappings* off his subject' to find its real essence, was the antithesis of idealized ancient Greek sculpture upon which his imaginative work was based.[12]

Watts's female portraits presented, as the *Evening Standard* put it, his 'most undisguised failures and most delightful successes'. If he could find sympathetic expression in the soul of his sitter, with the odd exception, beauty alone was not enough. He painted life-size and, whereas male portraits focused chiefly on the face and were rarely more than half-length to maximize the impact, women he had most loved and major aristocratic commissions were painted full length. The sumptuous Venetian-style portraits of Miss Ford as *Bianca*, Alice Prinsep playing the piano and Madeline Wyndham – were widely admired. That of the Countess of Rosebery – the former Hannah de Rothschild – her clear blue eyes directed at the viewer, was the most popular.[13] *Choosing*, the jewel-like picture of his young bride Ellen Terry, which Watts had asked for, was missing; its owner 'Eustacia' Smith, when accosted by Mrs Barrington at the private view, replied somewhat perversely that she had received no request, yet she lent two other paintings.[14]

The sight of his social realist pictures amongst the refined art at London's most aesthetic gallery jolted critics. No modern painter had confronted the problem of women's degradation as frankly. The woman shivering in *Under a Dry Arch* was not 'picturesque, sentimental wretchedness'[15], but a cruel fact of life in the gutter, of vice and drunkenness leading to death, and the tyranny of the rich over the poor; and *The Irish Famine* underlined worsening conditions and ferment in Ireland. The problems was still pertinent over thirty years later. 'Bad policy, Mr Watts, to confront these "curled darlings" with so vital a question', the *Spectator* objected. 'You come too close home Sir to our consciences, to be agreeable.'[16]

That was the essence of Watts, to stir the spectator's consciousness. Unpopularity and ridicule had never dented his resolve to tackle his subject matter, despite the damage to his respect, his nerves, and his bank account. The poor must be raised from misery. He never again painted the victims, but worked increasingly to open the nation's eyes to their plight; he sent his noblest art to inspire them in the slums, he would open his gallery to them and increasingly promote art and the revival of handicrafts to stimulate their lives. On canvas he now addressed poverty from a moral idealistic standpoint.

Alexander Ionides's gesture in releasing *Aurora*, the earliest work in the exhibition painted before Watts left for Italy, brought to an end the Greek's bitterness and marked his perceptive patronage.[17] The earliest cosmic subject *Time and Oblivion* still puzzled critics. Its harmonious composition prefigured Pater's dictum that 'All art constantly aspires towards the condition of music' and was seen as 'one of the grandest pieces of expressional form', but the obscure subject failed to please, except as decoration. If the picture seemed 'an incomplete dream', this was Watts's intention; seeing a fragment, the viewer is meant to imagine the greater whole. However, *Life's Illusions*, the nude embodiments of Hope and Ambition hovering over shattered symbols of greatness and power, which had signified 'nothing' to the *Athenaeum* in 1849, was now 'the delight of a mind poetical, speculative, and in love with leisure . . . at once learned and deliberate', and to Quilter it was '*immorally* beautiful',[18] but its complex messages still confused many.

Literary themes were clearer, if not always as successful. The overwhelming favourite and only work Watts acknowledged as 'entirely an illustration of another man's ideas' was the 1870s *Paolo and Francesca* with Virginia Somers as Francesca. Even the staid *Art Journal*, which had criticized Paolo's 'insufficiency of thigh' in 1879, now declared the picture 'one of the master's crowning achievements'.[19]

*The Eve of Peace*, a medieval knight at the close of battle and the heroic *Sir Galahad*, each figure in idealized contemplation, give the impression of moving on, more peace to achieve in a troubled world.[20] Throughout the gallery there was a sense of nineteenth-century unrest, questioning, sadness and uncertainty. The *New York Times* congratulated the artist for immortalizing, in *The Midday Rest*, 'the hulking heroes who thrashed Marshal Haynau' – notorious for flogging women in the capture of Brescia – and 'guided the steeds that dragged the Duke of Wellington's Funeral Car.'[21] Even in landscape, there was pathos. *All the Air a Solemn Stillness Holds*, a second version to the haystacks lit by the last flush of sunset, has a farmworker on a grey horse, rather than *Colleoni*, merging with nature in the foreground shadows. Particularly telling were areas of pure or increasingly atmospheric light colouring, as in the *Carrara Mountains from Pisa* and the poetic horizontal seascapes, *The Island of Cos*, which the *Athenaeum* noted 'has more than a touch of the power and sentiment of Gaspar Poussin' and the popular *Return of the Dove*, the cunning effect of the exhausted bird flying over the waves.[22]

Watts's stature as a Victorian Olympus was more controversial. Although meticulous as a draughtsman in studies and life-drawing, he avoided a conscious display of 'dexterity' in his painted poems; and with Long Mary's unusually elongated, small breasted body as his ideal female form, his

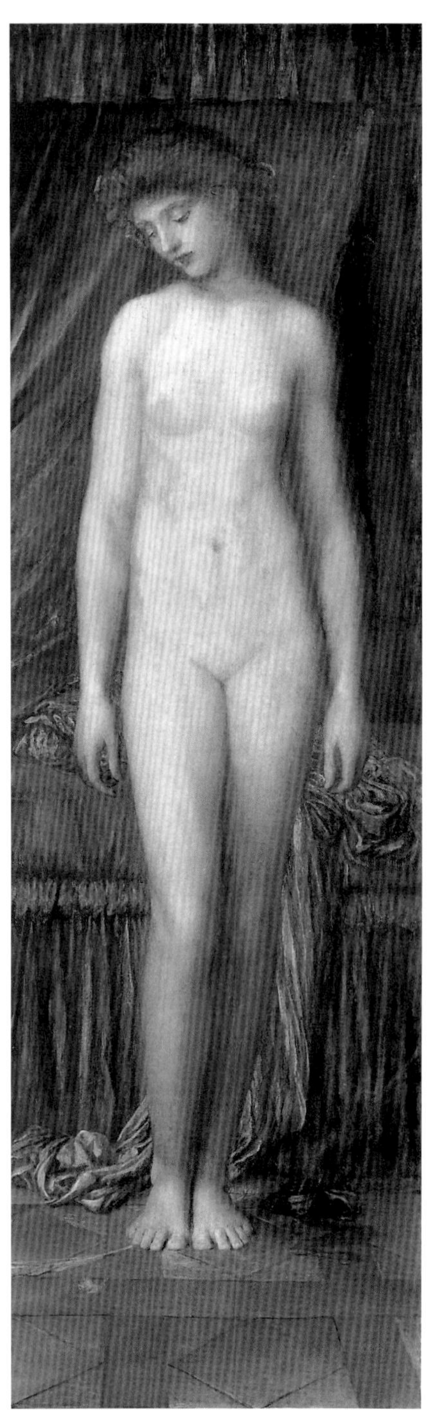

124    *Psyche*, 1880–82 (Tate, London).

figures stood out from contemporary figure-painting, their proportions often unpalatable, or simply disconcerting, when combined with 'the finest feeling for beauty of form', as in the triple nude study, retitled *The Three Goddesses*. Struck by 'the calm and powerful study', the French critic Ernest Chesnau saw Watts as 'the only painter of the English school who has treated the female nude simply from the point of view of style, and with no other object than to realize its purely plastic beauty.'[23]

*The Wife of Pygmalion* endured as 'an exquisite modern';[24] and *Ariadne in Naxos* and *Diana and Endymion*, admired by artists, were recognized by critics to be masterpieces of poetry, design and colour. In this 'most complete' *Ariadne*, Watts had given equal importance to the poetry of the light-filled island setting, to the expression and form of the Cretan princess, to the *mouvementé* folds of her drapery inspired by the Parthenon sculpture, to the playful panthers of the gods, and to the urgent direction of her companion that rescue is at hand – not to be confused with *Ariadne deserted by Theseus*, waking up to her plight and also exhibited. *Endymion* was noted for inventive, technical and suggestive power, the use of colour to create the mood, the phosphorescent ripples of drapery and cool other-worldly tones of the moon goddess.[25]

There were three versions of *Orpheus and Eurydice*: Madeline Wyndham's horizontal half-length of the late 1860s; a phantasmic *pas-de-deux* – the silver body of Eurydice collapsing in the arms of the Thracian poet – the 1872 design for the larger full-length of 1879, also exhibited. Its 'true poetic feeling', refined sentiment and elaborate design, to Chesnau, seemed reduced by the overpowering character. No doubt reawakened by these, the French artist Odilon Redon was tackling the Orpheus myth, though like Moreau he concentrated on the theme of his severed head.[26]

Watts was recognized as England's finest living painter of the idealized nude, in dignity of form and gesture, purity and, owing to his large-scale and subject matter, power. Whereas Burne-Jones produced gently drooping figures stylized in the manner of Botticelli and Mantegna, and Leighton portrayed more muscular, soft-contoured figures derived from later Greek sculptors, Watts, choosing the earlier school, treated the entire figure as an impression. 'You see, or fancy you see to this day,' Quilter wrote of Phidian sculpture, 'the play of the muscles under the skin, but the last thing that ever strikes you is their anatomy. It is all there when you look for it, but the whole work is so beautiful that you never feel tempted to notice the way it has been produced. It is exactly this which has been Mr Watts's aim – we should call it the human method as opposed to the scientific or the sensual . . . the body as a vehicle for expressing all high feeling.' Rather than present a typical woman, identifiable by her education or breeding, Watts expressed ideal truths through intensified emotion and the use of colour.[27] The tall mythological nudes *Daphne* and *Psyche* (fig. 124) are mysterious and strikingly impersonal. Both stand towards the viewer, their heads inclined to the left and one leg bent, yet the essence of each pose and expression is quite different. *Psyche*'s bowed head, rigid upper body and limp arms show a young woman dejected by grief, in the grey mist of early dawn; a broken lamp at her feet evidence that she has yielded to temptation. *Daphne*, glows with warm colour as she raises her arm above her head, beginning to merge with the laurel tree behind, under the protection of the gods. 'Apelles might have painted thus,' suggested the *Daily News*.[28]

More dynamic and integrated with nature, but, as yet, small studies for Watts's cosmic fresco scheme, were the biblical *Eve* trilogy. The first beautiful columnar figure stands with her head raised and palms facing down, linking Heaven and Earth – a decade later, she would be developed into an astonishingly Symbolist image *She Shall be Called Woman*. As *Eve Tempted*, she bows forward, 'enmeshed, enthralled', into the forbidden Tree of Paradise; overpowered by the scent of the flowers and luscious fruit, her head is thrown back and arm angled in ecstasy; and finally, in *Eve Repentant*, 'the Earthly paradise wrecked', she is seen in moonlight, pressing her entire body into the tree, her hands clasped over her hair, which falls to the earth.[29]

Leighton, in his address to Academy students on 10 December 1881, had emphasized that the prime purpose of art was to create aesthetical impressions that delight the viewer and offer escape from life's ills: 'What definite oral truth is taught by it with all its universality? What ethical proposition can it convey? What teaching or exhortation is in its voice?' he asked, challenging Watts's aims. 'None, absolutely none. The president insisted that the language of Art was not an appropriate vehicle for ethic truths, that only words should express ideas. 'It is not, then, it cannot be the foremost duty of Art to seek to embody that which it cannot adequately present, and to enter into a competition in which it is doomed to inevitable defeat.' However, he acknowledged that 'intellectual and ethical elements . . . added to the fundamental aesthetic sensation, having, like those stirred in us by Music, the power to raise us to the highest regions of poetic emotion, deserve to rank amongst the noblest delights of men.'[30] Privately their debate would continue, Leighton arguing that beauty was the only true mission of art and that a picture suffered if it suggested an unseen thought, that no art should be didactic. Watts agreed that neither painting nor poetry should be didactic, but there was a wide difference between being didactic and being suggestive. At times, he clearly did cross that boundary.[31]

Critics viewed Watts's allegorical work with varying degrees of doubt, suspicion and awe. All were struck by the overall sense of mystic sorrow. 'He lives in a strange air, which can hardly be breathed by healthy human art'. As Leighton warned, 'The meaning is often hard to seize, the beauty which we expect from art is not always present.'[32] The 'large sexless figure' in the clouds, calling for religious tolerance, but offering no solution, in *To All Churches: A Symbolical Design*, was all the more confusing for Watts's modern iconography presenting God as neither male nor female.[33] The artist attached particular significance to his reinterpretation of Death in the monumental sculptural *Time, Death and Judgment* and the much-admired *Love and Death*, but the grand, grave fourteen-foot-high *Angel of Death* presiding over her court, at the end of the gallery, was too unfinished.[34]

Watts was widely respected for his courage, for having forged and pursued a unique path in the face of censure and neglect, and praised for both strengths and weaknesses, 'the rich harvest of a genius still in its vigour'. His portraits were expected to stand the test of time and not look unworthy beside old masters, and Watts was acknowledged as England's most imaginative – if imperfect – modern artist. Sir Coutts's experiment had proved to be 'a vindication of the poetic genius and the executive power of a living master', an example of Leighton's advice to students, not to debase their self-respect for temporary popularity. How well Watts's monumental works would have looked at Burlington House, observed *The Spectator*, had the Academy, rather than the Grosvenor, chosen to hold the landmark exhibition and honour their most senior member, who was seen in France as 'the only Englishman who has an appreciation of the nude in art combined with the ability to portray it'.[35]

William Graham wrote to Watts as the exhibition opened: 'I must confess a new astonishment at the grandeur of it when presented en masse, as it is on these walls, and at the abundance of your productive power which the collection manifests.' Furthermore, the exhibition raised the standing of British art on the Continent.[36] Watts's reputation was enormously enhanced, though he doubted it was assured. Having worked so long without praise, he preferred to be undervalued than overrated, yet he needed to know that his ideas were affecting the public so that he could satisfy his yearning to guide his generation from materialism towards nobler thought and action. Members of the public were moved to seek his views on society's ills.[37]

The critics' verdict of his life's work now meant a great deal to Watts, who collected the reviews and discussed them with the Barringtons on his return from Brighton. Crushing superficial criticism of his figure painting and technique depressed him when there was so much more to the overall concept.[38] His contact with Quilter paid off, resulting in an usually informed response in *The Times*.[39] Leighton proposed *Psyche* as a Chantrey Bequest purchase by the Academy.[40] As purchasers requested prices, Watts engaged Russell Barrington to negotiate, advising him to consult Holman Hunt. (In the event Burne-Jones was consulted). He was quite clear how much he wanted: for *Carrara Mountains* one thousand guineas (bought by his sitter Horace Davey, QC), a thousand to fifteen hundred for *Greek Poetry* – or eight to nine hundred without copyright – and seven to eight hundred for *Esau*.[41]

A surprise dinner was to be held in his honour at the gallery on 25 January. Gladstone and Harcourt were among the hundred or so guests invited by Hallé, and a couple sent their regrets in congratulatory letters to Watts in Brighton.[42] Having publicly lambasted Academy dinners, he could hardly preside over a feast at the Grosvenor. The thought of a 'greenery-yallery' affair amongst his serious works of art appalled him. He sent an immediate veto to Sir Coutts and wrote to Burne-Jones as a member of the committee. 'I quite understand – of course it will be stopped at once and no harm done,' Burne-Jones replied, stung by the tactless Emilie Barrington who had pointed the finger alarmingly at him. 'This winter is a triumph for you isn't it?'[43]

The Gallery, not a little miffed, was left with the task of notifying guests. Touched to hear from the Earl of Lytton that 'eating and drinking appear to me grotesquely inappropriate modes . . . of expressing admiration for a man's genius or gratitude for his work', Watts invited the poet and former Viceroy of India to sit for the collection. Cloaking his monumental ambition with humility, the artist replied that what he really wanted was to be compared to the old masters. 'Those who while they ennoble their birthland enrich the world and ennoble humanity itself, from my childhood I have had a longing to be of that band, but I dare not think it is for me . . . By showing me what your own genius presents to you as mine, it is you who complete the strain if I strike the chord.'[44] He was thrilled by F. W. H.

Myers's response, a twelve-stanza poem in the *Fortnightly*: 'To be glorified by poetry! Sympathy with my strivings should be, & are, very dear to me.'[45] Browning attracted the crowds at the exhibition when he spotted the Prinseps' granddaughter standing, astonished, in front of the nude *Goddesses* and composed an 'amazed' couplet for her. Their laughter sent twelve-year-old Laura flying back into the artist's arms.[46]

Rickards and Mary Fraser Tytler  (fig. 125) rejoiced to see Watts's elevation of British art acknowledged at last.[47] Thornycroft gave a lecture to Academy students on his principle of the flattened curve, and the Princess of Wales and the prime minister joined the artist at Leighton's private view.[48] Longing to congratulate him, Mary called twice at Little Holland House in his absence – since her father's death she had been a more frequent visitor from her new home, 68 Eccleston Square. On 14 March, she wrote to tell him of her pleasure in his triumph: 'I have long perceived that whilst before some great master's pictures I feel wonder, before yours I always feel *better* . . . you must have had all the greatest of England thanking you worthily for your great and good work but I have also a feeling that you are too great not to be pleased to give pleasure to the least, and so I have told you of mine.'[49]

'My dear Miss Tytler,' he replied on 17 March, 'I think I am old friend enough and certainly am old enough in years to say My dear Miss Mary, or indeed, My dear Mary without the Miss! Your charming letter has given me great pleasure.' Delighted that his pictures awakened 'higher thoughts and feelings than is always the case even with some of the best' he invited her to bring him her work when she returned to town.[50]

Cambridge University commissioned portraits of its chancellor, the Duke of Devonshire, for the university and for the sitter,[51] and Watts was negotiating a portrait of the Marquess of Salisbury, the Conservative leader of the opposition in the House of Lords for his historical series,[52] when the *New York Times* reporter arrived at Little Holland House. As the artist showed him into the studio – 'a large and lofty room with but few luxurious accessories – the reporter noticed that his hair was now streaked with silver beneath the velvet skullcap, his beard shorter and quite grey. Cardinal Manning's portrait impressed him as 'a speaking likeness, with the keen, resistless, unflinching look in his blue eyes so familiar to us all'. The gallery was still denuded from the exhibition. Even so, the artist's achievements seemed immense. They left the studio and walked to the dark, narrow landing. Suddenly Watts released a blind on their left. 'There before us stood his colossal figure of *Hugh Lupus* . . . Below us to the right, was an open door leading to the garden; the sun struck across this and over the green turf; the effect was magical; the great warrior on his charger seemed alive.' A month later a review of Watts's life, art, and immense labour, reached the American public.[53]

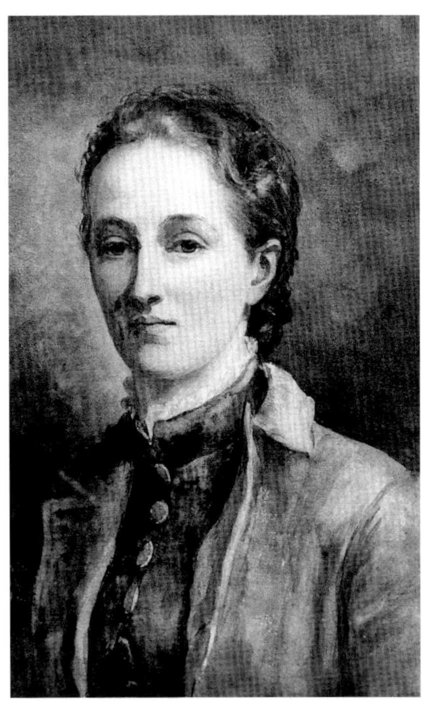

125    Mary Fraser Tytler, *Self-portrait*, 1882 (Watts Gallery).

## 14   Revelations

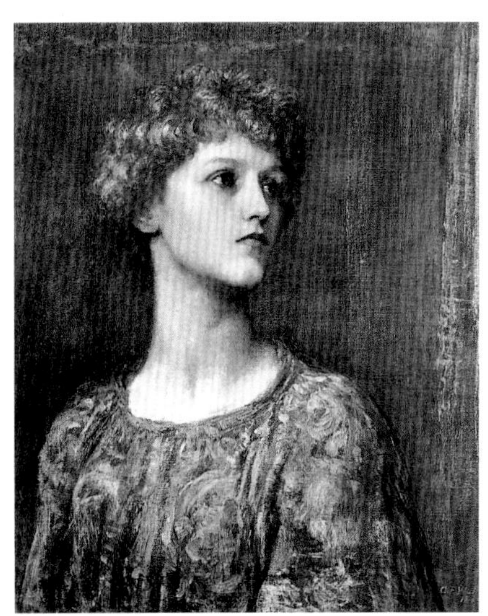

126   *Dorothy Dene*, 1888 (courtesy of the Fine Art Society).

THE REVEREND SAMUEL BARNETT SAW THE St Jude's Easter art exhibitions, and especially Watts's paintings, as a way of leading parishioners to the light. According to Henrietta Barnett's account of 'Pictures for the People' published in *Practicable Socialism*, the 4,600 catalogues sold at a penny in 1882 more than covered printing costs,[1] despite noisy threats to visitors from the Lord's Day Observance Society, demanding that the bishop order closure on Sundays. Barnett's vigorous defence won the day. 'Never in my intercourse with my neighbours have I been so conscious of their souls and their souls' needs as when they hung around me listening to what I had to say of Watts's picture *Time, Death and Judgment*', he wrote to the bishop, and convinced him that in revealing the spirit of the pictures, he was drawing slum parishioners away from degrading sights and closer to God.[2]

By chance Watts spotted Ellen Terry through his hedge in the garden next door, probably Val Prinsep's. On Easter Sunday, he sent a letter to Britain's best-loved actress at the Lyceum Theatre, where her performance as Juliet, opposite Irving's Romeo, was reported to be unusually low-key, following the departure of her second husband. 'I watch with eager interest your success rejoicing greatly in it. Will you shake hands with me (in spirit?) What success I may have will be very incomplete & unsatisfactory if you cannot do what I have long been hesitating to ask. If you cannot keep silence, if you can, one word "yes," will be sufficient. Signor.' She marked the envelope '1st after long years' and answered simply, 'Yes.'[3]

The Royal Academy summer exhibition catalogue announced the purchase of *Psyche*. 'I believe the design intellectually and graphically would place the picture if the craftsmanship were satisfactory among the valuable possessions of the world,' Watts wrote to Leighton, adding that 'if we do know when and how far we succeed we cannot know how we fail.' He wished to improve the picture and needed the summer to finish it. 'How proud I should be to see my work the property of the Academy and the nation,' an honour he nearly refused so as not to block Val, who had painted a large picture with an Academy purchase in mind. Hamo Thornycroft's heroic bronze archer *Teucer*, modelled with his advice, was also bought through the Chantrey bequest, but Val did not succeed that year.[4] Watts's unnamed *Portrait* of a lady in a saffron dress may have been Leighton's model of the 1880s, Ada Pullan, the 'vision of beauty' dressed in deep mourning, whom Mrs Barrington spotted outside Holland Park Studios. Leighton celebrated her dramatic expression and gestures in subject pictures, but could not capture her complexion for a portrait. In a two-hour sitting Watts encapsulated her clouded pallor, tinged with shell pink. As Dorothy Dene (fig. 126) she too would be groomed for the stage.[5]

As shockwaves from Manet's *Un Bar aux Folies-Bergeres* at the Paris Salon were reverberating in London – 'an ugly girl in glaring blue, surrounded by gaslights, champagne bottles . . . stares stupidly at a world which once knew better things,' cried the *Athenaeum*[6] – Watts's portraits of Cardinal Manning and HRH The Prince of Wales caused a commotion at the Grosvenor.[7] The Very Reverend Henry Edward Manning, Cardinal Archbishop of Westminster, much changed since his reputation at Oxford as one of Gladstone's three most handsome contemporaries, now led an ascetic life. Watts used a large format to present him like a Titianesque Renaissance pope (pl. XXII). Robed in scarlet, the cardinal sits on a red upholstered throne, facing the viewer's left in three-quarter profile. Beneath his biretta, his face is skeletal, the red-rimmed eyes glassy and concentrated, the nose strong and pointed, there is a hint of grey moustache on his clean-shaven face; from rich lace cuffs, his veined hands and attenuated fingers relax over the arms of the throne. The picture is a celebration of cardinal red, with fine attention paid to the ageing flesh and gaunt features Watts thought 'almost impossible to realize in any living man'.[8]

But the *Athenaeum*, which revered his 1860 portrait of Sir Benjamin Brodie in the light of the old masters, Holbein, Titian and Bellini, found the cardinal's 'strangely emaciated features loaded with thought . . . antithesis to *Sir B Brodie*. It is intensely powerful and pathetic, but by no means one of the most agreeable of Mr Watts's portraits.' Manning cut out the review, underlined the last phrase, and had it sent to Watts, reprimanding him for being true to life. As a teetotaller, he felt the picture libellous. 'It has made me a little tipsy about the nose!'[9]

His attitude to faith, published in *The Eternal Priesthood* the following year, was comparable to the artist's imaginative sketches in that the idea is more important than the finish: 'In the measure in which we realize the world of faith, the eternal truths, the nature of sin, the love of souls, their danger of perishing, we shall find no difficulty in speaking of them with sincerity and simplicity. It is the desire to be eloquent and to shine as orators that causes unreality, vain-glory and emptiness.' Watts would later refer to his visionary pictures as 'Eternal Truths',[10] but for the present he was hit by a terrible truth.

Criticism of his full-length portrait of the Prince of Wales (fig. 127) by Quilter in *The Times* may have been justified, but his claim that the Academy refused to exhibit it compelled the artist withdraw it from the Grosvenor. On 10 May 1882 Watts wrote to the benchers of the Middle Temple, returned their cheque for a thousand pounds and advised them to commission Frank Holl, not yet a full Academician, to produce a portrait 'more worthy of the subject'. Conditions were partly to blame. Sporadic sittings had taken place at Marlborough House, where lighting and conditions differed from those in the studio. The problem was surely that Watts's overriding concern was to reveal the inner man, largely through the face and head, which in itself looked well, but took up barely one-fifth of the picture space, otherwise filled by the prince's corpulent form, black cloak and refined feet. The following day the benchers banked the cheque, and acknowledged that 'as the genius of Mr Watts has been so frequently man-

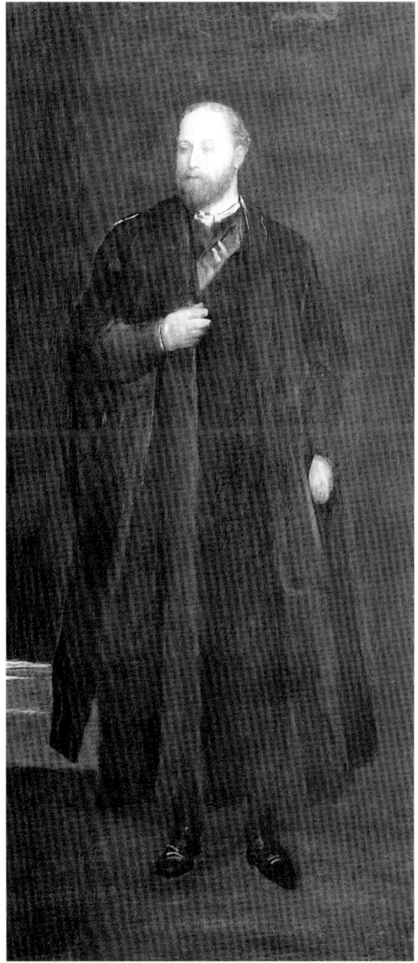

127   Study for *HRH The Prince of Wales*, 1874–82 (private collection).

ifested and is so generally acknowledged, they hope that their recognition of it may lend to console him for his disappointment in this instance'.[11]

The experience was all the more galling in view of his heightened resolve to create 'good things for the honour of the age and nation.' On Wednesday 14 June at the Sheldonian Theatre in Oxford, Watts accepted the honorary doctorate. The Barringtons had travelled with him by train to the midday ceremony and while they went on to the award-winners luncheon, he ate sandwiches in the meadows.[12] He had vowed to start nothing new until his old works were completed, but he could never suppress ideas, and was now developing *Love and Life* (pl. XXXI), a major metaphysical companion to *Love and Death*, in which Love, a winged youth, leads a timid nude maiden up the rocky path of life. Opening the gallery to the public freed him from interruptions, though he made time for close friends. 'Now that I have a gallery into which visitors can go I see no one except by appointment till 6 – nor do I ever make engagements for sittings till after 2 o'clock,' he explained to Lady Airlie. '*Certainly* before 1 o'clock you would always find me alone.'[13]

The Duke of Devonshire came for his first sitting on 22 June, to pose for Cambridge University's three-quarter-length portrait (fig. 128) in his gold-laced black chancellor's robe, with the ribbon of the Garter. Irish strife had come to a terrible head on 6 May, when his son the new chief secretary Lord Frederick Cavendish had been stabbed to death with his undersecretary in Phoenix Park in Dublin. The duke's dignity at this sad time impressed Watts. He kept every appointment and endured long sittings, while privately confiding in his diary on 15 July, 'When I look back to the last few weeks all seems like a dream.'[14]

However, the artist showed little nobility in negotiations to buy *The Birth of Venus* from Walter Crane, also bereaved, moving home after the death of his infant son. 'I have always desired to possess your picture', Watts began. Pleading that he had been 'crippled' by framing for the Grosvenor and building expenses, he asked to pay the three hundred pounds in instalments. Crane respectfully agreed, but had to wait four years for the final instalment, still fifty pounds short.[15] Watts was rather more gallant to the *Punch* cartoonist Linley Sambourne, when asked for a contribution to his autograph fan. These served as glamorous visiting books from the 1870s, and Sambourne's sandalwood *brisé* fan, decorated and signed by artists, would look well in his aesthetic Kensington home in Stafford Terrace. Watts, following Millais's palette, drew a bundle of paintbrushes, signed and dated 11 August 1882.[16] He had been overworking and wanted a change of air and amusement. The Briary was let and Brighton, too glaring in the summer, was 'too bare of trees'. While he entertained thoughts of taking a country cottage for fishing,[17] an accusation that his work was too grave drove him to paint an oddly comic picture, *BC*, of a naked couple sitting on the edge of the sea, the young woman looking with amused concern at her lover sickened by the taste of his first oyster.[18]

In September Lady Marian Alford was one of the last visitors to see *Hugh Lupus* (fig. 129) – 'full of vigour very rich and I thought as fine a statue as you could wish to see'[19] – before the mighty horse and rider, having been photographed from every viewpoint, was swathed in a sheet and driven away to be cast in bronze at the Thames Ditton statue foundry. Watts had set the entire group at an angle. The *Gros Veneur*, his rolls of fat indicated

128     *The Duke of Devonshire*, 1882 (Fitzwilliam Museum, Cambridge).

by a rippling tunic, stretches back in a high medieval saddle from which hangs a huge Norman sword; his legs are heavily armed, not stretched; his right hand, boldly ungloved, reaches up to cast off the falcon, while the horse, its body twisting with energy, left foreleg raised, strains to gallop up and over the rocky terrain. At last the sculpture trolley was available for the construction of the great symbolic equestrian statue that would absorb Watts for the rest of his life.[20]

Embarking on a third *Nineteenth Century* polemic, Watts prepared clear, focused notes the subject of 'Taste in Dress', in a portable five-inch notebook. Emilie Barrington's contribution, if any, would have been minimal, for Thornycroft had designed her a garden studio of her own. Here she installed casts of the Panathenaic riders and *Nike Athena*, from which Watts would instruct her while she copied or enlarged his designs; she also worked from models, among them, on 13 December, Dorothy Dene. A gate was erected in their dividing fence so that he could reach her without having to change out of his studio clothes for a formal entrance from the road – Mrs Barrington had given him a peasant smock from Somerset and an embroidered blue linen one from Brittany.[21] The young writer 'Vernon Lee', whom she took to Watts's and Leighton's studios through a succession of 'paddocks and back doors', recalled her as 'a rumpled, scrumpled little brown paper woman, of uncertain artistic pretensions, a sort of King Charles dog of the neighbouring studios.'[22]

'On Taste in Dress', published in January 1883, was largely a diatribe savaging the depraved, unhealthy fashion for stays and pipe waists, which destroyed the balance, beauty, pliancy and variety of nature, and forced the heart and lung cavity to contract, crumpling the ribs. Worse, ribs broken by tight-lacing had been known to pierce lungs and cause death. The refined lady defying the law of nature, declared Watts, was like a 'squaw who sticks a bone through her lip to make it hang down below her chin? A cynic might ask on which side the savagery is greater.' He called for action from the medical profession.[23] (In a Birmingham court six years later, the death of a servant would be pronounced as 'Death from pressure round the waist.')[24] Although Watts was not the first to urge doctors to speak out against the dangers of tight lacing, 'In Taste in Dress' gave rise to his most eccentric distinction. That spring, the Rational Dress Association held their first exhibition at the Prince's Hall in Piccadilly to encourage dress reform – there was a wonderful array of Liberty's Art Fabrics, boneless stays, a tricycle suit, a Greek costume, tea gowns, cricketing, calisthenic and walking dresses and, from Worth et Cie, a black satin 'Dress of the Future' – and the Norwood Anti-Tight-Lacing Society elected Watts their president.[25] He wrote to Ruskin of his wider concerns for educational reform, craftsmanship and progress.[26] On a visit to Walter Crane, he tried out a tricycle, wobbled happily over the lawn and wondered if it might be safer than a horse at negotiating slippery wooden pavements.[27]

That winter in Brighton, still fascinated by haystacks, which would inspire Monet's series at the end of the decade, Watts painted a study of stacks on the downs, as well as a life-size portrait of a young girl, who had captured his eye in the audience at the Aquarium. With her mother's permission, Katie came to sit in that same pose, in profile, absorbed and alert, as though listening to a performance; she wore a saffron pink dress trimmed with white lace banding, collar and cuffs, a white cap and black boots; her

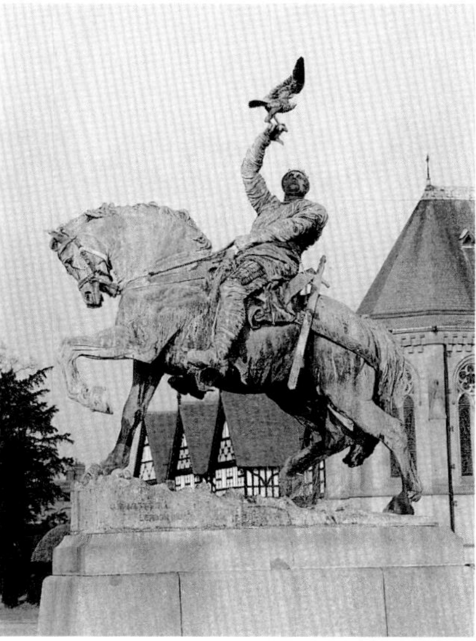

129   *Hugh Lupus*, bronze, 1870–83 (Eaton Hall).

white gloves, one crossed over the other, lay on the floor.[28] Meanwhile his portrait of Rossetti stood on an easel at the poet-painter's memorial exhibition of 84 pictures at the Academy – there were 153 at the Burlington Fine Arts Club. Watts thought the watercolours finer than the paintings in oil – 'his flesh was never good, no blood flowing under the skin' – and that had Rossetti followed Dante less, he might have achieved greatness for his individual style and poetic power.[29]

*Psyche* hung in the place of honour at the Royal Glasgow Institute's annual exhibition of English and Continental art.[30] In March Lady Ashburton's daughter Mary Baring sat for a full-length portrait; and Watts completed heads of Dorothy Dene and the Countess of Kilmorey for Rickards.[31] His ten pictures sent to St Jude's – more than any other colleague – included portraits of Garibaldi, Manning and Carlyle ('a man worn with the shams and sorrows of his age', Barnett explained in the catalogue), and a preview of his four paintings of the Horses of the Revelations.[32]

In a lecture at Oxford in May, Ruskin lauded Watts and Burne-Jones as leaders of the 'Mythic Schools of Painting'. Watts, he said, had been partly restrained and partly oppressed by his effort to achieve perfection: 'His constant reference to the highest examples of Greek art in form, and his sensitiveness to the qualities at once of tenderness and breadth in pencil and chalk drawing, have virtually ranked him among the painters of the great Athenian days'. Linking the two artists with Rossetti and Holman Hunt, he concluded "All great Art is Praise".'[33] Watts quoted that final dictum on his letterhead.[34]

His paintings of the apocalyptic horsemen were moved to the Grosvenor. Awesome, visionary studies of power and light, *The Rider on the Pale Horse* (fig. 78), *The Rider on the White Horse*, *The Rider on the Black Horse* and *The Rider on the Red Horse* of *Revelation* hung at the end of the west gallery. The *Pall Mall Gazette* deemed them unintelligible to all but 'those who are not offended by the extreme application of Mr Watts favourite theories about tone and finish'. On the other hand, his haystacks, stark and richly massed on a hilltop against puffs of cloud in a luminous pale sky in *Study on Brighton Downs* drew comparison with the watercolourist John Sell Cotman. The fifteenth-century *Condottiere*, a formidable figure inspired by the engineer Sir John Hawkshaw, dressed in armour lent by Sir Coutts Lindsay, attracted little notice, but study for the Hon. Mary Baring, likened to a Palma Vecchio, and *The Rain it Raineth Every Day* – a girl leaning over a chair gazing out of the window, longing for the rain to stop (Blanche and Rachel both posed) – and *Katie*, Watts's single contribution to the Academy, enchanted reviewers.[35]

Manet died at the age of 51 on 30 April and immediately his professional standing, eclipsed in his lifetime by a rebellious public image, began to rise. As his friend and colleague Edgar Degas observed in the funeral procession, 'He was greater than we thought.'[36] Watts was invited to represent England at an *Exposition Internationale de Peinture* at the Galerie Georges Petit in Paris. His seven pictures – *Ida, Paolo et Francesca de Rimini, La Denonciation de Cain* (a five-foot reduction from his Academy diploma picture), *Eve (La Création,* or *She Shall be Called Woman), Eve (Le Repentir), La Création d'Eve* and the portrait of Swinburne – impressed Huysmans. The novelist incorporated them into *A Rebours (Against*

*Nature*), in which the aesthete anti-hero Des Esseintes, planning a visit to London to escape the vulgarity of Parisian life, recalls modern English paintings he would like to see again:

> weirdly coloured pictures by Watts, speckled with gamboges and indigo, and looking as they had been sketched by an ailing Gustave Moreau, painted in by an anaemic Michael Angelo, and retouched by a blue-obsessed Raphael; among other canvases, he remembered a *Curse of Cain*, an *Ida*, and several versions of *Eve*, where, in the peculiar, mysterious amalgam of those three masters, one could sense the personality – at once sublimated and crude – of a learned, dreamy Englishman, tormented by a fixation on hideous colours.[37]

Watts himself wrote of the tormented Cain: 'For him no bird sings, no flower blooms, he does not feel the scent on the passing breeze. The mark is set upon him. No man shall kill him for no man is conscious of his presence.' *Ida* was an opalescent new grouping of the three Graces – later called *Olympus on Ida* (pl. XXVIII) – closer in design to the curtain folds that first inspired the subject.[38] A determined young American visitor to the exhibition was so excited by his pictures that she made her interest known to Watts, who wrote to Gertrude Mead in June, presumably to invite her to the studio.[39]

He agreed meanwhile to design one of a series of tableaux to illustrate a new translation of *The Iliad of Homer*. His scene was to show Thetis informing her son Achilles that he must relinquish Hector's body to Priam. Watts commissioned Henry Holiday, who designed embroidery for Morris, to supply fanciful details symbolic of the sea to be embroidered on to the classical drapery of Thetis and her Nereids. Promising Holiday full credit, he suggested, 'The subject might suit you afterwards for a picture.' The tableaux, also designed and probably masterminded by Leighton for Dorothy Dene, were first shown in Kensington, at the home of Lady Freake.[40]

'*My Blanche* is to be married to Mr Somers Cocks', the proud artist notified Rickards's secretary. Herbert Somers Cocks, a lieutenant in the Coldstream Guards, fought with great credit in Egypt – 'I believe the youngest officer there'. A second cousin of Lord Somers, he was reassuringly mature at only a year older than twenty-year-old Blanche or, as the artist called her, 'Daisy' (fig. 130).[41]

By early June he had finished Rickards's *Love and Life* and hoped it would be seen as 'the crown of his collection'.[42] The Duke of Devonshire had given the last sitting for his Cambridge portrait and on 13 June 1883 the university awarded Watts – in company with Matthew Arnold and eleven others – an honorary LL.D degree. While in Cambridge, he visited Eveleen and Frederic Myers, who was doubtless responsible for his subsequent election as an Honorary Member of the new Society for Psychical Research.[43]

A fortnight later, he led Blanche up the aisle of St Mary Magdalene, Reigate. Lady Henry Somerset and her mother Virginia Somers, presided over the wedding reception at The Priory, and the honeymoon was spent at Eastnor Castle. 'Darling Daisy', wrote the artist, 'I hoped when you married I should be able to give up feeling all anxiety about you, please let me think this may be.'[44] Three months later, Lord Somers died and was

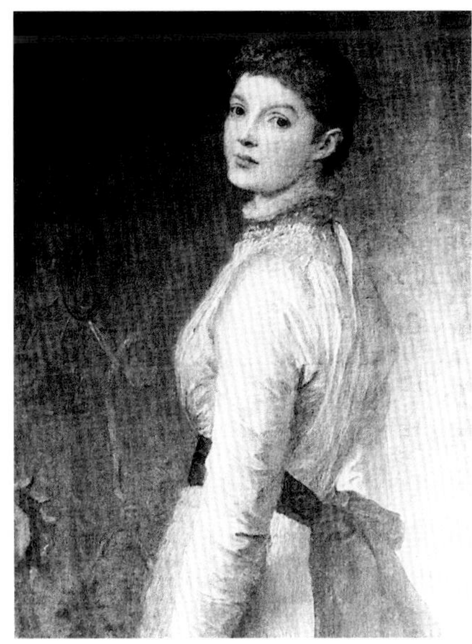

130   *Blanche Somers Cocks*, 1883–84 (Eastnor Castle Collection).

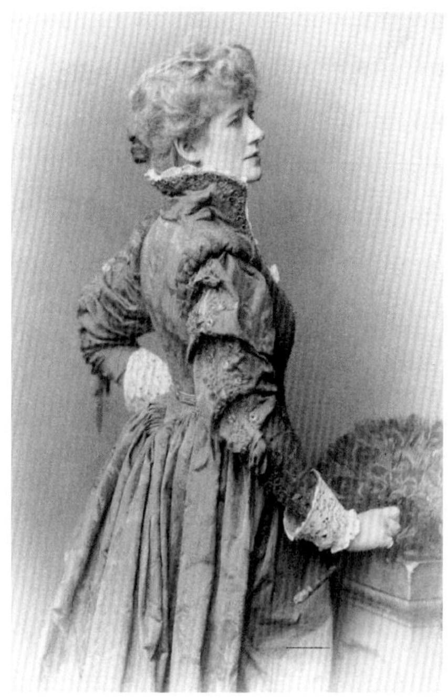

131    Ellen Terry as Beatrice in *Much Ado About Nothing*, 1882 (photo: Window & Grove).

painted on his deathbed by Watts. To Sara Prinsep, the picture showed 'that ineffable calm of death which Signor alone can give with his brush.'[45]

The artist himself, wracked with guilt and longing to see his former wife, whose triumphant performances as Beatrice in *Much Ado About Nothing* (fig. 131) were drawing to a close, had been writing to Nelly in secret. 'Every triumph gives me greater pleasure than I can say & the most profound satisfaction that your genius found its higher sphere & scope.' He very much admired Shakespeare, and his fateful reservation against the stage had vanished. Her happiness and prosperity would always be a chief joy in his life. 'Let the past be as you say a story in a book that we have both read. *As Artists* we can still wander hand in hand through the images of the beautiful'. Promising that he would never give her cause to regret the impulse, he repeated '*I should so much* like to hear from you occasionally. You say you would not want replies, & perhaps that would be best. Write to me when you feel discouraged or want a handclasp & affectionate interest. Pray do not talk about "offending." How can you do that.' On 10 July, he invited her to shake hands with him before she left for her American tour: 'If before you go you can do what I so much wish, if you come in your married name no one need know any thing about it.' Having heard on the grapevine that she wished for one of his pictures, he wanted to have the portrait of Nelly running framed for her. Could she send her address?[46] He had not touched it since she had modelled for him, but that if the picture revived unpleasant memories, she should sell it. Nelly sent her Earl's Court address the next day. 'It is impossible for me to stay away since you say you desire me to come. For what can I see in your request but an expression of *your life*, of beautiful gentle goodness. When you wrote to me last Easter twelvemonth you forbade me saying anything in answer, only "*yes*", but in truth your words made me dizzy with exquisite waves of feeling.' Her work gave her incessant *gratitude* and joy. Could she come immediately her engagement was over? 'I am worried & perplexed to think I can *say nothing* while the whole wish is so great to desire some words that could thank you & bless you. Nelly. Read between the lines of mine how sacredly I shall hold your letter.[47]

'Now that I think there shall be between us for evermore a tender kindness which the most worldly could hardly blame, my way down towards the dark unknown shall be much smoother and lighter', he replied.[48] Warning that social etiquette forbade their correspondence, he wrote letter after letter, warm, passionate, yearning, reiterating his constant, silent admiration for her and deep sorrow for the difficulties he had caused, that he could 'never for a moment lose the pain of feeling that I have spoilt your life. I never have forgiven myself & never shall.' She felt constrained, but replied freely, confiding in him and regretting steps she could not undo, asking 'do not forbid me to write.' Her words eased his troubled heart and set it racing, but they remained secret, for he burned her letters. Nelly kept his. 'Write to me (without constraint) whenever it would ease your mind to fall back on a sympathy I promise without stint or end. When it will encourage you to high resolve or check impulse to recklessness . . . a thread will steady when the narrowness of the path makes one dizzy.'

He rejoiced at her great reputation and determination to conquer difficulties. Her only real problem was her social position, with two failed marriages, and as the mother of children born while she was still formally

Watts's wife. He offered support for them should they ever need it, and encouragement. 'Victory is glorious in proportion to the might and strength of the enemy . . . the defeat of the morning has often been turned to triumph later in the day . . . you have a great future (not merely artistic) before you.'

> That you should feel constrained in writing to me is but too natural, but the qualities of heart & feeling shown in your letter in answer to mine expressing a wish to see you once more; broke down all constraint on my part, let my profound sympathy poor Nelly, break down constraint on yours as much as if we two stood face to face on the brink of a universal Grave.'

He had not been able to secure tickets to take Blanche (whom she knew), to *Much Ado*, and at his request she arranged seats in the centre stalls for a morning performance of *The Belles Strategem*. Every day for a week after the play closed, he remained in and alone between two and three o'clock, but Nelly did not come. 'I am sorry, very, very, very sorry, but cannot desire any thing that is not good for you,' he wrote on 8 October 1883, as she was about to sail for America. Nelly marked the letter 'important':

> I had set my heart upon exchanging a word, & a pressure of hand but you know I said it was to be all as you decided. God bless you, & give you every kind of success, do be careful, do be prudent. You have conquered much & conquer many. You said you would like to write to me. Do & any how you like or that may be a relief to you & never think that I will misconstrue a word or that any thing you write will ever be seen by any other person . . . All good attend you.'

The idea that 'this great man' still shouldered guilt for her seemed to the actress 'a chivalrous assumption of blame for what was, I think, a natural, almost inevitable, catastrophe'. Living apart had allowed their genius to develop. Renewed contact brought revived tenderness between them, though they would never meet.[49] Among the waving crowds at Liverpool docks as Henry Irving and Ellen Terry set sail were Oscar Wilde and Lillie Langtry, who was herself between tours of America. Not a great actress, she was beautiful and resolute, but self-conscious. She had since studied in Paris and could not resist relaying to Watts news of her success.[50]

Asked to lend pictures to augment the opening exhibition of the new Manchester Art Gallery, at which *Love and Life*, lent by Rickards, had its first public viewing, Watts was appalled to hear that *Midday Rest* was placed above the line.[51] Watts commissioned the art photographer Frederick Hollyer to record his portraits (including that of the Duke of Devonshire before it left for Cambridge to be hung in the Fitzwilliam Museum).[52] He had substantially improved Manning's portrait and *Love and Death* and produced powerful atmospheric landscapes when Gertrude Mead came to the Little Holland House Gallery on 21 October.[53]

Mary Fraser Tytler was in the gallery every day, copying a portrait, presumably after her appointment with Watts on the 27th.[54] As she recalled, the American walked in, met the painter by chance, struck up a friendship through her sympathy for his art and determined that it should be seen across the Atlantic.[55] He was given to understand 'that the Americans were quite unaware of the existence of any modern art other than Parisian, and that my pictures might be a useful corrective'. With a dash of romance, she wooed him with flowers. While he stayed home to master rheumatism and neuralgia, he encouraged Emilie Barrington to entertain her, he arranged her visit to Rickards's collection before she set sail for New York. He was tempted – 'No work of mine has been seen there, but a great many Americans come to see me' – but she was still playing her fish when she left and sent a letter on half the page, leaving the blank space for his reply.[56]

Mary Fraser Tytler, exhilarated at her growing contact with Watts, wrote to Hallam Tennyson of her joy at having wormed her way into the Little Holland House Gallery. Shortly afterwards, Watts wrote to Hallam, sending congratulations on his father's elevation to the peerage: 'One of natures noblemen he cannot be raised by the action of sovereigns or governments but I am glad that he should add distinction to a time honoured institution which I believe to be of no small value.' The artist was visiting Mary two or three times a morning.[57] Profoundly spiritual, she was moved that a man of his transcendent 'spirit of intelligence' should compel friends to confide even small concerns to him. She wrote in her commonplace book, 'His words follow me through the day, and are a new strength.'[58]

Morris's Socialist propaganda will not have escaped their notice. His Oxford lecture 'Art and Democracy' delivered on 14 November 1883 was widely reported.[59] While both endorsed his lament for England's loss of instinct for beauty, its environmental pollution, commerce and its plutocratic society, and may have argued his attack on middle-class liberals – Mary was a socialist – the vehemence of the artist-poet and his overriding political activity saddened friends and colleagues.[60]

Watts, pressed to pose for a formal photograph by Bassano (fig. 132) on 23 November, invited himself to lunch afterwards with Virginia Somers.[61] His artful strategy of allocating social time slots – Mary was received in the morning, Mrs Barrington in the evenings, leaving lunchtime for others – meant that women nurtured a special intimacy with him, each regarding him as her own genius, though the officious Emilie Barrington was too busy to notice. As for Watts, he responded with joy to empathy with his aims and ambitions for art and especially to an imaginative mind. Spreading the idea of beauty, musicality and spirituality of art was paramount, to be explored and shared. By December he was achieving mystical atmospheric effects through experiments with broken prismatic colour in both painting and sculpture. The dynamic plaster sketch for his symbolic equestrian group *Active Force* – later known as *Physical Energy* and even larger than its forerunner *Hugh Lupus* – now stood on the modelling trolley. *Active Force* was infused with 'world-subduing energy which conquers savagery and compels civilization,' noted the *Athenaeum*. The hero, one hand on the horse's reins, shading his eyes with the other, to scan distant lands yet to be conquered, represented for Watts 'a symbol of that restless physical impulse to seek the still unachieved in the domain of material things', and was destined for the nation. As a statement of his ambition, the statue could be seen as an idealized self-portrait. The innovative surface – broken like an Impressionist painting to catch the light and strengthen the sense of force – would never look traditionally 'finished'. He would work on the horse and rider for the rest of his life, with his assistant Thompson.[62]

The new *Island of Cos* (pl. XXVII), was larger, deeper and more mystical than Rickard's version. Asked by its purchaser, a prominent Glasgow civil engineer, James Mirrlees,[63] to explain the butterfly hovering over classical

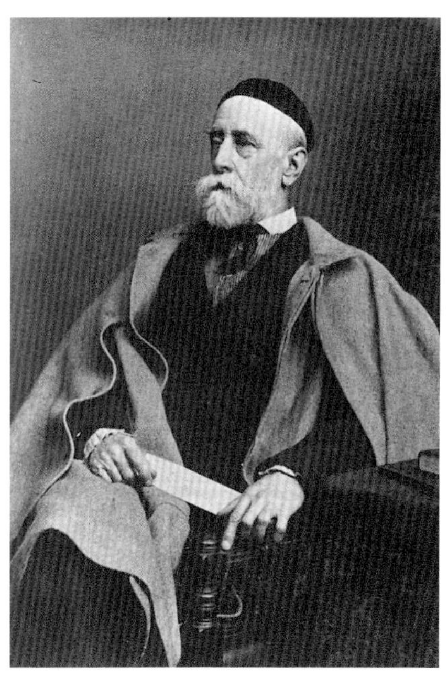

132    Watts, posing for Bassano, 23 November 1883.

ruins in the foreground, Watts replied that the finest art must offer more than beauty, that the suggestive element was crucial. The entire picture was in fact symbolic, contrasting the unchanging serenity of sky and sea with the decay and destruction resulting from man's achievement, and the butterfly symbolized the undying human soul: 'However little we may be able to certify respecting the spiritual side of man's nature, & however little he may be satisfied with any explanations of the unknown that have been put forth, a bare materialism does not recommend itself to me – I think the artist & the poet (I ought to have put the poet first, unless they are one & the same) may be allowed to dream'.[64]

Even more mysterious and a supreme example of Watts's atmospheric experiments was a painting of Uldra (fig. 133), the spirit fairy of ancient Scandinavian mythology, glimpsed through the rainbow mist and spray rising from a waterfall. For the larger universal *Love and Life* – the converse of *Love and Death* – he used unusually light tones for the mountainous background and virginal nude maiden, whom the adult Eros figure, Love, protects with purplish wings as he guides her up Life's rocky path. But the opalescent tints in the visionary *Uldra*, suggesting the features of Dorothy Dene, are no deeper those of a nautilus shell.[65]

As the year closed, Mary's regard for Watts was deepening beyond professional friendship. She had broken herself free from a dark love affair she had mourned in passionate poetry and prayer for over a decade. With unaccustomed boldness, she burst out: 'Signor, I think I have been looking for you all my life.' Ever a gentleman, he did not disillusion her at the time and she found in him sympathy and strength: 'A mind so broad & insight so far reaching that there is no small or great difficulty in my life . . . for which he would not have some simple words, so true, so direct & to the point, that they would become a power in my life'. Her love for him was strong. Mary knew that she was just one of the many people he had helped and on whom 'he looks with a great impersonal love, whose sorrows & cares he would like to soften with infinite tenderness . . . Ah me, I shall never look upon another human being at all like him – it's *genius* all that that great word includes, & with what it rarely joins, a most lovable personality.'[66]

Watts's concerns were directed across the Atlantic. He feared that Gertrude Mead's ambitions for him might be motivated by personal rather than artistic interest, and, worse, that his life's work might sink to the bottom of the Atlantic? 'I want your pictures to come to America for the sake of the people here, and not for your sake; I want them to come that the people may hear the voice of a great teacher', she replied. 'Please do believe me, many will listen. I feel sure they are hungering for a sight of such pictures as yours.[67]

The *Art Journal* opened 1884 with a four-page article on Watts's work to date. Edmund Gosse asked to write about him, to inaugurate a series on leading contemporary artists in the *Pall Mall Gazette*, interpreting for London readers the new large *Love and Life*, *Lady Godiva* and the triplenude *Olympus on Ida*, which the *Athenaeum*, illuminated for a wider public: Three goddesses . . . stand in an atmosphere of mist, which seems to shimmer, while golden light pulsates through it between the great dames and the spectator, thus becoming a magnificent veil . . . its margins are tinged with purple and merged with the cooler outer air.' *Uldra* was a study

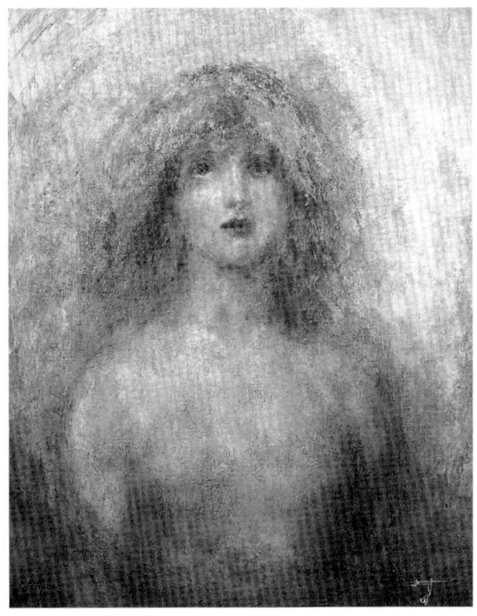

133    *Uldra*, 1883–84 (Watts Gallery).

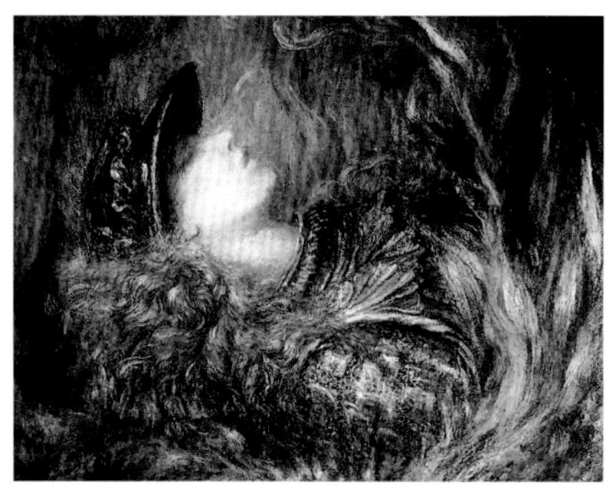

134   *Brunhild*, *c.*1880 (Leighton House Museum).

for the right-hand figure, Aphrodite, who stands erect where the celestial lustre is strongest, her hair shimmering down her legs.[68]

Watts was developing the ravished bare-breasted *Wife of Pluto* (pl. XII) into an erotic attack on the disease of wealth, with golden curls snaking over her shoulder in a looser treatment than his other half-nudes of the 1860s. He painted hair with even greater abandon in *Brunhild* (fig. 134). Recalling the music of Wagner – the composer had died in 1883 – the curls of the sleeping armed Valkyrie of the Niebelung appear to merge with the flames that almost engulf her.[69] When Mary brought Geraldine Liddell to play the piano to him, he leaped to his feet, crying 'She's full of music. She's full of music'. He loved her natural sound. As in painting, he could not abide conscious bravado.

Asked to design a monument to the former Lord Lieutenant of Anglesea, the Honourable William Owen Stanley, for Holyhead, he provided drawings for a recumbent figure and supporting angels and passed the commission to Hamo Thornycroft.[70] Meanwhile, having posed for Mayall's book on artists in their studios (fig. 135), he asked the photographer to record his pictures, and was painting on the prints in monochrome, with a view to sending them to the Americans in place of the originals.[71] Gertrude, busy marshalling the great and the good to promote an exhibition of his work in New York, was horrified. Louis Comfort Tiffany the Art Nouveau designer, wrote of his 'great desire' for the exhibition, which was endorsed by America's leading Impressionist painters, and Daniel Huntington, president of the Academy of Design and vice-president of the Metropolitan Museum of Art.[72]

Gertrude pleaded with Watts to send his originals.[73] Two days later, the president of the museum, John Taylor Johnston, proposed plans for a six-month loan exhibition opening in November, provided that there would be

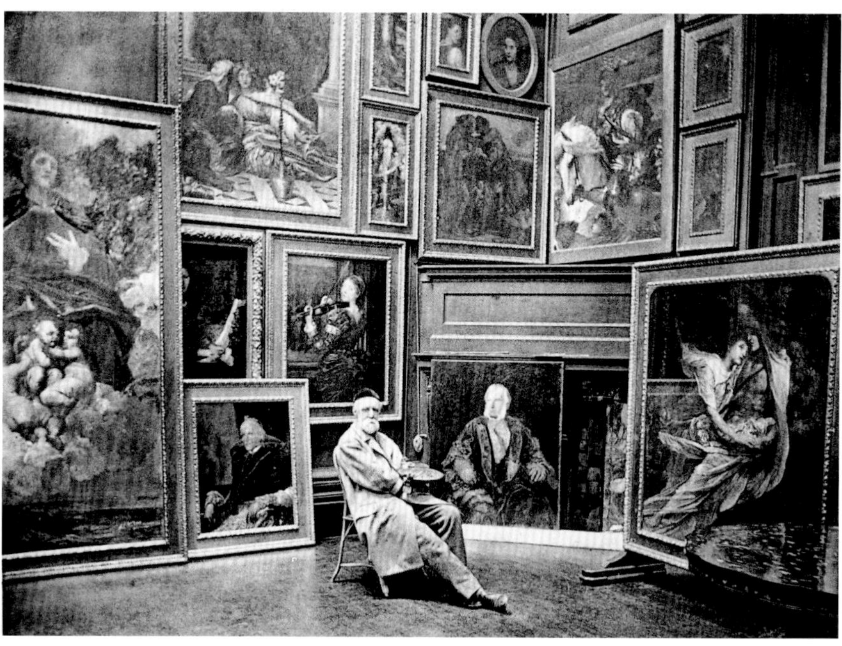

135   Watts in the painting studio at Little Holland House, 1884 (photo: J. P. Mayall).

no expense apart from transport and packing. The executive committee's resolution on 28 April 1884 'that the Trustees of the Museum heartily desire to make an exhibition of the works of the eminent English painter Mr G. F. Watts' was unprecedented. Never before had a living British artist been invited to exhibit in America. Subscribers were asked to donate up to a hundred dollars each to cover transport costs. The treasurer, Henry Marquand, appointed chairman of the Watts Exhibition Committee, sailed to London with a letter from the president requesting the artist's permission 'for the interests of Art in America, and the instruction of the American public.' But before the letter could be delivered, a major financial hurdle, the recent imposition of a thirty-three per cent import duty on works of art into America – a problem causing great concern in Europe – had to be resolved. Marquand could not deliver it. Meanwhile Frank Millet, an American artist resident in Kensington and member of the committee, liaised with Watts to list titles, dimensions, insurance value and transport costs and to secure a comprehensive display for America.[74]

Millais was unusually impressed by *Active Force*. 'It is quite *magnificent*, & as good as any of the best Sculpture of the past'. He advised Watts to strengthen the horses legs and hindquarters. 'Make the animal as fine as the man, & you will have done a really great statue for the country'.[75]

*The Magdalen at the Foot of the Cross* was sent to St Jude's with portraits of the social reformers Matthew Arnold, John Stuart Mill and Sir Charles Dilke, now president of the Local Government Board and chairman of a Royal Commission on Housing of the Working Classes. Each picture was explained to the growing crowds by Barnett, whose latest reform venture – to establish a University Settlement in Whitechapel to provide housing, education and amenities for the poor, under the guidance of resident and visiting graduates, initially from Oxford – would have had Watts's heartfelt backing. Construction of Toynbee Hall, named after the late Oxford historian Arthur Toynbee, whose principle was that 'the poorest class should be raised in the interest of all classes', would begin that summer.[76]

The ferment of ideas for the regeneration of craft and the unity of the arts, promoted by Ruskin, Morris and Watts, led to the foundation in March of the Art-Workers' Guild debating society – and of the Century Guild, a collective of designers headed by Arthur Heygate Mackmurdo, whose aim was that all branches of art – building, decoration, glass-painting, pottery, woodcarving and metalwork – should be regarded no longer as the sphere of the tradesman, but as honoured expressions of the artistic spirit, to 'stand in their true relation not only to sculpture and painting but to the drama, to music, and to literature.' To raise the status of craft, the Century Guild concentrated on design reform, their new aesthetic reflected in *Hobby Horse*, their first literary journal, which Mackmurdo inscribed for Watts: 'George F. Watts, offered with all respect to England's greatest painter, one who gains the Guild's unbounded esteem.'[77]

With the excitement, health troubles, London exhibition work, he splendidly refused Lady Dorothy Neville's invitation to meet a celebrated beauty. 'I have little interest in those who become famous from accident. The amusement you so kindly offer me . . . would be in the indulgence of curiosity, not a nice feeling to be encouraged towards anyone who wears a crinolette.'[78] Watts completed major new subjects for the Grosvenor, but at

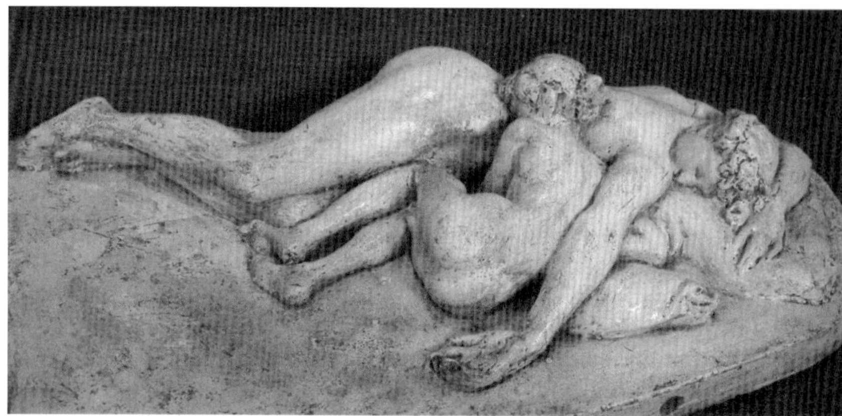

136  Sir Frederic Leighton's study for the sleeping girls in *Cymon and Iphigenia*, 1882–83, was treasured by Watts (Watts Gallery).

the last minute he ruined what he temporarily called *Prehistoric Pioneer* – the slight, squeamish *BC* – that he had, unusually, painted expressly for Burlington House. As Sir Coutts had taken pictures for the Grosvenor and he was anxious not to offend the Academy, he sent it nevertheless and wrote to George Richmond that, 'If you find the work in any way a discredit to the Academy as coming from one of its members please let me withdraw it . . . I prefer to be least among the best, to being best among the little!' For the first time in over a quarter of a century, he was not represented in the summer exhibition.[79] It was not a little embarrassing. As Frank Holl's portrait of the Prince of Wales was shown, he wrote to congratulate the Benchers of the Middle Temple on its success. He was thrilled to receive from Leighton a plaster model for the sleeping group in his Academy entry *Cymon and Iphigenia* (fig. 136), from Boccaccio's *Decameron*. 'Nothing more beautiful has ever been done!' – he thought it even better than Phidias. The shepherd Cymon owes much to his own *Aristides and the Shepherd*. Rodin's *Age of Bronze* seen for the first time in England and Alfred Gilbert's bronze statuette of the winged *Icarus* on the rocks aroused a sensation. Commissioned by Leighton, Gilbert's figure was not only reminiscent of *Love and Life*, but of Watts himself: in the artistic expression of an idea, furthermore, symbolizing Ambition, it was a conscious self-portrait, as the sculptor recalled in his autobiography: 'I was very ambitious: why not "Icarus" with his desire for flight?' Gilbert, inspired by Watts's visionary metaphysical works at the Grosvenor retrospective, was modelling an even more Wattsian composition, *Post Equitem Sedet Atra Cura* (Behind the Rider Sits Dark Care), a roundel clearly informed by *Life's Illusions* and the early *Fata Morgana*.[80]

Burne-Jones's *King Cophetua and the Beggar Maid* attracted most interest at the Grosvenor, bracketed in the press with Watts's powerful vertical cloudscape *Rain Passing Away*. In the pale blue firmament, a huge billowy white mass and distant clouds, illuminated from above, cast a deep shadow over the hills far below, suggesting 'an eternity of repose' as the rain passed, as though the landscape itself had soul. *Uldra* – hanging between his national portraits of the Marquess of Salisbury in his robes as Chancellor of Oxford University, and the more poetic *Earl of Lytton* – enchanted and mystified critics: But Lord Lytton has a neighbour . . . a delicious study of ideal female beauty, which Mr Watts has elected to christen *Uldra*. It seems to have been drawn with a fairy pencil and tinted from a fairy-set palette; but why *Uldra*, Mr Watts? The beauteous vision . . . is yet clothed in a kind of ethereal haze. She is a Child of the Mist, a Witch of the Alps'. Through the prismatic spray of the waterfall, they found it easier to see her as de la Motte Fouqué's water spirit Undine.

Even more puzzling was *The Happy Warrior* (fig. 137), a female spirit head hovering over the half-length armed knight, embodying the ideals for which he had fought. Named after Wordsworth's *Character of the Happy Warrior* and his patriotic endeavours in life, the head of Watts's knight is falling back at the point of death, as his spirit emerges.[81] 'I see a very noble expression of Art in the visionary, very monumental & even splendid, he wrote to the American journalist William Stillman, 'not religion in the ordinary sense . . . but touching the highest & I think the truest religious sensibilities, suggestively touching philosophical imagination.'[82]

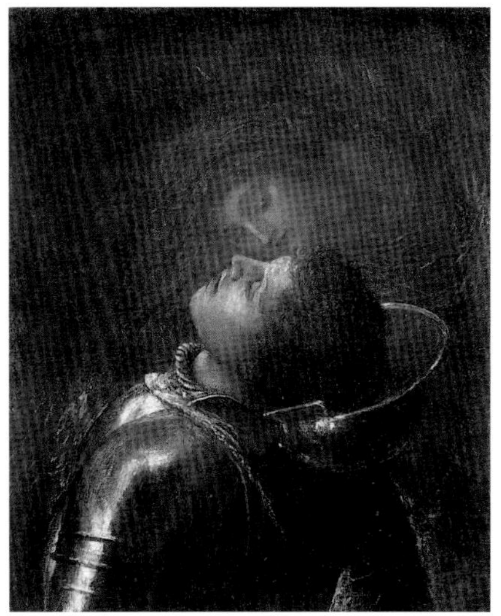

137  *The Happy Warrior*, 1884 (Bayerische Staatsgemäldesammlungen, Munich: Neue Pinakothek).

Watts had taken to riding along Piccadilly on the top of an omnibus after dinner, partly for the air and partly to help him sleep,[83] for the still unresolved Metropolitan exhibition, an enterprise that Watts had undertaken simply to thank Gertrude for her 'affectionate sympathy', was 'a terrible nightmare!' On 31 May he sent a Hollyer portrait of himself for the frontispiece to the catalogue, and he promised 'the best of my gallery' with wavering confidence: 'They are *most* disappointing to me but the idea of losing the results of so much real application & thought is very dreadful to me. From the moment the pictures depart (if the thing comes off) I shall regard them as lost.' He valued them at $500,000 and, coaxed by the ever attentive and reassuring Millet, agreed on 17 June to let the pictures go. (To raise the $3,535 insurance in time, the American subscribers now agreed to pay two hundred dollars and Tiffany was co-opted on to the exhibition committee.[84]) While Emilie Barrington worked closely with the artist, preparing for the exhibition, Mary Fraser Tytler had taken to wearing the artist's photograph in a locket on her bracelet.[85]

'What a possession to the world Mrs Cameron could have been by Pepys!' he wrote to Una Taylor, thanking her for her father's manuscript *Autobiography*, though he rebuked his old friend Sir Henry for not mentioning advances in art, and in particular, the Pre-Raphaelite movement. Though determined to pursue his own vision apart from the Pre-Raphaelites, he appreciated its significance in the history of English art.[86]

Ellen Terry had returned from her American tour. Watts, hearing that she was unwell, scanned the papers to see whether she would be fit for her opening night as Viola in *Twelfth Night*. Courageous as ever, she performed sitting down. 'Always believe my spirit shall be with you when it can aid,' he wrote, again inviting her to his gallery, with an interesting reminder that he himself used the back entrance, through Val Prinsep's garden.[87] Val married gloriously on 25 July. His bride Florence Leyland was the shipowner and art collector's daughter, and his best man was the president of the Royal Academy. Mary Wyndham, now Lady Elcho, spotted Watts among the guests at the wedding banquet at Prince's Gate. Leyland asked him back to see his collection. In return the artist invited him to Little Holland House Gallery before his pictures left for America, warning, as he offered to show Kate Holiday the almost finished *Time, Death and Judgment*, 'You may never see them again'.[88]

IN A RADICAL MOVE TO SECURE THE Watts exhibition, the trustees of the Metropolitan Museum of Art resolved to put the entire museum into bond for the sum of $206,000. This meant that no duty would have to be paid unless a picture was sold, but most were reserved for the nation.[1] Millet presented Johnston's official invitation to Watts in July 1884. Until then Watts had believed the exhibition to be the desire of a few misguided sympathizers. He was deeply moved. In his reply to the president, he outlined his motivation: that because art no longer served religion or state, and was 'in danger of losing its character as a great intellectual utterance', he had worked to encourage the respect for art, corresponding to that given to noble poetry and literature. He warned that many pictures were 'extremely incomplete', which did not matter in his own gallery, but 'I feel most strongly that to justify the presumption of coming before the American public . . . the works ought at least to have the merit of completion', and finally, that his 'very independent manner . . . can in no degree be considered as representing any section of the English School, & can have no interest from that point of view'. His frank words almost toppled the enterprise, which required nursing on both sides of the Atlantic.[2]

'I know his peculiarities so well that I am sure I understand precisely what he means', William Alexander, a trustee of the museum, reassured Marquand that the artist, a modest, yet proud and sensitive man, did not wish to send his pictures unless the American public was aware of these peculiarities. Whatever excuses Watts made to the contrary, 'he is a representative painter of the English, his individuality and the unique character of his work are among their chief recommendations.' In explaining Watts's habit of changing and retouching pictures in his gallery, which would be impossible if he finished them for sale or sent them away beyond his control, Alexander suggested that the artist's objections arose merely from his reluctance to be parted from them at such great distance. His stipulation that his solicitor, Martineau, should deal with the business side, would guard the museum from possible error. Alexander congratulated the chairman on achieving Watts's agreement. But fear of a 'dilapidation bill' from English solicitors reverberated between trustees, until Millet pointed out that Watts would never sanction a lawyer's claim for damages.[3] A prized picture had been cracked at Birmingham and Watts had said nothing: 'He simply grumbled and repaired it. His letter [to Johnston] is exactly like him. The pictures we all call done are to him only just begun. He is very queer about his pictures. He is loath to send them for fear they will be much criticized but he is very much pleased and flattered by the invitation and will do the right thing I am sure.'[4] When the artist, having agreed to lower valuations for insurance, insisted on legalities, Millet explained that Watts was 'anything but a grasping man' but considered the insurance a guarantee that the risk of losing his pictures was not as great as he feared; just in case, he asked for them to be sent in two successive ships.[5]

On 1 August, Watts consulted Gosse as to how he should enlighten the American public. His chief concerns were that his acceptance should not be seen as presumptuous, not least by his colleagues, and that many canvases represented work in progress and could hardly be regarded as pictures, but as expressions of moods and ideas. Because his paint surfaces bore none of the bravado of the French Impressionists, as he explained in the studio a day or two later, he hoped the Americans would understand that the focus of each painted poem was the idea, and that he preferred not to dilute its poetry with a show of dazzling skill. Gosse, soon to give a series of literary lectures in America, agreed to write an 'open letter' for the *Century* magazine. He sent a proof to Watts, who was irritated that Gosse had written as his 'mouthpiece', and he did not like the tone; nevertheless he approved the proof. ('I answered like Hotspur' – and forgot about it.)[6] In the meantime, the American press heralded Watts as the 'Dean of English painters', 'the greatest imaginative painter of his time in England', his works for the nation, 'in striking contradistinction to the showy school of the French . . . illustrate the highest range of the painter's art' – such a build-up fuelled Watts's fear that American art-lovers would be disappointed.[7]

Emilie Barrington, whose key role in producing the descriptive catalogue should not be underestimated, set off on holiday, leaving Emma, the housekeeper, to list the fifty-three pictures as they were packed into crates by his framers – W. A. Smith of Mortimer Street, who had taken over from the late Joseph Green. All but seven loans were from Little Holland House Gallery. The Academy would not release *The Denunciation of Cain* or *Psyche*; the Wyndhams could not bear to part with their portrait of Madeline; and the prime minister's was too precious to risk drowning. *Paolo and Francesca* and *Orpheus and Eurydice*, repainted since the Grosvenor retrospective, glowed through their final varnish; but illness prevented the artist finishing *Love and Death*, which he had been developing since the 1877 exhibition – it had to go with large areas painted out.[8] Once the Metropolitan pictures were packed, Millet, worried not only about rising costs and safety, but that Martineau could prevent their departure, arranged for them to sail aboard the *SS France* on 25 September, under the close supervision of his friend Captain Robinson. The ship's hatches were to be battened down so that in extreme rough weather there would be no danger of water damage.[9] On the other side of the Atlantic – after a valiant struggle to raise funds, largely contributed by the trustees themselves – the secretary, General di Cesnola, hoped that New Yorkers would appreciate how much good the *much abused* trustees were doing for the development of art in their city.[10]

'What will be, will be,' Watts wrote to Gertrude Mead. 'I shall wish them safe back because I want to present the best (carried as far as I can) to my own country but if they go down or are otherwise destroyed my regret will not be the death of me.' Much worse was 'my dread of the disappointment that may be felt, that swallows up every other feeling', the fear that undue press coverage might reflect on his colleagues.

Towards Gertrude herself he felt growing affection, untrammelled by the difference in years. (He had taken to addressing her as Mary, but would later revert to 'Gertrude'. As she signed herself 'M. Gertrude Mead', she will be referred to here by her middle name.) 'What are the few years of human life on the shore of the great sea of Time! One's spiritual existence has no age. It is part of the great unknown perhaps of the Eternal – It is that spiritual existence which you perceived in me that awakened the kinship with your own, so you will come to see as I see that we are but two children playing on that shore not unmindful of its mysteries.' To Watts 'childlike' characterized purity of thought: 'I encourage in myself childishness in aim & sympathy & simplicity knowing that so alone is there any chance of good from my life & safety from disappointment for myself. Thanks for the little account of your life & habits but I want more'[11]

As the seven-and-a-half-ton bronze huntsman *Hugh Lupus* sailed up the River Dee, to be positioned at the west front and gates of Eaton in time for the duke's fifty-ninth birthday on 13 October,[12] the sculptor heard that his pictures had arrived safely in New York, where Ellen Terry was playing Ophelia. 'This will find you I hope in the enjoyment of the triumphs, the good health & above all perhaps the society of amiable & loving friends. No one can rejoice in believing this more than I do,' he wrote, appreciating her gift of leaves and agreeing to help her son, Teddy. (In his memoirs, the artist and stage designer Edward Gordon Craig clearly loathed Watts.[13])

Watts advised Gertrude not to use modern artificial exhibition lighting, whereby spectators standing in the dark faced floodlit pictures, but to direct light across them, from above or behind; and Tiffany, responsible for the hanging, was informed to hang the pictures '*low, very* low'.[14] Watts had particularly asked that they be should shown alone in a single gallery, but at the last minute Sam Avery persuaded di Cesnolo to hang them with others, separated only by a screen. Millet, arriving after the exhibition opened, was appalled to find that the museum had broken their contract:. 'It is such an insult to Mr Watts as it stands that I can't think of it with any patience.' He insisted on a rehang, but the trustees would not yield.[15]

The 'epoch-making' collection of paintings by Watts – the Metropolitan Museum's first exhibition of an English artist, indeed, first living painter – opened on 1 November 1884 and aroused extraordinary interest.[16] From the catalogue entry for *Chaos* (fig. 138), Americans learned how the artist had long aspired to fill a hall with heroic frescoes, outlining the story of mankind, with an eye to Carlyle, from a broad modern perspective. That the scheme had not been carried out was the regret of his life, wrote Emilie Barrington: 'He feels he has never been able to express himself fully in his own special language of art . . . that instead of producing a complete work, only fragments remain to show the direction of his scheme.'[17]

The *Nation*, describing his work as 'magisterial', the portraits placing him 'among the greatest painters of all nations and times', forecast the controversy that followed. As his technique and ideal qualities were the antithesis of French painting, there would have to be a revolution in American taste to accept Watts's art 'as it really is, higher in aim, nobler in its sphere, and really of a stronger quality of workmanship than any modern painting, except the pictures of Millet'. [18]

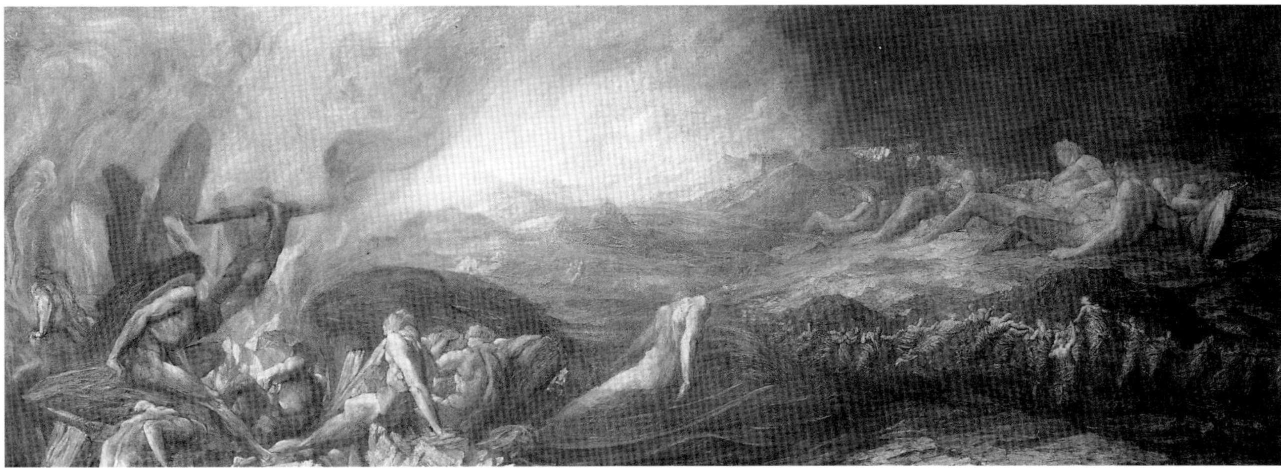

At home, Watts called on William Holman Hunt, who asked for advice in finishing *The Triumph of the Innocents*.[19] Salviati's mosaic of *Time, Death and Judgment* was now set into the façade of St Jude's Church (fig. 139) to commemorate the Barnetts' endeavours 'to make the lives of their neighbours brighter by bringing within their reach the influences of beauty'; Watts invited Matthew Arnold to unveil it, choosing him because of their shared quest to inspire the working classes through poetry and art. Arnold disliked speaking in public, 'but I cannot withstand a request from you . . . [and] to show my respect for such a worker as Mr Barnett'. Watts always intended the symbolism of his painting to stimulate thought. He wished the viewer to engage in an active process of interpretation rather than passively absorbing the image set before him – to take from the picture more than the artist had put into it. And in the opening address of the new Toynbee Hall on 29 November, Arnold did this, extending the powerful religious message of *Time, Death and Judgment* for use as a reforming tool. Describing Time as 'full of hope, energy, daring, venture, moving on to take possession of life', beside Death, 'the heartpiercing separations, from which the fullest life and the most fiery energy cannot exempt us', Arnold used Judgment – 'the Prince of the world is thus judged' – to attack the idle rich. 'More and more it is becoming manifest that the Prince . . . is a perpetual idolater, selfishly possessing'. He concluded his address: 'Brook no continuance of weak-mindedness; Great is the glory, for the strife is hard.' The mosaic was seen as 'an interesting development in mural decoration', better suited than fresco to withstand the London smoke, damp and fogs. A beacon in the grim streets, it inspired a sonnet by the Reverend Hardwicke Rawnsley; and the *Pall Mall Gazette* observed 'the bright and even dazzling effect which this reproduction of Mr Watts's picture has among the else unbroken ugliness and gloom of Commercial Street.' But for all his keenness to encourage craftsmanship, the artist could not bring himself to see the mosaic: 'I was unable to superintend its execution, and when so much in these days is left to purely mechanical workmanship one cannot expect the result to be satisfactory.'[20]

On 20 November, a committee headed by the Earl Brownlow met at his home in Carlton House Terrace, London, to plan a prospectus for the Home

138   *Chaos*, 1882 (Tate, London).

139   The mosaic of *Time, Death and Judgment* above the fountain at St Jude's Church, Whitechapel, 1873, engraving: Barnett 1918, I, 74.

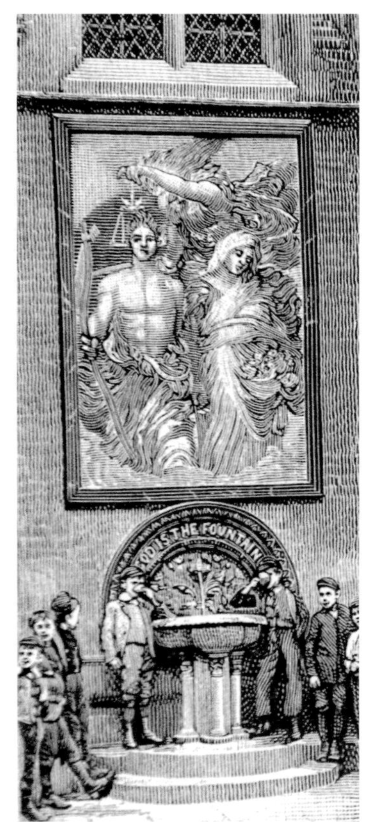

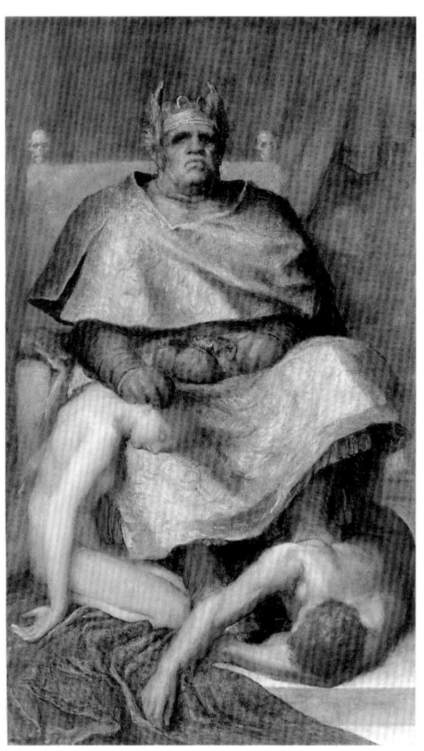

140    *Mammon*, 1885 (Tate, London).

Arts and Industries Association, to launch a nationwide handicraft revival movement dedicated to improving the lives of the poor. Among the committee were the novelist and social reformer Walter Besant as treasurer, the architect and designer W. A. S. Benson, Lady Brownlow and her sister Gertrude, now the Countess of Pembroke, Charles Leland, who ran classes in Philadelphia, and the prime mover, Eglantyne Jebb, who had founded the movement as the Cottage Arts Association in Ireland. Classes in woodcarving, metalwork, clay-modelling, leatherwork, flax-spinning and embroidery, to be run throughout the country by voluntary teachers – as Watts had proposed in 'The Present Conditions of Art' – would transcend social barriers, offer occupation, raise moral tone, and introduce a taste for beauty into the poorest homes.[21]

Watts stepped up his attack against the greed of the rich, with a grotesque personification of *Mammon (Dedicated to his Worshippers)* (fig. 140). Painted in similar pose, but the antithesis of the Manning portrait, the fat frowning figure in a crown of gold coins and ill-fitting golden robes, sits on a throne bearing finials of skulls. His features are not unlike those of *Hugh Lupus*; his neck crumples in heavy animal folds, and his donkey ears recall Carlyle's Ovidian reference to 'serious, most earnest Mammonism grown Midas-eared'. However, unlike his earlier representations of Ovidian themes, painted at the point of metamorphosis, Watts's *Mammon* does not move, except to press his cruel message. Moneybags sprawl in his lap as he deadens mankind, his blood-red left foot bears down on the prostrate body of a man, his fat right fingers, over the head of a kneeling nude maiden, crush her lifeless on to his richly draped knee.[22]

Watts began a portrait of Madeline Wyndham's dashing twenty-one-year-old son, George, a subaltern in the Coldstream Guards (fig. 141). Having volunteered for the expedition to join General Charles Gordon's forces and the Egyptian garrisons under attack at Khartoum, George was leaving with his regiment to serve initially in Egypt.[23] Before the artist could complete the portrait, he was struck down by bronchitis and the most disabling illness for years.[24] Gladstone, whose Reform and Redistribution Bills succeeded in extending the franchise to labouring men, failed to gauge the pulse in Khartoum. Watts feared annihilation of the Anglo-Egyptian forces, even before the dervishes beheaded General Gordon on 26 January 1885.[25] 'I go on with my work . . . amid the wreck of Empires', he wrote from Brighton. 'The greatest possessions the world has had & will ever have are not the achievements of Armies or even of statesmanship, all these become but historical ghosts. But the efforts of imagination, poetry, sculpture, painting, which if really worthy, are for all that . . . I try to do my work as each soldier in our little army performs his duty.[26]

Hamo Thornycroft commissioned Alfred Gilbert to execute a portrait bust of Watts. 'I hardly know how to reply to your proposal which confers so high an honour upon me, that I am quite overcome by it,' Gilbert replied on 2 January. 'If you can persuade Mr Watts to sit to me I should consider the value of such an honour far above any price I could name.' He could not be persuaded; but with Leighton and Millais he recommended Thornycroft to design the memorial to Gordon. (The general had refused to sit for the Hall of Fame – a rare rebuff for Watts.)[27]

The response to his Metropolitan exhibition took the artist by surprise – he had long been resigned to failure and to embarrassment at letting down friends and supporters. Crowds poured into the museum. Talk of extending the exhibition was clouded by bitter press correspondence, sparked by Gosse's article. Never before had a trusted critic, invited to his studio to discuss aspects of the artist's work, assumed to write as his 'mouthpiece'. Watts, accused of vanity and causing offence to the Americans, as though they could not judge his work for themselves, was 'greatly annoyed'. Stillman published his letter explaining that 'I certainly never desired that he [Gosse] or any one should cram my ideas about my pictures down the public throat', prompting Gosse to write angrily to the artist, who deluged Gertrude Mead with letters. 'This is the Nemesis in *Time, Death and Judgment* which is not Judgment but the Weigher! Judgment would come after', complained Watts. He hated coming before the public and simply wished to be seen as a bricklayer, building a wall with an enduring purpose.

There had been misunderstandings on both sides; his own failings he attributed to his 'dual nature' and even though he wished to make amends for the journalist's exposure – 'Poor Gosse seems to have got into such disgrace that I feel a Britisher's desire to help the one who stands against so many' – he was concerned that the American art world should know that his work was not a protest against any school, except art that had no intellectual purpose. But he did object to the exclusive admiration of the French School of Art 'because I think the vivacity of American intellect will rather lose than gain by the French element . . . I say this with all respect for that vivacity we English would be all the better for possessing.'[28]

The row did not deter him from inviting critics to discuss ideas, not least the controversial issue of his abstract technique. 'When you come to England I should like to have some talk with you upon the principles of Art, especially regarding The Ideal monumental subjects I have in mind, & particularly upon one point, viz how far *apparent* mastery in *brushwork* would be desirable,' he wrote to Stillman on the 14th:

I am not in this seeking to excuse a *want* in myself, *a want I very freely acknowledge*, but my idea is that the expression of art would only be the greatest in making the spectator forget the artists in the work. If the want of power is felt, the defect is great, but I think the pictures I have in my mind should look as if they had become, not been produced, but Phidias is an example of what I mean, nothing is displayed though every thing is there. Certainly the beauty of the brush & pleasure in artistic dexterity should be felt in portraits, & in domestic scenes, not I think in a painted invocation or Anthem.[29]

During his long recuperation in Brighton, he received a bold, sad letter from Mary Fraser Tytler. 'My very dear Signor, I have not been able to go to Little Holland House & hear any news of you lately & been feeling rather an outcast from it.' If he was not returning to London, would he please write. After her visits to him she observed beauty and nobility in people's faces. Now she just saw hideousness and vulgarity. She reminded him that when she told him in November, 'I grow when I am with you', that 'You said that it was fancy – "but if it was a good fancy it was all right" – It is good, a fact, really . . . Always yours, Mary.'

'My dear Mary, You are a silly child! & confound a certain atmosphere in my Studio arising from the intention of my work acting upon your artistic temperament with me the artist', he rebuked her. 'I would not leave

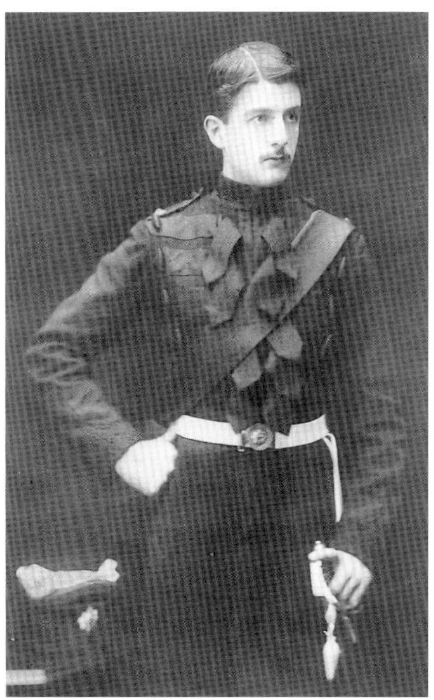

141   George Wyndham, aged twenty-one (photo: H. S. Mendelssohn).

this so for as it is an unreal thing it cannot be good.' He challenged her threat to remain an old maid and hoped instead that she would marry. Of course he must return to work as soon as his neuralgia subsided: 'I should like to know what you have been doing. Write me a line about it for I am not likely to be home for the next fortnight'.[30]

As Mary ventured out into the slums to give the first clay-modelling evening classes at a Whitechapel shoe-blacks club – she had joined Barnett's scheme to enrich the lives of the poor[31] – Watts replied grandly to Gertrude Mead across the Atlantic: 'It has not been given to me to influence peoples or to shape nations, nor to speak with the persuasive or prophetic voice of the Poet, but what I can, I would do.' He had 'great respect' for America and was keen to help 'strengthen a thoroughly vital stream of interest & relationship between us across the sea.' On 13 February 1885 the president of the Metropolitan Museum asked 'in view of the extraordinary interest which your paintings have developed in this country' to extend the exhibition until October. 'The exhibition of your works in this city has been a boon not only to the citizens of New York, but to the American people at large. Thousands are daily visiting our galleries and the general admiration your paintings have created is as genuine as it will be lasting . . . your name is today a household word in this great metropolis.' Watts replied, agreeing to the president's request:

> If my work can help to stimulate a regard for art which, appealing rather to the intellect and finer emotions than to the senses, can never be popular, I am too happy in being accepted as a pioneer in such a direction to hesitate. . . . That my name should find a place in the best known and cared for museum in America; that it should be among those Englishmen who have had the good fortune to aid in strengthening ever so little of interest in the concerns and welfare in the old country, connection in feeling which I, as a son of that old country, hope and trust may never diminish in America, is a greater distinction than I ever looked forward to, and of which I am indeed proud.'[32]

Gertrude Mead promising to guard the pictures and their copyright 'as a lioness would her whelps' in adoring letters to the artist, asked 'Who takes care of you, I wonder, & who reads to you?' to which she received no answer.[33] By no means coy to Marquand, she too pressed for a rehang, insisting that the screen was outrageous and 'the other pictures an insult to Watts.' The trustees refused, but they elected Watts an Honorary Fellow of the Metropolitan Museum for life.[34]

'As to Death, my friend Death!' he commiserated with Madeline Wyndham, 'The great power always walks by my side with full consciousness on my part' (Madeline advised her daughter on the death of a housekeeper to 'think of Mr Watts's beautiful angel who comes in love')[35] – 'I felt the touch and go of my pulse, and will show you my rendering of the visitation when I felt perhaps the time was come, but it was not yet. I am glad to find I did not feel afraid.' Mindful of George Wyndham, serving abroad with his regiment and at risk, he added, 'Doubtless your boy sees the friend (for in spite of all, I feel certain it must be called so), close by in a terrible shape . . . and even while you shrink . . . the nobility of your position, giving of your best for your country and helping, through the brave boy, to set the great example to future times.[36]

Watts divided his portraits of the Gurney sisters between the Grosvenor and the Academy. 'What lovely times you must have had painting those two girls? I think I shall set up in my old age for a portrait painter – Landscape is dull by itself,' Ruskin wrote on 23 May, looking forward with 'unmixed pleasure' to visiting Watts.[37] According to the *Art Journal*, the Academicians had hung his portrait of Laura Gurney (fig. 142) as a pendant to Leighton's picture of *A Young Girl* in blue, to provoke comparison. Laura, standing in a purple hat, her eyes questioning, quick and observant, wore a red brocade fur-trimmed cloak over a black gown, a juxtaposition that struck the *Athenaeum* as 'noble and original'. With the portrait of Rachel Gurney at the Grosvenor were two vertical mountainscapes: *Mount Ararat*, a 'poetic representation of the heights upon which the ark rested and was safe' and the large *Love and Life* painted for the nation (in tandem with the Metropolitan canvas), both subjects revealing the Wattsian theme that Love envelopes the entire universe. Wings on the male nude figure symbolized its universal rather than personal or carnal nature. His painting of 'naked, bare Life', a refinement of the purest classical genre he had determined to revive in British art, was one of an unprecedented number of female nudes in the London exhibitions that incited a protest letter to *The Times* from 'A British Matron'. The anonymous 'H' took up the cudgels, accused artists of 'violently' altering convention by portraying indecently real models as ideal subjects – John Callcott Horsley, the treasurer of the Royal Academy, would pursue the attack.[38]

'My dear Ned,' Watts wrote to Burne-Jones. 'I wish I might venture to hope you would accept the recognition the Academy has done itself the honour to show by becoming one of us. I believe you could help the cause of Art more effectually by doing so than by remaining outside.' Like himself, Burne-Jones had not sought membership of the Academy, but nor did he desire to exhibit there. On 4 June Briton Rivière surprised many Academicians by proposing him as an Associate and he was swept in with a huge majority. 'You must see how many friends and admirers you have among the body in the fact that the moment your name came up you were elected,' added Watts. 'Leighton and Poynter and myself know your opinions too well to think we should be giving you any pleasure by putting your name in the book. I must say I was delighted to find a stranger to you personally brought the matter suddenly to such (for the Academy) satisfactory end.'

Ever dear Signor

    Thank you for your long note: you know all I feel about it – have we not talked over these things many a day – I loved solitude & peace & isolation – & I give these up reluctantly – as I gave them up to exhibit at all, but I can't have my way – ever since you & Leighton are so affectionately kind about this I am bound to be glad too: I wish you had a better godchild to back so strenuously as you do.

    I am unfit for teaching or taking any part in the administration of that big society – I told Leighton all my disqualifications, how bound in honour I feel to the Grosvenor, how inconsistent my position could become – all that seemed to me needful to say I told him this morning – and I think you know all my innermost mind about it: and there I need not say it to you. Of course I like to be by your side – of course I feel

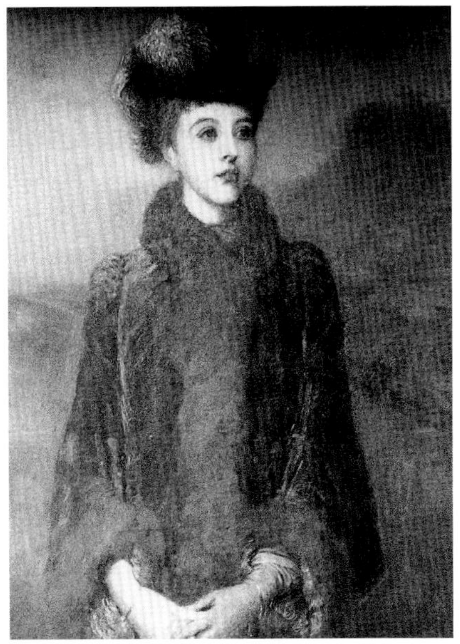

142  *Laura Gurney* (detail), 1883–85 (private collection).

proud that you & he are so glad, and if I now & then grieve over lost insignificance it is not because I am ungrateful to you both, Your affte Ned.[39]

Their warm support encouraged him to believe the Academy might now appreciate his work and aims. With a heavy heart, he accepted the 'unlooked-for honour', provided that it would not prejudice his association with its rival. After all, Watts still sent his best poetic works to the Grosvenor.[40]

The government, in deep trouble over the fall of Khartoum and the festering Irish problem, was defeated on a vote of censure on 8 June. Gladstone, replaced as prime minister by Lord Salisbury, graciously refused the Queen's offer of an earldom.[41] On the 24th, he wrote from Downing Street, 'My dear Watts, I have to request with the sanction of Her Majesty, that you will allow yourself to be enrolled among the Baronets of the United Kingdom. It gives me truly pleasure to have the means of thus doing honour to Art in the person of so distinguished a representation of the noble pursuit.'[42] The artist had been consulted by George Howard and agreed to an honour, but thought he meant a Companion of the Bath 'which would leave me really where I was' – because 'it would greatly please my adopted daughter'. He was startled by the title, which Millais happily accepted. That day, too, Sir George Watts accepted the congratulations of his brother artists for the unprecedented honour to 'ideal Art'.[43]

The following day he declined. (Privately he feared that his ugly surname might degrade their profession. If the Queen were to invest him with a new name, as an incentive, to create him the first of a new order, he would have accepted.) He explained to Gladstone that he was grateful to be honoured as a standard bearer for art, but that a baronetcy was excessive. His national artistic enterprise, 'the very course which alone could give me any claim' had prevented him earning the finances to support a baronetcy. The pictures were his only fortune and he was now even more determined to leave them to the nation.'[44] Just that week the *Athenaeum* announced that Watts had presented a *Portrait of a Boy*, then ascribed to the sixteenth-century French painter François Clouet, to the National Gallery.[45] Arnold wrote that 'To be associated with your noble and high toned art will give a new dignity to the name of Baronet' and hearing his decision planned 'to shake by the hand the highest and singlest-mindest artist of my acquaintance.[46] So highly did Watts value the honour that he felt he could not live up to it, but the social obligation was incompatible with the nature of his art and would disturb the harmony and tranquillity he needed to carry it out.[47] This time Leighton could not sway him. He apologised to Howard that he must have misheard the proposition and regretted that he may have prevented another recipient (he had: Leighton).[48] Congratulations continued to arrive, adding to Watts's discomfort. 'So you wont let them make you Sir George,' laughed Thomas Thornycroft. 'Ah never mind you shall [be] St George any how!'[49]

Watts spoke candidly to journalists, for publication.[50] 'Please don't let it be thought that I did so from any socialistic reasons, or that I flung back the offer,' he replied to F. G. Stephens, for the *Athenaeum*. 'The simple truth is that I could not help feeling the incongruity between my very restricted means (arising from want of sympathy with my aims in picture buyers). I have a strong desire for the dignity of proportion.'[51]

At least the publicity had served the cause of art well; and Watts resolved to focus only on the national character of his work. As he wrote to Lady Tennyson: 'The more I can get away from observation the better my chance will be of shaping out the character (at least) of my efforts.'[52] He told Anny Thackeray Ritchie that he would prefer to be remembered as a 'Poet and Pioneer'; and the Duke of Devonshire, sitting in July for his second portrait, noted in his diary that 'Watts told us today that this was the last portrait he would ever undertake.' To Nelly, who congratulated him warmly on his decision, her co-star Irving having refused a knighthood two years earlier, he asked that she disregard 'sublime notions' and expressed 'pleasure to think that we know each other well now'.[53]

A week later he was shocked out of his tranquillity by a sensational exposé of child prostitution in the *Pall Mall Gazette*, 'The Maiden Tribute of Modern Babylon', a problem Ruskin had touched on in *Fors Clavigera*. Asked to investigate claims by the Salvation Army, the editor W. T. Stead enlisted the aid of the social reformer Josephine Butler. Butler had established homes for work-girls and fallen women and was campaigning against the Contagious Diseases Acts; and she had revealed that thousands of children as young as thirteen – the legal British age of consent (compared to twenty-one in France) – were being procured. Many poverty-stricken mothers believed their children were going into domestic service or even thought prostitution less unappealing than the dreadful conditions in factories. Girls arriving from Ireland *en route* for convents were ensnared at the dockside by women masquerading as nuns. To press home the terrible truth, how easy it was to procure and sell a child, Stead's team bought a child for five pounds.[54] Emilie Barrington, noting that Watts worked best when his Celtic passion was roused, recalled his indignation at the unmentionable subject one evening. He drew furiously from five to eight o'clock the next morning and sent a note inviting her to see a vigorous, complete drawing of the Minotaur crushing an innocent bird in his brutal hand (fig. 143).[55] As he transformed this symbolic defence of innocence into paint, producing in addition a disturbing study of a child in the clutches of a monster, Watts entertained Henrietta Barnett and the Whitechapellians at Little Holland House; and his *Daughter of Herodias* – Salomé eyeing and pointing to Herod's ring to indicate his responsibility for the death of John the Baptist – was hailed as the connoisseurs' picture at the Royal Cambrian Academy in Cardiff.[56]

The monstrous *Minotaur* was revealed to the public on 25 July. Leaning on the angle of a parapet, his brawny human back to the viewer, the brute stares over land and sea; his bull's ears twitch at the approach of his victim, as he mindlessly crushes the bird beneath his fingers. 'Apart from the grim force of the design, the work is remarkable for the harmony and appropriateness of its colour and tone, its virile draughtsmanship, and the energetic modelling of the flesh', declared the *Athenaeum*, which the following week announced progress on *Europa* – combining the brutal beauty of the bull Jupiter who is about to ravish Europa – and the Cain cycle. *The Denunciation of the First Murderer*, developed since Paris, shows Adam's son standing defiantly above the body of Abel and called to account by God;

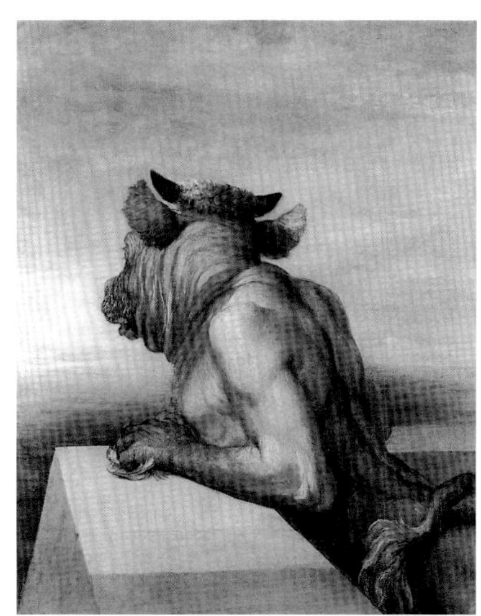

143   *The Minotaur*, 1885 (Tate, London).

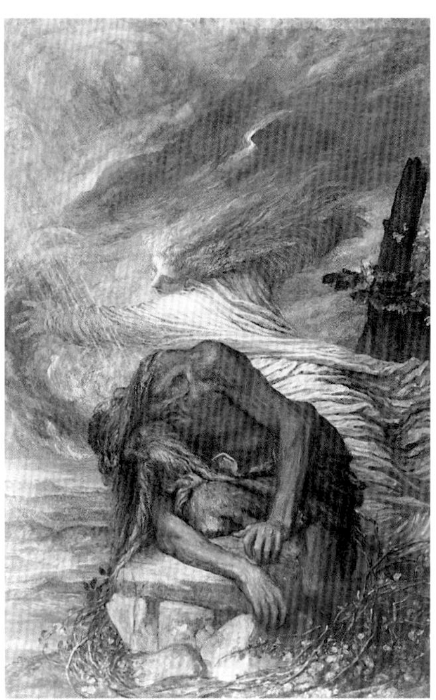

144    *The Death of Cain*, 1885–86 (Royal Academy of Arts, London).

in the second picture, the angel endeavours to break down Cain's selfish isolation and soften his heart; in *The Death of Cain* (fig. 144), he appears skeletal, his head and arms droop and he repents as the radiant angel removes the curse and his soul is received at the gates of heaven. Watts explained to Adolphus 'Doll' Liddell that, until that moment, as part of the curse, Cain was to be invisible, to travel the world with no feeling for other men. He also showed Liddell how a photograph had heightened the effect and mystery of a charcoal drawing by darkening the mass of figures and lightening the background.[57] In September he lent *Europa* to the Corporation Gallery in Birmingham and sent *The Minotaur* with *Love and Life* to the Walker Art Gallery, noting in the catalogue that 'the real mission of Art – not merely to amuse, but to illustrate and embody the mental form of the beautiful and noble, interpreting them as poetry does, and to hold up to detestation the bestial and brutal'.[58]

In gratitude for his Metropolitan exhibition, he wished to present a picture to the American people, to help start an art collection, for they had as yet no National Gallery. 'In token of the great interest I feel in the national progress . . . the importance & influence of Art, & knowing the value of a starting point, the hope of being in some small degree instrumental in forming a national collection of works of art in America', he wrote to Gertrude Mead, 'I wish to present not to the museum or to any particular Institution but to the Nation, one of the pictures which it gives me great pleasure to think have been so generously received.' *Love and Life*, he suggested, had the widest significance. The secretary of state, T. F. Bayard, confessing that he had never seen a more honourable and impressive record of an artist's life work – 'I hope the seed he proposes to sow may fall on good ground' – confirmed President Cleveland's appreciation and asked for the picture to be sent to Washington. The artist cabled agreement. However, on Gertrude Mead's advice (until the American government established responsibility for the cost of transport to Washington), *Love and Life* sailed for England with the rest of the Watts collection on 16 October. Nine years would pass before the president could take delivery of Watts's present to the American nation. In the meantime, Watts saw that Gertrude Mead needed employment and suggested that she direct her energies towards establishing a national art collection: 'Of all the great states America is the only one that does not possess such property.'[59]

Having willed The Briary to Blanche, Watts now gave it to her. She was pregnant and 'I thought it nicer to *see* the young people enjoying it.' He had calculated professional and household expenses against share income, did not need the income from rent and would earn nothing until the following spring. The decision to paint only for the nation made him feel liberated. He wrote again to Gladstone to thank him for his 'munificence' and wished he deserved a dukedom, but his mind was filled with visions of the universal conditions of Life and Death, Light and Darkness.[60] 'Labouring by the side of the Poet & the Statesman, the Artist may deal with those great visions & here I think the Art of England has been at fault'. Contrasting his limited means with the idea of making his art acceptable to the nation both before and after his death, he was grateful to the statesman for 'a most delightful feeling of freedom & independence'.[61]

Even so, Gladstone knew that Watts could not be tempted away from his studio to 'unfold this matter' beneath the trees at Hawarden Castle, in

Cheshire. 'You have adopted a resolution of the kind that makes the nine-teenth century stare or blank as though blink who found in a great right-ness and have not eyes for it. The course that you propose is indeed a self denying, an unworldly and a noble one, and will give you a place in the grateful recollection of your countrymen not less high than that which you hold in the annals of its Art.' The artist, in turn, suggested that 'when you renounce the fatigues of office & you have time to resume our discussions of Homer you will come & sit in my dentist's chair & let me try to make a portrait of you for the National Portrait Gallery. I want to have a ray of illumination thrown upon the great figure of Achilles.'[62]

Horsley's blistering attack, in a Church Congress paper, on the shame and immorality of nude painting, of models and the life class, and his demand for all models to be clothed, antagonized colleagues. Watts, as 'the foremost painter of the nude in England', was called by the *Pall Mall Gazette* to respond. Speaking for Leighton and others, he pointed out that he had seen no evidence of degradation in a model, whom he treated 'as I would treat any lady in the land', or crude conduct or immorality in a life class. He had never known a girl 'go wrong' after sitting in the nude; the very suggestion was insulting to her and 'only a bad or singularly consti-tuted mind would consider that the undraping of the figure for the purpose of art robbed a woman of her modesty or destroyed her respectability'. Warning against hypocrisy, he declared that, 'To abolish the model is to abolish all true art.' As for the insistence on clothes, 'the sight of a naked woman in the schools is not half so impure as the undressing that fash-ionable women subject themselves to [at] parties.' He directed the *Pall Mall* critic Marion Spielmann to his own work, the figures crushed by *Mammon*. 'Now, why have I painted these little victims naked? Because they are types of humanity, and had they been clothed the force of my meaning and teach-ing would be altogether gone.' 'The model is but the grammar of the higher language of art,' explained Watts. He would make twenty or thirty studies for future reference, 'when I want to be sure as to the play of a joint or a muscle, or the fall of light'. Had he not first drawn the draped *Angel of Death* as a nude figure – from a model – it might have looked grotesque; and 'to emasculate art by suppressing the study [of] the highest form of pictorial art – is simply prudery . . . setting narrow limits to our art and putting blinkers on our imagination.'[63]

Watts summoned every ounce of tact to tell his fellow Academician exactly where he was wrong. The issue should not have been directed to churchmen, unless it were purely a question of morals, which it was not. There was no evidence of scandal or degradation. To forbid the life class would drive students 'into the crookedest arts to obtain models, or a less evil, though I think a great one, into seeking in Paris the means of study not to be found here.' Horsley was entitled to his opinion, but he should address the profession, rather than outsiders. 'Certainly my idea of art is not the same as yours . . . Far from being indifferent to the morality of it. I even think I believe its utterances more important than you do. Conse-quently I believe its responsibilities to be greater. I cannot imagine that any sanely-minded individual would find it necessary to refocus his thought after looking at the *Theseus* or the *Milo Venus* before entering a drawing-room or even a church'. Horsley, caricatured by Sambourne in *Punch* as 'The model "British Matron" ', sent a rambling reply, which he asked Watts to forward to Leighton: 'The only drawback I felt in doing my duty was the conviction that *I should find my* views completely *à travers* with those for whom I have all regard & respect, notably yourself, Leighton, & Poynter.'[64]

The Metropolitan collection, augmented with pictures from London, transferred – by arrangement with his framer – to Birmingham for the inaugural exhibition of the Museum and Art Gallery, to be opened by the Prince of Wales on 28 November 1889,[65] Spielmann began to compile a catalogue of Watts's work to be published as a special issue of the *Pall Mall*. In writing the catalogue essay, the artist took the opportunity to reiterate his aims and to explain the meaning of his art – his cosmic work in particular. In addition to the work that he described as 'reality' (the portraits), he defined two other categories: '*types* as in *Orpheus & Eurydice*, & the figures on the sea shore . . . [and] *symbols* as in the abstractions!' He pointed out that the symbolical equestrian group, hereafter referred to as *Physical Energy*, did *not* represent youthful energy (too narrow), but 'Physical energy – as distinguished from the intellectual; Columbus was not a youth when he set out to discover the New World. Neither was Captain Parry a youth when he went to the North Pole. The energy of which my work is illustrative is of no age though of course more a characteristic of youth than of age.'

A significant example of his cosmic work, *Time, Death and Judgment*, was to go to the new National Art Gallery of Canada. The decision to donate the painting to the Canadian nation was part of his scheme to present his serious subjects to national institutions – both at home and abroad.[66] That winter, private grief spurred him to resurrect a picture that was to become his best-loved cosmic work.

'My poor Blanche . . . has lost her baby', Watts wrote to Madeline Wyndham.[1] He grieved for her loss, and, determined to see Egypt, planned to join the Somers-Cocks in Cairo. 'I am painting a picture of '*Hope* sitting on a globe with bandaged eyes playing on a lyre which has all the strings broken but one out of which poor little tinkle she is trying to get all the music possible, listening with all her might to the little sound, do you like the idea?' A friend of Emilie Barrington modelled for this iconic Wattsian image of a blindfolded auburn-haired figure bent double in her effort to make music (pl. xxix). Her luminous classical robe falls in multiple folds, her feet are bare; With her head bent close to her lyre, there is great pathos in her pose. Watts said of the single string, 'It is only when one supreme desire is left that one reaches the topmost pitch of hope.' His conception contrasts with Puvis de Chavannes's adolescent girl seated in the battle-fields, holding out a symbolic branch of oak after the Franco-Prussian War.[2]

In January 1886 Watts consulted his influential old friends, the Earl of Wemyss (now aide-de-camp to the Queen) and Lord Aberdare (Henry Bruce, the former home secretary) with a view to donating the portraits and best ideal works to the nation during his lifetime. To Lord Wemyss, who would also pursue the matter in the Lords, he explained, 'I shall make this gift not so much considering the things of any real value as for the sake of precedent.' He was concerned, that if unacceptable, it might be awkward to refuse. Lord Aberdare consulted Sir Henry Layard and Earl Spencer, the Lord President of the Council, and reported that portraits of deceased celebrities would be warmly welcomed by the National Portrait Gallery and the imaginative works by South Kensington Museum, but that the pictures should be kept together until the Portrait Gallery was available. Grateful that a temporary arrangement would serve to test public opinion, Watts sent a formal proposal to Lord Spencer. 'Such a gift would be of great value and importance to the country, and your munificence will be immensely appreciated,' replied the earl, who called at Little Holland House and sent a museum official Thomas Armstrong to see him.[3]

While his portrait *Sir John Millais* greeted visitors to Millais's exhibition at the Grosvenor Gallery that winter, Watts worked on *Hope* and repainted the American *Love and Life*. He invited Briton Rivière to come and criti-cize *Hope* – 'Pull it well to pieces' – and to compare a new version of *Love and Life* with that destined for America. He had presumably sent a third version to replace it in the travelling Watts Collection, which would transfer to Nottingham that year.[4] Bronchitis curtailed his work in February and jeopardized plans for Egypt. His assistant – either Fanny Cornforth's stepson Cecil Schott or Henry Moore[5] – produced drawings under his supervision for the *Pall Mall*'s catalogue of his works published in the spring. Efforts were made to save his frescoes, fast fading and blackened by the London smogs. *Christ and the Evangelists* at St James-the-Less was converted into mosaic, and Lord Wemyss headed an appeal for a similar conversion of the Lincoln's Inn *Hemicycle*; and that year the Watts collection transferred to Nottingham.[6]

Inside a Society for Psychical Research pamphlet advertising 'A Protest by Madame Blavatsky' on 6 March, the artist experimented with shadows for the face of Death in *Time, Death and Judgment* – an appropriate choice of subject. Even more apposite would have been his contribution to the Grosvenor, *The Soul's Prism* (later known as *Dweller in the Innermost*; pl. xxx), a vibrating embodiment of consciousness, encapsulated in a sonnet by Walter Crane. Moved that his subliminal 'stuttering' had been understood, Watts included the poem in the catalogue entry:

> Star-stedfast eyes that pierce the smouldering haze
>   Of Life and Thought, whose fires prismatic fuse
>   The palpitating mists with magic hues
> That stain in the glass of Being, as we gaze,
> And mark in transit every mood and phase,
>   Which, sensitive, doth take or doth refuse
>   The lights and shadows Time and Love confuse,
> When lost in dreams we thread their wandering maze.
> . . . Behind thy veil behold a heart on fire,
> Wrapped in the secret of its own unrest.[7]

Watts wrote to congratulate and argue with Ruskin on the first volume of his memoirs *Praeterita* in which the critic ranted against accusations that he had charged too much for his books. Suffering from a mental disorder after retiring as Slade Professor, he was 'deeply grateful' to hear from 'Dearest Watts', who had offered him a picture. 'Your writing which I constantly read gives the greatest pleasure I know & whether I agree with all your dogmas or not, I acknowledge your objects are always good & noble & sympathize with more than I can say.'[8] Writing to Gertrude Mead after a long silence from America, he feared that 'my unconventional style and habits' had deterred her.[9] A new British admirer was overwhelmed by his enthusiasm. Mrs Ann Budgett had seemed at once a friend, rather than an acquaintance because he knew her face well from Millais's portrait and she had worked with Stopford Brooke editing Turner's *Liber Studiorum*. Bemused by her reaction, he wrote in apology: 'I am at a loss to understand what thoughtlessness! unless absence of affectation & presence of sympathy with my efforts could be so construed, & I am afraid now that I really *did shock* you by my unconventionality.' He had hoped that she might model for a head study for a symbolic work.[10] Ann Budgett did return, but not at once. Theresa (Trees) Sassoon, herself an artist, felt no such qualms. The sister of Hamo Thornycroft and mother of the future poet Siegfried sent him her drawing of *The Fates* on 13 March and invited him to her home which she had filled with copies of his works, though he refused for fear of offending older friends whom he did not venture out to visit.[11]

Now finding Mary Fraser Tytler's slightly eccentric attitude more appealing, he wrote to invite her to his studio. 'Until you marry or engage yourself I . . . want you to feel that you may speak to me on any subject you like.' He assured her that he would neither misunderstand nor betray her confidence and that even when he was not expecting her, he would see her: 'It is a great pleasure & advantage to me to breathe an unconventional atmosphere.'[12]

While his exuberant flirtations with artistic young ladies would never stop, his letters to Mary urge intimacy, for despite her aristocratic roots, she preferred a creative atmosphere to society. Her classes for shoe-blacks, now part of the rapidly expanding Home Arts and Industries Association of which Watts was to be a vice-president, gave her a glorious sense of purpose. A natural teacher, she loved awakening her impoverished lads to the joys of creativity; and as she became more involved with the Home Arts, Watts approached colleagues – Walter Crane and Frederic Shields – on her behalf for ornamental designs to be copied in the classes. She painted chiefly portraits at her studio in Bloomfield Place, around the corner from the Grosvenor, and when her paintings were rejected by the gallery he offered sympathy. He consulted her about St Jude's. Could they accommodate without damage *Angel of Death* and the dozen other requested pictures he now considered national property, and could she bring some work? 'It is long since I have seen any', he wrote on 31 March. He wanted more.[13]

Blanche and her baby were staying at Little Holland House when Ellen Terry wrote to tell him how much she cared for *Hope*. She had seen a photograph taken by Henry Herschel Cameron, the son of their old friend Julia Margaret Cameron. 'You have made of it a picture of *your own painting*,' he replied. They exchanged family news and, as ever, he asked her to confide in him unreservedly. I always send *mentally* the utmost comfort & aid that it is within the power of my will to afford'. *Hope* was proving very popular at the Grosvenor, if not with Whistler. 'Well', he exclaimed. 'That is the hope that maketh the heart sick!' And he later caricatured *The Minotaur*.[14] Watts, meanwhile, encouraged that he was not losing power as he grew older, asked Cameron, now authorized to photograph his works, to send the actress copies of each one.[15] He casually offered to send some to Gertrude Mead, who had perplexed him by writing to Emilie Barrington, rather than to him directly; he wondered if his attraction had failed the test of time, that she had read too much about him.[16]

Leighton persuaded him not to send the *Eve* triptych to Burlington House and instead he resurrected his Pre-Raphaelite portrait of Jeanie and *The Death of Cain*. Visitors were struck by the skeletal outcast, his head falling at the moment of death, as a flaming angel sweeps away the cloud. 'Cain is, in my intention, a symbol of reckless selfish humanity (always killing his brother)', explained Watts. His picture inspired four statues, as well as a poem by the future headmaster Downside Edward Butler.[17] As he had forecast, 'Leighton will carry off all the honours this year with his ceiling [a rich symbolic decoration for a music room for Henry Marquand in New York] and two statues [*Needless Alarms*, a girl startled by a toad, and *An Athlete Awakening from Sleep*, or *The Sluggard*, the seminal languid pendant to *An Athlete Wrestling with a Python*].'[18] The chief event to col-

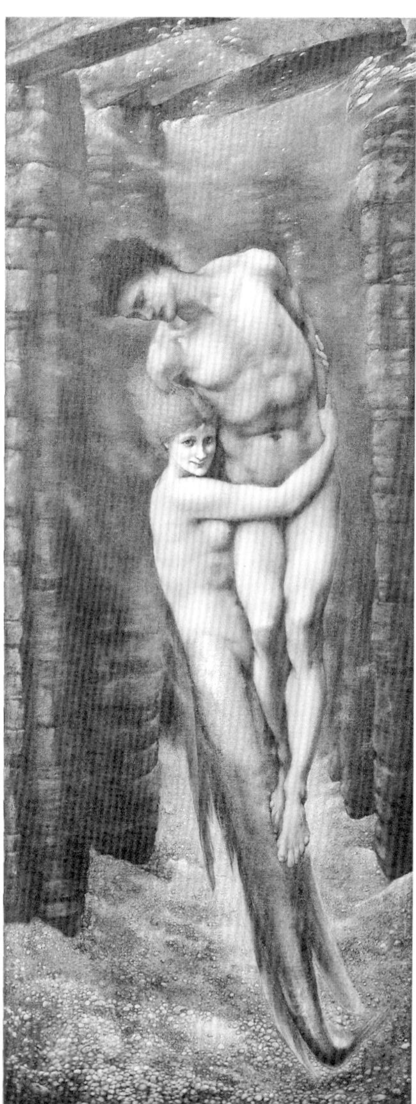

145    Edward Coley Burne-Jones,
*The Depths of the Sea*, 1886 (private
collection, courtesy of Julian
Hartnoll).

leagues, however, was Burne-Jones's first contribution, *The Depths of the Sea* (fig. 145), a macabre picture of a drowned youth in the clutches of a mermaid had taken the president aback. ('Such a thing seemed impossible five years ago,' Hamo Thornycroft noted in his diary.) The mermaid's face was seen to resemble that of Laura Lyttleton, the elder daughter of the collector Sir Charles Tennant, and all the more poignant because she died in childbirth after the Academicians' varnishing day.[19]

The death of Tennyson's younger son saddened both Watts – 'I have not words with which to express my sorrow' – and Mary Fraser Tytler.[20] Her imaginative spirit, embracing resurrection, rebirth, the eternal circle – and therefore at variance to his – delighted Watts, and news that she had received an offer of marriage so alarmed him that he mistook her elderly sitter General Frederic Cotton for her suitor. 'My dear Mary. What Genl Cotton? I may be going to Brighton in a few days for a short time. I wish very much indeed to have a little talk with you. He invited her to lunch and offered to be at hand for the general's sitting in her studio on 14 May, asking to arrive early, ostensibly for her opinion on drapery materials. That night, at the Prince's Hall in Piccadilly, Dorothy Dene appeared as Nausicaa in *The Tale of Troy*, a new translation by Professor Warr of King's College. Watts, with Leighton, Poynter, Holiday and Crane had provided designs and persuaded Violet Lindsay, now married to Henry Manners, and Margaret Talbot, the wife of his *Standard Bearer* Reginald, to take part.[21]

His truest standard bearer, the Earl of Wemyss, asked in the House of Lords for formal governmental recognition of Watts's bequest and for accommodation had to be found for the pictures. 'It would be of the utmost advantage of the nation to possess these', Earl Spencer acknowledged and promised that the South Kensington Museum would do all in their power to secure these valuable treasures for the nation. Lord Wemyss thought they should be at the National Gallery rather than South Kensington, but there was no space. 'This is not the way to induce [others] to follow Mr Watts's noble example.'[22] An enterprising lad, modelling to Mary for pocket money, called out from his high chair, 'Do you know what I calls Mr Watts?' The eight-year-old declared with pride, 'I calls him painter to the nation.'[23]

To comfort Emilie Barrington on the death of her mother, he drew a portait sketch in red and black chalk.[24] When at last he heard from Gertrude Mead, her 'unconventional affection' was equal to his, and sent confusing messages. He composed a 'rhapsodical' reply, but instead sent a considered response – addressing her, as usual, as 'My dear Mary': 'Since you wish it, I will say nothing about your original expression of deep interest & feeling.' He urged her to do more. She should create work, a cause. 'Find out what is best in humanity & endeavour to stimulate encourage & develop it. Find out what is bad & endeavour to root it out, dry it up & destroy it.'[25]

To test the public response to his mission, the *Time, Death and Judgment* destined for Canada was transferred from Kensington Palace to the South Kensington Museum on 22 June. Watts was invited to choose the distemper for the walls and to supervise hanging and lighting.[26] The second Home Arts exhibition was in full swing at St Andrew's parish room in Bethnal Green, where pupils and their teachers were selling embroideries, wood-carvings, metalwork, pots and woven objects; Morris lent 250 yards of fabrics, and Princess Christian was among the visitors; but most significant for Eglantyne Jebb was meeting Mary Fraser Tytler at the Home Arts garden party: 'A slightly made figure, a sweet thoughtful face – rather regular features – young – now here is a new friend – how these joys come wholly unexpectedly! We had some talk together – she holds a class. This meeting is perhaps the chief event of my visit to town this year – for I feel here is a treasure come into my life.'[27]

The two women met again that week at Bethnal Green and at the Grosvenor where Eglantyne was taken straight to *Hope* and *The Soul's Prism*. 'I looked at *nothing else* during our happy brief hour there . . . that I should know and see and understand these glorious pictures and hear about the artist from his friend . . . It seemed almost profanation to have them hanging there among poorer things, to be stared at foolishly criticized by a crowd – yet he who painted them wills it so – though he never comes to a gallery while his pictures are hanging there.' Eglantyne returned to the Home Arts headquarters for a meeting at Langham Chambers where Mary was elected to the Council. There seemed – as Eglantyne surmised – Hope for the Scotswoman, who had long despaired of love and did not expect it of Watts.[28] Nine days later, on 3 July, Mary noted in her commonplace book, 'He said "I want you".' Quite simply, he needed her; and as he returned Nelly's theatre tickets he was unable to use, he sent his first wife 'all good wishes now for ever more'.[29]

'I want you to tell me very distinctly when you are engaged or consider that to be within distance, or decided *probability*', Watts wrote on 12 July. Mary was taken aback at the idea that Watts thought she might soon be engaged to another.[30] Watts had also gleaned the impression that her engagement – if there was one – had arisen from financial considerations, which he deemed 'not nice'. (Nor was it likely, for Mary was a socialist, deeply religious, conscientious, and not hard up.) He was confused. 'When you have made up your mind as to that future, or even *that it may be*, I consider all things taken into account, that we should become strangers. But you know I shall always be yours affly Signor.'

Watts painted a bleak picture in order to appeal to her sympathy and strength – 'lumbago takes everything out of me' – to help complete his artistic mission. When he had given his pictures to the nation, he planned to go away, give up Little Holland House and for his last few years move, perhaps, to Wimbledon. 'How much I value & respect your great qualities & find how very dear you would become to me.'[31] Obsessed by her possible engagement, he deluged her with daily letters, raising doubt after doubt, warning her against committing herself unless she was certain, but 'If our intercourse (not our recollection – affectionate for so long) comes to an end . . . I must not have kept alive vain regrets I should condemn but be unable to repress! . . . I do grieve to lose the much that might have been thought, & done, & seen together.'[32]

In a panic on 16 July, he wrote 'I shall consider you have decided & cease to regret as much as I can, but if you can come to me after October (is it?) you will find me. Come next Saturday & after never! Unless your prospects fall through – I shall always feel you are the one in whom I have felt the greatest confidence.' Mary's later query – 'Why? Beloved Signor why?' – suggests innocence. Did she not after all tell him she was to marry in October? The next day, he proposed. She pleaded for time. He wrote again offering artistic guidance and won her over. For sixteen years their friend-ship had revolved around art; mutual interest as art reformers had brought them in closer touch. Watts was more than three decades older than thirty-six-year-old Mary and, as he said, he was not offering passion. Even as his wife in his noble ascetic studio home, would she have to be an 'old maid' nurse after all? On Sunday, 25 July 1886 Mary went to Little Holland House and told him her *life* was his: 'There are no words for an hour like this – only tears of joy at the feet of God – God, & the noblest heart all mine, all mine'.[33]

Marriage to Britain's most famous, if controversial, artist, carried immense responsibility. That day he offered to present *The Death of Cain* to the Academy, as a pendant to *The Denunciation*, which dominated the new Diploma Gallery.[34] Of course it was a privilege and her joy to share artistic and educational ideals, but it would require courage to marry the Signor, a man of his idiosyncratic genius, whose friends and sitters were the most remarkable figures of the age. Beautiful women still worshipped and flirted with him; some had felt honoured to be allowed to look after him and nurture his art, but they were safely married to wholesome, healthy men. They had never had to tie themselves entirely to him and could always escape.

Even the woman Mary came to see as her greatest adversary, Emilie Barrington, could find him maddening. 'There is a tendency to a species of mental inebriation in those possessed of the creative faculty . . . not only when he was inspired to create expressions in art, but also when he turned his imagination on to situations in real life.'[35] Outside his studio, when it came to dealing with a difficult everyday problem or a financial matter, 'the bare naked truth was not always what he cared to face', wrote Mrs Bar-rington. 'In the large things he was always right (providing he was not evilly influenced), in the small – scarcely ever!'[36] He would either leave matters vague, postpone dealing with them, or exaggerate each trifling problem and imagine all sorts of dangers. Mary had the strength and devotion to his ideals – her own would stretch further – would give him strength, con-fidence, ease his life and release him from his terrors; yet she too possessed the mysterious Celtic characteristics Mrs Barrington saw in Watts. Mary was the more diffident, but both were intensely though shyly emotional: 'The sensitiveness of the Celtic nature is often veiled, its emotional side being kept smothered under a curious kind of patient melancholy and secre-tiveness. It is rarely fully awakened except when a fire, seemingly outside its own consciousness, is lighted, and then with fervour it expresses itself.'[37]

For the time being, the engagement was to be kept secret, in the first instance because as a sixty-nine-year-old divorcé – the same age as her late father would have been – he might not be acceptable to the Fraser Tytlers: 'I cannot help thinking from what you say your family . . . would find me nothing but a jarring element'. But through his work he could claim: 'my mind has kinship with Tennyson, Browning Matthew Arnold and their fellows, who are led by Thought, and by whom Thought is led. You will see how far this is likely to be in harmony with those you most care for; and will ponder well *even now* while it is time.' His divorce was a stum-bling block for them both: 'The *subject* for disapproval to which you allude (and which I must forever decline to discuss even with you!) is one that cannot be denied or explained away. This much I will here add about it, the legal measure was not suggested by me, nor ever would have been so. It is for you to consider whether any set off can be sufficient to compensate for possible estrangement which might arise out of serious disapproval, do not let anything blind you to the pain of such a state of things, there is yet time!'[38] She asked whether he was sure about their marriage. 'Don't be a Goose!' he replied. Do not let us have either doubt or fear.'[39]

He had dispatched the American *Love and Life* to the Berlin International Exhibition, when he heard again from Gertrude Mead. Reminding her to destroy his letters, he wrote that 'sometimes I really feel life is such a burden that but for leaving so many things undone I could wish it to slip away altogether unawares! This is a sad confession of weakness.' Writing at length, he suggested enigmatically 'Read between the lines where my scribble is halting or unintelligible.' She should devote her energies to becoming the Prophet of Art in America, to raise it from preoccupations with material success and small inventions. 'You will soon have Mr Whistler among you, a man of remarkable ability but wholly given up to making an effect, not good preaching for America! He will appeal to the sense of admiration of effect which I cannot help feeling is a defect in one side of the American character. It cannot lead to real greatness. So young & great a nation should have for aim the ennobling of the human race!' Poetry and Art – 'one and the same' – were paramount to a nation's greatness.[40] 'Symbolic poetry', Jean Moréas declared in *Le Figaro* on 18 September 1886, 'attempts to clothe the Idea in a perceptible form which, though not itself the poem's goal, serves to express the Idea to which it remains subordinate'. Moréas was a minor poet, but his manifesto established the term 'Symbolist' adopted by French artists to describe Wattsian concepts that had mystified the British public for almost forty years.[41]

That month as South Kensington Museum prepared to receive his pictures, Mary went up to Inverness-shire to break the news to her brother Edward, now the laird of the family home, Aldourie Castle. Watts confided their 'very great secret' to Mrs Barrington. 'Lie', Mary later scrawled in the margin of her enemy's *G. F. Watts Reminiscences*. 'He wrote to no one till he had told the Prinseps thro' Julia Stephen.' Perhaps the wretched woman guessed. Mary's indignant response to the charge of secrecy – three heavy exclamation marks – suggested a wicked sense of triumph?[42]

Andrew and May Hichens did not yet know, although he had spent a couple of days with them at Monkshatch, their new Arts and Crafts country home in Surrey, taking 'the faithful Emma *to instruct the cook*'. Nor did Leighton, who was away. But Gerry Liddell sent 'beaming' encouragement, and Mary's family were intrigued. As her half-brother, William, put it, 'Let us know the day, and Ted and I will be there to give you to the Nation.'[43] Astonished by their warmth, Watts wondered whether they knew that he could offer her only twelve hundred a year – eight hundred until the nation's work was completed. 'I should like you to haggle & make a better bargain if you think you ought. I should like to leave you everything but no doubt Blanche has had good reason to think all outside various claims, would be hers but we will have that matter for the present.' His thirty-eight-year lease on Little Holland House would be transferred into her name, the Iron House (the 'Tinpot') was to be her studio, adapted to her requirements, and she could entertain friends in the gallery, which was open to the public only at weekends; he would relinquish everything outside his studios into her care.[44]

Up at Aldourie, Mary was happier than ever. 'The roots of my heart are very deep in here', she wrote and mused wistfully in Wattsian terms about Little Holland House, the work in the garden and studio 'in harmony with all I love here . . . I have grown to see the spiritual side of nature, & find it is of the same kind as the spiritual side of man'. Resolute about her chosen path, she did not need a financial settlement – 'I want when you take me on, to be just a sort of pillow, that helps you to rest, & perhaps something more too, but *not an anxiety*'. Promising to forgo luxuries, she assured her fiancé that falling into debt was worse than starving, and sent down some grouse for Ruskin's lunch.[45] Watts was amazed at her willingness to sacrifice 'half a life & probable enjoyment of social pleasures to look after a mere mammal in seclusion' and yearned to bring her joy, for her to 'feel that peace that confidence brings'.

> I shall be disappointed if you do not bloom out like a flower that is transplanted into favourable soil. I want you to feel if I do not profess the passionate feeling which would not be becoming to my age, I can love you very much with the love that joins itself closely round goodness & has its roots deep down in perfect trust, & that the door of your cage shall be wide open & there shall be no wires, but silver films instead! & I shall take no love or interest away that you have given or felt in any other direction.'[46]

He sent up grapes for her three-year-old nephew Charlie who had fallen from his horse, and in return Mary sent down some grey thistles, though packaging had presented a problem. 'No one seems to have an old corset box & yet we all wear them,' she despaired to her distinguished president of the Anti-Tight Lacing Society.[47] Her thorny gifts delighted him: 'If I were in Scotland . . . I could make a picture of the purple mountains in the deepening twilight with nothing for foreground but a group of these beautiful thistles. Wouldn't it be very scotch? You might try it.' He was painting another picture of *Hope*.[48] His daily endearments were sprinkled with anguish at the thought of her heavy undertaking – 'not all beer & skittles' – and taking her away from her family. 'Do you *believe* I love you?' she asked. On 7 October, Charlie died. With a lump in his throat, Watts drew a design of Death the Angel Crowning Innocence, as the child's memorial, which he suggested they made together. 'I think you might make the carrying out of it a consoling object.' He sent a drawing to comfort Edith, the boy's mother, and longed for Mary to come home.[49]

He began to experiment with pastels. One evening Emilie Barrington brought a roll of dark red flock wallpaper into his sitting room and watched, amazed, as he drew an old man's head in under five minutes.[50] Hamo Thornycroft called to consult him about the height of the statue of General Gordon, then planned for the empty pedestal in Trafalgar Square.[51] As far as Millais was concerned, *Physical Energy* was finished. 'Now leave it alone. Don't put another touch upon it,' he told Watts. 'It is a damned good thing, I tell you. Cast it at once!' The sculptor declined his generous offer to subscribe. By its very subject – seeking further tasks – Watts always envisaged improvements to his great horse and rider, amputating a limb, turning it about and refining it to capture the ideal position or fall of shadow.[52]

He was developing an astonishing picture of 'the hand of the Creator moving by light and by heat to recreate'. *After the Deluge: The Forty-First Day* (pl. XXXIX) shows the sun radiating over the waters as vapour trails disperse into the mist. Rather than a figurative portrait, it was an impression of enormous power; and when a visitor suggested he add the figure of the Creator, he refused, but was glad to have provoked the question. 'It is exactly what I would wish that makes those who look at it conceive for themselves'.[53] At South Kensington, the staircase wall leading up to the new art library had been, as requested by Watts, distempered 'rich reddish marone', which was also the colour used on the walls of Watts's gallery at Little Holland House. The first few pictures were hung by 16 October.[54]

'Loving Mary & dear Wife! For so I always think of you nor could 20 ceremonies make you more so to me,' he wrote. 'I wish the time were come.' As she was about to return south he told her that he had confided in Julia Stephen, who was delighted, 'so you see a big stone is laid'. Mindful of their age gap and the scandalous mishandling of his marriage and separation from Nelly, his letters notifying selected friends dwelt only on his 'selfish' needs, as he told Mary. They suggest a grim future for her as nurse and secretary to enable him to complete the nation's work. Passionate truths, 'the great problems of human life', flowed naturally from his brush, but he struggled to articulate them with his pen; and only after friends' response did he dare reveal their joy.[55] Blanche – responding to his anguished letter in which he hoped his 'ridiculous step, for it cannot be distinguished that I am now an old man!' would not seem painful or distasteful – hoped he was 'very happy'.[56] No further 'phospheric flicker[s] of aspiration' to Ellen Terry survive. He would have written one last letter, but she was desolate, mourning the death of Godwin, now inscribed on her crucifix as 'My love (and my only lover)'.[57]

Concerned that Sara Prinsep might feel he was deserting her family after thirty-seven years, Watts asked Mary to write that 'you wish she could look upon you as a sort of daughter'. This was a formidable task; for his former hostess, though ailing, was as impulsive and imprudent as ever. Mrs Prinsep told the Hichens. 'Thank God', wrote Andrew. 'No other woman I know deserves or is fitted for the trust she undertakes. It is a serious, solemn, and sacred thing which she has to do.' Julia Stephen urged Watts not to delay. 'If you don't take care I will make Leslie put on his cassock again and marry you off hand; you must get away from these cold winds.'[58] Mary found him in poor health and as Dr Bond recommended a warmer climate, she began to plan a visit to Egypt.

It was not the news, but the possible risk to Signor's health that almost pierced Leighton's heart. Watts greeted him on 3 November, 'I am going to surprise you very much & perhaps incur disapproval. You will feel doubtless that at my time of life the thing is out of harmony.' Mary admitted that the announcement did very likely surprise and distress him, but she understood. 'Signor was too precious a friend to give into unknown and untried hands without anxiety.'[59]

'So that is what he meant by a mysterious word,' Hallam Tennyson wrote to Mary, rejoicing at the marriage of 'the most loveable of men' to 'one of my oldest friends'.[60] Anny Ritchie's response – 'so *thrilled* . . . One does feel the marriage of true souls matters. I have always thought her and what this proves her to be – a sweet woman and a true artist'. Asked to describe Mary, Anny had said, 'Something between an aspiration and a regret', which Signor thought that might apply to him also. One of his reasons for secrecy was that he wanted no gifts. Instead they would love her trust and affection, which no burglar could steal, and perhaps Mary could choose one of her novels. He disapproved of possessions; and when Virginia Somers later sent Mary a necklace, he made her return it, saying that he had not permitted her family to give 'what added to the excess of life'.[61] She and her sisters had presented Edward and his bride with diamond earrings, ivory parasol, girandole and a brougham. Mary would enjoy Watts's paintings more. In her letter of 6 November, writing of her colour angel and the harmonies in her life, she recalled a dream from twelve years before:

> I was in a glorious cathedral quite alone – and thinking I had never seen anything so beautiful – when an angel came to me and said, 'So you think this beautiful? – it is much more beautiful above – I will show you' – and we went up to a sort of clerestory – very high almost on a line with the vaulted roof – and down its long vista I looked and saw not form though it was there, but the most marvellous harmonies of colour – only to be dreamt of – and could not help, from pure wonder, going down upon my knees – and the moment I had done so – I felt a hand – and it was yours and behind me *you*![62]

Her dream symbolized to Watts the full unity of their aspirations. 'Take your biggest moral Pallette knife & spread my love around where you are . . . Best & most permanent colours.' He told her about the beating wings and cries he had heard at Charles Street in 1849, the year of her birth. Mary was touched by his dream. It was no dream, he replied, but 'an impression . . . who knows of how much reality! Was it think you your soul seeking its fellow?'[63]

Unable to throw off a persistent cough and chill, he asked her to leave arrangements with P. & O. elastic, for he must recover before travelling. He did not want to leave her a widow, or let down the nation. She wondered how she would deal with his tetchiness. As Leighton well knew, he dreaded the ordeal. According to Ronald Chapman (the son of the Watts's ward Lilian), Mrs Barrington tackled Mary in the hall at Little Holland House and told her he would die on the voyage. Watts had said she might find his fiancée 'a little shy and reserved, but I don't think you will have any difficulty. We are both to have perfect confidence & freedom, & [as he repeated to "Mary" Mead] none of my habits are to be changed.' Little did he know. The two women argued furiously. Emilie Barrington, the rampant guardian of his muse hitherto, could terrify her targets, intimidating even Leighton, who complained to Luke Fildes, 'I scarcely dare to go to bed.' Fildes advised both men to marry. Leighton would never escape her clutches. Mary remained resolute, as unswerving as Watts to achieve her goal of making a happy marriage.[64]

He notified Marion Spielmann in November that he wished to draw public attention to the nine 'sample' pictures soon to be on show at South Kensington – *Love and Death, Love and Life, Time, Death and Judgment, Mammon, Dedicated to all Churches, The Minotaur, Hope* and portraits of Manning and Tennyson. *The Midday Rest* and *The Court of Death* (formerly the *Angel of Death*) would follow. They were there as to test opinion as to whether his collection would be acceptable. Rather than a complimentary review, he sought and received an explanatory statement. In persuading Spielmann to give him this, he wrote: 'My distinct object in painting these and others with the same destination has been to oppose the principle that "Art for Art" is the only principle or even the best. I do not deny that beautiful technique is sufficient to constitute an extremely valuable achievement but it can never alone place a work of art on the level of the highest effort in poetry and by this it should stand.'[65]

In an interview with Spielmann and a series of letters, he explained that his efforts 'arise from a desire to supply what I feel much wanted, not didactic art but art suggestive of consideration belonging to our higher natures' and hoped they would stimulate younger artists to aspire and help to elevate English taste. Even historical pictures were but costume pieces, valuable as fact, but they 'hardly awaken in the spectator any intellectual activity'.[66] He asked to see a proof, but Spielmann rushed the article into the *Pall Mall Gazette*, embarrassing the artist with what Watts perceived to be its 'Air of Presumptuousness'. Always anxious to avoid sudden, sensational interest, he had wished his influence to be 'quiet & lasting & you can understand how much I wish to avoid the slightest appearance of swagger or dogmatism in what I say'.[67]

While he saw the press as an important vehicle for his national mission and let it be known that his gallery would remain open while he was in Egypt, there was no advance notice of his marriage. 'My most dear Signor,' wrote Burne-Jones. 'I must have a word from you, or a look at you if it true what newspapers say that you are going away to Egypt – mostly they lie these newspapers – but you mustn't go without seeing me – for I do love you heartily.'[68] On Friday 19 November he was still coughing when he dashed round to Mrs Barrington, not exactly to say goodbye – 'so unnecessary between real friends! and fit only for acquaintances'. He sent a last-minute note to Lady Holland, the widow of his dearest patron and friend, to inform her that he was leaving to escape the fogs, with a companion, 'a first rate intellect & beautiful character – she is still young enough to make the office of nurse (for it won't be much else) a sacrifice, but she believes that sympathy with my work & objects will compensate for much'.[69]

A bundle of nerves, Watts arrived with Gerry Liddell to join the Fraser Tytler family at Mary's stepmother's home, Mounthill, in Epsom. He strolled with Mary in the afternoon and retired to his room. There was a momentary hiccup when his housekeeper, Emma, and Mary both tried to unlace his boots. On the morning of Saturday, 20 November 1886, the wedding party walked down the country lane to Christ Church for the ceremony; afterwards they returned by train to London for luncheon with the Hichens at Chester Street. The bride and groom spent their first night together at Little Holland House, '*my* home with *my* beloved,' wrote Mary (fig. 146).[70] His wedding gift to her, a highly charged picture of *Orpheus and Eurydice*, mirrored his mind. Their upper bodies fill the canvas; the nude Orpheus, clutches in his left hand the lyre of Hope and his right arm diagonally across the picture reaches over her shoulder as he yearns for the dying Eurydice. So sensual is the picture that Mary did not refer to the gift in her memoir of Watts.[71]

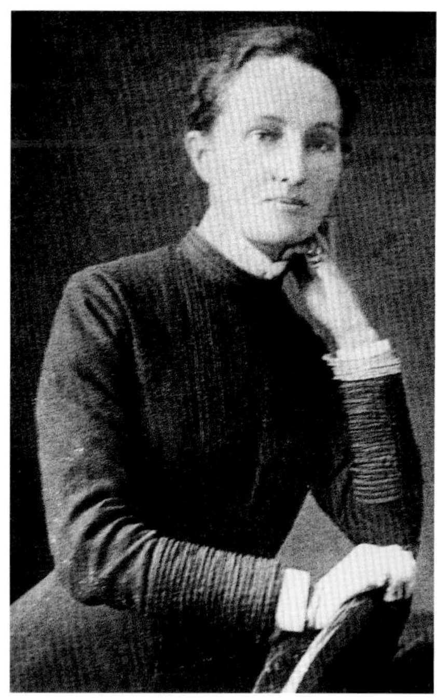

146   Mary Fraser Tytler, *c*.1886–87 (photo: Frederic Hollyer).

The next morning, he invited Mrs Barrington round for a discussion. She was to keep an eye on Cecil Schott, who would be copying pictures for St Jude's in the Iron House, if not on Aitchison, who was adapting the house to accommodate the new guardian of Watts's muse. It was fortunate that Emile Barrington had to leave before they set sail. Watts authorized William Agnew to take pictures for next year's Royal Jubilee exhibitions and for Nottingham, the next venue for the augmented Metropolitan collection. Warning Lord Wemyss as he embarked on a marble statue of *Venus*, 'Who takes up Art becomes her slave!', he had a nude figure drawn up, marking the Canon of Proportions, and asked his old friend for an introduction in Egypt.[72] Sir Frederic Leighton bid him an affectionate farewell and watched at the dockside with tears in his eyes as Mary took Signor aboard the steamer, leaving his countrymen to pass judgment on his gift.[73]

That Saturday, the twenty-three-year-old craftsman Charles Ashbee made his weekly visit from Toynbee Hall to the South Kensington embroideries. He recorded his impression of Watts's pictures: 'I was bewildered by their greatness . . . He seems to me without exception the greatest of modern painters, and Holman Hunt next to him, but in Watts there is more of the 19th century, & that is why he strikes home. His picture of *Mammon* is fearfully great.' As the hitherto sceptical French critic Robert de la Sizeranne passed them on his way up to the library, he was converted. 'By the time I had reached the last step I no longer believed that mythological painting was dead, nor that, in order to enlarge the figure of a fact to the sexless, impersonal universality of an idea, all warmth of feeling and all the drama of life must be extracted from it. What was there between these two opinions? Two pictures by Watts – *Love and Death* and *Love and Life*.'[74]

# PART II

# Love Triumphant

# 17 Apex of Art

Watts found in Mary not only a 'wise and gentle companionship' that eased his life, but, as he wrote to Emilie Barrington, an imaginative spirit that heightened their partnership. To throw off his chill from the cold seas, they broke the journey at Malta, where the governor, Sir John Simmons, arranged for them to stay at the Villa Micallef in Sliema. Watts so loved the warmth, colour and pure, clear lines of the seascape that he reserved the house for the next winter; and after a fortnight they resumed their honeymoon tour aboard the *Thames*, making tiny sketches of landscapes, of sailors hauling ropes and Egyptians in flowing robes.

'When you have seen Greece and Egypt', he had told Mary, 'you have got the keynote to all that is beautiful in art.'[1] She saw the crowds on the quayside at Port Said as apostles and prophets, and a mother and child on a donkey led by the father as a living, breathing old master picture: 'Here was the human being, not dressed but clothed, every line of each garment expressive of some dramatic or stately movement, the colours stained to harmonies unknown to Western eyes.' The couple left the steamer for a night at Suez, and from the roof of their hotel they watched the sun set over the Gulf. With the mountains of Sinai on their left, they looked down on the dark silhouette of a man standing so still in his boat he could have been a bronze sculpture. A call to prayer rang out from a minaret. He raised his hands together and 'went prostrate before the glory'.[2]

On Christmas Eve they arrived in Cairo and explored the city with an old friend, Charles Hamilton Aidé, a novelist, composer and amateur artist. Thanks to Lord Wemyss, the Sirdar Sir Francis Grenfell arranged for the couple to stay in the palace built by the Khedive Ismail for the Empress Eugenie for the opening of the Suez Canal.[3] Now deserted and infested with fleas, its position at the foot of the Great Pyramid enabled Watts to study the even greater Sphinx, as he viewed it, under various atmospheric conditions. Conscious that yellow and blue were the colours most prevalent in nature, forming light and atmosphere, he made watercolour sketches of the Sphinx in sand-coloured washes on blue-grey paper (fig. 147). The massive limestone creature fascinated Watts, as 'a symbol of time . . . strong calm & inexorable with a smile that is cruel,' the epitome of Egyptian art in its solemnity and mystery.[4]

'Signor put out his hand to me before daylight & told me it was a new year,' Mary began her first diary on 1 January 1887. Those words epitomize Watts. He lived for the light, loved to watch the breaking dawn and

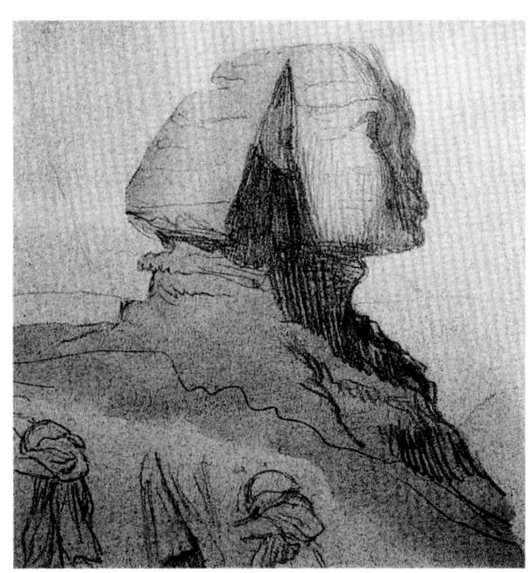

147  *The Sphinx*, 1887, private collection.

looked forward to work at his art each day. 'Pyramids & Sphinx by sunset & by moonlight,' she continued. 'I begin my life with Signor, by beginning the oldest history of the world.' Fearing at first that 'his light might mean *blindness* to me',[5] she would record in 'Fatima', as she named the diary, his aims, advice, daily struggles, his light sense of humour, and recollections, the dialogue with sitters and visitors, love of nature, plans for the nation and worldly thoughts. As she sat beneath the Sphinx in the burning sunlight, her husband preached a sermon to a young sheik: roughly, a good deed produces a feather, a bad one makes feet heavy, too much backsheesh makes gold in his shoes. The sheik, translating for his grinning companions, cried, 'We want to grow feathers to make wings, to get up to Allah!' Watts sketched the Sphinx in oil as it was darkening against the twilight.[6]

John Cook, the senior partner of Thomas Cook's, arranged for the couple to hire a dahabeeyah, and on 4 January, they set sail aboard the *Victoria* for a seventy-day cruise down the Nile. Watts drew on deck, making studies from the loosely draped fellaheen. He admired their fine, square shoulders and chest, which he had never found in England, but had modelled for the rider in *Physical Energy*. Their artistic perceptions heightened as they studied the physique of the fellaheen, the deep bronze colour of the Berbers, the rhythmic movements of figures loading sugar cane, and the majestic flight path of the kites and vultures. Rocky steeps rose both sides of the river, solid and grand in form, yet delicate in effect. Art could never render both qualities without neutralizing one, he said. The mountains in the almost pink light with magenta shadows looked beautiful, but appeared ugly in Hunt's picture because he had no sense of loveliness and mistook *colours* for *colour*. 'Colour, Signor thinks, is life.'[7]

'Do you feel you have seen more than you ever did before?' he asked Mary. He wanted her to feel 'the one law that runs through all nature . . . for all that is good in my work is due to my perception of that truth.' Drawings in a tiny sketchbook show the president of the Anti-Tight-Lacing Society advising his wife on undergarments that would not constrain the line of her waist – that would not offend against the laws of nature. Under his tutelage, she began to relate details of daily life, the majestic sweep of line, to the glory of the rising sun, as parts of a great design. Even his nightmares were visionary. He dreamed of an evil person in constant conflict with a good one, and when at last they fought, evil won; another was of a tall straight house to which the evil creature wanted to take him. Mary's devout Christianity, which both feared might be a problem, actually brought them closer together and would remain firm, however interested she was in civilizations of the world. No doubt her Sunday texts reminded him of the dark days of his childhood, though rather than threaten, hers – at the time Martineau, preaching spiritual socialism – provoked thought; and to Watts, the true spirit of religion was the most important intellectual idea; its hope lay in the development of universal brotherhood, free of dogma and creed. Keep that thought as a religious teaching, he advised, and she would recognize leading thinkers of the future.[8]

At Luxor, watching the colossal, recently excavated statue of Ramses II being towed by a string of workmen, Watts wanted to use the line of the king's arm and shoulder for his giants in *Chaos*. The temple of Karnak, marvellous though it was, did not move him as much as the Sphinx's cheek. This, he said, was where he differed from Ruskin, who found more beauty in almost everything but the human form.[9] Watts thought the Egyptian mind wonderfully monolithic. The Egyptians had sacrificed art to the abstract idea. There was no delicate detail in the form of the Sphinx or the coloured Ramses, but their Majesty and Mystery was superb. Mary, interested in the symbolic language, decided that her future artistic role would lie in creating highly ideal decorative art, starting with the Egyptian winged-sun motif. They planned to have the winged sun at Little Holland House. 'How happy we are to have interests & what are *more* than interests in common. It is very rare,' Watts said, noting privately 'Every good thought echoed, ordered, every effort encouraged & sustained.' As he proposed ships in full sail, symbolizing his motto 'Forward and Fear Not' for the mantelpiece at Little Holland house, she made flamboyant pencil sketches of boats beneath a winged sun and fearsome curvilinear asp.[10]

'Pray say *mille choses* from me to the Signora', wrote Leighton, delighted that his marriage was 'the right thing' after all. He sent Academy gossip. 'Hunt *who has cut Ned Jones for accepting* will gnash his teeth in wrathful scorn'. Gilbert's triumphant election as an associate pleased Watts, though he queried the sculptor's design of feet. Leighton, as chairman of the Jubilee Exhibition in Adelaide, secured Watts's agreement to send out *Orpheus and Eurydice,* for which he was awarded a diploma and medal for the First Order of Merit.[11]

The *Victoria* turned back down the Nile at Aswan. Sailing away from the sun, the symbol of unimaginable power and light, was difficult for Watts. At two in the morning on 23 February, his seventieth birthday, Mary kissed the man whose art had affected so many people, 'which is all my world now.' He calmed her fear that he might never love her, though he frankly acknowledged his lack of affection before their marriage. Their harmony transformed it into 'a bond that nothing can shake'.[12] But by 10 March, frustrated that the wind was blowing against them, wasting time and turning the river to mud, he wrote to Mrs Barrington, 'still on the Nile' in bad humour. Two days later they disembarked, spending three weeks at the sulphur baths in Helouan to alleviate lumbago, eczema and bronchitis. He drew a ridge of rocks highlighted by the shadows of flying cloud and sketched the Pyramid plain. Asked to paint a child's portrait, he refused, then changed his mind because the hundred pounds would enable them 'to buy things here' – not the embroideries and rugs that Mary hoped for, but a pair of trousers. Burne-Jones would later chide him for it.[13] Meanwhile, as she embraced her husband through the mosquito nets – 'the kiss through the veil' – Watts assured her there could never be a veil between them now. 'I have only to be myself, no need for me to feel in what was called "a very difficult position".'[14]

Leighton now chose '3 or 4 of your masterpieces' from South Kensington, at Agnew's request, for the Royal Jubilee Exhibition at Manchester. The museum curators, miffed at losing *Hope, Love and Life, Love and Death* and the Manning portrait, were obliged to despatch them 'for the honour and glory' of the display celebrating fifty years of English art. Margaret Burne-Jones, pleading for a portrait of the Spanish singing teacher Manuel Garcia, reported that Little Holland House Gallery had been besieged by visitors. Her father sent his love to Watts: 'I wish you ever back – all of us poor wretches have had a hard fight with preternatural darkness this winter.'[15]

Charles Rickards had died the previous year. His collection, auctioned at Christie's on 2 April 1887, aroused much interest because Watts's work rarely came on to the market. The artist received a news cutting. The fifty-seven pictures, for which Rickards had paid some £27,000 over two decades, were estimated to sell for £13–14,000; they realized £16,001. The Manchester Corporation acquired *Prayer* for 500 guineas. Sir Alexander Henderson paid a handsome 950 guineas for *The Eve of Peace* and 860 for *The Return of the Dove*, the latter originally purchased for 500. *Love and Death* fetched 1,100 guineas and the beautiful *Bianca* 510, both bought by Joseph Ruston. The replica Joachim portrait was acquired for 420 by Agnew, the major purchaser, for the Chicago Corporation. Twenty-year-old Roger Fry, a keen disciple, having first attended 'divine worship at Lincoln's Inn', left the auction house 'more fully convinced than ever that not only is [Watts] the greatest modern painter but one of the greatest men. His portraits are simply grand . . . his children I like more than Sir Joshua's.' Fry wrote to Ashbee, marvelling at the seascapes, *The Return of the Dove*, *The Island of Cos*, and, above all, the sculptures of *Clytie* and *Medusa*.[16]

The Wattses set sail from Alexandria, heading for Constantinople,[17] and an unscheduled stop at Piraeus enabled them to make an early visit to 'the Apex of Art'. On the train, Mary was trembling in anticipation, when, suddenly, around a curve the Parthenon came into view. The gates were closed. It was a holy day in Greece. Fortunately, the Indian princes in the carriage behind them, fellow travellers on their way to England for Queen Victoria's Golden Jubilee, allowed the couple to join their private visit. Looking through the pillars of the Parthenon, down to the Bay of Salamis, they marvelled at the vision of blue that had stirred Homer and Phidias. Now Mary understood *Genius of Greek Poetry*. 'It has the same palpitating depths of blue, and the fruits of nature seemed to take human shape in the air as we spoke.' Filled with emotion, Signor pronounced, 'We have got something for life' and turned away.[18]

En route for Constantinople, the ship docked briefly at Smyrna, triggering memories of Halicarnassus. Watts painted an oil sketch of Mary, 'straight off, in four colours', achieving her flesh tones in Venetian red, yellow ochre, raw umber and flake white. She posed in profile, looking away from him. In almost transparent burnt umber, he outlined her straw hat, her strong nose and chin, her auburn hair loosely coiled at the nape of her neck. There is a feeling of repose in the tender picture she called 'The Wife of his Eden' (fig. 148).[19] Mary had cried much since their marriage, over past sorrows, but chiefly through joy. 'It must be irrigation of my dried old heart I think – or the dew of his rich nature moistening my hard one! The very tears are a responsibility.'[20] He rebuked her for her 'far too exalted an idea of my place.'[21]

A portrait of five-year-old Bernard Caillard broke the monotony of hotel life in poor weather. Though Watts needed few sittings to finish it, he agonized. 'You cannot imagine what it has cost me.' It was not worth the fee, yet he felt he was cheating the boy's father, Vincent Caillard, the English financial administrator in Constantinople. Mary left her husband to rest. While she was out, he finished the picture and went off to buy himself a Gladstone bag.[22] No doubt he was feeling restless. The exhibitions had opened in London. He missed not seeing his brother Academicians beforehand and had sent nothing to Burlington House.

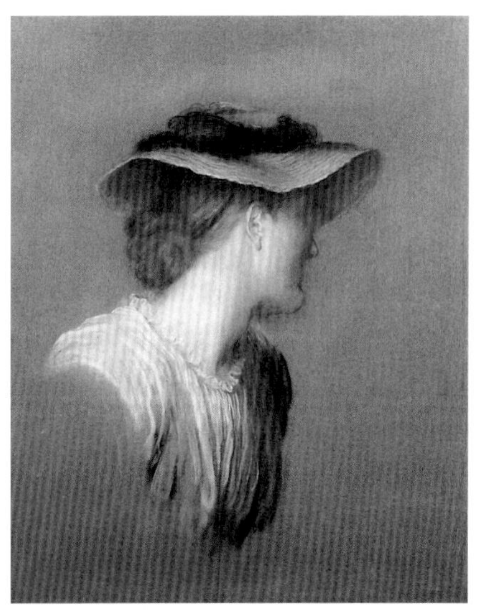

148   Mary Seton Watts, *The Wife of his Eden*, 1887 (Watts Gallery).

Leighton's news, however, made colourful reading; Burne-Jones had not been able to finish his Academy picture, John Singer Sargent had sent a 'startling bust' (*Mrs William Playfair*) and 'in *strictest confidence*' Millais's '*Mercy', St Bartholomew's Day* was 'dreadful', and he himself had taken 'an unconscionable time' over the Imperial Jubilee medal for Adelaide and had 'terrible trouble' with *The Last Watch of Hero* and *The Jealousy of Simoetha the Sorceress*, for which Dorothy Dene had modelled.[23] (There was a bronze triptych of *The Story of Psyche* by Harry Bates, not mentioned in the letter, clearly informed by *Hope* and *Love and Death*.[24]) Dene appeared again in Watts's single contribution to the Grosvenor, a new enlarged version of *Olympus on Ida*, exhibited as *The Judgment of Paris*. 'I have tried to express without attributes the different characteristics of the Goddesses, & by the qualities of surface to suggest a certain sense of the celestial purpose accompanying them.'[25] On the steamer returning to Athens, past the plains of Troy, he pointed out the snow-covered Mount Ida, and with tears in his eyes talked of the gods and heroes of *The Iliad* and Homer's conception of unrestrained power. More than ever he wanted to paint the landscape.[26]

Ionides's sister Euphrosyne Cassavetti found rooms for their last three weeks in Athens. Watts went straight to the Museum of Marbles to see the *Victory*.[27] To have carved that one statue, he enthused, 'is worth a lifetime'. Her head combined 'the beauties of the swan & the power of the horse in the neck, something more than a woman'.[28] The popular Greek prime minister Charilaos Tricoupi was sitting to him, as a commission for Ionides's son Alecco, when Watts was taken ill. He was appalled at being struck down in *Athens* – the 'Apex of Art.' At his most painful moments, he tested his beliefs, to see whether they were as instinctive as when he was happily pain free.[29] In Athens, alone with nature – not necessarily on mountains and rocks, but supported by elements of the earliest human productions – offered the finest imaginative scope. 'Perhaps you hardly know how much you have gained in these last months – the book of the world open from its earliest chapters,' he told Mary.[30]

They found the archaeologist Professor Francis Penrose measuring the Parthenon, presumably for the 1888 edition of his *Principles of Athenian Architecture*. The two men exchanged theories on the circle in Greek art, Penrose showing how the curve in the base and cornice of the Parthenon and the deeper carving at the top of the pillars, not quite perpendicular, created the harmonious illusion of straight lines. He placed his hat at one end of the base line and instructed the artist to stoop down at the other end, where he saw that the curve hid the hat. To Watts, this flexibility enhanced the impression that the building was growing out of the rock itself, that art and nature were one.[31] The emotional beauty of Phidias was comparable to nature, the rock, cloud, meadow; any extra emphasis, such as the strong emotion of Michelangelo, would detract from its serenity. ('Michel Angelo aimed at Spiritual qualities the great Greek did not dream of', he had written to Gertrude Mead. A conscious effort was a weakness, but – clearly speaking from the heart – 'we must appreciate the strength of the intention'.)[32] He revisited the Museum of Marbles. Casts of the *Fates* were displayed nearer the ground than the originals at the British Museum and he was struck by their volume, the ease and flow of their curves, infinite variety of planes and the way the drapery cut lightly into the flesh on their shoulders, 'No one understood how to give a kind of tremendous palpitating beauty in every line of drapery as the Greeks at this best period. It is the music of form light & colour.'[33]

Signor hoped that the beauty of Greece would penetrate his and Mary's future work.[34] They drove out to the Pnyx and discovered 'the most perfect view of the Acropolis' before setting sail for Marseilles. At Messina they picked up a stricken ship. They admired the lines of Mount Etna, and the distant view of Vesuvius, smoking vigorously. A summer sea-fog gave rise to two mystical pictures, *The Sea Ghost*, a vision of the ship looming up through the mist, and *Off Corsica*: 'Out of a veil of cloud out of a silvery pearl sea rose clear blue peaks with sunny snow upon them every line pure & clear against the sky, but tender like a dream – lost at the foot in a thin grey stretch of mist.' The vision vanished like breath on a mirror.[35]

After such marvels, Paris brought them back to reality. Haussmans' wide boulevards, which were being laid out when Watts visited in the 1850s, had transformed the city. He found Auguste Cains's sculpture in the Champs Elysées 'powerful – very unlike the Greek – quite modern'. At the Louvre, he enjoyed Veronese's *Marriage at Cana*, but, to Mary's consternation, not the *Mona Lisa*.[36] They spent all day at the Salon, where, apart from Alexandre Cabanel's naked *Cleopatre*, he preferred the sculpture, in particular, the Belgian Constantin Meunier's *Le padleur*. The awards he thought in surprisingly bad taste. Obliged to forego the temptations of the Paris shops, Mary felt a frustrated pang that Signor did not share her enthusiasm for 'the spangles of life'. They crossed the channel at Calais and arrived back at Little Holland House on the evening of Saturday 4 June 1887.[37]

At dawn, Watts dashed round to Leighton to exchange reminiscences of Egypt and Athens recalling, as Leighton's sketches of the 1860s show, 'the crystal keenness of the lights and the *reflected* lights which throw such a glow over everything Egyptian'. The two friends had been similarly affected, and Watts returned home exuberant. 'He loves him I think better than any other man alive', noted Mary. 'He has a different tone of voice for speaking of him.' She, too, was much moved. Having knelt 'like the Mahommedan before a sunset' at church, she sat in the gallery – 'my own cathedral!' – before *Chaos*, 'my dear ones mind, so spiritual & so creative glowed out upon me from the canvas – sunlight & all the impressions of nature are there'.[38]

An aura of noble simplicity permeated Little Holland House, where every daylight hour was devoted to art and elevated thought. The following morning, Watts awoke at 3.45. Mary need not get up, he said, 'but it will be very nice if you can' and by four they were drinking coffee in the studio. Emma had lit the fire. Outside, the lamplighter was extinguishing the lights in Melbury Road. Watts stepped lightly from one canvas to another, 'every movement full of enthusiasm and the expression of earnest endeavour'. They bathed at half past seven and had breakfast at eight in his Hall of Fame, the cool north ante-room with its dado of Watts's portraits. Doors opened on to the gallery, where the sun streamed through the glazed roof, highlighting the curves and lines of his iridescent canvases. He nurtured Mary's artistic development, offering advice, adding his own touches to her portrait of her great uncle, Field-Marshal Sir Patrick Grant, commissioned by the Royal Horse Guards for the officers' mess.[39] At any moment he would summon her to examine a detail, such as the texture he had achieved by dragging a dry brush over the windblown clouds of Helouan, splayed 'like uplifted arms about the moon'. He began to make a replica of the Tricoupi portrait to present to Athens;[40] and he had the great white horse and rider, *Physical Energy* (fig. 149), rolled out into the garden where he worked on it outside, with his assistant Thompson. The *Art Journal* described the setting:

> Out at the back of the house, on one side of the large garden, lies a paved courtyard, guarded by an old ivy-grown wall. At either end of this court-yard two buildings face one another – an erection of brick and an erection of glass – the one a working studio, and the other a huge transparent house, built to hold the gigantic figure on horseback . . . The group is fixed on a trolley, the trolley rests on a pivot table, and from the pivot table rails lead the way to the courtyard.[41]

The sculptor, protected by a full-length smock, hammered and chiselled at the gesso, while Mary painted on the lawn. He worked up to sixteen hours a day, retiring at nine on summer evenings. When he needed to rest, rather than sit, he would lie on a divan seat in the drawing-room alcove, which Aitchison had designed to focus the sound, while Mary read to him. Now despite the artist's increasing deafness he could pinpoint every mistake. After dinner, they relaxed in the gallery – 'his great soul hovering round me, a thousand different voices of his great mind seem speaking to me from my *cathedral* walls'[42] – and at bedtime he would glance at his watch and say, 'How I wish it was time to begin work again.'[43]

Buffalo Bill's Wild West Show (fig. 150) at Earl's Court offered a break in the schedule. And at the Grosvenor Watts admired Burne-Jones's unusually optimistic nude trio in *The Garden of Pan* above *The Baleful Head* of Medusa, from the Perseus series commissioned by the chief secretary for Ireland, Arthur Balfour. However, the duc d'Aumale's invitation to breakfast, and Blanche Lindsay's to meet the 'charming' princess and other social engagements, were sacrificed to art.[44] The colourful jubilee decorations cheered Watts as he returned from the Academy on 20 June. Brilliant bunting, flags, flowers, rugs, lamps and embroideries hung from the houses. He wished London looked as bright more often. Did he notice an advertisement on the omnibuses featuring Georgina Weldon, his mischievous songbird of the fifties, now a litigious lesbian – 'I am 50 today but, thanks to Pears' Soap, My *Complexion* is only 17.' As crowds gathered for the State procession to Westminster Abbey, the Wattses were at work in their studios.[45]

Among the newly weds' earliest visitors were Georgy Burne-Jones, Sir Frederic Burton, the director of the National Gallery, Edward Poynter, her professor at the Slade – to see *Mr* Watts ('I was not snubbed') – Hamo Thornycroft and the household's adored Lord Wemyss. 'Are you going to make my master a lord?' asked Emma. Her cheeky affection reveals the warm, relaxed atmosphere at Little Holland House. An heroic figure, six foot tall, with a fine straight back, square shoulders, his clean-shaven chin stylishly fringed by silver whiskers and beard, the earl 'carried his head like a challenge'. Watts used to say he was 'my severest critic'.[46] But his true critic, preoccupied during the week with presidential duties, invariably called on Sunday at nine, for a brisk interchange of ideas 'flowing with the rush of a mill-race'.[47]

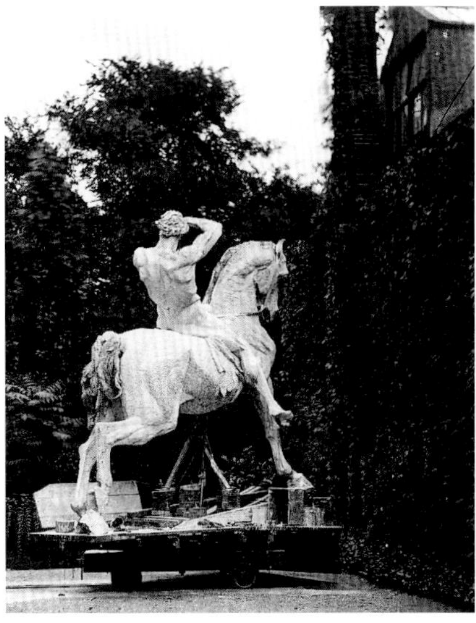

149   *Physical Energy* in the garden at Little Holland House.

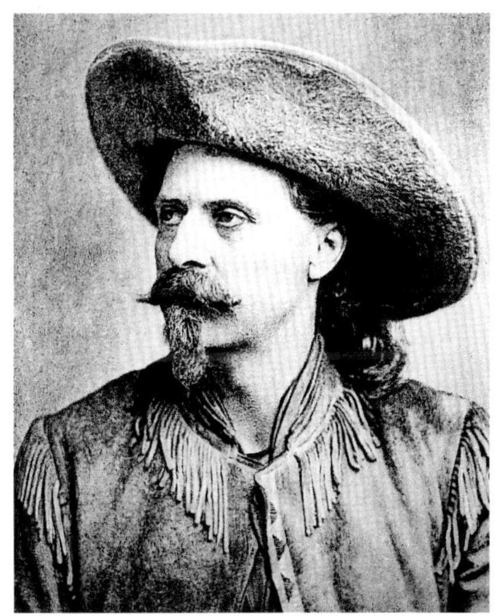

150   *Buffalo Bill*, 1887 (repr. in Victoria and Albert Museum, 2001, fig. 263).

Mary Olver, the secretary of the South London Fine Art Gallery, came to discuss new developments. Like Samuel Barnett, who sat that summer for his portrait, the gallery's founder, William Rossiter, aimed to educate the poor through art. A former student and teacher at the Working Men's College, he established the South London Working Men's College in 1868; ten years later, he opened the first Free Library in South London, where he held art exhibitions. Now that the Free Library Act had been adopted in Battersea, he was moving the enterprise to Camberwell; he wanted a permanent base and was enlisting influential artists to help achieve it. Leighton was taking over the presidency of the South London Fine Art Gallery from Gladstone, and Burne-Jones and Watts, as members of the Council, threw themselves into the enterprise. Rossiter's policy of keeping the gallery and library open in the evenings and on Sundays allowed workers and children (the latter were not allowed into Free Libraries) access to the collection, and would provide a social and educational focus for the deprived neighbourhood.[48]

Watts was heartened by the 'distinctly new place' now accorded to art, and pleased by F. D. Maurice's use of 'light' for 'intelligence' in *Religions of the World*. Yet, although poets and painters both expressed ideas in figurative language, 'the frowning mountain' was explicit and acceptable from a poet, on canvas it was derided as 'symbolical nonsense'.[49] Watts's face lit up when Burne-Jones arrived, always whimsical, even when demoralized about his work.[50] A visit to his studio left Watts so moved that he determined to improve his art.[51]

Mrs Barrington proprietorially burst in through the gate between their gardens at her usual hour. When Val Prinsep married, Watts returned his garden door key and visited his studio on an open Sunday. Returning from his own honeymoon, he had placed a wedge in the Barringtons' gate, as a 'hinting that we wished to be alone at least some part of the day'. Emilie Barrington threw away the wedge. He had said nothing would be changed. Her intrusion during the couple's quiet moment between work and dinner infuriated Mary. A trifle it may be, 'but one I must not ignore – as it has the possibilities that lie in the downy heads of a thistle! Cut them before they go to seed.' Seeds of jealousy began to sprout.[52]

At the Royal Jubilee Exhibition at Manchester – the first comprehensive review of contemporary English art – Watts's paintings were linked to Etty in the treatment of the nude. Centred by *Hope*, 'the key-note of his teachings', his thirty-four pictures (Leighton had sent eleven, Millais, nineteen) filled an entire wall of the gallery of poetic painters, opposite a fine display by Burne-Jones, who had advised on the wall colouring. The *Magazine of Art* ascribed Wattsian pathos not to disgust with humanity, but to profound, positive understanding. The chief defect of 'England's noblest idealist', echoing Leighton's argument, lay in attempting to express in paint 'thought proper to the written word alone, and, above all, to sermonize – to follow not only in the footsteps of Titian and Giotto, but in those of Blake – to be a Bunyan among painters, and to limn for us a new *Pilgrim's Progress* such as it is beyond the proper province of art to embody'. As Watts intended, art should stretch the mind.[53]

Mary, diffident in society, enjoyed the warmth of Signor's artistic friends – 'very different from any entertaining I have been accustomed to'.[54] Dolly Tennant, Lecky, Henry James, Mia Jackson and Julia Stephen, and the

German artist and critic Emil Heilbut called. Julia's daughter Vanessa, later recalled that en route, her mother suddenly sprang forward and clapped her hands, crying 'That was where it was!' at the memory of the old salon.[55] Anny Ritchie came for help with her article on Ruskin, for which Watts lent letters.[56] He and Mary were invited to luncheon at the home of the Earl and Countess of Pembroke, whose house in Carlton House Terrace was decorated with the frescoes that he created for the Somers when they had lived there. At the Wemysses in St James's Place, Mary noted that their Titian of *Venus and Adonis*[57] was finer than that at the National Gallery.

The sight of *Captive Andromache*, a sumptuous processional composition, in Leighton's studio, sent Watts home feeling awed and dejected that in comparison his work was disappointing. More objective later, he observed that in *The Last Watch of Hero* – soon to be on display with his *Prayer* as corporation purchases at the Manchester autumn exhibition[58] – the figure's dramatic stance at the window was too poised, 'neither quite natural nor positively ideal'.[59] At the Grange, Burne-Jones was painting a new *Rose Bower* from the Briar Rose series, less diaphanous than his Wattsian version painted for William Graham in 1871. Watts criticized Sleeping Beauty's arm: it was too thin at the elbow and showed no bone. From the finished work it is clear that as Ned advanced the picture he took note of Signor's observation.

Encouraging Mary's plans to model decorative reliefs, Watts sent Osmund Weeks to instruct her in *gesso duro*.[60] He wanted her to understand the principles of form: that all lines curved towards their object, a simple, natural truth, fundamental to the composition of art. As she modelled a saint, he showed her how monumental 'straight' drapery lines expressing the form of the limbs achieved quiet and reticence – by 'straight' he meant 'fine' or 'sharp'. He gave her Henry Moore's *Analysis of Drawing, Painting and Composing* to read and arranged for her to study with Moore. After her lesson, he came up behind and kissed her, saying, 'We may yet do some good work in the world.' Talking of Moore's scientific approach, he explained that 'Sir Fred reasons out his subject before he feels', whereas he himself felt compelled to paint a 'great & beautiful' design, which he afterwards tested against science.[61]

Out in the garden, Mary worked on her garden easel, designing Egyptian wings for the 'Forward and Fear Not' emblem on their porch. Her husband worked on *Physical Energy*, chiselling the rider and amputating an arm 'that it may be finished & made movable'. The *Athenaeum* announced on 6 August 1887 that 'Mr Watts has made great progress with the colossal equestrian group'. However, characteristic of the subject itself, the stalwart warrior restraining his horse, yet impelled to tackle a new enterprise, presented a constant challenge. A fortnight later he altered the rider's back, which was at last as he wanted it, but to Mary the head looked strained. 'He likes me to tell him what I think, & is a lesson to me in patience . . . His mind is so fair, so just & so humble, without the least loss of self-reliance.'[62]

He painted two quite different pictures of Mary. For both she wore a black dress, edged with a narrow white frill at the neck. In one, she is seated in three-quarter profile (fig. 151), her loosely coiled auburn hair a natural foil for her fine features and warm complexion, she appears to be contemplating her role as the painter's wife. The other, smaller painting, in which

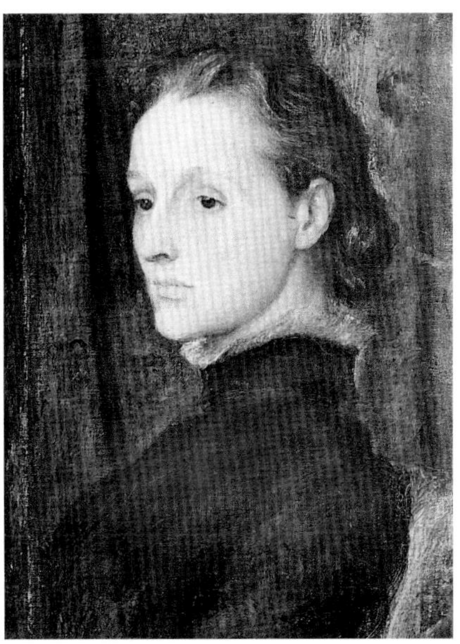

151  *Mary*, 1887 (Watts Gallery).

she is viewed from behind, her hair tightly knotted beneath a black ribbon, was presumably painted while she worked at her own art.[63] He had been improving Leighton's portrait and *Aspiration*, the young Arthur Prinsep idealized as a knight in armour and now in reality Lieutenant-General in command of the Eleventh (Prince of Wales's own) Bengal lancers.

Mary found a drawer of notes he had written in his bath, or when lying in bed, alone and ill. 'Take care,' he warned. 'You may come to think differently of me when you have read all those.' No doubt: for among them were letters apologizing for his marriage, which she thought she might read aloud to him.[64] Aubrey de Vere, observing the couple's unusual spiritual harmony, warmed her heart. 'You must feel you have set his life to music.' Lady Frances Baillie, whose father, the seventh Earl of Elgin, procured the Marbles, advised her, 'Be *absorbed* by him.'[65]

In preparation for the Centennial Exhibition at Melbourne, Watts was painting the small *Love and Life*, defining faces in the study of the *Court of Death*, and refining the second large *Love and Death*, which he brought out on to the easel in the Iron House (the 'Tinpot') to reassess the drapery. If only one subject could be preserved for future generations, this was the one he would chose. The figure of Death, Mary noticed, had lost weight, the drapery lines creating too quick a sense of movement. Day after day she watched him work to retrieve the strength, 'a hair's breadth of line or a breath of colour making the difference that a pause or an accentuated word would make in conversation'. Raising Death's outstretched arm, he softened the action from 'I shall' [crush Love] to the less severe, 'I am compelled'. Watts was touched by her growing understanding of 'the language of line' and proposed a joint enterprise to define its principles.[66] By mid-August, she had decorated Signor's reading niche with a golden symbolic design, 'the first page of a beautiful book,' he reflected. 'How aggressively happy you looked that evening, lolling on velvet and with a background of gold', wrote Burne-Jones. 'And having accounts simplified for you – cleared up simplified and dismissed from the mind for you.'[67]

Mary's support, both personal and secretarial, freed Watts's mind from pressure, enabling him to focus on matters of national interest. The Queen's Golden Jubilee seemed to him the perfect vehicle for his monument recording heroic acts of self-sacrifice in everyday life. He sent his valet Alfred Coleman to *The Times* office for a report of Alice Ayres, a maid who had died in April 1885 saving her master's children from a fire. Mary composed a letter based on phrases he had repeated so often, for publication in *The Times* on 5 September 1887, reprinted in the *Spectator*:

> The character of a nation as a people of great deeds is one, it appears to me, that should never be lost sight of. It must surely be a matter of regret when names worthy to be remembered and stories stimulating and instructive are allowed to be forgotten . . . It is not too much to say that the history of Her Majesty's reign would gain in lustre were the nation to erect a monument say here in London to record the names of these likely to be forgotten heroes – I cannot but believe a general response would be made to such a suggestion and intelligent consideration and artistic power might combine to make London richer by a work of Art and our nation richer by a record that is infinitely honourable.
>
> The material prosperity of a nation is not an abiding possession, the deeds of its people are.'

He sent copies of the letter to Gladstone and Lord Wemyss urging them to pursue the issue as a matter of national importance. These heroic acts, he told the *Pall Mall Gazette*, were more often than not enacted by the poorest people and recorded only in a newspaper paragraph: 'We want something more than this.' He had in mind a circular, covered colonnade, 'a kind of *campo santo*,' possibly in Hyde Park, and like the *Monument des Martyrs* in Brussels, with a marble wall, inscribed with the name, date and, most important, the story of each deed, in itself instruction for future heroism. There could be a central statue symbolizing Heroism, not necessarily to be carried out by himself. He was happy for others to carry out the enterprise, but if required he was ready. As ever, the idea was applauded – except by Leighton – and, if not forgotten, set aside.[68]

Mary was troubled. Before her marriage her sole object had been to succeed at her own art, but now, 'Instead of my *work* I focus *him*.' Under his shadow, any problem she faced in her own art often seemed insurmountable.[69] He told her how he added to his own difficulties experimenting with different qualities of line for each feature, rather than producing a particular line for a foot or hand, 'This perhaps explains the pathos of the hand of *Francesca* & the strength in the foot of [*Love and*] *Death*.'[70] Keen to make *Death Crowning Innocence* (pl. XXXII) as beautiful as *Hope* – to appeal to friends, to comfort the bereaved – he wanted the colour to be full of motion and the angel 'solemn, but tender & protecting'. The picture appeared as the frontispiece in the Century Guild's *Hobby Horse*.[71]

Barnett brought his wife to his final sitting in September, a second portrait on a yellow ground that made the picture luminous. Her teasing 'Now Samuel look as you do in Mr Watts's picture' presented no small challenge, for as Chesterton was to write, 'he scarcely ever paints a man without making him about five times as magnificent as he really looks,' and the sitters subsequently appeared 'mean and unsympathetic sketches from the Watts original':

> Watts does not copy men at all: he makes them over again. He dips his hand in the clay of chaos and begins to model a man named William Morris or a man named Richard Burton: he is assisted, no doubt, in some degree by a quaint old text-book called Reality, with its stiff suggestive woodcuts and its shrewd and simple old hints. But the most that can be said for the portraiture is that Watts asks a hint to come and stop with him, puts the hint in a chair in his studio and stares at him. The thing that comes out at last upon the canvas is not generally a very precise picture of the sitter, though, of course, it is almost always a very accurate picture of the universe.[72]

'The face is certainly like something in me', Barnett wrote to his brother. 'Yetta . . . is very pleased.' That day they were shown the four copies by Cecil Schott to be hung in St Jude's for the harvest festival.[73]

Mary was studying photography – with William Stillman and at Frederic Hollyer's studio – presumably in order to record her husband's works. Hollyer photographed the couple at Little Holland House – 'he all light himself *my* light. I sitting in the light' (fig. 152). Watts was amused when the Autotype Company staff recognized him from Stillman's photograph – 'Sir, it makes you fifteen years older than you are!'[74]

152   Signor and Mary at Little Holland House, 1887 (photo: Frederic Hollyer).

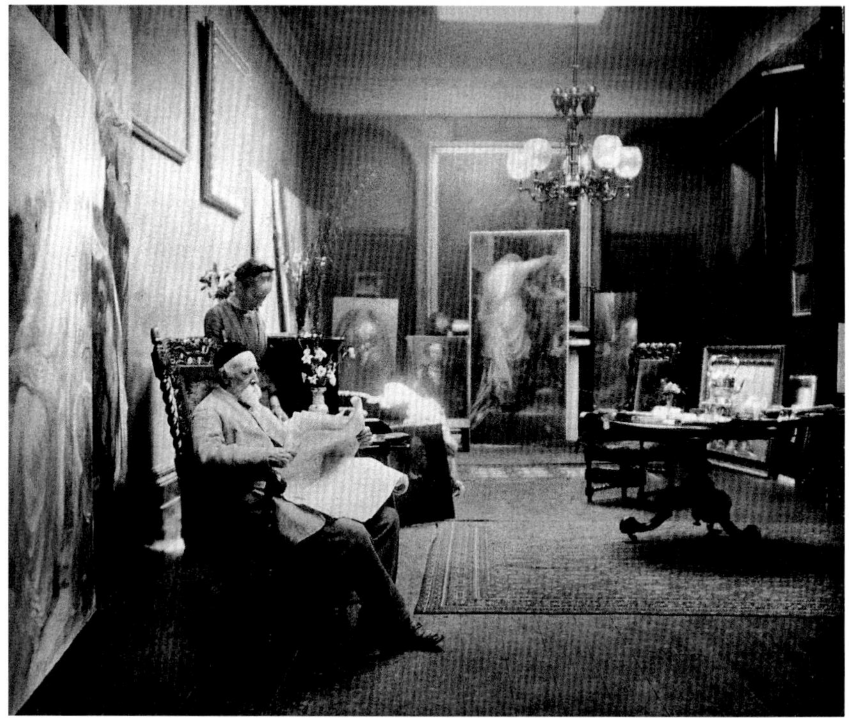

Strolling down Holland Walk, he decided to introduce Mary to Lady Holland. She was away, but the deaf old butler, Lane, proudly guided the couple into the most interesting rooms. There was evidence of Watts's brush on brackets, friezes, ceilings, as well as the portraits. In the evening she read to him from her old impassioned commonplace book. Having allowed her to examine his past, he was eager to discover her early life.[75]

They dashed up to Manchester to see the Royal Jubilee Exhibition. In the miserably grey half-light of day, the town seemed hideous. Rushing to the exhibition, the Watts found the end wall pictures shrouded in fog. They were especially moved by Orchardson's paintings, by Frederick Walker's 'glowing exquisite tender revelations of the spirit', and by Leighton's *The Summer Moon* and *Hercules Wrestling with Death for the Body of Alcestis*, painted in the seventies. The only one of his thirty-four pictures Watts acknowledged to be good was the portrait of Burne-Jones.[76] He showed *Aspiration* for the first time, with the now finished presidential portrait of Leighton and *The Spirit of the Ages* (exhibited the previous year as *The Soul's Prism*; pl. xxx) at the Royal Birmingham Society of Artists, of which Watts was president for 1887.[77]

Browning came to Little Holland House in October. In Watts's view, he was the only living poet with a taste for art or music, but his verse lacked 'the strong poetic wing that should lift him above humanity, above creation':

Browning digs deep, & finds light, but it is a volcanic flash – it is not the serene light of heaven. He is occupied only with humanity – with a dissecting knife he lays the human heart open – but he never takes one, as the true prophet should to verses that show us a something beyond . . . or rather to heights . . . each takes its place among the stars, & the air of heavens infinity is blown upon our faces . . . For a great work of art, altitude & depth are absolutely necessary – but there is much needed besides. Browning has been content to give his great thoughts to the world rough hewn & therefore incomplete, whether from want of power, or want of will, great though it is.[78]

That month Professor Jowett returned to sit. The artist had not been satisfied with his portrait, nor were his Balliol colleagues. Watts felt Frank Holl or Millais would have done better, for he was struggling to reconcile the master's swollen face with his wisdom, perceiving, too, a lack of imagination.[79] Nine years had passed since the first sitting. 'I shall have therefore the advantage of looking much younger than I am', wrote Jowett, happy to return for their discussions. While staying with Florence Nightingale, he came to the studio three days' running. His cheeks a little shallower perhaps, his hair no balder, with a hint of side-whiskers and sad, brown eyes, he stood for the three-quarter-length portrait in his crimson-edged black silk gown. Mary sat close by, to engage the kindly septuagenarian in conversation: 'Rather an exultation to be perched between these two.'[80]

Signor asked her to send his old portrait sketches of Florence Nightingale to the nurse. He spoke of her as 'the greatest woman in England' and was delighted when Mary received a reply and that through contact with his remarkable sitters he could enhance her life.[81] Jowett was taken ill, but was keen to return. Nightingale sent an anxious, insistent letter to Mary: 'Mr Jowett's physician has given him the strictest orders not to sit longer than an hour and a half altogether. Might I beg that you will not allow it? He is so tempted to transgress. His condition requires the greatest care – And he is incapable of any. He will telegraph tomorrow morning to Mr Watts. Pardon my caution, the caution of an old Nurse.' To force the artists' compliance, she quoted the doctor: ' "If he will not obey my orders, he must not go to Mr Watts at all!" '. The master did go one forbidden day, but completed the sittings at the end of the month. He thought the mouth still had 'an unsettled discontented look' but that 'the fault may be in the original'. He would miss the sittings.[82]

According to Emilie Barrington's *Reminiscences*, Watts visited her most mornings. Seeing her struggle over a portrait of her husband, he borrowed her palette and brushes and worked over it for half an hour. 'Never do I touch that again, Signor,' she cried, and he completed it for her birthday.[83]

A refreshing young American actress Mary Anderson, making her London debut at the Lyceum, had enchanted Watts before his marriage, and he now invited her to stand for a portrait. Gladstone, warning that the artist's 'captivating' talk would prolong the picture, said that he envied her, for 'I know no man who charms me in conversation as Watts does.' The actress breezed into Little Holland House with a bouquet of red roses. To Watts, she was like a breath of fresh mountain air, and he wished to capture this in the portrait. She saw the artist too as a free spirit, and welcomed his lack of pretension. Her description of him in his trademark white ruffles, scarlet ribbon and velvet skullcap is the only one to note his dark shining

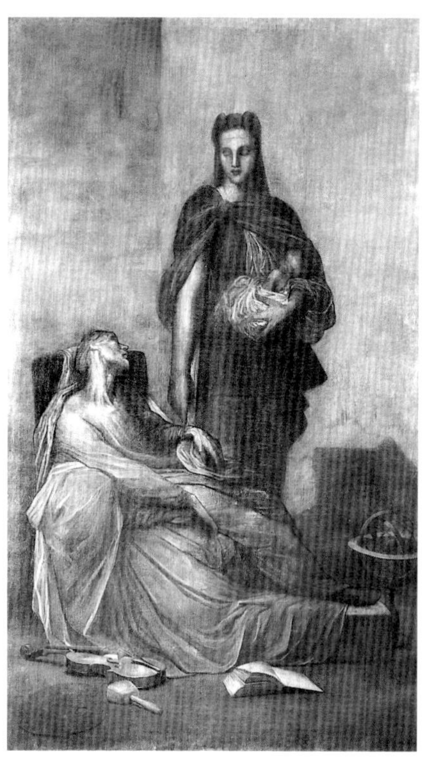

153    *The Messenger of Death*,
1884–85 (Watts Gallery).

eyes beneath bushy brows. She had been horrified by the morbid pictures at the Grosvenor painted by the Russian artist Vassily Verestchagin. By the time she came next, Watts had seen them. There were immense landscapes – the Wailing Wall in Jerusalem and grim scenes from the Russo-Turkish War. *All Quiet at Shipka* showed beds in a field hospital, each covered by a death sheet. The actress asked triumphantly if the lack of imagination had not shocked him. 'Some painters see. Some feel. Some imagine. The greatest do all', he replied. 'This one certainly *sees*!' He was moved by their vigour and truth.[84] Verestchagin himself came to the studio. A large cheery man, he was clearly impressed, except that he suggested Watts gave his new Angel of Death (fig. 153) a distinctive symbol. His host refused and Verestchagin roared with laughter and the following day proposed an article on 'The Aims of Art' to Spielmann, now editor of the *Magazine of Art*.[85]

*The Messenger* shows a serene robed woman standing against the light, an infant in her left arm, the other down by her side, stretched slightly towards a dying figure, ready to lead away the soul. Watts's conception of Death as a friend had come to him during a severe illness before his marriage when. as Mary Anderson put it, 'the calm, beautiful figure seemed ever standing by his side ready to release him from suffering . . . To have given to the world an emblem so consoling . . . cannot but inspire the deepest gratitude.' Gerry's cousin, Doll Liddell, described *The Messenger* as 'the Genius of Humanity.' He recorded that Watts had said he preferred people to interpret his pictures in their own way, as they would a poem; he simply hinted that the picture symbolized the genius in charge of the beginning and end of life. Like the actress, Liddell was struck by the new *Love and Death*, to which a crimson wing had been added, to make it 'glow in red & sunlight'.[86]

Mary Anderson had been sitting one Saturday when Julia Stephen arrived to find the house in turmoil. Due to watch Anderson perform in *The Winter's Tale* that evening, Watts was struggling to do up the evening dress he had not worn for years. He could not find a white tie, shirt or studs. Wardrobes were tearfully disembowelled. Clothes lay strewn about the floor. Alfred lent his tie and a frantic search round Kensington produced a dicky. Signor and Mary arrived at the Lyceum to find Anderson on stage. Her red and purple robe, designed by Lawrence Alma-Tadema for her role as Queen Hermione, was disappointing. Happily, also performing the youthful daughter Perdita, she appeared 'divinely beautiful' in pure white; and the artists loved her final scene as the statue of Hermione stepping from her pedestal to receive the arms of her living king, Leontes, played by Forbes Robertson.[87]

The Wattses were about to leave for Malta when Charles Hallé and Burne-Jones called on 31 October to discuss the worsening troubles at the Grosvenor Gallery. Without Lady Lindsay, now estranged from her husband, Sir Coutts, feeling the pinch had appointed a manager, whose commercial innovations – restaurant advertising boards in the gallery doorway and corporate evenings – lowered the artistic tone and seemed repulsive to the directors and artists. For Burne-Jones it was too much: 'One night we are a background for tobacco and another for flirting – excellent things both, but not there,' he wrote to Hallé. His anguished letter, shown to Sir Coutts, failed to move their unhappy old friend and patron. 'These artists are so unpractical, but why all this fuss about master and servants falling out?' he blustered.[88] The resignation of Carr and Hallé, and the withdrawal of Alma-Tadema and Burne-Jones, announced in *The Times* on 2 November 1887, was Sir Coutts's loss. As the avant-garde enterprise collapsed, plans for a new venue were afoot. The following evening, Burne-Jones came to Little Holland House and found Signor 'much too happy' in his golden niche to tell him that the former directors were planning a new gallery. After Watts and his wife had set sail, Burne-Jones wrote to reassure him that he would take no part in setting up the gallery, and would not commit Watts to the venture:

> Nor will I have your big name brought into the affair at all – I want to exhibit where you do – better still I should like never to exhibit at all – but to leave all that for people to deal with when I am over. I am afraid I shall never feel anything but a stranger at the Academy – and many & many a time I wish it had not occurred to them to elect me – for I am quite useless to them, and many would be glad to have my place, & I should like to yield it up – but I shall not trouble about this or the Grosvenor matter anymore at present.[89]

While Burne-Jones agonized, blaming himself for the catastrophic exodus, he was glad that his friend was kept well away from the argument. Mary's sole concern as the *SS Britannia* rolled to an angle of twenty degrees was whether her husband would live to finish his work. In the Mediterranean sun, Watts longed to see Burne-Jones. That society, the public and press sided with Sir Coutts, now in need of income, having spent £200,000 on the venture that launched the Continental careers of his avant-garde colleagues, was natural, if upsetting. 'I feel so anxious not to draw you into the affair,' wrote Burne-Jones. 'I keep remembering your words that you wanted to show your pictures side by side with mine and nothing that ever was said to me will be more remembered than these, and still I hope you will, though I dread to say a word to influence you. I never felt more right about anything.' By Christmas a prime site, 112 Regent Street, had been found for the new gallery. Watts would never again exhibit at the Grosvenor. Bereft of its stars, the Bond Street gallery struggled on until 1890, when it closed in with an overdraft of £111,000. But thanks to Sir Coutts's enterprise, Watts had been encouraged to pursue ideal subjects the public would not buy and, as the father figure of the English Symbolist movement, he had achieved an influential international voice.[90]

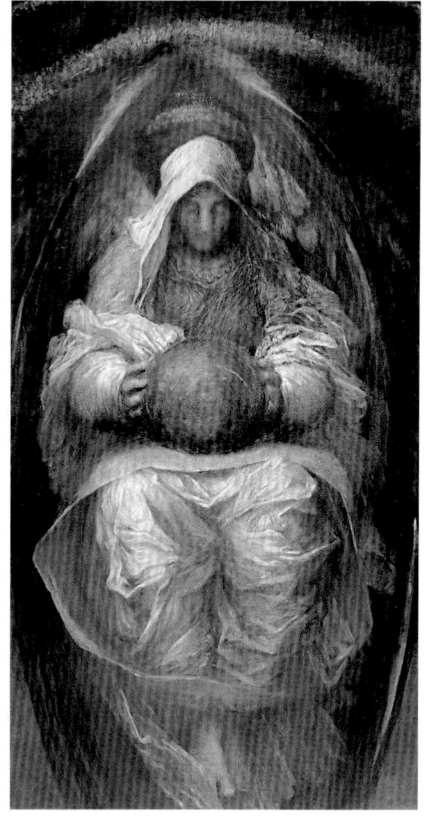

154 *The All-Pervading*, 1887–90 (Tate, London).



THE PALATIAL VILLA MICALLEF AT SLIEMA looked out over olive groves and pines, across Sliema Creek to the fortified capital of Valletta and every day, whether the air was calm or the wind blew – the warm, dusty *scirocco* from the Sahara, or the rainy *gregale* from Siberia – the two artists walked to the shore to watch the sea rolling and bucking over the rocks. Watts sat and gazed at the colours at their feet, 'the sharp golden sandstone, the emerald green water, and the converse opaque blue and purple', asking Mary to study this 'splendid opposition of life', which he said the early Germans captured, 'our modern painters many of them making the fleck on the wave like chips of wood!'[1]

In the light-filled drawing room that served as his studio in the winter of 1887, he painted two joyful *amorini* – *Love Knocking at the Door* (later renamed *The Habit Does Not Make the Monk*), and *Good Luck to Your Fishing*, the cupid kneeling in the whirling sea, a detail from his Carlton House Terrace fresco. The huge chandelier inspired a serious metaphysical subject, *The All-Pervading* (fig. 154), a mystical robed figure holding on its lap a globe of the universe, a blue sphere flecked with light. 'It promises to be most suggestive', noted Mary.[2] She read to him from Lacordaine, Milton, *The Arabian Nights*, Jane Austen, Martineau and English papers sent out to Malta, the *Pall Mall Gazette*, *Budget*, the *Antiquary*, and the *Athenaeum*.[3]

In the mornings he would lie without speaking, his mind 'occupied by some serene inward vision – too vague and spiritual to come into words'. Mary finished classifying his papers, discarding his doubtful pre-marital notes, began to learn Italian and modelled a group of *The Merciful*, but when she spent a morning picking and arranging flowers, her husband rebuked her gently for not having devoted even an hour to drawing.[4] He now relied very much on her, and if she went out without him, she would find him in a wretched state on her return. They vowed to be together as much as possible.[5]

To commemorate the recent Manchester Jubilee Exhibition, Agnew asked to purchase *Love and Death* through Sir Joseph Whitworth's bequest. Watts valued the major Symbolist subject at £3,000. He replied that he would give it, but married life – travel and six months' rental in Malta – incurred greater costs and he must still paint and preserve his best symbolic pictures for the nation. He therefore wished to keep back the better, second version, but Manchester could have the consistently improved version he had exhibited at the Grosvenor. Hearing from Agnew again on 12 December, he glanced wistfully at Mary. She read his mind: 'Darling, could you not give them the picture', and he offered Agnew the picture as their joint gift. 'I say *we*,' he said, 'You are associated with me in this.' He made her promise that if his work became feeble or bad, she would never let him exhibit it.[6]

Andrew Hichens wrote to say that Sara Prinsep, Watts's impulsive, warm-hearted friend of forty years, had died. As Mary opened the letter and gently broke the news, he lay his head on her shoulder and sobbed. 'I am glad she knew you were a darling', he said. 'How sad the dismemberment of that sisterhood seems to me, like pages of some beautiful book torn out one by one.'[7]

Two days later, they hurried along the Fort path to see a ship steam past the point, when Watts fell sideways on to the road and was knocked unconscious. Mary rolled up her cloak, placed it under his cheek, and ran until she found some soldiers. They raced back to the motionless artist. When he came to, Mary tied a handkerchief around his bleeding cheek. One soldier ran for water, another for a cab. Watts was violently sick and arrived home semi-conscious, ashen and retching. Alfred and Emma helped get him to bed. Mary administered brandy and felt a strong pulse. The doctor, fearing fever, came again and again. 'I had tasted death', Mary wrote after an anxious night, 'but it has passed.'[8] His old ailments returned, vertigo, eczema, sciatica, but subsided faster than the injury to his right hand that prevented his painting: 'Such a rickety machine I am. No sooner one part gets patched up, another falls to pieces.' Disgusted with himself, very deaf and in pain, he remained affectionate, addressing her as 'my best and dearest' and 'my pearl' and was eager to talk about inventions to power and purify London. One idea was a huge steam-powered pyramidal building to deal with sewage, waste and pollution, and run electricity: 'This and the idea of using sun in some way as a purifier of the atmosphere of London, a form brought to bear on fogs – is often in his mind.'[9]

At Sliema, the sight of wind blowing the spray back from the crests of the waves would inspire a future painting, *Neptune's Horses* (pl. XXXVI).[10] But he could not overcome the illness and doctors advised a change of climate. In February the household transferred to the Hotel Nobile at Naples. Within days he was up on the roof, watching the midday sun burst from behind the clouds and sprinkle the purple city with jewels of light. He found an artist selling gouache pictures in the vestibule, had lessons in gouache and, from his bedroom window, recorded impressions of Vesuvius and the bay of Naples. For a better view, the Wattses moved higher up to the Hotel Bristol. Looking down on to the Villa Rocella, he saw that the expanded city now surrounded Lady Holland's country home. He grumbled about the 'terrible expense of health and time and money' in letters to Emilie Barrington, expressing doubts about the new gallery, wondering whether Richmond, now an associate member of the Academy, would stay with the Grosvenor. In the run up to exhibitions, Watts was keen for news. He and Mary sailed for Cannes and settled at the Villa Baron at Mentone.[11]

Burne-Jones had written at length to tell them about Margaret's engagement to Jack Mackail, a classical scholar, and to report, after the 'sickenly and discouraging' Grosvenor quarrel, that work had begun on the New Gallery in Regent Street.[12] Signor, following developments in the papers, chiefly supporting Sir Coutts and blaming Burne-Jones as the instigator, had written anxiously to the latter. 'If I could have had a voice in the matter, not a whisper of it all should have reached you', Ned replied. 'There is not a step I regret and chiefly I am glad you have been saved all annoyance.' With some reluctance, Watts agreed to serve on the committee of the gallery, 'that miracle of energy', which was due to open in May. Burne-Jones was housing Watts's *Angel of Death* (ultimately, *Death Crowning Innocence*; pl. XXXII) which would be exhibited. Millais and Tadema were each sending two pictures, and Burne-Jones himself was showing three. 'Have you no sculpture to send? – do if you can', he asked Watts. Ned had been stung by the criticism and longed to be out of public view, never to exhibit another work. He was finishing the picture of Perseus fighting the monster, later called *The Doom Fulfilled*: 'I keep wondering if you will like it . . . I want to see you – I wish we were more together'.[13]

Burne-Jones was sorry to have upset Watts by sending nothing to Burlington House, but the Academy, having obliged him to become an associate, had failed to honour him with full membership, and Ned was offended: 'It's a rude old habit of theirs, this of offering unsolicited honours to men who can do without them and then instead of perfecting their act of grace, waiting till the day of graceful action is past – they did the same to you I remember, and a pretty fury I was in about it for your sake – but it is an infinitely little matter.'

Finally, mindful of last year's gaffes in Cairo and Paris, he spoke up for Mary:

> O my dear Signor – if there are any shops or marts of merchandise in Mentone, I beseech you, by all that is wide and experienced as in the sayings of the ancients let your wife have full licence to traffic, barter, chaffer and cheapen in those same marts – it is a natural, reasonable and necessary desire, which will unfailingly bring happiness to the household – that was a bitter story she told me, and I cannot forget it or cease to smite a little blow in my otherwise unqualified admiration for you.[14]

Sympathizing with Burne-Jones, Watts made the unusual decision to send just one picture to the Academy – a symbolic image, *Dawn* (fig. 155) – and he would no longer exhibit at the Grosvenor. As he explained to Henrietta Barnett, he refused to be identified with an organization that made art a financial issue. He had no wish to enter the dispute, and was sending just the one picture to the New Gallery.[15] On artistic grounds he would always go with Burne-Jones, for his artistic principles and his future standing in art. The Grosvenor squabble was trivial, but the principle was important and he would not be denied the right to protest against Mammon worship. He regretted the scandal, and the rush into press, 'screaming to the public about what the public cares nothing for' – except money-making. Watts, who used the press whenever he needed to explain his views or his art to the public, would surely have done the same. Indeed, a day or two later he would join the fray. His letters cried out for news and what with doctors' bills, a sick nurse, boats, trains and, worst of all, hotels, he felt he could never face such travel again. Yet, happily, Mary noted in 'Fatima': 'Tells me I have joy upon his moods'.[16]

He began two pictures of Naples. As the villa was not large he achieved distance by leaving a door open into the next room, which in itself gave

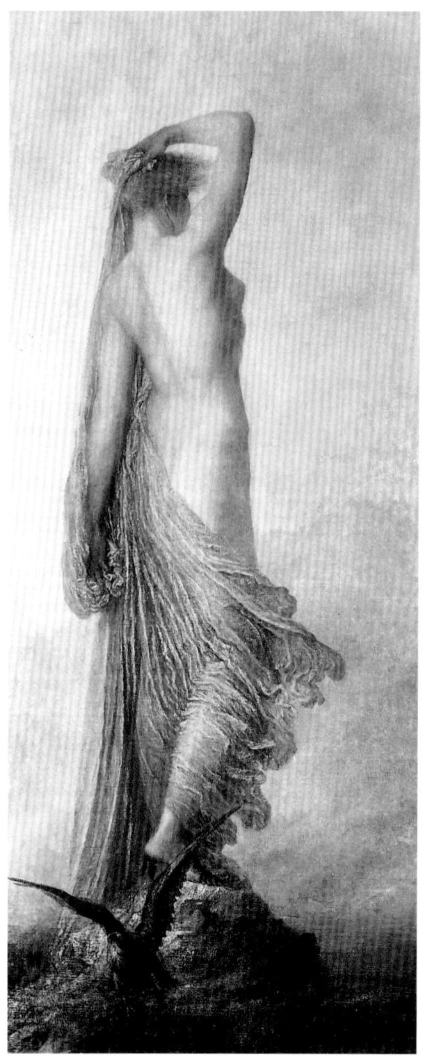

155   *Dawn*, 1887 (courtesy of the Fine Arts Society).

rise to *The Open Door*. Its message was universal, also symbolic of the Wattses' marriage. A woman, having opened the door to look at the storm, gazes down at a white butterfly, symbol of the soul, that flutters in, to seek shelter.[17] Villa Baron overlooked calmer shores of the Mediterranean, the light silver, rather than gold. They walked high up through the woods to an idyllic spot, looking across the valley to the forested mountain-top convent of Sant' Agnese and the even higher alpine ranges behind. Until that moment, Watts had thought of the Alps as 'cold ugly white masses devoid of colour'. Returning again and again with his pencil, to check each characteristic feature, Watts painted *Sant Agnese, Mentone* as he might a portrait. He drew the mountains' bony skeleton, added muscle and clothing, the flesh and folds of vegetation; however, when the structure was built up, detail would be subordinate to the atmosphere he wished to create, the glistening granite and astonishing light. To render nature truly – that is, to give her inward beauty, he explained, 'one must make careful studies first, either in pencil or monochrome, looking much and well at nature and then coming away and trying to paint the impression left on the mind'. This was why he preferred the backgrounds in Millais's pictures to his land-scapes painted from nature.[18]

Disappointed by the 'plodding materialism' of Morris's pamphlet, *The Aims of Art*, calling for art to elevate minutiae of everyday life, and appalled by the report of Sir Coutts Lindsay's farewell speech, 'Art is not a religious cult and has nothing to do with it', Watts dictated his manifesto for the elevating spiritual power of art to Mary, and sent 'The Aims of Art' to Spielmann for publication in the *Magazine of Art*. Watts saw himself as a standard-bearer leading his colleagues towards a nobler battle, to raise art from its derisory status, 'a mere ornamental fringe on the social garment'. In response to Morris, he endorsed the socialist desire for justice and rights. However, people needed not just contentment, but affiliation with the finest imaginative thought. Man's greatest faculty was the intellect, above all Imagination. 'In giving out the inspirations of this divine faculty he is at his best, and when he has been great in this, he has adorned his epoch and has made his country famous as no other human effort has the power to do.' Parallel with the undisputed mission of poetry to elevate and instruct, 'a stronger appeal through art might be made to some minds by impressive symbols of the mysteries that surround human life from its beginning to its close, and be more efficacious to keep alive simple faith than the accumu-lation of dogmatic utterances.' He continued:

> Profoundly deep in the human mind exists a spiritual yearning dependent on no special creed, questionings by nature left without response, yearnings the most perfect knowledge of material things will never stifle. The true prophet, be his language prose or poem, art or music, can transport to regions where earth takes its place among the stars and something beyond of heaven's infinity seems borne upon the air.

Yet figurative language, such as 'crowned with success' or 'arm of the sea', acceptable in poetry and speech, viewed unintelligible in art. 'To the discernment of truth and beauty, to the arousing of man's imagination, to the widening of the span of this celestial region, should Art be mainly dedi-cated', he concluded, 'for this most truly is its mission'.[19]

Spielmann had reproduced an engraving of Madox Brown's *Work*, a picture that Watts greatly admired. He asked for a proof, and advised that in the engraving of *Sir Frederic Leighton PRA*, the strong red colour of the robe should be indicated by 'a light mass with deep tones in the shadows in order to render the vivacity of the quality'.[20] The Academy portrait was one of eight of his pictures chosen by the president for next year's Exposition Universelle in Paris. Leighton asked him to 'pen your most eloquent epistles at once . . . *Please put the screw on at S. K.* – that is where the men will pinch – and write also to Nottingham.' His energetic, news-packed letter pressing Watts into action, reporting increased outsider entries to the Academy – 'in spite of the now added New Gallery we had 700 or 800 more works sent in here last year' – demonstrates the encouragement he offered artists. Keen to show avant-garde work at Burlington House, he was delighted by Watts's entries. Amongst these was a new portrait of Mary, executed in pastel to encourage the medium, especially for artists struggling with oils – as well as the promised idealized nude *Dawn*, standing on a rock against a saffron and purple background; seen in profile from behind, she stretches up her arm, a golden veil slips down her back and at her feet a bird begins to sing.[21]

Saddened by news of Matthew Arnold's death – 'a valuable man and personally delightful' – and the knowledge that near by, at San Remo, the German Emperor Frederick III was dying, he raged at the loss of two great liberals.[22] He heard from Hichens that Emilie Barrington wanted Octavia Hill's Red Cross Settlement hall in Southwark to be decorated with murals illustrating unsung heroism. (Leighton had vetoed the scheme, when she had proposed it the previous year for the new People's Palace in Mile End.) Hichens asked whether Watts minded that Mrs Barrington had not only hijacked his project, but that only the working classes would see it. It was not the simple record he now had in mind, but it could inspire them and would not affect his plans. In his view, artistic treatment would divert attention from the sacrificial act to be recorded. 'What I look forward to is the socialism of co-operation in all things,' he replied. 'Unless something of the kind can be brought about I feel we are done for as dominant nation.'[23]

During the last two winters abroad he had assessed England's position and now sent forceful proposals to Lord Wemyss: 'We are falling on evil days. Every nation stands by with unfriendly feeling. We are surrounded by the hostile, the hungry and the expectant. We are neither loved, which is a pity, nor trusted which is a disgrace, nor feared which is a disaster! . . . Prestige is the very breath of our nostrils and the loss of it leaves our reality nothing but a vapour a blast will destroy.' The country could be saved by a powerful Navy and a revival of patriotism. Moral sentiment should be stimulated. 'A real co-operation of all classes, that socialism which binds family life together is . . . the ultimate end of progress the only stable future, co-operation of individuals of states, of nations with each other . . . no riches or power will ever give permanence if there is disintegration or more than healthy opposition.' He saw life peerage as an incentive for improvement. 'I hope you are in favour of life peerages! I think the element so imported would be of infinite value.' Present hereditary peers, recruited from 'The Army, The Navy, The Bar and Wealth', did not represent the entire nation. Pointing out that his proposal referred only to men of mature experience, who would not swamp hereditary peers, he recommended Leighton, though he would be obliged to relinquish the presidency. His *Captain Andromache* hung in the place of honour at Burlington House. Watts wrote, 'I suppose you were at the Academy dinner. I wonder whether Leighton was great, his picture is I know. I fancy the show is a good one and am impatient to see it.'[24]

London's refreshing High Art venue, the New Gallery, opened on 9 May 1888. A fountain played in the marbled entrance hall, and pictures hung on gold leather walls in the ground floor galleries. Watts's *Angel of Death* (pl. XXXII) hung with Burne-Jones's *The Tower of Brass* and *The Rock of Doom* and *The Doom Fulfilled* from the Perseus series.[25] The design for *Angel of Death*, drawn originally to comfort Mary's family after the death of her nephew, now painted in moonshine, shows an angel cocooned within her own wings, tenderly placing a halo over a dying infant in her lap. Tender and mystical, it was admired and, to Watts's gratification, understood. More than ever he felt that a picture must refer to a 'great eternal truth' and that if, like this one and *Love and Death*, it was inspired by personal experience, the effect would be greater. Asked if he would sell *Angel of Death*, he thought of selling it to a serious collector of modern art, but at Mary's insistence he reserved it for the nation – 'Considering how anxious our expenses this year have made us she cannot be accused of a tendency to money grabbing!' he wrote to Hichens. As buyers pressed him to sell, he stood firm, 'not that the nation cares a dump!' But he would paint other versions and was obliged to refuse Spielmann permission to engrave it after Agnew advised its diminished copyright value might jeopardise a future sale.[26] In splendid contrast, Watts sent *Aspiration* and *Wealth* to the Royal Scottish Academy. Having sold the original *Hope* to Joseph Ruston, he declined an offer for the improved second version – reserved for the nation – which was sent to the Melbourne Centennial International Exhibition with *The Spirit of Christianity* and *Mammon* and the first *Tennyson*, bought by the government of Victoria for 600 guineas.[27]

To escape the heat in Menton, the Wattses travelled to Turin. He spent hours studying Veronese's masterpiece *Solomon and the Queen of Sheba*; and at the sight of peasant men and women in the galleries on Sunday afternoon, recalled the shepherd who had watched George Mason paint in the Roman *campagna*, crying out to leave the picture as it was: '*Ah, lascia stare!*'[28] Reading Émile Zola, Watts recognized their mutual desire to use their art 'for all time and for all people', though his 'terrible pictures of French peasantry' seemed quite the reverse of the courteous Savoyard.[29] He had moved to the Hôtel Thermal in Aix-les-Bains, to cure his gout. In the first week he was 'douched and thumpt'.[30] Still able to work, *Peace and Goodwill* (fig. 156), an ironic subject suggesting the reverse, had come to mind. Peace was to be a queen, a starving outcast from her kingdom: 'She will turn wearily towards a streak of light which may mean the dawn of better things. The son, her heir, is still only a young child upon her knee.' He mulled over the idea for a day or two; and in an illuminating letter, Mary described his method as he started the picture.

Signor is sitting now before a little wax figure we have twisted up together and draped in wet handkerchiefs. The wax lady is poised on the edge of the table, and he, a few feet off, is leaning back in his chair, one knee thrown across the other. All the lines are long and come so well,

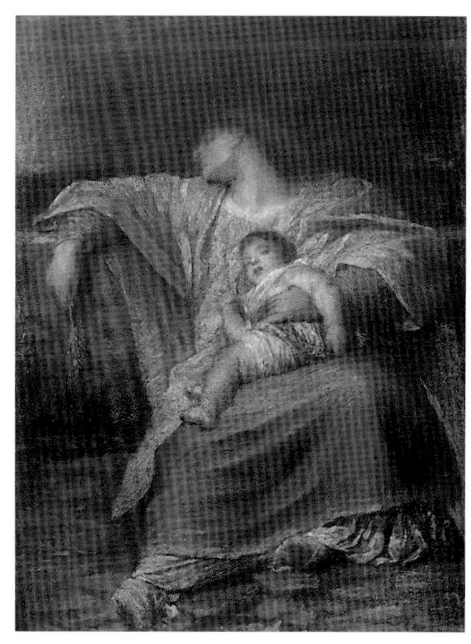

156 *Peace and Goodwill*, 1888–99 (Watts Gallery).

his figure reminds me of nothing so much as one of his own silverpoint drawings. His drawing-book, held at arm's length with one hand, is just supported by his raised knee, the other hand is working away busily. Then clear-cut against the window I see the small head moving up and down, as he sends that earnest direct glance of his from his model to his sketch.

He made gouache sketches, adding colour and regal robes. That the rough figure could suggest such beauty surprised her: 'Before Signor begins a new picture, he does not see the design very distinctly. He has first a very strong mental impression of the ideas he wishes to convey, then he is conscious of a certain nobility of outline in keeping with the idea, but nothing more than that. The rest comes as he works it out on paper or on canvas.'[31]

On his return, he planned to finish his sculpture and *The Court of Death*: 'those I imagine will about complete my work,' he wrote optimistically to Hichens. There was, of course, much more to do; and when Hichens invited him and Mary to stay at Monkshatch, he eagerly looked forward to painting his picture of an old white horse, outside in the Surrey woodland. 'I want a worn out draught horse and when they get to be useless the poor things are not turned out, but turned off! I may find one at an Institution for decayed horses which I believe has lately been established.'[32]

Hearing from Gertrude Mead, he warmly invited her to meet Mary, but to arrange with them, not through Emilie Barrington, who, he confided, was tactlessly bringing his friends to Little Holland House as if she were the hostess. 'My wife particularly wishes to make the acquaintance of my friends though me'.[33]

Mary, apparently unaware of Thornycroft's earlier proposal, commissioned Gilbert to execute a portrait bust of her husband. His acclaimed symbolic Fawcett Memorial of 1887, and now the reports of the Jubilee Memorial to Queen Victoria, no doubt stimulated the invitation. Like Rodin, who declared the model of *Queen Victoria* at the Academy to be the finest modern sculpture of its kind, Watts, when he eventually saw it, exclaimed, 'It is the finest thing since the *Colleone*!' Gilbert accepted at once: 'If Mr Watts will sit to me, it will not only give me much pleasure to endeavour to make his portrait but I shall esteem his doing so as an honour and a privilege.'[34] Despite his growing status, he was in awe of Watts, and the collaboration between the two innovative Symbolists seemed momentous.

At the last minute Doctor Blanc advised rest in more bracing air before the long journey home. The Watts headed north for a final week at Monnetier in the Haute Savoie, 2,000 feet above sea level. As their train steamed into La Roche-sur-Foron the station at sunset, they gasped at the Swiss alpine scenery, steeped in crimson. 'Suddenly, a line of snowy peaks blazed out upon a background of giant cumulous clouds.' Throughout the week he marvelled at the effects of sunlight and shadow on the mountains, the sapphire shadows, 'glittering as silver'. Armed with studies of the 'Celestial city' and impressions of the radiant '*Gloria in excelsis* of earth and sky', they spent a couple of days in Geneva and Paris, and on 14 June they arrived home to find Val and Florence Prinsep on the doorstep, waiting to greet them.[35]

Among their earliest visitors were Robert Browning and his daughter, Mrs Barrington, to discuss Red Cross Hall; Julia Stephen; Gertrude Mead; Auberon Herbert to discuss education and Lecky. Jowett gave portrait sittings, and Lord Wemyss brought his *Venus*, 'in triumph'. On 4 July 1888 the Metropolitan collection arrived back after four years, having travelled to Birmingham, Nottingham and Saltaire. Some had been sent on to Rugby School.[36]

Sales of *Dawn* to Agnew and the four *Riders* and, soon, *The Dove which Returned Not Again* to the Manchester collector William Carver alleviated travel and medical expenses. After catching up at the exhibitions, he thought Burne-Jones's red-robed Marie Stillman as Danae in *The Tower of Brass* at the New Gallery, 'the essence of loveliness'.[37] Watts determined to overcome his gout. He again tried the waters at Harrogate, to no avail, but while there he conceived an explosive vertical image confronting the response to spiritual and intellectual advance. In *Progress* (pl. XLI), the apocalyptic Rider on the White Horse leaps through a golden blaze, over the hunched figures of an old man reading, a rich man 'money-grubbing' in the dust, a sluggard shading his eyes, and one who sees the spirit of Progress in the air and begins to rise.[38]

Sixteen-year-old William Rothenstein arrived at King's Cross station, restless with excitement at being in the same city as Watts and Leighton. In his first year of study under Alphonse Legros at the Slade, he sent out an appeal for Legros, whose picture *Les Femmes en Prière* remained unsold at the New Gallery. Watts sent £50.[39] He pledged the early *Fata Morgana* to John Cook for the new Leicester Art Gallery and would rework the picture (pl. II) in the autumn, heightening the colour, adding impasto to the flat fresco-like surface.[40]

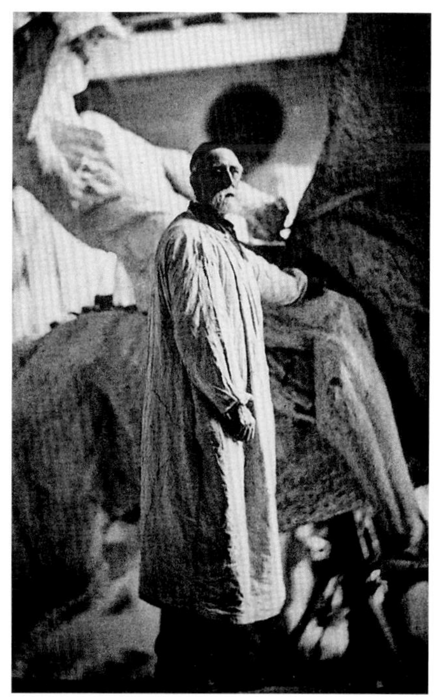

157 At work on *Physical Energy*, 1888 (photo: Henry Cameron).

Sir William Gregory, a trustee of the National Gallery, called on the 9 August to discuss Watts's gift to the nation. Faced with limited space and too many bequests from artists' widows, the trustees were about to institute a rule that no works were to be accepted until twelve years after a painter's death. Could Watts therefore add a codicil to his will before the new rule came into effect in November?[41] Adding the codicil, he placed at the disposal of the trustees thirty to forty paintings (including the nine at South Kensington), and described them 'national property by gift now'.[42] He sent his picture of the Alps at Mentone for exhibition in Manchester.[43] Hallé, who called after hanging an exhibition at the People's Palace, reported that fog had fallen over two portraits, apparently similar in tone, and that one had become invisible, but Watts's portrait shone, because his pure light ground reflected the dim rays.[44] Mary's brief diary notes at this time – 'Mrs Coronio lent his *Minotaur*' and 'Signor calls the Toynbee Hall workers "Crusaders who know what modern war should be"' – coincide with inquests on the gruesome mutilation of prostitutes in Whitechapel, murdered by 'Jack the Ripper'.[45]

Burne-Jones's son Philip, who painted the odd small-scale portrait in oil colour, was overjoyed when Watts agreed to be painted at work on *Physical Energy*. He arranged for Henry Cameron to take preparatory photographs of the sculptor standing in his long white smock on the scaffold with the giant gesso horse and rider looming in the background; the image (fig. 157) provides an interesting record of the scale and the musculature of the monument upon which Watts would continue to build.[46]

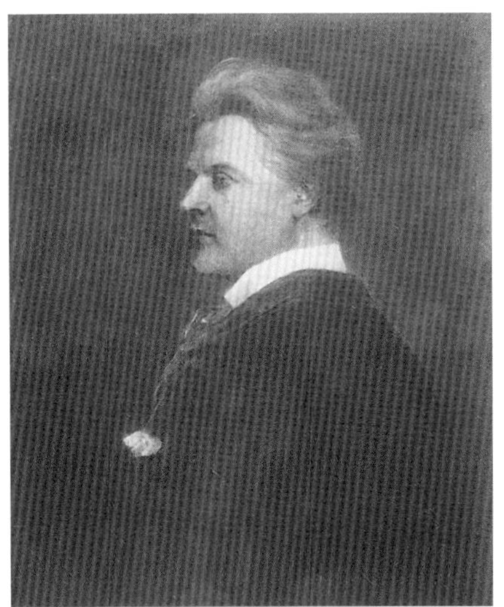

158   *Alfred Gilbert*, 1888
(whereabouts unkown; photo:
Frederic Hollyer).

Gilbert arrived by cab for the master's first sitting at midday on Monday
20 August. 'I cannot tell you how great an endeavour I shall make', were
almost his first words to Mary. She was struck by his youth. At thirty-four,
Alfred Gilbert (fig. 158) was barely five years her junior, of stocky build,
with square shoulders and chest, his hair combed back above his eager,
clean-shaven face. While his tools were arranged in her Iron House studio,
Watts took the sculptor into his gallery and they returned, engrossed in
earnest conversation. Gilbert, too, usually required five sittings, 'I want to
make it my best work – the portrait of a man who might have been great
in any profession, and by accident was an artist.'[47]

In this case, he would have eighteen sittings. At first he tried to show a
transient expression, 'that keen look of his, like a war-horse', but gradually realized that a graver look was more characteristic. After lunch, Gilbert
would look round the gallery, 'sweeping the air with his hand' to outline
the composition of the pictures.[48] 'He steals all the best subjects away from
the sculptors!' the sculptor shook his fist. 'Mr Watts tells me things that
are of such infinite value, and they are so simple!' He mentioned Thornycroft's earlier proposal,[49] 'Signor was touched,' Mary commented in *Annals*,
papering over an awkward situation Mrs Barrington was determined to
exacerbate.

Thornycroft, now a full Academician, noted in his diary on 4 September
1888 that Gilbert promised him a copy of the bust 'if I will give him a work
by myself, which bargain is so unequal that I am almost inclined to accept'.
On 26 September he wrote to Watts, Emilie Barrington and to Gilbert.
Delighted that his hope for 'a bust of Signor by you, bids fair to be realized now', Thornycroft assumed the commission to be his, for a fee of £150
to £200.[50] Mrs Barrington, infuriated by the Wattses, wrote to Thornycroft,
defiantly quoting Signor's earlier reaction to his original proposal – 'it
would only be a waste of Gilbert's time and misapplication of mine' – and
insisted that 'you should not have an expense entailed upon you (and which
I am afraid I brought about by my speaking to you)'. She demanded a visit.
Thornycroft complied.[51] The next day, Gilbert warmly acknowledging his
efforts, assured him that this portrait was for Mary and would ask her permission to make him a copy. 'Fate and circumstances ruled that a kind and
good lady should share your desire and that she should prevail with your
friend, her husband now to give me the sittings which at one time seemed
hopeless to hope for.'[52]

Emilie Barrington had become a thorn in Watts's side. Proprietorial and
intrusive, she irritated Mary and, spreading rumours that she was jealous
and cruel, attempted to alienate his friends. Alarmed that Gertrude Mead,
who had been silent since her visit in August, was about to visit Mrs Barrington, Watts wrote to explain their difficulty: 'She and Mary do not sympathize, but her grievance if finely stated comes to this only. That Mary
could not consent to have an intimacy, which could only, and should only
be won by mutual respects and sympathy, forced by actual violence. This
hardly calls for resentment on the part of mutual friends!' He did not wish
to influence the American against his neighbour, who spoke of Gertrude as
her most intimate friend. 'She has a thousand good qualities. I am in debt
for unvarying kindness and could count upon any aid, but this does not
give unlimited rights!' He kept the letter secret from Mary and on reflection, felt guilty about its tone.[53] Gertrude agreed to visit the Wattses in

Brighton where they were to spend the winter. That their friendship remained intact was a relief. Mary sent a warm reply.[54] Watts could not get the wretched woman out of his mind. While insisting to Gertrude that *'There is no war between us!'* he warned that Mrs Barrington had now offended someone else. 'Take care . . . she has a craze *to show how very much she knows about every body* and is sometimes injudicious to the extent of creating real trouble, also she has a curious tendency to think people *cracked.'*[55]

In October, his portrait collection was recorded by the fine art photographer Frederic Hollyer.[56] Invited to respond to Millais's paper, 'Thoughts on our Art of Today' in the *Magazine of Art*, he accepted eagerly – 'Sir John is too great an artist to quarrel with a difference of opinion'. Hoping that their colleagues would add their thoughts and challenge his own, he sent the first of a series of letters from his sick bed, with notes, which Spielmann collated for publication.[57] Millais had stated that the best modern art was as good of its kind as that of the old masters, that the best English art could hold its own against the world, and that although the Elgin Marbles were seen as the perfection of art, it must be asked how much of that reverence could be ascribed to the effects of Time, suggesting that the white marble of the Parthenon would have looked 'excessively crude' when it was first built. Time and varnish were two of the greatest Old Masters, declared Millais, for the artists themselves had painted in bright colours, which the nineteenth-century eye would consider vulgar. Greek painting, he imagined, was 'little more than *tinted outline*'.[58]

Watts, having witnessed the bright decoration at Halicarnassus, noted that 'the modern eye might at first have something to get over, but there could have been nothing harsh and crude'. Nor were the bright colours of the Venetians crude, nor would time turn white into colour; it would simply tone down, 'I wish so much to combat the idea that the Artist should paint his flesh White, leaving it to time to make the colour of it.' At the National Gallery, in Bronzino's allegory with Venus and Cupid, 'the colour is as crude and the surface as bare of mystery as if it had been painted yesterday', whereas the white sleeve of the Magdalene in Titian's restored *Noli Me Tangere*, was 'still a beautiful white', quite different from her fair flesh. Still more significant for Watts (and revealing today given the Venetian's influence on his own work) was the unrestored *Venus of Urbino* in Florence: 'It is an elaborately painted picture owing nothing to the brightness that slight painting often has and retains, the colours being untormented by repeated re-touching. This picture is a proof that when the method is good and the pigments pure, the colours change very little'. After 300 years the white sheet still looked white against the flesh, which, without strong colour or shadow, appeared to be lustrous on the surface with blood circulation beneath – 'an absolute triumph'. Young artists, he insisted, should use pure, rich colour.

He endorsed Millais's objection to over-elaborate art, but considered carelessness worse, because it suggested insincerity; and as for pictures that look as though they have been produced without effort, 'Nature never works in this way; and to make it appear that in imitation of her fullness and loveliness no heartbreaking pains have been taken, is to treat her with an irreverence to grieve over.' Mere dexterity could not give lasting pleasure. Ugly smears were unacceptable.

To provoke a response, he suggested that Gainsborough knew nothing of human form, and whereas Reynolds's drawing was not good, Gainsborough's was bad. He strongly disputed recent opinion that a portrait need have no interest except the figure and that there should be no background. The effect might work in the incongruous surroundings of an exhibition, but the picture would be dull to live with. Certainly the face should be more interesting than background detail. Raphael's portrait of Julius II seated on his papal throne was to Watts '*the* finished portrait in the world', and no elaboration in its background could distract attention from the portrait itself. A portrait was the most truly historical picture, 'The longer one looks at it the more it demands attention. A superficial picture is like a superficial character – it may do for an acquaintance but not for a friend.'[59]

By contrast, Gilbert felt a growing respect for him. Just one more sitting was needed, but he longed to begin the bust again: 'How I wish I had known Mr Watts when I first began as I do now,' he said. 'These hours have been priceless, they take me out of myself. I gain so much in every way.' Leighton ran his hand over the planes of the cheekbone, to the planes of the coat. He and Watts congratulated each other on the demise of the bathing-towel from the modern portrait bust.[60] Leighton had appointed Gilbert head of the sculpture section of the First Congress of the National Association for the Advancement of Art and Its Application to Industry (NAAAAI), set up under his presidency to co-ordinate the avant-garde factions of the craft revival with the fine arts. Meetings were to be held in principal manufacturing towns. Gilbert asked Watts to produce a paper for the first meeting in Liverpool. Other papers were to be delivered by Walter Crane, president of the applied arts section and, as Master of the Art-Workers' Guild, of its exhibiting arm, the Arts and Crafts Exhibition Society (Watts attended the private view of its first exhibition at the New Gallery on 29 September),[61] – Alma-Tadema, who headed the painting section and Aitchison, architecture. Before leaving for Brighton, Watts sent a long letter of support, which Gilbert was about to read on his behalf on 5 December 1888.[62] As Gilbert rose to read the letter, he broke out into an impassioned defence of Tom Lee, whose naked allegorical figures in marble frieze panels of *The Progress of Justice* at Liverpool's grand Greek Revival building, St George's Hall, was attacked at the Congress. He would have had the whole-hearted support of Watts, whose paper, the sculptor reported, had evoked keen interest. Gilbert promised some 'exquisite modelling wax' on his return to town.[63]

As *The Court of Death* was set up on a platform at his bright, spacious, Brighton studio, a former picture gallery at 31 Sussex Square, Watts despaired at the amount of work ahead and – his constant fear – that he might die before he had completed it. Within an hour his resolve returned. He took up *Ariadne* of 1860 (fig. 159) and transformed Miss Ford's white and golden robes into rippling folds. Anny Ritchie was staying with the Wattses when they learned in December of the sale of *Ganymede*, the Trojan cup-bearer modelled by the wide-eyed mischief, Demetrius Zambaco. Henry Holiday joined them for lunch that day and talked of the tableaux he was arranging to raise funds for a large crèche run by Emily Hughes for the children of serving girls and laundresses, but now closed with debts of £300. Since Princess Louise was no longer able to open the bazaar, affluent Brighton society and dignitaries had lost interest, which dis-

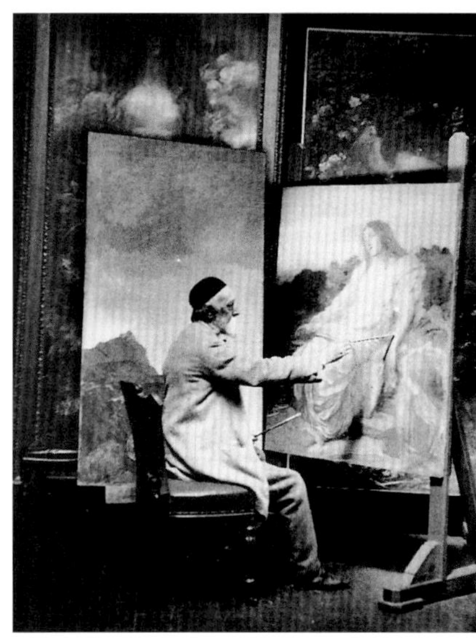

159   Watts painting *Ariadne* at Brighton, 1888–89 (Watts Gallery).

gusted Watts. He invited Mrs Hughes to tea, said quietly that he would like to help her reopen the crèche and slipped her a cheque for £300. Expecting £5 or £10, she wept with relief, 'I can open it next week.'[64]

Burne-Jones was buying a house in Rottingdean and promised to 'potter across like an ancient thing as I am and have talks with you both'. Leighton sent spirited letters about next year's Paris exhibition, and looked forward to seeing Watts's new work – 'the great sign and test that you are seeing good times' – and to having *The Court of Death* at the Academy. 'Don't let me catch you talking of *resigning*!!' He gossiped sadly about Val Prinsep's failures, more worrying now that he had a young family. 'Val has not begun *his* new *Eve* yet. Well may you ask . . . *Eve*?!' wrote Leighton, for Watts was developing two of his *Eve* series in Brighton.[65]

At his special request, Mary bought him a seal. They had chosen a Dutch seal; and on Christmas Eve, he composed motto for it – 'The Utmost for the Highest' – and for its engraved decoration Mary designed a pattern of a star reflected in a pool, inspired by their current reading, the *Autobiography of Benvenuto Cellini* (the new translation by John Addington Symonds). 'Remember the daisy' was one of his favourite sayings at home, meaning that even the smallest action must be in keeping with a great aspiration. Mary's exuberant, highly symbolic Art Nouveau design with a Tree of Life entwined with ears of corn, a heart and a Celtic triskele serving as a star, 'the highest of small things', was therefore centred by a daisy.[66]

As her husband painted over a gilded ground to recreate the glorious *Sunset on the Alps* (pl. XXXVIII) at La Roche-sur-Foron, he momentarily captured the diamond glitter, height and weight of the mighty peaks; but he worked on and she watched sadly as the grey English winter seemed to dim his impression. 'Brighton killed Alps', she noted starkly in her diary.[67] None the less, his composition of orange-red masses relates to landscapes by the modernist French painter Paul Gauguin and the Nabis movement. On the other hand, he was giving greater definition to *Love and Life* in preparation for Paris. Even if the weather in Brighton was bad, the light was much better than in London, where Leighton faced 'these hideous fogs – they are *constant* and make work for me nearly impossible. Happy you that you can *see* to work!'[68]

'Thoughts on Our Art of Today', published in the *Magazine of Art* in January 1889, was received too well. Shocked that nobody refuted his trenchant criticism of Gainsborough, Watts advised Spielmann to request papers from Armitage, Gilbert, Thornycroft, Val Prinsep and Richmond, who was finishing a statue in the iron studio.[69] Asked to name the finest painters of the day (for a miniature fan), he listed in order of merit Burne-Jones, Hunt, Millais Leighton, Orchardson, Alma-Tadema, Hook, Herkomer and Richmond.[70]

The columnar *Eve* emitting light and soon to be renamed *She Shall Be Called Woman* (pl. XIX) was not an apotheosis of womanhood but of feminine qualities, Watts explained to Mary. He therefore highlighted the heart and breast, the source of tenderness, goodness and love. As he added touches of ultramarine blue, he intensified the sense of teeming life and freshness of the first morning. Virginia Somers sat in front of the picture for a time and exclaimed, 'It is the greatest thing he has ever done!' In his quest to do even better, to Mary's frustration, he spoiled it. Only last summer she had seemed to worship his work, almost without question –

'She is a Goose I am afraid when the question is of my work,' he had written to Hichens.[71] Now, after two years of marriage, watching Watts achieve the perfect point, then overworking a picture, she longed to utter the shepherd's warning, but recognized, with frustration, that, 'The painter knows what he knows . . . And if he saw fit to go further, not twenty shepherds nor a whole Academy of artists would deter him.' *Sunset on the Alps* lost qualities he would never retrieve.

Heightening the visionary effect of the newly created Eve, whose outspread hands and upper body appear close to heaven, to direct attention to her torso, he wreathed the lower limbs in more and more cloud and fluttering birds, and concealed – or as Mary put it, 'deliberately sacrificed' their Phidian form. Only the foot is firmly planted.[72] As he lay in semi-darkness on 11 February, he spoke of a vivid dream, so vivid that she recorded it verbatim. The dream encapsulates his life and ambitious sense of purpose on his solitary path to raise the touchstone of art.

> I was climbing up the side of a steep mountain, and I knew that it was the mountain of Fame – Fame in the greatest sense of the word, all that is worthy of the best endeavour. It was so steep that I had to cut each step that I took, and I knew as I went on that the path I made closed up behind me, so that no one could follow where I went; and I could not find the trace of any one who had gone before me. From the foot of the hill I had seen quite clearly the paths made by other men – some rough, some smooth; but when I began myself to climb, I could not see them at all; they were all hidden under tangles of thorns and briars . . . I was suddenly lifted up . . . to . . . the very top of the mountain, so that I could see the whole distance laid out before me. It was more ethereal than I can describe, of a beauty that can only be imagined in a dream. I was looking over a sort of parapet, and there were pillars of some building beside me; and, though I heard voices, I could not lose one moment of the beauty by turning to see who spoke; but I was aware somehow that those people had reached the summit, and were to remain there for ever, themselves a part of that great beauty, giving out to it from their own being. And I said to myself, this is the sort of fame for which I have given my life.

The vision, infused with elements from *Love and Life* and *She Shall Be Called Woman* and the tangled briars of Ned Burne-Jones, had been even more beautiful than their first day looking out from the Parthenon; and he wished to keep it in mind. It was his most positive self-assessment so far.[73]

The moment his health returned, Watts was scrambling up and down scaffolding at work on *The Court of Death*. 'Is it not a lark!' he exclaimed, as he scrubbed red pigment over *The Messenger*.[74] While laid up, he had composed 'More Thoughts on our Art of To-day', partly because no one had challenged his 'arrogant' criticism of Gainsborough. A photograph of the Gilbert bust accompanied the paper;[75] the sculptor had not yet cast it in bronze, for he was waiting to make final retouches, to perfect his tribute to the master. Gilbert would not accept payment for the work; the honour of spending time with the Wattses and the lessons he had learned were more than sufficient recompense; and on 7 April, he asked Mary to accept the bust as his tribute to 'a master whose works impressed me as a boy and fill me with woe and admiration now that I am the manly representation of that boy, who never dreamt of the honour in store for him.'[76] The plaster was exhibited at the Academy, where Watts's sole contribution was the mischievous Cupid in *The Habit Doesn't Make the Monk*.[77] He had promised extra pictures to the New Gallery because Burne-Jones, preoccupied with the Briar Rose series, was unable to exhibit. John Singer Sargent had adopted Burne-Jones's suggestions for the colour of his portrait of *Ellen Terry as Lady Macbeth*, her hair falling in thick magenta plaits as she stands full length in a shimmering turquoise dress designed by Alice Comyns Carr, the wife of the director of the New Gallery, where the picture aroused a sensation.[78]

George Bernard Shaw, as art critic for the society journal the *World*, noted that 'Mr Watts this year distances every competitor'. His contributions spanned half a century: two mystical seascapes, *The Sea Ghost* and *Off Corsica*; and, as a vivid antithesis, the *amorino* kneeling over the waves in *Good Luck to your Fishing* – 'the vigour of the artist's fancy at its best'; the bronze *Clytie* – (the artist as sculptor was seen in Philip Burne-Jones's painting of Watts at work on *Physical Energy*); the ravished *Wife of Pluto* suffering from 'the dis-ease of wealth'; the granite peaks of *Sant' Agnese, Mentone*; and *The Wounded Heron* (which Watts had sold at the Academy in 1837 and purchased back from a Newcastle dealer for five pounds the previous autumn).[79] 'This reminds us that Mr Watts is no longer young, but his hand has not lost its cunning', declared the *Daily News*. Finally, *Fata Morgana*, the Leicester nude now heightened with 'sumptuous fleshtints', created a furore, though Watts, stung by snipes that it was an old painting and 'he can't do any thing like it now', urged Spielmann to stress that his new work – according to subject – was 'much more colourful than my former things'.[80] The Duke of Westminster had fallen in love with *Sant' Agnese* and the fishing cherub, but both recalled memories too happy for Watts to relinquish them.[81]

The Paris Exposition Universelle, celebrating the centennial of the French Revolution, opened on 5 May 1889. Outside the galleries in the Champs de Mars Gustave Eiffel's tower of wrought-iron latticework rose 1,000 feet high, the tallest structure in the world. 'I have taken no end of trouble to get my friends properly represented in Paris, sometimes with success and sometimes not, but where I have succeeded I don't grudge the labour I spend', Leighton wrote to Mary. 'It is my duty to do all I can to get England's credit upheld in each case.' He had liaised with four owners and South Kensington for Watts's eight pictures for the Paris exhibition and was disappointed that Eve was not among them, but they were awarded a first-class medal, stamped with the Eiffel Tower. 'Mr Burne-Jones with *King Cophetua and the Beggar Maid* and Mr Watts with his *Mammon, Hope, Three Graces* and other works, lift the tone of the exhibition to a very high level', reported the *Magazine of Art*.[82]

On 5 May, the prime minister announced at the Royal Academy banquet, that an anonymous donor (W. H. Alexander) had offered to finance the building of a National Portrait Gallery. Watts responded enthusiastically. The news surprised even Viscount Hardinge, chairman of the gallery's trustees, 'Salisbury took our breath away.' Within three weeks the ecclesiastical architect Ewan Christian was commissioned to design the gallery in St Martin's Place, adjacent to, but separate from, the National Gallery. A permanent home for the Hall of Fame was assured.[83]

Surprisingly, two days later, Leighton approached Watts for Mary's signature to an appeal against the extension of parliamentary suffrage to women, to be published in the *Nineteenth Century*. His sister, Alexandra Orr, was gathering signatures. Watts had long promoted careers for women. He and Mary, a keen suffragist, saw women's suffrage as a natural development of educational reform. Leighton accepted her refusal with characteristic grace, pointing out that 'an attitude which should seem hostile to the highest and fullest development of the intelligence of women is one which would not be endorsed by the supporters of the movement'. Many of the 104 signatories, wives of distinguished artists, aristocrats and men of letters, would later campaign for the suffrage, and, as Mary suspected, 'Sir Frederic himself was but a lukewarm opponent.'[84]

An exhibition of the works of Claude Monet opened at the Goupil Galleries. Watts, never an advocate of Impressionism, which he considered small-scale work – though he admired the French artists' conviction – advised the brother of an aspiring artist that he should attempt the style only as an experiment: 'No impressionist picture can be truer or freer in effect than Turner's best pictures many of which are elaborate. I must earnestly warn your brother against *beginning* by being impressionist. He may be one at the end of his career . . . but great work in poetry, in literature and in art is always *full* work.'[85]

He returned home in fighting form, determined to ask a colleague to design a statue to Mammon for Hyde Park, before which worshippers could be honest enough to bow. 'You make the statue', suggested Briton Rivière. 'You will find worshippers!'[86] Watts, very taken with Harry Bates's wax model for Lord Wemyss's statue *Hounds in Leash*,[87] was more than occupied with *Physical Energy*. To complete the St Paul's cathedral spandrels, he prepared wax models and sketches of *St Mark* and *St Luke* for W. E. F. Britten, who had them executed in mosaic by Salviati; the *St John* would be erected unaltered in 1890, a quarter of a century after Watts's original design.[88] Having advanced *Eve Tempted* and a bigger *Eve Repentant* (laid in by Britten), Watts was enlarging the radiant *Genius of Progress*.[89]

# 19 Limnerslease

THE NEW ARTS AND CRAFTS GUILDS looked to Watts to support their work and to endorse them in print. After C. R. Ashbee, the designer and founder of the Guild and School of Handicraft at Toynbee Hall, brought his boys to Little Holland House on 21 September 1889 to discuss a commission, Mary wrote, 'Little Holland House would be very incomplete till it has some specimen of the work of the Handicraftsmens Guild to show.'[1]

'The National Position of Art', a paper Watts was writing for the Edinburgh NAAAAI Congress, was all but complete when Arthur Heygate Mackmurdo, who had founded the Century Guild, brought his associate Selwyn Image to the studio. At Mackmurdo's request, the paper was printed in *Hobby Horse*, the literary journal that reflected the guild's organic aesthetic, its antipathy to mechanical symmetry and its intent to raise the quality and stature of design.

'In the haste to be rich', Watts pointed out, 'the very man, perhaps, who finds his most refreshing leisure within the walls of his private picture gallery is in his daily work assisting to extinguish the life of this very art ... turning his workmen into machines, and pouring hideous and badly made articles out upon the world, every one of which weighs in the scale against the chances of a national life for art, as it does against national reputation.' Only the wealthy could afford beautiful Arts and Crafts furniture. 'Is it asking you too much to give this cheer to the cottage, where it is of really far greater importance?' Not all aspiring artists could expect to create great painting or sculpture, but they could apply their gifts to creating valued, if not luxurious, decorative art.[2] He drew attention to the growing Home Arts movement, which was running 450 classes in England, Scotland and Ireland, with its headquarters and annual exhibition at the Albert Hall in London: 'In the activity of such work we have all that is most needed to revivify what was naturally artistic in the British Islands ... an art which shall truly express and illustrate by its originality all that is peculiar and best in our modern life.' Rivière reported that the 'eminently practical' paper had been a 'really useful' contribution to the association.[3] Watts became increasingly bound up with both the Home Arts and the South London project – for the new gallery he signed an appeal for £4,000 and contributed generously himself.[4]

Signor and Mary had a cast taken of their intertwined left hands (fig. 160). Hers is the firm neat hand of a craftsman – at the time she was modelling *Death Crowning Innocence* in terracotta. There is no hint of the

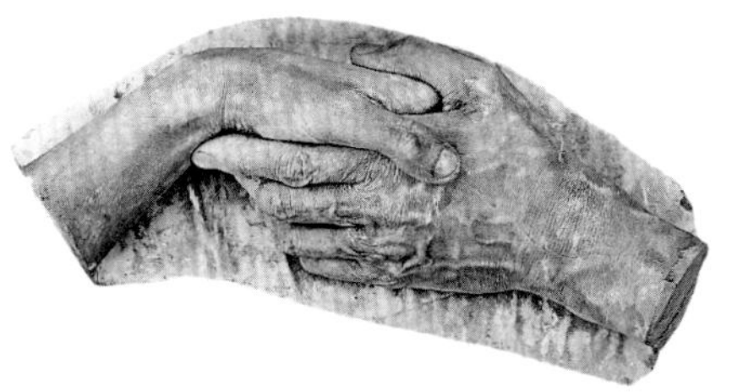

160 Plaster cast taken from the hands of Signor and Mary, 1889 (Watts Gallery).

dainty manicure befitting a lady of society in the thumb that curves over his fine, wrinkled, strong hand. His first finger stretches into the curve of her wrist, while his thumb rests upon her knuckles. Watts's hands, often sensitive and nervous, were to remain steady and strong. His sculpture assistant Thompson marvelled at the master's agile step. 'He is just as sharp as a pin, madam!'[5]

They spent the winter at the Hichens' home near Compton in Surrey. On a wooded plateau sheltered by the Hog's Back, the setting at Monkshatch was perfect. On 26 November an old grey horse came to stand for *Patient Life of Unrequited Toil*. The artist set up his easel beneath the chalk cliff (fig. 161), an old quarry, which reflected the sun's rays 'at compound interest'. He would walk along turf paths into the pit and gaze up at the vents and seams in its great white walls, at the splendour of the dark velvet yews lining the cliff edge. Watts steeped his mind in winter woodland, studying the growth structure in the hedgerows and copses, 'I have been nearly all the morning painting in three bramble leaves. With his keen eye and still steady hand, he needed little encouragement to play billiards in the evenings.[6]

Lady Holland had died on 20 September 1889. Watts had sent flowers in memory of '46 years of friendship'.[7] Then, to compound their sadness, they heard of Robert Browning's death in December from a heart attack in Venice. The loss of two old friends was a shock.[8] That summer, the poet had so enjoyed Emma's curry that he had asked to be invited back to Little Holland House. Lingering in the iron-house studio, he had said, 'I am looking at the little head that has done all this work.' His affectionate comment had touched a nerve. Watts had been self-conscious about the size of his head until he discovered that his sitter, Sir John Lubbock, the Liberal MP, scientist and banker, was similarly afflicted. Browning had pointed out that many poets had small heads, that Byron's brain weighed only seven pounds. He would miss the poet's 'vitality & vivacity' and signed his memorial for Hallam Tennyson. The Laureate sent his latest volume. 'Crossing the Bar' Watts thought especially lovely: 'I must also send my contribution to the public thanks for the accumulation of the debt England & English speaking peoples owe you.'[9]

*Love and Life* was despatched to Montreal. The South Kensington Museum, irritated at having once again been used as temporary agents for a bequest intended for another institution – the cramped National Gallery – circulated a flurry of memos: 'It is very difficult to deal with a man like this who has a very great idea of his own genius and in whom a *great many* of the public also believe.' The director Sir Philip Cunliffe-Owen was urged to see 'the Great man' and point out that 'we can't be always changing and leaving blank spaces on the walls . . . even for these inestimable works . . . that we are not merely carriers of pictures. In fact can't take any pictures unless they are to be left for a time.' *Love and Life* returned to South Kensington without further note. Watts, oblivious, was still in Compton.[10]

The artists longed for studios in the Surrey hills, where the tall Scots firs reminded Mary of her highland home, and Signor loved to listen to the wind blowing through their bows. A bolt-hole away from the London fogs and the prying eyes of Mrs Barrington would bolster his health. On 19 February 1890 Hichens breezed in from a walk to say he had found the ideal site. He led the Wattses down the hill and within fifteen minutes they were

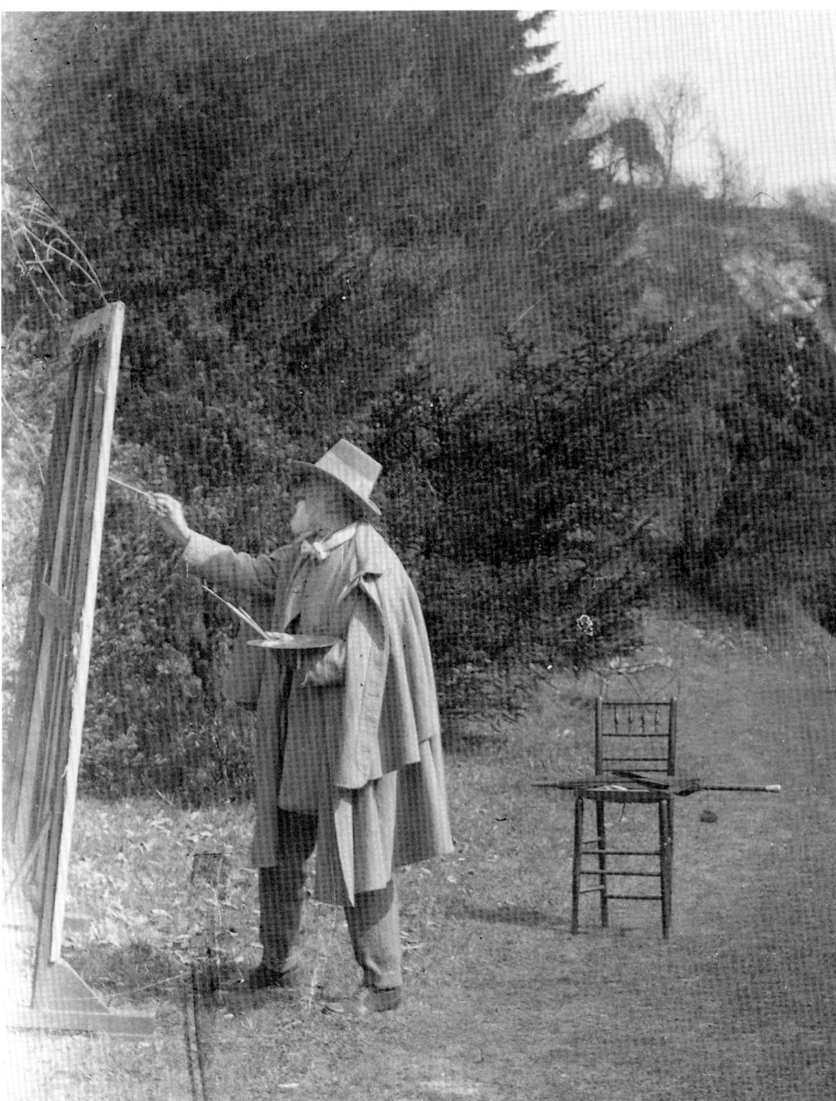



standing on a wooded knoll, above the Pilgrims' Way. 'Too delightful for accomplishment', sighed Signor. Almost, for William More Molyneux of Loseley, who owned the manor of Compton, felt duty bound to preserve rather than sell the land, but he agreed. Hichens, a trustee and manager of the Stock Exchange, insisted on paying for the site and house, to save 'the beloved little man' financial anxiety; and on 24 March he agreed terms with More Molyneux, at £200 an acre for the eight-acre plot. Six days later, the couple camped out on a rug under the trees, gazing up into the branches.[11]

Concerned that *Patient Life of Unrequited Toil* looked 'like a bottle of green pickles', he told Rivière, one of the Academy hangers, that his work should be assessed as though he were an outsider, and rejected if it risked disgracing the institution. However, Watts accepted Leighton's diplomatic criticism that it was not his typical subject, which proved he was not stuck

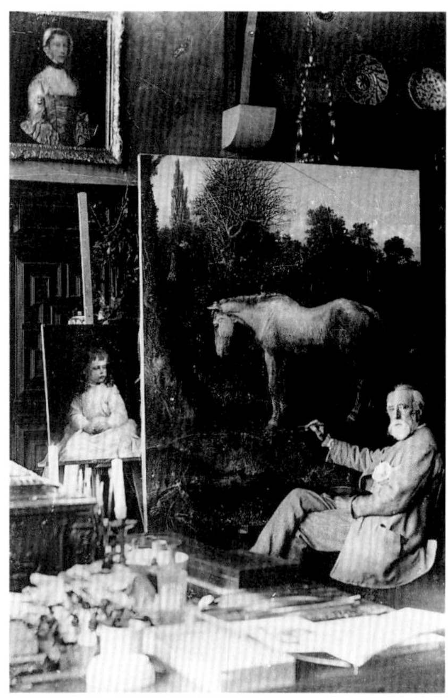

162    At Monkshatch, painting *The Life of Unrequited Toil*, with Hester's portrait on the easel, *c.*1889–90.

in a rut, and he sent it to the Academy with a portrait of Mary's three-year-old niece Hester Fraser Tytler (fig. 162).[12]

'Velazquez holds me', said Watts and travelled up to London in March to see *Venus and Cupid* on view at the Academy. Irresistibly drawn to an exhibition of armour at the New Gallery, he also went to Gilbert's studio and heard Joachim perform.[13] Leighton, struggling to complete his own pictures – notably, the standing nude *The Bath of Psyche*[14] – was delighted to see Signor 'in *splendid* form and . . . no worse for his junket'. He, too, needed to recharge his energies and, writing from the bracing sea air of Norfolk, relayed the selection committee's views on the picture of the old horse. Despite their disappointment that Watts had not sent works revealing 'the higher qualities of your artistic personality', which indicated that his ambition to raise to the level of music and literature had been achieved, the Academy none the less desired to hang his pictures. Their criticisms were trifling – Hester's highland bloom was too red and a yellow on the old horse's foreleg 'a little *out of key*'. Leighton had been especially struck by the woodland setting, which showed 'that you have been able to work *long & engagingly*; the result of that improvement in your thoughts in which we all so truly rejoice'.[15]

Christie's sale in March of a dozen imaginative subjects from the Manchester estates of Sam Barlow and William Carver attracted keen bidding. *Una and the Red Cross Knight* sold for over £1,700. Earl Pembroke paid £1,522 10s for the large *Rider on the White Horse* and £483 for *Hope. Love and Death* went to Agnew for £1,386. A Cheshire collector Charles Galloway snapped up the smaller *Rider on the Red Horse* for £236 5s, *The Dove which Returned Not Again* for £493 10s and *Rain Passing Away* for just £126. James Smith, a Liverpool wine merchant, bought the other two riders and the peeping Cupid 'A Villain, I'll be Bound'.[16] At last people were interested in intellectual art. Many letters encouraged him to believe that 'I have rightly estimated the best functions of the art I believe so much in'. Though he regretted the break-up of the Apocalyptic series, Smith would eventually complete the set, and in April paid 500 guineas for *The Wife of Pluto*.[17]

Hallam Tennyson wrote to say that Dr Henry Montagu Butler, Master of Trinity College, Cambridge, wished for a portrait of his father. A subscription committee had been formed, but the Poet Laureate would sit only to Signor. Would he come to Farringford? Watts agreed to honour his old friend. There would be no fee.[18] Madeline Wyndham asked him to sketch her second son, Guy, before he left with the 16th Lancers for India. The dashing young captain rode over to Monkshatch from Aldershot for two sittings in April;[19] and the architect Ernest George came down on 18 March to discuss the new house. He ran a versatile London practice in partnership with Harold Peto. Essentially an artist, George exhibited at the Academy. His poetic perspective drawings were executed in soft sepia pen with wash, and, unlike Norman Shaw's ruled black pen and ink perspectives, depicted natural textures; and the buildings angled from a low viewpoint, (the 'worm's eye view' emulated by his recent student Edwin Lutyens), appeared to be rooted in the countryside. His drawing of 'A House with Studio near Guildford' for the Wattses was published in *The Architect* of 16 May 1890 (fig. 163). In keeping with Ruskinian Arts and Crafts tradition, the lower section was to be built of local Bargate

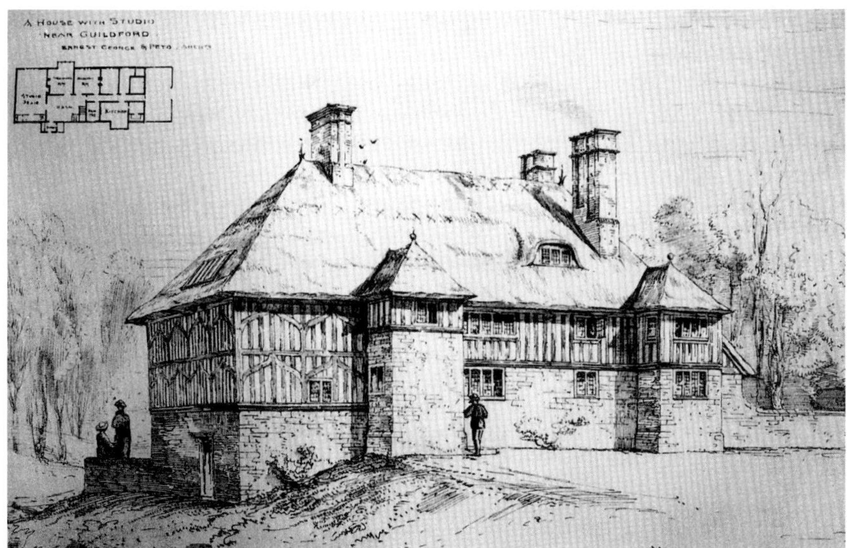

163 Ernest George's design for Limnerslease (*The Architect*, 16 May 1890).

stone, the upper storey of oak quartering, with a hipped roof of heather thatch; the galleries studio and canvas room beneath emerged from the hillside.[20]

On his return to Kensington for exhibition varnishing days, Watts received a visit from the Russian revolutionary officer Stepniak ('Son of the Steppe'), Sergei Mikhailovich Kravchinsky. An apostle of freedom with a violent past – he was said to have assassinated the St Petersburg police chief General Mesentzeff – Stepniak now lived in London, recruiting intellectuals to the Russian liberation movement. He published studies on the rise of despotism in *Russia under the Tsars* and a crusading novel, *The Career of a Nihilist*. Had illness not prevented him, he would have brought his revolutionary Nihilist colleague Prince Peter Kropotkin to Little Holland House.[21]

Watts asked Spielmann not to give advance notice of his exhibition pictures, especially the old horse: 'Being of a subject & character unusual to me I wish it [to] have its natural freshness.' Unable to work on more serious subjects away from home, he had completed two old subjects for the New Gallery: *Ariadne* and *Little Red Riding Hood*. For the popular *Little Red Riding Hood*, outlined at Freshwater from Julia Cameron's model Lizzie Keown, he recruited the Monkshatch gardener's daughter to pose for him over the winter, and painted her hugging her basket and spray of poppies, a red hood lavishly arranged over her blonde hair and country smock. Her soulful eyes express mild alarm as she stands against an ivy-covered tree, the Pilgrims Way curling around the fields into the distant hills. Watts felt that his exhibition pictures looked ineffective; and when the New Gallery asked for a price, to Mary's frustration, he dithered. The fee would have helped fund the new house. Privately depressed, he recommended that Spielmann review instead Burne-Jones's *Briar Rose* series at Agnew's and his 'wonderful' tapestry at Morris & Co in Oxford Street; he was amused by the critic's verdict of his *Patient Life of Unrewarded Toil* as 'the work of a barbarian, but a very learned barbarian'.[22]

His physician Dr Thomas Clifford Allbutt wondered how Watts maintained his great imaginative thoughts so constantly, how he cared for larger issues, brushing aside pettinesses: 'The great difference between him & many others is his sense of proportion – the *grand outline* is always kept even in his simplest thoughts.' In order to assess a point of view or problem, whether artistic or political – 'to sift out the dross of convention' – Watts would envisage the issue in a historical context centuries before, or in the future.[23] As Allbutt observed, the artist lived habitually in 'one vision, future, present, past . . . His familiar walk with the transcendental in his own language gave him a kinship or growth with it such that he could suggest much of it even in plain English. If now and then he found the need of rhetoric in his pictures it never appeared in his conversation, which . . . had the spontaneity of childhood.'[24]

Hallam Tennyson met Signor and Mary off the Yarmouth steamer on 16 May and drove them to The Briary. Blanche was away in the Riviera; and according to the caretaker George Andrews, Lord Tennyson had come several times to check that the house was warm enough. At Farringford the next morning, Emily Tennyson greeted them both tenderly, for Mary too, had known the family since she was eighteen; and Tennyson had held her trembling hand while he read her *Maud*, for she was shyer than Nelly four years before. Now the poet joined the artists: 'There was talk of everything but painting, and later we all, save the dear lady on her sofa, walked back to The Briary through the sweet old-fashioned garden, gay with spring flowers. Signor and Lord Tennyson walked in front, falling naturally into their old habits, recalling old days and stories that made them laugh.' But the poet despaired at a letter from a stranger, 'I wish I had never written a line in my life.' Watts remonstrated, 'Ah, now you would not have made your Arthur speak like that!', at which Lord Tennyson put out his hand. 'Well, there, look at my hand; it is the gout!'[25]

By the second evening, Watts had still not mentioned the Trinity portrait. Tennyson, reneging on his promise to let the artist broach the subject, demanded outright, 'When are you going to paint me?' The following morning, every symptom of anxiety that a portrait commission could provoke struck Watts. He was depressed for hours. Mary, fearing the day might be wrecked, wrote to Hallam and asked him to come in the carriage that the Tennysons were sending to collect the artist; she then had his canvas and paints hidden inside before he appeared. Hallam kept Watts talking during the brief ride to Farringford, and he was soon happily at work in the library, painting the poet for Trinity (pl. XXXV), not in a Cambridge gown, but in the crimson and scarlet robes of its rival, as his son explained to the Master: 'My Father once reached Weybridge on his way to receive the LL.D but became ill & could not go further. I think that Cambridge . . . ought to have passed a *special* grace granting him the LL.D. However he is in consequence of their red tape painted as an Oxford man for Cambridge'. Hallam was so impressed by the portrait that he asked Watts to paint another, assuming it to be for the nation.[26]

As the two portraits of Tennyson progressed – for the second, in the same pose, he was dressed in baronial ermine – Mary watched poet's natural grandeur developing on canvas. 'That is what a portrait painter should do, not by accentuating or emphasizing, but rather keeping in mind those lines which are the noblest', Watts told her. 'What I try for is the half-unconscious insistence upon the nobilities of the subject.' Hallam sat between the artist and sitter, reading aloud. Tennyson spoke of the way Edward Lear set his poems to music – 'he put a sort of diaphanous veil over them, that was all' – and that he himself did not, as a rule, take long to write a poem. The entire construction and most words were in his head before he wrote a line. 'Tears, idle tears, I know not what they mean,' which Watts thought 'consummate', had flown naturally from his mind, not unlike his own *Hope*.[27]

Gerry Liddell joined them at The Briary for the last week and set out with Mary to meet the artist, sitter and his son after their morning's work at Farringford. As they climbed towards a glade, the three men came into view; Mary's painterly record brings the scene to life:

> Down the great aisle of elms they came, a white Russian deer-hound flashing like silver through the sun or shade, and the central figure the poet, a note of black in the midst of the vivid green, grand in the folds of his ample cloak and his face looming grandly from the shadow of the giant hat. 'Monumental' Signor would have called him. The slight stoop and the heavier step of age made the youthful figure of the son look all the more . . . his father's vigorous staff and prop . . . the delicate grey figure of our beloved painter on the other side, the grey hat crowning silver hair, a grey cloak taking pleasant folds while he stepped like a boy, light and neat in every movement.

The poet smiled and playfully held out the crook of his walking stick for the women to shake hands with. Their talk became sombre, more contemplative, their thoughts turning 'to a life beyond this life'. Their last few hours together were spent in Tennyson's study, listening to his poetry. He stood under his portico, waving farewell until the carriage was out of sight; and Watts returned to London with one portrait complete, the other well advanced. It had been a special reunion, their elevated discussions more enriching than any social exchange. 'Signor & I ask each other often if we have ever had a happier time together I do not think even Egypt or Greece can outdo it', wrote Mary.

A month later the Master of Trinity called to inspect 'this most munificent gift',[28] in the autumn the Society of British Artists would borrow the prestigious portrait of Tennyson in ermine for their gallery in Suffolk Street, and the following year the *Daily Graphic* printed a cartoon of Watts painting Tennyson as 'The Choice and Master Spirits of this Age' (fig. 164). Watts earmarked this for the nation because the robe marked 'a distinctly historical event', the first elevation to the peerage for literature.[29] Meanwhile, in June 1890, he lent four pictures for exhibition with Sir Horace Davey's *Ariadne in Naxos* at the Corporation of London Art Gallery, and on 20 June dashed down to Compton, where building started, and a drive was cut through to the new house.[30]

George Howard, now the Earl of Carlisle, and Sir Frederic Burton – respectively, trustee and director of the National Gallery – came to discuss the search for a new National Gallery of British Art, a potential home for Watts's Symbolist works. The sugar magnate Henry Tate had offered his collection of modern pictures to the National Gallery in 1889 on condition that the sixty pictures were displayed together in Trafalgar Square. The controversial proposal, rejected on grounds of space, had led *The Times* to suggest in March 1890 the creation of a 'great British gallery' . . . 'that shall do for English art what the Luxembourg does for the French'. Rooms at

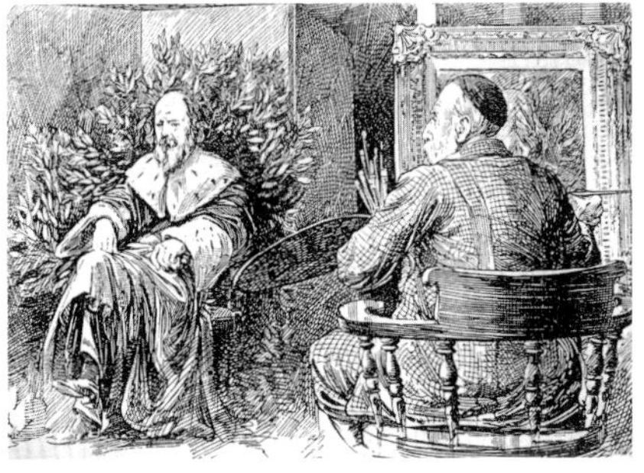

164   Tennyson sitting to Watts (cartoon by Reginald Cleaver in the *Daily Graphic*, 8 September 1891).

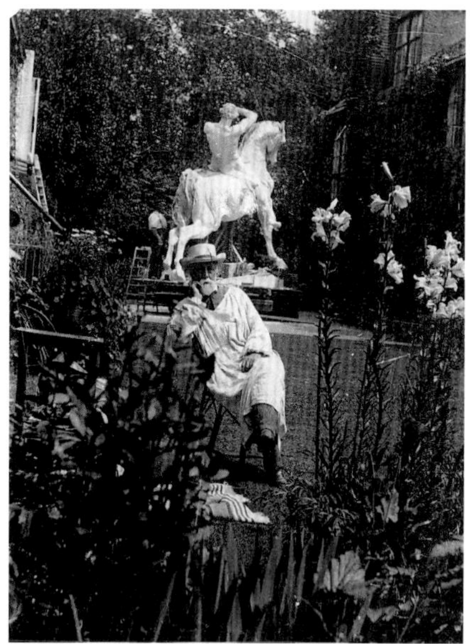

165   Watts in front of *Physical Energy* in the garden at Little Holland House, Melbury Road, 1890.

Kensington Palace and the South Kensington Museum were proposed, but these, Agnew pointed out in a letter to *The Times* in July, could only be makeshift.[31]

'Anyone who sheds a gleam of art on the wintry face of toiling poverty is a benefactor', declared the actor Henry Irving, in an appeal for the South London Fine Art Gallery. Calling for loans of works of art, he said: 'An admirable example has been set by Mr Watts, and Mr Burne-Jones, and Sir Frederick Leighton – [applause] – whose pictures have carried visions of ideal form and colour into many a soul which never before had any perception of the beautiful . . . I only wish it were possible to have a free theatre, for all art ranks amongst the missionary influences of civilization.' Georgie Burne-Jones and Mary had now joined their husbands on the Council; and both the Wattses were appointed vice-presidents of the Healthy and Artistic Dress Union, founded on 2 July.[32]

'I am to be Stanley's wife', wrote Dolly Tennant. Watts's portrait illustrated press notices announcing her marriage to the explorer Henry Morton Stanley. The artist, unable to go to the ceremony in Westminster Abbey on the 12 July, surprised friends by attending the reception at Richmond Terrace.[33] A couple of days later, he was photographed in a jaunty sun hat and sculpture smock in front of *Physical Energy* in the garden of Little Holland House (fig. 165). The horse and rider clearly dominates the view from the south-facing windows of the house. Thompson stands dwarfed beside the great white statue, the taller glass studio doors on the left are propped open by a ladder, and the sculptor himself is seated centre foreground, with Annunciation lilies in full bloom towering above his head on one side and, on the other, an empty chair not quite concealed by lush foliage, suggesting that the photographer was Mary. He worked vigorously at the statue that summer.

Creating the embodiment of health, power and strength had come naturally; his concern now, to perfect each part without losing the impact, was more difficult. As he raised the blind to inspect it from her dressing room window, he wondered if would ever achieve the figure, not as an individual, but what he called 'a type', representing five thousand years of activity and achievements. 'I should like to write the roll of great names on the pedestal: Genghis Khan, Timon the Tartar, Attila, and Mahomet.' Lady Davey and other friends had offered to subscribe to the casting of *Physical Energy*. Again he had declined: 'It may be a failure now for all I know, or never finished.' *Physical Energy* was in itself his mental and physical lifeline. Having to work on it in the garden kept him outside continuously in daylight hours. 'I must live in the light', Watts would say. The early start made him feel better, 'as if my mind was clearer, and as if I knew something more. Very often in the morning the perception seems to come to me that all this that I am doing is too small for me, – and then it goes!' After a sixteen-hour day – thirteen at work – he wondered why he was tired by eight o'clock.[34] On 15 July, Gilbert delivered his bust (fig. 166) as a 'commemoration of a time in your life, which will ever be memorable'.[35]

Hallam Tennyson requested a chalk drawing of the Trinity portrait for a popular edition of his father's poems to be published by Macmillan in October 1890. Were the portrait itself to be reproduced, he pointed out, Watts would lose the copyright. Increasingly now, Hallam took advantage.

He demanded the drawing as a gift to Lady Tennyson, and of course, the artist agreed, as a contribution to 'the debt the nation & the age owes to your Father . . . also to make a constant effort to bear in mind the best epitaph I know, "What I spent, I had, What I saved I lost, What I gave I have".' He sent belated birthday greetings to the poet, Mary having recorded her own message by phonograph.[36] 'My dear Signor & Signor's Mary, I stand amazed at my Hallam's boldness', wrote Lady Tennyson from their Surrey home, Aldworth, near Haslemere. 'I had no idea of the immense favour he had asked and I know not how to express my gratitude and his for the truly gracious manner of its granting. As to what such a possession will be to us it is fain to attempt to say – an heirloom precious indeed for all generations of our race.' Macmillan had requested the sketch. 'You are the only person in the world who could make it so Hallam. He and I hope you will forgive him.'[37] Aldworth was less than a dozen miles from Compton, where Watts, longing now for the new house, placed a sixpence and a stone in the wall near the larder window on 21 August.[38]

A portrait of Lady Katherine Thynne, which he was inspired to paint after she accompanied her mother, the Marchioness of Bath, to Little Holland House, was well under way by September,[39] when Horsfall again consulted Watts about the types of pictures he should show at his new Manchester Art Museum at Ancoats Hall, on the fringe of the slums of Manchester. Horsfall's enterprise, intended to educate the poor 'especially in great manufacturing towns', was on Watts's mind. He wrote at length, recommending that the children and workers be taught to perceive the beauty in objects, and when they recognized 'the infinite grace & charm in a tangle of tendrils, & the finish & beauty to be found in the apparent confusion in a bundle of weeds,' they could learn to understand the beauty of lines in art. 'The Artist might spring out of such an *awakening of a new sense*', Watts wrote, 'but the teaching would not have for its object the making of an Artist. Artists, like poets, are born not made'. Finally, he suggested that the galleries be separated into compartments showing just a few works of art '& those analogous in character so that the uninformed mind should not be confused'. Horsfall followed his and Leighton's advice, rather pursuing the president, who now had to summon every ounce of tact with Rossiter who was treating the South London as his personal preserve and whose outbursts were 'more righteous than politic'. 'The South London Gallery business is disastrous!' the president wrote to Mary. 'Little Mr Rossiter is indomitable.'[40]

Both the South London Gallery and Ancoats Hall projects were founded on principles established by Ruskin, whose books Watts prized more than any other possession. 'They could have taken nothing from me that I value more', he cried when Mary showed him the gap in their bookshelf. The books were retrieved again ten days later, but his distress was compounded when he discovered they had been stolen by his valet Alfred.[41] The shocked couple treated him as best they could. Keen as they were to improve the lives of the disadvantaged – even known criminals in Whitechapel – the discovery that a member of their own household had been deceiving them for some time was hard to take. 'Nothing astonishes me more in my daily life with Signor, than the large impersonal quality of his mind on all subjects,' wrote Mary. 'Whether it is in dealing with a servant who has betrayed the confidence & generous kindness of years or whether he is looking at larger

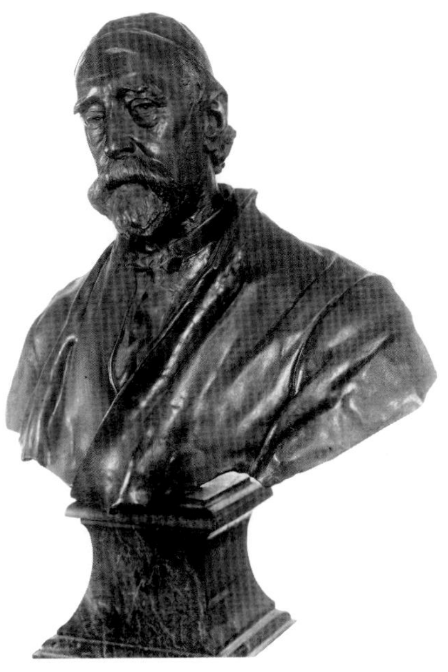

166 Alfred Gilbert's bronze bust of Watts, 1888–90 (Tate, London).

affairs, the same spirit is always there – I have never known him take a small or even personal view of any question – I do not think the return of his precious books has yet given him one moments pleasure.'[42] Worse still was the maliciousness of his neighbour, who accused Mary of being unkind to Alfred. Watts, exasperated at Mrs Barrington 'blistering our lives', summoned her to explain herself. Should she ever imply such falsehood, not only their friendship, but all intercourse must cease. It seems that the two women lunged at each other in a passionate clash of umbrellas in the hall of Little Holland House. On 2 October, the artist wrote again:

> You are to see me before you go on a visit . . . I acknowledge and am grateful for much and unvarying past kindness and more, but this could not justify your unwise persistent determination in the beginning to make Melbury House and Little Holland House joint concerns. My wife distinctly showed you that this was not agreeable to her and you must remember she was a stranger to you! You obliged a duel which distressed her for her nature is most kind, but she felt that either she or you must be master of the situation, however unreasonable she might have been (and few wives will think she was), you were wrong!

Furthermore, he complained to her sister Julia Greg about Mrs Barrington's conduct which was impeding his work. At 74, the loss of 'good spring', as he put it, could be serious.[43] Mary refused to see her again. Their antagonism led to a terse dismissal in Mary's biography of Watts: 'I met Mrs Barrington for the first time very shortly before our marriage. I never saw her after September 1890. She and I never really knew each other.' Worse, she skirted over key developments in her husband's career during Mrs Barrington's tenure as his assistant.[44]

He contributed with enthusiasm to an exhibition at the Galleria delle Belle Arti in Rome organized by *In Arte Libertas*, the innovative modern Italian movement, headed by Costa.[45] Queen Elisabeth of Roumania, the writer and poet who published under the pseudonym Carmen Sylva (fig. 167), was in London on a rare brief visit and invited Watts to dine. As ever, he declined; so the next day, she sent an invitation to a private reading, which tempted him, for he admired her writing. His refusal was probably owing to his knowledge that Ellen Terry would be present. Determined to meet Britain's poetic painter, the queen took her entourage – among them, the philologist and orientalist Professor Max Müller and Alma Strettell, who translated her poetry – to spend her last afternoon in England at Little Holland House. 'Here Carmen Sylva seemed really to have met her affinity – as far as English people go', recalled Strettell. 'She loved and understood all his work, both painting and sculpture; and he, for his part, could not make enough of her.' Watts showed her everything, even in his rough workshop; he talked of a picture he was about to begin, an *Epitaph* based on the motto he quoted to Tennyson, 'What I spent I had. What I saved I lost. What I gave I have' (fig. 179). Such words thrilled the royal poet. In passionate broken English she asked him about the symbols he planned for the epitaph of a nobleman: his ermine cloak, his spear, helmet and shield representing glory and honour in the battlefield; a pilgrim's staff and scallop shell (the holy search for happiness); a laurel crown, lute and book (poetry, music and learning); roses (joy and loyalty); and peacock feather (hope and immortality) – all to lie across a horizontal canvas

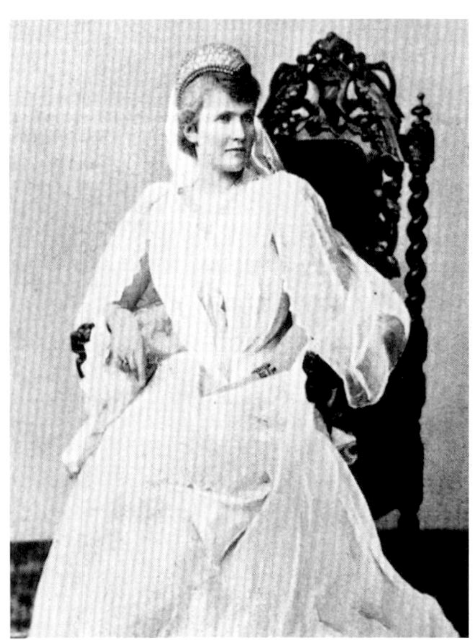

167    Carmen Sylva, Queen of Roumania (Burgoyne, 1941, p. 149).

beneath the shrouded figure. So affecting was the visit that Carmen Sylva had to be prised away to catch her train back to Roumania. To Watts, she was the epitome of a Ruskinian queen, 'royal in giving'. Charmed not only by her writings, but by her mind, her voice, beauty and gesture, he wished he could have painted her. 'It is sad they never met again', mused Strettell. 'They would have been real friends.'[46]

The Lincoln's Inn fresco was the chief work by which he himself believed he would be remembered in posterity, but veils of soot blown through the door had risen over three decades and were threatening to obliterate it. At last the benchers engaged the help of Professor Church, who painstakingly rubbed away the soot with cotton wool and a fine spray of methylated spirit and preserved the *Hemicycle of Lawgivers* with coatings of paraffin wax.[47] It may be no coincidence that one of the symbols in the *Epitaph*, the cup from which the golden waters of life run, was the silver-gilt cup presented to him by the Benchers (and graciously returned by Mary after his death, without the sovereigns, the golden waters of life having run dry.)[48]

In poignant contrast, for the romantic artist who valued the heroism of fighting for one's country, his new embodiment of *Faith* (fig. 168), a larger-than-life female figure wearied by persecution, seated on a rock, soaking her blood-stained feet in the stream of Truth, shows her loosening her sword. To Watts, Faith was 'the elevation of the material reason into the region of the spiritual idea'. Here, startled by the dawn chorus, she looks up, turns away from violent memories and listens instead to Nature 'the great voice of Eternity'.[49]

He was writing a series of essays to help revitalize craftsmanship. Worldly and political in a preface to Mackmurdo's *Plain Handicrafts: A Guide to Elementary Practice*, he warned that the safety of the nation was at risk from discontented people, deprived of beauty at home, ignored and degraded in the machine age. Thought and Imagination, the attributes of man alone, must be fostered or lost. 'To lead the weary toiler along the dreary road of everyday mechanical work into its wayside gardens, to open closed eyes to a world of loveliness and grace where every flower that blows and every tendril that twines enlist themselves in his service and become his friends, is the function of Plain Handicraft'. All should share in that appreciation, Watts added. 'The hunger for brotherhood is at the bottom of the unrest of the modern civilized world.'[50]

Here, and in his preface for Ashbee's *Transactions of the Guild and School of Handicrafts*, Watts evoked the *entrelac* patterns of Art Nouveau decoration. He directed the craftsman to 'the inexhaustible book of Nature, the only basis of all true decoration, ever open for reference', to Ruskin and advised 'never to forget in the noise of the workshop, or in the temptations of the market, that his work, well and beautifully done, may be the cradle of a superb art, and may win back for his country that great spiritual possession, the perception of Divine beauty, from which, by her blindness, she has been too long disinherited.' Mary separately contributed Egyptian style motifs of the winged sun and asp.[51]

'A visit from him is like fine old wine,' Mary noted after Sir Frederic Leighton's visit, shortly before his sixtieth birthday.[52] They left for Compton, having decided to name the new house Limnerslease – 'limner' as the home of an artist and 'lease' from the old English 'to leasen' or glean, reflecting 'our hope . . . that there were *golden years* to be gleaned in this

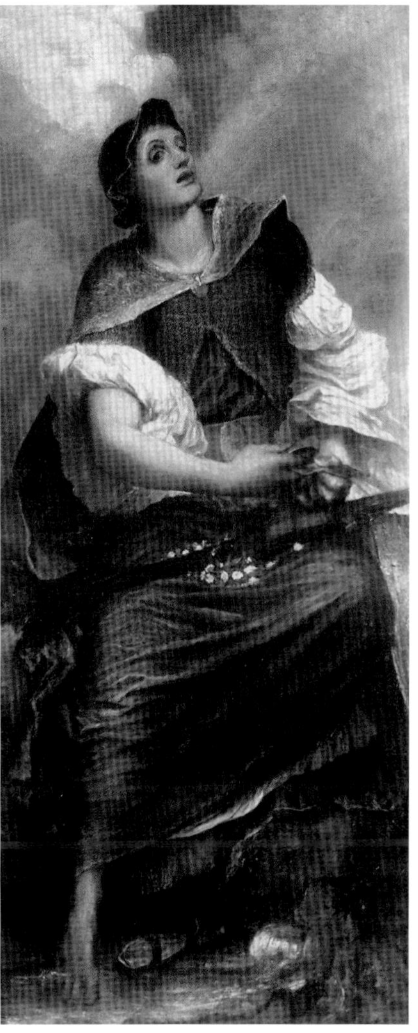

168    *Faith*, 1890–96 (Tate, London).

new home'.[53] Burne-Jones would dub it 'Dauber's Den' or 'Painter's Palette', Leighton's suggestion that 'it should be Limner's Ease should it not?' earned a swift rebuke from Mary. 'Ease' would not cheer her husband. 'Work work work' was his joyful anthem. 'Work is the life of life.'[54] The height of the doorways, only six foot three inches – 'a modern girl with a hat on must stoop to come in,' Mary observed[55] – reflects that sense of purpose.

Watts had repaid Hichens in November and was preparing a series of red chalk drawings for exhibition and sale through Agnew's in Bond Street. The series was to be sold in the spring as a synopsis of the Symbolist paintings designated to form the nucleus of a future National Gallery of purely British art.[56] While he worked on these to pay for the house, Mary threw herself into its interior decoration and to transforming the hillside stubble into a garden, for which her experience of the magnificent Aldourie estate had well prepared her. She explained to the tenant of her future gardener's cottage that they were sorry to evict him and would have liked to employ him in the garden, but it would be a waste of his carpentry education.'[57]

Harold Peto came down to Limnerslease in January 1891. He regretted the smooth interior plasterwork and would have preferred to leave it rough, as Americans did on occasion. Mary had been longing to try that texture in the drawing room and perhaps vary the colouring, 'a peacock green for instance, more green in part, more blue'. She was modelling highly symbolic clay panels for the ceiling, as a memorial to her husband's life and work. There was an architectural miscalculation to rectify – a new side porch was needed to avoid collisions between people coming down the back stairs and entering through the tradesmen's or garden entrance – and she had to organize carved mantelpieces, screens and minister to a demanding husband, enjoying his winter garden in snow boots sent by Peto.[58]

'There should be no loitering or haste in a well ordered life', he would preach. Happily guilty of both, his unheeding wife paid little attention, except to calm his life for work, read and stimulate him, keep him healthy as best she could, rubbing his legs with lanoline to ease cramp. Despite her upbringing, she was delighted to relinquish social position for artistic noblesse with Watts in a modest studio cottage, harmonizing with nature. Of society and staying in grand houses, she wrote 'Ruskin & Signor make one feel their smallness . . . the *crust* of things is what tells in society', whereas the artist and critic addressed the soul. But when he said, 'I do like my friends to be ladies and gentlemen,' his socialist wife retorted that she did not care whether they were dukes or dustmen.

Trees were a problem. To Mary, the new house, surrounded by scrub oaks, felt claustrophobic, and she feared that the loss of light and damp, decaying leaves would affect his health. 'Signor's tender heart won't allow more than three or four to go at a time.' He would not have a twig cut: 'His love of the birds & his love of trees are too strong for any argument.'[59] She showed him her symbolic plan for his drawing room ceiling. He suggested she insert 'Let there be light' around the central all-embracing winged sun – the only complete symbol at this stage – and bind the scheme together with a single cord, as 'the symbol of unity and fundamental law underlying all. She had yet to research and design the symbols, but like him, she did not veer from her initial idea, inspired not only by Watts, but by Ruskin and her own deeply spiritual mind.[60] 'It is to be the concrete expression of the spiritual atmosphere that Signor has round him – the aroma of his thought put into the silent language of my symbols.'[61]

Determined to overcome gout, Watts was following the rigid beef and hot water regime promoted by the American physician James Salisbury, who reasoned that as humans were two-thirds carnivorous, one-third herbivorous, this 'natural' diet would maintain bodily health and prolong life. Emma was instructed to broil cakes of lean minced beef, to be taken with a small piece of dry toast and black coffee at each meal. At first the diet made Watts feel tired and oddly chilly without cream. He gave in and had some for lunch. Its effect was like champagne, '*very* strange', Mary noted,[62] but he persevered and by the end of February Dr Bond found no trace of gout in his pulse, but the deafness remained.[63]

Journeys up to London – twice in February, for medical and business meetings – increased his nervous tension. He refused to let Mary leave Little Holland House until the fog lifted in case she became ill. At seventy-four, hoping for a new lease of life 'in a way I have no right to do', he said 'I want to live as long as I can to do good work yet in the little house . . . you must help me, give me no anxiety, running no risks of laying yourself up'.[64] They had a new will drawn up, bequeathing most of their fortune to the creation of the Monument to Everyday Heroes and the rest, after small bequests, to the Home Arts. Should he die first, Mary was comforted by the thought that she might build the colonnade for him, as a memorial. They might find it advisable to sell Little Holland House and live in greater comfort at Limnerslease, with a carriage: 'We might then ourselves carry out the "Heroes".'[65] Spielmann's otherwise excellent 'interview' in the *Daily Graphic* – which encapsulated his aims and revealed that Watts had willed twenty-six portraits and eleven epic pictures to the nation – implied that he referred to death as 'the great marauder', 'which Signor greatly resents'. Mitchell, their builder, bought a copy of the paper and was given a signed and dated print of Stillman's photograph of the artist seated in front of *The Wife of Pluto* and *Time, Death and Judgment*: 'I am very proud of working for Mr Watts'. Mitchell blushed, lowering his head: 'I like his principles.'[66]

The artist's headaches brought on by the Kensington fog lifted the moment Sir Frederick walked in. 'Delighted no fog in his mind!' wrote Mary. 'When he talks he reminds me of exquisitely skilful piano playing – The management of words is so deft . . . no false note'. He laughed at criticism of himself as 'the petted favourite of Royalty', but she felt he 'rather writhed', and was relieved that her husband was protected by his quiet life. 'It is best for the imaginative working out of poetic mind.' Even so, 'the world's ways are best for character.' Leighton had smoothed over Rossiter's outbursts and was hopeful of a £300 endowment from the Charity Commissioners for the South London.[67] Pinkerton, the young gallery architect came down to Compton to ask about the colour of the walls, and accepted Watts's deep full crimson.

At Monkshatch, where they stayed until Limnerslease was finished, Mary worked 'like a tiger' at her ceiling panels, the sun streaming in through open glass doors. Watts oiled his picture of *Naples* in preparation for the New Gallery and Marie Stillman brought Garibaldi's red shirt, to help finish his portrait.[68] The expense of Limnerslease preyed on the artist's mind. He hoped to sell *Uldra* and *Nixie's Foster Daughter* through Agnew's, but refused to accept less than £1,500 for these two prismatic pictures. Reluctantly, and to Mary's greater distress, he allowed Hichens to return his Watts's repayment and effectively own the house. He admonished his wife: 'We do not want possessions.' The next day, however, he spotted a bill for

*The Queen of the Air*, Ruskin's 1869 celebration of Athena in the Heavens (storm), in the Earth (vital force) and 'in the Heart' (imagination and will). 'Signor has been so cute & has smelt out my birthday present for him', she noted in her diary, '& is waiting with some impatience till Monday when he may have it! I am quite hard & unmoved when he says "lets have it at once".'[69]

They made the acquaintance of the ladies of the manor of Compton, Miss Hagart and her sister Mrs Ellice. After church on Sundays, Watts would stand waiting on the bank to greet Mary. His slim, nimble figure, dressed entirely in grey – hat, Inverness, trousers – and nut-brown tennis shoes reminded her of one of his silverpoint drawings.[70]

Violet Lindsay, now married to the Marquess of Granby, brought her four-year-old son 'Little-John' and cousin Nina Welby to Little Holland House on 4 March. Aglaia Coronio, in splendid spirits that day, told them how Morris had drawn from memory the carpet patterns from Holman Hunt's *The Awakening Conscience*; there was some discussion over the woman's head, she had shown the drawing to the astonished artist, who had repainted the head ten years earlier. Watts called on Sir Frederic to save the grand old trees in the High Street from demolition. 'Money buys against light, air, health – beauty – God's best gift & we fold our hands & are impotent to help.'[71]

To raise funds for their country home, Watts began another picture of *Hope*, but was ashamed of painting a potboiler and struggled to maintain interest in this – at least sixth – version. Keen to introduce something better into it, he added a rainbow – a symbolic link between heaven and earth – behind the blindfolded figure.[72] *Naples* was too often laid aside as he embarked on a new *Joan of Arc*. He had not painted a historical subject for some time, but, fascinated by its moral power, he wished to show the French that 'Englishmen . . . are capable of doing justice to greatness wherever it is to be found'. From a spiritual standpoint, Mary noted, 'Signor's hope is in further life, lives perhaps, moving on to final oneness in the vast soul that erected all – a conscious part of him once more now.' The idea of immortality, however, was really her interest, explored in her art, rarely his. As he drew *Joan of Arc* on brown paper, in watercolour over a plaster ground and in red chalk for Agnew's, she wrote, 'he seems to need the relief of something new while he works at things long in hand – he has never, I should think except in the case of a portrait – begun a picture & finished it right out of hand, or worked at it steadily for any length of time'; and yet he prepared no fresh surprise for the exhibitions or studio visitors: 'He lets his beginnings be seen, from year to year, till the world says he does nothing new.'

She stopped him sending a *Time, Death and Judgment* to the New Gallery, but despite her pleading he refused Hallé's request for the Cambridge *Tennyson*.[73] Absorbed by *Joan of Arc*, Watts could not finish *Naples* in time for the New Gallery and instead offered *After the Deluge* to accompany *Nixie* – both painted five years earlier. 'Surely my dear one is more inconsistent & lawless about his exhibition pictures than any one else,' thought Mary. He refused to send the fine finished portrait of *Tennyson* from Trinity, because newspaper critics had seen the unfinished replica – in peers robes and therefore with an altogether different aspect – at a small exhibition in the autumn. *After the Deluge*, which he refused to send to the New Gallery four years earlier, had been on view to the public in his own gallery. 'He works & works, year after year, yet seldom completes & now I feel *Naples* will be put away, the *Joan of Arc* begun, – put away.' Hoping that the new studio would impel him to complete more pictures, Mary begged him to have all future exhibition pictures finished by the end of the year.[74]

Thompson was now assisting with her ceiling panels and Watts helped her revise the scheme: 'Thinking & talking over the endless variety of ideas that they suggest – it seems to me that I am doing what I purposed to do, at the beginning of my life with Signor & it makes it the most delightful work I have ever done.'[75]

As Watts was finishing the last chalk drawings, *Faith* and *Conscience* in April, Mary noted, 'He is much inclined to like his youngest child best, & he thinks them the best he has done' – a phrase he repeated to many pur-chasers.[76] Forced to his bed one Sunday, he prepared a catalogue essay for Agnew's, presenting the drawings as his manifesto 'to identify art with the best in the conscience & action of the age' and alluding for the first time in print to his near lifelong ambition – 'What Michael Angelo did for theology in the Sistine Chapel, it has been the object of long years to do for the widest humanitarianism'. He rejected objections to symbolic or didactic art as 'fashion in opinion rather than sound judgment'. Sym-bolism was the only way to express abstract subjects; and although 'a too obvious intention to teach may reasonably be offensive', Homeric poems, as Ruskin pointed out, were 'didactic in their essence, as all good Art is'. To deny this, Watts continued, quoting *The Queen of the Air*, 'is one of the most curious errors of modernism – the peculiar and judicial blindness of an age which . . . studiously avoids collision with every prevalent vice of its day . . . [and which] has become equally dead to the intensely ethical conceptions of a race which habitually divided all man into two broad classes of worthy or worthless.'[77]

That even Hichens thought Watts's symbolism excessive concerned Mary, who was weaving multiple meanings into a single motif for the ceiling at Limnerslease.[78] On 17 April, she photographed her last ceiling panel before it was installed at Limnerslease. The winged sun radiates from the centre (fig. 169), the sun itself symbolizing Life and the Universe, its circular shape, Eternity, Unity of the law of Creation. Four pairs of wings and rays point-ing diago-nally to the corners of the earth, suggest Loving Shelter, Spiritual Life and Motion, 'the primary law of all Vitality'. This central motif alone appears to evoke Watts's *Love and Life*. Double panels stretching out from the Winged Sun like arms of a cross symbolize joys of the Soul (Faith), of the Heart, of Work and of the Senses. Dotted between them are daisy-shaped panels of the Blessing Hand interwoven with palms of Peace, recall-ing Watts's dictum 'Remember the Daisies of Life', the tiny flower trodden under foot, still growing towards the sun.[79]

Ernest George came down to Limnerslease to find a new garden laid out.[80] Watts had paced out the line of the oak fence, which was to be draped with soot-covered ivy, brought into the pure clean country air from Covent Garden. But he had no peace in mind for his architect: 'Signor pitched into him rather smartly about the soil pipe chiefly & architects who will try to hide things & make them look what they are not.' George denied the charge, saying that the only sham was the brick behind the stucco and oak (fig. 170), built in for warmth. The foreman had shown intelligent interest in the symbolism of the ceiling, but, 'Mr George who seems to have been

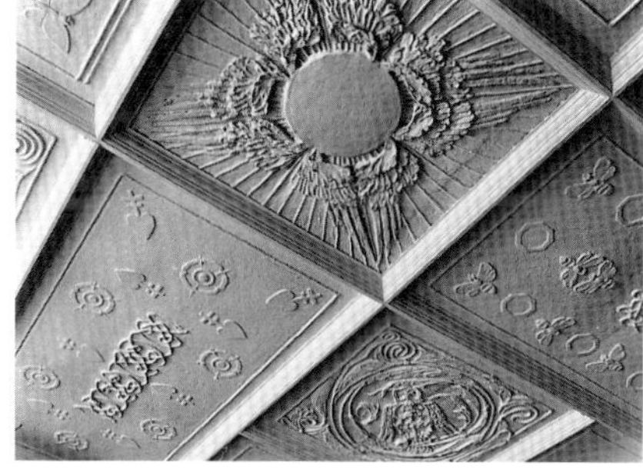

169   The winged sun in the centre of Mary's symbolic gesso ceiling at Limnerslease, 1891.

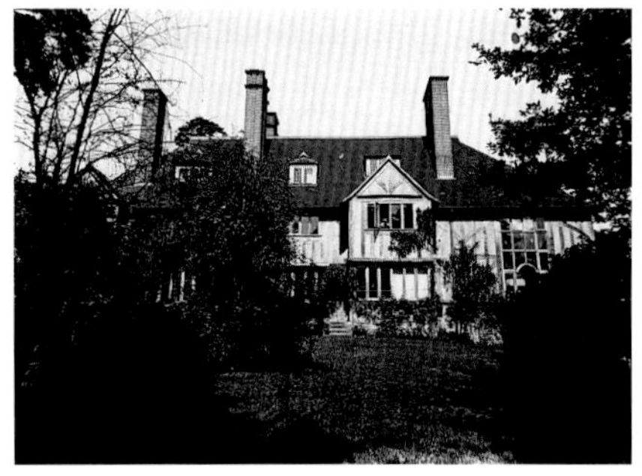

170   Limnerslease, *c.*1898.

in Egypt, had not known that their decoration has any significance beyond that – 'its very *raison d'etre*'.[81]

They returned to Kensington for the exhibitions and Emma's marriage to Thompson on 25 April. In the morning, Mary, having counselled them both, placed a white camellia in the bridegroom's buttonhole and told him the celebrations at Little Holland House were a token of their regard. After the service, Watts received the bridal party in the gallery for the wedding breakfast. That afternoon he had added last-minute touches to *Nixie*.[82] Varnishing at the New Gallery, he felt that *Nixie's Foster Daughter* and *After The Deluge* looked well. His conception of the radiant sun over the retreating waters was seen as sublime by reviewers, 'an invention such as only the modern Blake could have given birth to'.[83]

Watts agonized as the red drawings left for Agnew's. Relieved, but suddenly miserable, he felt they were bad, wished he had never done them or agreed to the exhibition, 'I feel it is so unlike myself, I *wish* I could just work on quietly & never show anything.' Leaving Mary to copy out the text for the catalogue text, arrange the labels in Bond Street, and supply guest lists for the private view (which they themselves would not attend), he enjoyed his 'yearly day of social dissipation' varnishing at the Academy. The half-length portrait of *Lady Katherine Thynne*, painted in silvery, opalescent tones, was his sole contribution, yet talking to Millais, Rivière, Alma-Tadema, he was moved by their intense – not flattering – appreciation of his work. *Lady Katherine Thynne* was well received. Lady Bath wrote to thank for 'the honour done their child. the *Magazine of Art* considered it one of his finest female portraits. 'To study it is an education in art' declared the *Athenaeum*. The veteran animal painter Sidney Cooper and Philip Calderon had stood in front of it for half an hour. 'No one uses paint as he does,' Cooper told Mary. She noticed a greater interest now in texture, not only brushwork.[84]

Rossiter selected simple subject pictures for the opening exhibition of the South London, among them *Red Riding Hood*, just back from St Jude's.[85] On his Sunday visit, Leighton was angry that William Richmond had abandoned the Academy for two years. However serious his work, he should participate. But Richmond, recently commissioned to decorate the choir and apse of St Paul's cathedral, was not so much boycotting his colleagues, as suffering from nerves, as he would explain to Watts the following year: 'An anxiety about my work, that I might not be before the world as a fool and a very real (I hope) feeling that you and others were far more fitted for the serious task before me than I could be – At the same time a certain strong feeling that if I *tried* I *might* do something worth doing, and which would not to discredit to my friends.'[86]

Watts and Mary left for Limnerslease, where he succumbed to influenza, too ill to leave his dressing-room sofa to receive Agnew. Determined to deliver his message, the dealer insisted on going upstairs to tell him that the Whitworth Gallery had bought the red chalk series for £2,000. This was excellent news, both as financial relief and because it ensured that the series would be kept together. Agnew even refused his commission.[87]

*Hope* – framed with an iris motif symbolizing, like the rainbow, a link between heaven and earth – was offered to Richard Budgett of Stoke Park, whose aesthetic art-loving wife Ann had admired the picture before her early death. Her grateful widower sent a cheque for 500 guineas.[88] Watts thought out new designs as he lay awake at night. He planned to add the story of Life, from her birth in a primeval dawn to a beautiful new sphere, where she was robed by Faith and Hope and crowned with an olive wreath by Love. 'How exquisite it might be', he said, turning to Mary, his face bright from the vision within. Longing to 'break the barriers of the flesh', she suggested he preserve the idea in chalk: 'Life is not long enough for anyone to paint all the pictures his mind teems with.' She went to view Holman Hunt's *May Morning on Magdalen Tower* and reported how lovingly Hunt looked upon his work, 'not as Signor does, when he has finished a picture, with almost pain.'[89]

Struck down for much of May with a serious bout of coughing and influenza, Watts believed his time had come. He held Mary in his arms and longed to recover for her sake. 'It is too much', he sobbed. 'I give myself up now. It is all done now.' Emma stayed up all night. Dr Bond, cheerful as ever, assured them he would pull through but called upon the services of a nurse and for Sir Andrew Clark, the president of the Royal College of Physicians, who attended Gladstone and Tennyson. As Thomas Bond rode up, the spirit of health, fresh from his gallop, with mud spattered over his riding boots and spurs, even the distraught Mary was moved by the doctor's manly vigour. 'Now look at my face Mrs Watts. I'll be in tears when there is any need for it.' The danger passed. 'I fancy it was near', said the artist quietly. 'It has no horrors for me . . . I have shown in my work what I feel about death.' He and Mary viewed life – whether in the creation of art, literary or political discussion, or observation of nature – as an ardent religious endeavour. As his figures of Death represented 'messengers of the Great Power', rather than the power itself, Mary agreed that a beautiful messenger would be sent for him, but not yet, not for years and not until they were safely in their new home. Nevertheless, she urged him to write his letter of personal wishes to attach to his will. He was determined to live to see the creation of his monument to everyday heroes, 'a beautiful semi-circular cloister, or triangular building round an open space – decorated with one fine group such as Gilbert can do.'[90]

Watts protested against the brandy prescribed by Dr Allbutt, who reported that his drawings were the talk of the Savile Club and that Thomas Hardy had declared after seeing them that he must begin art over again (Hardy's preference was for Monet). The *Graphic* was serializing his new novel *Tess of the d'Urbervilles* when Hardy made the pilgrimage to Little Holland House. He conversed only with Watts as they strolled round; he cared little for the art after all, and virtually ignored Mary and Marie Stillman's daughters, leaving a sour taste.[91]

Sir William Bowman called and held the artist's hand, fearing that neither of them had much time left. The kindly surgeon had bequeathed the Watts self-portrait to the trustees of the National Gallery to join his collection, wherever it was to be housed. Watts started to draw again, first his hand-kerchief, and, a day or two later, his sheets, and in June he drew a simpli-fied version of *The Court of Death* in chalk. Death sat with the infant Humanity, and alone at her feet Love held up rose leaves, their lingering fragrance symbolizing Life beyond the tomb, as 'The Genius of Rest.' A significant omission from the Symbolist series and nicknamed 'the influenza drawing' because it moved visitors to tears, it later went to the Whitworth.[92]

The London busmen, many of whom worked up to twenty hours a day, were striking for a maximum of twelve. The *Trade Unionist* sought Watts's support and published his response with letters from Cardinal Manning and Florence Nightingale on 13 June 1891. 'While I cannot pretend to understand how the bus arrangements of firms and companies should be carried out, I feel it is a monstrous thing to exact even as many as twelve hours' labour from any man', replied the artist who himself worked every daylight hour. His letter stood out as an attack against commercial greed. The principle of securing large returns for shareholders 'irrespective of every other condition' was unworthy, unwise and unsafe. No doubt to cover himself, for it was largely share income that funded his life, he added that he was not writing as a socialist, but on the principle of justice and consideration for others, and suggested 'co-operation' in future. The London General Omnibus Company conceded the twelve-hour working day.[93]

Leighton came to gossip about the French. Pierre Puvis de Chavannes had quarrelled with Ernest Meissonier, with whom he had co-founded the Société Nationale des Beaux-Arts as a progressive alternative to the Salon. Meissonier had died, and his grieving widow refused to allow Puvis de Chavannes to give the presidential graveside oration. Furthermore, the latter's work had deteriorated and lacked his grand composition of line, yet still Parisians were enraptured. Sir Frederic had seen exquisite gems but, alone with Signor, he spoke of pictures 'with all the necessities of nature dwelt upon! Horrible hideous women without clothes in a field with nothing to account for their being hideous, misshapen old charwoman!'[94] Sir Charles Newton also visited the patient, but was too weak himself to rise from the carriage, his chin collapsed on to his chest. Val Prinsep very much hoped to be elevated to full membership of the Academy. While he and Watts attended the election, Mary entertained Florence Prinsep, but the men returned despondent. 'Alas' sighed Val, mounting the steps. He had lost by six votes to Frank Dicksee.[95]

Her diaries record many welcome visitors, among them a Mr Arthur Leak who brought an album of Watts's childhood drawings. But Emilie Barrington, paying her first social call for a year – she had already seen Watts in the studio that morning – caused such misery that he again proposed giving up Little Holland House. 'He is so gentle he would not have me hurt a fly', wrote Mary, 'but I shall not let him be driven away by a foolish woman like that from all his friends.'

Far more appealing, unexpectedly, was Oscar Wilde. *The Picture of Dorian Gray*, now causing outrage for its homosexual innuendo, had attracted the young Lord Alfred Douglas, and their first fateful meeting had just taken place. 'Vice and virtue are to the artist materials for an art. From the point of view of form, the type of all the arts is the art of the musician', Wilde wrote in the preface. 'All art is at once surface and symbol. Those who go beneath the surface do so at their peril. Those who read the symbol do so at their peril. It is the spectator, and not life, that art really mirrors. Diversity of opinion about a work of art shows that the work is new, complex and vital.'[96]

Ashbee, preoccupied with symbolism himself, returned with members of the Guild of Handicraft to look at armour from which they were to design a reduced version to cover Watts's gesso model for *The Court of Death*. Both the armed model and Ashbee's design would be exhibited at the New English Art Club's first winter exhibition of modern pictures at the Dudley.[97]

'I DON'T SUPPOSE YOU WILL CARE A PIN for my opinion, but I cannot help writing to say how great I think your picture of your mother is, a real poem of the highest order, a most serene harmony, the impression of it remains with me like a strain of sweet & solemn music,' Watts wrote to Whistler. Their pictures hung side by side at the opening exhibition of the Society of Portrait Painters. The American drew a tiny trophy on the back of the blue-grey envelope and acknowledged 'the deep pleasure this flattering & warm expression of sympathy from a confrere so greatly distinguished as yourself'. Why, when Whistler sent one of his finest portraits, did Watts not contribute a national figure? Instead he sent an untitled portrait of the teenage Rachel Gurney, now engaged to the brilliant, difficult Earl of Dudley. That morning he had started to paint the epitaph picture.[1] He was enjoying a merry summer and had surprised the polo-playing fraternity at the Hurlingham Club in Fulham by his interest in horses and riders. He planned to have a Welsh pony to ride at Compton.[2] Hichens's birthday was celebrated with champagne in the kitchen of Limnerslease, 'Signor carousing too, and looking so well'. He wished to add a bath and window to the house. George would not approve, but Signor insisted, 'Depend upon it where art is divorced from reason it lacks a great deal.'[3] The epitaph and *Eve*, the newly awakened woman, also representing the mind of modern times, would preoccupy Watts until the exhibition season.

'He is thoroughly modern', Julia Cartwright observed after interviewing the artist at Little Holland House, for *Atlanta*. Looking thin and grey and still pale from his influenza, the 'great old man' impressed upon her: 'My intention has not been so much to paint pictures that will charm the eye as to suggest great thoughts that will appeal to the imagination & the heart & kindle all that is best & noblest in humanity.' He seemed above all a poet, teacher and prophet and hoped to start a Home Arts branch in Surrey. He spoke tenderly of Burne-Jones's *Briar Rose* and *The Days of Creation* and of Leighton as a fine draughtsman, though his work was too pale and elaborate. In his Leghorn hat and slippers Watts took the critic into the garden, and had *Physical Energy* pushed out and turned about so that she could see the fall of shadows on the rider's face.[4] In a radical change, he removed the front leg pawing the air, straightening it. 'He is now motionless' – for the moment.[5]

Signor walked up the hill to Limnerslease and stepped in through the garden window to take possession of the house under 'the blessing hand'

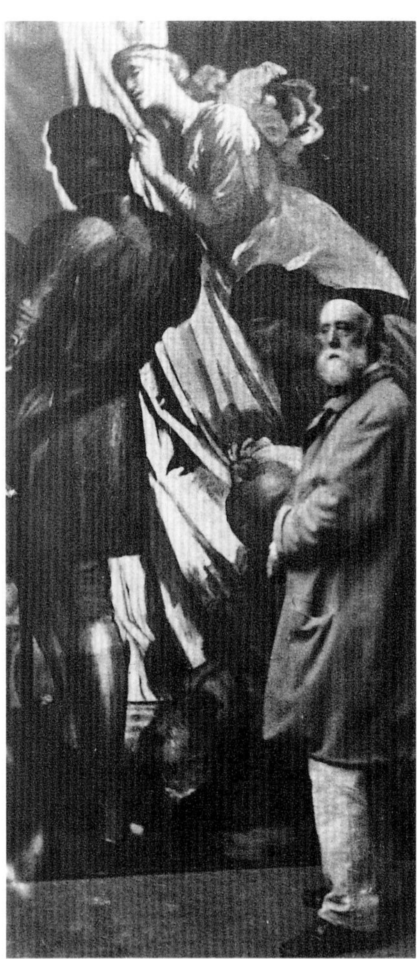

171   Watts painting *The Court of Death*, c. 1891.

of his wife's ceiling. The oaks overshadowing the house depressed Mary. He accused her of being 'dull as ditch water'. At least you knew where you were with him, she thought, 'as he snorts & kicks out directly something in the daily harness of life.' He soothed her with a walk, set to work on *Sunset on the Alps* and agreed to have two small trees felled. The large *Court of Death* was installed in the studio and as the Hichens arrived with saws and axes, Watts got out his long chair – a gift from Lady Lilian Yorke – turned its back to the window, while the blind was lowered and the trees were cut down. In the Limnerslease studio, light radiated on to *The Court of Death* (fig. 171), which he manipulated on pulleys that dropped down through the floor,[6] allowing him to reach the top of the canvas. With a clear view of the magnificent lines of three Scotch firs, he was consoled for the loss of the stately oaks. 'Women are patient in trial, but impatient in action', he pronounced, as his wife looked longingly at others 'whose death I thirst for to give us more light'.[7] The studio filled with pictures, including *Eve* and *The Good Samaritan*. He would paint on as many as six before lunch. Mary hung the walls with muslin, 'rosy red' in the drawing room and dining room and green in the hall. '*Eve* is Olive Schreiner's *Woman*, things grow beneath her feet – the light is from her!' Schreiner was a fiery socialist and feminist, whose imaginative writings were likened to his paintings, as he recognized in the breadth and simplicity of her *Dreams, the First of the Lost Joy*.[8]

As early as three in the morning Watts would lean out of the window, or sit among his pictures with his arms folded watching, waiting for the light he needed for work. He and Mary would breakfast in the studio. Both were designing in styles quite different from their contemporaries: she beat out an exotic Celtic-inspired design symbolizing the Prometheus story for the brass mantelpiece; while he painted a picture of the sea nymph Acis clasping Galatea – from his fresco of *The Elements*.[9]

Lord Wemyss sent his model of *Venus* to Little Holland House. 'It is really a most charming & graceful little figure! Surely you must have had no end of help!' replied Watts.[10] He received a visit from Margot Tennant. Her father, Sir Charles, owned *Endymion, Good Luck to Your Fishing!* and the study of an ass and foal. Margot was the wittiest, most indefatigable, tactless member of a vibrant coterie of friends known as the Souls, who included Arthur Balfour, Lord Wemyss's daughter-in-law Mary Elcho and her brother George Wyndham, George Curzon, Violet Granby, the Pembrokes, the Brownlows and Ettie Desborough. If Margot did not charm Signor as much as he hoped, it was because she called Sir Frederic 'a bore'.[11]

Their evening's reading about Wagner – one of P. T. Forsyth's lectures on religion in the art of Rossetti, Burne-Jones, Watts, Holman Hunt, and Wagner – sparked a pillow dispute. Watts ranked the composer as high as Tennyson, whereas Mary saw in him the medieval mysticism of Rossetti. As they lay in bed, Watts said that Wagner had the uplifting spiritual imagination of Tennyson. Mary linked the composer's concern for humanity to Browning. No, Wagner had a higher range, but then, as she rose to Browning's defence, 'the pillows began to charm me softly'.[12] Percy and Madeline Wyndham called at Little Holland House on their return from Bayreuth, where they had found *Parsifal* more of a religious service than an opera – much as people saw Watts's art. The French poet Stéphane Mallarmé's description of Wagner's music – 'An absolute which is at last understood emerges from the retreating waters; it is like a mountain peak which stands isolated and glittering in all its brilliance' – might well apply to *Sunset on the Alps*.[13]

Leighton called before leaving for the Alps himself, fearing that his holiday would be destroyed by preparation for the presidential discourse. Did he really loathe the idea, Mary wondered, when he does it with such ease? Among the bustle of visitors were Aubrey de Vere, Lord Wemyss's daughter Evelyn, Viscountess de Vesci, Sir Robert Morier, reminiscing about the Cosmopolitan Club, Lady Lothian Lady Pembroke and Lady Alice Gaisford, who photographed friends in the style of Julia Margaret Cameron. Now dying of cancer and thinking very much of Watts, Lady Alice wanted to have his self-portrait close by her, 'People find their mountain air in his pure lofty nature.' Mary made her take their copy and gave *The Recording Angel* to Lady Lothian.[14] Baron de Casson invited him to chose armour for *Joan of Arc* from his collection at South Kensington and lent him a helmet, which Watts painted into the foreground of the epitaph picture, beneath the bier. In the half-light – itself evocative of the subject – he repainted the helmet, turning its face to the ground. Stung by Henrietta Barnett's candid remark that she saw no beauty in the picture, he painted the peacock feathers to stretch from the crown of the helmet across the base of the canvas, almost to the edge, giving a sense of calm.[15]

Walter Crane came to sit for the nation. For this penetrating portrait (fig. 172), there were to be eight two-hour sittings, from eleven o'clock until one, the first on 19 August 1891. 'Now I am going to show what a fool I can be!' warned Watts, positioning the craftsman at some distance from the easel. His nerves vanished as he questioned the sitter about his ideal portrait at the National Gallery – a Holbein – and in turn marvelled at Van Dyck's *Gevartius* from his seventeenth-century series of eminent men.[16] He had laid in the portrait, 'gradually worked into it, getting solidity and modelling, and towards the last moved up his easel nearer, until he was quite close'. At the end of the sitting he rose and invited Crane to look. The fine head, painted in three-quarter profile, a slight fringe straggling over his forehead and a moustache and fine imperial both curling to a point, surprised even Mary. 'I like it now immensely. "One who never turned his back but marched straight forwards" rushed instantly into my mind. Mr Crane was pleased himself.'[17]

Seated in a brown-olive velvet coat, a jaunty cravat knotted at his neck, the craftsman talked of the Australian liner *Ophir*, being built for the Orient Company, its saloons decorated with his painted wooden panels of female figures symbolizing the seasons and times of the day.[18] One afternoon, Watts walked with Mary to Crane's studio in Shepherd's Bush. It was a cavern of delights, with designs for table linen, brass and leather, and tender poetical landscapes in watercolour so scattered about, like gems in a pigsty, that Watts wondered how he produced beauty.[19] The portrait, almost finished by the end of August, was turning out to be one of his finest. 'I have given it the forward look', he said. 'Well I always have looked to the future since I was quite a boy', replied Crane.[20] Mary saw in that look his patient courage and 'the sadness of one who has the sorrows of a suffering world upon his heart [his infant daughter had died], but who sees beyond and has hope'. The next day, the forward look had gone. 'The sorrows of the artist's wife are upon me. Yesterday Walter Crane's portrait

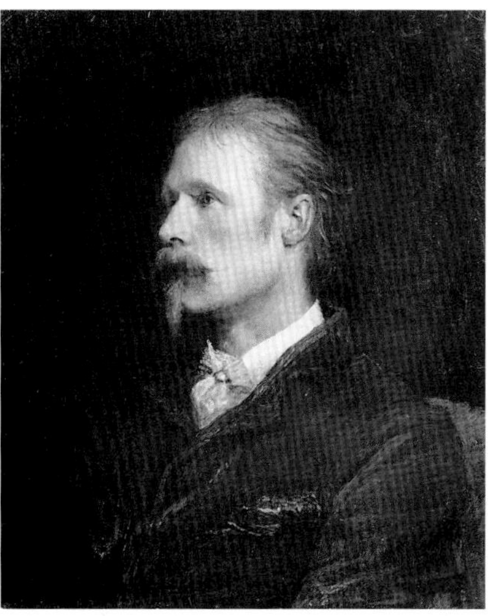

172    *Walter Crane*, 1891 (National Portrait Gallery, London).

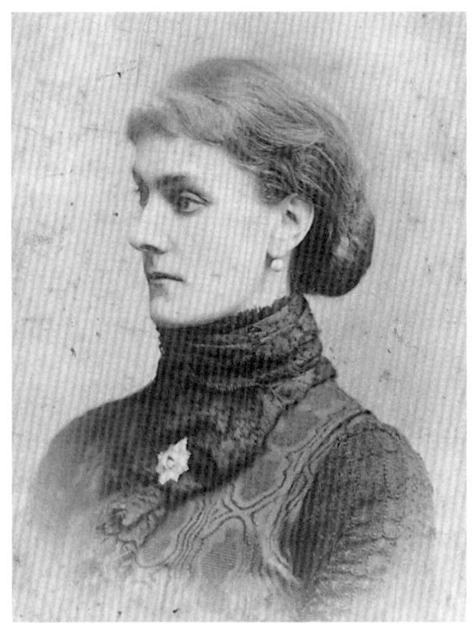

173    The Viscountess de Vesci
(photo: Lafayette).

was entrancing, an epitome of his life, that really a work of genius, today Signor had it in, worked of it – the glory of it is dead! The soul has gone out like a light – It is nothing more than an ordinary portrait. Will it ever come again?'[21]

Watts was, as ever, improving *Physical Energy* – the rider was now pulling away from the horse. He began a charcoal portrait of Evelyn de Vesci (fig. 173), whose 'lamp-like eyes' heightened her expression of worldly sorrow.[22] His *Roman Lady*, illustrated in *Hobby Horse*, exhibited at the Royal Scottish Academy and purchased by the Birmingham Art Gallery, was now on show with *Death Crowning Innocence* at the Modern English Exhibition.[23]

'What in the superstitious mind is mere dread, in Browning's & Tennyson's is aspiration – you cannot take away the mysterious, man cannot do without it,' said Watts.[24] It was the mystic element of Annie Besant's highly publicized conversion to theosophy – rather than her unconvincing supernatural claims – that interested him. 'Of course it is an illusion, but if you come to that almost everything we see is an illusion, the very colour we see is not the same to other eyes, it is a matter to bear in mind for till we do we shall never understand a truth spiritually', he said. Fascinated by the spiritual conditions of humanity, he believed that man evolved the idea of God and a moral conscience. 'The continuous aspiration of the human heart for that which is spiritual & outside itself as it passes through the ages, results now & again in a great revelation through one mind.' While Mary read him A. P. Sinnet's *Esoteric Buddhism*, which she was researching for her ceiling of civilizations, he was struck by the 'largeness of conception in the Buddhist theology'.[25]

Virginia Somers swept in to Little Holland House one September evening, saying, 'I have never been dazzled by anyone else . . . All other brushes are like boot brushes by his.' The two old friends teased each other, the countess, rushing girlishly at him. Her daughter Adeline, now the Duchess of Bedford, had visited the day before.[26] Mary's sister Christina brought her husband Edward Liddell, whose encyclopaedic mind Watts appreciated as he sketched his brother-in-law, testing the effect of diffused light without shadow.[27]

Walter Crane was sitting when Stillman brought news of a machine that was to fly against the wind. Watts said he had long thought engineers were too discouraged by weight. Crane forecast its use in wartime – 'dynamite dropped into the beleaguered town by one of these flying devils!' Watts, too deaf to join in, painted on. The Academician Briton Rivière, who harboured personal reservations against Crane, was riveted by the portrait. 'That man can never die".' But to Mary 'the eye *still* no longer looks beyond today, it looked before into 1000 unknown tomorrows'. She persuaded Watts to invite Crane back, for 'a breath makes or unmakes the spirit of a face'. Within half an hour, he recaptured much of the earlier magic – not quite all, she thought.[28]

A wide-ranging public now crowded his gallery at weekends. 'They looked like my own sort mostly. Didn't look so delicate as some m'am', Thompson reported.[29] Lady Brownlow wrote to ask Watts about a gravestone for Lady Waterford. He and Mary, now modelling *Love and Death* in relief for the memorial triptych at Aldourie, sent drawings. His angels kneeling above her cross-shaped gravestone were executed in stone for the memorial at Ford in Northumberland.[30]

Anxious for news of the ailing Jowett and Ruskin, Watts wrote to Sir Henry Acland, triggering memories of the 1850s, 'You were kind to me in the early days of the utmost happiness of home and of work. When Ruskin and Newton and Holman Hunt – Rossetti and Woolner and Alexander Munro brightened and beautified our young lives, and all of Art and of time seemed to be our daily life – And all that is broken – many – most gone. Ruskin practically.' Acland, too shy to sit at the time, now wished to be drawn for his children. Watts looked forward to rekindling their friendship in the studio.[31] He began to paint a vertical vision of *Neptune's Horses* (pl. XXXVI) racing forward over the green Malta seas; and, reworking *Sunset on the Alps* into a vivid shimmering colour, he forecast that man would master the power of the sun. 'Saturn might be a reservoir.'[32]

'He is well here, & his mind free, doing such good work,' Mary wrote at Limnerslease, where nature provided material for his pictures.[33] Smaller casts of the *Theseus* and *Illissus* stood on the studio mantelpiece. Watts, determined to avoid mannerism, wished to emulate their high points, in particular, their clean, sharp edges. 'Look at that', he said, pointing out the pectoral muscle of the *Theseus*, 'I should be glad to have that distinguishing feature in all I do.' Little Maud Collins, a waif Mary had brought down for the fresh country air, posing in her smock (fig. 174); he loved to see her flying about.[34] Maud's pose may have been inspired by a Belgian Symbolist drawing, *Silence* by Fernand Khnopff, at the Grosvenor pastel exhibition. For Lady Katharine's portrait, Watts accepted just half his 600-guinea fee, to fund a new cottage and stable.[35]

He joined the committee to raise funds for a public commission for Ford Madox Brown, asking Frederic Shields for news – 'I think you will excuse my ardent desire to know all that is being conscientiously done. In a few months I shall be 75 so have not much time to lose.'[36] Leighton co-opted him on to an international committee to erect a monument to Perugino at Perugia.[37] If appeals made Watts fret, Mary's instant cure was to show him his bank book. By and large he gave generously; he answered the letters in the half-light before dawn or at the end of a long day, and walked down with the post to Compton for a banter with Mrs Hart, the fat postmistress, bakeress and proprietor of the village wagonnette.[38]

Watts himself was a reluctant sitter. Results were generally disappointing: 'Lately people have been here trying to paint & draw him & have given me nothing to look upon but a face like a well fed alderman – no trace of Signor!' He sat in August to John McLure Hamilton, 'Nothing will come of it, but a little old man's head, with a red cap & beads for eyes, not Signor in the least.'[39] Another pencil sketch yielded only 'a good portrait of the velvet cap, as usual', not helped by his uncharacteristic pose in the sitter's chair. Leslie Ward's 'Spy' caricature for *Vanity Fair* (fig. 175) was closer to the mark. Presented as an artist, he stands in profile in his grey round-necked suit, narrow red necktie and suede slippers – apparently unlaced – one upon the oak footstool, his ruffle-sleeved right hand on a chair back, the other down at his side, holding a paintbrush. His expression is earnest and the eyebrows are bushier than expected, above a strong Roman nose and profuse white trimmed beard. Even Gilbert could not

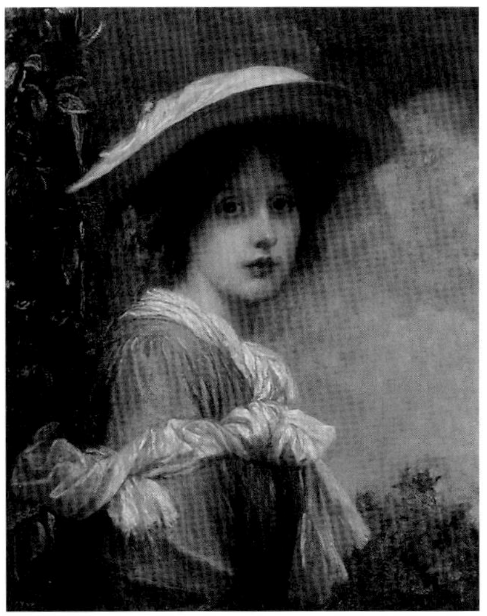

174   *Maud Collins*, 1891–92 (courtesy of Sotheby's).

175   Watts caricatured by Leslie Ward 'SPY' (*Vanity Fair*, 19 December 1891).

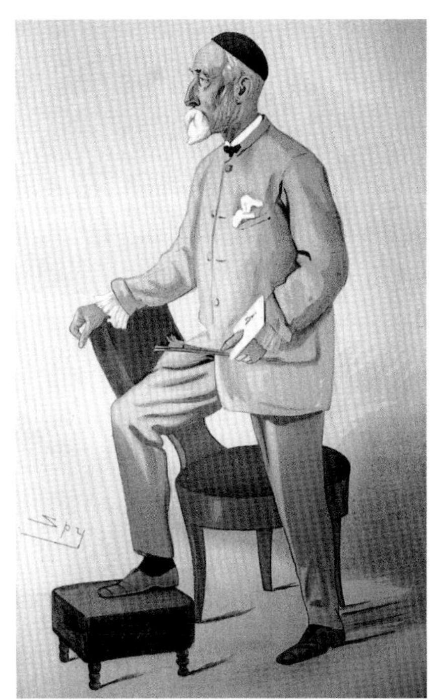

capture his spiritual serenity, 'He has a peculiar dependence on thought & circumstance for all the beauty of expression, even of line in his face. How can strangers know this? Shall I ever draw or paint him?'[40]

There was little serenity in November when Emma Cadwallader Guild came to Limnerslease to sculpt his portrait, apparently her first professional commission, requested by Agnew, to present to the Whitworth Gallery. The American was wildly enthusiastic, as the venerable master sat humbly in his sculpture smock, resting his arm on the table, his hand for a time under his head and feet crossed behind the footstool. She began a full-length portrait, then stopped at the bust. Watching her work, Watts could not resist offering advice; he urged her not to lose her clear edges. Highly strung, egotistical, and clearly overawed, she did not appreciate his guidance, and when he insisted, 'It makes the difference between refinement or vulgarity in work', she refused luncheon. He scolded her for being hysterical. To an extent Mary sympathized, for as his wife she herself had felt powerless to paint or sculpt. With a strange grimace, her hair streaming about, the sculptress found problem after problem at Limnerslease. Watts did his best to please her, wrote to Agnew and Lady Ashburton, seeking commissions for her, and she returned happily to work at his bust, while he, crippled again by lumbago, felt his studio was not his own and was uncomfortable in the constant presence of a stranger.[41]

He wanted the clay out of the studio by the end of the fortnight. When Mary explained that the clay was making him ill, Mrs Guild retorted that her presence was 'a stimulus to Mr Watts'. He sat until dusk, then begged her not to work in bad light. 'This has to last 2000 years & I must work at it as I like. I have been worried to death, she screamed. 'My good woman,' retaliated Signor. 'Who has worried you to death?' at which the sculptress yelped and fled upstairs. Watts calmed her. Having threatened to leave, she modelled, engrossed, until the Saturday, while he worked in the dining room. As her jaunty confidence returned, the Wattses, wretched and exhausted by her hysterics, longed to be alone. The wrinkle she added to the forehead that last morning was unsurprising, if not characteristic, 'He has no one particular wrinkle at any time, only several very mobile ones, accidents that fly across his brow now & then, but the habitual expres-sion is serenity.' Guild had achieved a refined literal image (fig. 176), Mary acknowledged, but it lacked the distinction of Gilbert's. After she had gone, leaving Brucciani's to cast the bust, the artists skipped round the studio, 'the only way in which, in spite of age, we could quite express our feelings.'[42]

The Victorian Exhibition of the great dead of the era – notably portraits by Watts and Millais – opened at the New Gallery in December 1891. The veteran *Lord Lawrence* was seen to be Watts's grandest. His 'one and only complete failure', according to the *Athenaeum*, was the second portrait of Rossetti, painted for the nation after the sitter kept the first. (James Smith, who bought the original at Leyland's sale at Christie's the following May, exchanged it for Watts's replica in 1893.) Yet William Rossetti was moved to write: 'You have made my brother shine forth pre-eminently among his contemporaries both for aspect of genius and for those attractive qualities of person which one might associate with mental superiority'. Watts, delighted, asked to paint a pendant portrait of their sister Christina. The

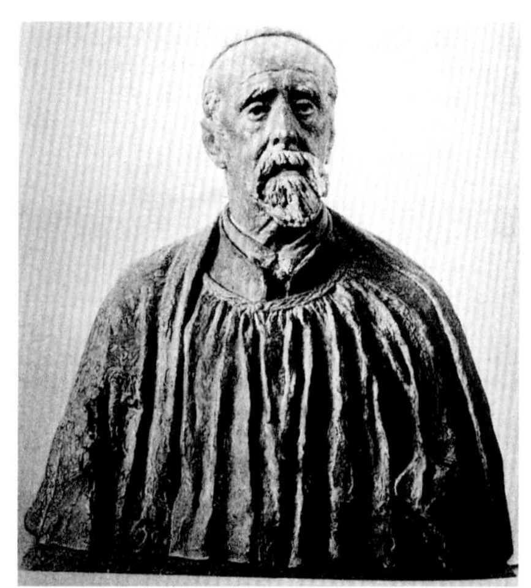

176    Emma Cadwallader Guild's terracotta bust of Watts, 1891 (*The Studio*, 1898, XII, p. 54).

poet agreed to conquer her shyness, but in the event was overcome by ill health.[43]

'Seigneur, Vos envoit à l'exposition universelle ont été une Révélation' began an ecstatic invitation from Joséphin 'Sâr' Péladan 'Grande Maîtrise' and his patron the Count Antoine de la Rochefoucauld 'Grand Prieuré' to join their exotic Salon of the Rose + Croix in Paris. Watts had been intrigued to read of Péladan's Rosicrucian order, and the rebel salon 'a temple dedicated to the Art-God', but saw it as a dying protest against realism, with no sense of progress.[44] Burne-Jones had received their 'funny high faluting sort of pamphlet . . . It was so silly a piece of mouthing that I was ashamed of it . . . I shall not at once promise to send there, but will make further inquiries & tell thee, my dear', wrote Ned.[45] Both sympathized with the idealistic swing of the pendulum, but neither wished to join. Watts, Burne-Jones and the French Symbolists abstained from the first Rosicrucian Salon, which did, however, attract the Dutchman Jan Toorop and the Belgian Symbolists Fernand Khnopff and Jean Delville. It opened at Durand-Ruel's gallery the following March.[46]

Among unfinished work in Watts's studio, was the large, almost complete *Temptation of Eve*, which needed finishing, yet he took up a discarded replica. *Eve Repentant* was still in monochrome and he had not touched the great *Court of Death* that winter. That he should waste months of energy on a replica he would then abandon tantalized Mary.[47] If his methodology seemed idiosyncratic, his fever for creating continued unabated.[48] She, too, having concentrated so much on him, yearned to begin 'real work'. His Christmas gift to her, Ruskin's *The Crown of Wild Olives*, reflected that passion: 'It is what I have been saying all my life,' enthused Watts. 'What we think or what we know, or what we believe is in the end of little consequence. The only thing of consequence is what we *do*.' Mary had rebound Ruskin's *Morte d'Arthur* and autobiography *Praeterita* for her husband. [49] 'Never let us be a week without reading something of his' exclaimed Watts. 'His is the true socialism'.[50] Their current reading, *War and Peace*, Watts thought shrewd, as fine as Zola, particularly Tolstoy's universal vision and comparison of a man to a rain drop which longs to reflect as much of God as possible, disappears into infinitude, returns to God, to reappear again. Pointing to a glass globe of water with drops around the outside, he said, 'God is in the midst & each drop tries to spread itself out so as to reflect him better, then it shrinks it disappears, & comes back to the surface again.'[51] For Mary this would have suggested resurrection, but for Watts it meant refreshing and revitalizing his powers.

As the year closed, his newly created Eve was growing radiantly – 'a wreath of clouds, of light, of wings, of her own golden hair, is girdling her, & the light & colour is becoming superb'. The *Modern Church* ranked Watts among the 'Teachers of the Century', expressing in his – albeit, generally unpopular – paintings, the great questions of life and destiny.[52] He began *Industry and Greed* (fig. 221) – a miser hugging moneybags with a hardy blacksmith carrying his tools, his face and arm bathed in sunlight – and declared that the true ideal of work should benefit all, 'We *must build* something.'[53]

William Blake Richmond, feeling out on a limb, invited Watts's opinion of the first two mosaics *in situ* at St Paul's: 'Your influence has been great upon me, and I would like (in my humble way) to carry out your tradition wherever it has been noble, while to the decorative spirit of early Italian Art I cling.'[54] These first two mosaics, reclining *Angels of the Passion* are lighter in colour than the later mosaics, the enrichment very likely suggested by Watts. In the absence of the 1892 diary, Mary's brief note at this time records that her husband would liked to have done for modern thought what Michelangelo did for theological thought.[55]

Delighting in the Compton air, he painted a rosy cupid, *Afloat*, 'on a wave "gold to its depths" with sunlight'. He bought a swing for the young servants, and regaled friends with episodes from Greek mythology. Watts was often goaded into telling the entire story of Troy. Like Gladstone, he believed a deeper meaning had been the foundation of the myths.[56]

'His whole life seems to me like a prayer', exclaimed the Countess of Pembroke when she came to stay at Limnerslease. She linked him with Carlyle in shaping the seriousness of the age. Watts had always been a high point in the Talbot sisters' lives. Gertrude Pembroke, accustomed to the grandeur of Wilton, was enchanted by the spiritual atmosphere in the artists' studio cottage: 'To be there is like being on the mountain tops with two flowers of nature about one & one feels that the spirituality & the intellect is a fact that cannot be materialized & reasoned away – that it is a power as great as any – his power of spirituality', she wrote to Constance Lothian, recommending that she too should come to Limnerslease: 'I think it cd do you good . . . his studio full of glorious pictures & grand ideas – gives me a sense of spiritual life that one gets nowhere else . . . his glorious *Eve* standing straight up with flowers & all living things about her.' He had spoken of the House of Life, for which he had now painted most of the pictures, as the dream of his life, but unfulfilled. 'How I wish it cd be begun before he dies.'[57]

Struck again by influenza for almost a month, he could not finish *Eve*. To show goodwill towards the Academy, he submitted her nevertheless, under the title '*She Shall Be Called Woman*', provided, as he explained to Calderon, that if it were deemed too unfinished he could withdraw it. Only at the last minute before show Sunday – that day his studio doors were firmly shut, for he abhorred the idea of showing off exhibition pictures – did he allow critics to preview the picture.[58] The instant he released a painting, he wanted to forget about it. He began an opalescent picture of *Iris, Messenger of the Gods* (fig. 177), descending through the air upon a rainbow and almost as transparent as raindrops. 'Art', he declared one evening, 'is a representation of a sensation.'[59]

Watts accepted an invitation to luncheon at Carlton House Terrace on 1 April 1892. Dressed in floating draperies – Lady Lothian in black, Lady Pembroke in white and Lady Brownlow in grey – the women looked like the Three Fates and asked questions in high-pitched voices. 'Life was constantly lived on the heights and conversation never dropped to a mere gossip; majestic, serene, yet strenuous.' Adelaide Brownlow, a close friend of the Princess of Wales and the most beautiful of the sisters, described Watts as the only man Lord Brownlow is jealous of'; Constance Lothian spoke of his Monuments to Heroes as 'something Signor wanted to build to Housemaids';[60] and Gertrude Pembroke was determined to launch the ship of his dreams. A week later, she drove Lady Brownlow to discuss Watts's House of Life series, the Symbolist works dedicated to the nation,

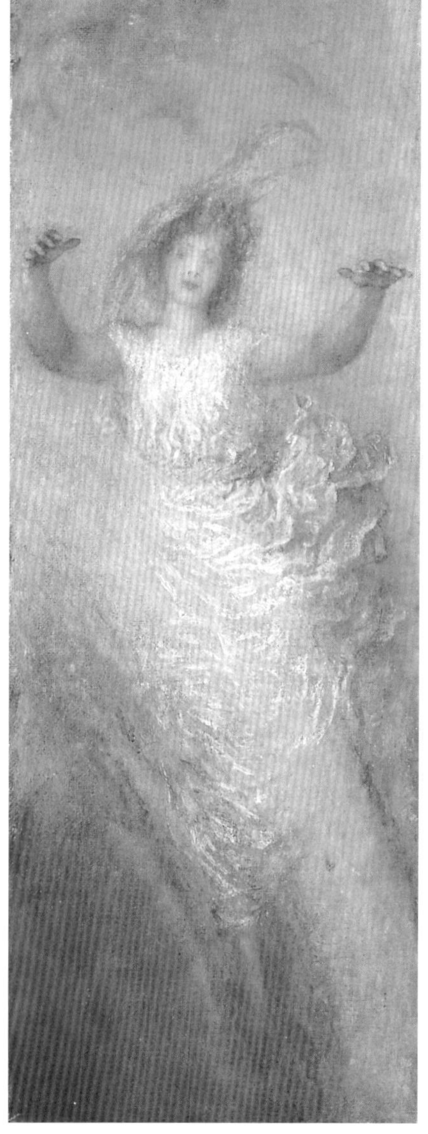

177   *Iris, Messenger of the Gods*, 1892–94 (private collection).

with Henry Tate in Streatham. Tate had offered to fund the building of a new National Gallery of British Art. As the government dithered he had withdrawn his offer, but now momentum was gathering pace and in *The Times* on 17 March Sir Edward du Cane had proposed the government-owned site of Millbank Prison. Lady Pembroke had spoken on Watts's behalf to the Chancellor of the Exchequer, George Joachim Goschen, and Tate was keen to allocate a room to him: 'If this offer had come to me 20 years ago, I would have left it complete' sighed the artist. 'It might have been a great work, worth giving all ones life to – now it can be but most fragmentary.'[61]

Thanks to the Edinburgh Social Union, an inspired Irishwoman had been commissioned to paint a symbolic mural scheme for the mortuary chapel of the children's hospital. Like Watts, whose tiny lunette portrait features amongst heroic poets, painters and philosophers – Carlyle, Ruskin, Tennyson, Browning, Burne-Jones, Rossetti and others – on the chapel walls, Phoebe Traquair believed that art should unite past with present and bear a moral message. In her decoration of the Song School of the Cathedral Church of St Mary in Edinburgh, now nearing completion, her heroes appear full-length in a life-size procession illustrating 'O ye powers of the Lord.'[62] Watts, dressed in a grey working smock, holds a scroll with a sketch of *Love and Life* (fig. 178), about which he had recently written to Traquair's father, Dr William Moss, who owned *Olympus on Ida* and was buying *When Poverty Comes in at the Door Love Flies Out of the window*.[63]

A new visionary idea sprang to his mind, 'And man became a living soul', a great figure becoming conscious of his surroundings.[64] However, all was not well with *She Shall Be Called Woman*. Rather than return the picture, the Academy hung her above the line. Leighton, exhausted after council business, escaped for a brief break, after discussing the picture with Calderon, about which they both agreed, and wrote to Watts about the display. The letter reveals an exceptional rapport between Watts and Leighton, and the frank and constructive criticism that he had given over the years:

> Whilst I cannot admit that his feelings towards you are the same as mine or that you are to him the same very dear and honoured friend that you are to me, he entertains for you a truly affectionate and *appreciative* friendship – we took therefore your letters warmly to heart . . . you know how keenly I appreciate and how deeply I acknowledge the high tone[65] and the dignity to say nothing of the other qualities, which are ever present in whatever comes from your mind, attributes too rare alas! in the Art of our day; I feel that this mobility of thought and imaginative force are fully present in your Eve.

Under the impression that Watts was worried about the picture's fresco-like look, both Academicians approved the texture, but the strong exhibition light revealed inequalities and the lack of finish that were Watts's real concern, and hanging the picture above eye level lessened the effect. In discussing its position, the president was contravening Academy rules, but he wished for Watts's opinion: 'It is *low* in the long room in one of those transverse angles (like your *Cain* a few years ago . . .) but *there is a* moderate sized *picture under it* – that the picture gains in finish where it is there *can*

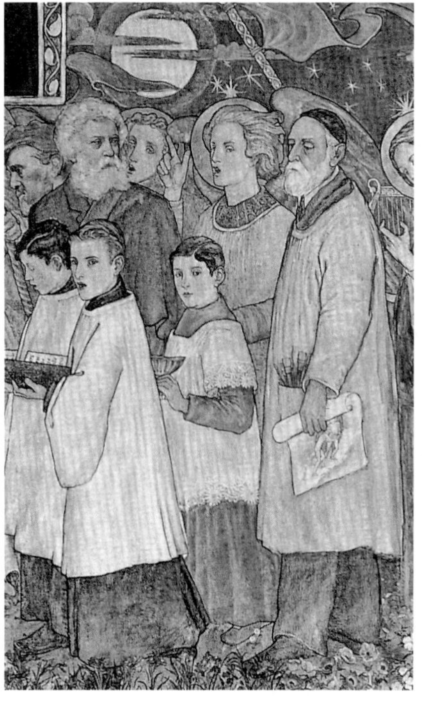

178   Detail from Phoebe Anna Traquair's decoration for St Mary's Cathedral Song School, Edinburgh, *c.*1888–90 (photo: Peter Backhouse).

*be no doubt'*. Watts proposed instead the long wall, but there, Leighton pointed out, the picture would have to be hung in the centre', and pushed even higher, whereas occupying the width of the transverse panel, the tall narrow canvas would be isolated from work 'of a different quality' and visible the entire length of the room from the central hall, 'We do trust my dear Signor that you will like the place when you see it.'[66]

Well, *She Shall Be Called Woman* was to hang unfinished, to be judged, Watts hoped, on the conception and intention. He thought the picture out of place at the Academy and would have preferred to have it criticized beside the Elgin Marbles, during a reading of the first two books of *Paradise Lost*, to the accompaniment of Beethoven's *Moonlight Sonata*.[67] His visionary Eve emitting light, nude but for her lustrous hair and the wildlife springing up around her, was not so much biblical, but 'an incarnation of the spirit of our own time, and a hope for the future . . . intended to suggest the very essence of life, strong, fresh, vital, electric'. The picture was seen as a failure. Watts said nothing. Leighton regretted exhibiting it.[68] He wrote to say that the Council were pressing to acquire his presidential portrait: 'Don't go *bedevilling it*'

Millais thought the portrait of Walter Crane 'sublime'. Highly praised at the New Gallery, the portrait was assumed to be an earlier work (Crane formally refuted this in a letter from America), partly because of the fine paint handling – too fine for a man of Watts's age – and because the craftsman looked unusually serene. Leighton, to Watts's surprise, preferred the epitaph picture *Sic Transit*. *Afloat* was his third contribution. In *Sic Transit* (fig. 179), 'WHAT I SPENT, I HAD, WHAT I SAVED, I LOST, WHAT I GAVE, I HAVE' is inscribed above the silver-grey shrouded body that stretches across the canvas; a wreath of poet's laurel has slipped from the head, and material emblems of his noble life lie beneath. Symbolizing the end of human life, the picture was 'very important', declared the *Athenaeum*.[69]

Watts explained to Forsyth why, unlike Holman Hunt, he avoided theological symbols, 'I indicate no church excepting the great church, the human conscience! my desire being to speak to all denominations, the Jew, the Mahomedan, the Christian of every shade of belief, even the materialist, the Methodist & every other ist.' Conscience he regarded the supreme spiritual force, 'the one revelation by which we should live . . . quite apart from

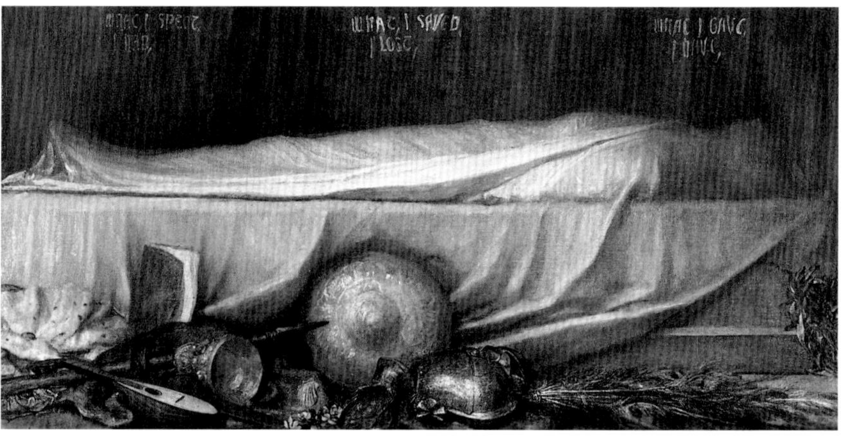


179   *Sic Transit*, 1891–92 (Tate, London).

mind or reason.' Relating Conscience to the mind of the Creator, he was applying boney structure to his personification *Dweller in the Innermost*.[70] On a purely artistic note, he was keen to promote the exhibition of Lady Waterford's works at Carlton House Terrace.[71] The *Pall Mall Gazette* quoted his exaggerated comparison to the greatest masters – 'in colouring she was a Tintoretto'. He admired the spontaneity and grace of her work.[72] That he thought her personal attachments weak might unseat Mary's diary extract that he was the 'only person I know who does not really enjoy a good pick at others failings & faults!'[73]

'Signor is so very radical when he meets a Tory!' she wrote, without qualification,[74] and this was no less true with Lord Wemyss. The octogenarian Earl of Selborne came to sit in June 1892, as a commission for Lincoln's Inn. Unusually, fearing the earl's head might not look well in a portrait, he agreed to paint the former Liberal lord chancellor in his wig, but at the first sitting, encouraged by the colour and character of his head, he dispensed with the artificial aid. Lord Selborne had sat to Sir Francis Grant, but spoke disparagingly of him as 'a coxcomb . . . not an artist'.[75]

'My contribution to the history of today . . . would be very incomplete without a portrait of Lord Rosebery!' The earl took Watts's invitation to sit for the nation as 'perhaps the highest compliment I have ever experienced'. Not that he had enjoyed the procedure: 'Sitting is very irksome to me, the more so as vanity tells me that the result can only be mortifying. Standing before Millais in a fur coat during the dog days of 1886 as a repose from hard work at the Foreign Office turned me off any wish to be a model again! But if you desire it I can only place myself at your disposal – the more so as your portrait of my wife is perhaps my most prized possession.'[76] The busy statesman forwarded photographs, squeezed in the odd sitting and after the autumn sat for a replica.[77] He wanted to see an Order of Merit established for literary and artistic men, to be elected by themselves. Lord Houghton, the late president of the London Library, had worked hard for it, said Lord Rosebery, and wore the honour, awarded by the Emperor of Mexico, on his watch-chain.[78]

Sir Andrew Clarke was also sitting for the national series at Little Holland House in June. Watts gave *Sant' Agnese, Mentone* to Evelyn de Vesci for her wedding anniversary.[79] Mourning the loss of five old friends and sitters – the beautiful Lady Lilford, Lord Lytton, Lady Alice Gaisford, Sir William Bowman and Julia Jackson[80] – he was determined to live on: 'I really do feel I may do some work yet'. Whereas Sir Frederic complained of 'having made a distinct drop' and needed rest, Watts struck Sir Andrew as exceptionally fit for his age. Attacking *Physical Energy*, he made two important changes to the horse's legs to achieve 'the arrested action and impatient trample'.[81] Some days could not command a single idea; on others they came to him so quickly he could hardly restrain them. All nature is rhythmical, replied Dr Albutt, talking of the ebb and flow in our minds and bodies. 'The greatest works can only be created at a high tide.'[82] On 25 July, Watts gave a study for *The Open Door* to Margot Tennant, who lived her life on the crest of a breaking wave and inscribed the label 'high standard be, the finest friends'. At exhibition, the caption asked, 'Does the picture mean that into the maiden's soul also the butterfly of hope, or awakening love, will shortly enter, or that a soul, tossed by the storms of passion, finds refuge in the home of innocence and peace?'[83]

Afflicted by a foot so painful that he had to be carried, he could barely work in late summer and accidentally daubed ultramarine on his coat sleeve. The old coat did not matter – it was nicknamed 'Squalid' – but the sight of the blue stain appalled him, 'I feel as if I had done something that has degraded me as an artist.' He now offered *Vindictive Anger* to Henrietta Barnett as a small picture to invite discussion at St Jude's. Designed as a companion to *Mammon*, it showed a vulture-headed figure, the destroyer of youth and beauty and even its own house, which it has set alight and will perish in the flames. In case he should die at any moment, Watts was painting every picture as if it was his last.[84]

News that Tennyson was dying hit him deeply. His last message to the Wattses had been, 'Give them my love ten times over.' He thought of writing a poem to the artist, on his imaginative paintings and on their shared love of the golden spring crocus.[85] Watts had recently suggested that he might write about the death of Simon de Montfort: 'The story of the great Patriot & the great Plantagenate culminating in the battle of Evesham, would make a magnificent subject, especially when it is remembered how much the history of England was shaped by the two men.'[86] Devastated that his dear friend, the nation's 'great Beacon', was failing, Watts lay his head on Mary's shoulder and sobbed, 'I feel as if life would never be quite the same to me.' The Poet Laureate died on Thursday 6 October 1892. That day, they read his last poems – each volume sent as a gift from Tennyson – and felt that 'the great poet talked with us'. The artist composed a verse himself. He could not paint. Sorrow, deeper than he had ever known, 'seemed to require a new expression', Mary explained to Lady Tennyson, and gave him the strange impulse divined by Browning, to 'forego his proper dowry, –

> Does he paint? He fain would write a poem . . .
> So to be the man and leave the artist,'[87]

Profoundly moved by the invitation to be a pallbearer at the funeral – 'the greatest honour I think I ever received' – he was bedridden, still unable to put his foot down and felt a lifelong sense of guilt that he could not pay 'the last outward act of homage to the greatest of the age'. Gladstone, too, was obliged to refuse. Watts sent a wreath of poet's laurel from Little Holland House garden. While Mary attended the service in Westminster Abbey, where Ellen Terry wept over Anny Ritchie's shoulder, [88] Watts marked Tennyson's verse in *In Memoriam*.[89] Afterwards the Tennysons sent Watts the lines the poet dictated on his deathbed:

> When the dumb hour clothed in black
> Brings the dreams about my back,
> Silent voices of the dead,
> Toward the lowland ways behind me
> And the sunlight that is gone!
> Call me rather, silent voices
> Forward to the starry track
> Glimmering up the heights beyond me
> And always on.[90]

The poet's words, Watts wrote to Hallam, would live 'as long as our language is spoken or known through the ages!' He became listless and took to his bed in mourning. While Lady Tennyson took comfort from his portrait of her husband, Sir Andrew Clarke – who had never witnessed a more glorious death scene – recalled the final moments: how beams of light fell upon the bed and played upon the features of the dying poet 'like a halo of Rembrandt'. The spirituality of Tennyson's poetry uplifted Watts.[91] He had felt very much in harmony with both Tennyson and Browning; seeing art, music and poetry almost as a single art form, he was at times angry at his struggle with words and that only in his dreams could he create music. Now as he read the poet's final volume, he exclaimed, 'Browning is like a mountain torrent, Tennyson like a flame!'[92] Roden Noel sent a copy of his poems. Admired by Tennyson and Traquair, he had been ignored by critics and sought words of encouragement.[93] Mary resumed her researches in their readings. 'With flying feet we step from Stone to Bronze, from Bronze to Egypt, Chaldea – Babylon Greece & Rome today! – following the torch of civilisation!' read her breathless notes. Existence, they felt, did not end with death.[94]

On 5 November, he was able to walk for the first time in two months, and rode on a borrowed horse.[95] Invigorated, he asked Lord Aberdare to find a couple of Welsh ponies fourteen hands high. Good shoulders, mouth and high withers were of paramount importance. 'I ride much with my legs in order to identify myself with my horse rather by knee indications than anything else. This puts me more in the middle of the saddle than a hunting man so that with low shoulders I am too much on the horses neck.'[96] By 17 December, Brenda, a Welsh cob, had arrived and the Wattses cantered joyfully down the Pilgrims' Way.[97]

'*Seriously* I do think I am improving! Of course this is what a young man in his seventy-sixth year may hope!' Watts assured Lord Aberdare.[98] He had been advancing the American *Love and Life*, which he intended to exhibit at the World's Fair at Chicago and then leave in the States to stimulate a permanent art gallery.[99] As the year closed Watts began to use larger brushes and more colour.[100] Sir William Harcourt confirmed that the Government had granted the Millbank prison site for Mr Tate's National Gallery of British Art.[101]

The interfering Emilie Barrington caused misery at Christmas. Watts painted portraits only from life, but she pressed Anny Ritchie to plead for a portrait of Thackeray for Trinity College, Cambridge, long after his death. 'Dearest Mary & Signor I know so well that it may be utterly impossible that don't even answer this except one day to tell me how you both are . . . I always feel in a jumble over EB. She is so clever so hankering & kind but Richmond cant get on with her.'[102] Watts had invited her father to sit several times, and it saddened him to refuse Anny, 'Now, more than every moment of a life that cannot be from time greatly extended must be given up to tasks which I have set myself, also I cannot undertake any pictures excepting such as are to be devoted to the object of helping to form a true National Gallery.'[103]

Blanche had been unwell for some time. Hearing that she was going abroad, away from her children again, Signor questioned her doctor's orders. 'I cannot think you have good advice . . . you are too active to live the bad life so many women do, half their time in bed & the rest in vitiated air.' He wished she would try a natural cure at Limnerslease, where he felt better than ever – 'bilious headaches gone, rheumatism almost forgotten indeed I think nothing but inherited fragility preventing me from doing & being as other people at 76! indeed much better than most . . . I feel I may hope to do more & better work yet than ever I have done in my life, owing to nothing but living as far as possible a natural life.'[104]

Strolling in the village, he and Mary marvelled at the colours of the blacksmith's elms, old bricks and velvet moss, and a tall young man ahead of them in weather-stained brown and green clothes. 'How like Walker!' exclaimed Watts, suddenly indignant that the late Frederick Walker had not received the respect he deserved, because critics had been blind to 'the poetry of nature' in his paintings;[105] and he was furious at the Academy's neglect of Burne-Jones, whose work, on exhibition at the New Gallery, he thought unrivalled in ancient or modern times. He regretted that there were no examples of Ned's stained glass – 'what Signor thinks his greatest work, for he made that art nothing like it having gone before.'[106] Urging Spielmann to see the exhibition, Watts wrote, 'Though a member I owe the Academy a great grudge for not electing him a full member on the occasion of the next election after his becoming an ARA. I think posterity will judge the body pretty hardly & I think it ought to be scarified on every occasion now.' Burne-Jones was one of the most scholarly, cultivated men of the day. Each year his name had been put forward for full membership and even now, with a highly acclaimed exhibition, he was rejected. Watts would have resigned the first time, and refrained only out of sensitivity towards Leighton and Rivière, 'I cannot but feel that the Academy has lost, for I regard it as lost! an opportunity of connecting its name with one that I believe will overshadow nearly all others of this time.'[107] To Ned, for the moment, he simply sent congratulations and an appraisal of his place in art.

> I always believe that you & Holman Hunt are the men the future will delight to honour. I ought not to leave out Rossetti, as for myself perhaps I may get the credit of having desired much, but though I am not conscious of imitation I feel that my *work* is too much in the old groove & not so good. Millais is of course a great *painter* but that is not quite enough. This is naturally only for your eye. There are many whom I really admire very much, but somehow feel that intellectual grasp is wanting.[108]

Georgie Burne-Jones confided to Mary that her husband, feeling sad and humble, said he was never 'brought up to believe that there were two Days of Judgment for him to go through'.[109] His resignation from the Academy on 10 February 1883 was felt by Leighton to be 'the one dark spot in the term of my Presidency, as your election was its brightest'. The men remained friends, and for fear of alarming Signor, to whom he had written before anyone else, Ned sent the letter disguised within humorous note to Mary: 'I hope he won't think it a Valentine from a pretty lady.'[110] Watts could not bear to read of his anguish, or indeed strife between friends. He put the letter aside and refused to open it, saying he would reply without reading it. Mary pleaded with him. Three days later, he read.[111]

> My dearest Signor
> I've been thinking & thinking many a day how best to end my impossible position in the Academy – when I am no good to them, can't help them, am a source of bother & difficulty for them – and for myself, find myself just when of all places in the world I am least at ease – when I am

competing with others year after year, against my will or desire – and I feel so old, my dear, so unfit for it all – & shall breathe more freely now I have left them.

You see I'm like a man who has been asked into a house as he was passing by, and being beckoned to he came in good naturedly & without much thought – & has been on the hall mat ever since – and I want to be away and free and out in the open air.

I love some of my brother artists, I like many, I want to be on pleasant terms with all – but an Academy says nothing to me – I don't really & never did care one button about it – & now that I see relations are growing difficult, & the newspapers in their charming way are at work I shall serve the Academy & myself most of what I have done –

So on Saturday I resigned, as courteously I hope as was possible – & wrote to Leighton & to Briton Rivière – from both of whom, I have had this morning lovely letters – from Leighton especially one so generous & warm hearted that I shall love him more than ever –

And you are not to be vexed my darling friend – there – things don't matter really a bit – nothing in all the world matters one bit except making a beautiful picture.

Your affectionatest Ned[112]

That he had felt obliged to explain saddened Watts: 'Dearest Ned . . . I care too much for Art to care about Academies'. The subject need never be discussed between them, 'excepting in so far as it has troubled you, it must be a matter of indifference to us both. We neither of us have more time or energy than we require for pressing expenditure in other directions.' He had never disguised his opinion of Academy blunders over Fred Walker and George Mason, 'so I need say nothing about its mistake (to put it in the mildest form!) in your case. Leighton & Briton Rivière are men too alive, too true as men & artists to take your action ill or to regret excepting from the point of view of losing, not a friend, but a colleague.' He invited Ned to stay at Limnerslease and agreed, above all, that 'nothing matters except making a beautiful picture because I connect the achievement with everything else that is beautiful'.[113]

Gertrude Jekyll came to Limnerslease on 15 February. Having devoted her artistic energies to embroidery and jewellery design, she was establishing a reputation for creating gardens imbued with colour harmonies and contrasting textures of Arts and Crafts ideology. Jekyll was creating her own artistic garden three and a half miles away. At an early stage of her association with the twenty-three-year-old architect Edwin Lutyens, a former apprentice in Ernest George's practice, whom she had commissioned to build her house Munstead House, she brought with her a root of poet's laurel.[114]

No quiet cob, Brenda provided a robust challenge. 'Steady,' he would cry as he trained her by the weight of the rein, to stop wanting to break into a gallop along the Pilgrims Way. 'Signor [gave] her a sharp trot out & in . . . It surprises me to see how quickly horses understand his words!'[115] Inspired by the Earl of Winchelsea's controversial Agricultural Union, which encouraged landlord, labourer and farmer to work together,[116] Watts proposed to take over Cook's farm on the perimeter of his estate and install a consumptive London gardener (whom Mary had brought to Compton to recover his health) to breed poultry. That the experiment was bound to incur loss would not dampen his desire to support a failing industry vital to the backbone of Britain. He saw the nation as apathetic, on the brink of losing prestige: 'We are surrounded with dangers, hated by every nation by the French openly so, Germany can't abide us. Russia is not likely to forget the Crimea. Spain would rejoice in our weakening. Portugal lately showed her teeth, and now Japan is up in arms against us . . . America . . . talks of stopping immigration which will increase the congestion in our towns,' he wrote to Hichens. 'Mary & I have been reading together the story of ancient days, how all the great Empires have fallen one after another from their high estate. . . . if we are to be only a nation of shop-keepers our fall will be sudden and terrible. Much I think may be done by a strong endeavour to resuscitate the Agricultural interest, but everyone must help, and many must give up something that may amount to more than a superfluity'.[117]

Watts was fascinated by Sir Robert Bell's illustrations of outer space and the idea that a message travelling at 180,000 miles per second would take three years to reach the star Alpha Centauri, 'Imagine the Creator of Allbeing made the sort of conjuror Man has made him!' To Watts, mindful of the unity of creation, 'every atom of it bound together by one great law into one whole', recycling waste seemed like good and evil interwoven; and he dreamed of a great furnace that would dispel the fogs and, endearingly 'cook all our dinners'. He considered installing electric light, but at £1,000 the cost was too great. However, he persuaded the rector Hugh Gillett to organize a telegraph office in Compton.[118]

On the death of his ninety-year-old stepsister Harriet, parcels arrived daily from Long Ditton – pictures and books, his old Ossian, Pope and his father's Shakespeare among them. The old man's portrait, cracked and blistered, painted with quills, brought tears to his son's eyes, 'He was very refined,' said Watts, his face quivering. Discovering a family name, 'Floris' repeatedly inscribed in their prayer book, he decided to substitute it for the less distinguished second name 'Frederic'. Mary rejoiced at his Welsh ancestry, 'I always felt sure he must be – he is *not English*.' She preserved the drawings, dating back to 1827, in an album.[119]

For the first time since their marriage, Watts made studies from a model, Mrs Stevenson. Mary's comment that referring to nature would improve his pictures implies that these studies were not only of arms and hands for the nude figure of *Eve Repentant*.[120] Having hung his Michelangelo prints up the staircase, she was working secretly, in her gallery above his, to complete her decoration for his niche, for his birthday.

To symbolize their joyful reading, 'peace of mind, rest of body, communion of thought suggestion, & over that sun earth moon & planets, & over that again the final end of a shaft of light', it was a fantastic illumination – effectively, their *Last Judgment* – inspired by her husband's work and the style of the *Book of Kells*, fertilized by her extraordinary spiritual imagination: 'I am trying to make my patterns express the whole range, flowers, trees, birds, beasts, man & his double nature spirit & flesh – sun stars moon – angels – & a light beyond from where they veil their faces! But that is not all *papyrus* comes in for books, *poppies* for rest – & then all I am longing to get in poetry art science, religion, history, fiction.'

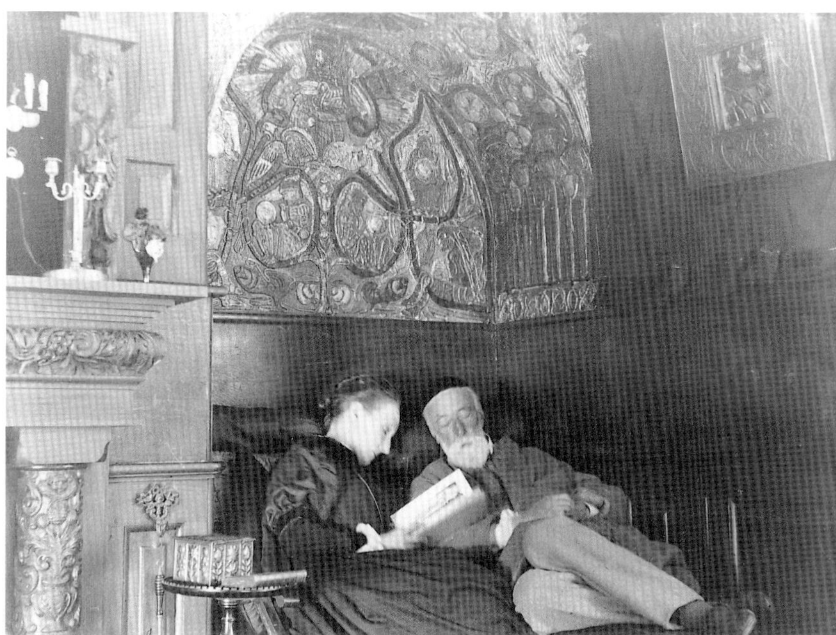



His *All-Pervading* was to be enveloped within Art Nouveau entrelac. 'Oh you *are* greedy!' he laughed, though he himself was plagued by 'too many ideas'.[121] Soon after midnight on 'St George's Day', he woke for his birthday blessing. Mary modelled for two hours more, and with her maid Phoebe and Andrews – The Briary caretaker, now looking after Limnerslease – manoeuvred the plasterwork downstairs and up into the niche. It was still to be painted, but that evening Watts lay happily 'under the banner' (fig. 180).[122]

Inspired by their evening readings, the history of the Chaldeans, their beliefs, the discovery of the Library at Nineveh, he marvelled at the lofty, reasonable philosophy of the Brahmins. 'There is no study like this.'[123] Samuel Laing's theories in *Human Origins* that spiritual civilization began not nineteen centuries ago, nor with Jewish belief or even Egyptian, but earlier still, impressed him: 'the soul of man . . . seeking its own science! as ours seek still.' These studies excited him, expanded his mind and soul.[124] Riding along the Pilgrims Way, he talked of death, of letting go material things. 'The older I get the more I agree that the only reality is the spiritual.' Mary replied, 'You will soon ask for a paintbrush when you get to the new life.' He laughed, 'That I am sure I shall.'[125]

Both were stimulated by Edward Carpenter's *Civilization: Its Cause and Cure*, the theory that in the fall of man is the development of self-consciousness, 'the dual self in conscious antagonism with each other – but will in time regain paradise by recognizing their *real unity*. How much better to think of God within man and nature, rather than God punishing man for sins. The Wattses were keen to interpret these ideas in art. When Mary suggested she would symbolize Adam and Eve reaching up to take the fruit to represent conscience, he wanted to steal the idea, but chose

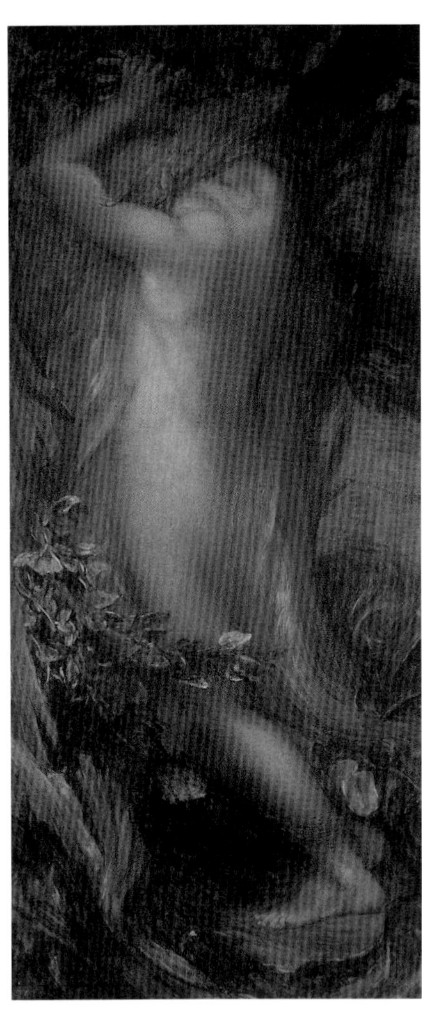

181   *Eve Repentant*, 1868–1903
(Tate, London; photo: Frederic
Hollyer).

instead to show the sudden awakening as man discovers himself to be *Naked and Ashamed*. A month later, he took a wax mould from his own leg for *Naked and Not Ashamed*.[126]

Watts called Mary down from her studio to look at *Promises* – a rainbow-winged Cupid gazing at the viewer, scattering roses (a birthday gift from Janet Ross, née Duff-Gordon). He had lost the mystical quality after painting from a real wing; for the reduced colour made the picture look sweet rather than noble. Within an hour he restored the mysticism; and Mary drove out to buy an orange tree for the background foliage.[127] Watts had taken up the *Alps Near Monnetier* and improved the sky and foreground. However, as she urged him to retrieve the sparkling, iridescent character of the icy peaks, she depressed him and made herself feel brutal.[128]

Léonce Bénédite, now acquiring foreign works of art for the Luxembourg in Paris, including Whistler's portrait of his mother, came to Limnerslease on 2 March 1893 to chose a Watts. He held Watts in high regard, talking of him as the head of the great English school of art. French curators and the younger artists, he said, were interested only in art that expressed ideas. Bénédite favoured *Eve Repentant* (fig. 181) and *Love and Life*. That Watts had painted several versions of the latter did not devalue them, for each was an expression of thought intended to stimulate international collections; and when the Luxembourg reopened the following January, *Love and Life* – given, of course, rather than bought – would be seen as the most important English contribution.[129] In Berlin, meanwhile, the Norwegian painter Edvard Munch, the protégé of Watts's friend Fritz Thaulow, was creating a stir, exhibiting uninhibited, emotional pictures for *The Frieze of Life*, a poem of life, love and death, with which – like Watts – he would long to fill a hall.[130]

At the inaugural exhibition of the Grafton Galleries, Degas's *L'Absinthe* of the 1870s whipped London critics into a frenzy, swearing outrage or ecstasy at the Frenchman's uncompromising portrayal of Parisian decadence: a dejected woman, said to represent a prostitute, slumped on a café bench, dulling her senses over a glass of the notorious, pale green absinthe.[131] 'The inexhaustible picture draws you back and back again', declared *The Studio* in its opening issue. 'The truth about it is that it is true. We see the absolute impression of an incident. The incident is unpleasant, and like many unpleasant things of fascinating interest, it is painted by a painter of genius. In the hands of a lesser man it would have been naught – even contemptible ... The New Critics ... have burned their ships. They have closed their Ruskins for ever.'[132]

Forewarned by F. G. Stephens about the 'vulgar' new school, the Wattses set out for London. They arrived at the steps of Burlington House to find Leighton and Calderon, and the Prince of Wales waiting to greet his sister the Empress Frederick. Inside, at the old masters exhibition, their vivacious younger sister and sculptress, Princess Louise spotted the artist, 'I thought I saw a friend!' and then teased him for wearing his fur coat in March. The following morning, Sir Frederick called, just after breakfast, for a gossip about the empress, who had eyes only for Van Dyck, and about the 'disgusting picture' at the Grafton – 'so cleverly painted that the young men are completely carried away by it and say what does it matter what he paints when it is so superb'.[133] Watts admired the subtle treatment of the woman's head but, according to Mary, little else.[134] He turned his attention to the role of women in modern society, their wider influence beyond loving self-sacrifice: 'Women like Florence Nightingale, like Ellice Hopkins & Mrs J. Butler may devote themselves to great principle without losing the grace & beauty which should distinguish their sex – splendid sentiment, not sentimentality . . . the pioneer must deal with the grander note in combination.'[135]

His campaigns to inspire a national appreciation for art and the revival of craftsmanship had born fruit – 'At no other period of the aesthetic history of this country has there been such an intelligent appreciation of the Fine and Applied Arts', declared *The Studio* – but Watts grew increasingly concerned at the displacement of the splendour of reticence by the new decadence, self-conscious exaggeration and ugliness in painting.[136]

# 21  Dual Forces

On Tuesday, 21 March 1893, Watts laid the foundation stone of the Free Library, Reading Room and Lecture Hall at the South London Fine Art Gallery. He and Mary drove in a stately barouche-landau to perform his first public ceremony. Greeted at Camberwell by the council and donor, John Passmore Edwards (the proprietor of *Building News*), Watts applied the mortar with a silver trowel presented by the architect Ernest George, and gave a short speech encouraging the admission of young children to the gallery.[1]

Among the many visitors to Little Holland House that spring were the Earl of Feversham's ravishing daughters, Lady Helen Vincent and the Duchess of Leinster, Lord Weymss, Lecky, Aglaia Coronio, Julia Stephen, Ladies Airlie, Granby, Lindsay, and Somers, and Mrs Wylie, who sparred playfully with the artist. Sir Frederick Burton, in buoyant spirits, called before retiring from the National Gallery.[2] George Meredith was reluctant to sit for the nation. 'I have no ambition to provoke an English posterity's question. Who is he? And my grizzled mug may be left to vanish', the novelist wrote to Julia Stephen. 'It is really painful to meet the dear and noble fellow's offer in such a manner.'[3] A wealthy admirer, Jean Palmer, drove him over to Limnerslease and persuaded him to stay with her at Loseley for the portrait. A bent, frail figure, Meredith said he must do Julia's 'portrait' – 'when I get her more by heart.' George Eliot had told Watts she never drew from life. 'Oh, I do,' said Meredith, 'but never till I know them by heart'.[4]

Watts was reading *Diana of the Crossways*, the novel he had modelled on Caroline Norton, when portrait sittings began on 3 April. Both agreed that Tennyson was the most natural and spontaneous living poet. Meredith, talking of Carlyle as the father of the earnestness of the era, believed future historians would regard it as the most heroically striving of any time. Watts wished he could exchange the dim visions of his aspirations for a more complete expression of them, 'You would rather be a man of aptitude than a man of genius,' countered Meredith. The artist thought a little genius was less useful than a great talent. 'To *yourself*, yes, for the world at large no,' replied the novelist, 'because even in an incompleted striving you give direction.'[5] His attitude to life, progress, balance, were very much in tune with Watts's views of universal brotherhood and equality of the sexes. Meredith's mind seemed like a spring of sparkling water to Mary. 'He hopes to see a freer intercourse between man and woman and would have boys and girls educated together at the same schools!' Even ugly new styles in art, music and poetry he saw as a revolt against artificiality.[6] Life was now so busy and without a guiding star, said the artist, 'We see too much & are dazzled.'[7] Like the Wattses, Meredith supported the Irish Home Rule Bill. He admired Gladstone for inaugurating a new spark in politics, but disapproved of his writing. 'No need for the prime minister, in the midst of a political struggle to write pamphlets to vindicate the character of Helen of Troy.' Artist and sitter had a set-to over Helen.

Meredith left behind him a sense of hope,[8] though Watts could see none for art. Mary insisted that the artistic instinct could not die and planned to thrash it out with him, let him lay bare his views. 'I feel an upward impulse now . . . I want him to be the standard bearer, not the panic-stricken laggard. Hope may well be the stimulant of life, but it could hardly reverse the surging trend.[9] Looking at his father's portrait, she recognized his strivings in Signor. 'He is the son of aspiration & of sorrow'. The picture had lost in the cleaning 'that very thing he is now giving Lord Selborne's which is the very life of the picture, the delicate films breathed over it, lost too easily, rubbed off even by the most careful hand'.[10] The earl opposed Home Rule and had therefore remained outside the cabinet. At his final sitting on 21 April, he was so anxious that Mary avoided the issue, almost as hotly debated at Little Holland House as in the Commons, which the next evening voted in favour of the Bill. As Lord Rosebery predicted, it would be overturned by the House of Lords.[11]

Gertrude Jekyll invited Watts and Mary to Munstead on 27 April. Her workshop was an Aladdin's cave of leather bottles and wrought-iron tongs, pincers in the shape of hands, an old hazel stick carved with a thatcher's account and wagon bells. Watts's favourite was an iron platter, whose blue tempered surface, silver edgings and inlays were reminiscent of fine old armour.[12]

*The Happy Warrior* (fig. 137) was among a large collection he was preparing for the first international exhibition of the Munich Artists Association. The Royal Cambrian Academy chose *The Creation of Eve* for their annual exhibition. *Love and Life* was shipped back across the Atlantic with *Love and Death*, *Paolo and Francesca*, *The Genius of Greek Poetry* and portraits of Robert Browning and Walter Crane for the World's Columbian Exhibition in Chicago, celebrating the 400th anniversary of the European landfall in America.[13] But as journalists pressed for advance notice of the London season, Watts asked Spielmann to announce that 'I do *not* & never *shall* paint pictures for exhibitions.'

Hallé and Carr, briefed by Burne-Jones about Watts's 'exquisite' new *Endymion*, arrived at Little Holland House to find Rivière selecting it for the Academy. They prowled the lower studio (fig. 182), choosing just *Jill* (Maud in her smock) for the New Gallery. 'I wish we could have snatched the *Endymion* from the jaws of the Academy which is very well able to take care of itself & where your beautiful little picture will be swamped in the thousands of works painted in quite a different sentiment', wrote Hallé – is it still too late to reconsider your decision?' Watts had painted *Endymion* for recreation. He loved the old myths, but used them as vehicles to suggest 'the thoughts that arise in me'. The crescent moon goddess

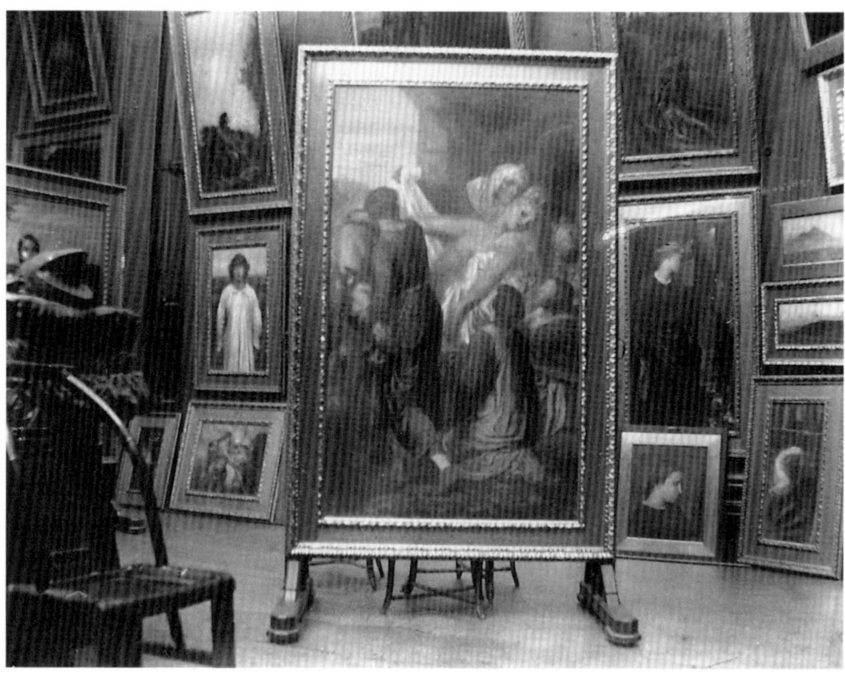

182  The studio, showing *The Open Door* and the new vertical *Endymion* to the right of *The Return of Godiva*.

was less effective in a vertical format. *The Open Door* and *Neptune's Horses* surging through the waves were widely admired at the New Gallery, where Crane's frieze of leaping horses suffered in comparison.[14]

'Mr Watts is in himself a whole epoch of English painting', declared *The Studio*,[15] but it was John Singer Sargent's sensuous portraits, *Lady Agnew of Lochnaw* at the Academy and *Mrs Hugh Hammersley* at the New Gallery, that made the greatest impact. Sumptuously seated, his elegant sitters engage the viewer. Mrs Hammersley, in velvet, seems about to spring up from her sofa, and the beguiling Lady Agnew poses in an opalescent white gown, her sleeves transparent against a floral bergère.[16] Although Watts admired the drawing of *Lady Agnew*, he was disturbed by Sargent's airy bravura 'theatre curtain' treatment. He could not bear to see quality of line dropped for an impressionistic 'smear' and turned his back on *Mrs Hammersley*. Leighton raised his hands in delight at the vitality of the picture. Watts rebuked him. Vitality was wonderful in a small humorous sketch, but wrong in portraiture, which should be seen as a monument. 'He can scold so wonderfully without making people angry', noted Mary. Rather than capture the soul of his sitters, Sargent caught their spirit. Watts's younger visitors were enraptured. He would explain how a fleeting expression, eternally fixed, violated the truths of nature. 'His background is soap.' Watts, proud that he never painted for effect, feared the influence of Sargent, whom he saw as a fine artist, flawed by his dextrous technique. He recognized sadly that people had lost all sense of the greatness of monumental art.[17] A bizarre advertisement appeared in the *Pall Mall Gazette* contributed by artists, dealers and critics, in memory of British art 'starved to death by official greed'.[18]

Passionate now that painting for the annual exhibition stifled imaginative art, Watts even criticized Leighton, whose painting was 'extremely fine', but carried out like fretwork: 'There is never anything unexpected in his work, consequently nothing that appeals to you. I deplore it for though imagination is not his strong point, he possesses it, & this painting by recipe, is the negation of it.' At the Academy Leighton would point to a picture and say, 'There look at that, they say the Academy does not teach – is not that good work'. As far as it went, it was good, but not enough, Watts thought: 'I feel so angry with dear Leighton for not giving himself a chance.' The leg in the president's exhibition picture *Hit* was badly executed, nothing like the legs in Meissonier's *La Rixe*, for example, 'Those were *legs* – Leighton's is not a leg at all'.[19]

Yet *Bellona*, Jean Léon Gérôme's ivory and bronze statue of the war goddess, at the Academy made Watts long to create his *Nemesis* from similarly varied materials. 'I feel sure Gilbert will catch fire from it', enthused Mary.[20] '*Faith* is growing & oh that head of George Meredith I am certain that reading bits of *The Egoist* to him has had some effect, he has worked in, that surgeon like sharp delicate cut of his.' He painted the head of the sorrowful man in *For He Had Great Possessions* (pl. XXXIV), bowed in shadow, to emphasize the misery of riches. Mary thought, 'None but my little man would have dared to trust to making a picture of it without a face.' To Watts, possessions were harmful as inward distractions. 'Our health even depends upon our mental capacities being drawn outwards & well expended, the constant supply of power goes on.'[21]

When the second pony, Rufus, arrived, the artist taught their groom to ride, instructing Harvey not to dawdle – 'It rots the character!' Rufus was a joy. To Spielmann, he looked like the Elgin marble, a worthy model for Phidias. Riding again, his mind seemed clearer, 'I get a glimmering of something much vaster & then it goes':

> If you can conceive the great spirit shutting up a portion of itself in a shell intending that it should make its own life – work its way, not to remain in happy indolence – then one understands that the turning out of Paradise was the beginning of life for humanity, the parable has been misunderstood. The human mind is greater than all creation it can travel to the end of space! But *there* it stops, it deals with everything that is, can govern most things, but it can't create, therefore there is something greater than itself – It is a part of that Creator – divine too.'[22]

Mary's nephew Neil came to stay at Limnerslease. The three-year-old was devoted to the artists. He rode Brenda, sitting in front of Uncle Signor, posed for his portrait and, at bedtime, if the artists failed to play bedtime games, he protested. Night after night, Watts, pretending to be a duck, frog or pelican, pranced up and down on the bed, but with such energy that he frightened the boy, who banished his mortified uncle from the room. 'Though Signors games of being the poaching eagle, vulture, pelican, etc are awfully fascinating, there is something of the terror in them too & he likes me as a protection.' Forty-four-year-old Mary would have loved children of her own (their dog Shag, a Dandie Dinmont featured in her diaries only when he was dying): 'Two delicious children would rightly fill both heart & mind, I think, so wonderful to help the right growth of character

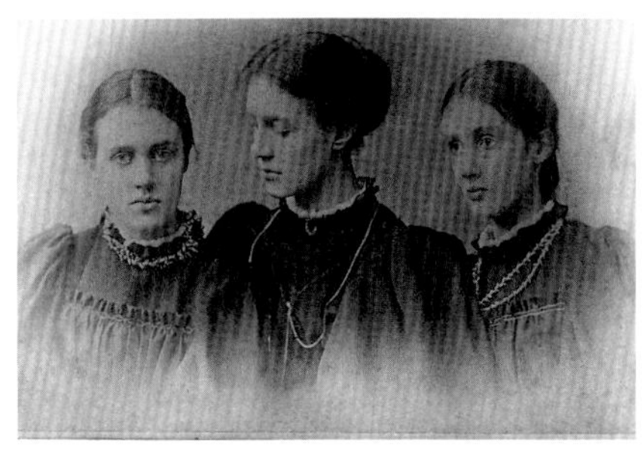

183   Vanessa, Stella and Virginia Stephen, *c.*1896.

– I suppose a real mother has less anxiety than the poor hen, who spreads her feathers over ducklings, goslings, egrets & who knows not what!' This was largely what she did, looking after her husband, nephews and nieces, bringing sickly waifs to flourish in Compton.[23] Julia Stephen's children, Vanessa and Virginia (fig. 183), and Watts's godson Adrian, were staying at Limnerslease when Walter Crane arrived with his wife and daughter.[24] Eleven-year-old Virginia wrote to her mother, 'I caught a fritillary this morning. Mrs Crane stayed quite late yesterday. We have breakfast and tea in our play room but dinner with Mr and Mrs Watts . . . The beds are so soft that you sink down ever such a way when you get in. Mr and Mrs Watts go to bed at about half past eight, and they get up about 5 . . . We gave Emma some wild roses, the place is simply swarming with them.'[25]

Virginia would later recall Meredith pointing out a flower 'that damsel in the purple petticoat' and her mother kissing Watts before he dipped his moustache into his bowl of cream.[26] For the final sitting, Meredith was obliged to miss the opening night of Arthur Pinero's *The Second Mrs Tanqueray*. He brought Admiral Maxse, in whose company he was funnier and cynical, joking that the artist had been cruel to his nose.[27] On seeing the portrait, Henry James recognized Meredith's dual nature, as a brilliant, worldly poseur, yet simple, generous and childlike. He studied many portraits, observing that 'a face passed through the mind of Signor, comes out like a better self of that sitter!'[28]

Evelyn de Vesci came to stay at Limnerslease for portrait sittings. It was unusual for the Watts to enjoy a guest as much. A beautiful, compassionate woman, she was exhausted from worry. As she sat by the artist, the lines of her soft white dress falling about her splendid figure, she feared chaos in Ireland if the Home Rule Bill were to be passed by the Lord's. She was devoted to the tenants at Abbeyleix, Viscount de Vesci's Irish estate.[29] The issue was tearing society apart. Margot Tennant declared that Gladstone had 'made a Balaclava blunder'.[30] Oscar Wilde, his hair elaborately waved, came to Little Holland House in June 1893. He too supported the Bill, and gloriously quashed an opponent, 'Ah, my own idea is that Ireland should rule England!'[31] Lord Wemyss's unconscious tribute, bemoaning the Wellington memorial in St Paul's, that the next one would be Burns 'who tends to free us from the *tyranny of capital!*', delighted the Watts. (John Burns, the founder of the Battersea Labour League, would sit for a portrait in October 1897.[32]) Hamilton Aidé brought news of the Italian actress Eleanora Duse and her triumphant London debut in *La Dame aux Camellias* at the Lyceum.[33] And a Scotswoman called. Inspired by *Love and Life*, she had approached Watts out of the blue for £20 to bring back her artist lover from Tangiers; now that he had found a patron, she wished to repay the debt with a hamper of symbolic flowers – heartsease and 'incorruptible' roses.[34] The diminutive writer Olive Schreiner, deeply moved by meeting Watts and especially by *She Shall Be Called Woman*, confided that she was to marry and that her fiancé had hung a print of *Love and Death* above his bed. When she returned to her South African farmhouse, its sole ornaments would be his pictures.[35]

In the blazing heat, Watts hammered at *Physical Energy*. 'He is wonderful in his energy & power', marvelled Mary. Two days later the rider was headless, armless, 'a maimed sad creature', destroyed in a fit of despondency. The rider soon had a new head and thickened torso, but Watts felt like hacking it all to pieces.[36] Gilbert, too, was devastated by the controversy that followed the unveiling of his memorial to the Earl of Shaftesbury. That day, the Wattses imagined Regent Circus with drapes hanging from every window, crowds carrying flags with mottos and a trilling oration to the social reformer, as Gilbert's masterpiece was revealed to a grateful public. Nothing could be further from their vision, the artists discovered to their horror, when they arrived for the ceremony amid wind and rain on 29 June.

> A wooden pen, covered with a grimy sail cloth rows of respectably hideous chairs tied together where people with pink tickets could go – outside the crowd were turned off, 'Pass along please pass along.' Inside the privileged few sat for more than an hour while one duller speech after another was stumbled out speaking for the most part of one of the greatest philanthropists of our day! The Duke of Westminster was best, & old Sir Harry Verney paid his schoolboy friend a tribute touching, in the little quavering voice of the man 91 years old!! 15 years older than my darling, standing bare headed there, & making his voice heard – It was the only bit of poetry in the whole thing.[37]

The tarpaulins were pulled back and *Eros*, one of the first public monuments in Britain to symbolize an idea – the virtue of Christian charity – was revealed to the drenched few. The first sight of Gilbert's swirling polychrome fountain topped by the glistening nude figure, a three-tiered Art Nouveau ensemble so bold that it stood out even in the London fogs, would have been startling. Above a great green octagonal cistern, provocative putti and dolphins writhed around a sinuous red-bronze basin, with water spurting from shell-like drinking fountains (to suggest abundant love for mankind; fig. 184), and at the top, about to fly off a nautilus shell, the wickedly sensual silver figure Eros (as selfless love), modelled in aluminium from Colarossi's son Angelo. Watts's wreath of golden lilies gleaming under the spray of the dolphins and made by Mary during Passmore Edwards's portrait sitting, cheered the otherwise funereal ceremony;[38] and while the Foreign Secretary sat at Little Holland House, she wrote a tribute for the Gallery portrait of Lord Shaftesbury.

*Eros*, feted at first, faced growing derision. Jets of water bursting from the mouths of the putti splashed spectators, and the flower girls needed umbrellas to shield themselves from the spray.[39] 'The dishonoured sculptor should be shot', one critic wrote to George Bernard Shaw. 'But for Gilbert shooting is too honourable a death. He should be drowned in the fountain with which he has disfigured Piccadilly.'[40] Watts called on Gilbert, who was thrown into debt by the memorial. His work in the studio, however – the monument to Queen Victoria's grandson the Duke of Clarence – was glorious. 'Well we have one artist now,' exclaimed Watts.[41] Lady Lothian, who had asked Gilbert to design her silver wedding present to Lady Brownlow, a key opening all the gates of Ashridge, their Hertfordshire home, wanted to found an art school with Watts as director. Mary dissuaded her.[42]

On 1 July 1893 the Munich Artists Association opened at the Glaspalast with twenty-four works by Watts on display. Elected an honorary member of the Munich Academy of Fine Arts, he, unusually, agreed to sell *The Happy Warrior*, the only version of this supreme symbolic subject, to the association, for half price.[43] Out of the blue, a grand piano was delivered to Little

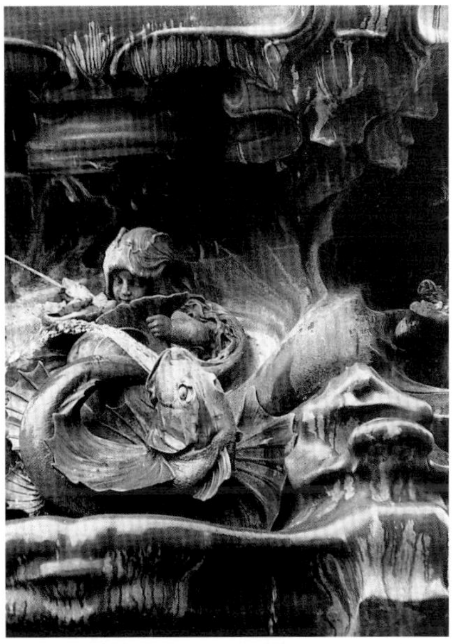

184  Alfred Gilbert, the Shaftesbury memorial (detail), 1886–93.

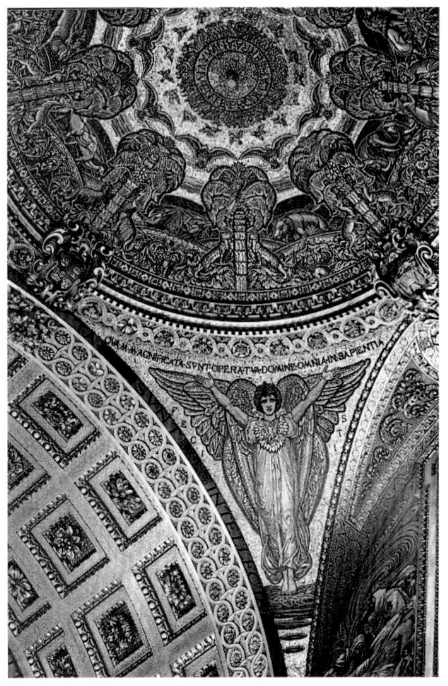

185   Detail of William Blake Richmond's mosaic ceiling at St Paul's cathedral, *Creation of the Beasts*, in the saucer dome, 1892, and *An Angel of the Pendentives*.

Holland House. The manager of Broadwood, Julian Hipkins, had written about the gift 'from friends and admirers of Mr Watts', but the artist thought it was a hoax and was embarrassed when the donors were gradually revealed. Kate Holiday was the instigator, supported by Gerry Liddell, Ruskin, Lord Wemyss, Evelyn de Vesci, Hipkins and the Ladies Pembroke, Lothian and Brownlow. The Holiday family christened the piano with Wagner's *Meistersinger* and the 'Slumber Song' from *Siegfried*. A young pianist Edie Reynolds played wild Hungarian dances and on 1 August gave a recital for their friends, Leighton, Lady Katie Thynne, Lord Archibald Campbell, and Rachel, Countess of Dudley, whose sister Laura had just married Sir Thomas Troubridge.[44] Watts was dipping into E. F. Benson's *Dodo*, a blatant satire of Margot Tennant and the Souls. As H. H. Asquith was wooing Margot, Lord Rosebery advised the Home Secretary to read it – 'there is a great deal of truth in it.'[45]

Lady Granby longed to draw Watts, and told him that Sargent wanted to paint her because he thought his picture of her in Prussian blue the finest portrait he had ever seen – 'Who would believe it!' wondered Mary. Watts's portrait of Violet Lindsay, now Lady Granby (pl. XXXIII), would dominate the opening exhibition of *La Libre Esthéthetique* in Brussels the following year. To the Belgian Symbolist Fernand Khnopff, it was 'a superb jewel . . . richness without parallel'.[46]

Despite Watts's antipathy to the 'smear' in art, his views broadened with age, 'Signor keeps younger than his friends, & as their ideas ossify, his remain elastic!'[47] Julia Cartwright found him in joyful spirits, with hoards of visitors, among them Sir Henry Layard, looking years older than his host, and the sculptor Joseph Swynnerton with his wife Annie, a women's rights activist and daring painter of the nude, influenced by Watts and Burne-Jones. '[Watts] declares he is just beginning to know how to paint and if he can only live another ten years he will yet accomplish something', wrote Cartwright. In the garden with Lady Katie Thynne, she learned the sad story of the riderless horse – 'Mr Watts having come home . . . in a most disconcerted mood this spring & destroyed all he could lay hands on.' Happily, at four in the morning the maid heard him singing and whistling as he chipped in the sculpture studio.[48]

One afternoon, Watts took Mary to see Richmond at work in St Paul's. They climbed up to the roof of the apse, above the altar, to find the artist suspended with his assistant, applying the mosaic decoration (fig. 185), almost two centuries after the cathedral was built. 'At last our 19th century has broken through the fogs, smoke, market price all the chains that bound it, & is to have its glorious roof', Mary enthused. 'Mr Richmond has found *himself*, has come out of the shadow of all other work'. Recognizing his pioneering achievement, they wanted to press forward: '*Surely* we must move on, kill smoke, kill ugliness outside – have a resurrected St Paul's with a green space about it, red gabled houses'. Elated that Richmond and Gilbert were developing Watts's life work, Mary saw that, 'Far from the torch falling from the hand of Mr Burne Jones Signor & others to turn out in flimsy clever portraits like *Mrs Hammersley* it was passing to men who will climb to light a beacon for the world.'[49] Watts was determined 'to make art a factor in *real* progress by suggestions in a beautiful & universal language of ennobling thoughts'.

He had agreed to sell further pictures to Smith, but *Ophelia*, among his eighteen pictures at the New English Art Club exhibition in Newcastle, was not for sale.[50] The original sitter, Ellen Terry, struck by a presentiment before leaving for America, urged Lady Leslie to deliver a message to her former husband and his wife. Greeted in the drawing room by Mary, Constance Leslie spoke kindly, clearly uncomfortable that she might upset her hosts, handed over Ellen Terry's note, saying Mary could bury it in her heart if she wished, but the actress had a strong sense she might never return: 'If I don't – now this is very private – see Mr Watts (the dear Signor) for me, & to him present my devotion & say, he, from first to last has been a beautiful influence in my life & that I pray God bless him, she too I bless for going into his life & cheering it – I have always had a great desire to tell her so, but feared it might not be seemly in her eyes'.

Mary, disinclined to break her promise not to mention his first marriage, for a presentiment she trusted would end in 'a most happy return', was deeply touched and copied every word into her diary. She composed a letter, imbued with sentiments Watts might have given, for Lady Leslie to forward. Her ladyship inscribed the envelope 'beautiful letter from Mrs Watts'. If the actress were taken ill or 'before *he goes* away from us altogether', Mary promised,

> Signor shall most surely have the loving words exactly & truly given him . . . He seems to me to live more & more in a deep wide impersonal love for every one . . . In those wider affections there is room for all – & whenever mistakes or misunderstandings have arisen, he never blames any one; only his own want of power in dealing with the difficulty is deplored . . . I send you this for you & one other only –
>
> I shall always like to think of the kind thought given to me & value it, though most I value the knowledge that whatever the mistakes were, in neither heart (for I have long read one), without word, does anything remain now, but a purified feeling best kept in a hallowed silence.[51]

Nelly had been brooding over their time together in Freshwater: 'I was 17 in years then, but scarcely 7, in wisdom,' she reminisced to Hallam Tennyson.[52] Though the actress survived her trip, that week the mayor of Chicago was murdered. She was performing there, and her former husband's paintings were on display at the World's Fair. To the *Tribune* Watts was 'decidedly a genius, the one Englishman in the Exhibition to whom such an epithet belongs', but his pictures 'triumph as far as ideas ever can triumph in such a struggle, over the stringy pigments and halting manner by which this painter's art is afflicted. It is a maimed art.' That he was not among the many medal-winners prompted the *Art Journal* to observe: 'it is more distinguished not to be in the list'.[53]

Watts woke one morning with the thought that art might bind nations together, as 'a great medicine giving vitality to that interchange of ideas – common to all nations . . . a titan language dwelling upon subjects that unite all mankind.' Scandinavia, Germany and Italy were represented in his pictures, notably the landscape *Vesuvius from Naples*, on show at Robert Dunthorne's gallery, the Rembrandt Head, in Vigo Street. That day, he received a visit from the German art critic Professor Emil Heilbut, who had stirred controversy by writing in a review of the Munich portrait painter Franz Lenbach that Watts was more spiritual.[54]

Sir Andrew Clark observed during a sitting that Gladstone was a cold man, his affections strong, but impersonal. The conversation spurred the artist to write to the prime minister's wife seeking an introduction for Mary, 'My wife very earnestly desires to have the honour & she is worthy of it, of shaking hands once in her life with Mr Gladstone. Could this be managed without intrusion upon time & attention so valuable? I also should like to have the same honour once more.'[55] An invitation came by return and on 9 August, the couple set out for an evening garden party at Downing Street. 'It is rather a plunge to go out once – in four of five years!' Mary noted. Passing Arthur Balfour, the Leader of the Opposition on his way from the House, they broke through the crowds outside Number Ten. The prime minister, having told Richmond that he enjoyed Watts's conversation more than any, greeted Mary warmly, then he and Watts sat side by side, their knees and heads together, arguing about Homer. He tackled Mary about his drawing of the *Ilyssus* promised long ago in lieu of *Orpheus and Eurydice*. Watts, who had given the apparently unwanted drawing to Leighton, was further embarrassed to receive a gift from the prime minister: 'I cannot say how much I am touched by your kindness in finding time & sending me the copies of your books especially after my own most extraordinarily bad conduct & forgetfulness for which I blush every moment. Some day however I hope while making amends, to call Phidias into court to support my view.'[56]

'Dear me! It's always harvest time wi Mr Watts!' exclaimed old Carpenter, an out-of-work bailiff digging paths for Mary at Limnerslease.[57] As the artist felt giddy in the heat, she suggested a trip to Coniston, to see Ruskin and revive in the fresh mountain air. No sooner had he agreed than travelling nerves set in, the giddiness and headaches worsened. Mary gave him sal volatile, but at dawn he asked for the curtains to be closed to hide his beloved light. The Coniston trip was cancelled. Yet he was well enough to work at the horse, and wrote to Ruskin, 'Dear old friend, Master and best teacher', that he had looked forward to their discussion and was sorry he had given up writing: 'There is so much to say & teach in these days of transition; I cannot feel but that civilization having gone so wrong very great & radical changes are inevitable, & perhaps very near, & I wish every voice that can be raised with authority should be heard.'[58]

Mary was concerned that if, as planned, they gave up Little Holland House, and lived only at Limnerslease, without variety Signor might sink into old age. He insisted that they could never be dull together, but she knew that they must keep the house. It was reassuring to see him attack *Physical Energy* with a new *desire* to complete it. By the end of the month the rider was back on the horse, and she wondered whether he needed to *lose* in order to regain. As the work neared completion, Watts, dissatisfied with himself, allowed no one to touch it.[59]

At the British Museum, researching Buddhist symbols for the Limnerslease ceiling, Mary was distracted by the art of the Celts. Watts was delighted by her reaction to their sharp-edged curves, that the early Celts felt beauty as much as the Greeks. The early artists, he explained, expressed a message; now art was merely ornament. In art, as in music and language, a pure line served a purpose. A clear edge in sculpture and metalwork was like a distinct order – the *clearness* of communication defined by the French actor Coquelin – whereas fudged edges, like the smear in painting, were like a flowery little speech.[60] 'Sunrise is to me a finer sight than sunset, that great glory coming up slowly from behind the darkened earth,' said Watts. Before dawn, he would survey his sculpture by candlelight, illuminating the great throat and breasts of *Dawn* while the horse loomed from the darkness overhead.[61]

Annie Swynnerton, who had slavishly followed Wattsian theories as a student, was distressed after his visit to her studio in Shepherds Bush. In his view, her vivid use of colour in ideal nudes betrayed her – *Cupid and Psyche*, for example, shows the influence of *Love and Life* and *Thetis*, but with a blush and lipstick. He had tried to demonstrate where ideal art differed from the realism of portraiture to give a general sense of the beautiful truths of nature.[62]

On 25 August, Watts began a portrait of 'Nellie' Agathonike Ionides, the fifth generation of the family he had been painting for over half a century. Her lively expression, such that he would never use in an adult portrait, shows how enchanted he was by the Greek child.[63] Una Taylor brought various little waifs to Little Holland House, among them, golden-haired Lily, now thirteen. Her mother Maud Macintosh had given up a wicked life and died long ago of consumption, and on the death of her natural father, Major General Henry Abbott, whom she believed to be her grandfather, his son – now her guardian – told her that she was illegitimate. Reluctant to return to the aunt who called her an 'incubus', Lily loved staying at Little Holland House.[64]

Watts's aims and position had brought Mary into the heart of the craft revival movement. She encouraged Conrad Dressler, a sculptor and former pupil of the late Sir Edgar Boehm, with his plan to train a brotherhood of artist-craftsmen to design English outdoor ceramic decoration, on a Lucca della Robbia ground. Liverpool merchants had offered financial support. In the spirit of Pugin, Watts, Ruskin and the Arts and Crafts Movement, materials would be dug from the earth, using no machinery other than that driven by water or a donkey. Unlike the lad from the People's Palace who came to Signor – 'hungry-eyed, dying to leave off being a machine' – hoping to go to Herkomer's to become another picture maker, but learn nothing, and unlike the wallpaper designer who created only the outline, which was coloured by someone else, Dressler's workmen were to be involved creatively from first to last. He brought his partner, the painter Harold Rathbone, to discuss the scheme with Watts.[65] Henry Ward, the editor of *Practical Photographer* brought photogravures produced by English craftsmen, an endeavour Watts was also keen to support, and introduced Frederick E. Ives, the American pioneer of the trichromatic half-tone process in colour photography.[66] The Home Arts badly needed funds and a new design secretary. Sweeping aside Signor's plea not to take advantage of his sitting captives, Mary put the case to Passmore Edwards. He promised to publish her appeal in the *Building News*.[67]

While she appealed to influential friends and patrons on behalf of the Home Arts, Watts fulminated about Joseph Chamberlain's attack against Home Rule. 'Mr Aidé & I laughed over the *non-political* position he always claims for himself'.[68] Lord Rosebery, sitting again for his portrait, made an impassioned plea for real union in Ireland, for England to admit guilt and Ireland to find her better self, but the Lords threw out the Home Rule Bill. Dynamic in the House and in letters to Watts, the earl was not at ease with

Mary in the studio, but his eyes, dark, dull and dreamy, lit up when he spoke to Watts of the future.[69]

Laing's study of the dual spiritual forces of good and evil, *A Modern Zoroastrian*, relating initially to Mary's studies, fascinated the Wattses: 'Those dim gropings after the Almighty Power seen through ourselves & through the universe.' Watts wanted to make his rider look like man, 'a part of the great creation! – cosmos in fact – his great limbs like rocks & roots, head like sun.' He had achieved this in *Chaos*, but he vowed *Physical Energy* should be his finest work. The most difficult part was 'trying to give a sense of deliberate largeness to the lines – No good music . . . is without that deliberateness of precision.'[70] He asked Rivière to check *Physical Energy* and *Love and Life*. Was his latest work good or bad? He had also had an idea for a statue of Tennyson.[71]

Canon Rawnsley and his wife came to luncheon at Little Holland House. Watts had contributed substantially to the new workshops and showroom for their Keswick School of Industrial Art, a particularly successful branch of the Home Arts, specializing in metalwork. He would support Rawnsley's latest venture – with Octavia Hill and Sir Robert Hunter – to form a National Trust, to preserve property and land for the enjoyment of the nation.[72]

As neither Watts nor Leighton could attend the royal opening of the South London Gallery buildings, Mary asked Val Prinsep to take their place. Val refused, not wishing to play second fiddle to Sir James Linton, the vice-president, an honour Rossiter had declined. Mary was indignant: 'My little Signor was trotting off cheerfully to take *any* place! – he does not know he has a dignity at all – blessedly.' Confined to his bed, he was missed, and their maids heard people in the crowds asking which was Mr Watts.[73]

Gertrude Mead brought her husband Edwin Abbey to Little Holland House. An illustrator, muralist and close friend of Sargent, Abbey had been motivated by the works of Watts and Leighton exhibited in Philadelphia to move to England; honoured to sit for a portrait head in charcoal, as a wedding gift, he was inexpressibly moved at 'talking all this while with one of the very great thinkers of our time – and to have listened to what I know is the expression of the very noblest artistic thoughts of this age.' That Watts's hand did not always carry out those thoughts, he wrote, did not detract from their greatness.[74] Sir Andrew Clark came for a final sitting on 13 October. Strong, masterful and illogical, he talked so heartily of building up a library that three weeks later the Watts could hardly believe that he had 'handed up his sword in the great Court of Death'.[75]

Returning to Limnerslease for the winter, Watts acquired a new field and regained his youth with a daily gallop. He exhausted himself trying to achieve sentiments of both power and meekness in *Repentant Eve*. His sense of counterbalance was more obvious in the twin nude boys, barely old enough to stand, representing 'the spiritual and the carnal' *In the Land of Weissnichtwo*, a butterfly alights on the hand of the fair, wide-eyed boy as his darker twin gorges on grapes. While Watts painted below, Mary worked on Indian symbols for her ceiling.[76] He was increasingly drawn to politics. His anger at the ungenerous, unchivalrous attitude of Home Rule opponents claiming all as a birthright, severely tested his friendship with Andrew Hichens, who called as he knocked at the door, 'May I come in although I am a wretched Tory.' Of course. 'It is *not* his being a Tory I object to, the more the different opinion of the same question are ventilated the better', said Watts. 'What I dislike & regret is that any man who does not agree with [him] is looked upon as an enemy.' Gradually the friends resumed political argument, Hichens attacking the demands of the striking miners, while Watts praised their fighting spirit and spoke up for Zola. As Mary woke, he stood by the bedside and stormed against apathy and ignorance, the cruelty of people who were themselves comfortable. 'Too much for me . . . every nerve in my body seemed on fire'. She protested 'Well, what am I doing?' Her working day was ruined. A ride helped, but she begged him not to dwell on hopeless issues.[77]

The foundation of 'The National Trust for Historic Sites and Natural Scenery' offered hope. Watts returned to London for the preliminary meeting under the presidency of the Duke of Westminster at Grosvenor House on 16 November 1893. Agreeing to join the Provisional Council, Watts wrote to Rawnsley:

> Providing for the needs interests & pleasures of those who are coming after us should exercise the minds not only of statesmen, but every one who has the well being of the nation at heart . . . Trades Unions must be supplemented, for they cannot be put down, by Unions among the thoughtful to promote pleasure & contentment – to keep alive interest in the history of the country is not one of the least happy of the means to be employed.[78]

Visitors again converged on Little Holland House. Books of drawings arrived from Phoebe Traquair. Evelyn de Vesci had been to see her painting brilliantly coloured murals at the Catholic Apostolic Church in Edinburgh. Thrilled to meet a friend of Watts, Traquair came down from her ladder and said that he had 'lighted the torch' for her. He admired the drawings, but her adulatory letter made him feel 'an impostor'. (When Traquair met him at Little Holland House the following March, he seemed to surpass her exalted expectations.[79]) Hollyer presented two huge volumes of photographs of all his work to date (fig. 186), portraits in one, subjects in the other – a splendid source of reference today. The Tintoretto effect of *The Court of Death*, which showed the grand masses, but blotted out the details, delighted Watts.[80] Hearing from William Spence, he replied eagerly, asking for the Florentine recipe for tempera colours, which he wished to apply rapidly on large elaborate designs: 'This would take too long in oil, for I have not time to lose! . . . I am impatient to begin these things.' Urgently striving for the nation, he was planning a new visionary subject, *Love Triumphant* (pl. XXXVII).[81] Even in the dark days of December, he rose at four, to light a candle and scribble down thoughts. Mary, who made him sleep summer and winter with the window open, attributed his vigour to the thimbleful of whisky he enjoyed at luncheon. Laughing, he put it down to animal magnetism, people liking him more than he deserved.[82] Either way, as he told Augustus Hare, he had no need of a maulstick.

Hare's biography of Lady Waterford and her sister Viscountess Canning was about to be published when he came to Limnerslease with his cousin Lady Victoria Rowe. Leaving their carriage at the bottom of the hill, they walked up the winding paths, through Scotch firs and bracken, to 'a rustic hermitage', where they found Watts, 'like a pilgrim, like a medieval hermit saint, in a brown blouse and slippers, with a skullcap above his white hair

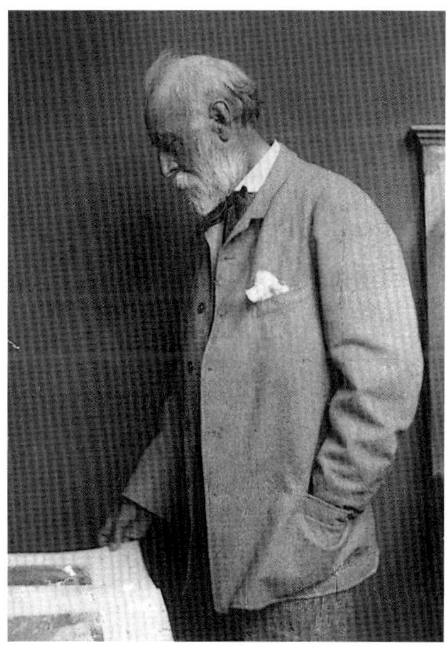

186    Watts studying Hollyer's photographs of his paintings, 1893 (photo: Frederic Hollyer).

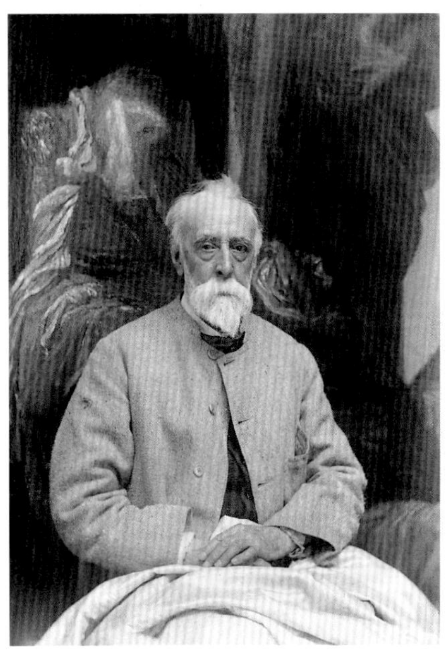

187   Watts seated in front of *The Messenge*, c.1895.

and beard, and his sharp eager features, in which there is also boundless tenderness and refinement'. They talked at once of Lady Waterford. Photographs of her works hung happily beside those of Titian. Watts wished he had painted her in later life, when she had more history, and his power of analysis had ripened. Walking from the colourful, low-ceilinged drawing room, the studio seemed immense. 'You wonder what that is?' asked Watts, pointing to a painting of the sorrowful man hiding his face in his rich Eastern costume. 'He has tried, but he *cannot* [relinquish his great possessions] . . . He is going out into the world again, and yet – and yet he is very sorry.' The artist had just to add rings and a gold chain to complete the story. His guests, fascinated by *The Messenger*, were told that the Angel of Rest was bidding the weary old man (fig. 187), by whom lay instruments of music and science, to come and rest. Hare's favourite portrait was the chalk head of Lady de Vesci, which encapsulated her dignity, sympathy and pity. Watts took them to the studio window to see 'the half-clothed trees of the winter world' and birds fluttering in and out of coconuts hanging from the branches, 'I like to see them enjoy it'.[83]

Mary was designing her first 'national work', a reredos for St Albans workhouse chapel, where her brother-in-law, Canon Edward Liddell, officiated. As Watts, who was donating a brass cross, advised against a richly coloured background, she chose a silvery tone. After much despair and 'a little lotus eating in the niche' with her head on his shoulder, he so admired it that she had to remember his tendency to over-praise. On her return from St Albans, he showed her the large version of *For He Had Great Possessions*. The drop of the man's head was far finer, thought Mary, but the smaller version was more reticent and poetic. 'He will get his music right by & by.' Feeling he needed help from a living model, she tied an orange silk turban around her head, threw on an old cloak edged with fur, and posed herself. Delighted, he made studies from her bowed head and back in pencil, but for the figure itself he created the impression of an older man who had enjoyed a long life of luxury.[84]

That evening, he claimed that of all his *confrères*, he was the most modern in thought and expression of thought.[85] Reading lectures on Buddhism, he compared the natural upward tendency of the man 'to a flower drawn to the sun', but disputed Buddha's ideal of immortality, feeling that the final return to unity with God need not be unconscious. 'One can imagine having the *extra* delight of the music of having left the world better for your life,' he said, Mary adding, 'as if he had heard that music dimly already!'[86]

Leighton's Christmas letter was delivered with a sad account from Dr Bond about the acrobat Zazel, who was paralysed after a fall when the scaffolding had collapsed in America. Wickedly, Mary wondered whether it might be asking too much to regret that their cultured friend had not trained to jump like Zazel. 'Find it rather a comfort to think there is something he does not do.' Sir Frederic was a splendid fellow, but she wished he would let himself go. His work was too perfect and showed none of his vitality. 'It his *cultured* self that is in it *only* & one longs for more life, even ugliness! – His work has probably done much to produce Degas & others of the brotherhood of ugliness.[87]

Across the Atlantic, *Love and Life* (pl. XXXI) was the subject of a tug of war. A Resolution in Congress to secure Watts's gift for the American people was delayed because Marquand, now president of the Metropolitan, was determined to secure it for the New York museum. 'Washington is a sort of provincial place & the center of art is New York & not at the seat of government – we have 8 or 10 times the number of visitors yearly that Washington has', he wrote to Watts, requesting formal letter of authority. The artist had understood that *Love and Life* was to be consigned 'to the museum in fact! in trust, as National property, to be dealt with hereafter according to the will of the Authorities'. It had been transferred to the Georgetown Custom House when he heard from the American Ambassador in London, T. F. Bayard, that 'the Government of the United States has no connection whatever with the Metropolitan', and would he therefore allow *Love and Life* to hang at the White House in Washington. The artist's motive was 'to help to form the nucleus of that Grand Gallery of Art with which, in the course of time, America will doubtless enrich herself, and which the characteristic expansion of American ideas will develop into the centre of the Artistic utterance of the English-speaking race'. For temporary public display, the museum was more appropriate than an official residence, but Watts did not refuse, and the ambassador gave Congress the go-ahead, assuring him that there was 'no reason to doubt that an American National Gallery of Art will, at no distant day, be called into being.'[88] Meanwhile, at the reopening of the Luxembourg in Paris on 1 January 1894, *Love and Life* was judged the most important English acquisition; and Edmund Gosse in his seminal reassessment in the *Art Journal* established Watts's *Clytie* – 'that swallow of 1868' – as 'the true forerunner of the New Sculpture'.[89]

'There is little doubt that this is not the age of enthusiasm', began L. T. Meade in the first of two papers on Watts in *Sunday Magazine*. 'We are smart, clever, and, as a rule, well-informed, but we are not enthusiastic. We pride ourselves on our realism . . . look coldly at mysticism, symbolism, allegory, and metaphor. Ours is a hard and money-making age . . . It is the fashion now to be real, to look without shuddering at ugliness.' Meade saw the artist as a prophet and seer – 'Like St John, he stands in the wilderness of the world, and points to eternal truths.' Undoubtedly his vision was unique. Watts saw himself as a beacon.[90]

On 27 January, the prime minister offered a baronetcy to Watts and Burne-Jones. Neither wished for a title, but Phil Burne-Jones persuaded his father to accept. Again Watts would not. He replied at length to Gladstone, acknowledging the renewed offer as 'a greater distinction than could be ten Baronetcies!', but still considered it inappropriate to 'purely intellectual efforts'. To reject – twice – an honour sanctioned by the Queen was highly embarrassing, but the artist, addressing his art to the public conscience, found the social honour unpalatable. He suggested to Gladstone that the title of 'Honourable' – like an honorary university degree – would be more fitting for men of art and letters. To Hichens, he went further, and proposed 'Right Honourable', because even as non-practising privy councillors men like Browning or Lecky could be consulted for valued opinions 'as students of men, manners, physiology, and psychology . . . I should not be sorry if you would ventilate my idea in any quarter likely to find interest in it, Mr Lyttleton or Mr Gladstone himself, not as coming from me, but as my idea.'

Like Hichens, Leighton was irritated by his refusal, 'I do feel that the *second* and more pressing offer of a title does emphasize the compliment offered to you'. Sir Frederic added, 'I of course entirely *understand* your feeling in the matter – mine was, and is purely a *great* unwillingness that there should be any honor held by an artist in this country that should not be yours.' Watts's perhaps most illuminating extant letter on the issue was to Spielmann, for the benefit of the *Magazine of Art*, 'I suppose the Burne-Jones Baronetcy surprised you a little. Some of his friends regret his having accepted the distinction but though it is nothing to him it is & will be valuable to his son.' Unlike Burne-Jones's commissions, Watts's most expensive and important work (dedicated to the nation) was not for sale, 'I never have had that object & cannot take it up now'. His primary concern was to stir people's conscience through the medium of art, rather than personal position: 'I am greatly pleased to find that in the letters I constantly receive (from strangers) that this is felt & that what I do is not regarded from the decorative or pictorial point of view. I get no praise for my pictures as works of Art & I am flattered, so often, by the proof that the Artistic is forgotten in the more important one'.[91]

Affectionate correspondence passed between him and Burne-Jones, from whom he asked to borrow – presumably for an educational venture – some 'lovely silverpoints, the most beautiful things I ever saw, illustrations I think of some of Morris's words, such a corrective to the splashing style of the day'. Burne-Jones replied, 'You dear thing of course I'll do anything you ever ask me . . . always & without cessation I am your loving old old Ned', and offered a special new drawing. 'Do you know what I would do to please you? or rather what I wouldn't do? Stand in a pillory at Charing Cross from morning till night if it could possibly be of any service to you – don't see how it could – but it would amuse some people. Anyhow tomorrow I will begin it – the drawing not the pillory . . . Your most affectionate unchanging Ned.'[92]

On his return from Biarritz, Gladstone came to the studio for a preview of the portrait of their late doctor, Sir Andrew Clark, and Watts began the promised drawing from Phidias 'to illustrate what I feel about the two great Epics over which I persevere to differ from you.'[93] Deeply moved by Mary's research into the symbolism of ancient civilizations, he had come to see it as a language expressing 'the highest ideas of man', beyond mere fact and the mere fringe of ornament. Both now influenced each other, as Watts acknowledged after reading a Zoroastrian article that echoed the symbolism of his own *Happy Warrior*, 'My work is in harmony with all that', he said, correcting himself, '*Our* work . . . for your work has taken you into the region of the greatest thought . . . this effort of the human mind, always trying to raise itself to its *own* origin.'[94] In a brief guide to female dress for *Aglaia*, the journal of The Healthy and Artistic Dress Union, he compared a simply robed Egyptian woman with a water-jar on her head, to a harem favourite in stiff black dress, hobbling on French high-heeled shoes: 'What a difference! That 'free creature with the water-jar', neither 'divinely fair' like an English maiden, nor 'divinely tall', moved majestically 'in God's own image'. Extending his attack on tight waists and the barrel skirt, he pointed to the grace of folds, the beauty of variety, light and shade, and the length of line that gave height and distinction to the human figure.'[95]

The dual forces in his art were splendidly apparent that Easter in the caption to *Europa*, her arms around bull carrying her over the seas with a glint in its eye, on exhibition among his thirteen wide-ranging pictures at St Jude's: 'The artist shows us the brutal beauty of the bull (Jupiter) and the frightened contentment of the woman (Europa).'[96] Out riding one morning with Mary, they discussed what Professor Friedrich Max Müller, editor of *The Sacred Books of the East*, called 'The Self', 'but we cannot divest that word from the My-Self'. To Watts it suggested much more. He felt instinctively a sense of the Eternal Self, that consciousness in the philosophy of India, the Parthenon fragments, the poetry of Wordsworth. 'In all great art I hear the organ tone – it makes me feel religious – in my own work I am always trying, trying for it!'[97]

'Your Titian of Limnerslease has made me by much the richer. It has the effect of a fine picture – on me, at least', wrote George Meredith. At the New Gallery exhibition of 1894, Meredith's portrait was admired by critics, especially the expression (fig. 188). His mind is engaged, possibly disputing an idea. (To the poet Siegfried Sassoon writing half a century later, it did not show the 'wind-blown sky of expressiveness and thought in action' encapsulated by Sargent. 'The beautiful face is there, but the daemon of genius has been tidied away.' Because he looked like 'a cross between a distinguished art-critic and a dilettante Ambassador', Sassoon suspected that sitting with Mary had made the novelist feel prim and proper.[98]) The portraits of Meredith, and Passmore Edwards and Sir Andrew Clark at the Academy with the acclaimed *For He had Great Possessions* were now formally bequeathed to the nation;[99] and after sixteen years as an associate, Val was elected to full membership.[100]

A fraudulent dealer was making mischief with a small nude painting, unusually realistic in Watts's oeuvre. Phil Burne-Jones came to the rescue; in a surprise swoop, he reduced the six-foot miscreant to wax and returned triumphant in a hansom cab with the picture.[101] Sir Henry Acland came to Little Holland House in May for the promised portrait in chalk. The old campaigner begged for the sketch of the fresco for the Taylorian Ceiling for the University Galleries.[102] 'Most of our old friends are gone', sighed Sir Henry Layard when the artist visited his sick bed. Within six weeks, he too had died.[103] Lady Vicky Rowe found that Watts's pictures dissolved her fear of death.[104] The Duchess of Leinster (fig. 189) was much inspired by his work. Trapped in marriage to a tyrannical husband, who had since died, she had taken up painting and sculpture when she came to Little Holland House for the last time in June. Watts began to paint her portrait. Unaware that the beautiful young duchess had less than a year to live, he was struck by the sight of her standing in front of the *Messenger*, 'the grandeur of the living form, even in competition with the ideal'.[105] As the artist rested, he appeared to Mary 'a sleeping angel . . . so far removed from the ordinary', and she felt a tremendous responsibility as his wife.[106]

Mrs Humphrey Ward consulted Watts about the foundation of her new educational settlement. His reply suggests she may well have asked him to paint frescoes, but as well as completing his national work he was stepping up efforts on behalf of the Home Arts. 'You may be sure I would eagerly aid in carrying out the scheme you propose it is the sort of thing I formerly would have given my time & every thing else in my possession to forward . . . I have so much on my hands in my self imposed task to carry out what I may call my essays on the art of living.' He invited Mary Ward to discuss the project and gave her an introduction to the architect Norman Shaw whom she engaged to judge a competition for the new building.[107]

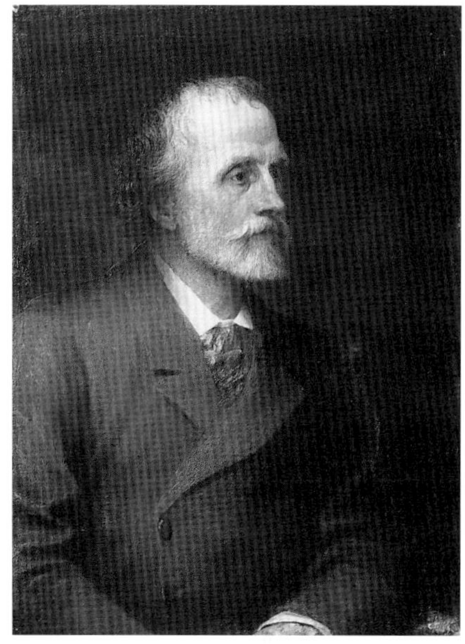

188   *George Meredith*, 1893 (National Portrait Gallery, London).

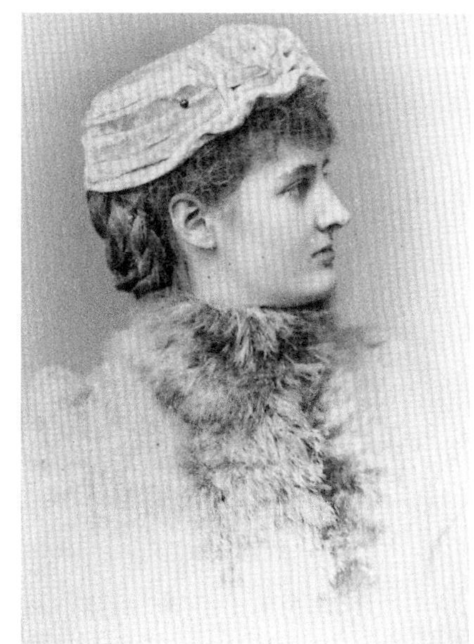

189   The Duchess of Leinster (photo: W. & D. Downey).

The Della Robbia pottery was one of the highlights at the annual Home Arts exhibition. Watts, spearheading a campaign to achieve financial security for the association, wrote to a hundred patrons and art lovers, requesting donations of £50 each. A group of workers, visiting from Stoke Newington, declared, 'We look upon him as national property', a sentiment echoed by Mary when Cosmo Monkhouse came to research an extensive article on Watts for *Scribner's Magazine* – 'I feel I have a National Trust!' Herkomer sent the first cheque and asked Watts to sit for a small, unsatisfactory portrait. Mary chased the appeal. In return for Agnew's donation, Watts drew his portrait in chalk; and the dealer, captivated by *Iris*, added the airy, luminous figure to his collection, promising that she would never leave his walls.[108] Max Müller, the scholar of Eastern philosophy, sat for the national collection in July. The two men were engrossed in conversation. Now and again the artist would look up and say, 'Now we must get on a little'; the professor would then rearrange his robe and pose briefly before resuming their discussion about the dual forces of light and darkness.[109]

Watts was planning to paint a lifeboat – Man, in conflict in the midst of forces he cannot control, sustained by Love at the helm – when Hunt came to Little Holland House in August. Hunt listened, but said nothing, though he too had been preparing a similar theme – a rare commission from the Gallery of Sacred Art for a triptych showing 'Christ in spirit at the helm in a boat'. Afterwards he wrote to Watts 'to explain a fact of some importance bearing on your purpose of painting a picture called *The Life Boat* with Our Lord as pilot'. The gallery manager had rejected his sketches and given the commission and, possibly his ideas, to another artist; as Hunt could not afford to waste time and money, he was reserving the sketches for future use. The two friends treated their unusual conflict with delicate magnanimity. 'There is no reason that you should not paint your excellent idea. Yours would I am sure be most interesting and novel,' added Hunt. 'I still feel that it would [be] wrong of me not to tell you to what degree the main idea is in prospect of being elaborated by me, and perhaps by another.' Watts replied:

> The subject *The life boat* which I think a very fine one has been in my mind a long time. I mentioned it in *confidence* to Richmond I think as long as a year ago. My wife thinks you would treat the subject better than I could & I agree with her & wish you would paint it in your noble & solid manner. Of course there can be no monopoly or copyright in choice of subject only it would be hardly in accordance with professional etiquette consciously to take a subject out of another's hands but your Friend of the Sacred Art Gallery can have no claims to originality if you choose to take a subject I have had so long in my mind & for which I have occasionally made scratches. I should like you to paint it & give it up to you most freely. I have more subjects in my mind & many in progress than I can ever hope to be able to carry out. Pray paint 'this' one if it is only with the object of preventing it from being done in a slapstick manner.

Their approach would, of course, be quite different. Watts planned to paint Love at the tiller and Hunt, Christ. Grateful for Watts's support after his presidential address to the Sunday Society, he too felt out on a limb –

'the orthodox people hate my words, as they hate my pictures, and the major part of the reforming world have a stronger disapproval of the point at which I stop,' Hunt had written. 'There would be more reason to grieve if you were deterred from carrying out fittingly your admirable conception.' He did not complete the picture, nor did Watts begin *Love Steering the Boat of Humanity* until the outbreak of the Boer War.[110]

Gilbert, now in dire financial straits, sent him a reduced version of his bust to present to Sir Charles Drummond – 'The making of the original was a great enjoyment and honour, and I could not spoil the recollection of the creation by making of it a market' – and began to sit for his own portrait in September 1894. Violet Granby, who had longed to draw Watts, came to record the event, and sent the sketch to Gilbert, jauntily inscribed: 'After Watts. Does This Amuse? It is to remind You of VG I couldn't finish it – cos' his sitter had to go, & I with him – Watts also wants you to remember him & 1 more sitting.'[111]

By early September he had decided to make up the £5,000 for the Home Arts himself by resuming portrait commissions. Mary was thrilled at her opportunity to start a Home Arts class in Compton. The parish council planned a new burial ground on a hill bordering the Limnerslease estate and she decided to teach villagers to model gravestones. 'My hope is that Terra Cotta shall be my Rita,' she noted, using her favourite Hindu expression.[112] Leaving Watts for a night in the care of Gerry Liddell, she returned to find that they had organised two 500-guinea portraits. Disheartened after painting them, he stacked the canvases out of sight, until his beloved critic Lord Wemyss lavished praise on one, calling out as he left, 'Long Live Mrs Rogers!'[113]

James Smith, like the late Rickards and Carver, found that building up a collection of Watts's pictures stimulated a new interest in life. The artist was therefore keen to sell to him, 'I should like you to have my pictures because I know you wish to buy from real pleasure in them & not with the view of turning them into money.' *For He Had Great Possessions* he would reduce from £700 to £600. *Ophelia* was not for sale, nor *Ganymede*, nor *The Sea Ghost*, which he was keeping to lend. Smith chose *Europa* at £800, and, after the Society of British Artists winter exhibition, *Arion* riding a dolphin. Watts explained that once he was financially secure and no longer needed to invest the proceeds from the sale of pictures not painted for the nation or given to provincial galleries, he would spend it on improving the lives of others, 'My wife has a peculiarly sympathetic nature & I should like her to have the means of gratifying her feelings in the direction most delightful to her . . . She is far more the spirit of generosity than I can profess to be but I cannot cross her in what I must approve, besides I remember the great text that I have endeavoured to illustrate "what I gave I have".'[114]

At exhibitions, he had been keeping an eye on the paintings of Frank Brangwyn, whose broad masses of colour he thought ideal for fresco. The Welsh artist was summoned to Little Holland House, which he found so daunting that when Phoebe opened the door he forgot his name and asked her to announce that 'a young man wanted to see him'. Brangwyn spoke of his struggles; and when Watts impressed upon him that he must paint a noble idea to help one's fellow man, the Welshman protested: 'I said, I wished it was possible – but one had to *live . . . I* had to do things which

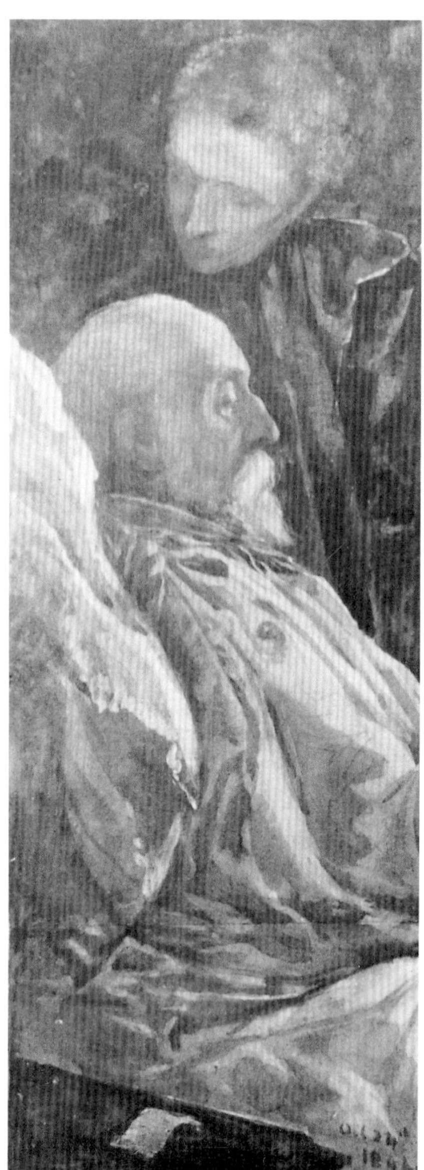

190    Mary's watercolour sketch of Signor, October 1894 (Watts Gallery).

were far from being noble.' So had Watts. Mary brought out an old pencil portrait. 'If you had to earn your living with such stuff today, you would starve, thought Brangwyn, who could not imagine the 'saintly old chap' painting a potboiler (*Hope* proved a valiant potboiler!). Watts had great hopes for Brangwyn, and after the visit wrote on his behalf to Briton Rivière, proposing a commission for one of the murals at The Royal Exchange, the first of which Leighton was now painting:

> Young Frank Brangwyn (the best eye for grand effects and colour out I think) came to see me to ask if I could help him to get a space on the walls of the Exchange which he is willing to cover without pay . . . we were much taken with the young fellow who has been a sailor I think before the mast & has still the sailor's roll. I am out of everything & can do nothing but you might speak a word for him, he has more originality than most, & it wont do for the Academy to let the best men slip whether students or others![115]

Watts, writing from his sickbed, was laid up again. Increasingly frustrated at the loss of time, he longed to improve and spoke of going along the right path, 'the silver way'. Burne-Jones sent a cheery note showing that it was hard work to be up; and Mary sketched him lying on his pillows: 'the spirit shining like a lamp thro' those beautiful brown eyes – the silver hair like wings about his head' (fig. 190).[116]

Once he was up and about, he pointed to his voluptuous figure of Mother Earth, supposedly unaware of her fecundity. Laughing, he asked if she liked it. '*I do much*,' though she found it strange, as indeed it is. 'There! You see nature has no outline, but I cannot do without one & that is just what happens in the spiritual world. To give anything form you must have boundary lines which do not really exist – Without the definite personal idea, one cannot well grasp it, do what you will the idea slips.'[117] Legros sent him some prepared paper and gold point; and in return he offered to draw his portrait 'in your style', a gesture that was doubly reciprocated by the Frenchman who drew separate portraits of Signor and Mary.[118] She had raised a princely £1,200 for the Home Arts. Not wishing her to send out more appeals, he sent a formal letter to *The Times*. A portrait study in blue stood on the easel at Limnerslease beside the *Outcast* child, *Goodwill*, a baby with a flower in one hand and holding out the other for alms with smoking factory chimneys in the distance, when the *Westminster Budget* reporter arrived. He was dazzled by Mary's decorations the instant the front door opened into a bright long room, where fantastic black oak carvings offset a wealth of tints and shades.

Watts arched niche, the richly coloured, gilded *Last Judgment* above his crimson couch, contrasted with the white symbolic ceiling panels; and as well as his pictures, flowers, Home Arts trays, copper, brass, pots, jars (fig. 191), there were mirrors all about and shimmering tinted glass. At the centre of 'this house beautiful', the veteran artist spoke of the Home Arts with astonishingly youthful fervour so soon after a serious illness. No, he insisted it was not a charity, nor a divine dividend, nor technical institution, 'or I would have nothing to do with it'. He deplored the decay of English taste, brutal working conditions and general discontent. To Watts, Home Arts classes were a power for good, patriotic and politically vital, resuscitating the best from the past to elevate the nation. Introducing a sense of beauty and new interest into humble households, they encouraged creativity in leisure hours and provided a joyful antidote to apathy and ruin.[119] 'Our day as a great nation is passed', he wrote to Horsfall. 'Machinery has, by making the activity of observation necessary in olden times unnecessary now resulted in a dullness in the labouring classes . . . If some means very effective are not discovered of checking the dreadful prevalence of drunkenness & gambling I fear the deterioration of the national character.' There should be a new direction in education, to encourage the observation of nature, and pure, original thought.[120]

He encouraged Andrews to photograph him in front of the large *Court of Death* (fig. 192). The monumental image, in which a fragment of the canvas towers over the seated artist, was significant for both men; and in December Watts sent a print to Horsfall. 'I send you a photograph taken

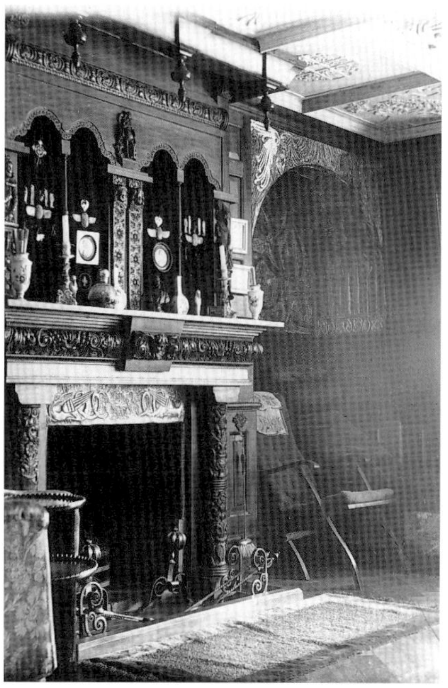

191     The Red Room at Limnerslease, *c*.1894.

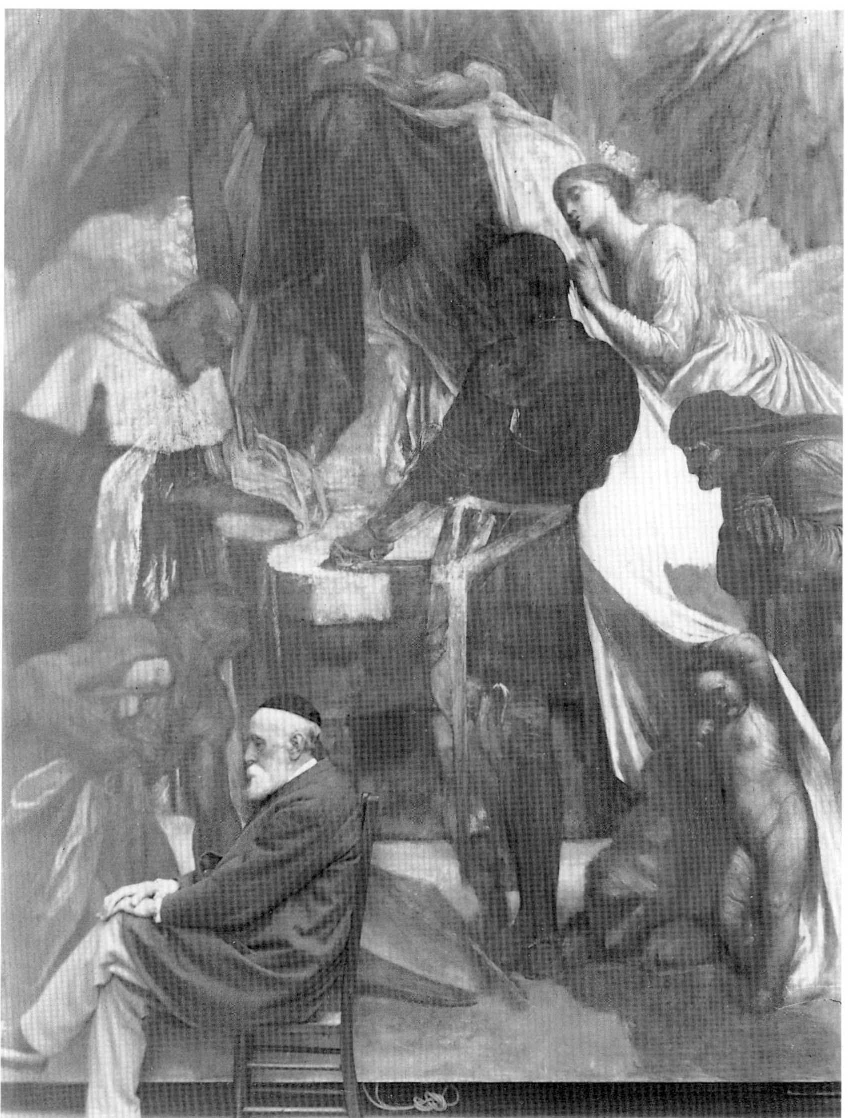

192     In front of *The Court of Death*, 1894.

by an amateur in my studio *here* by which you will see I am working on *The Court of Death* with hopes of completing it.'[121]

'When a man like Rembrandt or Watts paints either a portrait or a vision, he removes it to a sphere beyond the reach of mere physical sensation,' Cosmo Monkhouse wrote in the Christmas issue of *Scribner's Magazine*. 'Mr Watts . . . can make us feel either the presence of Death or the genius of Tennyson. In both cases he impresses our minds with a new image of the immaterial.' On the subject of portraits he captured Watts's intention absolutely – 'In the presence of his sitters he surrenders his own individuality. He has no wish to produce a fine picture sealed with his own artistic *cachet*, whereby everyone who looks may say, "This is a Watts"' – and observed 'a certain sense of the presence of a real person alone with his thoughts, secluded in a veil as of a special intellectual atmosphere.' Just as George du Maurier's wife finished reading the article aloud, he heard from Watts, who had enjoyed detecting voices of their old friends in the novel *Trilby*.[122]

However, although willing to be interviewed, the artist was disinclined to be the subject of a monograph, which William Graham's daughter Frances Horner had been commissioned to write by the publisher J. C. Nimmo. Burne-Jones, who had approached Mary to discover how his friend might view the idea, pointed out that a reliable chronological catalogue would be useful for a future biography. Nor did he accept Sir Henry Acland's proposal to take over from him as the Slade Professor in Oxford – 'if only for a year . . . to give a record of your thoughts'[123] – for he spoke best in paint.

*Love and Life*, his most significant, direct message to his generation, had been arousing stormy protests from the Women's Christian Temperance Union of the United States. Mrs Emily D. Martin, National Superintendent of Purity in Literature and Art, had urged her 300,000 members to write to President Cleveland objecting to the presence of 'two naked figures in atrocious postures' in the White House; when *Love and Life* was sent instead to the Corcoran Art Gallery she saw it as her victory. For Watts, too, it was an honourable decision. Though he let the gallery president know in no uncertain terms that the refusal to hang any picture because it was deemed immoral was so shocking he almost had it destroyed, he considered Washington's first art museum an admirable resting place, 'My notion was and is that it might possibly aid in giving stimulus to the idea of establishing a sort of Luxembourg. No great or wealthy Nation should be without the wealth represented by literature and art. I understand that the Corcoran Institution is intended to be of this kind.' Decades would pass before the foundation of America's National Gallery of Art. *Love and Life* may have come to rest, but it was still ascending its rocky path.[124]

## 22   Handover to the Nation

*JONAH* HUNG OPPOSITE SARGENT'S PORTRAIT OF the poet Coventry Patmore
at the Royal Academy Summer Exhibition of 1895, each a fierce visionary
male figure, the antithesis of the other. Watts's frenzied prophet preaching
with arms outstretched, fingers splayed, head thrust back against a background of friezes depicting gambling, drunkenness, horse-racing and figures
crawling up to moneybags, presented an image of such violent power that
no sinner in Nineveh could fail to don sackcloth and ashes and abandon
his or her evil ways (fig. 193). To the *Magazine of Art* the 'weird, ghastly,
screaming fanatic, the Solomon Eagle of an Oriental past, hideous in his
earnest gesticulation' was 'truly "great" . . . [but] to many it will be a repulsive picture.' *Jonah* did puzzle viewers. Over half a century later, however,
it would fascinate Evelyn Waugh. Watts also exhibited *The Outcast: Goodwill* – the infant symbolizing Trust, Innocence and Love cast out by the
fierce competitive commerce – the portrait of Professor Max Müller, and a
pastel head of Lady Mount-Temple.[1] His grand maternal Charity – begun
from Cameron's maid 'Madonna Mary' – hung at the New Gallery, with
the two Home Arts portraits of the Reverend Alfred Gurney and Mrs
Charles Coltman Rogers.[2] Watts would have to take on many more. Violet
Granby recommended a pretty young sitter, her future sister-in-law Norah
Bourke.[3]

Watts wanted English men and women to recognize that as members of
a great nation, taxes were their positive contribution to its needs. Were not
noblemen given their land by kings on the understanding that they should
bring men and arms into the field in an emergency? Too often they squan-
dered money at Monte Carlo, ' "Be sure of this," said our Jonah – "that
both for individual and for nations nemesis of their own deeds is certain
. . . Giving money is something – but giving ourselves is the one great and
necessary gift." '[4] Both the Watts were set to do just that.

'I very much wish you to see my wife's work', he wrote to Rivière. 'I
think she has a genius for symbolic decoration.' On 30 May, Compton
Parish Council discussed two letters: one from splendid old Mrs Ellice from
Eastbury Manor (now sitting for her portrait), who offered to give a further
quarter of an acre to improve the cemetery; and the other from Mary, offering 'on behalf of Mr Watts' to build a chapel. That day she drew a caricature of her husband holding out his upturned hat, as 'An Epsom Beggar,
drawn from Life by the Beggar's wife' (fig. 194), which she sent to the Earl
of Rosebery at The Durdans in Epsom. ('I have received your gruesome

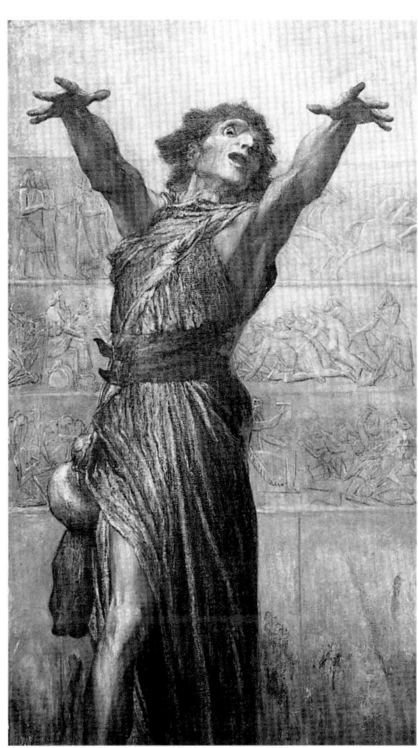

193   *Jonah*, 1894–95 (Tate,
London).

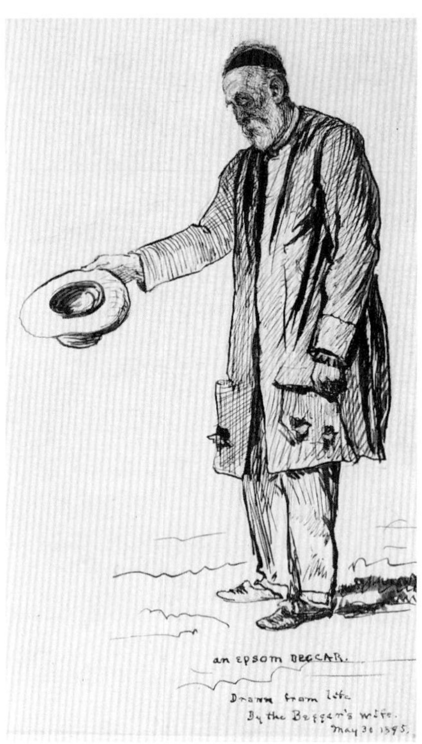



194   Mary's caricature of Signor as
'An Epsom Beggar, Drawn from Life
By the Beggar's wife', May 1895
(Watts Gallery).

portrait of my dear Mr Watts, and promise that you shall share in the spirits, but I can assure you that when the necessary presents are given there is little spoil to share! By the bye, does Apelles want any more sittings?'5) Her Terra Cotta Home Arts village class at Limnerslease was to model symbolic tiles for an extraordinary mortuary chapel, which she would design and Watts would fund with more portraits. He had urged, 'We *must build* something.' Suddenly he raised his hands to his heart, light flooded his face as he said 'Religion is the earnest endeavour of every moment'; and in that split second Mary felt she witnessed his inner life, 'the steady flame of aspiration'. Observers now spoke of the couple as artists of the same idealistic mind.6

Seriously ill again, he almost gave up. Death was never far from his thoughts, in the clear, calm manner he expressed in paint. But he grieved at the loss of Julia Stephen, whom he had known since she was four years old. He had loved her dearly, had photographs and drawings of her on display, and longed to write about her. Leighton, suffering from angina, missed the Academy dinner for the first time, and wrote cheerily from France, where he was enjoying 'the most irresponsible *restful* think', though 'I shall never be *quite* the old self again'. Watts sent his first drawing of *Love Triumphant over Time and Death* to comfort Lady Pembroke on the death of her husband and sent a red chalk drawing of *Charity* to Benjamin Waugh for the National Society for the Prevention of Cruelty to Children bazaar, where it raised 250 guineas.7

'All this might be made decorative,' said Watts, passing his hand over the handlebars of the bicycle that had conveyed John St Loe Strachey to Limnerslease to interview the artist for the *Spectator*. He decried Ruskin for having abused this excellent means of bringing town dwellers into the green fields, and wondered why the exercise should not be treated pictorially. (The new cycle posters would develop into a dynamic collaboration between art and commerce.) Watts hoped too, noted Strachey, that Oscar Wilde's recent trial for homosexuality had 'smashed the monstrous notion of "art for art's sake".' The English as a race had no artistic sense, he said. Though Reynolds, Wilkie and Turner had a greater understanding of atmosphere than did Titian, all three had used unsafe pigments – safety was paramount in his instructions to Winsor and Newton. When asked about the Home Arts, he said the state should take notice that he had written to Lord Rosebery. (He so felt strongly about the issue, he refused to let Mary apologize for having appealed to the prime minister to support the cause.) 'What I should like better than 'spoil' would be your attention to the matter', Watts wrote. He advised the prime minister to take action for the working classes, whose minds were dulled by machinery, warning, 'The average intellect of the Anglo Saxon does not contrast favourably with other nations & if it should be all shifted into the groves of money making & gambling the outlook would not be assuring'.8

A magnificent Lucca della Robbia *Madonna* roundel was given to Watts. Turning it to modern advantage, he and Mary had it inset, with her sgraffito border decoration, into a special shelter outside the studio at Limnerslease. Signor posed for Andrews in front of the Renaissance relic on 6 June (fig. 195), and gave friends and critics copies of the photograph, which he had enlarged by his framer's son J. Caswall Smith. The *Art Journal* highlighted its Venetian dignity and mastery of arrangement as an 'example of what is possible with the camera without special technical knowledge.'[9]

The Marquess of Ripon sat for the nation at the end of his term as Colonial Secretary. Watts was amused to see again the portrait he had painted before the marquess had achieved Cabinet rank, later to become Viceroy of India and First Lord of the Admiralty. The artist painted him in rich, red peer's robes.[10] Watts loved pomp and ceremony, to see a duke in ermine, driving in picturesque stagecoaches, just as he yearned for the working classes to retain their distinctive dress – 'infinitely more dignified than the present straining to imitate the clothes of the wealthy . . . buying what is cheap and ugly and machine-made'. Infuriated by the conservatism sweeping the country, ousting the Liberals, he wrote to Lord Rosebery, 'Now you are at leisure and I hope well, will you come and quietly reflect on the mutability of human affairs in my torture chair? I should like to press this as much as may be consistent with Humanity.' The London County Council had paid a young artist to copy the statesman's portrait. As Watts wished to add final touches to the copy, Lord Rosebery 'squeeze[d] a shabby sitting into a busy day'. Out of office, the earl looked quite different: 'I hardly knew the man again.' No longer tired and careworn, he was in 'wonderfully high spirits'.[11] However, at the Academy elections in July, at which Richmond achieved full membership, Watts noted how wearily Sir Frederic climbed the steps at Burlington House.[12]

That month, he gave a red chalk drawing of *Hope* to the Seamen's Mission in East India Dock Road,[13] and sent his early cricketing drawings and lithographs to Lord Harris for Lord's; he loved the sport, which he associated with the national character.[14]

While he attacked the hind legs of *Physical Energy* Mary designed her terracotta model of the mortuary chapel. The architect George Redmayne, inspecting the finished model at Little Holland House on 10 August – he would keep an eye on developments – observed that Watts's equestrian statue was impressionist. 'All art is impressionist,' replied Watts. 'The men who use the term do not carry out their own idea. The aim of their impression is to make evident their one dexterity. Something that is so far too great for expression, that it must be indefinite, the infinite looming large behind the finite, that is the impression which great art alone can convey.'[15]

All three trustees of his national gift – Sir William Gregory, Sir Henry Layard and Lord Aberdare – had died. 'If I dropt out of the world the nation would be left in great confusion', he wrote to Julia Cartwright, allowing her to chronicle his work and objectives in a special issue of the *Art Journal* before he handed over his 'unbroken series of ethical essays so to speak, and all my portraits of the makers of the Nation.' As there was no spare bedroom at Little Holland House, the artist invited her to stay at Limnerslease in the autumn. In the meantime Hulda Friederichs interviewed him for an extensive article in the *Young Woman*;[16] and Leighton wrote to Watts on behalf of Lionel Cust, the director of the new National Portrait Gallery:

A most important feature will be, of course, *your* magnificent contribution but here [Cust's] great perplexity steps in; – (he has consulted me privately) – in view of your having handed over certain works to S. Kensington at once he is uncertain whether your *Portrait Gallery* is to

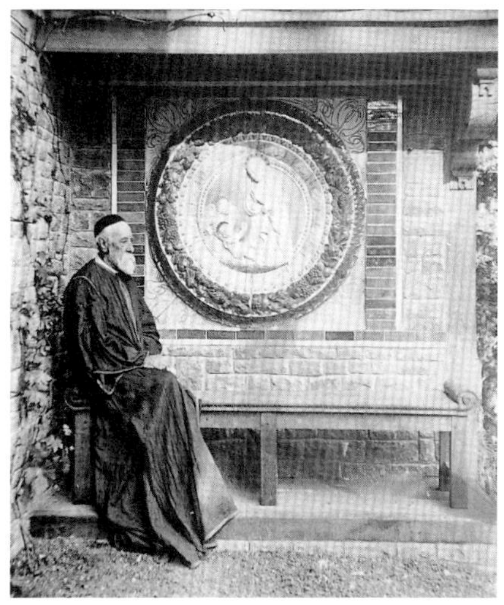

195 Watts seated in front of the Della Robbia tondo at Limnerslease, 6 June 1895 (photo: George Andrews).

be considered as a *gift* to be handed over to the Nation now that dignified provision is made for its housing, or as a *bequest*, which all earnestly and warmly hope to be a far off contingency; his arrangements would of course be made accordingly – will you let me have a word for him? Or, as I am wandering from pillar to post, would you send *him* just one line to solve his doubts . . . I am taking things *very* easily – and luxuriously – but am not in brilliant trim. *Ci vuol pazienza.*[17]

Watts invited Cust to the studio. 'I am delighted to find that you are willing to let the Nat. Port. Gallery have your splendid series of portraits at once', Leighton wrote from Dublin, putting a brave face on 'luxurious idleness'. 'You have this time fulfilled, and admirably, your aspiration to serve your country; we, at the Gallery, shall indeed be proud of our acquisition which will artistically and historically be a treasure to those who follow as well as to ourselves.' Nudged by the president, 'There is nothing to "*talk* over" with Cust – he wants the things very badly – he wants you to *hand* them over – do'. Finally, on 3 September Watts agreed to hand over the pictures. When Cust made his first selection on 18 September, Watts made it as easy as possible for him and arranged for Thompson to have the pictures ready. Advising Cust to have them cleaned and varnished by Dyer in Mount Street, he pointed out that all the important portraits were painted to help form a real National Gallery. 'I am glad to be associated with this inauguration.'[18]

Julia Cartwright arrived in October, from Paris where she was also researching an article on Puvis de Chavannes. The young American critic Bernard Berenson had described him as the greatest artist of the age, 'even superior to Watts', whom he considered 'far and away' Britain's finest artist. At Limnerslease, the studio was still dominated by *The Court of Death*. Cartwright saw the portrait of Mary Anderson raising her arm as though about to perform, a sketch for *Joan of Arc*, *The All-Pervading*, and two Surrey landscapes – the gaunt pine tree painted from his studio window in *Green Summer*, and the woodland and hills outside his bedroom window at dawn in *Under the Opening Eyelids Came the Morn*. 'I hope to do my best work yet,' was his constant refrain. In the dining room were sketches painted at Careggi and with Newton in Asia Minor, *Mount Ida* and *Chaos*. Prints of Michelangelo's Sistine frescoes lined the stairs, with Raphael's *Sedia* half-way up. 'I had the prettiest white-panelled and peacock blue room with old lacquered furniture and the most comfortable of beds.'[19] The next morning she set to work on the Hollyer albums, 'the master' popping in and out to explain the meaning of his pictures. When Mary told her about the chapel and that she would soon start teaching villagers to model its decorative tiles, Watts laughed at her extravagance, 'She thinks she can do it all for 1/9!' He too wanted to teach people to *live*, to escape drudgery and use their skills, to hope, work and enjoy life. As Cartwright left, inspired by his vision of a better country, Josephine Butler (fig. 196), arrived to stay for national portrait sittings.[20]

'Dreadful nonsense,' the reformer had said when she received his letter describing her as one of the people who 'had made the century.' She found Limnerslease cold and dull. The artist seemed like 'a small refined wizard'; he looked worn and thin in his graceful dressing-gown and she was amazed that with his small old hand he made such bold drawings, sitting far from

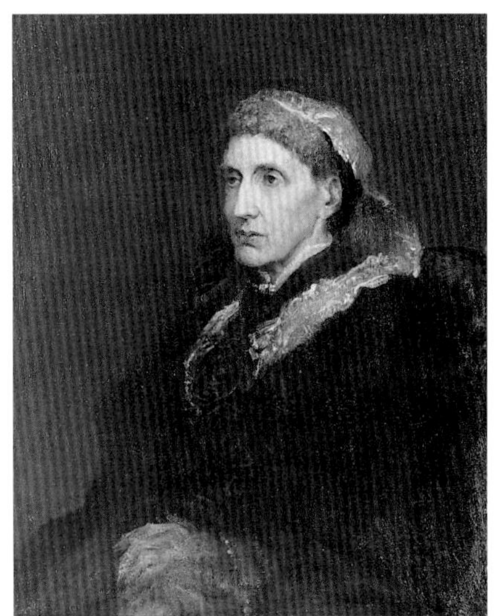

196   *Josephine Elizabeth Butler*, 1895–96 (National Portrait Gallery, London).

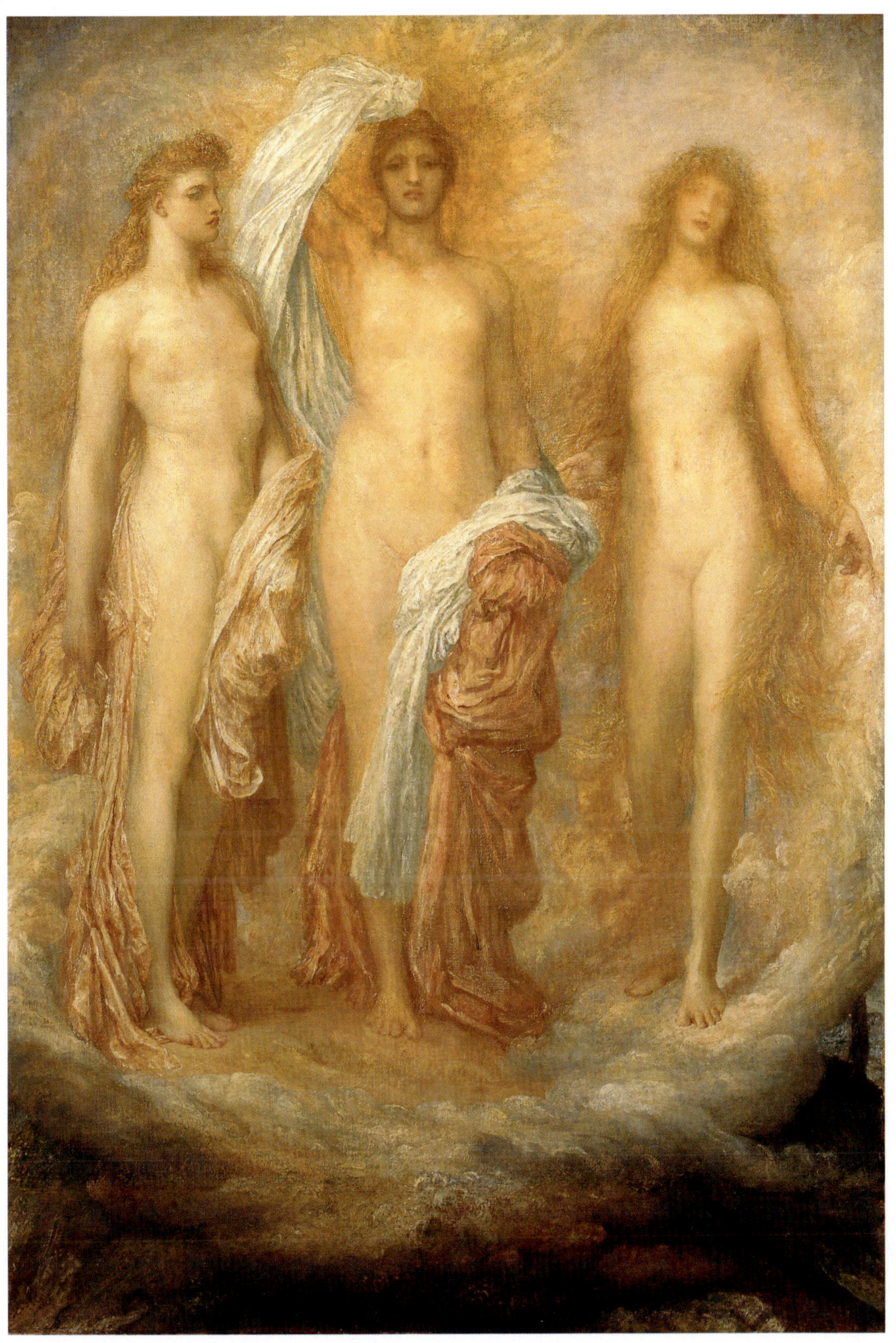

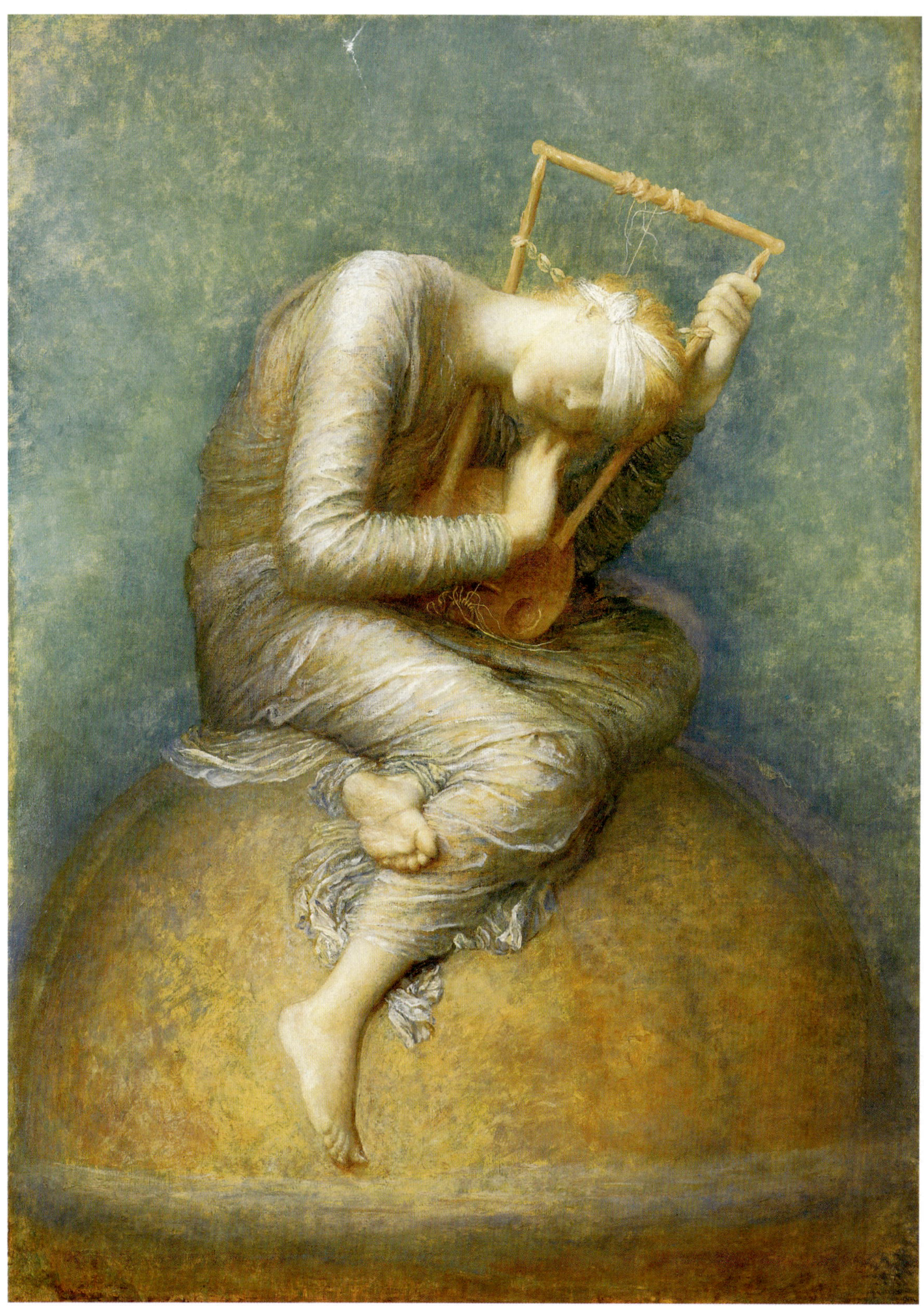

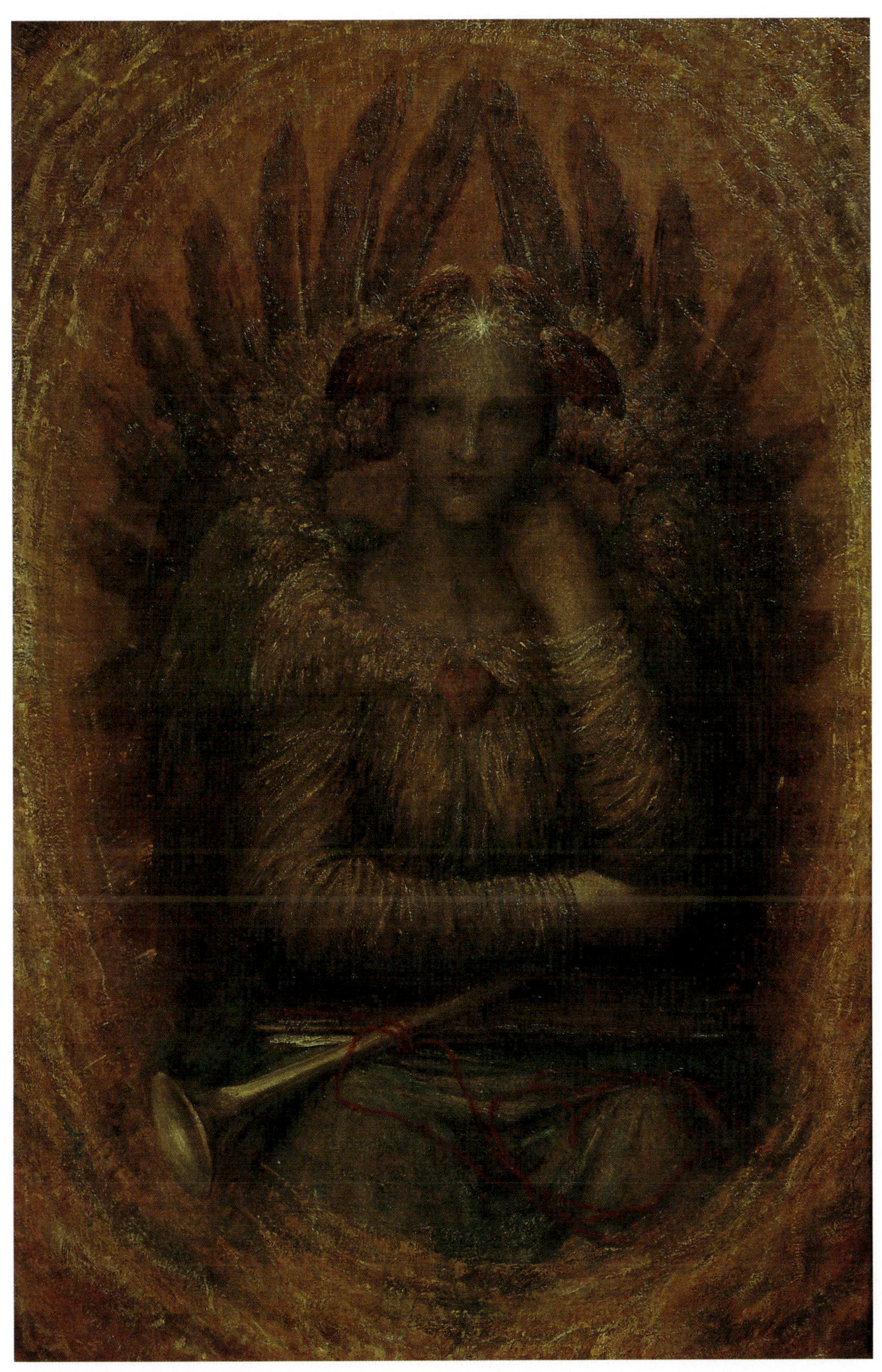

XXVIII (*previous page*) *Olympus on Ida*, 1884–85 (private collection).

XXIX (*facing page*) *Hope*, 1885 (private collection, courtesy of Christie's).

XXX *Dweller in the Innermost*, 1885–86 (Tate, London)

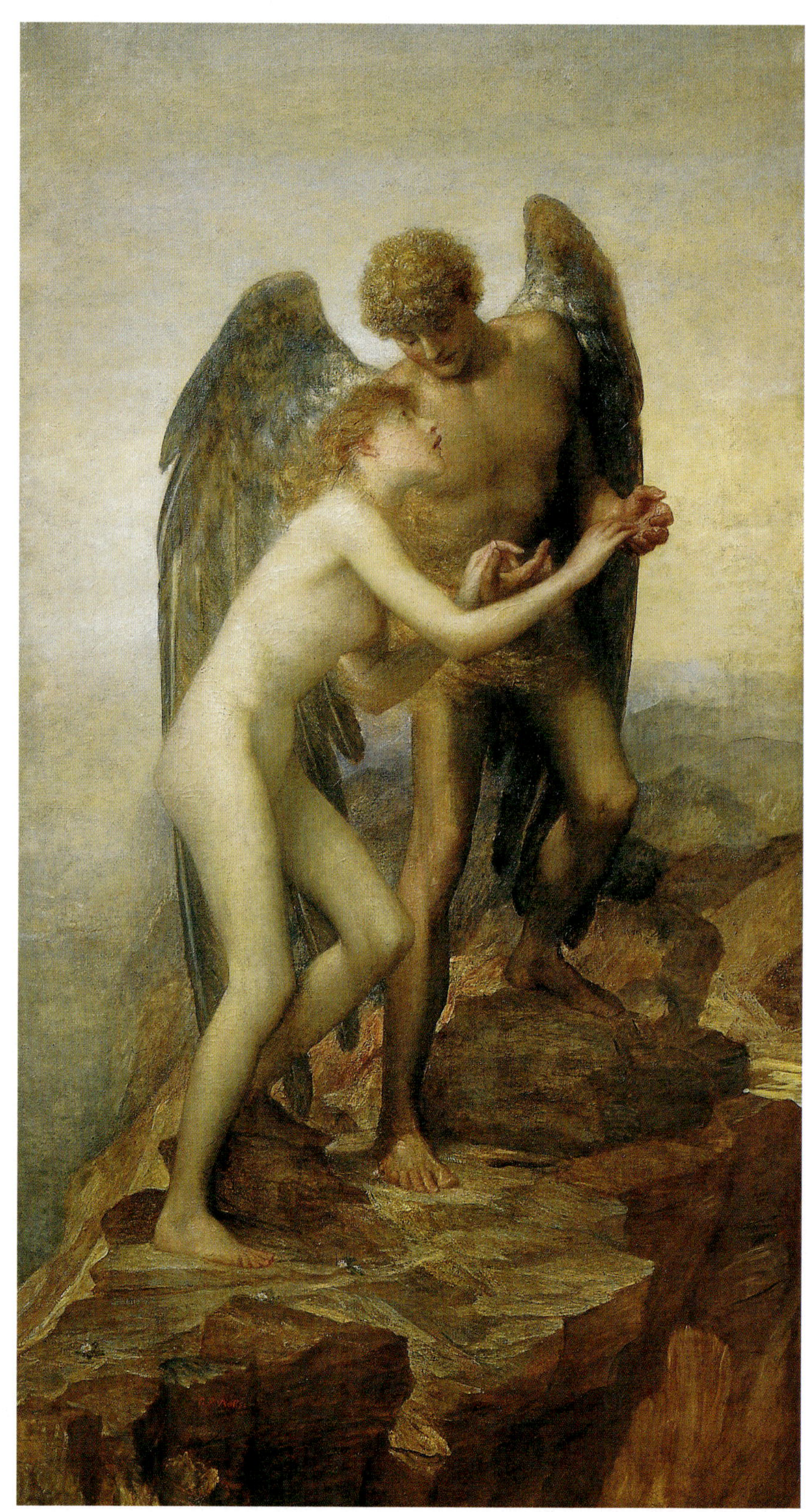

XXXI   *Love and Life* (private collection, courtesy of Nevill Keating Pictures Ltd).

XXXII (*facing page*)   *Death Crowning Innocence*, 1886–93 (courtesy of Bonhams).

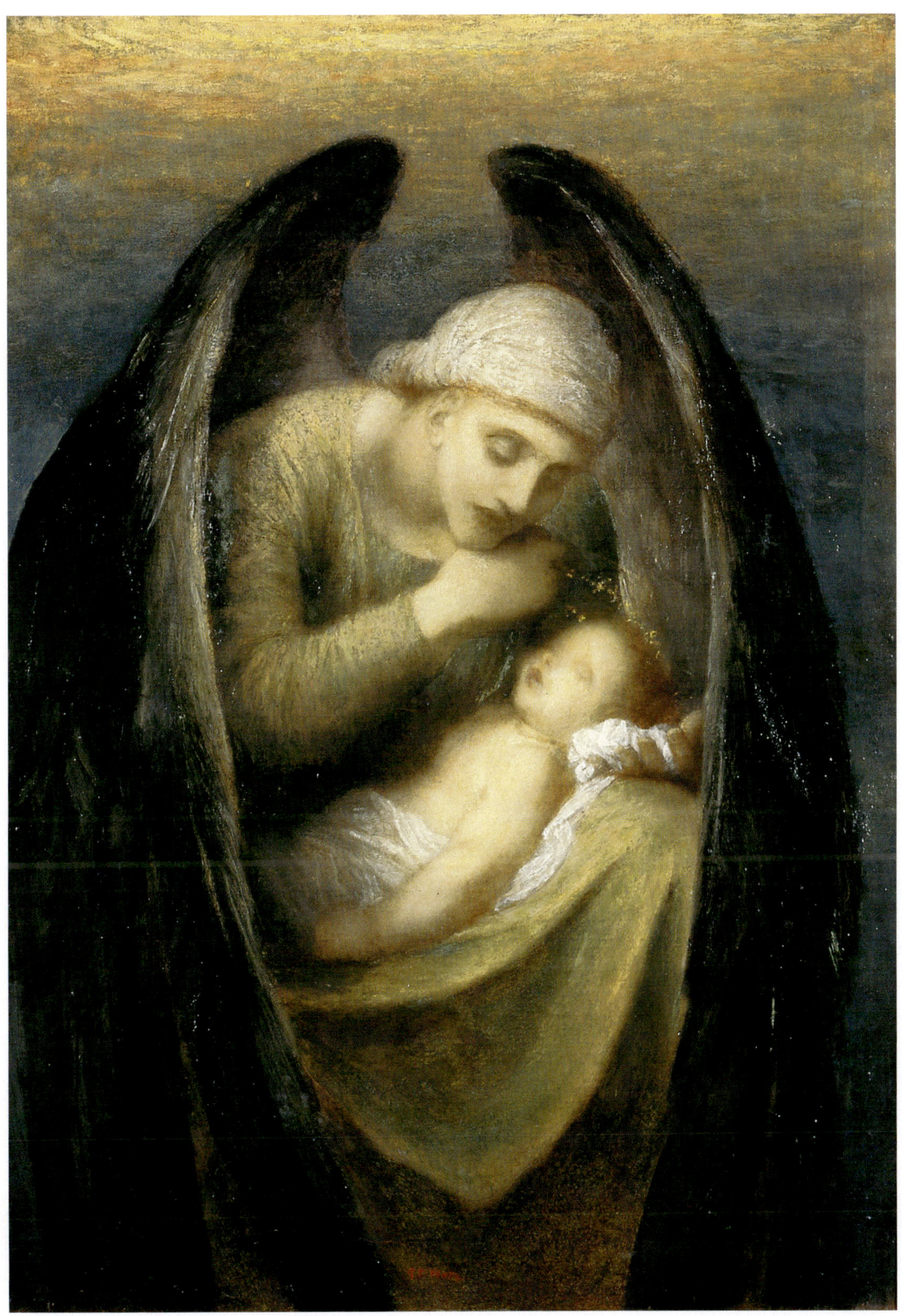

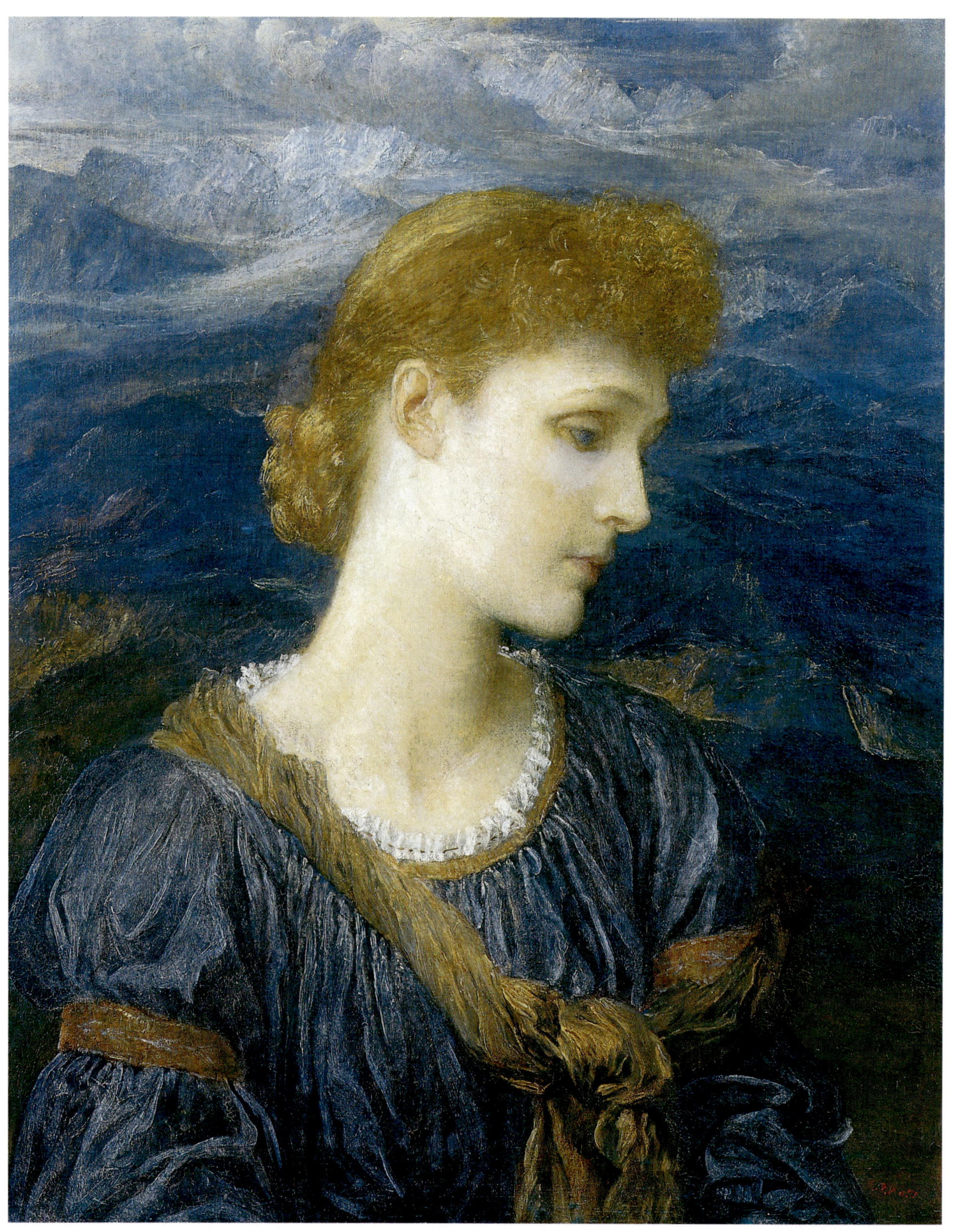

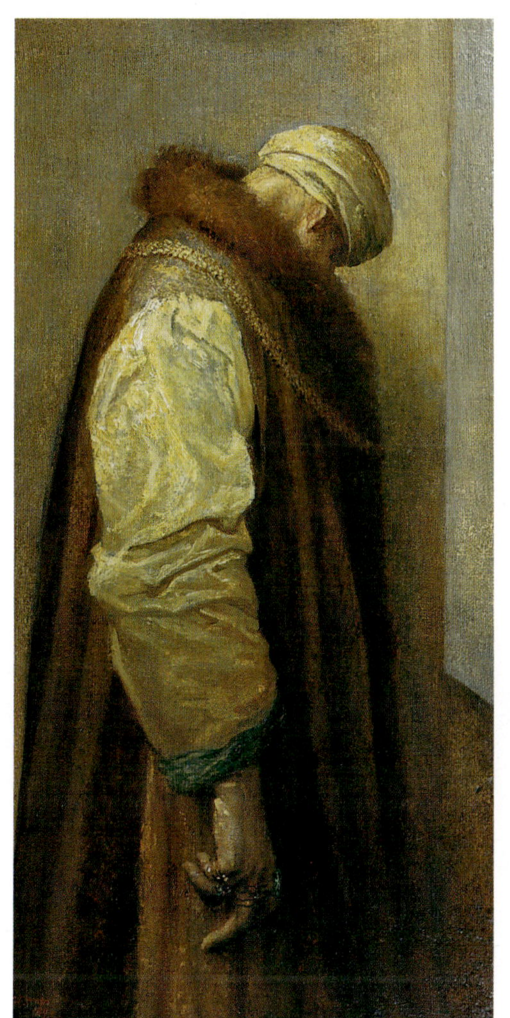 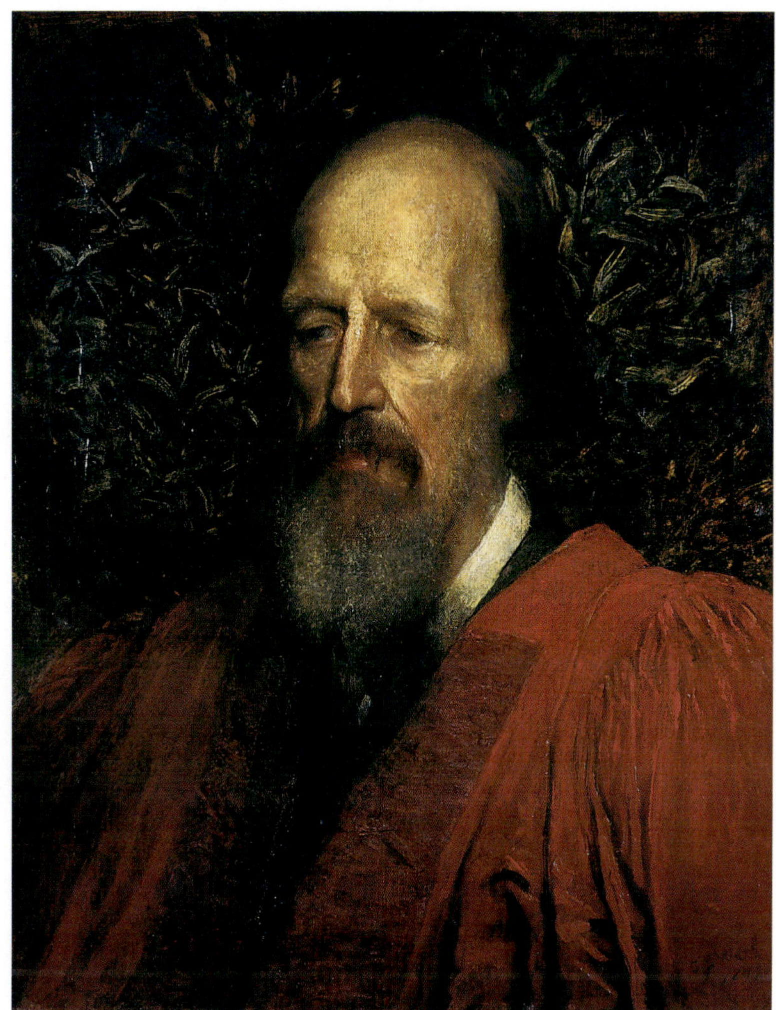



XXXIII (*facing page*)   *Violet Lindsay*, 1879 (private collection).

XXXIV (*above left*)   *For He Had Great Possessions*, 1893–94 (Watts Gallery).

XXXV (*above right*)   *Alfred, Lord Tennyson*, 1890 (Trinity College, Cambridge).

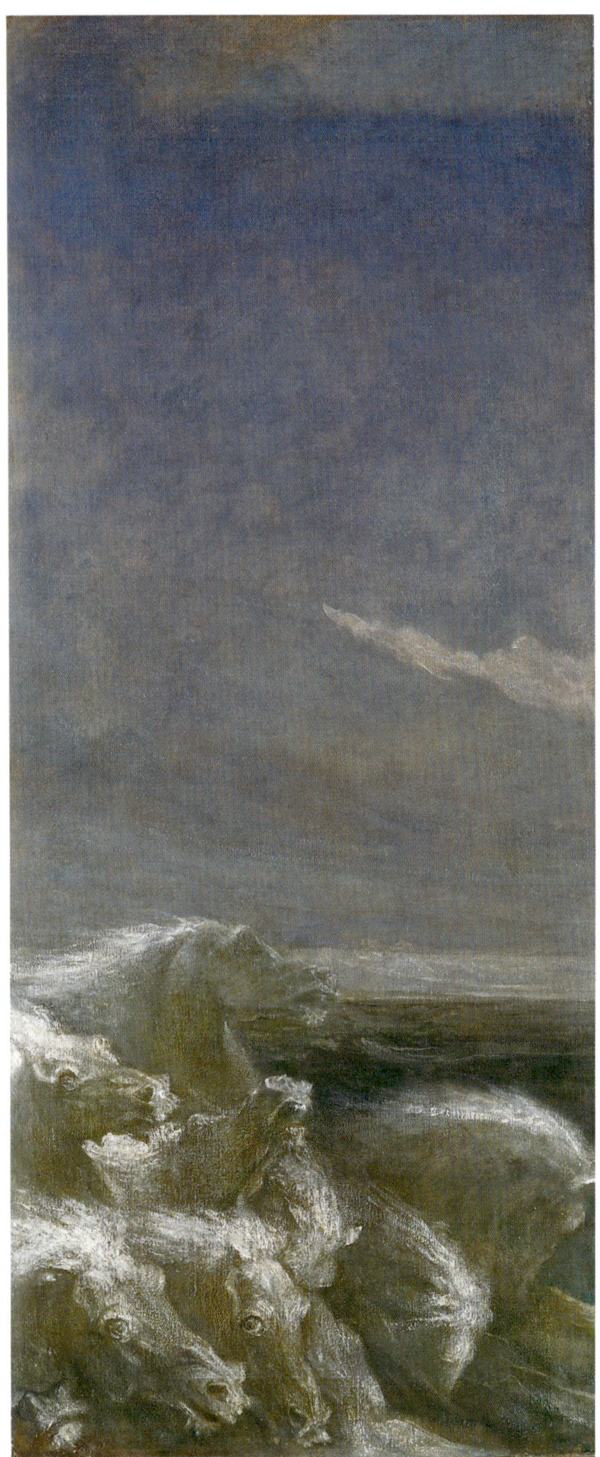

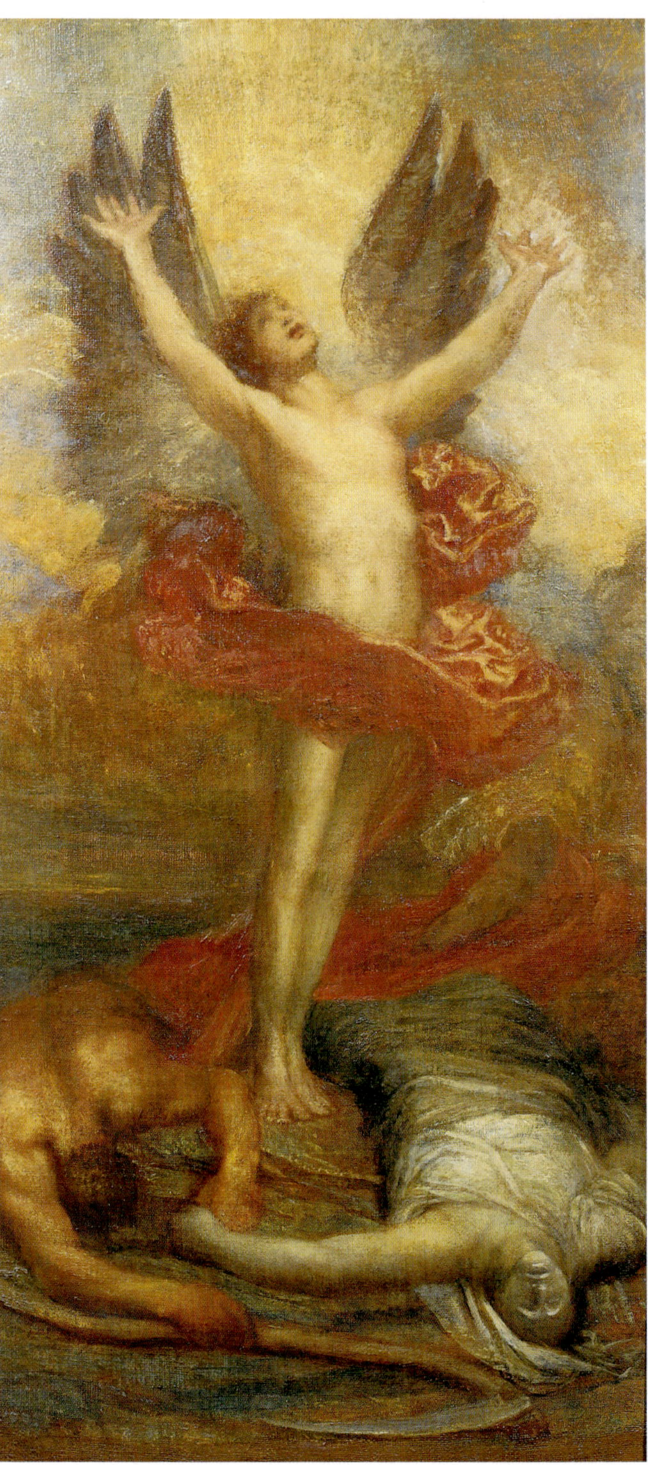

xxxvi (*above left*)   *Neptune's Horses*, 1891–93. (The National Trust, Fenton House).

xxxvii (*above right*)   *Love Triumphant* (Watts Gallery).

xxxviii (*facing page*)   *Sunset on the Alps*, 1888–94 (Watts Gallery).

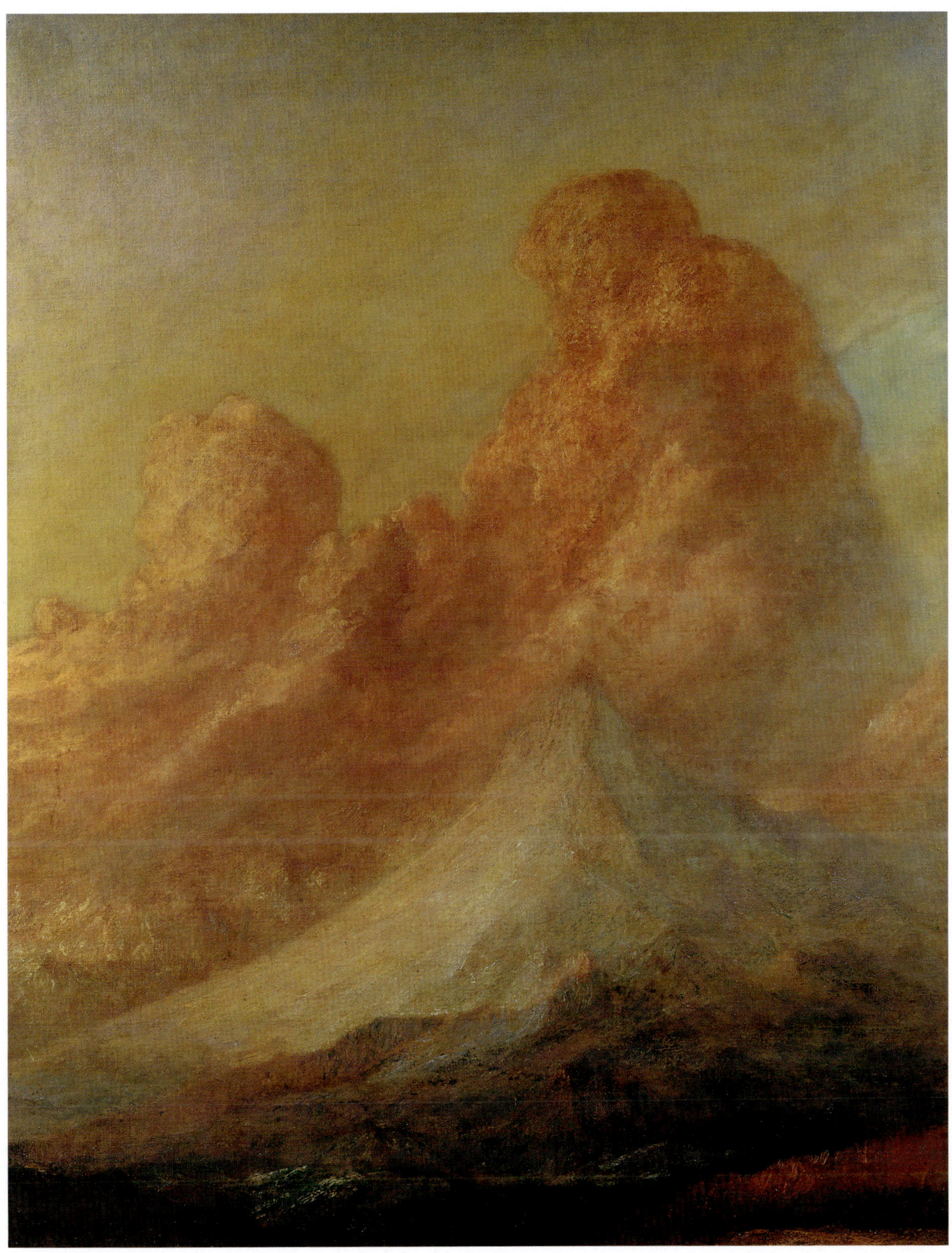

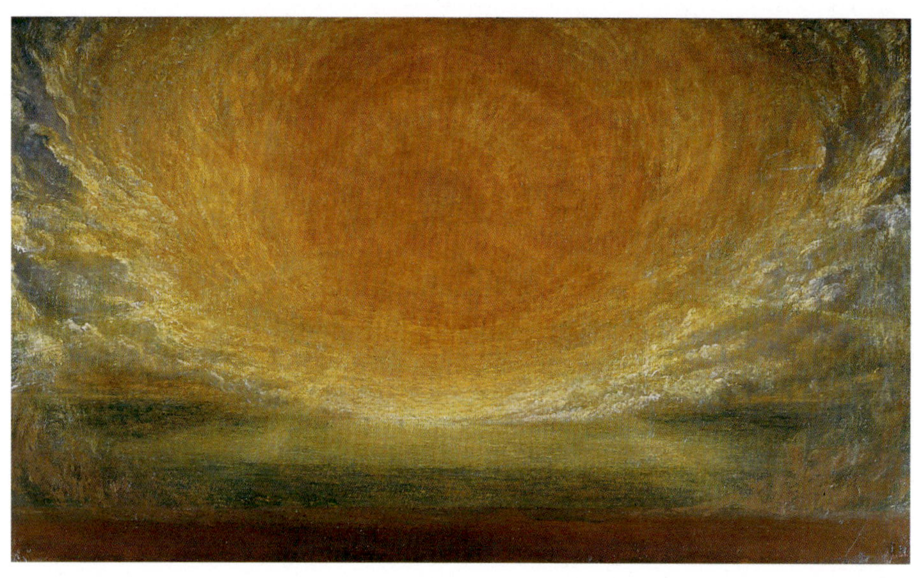

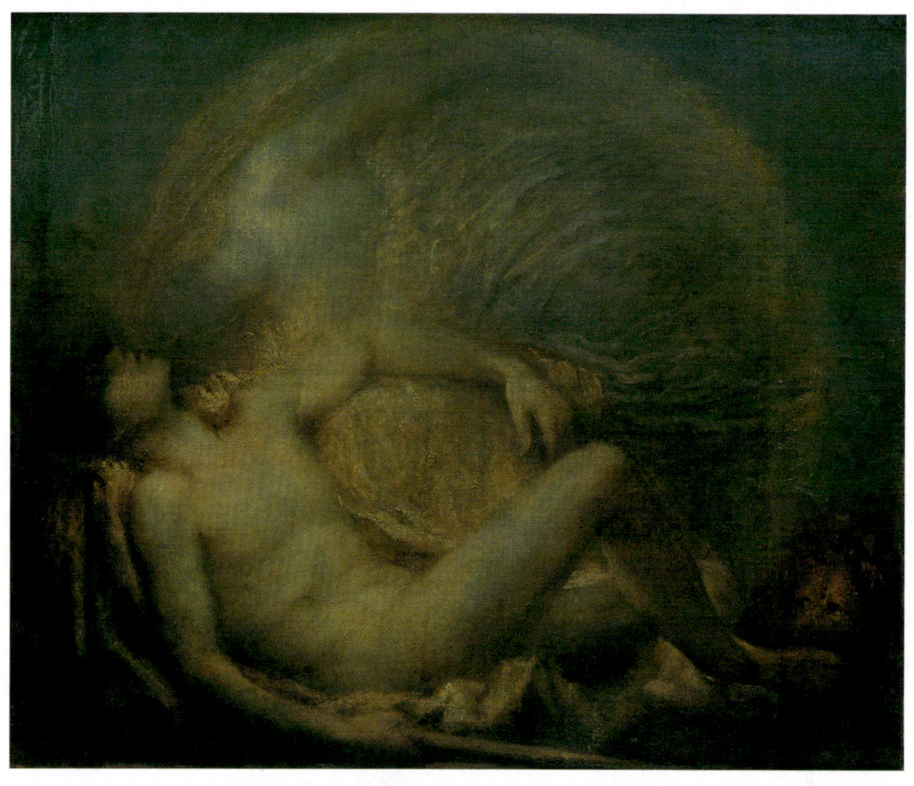

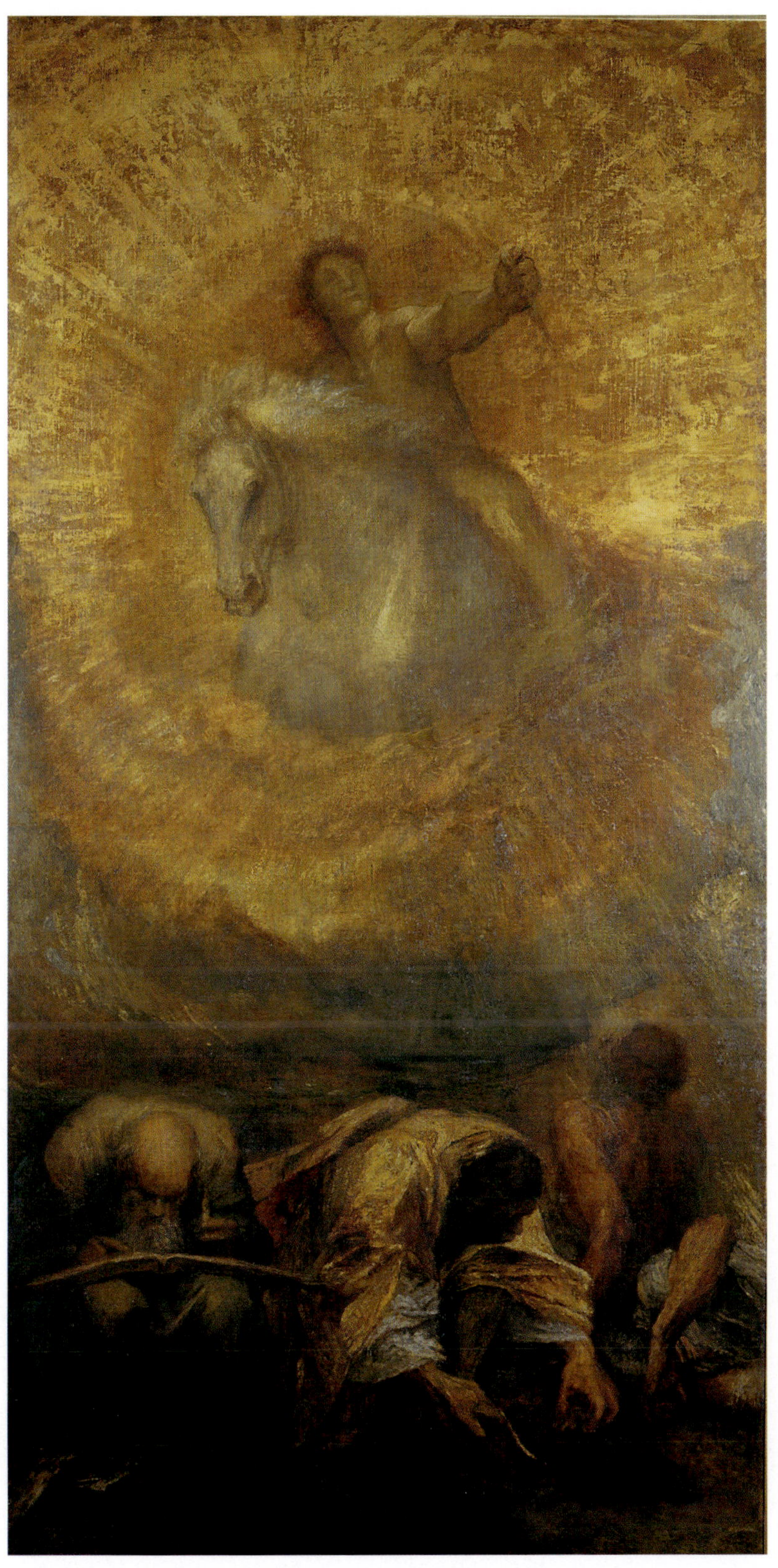

XXXIX (*facing page top*)   *After the Deluge: The Forty-First Day*, 1885–86 (Watts Gallery).

XL (*facing page bottom*)   *Endymion*, c.1869–1903 (Watts Gallery).

XLI   *Progress*, 1888–1904 (Watts Gallery).

XLII (*following page*)   *The Sower of the Systems*, 1898–1903 (Watts Gallery).

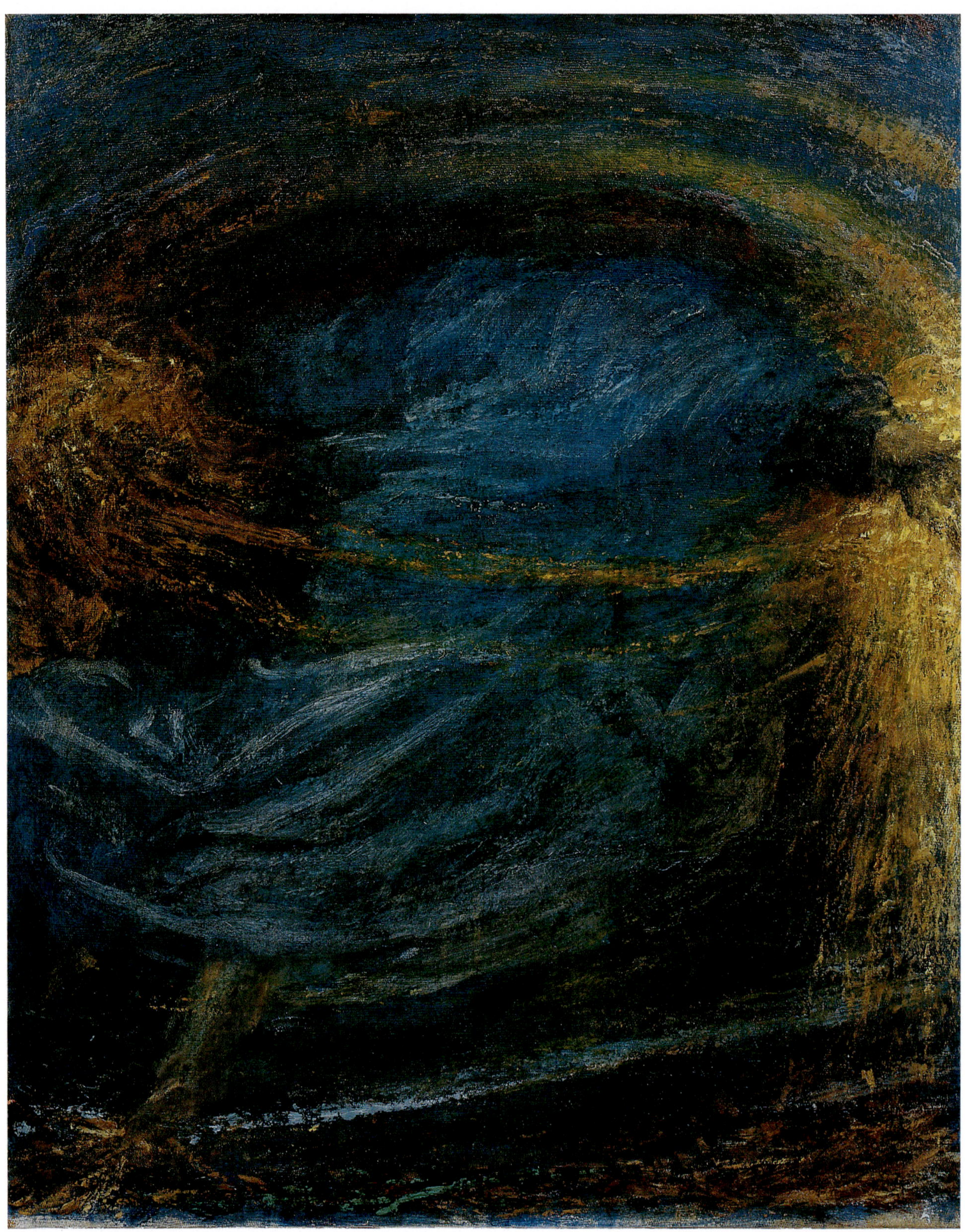

his easel, without a hand-rest. 'I remarked on it, and he took a glass of water and held it at arm's length. There was not the smallest movement in his hand or the water.' He admired her heroic crusades against the white-slave traffic and the Contagious Diseases Act, her efforts on behalf of fallen women, and for women's suffrage. Uncertain as to how much he knew of the seamier activities – he surely knew – Butler replied that she had not take it up willingly. 'I was *driven* into it by anger against injustice.' Recognizing that impulse, Watts insisted, 'But some people refuse to be driven; and you did not refuse.' Hers would be the only female portrait in his national series.[21]

On the third day he allowed Butler to see it. Her beautiful face was now ravaged by the marks of her crusades. The reformer was stunned. She could not trust herself to speak and fled upstairs to write to the artist: 'When I looked at that portrait which you have just done, I felt inclined to burst into tears. I will tell you why. I felt so sorry for her. Your power has brought up, out of the depths of the past, the record of a conflict which no one but God knows of. It is written in the eyes and whole face . . . Your picture has brought back to me all that I suffered.' She thanked him for not making her look severe or bitter, though sad, yet purposeful. 'If the portraiture speaks with such truth and power to me, I think it will in some way speak to others also.' Butler did not know what to make of the picture. She wrote to her son Stanley:

> It is rather terrible. It bears the marks of storms and conflicts and sorrow so strongly. The eyes are certainly wonderfully done. You know I have no brightness in my eyes now. He said he wanted to make me looking into Eternity, looking at something no one else sees, because – he says – I look like that; and he has certainly given that idea. It is not at all pretty, and the jaw and head are too strong and gaunt. I don't think my friends will like it. But then he is not doing it for us, but for posterity; and no doubt it will convey an idea of my hard life work. He is not finished. They say his pictures are seldom liked at first, but that they grow on people, on account of the power in them.[22]

At the Society of Portrait Painters exhibition, *Sympathy* – a portrait of Nurse Katherine Webster – was seen to be 'very tender and pathetically expressive . . . quite a masterpiece of harmony and colour'.[23] Hollyer was offering platinotypes from his paintings for 10s 6d per portrait, and 7s 6d for a $13\frac{1}{2}$-inch subject, up to two guineas for a $36\frac{1}{4}$-inch *Love and Death* or *Sir Galahad*,[24] when Watts began to paint *Paris on Mount Ida*. The Trojan prince, looking beyond the canvas to the unseen goddesses, is about to throw the apple of discord. Leighton admired Watts's 'beautifully drawn' head (similar to *Sir Galahad*) at the Centennial Exhibition of Lithography in Paris. The president looked dreadfully ill at Little Holland House on 5 November. Seeing his dearest friend wracked with pain, supposedly from a nervous condition, Watts, who had his own nervous attacks largely under control, sent a brochure recommending alternative treatment.[25]

In early morning discussion with Mary, he spoke of 'the flame that lives in each of us, all creation being the will of the Creator who Himself dwells beyond the threshold of the unthinkable,' but he wondered why he could never quite reach his ideal finishing point in his work, 'I have no grasp like Leighton.' Mary countered, 'You are trying for something more. He wishes to grasp the tangible and does so completely, you the intangible.' Watts would not be soothed, '*I feel so cut off.*' He pressed on, without a moment to lose, distraught when a studio lamp went out. 'I may live two more years or three but I can never get this hour back.'[26]

Mary's clay-modelling classes had begun. With the kiln to be paid for, and fees for assistants and labourers to dig the clay from their field, Watts was grateful for a visit from James Smith, now negotiating to buy *Arion*. Encouraged by his appreciation for *Time Death and Judgment* and *Jupiter*, he wrote to Julia Cartwright that his designs were not effective as mere pictures, especially in competition with popular works painted with technical skill and charm. 'My work is commonly a protest against the modern opinion that Art should have nothing to say intellectually. I think it might say a great deal!'[27]

Anny Ritchie arrived at the studio on Sunday 1 December to see the celebrity portraits before they were taken to the National Portrait Gallery. *Cardinal Manning* and *Tennyson* left South Kensington the next day, and were delivered to St Martin's Place on the Friday with portraits of Arnold, Browning, Carlyle, Sir Andrew Clark, Sir Charles Hallé, Lord Lawrence, The Earl of Lytton, John Stuart Mill, Panizzi, Rossetti, The Earl of Shaftesbury, Viscount Sherbrooke, Sir Henry Taylor, and two chalk drawings of Sir Henry Layard and Thomas Wright, adding to the four portraits (of Lord Lyndhurst, Admiral Lord Lyons, Earl Russell and Viscount Stratford de Redcliffe) already presented. 'If giving means sacrifice, giving something I shall miss then this is really *giving*. We shall miss them with all our hearts daily,' wrote Mary. Watts was delighted to have fulfilled the first part his lifetime ambition and gratified that the pictures were wanted and well received in the press; now he longed for the large Symbolist pictures to be housed. That morning Hichens brought *The Times* report of the 'munificent gift . . . representative of much of the best work of the last fifty years in England' – and Millais, battling against throat cancer, wrote, as a National Portrait Gallery trustee, to thank him for the 'really *Splendid Gift*'.[28] As Watts wished to retain copyright, he referred Cust to his business manager, J. W. Beck, the former New Gallery secretary; for reproduction, he recommended the Swan Electric Engraving Company. He stipulated that Hollyer should be granted exclusive photographic rights, and that no oil copies be painted from his portraits.[29]

Had Watts foreseen Mary's pottery enterprise he might have been more provident, he wrote to Spielmann.[30] He was disinclined to contribute 'a substantial cheque' to Sir Algernon West's appeal to support the Liberal party. Although by nature a sincere Liberal and eager for change, he could not be tied to a party. His continuous subscription over the last 40 years was intended to inspire 'a nobler set of conditions'.[31] In the lamplight he modelled a wax figure for *The Good Samaritan*. As Christmas drew near, he could not bear the 'little peddling way' religion was represented. 'Nothing grand about it – No reach.' To Watts, religion meant 'the constant desire to do right . . . like some powerful spring in machinery, keeping up the motion of the wheels into pressure.'[32]

On Boxing Day Blanche followed Herbert to an early grave, and was buried with Signor's photograph over her heart.[33] Strangely like the conscious counterbalance in his art, Lily Mackintosh, now seventeen years old, had grown to love the Wattses and her uncle asked Mary if she would be the teenager's guardian. Lily adored staying at Limnerslease, especially when Blanche's children, Arthur and Verena, were there; her aunt and uncle returned to India, and she made her home with Signor and 'Donna' (as she was encouraged to call Mary).[34]

Leighton's elevation to the peerage in the New Year honours delighted Watts, who envisaged an even greater career for him as a statesman. 'Best thanks in hot haste (piles and piles of letters!) from your very affectionate Fred Leighton' was the last note he received from his dearest friend, whom he had not seen since November.[35] On 23 January 1896 Lord Leighton, struck by a bronchial cold, awoke in agony. He rallied the next day, saying to his sisters, 'Would it not have been a pity if I had had to die just when I was going to paint better!' But on Saturday, refusing chloroform until he had signed a new will, he asked Val to 'Give my love to all at the Academy'. His sisters allowed Dorothy Dene to give thanks at her patron's bedside before he died,[36] courageous and perfect to the end. 'Half my life is gone with Leighton,' Watts cried out as the last of a stream of telegrams reached Limnerslease. 'This is dreadful!' In despair, he wrote to Mrs Barrington, 'No one will ever know such another. Alas! Alas! Alas!' He could not bear the thought of living in Kensington without him, or ever climbing the Academy steps again. He went to bed hoping it was all a bad dream, but sleep eluded him.

Watts had longed for Leighton to reach beyond the confines of the Academy – to serve art as never before through the House of Lords – and was mortified that his career had been cut short. 'I have seen it always rising, always going further, always successful.' In impassioned letters to Emilie Barrington, he praised the president's 'magnificent intellectual capacity, an unerring and instantaneous spring upon the point to unravel, a generosity, a sympathy, a tact (perhaps one of the most valuable qualities in our modern times), a lovable and sweet reasonableness, yet no weakness [a quality admirable in life, but not, to Watts, so admirable in the cool perfection of Leighton's paintings] . . . Life can never be the same to me again, my own grief is merged in the sense I have of the appalling loss to the nation.'

A tremendous light had been extinguished, thrusting Watts into a shadow of despondency. Leighton had coaxed, advised and laughed with him for forty-five years. He had been a tower of strength. Mary had always thought of Leighton as her husband's second self, 'the half that went into the thick of the battle of life, rejoicing in strength, and successful at every point'. No other man could appease him more sensitively when a picture whose textural quality was not up to scratch had been deservedly hung above 'the immediate *level of the eye*'. The president's wise counsel – even if Watts did not act on it – had been a powerful, reassuring influence. Until now, he knew that every daub of pigment would be seen by Leighton, although, as Emilie Barrington observed, Watts had disregarded his advice before taking the three most important steps in his personal life – presumably his two marriages and his divorce from Nelly. The diversity of their lives and attitudes to art had added sparkle to the friendship. 'Leighton has given us many noble pictures, but his life was the noblest of them all', he said. 'I admired and loved him as much as one man can another.' Burne-Jones sent a heartfelt note, 'Dearest Signor, This is a little hand grasp, that's all – just a squeeze of the hand from your Affectionest Ned.'[37]

The nation mourned. Crowds lined the streets as the cortège left Burlington House for the funeral at St Paul's cathedral. To Watts's further distress, his ankles were too painful to allow him to attend the funeral to pay public tribute. 'I am sad to feel that the last outward show of the affection and veneration I feel cannot be made by my presence on Monday . . . It is a blow I shall never recover from', he wrote to Rivière. He invited Rivière to Limnerslease in order to set in train his retirement from the Academy, which, had Meredith not pressed him to be a 'standard-bearer', he would have done long ago, 'As Leighton's career and mine as full members began together I should like it to end together.' He wished, too, to discuss his work and Mary's, about which he had hoped to consult 'my unspeakably lamented friend' and concluded, 'I am sadly exercised in my mind about seating anyone in that empty chair.'[38] After the funeral, he was appalled to learn that no death mask had been taken. He encouraged Millais to accept the presidency, 'It will not do to have less than the best.' Millais agreed 'for *the present*', but he was a sick man.[39] Now, when Watts needed a colleague's opinion of his work, he would turn to Rivière.[40]

Professor Herkomer came down to Limnerslease in March to finish his portrait of Watts, who rebuked him for referring to his Symbolist work as 'allegory'. 'The beauty of your Allegory is that it is articulate. When other men try allegory they are arabesques grotesque, unintelligible', the professor had said. 'Allegory is nonsense', said Watts. 'George III on a horse and a naked woman blowing a trumpet meant to represent fame! . . . I never mix the real and the unreal.' Louis Reid Deuchars was now working in his studio. The young Glaswegian had sent him a parcel of drawings in 1891 with a note – 'perhaps my mother was right when she said "leave that nonsense alane laddie" but I couldn't and I often feel I would go mad if I didn't paint something'. Watts had recommended him to friends, but Herkomer had rejected him after five minutes, 'He is not plastic enough. Won't have him at any price . . . I want only people with a future. . . . You are ruining him here. He will never do anything with his art.' Within months Deuchars was assisting Mary and her modellers.[41]

Meanwhile, Anny Ritchie came to stay at that 'most delightful working place', where 'everything was fragrant, kind, suggestive, the ceiling meant one thing the walls another I listened and seemed to be refreshed and redipped in the waters of life and hope . . . We saw the workshops where the villagers are taught to mould bricks for the Campo Santo . . . his pictures – painted at 79 and perfectly delightful and delight giving.'[42] She was making enquiries to preserve Leighton's studio and Arab Hall as a museum or music school for young painters,[43] and Watts was now able to give Gladstone the promised drawing from *Ilyssus*, 'It was in my dear friend Leighton's studio and not liking to ask him for it as he admired it very much I made several endeavours to do something else for you but could never satisfy myself.' He posted it to Hawarden Castle. 'The beautiful drawing has arrived. I cannot quite dismiss the idea that I have in a manner stolen it', replied Gladstone.[44]

Thousands of visitors poured into the new National Portrait Gallery at St Martin's Place on the opening day, Saturday, 4 April 1896. There was intense interest, but the pictures were cramped, either in dark, gloomy cellars, or raked with blinding beams. Burne-Jones was appalled: 'A pokey hole it is!' On the ground floor, opposite a line of naval heroes, 'Mr Watts's magnificent gift is as well seen as the place allows', reported the *Athenaeum*. But to Ned, even they seemed 'all gobs and ribs of canvas – there's not the least chance of a ray of sentiment penetrating them'. He did think that Watts's texture was sometimes 'over rough', but that his were the only portraits with any pretension to be art. In June, the First Lord of the Treasury, Arthur Balfour invited Watts to become a trustee of the National Portrait Gallery.[45]

Mary Anderson, having left the stage on her marriage to Antonio de Navarro, brought her husband to Limnerslease in April. They found 'the great painter more loveable than ever' and determined not to lose momentum, declaring as he retired before dinner, 'Light is the artist's treasure. Aurora his love.' So as not to disturb the servants at the crack of dawn, he now used a coffee-machine. Mary de Navarro seemed surprised that despite his quiet demeanour, 'he always surrounded himself with blazing colour. His rooms were aglow with it . . . tints he called "washed-out colour." ' As of old, they walked arm in arm up and down the studio, in intimate discussion. Despite his frail body, 'the spirit that shone through it was indomitable', de Navarro would recall in her memoirs, noting furthermore, that when Sargent used to visit her in Gloucestershire, he would stand before the large blue and gold oil sketch by Watts, and admire its workmanship.[46]

That summer Lily started her first term at Roedean. Watts stayed at Limnerslease until the last moment, apart from a brief trip to London for the varnishing days.[47] The primeval mother *Earth* with her fruits, the rich, smaller *Time, Death and Judgment, Naked and Not Ashamed* (fig. 197), and its silvery pendant *They Knew That They Were Naked*, were aired at the New Gallery. Portraits of Mrs Ellice and Walter Crane excited younger artists at the Royal Scottish Academy, while in London it was generally felt that his finest work was *The Childhood of Zeus* at the Academy – a large group of nude nymphs with the young god in the mischievous image of Dimmy Zambaco[48] – with portraits of Alfred Gilbert and the Marquess of Ripon and Leighton's *Clytie*, gloriously dynamic and unfinished.[49] By the time the exhibitions opened Watts was back at Limnerslease. Prince Eugen of Sweden called on 1 May 1896 to discuss pictures for the 1897 international exhibition in Stockholm. Outside Sweden, Norway, Denmark and Russia, only the greatest living foreign artists were invited to exhibit.[50]

As Leighton had meant to recommend a knighthood for Wyke Bayliss as president of the Society of British Artists, Watts added his signature to the testimonial.[51] Lord Salisbury's desire to offer him the title of Right Honourable appealed to Watts as a precedent, 'I should accept it, not because it would be anything to me personally but I should like to inaugurate this honour as suitable for literary and artistic labours.'[52] A dream, in which he was asked whether he minded being left behind when all his friends were honoured, and shown miles of sand representing the generations of man, with tiny points just high enough to catch the light, suggests that perhaps he had minded. But he wished the honour to reflect his intellectual aims and experience. Accordingly, the prime minister wrote to the Queen to recommend Watts and Professor Max Müller as privy councillors, citing the Professor Thomas Huxley as a precedent. Her private secretary Sir Arthur Bigge replied:

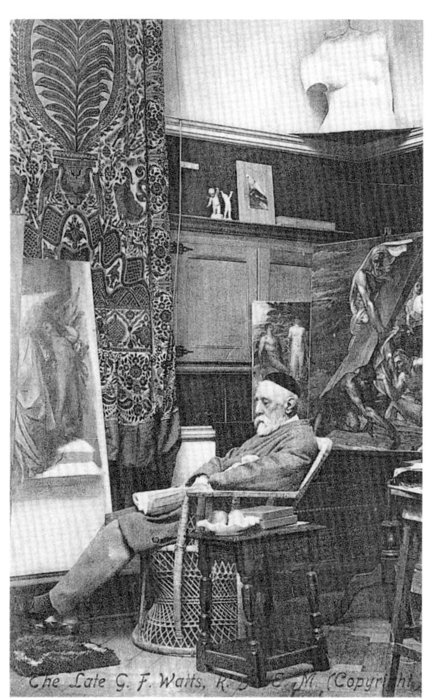


197   Watts reading in the studio at Limnerslease, with *Love and Death*, *Naked and Not Ashamed* and *Building of the Ark* on the easels, February 1896 (photo: George Andrews).

Her Majesty entirely approves of Professor Max Müller, as Man of Letters, as she did Professor Huxley, representing Science, for this honour. But the Queen cannot help feeling that there is something rather incongruous between the high position of a Privy Councillor . . . and that of an Artist who lives more or less by the sale of his works. Nor does Her Majesty consider professionally Mr Watts's standing is equal to that of either the late Lord Leighton or Sir J. Millais. Her Majesty would be ready to approve his being made a Baronet or the bestowal upon him of a suitable decoration.

Lord Salisbury, pointing out that Watts had declined the baronetcy 'for some reason unknown', had given no indication that he might now accept; neither did he state the nature and national aims of his art, nor present any real reason why the Queen should consent and risk further rebuff. This was a double blow, not so much, perhaps because Her Majesty saw Watts as an inferior artist, but that despite her interest in collecting, she clearly still regarded artists as inferior to scientists and men of letters.[53] He now feared that having refused the baronetcy, news of his willingness to accept a distinction – albeit intellectual – from Lord Salisbury might have offended Gladstone, to whom he wrote to explain 'how I came to decline your kind and flattering proposal and accept Lord Salisbury's'. For sixty-five years, his object had been to raise the standard of art from depression, and for the last forty he had 'sincerely endeavoured to the utmost of my restricted ability to give my efforts some National importance and have relinquished the wealth which successful professional practice might have given me'; and this year he had given up membership of the Athenaeum, 'my only luxury'. He had not worked for honours, and would leave the world without one – 'always taking off my hat to you' – but 'impelled by the desire to deserve the title Hon, I felt the wish to consider my efforts worthy, by Lord Salisbury's gratifying suggestion and accepted the attention . . . as constituting an example in a direction which seemed to me to be right. Her Majesty apparently disallowed the claim and I go on my way if not exactly rejoicing working in the same way and with the same objects.' Gladstone, dubbing him 'the Prince of British Art', replied generously that 'in forgoing your opportunities of fortune you have set a great example to an age which much needed it.'

However, the sense of guilt and confusion in the Watts household prompted a letter from Mary to Catherine Gladstone, explaining her husband's 'picturesque notions of the state necessary to weigh in the matter of the honour, he did not think himself entitled to' and to say that because of his philanthropic activities, he often feels the pinch, 'You will understand better why he saves and how he spends if I may tell you that he is just now giving our village here a little chapel for the new burial ground and he and I are getting immense pleasure out of the cheque by making the people work at the ornamental work themselves.'[54]

After only six months her Terra Cotta Home Arts class exhibited their symbolic terracotta tiles at the Royal Albert Hall, spotted at once by *The Studio*. 'The Compton branch showed some admirable capitals and surface fillings of modelled terracotta in rough clay baked in charcoal ovens to a most beautiful red. By mere chance, after noting these for marked approval, the designer was discovered to be Mrs G. F. Watts, the wife of the great artist, who has shown much practical interest in the movement.' He was indeed pursuing the cause with a vengeance and financing the enterprise, but this was Mary's project. She was the motivating force. Yet *The Studio* attributed her success to Watts. 'It is a curious thing, that in tracing the source of the design in the few instances of good and new work to be discerned in the gallery, in almost every case some artist of established reputation had supplied the motive power.'[55] Certainly, as Madeline Wyndham pointed out, many patterns produced by the Home Arts were ugly, but the success of chapel decoration was owed to Mary's fresh imaginative spirit. She did not discuss her symbols with Watts in detail, but as they explored world philosophy throughout the ages in their readings and discussions, they influenced each other. He painted and sculpted ideas and she modelled them into terracotta patterns. So that people of all creeds and civilizations could relate to the idea, Mary wove as many symbols as possible into the chapel friezes, whereas his pictures were sparse, unlimited by decoration.[56]

The first great mystery of Creation intrigued Watts. No longer was it appropriate to think of God as a kindly white-bearded old man, 'If I were ever to make a symbol of the Deity it would be as a great vesture into which everything that exists is woven.' He was referring simply to an all-embracing idea, unlike Mary's terracotta tapestries of symbols from the Celts, Egypt, Syria, Scandinavia, the Jews, Christians, Brahmins and Hindus, entwined in tendrils of the modern Art Nouveau. Universality, he said, was the pre-eminent quality that made Shakespeare acceptable to the world, 'It is that quality which makes nations great.'[57]

Lord Winterstoke had bequeathed his *Love and Death* to the Bristol Art Gallery. The white robe made Death look like an angel, thought Watts. 'I catch a glint of that white garment behind my shoulder and it seems to me to say "I am not far off".' He held Mary's hand and said, 'Now if I leave you, I know you will have your work, a definite life. Your work is a very important one – *remember* excessive grief is a very wicked thing.'[58] That day Lady Elcho noted that he had given a drawing to comfort her father-in-law Lord Wemyss after the death of his wife.[59] Watts decided that when his time came he wished to be cremated, telling Mary of a Hindu symbol used by the Swami – human life as a candle and the soul, a flame that disappears at last into the air. As he saw it, through cremation, the material being was 'compelled, as it were, to follow the spiritual' and the flame in his pictures '*will* live as long as paint and canvas can last'. Hallam Tennyson wrote that his father had wanted Watts to paint

> The face of Death is toward the Sun of Life,
> His shadow darkens earth: his true name
> Is Onward.[60]

So many friends were dying. On 13 August Millais succumbed to cancer and it was suggested on both sides of the Atlantic that Watts should – though he would not wish to – succeed him as president.[61] In due course, Poynter would accept the presidency. Josephine Butler returned to sit. She talked of her life, conflicts and vulnerability since the death of her husband, 'I never dare allow a single pessimistic thought for a moment.' Watts gave her a photograph of *Love Triumphant*. She held her hosts in her arms as she left. Her affection for Mary delighted him. 'You are an *accroche-coeur* – every one loves you', he said, beaming. When she had gone, the Wattses called on Violet Granby and watched her modelling the memorial to her nine-year-old son John, Lord Haddon.[62]

At the end of August, Watts formally notified the Royal Academy of his desire to become a retired member; and at his request the South Kensington Museum returned his Symbolist pictures in preparation for exhibition at the end of the year, before their presentation to the nation. He had hoped to show them at the Academy, 'especially as I wished in this case comparison with some of the best specimens by the old Masters'. But Hallé and Carr persuaded him to send them to the New Gallery, and with reluctance he agreed to another major retrospective.[63] Meanwhile, *The Creation of Eve* hung in the place of honour at the Royal Birmingham Society of Artists exhibition, with *Naked and Not Ashamed* and its pendant, flanked by panels by the society's president, Laurence Alma Tadema.[64]

Watts returned from Limnerslease to learn that *Sunset on the Alps* had come back from Toynbee Hall with a hole, the paint charred by a red hot poker, and no explanation. 'Signor takes it perfectly calmly!' Mary was furious. He must send no more pictures there. 'Well not anything important, I think', he replied; and when she insisted, he reproved her, 'The pictures are meant to be of service . . . I am always so terribly afraid in case we should allow *the best we have in us* to lapse.'[65] All too frequently now, he was called away from *Physical Energy* to sign pictures for descendants of his old patrons. Irritated at first, he was surprised by the rich painting of his youth – thirteen from the Jarvis family – and embarrassed by some of the Ionides/Cassavetti pictures. Aglaia Coronio came to help sort them out.[66]

The artist was under pressure to complete pictures for the New Gallery, and the house was streaming with visitors. Mary's niece Dorothy MacCallum sat for her portrait. She pursued her research at the British Museum, and took on an assistant, Miss Jackson, to help model her ceiling panels.[67] When gout forced Watts to stay in bed, Mary gazed at his shell-like forehead, the soft white flames of silver hair, his ethereal look, 'I must learn that vision by heart – I have never seen, and never will see its like again – The impression it gives is of some beautiful child's – he still trails his clouds of glory and yet he has the large experience of the man who has lived and worked and thought.'[68]

He agreed to join the Humanitarian League. Replying to the founder Henry Salt, Watts protested against 'the brutal fashion of docking horses . . . a disgrace to our civilization . . . more degrading than bull fighting' where, though in a bad cause, there was at least a sense of courage, but the brutality of docking horses' tails for 'the mere caprice of fashion' was not only painful, but destroyed the harmonious balance of Nature. 'Setting aside the disgusting cruelty, this want of taste which can prefer to see the noble creature changed by the destruction of the fine appendage into a thing that resembles the stump of a worn out broom, the noble creature made to resemble a pig or tapir is very lamentable when found among the classes that can boast of education and refinement.' Widely quoted by the League, Watts 'did great service in bringing an odious fashion into disrepute'.[69]

Gilbert was asked for another sitting. He thought the portrait 'absolutely *complete* . . . a portrayal that no amount of personal vanity could make me desire better' and did not want him to touch it, but 'Signor just breathed upon it – it is a fine rendering – resumé of him.' The sculptor spoke of the reredos he was modelling for St Albans; *The Resurrection of Christ* was to be of tinted marble, the angels' wings inlaid with shells. Commissioned six years earlier by Lord Aldenham, a director of the Bank of England and National Portrait Gallery trustee, whose silver-grey tones had fascinated Watts when he, too, sat in August. Gilbert was only now making the sketch for the reredos and would never finish the highly imaginative work.[70]

William Morris – as if forecast in 'The Doomed Ship' of *The Earthly Paradise* – caught a lung infection on a Norwegian cruise, from which he died on 3 October 1896. Mary kissed her husband, relieved that he was still safe with her. 'Yes, with all those strong men dropping around it is wonderful!' he said. Being 'a cracked pitcher' had its advantages, for he took took to his bed to deal with illness, whereas stronger colleagues carried on regardless and were dying in their sixties. That day Hollyer took a series of photographs of his most vigorous work, *Physical Energy*. The next morning they went to The Grange. Ned and Georgie Burne-Jones were deeply touched that Watts, who so seldom left his studio, had taken the trouble to visit them. Ironically, he was fit on the day of the craftsman's funeral, but he and Morris had not been close; instead he took Mary in the brougham to give Gilbert his portrait, stopping first at the Arts and Crafts Exhibition at the New Gallery, which was closed in memory of the society's president. But they slipped in and marvelled at the advances that had been made, the great art revival shaped by Morris, Gilbert and Burne-Jones. Crane's *Sonnet on the Death of William Morris* lay above the *Chaucer* in the Kelmscott book display. At Maida Vale, Gilbert bore scars of stress, though his 'wizard studio is more fascinating than ever'. On the way home they called to enquire after du Maurier and sadly, two days later, they saw the sandwich men proclaiming the 'DEATH OF THE AUTHOR OF *TRILBY*'.[71]

At Limnerslease that autumn, their reading was largely devoted to the writings of Claude Montefiore. The president of the Anglo-Jewish Association and co-founder of the movement for Liberal Judaism had come to Little Holland House in May. Watts had formerly felt little love for the Jews, believing that 'no nation had ever formulated such great truths as they had . . . side by side with these truths they had all the darkest side of half barbarian savagery, and superstition, and while they formulated the duty of God is to their neighbour for all the Christian world, they left it also the legacy of fanaticism, superstition, cruelty, a God who is a demon'. For a man with a broad, liberal mind, this seems extraordinary, yet, under the impression that Jews saw 'only the beauty of holiness and never the holiness of beauty', he was doubtless reminded of the orthodoxy he had rebelled against as a child. Montefiore's *The Children of the Ghetto* opened his eyes. 'We feel we know something of the Jews for the first time', wrote Mary.[72]

Montefiore drew universal parallels between Greek and Hebrew thought, discussing light and shade, good and evil, the palliative that turns pain to pleasure, sorrow to joy, and ultimately, that 'whatever the mystery behind all is the Infinite Love.' 'Signor says he does not know when he found a mind so entirely and perfectly harmonious with his own. He longed to meet the author to know his private belief, 'what fine wide mind accepts.' The following year he painted Montefiore's portrait. Meanwhile, as he worked,

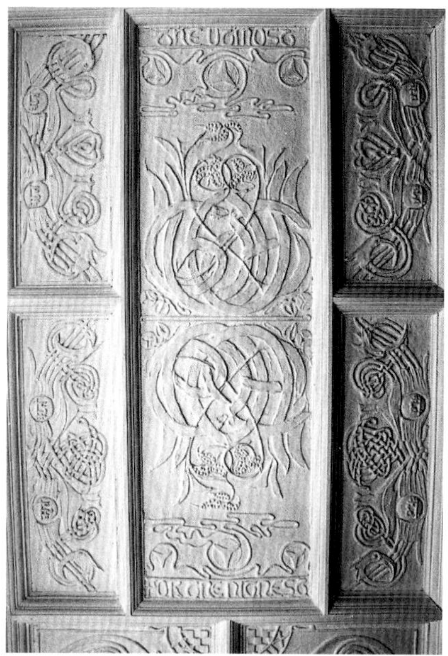

198    Detail of Mary's ceiling panels
dedicated to Signor at Limnerslease,
1896.

'a little flame flickering before his great canvasses,' Mary noted, 'He is
Greek in heart Celtic in his eyes! Mystery comes from Welsh strain'.[73] Inten-
sifying pictures for the exhibition, he spread Love's wing further round Life
and made Mammon so hideous that she hoped he was not going too far.

Madeline Wyndham came for luncheon in October. Stepping through the
front door she will have found much of the civilization ceiling in place; and
as she chatted to Watts on the niche sofa, above her head were the new
panels that bore emblems personal to Signor (fig. 198). He was astonished
by the chapel work, by the villagers' excellent modelling and Mary's complete and full idea. As she struggled to work out an inscription for the bell,
he suggested 'Be my voice neither feared, nor forgotten', making, as she put
it, 'his voice ring in the bell he gives'.[74] He was keen for her to have a bicycle
and loved watching Mary try it out at Limnerslease. Andrews held her, ran
about and finally rode it himself. 'I daresay as a *play* thing it may be good
for him', she wrote. 'I feel sure it will give me new power.'[75]

An intimate nocturnal interlude was recorded the next day; Watts having
been bedridden with gout, she may have been referring to his ankles – or
not: 'He proposed that I should rub him that soothing interchange of sleepy
activity that often sends me, the rubber, and he, who is the rubbed off into
the land of dreams – I rubbed in vain. We tried to sleep, he holding my
hand under his two upon his breast – I was wide awake, and knowing my
blessedness, to have his hands! to have mine above his heart! and know
that he wants it there.'[76] In the darkness, he brooded over the general view
that his technique was bad. Although the idea in his pictures was paramount, his aim was still to achieve this through beauty of colour, line and
effect. The artist spoke slowly, weighing his words, discussing the latest
critical comment that 'in spite of my shortcomings . . . I have achieved "a
commanding position".' The next morning, he read that Poynter had
been elected president of the Academy. In Watts's view, he was 'a good man
but *dry*'.[77]

'Ten years together. I hope you remember this is our wedding day', he
said. Mary's sleepy thoughts of her 'Spirit companion' were tinged with
foreboding of 'the dull vampires that suck and bleed all spirited life away';
and his comment that they were now seldom together saddened her. While
she frantically composed a tapestry of symbols to be modelled by her class
– 'pretty nearly the whole village of Compton', Watts wrote to Rivière[78] –
he composed a preface for the New Gallery exhibition catalogue. Together
they wandered down through the trees, across the lane and up on to
Budburrow Hill to check the height of the chapel. He gave considerable
time to the catalogue entries. The picture titles now seemed restrictive. 'You
can't label them, because they represent ideas much too far off, taking one
outside experience – I want them to take you as music might, and lead you
may be further even than I myself intended.' Watts, conscious that his range
of thought extended beyond the ordinary, believed his art would be better
understood in the future. In the catalogue preface he advised:

> The great majority of these works should be regarded rather as hiero-
> glyphs than anything else, certainly not as more than symbols which all
> Art was in the beginning, and which everything is, that is not directly
> connected with physical conditions. In many cases the intention is frankly
> didactic, excuse for this, generally regarded as exasperating . . . Whatever

type . . . the endeavour has been to impress distinctly the direction of modern thought.[79]

Giving Spielmann the go-ahead for an article in the *Nineteenth Century*, Watts asked the critic to focus on the ethical series, comparing them to 'a pictorial book of Ecclesiastes, or *Omar Khayyam* with I hope a little more Spirituality'. Yet he feared 'the Public will be disgusted with my name and will want to know nothing more about me for generations to come! . . . such apparent egotism.'[80] No other living British artist had had such exposure. The 155 pictures would include early works located by Mary, developments since the Grosvenor retrospective, and new work, but he felt obliged to print an apology for the familiar and unfinished pictures.[81]

As the paintings arrived in Regent Street, Watts instructed Thompson to look in and see whether they looked too unfinished. 'I want you to varnish the little *Blue Endymion* which I have sold, wash it very carefully first, and put as little varnish (mastic) as possible rubbing it on'; and Lord Wantage must be sent a good Hollyer photograph before the portrait of *Violet Lindsay* was sent to the New Gallery.[82]

Among visitors to Little Holland House on 1 December was the laird of Rothiemurcus. His eleven-year-old nephew Duncan Grant won as his preparatory school drawing prize Rawnsley's *Ballads of Brave Deeds*, published by J. M. Dent, with a preface and frontispiece, *The Happy Warrior*, by G. F. Watts. Mary, proud that Dent also chose *Love Triumphant* as a frontispiece for *Shakespeare's Sonnets*, which linked Watts with the great English bard, sent a copy to Lord Wemyss. 'When you look at it you will know that this is the picture going on now in the studio.' She too began to adapt her symbolic leather design *Hand and Soul* as a frontispiece.[83]

On Christmas Eve, there was a ripple on the waters of the Watts marriage. The artist received notice of his Royal Academy pension. He had tried to do away with this benefit years ago – most Academicians and their widows being too wealthy to appreciate the modest, almost insulting sum – and when he realized it was not a bill, refused to accept it, and sent instructions to have it paid to the Academy Benevolent Fund. In his frustration, he scolded Mary for not riding in the brougham to deliver her gifts round the village. 'I told him he had gone near to breaking our marriage contract, that when we were angry we were not to say things that could not be forgotten – threatening me to wish he may never have another birthday.' Peace returned on Christmas Day, which they celebrated with the Hichens at Monkshatch, walking home by lantern-light. 'It was something to have him walking up and down so vigorously!' As the year closed, the New Gallery was filled with his paintings, their uniquely rich, sombre tone out of tune with most modern art. [84]

Critics accepted his Symbolist challenge and many judged that his painting would rank in posterity with the masters. To be called 'a belated old master' was fine by Watts – 'that explains my work very well'. George Moore in the *Chronicle*, however, seemed determined to demolish him. The Wattses read the article to Hichens: it 'made him spurt, flume and flame . . . He would hang "George Moore".'[85] Burne-Jones confided his doubts to his assistant Thomas Rooke:

Why don't one's friends prevent one from exhibiting disasters . . . Most of the North Room is full of great weary things; there are 3 whacking

Eves which I can't abide, and a huge desolate *Court of Death* . . . But he does men better than women. The shoulders and all the torso he does splendidly, knows all about it, and that seems to be all he cares for – the heads are never very good. The hands not made nearly as interesting as they might be, and the legs seem always too hard and rigid, standing with a strong cutting light from the thigh. There is the most beautiful of all his pictures the *Dream of Endymion* . . . and his almost living portraits. The *Walter Crane* is a marvellous piece of painting.[86]

The muralist Heywood Sumner, astonished by Watts's variety, assurance and insight, acknowledged him to be 'far the highest of all our great painters, in conception, in style, in colour, in weight, in character, in every great quality he is so quietly supreme . . . Yes, we shall indeed have a great inheritance when his pictures belong to us.'[87] They inspired an early poem by twelve-year-old Siegfried Sassoon, who was taken to the exhibition by his mother. Growing up with a deep admiration for Watts, he envied his younger brother's privilege as his godson. Though Hamo Watts Sassoon – the boys were nephews of Hamo Thornycroft – showed no interest in the artist, Siegfried was moved by the lofty grandeur of *The Court of Death*. His impression appeared in his second volume of poetry given to his mother in March.

> There lay the lake of sleep: eternal sleep
>   That looked so still.
> And far beyond, the palace of King Death
>   Who hidden lay:
>
>        . . .
>
> The nobleman came up with bowed head
> The loyal knight came there to lay his sword
> There at the foot of death, who robed in black
> Looked on the people who came up to him
> To throw themselves, into the sea of gloom.
>
>        . . .
>
> And he spake thus: 'I hold the lives of men
>   From beginning to the end.'
>   And, yea, behind him angels stood
>   Guarding the things unknown, beyond the Tomb.[88]

Within days of Watts's exhibition opening, the Leighton retrospective opened at the Academy. Watts had been apprehensive, both for fear of comparison, and also on the part of his late friend, whose colour tones he felt were constrained by perfection; there seemed to be 'no birth pangs before the picture sprang full grown and *ready dressed* into the world'. He went to judge for himself in the new year, first to the New Gallery, where he went straight to *Time and Oblivion* and left feeling proud of only two pictures; the other, also painted half a century before, was *Life's Illusions*. 'Of *Time and Oblivion* I think Phidias would have said: 'Go on, you *may* do something.' At Burlington House, he too was taken aback by Leighton's variety. As a draughtsman, he could not be faulted, but on reflection, Watts confessed sadly, 'He does not move one, except perhaps in the *Summer Moon* and *The Sisters Kiss*. Millais does, and he also touches a wide range of sen-

timent – you may say Titian did not touch one from the sentimental side.
But then there was such splendour such a restrained mastery.'

Now that his national Symbolist works were in waiting for the nation,
he found it tiresome to send pictures to international exhibitions. 'I am
sick and tired of sending pictures about and really think I have done my
part', he wrote to Spielmann. Prince Eugen was asking for eight promised
pictures – notably, *She Shall be Called Woman*, *Time, Death and Judgement*, and the Burne-Jones portrait – which proved to be the highlight at
Stockholm.[89] *A Greek Idyll* (*Acis and Galatea*) and *Walter Crane*, constantly on the move, were off to Brussels. Manchester patrons had sent two
to the first Dresden International Exhibition of Fine Art, but Watts had to
find more for Munich and for British provincial galleries. Portraits of
Dorothy Dene and Lillie Langtry were going to an *Exhibition of Dramatic
and Musical Art* at the Grafton and to the Guildhall, and he had promised
the entire New Gallery collection to Barnett. 'I have made up my mind not
to come before the public anywhere any more,' he insisted to Spielmann.[90]
Barnett had asked Burne-Jones to lecture on Watts's pictures, both from a
personal viewpoint and to establish their place in world history. Ned had
clearly done so, for he told Rooke he could not have refused, 'One thing
would lead on to another until presently I should have no peace in life at
all'.[91]

Watts was fighting fit. Shortly before travelling up to Kensington for his
eightieth birthday, Mary followed breathlessly as he raced after the hounds.
A small deputation of the directors and secretary of the New Gallery came
to Little Holland House on Tuesday 23 February 1897, to deliver an illuminated address inscribed on vellum with a special sonnet by Swinburne
and signed by the Prime Minister, Cabinet Ministers, the Archbishop of
Canterbury, the great and the good from the arts and literature, including
every member of the Royal Academy – over 200 signatures. Carr recited
the sonnet:

> High thought and hallowed love, by faith made one,
>     Begat and bare the sweet strong-hearted child.
> Art, nursed by Nature; earth and sea and sun
>     Saw Nature then more godlike as she smiled.
> Life smiled on death, and death on life: the soul
>     Between them shone, and soared above their strife,
> And left on Time's unclosed and starry scroll
>     A sign that quickened death to deathless life.
> Peace rose like Hope, a patient queen, and bade
>     Hell's firstborn Faith, abjure her creed and die;
> And Love, by life and death made sad and glad,
>     Gave Conscience ease, and watched Good Will pass by.
> All these make music now of one man's name,
>     Whose life and Age are one with love and fame.

It was all the more moving, Mary noted, because of the informality
of the occasion. Their only other guests were her sister, Spielmann and
Geraldine Liddell. The New Gallery also gave a bronze portrait medal of
'Our Titian of Limnerslease', his image modelled by Hallé's sister Elinor. In
France '*Le père Corot*' had received a medal at a famous banquet the year

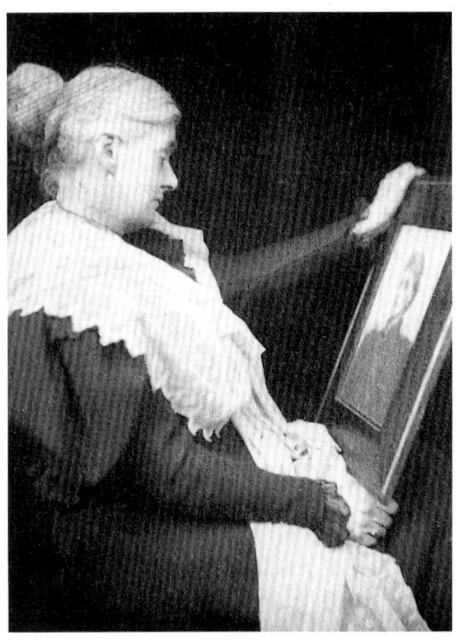

199   Madeline Wyndham looking at the portrait of Evelyn de Vesci, after 1897.

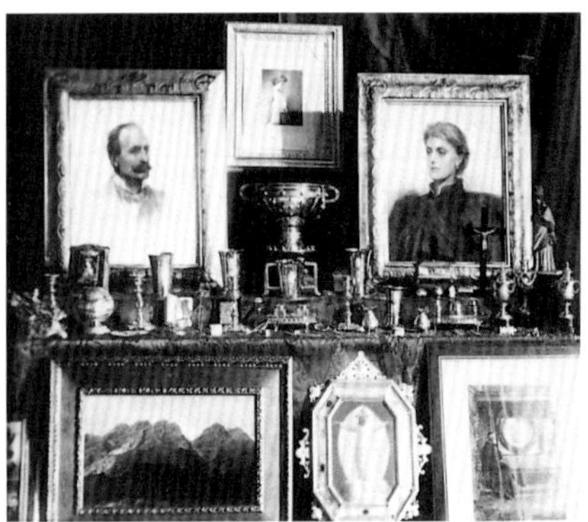

200   The Watts corner at Abbeyleix in Ireland, after 1897, with portraits of Visount and Viscountess de Vesci above *Sant Agnese, Mentone* and a photo of Signor by the tondo, with, presumably, Mary's *Hand and Soul* centred below (private collection).

before he died, but, declared *The Times*, never had an English artist received such a tribute, proving the width of his appeal and admiration for the high poetical mission of his art, 'He has often painted playful pictures, but he has never played with his art.' The Arts and Crafts Exhibition Society later presented their tribute 'to an artist peculiarly distinguished'; and in the afternoon the Watts held a children's party, largely dominated by the Burne-Jones's granddaughter Angela Mackail.[92] 'Dearest Ned, I think I am more shocked than pleased by success,' he wrote afterwards. 'We both of us find our days only look in upon us to nod and say goodbye. I return with interest your good wishes for health and power to work.'[93]

Gerry Liddell and Elinor Hallé were planning a musical soirée at the New Gallery, as a double celebration with Joachim. (Mary explained, 'There two Hamlets, possibly for fear one should fail). Watts promised to attend, but grumped that he hoped it would give as much pleasure to others as the misery it would cause him. Once there, he chatted happily to Ned and Joachim in the vestibule. The rooms filled with friends, many still as beautiful as their younger portraits around them – Virginia Somers, Lady Airlie, May Hichens, Violet Granby, Evelyn de Vesci, Madeline Wyndham and her daughter Mary Elcho, Arthur Balfour, Lady Wenlock – all attracted by the two veteran masters of art and music, seated side by side. Joachim's pupils opened the concert with Bach's concert suite for small string orchestra. As the maestro himself played the sonata in E for violin and harpsichord with the music critic John Fuller-Maitland, and Beethoven's *Frühling* sonata with Agnes Zimmerman on the piano, their music seemed to be echoed in rhythmic colour and harmony on the walls. [94]

A German critic Anna Wilmersdöffer thanked Watts for the joy his pictures had given her.[95] To De La Sizeranne, who encapsulated Watts's paintings better than most, the colours and sudden movement of the figures were disturbing, their discordance strangely compulsive. 'And yet you linger, for whilst Watts's colour distracts the eye, his ideas penetrate to the depths of the soul, and slowly arouse something that was sleeping there . . . [the figures] must be beings whose essence we ardently desire to look into.'[96] As for the artist himself, after a day's work he liked to stretch his range of vision and was found reading about astronomical discoveries.[97]

He invited the Viscount de Vesci to sit as a surprise silver wedding gift for Evelyn, and Mary designed a symbolic leather pouch to cover a volume of Rossetti's *Hand and Soul* (fig. 200). Evelyn's neice Cynthia Charteris came to the studio with Lord Wemyss, 'It was thrillingly full of scaffolding, pulleys and ropes, palettes and oozing tubes of paint.' Watching Watts paint, the nine-year-old was intrigued that 'Grandpapa, who usually told everyone how to do their own jobs, did not show the artist how he should hold his brush.' Cynthia recognized *Hope*, which was standard decoration in most schoolrooms. She had long been 'pleasurably terrified by those two nightmares of Watts's imagination, *Mammon* and *The Minotaur*' and was enchanted by *Paolo and Francesca*, imagining the lovers to be in a strange heaven, though her governess tartly corrected her: 'They are in Hell. They sinned.'[98]

Barnett had found a site for the new Whitechapel Art Gallery. The architect Charles Harrison Townsend had already exhibited a drawing for a dynamic twin-towered building with a bold mosaic frieze designed by Crane. Barnett needed a further £20,000. Watts campaigned on his behalf in *The Times* as *Punch* heralded the transfer of his pictures,[99] after which William Morris's portrait, chased round the exhibitions by Cust, was received by the National Portrait Gallery. He wanted a replica of his portrait of Millais, which, having given the original to the family, he would have undertaken to commemorate their friendship 'but I really have not time for all the tasks I have set myself'. According to Doll Liddell, who called at Limnerslease in May, he ranked Millais very highly among nineteenth-century English artists, second only to Walker for 'sheer natural ability'.[100] As a retired Academician his sole contribution to the Summer Exhibition was a portrait of Mary's vivacious niece, Dorothy MacCallum in a primrose and pink dress. The kneeling figure of *Paris on Ida* hung in a place of honour at the New Gallery. However, reviewers were more interested in his profile of Mary.[101]

*Sir Galahad* was installed in the chapel of Eton College in time for the Fourth of June celebrations. Watts had long wanted to present a picture to Eton as a teaching aid. Since his birthday when Henry Luxmoore, an assistant master, again asked after the picture, he had been working up the original six-foot watercolour sketch. The self-taught octogenarian was keen to identify himself with the institution that helped form 'the character of the youth of England'. His gift prompted a contemporary to claim Watts as an old Etonian, but, as the *Eton College Chronicle* suggested, if he had been, 'art would have been the loser'. Typically, he borrowed the picture back during the holidays to 'make it one of my very best'.[102]

He paid a return visit to St Paul's. Excited by the mosaics, he wrote to encourage Richmond and warn him not expect their excellence to be recognized yet, that Tennyson's best work had met with faint praise – '*Maud* was received with a shout of derision!' Richmond was knighted in the Queen's Diamond Jubilee honours.[103]

The National Gallery of British Art, a handsome classical building designed by Sidney Smith, was to be opened on 21 July 1897. Henry Tate invited Watts to meet Lord Carlisle and Sir Edward Poynter at Millbank on 29 June. Tate took him round the gallery, speaking only tentatively about his Symbolist collection. As he had not asked, nor would the artist presume to offer the pictures, Poynter consulted Mary. 'Oh, I am glad they want my pictures', said Watts. Inviting Poynter to collect them the following week, he explained that he had never regarded the pictures as his property, but had not expected a gallery to be available for them in his lifetime, 'I . . . only see now my Presumption and their defects, and shrink from the consequences of my temerity!' Charles Eastlake, Keeper of the National Gallery, formally accepted his 'interesting and valuable gift'.[104] On 13 July, the pictures left and Watts saw the accomplishment of his ambition.

'Signor lets his children go without a pang, except that "they are so bad".' His only agony was at the moment of departure, when he felt he should paint the pictures all over again; but a sense of bereavement hung over his household. 'The ropes hung down on our red walls like a decoration with suicide as a motif', wrote Mary. 'Thompson and I may be found hanging there tomorrow.' The next day was the private view and, after the royal opening, the gallery was crowded with visitors. Passing through the main entrance, into the central glass-domed octagon, turning left through the rectangular room of pictures from the Chantrey bequest, they came to an octagonal gallery, hung unlike any other with Watts's favourite rich red background, a perfect foil for his sombre Symbolist masterpieces. There were eighteen 'sonnets' so far – from *Chaos*, the first chapter of his hoped-for frescoed House of Life, through the finest *Hope*, *Love and Death*, *Love and Life*, and *The All-Pervading*, to the shocking *Mammon*, *The Minotaur* and *Jonah*, plus the self-portrait and *Psyche*, hanging separately amongst the Chantreys.[105] 'Do you think you could read any part of the *Intimations of Immortality* before most of the pictures in the Tate Gallery?' he wondered, comparing his painted poems to Wordsworth.[106] *Chaos*, painted in 1882, is much as he planned it in 1848. Swirling forms in rich blues and browns express 'the passing of our planet from chaos to order'. From the earliest fiery turbulence on the left, a single figure in the swollen tides of the central atmosphere of unborn creations marks the start of the strides of time and leads towards the 'colossal forms, silent and quiescent, symbols of mountain ranges' on the right. This disturbing composition of violence and tranquillity suggests a fraction of what might have been had Watts created the House of Life.[107]

The opening of the Tate Gallery was a landmark in the history of British art in that it accorded permanent status to native artists, charting their progress to the present day. In the Watts Room, the new keeper, Charles Holroyd, was filled with a sense of reverence, 'It is like entering a holy place to go into the room; all the pictures seem to express such a high spirit of endeavour after the best things.' For Watts himself, who had devoted his life to raising the standard of art, this was the summit. Whether the nation was grateful to him was not his concern: 'I have been right in my attempt', which he summed up for Spielmann, 'I endeavoured to give my pictures not only the direction of modern thought but also the stamp of our English Nationality, in character.'[108] Watts had challenged dogma that Art had nothing to do with ethics, and proved, as Holroyd put it, that Art can be didactic and lose none of its essentials. He had achieved his dual ambition. Yet there was more to complete for the nation. Presenting the collections in his lifetime would spur him to improve.[109]

# 23   The Colossus Sits

'THE SUN CALLS TO ME.' As eager to improve at eighty as he was as a young artist, Watts took Mary back to 'the great gods', the Elgin Marbles, and lovingly pointed out every rise and depression of muscle, the cast of the horse's nostril. The lower half of its head alone, he thought, showed the Greeks' sensitivity to the highest spiritual sense of beauty.[1] 'What a grand point could be made of the development of the psyche through the ages!' Watts suggested to Mary that she might incorporate 'the evolution of the idea of goodness in the mind of man, leading up to the knowledge that love is all' into the chapel decoration. As he developed *Love Triumphant*, he began to address the state of the nation, painting a sinister image. In his vision of Ezekiel, *Can These Bones Live?*, an English oak appears to be crushed by a golden pall, which covers symbols of destruction, death and corruption – broken tools borrowed from the village blacksmith.[2] Watts wondered if it might be possible for past, present and future to exist together. 'What we see is merely the slow process of development, some-thing lost, something gained. It is not all growth, for we do not get a mind bigger than Homer only in the turning of the wheel new facets are polished, & come into sight – There may be conditions where whatever has been, & is, takes visible form.' (Mary would transform this into a symbolic terra-cotta sundial for her husband.[3]) Ideas crowded his mind. Another was for a picture of *Crippled Reason giving her Epitaph*. 'Ah, you ought to have had a wall', exclaimed Mary.[4]

The great equestrian statue, photographed by Andrews in October,[5] was nearing completion. Watts offered to present *Physical Energy* to the nation, and, by January 1898, the Government had selected a site in Hyde Park, in the centre of the terrace at the foot of the Serpentine. Arthur Balfour (fig. 201), the First Lord of the Treasury, agreed to pay for the casting. Mary, and May and Andrew Hichens pressed him not to refuse. Announcements appeared in the press, but Watts had secretly turned down the offer. Having given everything else, he hoped to finance the statue himself, for it seemed unfair for the nation to pay before the public had had a chance to assess it. Ashbee recorded that here 'the little waxen nervous soul was as hard as steel'.[6] As Thompson would say, 'Oh he's remarkably hard to handle is Mr Watts! Nobody's going to *coax* him against his will.'[7] It was too soon. Health and weather permitting, Watts planned to finish the statue in the summer. 'I have I am afraid forfeited the approbation of my friends,' he wrote to Lord Wemyss. Returning the earl's

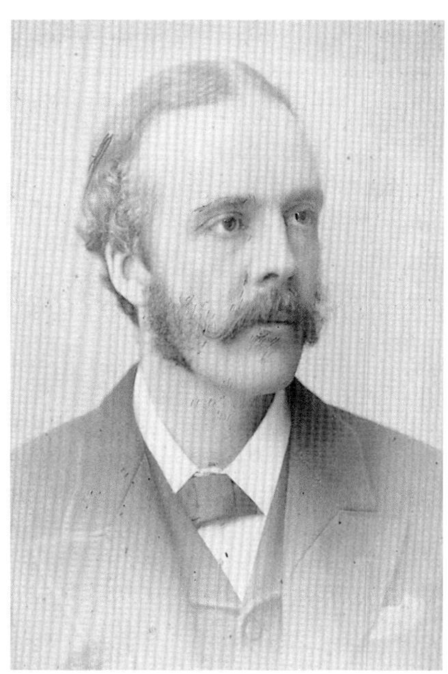

201   The Right Honourable Arthur James Balfour (photo: James Russell & Sons).

'lovely *Venus*', he warned: 'Pray do not think of doing anything *from the reality*. Study well the joints & movement & look at the best examples of Greek art, but make the figure your own.'

Watts was concerned for the nation. 'I see a great ship surrounded by threatening & advancing icebergs which must crush it. Are the officers & sailors aware of the danger & bracing up with courage & intelligence to meet it! Are the officers brave & wise! & the crew, what do we see? I fear gambling, drunkenness & endeavour to overreach one another, anything but combination to meet the peril for love of Position & the old ship.'[8] To Canon Barnett he reiterated the theme he and Hunt had both laid aside, of what was to become, *Love Steering the Boat of Humanity*: 'You ask me something! What can I say, excepting ask the question: "Watchman, what of the night?" Cometh the dawn or groweth still the dark night, does yet the Pilot's hand control the helm, or *drifts* the labouring wreck? But I will add my motto of which indeed I am rather proud! "The Utmost for the Highest".'[9]

Recently appointed an Associate of the Society for the Protection of Birds, he brought in a dead tit, admiring its plumage, just as he had for the heron he painted in 1837. 'When I look at that bird's wing . . . & see the exquisite adaptation of every bit of it to its purpose', he exclaimed, 'I know that that same care about everything we do should be the religion of our life. That is what I call the Love of God.' He was painting an angel weeping over an altar piled with iridescent birds' feathers, *A Dedication* – otherwise known as *The Shuddering* (or *Sorrowing*) *Angel* – as a protest against the destruction of life for millinery glory. The publisher Joseph Malaby Dent, lunching at Limnerslease, was keen to print the picture for the society.[10]

Lily's young friends were invited to Limnerslease in school holidays, but when a tactless maid upset Watts by suggesting Lily might be happier with Mary's sister, he agonized that his lifestyle might be too old for her teenage spirits and that she might prefer living with the Liddells – that she was 'rooted there, only a cut flower here'. Back at school Lily dispelled paternal anxieties, writing long, happy letters 'with just enough regret for home'. In return, she received a rare reply from the doting artist, writing as her 'great grandfather': 'You may love another, or others better but this place is mine & you must love me as much as you can (or as little as you will). I shall never change or give up that place, I think hardly if you wished it! No loving & loved friend you will ever have will be more anxious about your welfare & happiness than I . . . Your very loving old Signor.'[11]

Reading that Lady Sykes, whom he had painted as blue-eyed seven-year-old Jessica in the Cavendish Bentinck family group, had been found guilty of forgery, the Wattses reflected that many of his beautiful sitters had since had sad histories. Few could match the litigious Georgina Weldon, now sending provocative sympathy to Wilde. 'Yes', he replied. 'I have been able to strike a heavy and fatal blow at the monstrous prison system of English justice'.[12]

Watts's portraits of Burne-Jones, Walter Crane and Lady Granby were the talk of St Petersburg when the British Art Exhibition, arranged by the Grand Duchess Elizabeth, opened in the salons of the Imperial Society for the encouragement of Fine Arts.[13] The artist Charles Furse came to paint at Limnerslease before starting a series of murals for Liverpool Town Hall. Redmayne sat for a portrait drawing as a thanks offering for checking the chapel hinges.[14] For Mary, rushed off her feet with her class and now also designing vases, there was no social let up. The director of the Birmingham Art Gallery came to discuss loans, including that of *The Childhood of Zeus* and *Aspiration*. Watts, talking of the threefold mission of art, to 'delight the senses, touch the sympathies, & rouse intellectual & consequently spiritual activity', said that most art stopped at delighting the senses. Spielmann arrived, full of a book he planned to write on Watts. The artist, keen that the public should appreciate the pictures, rather than see them as an imposition, specified that the book should not be a biography. He and Mary answered numerous questions over the months. She offered her catalogue, but after Spielmann requested that it should be a definitive biography, Watts withheld consent, 'Nothing of the kind can be of real value during the life of the subjects or written without violating private confidence or giving annoyance to friends. As I said before I am sorry I cannot accede to the request but must beg the abandonment of the idea.'[15]

He wanted to finish *Love Triumphant* before his birthday. Not that he would stop there. 'It was glowing & glorious, when he called me in today to look at it. He has done much, the right arm of Love which gives it a great refinement & exaltation – every breath tells now – what a life of work *consecrated* to the highest', enthused Mary. 'You see, I want to plant his feet distinctly on the ground', he explained. 'All that is spiritual must get its impetus from the ground beneath our feet – That *must* be recognized, though many people would think it wrong.'[16]

'Oh my beloved, too fast the birthdays come!' Mary kissed him in the early hours of 23 February. 'Why has he all those wonderfully soothing essences!' Signor held out his hand to her, asking for more. 'My beloved, how great my love for you seems to me in these hours, & little fears grow great too – I was miserable because our night light went out. I knew it would! somehow, & dreaded it knowing the life candle thought in my mind, but I got up & relit it at one o'clock! – so I take it as a symbol of the year only.' Meredith wrote to 'let our beloved Signor know that I am among those many who on this his eighty-first birthday thank heaven that we count him as one of the living sons of Earth. It strengthens my sense of life to think that he is with us.'[17]

The following day, in France, Émile Zola was condemned to prison for libel for his open letter to the president published in the newspaper *L'Aurore* – 'J'Accuse!' – denouncing the French army, and therefore the government, for their anti-Semitic hounding of the Jewish army captain Alfred Dreyfus, who had been wrongly convicted of treason. Watts had followed every word of the trial. He admired Zola's defence of Dreyfus and believed that *The Times* spoke for the British in declaring that though the jury had not heard it, the ear of the world had, and justice-loving people had given Zola his case.[18] 'What I feel about the French is that as a nation you can not appeal to their conscience!' said the artist. He saw them as 'intelligently brilliant'; the Germans, in his view lacking in sympathy and a sense of justice, were the most intellectual; whereas England, less intelligently brilliant or intellectual, 'has a conscience that may be really and prominently touched – what she takes she is willing to give – with all our faults.'[19]

Watts had lent *'Stitch, Stitch, Stitch!'* to the Millais memorial exhibition at Burlington House. He believed the late president had rarely achieved as much as 'his splendid genius should have afforded': that Millais, like Landseer – 'the two Artists who ought to have raised the Banner of Art in England & planted it in the very noblest place' – had suffered from premature success. At the exhibition, Watts found *Speak Speak* 'puerile' and the head of Staunton in *Effie Deans* 'boneless'; but he lingered over *Leisure Hours* (he preferred Millais's female portraits), enjoying the fine blend of influences from old German masters with the best of the modern. 'What splendid strength of colour', he enthused, 'With such masterly execution!' Above all, he admired the early *Sir Isumbras at the Ford*.[20] 'That landscape always made me urge Millais to paint landscape long before he had done anything', he recalled. 'I hope I may have had something to do with his taking to it, though his life in Scotland actually led him to it.'[21] Millais's reputation had increased 'a thousand fold'. Watts wrote of him to Rivière, as 'the greatest painter we have ever had', especially in his rendering of maidenhood and childhood. 'Will the Academy ever have such Presidents again!'[22] He now felt his own work coming together. Subjects he cared about seemed easier; and he felt he saw more clearly. 'I fancy that must be very unusual at my age, is it not?'[23]

The American actress Florence Bligh, the future Countess of Darnley, thrilled her hosts when she stayed at Limnerslease for an expansive portrait (fig. 202). 'She ought not to quite shut up – her nature is too rich & beautiful & needs to warm the fire of others lives,' Mary observed. 'An Undine sort of creature, having found her soul she is living for the first time – Tonight she chose to be grave & sat by Signor in the niche'; and the following evening, she sat at their feet '& laughed & frivolled till we were made quite young again'. Her portrait, less sharply defined than the earl would have liked, characterized the actress's bright, gregarious spirit, 'an expression of my own feeling, a musical presentiment rather than a realistic one!' The contrasting components of character – temperament, training, heredity, circumstance and habit – fascinated Watts, who suggested this might be painted or woven into beautiful symbols.[24] Mary de Navarro came later that month. So regally did she address the pottery class that the artist chided her, took her hand and said 'always be a child.' In the autumn, she would return to pose for the radiant portrait he had started ten years earlier. De Navarro had talked of him to Prince Giovanni Borghese in Rome. 'Watts! I prefer him to any artist. He is a poet and gives one ideas', exclaimed the prince. 'I am his most devoted admirer.' Mary sent photographs of the prince's favourite pictures to the Palazzo Borghese.[25]

Watts had commissioned Ernest George to build four cottages under a single sloping roof in Compton; and Mary had summoned their old builder Mitchell to discuss the future of the pottery.[26] So popular were her terracotta Home Arts classes – their strange symbolic tiles acclaimed every year at exhibition – that with the chapel exterior complete she wanted to turn their enterprise into a professional business, producing terracotta tombstones, sundials and pots. In so doing, she would fulfil the highest ideal of the Home Arts: to train the working man or woman and equip them with skills to pursue a career as craftsmen in beautiful rural surroundings. Watts tossed and turned in bed: 'He could see nothing but misery – I had no head for business no nerve for extra work writing & worry, that I would probably go mad, or he would go mad & die – knowing that he would leave me to a miserable impoverished old age.' Finally, he agreed that she could

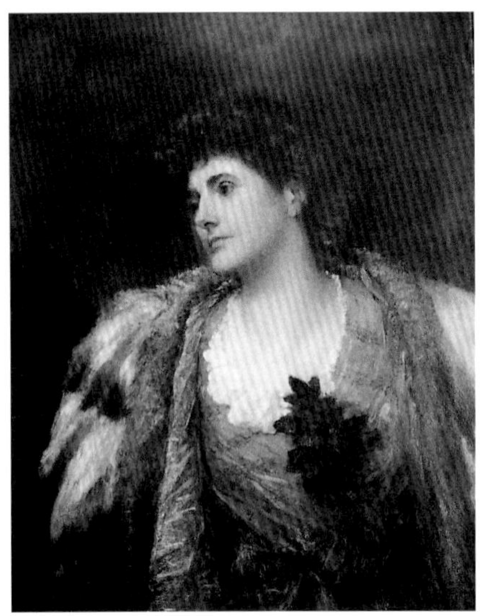

202    *Florence Bligh*, the future Countess of Darnley, 1897–98, (private collection).

take on Mitchell, Deuchars and a kiln-burner, and have a new pottery shed, but that if there was no profit she would give it up after a year. Mitchell accepted that night and the following morning helped produce a mould for the first tombstone. Two days later Deuchars modelled a capital for *The Winged Hours* sundial.[27] Watts advised her to make her patterns stronger and asked her to design a terracotta pedestal for *Clytie*.

Impressed by the way the village children had taken to modelling, he wrote to Horsfall urging strenuous efforts to educate the mind and body of the young, and thus restore the state of the nation. 'Inspiration . . . the equivalent of Light & Air, must come from a higher source than mere material conditions, but the roots of all earthly things are in the earth. No plant can thrive, no flower bloom in barren soil or with poisoned roots.' He wanted every child to feel the enjoyment of life. Recommending healthy meals, exercise, recreation, manual dexterity, he advised that they should be made aware that 'the divine quality of [the] Mind' that made people superior to animals, but if it were not exercised they were inferior, because they should be so much better.[28]

Lily was home for the holidays and amused to find Signor as eager to get to the sports at nearby Charterhouse school as she was. Miss Dymes, sacked for inefficiency as the Home Arts secretary, was invited to Limner-slease in April to research an article on Watts's portraits for the publisher J. M. Dent;[29] and the American contralto Madame Antoinette Sterling came to Little Holland House[30] when Watts was in town for the exhibition varnishing days. He was showing the portrait of Florence Bligh, *Early Spring* (Mrs Ellice's barefoot grandchild Isabel) and *Can These Bones Live?* at the New Gallery.[31] *Love Triumphant* was on exhibition at the Academy. Love, standing with arms soaring heavenwards above the collapsed figures of Time and Death, was both a sequel to *Time, Death and Judgment* and the supreme culmination of the Love trilogy, after *Love and Life* and *Love and Death*. 'In its solemnity and dignity the work stands alone', declared the *Art Journal*, 'an isolation akin to that which Sanzio saw in Michelangelo'. Watts planned to paint a replica for St Paul's cathedral.[32] The Belgian Symbolist painter Fernand Khnopff, reviewing the New Gallery for the *Magazine of Art*, highlighted Burne-Jones' *Saint George*, Sargent's *Portrait of Mrs Thursby*, and *Can These Bones Live?* Powerful and imposing, *Can These Bones Live?* was reminiscent of *Sic Transit*, though more disturbing. Angular golden drapery, broken branches and an ominous confusion of bones: 'sick gems, as one might fancy – all this forces itself on the attention of the most sceptical, and compels the mind to deep and gloomy meditation', wrote Khnopff. Preferring to ignore the meaning – the very point of the picture – the Symbolist suggested that as Watts's picture was well painted, 'Is it not wise, then, to admire in silence?'[33]

The imperialist Cecil Rhodes (fig. 203) arrived unannounced at the Little Holland House gallery and demanded to be painted by the master. Thompson advised him to write to the artist. A man of enormous ambition and ideals, Rhodes had set out for South Africa with little money and poor health, and amassed huge wealth setting up the De Beers Mining Company – in his view, vital to progress in South Africa – while spending half the year studying for a degree at Oxford. He was inspired by Ruskin's lectures: 'This is what she [England] must do or perish: she must found colonies as fast and as far as she is able, formed of her most energetic and worthiest of

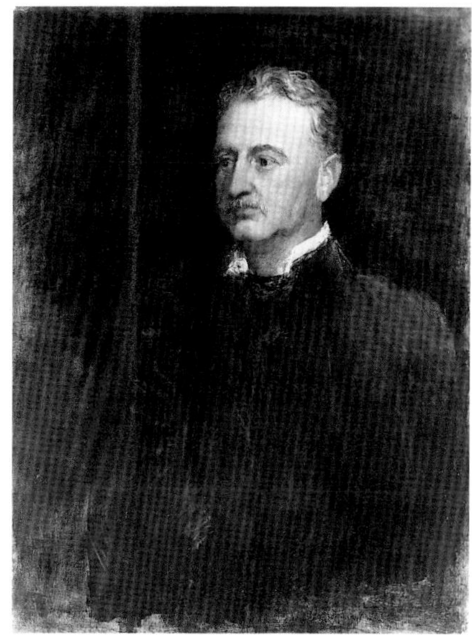

203   *Cecil John Rhodes*, 1898 (National Portrait Gallery, London).

men; – seizing every piece of fruitful waste ground she can set her foot on, and there teaching these her colonists that their chief virtue is to be fidelity to their country, and that their first aim is to be to advance the power of England by land and sea.'[34] With the proceeds of gold and diamond mining, Rhodes provided 'Homes, more Homes' for Britons in Africa, and planned to extend the railway the full length of the continent. The British government had supported his plans to enlarge the British Empire. However, Rhodes's ideal was for a federation of states. He had become prime minister of the Cape Colony, founded the nation of Rhodesia and sought to befriend the Boers – wandering farmers of Dutch origin – in the Orange Free State and the Transvaal. But President Kruger was opposed to progress and made life so difficult for the Uitlanders – chiefly British immigrants – in the Traansvaal, that Rhodes's administrator Dr Jameson planned a raid on their behalf. Rhodes had feared this would shipwreck friendship between Briton and Boer, his dreams for peace and progress, but returned too late to prevent the raid, assumed blame and resigned as premier. Meanwhile the Cape-to-Cairo railway had reached Bulawayo and he was in England to raise two million pounds to extend it to Lake Tanganyika.[35]

Watts, forewarned that Rhodes would be approaching him, wrote first (through Dorothy Stanley) to invite the imperialist to sit for the nation. Dolly would have preferred him to paint her husband. 'There is no one living who can give the *Soul* in men – *but you*, my dear Signor.' (That he would not paint Henry Stanley, the founder of the Congo Free State, was probably due to the brutal treatment of the Congolese people). Rhodes was lunching with the Stanleys when the invitation arrived.[36] The Colossus replied:

> I told Mrs Stanley I would like you to paint me as you are the best and I owe a likeness to Bulawayo to my people. I did not know you would do it as I was told you were particular . . . I will come on Wednesday at 9.30 if you agree . . . Herkomer has done me but he made me an alderman and that is just what I am not. I have sent photographs to your house so that you can begin on Tuesday without me. I dropped on the whole thing by accident as I saw the notice outside your house that the public might look at your pictures and your man was very kindly and thought you might like to paint me.[37]

Mary, worn to bits with her pottery enterprises, was juggling visits to the Home Arts exhibition when Earl Grey, the former Administrator of Rhodesia, brought Rhodes to Little Holland House at 9.30 on 18 May. Lady Granby arrived at ten, with pencil and paper to record the first sitting. The imperialist was asked to stand by the green chair near the studio door. Bearing signs of heart disease, his breathing sometimes laboured, his face beginning to purple, Rhodes looked older than his forty-five years. He stayed just long enough that day for the artist to block in his massive brow and head. As he had to return to South Africa on 21 May, there would not be time for the full five sittings.[38] For the first few, Watts was doubtful about Rhodes's plans to extend the Empire. Never before had he been pressed to paint a national portrait. This, too, would join the series of men 'who . . . may be said to make – or mar – England', he explained. 'I don't know which you are doing!' The imperialist, who saw himself as working for the benefit of humanity, admitted that the settlers he was bringing in would dominate the natives: 'People say, "Why can't we let the simple barbarian alone?" We can't help it. We can no more help the overflow of civilizations than prevent the overflow of water from a dam.' What Rhodes did regret was the barbaric way progress was achieved.[39] The aggressive colonization offended Mary's socialist instincts and, after preparing the studio for his next sitting, she turned to leave. 'Don't go away, Mrs Watts. I should like to talk to you,' ordered the imperialist, his voice breaking into a strange falsetto. 'I did stay, to talk and *stand* from nine [thirty] till eleven! – and learnt to know the spark of a man who can lead – Never have I known such a sudden conversion from all my former ideas of a man – I went in thinking I should not have anything in common. I stood there finding the minutes too short for all we had to talk about.'

No doubt the elevated spiritual atmosphere at Little Holland House induced Rhodes to talk as he did. He had extraordinary magnetic power and a highly imaginative mind. Earnest, honest, persuasive, he kept his eyes full upon his audience as he expounded his vision of the colonies as a haven from overcrowded Britain for the poor and his hope that the best British qualities would spread throughout the African continent. He cast aside Watts's pessimism. 'England extinct!' exclaimed Rhodes, 'No, I say she is only just going to begin to live' – echoing his own career forecast after Dr Jameson's fateful raid. Mary showed him *The Sphinx* and a letter from a stranger, who had been almost suicidal with despair until she saw a photograph of *Hope* in a shop window. The statesman was moved to tears that the picture had restored the woman's spirit.[40] Jameson, alarmed by his purple face after standing too long, accused Watts of plying him with alcohol, though he drank only coffee. The valiant Earl Grey brought him back again at 6.30 on Saturday the 21st. The artist, convinced of Rhodes' courage and force of character, took the men into the garden after breakfast, to see *Physical Energy*. 'That's what I should like to have to commemorate the completion of the Cape-to-Cairo railway', exclaimed the Colossus. Beneath the powerful rider seeking further lands to conquer, he wanted to inscribe the names of the first subscribers and the words, 'These people believed the scheme was possible.' The portrait continued until 1.30. Rhodes left for Africa that afternoon, Watts' pleading that he should be 'a maker not a marrer of the nation'. His mistrust had turned to admiration. For both men, each with an extraordinary vision, albeit very different, devoted every hour of the day from sunrise to the benefit of humanity as they saw it.[41]

Gladstone died of cancer on Ascension Day, 19 May 1898. Gerry Liddell had played soft soothing music for him. Watts had sent messages and on hearing the final news, responded in poetry, 'Whatever record leap to light / He never shall be shamed.' At Mary's request, he wrote out his tribute to stand with white lilies by his portrait. He told Julia Cartwright how Gladstone had lived his life by Watts's motto, to 'The Utmost for the Highest'. That evening, she learned that, unlike his timeless universal subjects, *Can These Bones Live?* was a modern message to England – 'the fall of Gold crushing and breaking down the old oak which yet springs up again with fresh life'. He enthused about ' "Johnny Millais' " fine show', and linked him with Velasquez as the best painters of a man's exterior. Millais's portrait of *Gladstone* did not show the depth of his character, but it caught his attitude and fire.[42] As always on the death a national sitter, Watts offered

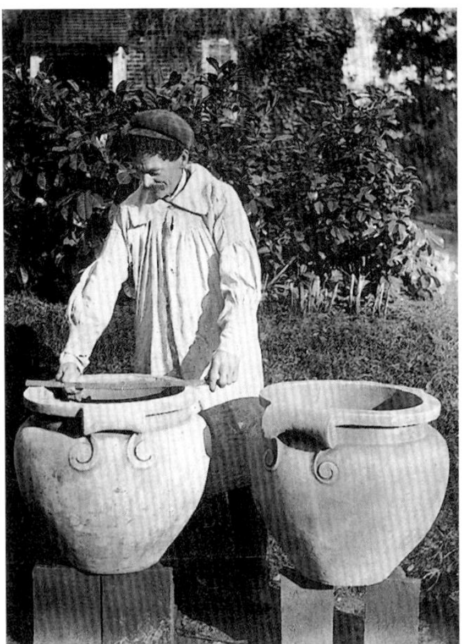

204   Louis Deuchars with Scroll Pots.

205   *Field Marshall Lord Roberts*, 1898 (National Portrait Gallery, London).

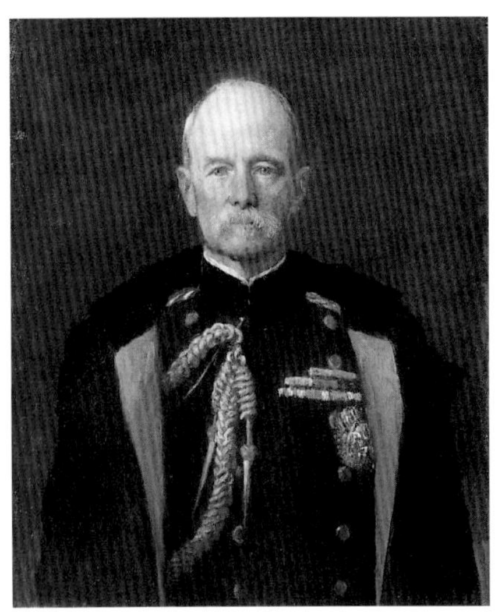

the earlier portrait to the National Portrait Gallery, but 'as Sir Charles Tennant has signified his intention of giving the fine & popular portrait by Millais', he wrote to Cust, 'I do not know whether the Trustees will think a second one desirable.' Both were accepted.[43]

Back at Limnerslease, visitors were entranced by the strange terracotta chapel in the Surrey hills. 'It is growing every day less red, & the green enfolds it all so beautifully now, the trees are in leaf, it looks a sweet resting place,' thought Mary; and, as indefatigable as her husband, on 1 June, training Mitchell at the wheel, she designed her elegant terracotta jardinière, the Scroll Pot (fig. 204).[44]

Signor was taken ill again and resented wasting time in bed. Frustrated, he felt as if he were sewn into clothes that were too small: 'I feel I ought to be more free, but I can't break the bonds.' 'They will crack some day like the dragonfly chrysalis,' exclaimed Mary. 'You will fly away with a flash on dragonfly wings from me, & then you will be happy.' 'No, for you will come too! If like the parable of my daisy we grow like the sun from looking at it, you will come too. It may be a little later, but you will come.'[45]

Lord Grey forwarded a note to her from Rhodes had written from Madeira. He had been extraordinarily moved by his visit to Little Holland House. Never in his rough life had he seen such a home. Even the maid who opened the door to him had seemed affected by the atmosphere. 'I felt it in her answer and her face.' He hoped that Watts was satisfied with his portrait. 'If not tell him from me to try the full face in the group and put in the eyes of the Sphinx looking over the desert into eternity for the picture, only in my case for empire of the race that I believe to be the best and which will be the best if we educate the youth to their responsibilities and teach them their work is paramount.' This was not personal conceit, he added, 'but the picture might help the cause one hundred years hence.'[46] Well, Watts was troubled. The portrait remained a sketch and he never allowed anyone to see it.[47]

Lord Grey brought his daughter Lady Sybil to breakfast at Little Holland House. The Colossus, he said, had been deeply moved by the atmosphere around Watts and had wished he had seen the cook too. Grey reported back to Rhodes that they had not been shown the portrait, that he had asked that he had suggested adapting *Physical Energy*, to give the rider's head '*some* resemblance to your features so that the Statue may go out to the World, as his conception of your character . . . It will be a far finer Monument to you than any that can be painted on canvas.' Walking over to the statue, the artist had said, 'Well, that is Rhodes!' As Lord Grey had brought his daughter specifically to learn about symbolism, Mary discussed the chapel and Signor demonstrated his symbol of the hand: the first finger he representing 'The Love of God', the second 'Faith', the third 'Hope', and the little finger 'Charity' – 'we cannot do much till we bring in the thumb of Reason & then we can do everything. But the thumb of Reason alone is also quite useless.'[48]

No sooner had they left, than Field Marshall Lord Roberts (fig. 205), former commander-in-chief in India and Ireland, arrived to stand in uniform for the nation. He was reassuringly upbeat about 'our dear Englishmen . . . "the best of men".' One of his most successful portraits, of the late Recorder of London, Russell Gurney, had been bequeathed to the National Portrait Gallery. Seeing it again, Watts challenged himself to outdo

it. He painted Roberts as a man of iron and steel – 'he looks *forged* out . .
. the eyes are a wonder of technique!'[49] Gertrude and Edwin Abbey came
on 11 June. He was about to become a full Academician, and sat for a new
drawing. Leighton's studio was to be preserved for the nation, and Emilie
Barrington, a leading force on the committee, was collecting his studies and
sketches to fill it, following the sale of his estate. She renewed contact with
Watts to ask for a painting of a nude male torso. He promised all his
Leightons, but refused her invitation to the house. The clay model of the
athlete was his most prized possession. 'In giving you this', he told her, 'I
give you the best thing I have.'[50]

Watts went down to Roedean. He loved watching the girls drill, the
master explaining what the Greeks called 'beautiful strength' in each
movement, so that they understood the beauty of a perfectly trained muscle,
of carriage and of bearing. At Brighton railway station, on the way home,
he bought a newspaper and was shocked to read that Ned Burne-Jones had
died. Having worked all day on *The Sleep of Arthur in Avalon*,[51] Ned had
suffered a severe attack of angina in the middle of the night. He, too, was
only in his sixties. Watts never thought he would outlive him.[52] Commis-
erating with Julia Cartwright at Little Holland House the next day, he dwelt
on 'poor Ned's' *great* intellect and the over-cultivation that made him paint
other men's ideas rather than express original thought, though he did it
supremely. He wished Ned had lived more in the present, nineteenth-
century England, rather than link himself with fourteenth-century Italy.
Had Burne-Jones painted a higher range of thought – subjects such as *Love
and Life* – he could have done so better than anyone and left a great
message behind him. Yet what marvellous imagination he had. He wished
they had seen more of each other in recent years and was glad that he had
painted Ned in his prime – 'my best picture'.[53]

Lady Betty Balfour arrived to make an appointment for her husband
Gerald. Cartwright noted that Watts said he was going to paint the Chief
Secretary because it would give him an opportunity to scold him for his
speech about not feeding the poor on champagne – 'It is a crime,' said the
artist, who made a point of sending fine pictures to exhibitions for the poor.
He would tell Gerald Balfour, as he had told Cecil Rhodes. 'I tell him he
is to educate all our statesmen!'[54] Madeline Wyndham came in, broken-
hearted over Burne-Jones, whose son Phil arrived; and after the funeral
Mary returned from Rottingdean to find Lady Granby.[55] One after another,
Ned's family and friends came to reminisce with Watts: Lord Carlisle. Lady
Wenlock, arriving in a collar of turquoise blue, seemed to Mary like a wood
nymph, 'not quite to belong to this time or place'. Professor von Oettingen
came, with a letter of introduction from Joachim, to acquire British art for
the Berlin Royal Academy of Arts.[56]

On Friday 1 July 1898, the Bishop of Winchester Randall Davidson consecrated the mortuary chapel in Compton. That morning the Watts were
up before sunrise at Limnerslease. Mary picked white poppies for the altar,
and a forget-me-not and the first rose from Leighton's rose tree, which she
dried to keep as a memento. Andrew Hichens accompanied her through
the wooden lych-gate and up the winding path, lined with tiny cypress trees,
to fill vases with poppies. May had embroidered an altar cloth. Every aspect
of the little Arts and Crafts chapel was symbolic, from the circular cruciform ground plan to the decoration. Only the exterior was finished so far.

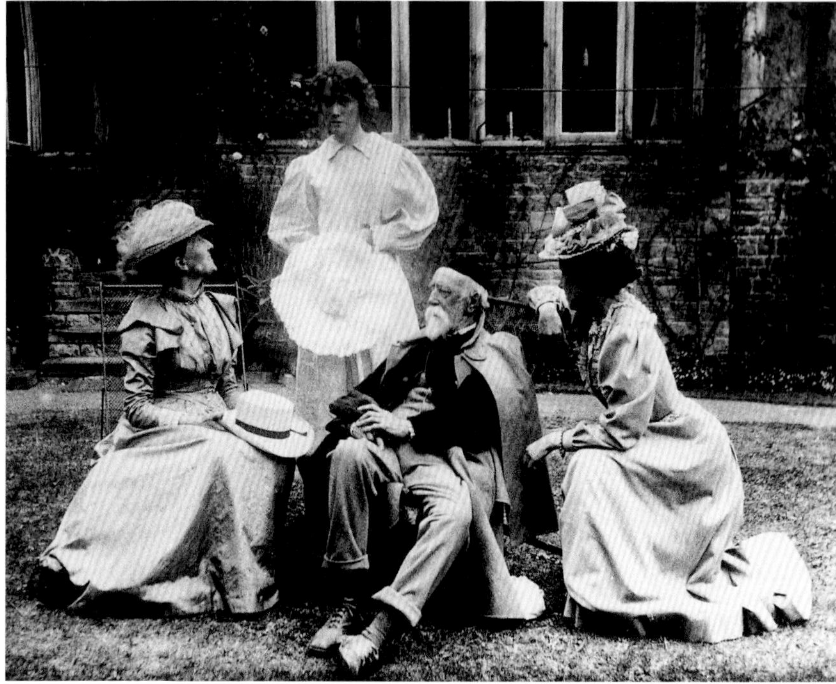

206    Mary, Lily, Signor and May Hichens in the garden at Limnerslease, 1898.

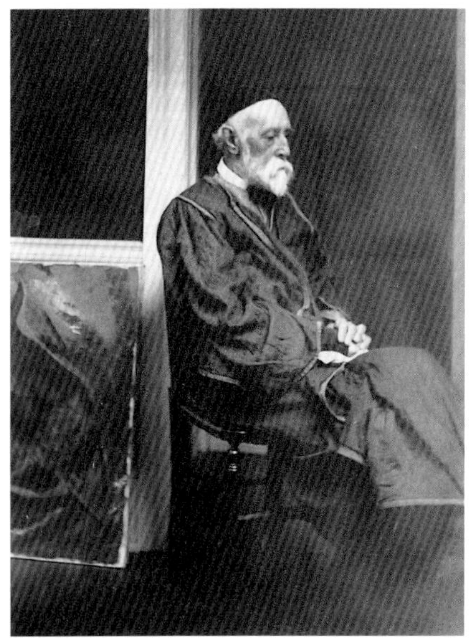

207    Watts seated in doctoral robes, presumably before the chapel ceremony on 1 July 1898, beside a study for *Love Steering the Boat of Humanity*.

Inspiration from her readings and early travels with Watts infused her terracotta tapestry of patterns. Modern Art Nouveau figures blend with ancient motifs from civilizations the world over, linked together with Celtic knotwork in an astonishing extravaganza. Like her husband, Mary referred to the terracotta patterns as 'hieroglyphs'. Their very exuberance seems to heighten the 'idea'. To represent the *Spirit of Hope*, for example, rather than his famous single figure sitting on top of the world, bent double over her lyre, her frieze is a riot of terracotta angels, their faces in the styles of Rossetti, Burne-Jones and Watts. The angels embrace Celtic-style roundels, doves symbolizing Comfort, the hart for Aim or Aspiration, the lion for Courage, the spider, Patience; and on each side of a double-armed cross and anchor, is a peacock, the symbol of Hope. The door alone, representing Man's Destiny, is a tour de force.[57]

Watts (fig. 207), his scarlet Oxford robes glinting in the sun, joined the bishop in the procession up to the little chapel and the assembled crowd (fig. 208). The choir of St Andrews, Wells Street in London, sang for the ceremony. 'The day was glorious', wrote Mary. Watts appears to have marked their gift with a symbolic drawing of three angels, now in the Royal Library at Windsor.[58] The central figure is bearing a gift of petals, a younger angel is peering over her right shoulder and on her left Mary, looking much as she did in Cameron's *Rosebud Garden of Girls*, gazes down at the petals. To commemorate Watts's generosity, the parish of Compton later presented him with a ceremonial book of the chapel illuminated by May Hichens. At a party at Monkshatch, kept secret from Watts until the last moment, Hugh Gillett, the rector of Compton, pointed out how beneficial the chapel work still was to the village. Seventy-three people – More Molyneux among them – had had a hand in the modelling. Even Watts was moved to speak, for enabling and teaching villagers to create their own heritage – albeit a mortuary chapel – was the ultimate Wattsian ideal.[59]

Mary, desperate for a change of air, left Watts happily in the care of their exuberant friend Gerry Liddell, while she travelled up to the highlands to refresh herself and recuperate for a month. She kissed him, absorbing the image of his face. 'I shall feel that you are very near,' he comforted her. 'Distance makes no difference to us.'[60] A doting guardian, Watts kept Lily back from school to recover from a cough and set to work with impatience.[61] 'I can't keep my hands off the canvas the moment I come down.' He loved to think of Mary at home in the hills: 'Do prize lying on your face on the bosom of mother Earth, then writing . . . you had better let designing alone & content yourself with the suggestion & inspiration the great mother & greater relations, Heavens, stars, & sun! will fill up all the crannies of your mind. They will all come out again without effort . . . I want you to do nothing, not even think but let the air & beautiful surroundings sink into your body & mind.[62]

While Mary wrote *The Word in the Pattern*, her guide to the symbolism of the chapel, and a paper for *The Studio*,[63] Gerald Balfour was sitting to her husband. He was tall, handsome and spoke with a deep voice. Watts admired his bone structure and saw him as a man with a future. 'The vulture is a cunning bird', quipped Phil Burne-Jones when he saw the portrait. However, although the sitter went on to become president of the Board of Trade, his brother Arthur, painted by Sargent, would have a finer career.[64] Hollyer photographed Gerald Balfour's portrait (fig. 209) in August and he took another of the artist posing in field-marshall's uniform.[65]

Chiselling *Physical Energy* by candlelight, Watts studied the colossal group under every possible lighting condition, 'with the eye of an enemy'. Lord Wemyss took him to look at the 'lovely *Venus*'. Too embarrassed to comment, Watts thought the statue pretty and refined, but could his intelligent friend not see that her legs were like sausages? The earl had no such qualms when criticizing Signor, writing in his memoirs that he 'certainly scored' when he suggested that a slight indentation below the bridge of Balfour's nose was excessive. Watts hotly disagreed, but Lord Wemyss noticed that by his next visit it had been filled in. He apologized for his criticism. 'My friend gave a great growl and shook his fist at me. It assuredly is a thing to be proud of that my *Venus* meets with his approval.'[66] Earlier in the year, at luncheon with the earl's daughter Lilian Yorke, daughter-in-law Mary Elcho and Godfrey Webb, the Clerk to the House of Lords, Watts had met the model for Venus. Grace Blackburn, the future Countess of Wemyss, was clever, proud of her pretty figure and – the family was stunned to learn – modelling for the nude statue.[67]

Rodin's statue of the novelist Honoré de Balzac, commissioned by Zola, had been the talk of the Paris Salon[68] when Lord Brownlow, the Lord-Lieutenant of Lincolnshire, visited Watts to discuss a memorial statue to Lord Tennyson. The octogenarian sculptor, undaunted, had seemed keen to take it on himself. In September, he offered to sculpt a large statue not as a commission, but as a gift, content this time for the county to bear the cost of casting. 'Now what I want is a cast of Woolner's fine bust which will be a great help', he wrote to Hallam. 'This is the best news I could possibly have heard from you – you are the only person living who could

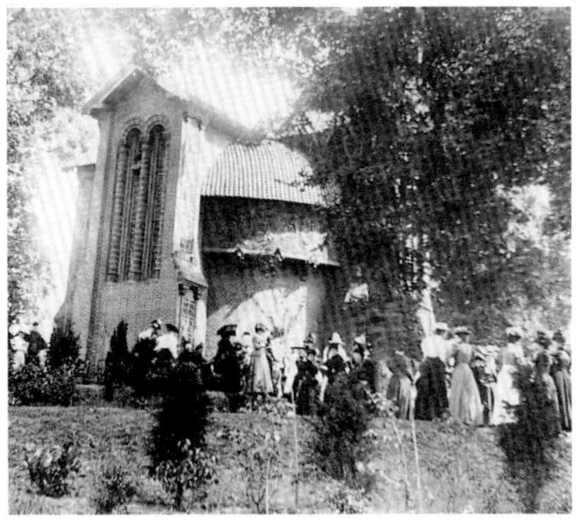

208   Consecration of the mortuary chapel at Compton, 1 July 1898.

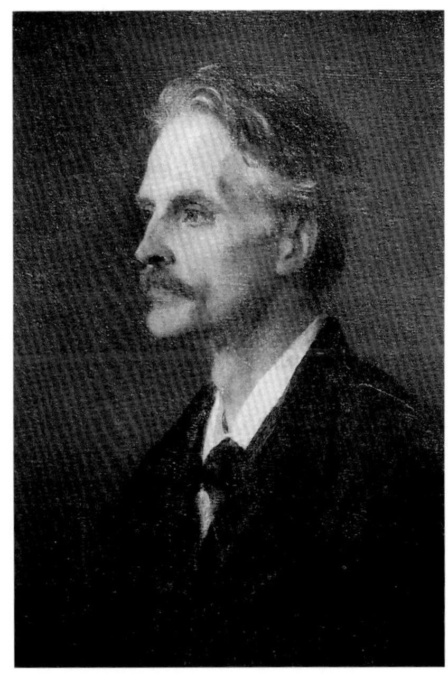

209   The Right Honourable Gerald William Balfour, Chief Secretary for Ireland, 1898–99 (Watts Gallery).

do this great work', Hallam replied, offering to lend his cast. Watts prepared a small wax model of the poet with his wolfhound, to present to the committee, and completed the purchase of the farm neighbouring Limnerslease, which had an old barn large enough to house the monumental sculpture.[69]

The labour politician John Burns, after lunching at Little Holland House in October, was driven by the Wattses through the Park to the station. 'The first carriage we met had Ellen Terry in it if I am not much mistaken. Watts was brimful of chaff and kindly fun which I developed, and by the time I was dropped at Charing Cross, in spite of age, work and worry we might easily have been taken for a jovial party returning from a festivity.' The artist had good reason for his merry frame of mind. He was on his way to discuss the fulfilment of a special aspiration.[70]

# 24 'Our Race as Pioneers'

IN *The Times* OF 13 OCTOBER 1898, St Botolph's, Aldersgate announced Watts's approval for the erection of a *Campo Santo* to commemorate 'lowly but noble' heroes in their extended churchyard, known as the Postman's Park. 'Mr Watts has himself promised to commence without further delay a covered way, in which memorial tablets may be affixed to the wall, recording the brave deeds of the miner, the fireman, the lifeboat-man, the policeman, the engine driver, the labourer, and the domestic servant.'[1] This was the format Leighton had proposed. Doubtless they had discussed it over the years. The *Art Journal* took up the cause and proposed a national art schools prize for illustrated memorial plaques. Lord Meath, chairman of the Metropolitan Public Gardens Association, protested that it was illegal to build on a disused burial ground and, although he recommended a more prominent position on the Thames Embankment, Hichens was outraged at the violence of his protests.[2]

The open space was crucial, for although Watts now had in mind a simple shelter, a wall of plaques, each one inscribed with the name, date and deed: an index of unsung heroes from the start of the reign of Queen Victoria, his intention was as didactic and symbolic as a picture. 'One soul's sacrifice is as great as another, for what can a man give more than his life?' he wrote to Gosse. The intelligentsia should be seen to acknowledge these noble deeds, he explained, and the plaques be read as a warning of the vices of their day. Monuments such as these should stand in public spaces where loiterers might pause, revere and be inspired.[3]

Watts had begun a sinister variant of the fresco of the mother and child in *Humanity in the Lap of the Earth* painted at old Little Holland House half a century earlier. The child remains alert, but the woman dozes in *The Slumber of the Ages*, as he subsequently named the picture, symbolizing the brevity of life and small human aims.[4]

Georgy Duff Gordon's great niece was staying at Limnerslease. That evening Lina wore her Florentine 'cloth of gold' gown. Modelled on a design from a painting by Leonardo, the deep rose silk brocade, interwoven with gold thread, had been presented to her mother by the leader of the Indian Mutiny Nana Sahib. As the lamplight fell on her golden hair, Watts felt he must paint her and invited her to stay. She devised a system to relieve the strain of standing in the heavy gown, sinking on to her heels whenever he looked away to refill his brush, rising back into position before he turned round; yet her three-quarter-length portrait exudes elegance and repose (fig.

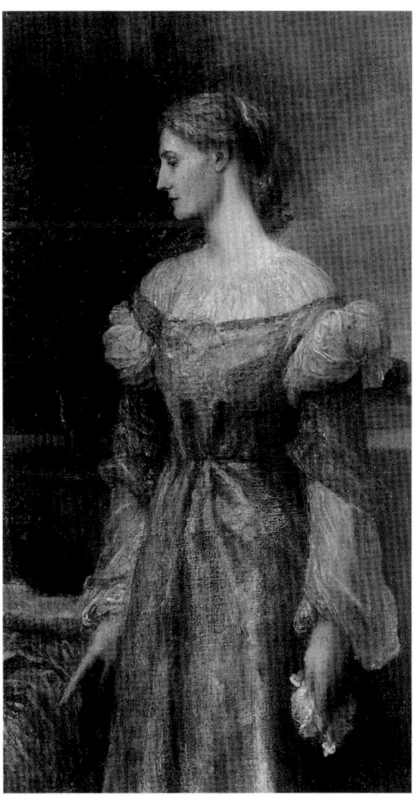

210 *Caroline Lucie 'Lina' Duff Gordon*, 1898 (private collection; photo Arthur Rust).

210). Lord Wemyss brought down Mrs Patrick Campbell. The actress, her luxuriant black hair, black eyes and creamy complexion quite different from Watts's auburn-haired sitters, threw herself at his feet and pleaded to be painted in her Lady Macbeth gown. 'What, what, my dear?' the deaf artist bent down towards her. Lina relayed her request. 'I am not a costume painter,' Watts replied frostily, nor would he emulate Sargent's spectacular portrait of Ellen Terry, but Mrs Pat treasured his sketch of Nelly as Ophelia.[5] Lina was amused by the bath notes, scraps of jottings of thoughts and images that sprang to mind, copied out by Mary. One queried the meaning of God's response when Moses asks, 'shew me thy glory'. The expression, 'Thou shalt see my back parts: but my face shall not be seen', was ridiculous, thought Watts, but thinking about it led to a remarkable abstract picture.

What the 'stupendous' Jewish law actually meant was that man cannot see God's face, but can find him collaterally, as it were, in Creation. Watts's view of 'the true religious conception of the Creator & his creation' was that: 'A Breath issuing forth becomes matter – controlling this matter are two laws: force which propels & gravitation which controls – & here in its enormity you have the whole thing – the conflict produced by these laws explains every phenomenon – The nebulous form of matter in its primitive conditions acted on by these two laws becoming the ordered universe.[6] It seemed unpaintable, absurd. Watts began by making circular scribbles and pierced the paper with his pencil, to create a void. Refracted rays thrown by a night light on to his bedroom ceiling suggested the form of *The Sower of the Systems* (pl. XLII), a veiled figure, impelled forward, projected through space while scattering stars, suns and planets – an astonishing advance from the bearded old man.[7]

Watts drove out to William More Molyneux, presumably to finalize negotiations for Cooks' Farm, which were concluded on 10 November 1898.[8] Facing heavy costs, his anxiety about funding the memorial to heroes was somewhat relieved by James Smith's purchases that winter: a portrait of Lily for 150 guineas and a sketch of *Orpheus and Eurydice* for 100; the more substantial *Chaos* was under discussion.[9] Smith also resolved to inaugurate a public collection for the memorial. Under the strain, Watts saw Death again, and once more felt on top of the world; he began writing a new essay about the English. On 13 December, Thompson came to Limnerslease to join him for the opening of the Great Barn Studio and the two men worked together from ten until four, building up the massive gesso figure of the late Poet Laureate – fatefully, upon the base of the abandoned sculpture *Aurora*. At sunset a pair of white legs shone out against the darker barn, and by 22 December the huge ghost of Tennyson had risen.[10] Like *Physical Energy* at Little Holland House, the staue of the poet was built upon a trolley wheeled out into the garden at Limnerslease, an ideal setting for the statue that was to reflect the poet's love of nature. Whereas Rodin's *Balzac*, swathed in a cloak, his huge face framed by flowing hair, gazes upwards with a commanding expression of pride and drama, Watts's *Tennyson* standing in his favourite Spanish cloak, the Freshwater wind blowing out its folds, was to be contemplative, with his wolfhound at his side. However, when Lord Wemyss mentioned that a place was reserved for him opposite the statue of Millais at Westminster Abbey, Watts would have none of it. He leaped furiously from his niche and swore that no man woman or child should be made to pay a farthing to raise any statue in his memory. Though he, too, would stand in his cloak in 1899, cast in bronze by Gilbert as *Edward King and Martyr* on the memorial to the Duke of Clarence.[11]

Watts began the year with an interview by the *London Argus* to discuss the heroes' memorial and the mission of art. The artist's 'bronzed and animated face' lit up at the thought of his favourite scheme. Creating monumental sculpture outside, winter and summer, kept him fit and seemed to rejuvenate him. Asked about the progress of art in the community, Watts reported great developments in artistic life, the dissemination of taste and ideas through illustrations in books and newspapers; and the abundance of promising young artists.[12]

'He is the greatest altogether, the greatest of any age!' enthused Watts, with loving exaggeration. Swept off his feet by the wave of admiration arising from the Burne-Jones memorial exhibition at the New Gallery, he had lent watercolours of *The Wheel of Fortune* and a scene depicting lovers kissing on the banks of a stream.[13] 'No doubt the splendid genius will stand in the future as the representative of great Art in the Victorian Era', he wrote to Georgie. 'You must be a proud woman.' In his view Burne-Jones had been constrained by the architectural conditions of modern work, the church or room: 'When he is more at large, where he feels something that suggests a sensation . . . [and] has painted flowers, his flowers give me the feeling that is more than his figures or his faces. He is very great, great like Spenser to me, or even greater for perhaps he has more colour.' The unfinished *Car of Love* was supreme, more human than *The Sleep of Arthur in Avalon*, which was spoken of as his finest design. Why had he not bullied Ned about those thin ankles! To Watts, *Avalon* failed to express monumentality, the grandeur of death, but Burne-Jones's female nudes were far better than Leighton's, the legs in *Morning with Her Cymbals*, he thought, excelled Botticelli, and his tapestry designs seemed greater than the Raphael cartoons.[14]

With the deaths of Leighton, Millais and Burne-Jones, Watts – already regarded as a seer and teacher – was seen as one of the great men and the greatest living artist of the closing epoch. Caswall Smith produced large photographs of him and his work, notably, the *Sir Galahad* presented to Eton and the artist relaxing in a wicker chair in his studio, later issued as a postcard. As the first president of the Pastel Society, Watts sent the half-length portrait of the late Lady Mount Temple and a *Study*, to its first exhibition at the Royal Institute of Painters in Piccadilly.[15]

In the studio at Limnerslease (fig. 211), he worked up the large national version of *Love Triumphant*. 'I feel I have been in paradise when I have been here,' enthused Gertrude Jekyll, moved more by his nature and sayings than by his art. Madeline Wyndham, whom Watts now described as a pomegranate – a symbol of fertility, with a sinful tinge in ancient Greece – encouraged him to accept a rare commission: to paint Wilfrid Scawen Blunt (fig. 212), her former lover, who had since had fathered a child with her daughter, Mary Elcho. The three Wyndham sisters were now sitting to Sargent, and Blunt noted with interest that in the background of the portrait was Watts's portrait of Madeline.[16] Blunt's long-suffering wife, Lady Anne Noel, had sat for a romantic drawing by Watts before her marriage (a union that perhaps owed much to Blunt's keenness to be associated with

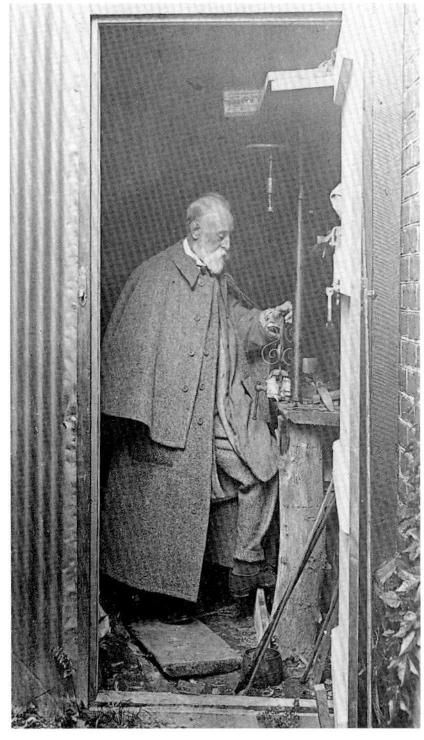

211   In the workshop at Limnerslease in the 1890s (photo: George Andrews).

212   *Wilfrid Scawen Blunt*, 1899 (photo: Frederic Hollyer).

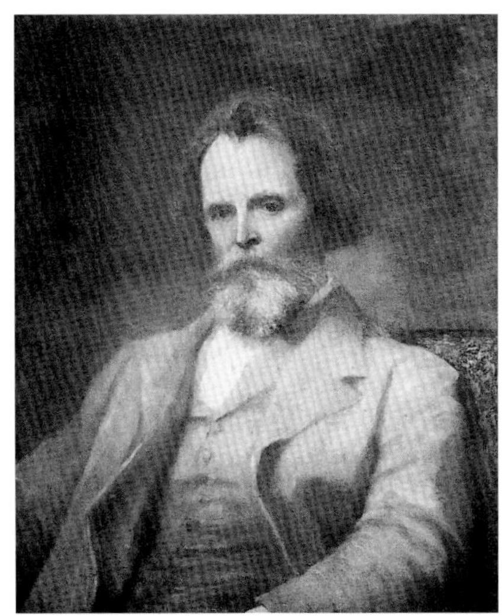

Lady Anne's grandfather, Lord Byron). That he too was a poet encouraged Watts. The two would find mutual ground in Blunt's rebellious political activities and in their interest in horses (Blunt bred Arabs). He was composing *Satan Absolved: A Victorian Mystery*, a poem attacking the crimes committed by the white man – amongst them dominance over primitive races and the killing of birds for their plumage – when he came down to Limnerslease in March.[17]

Watts set to work at once, blocking in the portrait in raw umber on a yellow ground. Unusually, he did all the talking – eloquently and without interruption – and found his sitter to be an intelligent listener who expressed interest throughout. The artist recalled how he had put Burne-Jones on a horse at Little Holland House and made him canter round a ride he had set up, forgetting that there were hurdles. Poor Ned fell off and never rode again. His was the best male portrait he had painted; but the most handsome, he told Blunt, was Sir Henry Taylor's, and his best female portrait was Madeline's. To Blunt, Watts's portrait of Thoby Prinsep, hanging at Monkshatch, was supreme, the finest in England.

From time to time, he would stop painting to illustrate a point. Blunt applauded his demonstration of the symbol of the hand; and when he quoted Rossetti's 'Lost Days of My Life', Blunt agreed that it was the finest of all sonnets. They spent emotional hours communing on Life and Death, the tragic Beauty of the world and the destruction of the weaker races by the strong. After visiting the philosopher Herbert Spencer, to whom he was dedicating *Satan Absolved*, Blunt asked whether Watts had painted him. No, he was too selfish, Watts replied, 'How could you expect me to paint a man with such an upper lip?' The two men parted on affectionate terms; and if Blunt's contemplative portrait was not, as the artist declared, his best ever, the sitter thought it very fine – 'I take some credit to myself in the result, for I never allowed his interest in our talk to flag for a moment.' Watts allowed him to reproduce the sorrowing angel, *A Dedication* 'to all who love the beautiful and mourn over the senseless and cruel destruction of bird life' as the frontispiece to *Satan Absolved* and was accordingly acknowledged as 'the first of living painters'.[18]

The picture would promote the Society for the Protection of Birds' appeal against the feather trade. At the New Gallery, the *Art Journal* found it so majestic that if the lesson were lost, its colouring alone proved the artist's genius. In any other hands the angel weeping over an altar of feathers 'would smack of hyperbole'. The reviewer, enraptured by the mystic, tender *Peace and Goodwill*, took the title at face value, but knew there must be a message. The gorgeously robed woman stretched across the canvas, her eyes searching the twilight, with a babe in her lap, 'in an attitude of ecstatic maternity', was clearly more than a Madonna and child – 'It is as if some prophet made a sign.' Quite the reverse, and not a little disturbing. The woman was an outcast and even Watts did not know whether the light at which she was gazing represented dawn or conflagration. A fearless gleam in the pale, blue eyes was the key to his portrait of Field Marshall Lord Roberts of Kandahar. To the Wattses' delight, Deuchars had two paintings accepted by the New Gallery, one a portrait of his master.[19]

At the Academy, Gerald Balfour's portrait was acclaimed as a resolute, penetrating, intellectual profile, his firmly composed lips suggesting a great deal of humour. Harry Bates's bronze, ivory and mother-of-pearl statuette,

*Mors Janua Vitae* – much influenced by *Love and Life*, except that the winged figure represented Death rather than Love – was exhibited posthumously. Watts had been shocked to hear of the early death that winter of the sculptor, a pupil of Dalou and Rodin, who had transposed his own sculptural painted figures into sculpture. Bates's apprentice Henry Poole would assist Watts at Compton.[20]

Watts presented his first large *Court of Death*, designed for the pauper chapel, to Horsfall's Manchester Art Museum;[21] and he sent to Agnew's a small, quite different *Good Samaritan*, depicting the victim lying at the road-side as his mounted rescuer touches his naked body to test whether he is alive.[22]

'Why should I not be your brother's tenant at Dalcrombie?' Signor suggested to Mary.[23] Working at a cracking pace to finish *The Court of Death*, *Love Triumphant* and *Time, Death and Judgment* for the Tate Gallery's new rooms, and the two huge statues, he was exhausted. He had never crossed the Tweed – nor had he ever expressed any wish to do so. Mary was surprised but elated at the proposition, and terrified for his health as they boarded the 8.15 train on 12 July. Lily, who had been asked to leave Roedean a little early for her daring use of slang words – notably, 'ripping'[24] – accompanied them. They spent the first night at Aldourie Castle, where he woke to a radiant view of the blue hills across Loch Ness. At eight o'clock they walked across the lawn to the shore and gazed down the length of the shimmering loch. This first picture Watts painted in a makeshift studio – a shelter that could be turned against the wind – set up on the moors near the lodge at Dalcrombie (fig. 213). There followed the evening

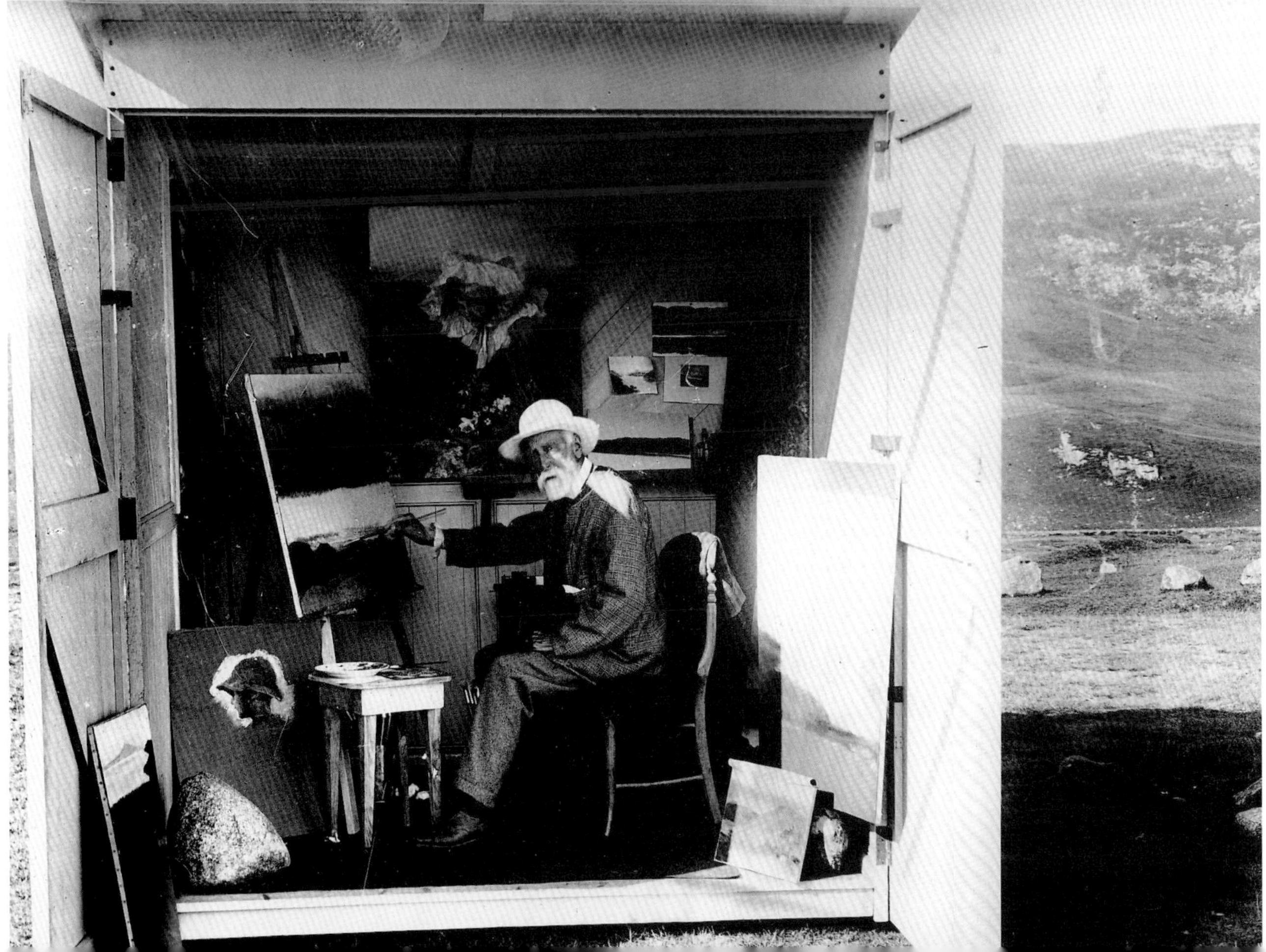

213   Watts painting in his shelter in the Highlands, 1899.

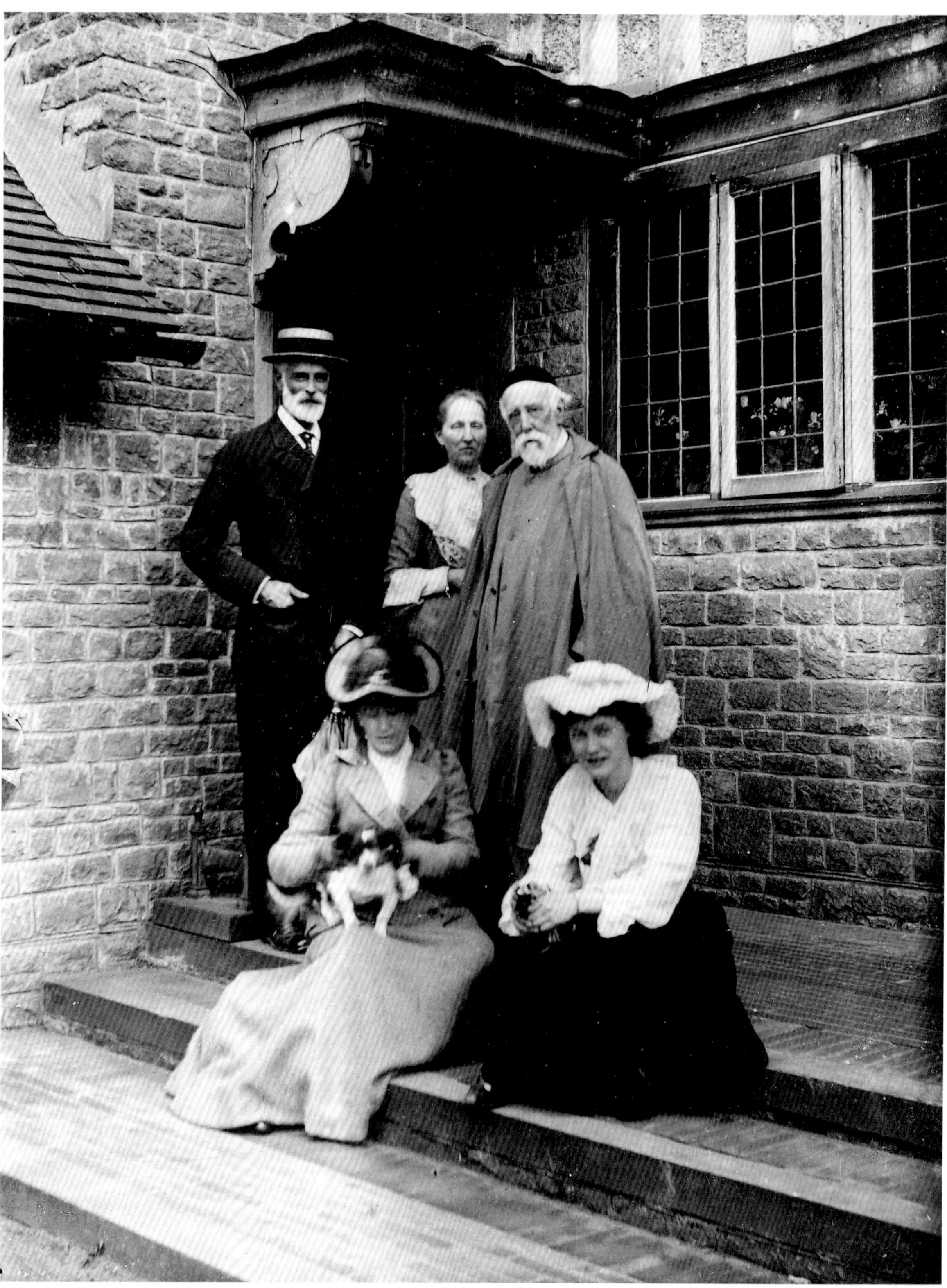

'Twilight of the Gods' or *An Afterglow* – in Egypt he had been fascinated by the sight of the grey sunless earth momentarily reflecting the sunlit sky[25] – *Loch Ruthven*, the gleaming Dalcrombie rocks, two pictures of Torness, and finally *In the Highlands* (fig. 215), of Lily gathering mountain flowers. To achieve the effect of the *Afterglow* he painted the rocky hillside in the sharp light and shade of midday. Mary queried this. 'I know, but it was *there*,' he replied. 'However much I may mystify it later, the anatomy must be there.' To suggest more than the viewer can see was – like nature itself – the key to real impressionism, but modern impressionists, he said, gave no hint of anything beyond.[26]

He tramped over the moors, admiring the strength and stride of the high-landers, and he rowed on Loch Ruthven, a small loch covered with waterlilies. Evelyn Heseltine invited him to sail on the *Leda* (fig. 216), dropping anchor now and again to show him the glens, rivers and falls. The weather was glorious, and if on occasion it rained Watts remarked happily that 'it was just to varnish the picture'; and of course it heightened the colour of the landscape. With a string of pilgrims, young and old, he and James Gow, a ninety-one-year-old crofter, rode up the legendary rock of Dunyardil. Leaving their ponies to graze on mountain grass, they climbed the last 40 feet to the summit on foot. So magnificent was the view that the old crofter, feeling 'one step nearer heaven', removed his blue bonnet, bowed his head in reverence and recited a Gaelic prayer. In their enthusi-asm for the wild bracing highlands, the Wattses stayed too long, the weather changed, and the artist caught pneumonia. He could not after all stay with Lord Wemyss at Gosford, the family seat in East Lothian, and only at the end of October was he well enough to return to Limnerslease.[27]

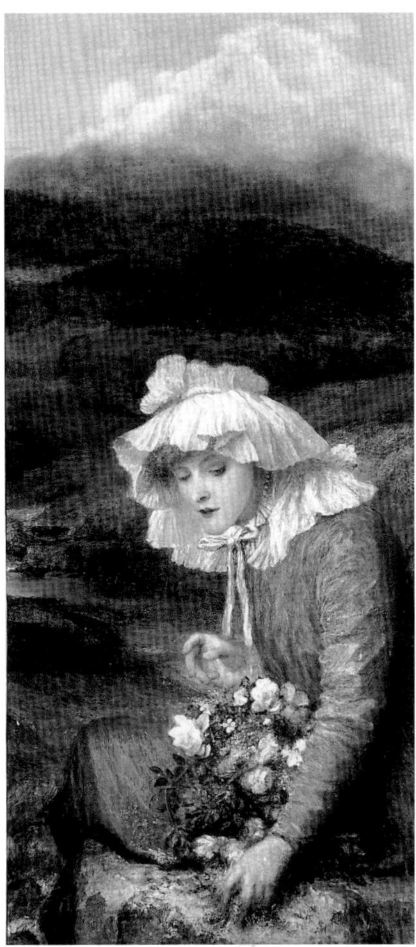

215   *In the Highlands*, 1899–1900 (courtesy of Sotheby's)

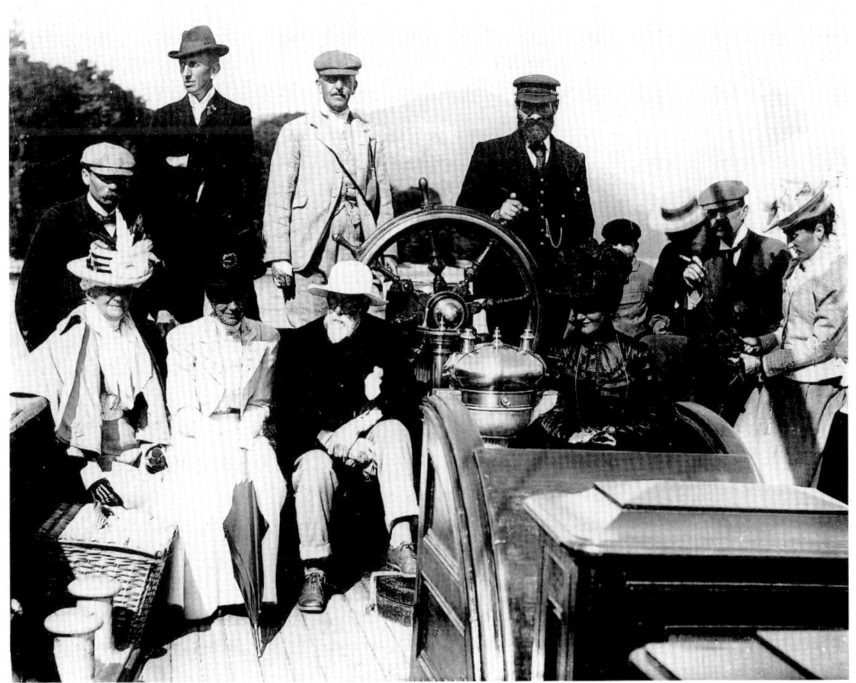

216 (*left*)   Watts and friends aboard Evelyn Heseltine's yacht, *Leda*, 1899.

214 (*facing page*)   Outside Limnerslease front door: standing, Andrew Hichens, Mary and Signor; seated, May Hichens and Lily, who wears the same hat as she wears in *In the Highlands* (fig. 215), 1899.

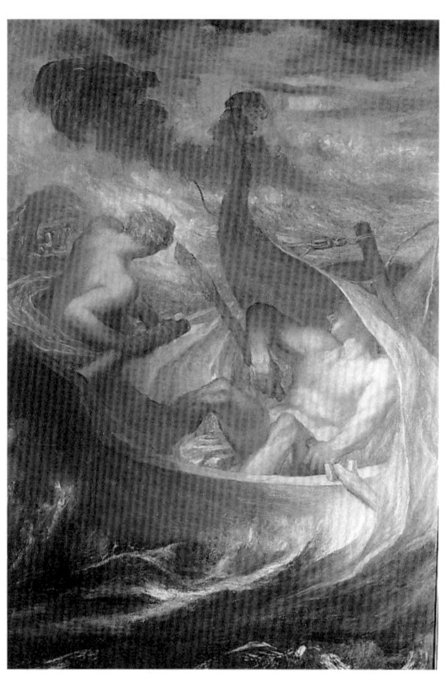

217  *Love Steering the Boat of Humanity*, 1899–1901 (Watts Gallery).

War had broken out in South Africa. Britain had been complacent and her troops, unprepared for the wily Boers, were suffering heavy defeat. Watts forecast a dreadful war and painted *Love Steering the Boat of Humanity* (fig. 217), to address Man's conflict in the midst of forces he is impotent to control. 'Poor humanity has caught a terrible crab,' he said.[28] He came to see in its horrors a redeeming patriotic grandeur, an opportunity for social reform and national service. Writing at length to Lord Grey and Lord Wemyss in December, he outlined a scheme that would strengthen the character of the people, reduce the pauper population, and make Britain fit for war. 'We are so tawdry with our preparations & indeed so unable to see a thing beyond the moment that we are likely someday . . . to find ourselves face to face with perils from which we may find it impossible to extricate ourselves with dignity & safety.' He proposed the establishment of training ships around the British coast, 'small vessels [that could] be strengthened into efficient little warships, a wasp squadron (the man whose rifle makes him more than a match for a lion could be utterly confounded by a swarm of Hornets)'. These would serve as protection against invasion, and schools for slum children, trained to naval and military standards that would fit them for any vocation.

My scholars might be soldiers, or sailors 'Tinkers Tailors' or anything else. I need say nothing about their splendid service in the field in orientation with the troops! After all what I propose is no more than what the Germans do, every man I believe . . . is obliged to serve two years in the Army. This does not prevent them from being infinitely better educated than our labouring classes. No doubt my scheme would be costly but it would be better to pay for security than for a reckless pauper population which in time of danger might prove to do our greatest!

This was no idealistic whim. Watts was speaking from experience, not simply from observation aboard a man of war. He and Mary had taken in the son of drunken and disreputable parents outside Compton – 'a boy who must have become a criminal or a tramp' – and sent him to a training ship at Portsmouth. He was back for the Christmas holidays. Rather than become a menace to society, he was bright, happy, popular with the servants, proud of his good conduct stripe, and keen to return to his ship.[29] His progress in two years suggested how several thousand boys might benefit, with wider training: 'Statistics tell us there are 270,000 yearly sent to prison and 100,000 tramps.' These were expensive and troublesome to the nation. His scheme, aiming to produce an immense national reserve of men with healthy bodies and active minds, would cost less than prisons and workhouses, 'I want the class that won for us Cressy & Agincourt. There was no standing army in those days but every man could be turned into a soldier at need.' And once trained the men could go out to the Colonies, into the Merchant Service. Warning that as Britain did not look into the future, 'Germany will soon be mistress I believe of all', he urged Lord Grey to air his scheme, which he himself would propose in a letter to *The Times*.[30] Watts, having always refused to take sides, took up politics with a vengeance. Writing to *The Times* in December, he re-enforced the case against the ruthless Boers, who in a single swoop had slaughtered 3,000 natives. More important than British supremacy, he declared:

The Boer has not in his character the elements of progress, or movement in intellectual activity – nothing that makes for civilization, which, however faulty, at present is the open door to all that is humanly best; and, supposing him successful against ourselves, the check to civilization on so large a portion of the habitable globe would be disastrous, could not be long permitted, and the result would be a war of still greater proportions and sanguinary character.[31]

Reinforcements were sent out to South Africa. Lord Roberts took over as commander-in-chief, with Sir Horatio Herbert Kitchener his chief of staff. At Aldourie, Lord Lovat and Mary's brother, Ted Fraser Tytler, discussed the idea of raising a body of highlanders, natural stalkers and marksmen, to defeat the Boers at their own game; and in the new year both Mary's brothers would leave to serve with the Lovat Scouts.[32] Luxmore wrote to Watts of a heartbroken mother, whose only child, 'an innocent knight' had been shot at Ladysmith – his favourite picture was his Eton print of *Sir Galahad*.[33]

When Ashbee called at Limnerslease, the dramatist Stephen Phillips was reading his new play *Paolo and Francesca*. Watts, though amused, seemed relieved by his arrival. Ashbee wrote in his diary that 'the dear Signior' [sic] was as sweet in his sublime humility as always. 'He surely is the hero in Art, if there ever was one in English painting. The majesty of the little old man, nervous, bright, sensitive & gentle is what always makes me dumb. He leads you up to his last piece of work & says 'that's what I'm working at now' in the most natural way, & whether the work be his least or his greatest it is always – as from God – take it for what it is 'tis all I can do.'[34]

The Glasgow collector John Reid had bought *Charity* in the spring. Keen to acquire the *Love and Death* on show at Dunthorne's, he wanted to know how many versions there were. At that time there were two large canvases, over eight feet high – one given to the Whitworth, the other to the Tate – a smaller unfinished canvas at Little Holland House, the Dunthorne version – nearly four feet high – and one destined for James Smith – three feet high. They were not exact replicas, for he had experimented with changes of colour and arrangement.[35]

On 20 January 1900 Watts heard of the death John Ruskin, whom he had loved and had respected as the most original thinker of the nineteenth century. The two men, born the same year, worked so long against the popular grain, with a vision for the betterment of humanity. His old sparring partner, whom he had never been able to paint, was laid to rest at Coniston. Watts sent a symbolic laurel wreath and contributed to the Westminster Abbey portrait medallion to be designed by the sculptor Edward Onslow Ford.[36] James Martineau had also died that month, and his portrait was washed and varnished for presentation to the National Portrait Gallery; and in February the Tate Gallery accepted the bronze *Clytie*.[37]

At the Paris Exhibition of 1900, Watts was represented by *Idle Child of Fancy*, *A View of Naples*, and portraits of Dorothy MacCallum, Lady Troubridge (painted as Laura Gurney), and George Meredith.[38] His quirky choice for the Academy was *The Return of Godiva*, the protest picture begun twenty years before. The *Athenaeum* saw poetic truth in his por-

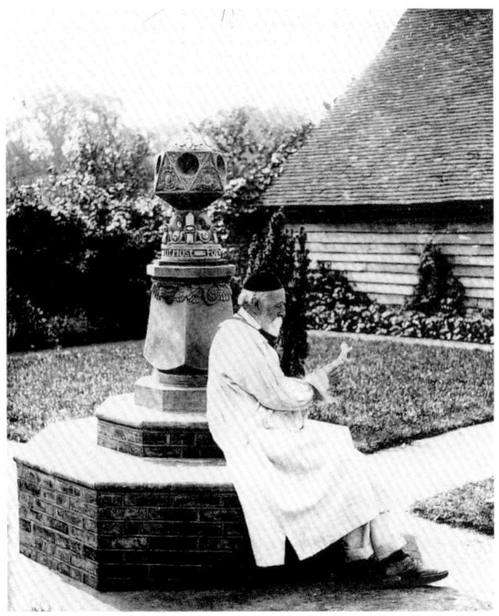

218   Watts seated beneath his sundial, 'The Utmost for the Highest', outside the barn studio at Limnerslease, *c*.1899–1900 (photo: Alexander Fraser Tytler).

trayal of a heroine past her prime, when the trial of riding naked would have been 'immeasurably greater'.[39] Watts reserved for the New Gallery his latest picture, Loch Ness seen through a misty haze – 'a landscape of supreme order of merit, with its unapproachable tones of blue' – and portraits of Wilfrid Scawen Blunt and Lina Duff Gordon in her golden dress.[40] Viewing the two exhibitions, Sargent's faults infuriated him, all the more so because critics talked of him as *the* painter of the age, which Watts hotly refuted, arguing that in Sargent's portrait of Victoria Stanley, the hands were different sizes, her white dress was like tin, her red coat a splash of ceiling wax. Shannon he thought an 'immeasurably better' painter. 'I don't feel the beat of the heart. I don't feel the circulation of the blood under the skin,' he complained to Sidney Colvin, who carried a torch for Sargent. While Watts agreed that presenting *The Wyndham Sisters*, at Burlington House, as magnolias blossoming from their mother's picture – painted by himself – was poetic, he was angry that Sargent, a fine artist, should be so uncivil – as he saw it – to the beauties and subtleties of nature. 'I wish he won't hustle art about as if she were a street hoyden.'[41]

Isadora Duncan raised the artist's spirits by dancing in his garden on 23 July. He would have been entranced by the young American's vision for the dance. She liked to express the emotions of humanity, but, like Watts struggling against the grain in his early career, her imagination was not appreciated by the theatre establishment. Struggling for money and armed with little but her Greek tunic and compositions for mythological dances *Narcissus*, *Ophelia* and *Water-Nymphs*, she and her family had travelled to England on a cattle-boat. Hallé had brought her to Watts. Isadora danced barefoot, in transparent Liberty veiling. She spent her days at the British Museum, studying Greek mythology and composing movements in harmony with poses and rhythms suggested by figures depicted on Greek vases. 'To express what is the most moral, healthful and beautiful in art . . . this is the mission of the dancer, and to this I dedicate my life', Isadora was to write three years later. 'Dancing naked upon the earth I naturally fall into Greek positions, for Greek positions are only earth positions.' As Narcissus, she looked 'first startled, then charmed' as she portrayed the Greek youth discovering his reflection in the water; Narcissus would grow more enamoured, lean forward, view himself from side to side, blow kisses to the liquid image, step across the shallow brook, still see the reflection, turning and bending in an ecstasy of delight. Watts told Isadora about his life and art, giving her the impression that '84 is quite the best age'. She had seen Ellen Terry's inspired performance in *Cymbeline* and was fascinated by his paintings of the actress as a teenager, but finding no theatre opening herself, she soon left for Paris.[42]

A week later, the Lord Mayor of London opened Watts's memorial loggia, a modest 50-foot lean-to shelter designed by Ernest George – inscribed 'in commemoration of heroic self-sacrifice 1899' – in the expanded Postman's Park. Watts had selected thirteen brave men and women, among them a bargeman who had drowned rescuing a boy at Blackfriars a fireman, a pantomime artist, a clergyman, the oilmonger's maid Alice Ayres, and an inspector who was run over by a train while saving a woman from suicide. Each incident was recorded on a series of ceramic tiles painted by William de Morgan (fig. 219). Watts could not attend the opening due to illness, but hoped to fill the remaining 131 spaces in his life-time.[43]

While Mary mediated with the National Gallery to preserve his copy-right and Hollyer's royalty and to ensure no further pictures were copied, the *Athenaeum* announced that Watts was painting a new composition of Joan of Arc on horseback and a huge picture 'to offer as the first of what may be many contributions from men of distinction in various capacities to the capital of that Federated Australia which is about to come into being'. This was a concession to Hallam Tennyson, now Governor of South Australia, who again appeared to be taking Watts for granted.[44] Four months later, Hallam wrote to explain that the young country wanted to own one of Watts's greatest works and 'are *anxious* to pay highly for it'. Delighted with their recent mythological purchase, the South Australians wished to buy his prized *Paolo and Francesca*. Watts sent the third large *Love and Death* to South Australia.[45]

Gerry Liddell and the Egyptologist Professor Flinders Petrie sat for their portraits in August.[46] 'He is doing a most delicious humming-bird portrait of *Lady Wenlock*,' Mary wrote to Lord Wemyss in September, before taking Deuchars up to Aldourie to start a pottery class nearby at Dores, because – as Watts explained to Lord Archibald Campbell – they feared the depop-ulation of the highlands might lead to the 'almost complete extinction of the fine race'.[47] Thompson was summoned to Limnerslease to help raise the statue of Tennyson, which Watts worked at until the end of the year.[48]

At the Society of Portrait Painters exhibition Roger Fry, for the *Athenaeum*, finding Watts's portrait of Andrews 'superb . . . perfectly in harmony with itself' and his unnamed *Study* 'one of the most artistic works here', pointed out that Shannon's *Mrs Mildmay and her Daughter Grace* 'reminds us of Watts'. He himself admired Sargent's portrait of a lady with a fan.[49] It was probably during this brief interlude at Little Holland House that Jacques-Emile Blanche called. The Frenchman had revered Watts's Symbolist pictures since the Paris exhibition of 1878 and now felt 'an unspeakable pleasure' in seeing them again at the Tate Gallery. Stepping into Little Holland House, he felt at once 'soothed, in the serenity of pure art.' A golden light shone in from the garden at the end of the day. 'Ladies like shadows' were arranging flowers in bowls and vases, and the heroic white horseman stood outside the window. When at last the artist entered in his ruby skullcap, he looked to Blanche, like a monk.[50]

The artist had despatched *Love Triumphant* and *Time, Death and Judgment* to the Tate, where his entire Symbolist collection was rehung in the new Watts Gallery, the large rectangular room VII.[51] He returned to Limnerslease, increasingly concerned about the state of the nation; in particular he deplored the reckless public jokes and sarcasm towards Presi-dent Kruger of the Boer Republic of the Transvaal – not for the president's sake but for that of British generosity and dignity. 'Whatever our faults acknowledged by the future historian want of generosity I hope will not be one', Watts wrote to Lord Rosebery, proposing an appeal to the British public. 'On the Continent we are regarded as a cancer in civilization. Is it to be a Surgeon or a Coroner!' The earl agreed: 'I loathe the tone about him – mainly because it seems to betray decadence' and suggested that Watts, 'being aloof from the suspicions and pettinesses of public life' should

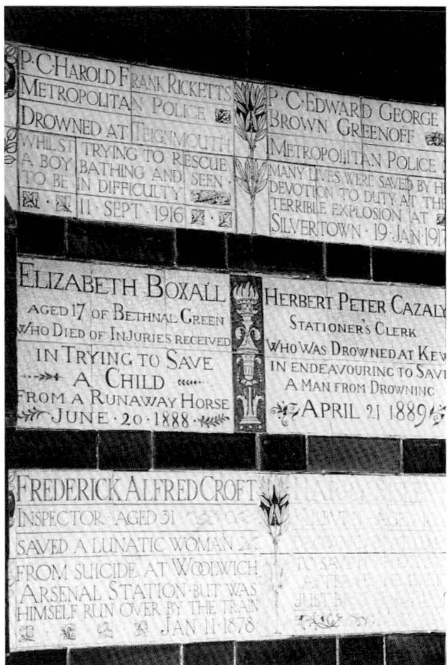

219   Heroic memorial plaques at St Botolph's, Aldersgate, designed for Watts by William de Morgan, 1900.

make the appeal himself: 'Bid Britons be generous. It is their best bait, and they are losing sight of it.'[52] The artist was writing his paper 'Our Race as Pioneers' when the textile manufacturer James Morton came to sit for his portrait: first, a charcoal portrait, a wedding gift to his fiancée, Beatrice Fagan, and now a full oil painting. Watts had offered these in gratitude for his advice on business, marketing and exhibition opportunities as Mary developed the Compton pottery enterprise.[53]

Queen Victoria died at Osborne in the early evening of 22 January 1901. Watts was invited to contribute a drawing to the Academy's presentation memorial album, and he made designs for the Victoria Memorial, ultimately undertaken by Thomas Brock. As Britain's matriarch, she had presided over an era of unprecedented advances; and, by and large, thought Watts, her sixty-three-year reign had been great: 'It will be felt everywhere that England is an orphan.'[54] His first professional successes had begun the year Queen Victoria ascended the throne. She had preferred to sit to German portraitists, but many of those whose vision had been instrumental in creating the Victorian age, he had recorded for the nation[55] – statesmen, social and education reformers, explorers, colonialists, scientists, engineers, poets, painters, philosophers, those who reflected the new morality, democracy and the rising power of modern Britain.[56] Although he had painted few men representing the expansion of trade, industry and commerce, he addressed these issues in 'Our Race as Pioneers', which was published in the May issue of the *Nineteenth Century and After*.

Watts, still pessimistic about the nation's future, believed that England had a vital role to play in South Africa. He emphasized the need to defeat the Boers for the benefit of world progress and civilization. Modern civilization was not exemplary, but as humanity was impelled to move forward it opened the way for better things, letting in light and air. 'In our ever probing onward, seeming to be so absolutely selfish', wrote Watts, 'we, the English people, are perhaps the agents of the great law – Movement, Progress, Evolution.'

In vehement Rhodesian terms, he declared, 'The Boers stop the way – they are unprogressive.' They were indolent, unproductive squatters, who had established themselves by savage conquest. In their hands the immense tract of South Africa would be lost to civilization. More active, progressive rulers should take their place, ' "Forward" is the voice of the law. Therefore it is almost an altruistic duty to explain that we as a nation must obey'. Watts insisted, 'we must be in South Africa, and later not we alone, but Germany and Russia, working to one end . . . in the interests of civilization.' England needed to provide for an expanding population. 'One of our greatest glories is the asylum, the freedom we offer, to even our enemies; but . . . The constant inflowing of strangers impels our already overflowing population abroad.' He forecast that commercial competition would lead to conflict and ambitious envy 'as fatal to peace as former mere love of power'; and unless pressure were diverted would generate unrest more sordid and destructive than lust of power had ever been, 'The goddess Trade, the modern Pandora, has in her box all the evils that can affect mankind.'

Conflict was the law of vitality, he went on, but the aim of the twentieth century should be to raise the standard of public morals and improve the mental and physical condition of the population. British advances in science, invention and discovery had contributed more to mankind than any other nation, 'Ill-mannered and wholly wanting in foresight, our aspirations have never been ignoble, nor have we been cruel in carrying them out. We have been in the van of the army of progress and freedom.' His concluding prayer of Ajax from Pope's *Homer* has Wattsian dual force: 'If we must perish, we thy will obey, But let us perish in the light of day.'[57]

The artist recognized that the sense of security and global power the nation had attained during the Victorian era was eroding, that England now lacked impulse and vision.[58] That he himself was seen by the world at large as an old master would not stop Watts moving forward in his art. Mary noted in her diary, 'Conscious of his soul always leading me upwards!'[59]

# 25 'How Fast the Days Go!'

'LIFE WITH YOU MELLOWS AND DOES NOT DECAY', wrote Lord Rosebery, wishing the artist 'a long lease' on his eighty-fourth birthday. Mary's gift was a gramophone.[1] Encouraging painters young and old, he awarded thirteen-year-old Brian Hatton the Royal Drawing Society's 'G. F. Watts Schools Prize' for the third year running. He held great hopes for the boy and would keep an eye on Brian's progress for the rest of his life.[2] Roger Fry, reviewing Richmond's exhibition at the New Gallery, extolled the 'glowing richness of the Wattsian influence'.[3] For his own part, Watts seemed proudest of pursuing his vision, 'The only quality that I can look back upon & say I *had* to save me from being nothing at all, is persistency. I never faltered.'[4]

The Whitechapel Art Gallery, designed by Charles Harrison Townsend, opened on 12 March 1901. Lord Rosebery spoke of it as 'the Coronation Day of the hope for which we had worked and waited', though Crane's striking mosaic frieze, a budget casualty, was missing from its innovative buff terracotta façade. Over 200,000 people visited the opening exhibition, to which Watts lent portraits, notably the *Canon Barnett, Earl Roberts* and *Commander-in-Chief*, and also the symbolic *Building of the Ark* – 'outside all fashions and periods', wrote Fry, 'It is one of his best works.'[5]

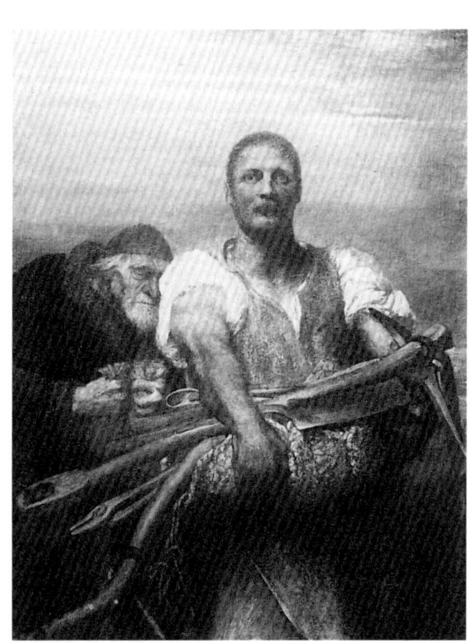

220 *Industry and Greed*, 1892–1901 (Watts Gallery).

Watts was important to the New Gallery. His admirers, who had feared that he might lose power, were astonished by the strength of his contributions. 'Signor's name is 1st in every mention of the New Gallery Ex', Mary noted. 'Mr Watts has prodigiously renewed his youth', enthused Roger Fry. He marvelled at the 'generous and massive forms, such grand and sweeping contours' of *Greed and Labour* (ultimately renamed *Industry and Greed*; fig. 220), which made even the most brilliant figures in the gallery look 'thin and shadowy' and at the magnificent line of the woman's neck, her head stretched to one side in the disturbing *Slumber of the Ages*. Between these two pictures, hung *Trifles Light as Air*, a study of naked babies drifting in the sunlit air: 'The aimless and wanton gaiety of the movement is beautifully suggested by the mazy rhythm of the design. It is one of the most purely delightful and winning conceits that Mr Watts has ever invented.' Fry had no idea what the pictures symbolized, yet he was convinced that 'Mr Watts is gifted beyond his ambitions and succeeds beyond his desire . . . [and] comes out at the end a pure and rapturous lover, not of truth or virtue, as he would have us believe, but of beauty . . . It is difficult to turn from such assured and definite creations as these to the ordinary fare of a modern exhibition.' The last sentiment was echoed by the *Art Journal*: 'He breathes a different air, interprets a nobler, more elemental spirit than any of his fellow contributors.'[6]

At the Glasgow International Exhibition, Fry highlighted Watts's 'noble *sensuality* which is the *fond* of his temperament' as against the 'expressionless charm' of Leighton's masterpiece *Hercules wrestling with Death for the Body of Alcestis*. Watts was represented by three highland paintings and ten pictures spanning the Victorian era, from the *Aurora* of 1842–43, lent by Scottish owners, to the most important, the weighty, sculpturesque *Charity*, which hung unhappily beside an evanescent *Nocturne* by Whistler. Both pictures of mood – diametrically opposed – they suffered in the clash.[7] Among Watts's four contributions to the Dresden International Exhibition was the highly symbolic *Love Steering the Boat of Humanity*, clearly a warning to Germany about the forces of conflict.[8] Mary's exotic terracotta sundial in memory of the late queen formed the centrepiece on the Compton stand at the Home Arts exhibition;[9] and she designed a terracotta chimneypiece for Watts's studio (fig. 221): exuberant Art Nouveau patterns intertwined with Anglo-Scandinavian, Brahmin, Egyptian and Celtic emblems, symbolizing *Love and Life* and *Love and Death* and surmounted by *Love Triumphant*.[10]

In July, the Right Honourable Charles Booth, the shipowner, sociologist, and (of particular interest to the artist), author of *Life and Labour of the People in London*, came to sit for the national series. 'Dodo' (Antonia) Booth – spoke of the sittings as 'all vigour, energy and enthusiasm'. Though the portrait was not finished, she saw in it an insight and dimension never achieved in his finished portrait by William Rothenstein.[11] Portraits of the late Friedrich Max Müller and the dashing Duke of Argyll were given to the National Portrait Gallery in August. Hallam Tennyson – soon to retire as Governor of South Australia – had written that the South Australians were overjoyed at owning *Love and Death* and wished to purchase a 'rough sketch of my Father'. Watts gave the grand portrait of the poet laureate in ermine to the National Gallery in Adelaide.[12]

In October, he began a sunny three-quarter profile portrait of Lily in a white dress, her amber scarf casually thrown round her neck and a soft red sash around her waist, a carefree young lady after her first ball.[13] The designer Charles Ricketts, 'greatly impressed' by his visit to Watts's studio at the end of the month, noted in his journal, 'He is of course the one great English colourist since Reynolds.'[14]

'What clothes would Mr Watts like me in?' enquired Major-General Robert Baden-Powell in October 1901. 'Shooting suit, General's red uniform, ditto dark blue, khaki uniform or what?' His defence of Mafeking had inspired the artist to paint a portrait for Baden-Powell's old school Charterhouse. 'It is putting me on a pedestal which I do not deserve', the general replied to the headmaster. Ordered home on sick leave, he came to sit in khaki uniform and broad-brimmed hat (fig. 222), with little time to spare, arriving for a twenty-four-hour stay at Limnerslease at three o'clock on 28 October. Watts painted until sundown, and after the next day's sitting, Baden-Powell saw more in the portrait 'than I know of in myself'. Mary, who was preparing the interior decoration for the chapel in the billiard room (fig. 223), noted how at ease he was among paints, gesso and clay. Lily, cheerily 'whistling and warbling', drove him to the station.

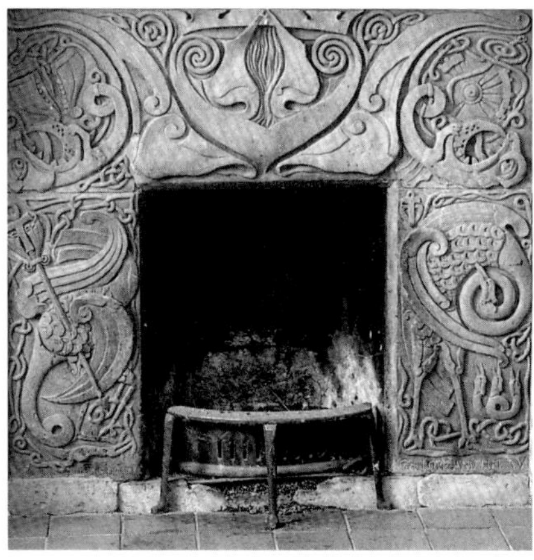

221   Mary's terracotta interpretation of *Love and Death* (left), and *Love and Life* (right), surmounted by *Love Triumphant* on the studio fireplace at Limnerslease, 1901.

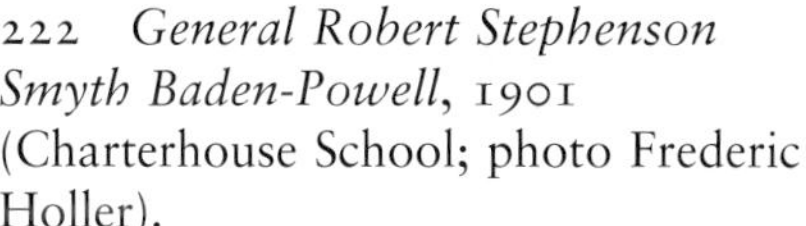

222   *General Robert Stephenson Smyth Baden-Powell*, 1901 (Charterhouse School; photo Frederic Holler).

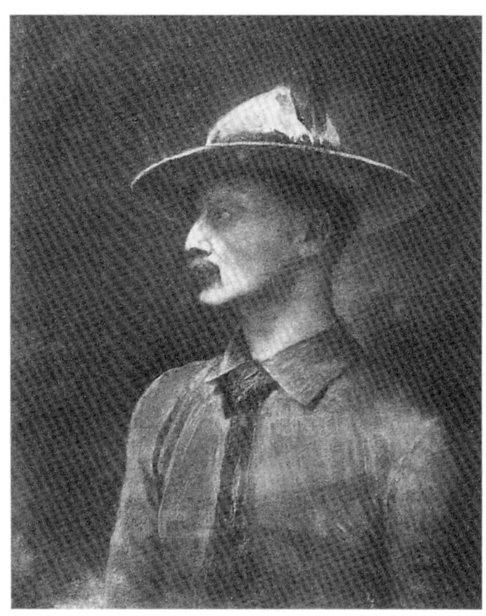

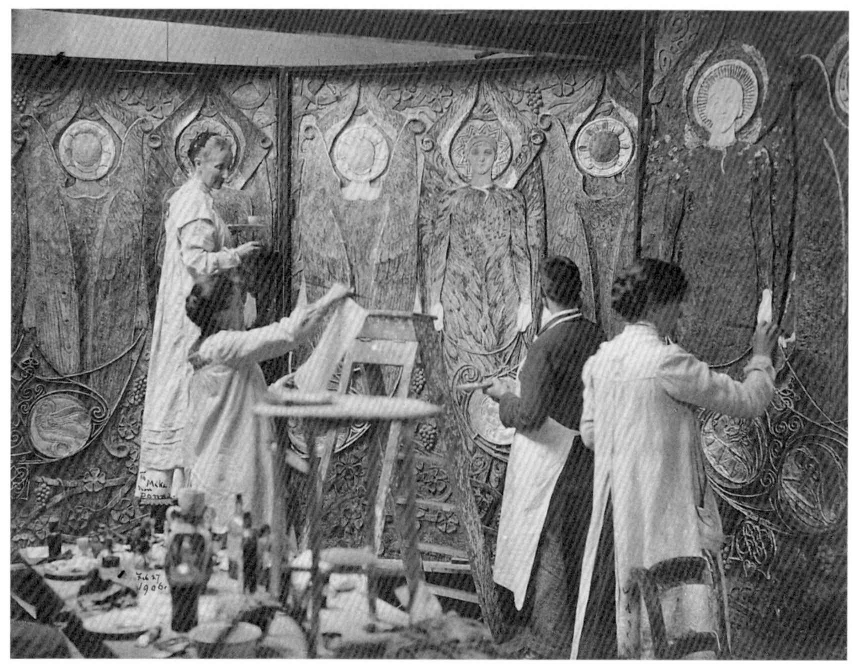

223 Mary (left) and assistants painting interior panels for the chapel, in the billiard room at Limnerslease, *c.*1901–03 (photo: Ernest Mills).

After picking up an Australian Sword of Honour in London, the general was summoned back to South Africa before his final sitting. Like Rhodes, Baden-Powell had felt soothed and refreshed by the Watts home. 'My mind often . . . wanders back to the delightful peep I had of a beautiful home life which I enjoyed at your house', he wrote from Johannesburg. 'How I envy every bit of it!' The artist, too, had been impressed by Baden-Powell and would have seen his foundation of the Boy Scouts as the most hopeful movement of the twentieth century.[15]

A sketch of Robert Dunthorne's daughter Marjorie in a splendid hat – most unlike Watts, but painted in appreciation of his encouragement for the art of mezzotint – was exhibited with portraits of Charles Booth, Professor Flinders Petrie and John Burns at the Society of Portrait Painters exhibition, where Fry highlighted the old-masterly picture of the Earl of Shrewsbury, painted in two hours four decades earlier. 'Every touch tells . . . The paint is not mere pigment, as in almost all the other pictures here; it is transfigured and raised to a higher power of expressiveness, as words are in a fine poem'.[16]

The Marquess of Dufferin wrote in December to tell the artist he had been sitting to Henrietta Rae. Watts had lent her his Little Holland House studio for the purpose. Sitting as Commodore of the Royal Ulster Yacht Club, Lord Dufferin was amused to occupy the very chair he had sat in for Watts some twenty years before. Like so many eminent sitters over the decades, he had recalled the studio as a haven from the stress of busy diplomatic life. Within months he had died and Watts's portrait of the late marquess joined the national collection.[17]

'I can think of no figure that emerges from the nineteenth century with steadier radiance of great achievement than the venerable figure of G. F.

Watts', Harold Begbie declared in the *Daily Mail*: 'He stands on the threshold of a new era with vigour unabated.' Mary, too, was attracting press interest. Interviewed for her pottery industry by *The Studio* and *Country Life*, her chief social, educational and artistic motivation was nevertheless inspired by her husband's exceptionally broad vision. Perpetuating his ideals and afterwards his memory would always predominate.[18] He was determined to finish the great *Court of Death*, its glow of light behind the throne reflecting the promise of a brighter dawn. In the February frost, he brought the *Tennyson* head and hands into the studio, and longed for the warm spring so that he could put the statue together and complete it.[19] When he heard that Blanche Airlie's son had died in the South African war, he sent her daughter-in-law, Mabel, his portrait of the gallant earl, painted as a baby.[20]

At last *The Court of Death* was finished. Watts summoned Thompson to Limnerslease for the lowering of the fourteen-foot-high canvas that stood at the end of the studio. On 19 March 1902 the ropes were loosened, and the picture was gradually tipped forward, offering a brief, better view before it sank on to its face across the floor. Holroyd arrived within minutes. By lunch time, the stretcher had been removed and the roll of canvas packed into the van. Mary had thought Watts would never live to see *The Court of Death* leave the studio. To her surprise, after having given so much time and thought to this seminal painting over the years, he did not miss it: 'I want my work to be of some use, & when it is done and gone, I don't think any more about it.'[21]

Rhodes died on 26 March. Watts had come to see him as the last Great Englishman. Though he did not care for imperialism, he admired Rhodes's ideal of a vast federation of self-governing English-speaking States. 'I have no objection to a Little England, if our Little England should live quietly, developing its own life and improving its own people side by side with other little States – a bright light in history for truth, generosity, courage and enterprise.'[22] The artist now felt profound sorrow. 'He was a great man even though making mistakes & perhaps to make mistakes I believe Alfred himself could make mistakes in an age so full of complications as ours,' he wrote to Lord Grey. At the earl's request he agreed that *Physical Energy* – 'my unfinished work, to commemorate poor Rhodes's unfinished work', as he described it to Anny Thackeray – could be cast over his tomb in the Matopo Hills, provided that he could preserve the gesso model to complete the work for Britain. Watts used to say as he chiselled at the gesso, 'I want it to belong to everything – roots and stones and trees and mountains.' And now the horse, symbolizing the restless physical impulse to seek the still unachieved goals would stand at the head of Rhodes Memorial – erected instead at his home in the mountains above Cape Town – looking out over the new country and beyond:

> My statue intended as an emblem of the energy & outlook so peculiarly characteristic of him shall be dedicated as you propose . . . I feel somehow, that its incompleteness has a pathetic appropriateness – It is only in this way that I can offer it for I must feel the completed work belongs to the Government, as the Government offered to cast it & find a site. I did not feel I ought to accept the generous offer in the unfinished state of the work but if I can ever finish it I shall look upon it as belong-

ing to those gentlemen whether in or out of office . . . the gift so far shall be my contribution & up to that point my identification with the great personality.[23]

When Lord Grey came to discuss casting the statue, he brought with him the imperialist's will. Outlining a vast imperial scheme to educate young colonists, the remarkable document endowed Oxford scholarships to American scholars, Germans, and English-speaking students from around the world. It astonished the Wattses – 'The same aims! The same boy-like simplicity', Mary noted, as her own husband.[24] Taken ill again and unable to check over the statue and watch it leave, Watts was back at Limnerslease. The next day, Thompson accompanied it from Little Holland House to Parlanti's Foundry at 59 Parson's Green. This time, Watts was depressed, ashamed of letting unfinished work go: 'It seems like presumption.'[25]

Alexander Fisher, the sculptor and pioneer enameller who was to supervise the casting of *Physical Energy*, estimated that it would cost up to £1,500 and take nearly seven months.[26] At the Academy Watts was exhibiting the portrait of *Major-General Baden-Powell*, inscribed, 'All may have, / If they dare try, / A glorious life or grave.' Fisher's bronze relief *Message to the New Century*, for Lord Grey, symbolizing 'the evolution of labour from slavery, through hirelingdom, to a full and perfect partnership with Capital', impressed Watts, who invited the young Symbolist to the studio. He warned Fisher never to heed adverse criticism, for it sprang from misunderstanding of the true aims of art,[27] advice he may have followed himself when Fry attacked *Love Steering the Boat of Humanity* at the New Gallery – 'The notion of Humanity catching a crab is almost comic' – and the *Art Journal* queried, 'Mr Watts may mean that under the guidance of Love, the craft of life can make progress even against a hurricane of wind and waters.' The *Spectator*, however, appreciated the significance. 'The falling sail, the rebellious oars, and the storm clouds all bode ill for the symbolic figure of Humanity, who tries to navigate the boat; but Love holds the rudder . . . How many painters are there now who could treat such a subject as this, and in such a grand and abstract manner, and yet retain that passionate force which is the life of a work of art?'[28]

*Physical Energy* was seen to represent kinship between two extraordinary idealists striving for humanity, 'the tribute of England's greatest living painter to Africa's greatest son'. Stead, writing in the *Review of Reviews*, declared Watts to be 'the greatest of all living Englishmen. Compared with his renown the fame of the King who is to be crowned this month cannot for a moment compare . . . Mr Watts, who is a monarch in the realm of art, sways a far more potent sceptre in his brush than the bejewelled staff which will be placed in the hand of Edward VII at the Abbey.'[29] The South African War ended on 31 May 1902 with the Treaty of Vereeniging, in which the Boers acknowledged Edward VII as their king.[30]

On 25 June, the king's private secretary Sir Francis Knollys wrote to Watts, 'I am commanded by the King to say that he hopes it may be agreeable to you to accept the Order of Merit.' The new Order, inspired by Frederick the Great's Order *Pour le Merit*, honouring servicemen, and civilians distinguished in the Arts, Sciences and Literature, was comparable to the Golden Spur awarded to Titian[31] and did indeed please the artist, though he hardly dared admit it. 'I rather liked the distinction of having none,' he quipped to Georgie Burne-Jones. 'My dear Friend,' wrote Richmond, 'I am glad that the King has recognized your genius – I cannot tell you how glad I am.' Among the first recipients were Lecky, Earl Roberts and Viscount Kitchener. That Watts was chosen augured well for the new Order, wrote the Lord Ripon: 'It is a proof of the king's good judgment.'[32] Anny Ritchie cheerily illuminated a newspaper cartoon of 'King Edwards *Round Table* where the Signor sits in his beloved place with other Knights around him each with their own particular gifts – He the only genius among them – Lord Kelvin [the scientist and inventor, William Thomson] perhaps . . . What a solemn coronation this has been. No crown of gold I think would have so bound the King to his people as this crown of thorns. But the sun shines and things look hopefuller.' Anny was glad of Leslie Stephen's knighthood, as president of the London Library and editor of the *Dictionary of National Biography*, for he was sad and lonely. In his memoirs Sir Leslie would recalled feeling shy when he visited Watts's studio, amongst artistic people, Leighton 'in all his glory, and Val Prinsep and his friends, who looked terribly smart to me.'[33] As Watts set out for the Athenaeum dinner on 25 July in honour of members of the Order, Mary noted how young and slim he looked. Her contribution to the nation, eight of her terracotta scroll pots, now stood around the fountain in the central hall of the Tate Gallery.[34]

At last, Watts allowed Andrews to photograph the *Tennyson* (fig. 224). 'The head is now down, being worked upon finally by Signor, who is wonderfully well this autumn & I hope will have the joy of hearing from you, on your return that you have seen the great bronze, & like it – It is very dignified, thoughtful & reverent,' Mary wrote to Hallam, enclosing a photograph in November.[35] Visitors young and old flocked to Limnerslease, among them the novelist Julian Sturgis, Mary Ward, the architect William Caröe and Lady Constance Leslie's daughter Mary Crawshay, who replaced Lillie Langtry as the face of *Summer*, for which the royal mistress had given so many sittings.[36]

The artist, who attuned his life to the daylight and never wished to acquire electric light, did, however, acquire a pioneering electric hearing aid. The Akouphone worked wonders. Watts thought he would never again hear birdsong, but now, even with the window closed, he could hear a thrush singing; and Mary could read without raising her voice.[37] He had *Progress* (pl. XLI) brought down from Little Holland House to hang in place of the great *Court of Death* at Limnerslease, where they celebrated their wedding anniversary with champagne and roses. She could hardly believe he was so well. He was now trying to establish 'the strength of the union – or possible touch with life beyond death . . . I rather feel and believe that all is one in the big scheme – mysteriously not lost, but not individual as we know it.'[38]

*Love and Life*, his tender metaphysical message to humanity, was arousing controversy again in America. Mrs Roosevelt had requisitioned the painting to hang at the White House. First there were those who quite rightly insisted that the artist had given it to inspire the American public, rather than to rest in privileged splendour in the presidential dining room. The Corcoran did not complain, but regretted losing it from their walls. Mrs Martin, horrified that her victory had been quashed, petitioned the

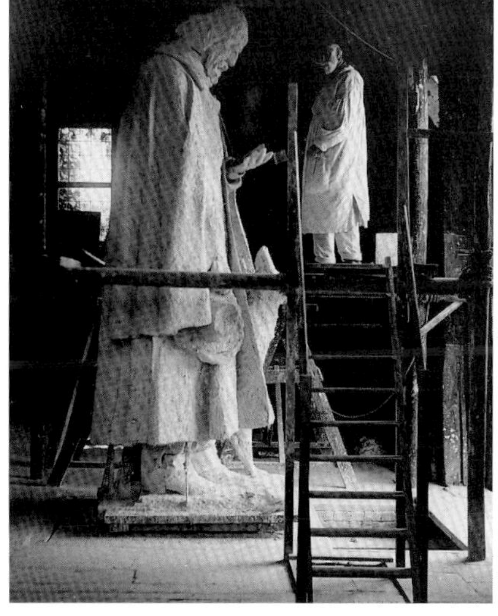

224   Watts working on the statue of Tennyson, 1902 (photo: George Andrews).

president and marshalled the women of Philadelphia to have the picture
removed, only to find herself ridiculed by American artists. 'Those who can
find anything sensual in the Watts picture', suggested one, 'must be anxious
to indulge themselves in overripe thoughts'.[39]

Dr Hugh Macmillan was preparing a biography of Watts for the Temple
series of men regarded – as the Italian patriot Joseph Mazzini put it – as
'God's born interpreters', when the writer G. K. Chesterton, who had
admired him since boyhood, began in January a more interpretative study
for Duckworth's Popular Library of Art.[40] Watts, in turn lent letters to John
Morley, OM, for his three-volume biography of Gladstone.[41]

Living for all but six weeks of the year at Limnerslease, he talked of
giving up Little Holland House and decided to build a rural art gallery
and hostel for Mary's apprentice potters in Compton. The Wattses bought
a further three acres of land adjoining the pottery buildings and commissioned a young friend Christopher Turnor as architect. Kit, an agricultural
reformer, was not a fully qualified architect, but he had trained in Lutyens's
office, working on Rosneath Castle in Scotland for Princess Louise, and
had built a house, Berthorpe, near Compton. A proud car-owner, he had
been motoring over to Limnerslease for over a year, talking and listening
to the artist, whom he regarded as a thinker far in advance of his time.
Watts, too, found that 'contact with a young fellow like that does me good'.
On 23 February 1903 he used the silver trowel, with which he had
performed a similar task for the South London Art Gallery, to lay the
corner-stone of the apprentice potters' hostel, the present Watts Gallery in
Compton.[42] It was his eighty-sixth birthday. Lily playfully threw one of his
gifts – a large laurel wreath – around her head, and looked, to Watts, like
a wood nymph in her white evening gown. He began a painting the following day.[43]

Lord Brownlow was becoming impatient. The *Tennyson* statue was
taking too long. Watts had had to begin again after the *Aurora* base
collapsed, he himself had a disabling rupture, and the winter weather had
blocked much outdoor work,[44] but by March, he was able to work at the
statue all day. Elected a foreign corresponding member of the Académie des
Beaux-Arts in Paris, he was approached by Evelyn, Countess Martinengro
Cesaresco, seeking to purchase the portrait of Garibaldi to for the Uffizi
Gallery. She had sent a photograph to his son Ricciotti Garibaldi, and both
agreed that it was the only portrait that revealed his soul. But the artist,
'an ardent well wisher of Italy' resisted the impulse even to give the picture
for he thought it unworthy of the Italian hero.[45]

Mary's *Pelican* rug was shown by Liberty & Co at the Grafton Galleries
exhibition *Founding a National Industry – Irish Carpets*, attracting attention in *The Studio*.[46] At the same time, Emilie Barrington mounted a small
retrospective of Watts's paintings at Leighton House, provocatively revealing in the catalogue his deep regard for Jeanie Senior – 'the Artist admired
not only the beauty but the character, the wide sympathies and unselfish
helpfulness of the nature of his sitter . . . In a sense, therefore, this picture
is more than a mere portrait.' Here in Leighton's studio, Fry saw that *Love
Steering the Boat of Humanity* was not a failure after all and hoped that
one day *Peace and Goodwill* and other monumental designs would be
properly placed as mural decorations.[47]

Vanessa Stephen (fig. 225) came to stay at Limnerslease on 14 March. Arriving with her half-brother George Duckworth, now private secretary to the Chancellor of the Exchequer Austen Chamberlain, she immediately changed for dinner into her favourite black velvet dress. (Vanessa and Virginia in their black dresses with white lace collars and wristbands looked to Rothenstein at this time, 'as though they had walked out of a canvas by Watts or Burne-Jones'.[48]) Twenty-three-year-old Vanessa was studying at the Royal Academy Schools, and Watts, having painted and influenced so many members of her family for over half a century, had promised to keep an eye on her artistic development. She recorded his every word in letters to her fellow student Margery Snowden. Though Watts had already dined, he sat beside Vanessa and asked after her studies. Had she tried the new solid oil colours? He had, and thought them useful for sketching, but they would make little difference to his own dry technique. What did students think of Rodin? No one had spoken about him, but Vanessa knew he was fashionable and thought she should make out that they worshipped him. He told her that he could not admire Rodin because his work was not beautiful: 'No art can be great unless it's beautiful any more than music could be great if it were all discords. The thing's an absurdity. Then he tries to express movement in sculpture & that's wrong.' Watts talked of Sargent, whose life-classes she adored.[49] 'Now Sargent makes his people move, but its more allowable in paint. Still none of the great old people painted their portraits moving', continued Watts. 'The whole idea of modern portrait painting is wrong – They try to make their sitters stand out from the frame and every picture should really seem to be some way inside and away from it.' He said that English caricatures were better than any other nation. In the evening they played the pianola. Vanessa promised Margery another letter the next day.[50]

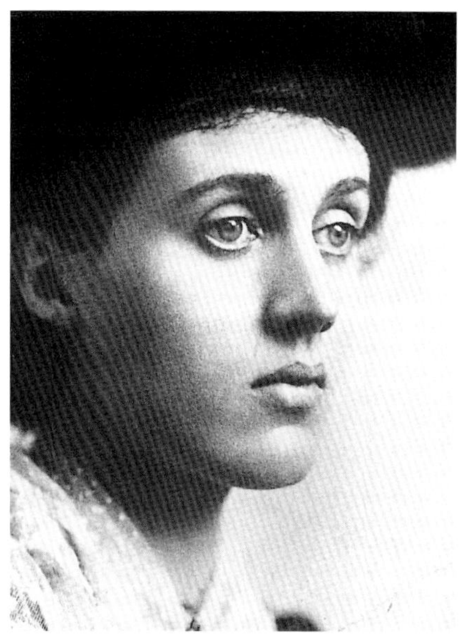

After breakfast, she went into the studio to find Watts finishing a picture of an ivy-covered oak. 'That's going to be sent to the Academy as a protest against Impressionism,' he said. *A Parasite* (fig. 226) – a tree trunk in the stranglehold of luxuriant waxy ivy leaves, painted in monumental close-up beside the spindly skeleton of a dead tree – seems to protest at a good deal more.[51] Because of his reservations about the quality of art education in Britain, he lectured to Vanessa purely on art. ' "You see every leaf is cleanly painted. There's no smearing, and cleanness is a great quality. Now what do you mean by style?" I gibbered feebly something about its being one's indi-vidual expression.' He taught her his chief principles, about the lines of nature returning on themselves, demonstrating the idea of the large circle on his Parthenon casts, 'You see how the lines stretch out into space, and in this cast of an arm . . . the forms are rounder and therefore not so grand.' She would learn this in the schools, he said, but the rule would help her gauge whether a picture had style, 'Now Rubens, though he has great vigour and movement and is admirable for those things, has not that quality at all, his forms are all rounded and like bubbles.'

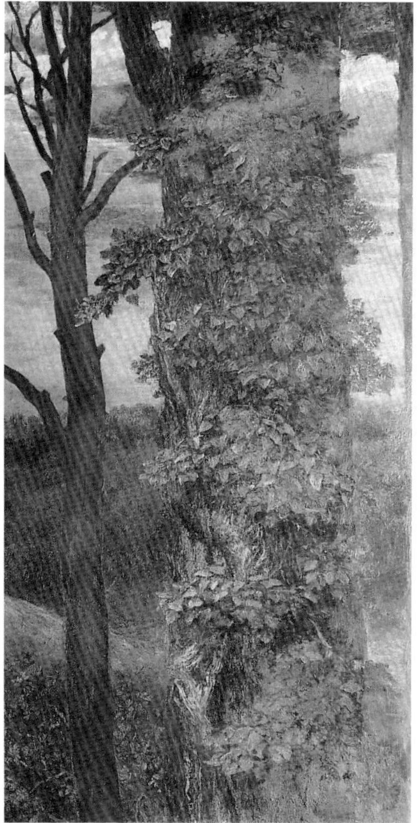

'Colour one can give no rule for – it's a matter of taste. Now look at this.' The 'brilliant green trees and grace' of *Surrey Woodland*, a general sense of colour and form, looking up from the bottom of their garden,[52] impressed Vanessa. 'There's no warm colour in it at all, it's all cold and I think that's the most difficult thing to make harmonious', he explained.

'Now this sunset [*End of the Day*][53] makes it look crude and of course it's much easier to make these warm colours into a picture . . . They suggest warmth and the blood circulating . . . If flesh were cold and like alabaster it would give one no pleasure, but when one sees a rosy child one wants to take it in one's arms and cuddle it.' Turning to the portrait *Mrs Crawshay* with Lillie Langtry's armful of roses, he demonstrated how all the movement was within the figure, in the blood circulation and the indefiniteness that makes one wonder whether it really is still: 'Of course Sargent's portraits are much greater in technical ability, and this makes no direct appeal to you as they do, but with him the movement is always in the attitude, and though his people jump you feel that they are quite incapable of jumping. They have no blood in them. Still I admire him for his great ability.' Telling Vanessa of all the great men he had known, the greatest genius of them all, he said, was Rossetti, and Millais was more loved than anyone – he was so hearty and kind. Watts gave Duckworth his bath notes on education, which he would discuss at length with Turnor. Vanessa came away thinking of Watts as a kind old gentleman with 'quite a sense of humour'. Her own portrait of her father, now suffering from cancer, was clearly influenced by Watts.[54]

At the New Gallery, lost freshness was, according to Fry, redeemed by Watts's four large paintings: the cosmic *The Sower of the Systems* (pl. XLII) and the landscapes *Green Summer, End of the Day* and *The Two Paths*, which dwarfed everything else. None of the critics could fathom *The Sower of the Systems*, but, asked Fry, 'Is there living in the whole world a single artist who could be trusted to paint a worthy companion to it?' *Green Summer*, the sky and trees seen from Watts's studio window, revealed the dead trunk of *A Parasite* – its message unrecognized at Burlington House – to be the upper part of the same tree. To Fry, *Green Summer* was 'as true and brilliant as an *impressioniste* could desire, and yet withal so gloriously harmonious in colour, comparable to the background of Titian's *St John*. By painting it over and again, rather than applying a 'dexterous swish of colour', Watts had given the picture what he called a breathing quality – 'our atmosphere, for beyond it there is no such thing as living and breathing for us'.[55] *The Two Paths*, itself remarkably atmospheric, had been inspired by a vivid dream in which the downward path had left a terrible impression, too dark to express in paint.[56] But the most extraordinary was *The Sower of the Systems*, Watts's suggestion of the Creator – 'a great vesture into which everything that exists is woven' – here, a veiled abstract figure of no definable sex, a dynamo sweeping through the stratosphere scattering flecks of Creation. No wonder critics were mystified.[57]

At the end of May 1903 he sent the sketch for *Neptune's Horses* surging through the waves – more abstract than the finished picture – to the Dutch Gallery, where it hung beside Whistler's *The Violinist*. Whistler died in July.[58] Watts battled on with the *Tennyson*, which was due at the foundry in August, 'I must try to get this thing off my hands, a terrible failure I am afraid!' he wrote to Rivière. With two months to go, he asked the Academician for proportions and drawings of the poet's dog Karenina, for Rivière had included her in a portrait of Lady Tennyson. The eleven-foot, four-inch statue was to be cast in very dark bronze. Kit Turnor made a model for the base and Watts checked the height of the pedestal with Thornycroft.[59]

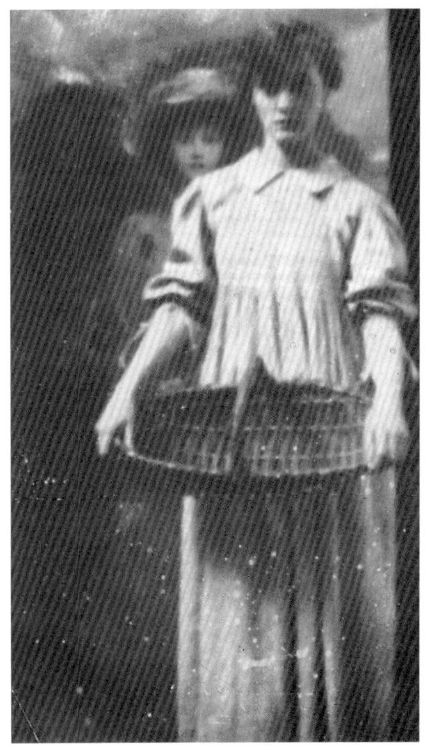

227    Lily posing for *Lilian*, August 1903.

However urgent the deadline, he needed the variety of other work to help him achieve it. One morning in June he took up the large canvas of *Endymion* (pl. XL), which he had laid in three decades before. This new large version was to be more visionary and mystic than the famous, sculptural original. Only the moon goddess would be luminously visible. Mary walked into the studio to find a 'blue wonder' on the easel. 'Oh what a dream for him to have!' Watts smiled sadly, 'Yes, and it was only moonshine after all.' She looked round the 'wizard's room' and saw that, as well as the sumptuous, glowing *Progress*, he was painting a blue and gold *Fugue* of babies and a landscape quite different from his usual work – just sky, cloud and struggling sunlight.[60]

The Cosmopolitan club presented the huge *Story from Boccaccio* to the Tate, where *Life's Illusions*, bequeathed by Mrs Alfred Seymour, now hung in the sculpture hall.[61] Watts invited Crane to make a small correction to the *Venus* (the painting that Watts had bought from Crane in 1882): he wished to present it to the gallery, as Crane was not yet represented there.[62] Amid the excitement of the Royal Horticultural Society Flower Show at Holland House, where Mary was exhibiting garden pots, Anny called on Watts and found him in his studio looking more like Titian than ever. He still rose at dawn, 3.30 on the longest day. 'Better to wear out than rust out,' he laughed. Admiring one of Brian Hatton's latest drawings, which he had shown to Rivière as 'the outlook of the future', he exclaimed, 'It is like Sargent'[63] Watts had exceptionally high hopes for Brian.[64] In July, the Hattons wore their finest togs for lunch at Little Holland House and a culture tour in the Watts's open carriage. Starting with Shields's murals in the Chapel of the Ascension, they went on to the crowded Greek Art Club, then to George Harcourt's works at the Doré Gallery, and finally to Caswell Smith's studio for tea. Here Mary introduced them to the actor Johnston Forbes Robinson. People made way for Watts everywhere they went. He rarely drove through London. '*We are* greatly honoured,' Amelia Hatton wrote to her husband.[65]

As vigorous as ever, the artist sang as he started work; and at six o'clock in the evening Lily's young man, Michael Chapman – expecting the octogenarian to be resting when he looked into the studio to say goodbye – discovered him standing on the top studio step, painting the large *Eve Repentant*. Watts worked furiously the next day to transform the wood nymph crowned with a wreath (which Mary disliked) into a portrait of Lily in her garden hat (figs 227 and 228). 'Come into the Studio. I have got something to show you,' he said to Mary when she returned from London. She knew he had been up to something, for he often surprised her when she was out. 'Suddenly in this one day a wonder had been wrought, the *Lilian*, our Lily, as she *is*, had come upon the tall upright canvas . . . her own sweet serious expression and beautiful eyes looked out upon me.' Mary exclaimed: 'You *are* a wizard!'[66]

On 6 August, Turnor photographed him working on the *Tennyson*. Mary went to inspect the site in Lincoln. Watts, chiselling until the last minute, watched in anguish six days later, as the great white statue of the poet laureate and his wolfhound, in his mind still only a sketch, was slowly lowered on to its back, laid upon a stretcher and carted away to Singer's foundry in Frome. 'I think what it ought to have been!' He confided to Rivière that

228  *Lilian*, 1903 (Watts Gallery).

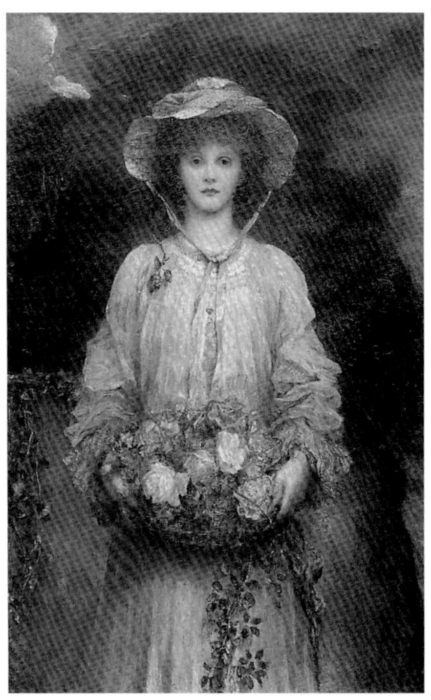

he could not think of the *Tennyson* without a shudder. 'I am seriously unhappy about it. Everything was against me forever a chapter of accidents, a fate against it.[67]

He returned to Little Holland House to finish *Physical Energy*. The torso stayed at the foundry for the time being, and the various parts filled the studio once more. At Parlanti's foundry, the bronze horse and rider looked '*magnificent*' to Mary, 'an heroic work for the frail-looking sculptor'. Even Watts was surprised. Seeing it in bronze indicated how he might improve the gesso, not least the bridle, which he asked Fisher to rearrange.[68] He sent portraits of the late William Lecky and Marquess of Salisbury to the National Portrait Gallery; and battling against a cataract in his eye, he painted a third picture of *The Messenger*, which the influential German director Karl Ernst Osthaus bought for the Folkwang Museum, an outstanding collection of modern and contemporary art at Hagen.[69]

'Signor feels a great change in his physical power, a marked sense of *growing old* & of enfeeblement,' Mary noted on 26 October. He was glad of her support when walking in the garden, and his step had grown heavier: 'Still is he not wonderful! His mind is as it was, & his heart & spirit still.' That day, inviting Spielmann to stay, he asked the editor not to bring Brian Hatton into the public eye yet – 'He has plenty of time before him & I want him to complete his growth & get strong.' The artist also wrote to James Smith, grateful for a cheque because 'my Wife's very active philanthropy sometimes outruns strict prudence so that our noses must not exactly be turned up at small sums'. But he was not well. Mary summoned Dr Albutt, who saw no visible sign of failure and confirmed that his mind was as vigorous as ever. The artist took a long slender cedar stem with a slim pointed brush at the end, held it at arm's length and, watching the steady point, said, 'When I see that point tremble my work will be done.' Allbutt later explained: 'Like his creative and analytic temper, those sensitive hands were as nervous as they were steady and strong. For such a finely strung instrument pain was intolerable; under pain only might his will or self-command be shaken.' Watts did take to his bed and again produced fine pencil studies of blankets folds.[70]

Little Holland House Gallery closed and the pictures arrived in Compton on 30 October. The next day, he returned to London to see Lina's exhibition. The *Art Journal*, pointing out his encouragement to rising artists, noted that he was also encouraging her husband Aubrey Waterfield and Dorothy Landau. That day, too, he bade farewell to the faithful servants on their retirement to Wandsworth. Emma had cooked for him for over thirty years. Her husband George Thompson, who had assisted Watts in the sculpture studio and gallery for twenty-four, planned to return to the studio the following summer.[71] (But barely had the new year begun when Thompson died of a heart attack. Watts would be devastated – 'Oh, I *have* lost a friend!'[72]

At Limnerslease Watts installed the larger Parthenon casts. Shortly before her birthday, Mary discovered in the studio a picture of a baby running from the sea with its arms reaching forward, towards the shore of life. 'Oh Signor!' she cried. 'Out of the nowhere! Into the here.' He had been painting it secretly in the early hours, 'I think I shall call it *Whence? Whither?*.'[73] He was still working extremely hard. There was so much he wanted to do, but he did get tired, and on 2 December admitted feeling unsteady on his feet.[74]

Auguste Rodin, in England as president of the International Society of Painters, Sculptors and Gravers, to organize their forthcoming exhibition at the New Gallery, came to see Watts at Limnerslease. Both men were moved by the meeting. The French sculptor afterwards asked for a photograph, which Mary had specially enlarged and posted on 10 December. Promising to enlarge a portrait of himself in return, he thanked her for the picture of 'the venerable English master of painting and sculpture, 'Il sera pour moi comme une image d'exemple à imiter pour le talent la fierté la générosité et la bonté.'[75]

With American electrical massage treatment, Watts's hearing was much improved. 'He is now aware that when we walk about there is noise – hitherto we seemed to slide.'[76] In the new year, the poet laureate Alfred Austin sent him a poem based on *Love and Death*;[77] and in January 1904 James Smith took delivery of the small *Love and Life*, commissioned ten years before. The artist was now painting with the auction room in mind, to fund his wife's activities.[78] He modelled a red foot in wax to get the twist he needed for *Endymion*. He liked the wax because he could reuse it. Refusing to listen to Mary, who begged him to preserve the beautiful foot, he insisted, 'It is such a waste of wax.' Both lost. Hoping to soften it, he put it too near the fire, and while he sat down to write a letter the twist he wished to paint melted away. As she grieved over the vanished spirit, he exclaimed jubilantly, 'The wax is not wasted!'[79]

That day Hallé came to luncheon. Watts happily offered five pictures to the New Gallery, all of them work in progress, as a competitive personal exercise, so as to improve. Desperately anxious about the direction of art, he said that painting and sculpture should cease altogether rather than sink into the cult of ugliness and obscenity. 'He begged me to close, or sell, or burn down the New Gallery, sooner than allow it to become a centre for everything he held to be most degrading in art,' Hallé recalled. 'His grief and rage that such things could not only be tolerated, but senselessly applauded, in a country where he, Burne-Jones, Leighton, Millais, and others had worked so hard to revive the sense of what was noble and beautiful, was a sad experience.'[80]

Watts was disappointed by Rodin's contemplative masterpiece, the large *Penseur* at the international exhibition. 'Signor feels that the *Penseur* is *no* thinker', Mary noted in her diary. Troubled by the monumentality of a non-ideal nude, and by the anatomy, he disliked the lumpy muscles and lack of shoulder blade – 'no fine long structure' – and thought the figure appeared to be suffering physical discomfort. *La Defense* he admired, with reservation; and *A Dream* was spoilt by the woman kicking up her heels. At least there was Charles Shannon. Even on reflection a few days later, he could not respect *Le Grand Penseur*. If it were to be seen as prehistoric man, he might approve, 'possibly it belongs to the order of the lumpy Hippopotamus – & such creatures. It is unintellectual – & that surprises me'. He had admired Rodin in the past, but this 'terrible' example, Watts wrote to Lady Wemyss, 'is a proof how necessary it is to keep a strict watch upon oneself, how easy it is to become a victim to fad'.[81]

The moment a purchaser expressed interest in Little Holland House, he began to fret, and Mary withdrew the house from sale. Her pioneering role

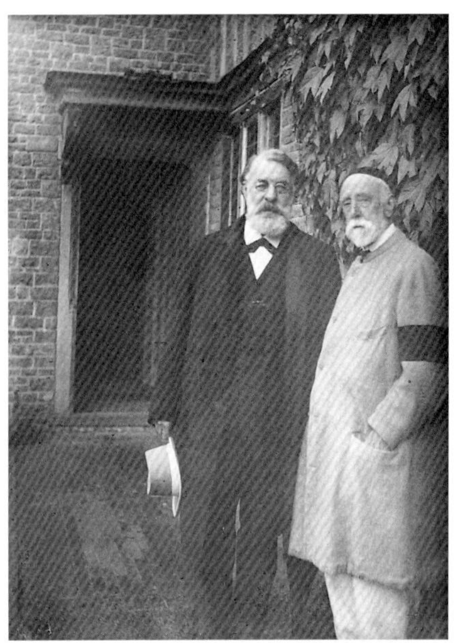

229    Watts with Joachim outside Limnerslease, *c*.1900.

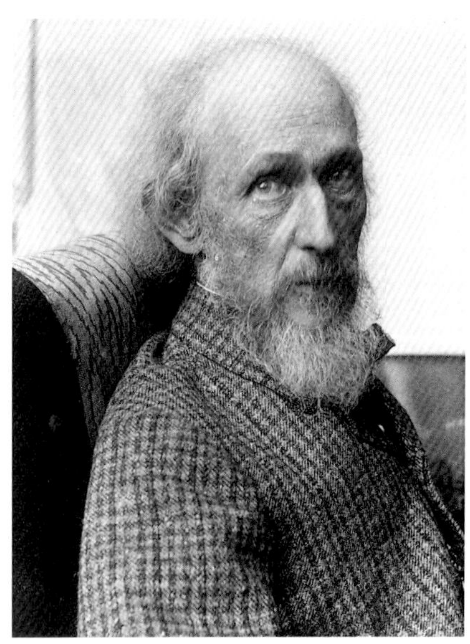

230    The octogenarian artist, *c*.1903–4.

231    The Watts Picture Gallery, 1906.

was acknowledged at Liberty's *Modern Celtic Art* exhibition, which displayed a wide range of Compton pottery in March: 'Never before, in this country at least, has the Garden Pot been treated as an item, *per se*, of decorative skill . . . the present exhibitors have struck out into untrodden paths, and, in this instance largely aided and advised by Mrs G. F. Watts, the talented wife of our greatest living artist, having shown us what notable results can be achieved with simple forms treated with bold designs.'[82] Both she and Watts exhibited at the St Louis World's Fair. She had designed pots made from Irish clay, and he sent the pictures *Brunhild* and *The Habit Does Not Make the Monk* and the portrait of Joachim.[83] A photograph with the violinist at Limnerslease shows the artist wearing a black armband (fig. 229). Watts explained to Turnor that he was in mourning for his countrymen, for their stupidity, apathy and failure to appreciate science. This he addressed in *Progress*.[84]

Rodin's photograph had arrived when Watts succumbed to painful eczema, and 'gathered in his sun', as put it.[85] 'I sometimes think my Lease is pretty nearly at its end', he wrote to Lady Wemyss, 'but I go on working.' He began *Destiny*, a seven-foot sequel to the running child; and he again experimented in tempera as groundwork for a contemplative, unfinished self-portrait, and designed a picture intended to symbolize his motto, 'The Utmost for the Highest'. He was fascinated by Chesterton's biography and posed for a medallion modelled by the American, Theodore Spicer-Simson. On 29 March, he resigned as a trustee of the National Portrait Gallery. It was becoming a struggle to rise at dawn, but when Mary protested that he need not do it he rebuked her: 'You are quite wrong. I know I *must* live in the light.'[86]

On Good Friday, 1 April 1904, the Watts Picture Gallery (fig. 231), the first British gallery devoted to a single artist, opened in Compton. Over a hundred paintings hung on his favourite blood-red arras cloth. Mary's intention was that the apprentice potters, who had been living in the hostel since August, should be inspired by his noble art. His motto 'The Utmost for the Highest' stands out in relief on the metal casing of the door. Visitors flocked to the picturesque gallery, which was open to the public free

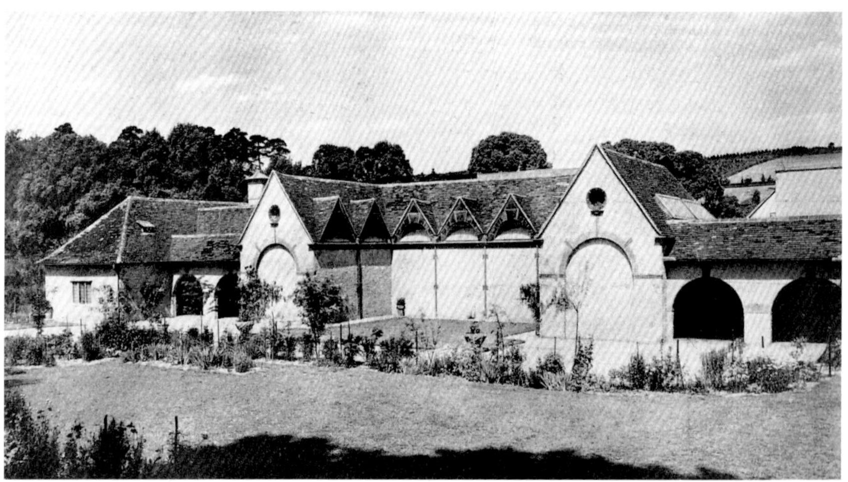

at weekends and on Wednesdays; there was an entrance charge of one shilling on Mondays, Tuesdays and Fridays, to cover the cost of the caretaker, Miss Hill.[87]

Over the next fortnight Watts finished a small arched version of *The All-Pervading*, which was placed over the golden altar (fig. 232), completing the interior of the most extraordinary, symbolic mortuary chapel in the country. Mary's exuberant Art Nouveau gesso decoration, painted in warm reds, blues and gold, with huge angels looking down in sorrow and up in hope, harmonizes in line and colour like the chords of music in his art and was designed to sympathize with and uplift mourners of all creeds. The veiled figure of *The All-Pervading* holds the universe, a blue sphere flecked with light, within the guiding Hands of Love. By insetting the picture into decoration symbolizing the soul and the Eucharist – the bird feeding on grapes – Mary seems to be acknowledging her husband's inspiration, though the design and decoration were entirely hers. He had doubtless seen the decoration in progress at Limnerslease, but when he wandered up to the chapel in early May, and saw the interior complete, he was astonished: 'He had not realized what I had aspired to in the matter of this glorified wallpaper.'[88] This little circular cruciform chapel celebrating life and death was surely inspired by his early desire to create a House of Life and his comforting modern reinterpretation of death in art.

*Physical Energy* – destined for the Cape – stood in the quadrangle of Burlington House (fig. 233). Walking up to the private view Hester Fraser Tytler thought Signor's horse looked gorgeous, but strange in bronze.[89] Fry warned readers of the *Athenaeum* to keep to the left-hand path to avoid 'an unpleasant first impression of what – even if it be a failure – is a great failure' and declared there to be more individuality at the Royal Academy than at the Champ de Mars in Paris. 'In the first place, we have Mr Watts.' Inside, *Lilian*, to the *Art Journal* and to Fry, asserted his unfailing power. After a lifetime shocking or alluring the spectator, this simple, direct image, delightfully out of touch with fashion in art, yet showing why the English aristocracy retained its power, was the concept of 'a singular genius.' Whereas Sargent painted aristocrats on their guard, 'socially on the defen-

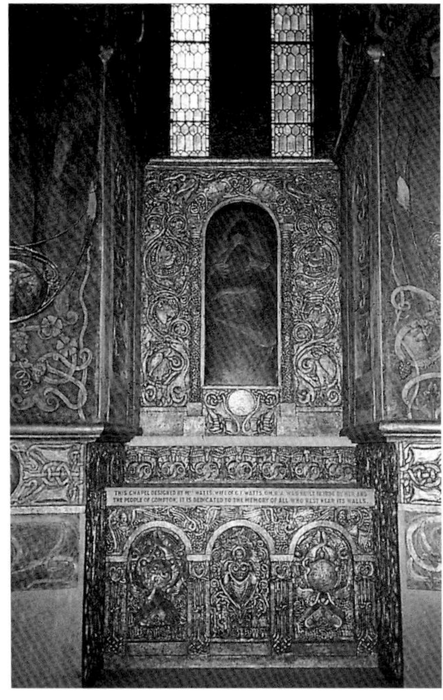

232   *The All-Pervading*, 1904, above the chapel altar.

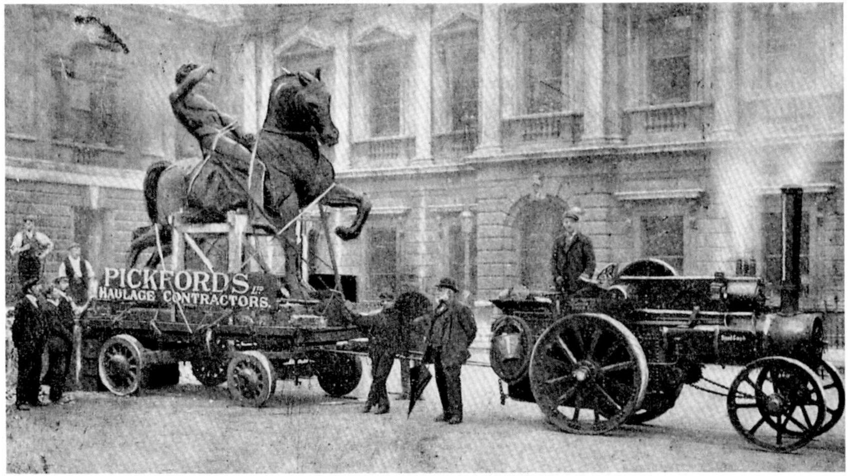

233   *Physical Energy* on Pickford's trolley in the quadrangle of Burlington House, 1904.

sive – supercilious and self-conscious [,] Mr Watts has given a type of distinction and breeding carried to the point of perfect simplicity and self-forgetfulness.' Neither Watts nor Lily was an aristocrat. *Lilian* was simply a loving family portrait, but the artist, having forged a unique path all his life to raise the standard of English art, would have appreciated Fry's appraisal as 'intensely English' in character.[90] At the New Gallery, Watts's five pictures – the small *Progress* (he was still working on the Limnerslease canvas); *A Fugue*; *Whence? Whither?*; the larger *Endymion* – more ethereal but not as fine as its classic predecessor – and *Prometheus*, stood head and shoulders above the rest.[91]

Watts was pretty tired, often in bed, but determined to finish *Physical Energy* in the summer. He doubted the success of the unfinished bronze now that the object of Art was to reproduce facts, rather than to suggest poetic ideals.[92] Studying the statue outside the Academy, however, he realized it was more finished than he had thought, and he saw how to improve the British version.[93]

On 16 May, Watts attended Joachim's Diamond Jubilee concert at the Queen's Hall. Sir Hubert Parry, Director of the Royal College of Music read the address, and afterwards the Prime Minister Arthur Balfour presented the violinist with his portrait painted by Sargent. The picture stood in the centre of the platform. As Watts rose from his front-row seat for a closer look, the audience began to clap. He assumed that the applause heralded the violinist's return, so he dashed back to his seat and refused to believe they were greeting him. That night he saw many friends for the last time.[94]

Returning to London on 25 May to make a change to *Physical Energy*, Watts took the rider off the horse, threw back his head and raised his outlook towards a higher viewpoint.[95] The weather was poor, and when his physician Doctor Archibald Keightley arrived on 4 June he was hard at work but beginning a chill. The artist had a slight sore throat and retired to bed early. He would never enter his studio again.[96] His chill developed into bronchitis and pneumonia, and Mary woke in the early hours of 16 June to find her husband in great pain, 'the whole face truly seeing the borderland between life and eternal life'. Both thought he was dying. 'I am not frightened', said Signor. 'I don't believe in the powers of darkness. *I believe in the Everlasting Light*.' He rallied the next day. Still weak and restless, he longed to tackle the rider's back, but he remained in bed, promising the doctor that he would paint his portrait if he recovered.

'I love art, and as I lie here, the present condition of it makes me miserable – The modern conception of art seems to me like the theology of the authorized creed, full of sound and fury signifying nothing.'[97] For decades he had celebrated death in his art. Now, lying beneath *Love Triumphant*, he summoned Mary and Gerry Liddell to his bedside to tell them what he had seen, but when he tried to talk of the 'glorious state . . . no place . . . no people, myself the only blot', he could only cover his face with his hands, moved to tears by its unutterable beauty.

> The Book of Creation was open – I saw the breath of the Creator acting on nebulous matter so that agitating waves and revolving lines flow from this in all directions and yet I saw that in all this violence and convulsion there was a restraining Force. The converging lines were evolution and the apparent conflict was a necessary part. Last night I was in one

of those spaces where collision had not taken place, all was clear and splendid.

'*Now I see that great Book. I see that great light*', he cried. 'Can we ever forget his face,' wondered Mary, 'So beautiful, spiritual, enraptured.'[98] 'It is not that I have no beliefs', he said, trying to describe that vivid Insight – 'but that I believe nothing is true that is not simple – If there is the Power that asks belief of its creatures, it cannot ask them to believe that which they cannot comprehend.' Again he rallied and asked to see Lord Grey, but when the earl came he was asleep.[99]

Gerry wired daily bulletins to Lord Wemyss. Signor asked for a peach; Lily ran to ask Val, and Gerry searched four shops. Shannon, hearing their quest, bought him seven.[100] Watts drifted in and out of consciousness. On Tuesday 28 June, he appeared to be on the mend. 'Oh Mary I have so *craved* for you.' But his temperature soared, the pain was intense and on the Thursday, as she buried her face in his hand, he said, 'There is nothing more to be said – nothing to explain, only goodbye goodbye goodbye – Bless everyone.' Startled, he called out, 'Where I am?' Huskily, his wife sobbed, 'Beloved you are quite safe.' 'Sister!' he cried, 'I cannot see faces distinctly – I want to see faces.' Someone had left a bunch of white flowers on the doorstep. George Duckworth arrived, knelt beside Signor and kissed his hand. He called for Lord Wemyss, who received a telegram: 'HE IS DYING QUITE QUIETLY – NO PAIN.' Mary moistened his parched mouth. They had slept apart during his illness, but now he called to her at midnight and they lay together hand in hand.[101] At 6.30 in the morning, he asked her to read to him. She had no book near by, so she began to recite the opening verses of *In Memoriam*. Lily ran out to borrow a copy. Hunt lent his precious first edition:

> Strong Son of God, immortal Love
> Whom we, that have not seen thy face,
> By faith, and faith alone, embrace,
> Believing where we cannot prove . . .[102]

The artist called the Messengers of Death to lead him away, crying again and again, 'Why, Why don't they come?' At 3.15 in the afternoon of Friday, 1 July 1904, he died.

Newspapers throughout the world mourned the passing of the 'Grand Old Man of English Art', 'The English Titian', 'England's Michael Angelo', 'The Great Symbolist', 'The Last of our Great Victorians'. The King sent his condolences.[103] Lord Wemyss instructed Henry Poole to arrange for casts to be taken of the artist's head and hands; and Alexander Fisher kept watch as Cantoni carried them out, promising in broken Italian English, that his death mask would be a '*splendide caste*' (fig. 234).[104] While his nurses were sent to Limnerslease to relax and 'see what a mark his life had made there', he lay beneath a pall in the barrel-vaulted studio. On Sunday evening, Randall Davidson, now the Archibishop of Canterbury, held a service in the studio and the choir from Holy Trinity sang 'Oh Strength and Stay' and 'Oh God our hope in ages past'.[105] Walter Crane sent a memorial sonnet.[106] Watts was cremated at Woking and his remains placed in a symbolic casket that Mary had exhibited the year before, with no thought

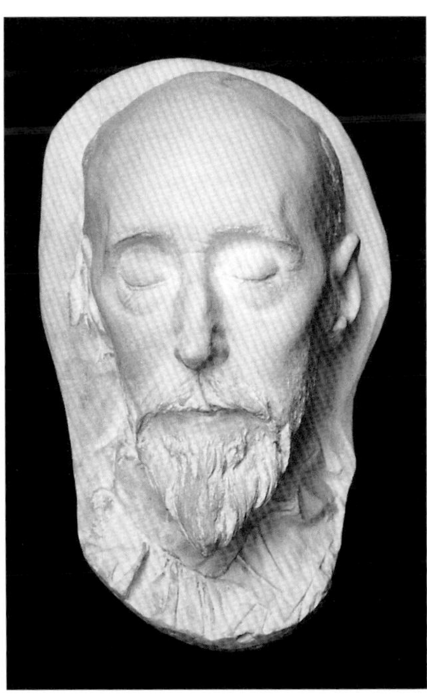

234  Death mask, 1904 (Watts Gallery).

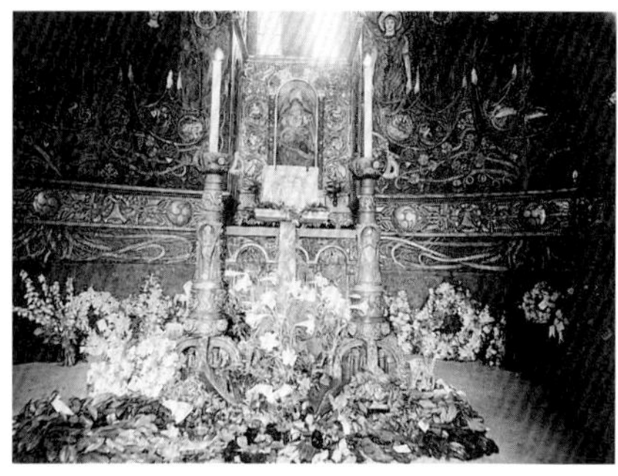

235   Watts's ashes inside the casket modelled by his wife on the stand above wreaths of flowers in the chapel at Compton, July 1904.

of its destiny, and since painted in the wax colours that would character- ize her pottery. The casket lay on the altar steps at the chapel in Compton, and the following morning stood on the central pedestal, surrounded by masses of flowers, lilies and wreaths (fig. 235), among them tributes from the Royal Academy, Eton, Charterhouse and the Art-Workers' Guild. Mary cut a wreath of poet's laurel, 'the victor's laurel'. Every day for seven days the chapel bell tolled at 3.15 until 3.30: 'Be my voice, neither feared nor forgotten.'[107]

On Thursday 7 July, the nation mourned his passing at St Paul's cathe- dral, where representatives from every walk of life, every social scale, sang 'Now the labourer's task is o'er'. The voice of his beloved Tennyson, 'Peace! Come away' from *In Memoriam*, set to music by Sir Charles Stanford, reverberated in a low affecting tribute, a luscious whisper of music and poetry that infused his art. Apprentice potters sang it again the next day at a memorial service in the mysterious pantheistic Watts Chapel, which like his pictures symbolized the timeless, universal spirit of humanity.[108]

Wearing his watch over her heart, Mary began to reply to some 500 friends, sitters, and strangers who wrote of his loss to the world, which was richer for his example.[109] In life and art Watts had challenged constraint and opened the eyes of his nation. Young and old, giants of the age, actresses, soldiers, bird-lovers, reformers, poets, painters, dukes, and labourers, felt strangely special in his company, inspired by his transcen- dental vision. The *Daily Telegraph* described Watts as 'the greatest of England's modern poet-painters – the greatest in aspiration, if not in achievement'. His pictures were not as finely finished as those of his dearest friends, Leighton and Burne-Jones, but his imaginative scope was far greater. 'If Watts failed at all his were brilliant failures, for his life-work stands forth as a monument of high thought, lofty purpose, and noble achievement,' concluded the *Westminster Gazette*. Quick to deride igno- rant critics, he summoned the press to spread his intellectual message. 'Men like Watts, men like all the great heroes, only breathe in public. What is the use of abusing a man for publicity when he utters in public the true and the enduring things?' Ellen Terry marked the passage in her copy of Chesterton's *G. F. Watts*.[110]

'Nature has been kind to me. She has made me respond to whatever is highest', Watts had said.[111] In so doing, he had forged a controversial new path throughout the Victorian era, to elevate his countrymen through art, but died in despair at the direction of twentieth century art. Yet, Picasso had recently reflected the imagery of *Hope* in his Blue Period paintings of *Life* and *The Old Guitarist*. Autotypes from Watts's Symbolist works were to hang in the opening scene of George Bernard Shaw's latest drama *Man and Superman*.[112] His early imaginative paintings had foreshadowed Continental Symbolism and *The Sower of the Systems* would herald future abstraction.

'Alas! the dear old "Signor" is dead', Ashbee wrote in his journal. 'To me he was always one of the fixed stars in the darkness. A kind of great redemption did he seem to give to an ugly and cruel age. Future times when they judge the Victorian period will perhaps say – "this is what Morris said of you, but because of Watts you shall go away honoured!"'[113]

# Epilogue

The future of his Compton gallery was thrown into confusion because the works it was built to house had been willed to provincial galleries, and Watts had not amended the will. Within days of his death, Hugh Lane was pleading for an 'Immortal' Watts picture for Ireland.[1] Mary took the case to the Attorney General. The three senior art experts, Sir Edward Poynter as the president of the Royal Academy, Sir Charles Holroyd as keeper of the Tate Gallery and Lionel Cust as director of the National Portrait Gallery, were appointed trustees of the Watts Gallery. From over one hundred paintings they selected just eight for the National Galleries of Scotland and Ireland, and for Manchester, Norwich and Nottingham. Come fashion or fad, Watts inspires a curious loyalty, for there have been only four curators of the Watts Gallery at Compton since the young artist, Charles Thompson, was appointed in 1906. An endowment of £6,000 from the artist's will still funds the gallery, and its trustees continue to represent the three art institutions.[2]

Alexander Fisher supervised the repositioning of the head and arms of *Physical Energy* in line with Watts's intended final change.[3] This supreme example of the Wattsian ideal, captioned by the *Daily Graphic* as 'London's Finest Statue', aroused ugly controversy when it was erected in Kensington Gardens in September 1907 (fig. 236). When the *Daily Telegraph* described it as a replica of the Rhodes Memorial, Mary dashed off a letter to the editor. On the contrary, the unfinished South African group was the equivalent of an engraver's proof, to which the artist 'returns, and works to perfect before publishing',[4] as Watts and Tennyson had viewed their work. To complete the statue of the poet, Mary modelled the 'flower in the crannied wall' upon which his gaze is directed. Lady Brownlow unveiled the *Tennyson* outside Lincoln cathedral in July 1905 (fig. 239).[5] Had Watts lived to see its 'resurrection' in bronze, thought Mary (he regarded the clay or gesso model as 'life' and a plaster cast 'death') its 'cosmic dignity of line' would have pleased him. The 'life' models of both statues are housed today at the Watts Gallery.[6]

Rooke was commissioned to record Watts's studio in watercolour before Little Holland House was sold.[7] His last unfinished self-portrait stood on Sir Joshua Reynolds's easel at the exhibition *Works by the Late George Frederick Watts*, RA OM, which opened at the Royal Academy in January 1905 and transferred to Edinburgh, Manchester and Newcastle, reaching Dublin in January 1906.[8] 'He is like a great eagle up above all of us, the

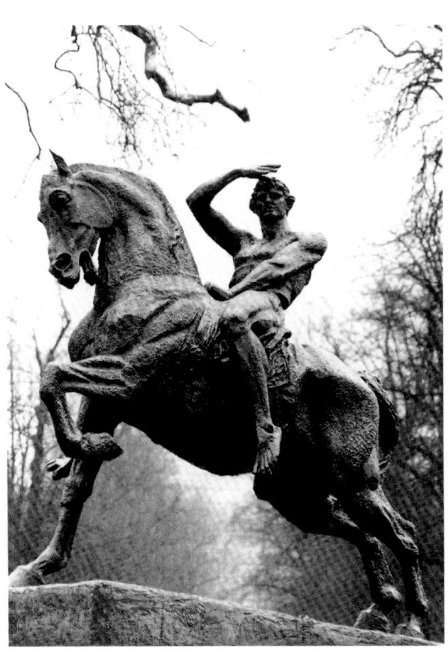

236 *Physical Energy* in Kensington Gardens.

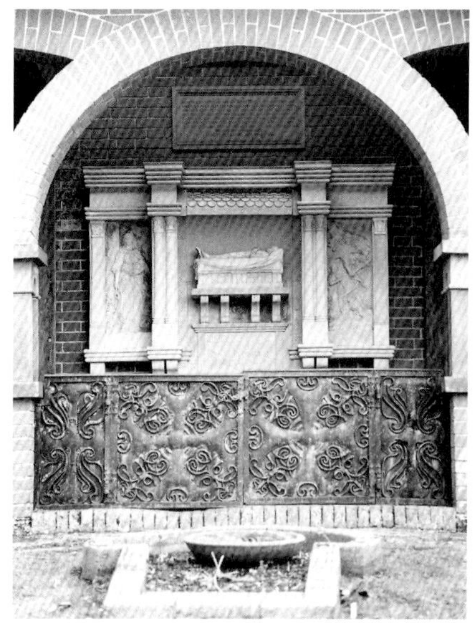

237   Watts's grave at Compton. The lower terracotta surround was designed in 1904 by Mary Seton Watts and the upper plaques in the cloister were modelled by Thomas Wren in 1907 after designs by Watts.

rest mere barn-door fowls and sparrows on the housetops only', Holroyd enthused.[9] That the memorial exhibition overlapped with Whistler's at the New Gallery sparked a lively debate. Whereas Fry attacked Whistler for attempting to separate art from life and supported Watts, Vanessa and Virginia Stephen abhorred Watts's work. Now living in Bloomsbury, they had broken away from their dark Victorian past after the death of their father. 'The Watts show is *atrocious*: my last illusion is gone. Nessa and I walked through the rooms almost in tears', wrote Virginia. Vanessa, appalled that Watts seemed to have neglected the art of painting, using it only as 'a half-learned language', penned an unpublishable critique, preferred Whistler and delighted in the abuse of *Physical Energy*.[10]

A terracotta birdbath was placed on Watts's grave, for his feathered friends to quench their thirst (fig. 237). In 1906 Mary designed a cloister to be built behind the grave, to house memorials to her husband and friends; and her Compton Potters' Arts Guild erected a tall symbolic cross at Limnerslease, on 'His Pilgrim's Way'.[11] The apprentices, otherwise destined to go into service, were sent by their families for an undreamed-of opportunity to become artist-potters. Bewildered at first, boarding under the lingering shadow of the world-famous artist, they enjoyed a healthy, rounded education essential to the Wattsian ideal. Visitors from all over the world making pilgrimages to Compton to see his strange cosmic visions, would find what a German newspaper described as 'The English Bayreuth'.[12]

Having fought tooth and nail to prevent colour reproductions being made from Watts's paintings in the national collection, Mary invited Emery Walker to produce negative plates and set up an etching press in a studio behind the gallery. Fine photogravure prints, faithful to his colours and printed on Japanese vellum under Thompson's supervision, sold for three

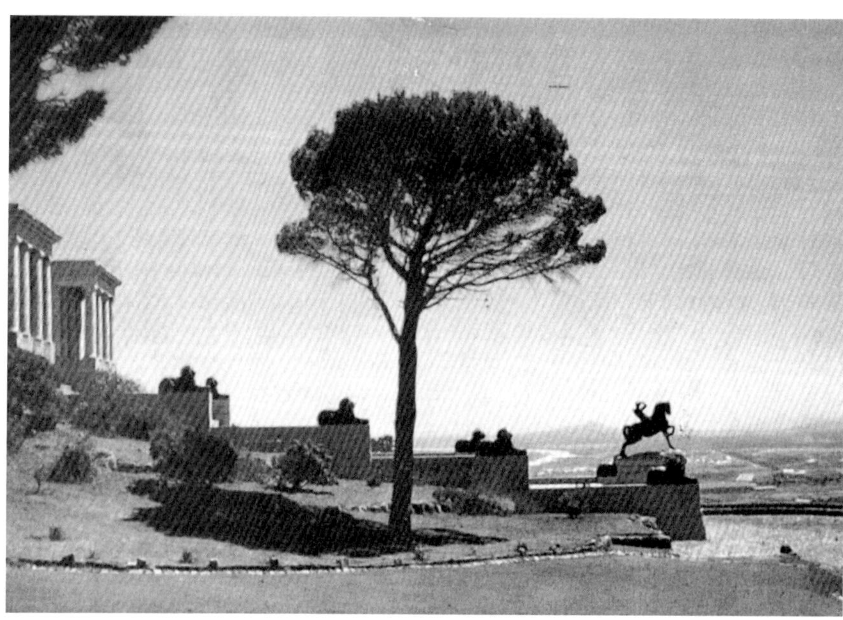

238   *Physical Energy* fronts the Rhodes Memorial (designed by Herbert Baker 1906–16) at Groote Schuur overlooking Table Bay, South Africa.

guineas at Compton and the Fine Arts Society in Bond Street. The Irish poet W. B. Yeats, who gave a lecture on Watts at the Dublin exhibition, kept a reproduction of *William Morris* over his mantelpiece, 'its grave wide-open eyes, like the eyes of some dreaming beast, remind me of the open eyes of Titian's *Ariosto*'.[13]

There was no sense of Wattsian 'organ chord swelling and powerful but unmodulated' in Sir Charles Stanford's sixth symphony *In memoriam G. F. Watts*, performed at the Queen's Hall on 19 January 1906. Mahler's eighth symphony of 1907 would have been more 'in keeping', as the artist would say. Mary installed a terracotta memorial to Watts and more heroic plaques at Postman's Park,[14] which a bronze *Minotaur* by Michael Ayrton overlooked in the middle of the twentieth century and was the setting for the play *Closer*, by Patrick Marber, performed at the Royal National Theatre in London and on Broadway in 1997.[15]

Emilie Barrington rushed into print with *G. F. Watts: Reminiscences*, an intimate, tactless record, published in Jeanie's memory by June 1905. Her insight during her reign as the artist's assistant in the 1880s is illuminating, but her assumptions after his marriage mislead.[16] Mary was preparing the definitive account of her husband's life, a three-volume biography, with his writings: *George Frederic Watts: The Annals of an Artist's Life*, published in 1912. She did not read her adversary's memoir until the year before, when she inscribed the title-page 'BY A POISONOUS SNAKE', made furious notes and unwisely omitted from her own work much with which Emilie Barrington was associated.[17] Lily married Michael Chapman, the son of Lutyens's first patron.[18] Her son Ronald, Superintendent of the Radcliffe Camera, Oxford, produced a definitive study of Watts, *The Laurel and the Thorn*, in 1945, followed in 1975 by *England's Michelangelo*, written by Wilfrid Blunt, a cousin of the amorist and curator of the Watts Gallery. Roger Fry came to lecture on Watts at Compton in 1909,[19] but the following year launched his seminal exhibition, *Manet and the Post-Impressionists*, at the Grafton Galleries, which took London by storm and diverted public attention from Watts.[20] Virginia Woolf (née Stephen) explained in her biography of Fry that the critic considered the transition from Watts to Picasso a natural continuation. Her comedy *Freshwater*, caricaturing the lives of her great aunt Julia Cameron, Tennyson, Watts and Ellen Terry, was enacted by family and friends at Bloomsbury parties in 1923 and revised for a performance in Vanessa Bell's studio in 1935.[21]

The artist Walter Sickert, writing in 1910, clearly admired Watts's portraits but was appalled by his 'turgid confusion of thought [which] lead him into the perpetration of such senseless monstrosities.' Sixteen years later, Sickert acknowledged 'Watts holds his own with time' and that 'A very curious thing about Watts is that his pictures on a large scale seem naturally to justify that large scale. They are better than the drawings for them, a thing that can be said of few paintings.' His late monumental figure-painting clearly influenced the sculptor Henry Moore.[22]

If the *cognoscenti* turned up their noses at Watts, Mary ignored them and made shopkeepers charge twopence – double the going rate – for post-cards of Watts in his studio. He had never been a slave to fashion; and she knew his light would shine again. But when, in 1931, the son of a former sitter let her know that he wished to sell his father's portrait, she replied that she could not afford it and, much as she would like to, could not rec-

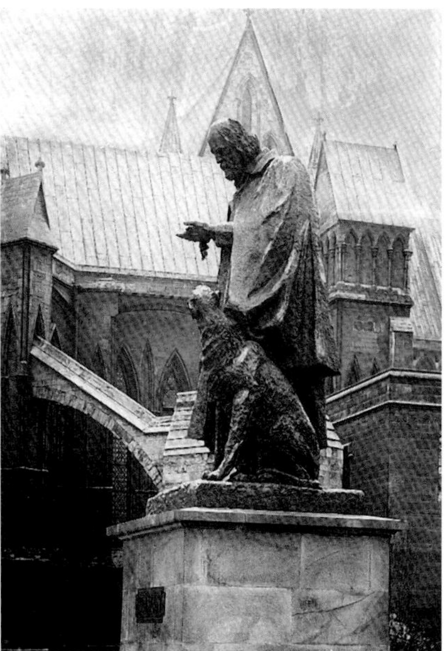

239   Watts's memorial to the poet laureate outside Lincoln Cathedral, *c*.1905.

ommend a purchaser, 'My husband's paintings are *no where* in the markets of today – I do not mind, except for those who wish to sell his paintings, because I feel a perfect trust in their future value.'[23] Mary died in 1938. Still today, the enchanting arts and crafts gallery she built to house them continues to offer an intriguing interlude to ramblers strolling along the Pilgrims' Way, and attracts ever more visitors worldwide.

In 1939 Lily sold a picture of herself, *In the Highlands*, for £7; in November 1999 it made £12,000. As most of Watts's major Symbolist works were presented as gifts to national and international galleries, few come on to the market. However, the American *Love and Life*, which was transferred from the White House to the National Collection of Fine Arts, Smithsonian Institution in Washington in 1832, was sold at Sotheby's, New York, on 21 March 1987 for $130,000 (£77,845) and at Christie's, London, in 1998 for £370,000. A large *Hope* went for a record £869,000 at Sotheby's on 26 November 1986; and the small half-length *Orpheus and Eurydice* for which Madeline Wyndham modelled rose from £62,000 in 1992 to £180,000 in 2003.[24]

'Our high estimate of Watts and his paintings I still feel to be justified', William Rothenstein recalled. His pictures were uneven. They were didactic, 'yet he is likely to take his place finally as one of the most richly endowed artists of the English school . . . his name evokes a luminous world of his own creation. This in itself is a proof of his genius,' continued Rothenstein. 'Watts may have painted more tedious pictures than men less copiously endowed, but he painted more splendid ones . . . Watts spoke to me more eloquently than did any other living artist.'[25] *The Times*, reviewing The Tate Gallery's partial reappraisal of Watts in the winter of 1954–55, noted that 'the cosmic visions which draw so many people to Compton would, it has evidently been felt, be too much for the cultivated visitor to the Tate'.[26] By 1974, when interest in Victorian art had begun to rise, only discerning critics noticed the Whitechapel Art Gallery's reappraisal in its exhibition *G. F. Watts: A Nineteenth Century Phenomenon*. To Marina Vaizey, writing in the *Arts Review*, his social realist pictures, landscapes and early works, were preferable to the 'inept and lifeless' Symbolist paintings. 'The art of this eminent Victorian is at its worst . . . And yet, Watts was also surprisingly daring: not in visible result, but in method and inspiration.'[27] His radical treatment of the nude was celebrated at the launch of Tate Britain, *Exposed: The Victorian Nude* in 2001, after his reemergence in the Tate Gallery's centenary exhibition of 1997, *The Age of Rossetti, Burne-Jones and Watts: Symbolism and Britain*. 'George Frederic Watts . . . is a revelation. I found him more impressive here than either Burne-Jones or Rossetti,' Richard Cork wrote in *The Times*. 'Anticipating science-fiction cinema in its wide-screen vision of turbulence in the cosmos, *Chaos* proves that Watts, at his best, does not deserve to be accused of Victorian vapidity.'[28] The artist himself would have kept an eager eye on unfolding developments as science unravels the secrets of the universe from its creation to the present day.

# APPENDIX I  A Projected Scheme for Frescoes Representing the Progress of the Cosmos

*Based on Watts's original manuscript before 1847 (NPG, ff. 54–60 and quoted in Mary Seton Watts,* George Frederic Watts: The Annals of an Artist's Life, *1912, vol. I, 100–04), with his later additions in parentheses, the scheme later known as 'The House of Life', was described by Mary as 'the ambition of one half of his life and the regret of the other'.*

The ceiling to [be] covered with the uniform blue of space, upon which should be painted the Sun the Earth, & the Moon, as it is by their several revolutions in connection with & depending upon each other that we have a distinct notion of & are able to measure (& estimate the magnitude of) Time. The progress of Time & its destroying (consequent) effects I would here illustrate for the purpose of conveying the lesson, the present moment is all that can be called our own &c. I would represent this globe with symbolical figures of the antagonistic forces Attraction & Repulsion, & half shadowed by progressing Time –

I would then give (perhaps upon half of the ceiling which might be divided by a gold band upon which the Zodiac might be painted) a nearer view of the Earth; & by a number of gigantic figures stretched out at length, represent a range of mountain, & typify the bony structure or skeleton. This I would make very grand & impressive in order to imply the comparative insignificance of man. The to us most important of the constellations should shine out of the deep ultramarine firmament. Silence & Mighty Repose should be stamped upon the character & disposition of my giants; & revolving centuries & cycles should glide in the form of female figures of great beauty beneath the crags upon which the mighty forms should lie, to indicate (as compared with its effect upon man & his works) the

non effect of Time upon them [*Titans*, a detail from *Chaos*].

Then I would begin with man himself, trace him through his moral & political life, First the hunter stage; gaining through the medium of his glimmering yet superior intelligence, advantages over the stronger yet inferior animals; almost his equal. Next the pastoral state, his intelligence more developed, to the consequent improvement in his condition, weak & serviceable animals domesticated, reclaimed by his intelligent care, the stronger & more savage subdued by the force of his will aided by all conquering intelligence. This is the golden age (the age of poetry). Of experience is born tradition of tradition, poetry, love performing its natural & legitimate function, instruction. This portion of the work might be rendered most beautiful since in this period of the existence of society we may perhaps reasonably suppose the human animal enjoyed the greatest amount of real happiness (equally removed from the penalties of ambition and degradation of a precarious and merely animal existence).

Next should be man the Tyrant, the insidious oppressor, & the Slave, the dweller in Cities, The Egyptians should raise the Pyramids, illustrating the story of Joseph & his brethren, from Egypt we would accompany the Jews of Palestine until the history becomes identified the Assyrians, history of that country principal illustration, Fall of Nineveh & Sardanapalus, History of Persia, principle illustrations, Cyre & Croesus, – India its mythology animal & . . . Greece, Mythology; general history, principal illustration, building of its Parthenon, portraits of the principal heroes.

. . . & here may be introduced the episode of Job, Alexander, Darius, Rome, history, illustrating Scipio, Labis, [maners] oration, combats of gladiators & wild animals in the amphitheatre, Achtesteus, Naval architects Seafight, Antony & Augustus, – Founding of the Christian era ... simply as a matter of history ... setting up the cross – destruction of Jerusalem, General history during the domination of the Popes, Gothic, invasion of Rome, Mahomet, Saracens ... history of Gaul – France, England, Peter the Hermit, crusades, Middle Ages.

*According to Mary, 'As the idea developed in his mind the scheme became more abstract, and less realistic and historic; it is certain that as the mythology of the races was traced by him [Mary read to Watts while researching ancient civilizations for a symbolic ceiling], its place would have been prominent, and possibly the whole scheme would have developed into the history of the progress of the spiritual side of man's mind; and he would simply have niched the men whom he considered most representative of all forward movement.'*

# Appendix II   A Poem by Watts Preserved by Ellen Terry

*The poem is preserved at Smallhythe Place (National Trust)*

Oh God, oh Father, by whatever name
Mortals upon Thee call in their distress
Or hail in their Thanksgiving;

If Thou dost look upon the little things of Earth
Which thou hast made; oh help my weakness
And illumine the darkness of my path
By the faint light of nature here I grope
I grope, and seek in vain a certain ray,
Far off I see the light but vainly strive to pierce
The gloom around; quicken though my sight,
And mould this unform'd spirit with form
Here like a little child I meekly ask the things
I deem most worthy, giving; oh instruct,
A better choice to make, and more complete,
Efface the aimless lives with which
The evil passions have deform'd my darken'd soul,
Expand & purify it to receive and to reflect the light,
Purge me of little longings, calm my anxious heart
Whose boding fears contract my spirits' room,
Broaden my sympathies, and strengthen my resolve,

That small misgivings may not gnaw my peace,
Give diligence and modesty to seek the truth,
Give steadfastness to hold thee right my
My conscience owns; with healthy eagerness
Mine object to pursue, with healthy cheerfulness
When failure spreads its gloom, & clogs the way
And with the knowledge of my littleness
To have a due reliance on myself;
And walk with firmness when I needs must think
My foot is planted on the solid ground,
Give me to know how far the serpents' while
May with the humourlessness of doves combine,
But if this knowledge be withheld from me,
Then rather let me be through life a pray
Than be myself a snare,
More I would ask, but know not how to ask
Except to cry for light, more light, more light!
Am I not weak within thine hands, mere clay!
To fashion as thou wilt! Oh take me then
My hear, my soul, my mind and all my being
And show me ever where my steps should tread
That when the great account shall come to be
Balanced & squared, I shall not dread the call.

APPENDIX III   An Outline by Watts for *Cain* as an Epic, Cantata or Oratorio

*Quoted in Mary Seton Watts,* George Frederic Watts: The Annals of an Artist's Life, *1912, vol. I, 258–59.*

IF I WERE A POET and musician like Wagner, I could make a fine cantata or oratorio of the subject. The first act would be to describe the innocence of the two brothers in their boyhood, the first shadow of the stain in the character of Cain just indicated; then, as the story grew, to mark the widening difference between them – the angelic guilelessness of Abel and the darkening of Cain's heart through the sin of jealousy, the ever-increasing desire to make himself greater than Abel ending in the madness of his wrath and the murder of Abel. The denouncing spirits, as I have painted them, represent the voices of conscience reproaching him with the many sins that culminated in the murder. The brand is set upon him; he is shut out from contact with all creation; he has closed the avenue of sympathy with his fellow-men; as he decides that they shall be unknown to him he becomes unknown to them. The brand, forbidding human vengeance ('No man may slay him'), constitutes the most terrible part of his punishment; he is driven out from all contact with created things – unseen, unacknowledged, unknown. Not only are his fellow-men unconscious of his presence, but all animate nature has cast him out: no bird or living creature acknowledges his being. For him no bird sings, no flower blooms, evil passions haunt and follow him, making discords in his ear; but all the while, one voice, as of an angel, is hear, and more and more prevails, until worn and weary nature can bear no more, and surrendering to the Voice, he returns to Abel's altar, there to give himself up a sacrifice; and there the angel removes the curse and he dies forgiven. I should have liked to have made a sort of psychological study of it all, not only of Cain and of Abel, but of the human beings who passed by Cain during his term of isolation.

# Abbreviations

<table>
<tr><td>A</td><td>Mary Seton Watts, George Frederic Watts: The Annals of an Artist's Life, 3 vols, 1912</td></tr>
<tr><td>AAD</td><td>Archive of Art and Design</td></tr>
<tr><td>ATRd</td><td>Diaries of Lady Ritchie, née Anne Thackeray</td></tr>
<tr><td>BCd</td><td>Diaries of Blanche Clogstoun</td></tr>
<tr><td>BL</td><td>British Library, London</td></tr>
<tr><td>B/L</td><td>Mrs Russell Barrington, The Life, Letters and Work of Frederic Leighton, 2 vols, 1906</td></tr>
<tr><td>B/W</td><td>Mrs Russell Barrington, G. F. Watts: Reminiscences, 1905</td></tr>
<tr><td>B/Y</td><td>Beinecke Rare Book and Manuscript Library, Yale University, New Haven, Conn.</td></tr>
<tr><td>Bod.</td><td>Bodleian Library, Oxford</td></tr>
<tr><td>Cat.P.</td><td>MSW Catalogue of the Portraits of G. F. Watts</td></tr>
<tr><td>Cat.S.</td><td>MSW Catalogue of the Subject Pictures of G. F. Watts</td></tr>
<tr><td>CDGd</td><td>Diaries of Lady Duff Gordon</td></tr>
<tr><td>CRAd</td><td>Diaries of C. R. Ashbee</td></tr>
<tr><td>GDGd</td><td>Diaries of Georgina Duff Gordon</td></tr>
<tr><td>D</td><td>MSW Diaries</td></tr>
<tr><td>DEVd</td><td>Diaries of the Duke of Devonshire</td></tr>
<tr><td>Dn</td><td>MSW Diary extracts</td></tr>
<tr><td>EBd</td><td>Diaries of Eliza Bagehot</td></tr>
<tr><td>EBJ</td><td>Sir Edward Coley Burne-Jones</td></tr>
<tr><td>EIB</td><td>Mrs Russell Barrington</td></tr>
<tr><td>ET</td><td>Ellen Terry</td></tr>
<tr><td>ETMM</td><td>Smallhythe Place</td></tr>
<tr><td>FC</td><td>Fondation Custodia, Institut Néerlandais, Paris</td></tr>
<tr><td>Fiche</td><td>Courtauld Institute microfiches of GFW correspondence (WG, NPG and Tate Britain)</td></tr>
<tr><td>Fitzwilliam</td><td>Fitzwilliam Museum, Cambridge</td></tr>
<tr><td>FL</td><td>Sir Frederic Leighton, PRA, later Lord Leighton of Stretton</td></tr>
<tr><td>GBJ</td><td>Georgiana Burne-Jones</td></tr>
<tr><td>GDGd</td><td>Diaries of Georgina Duff Gordon</td></tr>
<tr><td>GFW</td><td>George Frederic Watts</td></tr>
<tr><td>GG</td><td>Grosvenor Gallery</td></tr>
<tr><td>HAIA</td><td>Home Arts and Industries Association</td></tr>
<tr><td>Harpton</td><td>Harpton Court Papers at the National Library of Wales, Cardiff</td></tr>
</table>

| | |
|---|---|
| HFTd | Diaries of Hester Fraser Tytler |
| HH | The Holland House Papers |
| HR | Harry Ransom Humanities Research Center, Austin, Texas |
| HT | Sir William Hamo Thornycroft |
| HTd | Diaries of Hamo Thornycroft (L/HM) |
| Huntington | The Huntington Library, San Marino, Calif. |
| IMP | International Museum of Photography, New York |
| JCd | Diaries of Julia Cartwright (Mrs Henry Ady) |
| JMC | Julia Margaret Cameron |
| LHH | Little Holland House |
| L/HM | Leeds Museums & Galleries: Henry Moore Institute & Archive |
| LMA | London Metropolitan Archives |
| M | Mary Seton Fraser Tytler, later Mary Seton Watts |
| MAd | Diaries of Lady Marion Alford |
| Mc | Commonplace Book of Mary Seton Fraser Tytler |
| MEd | Diaries of Mary, Lady Elcho |
| M/JRL | John Rylands University Library of Manchester |
| MM | Metropolitan Museum of Art and archives |
| NAAAI | National Association for the Advancement of Art and its Application to Industry |
| NAL | National Art Library, Victoria and Albert Museum, London |
| NAS | National Archives of Scotland, Edinburgh |
| NG | National Gallery, London |
| NPG | National Portrait Gallery, London |
| RA | Royal Academy of Arts, London |
| RA/L | Royal Academy of Arts, *Frederic Leighton 1830–1896*, 1996 |
| RBKC | Royal Borough of Kensington and Chelsea Local Studies Library, London |
| RC | Ronald Chapman, *The Laurel and the Thorn: A Study of G. F. Watts*, 1945 |
| RCA | Royal Cambrian Academy of Art |
| Tate | Tate Gallery/Tate Britain/Tate Publishing |
| TRC | Tennyson Research Centre, Lincoln |
| V&A | Victoria and Albert Museum, London |
| V&A/MA | GFW papers in the V & A Archive, MA/1/W882 |
| WCA | Westminster City Archives, London |
| WG | Watts Gallery, Compton, Surrey |
| WGc | Watts Gallery cuttings book |
| WSBd | Wilfrid Scawen Blunt diaries (Fitzwilliam Museum, Cambridge) |

# Notes

## 1 Ambitious Youth (1817–1843)

1 *Hereford Journal*, 7 June 1815; D, 2 February 1893; A, 1: 87.

2 On 7 June 1816, the British Government paid Lord Elgin £35,000 for the sculpture. Michaelis, 1908, 39; Asleson, 1998, 167; Joliffe, 1990, 49.

3 The St Mary-le-Bone Church register records GFW's birth as 22 February 1817, baptism as 30 March and spells his second name with a 'k'. His date and time of birth inscribed in his prayerbook was 2 o'clock on 23 February, the date he celebrated. M quotes 1 o'clock that day in A, 1: 7. He spelled his name without a 'k' in the St Barnabas marriage register to Ellen Terry. Letter to F. G. Stephens, 4 March 1894 (Bod., MSS Don.. e.87; ff. 157–58); A, 1: 5.

4 GFW's father, who returned to Hereford offering his services as a superior London musical instrument repairer and tuner, was awarded freedom of the City of Hereford in 1818, the year his father, GFW's grandfather, died.

5 D, 2 February 1893.

6 A, 1: 12–13.

7 A, 1: 10, 14–17; Stead, 1902, 574.

8 D, 2, 12 February 1893; A, 1: 15–16.

9 B/W: 14; A, i: 10–11.

10 D, 4 July 1891; Stephens, 1884, 45.

11 In the early 1830s Behnes took a studio at 13 Osnaburgh Street. D, 4 December 1902; A, 1: 20.

12 A, 1: 21; D, 30 August 1891.

13 *The Times*, 28 June 1830; Richardson, 1966, 354; Anderson, 1972, 603; Joliffe, 1990, 126.

14 A, 1: 22–23; Dn, 25 May 1903.

15 A, 1: 22–25; D, 4 July 1891; B/W: 14, 48.

16 A, 1: 24.

17 Chesterton, 1904, 35 and 42.

18 A, 1: 22, 25; D, 14 February 1893 and 26 February 1898.

19 RA student registers, 1825–1905; York City Art Gallery, 1999, 9; Cat.S.153; J. St Loe Strachey, MS notes of a conversation with GFW, 21 October 1895 (Glasgow University Library, MS Laver S27); A, 1: 25.

20 D, 1 October 1891.

21 A, 1: 33–34; Cat.P.13a.

22 Cat.S.85b; A, 1: 31.

23 The first series of five lithographs was published by S. Knights and printed by W. Sharp in 1837. Wanostrocht, 1845 and 1850; Brodribb, 28–31; RC, 16–17; D, 12 July 1895; A, 1: 31. Five original drawings were presented to the Marylebone Cricket Club in 1895.

24 Ionides, 1927, 6; Ionides, 1996, 56; V&A, 1970; Catsiyannis, 1988, 8–9 and 41; A, 1: 32–33; Dakers, 1999, 7; D, 7 May 1887.

25 Cat.S.71a; Dn, 2 May 1889; Chesterton, 1904, 47; Reynolds, 1966, 11; RA, 1837, cats 257, 328 and 510; RA, *Critiques*, III, 1837.

26 Dn, 24 November 1897, 9 January 1901; Cat.S.23c, 69c, 70a; Cat.P.7b and c, 22b, 57c, 65b–66b, 81b, 82c–84b; A, 1: 27, 34; at RA 1840, cats 7 and 408, GFW also exhibited *Isabella e Lorenzo* from Boccaccio (Cat.S.78b; Cat.P.171c). Other portraits painted from 1836–1843, included those of Richard Edmonds, the Reverend A. O. Wellsted and Alice Spring Rice.

27 V&A, 1925, 63–65; Catsiyannis, 1988; Cat.P.72–77; *Mrs Constantine Ionides*, RA 1842, cat. 407.

28 RA and British Institution records cite GFW's studio addresses at 33 Upper Norton Street (1837), 1 Clipstone Street (1838), 14 Clipstone Street (1840), 41 Robert Street (1841), 48 Cambridge Street (1848). D, 2 September 1896 records a Jarvis canvas inscribed, 'G. F. Watts 14 Roberts Road, Hampstead Road'.

29 Rebuilt 1840–60, to designs by Sir Charles Barry and Augustus Welby Pugin, after the original 800-year-old palace burned down in 1834.

30 From 1843, the Royal Commission of the Fine Arts held competitions for frescoes and paintings to decorate the new Palace of Westminster (1840–60) still under construction, designed by Sir Charles Barry and A. W. N.

Pugin; V&A, 2001, 41; A, I: 41; Janet McLean, 'Watts, Historical Thought and the Schemes of Painting in the 1840s', in Trodd and Brown, 2004, 110.

31  Cat.S.12.

32  D, 3 September 1896; Cat.P.74 and 86; Ionides, 1925, 56–57.

33  Wilson, 2003, 14.

34  A, I: 42; Pope, 1963, V, 1840–46, 280.

35  D. G. Rossetti to Mrs Gabriele Rossetti, 7 July 1843, quoted in Doughty and Wahl, 1965–67, I, 13–1; Marsh, 1999, 12.

36  *Illustrated London News*, 8 July 1843, 18: 'The grand old man, firm as a riven rock, and in his barbaric pride, as grim and as unconquerable as a mastiff, strides through the crowded streets with more the air of victor than of vanquished. Nevertheless, it may be seen the iron has entered into his soul.'

37  *Athenaeum*, 8 July 1843, 633–34, 12 August, 738; *Art-Union*, August 1843, 207.

38  Letter to A. C. Ionides, 15 June 1846 (Fiche 37, A6–9).

39  A, I: 43–44. Family withdrawals were paid to Mr Macdonald, whom GFW later instructed Ionides to send payments for his sisters. He took out £40 3s circular notes on 23 August 1843 and made a last withdrawal on 2 September. John Callcott Horsley, a second prizewinner, who had broken the news to GFW, later asked him to join the group sale.

## 2   Florence (1843–1847)

1   A, I: 46; RC, 22.

2   Noted in his expense book on 11 September.

3   From this tiny sketch, in 1843 GFW painted monumental oil study of a bull's head, and his painting of bulls and peasants, *Dolce Farnienti*.

4   A, I: 47–48; Spielmann, 1905, 19.

5   The British Legation building was referred to as either the Palazzo or Casa Ferroni. A, I: 48; Ilchester, 1937, 320.

6   Journal of the 4th Lord Holland (HH/BL, Add. MS 52099).

7   Cat.P.115b; Nevill, 1906, 37–38. GFW painted a double portrait of Lady Dorothy and her sister Lady Rachel, and made a pencil sketch of the Earl of Orford for Lord Holland.

8   Ilchester, 1937, 320–21; A, I: 48.

9   Carlyle, 1907: 'The light which enlightens, a flowing light-fountain . . . of native original insight, of manhood and heroic nobleness – in whose radiance all souls feel that it is well with them.'

10  A, I: 57.

11  Gaja, 1995, 34; In A, I: 50, M was puzzled by the erroneous reference – as she saw it – to the Venetian artist Paolo Veronese; Lady Holland bequeathed the portrait to the future Edward VII. Cat.P.69a.

12  Gaja, 1995, 55–56; *Holland House Dinner Book* (HH/BL, Add. MS 52164); Gaia suggests the incident took place in 1843 when the Riccis visited, and GFW was absent from dinner. In 1846, however, he painted Countess Walewska's portrait and appears to have used her facial characteristics for Francesca in his earliest known oil painting of *Paolo and Francesca* (1846–47).

13  Letter to Tom Taylor, draft. NPG aII.

14  Ilchester, 1937, 321.

15  A, I: 114.

16  *Pictures at Holland House*, 1904; Erskine 1903, 176–88; A, I: 69; Gaja, 1995, 116.

17  Letter to Tom Taylor.

18  A, I: 51–52.

19  The Hon Francis Charteris (1818–1914) dined at Casa Ferroni on 28 and 31 October 1843. Wemyss, II, 253.

20  'Fresco Painting', *Quarterly Review*, October 1858, 277–325; A, I: 54–55; Vasari, 16. As the picture itself was afterwards damaged by 'restorations', Kirkup's tracing preserved a historic record of Dante before his melancholy exile.

21  Lord Holland to Lady Holland, 21 June 1844 (HH/BL, Add. MS 52031; f. 103).

22  Richard Cottrell, Chamberlain to the Grand Duke of Lucca, lived at Carregi on leaving the service of the Grand Duke; Cat.P.40b; A, I: 66.

23  Benjamin Haydon to Seymour Kirkup, 5 April 1844, quoted in Haydon, 1876, II, 207.

24  Lord Holland to Elizabeth, Lady Holland, March 1844, quoted in Ilchester, 1937, 325.

25  NG, 2003, 23.

26  The ancient fortress was converted into a villa for Cosimo de' Medici by the fifteenth-century architect Michelozzo Michelozzi.

27  Since GFW's day, it has been said that the doctor went mad and threw himself into the well. Acton, 1973, 43, 48, 53, 272.

28  Lord Holland to Lady Holland, 20 and 21 June 1844 (HH/BL, Add. MS 52031; ff. 100 and 103).

29  A, I: 61, 74; D, 21 February 1887; Lord Holland to Lady Holland, 28 June, 3, 4, 7, 16, 17, 20 Jul 1844 (HH/BL, Add. MS 520301).

30  Dn, 15 November 1895; A, I: 72; Lord Holland's Dinner Book (HH/BL, Add. MS 52105).

31  D, 9 December 1891; A, I: 71 and II: 215. 'I would like to have done for modern thought what Michael Angelo did for theological thought.' Lord Holland took GFW on a secret visit to his family mansion Holland House in Kensington, but they dined with Lady Holland at her residence in Stanhope Street.

32  Lord Holland to Lady Holland, 1 September 1844 (HH/BL, Add. MS 52031; f. 150); A, 1: 75.

33  *Ibid.* 28 April 1845 (HH/BL, Add. MS 52032; f. 29).

34  Spielmann, 1905, 20.

35  Lord Holland to Lady Holland, 10 June 1845 (HH/BL, Add. MS 52033; f. 59).

36  *Ibid.* 11 Jun 1845 (HH/BL, Add. MS 52032; f. 64); Gaia, 1995, 68n; *Pictures at Holland House*, 1904, cat. 58.

37  JCd, 8 October 1895; A, 1: 63; Pope-Henessy, 1945, 240.

38  The Villa Rocella had belonged to the Coventry family and was Lady Holland's favourite home. With Lord Walpole, GFW had climbed the smoking volcano of Vesuvius and peered into its crater. A, 1: 74–75; Dn, 1 December 1897.

39  Dn, 20 July 1888; A, 1: 64–65; Cat.S.41b, 54b and 138a; Letter to William Spence 28 November, December 1893, n.d. (Fiche 40, D8–9). GFW described the preparation of *Echo*: 'the general composition first, the figure (a second time painted as a careful skeleton) *then* the skin, all those carefully finished, lastly painted as an oil picture. The tints were prepared by Bonelli in Florence.

40  Gaia, 1995, 67–70. *Buondelmonte* or *The Origin of the Guelph and the Ghibelline Quarrel*, Cat.S.19c. GFW exhibited *Fata Morgana* and *Paolo and Francesca* at the 1848 exhibition of the British Institution, cats 82 and 95.

41  Letter to A. C. Ionides, 15 June 1846 (Fiche 37, A6–9).

42  John Flaxman's outline engravings were published in 1793, reprinted in London in 1853.

43  Letter to Ionides, 7 September 1846 (Fiche 37, A10–12).

44  GFW paid a total of £110 to Mr Macdonald between 1844 and 1845, but made no withdrawals 1845–46.

45  'I have not yet decided upon the subject for your picture, but have been thinking much about it & shall work upon this though at the same time you would oblige me greatly by letting my sisters have £25 upon account. I will ask a friend a Mr Macdonald to call for it', GFW wrote to Ionides on 29 October 1846, asking for a further £25 on 27 December (Fiche 37, B2). *The Ostracism of Aristides*, completed in England and renamed *Aristides and the Shepherd*, was exhibited at Lichfield House in 1851.

46  A Bill promoted in the Lords to enable George IV to divorce Queen Caroline was abandoned in November 1820.

47  CDGd, 12 August 1846 (Harpton: 15591).

48  *Ibid.*, 25 August 1846. *The Greek Slave* was first exhibited at the Graves Gallery in London in 1845. Powers produced a marble replica for the Great Exhibition and six other large-scale versions, Tate, 2001, 113, cat. 46.

49  A, 1: 65–66; CDGd, 2, 3, 19 September 1846; Lady Duff Gordon to Lord Holland, 19 September 1846 (BL, 52034). A photograph of the *Medusa* plaster is recorded in an album relating to his Italian works.

50  CDGd, 3 October 1846.

51  GDGd, 30 August 1846 (Harpton: 2911).

52  *Ibid.* 17 November 1846. GFW's verses on verso of a letter from Lady Duff Gordon (WG).

53  A, 1: 65.

54  Letter to A. C. Ionides, 27 December 1846 (FC, Copy, Fiche 37).

55  Letter to GDG, n.d. (Fiche 40): Alfred stands . . . in the centre of the picture, his foot upon the plank about to spring into the boat. I have endeavoured to give him as much dignity, energy and expression as possible without exaggeration. Long-limbed and springy, he is about the size of the Apollo. The other figures are bigger, so you see my composition is colossal.

'Near to Alfred is a youth who in his excitement rends off his cloak in order to follow his king and leader, by the richness of his dress, this figure evidently belongs to the upper class and I shall endeavour to make that also evident by the elegance of his form and the grace of his action. Next to him is a youth who is probably a peasant. He grasps a ponderous axe and threatens extermination to the whole Danish race. Contrasted with him you see the muscular back of an older man who turns towards his wife who with a child in her arms follows distracted at the thought that her child's father is about to rush into danger. He points upward and encourages her to trust in the righteousness of the cause and the justice of Heaven (Religion and Patriotism). Behind him two lovers are taking a hurried and tender leave, and beyond them a maiden with dishevelled locks (your sister's hair) whose lover or father has already departed with clasped hands is imploring the protection of Heaven.

'In the corner a youth is buckling on armour; his old mother, with trembling hands and tearful eyes, hangs about his neck a cross; the father, feeble, and no longer able to fight his country's battles, gives his sword with one hand, while with the other he bares his chest, points to his wounds, and exhorts his son not to disgrace his father's name and sword; while with glowing cheek and beating heart the young man responds to his father's exhortations with all the ardour characteristic of his age. This I think my most interesting group. I have made the parents old and infirm and the young man but a lad, in order to show that he is the last and youngest, the Benjamin of the family; his brothers, we will suppose, have already fallen fighting against the Dane, defending their country.

'You see I endeavour to preserve a rich base accompaniment of religious and patriotic feeling. A boy, carried away by the general enthusiasm, clenches his little fists, draws his breath, and rushes along with the excited warriors, which helps to indicate the inspiring effect of Alfred's harangue. In the foreground two men lift from the ground a bundle which has been provided by the prudence of the king.

'On the other side of the picture some men, impatient of delay, rush through the water and climb the vessel-side, while others are engaged in getting it under way . . . I have endeavoured to cast my figure [Alfred] in the most heroic mould, simple, grand and elegant. Phidias my adored Phidias shall reign throughout.'

56   Letter to Ionides, 2 January 1847 (Fiche 37, B8).

57   *Ibid.*, 28 January 1847 (Fiche 37); A, I: 77–78. According to Wilfrid Blunt, author of *England's Michelangelo: A Biography of George Frederic Watts*, Ionides quarrelled with Athens University for whom *Panthea* was to be painted. The unfinished picture was painted over and, although the artist returned the fifty pounds, the matter would later become the subject of a financial row. Letter to Aglaia Coronio, 6, 9 Oct 1875; Wilfrid Blunt, 1975, 47–48. On 18 January 1850 GFW repaid £50 to Ionides and from 1859 to 1872 paid him £15 per quarter.

58   Cat.P.134c; Dn, 3 April 1896.

59   Letter to Ionides, 28 January 1847 (FC, Copy, NPG aXIII).

60   Letter to GDG, 9 March 1847 (NPG aXIV, 84–88, Fiche 40); A, I: 85–86.

61   *Ibid.*

62   Queen Victoria gave the first version to Prince Albert. V&A, 2001, 34.

63   GDGd, 28 March 1847. Overbeck's cartoon, designed for Frankfurt, was bought by Prince Albert in 1847.

64   Letter to GDG, 15 April 1847 (Fiche 40); Dn, 15 June 1889.

65   A, I: 86. *Exhibitors of the British Institution.*

66   A, I: 85–86; To GDG, 9 March 1847 (NPG aXIV, 64–65).

67   Letter to Charles Eastlake, Secretary of the Royal Commission of the Fine Arts (10 July 1847) quoted in A, I: 88–89. GFW had also submitted *Echo* as a poetic subject accompanied by a quotation from Keats, but only *Alfred* was accepted. Adjustments requested by Eastlake on 12 July 1847, to make the right leg less straight and left more prominent, were carried out in November.

68   Thackeray, 1911, 92. *Our Street* was first published separately by Chapman Hall for Christmas 1847 (1848), under the pseudonym M. A. Titmarsh.

## 3   A Caged Eagle (1847–1849)

1   Holland House Dinner Book 1847 (HH/BL, Add. MS 52164); letter to GDG, 1847 (NPG aXIV, 92–93).

2   Anon. [Robert Chambers], *Vestiges of the Natural History of Creation*, 1844.

3   Secord, 2000, I, 3, 9, 38 and 168; Wilson, 2003, 104.

4   Carlyle, 1907, 7–14.

5   See Appendix I; Stewart, 1988, 63; A, I: 101–03. B/L, I: 224–25. GFW was inspired by universal concepts underlying the frescoes of Andrea di Cione Orcagna. D, 25 January 1887: Francis Charteris hoped to arrange a commission for the hall.

6   *The Giants*, later called *The Titans*, represented a detail of the introductory chapter to the scheme. Cat.S.25c. Sketchbook (WG 15/5).

7   D, 30 September 1891.

8   Spurred by press criticism of Turner, Ruskin 1843, I, was timed to coincide with the RA 1843. Tate, *Ruskin, Turner and the Pre-Raphaelites*, 2000, 11, 13–14.

9   'And the Lord said unto Satan: Whence comest thou? Then Satan answered the Lord and said, From going to and fro in the earth and from walking up and down in it'. Job I, 7. Cat.S.131b. letter from J. Ruskin, quoted in B/W: 24; Macmillan, 1903, 150.

10   Letter to GDG (Fiche 40).

11   *Ibid.*, 20 October 1847 (Fiche 40).

12   *Ibid.*, October 1847, quoted in RC, 39.

13   CDGd, 12 February 1849.

14   Letter to GDG, 20 November 1847 (NPG aXIV, 69).

15   Acquired in 1918 by the Fitzwilliam Museum. *Art Union*, 1847, 73.

16   Cat.P.122a and b; D, 21 August 1893. An Italian political refugee, employed on the recommendation of Lord Holland's father, Panizzi was appointed Chief Librarian in 1856. Panizzi wrote that 'before Watts goes to Italy, which he is going to do almost immediately, he is going to paint me'. Although Fagan dates the letter as '?1850', the NPG gives a more likely date of *c.*1847, when GFW had hoped to return. The museum commissioned a further portrait on his retirement in 1866. Fagan, 1970, I, 324; II, 265; Ilchester, 1937, 373–74.

17   The portraits of Guizot and Lady Holland were shown at RA 1848, cats 307 and 582. A, I: 100; Cat.P.59c, 69c; Lichtenstein, 1875, 249; Erskine 1903, 183–84.

18   M, 'Resume of discussion on further lease of LHH', MS book V.

19   Letter to GDG, 20 November 1847, quoted in RC, 44.

20   *Ibid.* 1847 (NPG aXIV, 92–93).

21   *Ibid.* Friday n.d. (Fiche 41, A2).

22   *Ibid.* quoted in RC, 45.

23   *Ibid.* 14 December 1848 (Fiche 41). GDG chose thebull's head and *Judas Returning the Thirty Pieces of Silver.*

24 Letter to Ionides, 13 March n.d. (FC, copy, NPG and Fiche 37); Cat.P.163a; S.159b.

25 Cope and Horsley had completed frescoes illustrating Chaucer, Milton and John Tenniel in the Poets' Hall, where John Rogers Herbert and Joseph Severn were now painting. Hay and Riding, 1996, 94–97; *Athenaeum*, 24 November 1849.

26 Collected by the 14th Earl of Arundel. Haynes, 1975.

27 Newton recorded details of the thirteen slabs removed from Bodrum Castle in 1846 by Viscount Stratford de Redcliffe, who presented them to the British Museum in the belief that they had formed part of a frieze from the Mausoleum. Newton, 1861–62, II, 80–81; 1865, 44 and 333.

28 An etching dated 1645 shows the head, now believed to be a Roman reflection of Phidias's gold and ivory statue of Aphrodite Ourania at Elis. Her torso may have been carved from ancient marble in the seventeenth century. Sold in 1691 to Sir William Fermor, she ornamented 'The Tomb of Germanicus' at Easton in Northamptonshire, before the Countess of Pomfret donated the Arundel statues to Oxford University in 1755. Michaelis, 1882, 555–56, cat. 59; Ian Jenkins, 'G. F. Watts's Teachers: George Frederic Watts and the Elgin Marbles', *Apollo*, September 1985, 176–81; Vickers 1991, 6–8; A, I: 237–38; Cat.S.160c; WG, 2004, 53, cat. 21.

29 William Dyce had turned down the commission before the GFW campaign. Grock and Curthoys, 1997, VI, *Nineteenth Century Oxford*, Part I, 636; C. Newton to S. Birch, 26 August 1849 (British Museum: 3854); Newton to Dr H Acland, 17 October 1849 (Bod., MSS Acland, d.79, ff. 116–17); letter to Acland, 25 Nov 1852 (Bod. MSS Acland, d.71; ff. 108–09); Atlay, 1903, 229–30.

30 John Ruskin to the Revd E. Coleridge, 9 June, quoted in Cook and Wedderburn, 1904, XI, 30n; XXX, 303. JR hung *Time & Oblivion* in his studio for two years, by which time he preferred the art of the Pre-Raphaelites. JR paid GFW £42 for *Michael the Archangel Contending with Satan for the Body of Moses* on 9 May 1851. Blunt, 1975, 56.

31 GFW referred to his metaphysical pictures as 'imaginative' or 'allegorical' in the 1860s. D, 15 March 1896: he considered that 'allegory' implied a mixture of the real and unreal and did not therefore apply to his art. In 1886 the term 'Symbolist' was first applied to poetry in an article by Jean Moréas published in the Parisian newspaper, *Le Figaro*, 18 September 1886, and was applied by W. B. Yeats to painting in 1898.

32 Cat.S.145a and b; D, 7 May 1893; WG, 2004, 48–49. Painted at Dorchester House, before realising his theory that a curve stimulates imagination if it extends beyond the picture. B/W: 47.

33 Wallace Collection, P316, purchased by the Marquess of Hertford in 1870.

34 D, 19 June 1891. GFW purchased the pony from Wimbledon dealers named Hewett, to whom he paid £200 payment on 10 Oct 1848. 'A wandering dealer brought a pony there lean as a hawk & took him out after hounds & he jumped everything & was up to the front at the last.'

35 *Athenaeum*, 19 May 1849.

36 Quarterly payments of £35 to Mr Denew from 28 June 1849 to 13 November 1852, were presumably rent for Charles Street.

37 Cat.S.131c. *Magazine of Art*, 1893, iv and 286–87; Dn, 1893: before Italy, GFW used materials from Davys of Great Newman Street. Couzens prepared copies of portraits, notably for the Ionides family and GFW added finishing touches. Payments to Couzens are recorded from August 1848 until November 1870. A, I: 106. Luke Ionides, 1996, 57.

38 D, 24 October 1887; A, I: 116–17; letter to M, 11 November 1886.

## 4 Crusade Against Bare Walls (1849–1856)

1 D, 3 September 1891; A, I: 125.

2 D, 18 March 1887; A, I: 121–22; letter to Mrs Nassau Senior.

3 James Pattle was a Senior Judge in the Court of Appeal at Murshidabad. Fitzpatrick, 1923, 13–15; Woolf, 1926, 1–3; Quentin Bell, 1972, 14–15; Troubridge, 1925, 6–7.

4 Of the Pattles' ten children, seven daughters reached maturity, but the eldest had died leaving a young family: Adeline Maria (1812–36, m. Colin Mackenzie), James Rocke Milford (1813), Eliza Ann (1814–18) Julia Margaret (1815–79, m. Charles Hay Cameron), Sarah Monckton (1816–87, m. Henry Thoby Prinsep), Maria (1818–92, m. John Jackson), Louisa Colebrooke (1821–73, m. Henry Vincent Bayley), Virginia (1827–1910, m. Viscount Eastnor, later 3rd Earl Somers, Harriet Trevor Charlotte (1823), Sophia Ricketts (1829–1911, m. Sir John Dalrymple, who succeeded to the baronetcy 1881).

5 A, I: 122.

6 Ritchie, 1893, 13.

7 D, 18 March 1887; A, I: 121–25.

8 Hill, 1973, 53.

9 C. Newton to Dr H. W. Acland, 21 February 1850 (Bod., MSS Acland, d.64; ff. 94–95).

10 From Acland, 21 June 1850 (NPG axi, 3–4), 8 July, quoted in Stirling, 1913, II, 258. Newton, encouraged by Acland, mentioned Stanhope's name to GFW.

11 GFW exhibited *Virginia Pattle, Adeline, Mrs Jackson*

and *The Good Samaritan* at the 1850 RA Summer Exhibition.

12   Cat.S.65a; Dn, 7 May 1897; A, I: 130–31. In 1851 Wright sat to GFW for a chalk portrait. Mrs Edward Liddell, 1905, 10.

13   *Art-Journal*, 1850, 169.

14   Troubridge, 1925, 57.

15   Letter to Mrs Senior, 1856; D, 18 March 1887; A, I: 125.

16   Fitzpatrick, 1923, 16–17, 20; A, I: 127.

17   Letter to Dr H. W. Acland, 1850, quoted in A, I: 127; Cat.S.129c; Dn, 16 October 1888. GFW gave *The Ruins* to Acland in 1852.

18   GFW painted four social realist pictures: Cat.S.58a *Found Drowned* (1848–50), Cat.S.78a *The Irish Famine* (1849–50), Cat.S.153a *Under a Dry Arch* (1850), Cat.S.134a *The Song of the Shirt* (1850).

19   Cat.S.153a, 58a and b; WG, 2004, 48, cat. 7; Stewart, 1988, 106, 111; Stirling, 1934, 92.

20   GFW had loaned his earliest notable Symbolist work to Ionides as security for the Greek commission. *Aurora*, painted before he went to Italy, was never returned and years later became the subject of dispute.

21   Jean-François Millet (1814–75), the social-realist painter born in Normandy of peasant stock, had studied under Delaroche in Paris before settling in 1849 in the forest of Fontainebleau where he came to be regarded as a leading member of the Barbizon school of landscape painters.

22   Letter to Viscount Eastnor, 23 October 1850.

23   Taylor, 1924, 210.

24   V&A, 2001, 265.

25   Letter to Mary O'Brien, 1851 (NPG aXII, 50, quoted in A, I: 108–12; Ward, 1904, 164.

26   D. G. Rossetti, 'The Modern Pictures of all Countries, at Lichfield House, *Spectator*, 1851 quoted in Rossetti, 1888, II, 476–84: 'The biggest is G F Watts' piece of dirty Titianism, entitled "The Ostracism of Aristides". It has something in it, however, which somehow proves what was certainly the one thing most difficult of proof, considering the general treatment of the picture, – namely, that the painter is not a fool.'

27   Ilchester, 1937, 239.

28   Indenture 21 November 1874. (HH/LMA: E/HOL/Ac.70.85/II).

29   Ilchester, 1937, 443–44; A, I: 127–29; Barrington, 1927, II, 119.

30   Hill, 1973, 54.

31   Troubridge, 1925, 20.

32   A, I: 122.

33   Fitzpatrick, 1923, 15.

34   A, I: 205.

35   GFW's portrait of Cameron was painted in 1850. Ritchie, 1919, 3–4.

36   Cecil, 1975, 1; A, I: 205.

37   Letter to Sir Henry Taylor, 18 September 1859 (Bod., MSS Eng. Lett. c.1, f. 326; A, I: 205).

38   A, I: 123.

39   A, I: 124.

40   Letter to C. H. Rickards, 10 January 1875 (NPG aIII, 2–5).

41   A, I: 155.

42   Spielmann, 1886, 13.

43   Presented to the NPG in November 1896.

44   The first meeting of the trustees of the future NPG, under the chairmanship of Earl Stanhope, took place on 9 February 1857. Acquisitions hung in temporary accommodation for 40 years. Saumarez Smith, 1997, 9–12.

45   Lord John Russell (1792–1873), created Earl Russell in 1861, became prime minister in 1865, on the death of Palmerston.

46   Dn, 10 November 1897; D, 26 August 1893.

47   Cook and Wedderburn, 1904, XI, 30n; Bradley, 1955, 3, 19; letter to John Murray, 22 November 1852, 12 March 1853 (John Murray archive).

48   WG, 2004, 49, cat. 10. D, 12 August 1891. Reduced casts from the Elgin Marbles were sold through P & D Colnaghi for one guinea, 12/6 to Society members. *Arundel Society, 1851*; A, II: 81; Stephen, 1906, 317; Wemyss, 1911, 113–14.

49   Hunt, 1905, I, 180.

50   Letter to Ruskin (draft, WG).

51   Ruskin, 1853, III, 26n; Rawnsley, 1923, 129.

52   Letter to W. H. Hunt, 25 February 1897 (Huntington: HM 589); B/W 77.

53   A, I: 234.

54   Virginia Somers also appeared as *Poetry, Science* and *Progress*, Julia Cameron as *Hindustan*, Sophia Dalrymple as *Art*, Maria Jackson as *The Assyrian Empire*, her daughter Adeline Vaughan as *Truth* and Emma Brandling as *Rome*. B/W: 47, 83, 101 and illustrations; Twistleton, 1928, 106–07.

55   D, 25 January 1887; A, I: 132.

56   Shaw, 1970, 193.

57   Dn, 28 July 1888; A, I: 131–32.

58   Stirling, 1916, 297.

59   *Ibid.* 300–02; A, I: 137. At the same time Stanhope practised fresco-painting on the walls of his father's house in Harley Street.

60   Stirling, 1916, 298.

61   Letter from Lady Elizabeth Spencer Stanhope, 16 April 1852; *ibid.* 307–09; A, I: 139.

62   St Catherine's College (now Liverpool Hope University). *Governesses' Benevolent Institution Report of the Board of Management*, 1848; Stewart, 1988, 123.

63   Stirling, 1916, 309; *The Fairie Queene*, I, 12; letter to the Royal Fine Art Commission (draft, WG). The Com-

missioners approached GFW, after rejecting Joseph Severn's design for *The Faërie Queen* commissioned while GFW was in Italy. Stanhope, writing in September 1852, expected the fresco to be finished soon. GFW's experimental fresco of *Britomart* was probably prepared for the Palace of Westminster.

64  D. G. Rossetti to Thomas Woolner, 8 January 1853, quoted in Woolner, 1917, 49.

65  *Quarterly Review*, October 1858, 322. The pure fresco technique showed early signs of decay in the London climate.

66  Letter to the Benchers of Lincoln's Inn, 11 June 1852 (draft, WG); *Illustrated London News*, 9 March 1867, 224.

67  *Ibid.* n.d. (WG). The fresco was later renamed *Justice, A Hemicycle of Lawgivers*. As promised, GFW gave his services. Like James Barry decorating the Great Room of the Royal Society of Arts (oil paintings on canvas, 1777–83), GFW charged only the cost of materials.

68  Taylor, III, 329–32, reprinted in A, III: 89–98.

69  *Ibid.*

70  From Charles Thomas Newton, 16 June 1852 (Fiche 13, F8–11); Letter to the British Museum Trustees, 30 January 1852 (BM, letter 3857); Newton, 1865, I, 1; Letter to Newton, 1852 (Fiche 13 F12–14).

71  Letter to Acland, 25 November 1852, 13 March 1853 (Bod., MSS Acland d.71, ff. 108–09, 111–12). Letter from Acland, 14 October 1891 (NPG aXII, 9). The academics also feared damage to books. Atlay, 1903, 229–30; Stewart, 1988, 68–69.

72  Letter to Acland, 13 March 1853 (Bod., MSS Acland d.71, ff. 108–09), 8 May 1852 (WG).

73  Stirling, 1913, II, 278. Stanhope's sister Anna Maria and Percival Pickering were the parents of Evelyn de Morgan and the author Wilhelmina Stirling.

74  Cat.S.29c–31b; WG, 2004, 85. The picture was ultimately renamed *The Court of Death*. D, 14 December 1891; Letter to Countess Somers, 27 January 1894; Twisleton 1928, 106; JCd, 10 July 1891.

75  Letter from Lady Elizabeth Eastlake, 1 August 1853 (Fiche 32, C5); Paston, 1932, 118–19; Ilchester, 1937, 390; *Pictures at Holland House*, 133.

76  Letter from Lady Elizabeth Spencer-Stanhope, February 1853: 'We shall have to have the High Art put out of the drawing-rooms that they may be thoroughly cleaned', Stirling, 1913, II, 278.

77  A, I: 56.

78  Letter to John Ruskin (draft, WG), quoted in A, I: 144.

79  GFW MS notes (WG); A, I: 144–46.

80  A, I: 146–50.

81  Letter to Mrs Nassau Senior (Fiche 28 D9).

82  Letter to Earl Somers, n.d.

83  Dn, 28 July 1888; letter to Benchers of Lincoln's Inn (draft, WG); A, I: 150–51, 183.

84  Letter to Ruskin, 5 March 1860 (draft, WG).

85  Letter to Countess Somers. Lady Waterford later decorated the school hall at Ford, Northumberland, with murals (1862–83). WG, 2004, 59–60; Fitzpatrick, 1923, 32–33; Joicey, 1991, 14.

86  His receipt for forty guineas, 18 November 1854 (Royal Archives: P.P2/8/5023); letter from Sir Edwin Landseer, 7 November (Fiche 42, A4–7).

87  Coutts & Co. bank statements; letter to Earl Somers, 15 April 1855.

88  Hewett, 1958, 47.

89  Letter to Mrs Senior (Fiche 28, D8), quoted in A, I: 162–63.

90  Letter to W. J. Stillman, 11 October 1891 (Schaffer Library Collection, Union College Schenectady, New York 12308, WJS 587).

91  Letter to Mrs Senior (Fiche 28, D8).

92  Letter to Earl Somers, Monday night, n.d. The frescoes, uncovered by Joachim von Ribbentrop when he lived at CHT as German Ambassador to Britain in 1936–38, now hang at Malvern College.

93  Letter to Giovanni Bezzi, 13 January 1855 (NPG s1, ff. 66–69); Harrison, 1954, 106 and 129; Darley, 1990, 47; A, II: 99.

94  Marsh, 1999, 135.

95  Letter to Lord Lansdowne (draft, WG). Sending sketches for *The Allegro*, GFW wrote, 'I have thought ... that the Allegro presented a succession of images essentially English & that companion designs morning & evening not illustrations of the poem itself so much as of its pastoral Character would be most in keeping with, & make most agreeable decorations for the Hall at Bowood.' The frescoes were postponed, the subject instead *Achilles Watching Briseis Being Led away from His Tent by the Messengers of Agamemnon* and *Coriolanus*, for which GFW received £300 on 16 July 1859.

96  B/L, I: 143–44, 22; A, I: 198; Ormonds, 1975, 17–18, 32; RA/L, 94.

97  Letter to Mrs Senior. The Paris exhibition continued until January 1856.

98  *Ibid.*

99  *Ibid.*

100  GFW used Arthur's head for *Sir Galahad*, *Aspiration*, *The Red Cross Knight* and other paintings.

101  *Pictures at Holland House*, 136, 55, 403; A, I: 158–62.

102  Notably, at the Palais Bourbon, the Palais du Luxembourg, the Louvre and the Hôtel de Ville.

103  Delacroix's studio in the rue Notre Dame de Lorette was in the quartier of *La Nouvelle-Athènes*. Wellington, 1951, 305–06, Paris, 14 October 1855; 312, 9 April 1856.

104  Ormonds, 1975, 34.

105  Her husband Edward Sartoris was an amateur artist. Letter to Mrs Senior, 2–5 November 1855.

106  Réunion des Musées Nationaux 1998, 84–85.

107  Princess Lieven, née Dorothea Benkendorff (1785–1857), *Pictures at Holland House*. cat. 24; Bingham, 1982 , 234.

108  Lichtenstein, 1875, 187; letters to Mrs Senior, November 1855–11 February 1856.

109  Letter to Mrs Senior (Fiche 28, D12).

110  RA/L: 109, cat. 11.

111  Ruskin, *Modern Painters*, III, 1856, Cook and Wedderburn, V, 137.


5  Breezy Bohemia (1856–1860)

1  Hunt, 1905, II, 165.

2  Stirling, 1916, 299. Mrs Stirling's description here is generally accepted as reliable.

3  Letter to Sir Robert Morier, 19 March 1855 (Balliol College).

4  The Thackeray sisters sat for their portraits in the late 1850s. Belinda Thackeray Norman-Butler, forward to Fuller, 1992, 6.

5  The Hon. Frederick Gerald Byng (1784–1871), youngest son of the fifth Viscount Torrington. Hill, 1973, 60.

6  A, I: 160.

7  Dn, 8 December 1897.

8  Hunt, 1905, II, 94, 122–23; Amor, 1989, 145; Cat.P.95a.

9  Burne-Jones, 1904, I, 159–60; Horner, 1933, 18.

10  Roxburgh, 1968, v, xl; M, note (WG); A, I: 136, 150; Blunt, 1975, 97. Sitters identified in *Justice: A Hemicycle of Lawgivers* include Minos (Tennyson), Servius (Val Prinsep), Solon (Roddam Spencer Stanhope), Ina King of Wessex (William Holman Hunt), a druid (Thoby Prinsep), Empress Theodora (Sophia Dalrymple), King Alfred (Emma Brandling, later Lady Lilford), Emperor Justinian (Sir Vernon Harcourt), Edward I (Sir Charles Newton)* and two barons (Lord Lawrence and Edward Armitage). *According Surtees, 1993, 89, Sir Coutts Lindsay modelled for the head of Edward I in 1857. Pythagoras bears a closer resemblance to Lindsay.

11  Letter to Mrs Senior (Fiche 28, D12); Ristori, 1907, 43.

12  Burne-Jones, 1904, I, 18; Maurice, 1928, 90; Fitzpatrick, 1923, 15.

13  Matthew James Higgins, known as 'Jacob Omnium' from the title of his first published article, 1845.

14  Lady Constance Leslie to M, 1856; A, I: 159–60. Her unfinished portrait began at about this time.

15  Twisleton, 1928, 105–08.

16  Ross, 1912, 40.

17  *Ibid.* 122.

18  From 1856 Hallé invited local, national and international players to form a special orchestra to perform in Manchester during the 1857 Art Treasures Exhibition; and after it closed the 60 players who stayed on formed the nucleus of the Hallé Orchestra. Letter to Mrs Nassau Senior; Hallé, 1896, 162. Hallé sat for his portrait c.1870. Cat.P.65a.

19  Hunt, 1905, II, 167–69.

20  Burne-Jones, 1904, I, 182; Horner, 1933, 19.

21  Adelaide Sartoris to Frederic Leighton, 25 June 1860, quoted in Antrobus.

22  George du Maurier to Tom Armstrong, March 1862, quoted in Du Maurier, 1951, 119.

23  GdM to his mother, February 1862, *ibid.* 111.

24  'Little Holland House', anonymous typescript, c.1898 (WG), 187. JMC gave GFW the Edward Moxon edition of Tennyson's *Poems* for Christmas 1857.

25  Euphemia Millais to Rawdon Brown, 27 October 1857, quoted in Fleming, 1998, 172.

26  Ormond, 1969, 103–04, 454, 499.

27  Letter to Mrs Senior.

28  *Ibid.* 18 August 1856.

29  *Ibid.* August.

30  *Ibid.* n.d.

31  Leighton subsequently carried out repairs. Henry Greville wrote to Leighton on 28 August 1856, 'With regard to Watts, he said he should be too happy to do *anything* for you, but he wished you to be thrown with Albert. He (Watts) is better and has left Malvern.' B/L: I: 259–62, 291; Millar, 1995, cat.5772.

32  Newton, 1865, I, 333–34, II, 67; A, I: 163.

33  Towsey 1856–57, 20, 25 November 1856.

34  *Ibid.*, 7–11, 17, 22–23 December 1856. Newton to Lord Stratford de Redcliffe, 15 February 1857, quoted in *Papers Respecting The Excavations at Budrum*, London, 1858, 9–10.

35  On 5 October 1891, GFW wrote to the *Daily Graphic*, suggesting commemorative plaques to heroic poets, notably Dibdin, whose 'manly lyrics give utterance to the best qualities of the English nation'.

36  Towsey reported day-by-day discoveries in his journal. Newton later backdated discovery of the site to 1 January.

37  Towsey, 16 January 1857; letter to Lord Stratford de Redcliffe, 25 February; George Aitchison, 'Colour', *Art Journal*, 1884, 297–300.

38  B/W: 27–28.

39  On Lord Lyons's death in 1858, GFW offered to make an etching or engraving from his portrait for Dominic Colnaghi. 'The likeness was considered good & none of the portraits I have seen about are like' (To Dominic Colnaghi, 7 December 1858 (Forster Coll MS, NAL, F.D.6.1.149).

40  Cat.S.63a and b; WG, 2004, 55–56. Towsey, 18 March

1857; Newton, 1865, II, 100–04; letter to the Earl of Clarendon, 19 March, quoted in *Papers Respecting the Excavations*, 10.

41 Towsey, 30 March 1857; Cat.P.50a; A, I: 166.

42 HMS *Gorgon* Log (PRO ADM 53/5759); Dn, 9 January 1897. When the *Gorgon* returned in July, GFW recommended that a draughtsman be sent out to record the finds. Letter to A. Panizzi, 21 July 1857 (BL, Add MS 70846; f. 122). Letter to Sir John Stuart, 14 June 1857, quoted in A, I: 168.

43 A, I: 167; letter to Georgina Treherne, 20 September 1857 (WG).

44 Dn, 2 October 1897.

45 Cat.S.61b.

46 Letter to Mrs Nassau Senior, May 1857 (Fiche 28, E3–4).

47 Stirling, 1926, 162.

48 Valentine Prinsep, 'A Chapter from a Painter's Reminiscences', *Magazine of Art*, no. 2, 1904.

49 GFW met the Count and Countess of Castiglione at a Holland House dinner in August 1856 and painted her portrait during her second visit, beginning on 1 July 1857. Ilchester, 1937, II, 414; Cat.P.34; MM, 2000, 17, 24–25.

50 Dn, 14 March 1892.

51 Letter to Lady Duff Gordon (draft, WG); A, I: 171–72.

52 Letter from John Ruskin, 18 October (Typescript, Bod., MSS Eng. Lett. c.50). From 1859 Val Prinsep attended Gleyre's studio in Paris.

53 Her father Morgan Thomas changed his surname to Treherne. Her mother was the daughter of John Dalrymple, a cousin of Sophia Dalrymple's husband, John. Thompson, 2000, 7.

54 Letter from Ruskin, 13 February 1873 (Bod., MSS Eng. Lett. c.590, ff. 195–96).

55 Letter to Mrs Senior (Fiche 28, E12–13).

56 RA, Summer Exhibition, 1858, cat.143, 167, 185; A, I: 175; Hunt, 1905, 180. In the portrait of Jeanie's mother *Mrs Hughes*, only the head itself has Pre-Raphaelite definition, Cat.P.70c.

57 Letter to Mrs Nassau Senior, 1857 (Fiche 28, E10).

58 'Poodle' Byng longed for a copy of the portrait. Letter from Richard Doyle, 11 August n.d. (NPG 253).

59 Letter to Georgina Treherne, n.d. (B/Y: GFW MS 2125; f. 3); Thompson, 2000, 21–29, 34, 46–50; Grierson, 1959, 11.

60 Letters to Georgina Treherne, 28 October, 9 November, 28 December 1857 (WG); letter to Mrs Senior (Fiche 28, E14). GFW warned Georgina against haste, but felt privately she should elope and that marriage might protect her from recklessness and trouble; Grierson, 1959, 19.

61 Letter to Mrs Senior (Fiche 28, E12–13). GFW paid £25 for his violin which he played for some years with adequate but not inspirational skill. A, I: 201.

62 Diaries of Sir Henry Cole, 11 January 1858 (V&A: 55.AA.02). Queen Victoria had laid the foundation for the new South Kensington Museum in 1857.

63 Albums, 12 February, 1858 (WG); A, I: 161.

64 Letter to Sir John Stuart, 13 October 1857; Philip Hardwick to the Treasurer of Lincoln's Inn, 25 October 1859 (Fiche 40, F2–3).

65 *Achilles Watching Briseis Being Led away from His Tent by the Messengers of Agamemnon*. Lord Lansdowne paid GFW £300 on 16 July 1859.

66 Letter to Mrs Senior. GFW stipulated that the horse should have a fine mouth. He did not use a snaffle bit, because it encouraged a heavy hand. 'I like to have plenty to do with a horse, except pulling against a hard mouth.'

67 Chedzoy, 1992, 53, 213, 220, 251–53, 273.

68 A, I: 191; Surtees, 1993, 59; Curtis, 1889, I, 242.

69 Ross, 1912, 46 and 49. Countess Somers posed for Briseis.

70 Letter to Mrs Senior, Saturday (Fiche 28). The LHH address was given in the catalogue.

71 *Ibid*. GFW was comforted to learn that King Alfred had been afflicted likewise, 'the relief of one hour was embittered by what he dreaded would come next. How well I know the feeling! Great, Good, dear Alfred!'.

72 Hunt, 1905, II, 180; *Athenaeum*, 1858, 630.

73 Bessborough, 1952, 83–85; Blunt, 1975, 85.

74 Barrington, 1927, 119–20.

75 Grierson, 2000, 19. In January 1860, Georgina married Harry Weldon, 18th Hussars.

76 Grierson, 2000, 36.

77 Burne-Jones, 1904, I, 187; Surtees, 1997, 42; Marsh, 1999, 137, 194 and 544 11.3n. 'Louisa Herbert' (Mrs Ruth Crabbe) whose beauty transcended her stage talent, was painted by Rossetti.

78 EBJ was forbidden to work in oil paint for the sake of his health and in an album of drawings produced in the summer of 1858 and dedicated to Sophia Dalrymple, his drawing illustrating Rossetti's poem *The King's Daughters* is said to feature Sara and her sisters in LHH garden. EBJ, 1981; Carr, 1914, 56.

79 The Hogarth Club met on Friday evenings at 8pm at 178 Piccadilly from July 1858 and from 1859 at 6 Waterloo Place. Members included William Burges, Burne-Jones, Hunt, Leighton, Prinsep, Rossetti, Ruskin and Woolner.

80 Burne-Jones, 1904, I, 180–87; *The Studio Diaries of Thomas Rooke* (NAL, 124–25); Horner, 1933, 18–19; Fitzgerald, 1997, 64–66; EBJ, 1981, 8–13.

81 Letter to John Murray, 30 October 1858 (John Murray archive); Cat.P.58c; Shannon, 1999, xv; Dn, 2 October 1897; D, 15 April 1898.

82 Cat.P.125a, Miss Isabella Prescott; *The Times*, 10 May 1859; Hunt, 1905, 181; Ruskin wrote in *Academy*

*Notes*, 'I cannot criticize my friend Mr Watts's picture *Isabella* (438); it is full of beauty and thoughtfulness. I have no doubt that he knows its faults better than I do; and they are so slight that the public ought not to see them but to admire it with all their hearts'; Cook and Wedderburn, 1904, XIV, 239–40.

83    Letter to Lord Elcho, 19 July 1859.

84    The Pitt-Rivers Museum, founded in 1865. Master-minded by Dr Acland, the museum was designed by Benjamin Woodward, a disciple of Ruskin and junior partner in the Dublin firm of Deane, Son and Woodward. Tate, 2000, 14.

85    Letter from W. E. Gladstone, 20 June 1859 (NPG); letter to Gladstone, 23 June, 6 August 1859 (Gladstone Papers, BL, Add MS. 44391; f. 378 and 44392; f. 117). Murray paid 80 guineas for the portrait delivered 28 December 1861. Letter to John Murray, 8 January 1862.

86    A, I: 169–70; Spielmann, 1886, 13.

87    'Lancelot and Elaine', *Idylls of the King*, lines 330–338.

88    Emily Tennyson to Alfred Tennyson, 26 March 1859 (TRC).

89    Tennyson, 1897, I, 428; A, I: 170; letter to Mrs Senior (Fiche 28, E14); MM, 1998, 6, 56–57; Darley, 1990, 41.

90    John Ruskin to Margaret Bell, 3–4 April 1859, Van Akin Burd, 1969, 149–50.

91    Letter to Emily Tennyson, 14 July 1859 (NPG 1859. B/Y: Alfred Tennyson Coll, MS. 276, GFW I, 246); Dn, 3 February 1891.

92    *Athenaeum*, 10 December 1859, 780.

93    *Quarterly Review*, October 1858, 323. The archaeologist was in between terms as under-secretary for Foreign Affairs.

94    Letter to the Benchers of Lincoln's Inn, quoted in A, I: 178.

95    D. G. Rossetti to Lord Aberdare (WG). Millais, 1899, I, 357.

96    At his bequest the bottles were given after his death to an aspiring artist, Brian Hatton. A, III: 61.

97    Letter to the Benchers of Lincoln's Inn, n.d. (drafts, WG exercise book).

98    Extract from Queen Victoria's Journal, 25 February 1860, quoted in Millar, 1995; D, 18 February 1898.

99    According to cat.P.112–13, the first portrait was begun in 1859. Soon after arriving in England in May 1858, Motley was taken to the Cosmopolitan Club, and introduced to members of GFW's circle. He dined at Holland House in July 1858, after which he left England, returning in mid-November 1859, staying until June 1861, when both portraits were completed. Motley was US Minister to Britain in 1869. Curtis, 1889, I, 227.

100    Letter to Mrs Prescott, 1 December 1859 (Fiche 38, F8).

101    Grant was knighted and elected PRA in 1856.

102    Letter to G. C. Bentinck, 22 June 1857, 27 March 1860 (University of Nottingham Library: PwM 159). Bank statements show an influx of 100-guinea and 200-guinea receipts, the former for a single portrait head.

103    *The Times*, 26 April 1860; Roxburgh, v, 86–87.

104    *Vestiges* was reissued in 1860 in its 11th edition. Alfred Russel Wallace, also determined to test the evolutionary theory of *Vestiges*, had abandoned surveying to become a naturalist, solved the theory and sent his views to Darwin and together they had published a joint paper in 1858.

105    Darwin, 1859, chapter 14, 490, echoes Watts's ideas for *Progress of the Cosmos*. 'The whole history of the world … will hereafter be recognized as a mere fragment of time, compared with the ages which have elapsed since the first creature, the progenitor of innumerable extinct and living descendants, was created … There is grandeur in this view of life, with its several powers, having been originally breathed into a few forms or into one; and that, whilst this planet has gone cycling on according to the fixed law of gravity, from so simple a beginning endless forms most beautiful and most wonderful have been, and are being evolved.'

106    *The Times*, 9 May 1859.

107    Letter from Lord Elcho, 14 January 1860; A, I: 197.

108    Letter to Countess Somers, c.1859–60. GFW found the low format and subject unsatisfactory. 'Indecision is not noble', he said of *Coriolanus*, the Roman general about to sack his own city until his family persuaded him not to. A, I: 195–96; Minneapolis Institute of Arts, 1978, cat. 11.

109    Letter from Lord Elcho, 14 January 1860; letter to M, June 1912, quoted in A, I: 197–98; Wemyss, 1912, I, 296, 302. The Elcho Shield was made for Elkington by Monsieur Mainfroid and drawings for the *repoussé* figures of Reginald Cholmondeley are preserved at the WG.

110    Muster Roll of the 38th Middlesex (Artists) Volunteer Corps.

111    Stirling, 1926, 164 and 167; MacCarthy, 1994, 170.


## 6    Choosing (1860–1864)


1    Letter from John Ruskin, 5 November 1860 (Bod., MSS Eng. Lett. c.50; f. 187).

2    Letter to Tom Taylor, 15 January 1861 (WG).

3    The portrait was exhibited at the Royal Academy in 1861, with *The Window Seat*, a French maid sewing at Little Holland House. Alice, who later married Jack Stacey-Clithero and her elder daughter, Rachel Gurney both had affairs with Prince of Wales. Rachel's sister, Laura, is the quoted memoirist Lady Troubridge. D, 30 June 1891.

4  Surtees, 1971, 104–05; 1980, 38; Spielmann, 1886, 35; Cat.P.71a and b; and S.15b; RA 1862, cat. 364. Mrs Huth, née Helen Rose Ogilvy, posed for a head in 1856 and a few years later for the full-length portrait.

5  Cat.P.4a; RA 1860, cat. 364; Cat.S.7a; New Gallery 1890, cat. 31.

6  According to censuses, Maria and Harriet Watts lived at Prospect Place from 1861–81. In 1891 Harriet still lived there, with her niece, Thomas's daughter Mary Anne and her husband Robert.

7  D, 19 June 1891, 2 February 1898.

8  A, 1: 185–87.

9  Dn, 13 May 1888; Read, 1982, 13.

10  Cat.P.25b and c; Spielmann, 1886, 32–33; Spielmann MS (WG).

11  Letter from Ruskin, 29 September 1860, quoted in Cook and Wedderburn, 1903–12, XIV, 471 (typescript, Bod., MSS Eng. Lett. c.50, ff. 183–84).

12  Browning, 'A Toccata of Galuppi's, *Men and Women*, 1855, verse II, 1.

13  A, 1: 205; Weld, 1903, 64.

14  Letter from JMC, 3 December 1860 (Fiche 14, ff. G3–6).

15  Letter to JMC, 3 January 1861 (Fiche 34, E10); Longford, 1979, 18.

16  Cat.P.163a.

17  Pennell, 1908, 1, 81 and 109.

18  Letter to A. C. Ionides, 6 December 1860 (Fiche 37, B8); Luke Ionides, 1996, 9. GFW paid Ionides quarterly instalments rising from £13 to £25 from 1860 to 1875.

19  Letter from Ruskin, 1863 (Bod., MSS Eng. Lett. c.50, f. 190; Fiche 26, B7–8); 5 February 1861, quoted in Cook and Wedderburn, XIV, 472. (Typescript, Bod., MSS Eng. Lett. c.50, ff. 188–89).

20  Letters from Newton and to Newton, 10 December 1860 (draft, Fiche 13, G6–11); A, 1: 209.

21  Dn, 2 March 1889; A, 1: 209; Spielmann, 1886, 4. Dean Milman had reservations about the proposed artist Alfred Stevens, who was devoting all his time to the cathedral's Wellington Memorial, though he had the full support of the architectural surveyor Francis Penrose. Previous proposals had been dogged by controversy. Rejecting James Barry's scheme the previous century, the Bishop of London had declared he would 'never suffer the metropolitan church to be opened for the introduction of Popery.' Cathedral authorities were still dithering. GFW later recalled that it was proposed that he should design a complete decorative scheme for St Paul's.

22  'The Proposed Decorations in St Paul's Cathedral', *Builder*, 30 April 1864, 318. Stevens, GFW, Leighton and Baron Henri de Triqueti were reportedly asked to compete for the scheme. Stevens declined. Leighton's designs were turned down. GFW sent drawings on *The Transfiguration of Christ* supported by Moses and Elias.

23  Alfred Stevens to design mosaics of the Old Testament prophets for the remaining four spandrels. *Proposal for Completing and Adorning St Paul's Cathedral*, May 1863. Towndrow, 1939, 176–77; 'Mosaic Work in St Paul's Cathedral', *Builder*, 30 July 1864, 567; Simon Reynolds, 1994, 1–2; A, 1: 209–10. GFW's *St Matthew*, catalogued by St Paul's cathedral as 'pre-1864'.

24  The decayed fresco of Christ and the Evangelists, *Come unto me all ye that are heavy laden, and I will give you rest*, was replaced under GFW's supervision in the 1880s by a mosaic reproduction. Letter to Countess Somers n.d.; *Athenaeum*, 6 July 1861; *Illustrated London News*, 1 February 1862, 121; *Art Journal*, 1 September 1861, 261; Watkins, 1994.

25  Alessandro Allori, *A Knight of San Stefano*, Italian, Florentine, after 1561 (NG 670); letter to the National Gallery, c.1861 (draft, WG). Sir Charles Eastlake to Ralph Wornum, 8 June 1861 (NG5/347/1861); NG Minutes of Board Meetings, 1 July 1861.

26  The Crystal Palace, re-erected at Sydenham Hill in 1854, burned down in 1936.

27  Letter to Sir A. H. Layard, 10 September 1861 (BL, Add. MS 38987 f. 96).

28  *Ibid.*; *Art Journal*, 1862, 152.

29  Letter to Henry Cole, 13 February 1862 (BL, Add. MS 4948; f. 14): GFW suggests a theme of 'Quarrying or Pottery'. Henry Cole noted in his diary on 22 June, 8 July and 20 September 1863 that GFW agreed to make a sketch for £105 and proposed to illustrate scenes of manufacture.

30  Letter to Sir A. H. Layard, 13 March 1862 (BL, Add. MS 38988 ff. 93–94).

31  V&A, 2001, 271. Japanese design, seen in England for the first time in 1862, subsequently influenced English and European art and design.

32  In July 1863 Henry Bruce bought an Italian sketch of oxen. Palgrave, 1862.

33  Cat.P.157b, 88b, 139a; Cook, 1913, II, 43. A third portrait was of Mrs William Russell. *International Exhibition*, 1862; *Exposition Universelle*, 1862, cat. 79.

34  Letters to Emily Tennyson, 13 and 19 February 1862 (TRC: 6263–64); letter from Mrs Tennyson, 17 February (University of Virginia).

35  RA 1862, cats 124, 141 and 364; Cat.P.12b, S.15b and 61c; *Athenaeum*, 3 May 1862, 502; the Metropolitan Museum of Art, 2003, 431, cat. 194.

36  Cat.P.101a.

37  Marsh, 1999, 374–75; MacCarthy, 1994, 253; *Poems*, published spring 1870.

38  John L. Bradley and Ian Ousby, eds, 1987, 73; D, 26 February 1898; A, 1: 272.

39   A, I: 211; Cat.S.88–91; WG, 2004, 15, 33 and 80, cat. 88.

40   Cat.P.154a and b; Cat.S.137c; letter to Lady Lothian, 5 April 1865: GFW writes that he is belatedly sending her the portrait of Lord Shrewsbury (NPG). Cat.P.144b; A, I: 211–12 and 222; Surtees, 1988, 80; Bailey, 1927, II, 29.

41   Members of the St John's Wood clique included D. W. Wynfield, P. H. Calderon, J. E. Hodgson, G. D. Leslie, H. S. Marks, G. A. Storey and W. F. Yeames. GFW was not a member but may have been an early visitor to the Arts Club. Denvir, 1989; Lamont, 1912, 18–21; Dakers, 1999, 72–73; Maas, 1975, 179.

42   'G. F. Watts in Venetian costume, bust, full face' (PRO, COPY 1/5/451). Wynfield's portfolio of photographs of ten artists reviewed in 'Fine Arts', *Illustrated London News*, 19 March 1864, registered at the Stationers' Hall on 8 December 1863. Other sitters included T. Prinsep, V. Prinsep, E. Armitage, F. P. Cockerell, W. H. Hunt, Sir C. Lindsay, G. Mason, J. E. Millais, Du Maurier, S. Solomon, and F. Walker. Leighton's *A Noble Lady of Venice*, 1866, illustrated in B/L, II, 10.

43   Letter to Alfred Tennyson, n.d. (TRC: 6261).

44   NG 636. Gould, 1975, 184–86.

45   Emily Tennyson's journal, November 1862. Letter to Mrs Tennyson, (TRC: 4510); Allingham and Paterson, 1905, 80. GFW made an earlier charcoal drawing of Mrs Tennyson in July 1858. Bateman, 1901, XIV, 14.

46   Letter from Emily Tennyson, 24 June 1863 (University of Virginia).

47   Anny Thackeray's portrait was painted on panel in 1859. Belinda Norman-Butler, introduction to Fuller, 1992, 6.

48   Letter to the Dalziel Brothers, 18 February 1863 (BL, Add. MS 39168, f. 52), 16 December 1863, quoted in Dalziel, 1901, 246; Cat.S.43b. At this time GFW worked up a number of biblical subjects as representative figures for *The House of Life* scheme.

49   Amor, 1989, 170–71.

50   Report of the Commissioners, 1863, 330–44, reprinted in A, III: 99–146.

51   *Ibid.*, 344–46: Supplementary evidence, letter to Lord Elcho, 24 April 1863.

52   *Ibid.*, 332, para. 3130.

53   1200 of the 4000 rejected works were shown in a separate section of the Palais de l'Industrie.

54   Pennell, 1908, 102–03.

55   The *Concert Champêtre* (c.1510) then attributed to Giorgione, was one of the pictures GFW had sketched in Paris in 1843.

56   Ernest Chesneau, quoted in Cachin, 1995, 49.

57   Cat.S.7a; Ovid, *Metamorphoses*, VIII; *Athenaeum*, 9 May 1863, 623.

58   Cat.S.6a and 115b. RA/L, 128–29, cat. 26.

59   Ben and Sarah Terry's eleven children were: Benjamin, followed by two who had died in infancy, Kate (grandmother of the actor Sir John Gielguid), Ellen, George, Marion, Florence, Charles, Tom and Fred. Steen, 1962, 47–48.

60   Terry, 1908, 48; Craig and St John, 1933, 39–40; RC: 64–65.

61   Steen, 1962, 92; Violet Hunt memoir, n.d. (Typescript, WG and ETMM).

62   WG, 2004, 12 and 60, cat. 41. ET's amended copy of *The Story of My Life*, 53. Isaiah XXI, 11–12.

63   ET's memoirs suggest that she was born a year after her actual birth, recorded as 1847 on her birth certificate. Her marriage certificate gave her correct age as 16.

64   Terry, 1908, 6–25; *ibid.* 29–30; Steen, 1962, 57; Cheshire, 1989, 121.

65   *Ibid.*, 45–46; Steen, 1962, 80–86; Blunt, 1975, 105; Craig and St John, 1933, 37–38.

66   Craig and St John, 1933, 37–39.

67   Scott and Howard, 1891, I, 277.

68   Violet Hunt memoir, *op. cit.*

69   Terry, 1908, 53; *ibid.* 43.

70   Letter to Earl Somers, 16 June 1863; Dn, 29 August 1892, recalling Somers valued support, notes that the earl paid £600 – 'a large sum for me at that time'. A bank statement records his deposit of £315 on 15 February 1864.

71   Cat.S.37c–38a; A, I: 282; B/W: 129; Barnard, 1889, I, 173.

72   Terry, 1908, 47–48; Craig and St John, 1933, 39–40.

73   Stirling, 1924, 219.

74   Cat.P.1c, 10c, 18c, 157c and 167c; letter from Bowman, 17 November 1863 (Fiche 16, B10–11), quoted in A, I: 216. Bowman also sat for a portrait. The founding president of the Ophthalmological Society, from 1880, Bowman was created a baronet in 1884.

75   Letter to Mrs [later Lady] Constance Leslie, n.d. (Leslie Papers K/6/1, typescript in WG).

76   Violet Hunt memoir, *op. cit.*

77   St John, 1949 edition, 111.

78   Edith Craig MS notes in Army Book 124 (ETMM). According to the baptismal records of St James Church, Hampstead Road (LMA), Kate, Ellen, George, Mary Ann, Florence, Thomas and Frederick were baptised on 17 February 1864.

79   D, 2 February 1893.

80   Letter to J. P. Martineau, 13 December 1876.

81   Beeton, 1859.

82   CDGd, 19, 21 January and 18 February 1864.

83   The manuscript diary of Harry Silver, quoted in Melville, 1987, 27. Charles William Shirley Brooks was editor of *Punch* from 1870, succeeded by Tom Taylor in 1874.

84  Hunt had served as an apprentice clerk at the London branch of Richard Cobden's calico printing firm. He created costumes for his painting *Valentine Rescuing Sylvia from Proteus*. Hunt, 1905, II, 349.

85  Lady Leslie's reminiscences (Leslie papers, K/3/3, 29).

86  Constance Leslie noted in a brief memoir, 'Was present at the marriage of Mr Watts to Ellen Terry' (Leslie Papers). Blunt, 1975, 105.

87  Lady Holland divided her time between Holland House, St Anne's Hill and Chertsey and spent the winter months at her Naples villa, Palazzo della Roccella. Edward Cheney to Lady Holland, 7 January 1865 (HH/BL, Add. MS 52118; ff. 72–74), quoted in Ilchester, II, 1937, 426.

88  Elliott and Fry photograph of ET in her going-away outfit illustrated in Cheshire, 1989, 29; Terry, 1908, 53; Craig and St John, 1933, 42–43.

89  Steen, 1962, 96.

90  Ruskin, shocked by the sight of female pubic hair, failed to consummate his marriage.

91  D, 1 October 1891, 30 June 1896; Cat.S.53a. 'Drawing from the model is like looking in the dictionary for a word, you will not write poetry till the words come to you without having to learn them up in the dictionary every time', GFW explained. Mary Bartley, the gardener's daughter, married from Little Holland House and died shortly afterwards.

92  Ellen Terry inscribed this last verse of Thoby Prinsep's poem inside her copy of Chesterton, 1904.

93  Boyce, on Sunday 7 February in Surtees, 1980, 39: 'To breakfast with Fred Leighton . . . In his studio was a large picture of Dante at Verona with many figures, and one of *Orpheus and Eurydice* and another of a girl and her lover (an artist).

94  Terry, 1908, 53; Craig and St John, 1933, 43.

95  *Athenaeum*, 7 May 1864, 651. *The Painter's Honeymoon* was rejected by the Academy. RA/L, 135, cat. 30; Surtees, 1980, 39.

96  B/W: 35.

97  WG, 2004, cat. 47. Sketches for *Edward and Phillipa* and *Knight and Maiden*. Loshak, 1963, 476–85.

98  Photographs registered at the Stationer's Hall on 30 June 1864 (PRO, COPY 1/6/943 and 948). Cheshire, 1989, 122: in November 1862, ET played Serena in William Brough's burlesque *Conrad and Medora* – based on Byron's poem *The Corsair* – at the Theatre Royal, Bristol.

## 7    Unbridled Passion (1864–1866)

1  JMC, *The Watts Album* (IMP).

2  'Fine Arts', *Illustrated London News*, 19 March 1864. Wynfield registered ten photographs of the artists R. E. Hodgson, E. Burne-Jones, F. Leighton, V. Prinsep, W. F. Yeames, J. Phillip, T. Faed, H. S. Marks, P. H. Calderon and G. F. Watts on 8 December 1863 (PRO, COPY 1/5/450–51). Cameron wrote that Wynfield had given her one lesson and that she consulted him, presumably by letter, over early queries.

3  JMC, *Annals of my Glasshouse*, 1874, reprinted in Ruth Chandler Williamson Gallery, 1996, 12.

4  JMC's wooden sliding box camera carried glass negatives eleven inches by nine and her French Jamin portrait lens had a short focal length of twelve inches, producing a diffused image with only six inches of the plate focused. Among the chemicals she used were collodion for exposure, polyposulphate of soda for fixing, cyanide of potassium, protosulphate of iron, pyrofallic and citric acid; and for printing: nitrate of silver, chloride of gold for toning. JMC to Sir John Herschel, March 20 (Royal Society: 158).

5  Ruth Chandler Williamson Gallery, 1996, 12. Prior to the 'Watts Album' (International Museum of Photography in New York), JMC had given GFW the 'Signor Album' of 1857, with prints she had made from photographs taken by others.

6  *Ibid.*, 1996, 11–16; JMC to Sir John Herschel, 26 February 1864 (Royal Society: 159); JMC, *The Watts Album*, International Museum of Photography, 1986, 8–12; Art Institute of Chicago, 1998, 226.

7  JMC to Sir John Herschel, March 20 (Royal Society: 158).

8  Ritchie, 1919, 22–23.

9  ET to Hallam Tennyson, March 1893 (TRC); Terry, 1908, 56; Craig and St John, 1933, 45.

10  Cat.P.158a; Cat.S.26b. He took up *Charity* again in the winter of 1894–95.

11  JMC registered 505 negatives in batches at the Stationers' Hall for one shilling per negative from 30 May 1864. On 30 June she registered six photographs of Mrs Watts, including two of the *South West Wind* image *Opera Box* and *Medusa* (both also with hand to necklace) and five of GFW, including *Opera Box* with a youth. (PRO: COPY 1/6/940–41, 30 June 1864). International Museum of Photography at George Eastman House, New York, 1986, 98: *Sadness*, exhibited at Colnaghi and Company, London, in July 1865. Cheshire, 1906, 28; IMP, 1906, 98.

12  Letters from Emily Tennyson, April 1864 and from Alfred Tennyson to the Duke of Argyll, quoted in Tennyson, 1897, 1–4.

13  Cat.P.57a records the early sittings. Spielmann, 1886, 13 reports that Garibaldi's portrait 'was painted in a four-hour sitting'. A, I: 220; Ridley, 1974, 546–50.

14  A, II: 100; D, 5 October 1887. Garibaldi called on Florence Nightingale on 17 April 1864. Sir Harry Verney persuaded Nightingale to receive GFW. Cook, 1913, II, 469; Quinn and Prest, 1987.

15   Letter from Ruskin 14 May 1864 (Bod., MSS Eng. Lett. c.50, f. 191); Cat.S.3a; A, I: 219.

16   Eastlake, 1895, II, 142.

17   Terry, 1908, 53–54, 57.

18   *Ibid.* 54.

19   George Williamson to M. H. Spielmann.

20   Stirling 1924, 220.

21   Letter to Mrs Senior, n.d.

22   Holland House Visiting Book (HH/BL, Add. MS 52166).

23   Letter from Lady Lothian, 21 September 1864 (NPG aIV, 86).

24   Letter to Mrs Senior, n.d.

25   Lord Torrington to John Delaine, 20 November 1864 (Royal Archives, VIC ADD C/24). According to Violet Hunt, ET ran away to her family and to Sir John and Lady Simon in Blackheath.

26   Letter to J. P. Martineau, 13 December 1876 (WG); Edward Cheney to Lady Holland, 8 February 1865 (HH/BL, Add. MS 52118; ff. 75–76).

27   Terry, 1908, 44–45. Her Cupid costume illustrated in Cheshire, 1989, 20.

28   J. W. Carlyle to Louisa, Lady Ashburton, 18 October 1864 quoted in Simpson, 1977, 81.

29   Letter from Lord Torrington, 20 November 1864 (Royal Archives, VIC ADD C/24).

30   Lady Duff-Gordon, 1932, 32; Steen, 1962, 100–01. Letter from Edward Cheney, 8 February 1865.

31   Tom Taylor to Mrs Ben Terry, 25 November 1864 (ETMM: Z1479).

32   Craig and St John, 46.

33   Thomas Eustace Smith, Liberal MP for Gosforth, married to Martha Mary Dalrymple – a distant cousin of Sir John – had seen *Choosing* in W's studio. According to a letter from Marion Rawson to Wilfrid Blunt, 4 May 1974 (WG), GFW had accepted Smith's offer, but asked to keep the picture for a time, probably because it was to be exhibited at the Royal Academy. *Choosing* hung in Mrs Smith's boudoir at 52 Prince's Gate (after 1874). In 1885, revelations of Mrs 'Eustacia' Smith's affair with Sir Charles Dilke prompted Smith to sell their house and art collection to Sir Alexander Henderson, later Lord Faringdon.

34   Cat.S.54c; Macmillan, 1903, 171–72.

35   B/W: 36 and 41.

36   *Ariadne*, not in Cat.S., but exhibited at the Dudley in 1869 (43), was closer to Long Mary herself. Wrongly catalogued as *The Wife of Plutus*, the picture was designed in 1865 and developed in the 1880s and was exhibited at the New Gallery in 1896 with the quotation from Ecclesiasted VI, 7: 'And yet the soul [appetite] is not filled' was referred to by Watts in a letter to its purchaser James Smith, as Pluto's wife; 11 April 1890

(NPG aXIV, 18). A study exhibited at the New Gallery in 1889 was described by the *Athenaeum*, 11 May 1889, 606, as 'a study, heroic size, of rich carnations…no more', suggesting that the jewels were added later. Cat.S.160b; WG, 2004, 45 and 73; Morris, 1996, 493; WAG 2135.

37   Surtees, 1993, 113.

38   Cheshire, 1989, 18.

39   See Appendix II.

40   Ellen Terry to Mary Ann Hall 1865 (ETMM: Z2201). 'Watts v Watts and Godwin' draft divorce petition, August 1876.

41   Since their marriage GFW had paid Ben Terry quarterly sums of £25, presumably as an allowance for ET. Bank statements show that in 1865 he paid two £100 maintenance instalments instead of three, but this seems to have been due to unclear instructions in the Deed of Separation, for which Benjamin and Kate Terry acted as Trustees. In or after July 1864, GFW had shown portraits of Tennyson, Henry Taylor and Garibaldi, and a large Cameron negative of *Choosing* to Dodgson. ET was not present. GFW offered to take ET to be photographed by Dodgson who asked instead to photograph GFW and friends at LHH. GFW was to consult Thoby Prinsep. Marital problems presumably intervened. Clarke, 1979, 145. GFW wrote to Tom Taylor, 7 May: 'Whatever is to be done or can be done must be only with reference to her advantage, that & that only will guide me, & that must be the one consideration.' (ETMM Z1, 570).

42   Edward Cheney to Lady Holland, 8 February 1865 (HH/BL, Add. MS 52118; ff. 75–76).

43   J. P. Martineau, later Walker Martineau, of 13 King's Road, Grays Inn.

44   Later the Liberal statesman Sir William George Granville Venables Harcourt QC.

45   'He has done her so serious an injury that no liberality in any arrangements can compensate for it', Tom Taylor wrote to Vernon Harcourt (Bod., MS Harcourt, dep 201; ff. 2–3).

46   D, 18 February 1898; Redgrave, 1891, 280.

47   Westmacott, 1864, 156–58; Newton, 1856, 132; 1865, 272–73; letter to Newton, 8 January 1865 (Fiche 13, G12); Atkinson, 1871, 27; Asleson, 1998, 181.

48   Letter to JMC (NPG sII, Fiche 34, E11–12; A, I: 208).

49   Letter to JMC 1864 (NPG sII, Fiche 34; ff. F1–2; A, I: 208). *Pose plastique*, or *tableau vivant*, was a form of entertainment in which actors impersonated works of art.

50   Letter to Emily Tennyson, 25 February, 2 March 1865 (NPG, TRC: 6266). According to Emily Tennyson's journal the portraits of Hallam and Lionel Tennyson were completed on 14 October 1865.

51  JMC to Sir John Herschel, 31 December 1864, quoted in Ford, 1975, 140–41.

52  Cameron's two negatives of GFW with his violin and Kate and Elizabeth Keown were registered at the Stationer's Hall on 3 May 1865 (PRO, COPY 1/8/545); Offentliche Kunstsammlung Basel Kunstmuseum, 2001, 224–25, cat. 41.

53  Thackeray died on 24 December 1863.

54  Colnaghi, 1990; Naef, 1996, 41; Fuller and Hammersley, 1951, 115; Ritchie, 1893; Gernsheim, 1975, 30.

55  ATRd; AT to Walter Senior, quoted in Ritchie, 1924, 125–56; Fuller and Hammersley, 1851, 113 and 115; Allingham, 1990, 108.

56  *Athenaeum*, 5 May 1866, 18.

57  Three photographs registered on 3 May 1865 (PRO, COPY 1/8/456).

58  Letter to JMC (NPG, Fiche 34; F7–10).

59  'Fine-Arts: Art in Photography', *Illustrated London News*, 15 July 1865, 50; IMP 1986, 98 and 100: from May 1864, JMC exhibited at the annual Photographic Society of London exhibitions. Photographic Society of Scotland, December 1864 (Hon. Mention), Berlin International Photographic Exhibition, May 1865 (Medal for 'Studies'), Dublin International Exhibition of Arts and Manufactures, May 1865 (Hon. Mention for artistic composition).

60  The photographs of Lindsay, Rossetti and Browning were registered at the Stationer's Hall on 18 July 1865 (PRO, COPY1/9/594–98) and the photograph of Hughes on 4 August (COPY1/9/485).

61  JMC to Henry Cole, 20 May 1865 (NAL); Burne-Jones, 1904, 1, 183.

62  *Ibid.* 1, 297–98. The first machine for home use was patented by Isaac Singer in 1851.

63  Cat.P.21c. Neither this portrait of Lady Adelaide Talbot, nor an earlier sketch were satisfactory. In October GFW wrote to Lord Lothian offering to repaint her. Sittings began again in the summer of 1868. Letter to Lord Lothian, 5 July 1858; Lady Adelaide to Lord Lothian (NPG); Masterman, 1930, 23. Leighton painted her portrait in 1879, after her marriage to Earl Brownlow (Belton House, The National Trust). Royal Academy of Arts, 1996, 187–88, cats 81–82.

64  Anne Anson, third daughter of the Earl of Lichfield.

65  Journal of Rosalind Howard, 19 May 1865 (Castle Howard); Wemyss, 1932. Photographs registered 18 July 1865 (PRO, COPY1/9/597).

66  GFW exhibited *Esau*, portrait of William Bowman and *Design for a Larger Picture* [*Love and Life*] at 1865 RA, cats 22, 251, 300; *Athenaeum*, 6 May 1865.

67  For the full text of GFW's draft proposal for *Progress of the Cosmos* or *The House of Life*. See Appendix 1 (NPG, s54–57) and A, 1: 101–03. His will, dated 19 July

1866, listed six bequests: '1st I bequeath my half sisters Maria and Harriet interest from investments. 2nd to Virginia Countess Somers, the small picture called *The Giants* [15$^{1}/_{2}$ × 9$^{1}/_{2}$ ins]. 3rd to Mrs Prinsep all pictures of her family, sketchbooks and other papers. 4th to Richard Doyle, small study for *The Good Samaritan*. 5th to the nation portraits of Tennyson, Lawrence, Lyndhurst, Gladstone and others. 6th remaining works and property to be sold to settle terms of separation, to Ellen Alice Watts.' The executors were to be Doyle and Val Prinsep and the will was witnessed by Dr John Jackson and Burne-Jones. Cat.S.24–25; Tate, 1997, 164–65, cat. 49; Metropolitan Museum of Art, 1885, 38–41, cat.108.

68  *Athenaeum*, 19 December 1863; *Eleventh Report of the Science and Art Department*, London, HMSO, 1864; *Art Museum Register 1864–65*; notes of letters from GFW 23 September 1864, 31 January, 19 and 24 May 1865; Physick, 1982, 71–72; *Art Journal*, 1866, 10. Later Leighton, who turned down the offer of student assistance, filled two lunettes with frescoes of *The Arts of Industry as Applied to War and Peace*.

69  Cat.P.109b; A, 1: 209–10; Reynolds, 1994, 1–2.

70  Letter to JMC, 21 June 1865 (NPG, Fiche 34, F12). Photographs registered on 17 July 1865 (PRO, COPY1/9/606–7).

71  Letters to JMC, Friday No. 2 and c.1865 (NPG, Fiche 34, G1–3). Photographs registered on 17 August 1865 (PRO, COPY1/9/428–29).

72  Ruth Chandler Williamson Gallery, 1996, 16.

73  Dakers, 1999, 78–81.

74  GFW had painted George Howard's grandfather Lord Wensleydale in 1864. The Countess of Airlie (née Blanche Stanley) was the eldest daughter and Rosalind Howard was the youngest daughter of the Second Lord Stanley of Alderley. According to RH's journal, George Howard's sittings began on 23 March 1865. Letter to Lady Airlie, 7 July 1865.

75  Lane, *Catalogue of Oxford Portraits*, 1912, 1, 123. Letter to The Hon. George Fortescue, 20 June 1865 (BL, Add. MS 69367, f. 156).

76  Cat.P.20c. John William, 2nd Earl Brownlow (1853–67), son of John Hume Cust, Viscount Alford and his wife Marianne Margaret (known as Lady Marian Alford).

77  Letters to The Hon. George Fortescue, 20 June and 30 September 1865 (HH/BL, Add. MS 69367, ff. 156 and 158).

78  Dakers, 1993, 25. Leighton had painted Percy Wyndham's portrait and was his first choice for Madeline's, but he was committed to five portraits and declined. Percy, whose cousin Lilla Wyndham-King was married to Stanhope, wrote on 5 July and 11 December

1865 (WG) to GFW, who agreed to paint a full-length portrait of Madeline for 600 guineas. Sittings were postponed until 3 May 1867. A, I: 239.

79   Letter to Tom Taylor, 10 June 1865 (NPG aII, 11); letters to C. H. Rickards, 20 and 23 August 1865 (NPG aII, 15 and 16).

80   The French Gallery, 1865. GFW exhibited *Portrait of The Rt Hon W E Gladstone MP*, *Portrait of Charles Hanbury*, *A Study with the Peacock's Feathers* (catalogued by M as *The Peacock Fan* and also known as *The Amber Necklace*) and *Portrait of a Lady*, cats 106–09; Maas, 1973, 184.

81   Marsh, 1999, 278; Tate, 1997, cat. 43.

82   Cat.S.115b; *Athenaeum*, 4 November 1865, 618; Maas, 1975, 184. Lithographs were made from *A Study with the Peacock's Feathers* and the same model sat for a companion picture *The Nymph*; National Gallery, 2003, cat. 23.

83   Maurice, 1928, 90; Darley, 1990, 54, 69, 96 and 98.

84   *The Beloved* was subsequently shown at the Arundel Club. Marsh, 1999, 257; MacCarthy, 1994, 218.

85   EW married Russell Barrington on 1 July 1867; B/W: 1–2; EBd, 20 February 1866; Westwater, 1984; Marsh, 1999, 294.

86   Ellen Watts to Mrs Sarah Terry, quoted in Steen, 1962, 108.

87   Cat.S.144b. *Thetis* (RA 1866, cat. 23) was followed by *Daphne* and *Psyche*; *Athenaeum*, 12 May 1866; Minneapolis Institute of Arts, 1978, 70–71, cat. 15. In 1867 GFW painted the larger version now in the WG.

88   Letter from DGR (NPG, from Princeton University, USA); Tate, 2001, 93, cat. 29.

89   Cat.P.109b; A, I: 209–10; Reynolds 1994, I; Penrose, July 1872; J. Mordaunt Crook, 'William Burges and the completion of St Paul's'. From Augustus Capello, mosaicist to Dr Salviati in 1863, to the sub-committee of the St Paul's Decoration, 25 June 1877, read at meeting on 26 July): wrote that he 'made alterations of the spandrel representing St Matthew under direction of Mr Penrose. . . The head of the Evangelist and the whole of the small angel was reproduced abroad not according to the *Cartoon* so that I was obliged to pick to pieces (after fixed) all the work which did not correspond and I did reproduce it as it stands'. Dean Milman died in August 1868.

90   Exhibited with portraits of Tennyson and Gennaro at French Gallery Winter Exhibition 1866, cats 222–24.

91   Dakers, 1999, 81.

92   Letter to the Earl of Airlie, 4 August 1866; Surtees, 1988, 49.

93   Letter to C. H. Rickards, 25 September 1866 (NPG aII, 29–31). GFW, who usually preferred red, wrote to Rickards: 'Any dark colour red or green & no matter how rich would do, & if possible the pictures should be hung with the light on the spectators left & not too near the window because the spectator should stand between the picture & the light'.

94   Letter to Rickards, 22 November 1866 (NPG aII, 32–34).

95   A special class of female mosaicists had been established by the Art School in 1862 and the designs planned for 36 niches were to be carried out by Minton, Hollins or in Italian glass mosaic by Salviati. The *Illustrated London News* reported on 18 May 1867 that GFW had completed his Titian design; his 8′ 8½″ arched 'oil painting on canvas: gold ground for execution in mosaic' was recorded by South Kensington in 1868, and executed in English ceramic mosaic by Kate Clarke and Mary J. Jennings, superintended by Samuel Cooper for Minton, Hollins, completed in 1869. Reg. No. 845–70, Paintings Acquisitions Register for 1870. (Cartoon, V&A Print Department): *Fifteenth Report of the Science and Art Department*, 1868, 197; 1870, 317; Physick, 1982, 62 and 66.

96   French Gallery, 1866: cats 222–24, including *Genaro, the head of a Venetian nobleman*; Cat.P.158a, 20b; Cat.S.63c; *Art Journal*, 1866, 374 and 1882, 62.

97   Letter to Lady Ashburton, 27 August 1866 (National Library of Scotland): 'I have absolutely given up portrait painting, positively declining to commence new ones, [but] as I so much admire & respect Lady Marion [Alford], & the picture you propose may be considered a subject picture, I will . . . endeavour to carry out your wishes'.

98   B/W: 16.

99   A. I: 208.

## 8   Royal Academician (1866–1870)

1   GFW first proposed the memorial in a letter to *The Times*, to commemorate the Queen's jubilee of 1857. Eliot, 1866, 170–71; Ward-Jackson, 2003, 296 and 298n.

2   Letter to C. H. Rickards, 17 August 1866 (NPG aII, 25–28).

3   Eliot, 1866, was set at the time of the first Reform Act of 1832.

4   Indenture 21 November 1874 records that on 22 August 1860 Lady Holland agreed with Henry Edward, Earl of Ilchester to sell Holland House Estate (HH/LMA: E/HOL/Ac.70.85/II).

5   Mrs Thoby Prinsep to Lady Holland, 4 January and 9 March 1866 (HH/BL, Add. MS 52158, ff. 223–24 and 227). Lady Holland to Mrs Prinsep, 5 January 1866 (BL, Add. MS 52158, f. 226); Ilchester, 1937, II, 439;

Dakers, 1999, 62; A, I: 251; *Athenaeum*, 4 January 1868, 23. The greenhouse sculpture studio was built 1867–68.

6 Letter to John Denison, 8 January 1867. Ellen Terry's annotated Chesterton, 1904. His first red velvet skull-cap, retained by the descendants of his ward Lilian Chapman, is inscribed, 'made by Miss A Prinsep 1874'. Letter to the Countess of Airlie; A, I: 198–99.

7 Grant proposed and J. P. Knight seconded GFW's nomination as an associate member of the Academy. *Athenaeum*, 9 March 1867, 327; A, I: 231–32.

8 Letter from Dante Gabriel Rossetti, 18 May 1866 (NPG).

9 Report from the Council of the Royal Academy, 1868, 15; *Athenaeum*, 2 February 1867, 161; Royal Academy Election Book. 1867–98; A, I: 231–32.

10 Letter to JMC (Fiche 34, E10); *Illustrated London News*, 18 May 1867, 487.

11 On a printed note, 'Mr G. F. Watts regrets to say that it is against a principle he holds with reference to the modern custom of Autograph collecting to accede to the request just made to him'. Spielmann explained, 'The above designed not out of courtesy alone, but to relieve him of the [unreadable] the keeping of threepenny stamps!' From 1865–70, $^{1}/_{2}$oz letters required a penny stamp and $1^{1}/_{2}$oz, a threepenny stamp.

12 Sending blank mounts with her letter to Sir John Herschel, 3 March 1868 (Royal Society: 168), JMC wrote that a photograph 'to my idea is doubled in value by *your* genuine autograph'.

13 A, I: 243. A preparatory chalk study shows the knight with head bowed, kneeling on one knee.

14 GFW exhibited at RA 1867, cats 82, 207, 419, 619: portraits of the Hon Mrs Seymour Egerton, The Dean of Westminster, May Prinsep, and *A Lamplight Study: Herr Joachim*. Cat.P.139a, 149a, 82a and Cat.S.119c; *Athenaeum*, 18 May 1867, 66. JMC registered *May Prinsep Draped as a Nun* on 23 March 1866 (PRO, COPY 1/10/301).

15 GFW's note on the reverse of RA members' *Notice for the Exhibition 1867* (NPG sIII, 65–66). Letter to George Richmond RA, 25 April 1867 (RA: acc.2000/17).

16 John Evelyn Denison, Speaker of the House of Commons 1857–72, created Viscount Ossington in 1872.

17 GFW's current rate for a half-length portrait.

18 *Athenaeum*, 30 March 1867, 426.

19 On 3 May 1867 GFW wrote, 'If Wed 10 might be agreeable 2pm I will be ready to begin then' (WG). Wilfrid Scawen Blunt manuscript, *Alms to Oblivion*, v: 'Proteus: Madeline', 3, 5, (Fitzwilliam), '. . . she is shown as a queen of womanhood, "Earth's archetypal Eve", for it was of her that word was written'.

20 Blunt, *ibid.* III, 'Juliet' 2, 43–49.

21 Son of James Fitzgerald, first Duke of Leinster.

22 Pamela Fitzgerald to Emily Eden, 1820, quoted in Dickinson, 1919, 60.

23 Blunt, *Alms to Oblivion*, v: 'Proteus', 5, 50.

24 The Wyndhams' five children were Mary (born 1861, who would marry Lord Elcho's heir), George (1863, the future statesman), Guy (1865), Madeline (1869, later Adeane), Pamela (1871, the future Lady Glenconner and later Viscountess Grey of Fallodon). GFW also painted Percy Wyndham's elder brother Henry, Lord Leconfield. Madeline Wyndham noted in a brief manuscript *Remembrances of the Children* (private collection): 'the precious saying of Guy over which *Time & Oblivion* have paced & glided'.

25 Henderson, 1974, 87, 106–9, 137; Burne-Jones, 1904, II, 45–46.

26 Swinburne to George Powell, 22 May 1867, quoted in Lang, 1959–62, I, 246.

27 Spielmann, 1886, 37.

28 Newton referred to Brucciani's casts in relation to Oxford in a letter to Dr H. W. Acland, 29 January 1851 (Bod., MSS Acland d.64, ff. 96–99) and had spoken of the bust in a lecture to the Royal Institution in 1862, *Athenaeum*, 24 May 1862, 697–98. Named 'Sappho' in the seventeenth century when the later torso was joined to the head, she was listed in the 'Handbook Guide for the University Galleries, Oxford 1862, 1865' quoted by Michaelis 1882, 555–56. A cast from her was already known to exist in France. *Athenaeum*, 20 July 1867, 91–92; Sir Charles Newton to Professor Percy Gardner, 17 May 1888 (Bod., MSS Eng. Lett. c.55, f. 91).

29 CDGd, 16, 20, 21 June 1867.

30 *Athenaeum*, 21 December 1867, 856; Report from the Council of the Royal Academy, 1868, 18 December 167; D, 14 August 1893. Landseer had earlier accused GFW of 'apparently getting a reputation, & in the cheapest possible way'.

31 Cheshire, 1989, 122; Coutts Bank statements; Hunt, 1905, II, 148–49.

32 Ovid, *Metamorphoses*, I, 452; (Daphne), IV, 190–270; (Clytie). *Dudley Gallery*, 1867. GFW exhibited cats. 127 and 206–7, including *Sans Merci* (later known as *Mischief*).

33 WG, 2004, cat. 33. B/W I, 246; RA/L, cat. 10.

34 *Metamorphoses*, X, 11–63; Cat.S.111–13; *Athenaeum*, 28 December 1867, 899.

35 Commissioned on 3 August 1866 by Hon. William Cowper-Temple, Commissioner of Works for 300 guineas, *Beata Beatrix* was completed in 1870 and presented to the NG in 1889. Rossetti began a duplicate begun 1867, chalk version for William Graham 1869. Marsh, 1999, 303; Tate, 1997, cat. 44.

36   Ovid, *Metamorphosis*, XI. *Jeune fille thrace portant la tête d'Orphée*, purchased from 1866 Salon by the Musée du Luxembourg. Réunion des Musées Nationaux, *Gustave Moreau 1826–1898*, exh. cat. (Geneviève Lacambre), 1998, cat. 32; Mathieu and Lacambre, 1997, 16. EBJ decorated William Graham's piano with medallions on the theme of *Orpheus and Eurydice* (1873–80).

37   WG, 2004, 45 and 79, cat. 84. In 1863 Alexander Gilchrist published a biography Blake, who was the subject of an essay by Algernon Swinburne in 1864.

38   Revelation 6: 7–8. *Athenaeum*, 4 January 1868, 23; Gilchrist, 1863; Swinburne, 1864.

39   B/L II, 202. Prince Albert had proposed the idea of frescoes at South Kensington as a Crimean War memorial. Letter to Cole, 7 Janurary 1868, and letter from Cole, 10 January, quoted in the Art Museum Register 1867–68, 315: 521. GFW and Leighton were officially commissioned in a letter from Cole on 14 July. GFW's reply, 'Will undertake lunette as proposed', 15 July 1868 and Cole's confirmation, quoted in the Art Museum Register 1868, 300: 25003. Ormond, 1975, 4.

40   Cat.P.99a and b. Louise de Fonblanque, wife of Captain Francis Lowther RN.

41   A, II: 45; Asleson, 1998, 186.

42   Letter to the Countess of Airlie; M's notes of Wyndham letters (WG) 3 December 1867; letter to Mrs Wyndham, 29 January 1868 (NPG aIX, 37); letter from The Hon. J. E. Denison, 10 December 1867 (NPG s8).

43   Letter to W. E. Gladstone, 3 May 1868 (Gladstone Papers, BL, Add. MS 44415, f. 7).

44   *Art Journal*, 1868, 110. Several bronze casts were made from the clay model of *Clytie*, notably at WG and Tate Britain, and one was given to George Eliot. GFW carved one in marble, and of the two other marble versions, one was carved for Rickards by Nelson, 1877–78. Letters to Rickards, 30 July, 9–10 August 1877 and 6 September 1878 (NPG III, 165–73, 205–08); letter from Rickards, 7 August (NPG IV 74–76); Minneapolis Institute of Arts, 1978, 73, cat. 16.

45   GFW paid Brucciani seven pounds, five shillings and sixpence for the cast.

46   WG, 2004, 53–54, cat. 22; letter to Mrs Eustace Smith, n.d. (Churchill Archives Centre, REND 12/1); Cat.S.77b. GFW also painted *Iris*, depicting a fair-haired, half-draped young woman holding an iris; *Venus Verticordia*, (1864–68), featuring the face of Alexa Wilding, was commissioned by John Mitchell of Bradford. Tate, 1997, 152–53, cat. 43; bank statement, 30 December 1867.

47   Portrait of Sir Anthony Panizzi, presented to the British Museum in July 1866, showed a sketch-plan of the Reading Room in the upper right corner.

48   Leighton exhibited *Jonathan's Token to David*, commissioned by Wardell as a companion piece to *The Meeting of Jacob and Esau*. 'Fine Art Supplement,' *Illustrated London News*, 9 May 1868, 462; WG, 2004, 67; RA/L 1996, cat. 56.

49   Rossetti in RA *Notes*, 1868, I, 11, cat. 323.

50   Letter to Mrs Eustace Smith (Churchill Archives Centre, REND 12/1); Matthew, 1978, VI, 594.

51   Letters to W. E. Gladstone, 2 and 3 May 1868 (Gladstone Papers, BL, Add. MS 44415, f. 7).

52   The other 1868 Academy picture that impressed Swinburne was Albert Moore's *Azaleas*.

53   Swinburne in RA *Notes*, 1868, II, 31–32.

54   Letter to the Marchionness of Lothian, 5 July 1868 (NPG).

55   M ms notes by RA *Notes*, 1868 (WG).

56   *Art Journal*, 1868, 58 and 95. Proposed by the Earl of Derby three chronological National Portrait Exhibitions of deceased figures, tracing the history and progress or decadence of English art were held annually from 1866–68.

57   Letter to John Forster, 7 May 1868 (V&A: Forster Coll. MS vol. XL, 48.F.65.14); letter from Thomas Carlyle, 20 May 1868; Carlyle, 1904, II, 249n; Saumarez Smith, 1997, 11–12.

58   John Leslie to his wife (Leslie Papers K/3/7). His *Reminiscences* were subsequently published in 1881.

59   A, I: 250.

60   Note from Thomas Carlyle, with contemporary extract from Silvester De Lacy *Bibliographie Universelle*, XXVI, 206, 8 June 1867 (Fiche 31, F11).

61   Ritchie, 1893, 12; JMC, 1926.

62   Allingham, 1990, 10 June 1867.

63   Queen Victoria met Carlyle at the Deanery, Westminster Abbey, in 1869. Bailey and Bolitho, 1930, 253.

64   Carlyle, having admired *Arrangement in Grey and Black: Portrait of the Painter's Mother* sat down in Whistler's studio one morning in 1872 and instructed, 'And now, mon, fire away!' quoted in Tate, 1994, 144, cat. 61.

65   Pennells, 1908, I, 180.

66   A, I: 248–50; Dn, 8 December 1897.

67   Carlyle wrote to Mrs Jean Aitken on 30 June 1869, 'Watts, too, the Painter, has not quite done with me, I fear; and seems to be making a monster than otherwise. Well, Well!', Carlyle, 1904, II, 249.

68   From Thomas Carlyle, 1 July 1868 (NPG s.78).

69   John Forster to Thomas Carlyle, 29 July 1868, quoted in Davies, 1983, 205–6.

70   *Mrs Alfred Seymour*, Cat.S.143b, was 'remarkable for its depth of tone'. 'A Critical Notice of the Fine Art Exhibition held at Ruthin from 4 August to 26 September 1868', Ruthin newscutting; Lord, 2000, 273.

71 Letter from Thomas Hughes, 13 August 1868 (NPG si, 113–14). The frontispiece to *Tom Brown's School Days by an Old Boy*, 1869, was engraved after Watts's portrait of Thomas Hughes MP by C. H. Jeens.

72 Lady Adelaide Talbot to Lord Lothian, 1868 (NPG). Her Carlylean language reveals how Watts's aspirations affected his aristocratic sitters: 'I always feel so refreshed & ennobled after having talked to him – he raises one up so high – all that is fine – that is lovely that is good, of good report & noble – *that* he cares for & nothing else – it is strange that ones estimate of things should be entirely altered by one person like that – very rarely this happens that the spirit of the world is not on us all in some way or another.'

73 Letter to the Marchioness of Lothian, 5 July 1868 (NPG).

74 Scott correspondence quoted in A, 1: 243–44. Lichfield Cathedral Chapter Acts. 13, 1866–76 records that on 6 January 1870, 'A drawing of the proposed monument to the late Bishop Lonsdale was laid before the Dean and Chapter and approved. Ordered that permission be given to place it in the arch on the north side of the choir adjoining the reredos.' Henry Hugh Armstead, who had worked on the Albert Memorial, was lined up as second choice for the Bishop. Scott received a knighthood in 1872; Richard Prentis, 'A Tale of Two Canopies: The Mutilated Monuments of John of Eltham, Earl of Cornwall, and John Lonsdale, Bishop of Lichfield', *Friends of Lichfield Cathedral, 62nd Annual Report*, 1999, 27–35.

75 B/W: 112; WG, 2004, 14–15, 79, cat. 85

76 Letter from C. H. Rickards, 21 January 1868 (NPG aiv, 24–17); letters to Rickards, 1, 13 February, 12 March, 12 April, 21 and 24 September 1868 (NPG aii, 43–59). GFW decided against purchasing from Burne-Jones, now that he was establishing influential patrons.

77 Letter to Rickards, 24 October 1868 (Fiche 4).

78 Stewart, 1994, xxii, 37–38.

79 Marsh, 1999, 362; Rosalind Howard's diary, 6 April 1869. *Endymion* was 'the finest thing produced in our generation'. WG, 2004, 15 and 55, cat. 25; *Catalogue of the Pictures forming the Collection of Sir Charles Tennant Bart*, 1896; letter from Ford Madox Brown, 7 April 1869 (Fiche 15, B8).

80 Letters to Mrs Percy Wyndham, 27 February, 4 and 21 March 1869 (Fiche 27). GFW wrote that had he not agreed to sell *Orpheus* to Mrs Wyndham, he would have exhibited it and sold it for £250. During negotiations, he invited her to make her own copy.

81 Horner, 1933, 6. Arthur Hughes to Alexander Munro, April 1869, 'Is it not strange Watts has a splendid Endymion this year, also bought by Mr Graham', quoted in Roberts, 1997. The picture, acquired in 1879 by Sir Charles Tennant, was engraved in 1891 by Frank Short RA.

82 *Athenaeum*, 30 January 1869.

83 The *Titian* lunette, carried out in ceramic mosaic by Kate Clarke and Mary Jennings and superintended by Samuel Cooper for Minton, Hollins, was completed in 1869. *Report of the Science and Art Department*, 1869, 317.

84 Professor Solomon Hart, the third member of the hanging committee, featured little in correspondence or criticism. Report from the Council of the Royal Academy, 1870, 18 and 25; *Athenaeum*, 19 February 1870, 268; letter to D. G. Rossetti, 30 March 1869 (NPG av, 113).

85 Letters to J. Forster, 20 February and 23 March 1869 (V&A, Forster Coll. MS, vol. xl, 48.F.65.17 and 18).

86 Letter to Rickards, 10 February 1869 (NPG aii, 75–78).

87 Chichester Fortescue, long-standing member of the Cosmopolitan Club, Secretary for Ireland, appointed President of the Board of Trade in 1870 and created Lord Carlingford in 1874.

88 Letter to F. G. Stephens (Bod., MSS Don. e.87); letter from Chichester Fortescue, 14 July (NPG aiv, 38); Stocker, 1988, 12, 15–16, 25; A, 1: 255. Boehm had five rooms of Carlo Marchetti's divided former studios, at 76 Fulham Road, where under GFW's supervision he subsequently worked on the large statue of *Lord Holland*.

89 Letter to D. G. Rossetti, 30 March 1869 (University of British Columbia. Typescript, NPG av, 113).

90 Royal Academy Annual Report, 1869, Appendix 1, 19.

91 Letter from F. M. Brown, 7 April 1869 (Fiche 15, B8): 'The World under Water is a most astonishing imaginative suggesting vastness, and endless ligned atmosphere & singularly happy in the way the dove detaches itself from and floats above the waters.' Cat.S.38c; WG, 2004, 75, cat. 76; GFW referred to the picture as *The Deluge* and renamed it for the RA 1869 *The Return of the Dove. Daily Telegraph*, 31 December 1881.

92 At Rickard's request GFW exhibited the portrait of May. He would later drop his price for Rickards, from 600 guineas to 500. Letters from Rickards, 18 and 27 March 1869 (NPG aii, 79–85); letter to Rickards, 18 July 1871 (aii, 154–56). The Revd. William Blake Atkinson sent a copy of the poem, 5 July 1869 (NPG xii, 19); *Athenaeum*, 7 January 1882, 23.

93 *The Dream*, based on Milton's *On His Deceased Wife*, was among profiles of Mary Hillier registered for Mrs Cameron by E. H. Hounsell on 8 March 1869 (PRO, COPY 1/15/87–91).

94 Registered as, 'Painting in oil The Red cross Knight & Una George rides on a horse Una on a donkey by his side – landscape Clear Sky. Size 4 ft 5 inches high by 4 ft

11 inches' (PRO, COPY 1/15/138). The models were Arthur Prinsep and Mary Jackson, the future Mrs Herbert Fisher and the picture, exhibited at the RA in 1869 was bought by Samuel Barlow. M catalogued two other versions, one acquired by Mrs Herbert Fisher and the smaller painting, exhibited at the Grosvenor Gallery in 1879, purchased by Louis Huth, Cat.S.152a. The industrialist Sir Charles Tennant purchased a related study of donkeys, *Mother and Daughter* in 1869.

95   Letter to Edgar Boehm (Royal Archives, ADD A17 1785).

96   *Saturday Review*, 5 June 1869, 743–44. There were 70 foreign works, including Rosa Bonheur, Corot and Daubigny.

97   Report from the Council of the Royal Academy, 1869, 9.

98   Gullick, 1869, 13 and 30. Gullick acknowledged the improved display of sculpture and landscapes and the hangers' restraint with regard to their own works and suggested that W had been swayed by Leighton. *Pall Mall Gazette*, 26 May 1869, 11.

99   Letter from Sir F. Grant, quoted in A, I: 233.

100  Letter from W. E. Gladstone, 1 May 1869 (NPG). GFW exhibited at RA 1869, cats 45, 125, 327, 700: *The Return of the Dove*, *The Red Cross Knight and Una*, *A Portrait* (May Prinsep), *Orpheus and Eurydice*; Cat.S.38c, 111b, 152a and Cat.P.128a. A study of donkeys, known variously as *Mother and Daughter* & *Ass and Foal*, relating to the *Red Cross Knight* was purchased by Rickards; Cat.S.11c–12a.

101  Letter to Mrs Wyndham, April 1869 (NPG a1x, 38).

102  Letter to W. E. Gladstone, 2 May 1869 (Gladstone Papers, BL, Add. MS 44420; f. 202); letter from W. Gladstone, 4 May 1869 (NPG). W. M. Rossetti, 1903, 'William Rossetti – Diary, 18 July 1869, 'new picture from the Greek head at Oxford, very lovely'. Cat.S.161a. Louis Huth purchased GFW's second *Wife of Pygmalion*.

103  Letter from Dean Stanley, 3 August 1871 (NPG a1v, 117); letter to Rickards, 23 September 1869 (NPG a11, 99–102); A, I: 243; Coutts Bank statement, 23 November 1869.

104  Letter to J. Forster, 11 October, 7 November 1869 (V&A, Forster Coll. MS, vol. XL, 48.F.65.20–21).

105  D, 3 April 1893; A, I: 248. Thomas Carlyle to his brother, quoted in *Collected Letters*, *Carlyle*, 1970; National Trust, 1979, 26. Carlyle noted in a letter Forster, 12 October 1868, quoted in Davies, 1983, 284, 132n: referring to 'Watts's Blotch-Portrait . . . "Last sitting" to be, Friday next, $2^{1}/_{2}$ pm to end at 4 forever – So distracted a monster of Painting I have never seen before: cross bet$^{n}$ a Lunatic & an Imposter: no feature of me recognizable in it. Fie!'

106  Chesterton, 1904, 154.

107  Mary Ann Cross (George Eliot (1819–80)), partner of George Henry Lewes from 1843. Letter from George Eliot, 11 January 1870, quoted in Haight, 1985, 370–71; Haight, vol. 56, April 1982, 65–69; A, I: 276–77; letter to 'Mrs Lewes' (draft, NPG s11).

108  Letter to Henry Bruce, 15 February 1869 (Glamorgan Record Office, D/d B: 161/4. Fiche 43, NPG axv).

109  Letters from Rickards, 1 and 18 September and 9 December 1869 (NPG, a1v, 22–38); letter to Rickards, 17 September (NPG a11, 95–98).

110  Cat.S.79b; WG, 2004, 56, cat. 29, and 52, cat. 20; RA/L, 80, fig. 54; *Athenaeum*, 30 October 1869, 567; *Illustrated London News*, 30 October 1869, 441.

111  The nude painting bears a resemblance to the figure of *Night* on Michelangelo's tomb for Giuliano in the Medici chapel, Florence. Whitechapel Art Gallery, 1974, cat. 66, dates GFW's first design for *Hope* from 1865–70.

112  Richard Home Shepherd, in RA *Notes*, 1870, 8.

113  Beattie, 1983, 147.


## 9    Calling Off These Studios (1870–1873)

1   Letters to Rickards, 4 and 18 April 1870 (NPG a11, 119–26).

2   MacCarthy 1994, 199–200.

3   *Ibid.* 270.

4   William Morris to Jane Morris, 15 April 1870, quoted in MacCarthy, 1994, 150, 256–57 and 270. JM was staying with Rossetti at the Sussex home of Barbara Bodichon, future founder of Girton College, Cambridge.

5   Cat.P.31–32, 175a, Cat.S.27a and b, 62b and c. GFW used studies from her son Demetrius Zambaco for *Ganymede and The Childhood of Jupiter*. Fitzgerald, 1997, 147.

6   Burne-Jones to Rossetti, 1869, quoted in Fitzgerald, 1997, 125; Rosalind Howard's diary, 29 January 1869 (Castle Howard papers: J22/27).

7   Letter from Burne-Jones, 11 February 1870 (Fiche 16, D12). At 18, Maria Zambaco, granddaughter of Constantine Ionides and daughter of Euphrosyne Cassavetti, married Greek physician Demetrius Zambaco, with whom she had a son and daughter. To console her after their separation in 1866, her mother commissioned EBJ to paint her portrait. She and EBJ wanted to elope and in January 1869 he had dramatically prevented her suicide. Crane, 1907, 84; Fitzgerald, 1997, 125–28.

8   Howell, who lost his job as secretary to Ruskin, was paid by GFW until 20 April 1870. They remained in correspondence until 4 December. Marsh, 1999, 415; Burne-Jones, 1904, II, 11.

9    Letter to GBJ, 4 December 1870 (Fitzwilliam, VIII; 8); letter from EBJ, December 1870. GBJ bequeathed the portrait to the Birmingham Art Gallery in 1895. Cat.P.23c.

10   R. H. Shepherd in RA *Notes*, 1870, 8.

11   *Athenaeum*, 21 May 1870, 680.

12   E. Poynter, 'Systems of Art Education', *Lectures on Art* 2 October 1871, Lecture III, 1879, quoted in Andrew Forge, *The Slade 1871–1960*, 1960–61, 33–34.

13   Cat.S.33a and 54c; letters to C. H. Rickards, 4 and 18 April 1870 (NPG aII, 119–26). *Daphne* was bought by Louis Huth in 1872. R. H. Shepherd in RA *Notes*, 1870, 29; *Athenaeum*, 30 April, 485, 21 May 1870, 680; *Art Journal*, 1870, 290. The original maiden's head and upper torso cut from *Knight Errant*, appears dressed Millais's *The Martyr of the Solway*, 1871. Tate, 2001, 70, cats 12 and 90–91, cat. 32.

14   Blunt, 'Proteus: First Eastern Travels', *Alms to Oblivion*, v 1873, 5 (Fitzwilliam).

15   Marsh, 1999, I, 399.

16   Sittings continued until July. As the portrait, originally intended for GFW's national series, was given to the Rossetti family (NPG), GFW made a replica (WAG). A, I: 267, 270; Morris, 1996, cat. 2134; MacCarthy, 1994, 114 and 219; Marsh, 1999, I, 408–9; Rossetti, 1895, I, 349; Minto, 1892, II, 215–16; *Athenaeum*, 30 April 1870, 573–74.

17   Cat.P.167b.

18   A, I: 288–89.

19   Now attributed to Andrea Meldolla Schiavone (1522–1564), the picture was borrowed for two or three years and exhibited at South Kensington in 1870.

20   Atkinson, 1871, 30, first published in *Portfolio*, 1870, I, V, 64; letter to Rickards, 27 June 1870 (NPG aII, 127–29).

21   *Art Journal*, 1870, 290; Sir Edwin Landseer to the Marquess of Westminster, 13 June 1870 (photocopy, WG); letters from Lord Westminster, 14 and 21 June 1870 (NPG aIV, 102–4, 111–13), and to Lord Westminster, 15 and 22 June 1870 (Grosvenor Estate.pp/13/159–60); A, I: 251, 254–55; letter to Rickards, 22 November 1870 (NPG aII, 137–39). GFW planned to begin the full-size group in spring 1871. *Cheshire Under the Norman Earls*, 83 (Grosvenor Estate Papers).

22   WG, 2004, 44 and 87–88, cat. 110; B/W: 12; A, I: 256.

23   M MS book v (WG).

24   Letters from Lord Fortescue, 14 and 23 July 1870 (NPG aIV, 121–22); letters to the Countess of Airlie, n.d. and 29 July 1870 (The Airlie Papers). EIB states that Fabrucci, an Italian sculptor, later his assistant, showed GFW how to model plaster. Banks statements show his first payment to Fabrucci on 27 June 1877; B/W: 51. On 28 July GFW paid half his six-hundred-pound fee (first instalment) to Boehm. GFW did not mention Fabrucci in his letter to F. G. Stephens, (Bod., MSS Don. e.87): 'Boehm put the large statue up in his Studio, & I then went over it, leaving him to carry it on under my direction, in the summer I worked at it in Boehm's studio for about two months, it was then cast & brought to the garden of LHH, where in plaster I may say I entirely remodelled it, & a precious job I had.'

25   Ilchester, 1937, 445. Moved to its present position in 1926 for the building of Melbury Court, the *Lord Holland* statue was erected in Holland Park in June 1872 and unveiled in October. Boehm's railing and decorative relief panels were decorated with Japanese-style fish. *Athenaeum*, 29 June 1872, 820 and 19 October 1872, 504.

26   Letter to C. H. Rickards, 26 February 1871 (NPG aII, 140–42). Had Miss Lonsdale delivered the two photographs earlier, GFW wrote, 'I would have made a great difference.' According to M, Scott apologized that his elaborate canopy (based on the tomb of John of Eltham, Earl of Cornwall, in Westminster Abbey) destroyed the figure. A, I: 243–44; *Athenaeum*, 8 October 1870; Prentis, 1999, 27–35.

27   Fitzpatrick, 1923, 89; Longford, 1991, 28–29.

28   William Schomberg Ker, the 8th Marquess of Lothian died on 4 July 1870. GFW was subsequently commissioned to sculpt his memorial for Blickling Church, and to paint a replica of his portrait of Lord Lothian to hang in the Bodleian Library, Oxford.

29   Réunion des Musées Nationaux, 1998, cat. 88; MM, 2003, cat. 92.

30   Tennyson 1830, 'Love and Death'; Minneapolis Institute of Arts, 1978, 77–78, cat. 20 and 86, cat. 28; Hunt, *Light of the World* (1851–53); Réunion des Musées Nationaux, 2002, cat. 50; letters to Rickards, 26 February and 1 March 1871, 27 December 1873 and 27 December 1874 (NPG aII, ff. 140–46, 273–75 and 363–66). GFW exhibited at the Dudley Gallery 1870, cats 108, 120 and 192: large *Love and Death, From My Studio Window* and *Francesca and Paolo (vide Dante)*, the only version to include Dante and Virgil, with Jeanie's head modelling as Francesca bought by Rickards Cat.S.88a and 116c.

31   Letter to Mrs Senior, 22 November 1870; letter to Rickards, 22 November 1870 (NPG aII, 137–39).

32   'The Fire at Holland House' (HH/BL, Add. MS 52169; ff. 16 and 92); Liechtenstein, 1875, 304–05.

33   *Inventory of Pictures* (BL, Add. MS 52169; ff. 47–49): portraits of Dr Playfair, Mr Binda, The *Duc d'Aumale* and *Lord Holland* which GFW believed ruined were to be restored by him for £10 each. Letter to Lady Holland, 30 January 1871 (BL, Add. MS 52169, f. 66).

34   Letter from Lady Holland, 31 January 1871 (WG).

35  Marsh, 1999, 313.

36  Letters to C. H. Rickards, 26 February, 2 July 1871, 9 October 1874 (NPG aii, 140–42, 151–53 and 345–47). Minneapolis Institute of Arts, 1978, 78–79, cat. 21; WG, 2004, 62, cat. 46.

37  D, 25 September 1887; *Athenaeum*, 28 January 1871, 119; A, i: 264–65; Wood, 1999, 295.

38  France had declared war in July 1870. Napoleon III was captured in September and his pretentious second Empire collapsed – GFW decried its 'cruel indifference to justice'. Letter to C. H. Rickards, 29 August 1870 (NPG aii, 133–36).

39  Pissarro to Dewhurst, 6 November 1902, quoted in Dewhurst, 1914, 32.

40  Henry Cole and the organizer Richard Redgrave went to LHH on 14 March 1871: 'In the afternoon with Redgrave at Watts who lent several pictures', Diaries of Sir Henry Cole (V&A). Cat.S.36c or 37a and portraits of Lord Lawrence, Lord Cambell, Gladstone and Carlyle. *Athenaeum* 29 April 1871, 533 and 20 May 1871, 629; *Art Journal*, 1871, 201 mistakenly identified *After the Transgression* (*The Denunciation of Adam and Eve*), as a representation of the crucifixion.

41  Monet showed *Meditation*, another portrait of his wife and a French landscape and Pissarro exhibited two London snowscapes at the German Gallery. Shanes, 1994, 19.

42  *Report from the Council of the Royal Academy*, 1871, 6 and 22.

43  Socialist revolutionaries controlled the Paris 'Commune' from March 1871 until they were overwhelmed in a savage attack in June. Dewhurst, 1914, 31–33.

44  *Royal Glasgow Institute of Art*, 1871, cats 161, 379: *Venus and Cupid* (lent by John Graham of Skelmorlie) and a portrait of the late Thomas Graham, Master of the Mint (lent by Mrs Reid).

45  GFW made drawings for *Britomart* and a fresco in 1851–52. Cat.S.17 and 47; *Athenaeum*, March 1871, 310.

46  Fitzpatrick, 1923, 92.

47  RA 1871, cats 75, 172, 177; portraits of Lady Isabella Somers Cocks, Millais, Leighton. Cat.P.91a, 109a, 146b; *Athenaeum*, 13 May 1871, 596; *Art Journal* 1871, 154 and 174.

48  According to Winsor and Newton's records GFW's absorbent ground canvases 'were prepared with Flour paste, Plaster of Paris, and Glue dissolved in water; afterwards Whiting soaked in water, and mixed with Patent size, Honey, and a small quantity of Pale Drying Oil. Letter from Robert Thrupp of W & N, 28 July 1892, quoted in A, iii: 69.

49  Letter to Mr Lawrence, 31 October 1871 (V&A/MA, 86WW.1).

50  Letter from P. E. Calderon, 1871 (WG).

51  GFW's bank account held £4,763, of which his income of £328 from shares would not cover 'just claims': £300 alimony and £80 quarterly to Alexander Ionides, let alone rent, payments to Charles Couzens for copies, and framing.

52  Letter to Ruskin, quoted in A, i: 263–64; and from Ruskin, 10 May 1871 (Bod., MSS Eng. Lett. c.50; f. 193); *The Times*, 8 May 1871; Ruskin 1906, 100–02.

53  Letter from Benjamin Disraeli, 5 July 1871 (NPG, Fiche 22, D8–11), letter to Lady Marion Alford, 30 June 1879 (NPG): 'When GFW enquired again through Lady Marion, the elevated Earl of Beaconsfield, then prime minister, replied that he had presumed GFW did not care about painting him when he was willing to sit, that he had given up the idea, and was now too old – at the time Millais was painting his half-length portrait.

54  Letter from Countess Spencer, 13 July 1871 (NPG); Cat.P.19c and 148a. *The Revd. Stopford Augustus Brooke*, minister of the proprietary chapel of St James, York Street, London, 1866–76.

55  Bank statements show a deposit £600 on 1 August (presumably for *Lord Holland* for he paid Boehm £210 on the 3rd) and payments to Burne-Jones, Legros, Mason and Mrs Cameron. On the 14th he sold £2,007 6s 11d London and Brighton stock and on the 16th bought £2,004 19s 6d Carnegie Railway shares. On 26 September he paid in 500 guineas (presumably Rickards's cheque for *The Return of the Dove*. M MS book v).

56  Cat.S.126c; *Precis of the Minutes of The Science and Art Department*, 1863–77, 3 August 1871 (V&A/MA). The Albert Hall opened on 29 March. Letters to Rickards, 4 October, 5 November and 10 December 1871.

57  *The Times*, 14 November 1871; *Art Journal*, 1871, 285. *A Vision of the Last Judgment*, 1808, Tate, 2000, cat. 59.

58  A, iii: 22.

59  *Dudley Gallery*, 1871, 132: *The Angel of Death* (finished design for a large picture). Letters to Rickards, 20 August, 20 September and 4 October 1871 (NPG aii, 159–61, 167–73). Rickards eventually purchased the picture in 1881. Cat.S.30a.

60  Cat.S.30b; D, 19 March 1902.

61  Letters to Rickards, 5 and 15 November 1871 (NPG aii, 174–84. Fiche 5). GFW considered moving out to Richmond.

62  Plan of proposed new road, Melbury Rd (HH/LMA: E/HOL/Ac 70.74, Box 2), illustrated in Dakers, 1999, 147.

63  A, i: 253–54. M's notes from Book v.

64  Letters from Disraeli, 5 July, annotated by M, and 3 December 1871 (NPG, 341). GFW asked again, after Disraeli's re-election as prime minister and subsequent

elevation, writing to Lady Airlie to remind Lord Beaconsfield that he did wish to paint his portrait: 'It cannot be doubted he will stand a conspicuous figure in history.' Letter to the Countess of Airlie, 1 January 1875.

65  'My punishment is greater than I can bear', Genesis IV, 11–13. First oil sketch *en brunaille* c.1867–68.

66  Letter to Rickards, 31 December 1871 (NPG aII, 186–89).

67  Fisher, 1940, 14. The statesman H. A. L. Fisher, who visited his great Aunt Sara at Little Holland House as a boy, recalled his excitement at seeing the background to the GFW's large imaginative canvasses being filled in by the brave Conrad, whom he understood had fled from military service in Prussia and was under sentence of death.

68  Letters to Lady Ashburton, 26 January and 24 July 1872; 3 and 8 June 1874; Surtees, 1984.

69  Dakers, 1993, 49; Swenarton, 1989; Jones, 'Philip Webb', *Victorian Architecture*, London, 1963, 260–61.

70  Troubridge, 1925, 19; Kirk, 1990, 250 and 467.

71  Emily Tennyson to Edward Lear, 22 February 1871 (TRC: 5526).

72  Letter to JMC, 19 February 1872 (NPG, Fiche 34, G9–35 A1). JMC registered photographs of Rachel as *Cupid Considering* and Laura as *Angel of the Nativity* on 8 November 1872 (PRO, COPY 1/20/192); Troubridge, 1925, 34.

73  Letter to Rickards, 18 February 1872 (NPG aII, 192–94).

74  Ormond, 1969, 239.

75  Pennells, 1908, I, 179. On occasion Whistler relieved her and allowed a model to stand in her gown: Tate, 1994, 148, cat. 63; *Athenaeum*, 20 April 1872.

76  Letter to Rickards, 10 May 1872 (NPG aII, 199–201); Jekyll's diary notes (NPG axv, 112).

77  Letter to the Countess of Airlie, 20 April 1872; letter to Rickards, 5 May 1872 (NPG aII, 195–98).

78  RA 1872, cats 57, 145, 153, 215, 266: *V. C. Prinsep Esq.*, *A Portrait: Study, Philip Calderon RA, Miss Virginia Dalrymple, R. H. W. Dunlop.* Cat.P.27c, 35c, 48c, 128b.

79  *Academy*, 15 May; Sutton, 1963, 72; Stirling, 1926, 271; *Athenaeum*, 4 May 1872; letter to Rickards, 5 May 1872 (NPG aII, 195–98).

80  RA 1872, cat. 658: '*My punishment is greater than I can bear.*' Cat.S.21a; A, I: 257–59; *Report from the Council of the Royal Academy*, 1872, 18; Tate Gallery, 1854, cat. 57; Cat.S.21b; WG, 2004, 68, cats 57 and 58; see Appendix III.

81  On 10 October Tyerman cashed the first of GFW's monthly cheques for £350. Kirk, 1990, 250.

82  Letter to Miss Norman, 9 June 1872 (Huntington, HM.31135); letter to Rickards, 25 July 1872 (NPG, AII, 207–09).

83  Blanche was born on 17 October 1862. Her father was Major Herbert Clogstoun, VC. Her grandmother Adeline, the eldest Pattle sister, died in 1836. Troubridge, 1925, 9–10; A, I: 266; letter to Rickards, 21 September 1872 (NPG aII, 213–15).

84  *Athenaeum*, 29 June 1872, 820 and 19 October, 504.

85  Report from the Council of the Royal Academy, 1872; B/L, II, 89–90; letter to Rickards, 28 October 1872 (NPG aII, 219–22). Richard Johnson and family, Samuel Barlow and Mr Weighly had commissioned portraits. GFW's fee was now 300 guineas.

86  Dudley Gallery, 1872, cats 70 and 216; *Athenaeum*, 2 November 1872, 568.

87  A, I: 221; Cheshire, 1989, 14; Steen, 1962, 123–24; Tom Taylor to J. P. Martineau, 2 August 1876 (WG).

88  Letters to Rickards, 20 and 25 November 1872 (NPG aII, 223–29).

89  Cat.S.83c; letter to Mrs Senior, 20 November 1872 (Fiche 29, A1); letter to Rickards, 18 December 1872 (NPG aII, 230–32); Blunt, 'Proteus: Madeline' *Alms to Oblivion*, v, 3, 5; letter to Mrs Wyndham, 12 February 1873 (Fiche 27, E2). GFW, having agreed to repay Huth, who concerned to reduce nudity in his gallery, offered the picture to Mrs Wyndham, but Huth owned the picture, afterwards bought by Sir Alexander Henderson, when it was exhibited at the Exposition Universelle in 1878.

90  Letter from Alfred Tennyson, 27 December 1872 (NPG); letter to AT, 28 December 1872, (TRC:6269); Cat.P.105b and c. GFW painted one portrait of Martineau for Manchester New College and the replica now in the NPG.

91  Jenkins, 1996, 60–66.

92  Letters to Sir Charles Dilke, 25 September 1872 (WCA: 365/1, f. 41) and 31 December (BL, Add. MS 43909; f. 323), 1 January, 7 and 9 March 1873 (WCA, ff. 42–43 and 11). Lady Dilke was ill and her less successful portrait was destroyed by Dilke after her death in 1874. Cat.P.45c.

93  Letters from Ruskin, 23 January and 1 February 1873 (Typescripts, Bod., MSS Eng. Lett. c.50, ff. 194 and 197).

94  *The Globe*, 10 February 1873.

95  Letter from Ruskin, 13 February 1873 (Bod., MSS Eng. Lett. c.50, ff. 195–96).

96  Letters to Rickards, 19, 23 and 25 March 1873 (NPG aII, 237–47). See Appendix I. *The House of Life.*

97  *Minutes of the General Committee of The Athenaeum*, 1873; *Athenaeum Candidates Book*, 1873.

98  Dilke's portrait was completed by 7 March; letters to Sir Charles and Lady Dilke, 7 and 9 March 1873 (WCA).

99  Letter to Rickards, 25 March 1873 (NPG aII, 244–47).

100  In January 1873, James Stansfeld, President of the Local Government Board appointed Mrs Senior temporary Inspector to carry out an enquiry into the barrack

schools for pauper children, to give, 'the woman's view . . . I did the thing which they hated the most. I imposed a woman on them.' Mrs Senior's appointment was made permanent in January 1874.

101   Stirling, 1926, 267.

102   *Correspondence Relating to the Portrait in Oils of John Stuart Mill, MP by G. F. Watts RA OM*, MS book bequeathed by Sir Charles Dilke (WCA: 365/1); John Stuart Mill to Dilke, 9 March 1873; letter from Mill, 13 March (NPG sII, 303, fiche 15, B5); letter from Dilke, 16 March; letter to Dilke, 28 August; A, I: 273–75), recommends that the picture is etched by a French engraver and reserves copyright of Mill's portrait. Cat.P.108a and b. Dilke bought the original portrait and GFW painted a replica for his national collection and a further replica.

103   Read, 1982, 39; Thornycroft sketch model RA 1874; letter to Madeline Wyndham, 12 February 1873 (Fiche 27, E2); Manning, 1982, 61.

104   B/L, II, 194n; RA 1873, cats 13, 36, 214, 281, 915: portraits of George Warde Norman, William Spottiswoode (mathematician, physicist and future president of the Royal Society), the Duke of Cleveland, Miss Mary Prinsep (Cat.P.37b, 117c, 148c, and S.120a), and *The Prodigal* (model Colarossi).

105   Letter to W. E. Gladstone, 4 May 1873; Newton to Gladstone, 16 May (BL, Add. MS 44438; ff. 252 and 276); Newton, 1874.

106   Leighton to W. E. Gladstone, February 1873; letter to Gladstone, 4 May (BL, Add. MS 44437; f. 238; Add. MS 44438; f. 252); Ormonds, 1975, 68; Asleson, 1998, 133.

107   Then called *Eve in the Glory of Her Innocence*.

108   A, I: 262–63; letter to Rickards, 1 February 1874 (NPG aII, 281–87).

109   Letter to Rickards, 2 and 6 June 1873 (NPG aII, 250–55).

110   *Dudley Gallery*, 1873, cat. 75. *Art Journal*, 1873, 367.

111   *The Republic of Plato*, trans. Benjamin Jowett, quoted in A, II: 138.

112   A, II: 138–39; Milton, *Paradise Lost*, I, III: 380; WG, 2004, 26 and 51.

113   Cat.P.98b2. G. Horsley Palmer to the 9th Marquess of Lothian, n.d. (National Archives of Scotland GD40/9/458/8), 9 July (GF40/9/458/3). GFW was also painting a second portrait of the marquess for 150 guineas for the Bodleian. Letter to Schomberg Henry Ker, Marquess of Lothian, 9 January 1873 (NAS: GD40/9/458/10).

114   Fragment of undated letter (NAS: GD40/9/458/11).

115   The alabaster monument was believed to have been installed at Blickling Church in 1878; a sandstone replica was made for Jedburgh Abbey. National Trust, 1987, 47.

116   The Dean and Canons of St George's Chapel, 1999, 6.

117   Cat.P.136a; letters to Rickards, 4 and 30 August 1873 (NPG aII, 256–62). Rickards's sale of 2 April 1887 lists three portraits of Blanche. Aglaia Coronio's daughter Caliope also sat at this time. Harry Quilter, *The Times*, 6 January 1882.

118   GFW did not identify the builder. Webb's letter of June 1874 complains about Waterfield's and Saunders's accusations. Hill & Co. 1871 trade directory lists the builders Henry Saunders of Easton & John George Kennet of Middleton. Thwaite, 1996, 451 and 475; M states in A, I: 278, that the house was finished that autumn, but Tyerman continued to receive payments until March 1874.

119   Letter to JMC, 3 October 1873 (NPG).

120   D, 3 October 1887; A, I: 278.

121   Letter to Richard Redgrave, 10 December 1873 (V&A/MA, 84/67.11995). Leighton sent two sketches for the south-eastern lunette in September. Physick, 1982, 73.

122   Letter to Leighton, 15 December 1873 (JRM, Spielmann: Eng. MS 1301).

123   Cat.P.151b; *The Ulster*, 198.7 cm high, was bought in 1874 by Rickards and exhibited at the RA in 1879.

124   'The first cap worn by G. F. Watts Esq RA (Signor) made by Miss A Prinsep 1874' measures 23.75 cm in diameter (private collection). Ellen Terry noted on her copy of Chesterton, 1904, 45: 'He wore it because the slightest draught on his head gave him excruciating pain.'


## 10   Sweet Briary (1874–1876)


1   Middle Temple, 23 and 30 January 1874 (MT.1/MPA/No18, 97 and 100).

2   Originally spelled 'The Briery'. Weld, 1903, 84; Fuller, 1992, 25.

3   GFW received Barlow's deposit for *The Angel of Death*, presumably the $100 paid in on 6 March. Letters to Rickards, 1 February and 5 March 1874 (NPG aII, 281–87 and 303–06).

4   Troubridge, 1925, 19; Kirk, 1990, 250 and 467.

5   Troubridge, 1925, 20; Fuller, 1992, 25.

6   Cat.S.59b. *Freshwater in Spring*, bought by Rickards. Letters to Rickards, 13 and 22 February 1874 (NPG aII, 292–94, 299–300).

7   Rossetti and Morris signed the joint lease for Kelmscott in June 1871. Marsh, 1999, 416.

8   Fitzgerald, 1997, 155; letter from EBJ, January 1874, quoted in Harrison and Waters, 1989, 110.

9   Fitzgerald, 1997, 153.

10   From EBJ (Fiche 16, D14).

11   Weld, 1903, 85.

12 Cat.P.10c and Cat.S.152b. Letter to Rickards, 5 March 1874 (NPG aII, 303–06).

13 Cat.P.59b, 37b and 144a. Sir John Peter Grant GC MG. GFW exhibited a portrait of the Duke of Cleveland at the RA in 1873. Hogan, 1893, 345; Martin 1893, II, 408.

14 Cat.P.141a.

15 Cat.P.67c.

16 Atlay, 1899.

17 Cat.P.38c.

18 Dakers, 1999, 151.

19 Letters to Rickards, 21 February, 5 and 15 March 1874 (NPG aII, 295–98 and 303–09).

20 Percy Wyndham, having agreed to pay £600 seven years earlier, paid £1,000, deposited into GFW's bank account on 10 July 1874. Letter to Mrs Wyndham (Fiche 27).

21 Letter to Mrs Wyndham, 30 March 1874 (Fiche 27, E2), quoted in A, I: 240.

22 Ilchester, 1937, II, 441.

23 Letter to Lady Holland in Naples, 31 March 1874 (HH/BL, Add, MS 52163; f. 132). On 17 January 1874 Lady Holland passed her estate to the Earl of Ilchester.

24 Letter to Alice Liddell, 27 March 1874; Cat.S.94c, completed 1875.

25 A, I: 294.

26 *Ibid.*, incorporating language correction from Wilfrid Blunt's copy of *Annals*. In June JMC registered photographs of a fish girl, sailor, old man and child.

27 Cat.P.85a, 90c, 105b, 108b, 138c; letters to Rickards, 21–22 February, 7 May 1874 (NPG aII, 295–300, 320–23), and from Rickards, 8 February (aIV, 41–45); *Art Journal*, 1874, 162; *Athenaeum*, 11 April 1874, 499, 9 May 1874, 637, listing Millais's *Winter Fuel, The North-West Passage, Still for a Moment, A Day-Dream, The Picture of Health*. Mill's portrait was engraved that summer by the Frenchman Paul Adolphe Rajon. P. A. Rajon to Sir Charles Dilke, 4 July 1874 (WCA: 365/1.f.23).

28 Middle Temple, 20 February, 6 March and 29 May 1874 (MT.1/MPA/No18, 104–05, 108–09 and 128–30). Cat.P.165a; A. I: 280–81; Lee, 1925, I, 330.

29 Letter to Mrs Wyndham (Fiche 27, E2).

30 Letter from Webb, 8 July 1874.

31 *Ibid.*, 17 July 1874. Tyerman received no further fee after £4,300 paid by 25 March, representing a loss – or saving to GFW – of £215. Webb had a similar difficulty that year with Lord Sackville Cecil at the Oast House and in both instances refused to take his five-per-cent fee.

32 George Howard to Charles Howard, 25 February 1875 (Castle Howard archives J20), quoted in Dakers, 1993, 64; 1999, 151. Although Webb proposed that Watts deal in future through Thomas Hughes, as Jeanie's

brother there was clearly a conflict of interest. Webb's letters, 18 and 23 July 1874.

33 Letter to Miss de Rothschild, 25 July 1874; letter to Rickards, 11 June 1874 (NPG aII, 327–30).

34 HH/LMA: E/HOL/Ac.70.74.

35 Dakers, 1999, 153.

36 He paid £4,402 13s 2d to Jackson and Shaw, 7 June 1875–1 August 1877.

37 Letter to Rickards, 12 August 1874 (NPG aII, 331–34), and from Rickards, 15 August 1874 (NPG aIV, 46–53). Rickards was planning to buy *Freshwater Landscape, The Mid-Day Rest* (replica) and one of two portraits of Alice de Bretton, daughter of Baron de Bretton of Copenhagen, before her marriage to Lord Garvagh (Cat.P.58a). He had commissioned a bust of his vicar Armstead, which Nelson was to model in clay (completed by 1 July 1875) and carve in marble under Watts's supervision.

38 Letter from W. W. Graham, 14 August 1874 (NPG aIV, 262–68).

39 *Royal Manchester Institution*, 1874: *The Rider on the Black Horse, Daphne and Blanche* (cats 55, 58, 70, lent by Rickards), *Love and Death* (unfinished), *Orpheus and Eurydice*, (cats 61 and 67), *The Revd. James Martineau* (cat. 62, Martineau Portrait Committee), *The Angel of Death* (cat. 64, Barlow), *Richard Johnson Esq* (cat. 65, Johnson). Barlow, who was on the hanging committee, also owned the Corot.

40 Cat.S.88a. WGc, 15 September 1874. Letters to Rickards, 1 October and 3 December 1874 (NPG aII, 356–58, 341–44).

41 Bought by Charles J. Galloway 1875. Rickards's copy of a letter from Mrs Young (NPG aII, 361–62).

42 Letter to Rickards, 27 December 1874 (NPG aII, 363–66).

43 George du Maurier to Thomas Armstrong, September 1874, quoted in Ormond, 1969, 225–27.

44 'A Reminiscence of Mrs Cameron by a Lady Amateur', *Photographic News*, 1 January 1886. At Tennyson's suggestion JMC published the first of two volumes of her full-size photographs with handwritten text from the poet's idylls at Christmas: Cameron, 1874–75; Gernsheim, 1975, 46.

45 Letters to Rickards, 15 September, 2 and 29 November 1874 (NPG aII, 335–38 and 348–55); Cat.P.66c, 67a; Cat.S.24a. GFW also gave the Hichens an earlier picture of May playing under the now demolished cedar tree in the old Little Holland House garden, and had watercolour views of the house drawn for Rickards.

46 Quoted in Sotheby's 2000, 47, cat. 54.

47 Letter to Mrs Senior, 21 November 1874; letters to Rickards, 1 October and 2 November 1874 (NPG aII, 341–44, 348–51).

48   Fuller, 1933, 28; Dn, 16 February 1889.

49   Letter to Rickards, 29 November 1874 (NPG aII, 352–55).

50   Cat.S.34c; Dudley Gallery, 1874, cat. 165, *Dawn and Day*.

51   *Art Journal* 1874, 358; *Athenaeum*, 1874.

52   Letters to Mrs Sidney Bateman, 3 December 1874 and 13 May 1875 (HR).

53   Letters to Mrs Senior, 1 and 7 January 1875; and from Mrs Senior, 28 July, quoted in A, I: 296–97.

54   Letter to the Royal Academy, 23 December 1874 (RA, RAC/1/WA 13).

55   Holland Estate – Plan Referred to in Agreement dated 15 July 1875, Studio For G. F. Watts RA Drawing No 1. Approved on behalf of the Freeholder (The Earl of Ilchester) by Robert C Drivers Surveyor, 9 January 1875. Architect F. P. Cockerell, November 1874 (HH/LMA: E/HOL (Ac 70.74, Box 2).

56   Memorandum of Agreement, 15 February 1875 between Rt Hon Henry Edward Earl of Ilchester and Valentine Cameron Prinsep of Holland Park Road (HH/LMA: E/HOL/Ac.70.85/II).

57   Letter to Rickards, 10 January 1875 (NPG aIII, 2–5).

58   *Ibid.* 13 and 17 January 1875 (NPG aIII, 6–13).

59   A, II: 166.

60   Cat.S.135–36. *The Spirit of Religion*, exhibited at RA 1875 as *Dedicated to All the Churches* was ultimately renamed *The Spirit of Christianity*. In October 1873, he began a reduced version for Rickards, who referred to it as *The Sacred Heart*. The figure was intended embody 'the divine spirit of the teaching, not the personality of the divine Teacher.

61   *Ibid.*, 19, 23 February 1875 (NPG aIII, 18–25); Amor, 1989, 204–05. Cat.S.135–36.

62   Cat.P.63b.

63   Weld, 1903, 77–78.

64   Troubridge, 1925, 22–24 and 52. Rickards bought portraits of Laura and Rachel Gurney painted at The Briary, c. 1875. Cat.P.62–63.

65   Letters to Rickards, 22 December 1874, 19 February 1875 (NPG aII, 359–60; aIII, ff. 18–21).

66   *Ibid.* 9 February 1875 (NPG aIII, 14–17).

67   The portrait was presented to the Dean by the college in summer 1876. Letter to Alice Liddell, 18 February 1875 (BL, Add. MS 46359; A, f. 210).

68   Edith Craig MS notes, 'Army Book' 124 (ETMM); Terry, 1908, 99–100 and 107; Steen, 1962, 139–40; *Daily Telegraph*, 19 April 1875 quoted in Cheshire, 1989, 39. Fitzgerald, 1997, 153.

69   Letters to Rickards, 24 April and 27 June 1875 (NPG aIII, 29–30 and 40–42); *Art Journal* 1875, 251; Cook and Wedderburn, 1904, XIV, 266; John Ruskin, 'Academy Notes', 1875, 584. Cat.S.135–56 lists four versions of *The Spirit of Christianity*.

70   *Athenaeum*, 5 June 1875, 756; Cat.P. 98b, 141a, 147b, 165c; *Art Journal* 1875, 218. The Oxford replica of *The Late Marquess of Lothian* was also exhibited. Royal Artillery, 1977, 90–91, cat. 50, records Sabine's portrait, presented in 1877, as one of the finest portraits in the Mess.

71   Letter to Rickards, 1 August 1875 (NPG aIII, 49–52); A, I: 303.

72   BCd: 6 October 1877.

73   EBd: 23 and 26 July 1975; Westwater, 1984, 126: Mrs Barrington took Eliza Bagehot to LHH on 23 July, and as GFW was out, returned on the 26th and 'saw many pictures'.

74   As dates quoted in B/W are unreliable ('1868' would have been six years before demolition), the subsequent Easter meeting in Freshwater, for which she also proffered an introductory letter and due to illness at The Briary Watts met her outside, probably happened the previous year. B/W: 4–6.

75   EBJ to M, Dn, 2 April 1892.

76   B/W: 4–6.

77   *The Times*, 30 June and 20 July 1875. Toulouse had been flooded.

78   Letter to Rickards, 4 August 1875 (NPG aIII, 53–54); *Athenaeum*, 10 July 1875, 38.

79   Cat.S.6a, 23b, 25; Cat.P.30c; Tate, 1997, cat. 49; letters to Rickards, 10 May, 17 July, 1, 8 and 15 August 1875 (NPG aIII, 31–34, 47–61); letter from Rickards, 22 August (NPG, aIV, 60–63).

80   Letter from D. G. Rossetti, 26 August 1875 (NPG photocopy, Princeton USA), quoted in A, I: 267–68. According to Barbara Bryant in Tate Gallery 1997, 67 Watts acquired Rossetti's *Study for The Roman Window* (1874, Fogg Art Museum).

81   Letter to Rossetti, 27 August 1875 (University of British Columbia. Typescript, NPG aV, 114). The portrait, later purchased from a pawnbroker by F. R. Leyland, was bought from Christie's on 28 May 1892, lot 47, by James Smith, and given in exchange for another picture to GFW, who presented it to the NPG in 1895. Cat.P.137a.

82   A, I: 290.

83   *The Wheel of Fortune*, a study in blue, with Fortune seated in the wheel, not standing near it (Carlisle Museum) is listed in the Limnerslease Inventory, September 1938 (WG, 2002). New Gallery, 1898–99, 53, cat. 76. A, I: 290; WG, 2004, 78, cat. 83; Harrison and Waters, 1989, 103, 147; Fitzgerald, 1997, 140; Walkley, 1994, 40–41.

84   A, I: 290; Harrison and Waters, 1989, 108–10.

85   B/W: 99–100; A, I: 290–91.

86   Where now five villas their broad fronts present
     . . . Stood heretofore a nest of gables, built
     Each to supply a want as it was felt:

And shaded lawns, mowed carefully and rolled,
Provided pastime for the young and old.
Here grew to manhood youths of honoured name,
And here their mentor WATTS achieved his fame.
… Its demolition many much regret,
For there are many who can ne'er forget
The genial spirit in which friends there met.
Written in July 1876, on receiving two watercolours of
the old house and grounds.

87  Letters to Mrs Coronio, 6 and 9 October (Fiche 28, C9–13); letter to Mrs Wylie, 16 September 1875 (Fiche 27, E12); Cat.S.12b.

88  Letter to Mrs Wylie, 22 September 1875 (Fiche 27, E14) quoted in A, I: 292.

89  A, I: 289–90.

90  A, I: 298. *Freshwater Farm Buildings*, Cat.S.59. Bank statement records $24 paid to Morris & Co. on 15 April 1875.

91  A, I: 255.

92  A, I: 298; Mc, 17 September 1875.

93  Mc: 30 September 1875.

94  Dante's *Inferno*, Canto v, Cercio II, 31–33; Cat.S.117a; WG, 2004, 64, cat. 50.

95  See Appendix 1 (NPG 54–57).

96  Lettesr to Rickards, 13 June and 11 October 1875 (NPG aIII, ff. 36–39, 62–64). *Royal Manchester Institution*, 1875: cats 43 and 94, lent by Rickards, *The Ulster Coat* and *The Violin Solo*, cats 74 and 704 lent by Johnson, *Titans* and *F. W. Walker Esq*, cat. 707 *Dr William Roberts*. A 50-guinea prize turned down by GFW in 1874 was awarded in his name in 1875 for poetic design, to E. J. Gregory for a drawing of *Sir Galahad*.

97  Letter to Mrs Senior, 15 October 1875; Darley, 1990, 179; Dulwich Picture Gallery, 1994, 20.

98  PRO, COPY 1/31/93–95, 18 October 1875.

99  A, I: 300–01; Ritchie, 1919, 30–31.

100  Nottidge Charles Macnamara, a Fellow of Calcutta University and founder of the Mayo Hospital, was Surgeon to Westminster Hospital. Portraits of Mia, daughter of Louisa Bayley and of their three followed. Cat.P.103; letter to Rickards, 9 November 1875 (NPG, aIII, 65–66); A, I: 301.

101  The children of Herbert and Julia Duckworth, née Jackson (Cat.P.46c): George, born 1868, Stella, 1869 and Gerald, 1870.

102  A, I: 298–99.

103  Letter to Mrs Senior, 16 January 1876; letter to Rickards, 24 January 1876 (NPG aIII, 72–75); letter to Lord Wharncliffe, 12 August 1875 (Sheffield Archives).

## 11    New Little Holland House (1876–1879)

1  Private collection.

2  GFW's earliest neighbours in Melbury Road were, to his west (nos 2 and 4), a pair of semi-detached studios designed by John Belcher for the Thornycroft family of sculptors. William Burges designed his Tower House (1876–78) at number 9 and Richard Norman Shaw designed 8 and 11 for GFW's eastern neighbour Marcus Stone and Luke Fildes.

3  Ilchester, 1937, II, 447.

4  A, I: 304–05. Plan agreed, 15 February 1875 (LMA, E /HOL/Ac.70.85/II); letter to Rickards, 24 January 1876 (NPG aIII, 72–75); B/W: 8. On 5 November 1875, GFW wrote to Mrs Wylie that 'two of the bedrooms may be converted into warehouse rooms' (Fiche 27, F2). A, II: 54–55. From old Little Holland House, GFW had installed a black mantelpiece inset with Dutch tiles.

5  Letter to Rickards, 6 February 1876 (NPG aIII, 76–79).

6  *Ibid.*, 24 January 1876 and from Rickards, 15 February 1876 (NPG aIII, 72–72 and aIV, 64–67).

7  Letters to Countess Somers, 15 February and 5 March 1876; Cat.S.146–47; *Philadelphia International Exhibition* 1876, 211, cats 183–84. GFW subsequently allowed both portraits to be engraved.

8  Sir Charles Hallé to his wife, 29 April 1862, Hallé, 1896, I: 267–68.

9  Burne-Jones, 1904, II, 70–71; Hallé, 1896, II, 99–103; Fitzgerald, 1997, 165–66.

10  Letters to Rickards, 6 February and 31 March 1876 (NPG aIII, ff. 76–82); RA 1876, cats 164, 181. 1275 (to hang in the Native Hospital, Calcutta).

11  EBd: 15 February 1876.

12  Westwater, 1984, 116–17.

13  Barrington, 1927, II, 142; Westwater, 1984, 4, 5, 16, 120–21, 124; Greg, 1869, 36.

14  B/W: 6.

15  Beattie, 1983, 32.

16  In October 1876 Hamo Thornycroft drew up initial plans. John Belcher was the architect of nos 2 and 4 Melbury Road. No 2 was named Moreton House after Little Moreton Hall in Cheshire where the Thornycroft family farmed in the 18th century. Manning, 1982, 65. Westwater, 1984, 6.

17  B/W: 7.

18  Letter to J. E. Millais, 19 July 1876, quoted in Millais, II, 83. RA, *Works by the late Sir John Everett Millais*, 1898, cat. 15.

19  Mc: 9 April 1876 (WG).

20  Letter to M, 24 May 1876, quoted in RC: 111.

21  Mc: 12 July 1876.

22  Cat.S.51; letters to Rickards, 10 and 25–26 May 1876 (NPG aIII, 83–90).

23  Letter from W. E. Gladstone, 11 May 1876 (NPG); and

to Gladstone, 12 May 1876 (BL, Add. MS 44450, l30); A, I: 305–06.

24  Val Prinsep was painting the huge *Proclamation of The Queen as Empress of India*, bought by Queen Victoria.

25  Jenkins, 1996, 400–04; Masterman, 1930, 109; Fitzgerald, 1997, 165.

26  Letters to Rickards, 28 May, 15, 21 and 29 June 1876 (NPG aIII, 91–102). At the same time GFW organized chair covers to 'harmonize with the best style of things'.

27  Tom Taylor to Ellen Terry, 29 May 1876 (ETMM: Z1482).

28  Tom Taylor to J. P. Martineau, 2 August 1876; petition brief, 8 November; letter to J. P. Martineau, 13 December 1876.

29  Letters to Rickards, 15 June and 3 August 1876 (NPG aIII, 94–96, 107–09); letter to Countess Somers, 22 August; A, I: 308.

30  Cat.P.50; S.116b; *Wrexham*, 1876.

31  *Royal Manchester Institution*, 1876, cat. 105, 139: *Esau, Ariadne. The Academy*, 21 October 1876.

32  Letter to Rickards, 17 September 1876 (NPG aIII, 113–16); letter to Mrs Senior, 27 October; A, I: 313; Cat.P.156.

33  Letter to Rickards, 5 November 1876 (NPG aIII, 124–27).

34  *Ibid.*

35  The picture, later exhibited as *Pallas, Juno and Venus*, and *The Three Goddesses*, was finally known as *Judgment of Paris*. Tate 1997, cat. 14; Deschamps Galleries, 187, cat. 55; Tate, 1994, 43.

36  Letter to Rickards, 16 November 1876 (NPG aIII, 132–34).

37  *Ibid.*, 13 October 1876 (NPG aIII, 120–23); Mills, 1912, 198–99; Dixon and Muthesius, 1978 edition, 166–67; Newman and Watkinson, 1991, 173; *The Architect*, xvi, 15 July 1876. The Belgian muralists, Guffens and Sweerts, had decorated Courtrai Town Hall and the Institute of Fine Arts in Prague.

38  Letter to Rickards, 12 November 1876 (NPG aIII, ff. 128–31).

39  *Ibid.* 23 November 1876 (NPG aIII, 135–38).

40  Undated fragment (National Archives of Scotland GD40/9/458/11); the Lothian memorial was completed in 1878. National Trust, 1987, 47. Before Mrs William Stanley's death in 1876, GFW had made designs for a memorial to her husband at Holyhead, who died in 1884, when GFW passed on the commission. W, 54–55; Cat.P.152; letters from the Duke of Westminster, 6 April and 11 July 1876 (NPG aIV, 147–51); A, I: 318; letter to Mrs Senior, 7 December 1876.

41  Ford Madox Brown to Frederic Shields, 25 December 1876, quoted in Mills, 1912, 209–10.

42  Crook, 1981, 167. Edmund Oldfield to the Dean of St

Paul's quoted in *Building News*, 22 December 1876, 617–18; *Architect*, xvi, 23 December, 364–65.

43  Newman and Watkinson, 1991, 174; Mills, 1912, 252.

44  Letter to Rickards, 4 March 1877 (NPG aIII, 146–49).

45  Terry, 1908, 137.

46  Letter to Rickards, 15 March 1877 (NPG aIII, 150–52).

47  Letter to May Hichens 26 March; letter to Rickards, 27 March 1877 (NPG aIII, 153–56); A, I: 322.

48  Rossetti to Hallé, January 1877, quoted in Burne-Jones, 1904, II, 71.

49  Letters to Rickards, 15 and 25 April 1877 (NPG aIII, 157–61).

50  Hallé, 1896, II, 110, *Grosvenor Gallery*, 1877, cats 22–23, 34–35; *Illustrated London News*, 12 May 1877, 450; Surtees, 1993 146–47; Aldington, 1948; Wilde, 'The Grosvenor Gallery', July 1877, 118.

51  A, I: 323–24.

52  James, 'The Picture Season in London', *Galaxy*, August 1877, in Sweeney, 1956, 142–43. portraits of Lady Lindsay and Burne-Jones hung in the East Gallery).

53  Cat.P.95, exhibited at the Walker Art Gallery Liverpool, 1877, cat. 32.

54  James, *op. cit.*

55  Letter to Mrs Wyndham, 13 March 1877 (Typescript, Fiche 37, F6); Dakers, 1993, 39–40, 52; Barbara Bryant, 'G. F. Watts at the Grosvenor Gallery: "Poems Painted on Canvas" and the New Internationalism', Susan Casteras and Colleen Denney, eds, 1996, 114–15.

56  Robertson, 1931, 47. Burne-Jones's eight pictures, cats 59–66, included five single figures, *Temperantia, Fides, Spes, St George* and *A Sybil*.

57  Walter Pater, *Studies in the History of the Renaissance* (1763), reprinted as *The Renaissance: Studies in Art and Poetry*, including 'The School of Giorgione', May 1877, published separately in *Fortnightly Review* (October 1877).

58  Wilde, 1877, 119: 'One foot is already on the threshold, and one relentless hand is extended, while Love, a beautiful boy with lithe brown limbs and rainbow-coloured wings, all shrinking like a crumpled leaf, is trying with vain hands, to bar the entrance. A little dove [a new addition], undisturbed by the agony of the terrible conflict, waits patiently at the foot of the steps for her playmate, but will wait in vain, for though the face of Death is hidden from us, yet we can see from the terror in the boy's eyes and quivering lips, that, Medusa-like, this grey phantom turns all it looks upon to stone; and the wings of Love are rent and crushed.'

59  Corporation of London, 2000, 14–15; Calloway and Colvin, 1997, 19.

60  Joseph Comyns Carr, 'La Grosvenor Gallery', *L'Art: Révue hebdomadaire illustrée*, 1877, III, 2–4, reprinted in Carr, 1878, 14–15; Burne-Jones, 1904, II, 75.

61  *Grosvenor Gallery*, 1877, cat. 36; Réunion des Musées Nationaux, 1998, cat. 64; Lucie-Smith, 1972, 66.

62  John Ruskin, *Fors Clavigera*, July 1877, VII, 119, letter 79, reprinted in Birch, 2000, 265.

63  Called to advise on the dining-room colour scheme, Whistler worked at 49 Prince's Gate, London, from the summer 1876, exceeded his commission, continuing after Leyland refused to pay his full fees in October; he gave press and private views without the consent of Leyland, who on 6 July banished him from Prince's Gate. Tate, 1994, 164–65.

64  Burne-Jones, 1904, II, 86.

65  Gosse, 1894, 140; Beattie, 1983, 3; Read, 1982, 289; RA/L, 182–83; Tate, 2001, cats 122, 238 and 153; B/L: II, 198. GFW presented the sketch to Mrs Barrington for Leighton House as 'the most beautiful thing I have in my place'.

66  Cat.P.41a and 156a and Cat.S.39a. WG, 2004, 75–76, cat. 72; letters to Rickards, 12 February and 27 March 1877 (NPG aIII, 144–45 and 153–56); *Athenaeum*, 5 May 1877, 581; Christie's 1998, cat. 36; MM: 1885, 156, cat. 136; *Eastlake*, 1895, II, 249; Genesis 8: 12.

67  Letter to Mrs Aglaia Coronio, 18 May 1877 (Typescript, Fiche 28, D1); Chancellor, 1978, 258; Gregor-Dellin and Mack, 1978, I, 962–67; Masterman, 1930, 123–24.

68  Letters from the Duke of Westminster, 22 October, 2 and 7 November 1875 (NPG aIV, 139–46): among the references sent by the duke was, a *Times* article on the Bayeux tapestry as a guide to armour of the Norman Conquest. GFW at first ignored his criticism of the horse's outstretched legs in the small model – 'it is one that a horse could not keep with a weight on his back and we know that Hugh Lupus was so fat that he was nicknamed in consequence' – and in the final model changed the attitude into an impatient trample. B/W: 51–52; drawings on Grosvenor House paper, envelope dated 26 July 1877 (NPG aIV, 152–53).

69  From the Duke of Westminster, 24 April 1873 (NPG aIV, 126–29); B/W: 51–52 and 63.

70  The Fabrucci brothers exhibited sculpture at the Academy from 1880, Luigi specialized in busts and Aristide in figures and groups; the latter, paid ten pounds a week, from 27 August, was presumably GFW's assistant.

71  Letter to Mrs Wyndham, 9 December 1879 (Fiche 26, F9). GFW told Madeline Wyndham, when she wished to learn how to use gesso, that he had adapted the old Italian technique – 'So far and so far only it is my own' – that he had passed on his method to William Richmond, who taught it to Walter Crane's assistant, Osmund Weeks, from whom she should seek advice. B/W: 51.

72  Letter to Rickards, 9 August 1877 (NPG III, 168–71); B/W: 51; A, I: 256.

73  *Middle Temple*, 30 June 1877 (MT.1/MPA/No18, 391).

74  *Vanity Fair*, 19 May 1877; Langtry, 1925, 38 and 42; Beatty, 2000, 35, 38, 40, 47, 57 and 60.

75  Ponsonby, 1988, 46, 99 and 101–02; Beatty, 2000, 83–85.

76  *Athenaeum*, 6 October 1877, 441; BCd: 2 October 1877.

77  B/W: 11–12.

78  *Ibid.* 49–50. Hamo Thornycroft sketchbook, notes 17 November 1880 (L/HM). Asleson, 1998, 195–96.

79  Letter to Countess Somers, 16 September 1877: GFW now agreed to paint a portrait of the earl.

80  BCd, 1, 2 and 6 October 1877; B/W: 7 and 96–97.

81  Letter from Professor Benjamin Jowett, 7 July 1872; Jowett to R. S. Wright, 27 July 1877; letter from R. S. Wright, 31 July; letter from Jowett, 14 August, 5 and 10 December (NPG I, 194–204).

82  Lecky, 1909, 127; Cat.P.89c.

83  Minny Stephen died on 28 November 1875. Garnett, 2004, 181.

84  Letter to Rickards, 3 March 1878 (NPG aIII, 177–78); A, I: 327; BCd: 12 and 14 February 1878; Stephen, 1906, 317; Garnett, 2004, 59; Quilter, 1892, 221–22; Cat.P.149b.

85  BCd: 2 April 78, Good Friday, 13 April and 12 May 1878.

86  Of his four Grosvenor entries, *Ophelia*, *Mischief*, *Time and Death* (later renamed *Time, Death and Judgment*), *Sir Galahad* and a portrait of W. Strickland Cookson, the first two were exhibited at the 1878 Autumn Exhibitions at Manchester Royal Institution; and the third at the Walker Art Gallery, Liverpool, cat.P.39a; Cat.S.61c, 101a, 110a, 146a; B/W: 35–36; Cheshire, 1989, 47.

87  Letter to Rickards, 26 May 1878 (NPG aIII, 184–87); Cat.S.146a; *The Times*, 2 May 1878; *Spectator*, 18 May 1878: the reviewer also drew attention to Burne-Jones's painting *Laus Veneris*.

88  Letter to Rickards, 26 May 1878.

89  RA 1878, cats 128, 189, 195, 343, 379 and 1392: portraits of W. E. H. Lecky, Lady Constance Lawley (later Lady Wenlock), Florence, Jacques Blumenthal, composer of popular songs, pianist to the Queen, and H. H. Gibbs, and *Britomart and her Nurse (Spenser)*, worked on until its purchase in 1900.

90  Beatty, 2000, 101; *Daily News*, 4 May 1878.

91  Beatty, 101; Langtry, 1925, 57–58.

92  Letter to Rickards, 19 May 1878 (NPG III, 182–83). Nobility was the quality GFW considered lacking in modern life and wished to express in his work.

93  Spielmann, 1886, 47.

94  Langtry, 1925, 58–59.

95  Letter to Lord Wharncliffe, 12 August 1878 (Sheffield Archives).

96  *Paris Universal Exhibition*, 1878, cats 29 and 48; *Art*

*Journal*, 1878, 174; *Athenaeum*, 11 May 1878, 608; Tardieu 1879, xvi, 7–8; Carr, *L'Art*, 1880, xxii, 176; MM: 1998, 171–72, cat. 64; Fitzgerald, 1997, 172; Millais and Herkomer were also awarded the *Légion d'honneur*. Lord Mount-Temple lent the original marble *Clytie* carved entirely by GFW.

97 BCd: 20 and 31 May, 1878; Smith, 1996, 52.

98 Letters to W. E. Gladstone, 24 May, 12 and 17 June 1878 (BL, Add. MS 44447; ff. 165, 221 and 230); and from Gladstone, 15 June 1878 (NPG S.1).

99 Letter to Rickards, 25 August 1878 (NPG III, 193–96).

100 *Ibid.* 6 September 1878 (NPG III, 205–08); Swanson, 1990, 196, cat. 219; Stirling, 1926, 13; Wood, 1999, 208–09.

101 Stirling, 1934, 296.

102 Letter from EBJ (Fiche 16); Holiday, 1914, 260.

103 Letter to Rickards, 19 May 1878 (NPG aIII, 181–83); Cat.S.81c.

104 B/W: 41n.

105 Letter to Rickards, 3 July–1 November 1878 (NPG aIII, 188–213).

106 Leighton's portrait was completed by March 1879. Letter to the Council of the Royal Academy, 19 November 1878 (RA, RAC/1/WA 14); letters from Thomas Huxley, 21 October, 7 November 1878 (NPG S.1, 248–52).

107 *Athenaeum*, 30 November 1878, 693–94; Whitechapel Art Gallery, 1974, cat. 32.

108 EBJ, W. P. Frith and Tom Taylor testified for Ruskin, and Albert Moore and W. M. Rossetti would for Whistler. Burne-Jones, 1904, II, 86; Tate, 1994, 136–38, cat. 58.

109 Balfour, 1932, 220.

110 Wilfrid Meynell, 'Our Living Artists: George Frederic Watts, RA', *Magazine of Art*, 1878, 241–45.

111 Letter to Rickards, 7 December 1878 (NPG aIII, 214–17).

112 B/W: 94.

113 M's notes from a letter to Madeline Wyndham, 3 January 1879 (Fiche 27, F6); letter to the Revd. T. W. Jex-Blake, 15 February 1879.

114 Cat.P.2c; RA/L, 174, cat. 68; Spielmann, 1886, 34.

115 Letter to Rickards, 7 December 1878 (NPG aIII, 214–17); Cheshire, 1989, 47; Irving, 1951, 310; BCd: 23 January 1879.

116 The artist and future wife of William de Morgan. EBd, 22 January 1879.

117 BCd: 17 March 1879; Cecil 1975, 5; *Magazine of Art*, 1878, 245; Tardieu, 1879, xvi, 7–8.

## 12 Polemicist (1879–1881)

1 W. H. Thornycroft notes 'Marble *Stepping stones* 29 March 1879 George Watts R. A.' in 'Poets Fountain' red manuscript book, f. 6 (L/HM): 'It is a most successful work I like it very much. The left hand is too long and would be criticized. It destroys the elegance of the line of skin. Particularly do I like the sharp cut at the bend of the left arm. You find that decision in the Elgin work always. The hand of the girl is sweet.' How, 1893, 272.

2 B/W: 61; Cat.S.136c and Cat.P.17c.

3 Cat.S.64b; WG, 2004, 36–37 and 73, cat. 69; *Athenaeum*, 11 January 1879, 58.

4 Letter to Madeline Wyndham, 20 March 1879 (Fiche 27, F6–7). MEd, 30 March 1879.

5 Julia Stephen's daughter, the future Vanessa Bell, was born on 30 May 1879.

6 MM, 1998, 240–41, cat. 104.

7 WGc: 'The Grosvenor Gallery' 1879. GFW wrote to Rickards, 19 August 1879 that *Dorothy* was to be engraved for *L'Art*, (NPG III, 230–31).

8 Cat.S.112c. *L'Art* 1879 xviii, ill. opp. page 178; WGc 15, 1 May 1879, and 17, 4 May 1879; Tate Gallery, 1997, 67.

9 Cat.S.117a. WGc: 4 May 1879. Minneapolis, 1978 86, cat 28.

10 WGc; Cat.S.117a, 112c, 125b and Cat.P.58c–59a, 167c. GG 1879: cats 73–76, 105 and 143–44. *Paolo and Francesca, Orpheus and Eurydice* (sent on to *The Royal Manchester Institution: Exhibition of the Works of Modern Artists*, 1879, as cat. 19), *Little Red Riding Hood* (lent by Bowman); *Enid and Geraint*; *Dorothy*, the portrait of Gladstone and the Bowman self-portrait); Masterman, 1930, 123–24 and 143.

11 Letter from W. E. Gladstone, 23 May 1879 (NPG s1, 32–33).

12 Bagehot, 'Mr Gladstone' *The National Review*, July 1860, XI, 219, reprinted in St John-Stevas, 1959, 402–08.

13 Letter from Dean Liddell, quoted in A, 1: 306. Masterman, 1930, 163, 18 August 1879.

14 *The Times*, 6 January 1882: Harry Quilter recognized Gladstone's expression, when the portrait was exhibited at the Grosvenor Gallery in 1881–82.

15 RA 1879, cats 645, 282, 288, 414, 486, 1442. Entries were portraits of May Hichens (seated in citron-coloured dress), Sir William Armstrong; Lieut Col. the Hon. C. H. Lindsay, presented by the Officers of the St George's Rifles (in Volunteer uniform); the late F. P. Cockerell; Earl Cadogan (then Under Secretary for War); the Reverend J. Percival (the first Headmaster of Clifton College); Cat.P.67a, 4b, 96a, 36a, 27a and 123c; *Athenaeum*, 3 May 1879, 572.

16 Letter to Lady Marion Alford, 30 June 1879 (NPG).

17  The sisters took possession on 27 March 1879. The lease was post-dated 9 July. EBd indicates that the Barringtons moved in before she did; Westwater, 1984, 87–89.

18  B/W: 23, 39 and 71. Alert to new ideas, notably American scientific studies, he might be a recent publication, or Ruskin, the *Essays* of Francis Bacon, the Old Testament, or, a particular favourite, Robert Burton's *Anatomy of Melancholy* (1621), which perhaps prompted his concern to unravel 'the dualities in my nature'.

19  *Ibid.*, 67–68.

20  *Ibid.*, 72.

21  *Ibid.*, 13.

22  *Ibid.*, 99–100.

23  *The Times*, 4 July 1879; *Art Journal*, 1879, 262.

24  Letters from the Duke of Westminster, 17 June and 8 November 1879 (NPG aIV, 161–65): The statue was delivered to Grosvenor House in June; the Duke of Westminster discussed it with Lord Elcho, and wrote in November that Hugh Lupus's shoe looked uncomfortable for an equestrian. 'Would not a boot coming just over the ankle fit him better? and carry its owner better?' The shoe was authentic and, like Colleoni's, would stay below the ankle bone. 'When the horse is a bit rounded and finished, I shall be more than proud to possess a work of such surpassing merit and which cannot be second to any equestrian statue of any time.' Letter to Madeline Wyndham, 14 November 1879 (Fiche 27, F8); MEd: 19 December 1879. The statue was back at Little Holland House by December.

25  BCd: 14 August 1879; Langtry, 1925, 57–59: 'In imaginative art I think no painter of the day could vie with George Frederick Watts', wrote Langtry. In 1902 GFW overpainted her *Summer* with the face of Mary Crawshay; Cat.P.42b.

26  GFW also carved *Daphne* in marble (Tate Britain, 1879–82)

27  Letters to Rickards, 19 and 22 August 1879, (NPG aIII, 230–36); Blunt, 1975, 190.

28  Letter to Marion Spielmann, 1 February 1889 (M/JRL).

29  EBd: 18 August 1879; B/W: 79–80.

30  Dn, 14 May 1889.

31  *Transactions*, Manchester Meeting, 1880: Sir Coutts Lindsay, Bart, 'Address on Art', 110–30, and GFW, 'What Subjects are most suitable for the Pictorial Decoration of Public Buildings in this Country, and with whom should the Selection rest?', 700–10.

32  Of the two other versions of Marion Margaret Violet Lindsay in a folded scarf, her own shows her in a golden dress; Cat.P.96, Cat.S.81c; *Athenaeum*, 29 November 1879, 700; *Art Journal*, 1884, 3; Jaffé, 2003, 35.

33  Letters to Rickards, 23 October, 16, 19 and 26 November 1879, (NPG aIII, 239–50); from Rickards, 14 November 1879, (NPG IV, 81–83); B/W: 87.

34  Letter to Madeline Wyndham, 9 December (Fiche 26, F9); MEd: 19 December 1879.

35  B/W: 30.

36  Cat.P.91. Rajon had recently engraved his preparatory drawing for the earlier presidential portrait.

37  Letter from Rickards, 31 December 1879 (NPG IV, 84–87); *Athenaeum*, 3 January 1880, 24.

38  GFW, 'The Present Conditions of Art', *Nineteenth Century*, February 1880, reprinted in A, III: 148–90.

39  Letter from Matthew Arnold, 13 April (NPGs, 84–86); letter to Arnold, 13 April 1880 (V&A MSL/1980/39/1/86.WW1).

40  Letter from EBJ, 16 February 1880 (Fiche 16, F2–3).

41  Letter Madeline Wyndham, 26 August 1880 (Fiche 27); D, 9 Feb 1904; A, II: 317.

42  Holiday added clinging drapery to the plaster statue, which was accepted by the RA in 1881. Holiday, 1914, 270–71,

43  Letter to Rickards, 12 April 1880, (NPG III, 264–66); A, II: 3; *Athenaeum*, 17 April 1880, 512.

44  Letter from Rickards, 24 May 1880 (NPG IV, 88–90); *Athenaeum*, 17 April 1880, 512.

45  GG 1880, cats 38, 42–47; an unnamed portrait and portraits of the reverend C. Beanlands and William morris; *Daphne*; *Watchman! What of the Night?'*; *Psyche* and *Laura*; Cat.P.12a, 112a and 139b and Cat.S.122 a and b; MacCarthy, 406–08; *Art Journal*, 1880, 188; *Athenaeum*, 1 May 1880, 575 and 8 May, 605; Emanuel, 111.

46  *The Times*, 1 May 1880.

47  Letter from the Bishop of Exeter, 2 February 1880 (NPG IV, 320–22). Dr Temple, an activist for educational, social and temperance reform.

48  RA 1880, cats 4, 181, 212, 270 and 597; *The Dean's Daughter*; portraits of his doctor's daughter, Lucy Bond, the Bishop of Exeter (for Rugby School museum), Eveleen Tennant (Mrs F. W. H. Myers); and the self-portait that was painted for the Uffizi Gallery; Cat.P.88a, 17b, 168c, 153b and 156b; *Art Journal*, 1880, 125 and 187; *Athenaeum*, 1 May 1880, 571; Ash, 1997, pl.36.

49  *Paris Salon*, 1880, 68, cat. 3888; J.-K. Huysmans 'Le Salon officiel de 1880', *L'Art Moderne*, Paris, 1883, 135; *Art Journal*, 1880, 246–47; Réunion des Musées Nationaux, 1998, 169, cat. 81; Bareau, 1991, 242; Cachin, 1995, 108–09.

50  Rosa Richter first performed at the Aquarium as 'Zazel' in 1877 at the age of fourteen and was recruited by P. T. Barnum for his 'Greatest Show on Earth'; Cat.P.175b; D, 23 July 1887 and 22 December 1893; B/W: 17n; Squire, 1943, 262–64.

51    Letter from The Very Revd. H. G. Liddell, 25–26 May 1880, quoted in A, II: 18–19; RA 1996, 190–91, cat. 84.

52    Letter to Ethel Coxon, 1 August 1881 (Typescript, NPG aXII, 137).

53    Letter to Matthew Arnold, 21 May 1880 (V&A MSL/1979/7896/86.WW.1); from Arnold, 25 May (NPG, 87–88); A, II: 117–18; Cat.P.4; Arnold, July 1867, 36–53; Collini, 1993; B/W: 37.

54    Cat.P.104a; from J. E. Millais, 2 November 1881 (NPG): Millais lent the cardinal's cap that he had used for his portrait of Cardinal Newman. In Manning's absence, EIB's brother-in-law Orby Shipley offered his elderly hands as models. B/W: 103.

55    Emanuel, 1989, 111; Cartwright recorded in her diary that day that Melbury Road, 'The trees and the red houses with their high roofed studios [seemed like] another world…The Barringtons' house, or rather Mrs Bagehot's, is quite a sight. Full of lovely Morris hangings, De Morgan lustred tiles and Persian tiled tables, papers and ceilings designed by Walter Crane. A sideboard of Morris charmed me and I was glad to find our willow-pattern carpet used as a hanging and my dear rush chairs, and there are velvet hangings over every door and sofa, and photos all about. The garden …overlooking Watts' and Leighton's new homes… has some old trees in it which make it quite like a bit of country.'

56    Letter to Rickards, 26 August 1880 (NPG aIII, 267–69); from Lady Brownlow, 6 August 1880, quoted in A, III: 191–92.

57    MEd, 5 and 28 July 1880; M's note from his letter to Madeline Wyndham 20 July 1880.

58    Letter from the Countess Brownlow, 6 August 1880, *op. cit.*

59    Letter to Mrs Wyndham, 26 August 1880 (Fiche 27, F11).

60    Letters to Mrs Percy Wyndham, 3 and 5 September 1880 (Fiche 27, F12–13).

61    Letter from Oscar Wilde, n.d. (Fiche 15 B13); *Saunders Irish Daily News* 5 May 1879, reprinted Wilde, 1908, xiv, 5–23.

62    As bank statements do not specify payment, proceeds of a picture presumably paid for the field. Octavia Hill to the Revd. Samuel Barnett, 19 September 1880 (LSE, Coll. Misc. 512).

63    Barnett, II, 151 and 170.

64    Letter to T. C. Horsfall, 13 February 1880 (NPG XII, 223); Harrison, 1985, 120–23.

65    Letter to Mrs Aglaia Coronio, n.d. (Fondation Custodia, Paris, 9007) and 23 September 1880 (Typescript, Fiche 28, D4); Cat.P.75–77.

66    With share income, GFW would receive $7,519 16s 8d for the year ending June 1881. Letter to Rickards, 8 October 1880 (NPG III, 270–73).

67    Letter to Dorothy Tennant, 22 November 1880 (Fiche 43 D11); B/W: 89; *Athenaeum*, 25 September 1880, 407; *Building News*, 7 October 1881; letter to Mrs Eveleen Myers, 13 December 1880 (Trinity College: 27, f. 25).

68    Letter to Dorothy Tennant, 1880 (NPG xv, 146; Fiche 43, D10): 'The brilliant and acute French intellect regards the art of painting and sculpture as a thing of passing interest – as embroidery on the intellectual needs and yearning of our nature…a great picture should be a thing to live with, to respond to varying moods and especially should have the power to awaken the highest of our small mental and intellectual sensibilities. To my mind it is nearer in its operation on these sensibilities to music than to anything else, but it must have also the power to sustain the awakened and elevated spirit in that pure atmosphere that we only breathe in our happiest and least earthly moments. This can never be achieved by technical merits alone, never except by the artist throwing his whole and best self into his work. Such work may say little to the hasty observer…but the few who linger and take in something more in the course of time become a many. It is to such I would speak.'

69    Spielmann, 1886, 41–42. According to Spielmann, GFW painted the second portrait in 1877. Cat.P.29 quotes the earlier date for both portraits and a sketch, rescued from destruction by M.

70    D, 3 April 1893.

71    GFW, *Nineteenth Century*, March 1881, 450–54, quoted in A, III: 193–201, preceding her report of the school, its development since 1872 and symbolic designs, with reference to the history of embroidery dating back to ancient Greece.

72    Design by George Aitchison, dated 19 July 1877; MEd: 25 March 1881; Chissell, 1983, 186–87; Findlater, 1996, 10–16.

73    Letter from the Revd. Samuel Barnett, April 1882, quoted in Barnett, 1918, II, 151 and 153; *Tower Hamlets Independent*, 9, 16 and 23 April 1881; *East London Observer*, 16 and 23 April.

74    Murray, 1996, 302–03; Arnold, 1867, 36–53; RA, 1881, cats 84, 156, 229, 278, 511 and 1391; *Matthew Arnold*; *Miss Ellen Constance Baldock* (The Countess of Kilmorey); *C. A. Ionides*; *Miss Molly Williams* (Mrs Blakeney Booth); *F. Pepys Cockerell Esq*; Cat.P.4c, 8a, 75c, 172a, and 38b; *Art Journal*, 1881, 185; *Athenaeum*, 30 April 1881, 596; RA, 1996, cat. 84; Ormond and Ormond, 1975, 111.

75    Gilbert and Sullivan, III, 1930, 65 and 127. *Patience* transferred to Richard Doyly Carte's new Savoy Theatre

for its opening on 10 October. Vernon Lee quoted in Ormond, 1969, 258; Fitzgerald, 1997, 173.

76  A, III: 50–51.

77  Cat.P.150b, Cat.S.63a, 42a, 160c and 5c. GG, 1881–82; MM: 1885, cat. 121; Tate Gallery 1997, cat. 78.

78  Chesterton, 1904, 135–36.

79  Cat.P.15b, Cat.S.126; Cat.P.160; *Wantage*, 1902, 179, cat. 254; Minneapolis Institute of Arts, 1978, cats 25 and 26. *Athenaeum*, 30 April 1881, 599 and 629. *Art Journal*, 1881. *Whitechapel Art Gallery*, cat. 31. WGc 21, 31 Dec 1881. GFW described *A Reverie* as 'the young girl with the Indian purple drapery and lapis lazuli background', B/W: 186.

80  B/W: 65.

81  Cat.P.47b. GFW had first approached Lord Dufferin two years earlier, on his return as Governor-General of Canada. 'I can't tell you how much I wish to paint you', he wrote on 10 November 1879. Dufferin replied, 'What pleasure it would give me to have such an excuse for spending a few hours in your society and renewing our ancient friendship.' Lyall, 1905, I, 323–38.

82  Balfour 1932, 219–21, mistakenly records the date as 1880. Letter to Rickards, 27 May 1881, (NPG III, 288–91); A, II: 9.

83  Letter from EBJ (Fiche 16, F7–9).

84  *Art Journal*, 1880, 118; *Athenaeum*, 9 July 1881, 56.

85  Letter to Kate Holiday, 23 May 1881 (NPG XII, 201); To Rickards, 27 May (NPG III, 288–91); B/W: 52.

86  MEd, 1 June. M notes from letters to Madeline Wyndham, 8 June and 7 July 1881.

87  Letters to Rickards, 24 August and 4 September 1881 (NPG III, 294–98); Cat.S.30a.

88  Letter to the Countess of Airlie, 27 August 1881.

89  Lago, 1981, 30–31.

90  Barrington, 1903.

91  Ibid., 17. EBd, 5 August 1881, B/W: 90–92.

92  *Tom Bowling*; *The Banks of Allan Water*; *The Vicar of Bray*; *Sally in our Alley*; *Tell me, my Heart* were favourites; B/W: 93–94.

93  B/W: 93 and 112.

## 13  Genius Exposed (1881–1882)

1  Harry Quilter, *The Times*, 6 January 1882.

2  Quilter, 1892, 202; *The Times*, 6 January 1882; *Evening Standard*, 11 January.

3  EBJ to DGR (photocopy, Bod., MS Facs. d..272); *Athenaeum*, 7 January 1882, 22; Marsh, 1999, 524–24.

4  Letter from Cardinal Manning, 31 October 1881 (NPG).

5  Letter to the Hon. George Howard, 6 November 1881 (Castle Howard, J22/96/1556).

6  D, 26 April 1891: M noted the artists' mediums after a discussion with Leighton, who used turpentine, Fildes painted with petroleum, whereas GFW had long used Rock oil, prepared by Bell in Oxford Street. He also mixed in a small quantity of linseed oil to prevent rapid deterioration. B/ W, 65–66.

7  Letter to Quilter, 22 December 1881, quoted in Davids, 2000, 196, cat.173; Hallé, 1896, II,124–25.

8  B/W: 66–67; Troubridge, 1925, 46; Spielmann, 1886, 14.

9  GG, 1881–82: Cat.P.56, 23, 160 and 59. *Pictures at Holland House*, 1904, 98, cat.133; letter to Rickards, 19 November 1881 (NPG III, 299–300). The three-month exhibition closed on 31 March 1882.

10  Cosmo Monkhouse, 'The Watts Exhibition', *Magazine of Art*, 1882, 177–82.

11  Dn, 9 January 1889; A, II: 142.

12  *Globe, Daily News*, 31 December 1881; *Athenaeum, Art Journal*, 1882, 61–62; *Evening Standard*: 7 January 1882; Quilter, *Contemporary Review*, 1882, 221–22 and 204; *Pall Mall Gazette* 9 January; *New York Times*, 21 May; Macmillan, 1903, 71–72.

13  MEd, 11 January 1882; *Globe*, 31 December 1881; *The Times*, 26 January 1882; Quilter, 1892, 223.

14  *Sir Galahad* and *The Wife of Pygmalion*.

15  Eliot, 1859, II, xvii, para 8.

16  *The Times*, 25 January 1882; Quilter; 1892, 217; Cecil, 1931, III, 45; *Spectator*, 7 January 1882.

17  WGc first review; Cat.S.12b; GG 178.

18  *Evening Standard*, 11 January 1882; *Athenaeum*, 7 January 1882; *New York Times*, 21 May 1882; Quilter, 1892, 203, 210 and 219; Walter Pater, 271.

19  *Globe*, 31 December 1881; WGc third review, 31 December 1881; *The Times*, 26 January 1882; *Art Journal*, 1882, 62; WGc, 21; Cat.S.116–17.

20  Cat.S.51a; *Athenaeum*, 7 January 1882; *The Times*, third review 1882; Quilter, 1892, 220. *Minneapolis Institute of Arts*, 1978, 67–68, cat. 12.

21  Ibid., *The Times*, 6 January 1882; *New York Times*, 21 May; Macmillan, 1903, 220–21.

22  *Spectator*, 7 January 1882; *Athenaeum*, 7 January; *The Times*, 6 and 26 January; WGc third review, 31 December 1881; WGc, 21; Quilter, 1892, 223.

23  Chesnau, 1885, 267–68.

24  *The Times*, 6 and 26 January 1882; *Daily News*, 31 December 1881; *Spectator*, 7 January 1882; *Evening Standard*, 11 January; *Edward Burne-Jones*: MM: 1998, 216–21, cat. 87.

25  Cat.S.6–7 and 42a; *Athenaeum*, 7 January 1882; *The Times*, 26 January; Whitechapel 1974, cat. 29.

26  *Globe*, 31 December 1881; *Athenaeum*, 7 January 1882; Art Institute of Chicago, 1994, 161, fig. 68, Redon, *Fallen Glory (Head of Orpheus on the Water*,

27   *The Times*, 6 January 1882; *Spectator*, 7 January; Quilter, 1892, 209.

28   Quilter, 1892, 205, 225; *Daily News*, 31 December 1881; *Spectator* and *Athenaeum*, 7 January 1882.

29   Cat.S.46–50; A, II: 138–41; Tate Gallery, 1997, cat. 124. WGc, 20.

30   Leighton, 1896, 54–55 and 61; Stewart, 1994, 33.

31   D, 17 May 1887.

32   *Daily News*, 31 December 1881.

33   Cat.S.136b, later known as *The Spirit of Christianity*. *London Quarterly Review*, 1882, cviii, 155–56, quoted in RC, 101; *Athenaeum*, 7 January 1882; *Art Journal*, 1882, 61–62; Quilter, 1892, 217 and 224.

34   Apart from Quilter, only the *Globe*, 31 December 1881 understood the conception of *Angel of Death*. Quilter reported: 'In dignity of form alone we should have to rank this work high among the masterpieces of modern art, but when we add to that the power of composition that is shown, the originality of the conception, and the grandeur of scale.' *The Times*, 26 January 1882; Quilter, 1892, 214.

35   Address of 10 December 1879, Leighton, 1–33; *Daily News*, 31 December 1881; WGc 21; *Evening Standard*; *Spectator*, 7 January 1882; *Contemporary Review*, 225; *L'Art*, 1882, xxix, 8–12.

36   From William Graham, 31 December 1881 (NPG aIV, 257–59).

37   Letter to Arthur Reade, 19 February 1882 (Huntington, HM 23523).

38   B/W: 110–12.

39   D, 4 March 1893; Quilter, 1892, 225.

40   B/W: 110.

41   Cat.S.160, 8a, 43b, 45b, 63a, 23a and 58c–59b; *When Poverty Comes in at the Window*; *Arion*; *Esau*; *The Creation of Eve*; *The Genius of Greek Poetry*; *Carrara Mountains*; two Freshwater scenes and an unspecified *Landscape Study*. Cat.P.44c; B/W: 108–9; GFW pointed out that his prices compared reasonably to those of Millais, who charged £3,000–£4,000 for landscapes, and of Alma-Tadema, who had sold *Sappho* for £3,000.

42   Letter from Henry T. Wells, 12 January 1882 (NPG IX, 87–90); letter to Wells, 15 January, quoted in A, II: 17.

43   Letter from EBJ, n.d., and 17 January 1882 (Fiche 16, F13–G2).

44   Letter from Lord Lytton, 21 January 1882, quoted in A, II: 11–12; letter to Lord Lytton, 23 January 1882 (typescript, NPG aXII, 141–42); letter to Sir A. H. Layard, 13 January 1882 (BL, Add. MS 39036 f.9).

45   Letter to F. W. H Myers, 7 January 1882; letter to Eveleen Myers, 3 February 1882 (Trinity College Library, Myers Papers, 4.133 and 25.5(1); Stanzas 1–3 and 12 were reprinted in A, II: 20–21.

46   Troubridge, 1925, 44–45.

47   Letter from Mary Chesworth, 16 March 1882 (NPG aIV, 91–93).

48   Thornycroft, draft for RA lecture 1882 (L/HM); EBd, 9 March 1882.

49   A, II: 53; letter from M, 14 March 1882; RC, 112.

50   Letter to M, 17 March 1882; RC, 112–13.

51   *Cambridge University Reporter*, 17 December 1883, 293; letters from Cardinal Manning, 22 February and 26 March 1882 (NPG Ia, 226, 1,15); Shannon, 1999, 293–94.

52   Letters to the Marchionness of Salisbury, 21 and 23 January 1882 (Hatfield House Library); Lord Salisbury came for his first sitting on Saturday 29 April.

53   *New York Times*, 21 May 1882.


## 14   Revelations (1882–1884)

1   Whitechapel, 1882, cats 134–36: GFW exhibited a *Study of a Head* – 'the archer, the heathen of love, it may be, is at bay; he has met one stronger than himself' – *The Dove Which Returned Not Again* (WG, 2004, 75, cat. 72) and *The Rider on the Black Horse*. Barnett, 1918, II, 151.

2   Barnett, 1918, II, 152–53.

3   Letter to Ellen Terry, Easter Sunday 1882 (ETMM: Z1, 555); Cheshire, 1989, 61; Terry, 1908, 59–60.

4   Letter to Leighton, 6 April 1882. The RA paid £1,200 for *Psyche*. GFW exhibited Cat.P.151c and Cat.S.122b an unnamed lady's portrait in a saffron dress (193); *Alfred de Stern* (216) and *Psyche*; *Athenaeum*, 29 April 1882, 544. Prinsep's four RA entries in 1883 included *Mrs W. H. Kendal in Tennyson's 'Falcon'*, painted for presentation to the Garrick Club; *After the Honeymoon*; *Bathing Ghats at Benares*; and *Titian's Niece*. His *Ayesha* was purchased for the Chantrey Bequest in 1887. HTd, 18 February 1881: 'Watts came in. He liked the Bowman much. V good statue. Thighs and legs a little short, remember that you are speaking in verse so you can offer to enforce and exaggerate all that will give dignity devotion. Legs to stride, arms to reach, hands to grasp. Neck to raise the head. Keep your masses large . . . Spread the toes more.'

5   Cat.P.45a; B/L, II 267–68; B/W: 88.

6   *Athenaeum*, 6 May 1882, 579.

7   Less controversial were his earlier portraits of the late president of the Royal College of Surgeons Sir Benjamin Brodie, 1859, and of John Lothrop Motley of 1860; and

*The Dove Which Returned Not Again*, exhibited at RA, 1877, cats 125, 267 and 566; Cat.P.19b, 104a, 113a, 165a and S.39a.

8　*New York Times*, 21 May 1882.

9　Leslie, 1921, 328; *Magazine of Art*, 1893, 364–65; *Athenaeum*, 20 May 1882, 641; Minneapolis Institute of Art, 85, cat. 27.

10　H. E. Manning, *The Eternal Priesthood*, 1883, 184, quoted in Gray, 1985, 270.

11　Middle Temple Minutes, 12 May 1882, 9MT 1/MPA/ no. 19, 116–17); letter to F. G. Stephens, 14 May (Bod., MSS Don. e.87, ff. 141–42; Cat.P.165a; A, I: 280–81; *The Times*, 8 and 25 May; *Pall Mall Gazette*, 8 May, also reported the portrait 'a failure'.

12　*Oxford University Gazette*, 13 June 1882; B/W: 28n.

13　WG, 2004, 18 and 82, cat. 96; letter to the Countess of Airlie, 11 July 1882.

14　Cat.P.45; Goodison, 1955, I, 115; DEVd (Devonshire MSS, Chatsworth), vol. 22, 30 June, 6, 11, 15, 27 July and 3 August 1882; vol. 27, 14 March 1883.

15　Letters to Walter Crane, 5, 8, 25 July and 25 September 1882; 18 March 1886 (RBKC); Crane, 1907, 230–34. His investment income that month, including a £1,200 cheque, more than covered the £300 cost. GFW paid in £50 instalments and later presented the picture to the Tate.

16　Letter to Linley Sambourne, 11 August 1882 (Leighton House).

17　Note from letter to Madeline Wyndham, 7 August 1882 (Fiche 27, F13).

18　Cat.S.14c; *BC* was exhibited at the Liverpool Autumn Exhibition; *Athenaeum*, 13 September 1884, 134.

19　MAd, 12 September 1882; to Mary Chesworth, 26 September 1882 (NPG aIII, 304–6); having proposed a replica of *Love and Life* for Rickards, he wrote to check the size of its pendant *Love and Death*.

20　B/W: 51–52; Dn, 12 August 1903. Bank drafts for £1,300 and £200 from the Duke of Westminster were received on 5 and 13 October 1882. The symbolic equestrian statue, known first as *Active Force, Vital Energy*, was ultimately named *Physical Energy*.

21　EIB wrote that the studio and gate were GFW's idea; her sister stated that Russell proposed the studio. HTd, 5 September 1882; Ebd, 27 April and 8 December 1882; B/W: 63.

22　Gunn, 1964, 87–88.

23　*Nineteenth Century*, 1883, 45–57, quoted in A, III: 202–26. On ladies' hair, GFW criticized the high mass and fringes hiding the outgrowth of hair from the forehead; he criticized also the unhealthy fashion for tiny feet, unbalanced high heeled shoes, men's coat collars that obliterated the spring of the throat from the shoulders, the characteristic that distinguished Man from birds and animals.

24　The trial on 20 July 1889, reported in Thompson 'Fashion and Folly', n.d.

25　Prince's Hall, 1883; Duckworth, 24 January 1880, 11–15; Farrar, 1880, 202–5; RC, 1945, 138–39.

26　Letter to Ruskin, 3 March 1883 (private collection).

27　Crane, 1907, 235.

28　Cat.P.85a; *Athenaeum*, 1883, 575.

29　D, 29 January 1898; letter to Maria Earle (NPG aIX, 50); letter to W. J. Stillman, 14 January 1885 (Schaffer Library, Union College, WJS 584); Marsh, 1999, 533; A, I: 270; A, II 166.

30　*Art Journal*, 1883, 129.

31　Cat.P.9a. Letter to Lady Ashburton, 26 March; letters to Mary Chesworth, 21, 26 and 29 March (NPG aIII, 307–12).

32　*Whitechapel* 1883, cats 137–46: *Love and Death*; *The Four Horses of the Revelations*; *Poverty and Love*; portraits of Thomas Carlyle; Garibaldi; Cardinal Manning; and *Esau*. Cat.S.88c, 127–28, 160a, 43b/c; Cat.P.29a, 57a, 104a. EBJ and Millais sent one each, Hunt two and Rossetti's three included *The Annunciation*, *Fra Pace* and *Head of Dante*.

33　Ruskin 'Mythic Schools of Painting', *The Art of England*, reprinted in Cook and Wedderburn, The Complete Works of John Ruskin, XXX, 1903–12, 302–5.

34　Ruskin, *The Laws of Fésole*, 1879; Cook and Wedderburn, XV, 351.

35　GG 1883, cats 59, 73, 96, 103–6 (see WG, 2004, 45 and 79, cat. 84) and 204; *Study on Brighton Downs* (admired by and later given to Leighton); *A Condottiere, Early part of 15th Century*; portrait study of the Hon. Mary Baring, 103–6; 'For the rain, it raineth every day'; Cat.S.16c, 28b, 127b–128b and 124c; *Athenaeum*, 28 April 1883, 547, 21 April 1883, 514 and 5 May 1883, 575; *Pall Mall Gazette*, 2 May 1883.

36　Cachin, 1995, 127; Denvir, 1989, 411.

37　Huysmans, 1998, 108.

38　Galerie Georges Petit, 1883; Cat.S.109b, 117a, 22a, 46b, 50b and 45b and Cat.P.150c. The only other English artist was GFW's Melbury Road neighbour, the genre painter Colin Hunter. M inscribed a pen and ink drawing of *Olympus on Ida* 'suggested by Bed curtain when staying with Dr Cheyne at Brighton'. Whitechapel Art Gallery, 1974, cat. 64 ascribes this to GFW's leg injury of 1872, when he was working on the earlier version.

39　Only his envelope dated 28 June 1883 survives of this early correspondence (NPG aX, 23). Mary Gertrude Mead, born in Torquay, Devonshire, of US parentage, was educated in New York. Lucas, 1921, II, 183.

40　Letter to Henry Holiday, 9 May 1883; letter to Kate Holiday, 14 May (NPG aXII, 204–5); Parry, 1997, 128; *The Times*, 12 July 1883. Walter Crane and Poynter designed further tableaux. The Kensington series illustrated a new translation by Andrew Lang, Walter Leaf and Ernest Myers. In May 1886 their tableaux, illustrating Prof George Warr's translation was staged at the Prince's Hall, starring Dorothy Dene. Crane, 1907, 284; Ormond and Ormond, 1975, 136.

41   Letter to Mary Chesworth, 29 March 1883 (NPG aIII, 311–12).

42   *Ibid.*, and 24 May 1883 (NPG aIII, 311–15).

43   DEVd, vol. 27, 4 June 1883; *Cambridge University Reporter*, 19 June 1883, 943 and 947; letters to Eveleen Myers, 11 and 15 June 1883 (Trinity College Library, Myers Papers: 25, ff. 8(1) and 9(1). Ruskin and Tennyson were similarly listed in the *Journal for the Society for Psychical Research*, 1, April 1884, 33–34.

44   Letter to Blanche Somers-Cocks, 13 September 1883; *Surrey Advertiser*, 30 June.

45   Blanche married 26 June. GFW attempted to paint a formal portrait of the earl from photographs, after his death on 26 September. Cat.P.145a.

46   NPG 2274; letters to ET, n.d. and 10 July 1883; Edith Craig MS, *Army Book 124*, 18 July 1883 (ETMM: Z 1,574 and 556); Loshak, 1963, 480; Terry, 1908, 60.

47   Letter from ET, 11 July 1883 (draft, ETMM, 1, 498).

48   Letter to ET, 12 June [?July] 1883 (ETMM, Z1, 556a).

49   Letters to ET, 10, 12, 19, 21 July, 2 August and 8 October 1883; letter from ET 11 July (ETMM, Z1, 556–60, 571 and 1, 498); Terry, 1908, 60–61.

50   Letter from Lillie Langtry, n.d.; Terry, 1908, 252–53: 'My company is very much liked this year and I have gained a great deal of credit for putting my pieces so well on the stage – altogether I am a very happy woman and more earnest in my work than ever.'

51   Letter to Mary Chesworth, 17 September 1883 (NPG aIII, 316–18); *Manchester Art Gallery, Royal Institution*, 1883, cats 437, 441 and 761 list *Noon-day Rest*, *Katie* and *Love and Life*.

52   *Cambridge University Reporter*, 17 December 1883, 294. Subscribers raised £1,050 for the two portraits of the duke.

53   Note from letter to Madeline Wyndham, 15 October 1883; *Athenaeum*, 20 October 1883, 502, and 27 October 1883, 539. Cat.S.124a and 79c; *Athenaeum* specified *Rain Passing Away* as one of two new landscapes. GFW described *The Island of Cos* to J. B. Mirrlees on 29 December. Letter from Hubert Herkomer, 23 August 1882 (NPG aXI, 147).

54   Letter to M, 25 October 1883.

55   'An Interview with Mr G. F. Watts RA', *Pall Mall Gazette*, 9 May 1885.

56   Letter to M. Gertrude Mead, 4 November 1883; letter to Mary Chesworth (c/o Rickards), 21 November (NPG aX, 24–26); A, II: 25; of Madox Brown's murals 'I have not seen them, but know him as a remarkable though somewhat uncertain designer, very inventive but I think not sufficiently sensible of the value of beauty in Art.'

57   Letter from M to HT, 5 December 1883; letter to the Hon. Hallam Tennyson, 23 December (TRC, 4919 and 6272). James Beadle, the future military artist and cousin of the Prinseps, was also studying in the gallery, preparing his first Academy picture. A, II: 55.

58   A, II: 54–55; Mc.

59   Later published as 'Art and Plutocracy'.

60   MacCarthy, 1994, 477–79; Fitzgerald, 1997, 192; Tate Gallery, 2000, 125, cat.110; ATRd, 16 January 1884.

61   Letter to Countess Somers, 20 November 1883. Alexander Bassano (1829–1913), photographer, of 25 Old Bond Street, London.

62   Dn, 2 July 1892. A, II: 265; A, III: 270a. *Athenaeum*, 29 December 1883, 874. 'George Frederick Watts, RA', *Art Journal*, 1884, 1–4. GFW rejected his initial plan to design the *Theseus* as rider because its form was more suited to reflection than action.

63   Cat.P.114b and S.79c (see WG, 2004, 56, cat. 50): Mirrlees sat for his portrait in 1883.

64   Letter to James Buchanan Mirrlees, 27 December 1883 (copy, NPG aXII, 6)

65   Cat.S.151a; WG, 2004, 65, cat. 52. B/W: 88, 133 and 204. M refuted EIB statement that Dene was the model, insisting on the future Mrs Bates as model. Both may have been used. Jefferies, 1995, 79, cat. 4155. Letter to Edmund Gosse, 15 December 1883 (Brotherton Collection, Leeds University Library). *Pall Mall Gazette*, 20 March 1884.

66   Mc notes beginning 31 December 1883.

67   A, II: 26.

68   Cat.S.109a/b, 92a/b, 64b and 160b; from Edmund Gosse, 23 February 1884 (NPG aXIII, 89–91). *Pall-Mall Gazette* 24 March; *Art Journal* 1884, 1–4, *Athenaeum*, 12 April 1884, 482.

69   Cat.S.18a; B/W: 36–37: Emilie Barrington, who bought *Brunhild*, states that the subject struck the artist one dark winter afternoon when he sat by the fire, a green velvet hat suggesting the helmet and facial shadow.

70   B/W: 54–55.

71   A, II: 26 and 56; F. G. Stephens, June 1884.

72   Daniel Huntington, quoted in 'Opinions from Various sources upon the Proposed Exhibition of Paintings by Mr G. F. Watts, RA' (MM): The whole course of [Mr Watts's] studies has been a protest against a superficial and merely naturalistic view of his art. His pure and high aims, his imaginative and poetical conceptions and his severe study and discipline applied to the noblest ideal walks of art render his example one of great value to the student, and his achievements of rare interest and encouragement to those who hope for great and beautiful fruit in our future of Art.'

73 Letter from M. Gertrude Mead, 15 March 1884 (NPG aXIII, 65–68).

74 *Metropolitan Museum of Art: Board of Trustees Meetings*, II, 1873–88, 251–22, 17 March 1884. *Executive Committee Meetings*, II, 1881–90, 112–14, 28 April 1884. Draft invitation from the museum trustees to GFW, copy of letters from H. G. Marquand to F. D. Millet, 15 May, from William Alexander to Millet, 17 and 19 May. 'The United States: New Tariff on Works of Art', *Art Journal*, 1883.

75 Letter from Millais, 6 April 1884 (NPG); letter to Millais, 8 April (typescript, NPG aXIII, 149).

76 Letter from Samuel Barnett to Frank Barnett, 19 April 1884 (LMA, F/BAR/8); *The Times*, 9 April 1884; Barnett, 1918, I, 308; Darley, 1990, 234–37; Briggs and Macartney, 1984, 7–9; Jenkins, *Dilke*, 1996, 173–76.

77 Masse, 1935, I; *Hobby Horse*, April 1884, no. I; Cumming and Kapland, 1991, 22–24.

78 Letter to Lady Dorothy Neville, 28 March 1884 (NPG aXIII, 160).

79 Cat.S.14c: GFW realized that the frivolous subject did not suit a large canvas. Letters to George Richmond, 8 April 1884 (RA, acc.2000/17), and F. G. Stephens, 23 April (Bod., MSS Don. e.87, ff. 143–44).

80 *The Honourable Society of the Middle Temple Minutes of Proceedings*, 25 April and 13 June 1884 (MT.1/MPA/No. 19, 255 and 267). *Athenaeum*, 24 May 1884, 667; RA, *Leighton*, cat. 89; WG, 2004, 39 and 56, cat. 105; B/L, 198 and 258–59; Cat.S.9a; Dorment, 1985, 51–55; RA 1986, 14; Beattie, 1983, 138.

81 Cat.S.1c, 69b, 124a, 151a and Cat.P.101b and 141b; WG, 2004, 2, 19 and 77, cat. 78; Tate Gallery, 1997, cat. 77; WGc 30–32; *Athenaeum*, 20 October 1883, 502 and 10 May 1884, 603–4; *Art Journal*, 1884, 189–90, 132–36 and 573; A, II: 244. Alice Graver, a cousin of GFW's housekeeper, Emma, and the subject of *Alice*, was his fifth picture.

82 Letter to W J Stillman, 14 January 1885 (Schaffer Library, Union College, WJS 584). Stillman was married to Marie Spartali.

83 Letter to Blanche, 22 May 1884.

84 M MS notes for A; letter to L. C. Tiffany, n.d. (MM); letter from F. D. Millet to Henry Marquand, 16 June 1884 (MM); General di Cesnola to HM, 19 June (MM); Johnston, Stuyvesant, Bishop, Mills, Vanderbilt and Marquand were prepared to pay $200. GFW was later persuaded to reduce insurance values.

85 Letter to M. G. Mead, 31 May 1884 (NPG albx, 30); Mc. B/W: 115.

86 Letter to Miss Taylor, 15 June 1884; to Sir Henry Taylor, 29 June; from Sir Henry, 3 July (Bod., MSS Eng. Lett. c.2, ff. 251–52, and c.1, ff. 329–30, 331–34; D, 21 March 1887; Taylor, 1885.

87 Letter to Ellen Terry, postmark 9 July 1884 (ETMM, 1, 561).

88 MEd, 25 July 1884; letter to Mrs Percy Wyndham, 21 July 1884 (NPG aIX, 84); letter to F. R. Leyland, 2 August (B/Y, GFW MSS 2125.F3), GFW writes of his plan to assist Fanny Cornforth's stepson, Cecil Schott, an aspiring artist – 'I suppose I had better be cautious how I have dealings with the family!'

88 Letter to Mrs H. Holiday, 10 August (NPG aXII, 206); Marsh, 1999, 508.

## 15    New York Sensation (1884–1885)

1 Letter from General L. P. di Cesnola to the Hon. Daniel Manning, Secretary of the Treasury, Washington D.C., 6 March 1885 (MM); B/W: 115.

2 Letter to John Taylor Johnson, 22 July 1884 (MM); letter from F. D. Millet to H. Marquand, 25 July (MM); Howe, 1913, I, 214–15; MM: 1885, 10–11.

3 Letter from William Alexander to H. Marquand, 6 August 1884 (MM).

4 Letter from F. D. Millet to H. Marquand, 20 August (MM).

5 *Ibid.*, 19 and 29 August (MM).

6 Letter to Edmund Gosse, 1 August 1884 (Brotherton Collection, Leeds University Library); letter to M. G. Mead, n. d., and 20 January 1885 (NPG ax, 77 and 70–75); *Century*, October/November 1884, 156. On 24 March he wrote to Gosse 'I should not have considered myself possessing a right to complain (this I say in case you may have to speak of my work on any future occasion) for those who come before the public become in a way public property, and as long as criticism is not ill-natured and the critic abstains from personalities I for one shall always accord full licence.' *Pall Mall Gazette*, 9 May 1885.

7 *New York Commercial Advertiser*, 26 August 1884; *Boston Herald*, 13 September. 'I do so much hope it is and will be understood that I do not presumptuously consider myself here a representative or Champion of English Art but that having been called, I simply step out of the ranks and come', he wrote to MGM on 15 November. 'You know this I think and you know also (I hope) with what aspiration I work, that, when, subject to the laws that govern the fate of nations, states, and individuals, England shall lose her place among the living, it will be found she has always had sons who had her honour at heart and who strove to uphold her real dignity in feeling and aim at least' (NPG ax, 49–52). Charteris, 1931, 159–66.

8 M. G. Mead to H. Marquand, 24 August 1884 (MM); F. D. Millet to Marquand, 10 September (MM).

Leighton, Burne-Jones and Leslie Stephens lent their portraits; *Ariadne* was lent by Louisa Lady Ashburton; *Endymion* by William Graham; and *Bianca* and the portrait of Virginia Dalrymple by Rickards. Neither Horace Davey, QC, nor James Mirrlees were prepared to part with *The Carrara Mountains* or *The Island of Cos*. MM: 1885, 42 and cats 91, 94, 101, 107, 120, 127 and 131; letters to Rickards, 2 and 5 September 1884; Emma Graver's picture list (NPG ax, 37–40 and aIII, 322–27).

9 Letter from F. D. Millet to H. Marquand, 18 and 24 September (MM); National Steamship Company, 25 September 1884, confirms that the thirteen cases were shipped on the *France*. A telegram from General di Cesnola states, 'Watts pictures will go by Steamer Greece of the National Line which leaves on Wednesday morning' [after 9 October 1884] (MM).

10 General di Cesnola to Dr W. C. Prince, 27 September 1884 (MM).

11 Letters to M. G. Mead, 12 and 24 September 1884 (NPG ax, 32–36 and 41–43).

12 The gesso model presented by the duke to the cast collection at Crystal Palace was destroyed in the palace fire of 1936. Dn, 12 August 1903; A, I: 256; *Chester Chronicle*, 18 October 1884; *Art Journal* 1884, 192–93.

13 Letter to Ellen Terry, 31 October 1884 (ETMM, Z1, 562); Craig, 1957.

14 Louis C. Tiffany's copy of letter from EIB to M. G. Mead, n. d. (MM).

15 Letter from S. P. Avery to General di Cesnola, 16–17 October 1884 (MM); letter from H. Marquand to General di Cesnola, 17 October 1884; letters from F. D. Millet to H. Marquand, n.d. and 28 December 1884.

16 Letter from General di Cesnola, 12 August 1884 (MM); letter to M. G. Mead, 19 October 1884 (NPG ax, 44–48), quoted in A, II: 29–30; Howe, 1913, I, 213–15.

17 MM: 1885, 38–41.

18 *The Nation*, 20 November 1884.

19 Amor, 1989, 233. GFW later supplied a testimonial urging the Walker Art Gallery to purchase *The Triumph of the Inocents*. Landow, 1980, I, 80.

20 Letter from Matthew Arnold, 11 November 1884; letter to Arnold, 14 November (NPG s1, 96–100; NAL MSL/1980/39/2/86.WW.1); EBd, 29 November 1884; Barnett, 1918, II, 170–71; A, II: 57–58; Mr and Mrs Rawnsley founded the School of Industrial Art in Keswick that year. *Pall Mall Gazette*, 1 December 1884 and 9 May 1885.

21 Eglantyne Jebb to 'Laura', 27 November 1884, in Jebb's diary; *Magazine of Art*, 1888, 294–98.

22 Cat.S.97c; WG, 2004, 38–39 and 74, cat. 70; Tate Gallery, 1997, cat. 52; *Athenaeum*, 15 November 1884, 631; Carlyle, 1912, 163; Ovid, *Metamorphoses*, XI, 93–180.

23 Cat.P.173b; Egremont, 1977, 36–37.

24 Letter to M. G. Mead, 21 December 1884 (NPG ax, 53–55). GFW asked her to destroy his letters, but suggested she might keep this one as 'my profession of faith'.

25 Pollock, 1993, 316–17. Jenkins, *Gladstone*, 1996, 497–99.

26 Letter to M. G. Mead, 9 January 1885 (NPG ax, 57).

27 Letter from Alfred Gilbert to Hamo Thornycroft, 2 January 1885 (L/HM 268); Dorment, 1985, 59; Manning, 1982, 99. The Commissioner of works David Plunket, consulted Millais, Watts and Leighton who proposed an 'allegorical group of sculpture'. A statue of Gordon himself was preferred and Thornycroft's commission was announced in *The Times*, 8 September 1885; White, 1991, 11; *Hansard*, 3rd series, vol. 300, 1885, col. 384, 548–49 and 553–54; Spielmann, 1886, 13.

28 Letters to M. G. Mead, n.d., 15, 18 and 20 January 1885 (NPG ax, 60–77); letter to Edmund Gosse, 20 January (Brotherton Collection, Leeds University Library); B/W: 117 and 138.

29 Letter to W. J. Stillman, 14 January 1885 (Schaffer Library, Union College: WJS 584).

30 Letter from M, 26 January 1885, draft; letter to M, 27 January 1885; RC, 113–14.

31 A, II: 57–58.

32 Letter from J. T. Johnston and L. P. di Cesnola, 13 February 1885; letter to the President and Directors of the MM: 23 February 1885, reprinted in the New York *Commercial Advertiser*; MM, *Annual Report*, 1885, 14–15.

33 Letter from M. G. Mead to H. Marquand, 5 February 1885 (MM); letter to Mead, 10 February 1885 (NPG ax, 81–83); letter from Meaf, 2 March 1885 (axIII, 96–101); B/W: 117–18. Di Cesnola planned to close the exhibition for rehanging in April, but the trustees voted against it.

34 *Board of Trustees Meetings*, II, 1873–88, 18 May 1885, 292; letter to General L. P. di Cesnola, 4 June 1885. In view of Watts's success, the Metropolitan invited Leighton to send a collection. He did not do so, but in 1886 completed important ceiling decorations for Marquand. Letter from general di Cesnola to Sir Frederic Leighton, 24 March 1885. Ormond and Ormond, 1975, 168 (323).

35 Letter from Madeline Wyndham to Lady Elcho, 14 February 1885; Cat.S.99–100.

36 Letter to Madeline Wyndham, 4 April 1885 (Fiche 27, F14).

37 Letter from John Ruskin, 23 May 1885 (Typescript, Bod., MSS Eng. Lett. c.50, f. 201).

38 Cat.P.61c; Dn, 19 June 1887; *Art Journal*, 1885, 190

and 227; *Athenaeum*, 18 April, 512; 25 April, 540; 2 May, 572; 23 May, 670; GG, 1885, cats 30, 62, 140, 172, 256 and 344, including potraits of Eveleen Myers and Lord Hobart and a photograph of *Hugh Lupus*; cat.S.5a, 9b and Cat.P.62b, 68a and 156c; *The Times*, 20 and 25 May; Tate, 2001, 122.

39  Letter to EBJ, 5 June 1885 (Fitzwilliam, VIII, 3); from EBJ, n.d. (Fiche 16, G4–6).

40  Burne-Jones, 1904, II, 150–55; Fitzgerald, 1975, 207–9; *Athenaeum*, 13 June 1885, 767.

41  Morley, 1905, II, 442–44; Jenkins, *Gladstone*, 1996, 514–56.

42  Letter from W. E. Gladstone, 24 June 1885 (NPG).

43  Letter to Briton Rivière, 24 June 1885 (NPG aXIII, 193).

44  Letter to W. E. Gladstone, 25 June 1885 (BL, Add. MS 44491, ff. 193–94). Leighton was elevated from knight to baronet. Millais, 1899, II, 174.

45  *Portrait of a Boy*, now listed as sixteenth-century French, had been given to GFW by William Russell in 1862. Davies, 1957, NG 1190; *Athenaeum*, 20 June 1885, 798.

46  Letter from Matthew Arnold, 29 June and 18 August 1885 (NPG SI, 90–93, 101–2).

47  Letter to W. E. Gladstone, 28 June 1885 (BL, Add. MS 44491, ff. 221–22); A, II: 39.

48  Letter from the Hon. George Howard to W. E. Gladstone, quoted in Surtees, 1988, 143: 'I put the question to Watts twice and so can have no doubt about his answer. The second time he said that he thought that there would be conceit in refusing such an offer. I am very much vexed that this indecision of Watts has prevented you from honouring Leighton.'

49  D, 4 September 1887.

50  Letter to Sir George F. Watts, Bart, from Edmund Gosse, 26 June 1885 (NPG aXIII. 105–6); to Gosse, 5 July 1885 (Brotherton Collection, Leeds University Library).

51  Letter to F. G. Stephens, 1 July 1885 (Bod., MSS Don. e.87, ff.145–46); *Athenaeum*, 4 July 1885, 23.

52  Letter to the Hon George Howard, 30 June and 1 July 1885; letter from Howard to W. E. Gladstone, 2 July 1885 (BL Add. MS 44491, ff. 236–40); letter to Lady Tennyson, 8 July (TRC, 6275); letter to Lord Aberdare, 22 July (Glamorgan Record Office, D/d B 161/6).

53  Letter to Anne Thackeray Ritchie (Eton College Library, Ritch 11). Anny married her cousin Richmond Ritchie in August 1877; DEVd, 2 and 10 July 1885; to M G Mead, 29 October 1885 (NPG ax, 98–101, ts XIII, 118); to ET, 30 June 1885 (ETMM, Z1, 564); Irving, 1951, 410.

54  Pearson, 1972; Ruskin, 1906; Stead, 6–10 July 1885; Bell, 1962, 177–80; Wilson, 2003, 474–75: the subsequent trial revealed the sale to have been fabricated, for the child's mother, a retired prostitute in the care of the Salvation Army, had been Butler's maid.

55  Cat.S.100c; *Pall Mall Gazette*, 6–10 July 1885; WG, 2004, 19, 25 and 70, cat. 63; B/W: 38; Mathews, 23 May 1986, 338–41.

56  Ebd, 22 July 1885; GFW exhibited Cat.S.35a, 31c and 16a; *The Daughter of Herodias* (39); *Cupid* (41); *Little Bo-Peep* (55) at the RCA 1885; Lord, 2000, 303; unidentified press cutting, 18 July 1885, National Library of Wales HRC 8.

57  Cat.S.100c, 21–22 and 44b; *Athenaeum*, 25 July 1885, 120; 1 August, 152–53 and 29 August, 279; Liddell, 1911, 231, 15 June 1885.

58  *Magazine of Art*, September 1885, 360 and xlvii. GFW also sent *Mrs F. Myers* (140) and *Miss Rachel Gurney* (402) to Manchester Royal Institution, third Autumn Exhibition. Walker Art Gallery, 1885, cats 174 and 175.

59  Letters to M. G. Mead, 15 September and 29 October 1885; letter from Secretary of State T. F. Bayard to Mead, 1 October 1885; letter from Mead, 20–21 October (NPG ax, 96–101, typescripts, aXIII, 107–14; fiche 38 A11–B8). The pictures were shipped on the *Greece*. National Steamship Co., 16 October 1885 (MM).

60  Light referring to goodness and beauty, Darkness to ugliness and evil.

61  Letter to W. E. Gladstone, 4 October 1885 (BL, Add. MS. 44492, f. 143; Fiche 1 D8–9). His bank balance reduced from £7405 15s 2d in June 1885 to £4772 13 11d in 1886, the lowest level since 1871.

62  Letter from W. E. Gladstone, 9 October 1885 (NPG); To Gladstone, 11 October 1885 (BL, Add. MS. 44492, f. 167); Spielmann, 1886, 13, noted that Gladstone, inspired by the success of *Cardinal Manning*, had wished to sit again, but further sittings were not recorded.

63  Horsley read the paper on 'Art Schools and Art Practice in their Relation to a Moral and Religious Life' to the Church Congress in Portsmouth on 7 October 1885; *Pall Mall Gazette*, 9 October; *The Times*, 10 October, 10; Spielmann, 1886, 18.

64  *Punch*, 24 October 1885, 195; Tate, 2001, 122; to Horsley, 1885, quoted in A, II: 40–44; letter from Horsley, 12 November 1885 (NPG SI, 10).

65  Letter from Miss Mary Chesworth, 3 November 1885 (NPG IV, 94–96). M MS notes, September 1885. Birmingham, 1885–86, 181–85, cats 108–87. Spielmann, 1886, 1.

66  Letters to Marion Spielmann, 17, 21, 25 November and 7 December 1885 (M/JR).

16  Hope (1886)

1  GFW was presumably unaware that the pregnancy was proceeding. Blanche gave birth to Verena three months later.

2  Cat.S.71b; to Mrs Percy Wyndham, 8 December 1885 (Fiche 27, G1); letter to M. G. Mead, 29 October 1885 (NPG ax, 98–101, ts XIII, 118); letter to ET, 26 April 1886 (ETMM, Z1, 568); Blanche gave birth to a child in March 1886; B/W: 37; Troubridge, 1925, 24; Puvis de Chavannes painted two versions of *L'Espérance*, one nude, the other clothed in 1872, Walters Art Gallery, 2000, 120–21, cat. 41.

3  Letter to Lord Aberdare, 9 January 1886 (Glamorgan Record Office, D/d B: 161/7 and 8, typescript, NPG axv, 141–42, Fiche 43 D5–6); letter from Lord Aberdare, 20 March, quoted in A, II: 46. He had written to Earl Spencer by 21 May. Letter from Earl Spencer, 23 March 1886, quoted in A, II: 47–48'; letter to the tenth Earl of Wemyss, January 1886; *Art Journal*, 1886, 127; *Athenaeum*, 27 February 1886, 304; *The Times*, 18 May 1886.

4  *Athenaeum*, 9 January 1886, 75; to Briton Rivière, n.d. (*c*.1886) (NPG axIII, 193, quoted in A, II: 150).

5  GFW mentioned to Leyland, 2 August 1884, his plan to assist Schott, an aspiring artist (B/Y, GFW MSS 2125, F3). GFW encouraged Henry Moore, author of *Analysis of Drawing, Painting, and Composing*, to engage models and run an art class in the Iron studio. The students were chiefly friends of EIB. B/W: 166.

6  Letter to Mrs Holiday, 13 February 1886 (NPG axII, 207); letter to Mrs Stephen Coleridge, 26 February 1886 (ETMM, Z1, 567); Nottingham Museum and Art Gallery, 1886; *Athenaeum*, 6 March 1886, 335; letter from the Earl of Wemyss to Madeline Wyndham, 30 May 1886; the *Hemicycle* fresco itself was restored.

7  Cat.S.40a; letter to Walter Crane, 23 March 1886 (RBKC), quoted in Crane, 1907, 252–53.

8  Letter to John Ruskin (draft, WG exercise book); from Ruskin, 4 March 1886 (typescript, Bod., MSS Eng. Lett. c.50, f. 203).

9  *Art Journal*, 1886, 160. Letter to M. G. Mead, 5 February and 12 March 1886 (NPG ax, 102–4 and 106–9).

10  Letter to Ann Budgett, 20 May 1886, quoted in Sotheby's sale catalogue, 4 June 1997, 98, lot 157; *Athenaeum*, 3 July 1886, 524. Brooke 1885. Millais's portrait of Budgett was exhibited at RA, 1882. She had shown strong interest in a picture, which he could not part with (said to be *Hope*), and did not purchase his alternative offer, *The Happy Warrior*. She returned to LHH at least twice that summer.

11  Letter to Mrs A. Sassoon, 13 March 1886 (Davids, 2000, 195, cat. 172).

12  Letter to M, 13 March 1886.

13  *Ibid.*, 17, 23, 31 March and 3 April 1886; letter to Walter Crane, 18 March 1886 (RBKC), enclosing £100 for *The Birth of Venus*, for which he still owed £50. A, II: 55.

14  Macdonald, 1995, cat. 1483.

15  Letters to ET, 26 April and 11 May 1886 (ETMM, Z1, 568–69); *Athenaeum*, 24 April 1886, 561; 1 May 1886, 591; *Art Journal*, 1886, 188; Cat.S.40a and 71b; GG, 1886, cats 10, 61: *The Soul's Prism, Hope*.

16  Letter to M. G. Mead, 29 April 1886 (NPG ax, 110–13).

17  Cat.P.142c, Cat.S.21a and b: *The Death of Cain* (158) and *The Late Mrs Nassau Senior* (1493); *Athenaeum*, 20 March 1886, 399; *Art Journal*, 1886, 221 and 329; Fitzgerald, 1975, 211; letter to Edward Butler, 25 May 1886.

18  B/L, II: 259–60; Royal Academy of Arts, 1996, 39, 83 and 202, cat. 93; Tate, 2001, cats 50 and 124.

19  *Athenaeum*, 1 May 1886, 591; MM: 1998, 264–65, cat. 119; Fitzgerald, 1975, 211; HTd, 22 April 1886; Bonham Carter, 1995, 34–38.

20  *Athenaeum*, 1 May 1886, 584; letter to Hallam Tennyson (TRC 7566); letter from M to Tennyson, 5 May 1886 (TRC 7525).

21  Letters to M, 6 and 10 May 1886; A, II: 59; letters to Margaret Talbot, 8 and 13 April (Huntington, HM 44157–58); Crane, 1907, 284; Holiday, 1914, 312; 'Aeschylus in Picadilly', *The Era*, 15 May 1886, quoted in Ormond and Ormond, 1975, 136; Warr's Homeric translations, *Echoes of Hellas* were published by Marcus Ward, with illustrations by Walter Crane.

22  The Earl of Wemyss's draft for speech (NAS RH4/40/reel 11, 161); *The Times*, 18 May 1886.

23  Letter to M, 20 May 1886; A, II: 49–50.

24  EBd, 22–23 May 1886; B/W: 103.

25  Letter to M. G. Mead, 6 June 1886 (NPG ax, 114–17).

26  Letter to Thomas Armstrong, 15 June 1886; letter from Thomas Armstrong to R. Thompson, 18 June; letter from R. Thompson, 19 and 21 June, notes 22 and 24 June (V&A/MA).

27  Eglantyne Jebb's diary, IV, April 1885–August 1886 and 20–23 June 1886.

28  *Ibid.*, 25 June 1886; Dn, 16 November 1897. On 8 July, M was appointed to the design committee. *Home Arts and Industries Association Minute Book*, 1884–90, 33 and 35 (RIBA, HAIA/1).

29  Mc, 3 July 1886; letter to Mrs E. Wardell (ET), envelope postmarked 6 July 1886 (ETMM, Z1, 579). He arranged for a picture to be sent to her from his frame-maker. (Only the portrait and drawing of ET as *Ophelia* are recorded by ETMM.)

30  Chapman, 1945, 115–16 and Blunt, 1975, 174–75 suggest that her sitter was the fiancé, but the only sitter

Mary mentions in A, II: 58–59 was the elderly, married General Frederick Cotton.

31    Letter to M, 12–13 July 1886. His declaration that 'I may reckon on between £1,000 and £1,500 a year which would be quite enough' – a conservative estimate of his investment income alone – would have had no effect on Mary. Having pledged to take on no new commissions, his bank balance for the financial year after rejecting the baronetcy fell from £7,405 15s 2d to £4,772 13s 11d, but would never again be as low. According to Teresa Chapman, the some of the M correspondence published in RC, 115–26, was afterwards torn up by his mother, Lily. D, 25 December 1887: Blunt, 1975, 173–74.

32    Letter to M, 15 July 1886; RC, 1945, 116.

33    Letters to M, 16 and 23 July 1886; RC, 117; Blunt, 1975, 175; Mc.

34    Letter to the Council of the Royal Academy, 25 July 1886 (RA, RAC/1/WA 19), he added, 'I am unwilling to encumber the Institution with a white elephant and I shall not feel hurt if my gift is "declined with thanks" … "for want of" space'; WG, 2004, 68.

35    B/W, 143.

36    Ibid., 142.

37    Ibid., 39.

38    Letter to M, 8 August 1886; RC, 117–18.

39    Letetr to M, 1 September 1886, 118: RC, 118.

40    Letter to M. G. Mead, 16 August 1886 (NPG ax, 122–28).

41    Literary supplement to Le Figaro, 18 September 1886, quoted in Gibson, 1995, 31; Lucie-Smith, 1995 edition 54.

42    B/W: 39; M 'Reminiscences of GFW by a Poisonous Snake', MS dated 13 December 1911 (WG).

43    Letter to M, 6 August 1886; letter from M, 12 September; B/W, 163; A, II: 63. George Devey was the architect of Monkshatch.

44    Ibid., 12 September, 5 and 18 October 1886.

45    Letter from M, 15 September 1886; RC, 118–19.

46    Letters to M, 19 and 21 September 1886; RC, 119–20; letter from M, 20 September 1886.

47    Letter from M, 28 September 1886. Ibid., 121.

48    Letter from EIB to M. G. Mead, quoted in A, II: 106.

49    WG, 2004, 89, cat. 92; letters to M, 5, 8 and 10 October 1886; letter from M, 9 October; RC, 122–23.

50    B/W, 163–64.

51    HTd, 12 October 1886. The ten-foot statue planned for Trafalgar Square, was erected in Victoria Embankment gardens in 1888 (GFW had suggested a height of eight feet, Waterhouse eight foot six to nine feet). Beattie, 1983, 205; Manning, 1982, 103.

52    D, 16 August 1898; A, II: 172.

53    Letter to Mrs Holiday, 30 October 1886 (NPG axII,

208); Cat.S.1b; WG, 2004, 88, cat. 113; D, 17 July 1887.

54    Letters from Thomas Armstrong to Thompson, 3 September and 16 October 1886; letter from the High Commission for Canada to W. A. Smith, 8 September 1886; letters from R. Lackey, 13 and 15 September 1886; letter to Thomas Armstrong, 14 September 1886 (V&A/MA); Athenaeum, 27 November 1886, 174.

55    Letters to M, 18 and 24 October 1886. RC, 123–25; A, II: 60. He attributed the odd forgotten word or letter to aphasia, but there is no evidence of this in his letters. Letter to M. G. Mead, 21 October 1886 (NPG ax, 129–33).

56    Letters to Blanche Somers-Cocks, 24 October and 4 November 1886.

57    ETMM, Z1, 573 and Z2, 023.

58    Letter to M, 24 October 1886; letter from Andrew Hichens, 27 October; A, II: 60–62; RC, 125.

59    Letter to Sir Frederic Leighton, 3 November [1866] quoted in A, II: 62.

60    Letter from Hallam Tennyson to M, 11 November 1886 (NPG, 94).

61    Letter from ATR (NPG s260–63); letter to ATR, 10 November 1886; D, 20 July 1887.

62    Letter from M, 6 November 1886; RC, 126.

63    Letters to M, 11 and 12 November 1886; RC 126.

64    To raise funds for the honeymoon, GFW sold Brunhild to EIB; B/W: 165–67; RC, 127; Stirling, 1934, 294; letter to M. G. Mead, 13 November 1886 (NPG ax, 134–38).

65    Letters to Marion Spielmann, 5 and 8 November 1886 (M/JR); Science and Art Department General Stores report, 5 November 1886 (V&A/MA).

66    Letter to Marion Spielmann, 12 November 1886 (M/JR).

67    Ibid., 14–15 November 1886 (M/JR).

68    Letter from EBJ, November 1886 (Fiche 16, G7).

69    Letter to Lady Holland, 19 November 1886 (BL, Add. MS 52163, ff. 132).

70    A, II: 63; B/W: 167; RC, 127.

71    Cat.S.11c, catalogued as unfinished because the figures were too large; MM: 2003, 434–36, cat. 195; Birnbaum, 1960, 206–8.

72    Note of authority for W. Agnew, 6 November 1886 (V&A/MA). The Metropolitan collection would transfer from Nottingham to the Royal Yorkshire Jubilee Exhibition at Saltaire; to the Earl of Wemyss, 23 November 1886; B/W: 167.

73    A, II: 62; RC, 127; Athenaeum, 20 November 1886, 678; 27 November, 714.

74    The Ashbee Journals, 28 November 1886, f. 377 (King's College Library, Cambridge); Sizeranne, 1896.

17    Apex of Art (1886–1887)

1    A, II: 71.

2    A, II: 63–65; B/W: 168.

3    The converted palace today forms the central portion of the Cairo Marriott Hotel. A, II: 65.

4    D, 4 March 1887; A, II: 65.

5    D, 24 January 1887.

6    D, 1–3 January 1887; A, II: 65–66; B/W: 16; Cat.S.135b.

7    D, 31 January, 5 and 12 February 1887; A, II: 67–68.

8    D, 25, 28–30 January and 5 February 1887; sketchbook 14/9 (3).

9    D, 3 February 1887.

10    D, 11, 15–17 February 1887; M exercise book (WG).

11    B/W: 170–71; letter from Sir Frederic Leighton, 17 February 1887 (Fiche 19, B10–13). GFW exhibited an unidentified portrait (85) and *Orpheus and Eurydice* (86). Adelaide, 1888, 288.

12    D, 14 February and 7 March 1887; A, II: 71.

13    Letters to Blanche Somers Cocks, 18 February and March 1887; D, 25, 29 March; Cat.S.52a; letter from EBJ (Fiche 17, B13–C5).

14    D, 29 March, 3 and 5 April 1887.

15    Letter from Sir Frederic Leighton, 9 April 1887 (RBKC, 12722); letters from William Agnew to Thomas Armstrong, 6 and 9 April; letter from Amstrong to Thompson, Science and Art Department General Stores, 13 April (V&A/MA). The pictures were transported by R. Dolman and Sons. From Margaret Burne-Jones, 8 April 1887 (Fiche 17, A 4–9).

16    D, 12 April 1887; Christie, Manson and Woods, 2 April 1887; *The Times*, 1 April. *Pall Mall Gazette*, 2 April; letter from Roger Fry to C. R. Ashbee and G. L. Dickinson, 4 April, quoted in Sutton, 1972, I, 113–14.

17    A, II: 73.

18    D, 15 April 1887; A, II: 73–74.

19    D, 26 April and 26 May 1887; A, II: 77.

20    D, 22 April 1887.

21    D, 27 April and 5 May 1887.

22    Cat.P.27b; D, 2–3 May 1887.

23    Letter from Sir Frederic Leighton, 9 April 1887 (LH/1/6); Tate, 1998, 181, cat. 175. Sargent also exhibited *Carnation Lily, Lily, Rose*, Tate, 1998, 274. Ormonds, 1975, 125, 168–69, cats 329—30.

24    Beattie, 1983, 155.

25    Cat.S.109a; WG, 2004, 57; Art Gallery of New South Wales, 2001, 32; *Athenaeum*, 7 May 1887, 612; letter to William Moss, 5 January 1890 (NPG aXIII, 155–56).

26    D, 5 May 1887.

27    GFW had a cast of the *Victory* in his studio.

28    D, 6–7 and 14 May 1887; A, II: 78–79.

29    Cat.P.160b; D, 7, 9 and 13 May 1887; A, II: 81.

30    D, 15 May 1887.

31    D, 17 May 1887; A, II: 79–80.

32    Letter to M. G. Mead, 16 August 1886 (NPG ax, 122–28).

33    D, 16 and 20 May 1887.

34    D, 17 and 20 May 1887.

35    Cat.S.29b and 132b; D, 29–31 May 1887; A, II: 83.

36    D, 2 June 1887.

37    D, 3–4 June 1887; *Athenaeum*, 7 May 1887, 614.

38    D, 5 June 1887; A, II: 84; letter from Sir Frederic Leighton, 9 April.

39    D, 21 June 1898.

40    D, 5–7 June 1887; A, II: 84–85.

41    *Art Journal*, 1890, 135.

42    D, 13 July 1887.

43    Cat.S.52a; D, 12, 16 June and 7 July 1887.

44    D, 11, 13 June and 30 July 1887; A, II: 85. Tate, 2001, 269; MM: 1998, 221, 232–33, 266–67, cats 97 and 120; letter to Lady Lindsay, 15 June (Huntington, HM 31122); letter from Henri d'Orléans, duc d'Aumale, 16 June (Fiche 33E).

45    D, 20–22 June 1887; HTd, 21 June. Marshall, 1972, 210–11; Thompson, n.d., 272.

46    D, 7, 12, 26 June 1887; HTd, 26 June; Wemyss, 1932, 11–13.

47    A, II: 97.

48    D, 22 June, 15 and 18 July 1887; Dulwich Picture Gallery, 1994, 12–13, 19, 31 and 35; *South London Fine Art Gallery Report for 1890*.

49    D, 21 August 1887.

50    D, 18 July 1887; A, II: 98.

51    D, 25 June 1887.

52    D, 25 and 28 June 1887; letter to EIB, 2 October 1890 (draft, WG).

53    D, 10 July 1887; *Athenaeum*, 16 July 1887, 90–92 and 94. Armstrong, 1887, 4–5, 22–23. *Art Journal*, 1887, 249; Claude Phillips, 'The Progress of English Art as Shown at the Manchester Exhibition, *Magazine of Art*, 1888, 44.

54    D, 26 June 1887.

55    Spalding, 1983, 15.

56    Letter from M to ATR, n.d.

57    Formerly in the collection of the Earl of Bristol.

58    *Manchester Art Gallery, Royal Institution*, 1887, cats 320 (*Prayer* (purchased at Rickards's sale)) and 10 (*Hope*).

59    D, 20–21, 31 July 1887; Ormond and Ormond, 1975, cat. 330, pl. 166.

60    D, 29 July 1887; MM: 1998, 161–62. *The Faringdon Collection*, 1998, 56–57.

61    D, 29 June, 5–8 July 1887.

62    D, 29–30 July, 23 and 26 August 1887; *Athenaeum*, 6 August 1887, 189.

63    D, 3 July and 28 August 1887; *Athenaeum*, 22 October

1887, 543, announced completion of M's portrait, front or back view unspecified.

64  D, 28–31 July, 4 September 1887; Cat.P.91c and Cat.S.11a; Prinsep, *1770–1904* (India Office, BL, MSS Eur. C.97.).

65  D, 9 August 1887.

66  D, 7, 24 July and 1 August 1887; letter to Marion Spielmann, 6 August (M/JR); A, II: 87.

67  D, 20 August 1887; Dn, 27 August 1895; letter from EBJ (Fiche 16, G10–17, A2).

68  D, 25–26, 29 August and 11 September 1887; letter to the Earl of Wemyss, 7 September; letter to W. E. Gladstone, 10 September (BL Add. MS 44501, f. 81); *The Times*, 5 September 1887; *Pall Mall Gazette*, 1 November 1887, 1; A, II: 102; Corkran, 1904, 157–59.

69  D, 7 September 1887.

70  D, 12 September 1887.

71  D, 3 September 1887; *Hobby Horse*, II, 1887; WG, 2004, 82, cat. 93; *Athenaeum*, 22 October, 543, reported that the picture was nearing completion.

72  Chesterton, 1904, 144–45.

73  D, 18 July, 13 September 1887; Cat.P.9c; A, II: 99; letter from Samuel Barnett to Frank Barnett, 17 September 1887. (LMA, F/BAR/22, quoted in Barnett, I, 378–79). A second portrait was presented to Wadham College (Barnett, II, 391).

74  D, 11–12 August, 16, 19 and 21 September 1887.

75  D, 18 September 1887.

76  D, 24–25 September 1887; letter from Ford Madox Brown, 24 September 1887 (Bod., MSS Eng. Lett. e.118, ff. 33–34).

77  *Art Journal*, 1887, 350; Cat.S.11a and Cat.P.91c.

78  D, 25 February, 3 March and 16 October 1887.

79  D, 22 August 1891.

80  D, 3–5 October 1887; Cat.P.85b; A, II: 100; letter from Professor Jowett, 1 March 1885, 10 July 1886, 25 September 1887; letter from Jowett to R. S. Wright, 23 September 1886 (NPG s1, 212–13, 215–18 and 222); Darwall-Smith, 1993, I, H70,ff. 56–58.

81  D, 6 and 18 October 1887.

82  D, 11, 26–27 October 1887; Florence Nightingale to M, 9 October (Bod., MSS Eng. Lett. e.118, f. 35); letters from Professor B. Jowett, 22 and 30 October (NPG s1, 224–26).

83  B/W: 102–3; EIB exhibited the portrait as though painted by GFW at the St Louis World's Fair.

84  De Navarro, 1896, 175–78.

85  D, 21, 24–25 October and 2 November 1887; Cat.P.3a and b; A, II: 100–1.

86  D, 22 July, 10, 23 October and 2 November 1887; Cat.S.99; Jowett, 1993, 57; Liddell, 1911, 253; De Navarro, 1896, 176.

87  D, 29–30 October 1887; *The Times*, 5 September, 14.

88  D, 31 October and 3 November 1887; letter from EBJ to Charles Hallé, 3 October, quoted in Burne-Jones, II, 1904, 179; Hallé, 1896, II, 152–53 and 158; *Magazine of Art*, 1887, v; *Athenaeum*, 5 November, 610; *Art Journal*, 1887, 414; Carr, 1925, 157–60; Surtees, 1971, 176–77.

89  Letter from EBJ, n.d. (Fiche 16, G10–17 A2).

90  *Ibid.*, February 1888 (Fiche 17, A14–B6); Surtees, 1971, 178.


18  'The Utmost for the Highest' (1887–1889)

1  D, 12–13, 18 and 29 November 1887.

2  D, 17 and 29 November and 6 December 1887; Cat.S.69a, 64c, 2b; A, II: 104–5.

3  D, 12 October 1887.

4  D, 13 and 24 November, 1, 3, 7 and 10–11 December 1887.

5  D, 17 and 19 November and 11 December 1887.

6  D, 12–13 and 29 December 1887; A, II: 105–9. He wished to work on the picture and make the final choice after his return. The *Athenaeum* announced on 7 January 1888, at GFW's request, that as the original version belonged to the nation, Manchester would receive the new duplicate. Letter to Andrew Hichens, 15 May 1888 (NPG axII, 190–91).

7  D, 21 December 1887.

8  D, 23–25 December 1887.

9  D, 30 November, 27–31 December 1887.

10  Dn, 14 January 1888; Cat.S.106a and b; A, II: 104.

11  Dn, 16, 21, 27 February, 1–3 March 1888; A, I: 4, A, II: 110–11; B/W: 175–76.

12  Letter from EBJ, February 1888 (Fiche 17, A14–B6); Burne-Jones, 1904, II, 181–82.

13  Letter from EBJ, n.d. (Fiche 17, B7–12); Fitzgerald 1997, 213; MM: 1998, 231, cat. 96.

14  Letter from EBJ, [March 1888]; letter from EBJ to MSW, November 1887 (Fiche 17, B13–C5 and A12–13); Burne-Jones, 1904, II, 181.

15  Letter to Mrs Henrietta Barnett, 15 March 1888 (NPG axII, 30–31).

16  B/W: 176–77; Dn, 27 March 1888.

17  Dn, 16 March 1888; Cat.S.109c, 104c–106a; A, II: 113.

18  Cat.S.4a: *Alps behind Menton*; Dn, 8 April 1888; A, II: 114–15; JCd, 25 July 1893.

19  GFW, June 1888, 253; D, 16 December 1887; letter to Marion Spielmann, 2 April 1888; MSW to Spielmann, Easter Monday (M/JR).

20  Letter to Spielmann, 9 and 27 April 1888 (M/JR).

21  Dn, 16–17 March 1888; letter from FL, 15 April 1888 (RBKC, 12727); *The Spirit of Christianity* and *Hope* (hanging at South Kensington), small *Love and Life*,

*Rachel Gurney, Tennyson*, the presidential portrait of Leighton (LHH studio), and portraits of Browning and Carlyle (Not-tingham); Cat.S.34a; letter to Andrew Hichens, 22 April 1888 (NPG aXII, 188); Ormonds, 1975, 102.

22  A, II: 118.

23  Letter to Hichens, 22 April 1888 (NPG aXII, 188–89). The Red Cross Hall opened in June 1888. Walter Crane designed 3 cartoons in pastel, the first featuring Alice Ayres, was subsequently enlarged and painted on to a fibrous plaster panel by Mrs Barrington. Crane, 1907, 358–59; A, II: 103; Ward-Jackson, 2003, 296; Darley, 1990, 240–41; letter from FL to EIB, September 1887, quoted in B/W: 19, and Corkran, 1904, 157–59: 'You will have to consider (supposing first you are able to command the hands and brains needed) how far the idea of purely and directly didactic painting such as is proposed by Watts is compatible with the adornment of the spaces, with a view to training the eye of the people to sense of Beauty.'

24  Letter to the Earl of Wemyss, 8 May 1888. The Life Peerage Act was introduced in 1958.

25  *Athenaeum*, 19 May 1888, 635; Emanuel, 1989, 151.

26  Spielmann accordingly registered *Death Crowning Innocence*; Cat.S.35c; Dn, 20 May 1888; New Gallery, 1888, cat. 30. *Athenaeum*, 22 October 1887, 543, and 19 May 1888, 635; *Art Journal*, 1888, 221; to Hichens, 15 May 1888 (NPG aXII, 190–91); *The Times* and *Standard*, 9 May 1888; letters to Spielmann, 22, 25 and 31 May and 4 June 1888 (M/JR).

27  Dn, 3 May 1888; A, II: 106; Cat.P.157a; Cat.S.71b and c. Science and Art Department General Stores, 7 May 1888 (V&A/MA); *Art Journal*, 1888, 192. RCA, 1888, cats 24–25, 129: *Miss Gurney, The First Whisper of Love*, the original study for *Love and Life*.

28  A, II: 119.

29  Dn, 8 June 1888; A, II: 121.

30  Dn, 14 May and 5 June 1888; To Hichens, 15 May 1888 (NPG aXII, 190–91).

31  Dn, 16–18 May 1888; Cat.S.118a; MSW, 'Babblings', MS notebook, 1883–84 (WG); A, II: 124–25; WG, 2004, 19 and 71, cat. 65.

32  Letters to Hichens, 15 and 24 May 1888 (NPG aXII, 190–92).

33  Letter to MGM, 29 May 1888 (NPG aXIII, 136).

34  Letter from Alfred Gilbert, 29 May 1888; letter from EIB to Hamo Thornycroft (L/HM, 72); A, II: 133–35; Dorment, 1985, 67 and 77; RA, 126–27.

35  Dn, 5 and 10 June 1888; Cat.S.139a (*Sunset on the Alps*), Cat.S.3c (*Alps near Monnetier*); A, II: 126–27.

36  Dn, 20–21, 25, 27 June, 2 and 4 July 1888; A, II: 132.

37  Dn, 1, 9 July and 13 August 1888.

38  Dn, 22 July 1888; Cat.S.121a; Alston, 1929, pl. VII.

39  Rothenstein, 1931, I, 21, 254–55.

40  Cat.S.54b; Dn, 3 August 1888; A, II: 151–52; letter to Speilmann, 11 October 1888 (M/JR).

41  Dn, 9 August 1888; A, II: 131; B/W 79 f/n.

42  Letter to Sir William Gregory, 22 September 1888 (copy, WG); letter to G. F. Dunscombe, Fine Arts Department, South Kensington Museum, 23 December 1889 (V&A/MA).

43  *Sant' Agnese, Mentone*, catalogued as *The Higher Alps, Mentone*, Manchester Royal Institution, 1888, cat. 114, and as *Alps behind Mentone* in Cat.S.4a.

44  Dn, 29 August 1888; A, II: 88–89, 126.

45  Dn, 30 August and 19 October 1888; Wilson, 2003, 525–27.

46  Letter from Philip Burne-Jones to MSW, 30 August 1888 (Fiche 17, C6–6); Dn, 13 September 1888; A, II: 101. *Athenaeum*, 17 November 1888, 670.

47  Letter from Alfred Gilbert to MSW, 15 August 1888; A, II: 133–34; Dorment, 1985, 18–19.

48  Letter from MSW to Brian Hatton (Hereford County Archives).

49  Letter from Alfred Gilbert to Hamo Thornycroft, 2 January 1885 (L/HM 268).

50  Letter from Hamo Thornycroft to Gilbert, 26 September 1888 (L/HM, Th/C/636A).

51  Dn, 20, 21, 27 August, 4 and 12 September; letter from Hamo Thornycroft to Alfred Gilbert, 26 September 1888. HTd 4, 13, 26–27 September; letter from AG to HT, 28 September, quoted in Dorment, 1985, 91 (L/HM, 636 and c.276); EIB to HT (L/HM, 72); A, II: 134.

52  Letter from Gilbert to Hamo Thornycroft, 28 September 1888 (L/HM, Th/C/276).

53  Letter to M. G. Mead, 27 and 29 September 1888 (NPG ax, 139–45).

54  Letter from MSW to M. G. Mead, 19 October 1888 (NPG aXIII, 142).

55  Letter to M. G. Mead, 19 October 1888 (NPG ax, 146–48).

56  Letter to Spielmann, 11 October 1888; letter to Col Donnelly, South Kensington Museum, 17 October. (V&A/MA).

57  Letter to Spielmann, 4 June, 22 Jul, 12, 17 and 22 October 1888 (M/JR).

58  Millais, 1888, XI, 289–90; GFW, 1889, XII, 90.

59  Letter to Spielmann, 12, 17 and 22 October 1888 (M/JR); GFW, 1889, XII, 90–92.

60  A, II: 133–35.

61  Anscombe and Gere, 1978, 112–13; *Diary of Sydney Carlyle Cockerell*, 7 December 1920 (FC).

62  'All over the world, joy in beauty as an instinct is coming to an end, as in our own country, crushed by the wheels of machinery and forgotten in the competition for

wealth [William Morris pleaded, too, for human beings ground down by the monotony of machines]. . . . now our factories, our villas, and our cottages are sores upon the face of nature. . . . so much real and ennobling pleasure [was] denied to the eye of the modern man, whose life is already made too pleasureless, if not absolutely painful by its toil and struggle. While he is deprived of this pleasure the vitality of art languishes to extinction. . . . The stumbling-block to the English is the practical. Everything that does not present the idea of immediate advantage seems to be unpractical . . . a bogey from which it is necessary to escape without a moment's hesitation. We must not stop an instant to look behind the spectre, which would often prove only a white sheet and a turnip. [He hailed the growing number of Home Arts volunteers] teaching the boys and girls of our villages and towns to take a delight in some simple artistic occupation, showing the beauty of a sweep of landscape, or the grace to be found in the lines of a coil of rope. Till the love of beauty is once more alive amongst us there can be little hope for art. It is a universal language – everything we use or wear is an expression of it, or absence of it . . . 'the future will know us better from the impress we leave by moral character, intellectual efforts – by poetry and by art – than by wealthy and political position . . .'; Transactions, Liverpool, 1888, 108–11; *Magazine of Art*, XI, 1888, xxxvii; Emanuel, 1989, 154, 5 December 1888; A, II: 136.

63   Letter from Gilbert, 27 December 1888 (Bod., MSS Eng. Lett. e.118, ff. 7–9); Dorment, 1985, 95; Beattie, 1983, 43–44. As GFW's paper focussed on craft revival for the poor, Gilbert may have felt obliged to raise a specific sculptural issue.

64   Dn, 4 and 6 December 1888; ATRd, 1 December; Cat.S.62c; *Ganymede*, exhibited by the Royal Society of British Artists, was bought from the Suffolk Street Gallery by Henry Makins. *Magazine of Art*, 1888, XI, 126; A, II: 136–37; Holiday, 1914, 33–34.

65   Letter from EBJ to MSW, 7 December 1888 (Fiche 17, C9–10); letters from FL, 8 and 24 December 1888 (RBKC 12731–32. Fiche 19 D2–D8); letter to Andrew Hichens, 15 May 1888 (NPG aXII, 190–91); A, II: 138–39.

66   A, II: 137–38; WG, 1998, 33; Dn, 1 April and 10 May 1889.

67   Dn, 20 May; A, II: 126–27; GFW later reworked *Sunset on the Alps*, WG, 2004, 66, cat. 53.

68   Cat.S.39c; from FL, n.d. and letter to MSW, 7 January 1889 (RBKC 12729 and 12734); letter to Spielmann, 24 January 1889 (JR/M); letter to unnamed recipient, 26 January 1889 (Brotherton Collection, University of Leeds).

69   Letters to Spielmann, 26 January and 1 February 1889 (M/JR); letters from W. B. Richmond, 10 and 13 December (Bod., MSS Eng. Lett. d.275, ff. 148–51).

70   Dn, 31 January 1889.

71   Letter to Hichens, 22 April 1888 (NPG aXII, 188–89).

72   Cat.S.46–50; A, II: 138–41; Tate, 1997, cat. 124.

73   Dn, 11 February 1889; A, II: 142–44.

74   Dn, 18 March 1889.

75   Dn, 7 March 1889. Letters to Spielmann, 13, 17 and 29 March, 6 April (M/JR); *Magazine of Art*, 1889, 253–55.

76   Letter from Gilbert to MSW, 7 April 1889 (Bod., MSS Eng. Lett. e.116, ff. 78–79).

77   Cat.S.69a; RA, 1889, cat. 318; RA, 1986, cat. 2153.

78   Ormond and Kilmurray, 1998, 186–88, cat. 183; Terry, 1908, 35–37; Irving, 1951, 501–2; *Art Journal*, 1889, 191.

79   Dn, 17 September 1888; Cat.S.71a.

80   Dn, 17 and 27 September 1888; letter to Spielmann, 6 April and 2 May 1889 (M/JR); letter to James Smith, 11 April 1890 (NPG aXIV, 18); Cat.S.4a, 29b, 54b, 64c, 71a, 132b and 160b; New Gallery 1889, cats 1, 2, 17, 33, 57, 162, 184 and 403, Philip Burne-Jones, cat. 130: *The Wounded Heron, Fog Off Corsica, The Sea Ghost, Good Luck to Your Fishing, Fata Morgana, Sant Agnese Mentone, The Wife of Pluto, Clytie*; Tate 2001; *Athenaeum*, 11 May 1889, 60; G. B. Shaw, 'In the Picture-Galleries', *World*, 8 May 1889, quoted in Weintraub, 1986, 490; *Daily Telegraph, Daily News*, 2 May 1889; *Magazine of Art*, 1891, 12.

81   Letter from the Duke of Westminster, 1 July 1889 (NPG aIV, f. 166). *Good Luck to Your Fishing* was later purchased by Sir Charles Tennant and *Sant Agnese* given to Evelyn, Viscountess de Vesci.

82   Letter from FL, 25 April 1889 (RBKC, 12743. Fiche 19 F9–10); *Magazine of Art*, 1889, XII, xxxii; Art and Industries Supplement to *Art Journal*, 1889. 'The Paris Exhibition' 1889, iv, xii. *Paris Universal Exhibition*, 1878, cats 157–64; *Endymion, The Judgment of Paris, Love and Life*, portraits of C. A. Ionides and Leighton, and *Uldra, Hope* and *Mammon*.

83   Dn, 6 May 1889; *The Times*, 6 May; Hulme, Buchanan and Powell, 2000, 53–54; Saumarez-Smith, 1997, 15 and 19.

84   Letter from FL to MSW, 23–24 May 1889 (RBKC, 12742 and 12744; Fiche 19 F 7–8). Dn, 23–24 May 1889; 'An Appeal Against Female Suffrage', *Nineteenth Century*, CXLVIII, June 1889, 781–88; A, II: 145–46; Sutherland, 1990, 198. EIB signed the appeal.

85   Letter from GFW, 1 April 1889 (Huntington, HM 31142); *Magazine of Art*, 1889, XII, xxxiv.

86   Dn, 3 June 1889; A, II: 149.

87   Dn, 29 May 1889; Beattie, 1983, 156.

88   Dn, 25 August 1889; Towndrow, 1939, 177; Crook,

1981, 168; Reynolds, 1994; Britten added two cherubim to GFW's single praying angel in the *St Matthew* spandrel; *Athenaeum*, 14 February 1891, 224–25.

89   Dn, 8 May 1889; *Athenaeum*, 13 July 1889, 73; WG, 2004, 87, cat. 108.


19   Limnerslease (1889–1891)

1   Dn, 21 September 1889; letter from M to C. R. Ashbee, 5 October 1889 (Album of Correspondence addressed to C. R. Ashbee (V&A, 86.DD.17a); Crawford, 1985, 29–36.

2   Letters to A. H. Mackmurdo, 4 October, 12 November and 12 December 1889 (Huntington, HM 31128–30); *The Hobby Horse*, no. 17, January 1890, 2–10; MacCarthy, 1994, 591; *Art Journal*, 1889, 363.

3   Letter from Briton Rivière, 3 November 1889 (Bod., MSS Eng. Lett. d.275, ff. 156–57).

4   Dn, 18 November and 17 December 1889; letter to C. A. Ionides, 13 January 1890 (NPG axiii, 24); *South London Fine Art Gallery Report*, 1890. GFW gave £200, the highest donation to date; compare this with £25 from the Duke of Westminster and £10 from Constantine Ionides.

5   Dn, 16–20 November 1889.

6   Dn, 21, 26, 29 November 1889 and 3 March 1890. Cat.S.117c; A, ii: 153–56.

7   Dn, 23–24 September 1889; Ilchester, 1937, ii, 449.

8   Dn, 23 July, 13 and 24 December 1889; A, ii: 152–53.

9   Letter from Hallam Tennyson to M, 15 December 1889 (NPG 102); letter to HT, 16 December 1889; letter to Lord Tennyson, 26 December 1889 (TRC, 6279–80); letter from FL, Monday (RBKC, 12745; fiche 19 G4–7).

10   Letter to the Secretary, Fine Arts Department, S. Kensington Museum, 22 October 1889; memos from Mr Thompson to Sir P. Cunliffe-Owen, 8 January 1890; letter from Cunliffe-Owen to Thomas Armstrong, 8 January; letter from Armstrong to Cunliffe-Owen, 10 January; letter from General Donnelly to Cunliffe-Owen, 17 January (V&A/MA).

11   Dn, 3, 19 and 28 February, 1, 24 and 30 March 1890; A, ii: 157–58; RC, 132–33.

12   Dn, 21 August 1889; Cat.P.55c; letters to Briton Rivière, 22 February, 21 March 1890 (NPG axiii, 196–97).

13   Dn, 19 February, 5–6 March 1890; RA, *Exhibition of Works by the Old Masters*, 1890, 29, cat. 135, (*Venus and Cupid*), loaned from R. A. Morrit (National Gallery, NG2057); letter from FL, Monday, n.d. (RBKC 12745/87).

14   Ormond, 1975, 170, cat. 348 (*Solitude*), 350 (*The Bath of Psyche*), 352 (*Tragic Poetess*).

15   Dn, 11 March; letter from FL, n.d., 7, 13 March and

10 April 1890 (Fiches 19 G 4–7, and 20 A6–13; RBKC, 12750).

16   Christie's sale, 22 March 1890, lots 121–33. Carver had owned 13 Watts; *Athenaeum*, 15 March 1890, 347 and 29 March, 411.

17   Letters to James Smith, 3 and 11 April 1890 (NPG axiv, 16 and 18); WG, 2004, 23–24 and 18, cat. 53; Morris, 1989, 67–73.

18   Dn, 3 April 1890; A, ii: 158–59; Cat.P.158b.

19   Cat.P.173c.

20   *Architect*, xliii, 16 May 1890, 311; *Journal of the Royal Institute of British Architects*, 1923, xxx, 3rd series, 9 December 1922; Arts Council of Great Britain, 1981, 61.

21   Letter from Emily Ford, 29 April 1890; G. S. Stepniak to E. S. Ford, 28 April 1890 (NPG aiv, 272–73); Hulse, 1970, 8, 29–30, 41–44.

22   D, 23 January 1891; Cat.S.7, 117c and 126a; New Gallery, 1890, cats 31 and 47; letters to Marion Spielmann, 19 and 29 April 1890 (M/JR); Dibdin, 1923, 13; *Athenaeum*, 3 May 1890; A, ii: 156. 577; *Art Journal*, 1890, 166.

23   Dn, 14 May 1889.

24   Dn, 14 May 1889 and 13 May 1890; A, ii: 179.

25   Dn, 16–28 May 1890; A, ii: 159–60.

26   Letter from Hallam Tennyson to H. M. Butler, 25 May 1890 (Trinity College Library, Add. MS a233, f. 43).

27   A, ii: 162–63; Tennyson, *In Memoriam*, lxxxiii, 12.

28   Cat.P.158b and c; letter from M to Hallam Tennyson, 31 May 1890 (TRC 6281); A, ii: 164–67.

29   Letter to Spielmann, 25 October 1890 (M/JR); *Daily Graphic*, 8 September 1891, 1 (caricature by Reginald Cleaver) and 9.

30   *Corporation of London Art Gallery*, June 1890, cats 14–15, 19–21: *Fata Morgana*, *Violet Lindsay* and *William Morris*, *Ariadne in Naxos*, *Mischief*; *Athenaeum*, 30 August 1890, 298; Cat.S.6a.

31   Dn, 15 May and 12 July 1890; Spalding, 1998, 13–14; *Athenaeum*, 8 March 1890, 314; *The Times*, 13 March and 22 July 1890; *Report of the National Gallery 1890*.

32   *South London Fine Art Gallery Report of a Public Meeting*, 18 July 1890; Dulwich Picture Gallery, 1994, 12–13, 22 and 53; *Aglaia*, July 1893.

33   Letter to Dorothy Tennant, 2 July 1890; Dn, 12 July; A, ii: 167–68.

34   Dn, 3 July 1889, 5 January, 28 June and 14 July 1890; A, ii: 171–72.

35   Letter from Alfred Gilbert to M, 15 July 1890.

36   Letter from Hallam Tennyson, Aldworth, 11 August 1890 (NPG 106); letter to Hallam Tennyson, 12 August (TRC 628A).

37   Letter from Lady Tennyson, 15 August 1890 (NPG 107).

38  Dn, 21 August 1890.

39  Dn, 8 September 1890; Cat.P.159c.

40  Letters to Mr Horsfall, 6 and 12 September 1890 (NPG aXII, 226–30); FL to M, 9 September 1890 (RBKC 12753/111, Fiche 20 B4–5); D, 25 February 1891; B/L II, 275–83; Harrison, 1954, 127 and 29; Dulwich Picture Gallery, 1994, 31.

41  D, 20 June 1893: 'Bailey Bros of Nerrington Bath . . . got us back our *Modern Painters*'.

42  D, 6, 16, 17 and 21 September 1890.

43  Letter to EIB, n.d. and 2 October 1890 (draft, WG); letter to Mrs Julia Greg (draft, NPG 14).

44  D, 2 January 1891; A, I: 329. M preferred to ignore EIB's subsequent intrusions.

45  Dn, 28 September 1890; Agresti, 1907, 217 and 220.

46  Dn, 7 October 1890. *The Epitaph*, exhibited and catalogued *Sic Transit*; Cat.S.133a; A, II: 189–90; Adam, 1925, 195–97; Burgoyne, 1941, 149; Friederichs, December 1895, 79.

47  Dn, 30 May and 17 October 1890; A, II: 188–89.

48  Roxburgh, 1968, xii.

49  Dn, 21 October and 21 December 1890; Cat.S.53b and 54a; Sketchley, 1904, 101; Agnew, May 1891, cat. 2; New Gallery Winter Exhibition, 1896–97, 5 and 53, cat. 123.

50  Letter to A. H. Mackmurdo, 25 March, n.d., and 29 November 1890 (Huntington: HM 31132–34); Mackmurdo, 1890, reprinted in A, III: 272–76.

51  Dn, 22 October, 10–11 November and 8 December 1890; Ashbee, I, 1890, 9–11, 87 and 98; *The Guild of Handicraft Minute Book*, I, 1889, 15. He had also written a preface for the HAIA recreation classes.

52  Leighton was born on 31 December 1830.

53  Dn, 2 and 4 December 1890; A, II: 190.

54  Letter from FL, 2 December 1891; D, 10 December; Dn, 28 June 1892 (RBKC 12761).

55  D, 1 January 1891.

56  Dn, 14 November 1890; Agnew, May 1891; A, II: 192.

57  D, 5 January 1891; A, II: 198.

58  D, 6, 10, 14 and 25 January 1891; Watts Gallery, 1998, 36.

59  D, 12 January, 4 February and 13 March 1891.

60  D, 13–18 January 1891.

61  D, 25 January 1891.

62  D, 5–6, 11 February 1891; A, II: 191; Salisbury, 1950, 352–70.

63  D, 3 and 5 February, 1 March 1891.

64  D, 2 and 24 February 1891.

65  D, 2 and 8 February, 23 May 1891.

66  D, 19–20 February 1891; Spielmann, 19 February 1891, 4.

67  D, 3, 7 and 25 February 1891.

68  Cat.S.104c–106a and Cat.P.57; D, 8 and 10, 11 February 1891.

69  D, 23 January, 13 February 1891; Cat.S.107a and 151a.

70  Dn, 13 May 1889, and D, 15 February 1891.

71  D, 2, 3 and 5 March 1891. GFW drew a portrait head of Nina Welby on 9 July.

72  Cat.S.72c; D, 11 March 1891.

73  D, 9–1 and 31 March 1891.

74  D, 31 March, 15 April 1891. *Naples* was finished on 30 April 1892.

75  D, 9 and 12 March 1891.

76  D, 5, 7, 9 and 13 April 1891.

77  D, 12 April, MS 'April 1891' (WG Box 14/9); Agnew, May 1891; Ruskin, *The Queen of the Air*, 1869, 18, reprinted in Cook and Wedderburn.

78  D, 12 April 1891.

79  M exercise book (WG); WG, 1998, 36–37.

80  D, 4, 6 and 10 April 1891.

81  D, 17–18 April 1891.

82  D, 25 April 1891.

83  D, 27 April 1891; Cat.S.1b and 107a; New Gallery 1891, cats 9 and 238; *Art Journal*, 1891, 189. He was also contributing to the Berlin Artists Union Jubilee Exhibition and had *Love and Death*, *Live and Life*, *Hope*, and the portraits of Cardinal Manning and Tennyson sent from South Kensington to the Free Exhibition in Glasgow. Letter to the Corporation of Galleries of Art, Glasgow, 22 March 1891. Memo from Thompson, (V&A/MA).

84  D, 23 March, 23 and 26 April 1891; Cat.P.159c; *Magazine of Art*, XIV, 1891, 220; *Athenaeum*, 2 May 1891, 573.

85  D, 20–23 April 1891. The South London Art Gallery opened on 4 May.

86  Letter from William Blake Richmond, 6 January 1892; Reynolds, 1994, 2.

87  D, 2–3 May 1891. In a letter to Marion Spielmann, 25 April (M/JR), GFW pointed out that all but two of the twelve drawings (*Conscience Dweller in the Innermost*, *Faith, Hope, Love* [*and Life*], *The Spirit of Christianity*, *Mammon – the Spirit of the Age*, *Love and Death*, *Death Crowning Innocence*, *A Message from the Unseen* [*The Messenger*], *Time, Death and Judgement*, *Paolo and Francesca*, *Out of the Storm*) were studies of his designs for the nation, but excluded, notably, the important *Court of Death*. The Whitworth exhibited the drawings in July (*Athenaeum*, 13 June 1891, 774), and sold them at Christies, 26 April 1935, lots 78–84, retaining only *Love and Death*.

88  D, 6 May 1891.

89  D, 9 May 1891; A, II: 213; JCd, 10 July 1891.

90  D, 14–23 May 1891; Dn, 28 October 1895.

91  D, 26 May and 16 July 1891; Seymour-Smith, 1994, 410, 414, pl. 7.

92  D, 10, 27–30 May, 3 June, 5 July 1891; JCd, 10 July; A, II: 195–96.

93  D, 7 June; *Trade Unionist*, 6 and 13 June 1891; *The Times*, 13 June 1891, 14.

94  D, 9 June 1891.

95  D, 23 June 1891.

96  D, 21, 28 and 30 June, 1, 4–6, and 9 July 1891; 'The Picture of Dorian Gray', *Collected Works of Oscar Wilde*, Hertfordshire, Wordsworth Editions, 1997, 3; Calloway and Colvin, 1997, 60 and 66. M, very taken with Wilde, failed to note GFW's response in her diary.

97  D, 15 June 1891; Dudley Gallery, November 1891, cats 116 and 118; Crawford, 1985, 70 and 221.

## 20  *Sic Transit* (1891–1893)

1  D, 11, 14 July, 12 August 1891; letter to James McNeill Whistler, 14 July 1891; letter from Whistler, n.d. (Glasgow University Library, MS Whistler W67–68); *Society of Portrait Painters*, 1891, cats 224 and 244; MacDonald, 1995, 477, cat. 1318.

2  D, 21 and 27 June 1891.

3  D, 17 June and 3 July 1891.

4  D, 10 and 12 July 1891; JCd 10 July (Herefordshire Record Office); Emanuel, 1989, 167–68; Julia Cartwright, 1891, 13.

5  D, 13 August 1891.

6  'The Surrey Home of Mr G. F. Watts RA' news cutting (RBKC).

7  D, 18–22 July and 6 August 1891.

8  D, 14, 20 and 23 July 1891.

9  D, 2–7, 23 August 1891; Cat.S.66a.

10  D, 14 July, 16 August 1891; letter to the Earl of Wemyss, 25 July 1891. To GFW the space between the breast and stomach was too long: 'The breasts are too high, and it does not give a sufficient breathing room. The Greeks he said (getting up and going to the *Ilissus*) knew it belonged to the strong and grand development of the human frame and so they shortened the space between the chest and stomach and lengthened it from the throat to below the breast in man and woman.'

11  D, 29 July 1891; Cat.S.11c, 42a, 62c; *Catalogue of the Pictures forming the Collection of Sir Charles Tennant*, 1896; Abdy and Gere, 1982, 17–18; The name 'Souls' derived from verses composed by George Curzon at a dinner in 1889: 'Souls sparkled and spirits expanded.'

12  D, 2 August 1891; Forsyth, 1889.

13  D, 18 August 1891; Jullian, 1973, 14.

14  D, 8–11 August 1891; Cat.S.125a. Spielmann commissioned a small painting from his design of the *Recording Angel*. Letter to Marion Spielmann, 29 July 1891 (M/JR).

15  D, 11, 15–21, 24 August, 30 September and 6 October

1891; A, II: 197; GFW painted a separate study of the armour on 4 September.

16  A half-length portrait of Jan Caspar Gevaerts – Gevartius, secretary of the City of Antwerp – dressed in a loose cloak, dark doublet, white lace collar, his fingers splayed over a book.

17  D, 19 August 1891; Cat.P.41c; Crane, 1907, 360–61.

18  D, 22 and 24 August 1891; Crane, 1907, 323–34 and 360–61.

19  D, 29 August 1891.

20  D, 30 August 1891.

21  D, 4–5 September 1891; Cat.P.41c.

22  D, 26–27 August, 8–9, 29 September and 2 October 1891.

23  Cat.S.129b and 35–36; D, 24 June 1891; *Hobby Horse*, 1891; *Magazine of Art*, XIV, March 1891, xiii; *Athenaeum*, 10 October 1891, 491.

24  D, 22 August 1891.

25  D, 5–6, 8 and 17 September 1891; Dn, 25 January and, 19 November 1892; Mme Helena Blavatsky, who founded the Theosophical Society in 1875, died on 8 May 1891.

26  D, 10–11 September 1891.

27  D, 15–18 September 1891.

28  D, 26–28 September and 5–6 October 1891.

29  D, 28 September 1891.

30  D, 29–30 September, 5–6 and 22 October 1891.

31  Letter to Sir Henry Acland, 13 and 16 October 1891 (Bod., MSS Acland, d.71, ff. 116–17); letters from Acland, 14 and 17 October 1891 (NPG aXII, 7 and 9).

32  D, 13, 15 and 22 October 1891.

33  D, 23 October 1891.

34  D, 8–9 November 1891; Dn, 30 March 1892.

35  D, 28–29 October, 8–9 November and 1 December 1891; Cat.S.81. The picture of Maud standing in the smock was named *Jill*. Royal Museums of Fine Art, Belgium, 88–89, 2004, cat. 21; Tate Gallery, 1997, 78 and 240, cat. 107. *The Third Pastel Exhibition*, Grosvenor Gallery, 1890, cat. 180.

36  Letter to Frederic Shields, 12 November 1891; *Art Journal*, 1892, 95, and *Athenaeum*, 30 January 1892, 158, announced that artists had raised £900 (GFW gave £50) for Ford Madox Brown to paint *Wicliffe on his Trial in the Presence of John of Gaunt* for NG.

37  Letters from FL, 27 November and 2 December 1891 (RBKC 12759/122 and 12761/128, Fiche 20, B14–C3 and C7–8).

38  D, 31 October 1891; A, II: 206.

39  D, 21 and 26 August 1891. The McLure Hamilton portrait was shown in the *Society of Portrait Painters Second Exhibition*, 1892, cat. 152.

40  D, 1, 5, 14 October and 17 November 1891; *Vanity Fair*, 19 December 1891.

41   D, 14–24 November 1891.

42   D, 25–28, 30 November, 1 December 1891. The bust, praised at exhibition at Agnew's in March, was presented to the Whitworth by November 1892. *Athenaeum*, 19 March 1892, 380; 26 November 1892, 748.

43   D, 29 December 1891; Dn, 26 May 1892; D, 6 and 10–11 January 1893: Smith bought the replica, signed by GFW on 11 January, for the same price he paid for the original (valued at £500) which he exchanged for *Afloat* (£800); A, I: 270; *Athenaeum*, 5 Dec 1891, 768; letter to William Rossetti, 30 December 1891 (University of British Columbia); letters from W. M. Rossetti, 14 April and 12 June 1892 (Bod., MSS Eng. Lett. e.118, ff. 85–86). GFW was on the committee of *The Victorian Exhibition Illustrating Fifty Years of Her Majesty's Reign 1837–87*, The New Gallery, 1891–92, cats 22, 23, 171, 205, 212–13, 219–20, 227, 230, 233, 278, 286 and 375: *Earl of Shrewsbury, Lord Lawrence, Louisa, Marchioness of Waterford, Sir Henry Taylor, T. Carlyle, R. Browning, M. Arnold, G. C. D. Rossetti, J. S. Mill, W. Spottiswoode, Sir A. Panizzi, Baron Charles Marochetti, Earl Russell, Lord Campbell*; Cat.P.137a and b. GFW acknowledged receipt of the original *Rossetti* and a cheque (200 guineas for *Afloat*) in a letter to James Smith, 10 January 1893 (NPG axiv, 21); *Catalogue of . . . Ancient and Modern Pictures of Frederick Richards Leyland, Esq.*, Christie, Manson and Woods, 28 May 1892, lot 47.

44   D, 3 September 1891.

45   D, 9 December 1891; letter from EBJ, 1891 (Fiche 17, D3–10); Lucie-Smith, 1995, 114.

46   Lucie-Smith, 1995, 119–24; Ellridge, 1995, 141.

47   D, 14 December 1891.

48   *Ibid.*, and 21 December 1891.

49   D, 4, 7, 25 December 1891; 'The Crown of Wild Olive' Lecture 1, 1865, Cook and Wedderburn, 1903–12, XVIII, 401–32.

50   Dn, 25 March 1892.

51   Dn, 9 January 1892.

52   D, 18, 22, 26 and 28–30 December 1891; McLean, 'Teachers of the Century: G. F. Watts RA', *The Modern Church*, 31 December 1891, 635.

53   Cat.S.80a; Dn, 11 and 13 January 1892; Cartwright, 1896, 10.

54   Letter from W. B. Richmond, 6 January 1892.

55   Dn, 5 March 1892; A, II: 215. The first two mosaics of *Angels of the Passion holding the 'Nails' and the 'Lance' of the Passion* are in the north-eastern choir spandrels. Reynolds, 1994, 9; Stirling, 1926, 431.

56   Dn, 25 January, 3 and 6 February and 20 March 1892; Cat.S.1a; A, II: 199.

57   15 August 1891; Dn, 17 February 1892. Letter from the Countess of Pembroke to Lady Lothian, 20 February 1892; letter to the Hon. Mrs Reginald Talbot, 28 February 1892 (Huntington, HM 44161).

58   Letters to Marion Spielmann, 23 and 31 March, 5 and 17 April 1892 (M/JR).

59   D, 7 February 1891; Dn, 30–31 March 1892; Cat.S.77c; A, II: 220.

60   Dn, 1 April 1892; A, II: 203; Paget, 1923, quoted in Abdy and Gere, 1984, 164; Sitwell, 1942, 30–36.

61   Dn, 9–10 April 1892; A, II: 203; Rothenstein, 1962; Holroyd, 1907, 12.

62   'O all ye powers of the Lord' is the actual quote from Azariah's Prayer in the Apochrypha.

63   Cumming and Kaplan, 1993, 14–20; *Journal of Decorative Art*, supplement, May 1892, 33; *Builder*, 2 April 1892, 259.

64   Dn, 11 April 1892. Perhaps the inspiration for *Naked and not ashamed*, Cat.S.104b.

65   Letter from FL, n.d. (RBKC, 12746) GFW had earlier proposed a Wattsian subject to Leighton, and the president had felt paralysed by the idea.

66   Letters from FL, 8 and 12 April 1892 (RBKC, 12766 and 12768/143 and 151).

67   Letters to Spielmann, 5 April and 1 May 1892 (M/JR).

68   Dn, 30 April 1892; A, II: 200–03; *Athenaeum*, 30 April 1892, 571; *Art Journal*, 1892, 190; *Pall Mall Gazette*, 30 April 1892, 2; Tate Gallery, 1997, cat. 124.

69   Letter from FL, 26 April 1892 (RBKC 12769.154); *Athenaeum*, 30 April 1892, 574; *Art Journal* 1892, 190; Tate Gallery, 1997, cat. 126; A, II: 200; Cat.S.1a and 133a, Cat.P.41c. Professor Herkomer applied in September for his student D. A. Wehrschmidt to engrave the portrait 'for art's sake'.

70   Dn, 21 and 28 June and 29 July 1892.

71   Letter to Mr Forsyth, 11 June 1892.

72   *Ibid.*, Dn, 25 May, 17–18 June 1892; letter from Hallam Tennyson to M, 31 May 1892 (NPG 122); *Pall Mall Gazette*, 17 June 1892, 2; letter to Spielmann, 16 August 1892 (M/JR).

73   Dn, 8 April and 16 August 1892.

74   Dn, 11 April 1892.

75   Dn, 1, 15, 18 and 25–27 June 1892; D, 17 March 1893; Cat.P.141c; letter to Mr Gibbs, 2 June 1892 (Huntington, HM 31119); letter to the Earl of Rosebery, 9 March 1892; Palmer, 1898, II, 391.

76   Letter from Lord Rosebery, 10 March 1892 (NPG 165).

77   Cat.P.136b; letters from Lord Rosebery, 20 May, 23 July, 16 and 26 August, 13 September and 5 October 1892 (NPG 168, 171, 173, 175, 177 and 178); letter to Lord Rosebery, 22 May 1892; Lord Rosebery's diary 31 May and 23 August 1892; Dn, 31 May and 23–24 August 1892.

78   Dn, 24 August 1892.

79  Cat.P.37a; Dn, 11, 15, 21 and 28 June 1892; A, II: 204–5; letter to Sir Andrew Clark, 23 June 1892 (NPG axv, 115).

80  ATRd, 1 April 1892; letter to Hallam Tennyson, 6 April 1892 (TRC, 6285).

81  Dn, 12 and 18 June and 31 July 1892.

82  Dn, 3 July 1892.

83  Dulwich Picture Gallery, 1994, 97, cat. 63; *Open Door* (South London Gallery), inscribed 'Margot Asquith, given to her by G. F. Watts, 25 July 1892 (Sotheby's sale, 20 June 1989, lot. 74), was exhibited, though with no reference to the then Margot Tennant, at Manchester Art Gallery 1892, St Jude's and New Gallery 1893.

84  Dn, 6 September and 1 October 1892; Cat.S.156b and c; letter to Mrs Henrietta Barnett, 11 September 1892 (NPG axII, 32). A figure of Intemperance was added to the large version, later known as the *House of Wrath*.

85  A, II: 210; Tennyson, 1897, II, 205n.

86  Letter to Hallam Tennyson, 6 April 1892 (TRC, 6285).

87  'One Word More', Worsfold, 1904, II, 233, ix.

88  Dn, 5–6, 12 October 1892; letter to Audrey, Lady Tennyson, 8 October 1892 (TRC, 6286); letter from M to Emily Tennyson, 9 November 1892 (TRC, 4513); letter from M to Hallam, Lord Tennyson, 7 October (TRC, 6287); letter to F. G. Stephens, 9 October 1892 (Bod., MSS Don. e.87, f. 151–52); ATRd, 12 October 1892; Thwaite, 1996, 9; Hunt, 1982, 409.

89  Alfred Tennyson, *In Memoriam AHH*, xli, 1–4: 'Thy spirit ere our fatal loss/Did ever rise from high to higher;/As mounts the heavenward altar-fire,/As flies the lighter thro' the gross.'

90  'Silent Voices', reprinted in West, 1922, 66.

91  GFW was particularly moved by the following lines from *Ulysses*: 'It may be that the gulfs will wash us down:/It may be we shall touch the Happy Isles,/And we see the great Achilles whom we knew'.

92  Dn, 28 June, 17, 22 and 31 October 1892; letter to Hallam Tennyson, 9 November 1892 (TRC, 4511); A, II: 210–11; *Illustrated London News*, 15 October 1892, 476.

93  Letter from Roden Noel, 7 November 1892 (NPG s1, 18).

94  Dn, 11 and 16 November 1892.

95  Dn, 4 April, 5 and 10 November 1892.

96  Letters to Lord Aberdare, 21, 24, 25 November, 2 and 25 December 1892 (Glamorgan Record Office, D/d B: 161/10–11; NPG axII, 3–5, axv, 145).

97  Dn, 22 November and 17 December 1892.

98  Letter to Lord Aberdare, 28 November 1892 (NPG axv, 145).

99  Letter to Spielmann, 24 November 1892 (M/JR); Dn, 8 December 1892.

100  Dn, 29 December 1892.

101  *Athenaeum*, 3 December 1892, 786; *The Times*, 5 December 1892, 6; *Art Journal*, 1893, 30.

102  Letter from ATR, 25 December 1892 (NPG 280–82); Dn, 28 December 1892.

103  Letter to ATR, 28 December 1892. GFW recommended Millais, but ATR had the portrait painted by W. L. Bogle; letter from ATR, 30 December 1892 (NPG s283). GFW's posthumous portrait of the 18th Lord Lovat, painted from photographs in 1892–93 as a favour to M's cousins, was not a success; Cat.P.98c.

104  Letters to Blanche Somers Cocks, 11 December and January 1893.

105  D, 11 January 1893.

106  New Gallery, 1892–93; D, 17 March 1893; *Art Journal*, 1893, 1–9 and 60.

107  Letter to Spielmann, 6 and 11 January 1893 (M/JR).

108  Letter to EBJ, 15 January 1893 (Fitzwilliam, vIII, 4. Ts. Fiche 17, E3).

109  Letter from EBJ (Fiche 17, E4–6); D, 25 January 1893.

110  Letter from EBJ to M, 12 February 1893 (Fiche 17, E7); Burne-Jones, 1904, II, 232–34.

111  D, 14 and 17 February 1893.

112  Letter from EBJ, 12 February 1893 (Fiche 17 E8–11).

113  Letter to EBJ, 10 February 1893 (Fitzwilliam, VIII, 5; Ts, Fiche 17 E8). On 3 February GFW had written to Riviere for his impression of EBJ's exhibition (NPG axIII, 197).

114  D, 15 February 1893; Arts Council of Great Britain, 1981, 19–20; Brown, 1982, 33–37.

115  D, 24–27 January and 18 February 1893.

116  D, 7 January 1893; *Pall Mall Gazette*, 6 January 1893, 1.

117  Letters to Andrew Hichens, 2 and 5 February 1893 (NPG axII, 195–97).

118  Dn, 15 and 24 December 1892; D, 4, 14 and 22 January and 12 February 1893.

119  D, 2, 13–15 February and 7 May 1893. Drawings from another early album, formerly owned by Arthur Leak (WG); to F. G. Stephens, 26 January 1894 (Bod., MSS Don e.87, ff. 153–54).

120  D, 6–11 February 1893; WG, 2004, 63, cat. 49.

121  D, 6 August 1891 and 3, 31 January and 1 February 1893; WG, 1998, 38–40.

122  D, 20 and 22–23 February 1893.

123  D, 9–10, 15, 16 and 29 January 1893.

124  D, 6, 10–12 and 24 February 1893.

125  D, 20 February 1893.

126  D, 27, 29 January, 4 February and 6 March 1893; Cat.S.104b.

127  *Promises*, Cat.S.121c, was exhibited at the RA in 1893; D, 16 January and 14 March 1893.

128  Cat.S.3c; D, 27 February 1893; letter from M to Janet Ross, 26 April 1893, quoted in Ross, 1912, 330–31.

129  D, 2 March 1893; Bénédite, 1894–95, 92; *Art Journal*, 1893, 62 and 1894, 6. English purchases included Leighton's *Andromache* and three drawings by Burne-Jones for *The Wheel of Fortune*. MM: 1998, 201. Letter to H. G. Marquand, 15 November 1893 (MM).

130  Hodin, 1993, 20 and 55–56.

131  Henry Osborne Havemeyer sale, Christie Manson and Woods, 1892; Denvir, 1989, 22.

132  'Studio Gossip', *The Studio*, 1893, I, 36.

133  D, 6 and 10–11 March 1893; *Athenaeum*, 4 March 1893, 287.

134  D, 17 March 1893; Cat.S.33a and 144c; Grafton Galleries, 1893; *Art Journal*, 1893. 145–47; Tate Gallery, 1994, 201–3, cat. 124; Blanche, 1937, 28.

135  GFW and M MS notes, February 1893 (WG).

136  D, 30 January and 2 July 1893; *The Studio*, 1893, I, 36.


21   Dual Forces (1893–1894)

1   D, 21 March 1893; A, II: 228–30; *The Times, Daily Graphic*, 22 March 1893; *South London Press*, 25 March, quoted in Dulwich Picture Gallery, 1994, 15.

2   D, 12–20 March 1893; Abdy and Gere, 1982, 175.

3   Letter George Meredith to Mrs Leslie Stephen, 25 December 1892, quoted in Cline, 1970, II, 1114.

4   D, 1–2 March 1893; A, II: 232; Williams, 1977.

5   D, 3 April 1893; A, II: 230–32.

6   D, 4–6 and 9 April 1893;

7   D, 2 April 1893; A, II: 231.

8   D, 7–8 April 1893; George Meredith to Sidney Lysaght, 12 April 1893, quoted in Meredith, 1912, II, 1882–1909, 458.

9   D, 15–16 April 1893.

10  D, 20 April 1893.

11  D, 7, 21–22 April 1893; Morley, 1905, II, 744; Jenkins, *Gladstone*, 1996, 606.

12  D, 27 April 1893; Gertrude Jekyll's diary notes, 27 April 1893.

13  D, 23 April, 3–4 1893; letter to Spielmann, 27 March 1893 (M/JR); Chicago, 1893, 308, cats 486–91; *Art Journal*, 1893, 307.

14  Letter from Charles Hallé, 27 March 1893; letter to Spielmann, 27 March 1893; D, 30 April 1893; Crane, 1907, 408; New Gallery 1893, cats 55, 78, 230: *The Open Door, Neptune's Horses, Jill*; Tate Gallery, 1997, 181, cat. 61; *Athenaeum*, 29 April 1893, 544 and 6 May 1893, 577; *Art Journal*, 1893, 190; *Magazine of Art*, 1893, 256, 258 and 292.

15  *Studio*, 1893, I, 111.

16  *Athenaeum*, 6 May 1893, 578; Tate Gallery, 1998, 34 and 144–45, cat 50.

17  D, 8, 19, 25 June and 2 July 1893; A, II: 213.

18  *Pall Mall Gazette*, 8 May 1893, 2.

19  D, 3 May 1893; Ormonds, 1975, 172, cat. 374.

20  D, 8 June 1893; letter to Spielmann, 26 April 1893 (M/JR).

21  D, 3 May 1893; Dn, 4 February 1894; Cat.S.57c; Matthew 19: 22; WG, 2004, 74, cat. 70a.

22  GFW believed the horse's head was the only Elgin fragment carved by Phidias himself; Dn, 23 October 1892. D, 5–6, 8–9, 19 May, 24 July, 2 and 6 September 1893; Spielmann, MS notes (WG).

23  D, 2, 15 April, 14, 16–17 and 28 May 1893; Cat.P.55b; GFW began a second, smaller portrait of Neil on 1 June.

24  D, 20 May 1893; GFW's will, 21 November 1899.

25  Virginia Stephen to Julia Stephen [21 May 1893] quoted in Bell, 1972.

26  George Meredith to Arthur Wing Pinero, 4 May 1893, quoted in Meredith, 1912, II, 1882–1909, 459; Schulkins, 1985, 158; D, 24 May 1893.

27  D, 24–25 May 1893.

28  D, 12 June 1893.

29  D, 29–31 May 1893.

30  Asquith, 1920, 138.

31  D, 4 June 1893; Oakley, 1994, 196.

32  Dn, October 1897.

33  D, 11 June 1893; *The Times*, 25 May, 5; Weaver, 1984, 105.

34  D, 13–14, 17 June 1893.

35  D, 20 June and 4 October 1893. Schreiner was subsequently sent photographs of *She Shall Be Called Woman* and of GFW with *Physical Energy*. She hoped GFW would send pictures to encourage the South African government to build a national gallery. (The S.A National Gallery, founded in 1871, did not have its own premises until 1930. Their three paintings by GFW were acquired later.) Olive Schreiner (1855–1920), author of *The Story of an African Farm*, married Samuel C. Cronwright in 1894. Letters from Schreiner, 23 and 30 September 1893 (NPG axi, 190–206); letter from Schreiner to M, 5 October 1893 (NPG axi, 208–12).

36  D, 14, 16 and 19–20 June 1893; JCd, 25 July, 1893.

37  D, 18, 21–23, 29 June 1893;

38  D, 28–29 June 1893; Gilbert referred to the figure as 'Anteros'. RA, 1986, 135; Dorment, 1985, 112–13; *Art Journal*, 1893, 249; *Magazine of Art*, 1893, 394 and 428. *Athenaeum*, 8 July 1893, 73; Cat.P.51b; Edwards, editor of the *Building News* and halfpenny *Echo*, sat for his portrait on 21, 28 June, 1, 3, 6, 13, 21 July, 12 and 17 October.

39  D, 27 June and 3 July 1893; Dorment, 1985, 108–11; The Fine Art Society, May 1987.

40  Quoted by Lucinda Lambton on *A is for Art Nouveau*, BBC 2.

41  D, 29 July 1893. The 1899 face of *Edward King and*

*Martyr* added to the tomb in 1899 was modelled from GFW. Dorment, 1985, 173, fig. 110.

42  D, 22–23 June 1893; RA, 1986, 206.

43  Cat.S.69b. Munich, 1893, cats 1635–54c and 2253b, *Clytie*, bronze. GFW having refused payment, the German artist Max Nonnenbruck persuaded him to compromise. Other pictures included *Denunciation of Cain, Fata Morgana, Love and Death, Love and Life, Mischief, Psyche, Sic Transit, Time Death and Judgment, Lord Lawrence, Lady Lilford, Violet Lindsay, Cardinal Manning, Rossetti. Magazine of Art*, November 1893, VIII.

44  D, 7–8, 23–26 July, 1 and 18 August 1893; A, II: 209. Letter to the Marchionness of Lothian, 20 August 1893.

45  D, 19–23 July 1893; Abdy and Gere, 1982, 147 and 175. Benson, 1893.

46  D, 27 July 1893; Khnopff, May 1894, III, 32; Crawford, 1985, 410.

47  D, 4–5 and 10 August 1893; Dn, 3 June 1894.

48  D, 25–26, 28 July 1893; JCd, Emanuel, 1989, 178.

49  D, 31 July 1893.

50  Letter to James Smith, 31 July 1893 (NPG AXIV, 23–24). *The Studio*, 1893, 257.

51  D, 2–3 August 1893; letter from M to Lady Constance Leslie, 2 August 1893.

52  Dn, 7 May 1897; letter from ET to Lord Tennyson (TRC).

53  Irving, 1951, 562; 'An American Critic on English Art at the Chicago World's Fair', *The Studio*, November 1893, II, 45–50; *Art Journal*, 1893, 306.

54  D, 5, 10–11 August 1893; *Uldra, Joachim, Cupid with Butterfly, Naples* and *Cupid Asleep* were at Dunthorne's, the last two, Cat.S.32a and 104c, were bought by the Revd S. A. Thompson Yates. Frank Short was to produce a mezzotint from *Naples. Athenaeum*, 5 August 1893, 201; *The Times*, 2 August 1893, 13.

55  D, 1 August 1893; letter to Mrs Catherine Gladstone, 4 August 1893 (BL, Add. MS 46229, f. 105).

56  D, 6 and 9 August 1893 and 15 April 1898; letter from Catherine Gladstone, n.d. (NPG SI, 59); letter to W. E. Gladstone, 12 August 1893 (BL, Add. MS 44517, f. 217). Gladstone, who had accepted the offer of *Ilyssus*, said the drawing had been given to him, but he was asked to give it back. GFW recalled that the unwanted drawing of *Theseus* was admired years later and given to Leighton.

57  D, 12 and 15 August 1893.

58  Letter to John Ruskin, 28 August 1893 (Fiche 16, D11).

59  D, 17–20 and 30 August 1893.

60  D, 21 August, 5 and 20 September 1893; A, II: 235.

61  D, 23 August 1893; Dn, 8 February 1895.

62  D, 26 August and 3 October 1893; Tate, 2001, 144–45, cat. 68.

63  D, 25, 31 August, 1 September and 3 October 1893; Cat.P.77b; V&A, c1970, 65, cat. 1146.

64  D, 30 August 1893; Lilian Abbott Macintosh birth certificate. Maud Macintosh death certificate. Lilian Chapman's MS memoir notes (WG).

65  D, 3, 13, 15, 17, 28 August, 17, 21, 24 September and 29 October 1893.

66  D, 2 August and 14 September 1893.

67  D, 26, 28 June, 3–8 and 18 July 1893.

68  D, 8 September 1893; Jenkins, *Gladstone*, 1996, 602–4; M to James Smith, 8 and 11 September 1893.

69  D, 9 and 11 September, 16 October 1893.

70  D, 17–18 and September 1893; A, II: 235; Laing, 1887, reprinted in *Nineteenth Century*, January 1894.

71  Letter to Briton Rivière, 21 September 1893; M's note from a letter to BR, 6 October (NPG AXIII, 199). BR visited on 19 October.

72  D, 8 October 1893; Rawnsley, 1923, 66 and 98; Anscombe and Gere, 1978, 117; Darley, 1990, 300.

73  D, 10 July, 9 October 1893; letter from FL to M, 10 July 1893 (RBKC, 12777.171). The Burne-Joneses did not attend. M and GBJ had worked long and hard with Leighton over a change in the Trust Deed demanded by the City Trustees. As Rossiter was now salaried and the Gallery buildings were paid for by the Trustees, he and Miss Olver were no longer to hold life appointments. Rossiter had refused the position of Honorary Life-President.

74  D, 15 October 1893. The drawing was signed and sent to the Abbeys in June 1895. Lucas, 1921, 266–67.

75  D, 13 October and 7 November 1893.

76  D, 20, 23, 26–27 October, 5–6, 9 November and 5 December 1893; Cat.S.76c; A, II: 220; GFW had not yet named the twin boys, first mentioned in D, 1 April 1893 as *Gemini*.

77  D, 2–3, 9–11 November 1893.

78  Letter to Canon Rawnsley, July 1894 (typescript, Fiche 41, A12); Rawnsley, 1923, 110; Darley, 1990, 300; 'National Trust Milestones' (NTms); *The Times*, 17 November 1893, 17 July 1894; *National Trust*, 1895; Waterson, 1994, 14.

79  D, 2, 15 and 16, 18 and 28 November 1893; Dn, 20 March 1894; Cumming, 1993, 25–28.

80  D, 25 November 1893; Hare, 1896–1900, VI, 327–28.

81  D, 29 November 1893; letters to William Spence 28 November and December 1893 (Fiche 40, D8–9); GFW also asked Spence to trace *Della Storia di Firenzi*, a favourite textbook provided by his Italian master.

82  D, 2, 5 and 19 December 1893; Spielmann MS notes (WG).

83  D, 6 December 1893; Cat.S.30b, 57 and 99b; Hare, 1896–1900, 326–30.

84  D, 4 August, 1, 3–9, 12, 27 December 1893; Dn, 8

January 1894. His excessive praise applied only to amateur work: 'Once it passes beyond that name it becomes taught in a school, he is much harder to please – and satisfy.' Dn, 6 October 1894.

85  D, 12 December 1893.

86  D, 10 and 13 December 1893.

87  D, 9 July, 22 December 1893.

88  Letter from H. G. Marquand, 7 November 1893; to Marquand, 15 November 1893; Marquand to Hon Walter Greatman, Secretary of State, Washington D.C. Letter from C. R. Sherman to Marquand, 26 December 1893; letters from T. F. Bayard, 11 and 23 January 1894; letter to Bayard, 22 January 1894 (copies, MM). The National Gallery of Art was founded in Washington in 1937.

89  *Art Journal*, 1894, 60, 158; Edmund Gosse, 1894, 138–42.

90  Dn, 26 January 1894. Meade, January 1894, 15–16, the title proposed by the editor, Benjamin Waugh.

91  Dn, 29 January 1894; letters from the Rt Hon. W. E. Gladstone, 26 January and 21 February 1894 (NPG si, 65); letters to Gladstone, 30 January and 22 February 1894 (BL, Add. MS 44518, f. 24–25 and 44–45); to Hichens, 30 January 1894, (NPG axii, 198); from FL, 3 February 1894, (RBKC 12793); to Spielmann, 10 February 1894 (M/JRL); A, ii: 239–42; Burne-Jones, 1904, ii, 240–41; Fitzgerald, 1997, 251.

92  Letter from EBJ; letter to EBJ (Fiche 17, E13–F4).

93  Letter to W. E. Gladstone, 22 February 1894 (BL, Add. MS 44518, f. 44–45).

94  Dn, 2 January 1894; A, ii: 243–44; Mills, January 1894, 44–57.

95  'Women's Dress', *Aglaia: The Journal of the Health and Artistic Dress Union*, no. 2, spring 1894, 23–27; Leonée Ormond, 1969, 268.

96  Cat.S.44b; Alston, 1929, pl. xii; Whitechapel, 1894, cats 31–38, 84, 129, 154, 156 and 225: *Sic Transit, Europa, Capri, Death Crowning Innocence, She Shall Be Called Woman, Walter Crane, Lord Dufferin, Donkey's Head, Ariadne in Naxos, Blanche*, a sketch for *Court of Death, The Dweller in the Innermost, All the Air a Solemn Stillness Holds.*

97  Dn, 11 and 15 April 1894.

98  Letter from George Meredith to M, 13 December 1895 (NPG 218–20); New Gallery 1894, cats 76, 111 and 114 included *A Greek Idyll* and a small *Ariadne* (Cat.P.107a and Cat.S.66a and 7c); *Athenaeum*, 12 May 1894, 619; *Magazine of Art*, 1894, 306; Sassoon, 1948, 216–17.

99  *Athenaeum*, 5 May 1894, 587; *Magazine of Art*, 1894, 269, 272 and 291–92; RA, 1894, cats 221, 251 and 259.

100  Dn, 28 May 1894.

101  Cat.S.162b. After GFW's death M named the picture *When the Earth Was Young.* Dn, 4 and 5 June 1894; A, ii: 101–2.

102  Dn, 24 and 28 May 1894; letter to Sir Henry Acland, 20 May 1894 (Bod. MSS Acland, d.71, f. 118); letter from Acland, May 27 1894 (NPG xii, 37).

103  Dn, 1 June 1894; A, ii: 254.

104  Dn, 30 March 1894.

105  Lady Hermione FitzGerald, widow of the 5th Duke of Leinster. D, 8 March 1893; Dn, 8 June 1894; A, ii: 252–53; Estorick, 1981, 29, 71 and 99–100.

106  Dn, 29 May 1894.

107  Letters to Mrs Humphrey Ward, 15 June 1894, 20 and 24 January 1895 (HR).

108  Dn, 1 and 19 July, 11 August 1894 and 2 September 1894; JCd, 8 July 1894; letter from GFW, 25 June 1894; letters from Professor Hubert Herkomer, 22 June, 6 and 23 July 1894 (NPG axi, 161–63); letter from M to Charles Lees, 7 July 1894; *The Studio*, iii, 1894, 151; *Athenaeum*, 2 June 1894, 718; 30 June 1894, 844. Cat.S.77c.

109  Dn, 30 July 1894; Cat.P.113b; *Max Muller*, 1902, ii, 319.

110  Cat.S.95a; letters from W. Holman Hunt, 25 June, 13 and 20 August 1894 (Bod., MSS Eng. Lett. e118, ff. 3–5, 39–40 and e.116, ff. 92–93); letter to Hunt, 18 August 1894 (Huntington, HM 588); Landow, November 1980, 79–91; Amor, 1989, 248–49.

111  D, 27 July 1893; Dn, 5, 19–20 September 1894; Cat.P.58b; letters from Alfred Gilbert to M, 12 and 31 August 1894 (Bod., MSS Eng. Lett. e.118, ff. 37–38 and d.275, ff. 164–65); RA, 1986, 211, cat. 122; The Jean van Caloen Foundation, Loppem, Bruges.

112  In Hindu mythology, Rita designates the cosmic, liturgic and moral order of the world.

113  Dn, 4 and 9 September 1894; letter to James Smith, 1 October 1894 (NPG axiv, 32); A, ii: 252–53; Compton Burial Board minute, 25 May, *Compton Parish Council, 1894–1911*, i, March 1895; WG, 1998, 44.

114  Letters to James Smith, 5, 11 August, 1 and 4 October 1894 (typescripts, NPG axiv, 28–33); *Athenaeum*, 3 November 1894, 612.

115  Letter to Briton Rivière, 11 October 1894 (typescript, NPG axiii, 200); Belleroche, 1948, 67–68; Shaw-Sparrow, 1910, 64–67; Macer-Wright, 1940, 75, 86, 132, 137 and 139; Ormond and Ormond, 1975, 124 and 172, cat. 381. Brangwyn was not then accepted; in 1906 the Worshipful Company of Skinners presented his mural to the Royal Exchange.

116  Dn, 19, 21 and 27 October 1894; to Briton Rivière, 11 October and 1 November 1894 (typescript, NPG axiii, 200).

117  Dn, 13 November 1894; Cat.S.41a.

118  Letter to Alphonse Legros, 17 November 1894 (FC,

1994–A.657). Legros's earlier portrait of GFW, *c.*1877–78, owned by Leighton, was exhibited at the Grosvenor Gallery in May 1922, cat. 69.

119  *Westminster Budget*, November 1894; JCd, 7 October 1895.

120  Dn, 4 and 17 September 1894; to Mr Horsfall, 5, 15 and 21 December 1894 (NPG aXII, 231–352). Letter to the Editor of *The Times*, 26 November 1894; *Westminster Budget*, 27 November 1894; A, II: 252–53. Cat.P.60a and 135b, In January 1895 GFW gave the HAIA, 1000 guineas, the proceeds of portraits of the Reverend Alfred Gurney, vicar of St Barnabas, Pimlico, and Mrs Charles Coltham Rogers, for what became known as The Watts Endowment Fund. *Home Arts and Industries Association Report for 1894.*

121  Dn, 13 September and 6 December 1894; letter to Countess Somers, 27 June 1894; Cat.S.30b and 113c. His letter of 6 May 1894 to an unnamed recipient is the first reference to *Outcast Goodwill* (Huntington, HM 31144). Letter to Mr Horsfall, 21 December 1894 (NPG aXII, 236).

122  Letter from George du Maurier, 11 December 1894 (NPG fol 30); Monkhouse, Christmas 1894, 706–7.

123  Letter from EBJ to M, 17 December 1894 (Fiche 17 F 6–G2); from Sir Henry Acland, 1 January 1895 (NPG aXII, 26).

124  Letter to the President of the Corcoran Gallery of Art, 23 January 1895 (WGc); *Philadelphia, Press*, 15 December 1902; Blunt, 1975, 155; Tate, 2001, 224, cats 145–46.


22  Handover to the Nation (1895–1897)

1  Dn, 26 March 1895; Cat.S.83a, 113c and Cat.P.113b; RA cats 127, 258, 343 and 1334. *Magazine of Art*, 1895, 283; *Art Journal*, 1895, 162 and 166; *Athenaeum*, 4 May 1895, 578; Macmillan, 1903, 161–62; Blunt, 1975, 214; Tate Gallery, 1998, 36, fig. 37; Friederichs, December 1895, 75.

2  At the New Gallery's Venetian Exhibition in March, GFW's *Portrait of a Lady* was ascribed to Titian. New Gallery 1895, cats 246, 250 and 254; *Athenaeum*, 30 March 1895, 414, 4 May 1895, 579, and 27 July 1895, 135; *Magazine of Art*, 1895, 286 and 288. At the Goupil Gallery, *A Connoisseur's Treasures*, May 1895, cats 3–4, 15 and 22, Aleco Ionides included GFW's portrait of M. Tricoupi, *Amphion, Joan of Arc* and *The Baby*; Dn, 10 June 1895.

3  Dn, 13 August, 13 September 1895; Cat.P.25c.

4  Dn, 24–25 November 1895.

5  Letter from Lord Rosebery at The Durdans, Epsom, to M, 31 May 1895 (NPG 180).

6  Dn, 13 January 1892, 3 February, 16 April, 6 and 18 May 1895; letter to Briton Rivière, 23 January 1895 (typescript, NPG aXIII, 201); Dn, 21 March 1895; Cat.P.51c; *Compton Parish Council*, 30 May; Friederichs, December 1895, 74.

7  Dn, 6–7, 12, 21, 25 May, 25 June 1895; letter from FL, 29 March and 2 June 1895 (RBKC, 12803–4). John St Loe Strachey's MS notes of interview with GFW, 1 June 1895 (NPG aXIV, 59–62); JcD, 7 October 1895.

8  Letter to the Earl of Rosebery, 2 June 1895; Strachey, 1948. The trial opened on 26 April 1895 and Wilde was sentenced to two years' imprisonment on 25 May. Barbican Art Galleries, 2000, 138.

9  Dn, 6 June 1895; JCd, 8 October; photo J. Caswall-Smith. *Art Journal*, 1895, 350–51; Friederichs, December 1895, 74 and 81; Cartwright, Easter 1896, 30; *The Studio*, 1897, XI, 50; letter from George Williamson to M. H. Spielmann, 11 February 1898.

10  Dn, 25 June, 10 and 12 July 1895.

11  Dn, 16 August 1895; letter to the Earl of Rosebery, 9 July 1895; letter from Lord Rosebery, 15 August (NPG 183); Friederichs, 1895, XXXIX, 78; Dn, 16 August 1895.

12  Dn, 26 July 1895. Cartwright, 1896, 20.

13  Dn, 13, 18–19 July and 1 August 1895.

14  Dn, 12 July 1895.

15  Dn, 28 June, 3, 5 July and 9–10 August 1895; *The Studio*, XIV, 1898, 239.

16  Letter to Mrs Ady, 13, 18 July, 4, 17 August 1895 (Northamptonshire Record Office). GFW had been interested in her biography of *Sir Edward Burne-Jones, Bart*, 'The Art Annual', *Art Journal*, Christmas 1894, but had thought the idea of one on himself 'very distasteful'. Friederichs, 1895.

17  Letter from FL, 31 August 1895 (RBKC, 12815); Dn, 1 September.

18  Dn, 3, 8 and 18 September 1895; letter from FL, 3 September 1895 (RBKC, 12810); letter to G. Scharf, 14 February 1892; letters to Lionel Cust 2, 5, 18–19 September and 9 November; letter from M to Cust, 29 September (NPG).

19  Dn, 12 August and 7 October 1895; JCd, 21 September, 7–8 October 189; Cat.S.66c; Alston, 1929, XXIV.

20  Dn, 8–9 October 1895; JCd, 8–9 October.

21  GFW would have liked to include Elizabeth Barrett Browning, had he met her, and, as stated, distracting facial qualities had prevented him from painting George Eliot and finishing earlier sketches of Florence Nightingale.

22  Dn, 9–10 October 1895; letter from Josephine Butler, 12 October 1895, quoted in *The Times* 7 July 1928, and A, II: 250–51. Butler, 1954, 186–87.

23  Cat.S.141b and P.51c; *Athenaeum*, 19 October 1895, 540. *Mrs E. Ellice* was shown with *Sympathy*, for which

GFW had used an elaborate system, preserving the drawing while rubbing off pigment. Warm ochre over a monochrome of raw sienna and white was rubbed almost entirely with finger or paper, the surface scraped by a horn palette knife; flesh tones were applied and partly removed, leaving a thin film of colour.

24 Hollyer, October 1895.

25 Dn, 22 October 1895; Cat.S.123b; Dn, 5 November 1895; letters from FL, 2, 8 and 20 November 1895, (RBKC, 12811–13); Rembrandt Head Gallery, 1895, cat. 22; *The Studio*, 1896, VI; *Art Journal*, 1896, 43; Dorment, 1985, 180.

26 Dn, 25 October, 8 and 27 November 1895.

27 Letters to James Smith, 19 November and 9 December 1895 (typescript, NPG AXIV, 34–35); Cat.S.8b; Morris, 1996, 495–96; Dn, 14 November 1895; letter to Mrs Henry Ady, 29 November 1895 (Northamptonshire Record Office).

28 Dn, 8 September, 29 November and 6 December 1895; ATRd, 1 December; Memo, 2 December (V&A/MA); letter from J. Everett Millais, 6 December (NPG); *Athenaeum*, 7 December 1895, 799; Millais, 1899, II, 299; *Magazine of Art*, January 1896, 119.

29 Letters to Lionel Cust, 8, 10 December and n.d. 1895 and 1 April 1896 (NPG); letter from Cust, 1 May 1896.

30 Letter to Spielmann, 14 December 1895 (M/JR).

31 West, 1922, 312–13.

32 Dn, 16 December 1895 and 13 January 1896.

33 Dn, 26 December 1895.

34 A, II: 208–9; Lily Chapman's MS memoir.

35 Letter from FL, 2 January 1896 (RBKC, 12817); letter from M to Janet Ross, 16 February 1896 (quoted in Ross, 1912, 350–51); A, II: 254; B/W: 194; B/L, II, 331; *Athenaeum*, 4 January 1896, 25.

36 Lord Leighton's death certificate A 6247.

37 Dn, 25 January and 15 February 1896; letter from FL, 8 April 1892; letter from EBJ, Tuesday (Fiche 17, G3); letter to Ross, 1912; A, II: 254–55; B/W: 193–94; B/L, 333–34; *Illustrated London News*, 8 February 1896, 163; Ormond and Ormond, 1975, 144–46.

38 Letter to Briton Rivière, 31 January 1896 (ts, NPG AXIII, 202).

39 Letter to Sir J E Millais, 6 February 1896 (typescript, NPG AXIII, 150); letter from Millais, 8 February 1896 (NPG); *Athenaeum*, 8 February 1896, 188.

40 Letter to Briton Rivière, 19 July 1896 (typescript note, NPG AXIII, 203).

41 D, 26–27 September 1891, 11 and 15 March and 11 November 1896; letter to Spielmann, 11 March 1892 (M/JR); *Strathearn Herald*, 2 November 1895.

42 Dn, 18–19 March 1896; ATRd, 18–19 March.

43 Letters from ATR, 21 and 23 March 1896; letter from D. W. Freshfield to ATR, 22 March (NPG SI, 287–90,

295–98, 306–8). The RA declined FL's offer of the house as the official residence of the president. Findlater, 1996, 4.

44 Letter to Gladstone, 26 March 1896; letter from Gladstone, 28 March 1896 (NPG SI, 74).

45 Dn, 18 June 1896; NPG, 1896; Burne-Jones, 1904, II, 79; Lago, 1981, 101; A, II: 250; *Athenaeum*, 11 April 1896, 485; *Art Journal*, 1896, 153; *Illustrated London News*, 11 April 1896, 452.

46 Dn, 14 April 1896; De Navarro, 1896, 60–62.

47 Lilian Chapman MS memoir (typescript, WG); *The Times* 19 June; letter to Briton Rivière, 13 March 1896 (typescript, NPG AXIII, 203).

48 For the goat's head, GFW had borrowed a study from Briton Rivière; The picture, catalogued under various titles in Cat.S.27a, was exhibited at RA, 1895, cat. 220 as *The Infancy of Jupiter*, at NG 1896–97, cat. 60 as *The Childhood of Jupiter*, at RA, 1905 as *The Childhood of Zeus*. Letter to Briton Rivière, 17 July 1895 (typescript, NPG AXIII, 201).

49 New Gallery, 1896, cats 67, 79, 136 and 141; RA, 1896, cats 90, 220 [see n.16] and 305; Dn, 31 August 1895; *Magazine of Art*, 1896, 93, 292 and 298; *Art Journal*, 1896, 166, 174, 182, 188; Cat.S.41a, 104b, 144c and 146c; *Athenaeum*, 28 September 1895, 424–25; 2 May 1896, 587–88; RA, 1996, 240, cat. 125. *Mrs Ellice* was first exhibited with *Sympathy* at the Society of Portrait Painters.

50 Dn, 23 April and 1 May 1896; *The Studio* 1897, XI, 267–68.

51 Letter from EBJ, Monday (Fiche 17, G5–9); letter to EBJ, 17 April 1896 (Fitzwilliam, VIII, 6).

52 Dn, 6 May 1896.

53 The Marquess of Salisbury to Her Majesty the Queen, 14 May 1896; Sir Arthur Bigge to Lord Salisbury, 16 May 1896 (The Royal Collection Trust, A 72–73); Dn, 18 January, 17 and 19 May.

54 Letter from Gladstone, 25 May 1896 (NPG SI, 80); letter to Catharine Gladstone, 27 May (BL, Add. MS 46229 f. 110).

55 Gleeson-White, 1896, vol. VIII, 99.

56 Dn, 2 August and 22 October 1896.

57 Dn, 27 February, 5 and 21 July 1896.

58 Dn, 15 and 22 July 1896. George Leonard, ' "Love and Death" by G F Watts: An Appreciation', *Daily Press, Bristol* (WGc 1896).

59 MEd, 22 July 1896.

60 Dn, 10, and D, 1 September 1896; letter to Hallam, Lord Tennyson, 11 August 1896 (TRC, 4512); letter from Hallam Tennyson, 12 August 1896 (quoted in Tennyson, 1896).

61 Millais, 1899, II, 334; *Athenaeum*, 15 August 1896, 232; *Art Journal*, 1896, 350.

62    Dn, 20 August; D, 26–27 August and 19 October 1896.

63    Letter to the Council of the Royal Academy, 30 August 1896 (RA, RAC/1/WA 20); letter to South Kensington Museum, 29 August 1896; A. B. Skinner to South Kensington Secretarial, 2 September; letter to A. I. R. Trendell, S. Kensington, 7 September (V&A/MA); D, 14 September 1896; letter to Spielmann, 4 December 1896 (M/JR); letter to Briton Rivière, 31 December 1896 (typescript, NPG aXIII, 204).

64    *Art Journal*, 1896, 350.

65    D, 31 August and 2 October 1896; GFW had first exhibited *Sunset on the Alps* at the Alpine Club in 1894, cat. 114, as *An Alpine Peak*.

66    Dn, 10 January; D, 1–3 September 1896; MacCarthy 662–67.

67    D, 7–8 September and 2 October 1896.

68    D, 26 October 1896.

69    Letters to Henry Salt, 13 and 17 September 1896 (typescript, Fiche 40, A5–7); Salt, 1921, 204.

70    Letter from Alfred Gilbert, 22 September. RA, 1986, 19–20, 76; Dn, 24, 26 and 28 August and 29 September 1896; Cat.P.2b and c: created Baron Aldenham in 1896, Henry Hucks Gibbs had sat for a portrait in the 1870s.

71    D, 3–4 and 6–8 October 1896; M to Miss Courtenay Bell; Hunt, 1905, 387; MacCarthy, 1994, 670; Crane, 1907, 439–40.

72    D, 1 April, 20 May 1887, 31 August 1891; Dn, 1 May 1896; D, 9–13 and 17–19 October 1896.

73    D, 8–9, 11, 25, 27 and 29–30 November 1896; Dn, 4 December 1896; Montefiore sat 8–13 October 1897.

74    D, 13–14, 19, 21, 26 October and 3 November 1896; MEd, 21 October.

75    D, 3 November 1896; letter to George Thompson, 23 October 1896 (NPG aIX, 31); letter from Professor Hubert Herkomer, 30 October 1896 (NPG aXI, 169–71).

76    D, 4 November 1896.

77    D, 4–5 November 1896.

78    Letter to Briton Rivière, 6 February 1897 (NPG aXIII, 202).

79    D, 7, 20, 24, 26–27, 29 November and 20 December 1896; New Gallery, 1896–97, 3–5; Rooke, 1900, 312; Lago, 1981, 124.

80    A, II: 235–57; letters to Spielmann, 4, 8, 13, 15 December 1896 and 4 and 11 January 1897 (M/JR); Dn, 10 January 1897; Spielmann, January 1897, 161–72; GFW approved the tone of the article, but objected to the statement 'one creed is as good as another' which misrepresented his religious reverence, as opposed to his disapproval of rigid orthodoxy.

81    Rooke, 1900, 124.

82    Letters to George Thompson, 9 December 1896 (B/Y, GFW MSS 2125, F3), and Monday, n.d. (NPG aIX, 29); Cat.P.2c and 97a.

83    D, 26 October, 10 November and 27 December 1896; letter from M to the Earl of Wemyss, 28 December. Rawnsley, 1896; Gollancz, 1897; Rawnsley, 1923, 126–27; Spalding, 1997, 12–13; WG, 2004, 83–87, cats 98–99. *The All-Pervading* appeared as a frontispiece to Watson, 1896.

84    D, 24–25, 31 December 1896; Hallé, 1896, II, 213–14.

85    D, 29–30 December 1896; *The Times*, 29 December 1896; *Standard*, 30 December 1896; *Athenaeum*, 2 January 1897, 23–24; *Art Journal*, 1897, 62; *Magazine of Art*, January 1897, 201; letter to Spielmann, 7 February 1897 (M/JR).

86    Lago, 1981, 130.

87    Letter from Heywood Sumner to Julia Cartwright, 14 February 1897 (Northamptonshire Record Office).

88    The boys were nephews of Hamo Thornycroft. 'The Court of Death', *More Poems*, 1897, quoted in Wilson, 1998, 65–66. Rawnsley's poem on the exhibition, 'The Eve of Peace', was quoted in *The Studio*, 1897, X, 131.

89    Tate Gallery 1997, 32 and 289, n.95; Stockholm, *L'Exposition Générale des Arts et de l'industrie*, 1897.

90    Letter to Spielmann, 7 February 1897 (M/JR); letter to Walter Crane, 3 December 1896 (RBKC). Brussels International Exhibition, 1897, cats 134 and 170; Grafton Galleries, 1897, cats 182 and 198; *The Studio*, 1898, XIII, 50.

91    Rooke, 1900, 339.

92    Dn, 17 and 23 February 1897; A, II: 258–60. Fitzgerald, 1997, 272; Hallé, 1896, II, 214; *The Times*, 24 February 1897; *Athenaeum*, 27 February 1897, 286; *Art Journal*, 1897, VII.

93    Letter to EBJ, 25 February 1897 (Fitzwilliam, VIII, 7).

94    Dn, 7 March 1897; A, II: 260–61; MEd, 7 March 1897; Hallé, 1896, II, 215; Burne-Jones, 1904, II, 302.

95    Dn, 11 April 1897;

96    Sizeranne, 'A French View of English Art: Mythic Art – G F Watts', trans. H. M. Poynter, *The Artist*, XIX, April 1897, 150–55.

97    Dn, 3 March 1897.

98    Dn, 26 February, 4 and 30 March 1897; A, II: 261–62; Asquith, 1950, 83–84.

99    *The Studio*, 1897, X, 130–31; letter to the Editor of *The Times*, 16 April 1897, 6.

100   Letters to Cust, 22 November 1896, 5 May, 8 May 1897 (NPG 1078); *Art Journal*, 1897, 160; Liddell, 1911, 311.

101   *Athenaeum*, 17 April 1897, 517, and 1 May, 584–85; *Art Journal*, 1897, 162, 168 and 189; New Gallery, 1897, cats 106 and 140.

102   Letter to H. E. Luxmoore, 28 February, 16 May and June 1897 (typescript, NPG aXIII, 52–55); letters from Luxmoore, 17 and 23 May (Bod., MSS Eng. Lett. d.275, ff. 180, 182–83); letter from J. J. Hornby, Provost of Eton, 7 June 1897 (ff. 186–87); Dn, 17 April 1897; *Eton*

*College Chronicle*, no. 765, 17 June 1897; A, II: 262–64.

103  Letter to W. B. Richmond, 1 June 1897, quoted in Stirling, 1926, 399; letters from Richmond, 1 June and 23 June (Bod., MSS Eng. Lett. e.118, ff. 14–16).

104  Dn, 29–30 June, 2 July 1897; letter to Sir Edward Poynter, 4 July 1897 (Tate, NG 7/209/1897); letter from Charles Eastlake, 8 July (*National Gallery Minutes*, VII, 8).

105  Dn, 13 July 1897; letter from Sir Edward Poynter, 9 July 1897 (WG); *Love and Life, Love and Death, Death Crowning Innocence, Hope, The Dweller in the Innermost, Faith, The Messenger, Sic Transit, She Shall Be Called Woman, Eve Tempted, Eve Repentant, Chaos, The Minotaur, Mammon, Jonah, For He had Great Possessions, The Spirit of Christianity, The Dray Horses; Report of the Director of National Gallery 1897*, 5 (Tate archives). Frances Spalding, 1998, 20; *The Times*, 15 July, 11; *Athenaeum*, 24 July 1897, 138.

106  Dn, 29 August 1897.

107  Cat.S.24b; New Gallery 1896–97, cat. 148.

108  Letter to Spielmann, 8 December 1896.

109  Sir Charles Holroyd, 1907, 8, 97; letter to Frederick A. Eaton, Secretary of the Royal Academy, 27 November 1896 (RA, RAC/1/WA 21); *Art Journal*, 1897, 287; Dn, 1 March 1892.


## 23  The Colossus Sits (1898)

1  Dn, 17 June, 28–29 and 31 August 1897.

2  Dn, 9 November 1897; D, 25 February 1898; Cat.S.22c and 95c; WG, 2004, 86, cat. 106. Ezekiel 37: 3.

3  D, 6 January 1898; 'The Utmost for the Highest' sundial at Limnerslease, shown at the 1900 Home Arts exhibition. *The Studio*, 1900, XX, 83; *Art Journal*, 1900, 255.

4  D, 11 January 1898.

5  Dn, 13 October 1897.

6  D, 2 February 1898; CRAd, 5 December 1899 (King's College Library, Cambridge, 1898–99, ff. 100–01).

7  D, 7, 11 and 21 January 1898; *The Times*, 20 January 1898, 9e; *Art Journal*, 1898, 94; letter to Andrew Hichens, 9 January 1898 (typescript, NPG aXII, 199); A, II: 266–67.

8  Letter to the Earl of Wemyss, 27 January 1898.

9  WG, 2004, 85–86, cat. 103; letter to Canon and Mrs Samuel Barnett, 30 January 1898 (NPG aXII, 33).

10  D, 14 January and 5 February 1898; *Society for the Protection of Birds*, 1897, 8–9: Cat.S.36b; WG, 2004, 69–70, cat. 62.

11  D, 13, 15, 20 January 1898; letter to Lilian Mackintosh, 6 February 1898.

12  D, 19 January 1898; Cat.P.14c–15a, 161b–c; Thompson, 2000, 292–93.

13  D, 4 February 1898; *The Times*, 20 January 1898, 6.

14  D, 27 and 31 January 1898; Furse, 1908, 99.

15  D, 1, 3, 5, 9 and 11 February, 5 April 1898; letter to Spielmann, 5 April 1898 (M/JR).

16  D, 22 February and 13 March 1898.

17  D, 23 February 1898; letter from George Meredith to M, 23 February 1898 (NPG 214–17).

18  D, 9, 19, 22 and 24 February 1898.

19  D, 25 February 1898.

20  Spielmann, 1898, cats 6, 12, 15 and 47.

21  D, 1 January, 26, 28 February, 1 March 1898; letter to F. A. Eaton, 15 December 1897 (B/Y, GFW MSS 2125, F3); letter to Briton Rivière, 24 January 1898 (typescript, NPG aXIII, 206); RA, 1898.

22  Letter to Briton Rivière, 1 March 1898 (typescript, NPG aXIII, 207).

23  D, 21 March 1898; *Athenaeum*, 19 March 1898, 380.

24  D, 20 February and 4–7 March 1898; Cat.P.16a; letter to the Hon. Mrs Ivo Bligh, 24 May 1898.

25  D, 24 March, 6 September 1898; De Nevarro, 1896, 60–61.

26  *Architect*, 27 May 1898.

27  D, 22, 24 and 26–28 March 1898.

28  Letter to Horsfall, 20 March 1898.

29  D, 10–11, 13–16 April 1898.

30  D, 22 April 1898.

31  Cat.P.16a, Cat.S.22c and 137b; New Gallery, *Summer Exhibition*, 1899, cats 91, 113, 167. Deuchars exhibited *Robert Burns*; *Athenaeum*, 7 May 1898, 694.

32  Cat.S.95c; *Art Journal*, 1898, 163 and 172; *Athenaeum*, 30 April 1898, 572 and 4 June 1898, 731; *Magazine of Art*, 1898, 426, 464; JCd, 19 May 1898. Presumably it was this painting that later hung at St Paul's.

33  Khnopff, 1898, 428.

34  Millin, 1933, 31; Ruskin, 1903, 37.

35  Millin, 1933, 337 and 344; Melville, 1981, 4; McDonald, 1943, 9, 17–32.

36  JCd, May 1898; letter from Dorothy Stanley, 10 May 1898 (NPG 201).

37  Letter from Cecil Rhodes, 12 May 1898 (NPG sI, 205–9, Fiche 14, B2–6).

38  D, 13, 16–18 May 1898; letter to Cecil Rhodes, 13 May 1898 (University of Durham Library, 181/1).

39  D, 19 May 1898; A, II: 268. McDonald, 1943, 24.

40  D, 20 May 1898; A, II: 269–70; letter from Margaret Miller, n.d.; Millin, 1933, 293. After leading Uitlander troops on a precipitate Raid at Krugersdorp in 1896, against Rhodes's orders, Dr Leander Starr Jameson was forced to surrender to the Boers and briefly imprisoned in London.

41  A, II: 270–71; JCd, May 1898; McDonald, 1943, 151;

Baker, 1938, 82. As GFW had been dissatisfied with Rhodes's unfinished portrait, M released it to the NPG with reservations. Letter M to Lionel Cust, 9 July 1905 (NPG 1407).

42  D, 26 January, 1 April, 8, 19 and 22 May 1898; JCd, 19 May; A, II: 273.

43  Letter to Lionel Cust, 23–25 May 1898 (NPG 1126). At the same time GFW pressed the gallery to accept his portrait of Sir John Peter Grant for 'very distinguished work in Jamaica.' National Portrait Gallery, 1999, 166, cat. 40.

44  D, 28 May and 1 June 1898.

45  D, 30 May 1898.

46  Letter from Cecil Rhodes, Madeira, to M, 1898 (NPG si, 211).

47  Letter from M to Mrs Goldmann, 9 July 1905 (NPG); Cat.P.133a; A, II: 271.

48  Letter from Earl Grey to M, 4 June 1898 (NPG axii, 174–75; Fiche 35, F10–11); letter from M to Lord Grey, 7 June (University of Durham Library, 203/3); letter from Lord Grey to Cecil Rhodes, 11 June (University of Durham Library, 181/1).

49  D, 10–11, 14 June and 26 August 1898; Cat.P.135a.

50  D, 12 June 1898; B/W: 201; *Athenaeum*, 19 March 1898, 380; 6 August 1898, 98, announced that FL's sisters handed over the house in trust to the Committee and that GFW supported the acquisition of *Clytemnestra*. Mrs Russell Barrington, 'Lord Leighton's House, and What it Contains', *Magazine of Art*, 1899, 531; RA, 1897, cat. 142.

51  New Gallery, 1898–99, cat. 124.

52  D, 15–18 June 1898; Burne-Jones, 1904, II, 350; Fitzgerald, 1997, 283; A, II: 274; New Gallery, 1898–99, cat. 124.

53  D, 30 January 1898; JCd, 19 June; Dn, 5 February 1899.

54  JCd, 19 June 1898.

55  D, 20–21 June 1898.

56  D, 23 June 1898; letter from Professor Joseph Joachim, 4 June 1898 (NPG si, 180–81).

57  D, 5 June, 1 July 1898; letter from M to Mr Gleeson-White, 31 July; Gleeson-White, 1898, 235–40; Franklin Gould, 1993, 24; Mary Seton Watts, 2000, 18; WG, 1998, 45–48; *Surrey Advertiser*, 4 July 1898.

58  Royal Library, 14757.

59  D, 17 and 24 December 1898; Mary Seton Watts, 2000, 36; Bateman, 1901, 12.

60  D, 4 July 1898.

61  Letter to Lilian Mackintosh, 6 July 1898; letter to M, n.d.

62  Letter to M, 10 July 1898.

63  Mary Seton Watts, 2000; *The Studio*, XIV, 1898, 235–40.

64  J. S. Sargent *Portrait of Arthur Balfour* (NPG).

65  D, 15–17 July, 19 August 1898; Cat.P.8c; letter from Gerald Balfour to Lady Betty Balfour, 1898 (NAS GD433/2/25).

66  Wemyss and March, 1912, II, 253.

67  Letter to Lord Wemyss, 27 January 1898; D, 25 May 1898; MEd, 25 May.

68  D, 23 May 1898; A, II: 283; *Athenaeum*, 21 May 1898, 668.

69  Letter to Lord Tennyson, 5 September 1898 (TRC, 7031); letter from Lord Tennyson, 6 September 1898 (NPG 144); A, II: 283.

70  D, 4 October 1898; Kent, 1950, 89.

## 24  'Our Race as Pioneers' (1898–1901)

1  *The Times*, 13 October 1898, 13.

2  *Art Journal*, 1898, 352; letters from Lord Meath to the Editor of *The Times*, 21 October 1898, 8, and to *City Press*, 26 October 1898; D, 29 October 1898; Ward-Jackson, 2003, 297 and 298n; Corkran, 1904, 157–59.

3  Letters to Edmund Gosse, 6 November and 4 December 1898 (Brotherton Collection, University of Leeds); letter to Mrs Annie Bryans, 28 April 1899 (NPG axii, 56); A, II: 103–4.

4  D, 22 October 1898; Cat.S.133c; Mrs Wylie had laid in the canvas in watercolour.

5  D, 17, 27 and 28 October, 11 and 17 November 1898; Cat.P.48a; A, II: 253. Frank, 1994, 181 and 356–57; Waterfield, 1961, 81–82. Caroline, the daughter of Lucie Duff-Gordon, married Aubrey Waterfield in 1902. Peters, 1984, 99.

6  D, 10 and 16 November 1898; Exodus 34: 18–23.

7  Cat.S.134b; A, II: 105, 302; WG, 2004, 27 and 89, cat. 115.

8  D, 26 October 1898; letter to Lilian Mackintosh, 10 November 1898.

9  D, 17 and 25 November 1898; Cat.P.114c and Cat.S.111a; letters to James Smith, 17 October, 1 December 1898, 16 January 1899 (NPG axiv, 27, 37–38); Morris, 1996, 471–72, cats 2111 and 504, cat. 2109.

10  D, 28 November, 11, 13, 22 December 1898; A, II: 284. 'Mr G F Watts, RA, on Humble Heroes, and the Mission of Art', *London Argus*, 21 January 1899, 240.

11  Dn, 28 February 1899; Dorment, 1985, 173 and 175.

12  *London Argus*.

13  Dn, 1, 5, 6 January 1899; New Gallery, 1898, cats 3 and 76; WG, 2004, 78, cat. 83.

14  Letter to Georgiana Burne-Jones, 7 January 1899 (typescript, NPG av, 99). Dn, 7–8 January 1899.

15  Dn, 2–3 February 1899; Pastel Society, 21 September

1898; Pastel Society, 1899, cats 106 and 111; *Athenaeum*, 11 February 1899, 184–85; *The Studio*, 1899, XV, 275. *Art Journal* 1899, 62, 114 and 214.

16   Ormond and Kilmurray, 37, fig. 38.

17   Dn, 3 and 7 March 1899; Cat.P.16/17c; WSBd, 20 February and 7–8 March 1899; Longford, 1979, 334; Blunt, 1899.

18   Dn, 10 March 1899; Blunt, 1832, 315–19; WSBd, 10–11, 17 March and 11 April 1899.

19   Cat.S.36b and 118a; Cat.P.135a; New Gallery, 1899, cats 103, 115, 126, 197 and 318; *Art Journal*, 1899, 185–86; *Athenaeum*, 6 May 1899, 568 and 602; *The Times*, June 1899; *Bird Notes and News*, VII, October 1904.

20   Dn, 1 February 1899; *Athenaeum*, 4 February 152, 8 April, 441 and 29 April, 536; A. C. R. Carter, *Art Journal*, 1899, 178, illus. 180; RA, 1899, cat. 2050, *Mors Janua Vitae*; *Magazine of Art* 1899, 240; Leicester Galleries, 1929, 7; Beattie, 1983, 249. Poole's name appears in bank statements from May 1902.

21   Cat.S.29c; letter to Horsfall, 21 June 1899 (NPG aXII, 237).

22   *Athenaeum*, 24 June 1899, 793; Cat.S.65c; Christie's sale, 6 November 1995, lot 131.

23   Dn, 28 May 1899.

24   Lilian Chapman MS memoir.

25   D, 2 March 1887.

26   Dn, 12 July–23 August 1899; Cat.S.4b, 77a, and 87; A, II: 289–93; letter from M to Lord Wemyss, n.d. GFW exhibited *In the Highlands* at the Royal Academy, 1901, cat. 156.

27   Dn, 4 August–27 October 1899; A, II: 291–94; letter from M to Lord Wemyss, n.d.

28   Cat.S.95a.

29   Letter to the Earl of Wemyss, 14 December 1899.

30   Letters to the Rt Hon. the Earl Grey, 15 December 1899 and 27 February 1900 (University of Durham Library, 203/3) (typescript, NPG aXII 176–81), quoted in A, II: 296–98; letter to the Editor of *The Times*, 16 May 1900, printed 18 May.

31   Dn, 21 December 1899; letter to the Editor of *The Times*, 20 December 1899, printed 22 December 1899.

32   Melville, 1981, 3–6; Lindley, 1944, 76–77; Aldourie Game Book.

33   Letter from H. E. Luxmoore, Eton College, Windsor, to GFW, 15 January 1900 (NPG s166–68).

34   Dn, 5 December 1899; CRAd, 5 December (1898–99 ff. 100–01, King's College, Cambridge).

35   M catalogued eleven versions in all. Sketches bring the total higher still. At the same time Reid purchased *Spring*; Cat.S.26b, 88–91, 137b and 146c; letters to John Reid, 1 April, 7 and 14 December 1899, quoted in Caw, 1913, 39.

36   D, 14 February 1898; Dn, 22 January 1900; letter to E. T. Cook, 2 March 1900; letter from M to Mr Whitehouse, 6 February 1919 (Ruskin Library, University of Lancaster, RF L66 and B XXIII); *Daily Graphic*, 26 January 1900; John Dixon Hunt, 1982, 409; Dearden, 1999, 197–99, cats 295–96; *Athenaeum*, 27 January 1900, 120.

37   Letter to George Thompson, 22 January 1900 (NPGa IX, 35); NG Minutes VII, 93.

38   Cat.S.76a, 104–6; Cat.P.61c, 106b and 107a; Thomson, 1901, 76.

39   Cat.S.64b; *Athenaeum*, 12 May 1900, 598; *Art Journal*, 1900, 164.

40   Cat.S.87a; Cat.P.16c and 48a; New Gallery, 1900, cats 133, 139 and 145; *Athenaeum*, 28 April 1900, 535; *Art Journal*, 1900, 186.

41   Dn, 19 June 1900; New Gallery 1900, cat. 248.

42   Dn, 23 July 1900; Duncan, 1928, 33, 44, 49, 56, 61, 63, 68 and 72–73; Jurth, 2002, 23, 47, 59–60, 64 and 66; Terry, 1908, 316.

43   Dn, 30 July 1900; A, II:103–4; *The Times*, 31 July 1900, 2; Dagnall, 1987; *Art Journal*, 1900, 288; Ward-Jackson, 2003, 297.

44   Letter to Hawes Turner, 3 July 1900; letters from Turner, 31 July and 4 August; letter from Charles Holroyd, 1 August. Letter from M to Turner, 2 August 1900; NG Minutes CII, 119 (NG archives); Cat.S.53c and 82a; *Athenaeum*, 4 August 1900, 162, and 11 August 1900, 194; letter from Hallam, Lord Tennyson to M, 13 June 1900 (NPG 147).

45   Letter from Lord Tennyson to M, 3 October 1900 (NPG 151); Cat.S.90c. The mythological work was of a 'nymph', which was not catalogued M in the ownership of South Australia.

46   Dn, 9 and 19 August 1900; Cat.P.96b and 124a.

47   Letter from M to the Earl of Wemyss, 23 September 1900; HFTd, 23, 25 September, 2 October 1900; letter to Lord Archibald Campbell, 15 November 1900 (NPG aXII, 62).

48   Letter to George Thompson, 2 November 1900 (NPG aIX, 35); letter from M to Hallam, Lord Tennyson, 17 May, n.d. (B/Y, Alfred Tennyson Collection, General MSS 276, G. F. Watts, I, 202).

49   Ratcliff, 1982, 161 and 164. This brief reference in Dn, 21 November 1900 may refer to Sargent's portrait of the actress *Ada Rohan* of 1894–95, but he did not exhibit at the Society of Portrait Painters, 1900. Cats 8, 87 and 32; *Athenaeum*, 24 November 1900, 689.

50   Blanche, 1937, 28. Piper, 1955, 63.

51   Letter to Sir E. Poynter, 26 November 1899 (NG); National Gallery of British Art, 29 November 1900.

52   Letter to the Earl of Rosebery, 10 December 1900; letter from Lord Rosebery, 16 December 1900 (NPG 107).

53  Cat.P.112b. Dn, 24 and 29 December 1900, 1–2 and 9 January 1901; letters from M to James Nicol, 10, 11–12 December 1900; letters from James Morton to Nicol, 14, 23 and 29 December 1900, 6, 10 and 15 January 1901 (WG). Morton, 1971, 175, 177 and pl. VII.

54  Dn, 22 January 1901.The three mistakes of her reign, noted GFW, were 'Ireland, pain and sorrow, and Prince of Wales'. *The Art Journal*, 1901, 97.

55  To his regret, GFW had not painted Darwin, Herschel, Ruskin, Disraeli or General Gordon.

56  V&A, 2001, 24; *Art Journal*, 1901, 97.

57  GFW, May 1901, 849–57, reprinted in A, III: 277–94; Dn, 2 February 1901; A, II: 299.

58  Dn, 8 January and 1 April 1901; V&A, 2001, 24.

59  Dn, 7 March 1901; Sotheby's sale, 3 February 1981, lot 27; letter to Briton Rivière, 26 December 1901 (typescript, NPG AXIII, 214).


25  'How Fast the Days Go!' (1901–1904)

1  Letter from Lord Rosebery, 1 February 1901 (NPG s178); HFTd, 29 January 1901; Dn, 2, 19 February 1901.

2  Davies, 1978, 25 and 44.

3  New Gallery, *Richmond*, 1900–01; *Athenaeum*, 16 February 1901, 218.

4  Dn, 27 January 1901.

5  Whitehapel Art Gallery, 1901, cats 44, 50 and 298 (*Lady Dorothy Nevill*), 307 (*Claude G. Montefiore*), 311 (*Building of the Ark*); Cat.S.18b; Barnett, 1918, II, 175–76; *The Studio*, 1899, XVI, 196–98; Dulwich Picture Gallery, 1992, 96; *Athenaeum*, 6 April 1901, 440; 20 July 1901, 100–01.

6  Dn, 5 April, 22 April 1901; Cat.S.76b, 133c, 147c and Cat.P.94b; WG, 2004, 38-39 and 86, cat. 105 New Gallery, 1901, cats 123, 124, 127 and 128 (*Miss Geraldine Liddell*); *Athenaeum*, 27 April 1901, 536–37; *Art Journal*, 1901, 183–84.

7  Glasgow International Exhibition, 1901, cats 365–66, 377, 396, 401, 419, 442, 533–34, 635–36, 639 and 641; *Art Journal*, 1901, 324; *Athenaeum*, 17 August 1901, 227, and 14 September 1901, 357.

8  Dresden, 1901, cats 739–42 (*Love Steering the Boat of Humanity*, *The Meeting of Jacob and Esau*, *John Stuart Mill* and *Lady Somers*).

9  *The Studio*, XXIII, 1901, 66ff; Gregory, 1901, 135–36.

10  Letter from M to James Morton, 15 March 1901 (AAD). WG, 1998, 43.

11  Cat.P.18b; Dn, 6 July 1901; Norman-Butler, 1972, 156.

12  Letter to Lionel Cust, 21 August 1901 (NPG 1407); *Athenaeum*, 10 August 1901, 199; Cat.P.158c. Letter from Hallam, Lord Tennyson to M, 23 February 1901 (NPG 158); letter from M to Hallam Tennyson, 17 May, n.d.; letter to Hallam Tennyson 14 August 1901 (B/Y, Alfred Tennyson Collection, General MSS 276, GFW, 1, ff. 201–2); letter from Hallam Tennyson, 24 December 1901 (NPG 154).

13  Dn, 2 October 1901; Cat.P.116a.

14  Dn, 27 October 1901; Lewis, 1939, 70. Exhibited at the Royal Society of British Artists 1902. *Art Journal*, 1902, 387.

15  Cat.P.25a; letter from General R. S. S. Baden-Powell to Revd. Dr Gerald Rendall, 21 February 1901; letter from Baden-Powell to Mr Davis, 20 October 1901 (Charterhouse Archives 0337/1–38); Dn, 13 September and 28–29 October 1901; letter from Baden-Powell to M, 30 October 1901; letter from Baden-Powell, 3 November 1901 (Bod., MSS Eng. Lett. e.116, ff. 97–101); A, II: 299–301; *The Greyfriar*, IV, 54, April 1902, 41.

16  Cat.P.49b; *Society of Portrait Painters*, 1901, cats 15, 16, 19, 28, 38, 122 and 124: *The Earl of Shrewsbury, Miss Margery Dunthorne, John Burns*, MP, *The Marchioness of Northampton, Sir Benjamin Brodie, 1st Bt, Charles Booth, Professor Flinders Petrie*; *Athenaeum*, 16 November 1901, 670 and 30 November, 740.

17  Letter from the Marquess of Dufferin and Ava, 6 December 1901 (NPG s1, 46); Fish, 1905, 106–7; letter to Lionel Cust, 13 February and 24 March 1902. Henrietta Rae and her husband, the artist Ernest Normand had studios in Holland Park Road; GFW used to keep an eye on their work and, spotting a flaw in the foreshortening of her Academy picture *Zephyrus wooing Flora*, he drew a complete foreshortened skeleton over the figure of Zephyrus, to show where she should alter the swing of the figure to comply with nature. Fish, 1905, 47 and 49.

18  Dn, 4 January and 4 February 1902; 'The Potter's Wheel', *Country Life*, 15 March 1902, 328–30; Erskine, 1902; Begbie, 1902, 152–58.

19  Letter from M to Hallam, Lord Tennyson, 14 February 1902 (B/Y, folder 202).

20  D, 21 January and 8 February 1902; letter to Lady Airlie, 2 February 1902; Cat.P.2a; letter to James Smith, 25 January 1902 (typescript, NPG AXIV, 40).

21  D, 19–20 March 1902; A, II: 302–3; *National Gallery Minutes*, VII, 157; Bateman, 1901, 10.

22  McDonald, 1943, 9; W. T. Stead, 10 June 1902, 576.

23  D, 26 March 1902; ATRd, 14 February; letter to Earl Grey, 5 April 1902; letter from M to Earl Grey, 10 February 1903 (University of Durham Library, 203/3; ts, NPG AXII, 183–85); A, II: 271–73; A, III: 271; McDonald, 1943, 151.

24  D, 13 April 1902; McDonald, 1943, 102–11; Cat.S.53c.

25  D, 15 April 1902; Dorment, 1985, 58.

26  Letter from Alexander Fisher to Earl Grey, 18 April 1902 (University of Durham Library, 206/7).

27  Letter from Fisher to Earl Grey, 30 April 1902; letter to Fisher, 25 April 1902 (copy, University of Durham Library, 206/7); *Art Journal*, 1902, 206.

28  *Athenaeum*, 17 May 1902, 632; *Art Journal*, 1902, 222; *Spectator*, May 1902.

29  Stead, 10 June 1902, 567.

30  Melville, 1981, 19; *The Times*, 2 June 1902, 7.

31  Letter from Sir Francis Knollys, 25 June 1902 (WG); A, II: 303; St Aubyn, 1979, 369; NG, 2003, cat. 33 *Self-Portrait*; letter to Briton Rivière, 27 June 1902 (typescript, NPG aXIII, 215); St Aubyn, 1979, 369.

32  Letter from Sir W. B. Richmond, 26 June 1902 (Bod., MSS Eng. Lett. e.118, ff. 18–19); letter from the Marquess of Ripon, 28 June 1902 (NPG sI, 62); letter to Lady Burne-Jones, 12 July 1902 (Fitzwilliam, VIII, 14); *The Times*, 26 July 1902, lists the OM recipients as Lords Roberts, Wolseley, Kitchener, Rayleigh, Kelvin, Lister, Sir Harry Keppell, Sir F. Seymour, Sir W. Huggins, Morley, Lecky and GFW.

33  Letter from ATR to M, 26 June 1902 (NPG s.325–28); Maitland, 1906, 317.

34  D, 25 July 1902; letter from Charles Holroyd to Sir Edward Poynter, 14 July 1902 (NG7/266/1902).

35  Letter from M to Hallam Tennyson, 6 November 1902 (TRC, 7442).

36  D, 9–10 November 1902; Cat.P.42b; Langtry, 1925, 57–59.

37  D, 16 and 19 November 1902; A, II: 305; Berger, 1984, 53–54.

38  Letters to George Thompson, 14 and 23 November (NPG aIX, 37); D, 20 November 1902.

39  *Philadelphia Press*, 15 December 1902; Blunt, 1975, 156; Turnor, 1902–4 MS, 1.

40  Macmillan, 1903; Dn, 17–18 January 1903; Dale, 1985, 26; *Athenaeum*, 6 June 1903, 729.

41  Letter from John Morley, 13 and 20 February 1903 (NPG sI, 53–54); John Morley, 1905.

42  Dn, 9 January 1902, 4 January and 23 February 1903; A, II: 305; Turnor, n.d., 54, 215 and 221. The corner stone is inscribed 'BENISON ON THE HOUSE / BENISON IN THE HOUSE / BENISON FROM THE HOUSE.'

43  Cat.S.86b; A, II: 313–14; Lilian Chapman MS.

44  Letter to the Earl Brownlow, n. d. (NPG aXII, 45, Fiche 34, D4).

45  *Magazine of Art*, March 1903, 260; letter to Evelyn, Countess Martinengro Cesaresco, 5 March 1903; letter Cesaresco to M, 13 July 1905 (NPG aXIII, 58–59).

46  Dn, 1 March 1903; Grafton Galleries, 7–13 March 1903, cat. 80; *The Studio* 1903, XXVIII, 286.

47  Leighton House, March 1903, 6; *Athenaeum*, 4 April 1903, 440–41.

48  Spalding, 1996, 1–2 and 26; Rothenstein, 1931, I, 97.

49  Spalding, 1996, 35.

50  Letter from Vanessa Stephen to Margery Snowden, Saturday [14 March 1903] (Tate, 8010.11.3.VBms2).

51  Cat.S.116a; WG, 2004, 72, cat. 66. Having exhibited the picture as *A Parasite*, GFW wrote to J. K. Preston on 31 October 1903 that he was not 'always on stilts or riding the High Horse!' – this picture was only a study from nature. 'Nature of course is full suggestions. Symbolism is to be found in everything!' (NPG aIX, 42).

52  Cat.S.141a.

53  Cat.S.41c.

54  D, 15 March 1903; letter from Vanessa Stephen to Margery Snowden, Sunday, quoted in Marler, 1903, 8–11; Tate Gallery, 1999, 25, 55, 278, fig. 147; Bell, 1972, 73.

55  D, 3 June 1898.

56  A, II: 313; Cat.S.66c and 148c; WG, 2004, 66, cat. 54; *Athenaeum*, 2 May 1903, 569 and 16 May, 632; *Art Journal*, 1903, 184; *Magazine of Art*, 1903, 379, 425 and 432.

57  Cat.S.134c; D, 5 July 1896; A, II: 245; Tate Gallery, 1997, 280.

58  Cat.S.106c; *Exhibition of Pictures by Living Artists*, London, Dutch Gallery, 1903, cats 1 and 11; Morris, 1996, 500, WAG, 2110; *Athenaeum*, 30 May 1903, 697, and 6 June, 728; Tate Gallery, 1994, 317; *Athenaeum*, 18 July 1903, 133.

59  Dn, 11 June 1903; letters to Briton Rivière, 8 and 12 June 1903 (typescript, NPG aXIII, 216); letters to Hamo Thornycroft, 14 and 29 June 1903 (L/HM: 700–01).

60  Dn, 12 June 1903; A, II: 313; Cat.S.42b, 60a. 120c.

61  National Gallery of British Art, 176 and 184; *Art Journal*, 1903, 386.

62  Letter to Crane 24 October 1902, 8 July 1903 (RBKC), quoted in Crane, 1907, 233–34.

63  Ritchie, *Notes of Happy Things*, MS Ritchie, 1924, 264–65; letter to Rivière, 23 June 1903 (typescript, NPG aXIII, 216).

64  Letter to Mrs Amelia Hatton, 13 May 1903 (Hereford Archives, AD3/26/165), quoted in Davies, 1978, 60.

65  Letter from Mrs Amelia Hatton to Alfred Hatton, 28 July 1903 (Hereford Archives, AD3/26/63); Davies, 1978, 61.

66  Cat.S.86b; Dn, 4–5 August 1903; A, II: 313–14.

67  Dn, 6 and 11–12 August 1903; A, II: 305–6; letter to Briton Rivière, 30 August 1903 (typescript, NPG aXIII, 217).

68  Dn, 30 September 1903; letter from M to Mrs Hatton, 30 September (Hereford Archives, AD3/26/21); letter to Lord Wemyss, 23 December 1903; letter to Hamo Thornycroft, 28 February 1904 (HM 702).

69  Cat.S.100a; Dn, 31 August, 5 and 22 September 1903;

letters to Lionel Cust, 27 August, 10 and 13 September 1903 (NPG); Roberts, 1997, 831; *Magazine of Art*, 1903, 144; Röder, 1998, XXII, 5.

70  Dn, 26 October 1903; letter to Spielmann, 26 October 1903 (M/JR); letter to James Smith, 26 October 1903, (copy NPG AXIV, 39); letter from M to Lord Tennyson, autumn 1903 (note); letter from M to Mrs Hatton (Hereford Archives, AD3/26/22); A, II: 183.

71  Dn, 30–31 October 1903; A, II: 317.

72  Dn, 9 February 1904; A, II: 318.

73  Cat.S.159c; Dn, 11 and 13 November 1903; A, II: 318–19.

74  Letter to Verena Somers Cocks, 29 November 1903; Dn, 2 December.

75  Letter from M to Auguste Rodin, 10 December 1903 (Musée Rodin); Rodin to M, 17 December 1903 (Fiche 42, E2–5).

76  Dn, 25 December 1903.

77  Letter from Alfred Austin to M, 6 January 1904:
    'Enter you may not here; here Love doth dwell,'
    Love said to Death. But Death to Love replied,
    'No tenant may his Sovran Lord repel,
    And I am Lord wherever men abide.'
    Then, deaf to supplication, prayer, and tears,
    With Love's dwelling-place Death forced his way,
    Filled it with wailing, waverings, and fears,
    And chilled round limbs to unpalpitating clay.
    Then Love thus spake: 'Because you forced my door,
    Lo! you have fixed my occupancy now;
    Now am *I* Lord, that tenant was before
    And you my claim would vainly disallow;
    You have but strengthened what you sought to sever,
    And Love, once fragile, now is Love forever.'

78  Letter to James Smith, 15 January 1904, NPG AXIV, 45; Cat.S.94b; Morris, 1996, 503, WAG 2132.

79  Dn, 23 and 25 January 1904.

80  Hallé, 1896, II, 68–69.

81  Dn, 11 and 17 February 1904; International Society of Sculptors, Painters, and Gravers, 1904, cats 123, 331, 333, 334, 350, 352 and 355: *La Defense, Bellona, Le Penseur, Torso of St John, A Dream, Illusion, fille d'Icare, Le Grand Penseur*. Shannon, cats 182, 188, 240: *The Toilet, The Lady with a Feather, The Bathers*; letter to Grace, Countess of Wemyss, 30 March 1904 (NPG AIX, 112).

82  *Irish Industrial Exhibition, World's Fair, St Louis 1904, II: Handbook and Catalogue to the Industrial Section*, cats 120–21 and 35. Grafton Gallery, 1904.

83  Spielmann, 1906, 127; *Irish Industrial Exhibition, Worlds Fair, St Louis, 1904, II: Handbook and Catalogue to Industrial section*, 30–36; Grafton Gallery, 1904.

84  Turnor, 8 April 1904; *Enquirer*, 30 July 1904.

85  Dn, 20 March 1904.

86  Dn, 6–7, 13 and 28 March and 26 July 1904; letter to Lady Wemyss, 30 March; Theodore Spicer Simson to Auguste Rodin, 5 April; A, II: 319–20; Cat.S.39b, 46a and 169a; NPG, 1905, 2.

87  D, 1 April 1904; A, II: 320; letter from Lily Mackintosh to Lord Wemyss, 2 May 1904; 'Lady Artists of the Day, Mrs G. F. Watts', newscutting, n.d.; 'Mr G. F. Watts' Picture Gallery', *Surrey Advertiser*, March 1904.

88  D, 15 April 1904; Cat.S.2c; A, II: 320–21; M, 2000, 35–36; Franklin Gould, 1993, 37–38.

89  HFTd, 29 April 1904.

90  Cat.S.86b; *Athenaeum*, 7 May 1904, 597; *Art Journal*, 1904, 181.

91  New Gallery, 1904, cats 39, 45, 50, 132, 193; *Athenaeum*, 23 April 536; *Art Journal*, 1904, 193.

92  Letter to Briton Rivière, 6 May 1904 (typescript, NPG AXIII, 219).

93  A, II: 322.

94  A, II: 321; *The Times*, 17 May 1904, 11; *Athenaeum*, 21 May 1904, 664.

95  25 May 1904; A, II: 322.

96  A, II: 322.

97  D, 16–17 June 1904; JCd, 17 June 1904.

98  D, 19 June 1904.

99  D, 23–24 June 1904.

100  D, 26 June 1904.

101  D, 29–30 June 1904; letter from G. Liddell to Lord Wemyss, 30 June 1904.

102  Tennyson, 1849, lvii.

103  Letter from Lord Knollys to M, 2 July 1904 (Bod., MSS Eng. Lett. d.275, ff. 195–96).

104  Letter from Henry Poole to Lord Wemyss, 2 July 1904; letter from M to Lord Wemyss, 2 July 1904; D, 2 July 1904.

105  D, 3 July 1904.

106  Letter from Walter Crane to M, 3 July 1904 (Bod., MSS Eng. Lett. d.275, ff. 174–75), with sonnet: 'Lo! Regal death hath set his seal, and crowned/The Master's work whose sentient hand hath limned/The shadow on Love's threshold, who with eyes undimmed/Through Life's prismatic veil hath seen enthroned/Majestic Form with Truth and Beauty bound/In art's bright record, by the fountain brimmed/With dreams immortal, and in triumph hymned/To unheard music on celestial ground.'

107  D, 3 November 1896, 4–5 July 1904; *Art Journal*, 1903, 218, illustrated the casket at the Home Arts exhibition; *Graphic*, 16 July 1904; *In Memoriam: G. F. Watts*, 1904.

108  D, 7–8 July 1904; St Paul's cathedral, 7 July 1904; Liddell, 1911, 345.

109  D, 9 July 1904.

110  *Daily Telegraph* and *Westminster Gazette*, 2 July 1904.

111  D, 26 March 1898.

112  Tate, 1997, 33. Lucie-Smith, 204 and 207.

113  CRAd, *c*.12 July 1904 (King's College Library, *Ashbee Journals*, 1904, f. 33).

## Epilogue

1  D, 2, 31 July 1904; letter from Hugh Lane to MSW, 19 July 1904 (Bod. MSS Eng. Lett. d.275, ff. 197–98).

2  Will of GFW, Walker Martineau, 21 November 1899; 'The Executors and Trustees of the Will of the late GFW and MSW, Conditional Agreement', 24 May 1905; letters to Lionel Cust, 7–16 March 1905 (NPG 1407); letter from Sir Charles Holroyd, 8 March 1905; letter from Sir Edward Poynter, 12 March 1905; 'Bequests to the Nation by the late Mr Watts', *The Times*, 6 June 1905; *Minutes of the Watts Picture Gallery*; D, 31 October 1904; letter from Charles Thompson to Sir Charles Holroyd, 6 July 1906 (WG).

3  D, 25 and 27 July 1904.

4  Letter to the Editor of the *Daily Telegraph*, 6 March 1907; letter to James Smith, 14 June 1907. The head of the rider was put back two inches. This second version of *Physical Energy* was cast at Burton's foundry in Thames Ditton. A third cast stands as Rhodes's memorial at the National Archives at Harare.

5  D, 13–17 October 1904; A, II: 306; Read, 1982, 282–86.

6  Dn, 11 June, 6 and 12 August 1903; A, II: 306.

7  D, 12, 16, 19 August, 1 September and 16 December 1904.

8  D, 28 December 1904; RA, 1905. The memorial exhibition transferred to the Royal Scottish Academy, Manchester City Art Gallery, Laing Art Gallery, Newcastle, 1905, and the Royal Hibernian Academy in 1906; *Athenaeum*, 14 January 1905, 57–58.

9  Letter from Sir Charles Holroyd, 8 March 1905.

10  Virginia Stephen to Madge Vaughan, January 1905; Nicolson, 1993, 173; Spalding, 1983, 2, 46; 1980, 73; Lee, 1997, 205; Leaska, 218; 7 January 1905; Clausen, 1905, 8.

11  D, 5 August 1904, 23 February 1906. Tom Wren modelled the grey terracotta memorial to GFW – and M – with relief panels of *Destiny* and *Messenger*.

12  Thompson, 15 November 1913 (WG).

13  Yeats, 1955, 141–42, 550; Frayne and Johnson, 1976, II, 343–54; 'Colour Reproductions from the Pictures of G. F. Watts', typescript (WG); letter from Sir Charles Holroyd, 22 January 1908; letter from Hawes Turner, National Gallery, 22 January 1908; letter from G Moore to MSW, 21 June 1908.

14  Wren's memorial to Watts was unveiled by W. B. Richmond on 13 December 1905. After 1907 the plaques were produced by Doulton & Co, with decorative emblems replacing De Morgan's incense burners, the last four installed on 15 October 1930. Ward-Jackson, 2003, 297.

15  B/W; *Athenaeum*, 24 June 1905, 790–91.

16  MSW, MS notebook 5 (WG).

17  In 1889, Lutyens built Crooksbury, near Farnham for Arthur Chapman.

18  Woolf, 1940, 115–16.

19  Spalding, 1983, 91–92.

20  Woolf, 1976.

21  As has been stated, Watts painted Symbolist pictures directly on to canvas, making only the odd doodle in tiny sketches. For his portraits he made fine pencil studies; Sickert, *Art News*, 12 May 1910, quoted in Sitwell, 1947, 207. Sickert added in the *English Review* that month, quoted in Sitwell, 126: 'If in the eighties anyone had so much as squeaked in presence of a Watts he would have been apostrophised on all sides, somewhat thus: "But, disgusting personage, you are, then, in favour of rapine and oppression! Learn that, on *this* side of the Channel, etcetera."' *Manchester Guardian*, 2 March 1926, quoted in Sitwell, 211. Royal Academy, 1988, 39.

22  Letter from MSW to Mr Wallace-Dunlop, 30 July 1931.

23  Art Sales Index; Christie's sale catalogue, 24 June 1998, lot 33; 12 February 2003, lot 138; Sotheby's sale catalogue, 10 November 1999, lot 150.

24  Rothenstein, 1931, I, 32–33.

25  Woolf, 1940, 152–53; Tate, 1954; *The Times*, 9 December 1954, 7.

26  Whitechapel Art Gallery, 1974; *Arts Review*, 8 February 1974, XXVI, no 3, 51.

27  Tate Gallery, 1997; *The Times*, 14 October 1997.

# Bibliography

Jane Abdy and Charlotte Gere, *The Souls*, 1982.

Harold Acton, *Tuscan Villas*, 1973.

Eve Adam, ed., *Mrs J. Comyns Carr's Reminiscences*, 1925.

Adelaide Jubilee International Exhibition of 1887, exh. cat., 1888.

*Aglaia: The Journal of the Healthy and Artistic Dress Union*, July 1893.

Thomas Agnew, *Twelve Drawings by Mr Watts*, exh. cat., May 1891.

Olivia Rossetti Agresti, *Giovanni Costa: His Life, Work & Times*, 1904, 1907 edition.

Richard Aldington, ed., *Walter Pater: Selected Works*, 1948.

Helen Allingham and Arthur Paterson, *The Homes and Haunts of Tennyson*, 1905.

William Allingham, *The Diaries*, ed. H. Allingham and D. Radford, 1907, 1990 edition.

Rowland Alston, *The Mind and Work of G. F. Watts*, 1929.

Anne Clark Amor, *William Holman Hunt: The True Pre-Raphaelite*, 1989.

W. E. K. Anderson, ed., *The Journal of Sir Walter Scott*, 1972.

Isabelle Anscombe and Charlotte Gere, *Arts & Crafts in Britain and America*, 1978.

Lady Antrobus, ed., *A Few Letters and Recollections of Mrs Edward Sartoris*, n.d.

Walter Armstrong, *Fine Art at the Royal Jubilee Exhibition, Manchester*, exh. cat. 1887.

Matthew Arnold, 'Culture and its Enemies', reprinted in the *Cornhill Magazine*, xvi, July 1867.

——, *Culture and Anarchy and Other Writings*, ed. Stefan Collini, 1993.

Art Gallery of New South Wales, *Pre-Raphaelites and Olympians*, exh. cat., 2001.

Art Institute of Chicago, *Julia Margaret Cameron's Women*, exh. cat., 1998.

——, *Odilon Redon 1840–1916*, exh. cat., 1994.

Arts Council of Great Britain, Hayward Gallery, London, *Lutyens: The Work of the English Architect Sir Edwin Lutyens (1869–1944)*, exh. cat., 1981.

*Arundel Society, or Society for Promoting the Knowledge of Art: Report of the Council*, 1851.

Russel Ash, *John Everett Millais*, 1997.

C. R. Ashbee, ed., *Transactions of the Guild & School of Handicraft*, I, 1890.

Asleson, Robyn, 'Classic into Modern: The Inspiration of Antiquity in English Painting 1864–1918', PhD dissertation, York University, 1998.

Cynthia Asquith, *Haply I May Remember*, 1950.

Margot Asquith, *Autobiography*, 1920.

T. H. Aston, ed., *The History of the University of Oxford*, 8 vols, 1984– , VI: *Nineteenth-Century Oxford*, ed. M. G. Grock and M. C. Curthoys, 1997.

J. B. Atlay, *Famous Trials of the Century*, 1899.

——, *Sir Henry Wentworth Acland, Bart KCN FRS: Regius Professor of Medicine in the University of Oxford: A Memoir*, 1903.

J. Beavington Atkinson, *English Painters of the Present Day*, 1871.

Walter Bagehot, 'Mr Gladstone' *National Review*, July 1860, XI, 219, reprinted in Norman St John-Stevas, *Walter Bagehot*, 1959.

Albert Victor Bailey and Hector Bolitho, eds, 'A Victorian Dean': A Memoir of Arthur Stanley, Dean of Westminster*, 1930.

J. Bailey, *The Diary of Lady Frederick Cavendish*, 2 vols, 1927.

Herbert Baker, *Cecil Rhodes*, 1938.

Lady Frances Balfour, *Ne Obliviscaris: Dinna Forget*, 1932.

Barbican Art Galleries, *The Wilde Years: Oscar Wilde and the Art of his Time*, exh. cat., 2000.

Juliet Wilson Bareau, *Manet by Himself*, 1991.

Alfred Barnard, *Noted Breweries of Great Britain & Ireland*, 2 vols, 1889.

Henrietta Barnett, *Canon Barnett: His Life, Work, and Friends*, 2 vols, 1918.

Tim Barringer and Elizabeth Prettejohn, eds, *Frederic Leighton: Antiquity, Renaissance, Modernity*, 1999.

Mrs Russell Barrington, *Leighton and John Kyrle ('The Man of Ross')*, 1903.

——, *G. F. Watts: Reminiscences*, 1905.

——, *The Life, Letters and Work of Frederic Leighton*, 2 vols, 1906.

——, *The Servant of All: Pages from the Family, Social & Political Life of My Father James Wilson*, 2 vols, 1927.

Charles T. Bateman, 'Mr G. F. Watts and His Art', *Windsor Magazine*, 1901, XIV.

Susan Beattie, *The New Sculpture*, 1983.

Laura Beatty, *Lillie Langry: Manners, Masks and Morals*, 1999, 2000 edition.

Isabella Beeton, *Beeton's Book of Household Management*, 1859.

Harold Begbie, 'Life at Eighty-Five: An Interview with Mr G. F. Watts', *Daily Mail* (interview 8th) March 1902.

E. Moberly Bell, *Josephine Butler: Flame of Fire*, 1962.

Quentin Bell, *Virginia Woolf: A Biography*, 1972.

William de Belleroche, *Brangwyn's Pilgrimage: The Life Story of an Artist*, 1948.

Léonce Bénédite, *Le Musée du Luxembourg*, 1894–95.

E. F. Benson, *Dodo*, 1893.

K. Berger, *The Hearing Aid: Its Operation and Development*, 1984.

The Earl of Bessborough, ed., *Lady Charlotte Schreiber: Extracts from her Journal 1853–1891*, 1952.

Madeleine Bingham, *Princess Lieven: Russian Intriguer*, 1982.

Dina Birch, ed., *Fors Clavigera: Letters to the Workmen and Labourers of Great Britain*, The Whitehouse Edition of John Ruskin, 2000.

Birmingham, *Handbook to the Art Exhibition at the Inauguration of the Museum & Art Gallery*, exh. cat., 1885–86.

Jacques-Émile Blanche, *Portraits of a Lifetime*, 1937.

Wilfrid Blunt, *England's Michelangelo: A Biography of George Frederic Watts*, 1975.

Wilfred Scawen Blunt, *Satan Absolved: A Victorian Mystery*, 1899.

——, *My Diaries: Being a Personal Narrative of Events 1888–1914*, 1932.

Mark Bonham-Carter, ed., *The Autobiography of Margot Asquith*, 1920, 1995 edition.

John Lewis Bradley, *Ruskin's Letters from Venice, 1851–1852*, 1955.

—— and Ian Ousby, eds, *The Correspondence of John Ruskin and Charles Eliot Norton*, 1987.

Asa Briggs and Anne Macartney, *Toynbee Hall: The First Hundred Years*, 1984.

Martin Brinbaum, *The Last Romantic: The Story of More than a Half-Century in the World of Art*, 1960.

Gerald Brodribb, ed., *Felix on the Bat, with A Memoir of Nicholas Felix*, 1961.

Jane Brown, *Gardens of a Golden Afternoon: The Story of a Partnership: Edwin Lutyens and Gertrude Jerkyll*, 1982.

Brussels International Exhibition, *Catalogue of the British Fine Art Section*, exh. cat., 1897.

Van Akin Burd, ed., *The Winnington Letters*, 1969.

Elizabeth Burgoyne, *Carmen Sylva: Queen and Woman*, 1941.

Sir Edward Burne-Jones, *The Little Holland House Album*, 1981.

Georgiana Burne-Jones, *Memorials of Edward Burne-Jones*, 2 vols, 1904.

A. S. G. Butler, *Portrait of Josephine Butler*, 1954.

Françoise Cachin, *Manet: Painter of Modern Life*, 1995.

Stephen Calloway and David Colvin, *Oscar Wilde: An Exquisite Life*, 1997.

Julia Margaret Cameron, *Alfred Tennyson's Idylls of the King and Other Poems Illustrated by Julia Margaret Cameron*, 1874–75.

A. Carlyle, ed., *New Letters of Thomas Carlyle*, 2 vols, 1904.

*The Collected Letters of Thomas & Jane Welsh Carlyle*, 1970.

Thomas Carlyle, *On Heroes, Hero-Worship and The Heroic in History*, 1907.

——, *Past and Present*, 1843, 1912 edition, vol. III, vi.

J. Comyns Carr, *Examples of Contemporary Art: Etchings from Representative Works by Living England and Foreign Artists*, 1878.

——, *Coasting Bohemia*, 1914.

Mrs J. Comyns Carr, *Reminiscences*, 1925.

Julia Cartwright, 'G. F. Watts RA', *Atlanta*, V, no. 49, October 1891.

——, 'The Life and Work of George Frederic Watts RA', *The Art Journal Easter Annual*, 1896.

Susan Casteras and Colleen Denney, eds, *The Grosvenor Gallery: A Palace of Art in Victorian England*, exh. cat., 1996.

*Catalogue of the Pictures forming the Collection of Sir Charles Tennant Bart of 40 Grosvenor Square and The Glen, Innerleithen*, 1896.

Timotheos Catsiyannis, *Constantine Ionides-Ipliktzis 1775–1852 & The Ionidi Family*, 1988.

James L. Caw (notes), Glasgow, James Maclehose, *Catalogue of the Collection of Pictures of the British French & Dutch Schools belonging to John Reid*, exh. cat., 1913.

Lord David Cecil, introduction to *A Victorian Album: Julia Margaret Cameron & Her Circle*, 1975.

Lady Gwendolen Cecil, *Life of Robert Marquis of Salisbury*, 3 vols, 1931.

Anon. [Robert Chambers], *Vestiges of the Natural History of Creation*, 1844.

John Chancellor, *Wagner*, 1978.

Ronald Chapman, *The Laurel and the Thorn: A Study of G. F. Watts*, 1945.

Evan Charteris, *The Life and Letters of Sir Edmund Gosse*, 1931.

Alan Chedzoy, *A Scandalous Woman: The Story of Caroline Norton*, 1992.

David Cheshire, *Portrait of Ellen Terry*, 1989.

Ernest Chesnau, *La Peinture Anglaise*, Paris, 1882, trans. L. N. Etherington, *The English School of Painting*, London, 1885.

G. K. Chesterton, *G. F. Watts*, 1904.

Chicago, Royal Commission for the Chicago Exhibition, *Official Catalogue of the British Section*, exh. cat., 1893.

Joan Chissell, *Clara Schummann: A Dedicated Spirit*, 1983.

Christie's, *Impressionist & 19th Century Art*, sale catalogue, 24 June 1998.

Christie, Manson & Woods, *Catalogue of the Valuable Collection of Modern Pictures of Charles Hilditch Rickards Esq*, 2 April 1887.

Anne Clarke, *Lewis Carroll: A Biography*, 1979.

G. Clausen, *The Art of G. F. Watts, RA OM*, 1905.

C. L. Cline, ed., *The Letters of George Meredith*, 3 vols, 1970.

Colnaghi, *Whisper of the Muse The World of Julia Margaret Cameron*, exh. cat. (Jeremy Howard), 1990.

Compton Parish Council, 1894–1911.

Sir Edward Cook, *The Life of Florence Nightingale*, 2 vols, 1913.

E. T. Cook and Alexander Wedderburn, eds, *The Works of John Ruskin*, Library Edition, 39 vols, 1903–12.

Alice Corkran, *Frederic Leighton*, 1904.

Corporation of London, Barbican Centre, *The Wilde Years: Oscar Wilde & The Art of his Time*, 2000.

Corporation of London Art Gallery, *Loan Collection of Pictures*, June 1890.

Edith Craig and Christopher St John, eds, *Ellen Terry's Memoirs*, London, 1933.

Edward Gordon Craig, *Index to the Story of My Days*, 1957.

Walter Crane, *An Artist's Reminiscences*, 1907.

Alan Crawford, *C. R. Ashbee: Architect, Designer and Romantic Socialist*, 1985.

J. Mordaunt Crook, *William Burges and the High Victorian Dream*, 1981.

Elizabeth Cumming, 'Patterns of Life: The Art and Design of Phoebe Anna Traquair and Mary Seton Watts', in *Women Artists and the Decorative Arts 1880–1935: The Gender of Ornament*, ed. Bridget Elliott and Janice Holland, 2002.

——, and Wendy Kaplan, *The Arts & Crafts Movement*, 1991.

George William Curtis, ed., *The Correspondence of John Lothrop Motley DCL*, 2 vols, 1889.

H. Dagnall, *Postman's Park & its Memorials*, 1987.

Caroline Dakers, *Clouds: The Biography of a Country House*, 1993.

——, *The Holland Park Circle: Artists and Victorian Society*, 1999.

Alzina Stone Dale, *The Art of G. K. Chesterton*, 1985.

George Dalziel, *The Brothers Dalziel: A Record of Fifty Years' Work*, 1901.

Gillian Darley, *Octavia Hill: A Life*, 1990.

Robin Darwall-Smith, ed., *The Jowett Papers*, Balliol College Library, Oxford, 1993.

Charles Darwin, *On the Origin of Species by Means of Natural Selection or the Preservation of Favoured Races in the Struggle for Life*, 1859.

Roy Davids, *The Artist as a Portrait*, Fine Art Society, London, exh. cat., 2000.

Celia Davies, *Brian Hatton: A Biography of the Artist (1887–1916)*, 1978.

James A. Davies, *John Forster: A Literary Life*, 1983.

Martin Davies, *National Gallery Catalogues: French School*, 1957.

James S. Dearden, *John Ruskin: A Life in Pictures*, 1999.

Bernard Denvir, *A Most Agreeable Society: 125 Years of the Arts Club*, 1989.

Deschamps Galleries, *Winter Exhibition of Oil Paintings by British Artists*, exh. cat., 1876.

Wynford Dewhurst, *Impressionist Painting: Its Genesis and Development*, 1914.

E. Rimbault Dibdin, *George Frederick Watts*, 1923.

Violet Dickinson, ed., *Miss Eden's Letters*, 1919.

Richard Dorment, *Alfred Gilbert*, 1985.

O. Doughty and J. R. Wahl, eds, *The Letters of Dante Gabriel Rossetti*, 4 vols, 1965–67.

Dresden, *Offizieller Katalog der Internationalen Kunstausstellung*, exh. cat., 1901.

Dyce Duckworth, 'On Tight-Lacing', *The Practitioner*, 24 January 1880.

*Dudley Gallery Winter Exhibition of Cabinet Pictures in Oil*, exh. cat., 1867–74.

Dudley Gallery, *Catalogue of the First Winter Edition of Modern Pictures, New English Art Club*, exh. cat., 1891.

Lucie Duff Gordon *Discretions and Indiscretions*, 1932.

Dulwich Picture Gallery, *Palaces of Art, Art Galleries in Britain 1790–1990*, exh. cat., 1992.

——, *Art for the People: Culture in the Slums of Late Victorian Britain*, exh. cat., 1994.

Daphne Du Maurier, ed., *The Young George du Maurier: A Selection of Letters 1860–67*, 1951.

Isadora Duncan, *My Life*, 1928.

Lady Eastlake, *Journals and Correspondence*, 2 vols, 1895.

Edinburgh National Galleries of Scotland, *Phoebe Anna Traquair*, exh. cat., 1993.

Max Egremont, *The Cousins: The Friendship, Opinions and Activities of Wilfrid Scawen Blunt and George Wyndham*, 1977.

George Eliot, *Adam Bede*, 3 vols, 1859.

——, *Felix Holt: The Radical*, 1866, 1983 edition.

Arthur Ellridge, *Gaugin and the Nabis: Profits of Modernism*, 1993, 1995 edition.

Mrs Steuart Erskine, 'Mrs G. F. Watts' Terracotta Industry', *The Studio*, February 1902, 152–58.

——, 'Mr Watts' Portraits at Holland House, *The Studio*, XXIX, 1903.

Angela Emanuel, ed., *A Bright Remembrance: The Diaries of Julia Cartwright 1851–1924*, 1989.

Michael Estorick, *Heirs & Graces*, 1981.

*Exposition Universelle de 1862 à Londres: Section Française, Catalogue Officiel*, exh. cat., 1862.

L. Fagan, *The Life of Sir Anthony Panizzi KCB*, 2 vols, 1970.

Joseph Farrar, 'Lung Capacity and Tight Lacing', *Good Words*, 1880.

*Felix on the Bat: Being a Scientific Enquiry into the Use of The Cricket Bat, together with the History and Use of the Catapulta*, 1845 and 1850.

Julia Findlater, '100 years of Leighton House', in Robin Simon, ed., *Lord Leighton 1830–1896 and Leighton House: A Centenary Celebration*, 1996.

The Fine Art Society, '*The Shaftesbury Memorial: Alfred Gilbert & Joseph Edgar Boehm, Eros by Sir Alfred Gilbert*, exh. cat., 1987.

Arthur Fish, *Henrietta Rae (Mrs Ernest Normand)*, 1905.

H. A. L. Fisher, *An Unfinished Biography*, 1940.

Penelope Fitzgerald, *Edward Burne-Jones*, 1975, 1997 edition.

Kathleen Fitzpatrick, *Lady Henry Somerset*, 1923.

G. H. Fleming, *John Everett Millais: A Biography*, 1998.

Colin Ford, *The Cameron Collection: An Album of Photographs by Julia Margaret Cameron Presented to Sir John Herschel*, 1975.

Andrew Forge, *The Slade 1871–1960*, ts, n.d.

Peter Taylor Forsyth, *Religion in Recent Art: Being Expository Lectures on Rossetti, Burne-Jones, Watts, Holman Hunt and Wagner*, 1889.

Katherine Frank, *Lucie Duff Gordon: A Passage to Egypt*, 1994.

J. P. Frayne and Colton Johnson, eds, *Uncollected Prose by W. B. Yeats*, 1976.

Hulda Friederichs, 'An Interview with Mr G. F. Watts, RA', *The Young Woman*, XXXIX, December 1895.

Veronica Franklin Gould, *The Watts Chapel: An Arts and Crafts Memorial*, 1993.

The French Gallery, *Thirteenth Annual Winter Exhibition of Pictures: The Contributions of British Artists*, exh. cats., 1865–66.

James Anthony Froude, 'A Siding at a Railway Station', *Fraser's Magazine*, 1879, reprinted in *Short Studies on Great Subjects*, 4 vols, 1905.

Hester Thackeray Fuller, ed., *Three Freshwater Friends*, 1933, 1992 edition.

—— and Violet Hammersley, eds, *Thackeray's Daughter*, 1951.

Charles Wellington Furse, *Illustrated Memoir*, 1908.

Katerine Gaja, *G. F. Watts in Italy: A Portrait of the Artist as a Young Man*, 1995.

Henrietta Garnett, *Anny: A Life of Anne Isabella Thackeray Ritchie*, 2004.

Galerie Georges Petit, Paris, *Exposition Internationale de Peinture*, exh. cat., 1883.

Winifred Gérin, *Anne Thackeray Ritchie*, 1983.

Helmut Gernsheim, *Julia Margaret Cameron: Her Life and Photographic Work*, 1975.

Michael Gibson, *Symbolism*, 1995.

W. S. Gilbert and Arthur Sullivan, *The Immortal Operas*, 4 vols, 1881, 1930.

Alexander Gilchrist, *Life of William Blake*, 1863.

Glasgow International Exhibition, *Fine Art*, exh. cat., 1901.

J. Gleeson-White, 'A Mortuary Chapel, Designed by Mrs G. F. Watts', *The Studio*, XIV, 1898.

Israel Gollancz, ed., *Shakespeare's Sonnets*, 1897.

J. W. Goodison, *Catalogue of Cambridge Portraits*, 1955.

Cecil Gould, *The Sixteenth Century Italian Schools*, National Gallery, London, 1975.

Edmund Gosse, 'The New Sculpture', *Art Journal*, 1894.

The Grafton Galleries, *First Exhibition consisting of Paintings and Sculpture by British and Foreign Artists of the Present Day*, exh. cat., 1893.

——, *Exhibition of Dramatic & Musical Art*, 1897.

——, *Founding a National Industry: Irish Carpets*, 7–13 March 1903.

——, *Exhibition of Modern Celtic Art*, 1904.

Algernon Graves, *The British Institution, 1806–1867: A Complete Dictionary of Contributors and their Work from the Foundation of the Institution*, 1969.

Robert Gray, *Cardinal Manning: A Biography*, 1985.

W. R. Greg, *Why are Women Redundant?*, 1869.

Martin Gregor-Dellin and Dietrick Mack, eds, *Cosima Wagner's Diaries*, 2 vols, 1978.

Edward W Gregory, *The Artist*, 1901.

Edward Grierson, *Storm Bird: The Strange Life of Georgina Weldon*, 1959.

——, ed., *A Choice of William Morris's Verse*, 1969.

*Grosvenor Gallery Winter Exhibitions*, exh. cats., 1881–82.

Grosvenor Gallery, *Summer Exhibitions*, exh. cats., 1877–87.

Thomas John Gullick, 'The Royal Academy: "The Outsiders" and The Press', 1869.

*The Guild of Handicraft Minute Book*, I, 1889.

Peter Gunn, *Vernon Lee: Violet Paget (1856–1935)*, 1964.

Gordon S. Haight, 'George Eliot and Watts' *Clytie*', *Yale University Library Gazette*, 1982.

——, *George Eliot's Letters*, 1985.

C. E. and Marie Hallé, eds, *Life and Letters of Sir Charles Hallé*, 2 vols, 1896.

Augustus Hare, *The Story of Two Noble Lives: Charlotte Countess Canning and Louisa Marchioness of Waterford*, 1893.

——, *The Story of my Life*, 6 vols, 1896–1900.

J. F. C. Harrison, *A History of the Working Mens College 1854–1954*, 1954.

Michael Harrison, 'Art & Philanthropy: T. C. Horsfall and The Manchester Art Museum', in *City, Class and Culture: Studies of Social Policy & Cultural Production in Victorian Manchester*, ed. Alan Kidd and K. W. Roberts, 1985.

Martin Harrison and Bill Waters, *Burne-Jones*, 1989.

Malcolm Haslam, *Arts & Crafts Carpets*, 1991.

Malcolm Hay and Jacqueline Riding, *Art in Parliament: The Permanent Collection of the House of Commons*, 1996.

F. W. Haydon, ed., *Benjamin Robert Haydon: Correspondence and Table Talk*, 2 vols, 1876.

D. E. L. Haynes, *The Arundel Marbles*, 1975.

Philip Henderson, *Swinburne: The Portrait of a Poet*, 1974.

Osbert Wyndham Hewett, ed., 'And Mr Fortescue': *A Selection from the Diaries from 1851 to 1862 of Chichester Fortescue, Lord Carlingford, KP*, 1958.

Brian Hill, *Julia Margaret Cameron: A Victorian Family Portrait*, 1973.

*Hobby Horse*, April 1884–April 1991.

J. P. Hodin, *Edvard Munch*, 1972, 1993 edition.

James Francis Hogan, *Robert Lowe, Viscount Sherbrooke*, London, 1893.

Henry Holiday, *Reminiscences of My Life*, 1914,

Holland House, *Pictures at Holland House*, 1904.

Frederick Hollyer, *Catalogue of Platinotype Reproductions of Pictures &c Photographed and Sold by Mr Hollyer No 9 Pembroke Sq^r, London W*, October 1895.

Sir Charles Holroyd, ed., *The National Gallery of British Art (The Tate Gallery)*, 1907.

*Home Arts and Industries Association Minute Book*, 1884–90.

Frances Horner, *Time Remembered*, 1933.

William Holman Hunt, *Pre-Raphaelitism and the Pre-Raphaelite Brotherhood*, 2 vols, 1905.

Harry How, 'Mr Hamo Thornycroft, RA', *Strand Magazine*, 1893.

Winifred E. Howe, *A History of the Metropolitan Museum of Art*, 2 vols, 1913.

John Dixon Hunt, *The Wider Sea: A Life of John Ruskin*, London, 1982.

Graham Hulme, Brian Buchanan and Kenneth Powell, *The National Portrait Gallery: An Architectural History*, 2000.

James Hulse, *Revolutionists in London: A Study of Five Unorthodox Socialists*, 1970.

Joris-Karl Huysmans, 'Le Salon official de 1880', *L'Art Moderne*, 1883.

——, *A Rebours*, 1884, translated as *Against Nature*, 1998.

The Earl of Ilchester, *The Chronicles of Holland House 1820–1900*, 1937.

*The International Exhibition, Penny Guide*, 1862.

International Museum of Photography at George Eastman House, New York, *Cameron: Her Work and Career*, exh. cat., 1986.

International Society of Sculptors, Painters, & Gravers, exh. cat., 1904.

Alexander C. Ionides, *Ion: A Grandfather's Tale*, 1927.

Luke Ionides, *Memories*, 1925, 1996 edition.

Laurence Irving, *Henry Irving: The Actor and His World*, 1951.

Anna Jameson, *Commonplace Book of Thoughts, Memories, Fancies*, 1854.

Richard Jefferies, *National Art Collections Fund Review*, 1995.

Roy Jenkins, *Sir Charles Dilke: A Victorian Tragedy*, 1958, 1996 edition.

——, *Gladstone*, 1996.

John Joliffe, ed., *Neglected Genius: The Diaries of Benjamin Robert Haydon 1808–1846*, 1990.

Michael Joicey, *Louisa Anne Marchioness of Waterford*, Ford, Lady Waterford Hall, 1991.

John Brandon Jones, 'Philip Webb', in *Victorian Architecture*, 1963.

Philippe Jullian, *The Symbolists*, 1973.

Peter Jurth, *Isadora: A Sensational Life*, 2002.

William Kent, *John Burns: Labour's Lost Leader*, 1950.

Fernand Khnopff, *The Magazine of Art*, 1898.

——, 'Some English Art Works at the Libre Esthétique at Brussels', *The Studio*, May 1894.

Sheila Kirk, 'Philip Webb 1831–1915, Domestic Architecture', PhD dissertation, University of Newcastle-upon-Tyne, 1990.

Mary Lago, ed., *Burne-Jones Talking: His Conversations 1895–98, preserved by his Studio Assistant Thomas Rooke*, 1981.

L. M. Lamont, ed., *Thomas Armstrong, CB, A Memoir*, 1912.

George P. Landow, 'Christ the Pilot', a Panel for William Holman Hunt's Unfinished Triptych', *Journal of Pre-Raphaelite Studies*, November 1980, 2 vols.

Rachel Poole Lane, *Catalogue of Oxford Portraits*, I, 1912.

Cecil Lang, ed., *The Swinburne Letters*, 6 vols, 1959–62.

Lillie Langtry, *The Days I Knew*, 1925.

Mitchell A. Leaska, ed., *A Passionate Apprentice: The Early Journals 1897–1909 of Virginia Woolf*, 1990.

Mrs Lecky, *A Memoir of the Rt Hon W. E. H. Lecky by his Wife*, 1909.

Hermione Lee, *Virginia Woolf*, 1996, 1997 edition.

Sir Sidney Lee, *Edward VII, A Biography*, 2 vols, 1925.

Shane Leslie, *Henry Edward Manning, His Life and Labours*, 1921.

The Leicester Galleries, *Catalogue of the Memorial Exhibition of Sculpture by the Late Henry Poole RA*, 1929.

Lord Leighton, *Addresses Delivered to the Students of the Royal Academy*, 1896.

Leighton House, *Loan Collection of Works by G. F. Watts RA*, March 1903.

Cecil Lewis, ed., *Self Portrait Taken from the Letters & Journals of Charles Ricketts*, 1939.

Princess Marie Lichtenstein, *Holland House*, 1875.

A. G. C. Liddell, *Notes from the Life of an Ordinary Mortal*, 1911.

Mrs Edward Liddell, *George Frederic Watts*, London, 1905.

Sir Francis Lindley, *Lord Lovat: A Biography*, 1944.

Elizabeth Longford, *A Pilgrimage of Passion, The Life of Wilfrid Scawen Blunt*, 1979.

——, ed., *Darling Loosy: To Princess Louise 1856–1939*, 1991.

Peter Lord, *The Visual Culture of Wales: Imaging the Nation*, 2000.

David Loshak, 'G. F. Watts and Ellen Terry', *Burlington Magazine*, November 1963.

E. V. Lucas, *Edwin Austin Abbey RA: The Record of His Life and Work*, 2 vols, 1921.

Edward Lucie-Smith, *Symbolist Art*, 1972, 1995 edition.

Sir Alfred Lyall, *The Life of the Marquis of Dufferin and Ava*, 2 vols, 1905.

Jeremy Maas, *Gambart, Prince of the Victorian Art World*, 1975.

Fiona MacCarthy, *William Morris: A Life for our Time*, 1994.

Margaret F. Macdonald, *James McNeill Whistler: Drawings, Pastels and Watercolours: A Catalogue Raisonné*, 1995.

Philip Macer-Wright, *Brangwyn: A Study of Genius at Close Quarters*, 1940.

A. H. Mackmurdo, ed., *Plain Handicrafts: A Guide to Elementary Practice*, 1892.

Hugh Macmillan, *The Life-Work of George Frederick Watts*, 1903.

Frederic William Maitland, ed., *The Life and Letters of Leslie Stephen*, 1906.

Manchester Royal Institution, *Corporation of Manchester Art Gallery, Royal Institution, Autumn Exhibitions*, exh. cats., 1883, 1888.

Elfrida Manning, *Marble & Bronze: The Art and Life of Hamo Thornycroft*, 1982.

H. E. Manning, *The Eternal Priesthood*, 1883.

Regina Marler, ed., *Selected Letters of Vanessa Bell*, 1903.

Jan Marsh, *Dante Gabriel Rossetti, Painter and Poet*, 1999, vol I.

Dorothy Marshall, *The Life and Times of Victoria*, 1972.

A. Patchett Martin *Life & Letters of the Rt Hon Robert Lowe, Viscount Sherbrooke GCG DCL*, 2 vols, 1893.

H. J. L. Masse, *The Art-Workers' Guild 1884–1934*, 1935.

Lucy Masterman, ed., *Mary Gladstone: Her Diaries and Letters*, 1930.

Patricia Mathews, 'The Minotaur of London', *Apollo*, 23 May 1986.

Pierre-Louis Mathieu and Geneviève Lacambre, *The Gustave Moreau Museum*, 1997.

H. C. G. Matthew, ed., *The Gladstone Diaries*, Oxford, 1978, vol. VI.

Emily Southwood Maurice, ed., *Octavia Hill: Early Ideals*, 1928.

Max Müller, *Life and Letters of the Rt Hon Friedrich Max Müller*, 2 vols, 1902.

J. G. McDonald, *Rhodes: A Heritage*, 1943.

L. T. Meade, 'The Painter of the Eternal Truths: First Paper', *Sunday Magazine*, January 1894.

Joy Melville, *Ellen and Edy: A Biography of Ellen Terry and her Daughter, Edith Craig, 1847–1947*, 1987.

Michael Leslie Melville, *The Story of the Lovat Scouts 1900–1980*, 1981.

George Meredith, *Letters of George Meredith, edited by his Son*, 1912, vol. II.

Metropolitan Museum of Art, New York, *Board of Trustees Meetings*, 1873–88, 2 vols.

——, *Annual Report of the Trustees of the Association*, 1885.

——, *Catalogue of The Loan Collection of Paintings by George Frederick Watts RA of London*, 1884, 1885 edition.

——, *Paintings by G. F. Watts RA*, exh. cat., 1885.

——, *Edward Burne-Jones: Victorian Artist-Dreamer*, exh. cat., 1998.

——, *La Divine Comtesse*, exh. cat., 2000.

——, *A Private Passion: 19th Century Paintings and Drawings from the Grenville L. Winthrop Collection, Harvard University*, ed. Stephan Wolohojian, exh. cat., 2003.

Adolf Michaelis, *Ancient Marbles in Britain*, 1882.

——, *A Century of Archaeological Discoveries*, 1908.

Middle Temple, *The Honourable Society of the Middle Temple Minutes of Proceedings*, 1874–84.

Sir John Everett Millais, 'Thoughts on our Art of To-day', *Magazine of Art*, 1888, XI, 289–90.

J. G. Millais, *The Life and Letters of Sir John Everett Millais*, 2 vols, 1899.

Delia Millar, *The Victorian Watercolours in the Collection of Her Majesty The Queen*, 1995.

Sarah Gertrude Millin, *Rhodes*, 1933.

Ernestine Mills, ed., *Frederic Shields*, 1912.

The Revd L. H. Mills, 'Zoroaster & the Bible, *The Nineteenth Century*, January 1894.

Minneapolis Institute of Arts, *Victorian High Renaissance*, exh. cat., 1978.

W. Minto, ed., *Autobiographical Notes of the Life of William Bell Scott*, 2 vols, 1892.

Cosmo Monkhouse, 'George Frederick Watts RA', *Scribner's Magazine*, Christmas 1894.

John Morley, *The Life of William Ewart Gladstone*, 2 vols, 1905.

Edward Morris, 'James Smith of Liverpool and Auguste Rodin', in *Patronage and Practice: Sculpture on Merseyside*, ed. Penelope Curtis, 1989.

——, *Victorian & Edwardian Paintings in the Walker Art Gallery and at Sudley House*, 1996.

Jocelyn Morton, *Three Generations in a Family Textile Firm*, 1971.

Munich, *Münchener Jahresausstellung von Kunstwerken aller Nationen im Glaspalaste 1893. Offizieller Katalog*, exh. cat., 1893.

Nicholas Murray, *A Life of Matthew Arnold*, 1996.

Michael Musgrave, 'Leighton and Music', in Barringer and Prettejohn, 1999.

Roger Dixon and Stefan Muthesius, *Victorian Architecture*, 1978, 1995 edition.

Weston Naef, ed., *Julia Margaret Cameron: Photographs from The J. Paul Getty Museum: In Focus*, 1996.

National Gallery, London, *Report of the Director of the National Gallery*, 1899.

——, *Titian*, ed. David Jaffe, exh. cat., 2003.

National Gallery of British Art, *Descriptive and Historical Catalogue of the Pictures and Sculpture*, 1897 and 1900.

——, *Minutes of the Board*, 176 and 184 (*Art Journal*, 1903).

——, *Minutes of the Board*, 29 November 1900.

National Portrait Gallery, *Annual Reports*, 1896, 1905.

——, *Millais: Portraits*, exh. cat., 1999.

National Trust for Places of Historic Interest or Natural Beauty, *Report of the Provisional Council*, 1895.

National Trust, *Blickling Hall*, 1987.

——, *Carlyle's House*, 1979, 1990 edition.

——, *The Faringdon Collection*, 1998.

Mary De Navarro, *A Few Memories*, 1896.

Ralph Nevill, ed., *The Reminiscences of Lady Dorothy Nevill*, 1906.

New Gallery, *Exhibition of the Works of Sir Edward Burne-Jones, Bart*, exh. cat., 1898–99.

——, *Exhibition of the Works of Sir Edward Burne-Jones, Bart*, exh. cat., 1892–93.

——, *Summer Exhibition*, exh. cats., 1888–1904.

——, *Winter Exhibition: The Works of G. F. Watts RA*, exh. cat., 1896–97.

——, *Winter Exhibition: The Works of Sir W. B. Richmond*, exh. cat., 1900–01.

Teresa Newman and Ray Watkinson, *Ford Madox Brown and the Pre-Raphaelite Circle*, 1991.

C. T. Newton, *A History of Discoveries at Halicarnassus, Cnidus and Branchidae, being the results of an Expedition sent to Asia Minor by HM Government in 1856*, 1861–62, 2 vols.

——, *Travels & Discoveries in the Levant*, 1865, 2 vols.

——, *The Castellani Collection*, 1874.

Nigel Nicolson, ed., *The Flight of the Mind: The Letters of Virginia Woolf*, vol. I, 1975, 1993 edition.

Belinda Norman-Butler, *Victorian Aspirations: The Life and Labour of Charles and Mary Booth*, 1972.

Nottingham Museum & Art Gallery, *Handbook to the Collection of Pictures by G. F. Watts, RA*, 1886.

Offentliche Kunstsammlung Basel Kunstmuseum *Arnold Bocklin*, exh. cat., 2001.

Wrexham, *Official Catalogue of the Art Treasures Exhibition of North Wales & the Border Counties at Wrexham*, exh. cat., 1876.

Davis Oakley, *Oscar Wilde: The Importance of Being Irish*, 1994.

Leonée Ormond, *George du Maurier*, 1969.

Leonée and Richard Ormond, *Lord Leighton*, 1975.

Richard Ormond and Elaine Kilmurray, *John Singer Sargent: The Early Portraits*, 1998.

Richard Ormond, *Leighton's Frescoes in the Victoria and Albert Museum*, 1975.

Lady Walburga Paget, *Embassies of Other Days*, 1923.

Francis Turner Palgrave, *Handbook to the Fine Art Collections in the International Exhibition*, 1862.

Roundell Palmer, Earl of Selborne, *Memorials*, 2 vols, 1898.

Paris Salon, *Illustrated Catalogue*, 1880.

*Paris Universal Exhibition of 1878: Catalogue of the British Fine Art Section*, exh. cat., 1878.

Linda Parry, *Textiles of the Arts and Crafts Movement*, 1988, reprinted 1997.

The Pastel Society, *Catalogue of the First Exhibition of the Pastel Society*, The Galleries of the Royal Institute of Painters, Piccadilly, 1899.

The Pastel Society, *Minutes*, Preliminary Meeting, 21 September 1898.

George Paston, *At John Murrays: Records of a Literary Career, 1843–1902*, 1932.

Walter Pater, 'The School of Giorgione', *Fortnightly Review*, October 1877, reprinted in *Walter Pater Selected Works*, ed. Richard Aldington, 1948.

Michael Pearson, *The Age of Consent: Victorian Prostitution and its Enemies*, 1972.

F. C. Penrose, 'Surveyor to the Fabrick', *Description of a Scheme for the Internal Embellishment of St Paul's*, July 1872.

E. R. and J. Pennell, *The Life of James McNeill Whistler*, 2 vols, 1908.

Margot Peters, *Mrs Pat: The Life of Mrs Patrick Campbell*, 1984.

*Philadelphia International Exhibition 1876: Official Catalogue of the British Section*, 1876.

John Physick, *The Victoria & Albert Museum: The History of its Building*, 1982.

David Piper, 'In Defence of G. F. Watts', *The Listener*, 13 January 1955.

John Pollock, *Gordon: The Man behind the Legend*, 1993.

Sir Frederick Ponsonby, *Recollections of Three Reigns*, 1988.

Willard Bissell Pope, ed., *The Diary of Benjamin Robert Haydon*, 1963.

Una Pope-Henessy, *Charles Dickens 1812–1870*, 1945.

Prince's Hall, Piccadilly, *The Exhibition of the Rational Dress Association*, exh. cat., 1883.

Richard Prentis, 'A Tale of Two Canopies: The Mutilated Monuments of John of Eltham, Earl of Cornwall, and John Lonsdale, Bishop of Lichfield', *Friends of Lichfield Cathedral, 62nd Annual Report*, 1999.

Sir Henry Thoby Prinsep, *Three Generations in India, 1770–1904*.

*Journal for the Society for Psychical Research*, 1, April 1884.

Harry Quilter, 'The Painting of George Frederick Watts, RA: A Comparative Criticism', *Contemporary Review*, February 1882, reprinted in *Preferences in Art, Life and Literature*, 1892.

Vincent Quinn and John Prest, ed., *Dear Miss Nightingale: A Selection of Benjamin Jowett's Letters to Florence Nightingale*, 1987.

Carter Ratcliff, *John Singer Sargent*, 1982.

Eleanor Rawnsley, *Canon Rawnsley: An Account of his Life*, 1923.

H. D. Rawnsley, *Ballads of Brave Deeds*, London, 1896.

Benedict Read, *Victorian Sculpture*, 1982.

F. M. Redgrave, *Richard Redgrave CP RA: A Memoir, Compiled from his Diary*, 1891.

Rembrandt Head Gallery, *Catalogue of Original Lithographs exhibited at the Rembrandt Head Gallery*, exh. cats., 1895.

*Report of the Commissioners appointed to inquire into the Present Position of the Royal Academy in relation to the Fine Arts*, 1863.

*Reports from the Council of the Royal Academy to the General Assembly of Academicians*, 1867–72.

*Report of the Science and Art Department*, 1868–70.

Réunion des Musées Nationaux, Paris, *Delacroix: 'Une Fête pour l'Oeil'*, exh. cat., 1998.

——, *Gustave Moreau 1826–1898*, exh. cat., 1998.

——, *Chasseriau: Un autre romantisme*, exh. cat., 2002.

Graham Reynolds, *Victorian Painting*, 1966.

Simon Reynolds, *A Companion to the Mosaics of St Paul's Cathedral*, 1994.

Joanna Richardson, *George IV: A Portrait*, 1966.

Jasper Ridley, *Garibaldi*, 1974.

Adelaide Ristori, *Memoirs and Artistic Studies*, 1907.

Anne Thackeray Ritchie, *Alfred, Lord Tennyson and His Friends*, 1893.

——, 'Notes of Happy Things', MS.

——, *From Friend to Friend*, 1919.

Hester Ritchie, ed., *Letters of Anne Thackeray Ritchie*, 1924.

L. Roberts, *Arthur Hughes*, 1997.

W. Graham Robertson, *Time Was*, 1931.

Sabine Röder, 'Moderne Baukunst 1900–14: The Architectural Collection of the Deutscher Werkbund', *The Decorative Arts Society Journal*, 1998.

Thomas Matthews Rooke, 'Notes of Conversation' (photocopy in NAL), 1900.

Janet Ross, *The Fourth Generation: Reminiscences*, 1912.

William M. Rossetti, ed., *The Collected Works of Dante Gabriel Rossetti*, 2 vols, 1888.

——, ed., *Dante Gabriel Rossetti: His Family Letters*, 1895, 2 vols.

——, ed., *Rossetti Papers 1862–70*, 1903.

William Rothenstein, *Men and Memories: Recollections*, 1931, 3 vols.

——, *The Tate Gallery*, 1962.

Sir Ronald Roxburgh, ed., *The Records of the Honourable Society of Lincoln's Inn: The Black Books*, 1968.

Royal Academy of Arts, London, *Summer Exhibition*, exh. cats., 1837–1904.

——, *Notes on the Royal Academy Exhibition 1868*, 1868.

——, *Exhibition of Works by the Late Lord Leighton of Stretton, Winter Exhibition*, exh. cat., 1897.

——, *Exhibition of Works by the Late Sir John Everett Millais, Bart*, exh. cat., 1898.

——, *Exhibition of Works by the Late George Frederick Watts, RA OM, Winter Exhibition*, 1905.

——, *Alfred Gilbert: Sculptor and Goldsmith*, exh. cat., 1986.

——, *Henry Moore*, exh. cat., 1988.

——, *Frederic Leighton 1830–1896*, 1996.

Royal Artillery, *A Catalogue of Pictures, Sculpture & Models in the collection of the Royal Artillery Mess Woolwich*, 1977.

Royal Institute of Painters in Watercolours and New Gallery, Society of Portrait Painters, exh. cats., 1891, 1900, 1901.

*The Royal Manchester Institution: Exhibition of the Works of Modern Artists*, exh. cat., 1874–76.

*Royal Cambrian Academy of Art: Sixth Annual Exhibition of Works*, exh. cat., 1888.

Royal Museums of Fine Art of Belgium, Brussels, *Fernand Khnopff (1858–1921)*, 2004.

John Ruskin, *Modern Painters*, 5 vols, 1843–60.

——, *The Stones of Venice*, 3 vols, 1851–53.

——, *The Queen of the Air: Being a Study of the Greek Myths of Cloud and Storm*, 1869 and 1904.

——, *Lectures on Art Delivered before the University of Oxford in Hilary Term, 1870*, 1903.

——, *Fors Clavigera: To the Workmen and Labourers of Great Britain*, vol. V, 1906.

Don Russell, *The Lives and Legends of Buffalo Bill*, 1960.

Ruth Chandler Williamson Gallery, Scripps College, *Annals of my Glass House*, exh. cat., 1996.

The Dean and Canons of St George's Chapel, *Albert Chapel, Windsor Castle*, 1999.

Giles St Aubyn, *Edward VII: Prince and King*, 1979.

Christopher St John, ed., *Ellen Terry and Bernard Shaw: A Correspondence*, 1931, 1949 edition.

St Paul's Cathedral, *Memorial Service held on the Burial Day of George Frederic Watts RA*, 7 July 1904.

Dr James H. Salisbury, *The Relation of Alimentation and Disease*, 1888, reprinted in *Ohio State Archaeological and Historical Quarterly*, LIX, October 1950.

Henry Salt *Seventy Years Among Savages*, London, 1921.

Siegfried Sassoon, *Meredith*, 1948.

Clement Scott and Cecil Howard, eds, *The Life and Reminiscences of E. L. Blanchard*, 2 vols, 1891.

James A. Secord, *Victorian Sensation: The Extraordinary Publication, Reception, and Secret Authorship of Vestiges of the Natural History of Creation*, 2000.

Martin Seymour-Smith, *Hardy*, 1994.

Alan and Mary Mcqueen Simpson, eds, *I Too am Here: Selections from the Letters of Jane Welsh Carlyle*, 1977.

Charles Saumarez Smith, *The National Portrait Gallery*, 1997.

Jeanne Schulkins, ed., *Virginia Woolf, Moments of Being*, 1985.

Eric Shanes, *Impressionist London*, 1994.

Richard Shannon, *Gladstone: Heroic Minister 1865–98*, 1999.

George Bernard Shaw, *An Autobiography 1898–1950*, 1970.

Walter Shaw-Sparrow, *Frank Brangwyn and His Work*, 1910.

Robin Simon, ed., *Lord Leighton 1830–1896 and Leighton House: A Centenary Celebration*, 1996.

Constance Sitwell, *Bright Morning*, 1942.

Osbert Sitwell, ed., *A Free House! Or The Artist as Craftsman: Being the Writings of Walter Richard Sickert*, 1947.

Robert de la Sizeranne, 'A French View of English Art: Mythic Art' (trans. H. M. Poynter, from *La Peinture Anglaise Contemporaine*, 1895), *Artist*, April 1896.

R. E. D. Sketchley, *Watts*, 1904.

Alison Smith, *The Victorian Nude: Sexuality, Morality and Art*, 1996.

*Society for the Protection of Birds, Seventh Annual Report*, 1897.

Sotheby's, *English Literature & History*, sale catalogue, 19 December 2000.

South London Fine Art Gallery, *Report of a Public Meeting*, 18 July 1890.

France Spalding, *Roger Fry: Art & Life*, 1980.

——, *Vanessa Bell*, 1983, 1993 edition.

——, *Duncan Grant*, London, 1997.

——, 'The Tate: A History', 1998.

Sir Isidore Spielmann, *St Louis International Exhibition 1904: The British Section*, 1906.

M. H. Spielmann, *The Works of Mr G. F. Watts RA*, London, Pall Mall Gazette, 1886.

——, *Supplement to the Daily Graphic*, 19 February 1891.

——, 'Mr G. F. Watts: His Art and His Mission', *The Nineteenth Century*, January 1897.

——, *Millais and his Works, with Special Reference to the Exhibition at the Royal Academy*, 1898.

——, *G. F. Watts, RA, OM, as a Great Painter of Portraits: A Lecture Delivered in the Memorial Hall Manchester*, 1905.

Sir John Squire, *Solo and Duet*, 1943.

Norman St John-Stevas, *Walter Bagehot*, 1959.

W. T. Stead, 'The Maiden Tribute of Modern Babylon', *Pall Mall Gazette*, 6–10 July 1885.

——, 'Mr G. F. Watts, RA', *Review of Reviews*, 10 June 1902, 566–79.

Marguerite Steen, *A Pride of Terrys*, 1962.

F. G. Stephens, *Artists at Home*, London, Sampson Low, 1884.

David Alan Stewart, 'G. F. Watts: The Social and Religious Themes', PhD dissertation, University of South Carolina, 1988.

——, 'Of Angst and Escapism: George Fredric Watts and Frederic, Lord Leighton,' *Victorians Institute Journal*, 1994, vol. XXII.

A. M. W. Stirling, ed., *The Letter Bag of Lady Elizabeth Spencer-Stanhope, Compiled from the Cannon Hall Papers 1806–73*, 2 vols, 1913.

——, *A Painter of Dreams*, 1916.

——, *Life's Little Day*, 1924.

——, *The Richmond Papers from the Correspondence and Manuscripts of George Richmond RA and his Son Sir William Richmond RA, KCB*, 1926.

——, *Life's Mosaic*, 1934.

F. G. Stephens, *Artists at Home*, 1884.

Mark Stocker, 'Royalist and Realist: The Life and Work of Sir Joseph Edgar Boehm', 1988.

Lytton Strachey, *Eminent Victorians*, 1918, 1948 edition.

Virginia Surtees, *The Paintings, Drawings of Dante Gabriel Rossetti: A Catalogue Raisonnée*, 1971.

——, ed., *The Diaries of George Price Boyce*, 1980.

——, *The Ludovisi Goddess: The Life of Louisa Lady Ashburton*, 1984.

——, *The Artist and the Autocrat: George and Rosalind Howard, Earl and Countess of Carlisle*, 1988.

——, *Coutts Lindsay 1824–1913*, 1993.

——, *The Actress and the Brewer's Wife*, 1997.

John Sutherland, *Mrs Humphrey Ward: Eminent Victorian, Pre-Eminent Edwardian*, 1990.

Denys Sutton, *Nocturne: The Art of James McNeill Whistler*, 1963.

Denys Sutton, ed., *Letters of Roger Fry*, 1972.

John L. Sweeney, ed., *The Painter's Eye: Notes and Essays on the Pictorial Arts by Henry James*, 1956.

Vern Swanson, *The Biography and Catalogue Raisonné of the Paintings of Sir Lawrence Alma-Tadema*, 1990.

Mark Swenarton, *Artisans and Architects: The Ruskinian Tradition in Architectural Thought*, 1989.

Algernon Swinburne, *William Blake: An Essay*, 1864.

Charles Tardieu 'La Peinture à l'Exposition Universelle de 1878', *L'Art*, 1879.

Tate, London, *George Frederic Watts OM RA, 1817–1904*, exh. cat., 1954.

——, *James McNeill Whistler*, exh. cat., 1994.

——, *The Age of Rossetti, Burne-Jones & Watts: Symbolism in Britain 1860–1910*, exh. cat., 1997.

——, *John Singer Sargent*, exh. cat., 1998.

——, *The Art of Bloomsbury*, exh. cat., 1999.

——, *Ruskin, Turner and the Pre-Raphaelites*, exh. cat., 2000.

——, *William Blake*, exh. cat., 2000.

——, *Exposed: The Victorian Nude*, exh. cat., 2001.

Sir Henry Taylor, *Autobiography of Henry Taylor, 1800–75*, 2 vols, 1885.

Tom Taylor, ed., *Life of Benjamin Robert Haydon, Historical Painter from his Journals*, 3 vols, 1853.

Una Taylor, *Guests and Memories: Annals of a Seaside Villa*, 1924.

Alfred Tennyson, *Poems Chiefly Lyrical*, 1830.

——, *In Memoriam AHH, OBIT MDCCCXXXIII*, 1849.

Hallam Tennyson, *Alfred Lord Tennyson: A Memoir*, 2 vols, 1897.

Ellen Terry, *The Story of My Life*, 1908.

Anne Thackeray, *From an Island*, 1877, 1996 edition.

William Makepeace Thackeray, 'Our Street', *Christmas Books*, 1911.

Brian Thompson, *A Monkey Among Crocodiles: The Life, Loves and Lawsuits of Mrs Georgina Weldon*, 2000.

Charles Thompson, *Watts Picture Gallery Curator's Report*, 15 November 1913.

John Thompson, 'Fashion and Folly: A Dissertation on Dress Reform, embracing Tight-Lacing and other Fallacies', *Women's Library*, Scarborough, c.1890.

D. Croal Thomson, ed., *The Paris Exhibition 1900*, 1901.

Ann Thwaite, *Emily Tennyson: The Poet's Wife*, 1996.

Kenneth Romney Towndrow, *Alfred Stevens, Architectural Sculptor, Painter and Designer*, 1939.

Captain George Towsey, 'Narrative of the Expedition to Asia Minor in 1856–57', MS, British Museum.

*Transactions of the National Association for the Advancement of Art and its Application to Industry*, Liverpool Meeting, 1888.

*Transactions of the National Association for the Promotion of Social Science*, Manchester Meeting, 1879, 1880.

Colin Trodd and Stephanie Brown, eds, *Representations of G. F. Watts*, 2004.

Laura Troubridge, *Memories and Reflections*, 1925.

Christopher Turnor, *Journal*, nd.

——, *Notes of Conversations I had with Mr Watts from 1902 to 1904*, 1904.

Mrs Edward Twisleton, *Letters of the Hon. Mrs Edward Twisleton written to her Family 1852–62*, 1928.

Giorgio Vasari, *The Lives of the Artists*, 1550, 1991 edition.

Michael Vickers, 'The "Oxford Bust",' *The Ashmolean*, 20, 1991.

Victoria and Albert Museum, *The Catalogue of the Constantine Alexander Ionides Collection*, vol. 1, 1925.

——, *The Ionides Collection*, 1970.

——, *The Victorian Vision: Inventing New Britain*, exh. cat., 2001.

Walker Art Gallery, Liverpool, *The Seventh Exhibition of Modern Pictures*, exh. cat., 1877.

Giles Walkley, *Artists' Houses in London 1764–1914*, 1994.

Walters Art Gallery and the Baltimore Museum of Art, *The Triumph of French Painting, Ingres to Matisse*, 2000.

Nicholas Wanostrocht, *Felix on the Bat: Being a Scientific Enquiry into the Use of The Cricket Bat, together with the History and Use of the Catapulta*, 1845 and 1850.

Wantage, *Catalogue of Pictures forming the Collection of Lord and Lady Wantage at 2 Carlton Gardens, London & Lockinge House, Berks & Overstone Park and Ardington House*, 1902.

Wilfrid Ward, *Aubrey de Vere, A Memoir*, London, Longmans, Green & Co, 1904.

Philip Ward-Jackson, *Public Sculpture of the City of London*, 2003.

Lina Waterfield, *Castle in Italy: An Autobiography*, 1961.

Merlin Waterson, *The National Trust: The First Hundred Years*, 1994.

Philip Watkins, *St James the Less Westminster: The Church and Its History*, 1994.

William Watson, *The Purple East: A Series of Sonnets on England's Desertion of Armenia*, 1896.

George Frederic Watts, 'The Present Conditions of Art', *Nineteenth Century*, February 1880.

——, 'Letter to Lady Marian Alford', 'Art Needlework II', *Nineteenth Century*, March 1881.

——, 'The Aims of Art', *Magazine of Art*, June 1888.

——, 'Thoughts on our Art of To-day', *Magazine of Art*, 1889, XII, 90.

——, 'Our Race as Pioneers', *The Nineteenth Century and After*, May 1901.

Mary Seton Watts, *The Word in the Pattern: A Key to the Symbols on the Walls of the Chapel at Compton*, 1904, 2000 edition.

Watts Gallery, *Mary Seton Watts (1849–1938): Unsung Heroine of the Art Nouveau*, exh. cat., 1998.

——, *The Vision of G. F. Watts* OM RA *(1817–1904)*, exh. cat., 2004.

William Weaver, *Duse: A Biography*, 1984.

Stanley Weintraub, ed., *Bernard Shaw: The Diaries 1885–97*, 1986.

Agnes Grace Weld, *Glimpses of Tennyson and of Some of His Relations and Friends*, 1903.

Hubert Wellington, ed., *The Journal of Eugène Delacroix*, 1951.

The Countess of Wemyss and March, *A Family Record*, 1932.

The Earl of Wemyss and March, *Memories, 1818–1912*, 2 vols, 1912.

Rosslyn Wemyss, ed., *Memoirs of Sir Robert Morier*, 1911.

Richard Westmacott, *Handbook of Sculpture Ancient and Modern*, 1864.

Sir Algernon West, *Private Diaries of the Rt Hon Sir Algenon West*, 1922.

Martha Westwater, *The Wilson Sisters*, 1984.

Adam White, *Hamo Thornycroft and the Martyr General*, The Henry Moore Centre for the Study of Sculpture, Leeds City Art Galleries, 1991.

Whitechapel, St Jude's School House, *Fine Art Loan Exhibition*, exh. cats., 1882, 1894.

Whitechapel Art Gallery, *G. F. Watts: A Nineteenth Century Phenomenon*, exh. cat., 1974.

——, *Spring Exhibition*, exh. cat., 1901.

Oscar Wilde, 'The Grosvenor Gallery', *Dublin University Magazine*, xv, July 1877.

——, 'Miscellanies', in *Collected Works*, 1908.

——, *Collected Works*, 1997.

David Williams, *George Meredith: His Life and Lost Love*, 1977.

A. N. Wilson, *The Victorians*, 2002, 2003 edition.

Jean Moorcroft Wilson, *Siegfried Sassoon: The Making of a War Poet: A Biography (1886–1918)*, 1998.

Christopher Wood, *Victorian Painting*, 1999.

Virginia Woolf, introduction to *Victorian Photographs of Famous Men and Fair Women by Julia Margaret Cameron*, 1926.

——, *Roger Fry: A Biography*, 1940.

——, *Freshwater: A Comedy*, 1976.

Amy Woolner, *Thomas Woolner RA, Sculptor and Poet: His Life in Letters*, 1917.

Basil Worsfold, ed., *Browning's Men and Women*, 2 vols, 1904.

W. B. Yeats, *Autobiographies*, 1914, 1955.

York City Art Gallery, *The Artist's Model from Etty to Spencer*, exh. cat., 1999.

# Photograph Credits

Ashmolean Museum, Oxford: 77; Birmingham Museums and Art Gallery: 90; Bridgeman Art Library: 11, XXVI; British Library: 39; Christie's, XXVII–XXIX, 74, 102, 109; Courtauld Institute of Art: 14, 22, 89, 129; The Faringdon Collection Trust, Buscot Park: 79, 82; Fine Art Society: XIII, 69, 97, 126, 155; Fitzwilliam Museum, Cambridge: 128; Garrick Club Library: 131; Gernsheim Collection, Harry Ransom Humanities Research Center, The University of Texas at Austin: 63; Paul Greenhalgh: 150; Julian Hartnoll: 74, 104, 145; Richard Jefferies: 26; Robert Jefferies: 136; Leighton House Museum: 134; Lincoln's Inn: V; Manchester City Council: 78; National Museums Liverpool, XII, 67, 108; National Portrait Gallery: IV, XI, XXI, XXII, 172; NTPL/John Hammond: VII, Jonathan Gibson: XXXVI; Nevill Keating Pictures Ltd: VI, VIII, XXIII, XXXI, 81, 182; Palace of Westminster: 19, 32; The Paul Mellon Centre for Studies in British Art: 21; private collections: XVIII, 9, 47, 75, 123, 141, 174, 184, 202, 227; Royal Academy of Arts: XX, 52, 144; Royal Borough of Kensington and Chelsea Libraries and Arts Service: 27, 121; The Royal Collection © 2004, Her Majesty Queen Elizabeth II: 10; Royal Photographic Society Collection at National Museum of Photography, Film and Television: 61; St Mary's Cathedral, Edinburgh: 179; Sotheby's: 18, 41, 91, 127, 175, 217; © Tate, London 2004, IX, XVII, XIX, XXX, 24, 57, 124, 140, 143, 154, 167, 180; Tennyson Research Centre, Lincoln County Council: 53; Trinity College, Cambridge: XXXV; Victoria and Albert Museum, V&A Images: 66; Watts Gallery:I, X, XV, XVI, XXIV, XXV, XXXIV, XXXVII–XLI, 3–6, 12, 16, 20–21, 23, 25, 27–29, 33–35–37, 43–44, 49, 56–59, 61, 64, 66–67, 69, 71–72, 75, 77, 82, 88–89, 91, 94, 96–97, 100, 105–7, 111–13, 115–17, 119, 121, 125, 131–32, 137–38, 151–53, 156, 159, 162, 169, 171–73, 178, 180–82, 184–85, 190–95, 197, 205, 207–8, 211–12, 214, 218, 222–25, 227–31, 234–41.

# Index